GREAT WORLD THEATER

**Illinois Central College
Learning Resource Center**

HARPER & ROW, PUBLISHERS
New York, Evanston, and London

GREAT WORLD
THEATER

An Introduction to Drama

edited, with introductions, by

ALAN S. DOWNER
Princeton University

PN
6111
.D6

GREAT WORLD THEATER: An Introduction to Drama
Copyright © 1964 by Alan S. Downer.
Printed in the United States of America. All rights reserved. No part of
this book may be used or reproduced in any manner whatsoever without
written permission except in the case of brief quotations embodied in
critical articles and reviews. For information address Harper & Row,
Publishers, Incorporated, 49 East 33rd Street, New York 16, N.Y.

LIBRARY OF CONGRESS CATALOG CARD NUMBER: 64–18487

CONTENTS

V

PREFACE

THE TITLE OF THIS ANTHOLOGY, adapted from the Spanish playwright, Calderón (see p. 244), indicates both the scope of the selections and the principle by which they were chosen. The repertory spans 2500 years of playwriting, fourteen authors and nine countries. It includes examples of the major genres and the variations within those genres demanded by different periods and cultures. It is, of course, the merest sampling of a thousand plays that could be studied with equal profit and pleasure by the student in search of the dramatic experience. But the principle behind this selection has not been to present a mere sampling.

The modern trend toward studying drama as a highly specialized art form, giving due attention to the non-literáry elements that contribute to the total experience, is reasonable and proper; at the very least it provides the student with a method of approaching the play as a work of art rather than a vehicle for ideas, or the skeleton of a novel, or an awkwardly printed poem. There is, however, a point beyond which the non-professional student does not need to go, a point at which the minutiae of theatrical production or dramatic technique intrude upon his experience of the work.

The introductory comments to each of the plays are inductive and sequential, and are designed to present to the reader certain elements which are the unique property of the dramatic form, or which the dramatist uses in special ways. They should enable the student to penetrate step by step into the nature of the dramatic experience without insisting too much on matters which are primarily of concern to historians of the arts of the stage.

To assist the student to develop a fuller response to dramatic art in general, the plays have been arranged in chronological order, rather than grouped as genres within the major form. But because of the theme of the collection, there are two exceptions to strict chronology: Euripides is permitted to precede Sophocles, and Pirandello to follow Arthur Miller. Euripides' *The Bacchae,* whatever else it may be, is an effective statement of one of the basic and characteristic elements of drama, and Pirandello, in *Six Characters in Search of an Author,* re-examines these elements in terms of the modern world. Euripides and Pirandello are thus the two *metae,* the turning-posts around which the argument of *Great World Theater* proceeds: the nature of dramatic art in terms of the relation between the actor and his role, and between the actor and the spectator.

I wish to express my thanks to W. David Kay for preparing the Glossary of Dramatic Terms. While this occasionally supplements or defines terms used in the introductions, it is intended to have a wider usefulness to students who pursue the study of drama beyond the present collection. The Bibliography is designed with the same purpose: while offering more information about critical approaches, national repertories, and the authors represented, it can serve as a bridge to the theater of the great world which can only be hinted at in an anthology.

A. S. D.

EURIPIDES

THE BACCHAE

GOD OF MANY NAMES

THE POPULAR DRAMA is so much a part of our common experience that, like eating, or sleeping, or driving to work, we are scarcely aware of it until something goes wrong. Habitually we settle down in an armchair before the television set or sink into the ionized darkness of a movie theater and—so far as consciousness goes—do nothing. But should the film break or a commercial be particularly intrusive, we are made annoyingly conscious of theater or living room; we are impatient to return to Montmartre or Dodge City. Our annoyance is a clue to the peculiar nature of the drama and the particular value, for the spectator, of the experience of playgoing. Coleridge once wrote that the full enjoyment of drama required a willing suspension of disbelief, a desire to pretend, on the part of the spectator. But the suspension, the pretending, is seldom really *willed*. The very nature of the art of the drama, the way it is created, the form that it takes, and the relationship between performer and observer, so involves the spectator in the experience that his only conscious, willed action has been in his commitment to be present.

The nature of the art of the drama has been an enduring and intriguing puzzle for philosophers and aestheticians over many centuries. Even primitive man, before the discoveries of psychology and the exact sciences, tried to resolve it in the conventional primitive way—he translated the abstract idea into a concrete myth. The date is unknown, the details and the process hypothetical, but the fact is demonstrable and the myth perhaps more illuminating than the conclusions of sober scientific research.

In all primitive societies, drama grows out of and is an attempt to give expression to the eternal and fundamental concerns of man: death and life, the maintenance of order, invoking the beneficent forces of nature, immobilizing the hostile forces. To enact the resurrection of Osiris at the funeral of an Egyptian noble was to assure his triumph over death. To mime the germination and growth of corn or barley was to attract the sympathetic presence of the rain gods and insure a prosperous harvest. To imitate the actions of a victorious army before going into actual battle was to insure victory. If such performances are more ritual than theatrical they contain the seeds of drama, complete actions performed by actors impersonating gods, natural forces, or other men.

The word *impersonation* is one of the keys to the nature of drama. Derived from the Latin *persona*, a mask, it is a reminder that the first performers of drama disguised their faces with linen cloth or paint to indicate the characters or qualities they were assuming. The mask was not, however, simply to assist the spectators in identifying the persons of the play. More important, the mask assisted the performer in possessing, or being possessed by, the rôle assigned to him. The Greek word for this degree of total impersonation is *enthousiasm*, to be possessed by the god (*Theos*); in the earliest dramatic rituals, the performers felt themselves to be the gods, or the disciples of the gods. To be so possessed was necessary for the correct performance of the rite, and correct performance alone could assure the desirable end.

Of the many rituals and mysteries in ancient Greece, where the theater of the Western world first came to full expression, those associated with Dionysos, god of wine, were particularly suited for development into drama. To begin with, Dionysos was a late-comer to the Greek pantheon and both epic and lyric poetry (that is, the conventions of narrative and choral-rythmic expression) were highly developed arts. Further, he was not only, as Sophocles calls him, a "god of many names," but also a god of many adventures—his birth was miraculous, his upbringing mysterious, his ministry full of conflicts and violence. Most important, his religion was ecstatic; his cultists induced religious rapture by drinking the wine which was his gift to man, and felt themselves changed into skin-clad satyrs and Maenads, the original "herd" that had followed Dionysos into Greece.*

* See Margarete Bieber, *The History of the Greek and Roman Theater*, Princeton, 1961, pp. 1–3.

The celebration of Dionysos, then, involved impersonation and costuming, both necessary elements in drama. But the subject, the life of the god, encouraged development away from ritual, which depends upon the rigid and unvarying repetition of a formal pattern. Dionysos was the son of Zeus, king of the gods, and Semele, daughter of Cadmus, king of Thebes. The jealousy of the goddess Hera, wife of Zeus, brought about the premature birth of Dionysos, whom Zeus concealed in his thigh until the proper time for his birth should occur. Zeus entrusted the infant to Ino, sister of Semele, but Hera's persistent wrath drove her to commit suicide with her own child. Dionysos was then put in the care of certain woodnymphs who protected him until he was ready to journey into the world to bestow the gift of the vine on those who accepted his divinity. His whole history is a series of persecutions and conflicts, generally ending in madness and catastrophe for those who rejected him. Dionysos thus provided playwrights with a generous fund of stories, each centering on a situation of conflict to be resolved only by victory or defeat, the essence of tragedy, never by compromise, the essence of comedy.

According to a generally accepted legend, the first playwright to recognize the dramatic potential of the festival of Dionysos was Thespis of Ikaria (*fl.* 534 B.C.). Thespis is credited with "inventing" the protagonist, an actor separated from the group of followers of the god, who impersonated a mythical or historical character and delivered previously composed speeches. While such speeches may have been originally narrative—the protagonist recounting an experience to the chorus—at some point in time they must have assumed the nature of a debate or argument between the protagonist and the chorus leader with the full chorus becoming more and more of an observer or commentator on the discussion.

By the time of Aeschylus (525–456 B.C.), the first playwright whose work survives in other than fragments, the form and subject matter of Greek serious drama was firmly established. Basically it consisted of five episodes, passages of dialogue between two or more actors, interspersed with long choral odes (see Glossary: Greek tragedy). Each episode involved a conflict developed in discussion or debate, and each conflict led to one of increasing ntensity, culminating in a decisive action, generally taking place behind the scenes.

From the point of view of the modern playgoer, it may seem strange that the climactic moment of a play should be hidden from view, and a number of reasons have been advanced to explain a convention that the Greeks apparently never questioned. It has been suggested that the death of the hero derives from the primitive practice of human sacrifice, that the convention was a discreet means of satisfying the demands of the ritual without bloodletting (to strengthen this hypothesis, it should be observed that the "corpse" of the victim was conventionally displayed to the spectator in the concluding episode). It has also been suggested that the Greek tragic costume, a full-length robe, boots with elevated soles and heels, and an enormous mask, permitted only the most stately movements. But the reasons are less important than the effect.

The effect of the conventions of Greek dramaturgy was to emphasize not action but reaction, not what happened but the characters' response to the unfolding situation. Actors thus found themselves concerned with doing, but more importantly with the reasons for doing, with motivation. And since the plots in which they are involved represent the great archetypal relations of man and man, man and the state, man and the gods, the motivations assume the aspect of universality. They are as recognizable, as valid, for the contemporary audience as for their original spectators in Athens, five centuries before the Christian era. Indeed, psychology, the most recent scientific attempt to explain man to himself, has drawn much of its iconology from these dramatic extrapolations of primitive myths.

Of the hundreds of plays written and performed at the dramatic festivals in the fifth century, only thirty-two survive in a more or less complete state. Of these, seven are by Aeschylus (525–456 B.C.), seven by Sophocles (496–406 B.C.), and eighteen by Euripides (480–406 B.C.). Each play is based on a history or legend whose outlines were familiar to the audience, and each adheres with considerable faithfulness to the original story. The playwright was at liberty, however, to alter details and shift emphases to accord with the theme, the central meaning, of the action as he understood it. Thus Aeschylus can structure the action of *The Libation-Bearers* to portray Electra (and her brother Orestes) as victims of an unreasonable tribal law of blood vengeance, while Sophocles will rearrange the structure to reveal Electra as the captive of what might today be labeled a neurotic obsession, and Euripides in his turn will rearrange the incidents to expose the wayward cruelty growing out of passion and emotion.

It is a significant accident that more plays of Euripides have survived than those of Aeschylus and Sophocles combined. The youngest of the three masters, he is less concerned with moral and philosophical issues than with the pain and terror and rage that are to some degree the daily temptations of all men. There is wisdom in Aeschylus, and irony in Sophocles, but the exaltation of Euripides is in the struggle against overwhelming forces, human or divine, and the depiction in infinite detail of the capacity for irrational self-assertion.

Although one of the last plays of the great repertory of Greek tragedy to be produced, *The Bacchae* (405 B.C.) is the proper introduction to the understanding of dramatic art. It is the one surviving serious play in which Dionysos himself is a central figure and it represents, not altogether favorably, the ecstasies of his followers, the Bacchantes. King Pentheus, the opponent and victim of the god, can be taken as a conventional figure, the man of pride (*hubris*), the shortsighted ruler with complete conviction of farsightedness. However the two old men who capitulate to Dionysos, as much from caution as conviction, must have appeared ridiculous as they draped their aging bones with ceremonial skins, tottered into the bacchic dance, and raised their cracked voices in dithyrambic chants. And Pentheus is not presented without sympathy.

Rigid he is, and full of the assurance of position, yet if we compare him with the Creon of *Antigone* we are permitted to see in Pentheus' reactions certain lesser human failings (curiosity, for instance) that invoke our tolerance. But most important for understanding drama, Euripides is careful to show us—in the third episode—how a man becomes possessed by a god, how he becomes an impersonator, how he assumes a character quite other than his own. The degree, the absoluteness, of Pentheus' possession should be contrasted with the "acting" of Cadmus and Tiresias who go through the expected motions while remaining carefully aware of what they are about.

It is hardly appropriate at this point to do more than indicate that Euripides has here made the earliest presentation of the argument growing out of what was later to be called the "Paradox of the Actor." Is the actor at all times the self-conscious artist? Does he lose himself in the character he assumes? Is he, paradoxically, character and artist at the same time? It is, however, not inappropriate to observe that Euripides has captured for all time the origin of drama when his proud, masculine autocrat is willingly/ unwillingly transported into a frenzied female devotee before being torn apart by his own mother and her fellow enthusiasts.

The god of many names was omnipotent, and the gift he bestowed on his followers could mean ecstasy, the release from pain and fear; but it could also mean frenzy, the irrational pursuit of wanton violence. The drama has equal potential for good or ill, for ecstasy or frenzy, for exaltation or destruction. The association of the drama with Dionysos is too lacking in detailed records to be acceptable to scientific historians, but the mythic relationship is too illuminating to question.

The translation reprinted here was originally made at the end of the nineteenth century by Professor Alexander Kerr. It has been revised by the present editor in the light of the discoveries of recent scholarship and modern principles of translation.

Characters

DIONYSOS

TIRESIAS
a blind prophet

CADMUS
former king of Thebes

PENTHEUS
his grandson, king of Thebes

AGAVE
daughter of CADMUS, *mother of* PENTHEUS

SEVERAL MESSENGERS

CHORUS OF WOMEN
followers of DIONYSOS

SCENE: *Thebes, before the palace of* PENTHEUS. *At the center a smoldering altar, the tomb of* SEMELE, *mother of* DIONYSOS.

THE BACCHAE

Euripides

PROLOGUE

DIONYSOS. Hither to Thebes I, Dionysos, come
      Whom the daughter of Cadmus, Semele,
      Brought down by fiery lightning, bore to Zeus;
      And now a god in mortal shape I stand
      By Dirce's fountain and Ismenos' flood.
      And here my thunder-smitten mother's tomb
      I see hard by the house whose crumbling halls
      Still smoulder with celestial fire unquenched,
      Hera's[1] eternal cruelty to my mother.
      All praise to Cadmus who hath made this place   10
      His daughter's shrine; but I have wreathed it round
      On every side with foliage of the vine.
        Quitting the fields of Lydia rich in gold
      And Phrygia, through the Persians' sunburnt plains,
      The Bactrian walls, the Mede's inclement land,
      I took my way, through Araby the blest,
      And through all Asia which by the salt sea
      Extends, with teeming fair-towered cities holding
      Greek and barbarian tribes together blent;
      And there my choral dance and mystic rites   20
      Giving, that men might own me for a god,
      I visit first of all this land of Hellas.
        But here in Greece Thebes first I filled with shouts
      Of revelers, their forms in fawn-skins robed,

---

[1] Hera (Juno), the wife of Zeus (Jupiter), suspecting the god's infidelity with Semele, caused Zeus to visit his mistress in "all the splendor of a god." The earth maiden was consumed by the god's lightning, but her unborn child (Dionysos) was rescued by his father and placed in his thigh until the appointed time for his birth. Later in the play, Euripides disputes this story, but it is the common explanation of the meaning of the hymns to Dionysos, the dithyrambs (i.e., twice-born).

And put into their hands the thyrsus wreathed
With ivy, since my mother's sisters basely
Said Dionysos was no son of Zeus,
But Semele wedded to a mortal lover
Charged upon Zeus her fault, unchastity,
By craft of Cadmus, and for this, the lie
About her marriage, Zeus, they vowed, destroyed her.
Therefore I drove them raging from the house,
And frenzied now they hold the mountain height;
Robes of my worship I forced them to wear,   10
And all of womankind among the Thebans,
All women maddened from their homes I sent;
And there together joined with Cadmus' daughters
They sit beneath green pines on roofless rocks.
For to her sorrow must this city learn
That she knows nothing of my Bacchic rites;
And my mother Semele I must defend
By showing men the god she bore to Zeus.

   Now Cadmus his prerogative and power
Bestows on Pentheus, from his daughter[2] born,   20
Who fights against the gods in slighting me,
Depriving me of offerings and prayers.
Wherefore I'll prove myself a god to him
And all the Thebans; then to other lands,
Leaving my labors here well done, depart,
Showing myself; but if Thebes angered seek
To drag the Bacchanals from the mountain down,
Leading my Maenads I will join the fray.
And to this end, transformed in shape and figure,
I have assumed the likeness of a man.   30

   Exiles from Tmolos, Lydia's mountain wall,
My revel-band, my women, whom I brought
From lands barbaric as my ministers,
Take ye the timbrels of the Phrygian realm,
Devised by mother Rhea[3] and myself;
And marching here around the royal house
Of Pentheus, beat them, so that Thebes may heed.
But with the Bacchanals I will join the dance,
Seeking Cithaeron's dells where they are hid.

[2] Agave.
[3] The mother of Zeus, frequently identified with the Asiatic goddess, Cybele.

PARODOS

[Enter CHORUS, *Asian women, followers of Dionysos.]*

STROPHE I

CHORUS.   Away from the Asian land,
Departing from Tmolos divine, I urge on
For Bromios[4] labor delightful and toil
All painless, with revel-shouts honoring Bacchus.

ANTISTROPHE I

Who is this in the way? Who is this?
To the palace in haste let him go, and let all
Keep silence and worship, for I will exalt
Dionysos with song, as my custom has been.

STROPHE II

O blest the happy man who knows
The mysteries divine,   10
Who is sincere in life
And consecrate in soul,
With holy purifyings
Upon the mountains keeping Bacchic rites,
Keeping the lawful orgies too
Of the great mother Cybele,
And brandishing the thyrsus,
And with the ivy crowned,
Thus Dionysos serves.
Go, go, ye Bacchanals,   20
Restoring Dionysos,
The god-descended god,
Yea from the Phrygian mountains Bromios
To the broad highways of the Grecian land:

ANTISTROPHE II

Whom erst his mother, in the stress
Of childbirth's pangs brought on
By the winged shaft of Zeus,
An outcast from the womb
Brought forth, and quitted life
Touched by the thunderbolt's descending stroke.   30
But straightway in a cell of birth
Zeus Cronides[5] received him then,
For he hides him in his thigh
And with clasps of gold confines him,

---

[4] Another name for Dionysos. Sophocles, in *Antigone*, properly calls him "god of many names."

[5] i.e., the son of Cronos.

From Hera safe concealed.
And he bore the hornèd god
What time the fates matured him,
And wreathed his head with crowns
Of serpents, whence the Maenads round their hair
Fling this wild booty captured in the chase.

STROPHE III

Thebes, nurse of Semele,
Put on the ivy crown;
Bloom, bloom, with garlands green,
With smilax fruited fair,   10
And with boughs of oak or fir
Revel in Bacchic rage,
And your robes of dappled fawn-skins deck
With tufts of silvery locks of wool:
And round the wanton thyrsi consecrate
Yourselves; soon all the land shall join the dance,
When Bromios shall lead his revel-bands
Up to the mountain's summit, where awaits
A multitude of women
From looms and shuttles driven,   20
Made mad by Dionysos.

ANTISTROPHE III

O home of the Curetes,[6]
And ye all-sacred haunts
Of Crete where Zeus was born,
Where the tri-plumed Corybantes
In caves for me devised
This leathern drum tight drawn;
Then with its furious sound they joined
Wild notes of sweet-toned Phrygian flutes,
And in the mother Rhea's hands they placed it,   30
A din to match the Bacchanals' revel-shouts:
And by entreaty from the goddess mother
The raging satyrs gained the tympanum,
And in the dances joined
Of the trieteric[7] feasts,
The delights of Dionysos.

EPODE

Glad on the mountains is the worshiper
When from swift revel-bands
Upon the earth he falls,

---

[6] Demigods who protected the infant Zeus against his father Cronos, who swallowed his children to guard against their overthrowing him.
[7] Triennial.

Wearing the sacred fawn-skin robe, and thirsting
For blood of goats, eating with joy raw flesh,
Climbing the Phrygian and the Lydian mountains.
But Bromios the leader is, Evoe!
Earth flows with wine, milk, nectar of the bees,
And smoke of Syrian frankincense ascends.
And the Bacchant leader, holding
His flaming torch of fir
Upon the thyrsus, darts
Inciting to the race and to the dance   10
The wanderers, and rousing them with shouts,
As to the air he tosses his bright tresses.
And added to the revel-cries
Such words as these he shouts aloud:
On! On! ye Bacchanals,
Beauty of Tmolos with its streams of gold,
Sing ye of Dionysos,
Your voices with the deep-toned timbrels joined,
The Evian god in Bacchic strains exalting
With Phrygian shouts and cries,   20
Whene'er the sweet-toned holy flute
Sounds forth its sacred sportive airs,
Responsive to the Maenads as they wander
Off to the mountains; and right gladsome then,
As a young colt beside its grazing mother,
The Bacchanal bounds forward with swift foot.

SCENE ONE

[*Enter* TIRESIAS, *a blind old man.*]

TIRESIAS. Hail, porter! from the palace summon forth
Cadmus, Agenor's son, who quitting Sidon
Girded with towers this city of the Thebans.
Go, tell him that Tiresias is waiting.   30
He knows why I am come, the convenant
Which I who am old have made with him still older,
To bind the Bacchic wands, to wear the fawn-skins,
And with the ivy-sprays to crown the head.
[CADMUS *enters from the palace.*]

CADMUS. O dearest friend! for hearing in the house
Thy voice, I knew it, the wise voice of a sage!
Lo! here I come wearing the sacred garb;
For needs must he who is my daughter's son,
Lord Dionysos, shown to men a god,

As far as in me lies be raised to greatness.
Where must we lead the dance? Where stay the foot
And shake the hoary locks? Both aged men
Are we, Tiresias: as thou art skilled,
Expound to me; for I will never weary
By night or day the earth with the thyrsus smiting;
In our delightsome pleasure we have grown
Forgetful of our years.
TIRESIAS. Thy joy is mine;
I too grow young, I will attempt the dance.   10
CADMUS. Shall we then go in a chariot to the mountain?
TIRESIAS. The god would not have equal honor thus.
CADMUS. We both are old, but I will be thy guide.
TIRESIAS. The god will lead us thither without toil.
CADMUS. Shall we alone of the city dance to Bacchus?
TIRESIAS. Yes, we alone are wise, the others foolish.
CADMUS. Too long we linger; hold my hand in thine.
TIRESIAS. Well spoken; firmly grasp my hand.
CADMUS. I born a mortal do not scorn the gods.
TIRESIAS. Against the gods we do not match our wisdom.   20
Our sires' traditions of a faith as old
As time no argument shall overthrow,
Not even when wisdom comes from subtle thought.
Some one will say that I disgrace my age,
In that with ivy crowned I go to dance.
Not so, the god hath fixed no test of age,
Both young and old must mingle in the rite;
But equal honor he would have from all,
Nor chooses worshipers from favored classes.
CADMUS. Since thou, Tiresias, dost not see the light,   30
I shall become thy seer, to speak for thee.
Lo, to the palace hastes Echion's son,
Pentheus, by me made ruler of the land.
He shudders! what mischance will he recount?
[Enter PENTHEUS. *He does not see the old men.*]
PENTHEUS. Late absent from this land and just returned,
I hear of strange trouble in the city.
Our women have departed from their homes
For their feigned revels; on thick-shaded mountains
They rush like furies, honoring with dances
Bacchus, the new-made god, whoever that is;   40
Amid each festive throng the mixing-bowls
Stand crowned, while cowering in the wilderness,
One here, one there, they yield to secret love,
Pretending to be Maenads, but in truth

They worship Aphrodite more than Bacchus.
All whom I've captured, my servants keep
Safe in the prison, with fettered hands;
But those still free I'll hunt down from the mountain,
Agave, her who bore me to Echion,
Autonoë, the mother of Actaeon,
And Ino—these made fast in iron bonds
I soon from their vile orgies will restrain.
    They say there is a stranger hither come,
A juggling wizard from the Lydian land,   10
With ruddy face, with fragrant golden curls,
The grace of Aphrodite in his eyes,
Who day and night holds converse with the throng,
Feigning to teach young maidens Bacchic rites.
But if I capture him within this house,
From making the thyrsus ring and his hair stream back
I'll stop him, severing his neck and trunk.
He claims that Dionysos is a god,
Sewn up of old within the thigh of Zeus;
But the flaming bolt consumed the child with the mother,   20
Who falsely called herself the wife of Zeus.
Do not these deeds, this outrage of the stranger
Whoe'er he be, deserve the fatal halter?
[*Notices* TIRESIAS *and* CADMUS.]
    But here another wonder I behold,
The seer Tiresias wearing dappled fawn-skins,
My mother's father too, great cause of mirth,
With a ferule reveling—father, I'm ashamed
To see your hoary age bereft of sense.
My mother's sire, the ivy from thy head
Cast off, and from the thyrsus free thy hand.   30
Thy counsel this, Tiresias; thou wilt reap
More gain from auspices and offerings
By introducing this new god to men.
Did not thy hoary age deliver thee,
Thou wouldst be sitting 'mid the Bacchanals bound,
For bringing in vile mysteries: for where
To women at the banquets wine gives joy,
Naught in their worship call I good and pure.
CHORUS. Words impious! dost not, sire, revere the gods,
    Or Cadmus, sower of the earth-born crop?   40
    Dost thou born of Echion shame thy race?
TIRESIAS. When the sage gains fair subject for discourse,
    'T is no hard task for him to reason well;
    But thou appearing wise hast a glib tongue,

Yet in thy words there is no wisdom found.
But the man bold of speech and eloquent
Proves a bad citizen for want of sense.
   Now this new deity, whom thou dost mock,
Shall have such power as I can ne'er express
In Hellas. Youth! there are two things by man
Accounted first; the deity Demeter
(Or Mother Earth perchance thou fain wilt call her)
With solid food sustains the life of man;
But other needs this son of Semele   10
Has met, has found and introduced to mortals
The flowing draught which brings release from pain
To wretched men when they are filled with wine,
And gives them sleep, relief from daily ills,
Nor is there other remedy for troubles.
'T is he, a god, makes peace with the other gods.
And thus through him do men enjoy rich blessings.
Him dost thou mock as sewn up in the thigh
Of Zeus? I will reveal to thee this truth.
What time Zeus snatched him from the lightning's flame,   20
And to Olympos bore the infant god,
Hera desired to cast him forth from heaven;
But Zeus contrived against her like a god:
He took a part of the earth-encircling ether
And made of this a pledge, but Dionysos
He saved from Hera's rage; and men soon tell
That he was nurtured in the thigh of Zeus;
By interchange of words they made the fable,
Because the god had been a pledge to Hera.
A prophet is this god; for Bacchic rage   30
And madness hold large gift of prophecy;
And when the god in power enters the body,
He makes the enthusiast[8] tell what is to be.
And in the might of Ares too he shares;
For a host standing armed in line of battle
Panic oft scatters ere they touch the spear;
And this is also madness sent from Bacchus.
Thou yet shalt see him even on Delphic rocks,
Bounding with pine torch o'er the twin-peaked summit,
Swaying and brandishing his Bacchic wand,   40
Grown great in Hellas. Pentheus, heed my words!
Presume not that mere power prevails with men,
Nor, even if with thy mind diseased thou think it,

---

[8] Literally, the man into whom the god has entered.

Think thyself wise at all; within the land
Receive the god, honor him with libations,
Join in the sacred dance and crown thy head.
It is not Dionysos who will force
The women to be chaste, but self-control,
Constant in all things, this is nature's gift:
Consider this: even in the Bacchic revels
She who is modest will be undefiled.
Lo, thou art glad when many throng the gates,
Glad too when Thebes exalts the name of Pentheus;   10
So he, I think, delights in being honored.
    I then and Cadmus, whom thou dost deride,
Will crown our heads with ivy and will dance,
A hoary pair, yet must we join the dance,
Nor heeding thee will I assault the god.
The fell disorder of thy mind no drugs
Can cure, yet shalt thou not lack remedies.

CHORUS. Thou dost not with thy words, old man, shame Phoebus,[9]
    And honoring Bromios, that great god, thou art wise.

CADMUS. My son, well hath Tiresias counseled thee;   20
    Abide with us, within the pale of custom,
For now thy mind's distraught, thy wit is folly.
If as thou dost say, he is no god,
Yet call him god, and tell the glorious falsehood,
That the child of Semele may be thought divine,
And honor come to us and all our house.
Thou dost behold Actaeon's wretched fate,
Whom ravenous hounds which he had fed and fondled
Tore in the meadows limb from limb for boasting
That in the chase he distanced Artemis.   30
Lest thus thou fare, let me with ivy crown
Thy head; with us give honor to the god.

PENTHEUS. Lay not thy hand on me, thyself go revel,
    Nor make me share thy imbecility.
But on this teacher who hath made thee mad
I will take vengeance. Quick! let some one haste,
Approach his seat where he takes auguries,
With levers lift it, turn it upside down,
And all things in confusion throw together,
Giving his fillets to the winds and storms;   40
For by this course I best shall torture him.
    Go others of you through the town, seek out
The effeminate stranger who with new disease

[9] Apollo, the god of the sun.

Afflicts our women and dishonors marriage.
And if ye catch him, bring him hither bound,
To die by stoning, righteous penalty,
When he has seen in Thebes a bitter revel.
TIRESIAS. O wretched man! thou knowest not what thou sayest,
Now art thou crazed and thou wast daft before.
Let us go, Cadmus, and beseech the god,
Both for this brutish prince and for the city,
To bring upon us no calamity.
Follow me, bring the staff with ivy wreathed;   10
And hold me upright, as I'll do for thee.
Two old men fallen were shame; but let it pass;
For we must worship Bacchus, son of Zeus.
    But see that Pentheus bring not sorrow, Cadmus,
Into thy palace:—not as prophet now
Deal I with oracles, but with simple facts;
For folly is the language of a fool.
[*They hobble away.*]

STASIMON ONE

STROPHE I

CHORUS. Thou holy one, queen in the heaven,
Thou goddess, who over the earth
Art borne on thy pinions of gold,   20
Dost thou hear what this Pentheus hath said,
Dost thou witness the impious crime,
The outrage on Bromios wrought,
On Semele's son, who, where garlands are bright
At banquets, is first of the gods,
The immortals? And this is his task,
In the revels to order the dance,
To rejoice at the sound of the flute
And to banish all harassing cares,
When joy that is born of the wine   30
Comes in at the feast of the gods,
When at banquets with ivy bedecked
The bowl round the guests throws the spirit of sleep.

ANTISTROPHE I

Of speech that defies all restraint,
Of folly that violates law,
The outcome is ruin at last.
But a life filled with quiet and peace
And prudence with reverence joined
Unruffled and steadfast remain,

And a house in security keep; for afar
Though the gods have their homes in the ether,
Yet behold they the doings of men.
'T is not wisdom to be overwise
And to dwell on the thoughts that to man
Are forbidden; for short is our life,
And so he who pursues lofty ends
Shall fail of the good that is near.
These ways are the ways of the fools,
Of the mortals, I trow, of right reason bereft.   10

STROPHE II

O might I betake me to Cyprus,
The island of Aphrodite,
Where, filling with joy the soul
Of mortal man, dwell the Loves;
Come to the land which the manifold
Streams of a river remote,
Streams never fed by showers enrich.
But where is the fairest realm of all,
Pieria, home of the muses,
Majestic slope of Olympos?   20
Thither conduct me, O Bromios, Bromios,
Leader of Bacchanals, Evian god.
There are the Graces, and there dwells Desire;
And there too it is lawful to celebrate Bacchic rites.

ANTISTROPHE II

This deity Zeus-descended
Ever in feast rejoices,
And wealth-bringing Peace he loves,
Savior of young lives.
Both to the rich gives he equally
And to the poor to enjoy   30
The pleasures of wine that banish pain;
But hateful to him the man who scorns,
In the day and the glad night seasons,
To live the life of the blessed;
Wise is it mind and heart safely to guard against
Men who have over-much learning attained.
But what the scantly taught multitude
Always sanctions and practices, this I too would accept.

SCENE TWO

[*A* SERVANT *enters, followed by* DIONYSOS *surrounded by* GUARDS.]
SERVANT. Here are we, Pentheus, we have caught this game
        For which you sent us, not in vain we followed,
        We found our quarry mild; he did not flee,
        But offered willingly his hands, nor paled
        Nor changed the color of his ruddy cheek,
        But laughing bade us bind and lead away,
        And waited, making thus my task no burden.
        Awe-struck I said: "Sir, I arrest thee not
        Of my free will, but by command of Pentheus."
        But all the Bacchanals whom thou hadst seized,   10
        Confined and fettered in the common prison,
        Released from bonds far off unto the groves
        They bound, invoking Bromios the god;
        Self-moved from off their feet the fetters dropped,
        And keys without mortal hand unlocked the door.
        So, filled with many wonders comes this man
        Hither to Thebes. The rest must be thy care.
PENTHEUS. Let loose his hands; for hemmed in by my toils,
        Swift as he is, he never can escape me.
        Stranger, the women think thee fair of form,   20
        And to seduce them thou art come to Thebes;
        Unlike those of a wrestler, thy locks are long,
        Beside thy cheek thick showered, warm with desire;
        Thy skin too thou with care preservest white,
        Not by the help of sunlight but of shade,
        By thy beauty making Aphrodite captive.
        First then declare to me thy name and race.
DIONYSOS. I need no boast—easy is that to tell.
        Perchance thou knowest by hearsay flowery Tmolos.
PENTHEUS. Yes; that which girds around the city of Sardis.   30
DIONYSOS. Thence do I come, Lydia my fatherland.
PENTHEUS. Why dost thou bring these mystic rites to Greece?
DIONYSOS. 'T was Dionysos, son of Zeus, who brought me.
PENTHEUS. And is there yonder a Zeus who gets new gods?
DIONYSOS. No, 't was the Zeus who married Semele here.
PENTHEUS. By night, or openly, did he compel thee?
DIONYSOS. 'T was eye to eye, and he taught me sacred rites.
PENTHEUS. What is the nature of thy mysteries?
DIONYSOS. The god's initiates alone can know.
PENTHEUS. What profit bring they to the worshipers?   40
DIONYSOS. Thou canst not hear, but it is worth the knowing.

PENTHEUS. Well hast thou tricked this out to make me eager.
DIONYSOS. The mysteries abhor an impious man.
PENTHEUS. Thou plainly saw'st the god, thou say'st, how looked he?
DIONYSOS. Just as he wished; 't was not for me to order.
PENTHEUS. This too thou hast neatly turned, declaring naught.
DIONYSOS. He who speaks wisdom shall to a fool seem foolish.
PENTHEUS. Hast thou brought the god to Thebes, his first abode?
DIONYSOS. All the barbarians honor him with dances.
PENTHEUS. Yes, they in folly far surpass the Greeks.
DIONYSOS. In this they are wiser, though their customs differ.   10
PENTHEUS. Dost thou worship in the night or in the day?
DIONYSOS. By night most often; darkness bringeth awe.
PENTHEUS. This for the women is a cheat and bane.
DIONYSOS. By day too one may compass wantonness.
PENTHEUS. For thy base juggling thou must make amends.
DIONYSOS. For thy folly thou, and thy sin against the god.
PENTHEUS. How bold our Bacchant is, how skilled in speech!
DIONYSOS. Declare my fate; what evil wilt thou do me?
PENTHEUS. First then thy delicate curls I will cut off.
DIONYSOS. My locks are sacred, to the god devoted.   20
PENTHEUS. Out of thy hands next yield that thyrsus up.
DIONYSOS. Take it thyself; I bear the wand of Bacchus.
PENTHEUS. I'll guard thy body too in prison walls.
DIONYSOS. The god himself will free me when I wish.
PENTHEUS. Yes, when thou call'st him mid thy Bacchanals.
DIONYSOS. Even now what I endure, being near, he sees.
PENTHEUS. But where? for he is hidden from my eyes.
DIONYSOS. With me; but thou being impious dost not see him.
PENTHEUS. Seize him—this man jeers at me and Thebes.
DIONYSOS. I sound of mind bid thee insane not bind me.   30
PENTHEUS. But I outranking thee in power say, Bind him.
DIONYSOS. Scornful, thy deed thou know'st not nor thyself.
PENTHEUS. Pentheus, Agave's son, my sire Echion.
DIONYSOS. Thou hast a name to match a hapless fate.
PENTHEUS. Go—near the horse-stalls make him prisoner,
That on thick darkness he may set his eyes.
There dance; but these the women thou hast brought,
Partners in crime, I will either sell apart,
Or, stopping from this din and noise of the drum
Their hand, I'll keep them servants at the loom.   40
DIONYSOS. I go; for what is not my fate I ne'er
May suffer. For these insults Dionysos,
Whose being thou deniest, shall requite thee.
For in wronging me, thou art dragging him to prison.
[*Exeunt.*]

STASIMON TWO

CHORUS. Hail! thou, Acheloös' daughter,
　　Hail! Dirce[10], fair maiden adored;
　　Yea thou in thy fountains of yore
　　The scion of Zeus didst receive,
　　When him in his thigh from the fire
　　Immortal the Father Zeus
　　Hid away, giving voice to these words:
　　Come, my Dithyrambos, and enter
　　This retreat which thy father provides;
　　I proclaim thee, O Bacchus, to Thebes   10
　　To be called by this name Dithyrambos.
　　But thou, O Dirce, the blest,
　　Dost reject me who hold in thy land
　　My revels with garlands adorned.
　　Why repel me? why flee from my sight?
　　By the grace of the clustering vine,
　　By the gift of the lord Dionysos,
　　Hereafter for Bromios yet shalt thou care.

　　Ah me! what implacable wrath
　　Does the child of the earth now display,   20
　　The child from the dragon erst born,
　　Even Pentheus, he whom Echion,
　　His earth-born father, begot,
　　A savage-eyed monster, no man
　　In humanity's likeness, but fierce
　　As a giant at war with the gods.
　　Since myself, who our Bromios serve,
　　With cords he will quickly bind fast,
　　And already within he detains
　　My own fellow-reveler deep   30
　　In the gloom of the dungeon concealed.
　　Dost thou see this, divine son of Zeus,
　　Dionysos, thy heralds involved
　　In a warfare 'gainst violence waged?
　　Come, waving thy golden-hued wand,
　　O king, down the slopes of Olympos,
　　And restrain thou the pride of the furious man.

　　O where on Nysa, the lair

10 Antiope, like Semele, was an earth maiden beloved of Zeus.

Of wild beasts, art thou wielding thy wand
While thy revelers dance, Dionysos,
Or on the Corycian heights?
Or perhaps in the shady retreats
Of Olympos, the thick-wooded haunts,
Where Orpheus once playing the lyre
With his music assembled the trees,
Called round him wild beasts of the wood.
O happy Pierian land,
The Evian god honors thee,   10
And he in the chorus will come
With revels, and, passing beyond
The Axios-torrent, will lead
The Maenads that whirl in the dance,
And will pass o'er the Lydias, source
Of prosperity, giver of wealth
Unto mortals, the stream which I hear
With its waters the brightest of all
Enriches the land famed for steeds.

DIONYSOS [*within the palace*]. Attend, attend to my voice;   20
    Ho Bacchanals, Bacchanals, hear!
FIRST SEMICHORUS. Who is here? Whence and what is this voice,
    This summons to me from the Evian god?
DIONYSOS. What ho! Give ear! I call again,
    The son of Zeus and Semele.
SECOND SEMICHORUS. All hail to thee, our lord and master!
    O Bromios, our Bromios,
    Come thou and join our revel-band.
CHORAGOS. O, awful quaking of Earth's floor!
    Alas! alas!   30
    Soon shall the house of Pentheus
    Be shaken to its fall.
    In the palace Dionysos walks;
    Honor him as a god.
CHORUS. Oh! him we do adore.
FIRST SEMICHORUS. See where the marble architraves
    Are reeling yonder; Bromios
    Within the house will raise the shout of triumph.
DIONYSOS [*within*]. Kindle the lurid lightning torch;
    Burn with devouring fire the halls of Pentheus.   40
SECOND SEMICHORUS. Alas! alas!
    Dost thou not see the burning, nor behold
    Around the sacred tomb of Semele
    The flame of the lightning's bolt sent down by Zeus,
    Which she the thunder-stricken left at death?

PENTHEUS. Each gate around I bid you close and bar.
DIONYSOS. But why? do not the gods o'erleap the walls?
PENTHEUS. Wise, wise art thou, save where thou shouldst be wise.
DIONYSOS. Where need is greatest, there am I found wise.
　　　　　But first attend and learn the words of him
　　　　　Who from the mountain tidings brings to thee;
　　　　　Here, be assured, I wait, I will not fly.
　　　　　[*A* MESSENGER *enters in the costume of a shepherd.*]
MESSENGER. Pentheus, thou ruler of this Theban land,
　　　　　I come before thee, from Cithaeron yonder,
　　　　　Where the glistening flakes of pure snow never cease.   10
PENTHEUS. With what urgent message art thou come?
MESSENGER. The furious Bacchanals, who from your gates
　　　　　Darted in frenzy forth with naked limbs,
　　　　　I have beheld, and now am come, O king,
　　　　　To tell thee and the state how strange their deeds.
　　　　　But I would learn if boldly I shall speak,
　　　　　Or with reserve, to thee of things done yonder.
　　　　　For I do fear, O king, thy fiery spirit,
　　　　　Its keen resentment and imperiousness.
PENTHEUS. Speak, since from me thou shalt not suffer harm;   20
　　　　　But the worse thy story of the Bacchanals
　　　　　Shall be, so much the more I'll punish him,
　　　　　This man who has with his arts beguiled our women.
MESSENGER. The herds of grazing cattle had begun
　　　　　To climb the mountain crag just when the sun
　　　　　Sent forth his morning rays to warm the earth,
　　　　　When I saw three bands, three choruses of women:
　　　　　One troop Autonoë marshaled, thy own mother
　　　　　Agave led the second, Ino, the third.
　　　　　They all were slumbering with limbs relaxed,   30
　　　　　Some leaning 'gainst the boughs of the silver fir,
　　　　　Some with their heads upon the oakleaves resting,
　　　　　In careless guise but modest, nor are they
　　　　　Drunk, as thou say'st, with wine and flute-notes, roaming
　　　　　The forest wilds alone in search of Cypris.
　　　　　Then stood thy mother 'mid the Bacchanals,
　　　　　And raised the cry to rouse themselves from sleep,
　　　　　As she heard the lowing of the hornèd steers.
　　　　　And from their eyes shaking off balmy sleep
　　　　　They sprang erect, a sight of marvelous grace,   40
　　　　　The young and old, the virgins still unwed.
　　　　　And first their locks they showered upon their shoulders,
　　　　　Tied up their fawn-skins—all of those whose bands
　　　　　Had been unloosed—and girt the dappled skins

With wreaths of serpents that did lick their cheeks.
And others, holding in their arms a roe
Or wild wolf's cubs, with white milk suckled them,
Those who from recent childbirth had swollen breasts
Leaving their babes; and on their heads they placed
Garlands of ivy, oak and flowery smilax.
And one her thyrsus taking smote the rock,
Whence gushed a spring of sparkling water forth;
Another with her ferule struck the earth,
And the god set up for her a fount of wine.   10
And all who for a white draught had desire
Scraped with their fingertips the earth and found
Rich streams of milk; while from their ivy wands
Sweet drops of liquid honey were distilled.
Hadst thou been there, the god whom now thou blamest
Thou wouldst, on seeing this, have sought in prayer.
    And now we herdsmen with the shepherds met
For mutual debate among ourselves,
Since what they did was strange and marvelous.
A city stroller, skilled in the art of speech,   20
Said before all: "O, ye whose dwelling is
On the sacred upland levels, shall we chase
Agave, mother of Pentheus, from her orgies,
And do the king a pleasure?" This we thought
Well said; so, hidden by the leaves of shrubs,
We lay in ambush. They at the set time
Brandished the thyrsus in their revelries,
Iacchus, Bromios, the son of Zeus
With one voice calling; with them danced the mountain,
Danced the wild beasts; all was awake and moving.   30
    By chance near me Agave leaps and dances;
And forth I sprang intent on seizing her,
Leaving the thicket where we had lain concealed.
And loud she cried: "Ho, my fleet-footed hounds!
We are hunted by these men: come follow me,
Follow ye, armed with the thyrsi in your hands."
We therefore fleeing them escaped being torn
In pieces by the Bacchanals. They then,
Their hands unarmed, rushed on the pasturing cattle.
One, by her strength of hands, you might have seen   40
Hold fast a bellowing cow with swollen udder,
And some were tearing heifers into fragments.
You might have seen their ribs or cloven hoofs
Tossed up and down, while pieces which hung suspended
All stained with blood, dripped 'neath the silver firs.

The wanton bulls, that glared along their horns
Erstwhile in fury, then were flung to earth,
By the countless hands of maidens overpowered.
And the flesh that covered them was torn asunder
Ere thou couldst close the lids of thy royal eyes.
And they go uplifted in their flight like birds
O'er the low plains that by the Asopus' streams
Produce abundant harvests for the Thebans;
Next Hysiae and Erythrae, nestling low
Beneath Cithaeron's crag, like enemies   10
Assaulting, all things there pell-mell they scattered;
The children from their homes they snatched away;
Whate'er they placed upon their shoulders clung
Unbound with cords, nor fell to the black earth,
Not even brass or iron; on their locks
They carried fire that burned not. But the people,
Robbed by the Bacchanals, furious rushed to arms;
What now befell was a strange sight, O king.
For the men's pointed weapons drew no blood;
But they, shooting the thyrsi from their hands,   20
Gave wounds and turned the enemy in flight,
Women pursuing men, with help divine.
So to their starting place they went again,
Back to the fountains which the god sent up;
Washed off the blood; while from their cheeks the snakes
With their tongues licked clean the blood-drops on their skin.
    This god, whoe'er he is, receive, O master,
In our city. Great in other things is he,
And this too, as I learn, they tell of him,
That he gave the pain-assuaging vine to mortals.   30
But when we have no wine, no love is left
Nor other pleasure to the race of men.
CHORUS. I shrink from speaking freely
    Before the king, yet I must speak:
    Dionysos is the peer of any god.
PENTHEUS. Already is this Bacchic insolence kindling,
    Like fire hard by, a shame in the eyes of Hellas.
    We must not halt: On to the Electran gate!
    Bid muster all the men that bear the shield
    And all the warriors mounted on fleet steeds   40
    And all who brandish bucklers, those who twang
    The bowstrings, since against the Bacchanals
    We go to war: for it is past enduring,
    From women's hands to suffer what we suffer.
DIONYSOS. My words, no doubt, do not convince thee, Pentheus;

Yet I, ill used by thee, advise thee well,
Bid thee desist from warfare with the god.
Be quiet! Bromios will not brook thy driving
His Maenads from the mountains where they revel.
PENTHEUS. Counsel me not! thou art free from bonds; let this
Content thee! Else I fetter thee again.
DIONYSOS. I would bring him offerings, rather than in anger
Kick 'gainst the pricks, a man at war with a god.
PENTHEUS. I'll offer—my offering: women, as they merit,
Stirring up war within Cithaeron's dells.   10
DIONYSOS. Ye all shall flee: shame would it be to turn
Your bronze-wrought shields before the Bacchanals' wands.
PENTHEUS. Awkward to manage is our stranger here,
Doing or suffering he will not be quiet.
DIONYSOS. This still admits, my friend, a happy issue.
PENTHEUS. How shall I gain it? Serving my own slaves?
DIONYSOS. I will bring the women hither without weapons.
PENTHEUS. Ah me! thou art planning now some wile against me.
DIONYSOS. But what if I would save thee by mine arts?
PENTHEUS. Your compact this, that you may always revel.   20
DIONYSOS. Well, be assured my league was with the god.
PENTHEUS. Bring ye my armor; and do thou cease speaking.
DIONYSOS. Ha! wouldst thou see them seated on the hills?
PENTHEUS. Yes, for the sight I'd give vast weight of gold.
DIONYSOS. Why has such eagerness for this possessed thee?
PENTHEUS. To their sorrow I would see them drunk with wine.
DIONYSOS. Yet wouldst thou gladly see what will bring thee pain?
PENTHEUS. Yes, sitting in silence 'neath the silver firs.
DIONYSOS. They will trace thee out, e'en though thou go in secret.
PENTHEUS. Openly then; this thou hast spoken well.   30
DIONYSOS. Well, shall I guide thee? Wilt thou attempt the way?
PENTHEUS. With all speed guide me, for I grudge delay.
DIONYSOS. Then robe thyself in a peplus of fine lawn.
PENTHEUS. Why so? Shall I, a man, become a woman?
DIONYSOS. Lest they should slay thee, seeing thee there a man.
PENTHEUS. Thou speakest well and hast a practiced wit.
DIONYSOS. My teacher in this art was Dionysos.
PENTHEUS. How can we fitly do what thou advisest?
DIONYSOS. Going within the palace I will robe thee.
PENTHEUS. And in what dress dost thou propose to array me?   40
DIONYSOS. Thy flowing locks I'll smooth upon thy head.
PENTHEUS. What is the second part of my adorning?
DIONYSOS. Long trailing robes, a snood upon thy head.
PENTHEUS. I cannot dress myself in women's garments.
DIONYSOS. Thou hast lost thy eagerness to see the Maenads.

PENTHEUS. Wilt thou add aught else than this to my attire?
DIONYSOS. A dappled fawn-skin, and in thy hand a thyrsus.
PENTHEUS. Anything save the Bacchanals' mockery.
DIONYSOS. Fighting the Bacchanals thou wilt shed thy blood.
PENTHEUS. 'T is true, first I must go and spy them out.
DIONYSOS. A wiser course than chasing ills with ills.
PENTHEUS. And how am I to walk through Thebes unseen?
DIONYSOS. We'll go by lonely streets, and I will lead thee.
PENTHEUS. Come in, and what is best I will consider.
DIONYSOS. So be it: I at least am ready here.   10
PENTHEUS. Well, I will go; I will then either march
         In arms, or else thy counsels will obey.
         [Exit.]
DIONYSOS. Women, our man within the net is coming.
         He will go forth against the Bacchanals,
         Where dying he will pay the penalty.
         Dionysos, to thy task, for thou art near;
         Let us take vengeance. First unsettle him,
         Implanting a mild madness; since, being sane,
         He'll ne'er consent to wear a woman's dress,
         But lost to reason he will put it on.   20
         Now I would have him laughed at by the Thebans
         After those threats, in which he was terrific,
         Led habited like a woman through the city.
             But I will go to clothe the form of Pentheus
         With the very robe in which he shall meet his doom,
         Slain by his mother's hand; and he shall know
         Bacchus, the son of Zeus, who is a terror
         To wicked men, though to the just most gentle.
         [Exit into the palace.]

STASIMON THREE

STROPHE

CHORUS. Oh! shall I ever my gleaming foot set
         In the dances prolonged all the night   30
         As I shout aloud in my revel,
         Flinging back my neck to the dewy air,
         As a sportive fawn exults
         In the green expanse of the meadow,
         When she flees from the dreaded chase
         Away from the watcher's beat,
         O'erleaping the well-woven toils,
         While the hunter with many a cheer

Urges on his hounds to their utmost speed;
And she with fleet laboring steps
As swift as the wings of the wind
Bounds over the riverside plain,
Rejoicing in lonely solitudes
'Mid the sheltering boughs of the shady wood.
   What wisdom is most to be prized,
Or what among men is the gift of the gods
That is fairer than holding the hand
In victory over a foe?   10
What is noble is ever dear.

                                              ANTISTROPHE
Slowly, but yet very surely withal,
Moves onward the power of heaven,
And punishes those among mortals
Who are servants in bondage to folly and pride,
And forget to exalt the gods,
Led astray with infatuate mind.
And with cunning intent do they lie in wait
While the long seasons roll,
And capture the impious man.   20
It is never right to overpass
The limits of law in our thoughts and deeds.
Slight is the cost to believe
That this has the sovereign power,
Whate'er it be that is divine,
And in the long ages supported by law,
And whose source is found in nature itself.
   What wisdom is most to be prized,
Or what among men is the gift of the gods
That is fairer than holding the hand   30
In victory over a foe?
What is noble is ever dear.

                                                    EPODE
Happy the man who has escaped
From the storm at sea and has found the port;
And happy is he who has finished his toils.
In the struggle for wealth and power
One here, one there, leaves his neighbor behind.
Besides there are myriads more
Who by numberless hopes are lured on;
And of these some end to mortals in bliss,   40
While others vanish away.
But blest do I deem the man
Whose life is found happy day by day.

SCENE FOUR

DIONYSOS [*entering*]. Thou, mad to witness what were best unseen,
   Who cravest what thou shouldst not crave, O Pentheus,
   Come forth from the house and show thyself to me,
   Wearing the dress of a mad Bacchanal,
   A spy upon thy mother and her band;
   Thou art like in form to one of Cadmus' daughters.
PENTHEUS [*entering, dressed as a Bacchanal*]. But now indeed I seem to
      see two suns,
   A double Thebes; two cities of seven gates;
   Thou seem'st like a bull to lead me; horns appear   10
   Upon thy head to have sprouted. Wast thou then
   Truly a bull? Thou hast the form of one.
DIONYSOS. The god attends us, who before was angry,
   At peace with us; now thou dost see aright.
PENTHEUS. How do I look? Have I the mien of Ino,
   Or like Agave do I bear myself?
DIONYSOS. Methinks in seeing thee I see them both.
   But stop! this lock of hair is out of place.
   [Not as I smoothed it down beneath the snood.]
PENTHEUS. Within the house, shaking it up and down,   20
   I, in my frenzy, loosed it from its place.
DIONYSOS. But I, whose care it is to be thy servant,
   Will rearrange it. Come, hold up thy head.
PENTHEUS. Well, do thou deck me; I depend on thee.
DIONYSOS. Thy girdle too is loose, and round thy ankles
   The folds of thy garment hang in disarray.
PENTHEUS. Beside the right foot, yes; but, as I think,
   On the left side the fall of the robe is perfect.
DIONYSOS. Wilt thou think me thy best friend when thou shalt see
   To thy surprise that the Bacchanals are chaste?   30
PENTHEUS. With the thyrsus in my right hand or in this,
   Shall I appear more like a Bacchanal?
DIONYSOS. With thy right hand thou must raise it, keeping time
   With thy right foot; I praise thy change of mind.
PENTHEUS. Pray, could I not upon my shoulders carry
   Cithaeron's glens, with its crown of silver firs?
DIONYSOS. If 't were thy will thou couldst; thou hadst before
   A mind diseased; now it is as it should be.
PENTHEUS. Shall we bring levers, or, putting 'neath its peak
   My arm or shoulder, shall I with my hands uptear it?   40
DIONYSOS. Do not, I pray thee, wreck the shrines of the nymphs
   And the haunts of Pan, where he doth play the pipes.

PENTHEUS. Well said; we must not by force overcome
  Women; I'll hide among the silver firs.
DIONYSOS. Thou shalt be hidden where 't is thy fate to hide,
  Coming a crafty spy upon the Maenads.
PENTHEUS. And they, I think, are held, like birds in a copse,
  Entangled in the pleasant snares of love.
DIONYSOS. Dost thou then go a spy of that? Perhaps,
  Unless first caught thyself, thou wilt catch them.
PENTHEUS. Escort me through the midst of the Theban city;
  For I alone am the man who dares this deed.   10
DIONYSOS. Alone thou toilest for this land, alone;
  Therefore the battles which are meet await thee.
  Follow thou me: I am thy saving guide,
  Another shall return you home.
PENTHEUS.   My mother.
DIONYSOS. A spectacle to all.
PENTHEUS.   For this I am going.
DIONYSOS. Thou wilt be carried back—
PENTHEUS.   That will be pure delight!
DIONYSOS. In thy mother's hands.   20
PENTHEUS.   Thou wilt force luxury on me.
DIONYSOS. Yes, a strange luxury.
PENTHEUS.   'T is what I merit.
  [Exit.]
DIONYSOS. Strange, strange art thou, and destined to strange woes,
  Thou shalt find glory rising up to heaven.
   Stretch forth thy hands, Agave, and ye her sisters,
  Daughters of Cadmus; this young man I bring
  To a great contest; I, the victor, am
  Even Bromios: The event will show the rest.
  [Exit.]

STASIMON FOUR

STROPHE

CHORUS. Ye swift hounds of Frenzy, on, on to the mountain, 30
  Where the daughters of Cadmus their wild revel hold,
  And goad them to madness
  Against him that is robed in the guise of a woman,
  That raging spy of the Maenads.
  Him first shall his mother behold as he watches
  From the lookout place of a level rock,
  And shall cry aloud to the Maenads:
  Who comes here as a hunter
  Of Thebans upon the hills,
  To the mountain, the mountain, O Maenads, who comes? 40

Who can have been his mother?
For he is not born of a woman,
But either sprung from a lion,
Or is child of a Libyan Gorgon.
  Let Justice come openly, come sword in hand,
To slay, as she pierces his throat through and through,
The godless, the lawless, the unjust man—
The earth-born child of Echion.

ANTISTROPHE

For he, with perversity, lawless in temper,
At the revels of Bacchus and Cybele's rites,   10
With mind all distracted,
And with spirit insane, rushes thinking to win
The victory not to be conquered.
To keep the whole mind in control, to man's nature
Conformed, brings a painless life to mortals
Who obey the mandates of Heaven.
False wisdom I do not envy:
Delightful to me is the quest
Of those other things, manifest, great, that a man
Should aim at noble ends always,   20
Ever living a life pure and holy,
And honoring God by rejecting
Those customs that violate justice.
  Let Justice come openly, come sword in hand,
To slay, as she pierces his throat through and through,
The godless, the lawless, the unjust man—
The earth-born child of Echion.

EPODE

Appear as a bull to our sight,
Or a dragon with many heads,
Or a lion with fiery glare.   30
O Bacchus, come, and with smiling face
Cast thy snare around the man
Who pursues the Bacchanals, when he shall fall
On the deadly band of the Maenads.

SCENE FIVE

[*Enter a* MESSENGER.]
MESSENGER. O house, that once wast prosperous in Hellas,
        House of the sage from Sidon, who in the soil
        Of the serpent-dragon sowed the earth-born crop,
        How I deplore thee, albeit I am a slave.

CHORUS. What bring'st thou? Tidings from the Bacchanals?
MESSENGER. Pentheus is dead, the son of Echion.
CHORUS. Thou show'st thyself a mighty god, King Bromios.
MESSENGER. What say'st thou? why dost thou speak thus? dost thou
      Exult over my master's fall, O woman?
CHORUS. A stranger, in foreign hymns, I honor Bacchus;
      For I no longer cower in fear of fetters.
MESSENGER. Dost thou deem Thebes so destitute of men?
CHORUS. Not Thebes, but Dionysos, son of Zeus,
      Has mastery of me.   10
MESSENGER. I cannot blame thee, but it is not noble,
      Ye women, to rejoice over violence done.
CHORUS. Relate to me, declare, by what fate perished
      The unjust contriver of unrighteous deeds.
MESSENGER. When we had left the abodes of this Theban land
      And had passed beyond the Asopus' flowing stream,
      We three began to ascend Cithaeron's steep,
      Pentheus and I (for I was with my master)
      And the stranger who was leader of our quest.
      First then we rested in a grassy glen,   20
      Making no sound of footsteps or of words,
      That we might see, and be ourselves unseen.
      There was a cliff-girt vale, with streamlets moist,
      With pines thick shaded, where the Bacchanals
      Sat with their hands employed in pleasant toil.
      For some of them were garlanding anew
      A thyrsus which had lost its ivy crown,
      And some, like colts released from the painted yokes,
      Alternate sang their Bacchic melody.
        Unhappy Pentheus, when he could not see   30
      The women's band, spake thus: "Where we stand, stranger,
      I have no view of the Maenads' place for dancing;
      But climbing a bank or a towering silver fir
      I could see well the Maenads' shameless conduct."
      A miracle then I saw the stranger do;
      He seized a heaven-piercing fir tree's top,
      And drew it down, down, down, to the dark earth;
      Just like a bow it bent, or circling wheel,
      When its curvèd disk is marked by compasses.
      The stranger thus that mountain branch did bend   40
      Down to the earth, a superhuman deed.
      And seating Pentheus on the boughs of the fir,
      Up through his hands he let it rise erect
      All gently, lest the rider should be thrown.
      Upright it rose aloft into the air,

Bearing my master seated on its back.
And he saw the Maenads less than they saw him;
For he scarce was visible seated there on high
When the stranger from our view had disappeared;
But a voice from out the sky, 't was Dionysos,
As we supposed, shouted aloud: "Ho! maidens,
I bring the man who laughs to scorn yourselves,
Me, and my orgies; now take vengeance on him."
   And calling thus, between the earth and heaven
He stretched a shining belt of awful flame.   10
Silent the air, no leaf in the grassy dell
Rustled, the cry of beasts you could not hear.
But the Maenads catching an uncertain sound
Pricked up their ears and round about them glared.
Again he shouted; and the daughters of Cadmus,
What time they knew the clear command of the god,
Then forward sprang, vying with doves in swiftness.
The mother Agave, her sisters too, and all
The Bacchanals; on through the torrent dell,
Over crags they sped, filled with a heaven-sent fury.   20
But when on the fir they saw my master seated,
First they attacked him furiously with stones,
Climbing a rock that rose like a tower in front,
And they darted at him boughs of silver fir,
While others shot, with sorry aim, at Pentheus
Their thyrsi through the air, but did not strike him.
For on a height too lofty for their striving
He sat, a wretched, baffled prisoner.
At last they tried, rending with boughs of oak,
To rive the roots with levers, not of iron.   30
But when their labors brought them no advantage,
Agave said: "Now, Maenads, stand around
And grasp the tree, that we may catch the beast
Upon its top; and he shall not reveal
The god's mysterious rites." A thousand hands
Grappled the fir and tore it from the earth.
And earthward plunging from his seat on high
With myriad lamentations to the ground
Falls Pentheus, well aware of his coming doom.
And his priestess mother first began the slaying   40
And fell on him: his headband from his hair
He threw, that sad Agave knowing him
Might spare his life; and touching then her cheek
He said: "Mother, I am thy own son, Pentheus,
Whom thou didst bear in the palace of Echion;

Pity me, O my mother, I entreat thee,
And do not for my sins murder thy son."
She, foaming at the mouth and wildly rolling
Her startled eyeballs, and with mind distorted,
By Bacchus held in thrall, heeded him not.
But his left hand holding fast with both her hands,
Pressing her foot against the victim's side,
Tore out his shoulder, not with human strength—
The god it was who taught her hands to war.
And on the other side toiled Ino, rending   10
His flesh; Autonoë and all the band
Of Bacchanals pressed on; while mingled cries
Arose, he groaning while he still drew breath,
They shouting victory; one bore an arm,
And one a foot with its sandal shod; his sides
Lay open, torn, while each with bloody hands
Tossed to and fro the mangled flesh of Pentheus.
   His body lies, here under rugged rocks,
There 'mid the wood's thick foliage, strewed around
In fragments hard to find. The wretched head,   20
Which in her hands his mother seized and held
Transfixed upon the thyrsus-point, she carries
As a fierce lion's o'er Cithaeron's wilds,
Leaving her sisters in the Maenad chorus.
She comes exulting in her ill-starred prey
Within these walls, still calling upon Bacchus,
The conquering partner in the chase with her
Who wins but tears, the victor's only prize.
   I therefore turn from this calamity
Before Agave to the palace comes.   30
To curb our passions and revere the gods
I deem the noblest and the wisest course
For men who in their conduct follow it.
[*Exit.*]
CHORUS. In the dance let us glorify Bacchus,
   Let us sing of the fate that has come
   Upon Pentheus born of the dragon,
   Who put on the garb of a woman,
   Took the ferule with goodly shaft,
   The certain pledge of his doom,
   With the bull as his fatal guide.   40
   O ye Cadmaean Bacchanals,
   Renowned is the triumph song ye have won,
   But it leads you to mourning and tears;
   It is indeed a glorious game

To clasp a son with a blood-dripping hand.
But now I see Agave, Pentheus' mother,
With wildly rolling eyes approach the palace.
Give ear to the revel of the Evian god.
[AGAVE *enters, bearing the head of* PENTHEUS *in her arms.*]

STROPHE

AGAVE. Ye Asiatic Bacchanals,
CHORUS.   Why dost thou urge me on?
AGAVE. See! from the mountain we bring to the palace
          A freshly cut tendril,
          Our fortunate capture.
CHORUS. I behold and receive thee to join in the revel.   10
AGAVE. Without the snares of the huntsman
          I have caught this lion's cub,
          As you may see.
CHORUS. In what desert place didst thou catch him?
AGAVE. Cithaeron—
CHORUS.   Why say'st thou Cithaeron?
AGAVE.   Slew him.
CHORUS. Who was the first to smite him?
AGAVE.   Mine the honor.
CHORUS. O happy Agave!   20
AGAVE.   So call they me amid the revelers.
CHORUS. Who else?
AGAVE.   Of Cadmus—
CHORUS.   What of Cadmus?
AGAVE.   His daughters
          Next after me, next after me
          Attacked this beast.
CHORUS.   Thrice happy in this prize.

ANTISTROPHE

AGAVE. Be thou partaker in the feast.
CHORUS.   Ah me! what shall I share?   30
AGAVE. The whelp is still young and his downy cheek
          Just under the crest of soft-flowing hair
          Is beginning to bloom.
CHORUS. With his mane he resembles a roaming wild beast.
AGAVE. It was Bacchus, the mighty hunter,
          Who skilfully urged on the Maenads
          To capture this game.
CHORUS. Yes, our king knows the hunter's art.
AGAVE. Dost thou praise?
CHORUS.   What? I do.   40
AGAVE. Soon the Cadmeans
CHORUS. And thy son Pentheus will his mother

AGAVE.   Praise
CHORUS. For taking booty,
AGAVE.   This, the lion's whelp,
CHORUS. A wondrous booty!
AGAVE.   Wondrously.
CHORUS.   Rejoicest thou?
AGAVE.   I do exult
    In my exploits, yea deeds of might and valor
    Made famous in this land, that I
CHORUS.   Have wrought.   10
CHORAGOS. Show now, O wretched woman, to the Thebans
    The prize of victory with which thou comest.
AGAVE. Ye dwellers in the fair-towered Theban city,
    Come and behold this prize, this savage beast,
    Which we, the daughters of Cadmus, made our prey,
    Not with the looped Thessalian javelins,
    Not with the hunting-nets, but with the fingers
    Of our fair hands. Must one then idly boast
    And get one weapons of the armorer's craft?
    With our hands alone, unaided by the spear,   20
    We have caught this beast and torn his limbs asunder.
    Where is my aged sire? Let him come near.
    And where is my son Pentheus? Let him take
    And lift against the palace the firm ladders,
    That to the triglyphs he may nail this trophy,
    This lion's head, my capture in the chase.
    [*Enter* CADMUS, *and servants bearing the corpse of*
    PENTHEUS.]
CADMUS. Follow me, servants, bearing your sad burden.
    Follow before the house, with Pentheus,
    Whose body, after many a weary search,
    I carry here, finding it torn asunder   30
    Within Cithaeron's dells, not in one place,
    But lying scattered in the trackless wood.
    My daughter's awful doings I had learned
    On entering through the gates into the city,
    Home from the Bacchanals with old Tiresias;
    And back returning to the mountain, hither
    I bear my son slain by the frantic Maenads.
    Autonoë, her who bore to Aristaeus
    Actaeon, there I saw, and Ino too,
    Still frenzied, woe is me, amid the copses;   40
    But the third, Agave, I am told, approaches
    With frantic step, nor did I hear in vain;
    I see her now—O sight most pitiful!

AGAVE. Father, 't is thine to make the greatest boast,
    That thou hast begotten daughters best of all—
    Noblest by far, and me the peerless one.
    For I have left the shuttle and the loom
    For higher things, to capture with my hands
    Wild beasts. Behold within my arms I bear
    These trophies of the chase, to be suspended
    Upon thy house; with thy hands, father, take them;
    Exulting in the booty I have captured,
    Call thy friends to a feast; thou art twice blest   10
    In us who have done these wonderful exploits.
CADMUS. O boundless woe, not to be looked upon,
    Since murder foul your wretched hands have wrought.
    Glorious thy victim offered to the gods!
    All Thebes and me thou biddest to the feast.
    Alas! alas! our miseries, mine and thine!
    How justly, more than justly, hath the god,
    King Bromios, to our house akin, destroyed us.
AGAVE. Ah me! how crabbèd is old age in men,
    How sad in people's eyes. O that my son   20
    May, like his mother, prove a skillful hunter,
    When with the Theban youths he plies the chase.
    But he displays his power alone in fighting
    Against the gods. From thee, O sire, must come
    His warning. Who would summon him to our presence
    That he may look on me, the blessèd one?
CADMUS. Alas! when ye shall come to know your deeds,
    Ye will grieve deeply; but if to the end
    Ye shall continue in your present state,
    Not being blest, ye will seem not unblest.   30
AGAVE. Why, what is wrong or sorrowful in this?
CADMUS. First fix thy gaze upon the sky above us.
AGAVE. Well; why hast thou thus bidden me look up?
CADMUS. Is it still the same or dost thou think it changed?
AGAVE. 'T is brighter, clearer than it was before.
CADMUS. Is this distraction still within thy soul?
AGAVE. This word I know not, but I do become
    Conscious, freed from my former state of mind.
CADMUS. Canst thou give ear to me and answer clearly?
AGAVE. I have forgotten, father, all we said.   40
CADMUS. To what house didst thou come with marriage songs?
AGAVE. I was bride of Echion called the dragon-born.
CADMUS. What son was born to thy husband in the house?
AGAVE. 'T was Pentheus, from my union with his sire.
CADMUS. Whose head then art thou holding in thy hands?

AGAVE. A lion's, as our band of hunters said.
CADMUS. Observe with care, 't is no long task to look.
AGAVE. What see I? What is this my hands are holding?
CADMUS. Now gaze upon it and observe more closely.
AGAVE. Ah me! I look on grief unspeakable.
CADMUS. Think you it has the semblance of a lion?
AGAVE. Nay; woe is me! I hold the head of Pentheus.
CADMUS. Dabbled in blood ere thou didst recognize it.
AGAVE. Who slew him? How into my hands did he come?
CADMUS. Sad truth! how ill-timed is thy presence here! 10
AGAVE. Speak, for my heart throbs with a dread foreboding.
CADMUS. His slayers were thy sisters and thyself.
AGAVE. Where did he die? At home? Or in what place?
CADMUS. Where once Actaeon's hounds tore him in pieces.
AGAVE. Why to Cithaeron went this hapless man?
CADMUS. He went to mock the god and mock your revels.
AGAVE. But we—how was it that we thither sped?
CADMUS. Ye were insane, and all the city frenzied.
AGAVE. Bacchus hath ruined us, now I understand.
CADMUS. Outraged by you; for you denied his godhead. 20
AGAVE. Father, where can I see my son's dear body?
CADMUS. Here do I bear it, found with painful search.
AGAVE. Is it all well compact, with the parts unsevered?
CADMUS. [As well as haste and fear allowed.]
AGAVE. And in my madness how did Pentheus share?
CADMUS. Like you he did not reverence the god.
　　　　He therefore in one ruin all involved,
　　　　Both you and him, destroying utterly
　　　　The house and me, who, left without male offspring,
　　　　Now see—alas!—this one child of thy womb 30
　　　　Most shamefully and miserably slain,
　　　　To whom the house looked up; thou wast, O son,
　　　　The guardian of my hall, born of my daughter,
　　　　And the people feared thee; no one wished to flout
　　　　The aged man while he beheld thy face;
　　　　For thou the proper punishment wouldst inflict.
　　　　But now I shall be driven from home dishonored,
　　　　Cadmus the great, who sowed the Theban race,
　　　　And after sowing reaped the glorious harvest.
　　　　　O dearest one!—for though no longer living 40
　　　　Thou shalt be counted best beloved, my child—
　　　　No more this beard caressing with thy hand,
　　　　Calling me grandsire, wilt thou clasp my neck,
　　　　O child, and say: "Who wrongs, who flouts thee, sire?
　　　　Who, grieving thee, disquiets thy sad heart?

Speak, and I'll punish him who wrongs thee, father."
But I am wretched now, and thou art hapless,
Thy mother pitiable, and her sisters sad.
Lives there a man who scorns the might of heaven,
Let him mark this death and in the gods believe.

CHORUS. Cadmus, I mourn thy fate; thy daughter's son
Has his reward, a bitter thing to thee.

AGAVE. Father, thou see'st how my lot is changed.
. . . . .¹²

DIONYSOS. Thou shalt become a dragon, and thy wife,
Harmonia, Ares' child, married to thee,   10
A mortal, shall assume a serpent's form.
Thou with thy wife shalt drive a chariot drawn
By oxen, as the oracle of Zeus
Declares, and leader of barbarians shalt be.
Many the cities with thy countless host
Thou wilt sack; but when Apollo's shrine they plunder,
Returning backward they shall meet disaster.
But thee and Harmonia Ares will deliver
And bear thee to the Islands of the Blest.
This say I, from no mortal father sprung,   20
Dionysos, son of Zeus; had ye known wisdom
When ye would not, your ally then had been
This child of Zeus, and you would yet be happy.

AGAVE. Dionysos, we beseech thee, we have sinned.

DIONYSOS. You know me late; when you should have known, you
would not.

AGAVE. We are convinced; yet too great is thy vengeance.

DIONYSOS. Yes, for you outraged me; I am a god.

AGAVE. Gods in their wrath should not resemble men.

DIONYSOS. My father Zeus sanctioned this long ago.   30

AGAVE. Alas, old man! sad exile is decreed.

DIONYSOS. Why then delay what cannot be averted?
[*Exit.*]

CADMUS. Ah me, my child, sore evil hath befallen us,
Wretched art thou, and wretched too thy sisters!
But I, alas, who am old, must go to sojourn
Among barbarians; yet my lot shall be
To lead to Greece a motley host of strangers.
And Ares' child, Harmonia, my wife,

¹² At this point several pages are missing. Although scholars have found
fragments of the missing passages quoted in other classical works, the assembled
text remains hypothetical. The situation, however, is clear: Agave's grief and
resignation, Cadmus' pity, and a final appearance of Dionysos (perhaps in a
machine) to prophesy the future of the central characters.

> Herself assuming a fierce dragon's form,
> Shall I, a dragon in command of spearmen,
> Lead to the tombs and altars of the Greeks;
> Nor shall I cease from woes and be at rest
> When I have crossed the nether Acheron.

AGAVE. O father, torn from thee I shall be exiled.

CADMUS. Unhappy daughter, why dost thou embrace me,
  As a white swan by hoary age enfeebled?

AGAVE. Whither am I, banished from home, to turn?

CADMUS. I know not, child, thy sire is a feeble helper.   10

AGAVE. Farewell to thee, O palace, and farewell,
  O city of my fathers, leaving thee
  I go a hapless wanderer from my home.

CADMUS. Escape, my child, to the house of Aristaeus.

AGAVE. I weep for thee, my father.

CADMUS.   And for thee,
  My child, and for thy sisters I lament.

AGAVE. A terrible outrage this
  That Dionysos the king
  Upon thy house hath wrought.   20

CADMUS. Yes, dire was the wrong that he suffered from you,
  For he found his name unhonored in Thebes.

AGAVE. Farewell, my father.

CADMUS.   Fare thee well, sad daughter.
  And yet 't were hard for thee to come to this.

AGAVE. Ye attendants, conduct me where I shall receive
  As companions in exile my sisters forlorn.
  O let me depart
  Where accursed Cithaeron may see me no more,
  And my eyes may not look on Cithaeron again;   30
  Where no thought of the reveler's wand haunts the place;
  But let others care for the orgies.

  [*Exeunt.*]

SOPHOCLES

ANTIGONE

IRONY

IN "THE BACCHAE", Euripides is, of course, concerned with larger matters than the nature of the art of the drama. But it does his work no injustice to observe that some of the effect of his tragedy depends upon the spectators' awareness of the analogy between acting on the stage and living in the social group. The fifth-century Athenian would recognize and understand the complete impersonation or possession of Pentheus from his own experience or observation in the rituals and mysteries of the various religious cults, and he would recognize and understand the time-serving impersonation of Cadmus and Tiresias from his own experience or observation of the lesser or greater hypocrisy of everyday human behavior. Of these two kinds, or degrees, of acting the entire audience must be aware, or the play becomes a story of inexplicable horror and catastrophe which, like a newspaper account of an earthquake in a far-off land, causes the reader to shake his head and turn to the sports pages without further thought.

That this awareness was a fact can be deduced from Greek theatrical terminology. The original word for an actor, the protagonist, was *hypocritēs*, which simply meant one who makes an answer to a question. As the drama developed, the concept expanded to mean one who plays a part, an actor in the sense of impersonator. Somewhat later the meaning of the term was metaphorically extended to one who feigns or dissembles, hence the modern word *hypocrite*.

There is, however, a third degree of impersonation in *The Bacchae* which depends not on a clear-cut distinction between possession (being) and feigning, but on ambiguity. For the audience, as for Agave and the Maenads, Dionysos is a divinity; for Pentheus he is a charlatan. The god's behavior is constant and consistent throughout the play, yet his nature can be understood one way by the audience and another way by the king. Pentheus' reaction in the second episode to the presence of "Dionysos" is logical and justifiable: he sees him as a rabble-rouser, a corrupter of women, and instrument of disorder. Note that the confrontation occurs in the *second* episode, following the first episode in which Pentheus has mocked, with reason, the grotesque attempts at *enthousiasm* of the two old men. Had the play begun with these two episodes, the audience might have sided with the king and declared for order and reason over chaos and frenzy.

But the play does not begin with these two episodes and the audience is never permitted to question the identity of the god. The performance begins with a prologue, a personal address to the spectators by Dionysos. He reveals himself, his history, and his purpose, directly. He explains his assumption of human form, and his intention of converting Pentheus. One function of the prologue is, of course, expository, to give the audience information about past actions not enacted in the play, so that they may follow the actions that are performed. But a more important function is to create an attitude in the audience, a point of view from which they may evaluate the action to be shown to them. Because we are secure in the knowledge that Dionysos is a god and not an imposter, we will understand Pentheus as a proud and self-righteous tyrant, rather than a conscientious governor properly concerned about the welfare of the state. To provide the audience with information withheld from one or more characters in the play is to create a situation of *dramatic irony*.

In a sense, irony was inherent in Greek drama from the beginning. The subjects chosen by the playwrights were legends or histories whose main outlines were well-known to the spectators. Suspense about the ultimate end of the protagonist was impossible. The spectator knew that Agamemnon would return from Troy to be murdered by his wife, that Orestes would return from exile to assist Electra in her revenge against their mother, that Pentheus would be ruthlessly punished for resisting the god. These stories, in themselves, are exciting and horrible enough, but the difference between relating an event and dramatizing it lies in the necessity of involving the spectator, that it be not just a story but an experience for him. Dramatic irony is one of the ways to turn narrative into experience.

The effect of foreknowledge on the audience can be illustrated from so common an experience as the unfolding of a murder trial by the daily reports of the local press. Since he knows nothing in advance about the real character of the persons involved, the reader directs his attention to the evidence as it is produced, his interest being almost entirely in what will happen next. However, let one of the principals be a member of the reader's family, or his next-door neighbor: a person well-known to the reader through daily encounters in varying circumstances, a person physically and psychologically incapable of violent action. Now the reader will follow the account of the trial with a point of view. He will react to each incident revealed, each piece of evidence produced, with outrage or pity or a sense of vindication. Knowing the truth, he not only sympathizes with the protagonist, but becomes acutely aware of the characters and motives of the other participants, and he will thus become emotionally involved in the conclusion of the trial, the verdict, for he will wish it to express his conviction that the moral laws of the universe operate to secure justice.

From the earliest attempts at dramatic criticism, it has been recognized that Sophocles was a master of the use of dramatic irony. Like most developments in the history of an art, this was first the incidental result of a radical change of pattern. The earliest Greek plays (for example, those of Aeschylus) were composed in units of three, that is, they required three consecutive dramatic actions to relate their story and a full morning for performance. Thus the *Oresteia*, the one surviving three-part play, or trilogy, tells of the ending of the Trojan War and the return of Agamemnon to be slain by his wife, *presenting in action* the motives for the second play, in which Orestes and Electra plot and achieve vengeance, *presenting in action* the motives for the third play in which Orestes is pursued by the primeval punishers of crime until the Olympian gods finally put an end to the chain of sin and expiation.

The plays of Sophocles, however, are single plays encompassing their entire story in one complete action; in his *Electra* he compresses into five episodes the first ten episodes of the *Oresteia*. Since the actions of Electra and her brother depend, for evaluation, on a knowledge that their father has been killed by treachery, exposition becomes of major importance to the spectator and requires tactful handling on the part of the playwright to insure that, while the spectator is being instructed in the past, he does not lose his involvement with the present. The Sophoclean solution is a prologue which immediately introduces a conflict between the characters of the play, into which a portion of the exposition can almost imperceptibly be worked. The play thus begins moving forward almost from the opening lines and the spectator finds himself in the position of wondering what will happen next. Thus in *Antigone*, which may be the earliest of Sophocles' extant plays, the heroine and her sister debate the propriety of paying funeral honors to their brother Polyneices, proclaimed a traitor by King Creon. The audience is reminded of the story of Oedipus and of the civil war set off by his two sons. But more important, from the argument emerges Antigone's decision to bury her brother, and her justification that the laws of heaven are on her side.

When Creon enters in the first episode to make his statesmanlike defense of his order he does so against the audience's knowledge that the loyal and dedicated sister is at that very moment defying him and that he is unwittingly pronouncing the doom of his own niece. As in the case of Pentheus, the audience, uninformed, could quite properly applaud his decision to punish traitors and honor patriots that the ship of state maintain an even keel. Informed by the prologue, however, the audience knows that the situation is not as simple as Creon chooses to observe, and awaits with increasing tension the confrontation of convictions. The abstract issues of religion and state become concrete human concerns.

This is only the first, or basic, irony of *Antigone*. Because of the Sophoclean technique of keeping the audience constantly informed of things unknown to Creon, there are long passages where every sentence has an ironic significance. This is particularly true of the episode with Tiresias, the blind prophet, a conventional character in Sophoclean drama, conventionally accepted by the audience as in possession of the ultimate facts. Here, as in *Oedipus Rex*, Sophocles makes much of the additional irony that the man who can foresee events should be blind while those that have eyes see not.

In its largest and most dramatic sense, irony is a function of structure—the selection and arrangement of incidents for presentation by the performers. Selection is necessary, for the economy of the theater, in terms of available time, the reasonable number of actors employed, the patience of the audience, will not permit the presentation of a complete action from its inception to its conclusion. Yet the audience must be informed of every important fact in the entire story if they are to understand its conclusion. The playwright, therefore, selects certain events to be shown in action and relegates other events to be revealed through exposition. In primitive drama the exposition is narrated at the beginning and the action then follows, chronologically, to the end. By the time of Aeschylus, however, playwrights had discovered that the effectiveness of the action, the experience of the playgoer, could be intensified if the exposition were handled more subtly. Thus, in the first play of the *Oresteia*, the queen who is to murder her husband advances several cogent justifications for the deed based upon the king's actions in the past before she commits it; only after the slaying does she reveal her true motive, her own past adultery with Aegisthos. The supreme example of dramatic irony in the classical theater is Sophocles' *Oedipus Rex*, the account of a king who searches for the cause of the plague which has descended on his city; as he pursues his inquiry, episode by episode, more and more of his own past history is narrated until the climactic scene reveals the incident at his birth which identifies him as the fatal agent whose doom he has pronounced at the opening of the play.

In *Antigone* the ironic structure is less perfect, perhaps because the issues are less clear-cut. The audience, nevertheless, would know Creon as the brother-in-law of Oedipus and, in the earlier story, the man of reason who constantly urged moderation and consideration on the king. They would meet him now in the position of authority still speaking reasonably and persuasively, but because of the dramatic structure, unconsciously betraying himself as having yielded to the assurance and shortsighted decisiveness that seems to go with authority in the theatrical capitals of ancient Greece. The structure of the play is so patterned that the audience, from its godlike foreknowledge, sits constantly in judgment on the protagonist (Creon, not Antigone), watching his vigorous efforts to assert his convictions and effect his decisions against odds which we know will bring about his ultimate defeat.

Yet it was only in the theater that the Greek spectator could be so fortunately foresighted. The experience of watching the fall of Pentheus or Creon is only in part to condemn those who act unjustly, unreasonably. The enduring experience, the larger irony, is that those who, for a few brief hours, have been permitted foresight must leave the theater to pick up their own lives with an intensified sense of the blindness with which they will themselves act, make decisions and commitments. Once again, in inviting the spectator to "suspend disbelief," to accept as true the fictive action of his imaginary world, the playwright so devises his action that we must be aware of the analogy between what is acted in the *orchestra* and what is lived in the *agora*, the market-place, or at the domestic hearth. The serious dramatist does not invite his audience to escape from their own lives; rather he challenges them to live with deliberately increased consciousness.

Characters

ANTIGONE
daughter of OEDIPUS

ISMENE
her sister

CREON
king of Thebes

EURIDICE
his wife

HAIMON
his son

TIRESIAS
a blind seer

A SENTRY

A MESSENGER

CHORUS OF OLD MEN

SCENE: *Before the palace of* CREON, *king of Thebes. A central double door, and two lateral doors. A platform extends the length of the façade and from this platform three steps lead down into the orchestra, or chorusground. Time: dawn of the day after the repulse of the Argive army from the assault on Thebes.*

ANTIGONE

Sophocles

Translated by Dudley Fitts and Robert Fitzgerald

PROLOGUE

[ANTIGONE *and* ISMENE *enter from the central door of the palace.*]

ANTIGONE. Ismene, dear sister,
    You would think that we had already suffered enough
    For the curse on Oedipus:[1]
    I cannot imagine any grief
    That you and I have not gone through. And now—
    Have they told you the new decree of our King Creon?

ISMENE. I have heard nothing: I know
    That two sisters lost two brothers,[2] a double death
    In a single hour; and I know that the Argive army
    Fled in the night; but beyond this, nothing.   10

ANTIGONE. I thought so. And that is why I wanted you
    To come out here with me. There is something we must do.

ISMENE. Why do you speak so strangely?

ANTIGONE. Listen, Ismene:
    Creon buried our brother Eteocles
    With military honors, gave him a soldier's funeral,
    And it was right that he should; but Polyneices,
    Who fought as bravely and died as miserably,—

[1] Father of Antigone and Ismene. Fated to murder his father and marry his own mother, he had become king of Thebes and brought a plague on the city. When he discovered the truth about his situation, he blinded himself and went into exile, leaving the government in the hands of his brother-in-law, Creon.

[2] Eteocles and Polyneices, the sons of Oedipus. The latter organized an attack on the city, the former defended it; in the battle each was slain.

They say that Creon has sworn
No one shall bury him, no one mourn for him,
But his body must lie in the fields, a sweet treasure
For carrion birds to find as they search for food.
That is what they say, and our good Creon is coming here
To announce it publicly; and the penalty—
Stoning to death in the public square!
                              There it is,
And now you can prove what you are:
A true sister, or a traitor to your family.   10
ISMENE. Antigone, you are mad! What could I possibly do?
ANTIGONE. You must decide whether you will help me or not.
ISMENE. I do not understand you. Help you in what!
ANTIGONE. Ismene, I am going to bury him. Will you come?
ISMENE. Bury him! You have just said the new law forbids it.
ANTIGONE. He is my brother. And he is your brother, too.
ISMENE. But think of the danger! Think what Creon will do!
ANTIGONE. Creon is not strong enough to stand in my way.
ISMENE. Ah sister!
Oedipus died, everyone hating him   20
For what his own search brought to light, his eyes
Ripped out by his own hand; and Iocaste died,
His mother and wife at once: she twisted the cords
That strangled her life; and our two brothers died,
Each killed by the other's sword. And we are left:
But oh, Antigone,
Think how much more terrible than these
Our own death would be if we should go against Creon
And do what he has forbidden! We are only women,
We cannot fight with men, Antigone!   30
The law is strong, we must give in to the law
In this thing, and in worse. I beg the Dead
To forgive me, but I am helpless: I must yield
To those in authority. And I think it is dangerous business
To be always meddling.
ANTIGONE.   If that is what you think,
I should not want you, even if you asked to come.
You have made your choice, and can be what you want
      to be.
But I will bury him; and if I must die,   40
I say that this crime is holy: I shall lie down
With him in death, and I shall be as dear
To him as he to me.
                    It is the dead,
Not the living, who make the longest demands:

We die for ever . . .
                  You may do as you like,
Since apparently the laws of the gods mean nothing to you.
ISMENE. They mean a great deal to me; but I have no strength
    To break laws that were made for the public good.
ANTIGONE. That must be your excuse, I suppose. But as for me,
    I will bury the brother I love.
ISMENE.   Antigone,
    I am so afraid for you!
ANTIGONE.   You need not be: 10
    You have yourself to consider, after all.
ISMENE. But no one must hear of this, you must tell no one!
    I will keep it a secret, I promise!
ANTIGONE.   Oh tell it! Tell everyone!
    Think how they'll hate you when it all comes out
    If they learn that you knew about it all the time!
ISMENE. So fiery! You should be cold with fear.
ANTIGONE. Perhaps. But I am doing only what I must.
ISMENE. But can you do it? I say that you cannot.
ANTIGONE. Very well: when my strength gives out, I shall do no   20
        more.
ISMENE. Impossible things should not be tried at all.
ANTIGONE. Go away, Ismene:
    I shall be hating you soon, and the dead will too,
    For your words are hateful. Leave me my foolish plan:
    I am not afraid of the danger; if it means death,
    It will not be the worst of deaths—death without honor.
ISMENE. Go then, if you feel that you must.
    You are unwise,
    But a loyal friend indeed to those who love you.   30
    [*Exit into the palace.* ANTIGONE *goes off, left. Enter the* CHORUS.]

PARODOS

STROPHE I

CHORUS. Now the long blade of the sun, lying
    Level east to west, touches with glory
    Thebes of the Seven Gates. Open, unlidded
    Eye of golden day! O marching light
    Across the eddy and rush of Dirce's stream,
    Striking the white shields of the enemy
    Thrown headlong backward from the blaze of morning!
CHORAGOS. Polyneices their commander
    Roused them with windy phrases,
    He the wild eagle screaming   40

        Insults above our land,
        His wings their shields of snow,
        His crest their marshaled helms.

                          ANTISTROPHE I

CHORUS. Against our seven gates in a yawning ring
        The famished spears came onward in the night;
        But before his jaws were sated with our blood,
        Or pinefire took the garland of our towers,
        He was thrown back; and as he turned, great Thebes—
        No tender victim for his noisy power—
        Rose like a dragon behind him, shouting war.   10
CHORAGOS. For God hates utterly
        The bray of bragging tongues;
        And when he beheld their smiling,
        Their swagger of golden helms,
        The frown of his thunder blasted
        Their first man from our walls.

                          STROPHE II

CHORUS. We heard his shout of triumph high in the air
        Turn to a scream; far out in a flaming arc
        He fell with his windy torch, and the earth struck him.
        And others storming in fury no less than his   20
        Found shock of death in the dusty joy of battle.
CHORAGOS. Seven captains at seven gates
        Yielded their clanging arms to the god
        That bends the battle-line and breaks it.
        These two only, brothers in blood,
        Face to face in matchless rage,
        Mirroring each the other's death,
        Clashed in long combat.

                        ANTISTROPHE II

CHORUS. But now in the beautiful morning of victory
        Let Thebes of the many chariots sing for joy!   30
        With hearts for dancing we'll take leave of war:
        Our temples shall be sweet with hymns of praise,
        And the long night shall echo with our chorus.

SCENE ONE

CHORAGOS. But now at last our new King is coming:
        Creon of Thebes, Menoiceus' son.
        In this auspicious dawn of his reign
        What are the new complexities
        That shifting Fate has woven for him?

What is his counsel? Why has he summoned
The old men to hear him?

[*Enter* CREON *from the palace. He addresses the* CHORUS
from the top step.]

CREON. Gentlemen: I have the honor to inform you that our Ship of
State, which recent storms have threatened to destroy, has come
safely to harbor at last, guided by the merciful wisdom of Heaven.
I have summoned you here this morning because I know that
I can depend upon you: your devotion to King Laïos was absolute;
you never hesitated in your duty to our late ruler Oedipus; and
when Oedipus died, your loyalty was transferred to his children.
Unfortunately, as you know, his two sons, the princes Eteocles   10
and Polyneices, have killed each other in battle; and I, as the
next in blood, have succeeded to the full power of the throne.

I am aware, of course, that no Ruler can expect complete loyalty
from his subjects until he has been tested in office. Nevertheless,
I say to you at the very outset that I have nothing but contempt
for the kind of Governor who is afraid, for whatever reason, to
follow the course that he knows is best for the State; and as for
the man who sets private friendship above the public welfare,—
I have no use for him, either. I call God to witness that if I saw
my country headed for ruin, I should not be afraid to speak out   20
plainly; and I need hardly remind you that I would never have
any dealings with an enemy of the people. No one values friendship more highly than I; but we must remember that friends made
at the risk of wrecking our Ship are not real friends at all.

These are my principles, at any rate, and that is why I have made
the following decision concerning the sons of Oedipus: Eteocles,
who died as a man should die, fighting for his country, is to be
buried with full military honors, with all the ceremony that is
usual when the greatest heroes die; but his brother Polyneices,
who broke his exile to come back with fire and sword against his   30
native city and the shrines of his fathers' gods, whose one idea
was to spill the blood of his blood and sell his own people into
slavery—Polyneices, I say, is to have no burial: no man is to
touch him or say the least prayer for him; he shall lie on the plain,
unburied; and the birds and the scavenging dogs can do with
him whatever they like.

This is my command, and you can see the wisdom behind it.
As long as I am King, no traitor is going to be honored with the
loyal man. But whoever shows by word and deed that he is on

the side of the State,—he shall have my respect while he is living, and my reverence when he is dead.

CHORAGOS. If that is your will, Creon son of Menoiceus,
     You have the right to enforce it: we are yours.

CREON. That is my will. Take care that you do your part.

CHORAGOS. We are old men: let the younger ones carry it out.

CREON. I do not mean that: the sentries have been appointed.

CHORAGOS. Then what is it that you would have us do?

CREON. You will give no support to whoever breaks this law.

CHORAGOS. Only a crazy man is in love with death!   10

CREON. And death it is; yet money talks, and the wisest
     Have sometimes been known to count a few coins too many.
     [*Enter* SENTRY.]

SENTRY. I'll not say that I'm out of breath from running, King, because every time I stopped to think about what I have to tell you, I felt like going back. And all the time a voice kept saying, "You fool, don't you know you're walking straight into trouble?", and then another voice: "Yes, but if you let somebody else get the news to Creon first, it will be even worse than that for you!" But good sense won out, at least I hope it was good sense, and here I am with a story that makes no sense at all; but I'll tell it anyhow,   20 because, as they say, what's going to happen's going to happen, and—

CREON. Come to the point. What have you to say?

SENTRY. I did not do it. I did not see who did it. You must not punish me for what someone else has done.

CREON. A comprehensive defense! More effective, perhaps,
     If I knew its purpose. Come: what is it?

SENTRY. A dreadful thing . . . I don't know how to put it—

CREON. Out with it!

SENTRY.   Well, then;   30
     The dead man—
               Polyneices—
     [*Pause. The* SENTRY *is overcome, fumbles for words.*
     CREON *waits impassively.*]
                         out there—
                              someone,—
     New dust on the slimy flesh!
     [*Pause. No sign from* CREON.]
     Someone has given it burial that way, and
     Gone . . .
     [*Long pause.* CREON *finally speaks with deadly control:*]

CREON. And the man who dared do this?

SENTRY.   I swear I
     Do not know! You must believe me!   40

                                    Listen:
The ground was dry, not a sign of digging, no,
Not a wheeltrack in the dust, no trace of anyone.
It was when they relieved us this morning: and one of them,
The corporal, pointed to it.
                                    There it was,
The strangest—
                    Look:
The body, just mounded over with light dust: you see?
Not buried really, but as if they'd covered it   10
Just enough for the ghost's peace. And no sign
Of dogs or any wild animal that had been there.
And then what a scene there was! Every man of us
Accusing the other: we all proved the other man did it,
We all had proof that we could not have done it.
We were ready to take hot iron in our hands,
Walk through fire, swear by all the gods,
It was not I!
I do not know who it was, but it was not I!
[CREON's *rage has been mounting steadily, but the* SENTRY
is too intent upon his story to notice it.]
And then, when this came to nothing, someone said   20
A thing that silenced us and made us stare
Down at the ground: you had to be told the news,
And one of us had to do it! We threw the dice,
And the bad luck fell to me. So here I am,
No happier to be here than you are to have me:
Nobody likes the man who brings bad news.
CHORAGOS. I have been wondering, King: can it be that the gods have
        done this?
CREON [*furiously*].   Stop!
        Must you doddering wrecks   30
Go out of your heads entirely? "The gods!"
Intolerable!
The gods favor this corpse? Why? How had he served them?
Tried to loot their temples, burn their images,
Yes, and the whole State, and its laws with it!
Is it your senile opinion that the gods love to honor bad
        men?
A pious thought!—
                    No, from the very beginning
There have been those who have whispered together,   40
Stiff-necked anarchists, putting their heads together,
Scheming against me in alleys. These are the men,
And they have bribed my own guard to do this thing.

[*Sententiously.*]
Money!
There's nothing in the world so demoralizing as money.
Down go your cities,
Homes gone, men gone, honest hearts corrupted,
Crookedness of all kinds, and all for money!
[*To* SENTRY.]

                                          But you—!
I swear by God and by the throne of God,
The man who has done this thing shall pay for it!
Find that man, bring him here to me, or your death
Will be the least of your problems: I'll string you up   10
Alive, and there will be certain ways to make you
Discover your employer before you die;
And the process may teach you a lesson you seem to have
    missed:
The dearest profit is sometimes all too dear.
That depends on the source. Do you understand me?
A fortune won is often misfortune.
SENTRY. King, may I speak?
CREON.   Your very voice distresses me.
SENTRY. Are you sure that it is my voice, and not your conscience?   20
CREON. By God, he wants to analyze me now!
SENTRY. It is not what I say, but what has been done, that hurts you.
CREON. You talk too much.
SENTRY.   Maybe; but I've done nothing.
CREON. Sold your soul for some silver: that's all you've done.
SENTRY. How dreadful it is when the right judge judges wrong!
CREON. Your figures of speech
    May entertain you now; but unless you bring me the man,
    You will get little profit from them in the end.
    [*Exit* CREON *into the palace.*]
SENTRY. "Bring me the man"—!   30
    I'd like nothing better than bringing him the man!
    But bring him or not, you have seen the last of me here.
    At any rate, I am safe!
    [*Exit* SENTRY.]

STASIMON ONE

STROPHE I
CHORUS. Numberless are the world's wonders, but none
      More wonderful than man; the stormgrey sea
      Yields to his prows, the huge crests bear him high;

Earth, holy and inexhaustible, is graven
With shining furrows where his plows have gone
Year after year, the timeless labor of stallions.

ANTISTROPHE I

The lightboned birds and beasts that cling to cover,
The lithe fish lighting their reaches of dim water,
All are taken, tamed in the net of his mind;
The lion on the hill, the wild horse windy-maned,
Resign to him; and his blunt yoke has broken
The sultry shoulders of the mountain bull.

STROPHE II

Words also, and thought as rapid as air,   10
He fashions to his good use; statecraft is his,
And his the skill that deflects the arrows of snow,
The spears of winter rain: from every wind
He has made himself secure—from all but one:
In the late wind of death he cannot stand.

ANTISTROPHE II

O clear intelligence, force beyond all measure!
O fate of man, working both good and evil!
When the laws are kept, how proudly his city stands!
When the laws are broken, what of his city then?
Never may the anarchic man find rest at my hearth,   20
Never be it said that my thoughts are his thoughts.

SCENE TWO

[*Re-enter* SENTRY *leading* ANTIGONE.]
CHORAGOS. What does this mean? Surely this captive woman
         Is the Princess, Antigone. Why should she be taken?
SENTRY. Here is the one who did it! We caught her
         In the very act of burying him.—Where is Creon?
CHORAGOS. Just coming from the house.
         [*Enter* CREON, *center.*]
CREON.   What has happened?
         Why have you come back so soon?
SENTRY [*expansively*].   O King,
         A man should never be too sure of anything: 30
         I would have sworn
         That you'd not see me here again: your anger
         Frightened me so, and the things you threatened me with;

But how could I tell then
That I'd be able to solve the case so soon?

No dice-throwing this time: I was only too glad to come!

Here is this woman. She is the guilty one:
We found her trying to bury him.

Take her, then; question her; judge her as you will.
I am through with the whole thing now, and glad of it.
CREON. But this is Antigone! Why have you brought her here?
SENTRY. She was burying him, I tell you!
CREON [*severely*].   Is this the truth?   10
SENTRY. I saw her with my own eyes. Can I say more?
CREON. The details: come, tell me quickly!
SENTRY.   It was like this:
After those terrible threats of yours, King,
We went back and brushed the dust away from the body.
The flesh was soft by now, and stinking,
So we sat on a hill to windward and kept guard.
No napping this time! We kept each other awake.
But nothing happened until the white round sun
Whirled in the center of the round sky over us: 20
Then, suddenly,
A storm of dust roared up from the earth, and the sky
Went out, the plain vanished with all its trees
In the stinging dark. We closed our eyes and endured it.
The whirlwind lasted a long time, but it passed;
And then we looked, and there was Antigone!
I have seen
A mother bird come back to a stripped nest, heard
Her crying bitterly a broken note or two
For the young ones stolen. Just so, when this girl   30
Found the bare corpse, and all her love's work wasted,
She wept, and cried on heaven to damn the hands
That had done this thing
                        And then she brought more dust
And sprinkled wine three times for her brother's ghost.
We ran and took her at once. She was not afraid,
Not even when we charged her with what she had done.
She denied nothing.
                    And this was a comfort to me,
And some uneasiness: for it is a good thing   40
To escape from death, but it is no great pleasure

            To bring death to a friend.
                                    Yet I always say
            There is nothing so comfortable as your own safe skin!
CREON [*slowly*, *dangerously*]. And you, Antigone,
            You with your head hanging,—do you confess this thing?
ANTIGONE. I do. I deny nothing.
CREON [*to* SENTRY].   You may go.
            [*Exit* SENTRY.]
            [*To* ANTIGONE.]
            Tell me, tell me briefly:
            Had you heard my proclamation touching this matter?
ANTIGONE. It was public. Could I help hearing it?   10
CREON. And yet you dared defy the law.
ANTIGONE.   I dared.
            It was not God's proclamation. That final Justice
            That rules the world below makes no such laws.

            Your edict, King, was strong,
            But all your strength is weakness itself against
            The immortal unrecorded laws of God.
            They are not merely now: they were, and shall be,
            Operative for ever, beyond man utterly.

            I knew I must die, even without your decree: 20
            I am only mortal. And if I must die
            Now, before it is my time to die,
            Surely this is no hardship: can anyone
            Living, as I live, with evil all about me,
            Think Death less than a friend? This death of mine
            Is of no importance; but if I had left my brother
            Lying in death unburied, I should have suffered.
            Now I do not.
                              You smile at me. Ah Creon,
            Think me a fool, if you like; but it may well be   30
            That a fool convicts me of folly.
CHORAGOS. Like father, like daughter: both headstrong, deaf to reason!
            She has never learned to yield.
CREON.   She has much to learn.
            The inflexible heart breaks first, the toughest iron
            Cracks first, and the wildest horses bend their necks
            At the pull of the smallest curb.
                                        Pride? In a slave?
            This girl is guilty of a double insolence,
            Breaking the given laws and boasting of it.   40
            Who is the man here,

She or I, if this crime goes unpunished?
Sister's child, or more than sister's child,
Or closer yet in blood—she and her sister
Win bitter death for this!
[*To* SERVANTS.]
                                        Go, some of you,
Arrest Ismene. I accuse her equally.
Bring her: you will find her sniffling in the house there.

Her mind's a traitor: crimes kept in the dark
Cry for light, and the guardian brain shudders;
But how much worse than this   10
Is brazen boasting of barefaced anarchy!
ANTIGONE. Creon, what more do you want than my death?
CREON.   Nothing.
        That gives me everything.
ANTIGONE.   Then I beg you: kill me.
This talking is a great weariness: your words
Are distasteful to me, and I am sure that mine
Seem so to you. And yet they should not seem so:
I should have praise and honor for what I have done.
All these men here would praise me   20
Were their lips not frozen shut with fear of you.
[*Bitterly.*]
Ah the good fortune of kings,
Licensed to say and do whatever they please!
CREON. You are alone here in that opinion.
ANTIGONE. No, they are with me. But they keep their tongues in leash.
CREON. Maybe. But you are guilty, and they are not.
ANTIGONE. There is no guilt in reverence for the dead.
CREON. But Eteocles—was he not your brother too?
ANTIGONE. My brother too.
CREON.   And you insult his memory?   30
ANTIGONE [*softly*]. The dead man would not say that I insult it.
CREON. He would: for you honor a traitor as much as him.
ANTIGONE. His own brother, traitor or not, and equal in blood.
CREON. He made war on his country. Eteocles defended it.
ANTIGONE. Nevertheless, there are honors due all the dead.
CREON. But not the same for the wicked as for the just.
ANTIGONE. Ah Creon, Creon,
        Which of us can say what the gods hold wicked?
CREON. An enemy is an enemy, even dead.
ANTIGONE. It is my nature to join in love, not hate.   40
CREON [*finally losing patience*]. Go join them, then; if you must have
        your love,

Find it in hell!
CHORAGOS. But see, Ismene comes:
    [*Enter* ISMENE, *guarded*.]
    Those tears are sisterly, the cloud
    That shadows her eyes rains down gentle sorrow.
CREON. You too, Ismene,
    Snake in my ordered house, sucking my blood
    Stealthily—and all the time I never knew
    That these two sisters were aiming at my throne!
                                              Ismene,
    Do you confess your share in this crime, or deny it?   10
    Answer me.
ISMENE. Yes, if she will let me say so. I am guilty.
ANTIGONE [*coldly*]. No, Ismene. You have no right to say so.
    You would not help me, and I will not have you help me.
ISMENE. But now I know what you meant; and I am here
    To join you, to take my share of punishment.
ANTIGONE. The dead man and the gods who rule the dead
    Know whose act this was. Words are not friends.
ISMENE. Do you refuse me, Antigone? I want to die with you:
    I too have a duty that I must discharge to the dead.   20
ANTIGONE. You shall not lessen my death by sharing it.
ISMENE. What do I care for life when you are dead?
ANTIGONE. Ask Creon. You're always hanging on his opinions.
ISMENE. You are laughing at me. Why, Antigone?
ANTIGONE. It's a joyless laughter, Ismene.
ISMENE.   But can I do nothing?
ANTIGONE. Yes. Save yourself. I shall not envy you.
    There are those who will praise you; I shall have
        honor, too.
ISMENE. But we are equally guilty!   30
ANTIGONE.   No, more, Ismene.
    You are alive, but I belong to Death.
CREON [*to the* CHORUS].   Gentlemen, I beg you to observe these
        girls:
    One has just now lost her mind; the other
    It seems, has never had a mind at all.
ISMENE. Grief teaches the steadiest minds to waver, King.
CREON. Yours certainly did, when you assumed guilt with the
        guilty!
ISMENE. But how could I go on living without her?   40
CREON.   You are.
    She is already dead.
ISMENE.   But your own son's bride!
CREON. There are places enough for him to push his plow.

I want no wicked women for my sons!
ISMENE. O dearest Haimon, how your father wrongs you!
CREON. I've had enough of your childish talk of marriage!
CHORAGOS. Do you really intend to steal this girl from your son?
CREON. No; Death will do that for me.
CHORAGOS.   Then she must die?
CREON. You dazzle me.
                       —But enough of this talk!
       [To GUARDS.]
       You, there, take them away and guard them well:
       For they are but women, and even brave men run   10
       When they see Death coming.
       [Exeunt ISMENE, ANTIGONE, and GUARDS.]

STASIMON TWO

CHORUS. Fortunate is the man who has never tasted God's vengeance!
       Where once the anger of heaven has struck, that house is
             shaken
       For ever: damnation rises behind each child
       Like a wave cresting out of the black northeast,
       When the long darkness under sea roars up
       And bursts drumming death upon the windwhipped sand.

                                                      ANTISTROPHE I
       I have seen this gathering sorrow from time long past
       Loom upon Oedipus' children: generation from generation   20
       Takes the compulsive rage of the enemy god.
       So lately this last flower of Oedipus' line
       Drank the sunlight! but now a passionate word
       And a handful of dust have closed up all its beauty.
                                                      STROPHE II
             What mortal arrogance
             Transcends the wrath of Zeus?
       Sleep cannot lull him, nor the effortless long months
       Of the timeless gods: but he is young for ever,
       And his house is the shining day of high Olympos.
             All that is and shall be,   30
             And all the past, is his.
       No pride on earth is free of the curse of heaven.
                                                      ANTISTROPHE II
             The straying dreams of men
             May bring them ghosts of joy:

But as they drowse, the waking embers burn them;
Or they walk with fixed eyes, as blind men walk.
But the ancient wisdom speaks for our own time:
    Fate works most for woe
    With Folly's fairest show.
Man's little pleasure is the spring of sorrow.

SCENE THREE

CHORAGOS. But here is Haimon, King, the last of all your sons.
    Is it grief for Antigone that brings him here,
    And bitterness at being robbed of his bride?
    [*Enter* HAIMON.]
CREON. We shall soon see, and no need of diviners.   10
                       —Son,
    You have heard my final judgment on that girl:
    Have you come here hating me, or have you come
    With deference and with love, whatever I do?
HAIMON. I am your son, father. You are my guide.
    You make things clear for me, and I obey you.
    No marriage means more to me than your continuing
        wisdom.
CREON. Good. That is the way to behave: subordinate
    Everything else, my son, to your father's will.   20
    This is what a man prays for, that he may get
    Sons attentive and dutiful in his house,
    Each one hating his father's enemies,
    Honoring his father's friends. But if his sons
    Fail him, if they turn out unprofitably,
    What has he fathered but trouble for himself
    And amusement for the malicious?
                    So you are right
    Not to lose your head over this woman.
    Your pleasure with her would soon grow cold, Haimon,   30
    And then you'd have a hellcat in bed and elsewhere.
    Let her find her husband in Hell!
    Of all the people in this city, only she
    Has had contempt for my law and broken it.

    Do you want me to show myself weak before the people?
    Or to break my sworn word? No, and I will not.
    The woman dies.

I suppose she'll plead "family ties." Well, let her.
If I permit my own family to rebel,
How shall I earn the world's obedience?
Show me the man who keeps his house in hand,
He's fit for public authority.
                        I'll have no dealings
With law-breakers, critics of the government:
Whoever is chosen to govern should be obeyed—
Must be obeyed, in all things, great and small,
Just and unjust! O Haimon,   10
The man who knows how to obey, and that man only,
Knows how to give commands when the time comes.
You can depend on him, no matter how fast
The spears come: he's a good soldier, he'll stick it out.

Anarchy, anarchy! Show me a greater evil!
This is why cities tumble and the great houses rain down,
This is what scatters armies!

No, no: good lives are made so by discipline.
We keep the laws then, and the lawmakers,
And no woman shall seduce us. If we must lose,   20
Let's lose to a man, at least! Is a woman stronger than we?
CHORAGOS. Unless time has rusted my wits,
        What you say, King, is said with point and dignity.
HAIMON [boyishly earnest]. Father:
        Reason is God's crowning gift to man, and you are right
To warn me against losing mine. I cannot say—
I hope that I shall never want to say!—that you
Have reasoned badly. Yet there are other men
Who can reason, too; and their opinions might be helpful.
You are not in a position to know everything   30
That people say or do, or what they feel:
Your temper terrifies them—everyone
Will tell you only what you like to hear.
But I, at any rate, can listen; and I have heard them
Muttering and whispering in the dark about this girl.
They say no woman has ever, so unreasonably,
Died so shameful a death for a generous act:
"She covered her brother's body. Is this indecent?
"She kept him from dogs and vultures. Is this a crime?
"Death —She should have all the honor that we can give   40
        her!"

This is the way they talk out there in the city.

You must believe me:
Nothing is closer to me than your happiness.
What could be closer? Must not any son
Value his father's fortune as his father does his?
I beg you, do not be unchangeable:
Do not believe that you alone can be right.
The man who thinks that,
The man who maintains that only he has the power
To reason correctly, the gift to speak, the soul—
A man like that, when you know him, turns out empty.   10

It is not reason never to yield to reason!

In flood time you can see how some trees bend,
And because they bend, even their twigs are safe,
While stubborn trees are torn up, roots and all.
And the same thing happens in sailing:
Make your sheet fast, never slacken,—and over you go,
Head over heels and under; and there's your voyage.
Forget you are angry! Let yourself be moved!
I know I am young; but please let me say this:
The ideal condition   20
Would be, I admit, that men should be right by instinct;
But since we are all too likely to go astray,
The reasonable thing is to learn from those who can teach.
CHORAGOS. You will do well to listen to him, King,
        If what he says is sensible. And you, Haimon,
        Must listen to your father.—Both speak well.
CREON. You consider it right for a man of my years and experience
        To go to school to a boy?
HAIMON.   It is not right
        If I am wrong. But if I am young, and right,   30
        What does my age matter?
CREON. You think it right to stand up for an anarchist?
HAIMON. Not at all. I pay no respect to criminals.
CREON. Then she is not a criminal?
HAIMON. The City would deny it, to a man.
CREON. And the City proposes to teach me how to rule?
HAIMON. Ah. Who is it that's talking like a boy now?
CREON. My voice is the one voice giving orders in this City!
HAIMON. It is no City if it takes orders from one voice.
CREON. The State is the King!   40
HAIMON.   Yes, if the State is a desert.
        [*Pause.*]
CREON. This boy, it seems, has sold out to a woman.

HAIMON. If you are a woman: my concern is only for you.
CREON. So? Your "concern"! In a public brawl with your father!
HAIMON. How about you, in a public brawl with justice?
CREON. With justice, when all that I do is within my rights?
HAIMON. You have no right to trample on God's right.
CREON [*completely out of control*]. Fool, adolescent fool! Taken in by a
          woman!
HAIMON. You'll never see me taken in by anything vile.
CREON. Every word you say is for her!
HAIMON [*quietly, darkly*].   And for you.   10
    And for me. And for the gods under the earth.
CREON. You'll never marry her while she lives.
HAIMON. Then she must die.—But her death will cause another.
CREON. Another?
    Have you lost your senses? Is this an open threat?
HAIMON. There is no threat in speaking to emptiness.
CREON. I swear you'll regret this superior tone of yours!
    You are the empty one!
HAIMON.   If you were not my father,
    I'd say you were perverse.   20
CREON. You girlstruck fool, don't play at words with me!
HAIMON. I am sorry. You prefer silence.
CREON.   Now, by God—!
    I swear, by all the gods in heaven above us,
    You'll watch it, I swear you shall!
    [*To the* SERVANTS.]
                  Bring her out!
    Bring the woman out! Let her die before his eyes,
    Here, this instant, with her bridegroom beside her!
HAIMON. Not here, no; she will not die here, King.
    And you will never see my face again.   30
    Go on raving as long as you've a friend to endure you.
    [*Exit* HAIMON.]
CHORAGOS. Gone, gone.
    Creon, a young man in a rage is dangerous!
CREON. Let him do, or dream to do, more than a man can.
    He shall not save these girls from death.
CHORAGOS.   These girls?
    You have sentenced them both?
CREON.   No, you are right.
    I will not kill the one whose hands are clean.
CHORAGOS. But Antigone?   40
CREON [*sombrely*].   I will carry her far away
    Out there in the wilderness, and lock her
    Living in a vault of stone. She shall have food,

As the custom is, to absolve the State of her death.
And there let her pray to the gods of Hell:
They are her only gods:
Perhaps they will show her an escape from death,
Or she may learn,
             though late,
That piety shown the dead is pity in vain.
[*Exit* CREON.]

STASIMON THREE

                    STROPHE

CHORUS. Love, unconquerable
    Waster of rich men, keeper
    Of warm lights and all-night vigil   10
    In the soft face of a girl:
    Sea-wanderer, forest-visitor!
    Even the pure Immortals cannot escape you,
    And mortal man, in his one day's dusk,
    Trembles before your glory.

                 ANTISTROPHE

    Surely you swerve upon ruin
    The just man's consenting heart,
    As here you have made bright anger
    Strike between father and son—
    And none has conquered but Love!   20
    A girl's glance working the will of heaven:
    Pleasure to her alone who mocks us,
    Merciless Aphrodite.

SCENE FOUR

[*As* ANTIGONE *enters guarded.*]
CHORAGOS. But I can no longer stand in awe of this,
    Nor, seeing what I see, keep back my tears.
    Here is Antigone, passing to that chamber
    Where all find sleep at last.

                 STROPHE I

ANTIGONE. Look upon me, friends, and pity me
    Turning back at the night's edge to say
    Good-bye to the sun that shines for me no longer;   30
    Now sleepy Death

Summons me down to Acheron, that cold shore:
There is no bridesong there, nor any music.
CHORUS. Yet not unpraised, not without a kind of honor,
You walk at last into the underworld;
Untouched by sickness, broken by no sword.
What woman has ever found your way to death?

ANTISTROPHE I

ANTIGONE. How often I have heard the story of Niobe,[3]
Tantalos' wretched daughter, how the stone
Clung fast about her, ivy-close: and they say
The rain falls endlessly   10
And sifting soft snow; her tears are never done.
I feel the loneliness of her death in mine.
CHORUS. But she was born of heaven, and you
Are woman, woman-born. If her death is yours,
A mortal woman's, is this not for you
Glory in our world and in the world beyond?

STROPHE II

ANTIGONE. You laugh at me. Ah, friends, friends,
Can you not wait until I am dead? O Thebes,
O men many-charioted, in love with Fortune,
Dear springs of Dirce, sacred Theban grove,   20
Be witnesses for me, denied all pity,
Unjustly judged! and think a word of love
For her whose path turns
Under dark earth, where there are no more tears.
CHORUS. You have passed beyond human daring and come at last
Into a place of stone where Justice sits.
I cannot tell
What shape of your father's guilt appears in this.

ANTISTROPHE II

ANTIGONE. You have touched it at last: that bridal bed
Unspeakable, horror of son and mother mingling: 30
Their crime, infection of all our family!
O Oedipus, father and brother!
Your marriage strikes from the grave to murder mine.
I have been a stranger here in my own land:
All my life
The blasphemy of my birth has followed me.
CHORUS. Reverence is a virtue, but strength
Lives in established law: that must prevail.
You have made your choice,
Your death is the doing of your conscious hand.   40

[3] When her children were killed by Apollo and Artemis, Niobe wept until she
was turned into a column of stone.

ANTIGONE. Then let me go, since all your words are bitter,
    And the very light of the sun is cold to me.
    Lead me to my vigil, where I must have
    Neither love nor lamentation; no song, but silence.
    [CREON *interrupts impatiently.*]
CREON. If dirges and planned lamentations could put off death,
    Men would be singing for ever.
    [*To the* SERVANTS.]
                                    Take her, go!
    You know your orders: take her to the vault
    And leave her alone there. And if she lives or dies,
    That's her affair, not ours: our hands are clean.   10
ANTIGONE. O tomb, vaulted bride-bed in eternal rock,
    Soon I shall be with my own again
    Where Persephone⁴ welcomes the thin ghosts underground:
    And I shall see my father again, and you, mother,
    And dearest Polyneices—
                            dearest indeed
    To me, since it was my hand
    That washed him clean and poured the ritual wine:
    And my reward is death before my time!

    And yet, as men's hearts know, I have done no wrong,   20
    I have not sinned before God. Or if I have,
    I shall know the truth in death. But if the guilt
    Lies upon Creon who judged me, then, I pray,
    May his punishment equal my own.
CHORAGOS.   O passionate heart,
    Unyielding, tormented still by the same· winds!
CREON. Her guards shall have good cause to regret their delaying.
ANTIGONE. Ah! That voice is like the voice of death!
CREON. I can give you no reason to think you are mistaken.
ANTIGONE. Thebes, and you my fathers' gods,   30
    And rulers of Thebes, you see me now, the last
    Unhappy daughter of a line of kings,
    Your kings, led away to death. You will remember
    What things I suffer, and at what men's hands,
    Because I would not transgress the laws of heaven.
    [*To the* GUARDS, *simply.*]
    Come: let us wait no longer.
    [*Exit* ANTIGONE, *left, guarded.*]

---

⁴ The wife of Hades (Pluto), the god of the underworld.

STASIMON FOUR

STROPHE I

CHORUS. All Danae's[5] beauty was locked away
    In a brazen cell where the sunlight could not come:
    A small room, still as any grave, enclosed her.
    Yet she was a princess too,
    And Zeus in a rain of gold poured love upon her.
    O child, child,
    No power in wealth or war
    Or tough sea-blackened ships
    Can prevail against untiring Destiny!

ANTISTROPHE I

    And Dryas'[6] son also, that furious king,   10
    Bore the god's prisoning anger for his pride:
    Sealed up by Dionysos in deaf stone,
    His madness died among echoes.
    So at the last he learned what dreadful power
    His tongue had mocked:
    For he had profaned the revels,
    And fired the wrath of the nine
    Implacable Sisters that love the sound of the flute.

STROPHE II

    And old men tell a half-remembered tale
    Of horror done where a dark ledge splits the sea   20
    And a double surf beats on the grey shores:
    How a king's new woman[7], sick
    With hatred for the queen he had imprisoned,
    Ripped out his two sons' eyes with her bloody hands
    While grinning Ares watched the shuttle plunge
    Four times: four blind wounds crying for revenge,

ANTISTROPHE II

    Crying, tears and blood mingled.—Piteously born,
    Those sons whose mother[8] was of heavenly birth!
    Her father was the god of the North Wind
    And she was cradled by gales,   30

---

[5] Because of a prophecy that he would be murdered by his grandson, Danae's father imprisoned her in a tower. Zeus visited her in the form of a shower of gold and she became the mother of Perseus.

[6] Lycurgus, for persecuting Dionysos, was driven mad and killed his own child.

[7] The second wife of Phineus, jealous of her stepsons, prevailed upon him to blind them.

[8] Cleopatra, daughter of Boreas, the north wind.

She raced with young colts on the glittering hills
And walked untrammeled in the open light:
But in her marriage deathless Fate found means
To build a tomb like yours for all her joy.

SCENE FIVE

[*Enter blind* TIRESIAS, *led by a boy. The opening speeches of* TIRESIAS
should be in singsong contrast to the realistic lines of CREON.]

TIRESIAS. This is the way the blind man comes, Princes, Princes,
 Lock-step, two heads lit by the eyes of one.
CREON. What new thing have you to tell us, old Tiresias?
TIRESIAS. I have much to tell you: listen to the prophet, Creon.
CREON. I am not aware that I have ever failed to listen.
TIRESIAS. Then you have done wisely, King, and ruled well.   10
CREON. I admit my debt to you. But what have you to say?
TIRESIAS. This, Creon: you stand once more on the edge of fate.
CREON. What do you mean? Your words are a kind of dread.
TIRESIAS. Listen, Creon:
 I was sitting in my chair of augury, at the place
 Where the birds gather about me. They were all a-chatter,
 As is their habit, when suddenly I heard
 A strange note in their jangling, a scream, a
 Whirring fury; I knew that they were fighting,
 Tearing each other, dying   20
 In a whirlwind of wings clashing. And I was afraid.
 I began the rites of burnt-offering at the altar,
 But Hephaistos[9] failed me: instead of bright flame,
 There was only the sputtering slime of the fat thigh-flesh
 Melting: the entrails dissolved in grey smoke,
 The bare bone burst from the welter. And no blaze!

 This was a sign from heaven. My boy described it,
 Seeing for me as I see for others.

 I tell you, Creon, you yourself have brought
 This new calamity upon us. Our hearths and altars   30
 Are stained with the corruption of dogs and carrion birds
 That glut themselves on the corpse of Oedipus' son.
 The gods are deaf when we pray to them, their fire
 Recoils from our offering, their birds of omen
 Have no cry of comfort, for they are gorged
 With the thick blood of the dead.
            O my son,

[9] The god of fire (Vulcan).

These are no trifles! Think: all men make mistakes,
But a good man yields when he knows his course is wrong,
And repairs the evil. The only crime is pride.

Give in to the dead man, then: do not fight with a corpse—
What glory is it to kill a man who is dead?
Think, I beg you:
It is for your own good that I speak as I do.
You should be able to yield for your own good.

CREON. It seems that prophets have made me their especial province.
All my life long   10
I have been a kind of butt for the dull arrows
Of doddering fortune-tellers!
                              No, Tiresias:
If your birds—if the great eagles of God himself
Should carry him stinking bit by bit to heaven,
I would not yield. I am not afraid of pollution:
No man can defile the gods.
                            Do what you will,
Go into business, make money, speculate
In India gold or that synthetic gold from Sardis,   20
Get rich otherwise than by my consent to bury him.
Tiresias, it is a sorry thing when a wise man
Sells his wisdom, lets out his words for hire!

TIRESIAS. Ah Creon! Is there no man left in the world—

CREON. To do what?—Come, let's have the aphorism!

TIRESIAS. No man who knows that wisdom outweighs any wealth?

CREON. As surely as bribes are baser than any baseness.

TIRESIAS. You are sick, Creon! You are deathly sick!

CREON. As you say: it is not my place to challenge a prophet.

TIRESIAS. Yet you have said my prophecy is for sale.   30

CREON. The generation of prophets has always loved gold.

TIRESIAS. The generation of kings has always loved brass.

CREON. You forget yourself! You are speaking to your King.

TIRESIAS. I know it. You are a king because of me.

CREON. You have a certain skill; but you have sold out.

TIRESIAS. King, you will drive me to words that—

CREON.   Say them, say them!
Only remember: I will not pay you for them.

TIRESIAS. No, you will find them too costly.

CREON.   No doubt. Speak: 40
Whatever you say, you will not change my will.

TIRESIAS. Then take this, and take it to heart!
The time is not far off when you shall pay back
Corpse for corpse, flesh of your own flesh.

You have thrust the child of this world into living night,
You have kept from the gods below the child that is theirs:
The one in a grave before her death, the other
Dead, denied the grave. This is your crime:
And the Furies and the dark gods of Hell
Are swift with terrible punishment for you.
Do you want to buy me now, Creon?
                                        Not many days,
And your house will be full of men and women weeping,
And curses will be hurled at you from far   10
Cities grieving for sons unburied, left to rot before the
        walls of Thebes.
These are my arrows, Creon: they are all for you.
[*To* BOY.]
But come, child: lead me home.
Let him waste his fine anger upon younger men.
Maybe he will learn at last
To control a wiser tongue in a better head.
[*Exit* TIRESIAS.]
CHORAGOS. The old man has gone, King, but his words
        Remain to plague us. I am old, too,
        But I can not remember that he was ever false.   20
CREON. That is true. . . . It troubles me.
        Oh it is hard to give in! but it is worse
        To risk everything for stubborn pride.
CHORAGOS. Creon: take my advice.
CREON.   What shall I do?
CHORAGOS. Go quickly: free Antigone from her vault
        And build a tomb for the body of Polyneices.
CREON. You would have me do this?
CHORAGOS.   Creon, yes!
        And it must be done at once: God moves   30
        Swiftly to cancel the folly of stubborn men.
CREON. It is hard to deny the heart! But I
        Will do it: I will not fight with destiny.
CHORAGOS. You must go yourself, you cannot leave it to others.
CREON. I will go.
                —Bring axes, servants:
        Come with me to the tomb. I buried her, I
        Will set her free.
                        Oh quickly!
        My mind misgives—   40
        The laws of the gods are mighty, and a man must serve them
        To the last day of his life!
[*Exit* CREON.]

PÆAN

CHORAGOS. God of many names
CHORUS.   O Iacchos[10]
                                        son
of Cadmeian Semele
                    O born of the Thunder!
Guardian of the West
                    Regent
of Eleusis' plain
                    O Prince of mænad Thebes
and the Dragon Field by rippling Ismenos: 10

CHORAGOS. God of many names
CHORUS.   the flame of torches
flares on our hills
                    the nymphs of Iacchos
dance at the spring of Castalia:
from the vine-close mountain
                                come ah come in ivy:
Evohé evohé! sings through the streets of Thebes

CHORAGOS. God of many names
CHORUS.   Iacchos of Thebes   20
heavenly Child
                    of Semele bride of the Thunderer!
The shadow of plague is upon us:
                                come
with clement feet
                    oh come from Parnasos
down the long slopes
                    across the lamenting water

CHORAGOS. Io Fire! Chorister of the throbbing stars!
O purest among the voices of the night!   30
Thou son of God, blaze for us!

CHORUS. Come with choric rapture of circling Mænads
        Who cry *Io Iacche!*
                    God of many names!

[10] i.e., Dionysos.

EXODOS

[*Enter* MESSENGER.]

MESSENGER. Men of the line of Cadmos, you who live
　　　Near Amphion's citadel:
　　　　　　　　　　　　　I cannot say
　　　Of any condition of human life "This is fixed,
　　　This is clearly good, or bad." Fate raises up,
　　　And Fate casts down the happy and unhappy alike:
　　　No man can foretell his Fate.
　　　　　　　　　　　　　Take the case of Creon:
　　　Creon was happy once, as I count happiness:
　　　Victorious in battle, sole governor of the land,   10
　　　Fortunate father of children nobly born.
　　　And now it has all gone from him! Who can say
　　　That a man is still alive when his life's joy fails?
　　　He is a walking dead man. Grant him rich,
　　　Let him live like a king in his great house:
　　　If his pleasure is gone, I would not give
　　　So much as the shadow of smoke for all he owns.

CHORAGOS. Your words hint at sorrow: what is your news for us?

MESSENGER. They are dead. The living are guilty of their death.

CHORAGOS. Who is guilty? Who is dead? Speak!   20

MESSENGER.   Haimon.
　　　Haimon is dead; and the hand that killed him
　　　Is his own hand.

CHORAGOS.   His father's? or his own?

MESSENGER. His own, driven mad by the murder his father had
　　　done.

CHORAGOS. Tiresias, Tiresias, how clearly you saw it all!

MESSENGER. This is my news: you must draw what conclusions
　　　you can from it.

CHORAGOS. But look: Eurydice, our Queen: 30
　　　Has she overheard us?

[*Enter* EURYDICE *from the palace, center.*]

EURYDICE. I have heard something, friends:
　　　As I was unlocking the gate of Pallas'[11] shrine,
　　　For I needed her help today, I heard a voice
　　　Telling of some new sorrow. And I fainted
　　　There at the temple with all my maidens about me.
　　　But speak again: whatever it is, I can bear it:
　　　Grief and I are no strangers.

---

[11] Athene, goddess of wisdom.

MESSENGER.   Dearest Lady,
 I will tell you plainly all that I have seen.
 I shall not try to comfort you: what is the use,
 Since comfort could lie only in what is not true?
 The truth is always best.
        I went with Creon
 To the outer plain where Polyneices was lying,
 No friend to pity him, his body shredded by dogs.
 We made our prayers in that place to Hecate
 And Pluto, that they would be merciful. And we bathed 10
 The corpse with holy water, and we brought
 Fresh-broken branches to burn what was left of it,
 And upon the urn we heaped up a towering barrow
 Of the earth of his own land.
       When we were done, we ran
 To the vault where Antigone lay on her couch of stone.
 One of the servants had gone ahead,
 And while he was yet far off he heard a voice
 Grieving within the chamber, and he came back
 And told Creon. And as the King went closer,   20
 The air was full of wailing, the words lost,
 And he begged us to make all haste. "Am I a prophet?"
 He said, weeping, "And must I walk this road,
 "The saddest of all that I have gone before?
 "My son's voice calls me on. Oh quickly, quickly!
 "Look through the crevice there, and tell me
 "If it is Haimon, or some deception of the gods!"

 We obeyed; and in the cavern's farthest corner
 We saw her lying:
 She had made a noose of her fine linen veil   30
 And hanged herself. Haimon lay beside her,
 His arms about her waist, lamenting her,
 His love lost under ground, crying out
 That his father had stolen her away from him
 When Creon saw him the tears rushed to his eyes
 And he called to him: "What have you done, child? Speak
  to me.
 "What are you thinking that makes your eyes so strange?
 "O my son, my son, I come to you on my knees!"
 But Haimon spat in his face. He said not a word, 40
 Staring—
     And suddenly drew his sword
 And lunged. Creon shrank back, the blade missed; and the boy,
 Desperate against himself, drove it half its length

Into his own side, and fell. And as he died
He gathered Antigone close in his arms again,
Choking, his blood bright red on her white cheek.
And now he lies dead with the dead, and she is his
At last, his bride in the houses of the dead.
    [*Exit* EURYDICE *into the palace.*]
CHORAGOS. She has left us without a word. What can this mean?
MESSENGER. It troubles me, too; yet she knows what is best,
    Her grief is too great for public lamentation,
    And doubtless she has gone to her chamber to weep
    For her dead son, leading her maidens in his dirge.   10
CHORAGOS. It may be so: but I fear this deep silence.
    [*Pause.*]
MESSENGER. I will see what she is doing. I will go in.
    [*Exit* MESSENGER *into the palace.*]
    [*Enter* CREON *with attendants, bearing* HAIMON's *body.*]
CHORAGOS. But here is the King himself: oh look at him,
    Bearing his own damnation in his arms.
CREON. Nothing you say can touch me any more.
    My own blind heart has brought me
    From darkness to final darkness. Here you see
    The father murdering, the murdered son—
    And all my civic wisdom!
    Haimon my son, so young, so young to die,   20
    I was the fool, not you; and you died for me.
CHORAGOS. That is the truth; but you were late in learning it.
CREON. This truth is hard to bear. Surely a god
    Has crushed me beneath the hugest weight of heaven,
    And driven me headlong a barbaric way
    To trample out the thing I held most dear.

    The pains that men will take to come to pain!
    [*Enter* MESSENGER *from the palace.*]
MESSENGER. The burden you carry in your hands is heavy,
    But it is not all: you will find more in your house.
CREON. What burden worse than this shall I find there?   30
MESSENGER. The Queen is dead.
CREON. O port of death, deaf world,
    Is there no pity for me? And you, Angel of evil,
    I was dead, and your words are death again.
    Is it true, boy? Can it be true?
    Is my wife dead? Has death bred death?
MESSENGER. You can see for yourself.
    [*The doors are opened, and the body of* EURYDICE *is
    disclosed within.*]

CREON. Oh pity!
  All true, all true, and more than I can bear!
  O my wife, my son!
MESSENGER. She stood before the altar, and her heart
  Welcomed the knife her own hand guided,
  And a great cry burst from her lips for Megareus dead,
  And for Haimon dead, her sons; and her last breath
  Was a curse for their father, the murderer of her sons.
  And she fell, and the dark flowed in through her closing eyes.
CREON. O God, I am sick with fear.   10
  Are there no swords here? Has no one a blow for me?
MESSENGER. Her curse is upon you for the deaths of both.
CREON. It is right that it should be. I alone am guilty.
  I know it, and I say it. Lead me in,
  Quickly, friends.
  I have neither life nor substance. Lead me in.
CHORAGOS. You are right, if there can be right in so much wrong.
  The briefest way is best in a world of sorrow.
CREON. Let it come,
  Let death come quickly, and be kind to me.   20
  I would not ever see the sun again.
CHORAGOS. All that will come when it will; but we, meanwhile,
  Have much to do. Leave the future to itself.
CREON. All my heart was in that prayer!
CHORAGOS. Then do not pray any more: the sky is deaf.
CREON. Lead me away. I have been rash and foolish.
  I have killed my son and my wife.
  I look for comfort; my comfort lies here dead.
  Whatever my hands have touched has come to nothing.
  Fate has brought all my pride to a thought of dust.   30
  [As CREON is being led into the house, the CHORAGOS advances
  and speaks directly to the audience.]
CHORAGOS. There is no happiness where there is no wisdom;
  No wisdom but in submission to the gods.
  Big words are always punished,
  And proud men in old age learn to be wise.

PLAUTUS

THE LITTLE GHOST
[MOSTELLARIA]

VIA PLAUTUS

"ANTIGONE" AND "THE BACCHAE" represent very fairly the thirty-two extant plays of the Greek serious repertory. But the spectator in the classical theater expected to be moved to laughter as well as to pity by the actions impersonated before him. True, he kept his experiences carefully separated: one dramatic festival was appropriated to serious drama, another to comedy. But even a day's program of tragedies would be followed by a "satyr" play whose mythical subject was more grotesque than terrifying, and there are moments (like the Tiresias-Cadmus episode in *The Bacchae*, or the reluctant Sentry in *Antigone*) where the seriousness of the main action is lightened.

The earliest fully developed comic actions are to be found in the plays of Aristophanes (c. 448–380 B.C.) whose main weapon was satire and whose targets are so topical that much of the fun must be conjectured from industrious (and dubious) footnotes (see Glossary: Greek comedy). In several of his plays, however, the subject is sufficiently universal or sufficiently fanciful to evoke laughter without explication. *The Frogs* centers on a contest between the (deceased) tragic poets, with Dionysos as judge to decide which shall be brought back from Hades to revive the drooping stage. In *Lysistrata* the women of a city at war with its neighbor, frustrated and disgusted by the dislocation of their lives, enforce a peace by a highly successful, if somewhat bawdily presented, campaign of passive resistance. Even when dealing with such subjects as peace and war, however, these works are outside the traditional development of dramatic art; they present a comic dilemma, follow it with a number of scenes exploiting situations related to, or growing out of it, and contrive a conclusion. Of the careful structure of serious drama, with its pattern of action and exposition, the Old Comedy knows or cares nothing.

However, about 336 B.C. another kind of comedy, New Comedy, displaced the Aristophanic. It is chiefly associated with Menander (c. 342–292 B.C.), but, since until very recently his works were available only in fragments, most of our knowledge of the form derives from imitations of Menander and his fellows by two Roman comedians, Terence and Plautus. From the Roman plays and from the Greek remains, it is possible to see the very close connection between serious and comic drama.

In general, tragedy dealt with a protagonist following a self-determined course of action in opposition to the course decreed (without his knowledge) by the gods or some other supernatural force, and concluded with his defeat, sometimes after recognizing, too late, his error. The finality of the conclusion is well-represented in the fifth episode of *Antigone*, in which the baffled tyrant crosses the orchestra bearing the corpse of his only son, his only heir, into the house where his dead Queen awaits him. The later tragedies of Euripides, however, present a shift away from heroic struggle and final doom to the pathos of human suffering and the promise of some forgiveness. Agave, in *The Bacchae*, arouses pity because the playwright insists on presenting her as a mother; Cadmus is promised eventual salvation and immortality. In his version of the story of Electra, Euripides directs his audience to consider human suffering rather than superhuman justice. And as the years moved on from the days of Sophocles to the days of Menander, the stage reflected a change in the interest of the audience. Myth and legend became less and less attractive; the long war with Sparta finally ended, there was perhaps less urgency to be reminded of the archetypal struggles of the past. The concerns of the middle-class, family life, commercial success, became more and more the preoccupations of the audience, and hence of the dramatic experience they sought.

The characters of Menander, and therefore of Terence and Plautus, are young men and their sweethearts, miserly or stubborn old men who oppose them, clever servants who aid them, and professional types (soldiers, moneylenders) who are introduced to be made sport of. The setting is realistic and contemporary, a city street lined with the houses of the principal characters; the sentiments are homely and proverbial; and the action is complex enough to hold the interest of the audience but not so complex as to leave them in doubt of a happy outcome.

Plautus' *Mostellaria* is derived from a Greek comedy by Philemon, a contemporary of Menander, and makes no attempt to disguise its origin. The setting and the characters are Greek, though the attitudes are bourgeois Roman. The situation is highly conventional: in his father's absence (on business) the young hero has recklessly wasted the family property and income in riotous living. Unexpectedly the father returns and it becomes the responsibility of the clever slave, Tranio, to keep him in the dark as long as possible. Most of the comedy comes from Tranio's inexhaustible inventiveness: whenever the truth is about to be revealed, he discovers a new trick to deceive the Old One. In the end, a compromise is forced on the father, and the play ends with no hint of the characteristic finality of tragedy.

Yet, aside from the ending, the differences between tragedy and comedy are more of degree than kind. The tragic protagonist was often the political tyrant, stubborn in his pride of judgment; his comic counterpart is the domestic tyrant, the merchant blinded to the true nature of things by his success or his position. The clever servant or slave is a descendant of that god-in-the-machine (see Glossary) who appears so often in Euripides to help the characters (and the playwright) out of the tangled web they have spun. The climactic episode of tragedy comes when the hero, Creon, for instance, is finally brought to recognize his own responsibility for the state of affairs; in comedy, it comes when the father discovers that the young lady he has been opposing is the long-lost daughter of his respectable best friend or that, as in the *Mostellaria*, the young men intend to make good his financial losses. Tragic conflict often turned on the maintenance of order in the state or on some ethical problem; comedy is concerned with the proper relationships of men and women in the family, and on the accumulation of money that ensures security.

As in tragedy, irony plays an important part in the comic experience: the young lover overhearing his sweetheart and her nurse as they discuss what her manner and conduct ought to be;

more grossly, the clever servant directing jokes to the audience as he makes fools of the two householders. This is perhaps the clearest example of how comedy diminishes the conventional devices of tragedy and at the same time broadens them for the pleasure of the audience.

For the pleasure of the audience is of great importance to the comedian. Plautus (254–184 B.C.) was first and last a professional man of the theater; the theater was his life and his livelihood. Unlike his tragic predecessors he did not have the state or a religious cult to support him, but only his own talents and an acute sense of what the audience wanted. Hence, he adopted and extended the use of dramatic irony in which the audience participated with delight. Hence, the comic adaptation of the recognition scene: in tragedy this had come at the climax of the action and led to a reversal of the actor's fortunes (Agave recognizes that she has killed her son and is changed from Queen Mother to outcast); in comedy, there are as many reversals in each act as the playwright can devise: a situation is established only to be overthrown by the next character to enter. Such modifications of tragedy were in the New Comedy of the Greeks.

But Plautus had some elements of his own to introduce into the comic pattern. He was himself of humble origin and must have been aware of the popular amusements of the country people, plays burlesquing the pomp of heroic legends, comic skits sporting with the supposed peculiarities of the natives of particular towns or districts, folk songs. At any rate, he imported these elements into the comic actions borrowed from the Greek, and created a kind of drama which can properly be called Plautine. Instead of long episodes in more or less regular poetic dialogue (the traditional chorus disappeared in New Comedy), Plautus freely interrupts his poetic dialogue—*diverbia*— with musical passages—*cantica*—presented as solos, duets, or group numbers. *Mostellaria* is, in fact, a kind of musical comedy, mingling songs, deliberate parodies of tragic pomp, and a plot about the defeat of a tyrant through the ingenuity of a very earthbound god indeed. For the reader with any knowledge of the later history of dramaturgy, the play will seem like an old friend; the Plautine combination of a debased tragic plot providing opportunities for extended comic situations is the most durable of all dramatic structures. It would not be too extreme to say that it was by way of Plautus that a drama devised for an ancient culture, and reflecting the myths and ethics of vanished cults, found its place in the enduring traditions of the living theater of succeeding centuries. The Broadway stage, the movie screens, and the television sets of this century attest to its durability and, in the proper hands, its vitality.

The present translation is based on the text edited by W. M. Lindsay and published by the Clarendon Press, Oxford (*n.d.*). The translator has been guided by a desire to make a faithful approximation of the Plautine form, shifting with the original— from dialogue to song and, in the *cantica*, to suggest the freedom of Plautine patterns from the "shambling mass of hirsute bacchaics" to the rigid simplicity of folk song. For those readers who (unlike the translator) detest puns, it should be pointed out that here, too, the English text attempts to be conscientious.

Characters

THEOPROPIDES
an old man

PHILOLACHES
his son

PHILEMATIUM
PHILOLACHES' *mistress*

SCAPHA
her maid

TRANIO
THEOPROPIDES' *servant*

SPHAERIO
another servant

GRUMIO
a farm hand

CALLIDAMATES
PHILOLACHES' *friend*

DELPHIUM
his mistress

PHANISCUS
PINACIUM
his servants

SIMO
THEOPROPIDES' *neighbor*

MISARGYRIDES
a moneylender

SLAVES

SCENE: *A street in Athens. The stage is narrow, and so long that it seems plausible for characters at one end not to notice characters at the other end, or to overhear their conversations. At the back on the right, the house of* THEOPROPIDES; *on the left, the house of* SIMO, *whose porticoed doors open onto the street. Between the houses, a narrow alleyway. At the front of the stage, in the center, a small altar.*

THE LITTLE GHOST
[MOSTELLARIA]

Titus Maccius Plautus

Translated by Alan S. Downer

ACT ONE

[*From the house of* THEOPROPIDES *comes an exchange of unintelligible curs-ings, and a great clashing of pans. The door opens and* GRUMIO, *dressed in farmer's clothes, bursts out, yelling at the enemy within.*]

GRUMIO. Come out of the kitchen, you scoundrel, so saucy 'mong your saucepans. Come out of that house, you termite! By heaven, when I git you back on the farm, I'll *git* you, sure as shootin'. Come out! Come on out, I tell you, kitchen-stink! What're you hidin' fer?

[TRANIO, *a very superior and self-sufficient slave, foppishly dressed, poses in the doorway.*]

TRANIO. Why on earth are you making all this uproar in front of the door? Maybe you think you are still in the country? Get away from the house. Back to the country; back to—hell. Go away from the door. There. [*He slaps* GRUMIO.] Is that what you were after?

GRUMIO. Ouch! What're you hittin' me fer?

TRANIO. For living.

GRUMIO. All right, but just wait'll the Old Man gits back. Just let him git safely back. Your belly's got fat with him gone.

TRANIO. Well, that's not the truth or anything remotely like it, you squash-head. How can anyone grow fat on something that isn't there?

GRUMIO. So, you city-slicker, you crowd-pleaser, you're throwin' it in my face I'm a stupid country boy? I bet I know why, Tranio. You know you're headed for the grindin' mill pretty soon. In just a few days, Tranio, you be an added link in the chain gang down on the farm. So while you still got the chance, bottoms up, and burn the candle, and lead the Old Man's son astray. Drink all day and drink all night, live like

Greeks, buy up whores and set 'em free, feed parasites, and stuff your-self with fancy food. Is that what the Old Man told you to do when he went abroad? Is that how he's going to find his property's been took care of? This your idea how a good servant acts—ruin the Old Man's property and his son at the same time?

I can tell the boy's ruined from the sort of things he's up to. And to think, once there wasn't a boy in the whole of Attica who had a better reputation for thrift or clean livin'. Now he takes the prize in the other direction. Thanks to you and your teachin'.

TRANIO. It's no business of yours what I am or what I do. Haven't you enough to do, taking care of the cows down on the farm? If I like to drink and flirt and bring home women, I'm risking my skin not yours.

GRUMIO. Listen to loudmouth talkin'!

TRANIO. May Jupiter and all the other gods damn you. You smell of garlic, you attar of sewage, barnyard, goats, pigsty, and manure.

GRUMIO. Well, what d'you expect? We can't all smell of imported perfumes just because you do. We can't all sit at the head of the table and eat fancy because you do. You take your squab and fish and fowl, and leave me my garlic and my fate. You're in luck and I'm not, and that's the way it is. For me things c'n only get better—for you they c'n only get worse.

TRANIO. Don't tell us you're jealous, Grumio, because things go well for me and bad for you. Things are just the way they ought to be: I chase the girls and you chase the cows. Chops for me and slops for you. And quite right, too.

GRUMIO. The public executioners will make you look like a sieve, I be willin' to bet, chasin' you through the streets with pitchforks . . . if the Old Man gets back.

TRANIO. How do you know that won't happen to you before it does to me?

GRUMIO. Because *I* never earned it; you did and do.

TRANIO. Save your breath to cool your porridge, unless you'd like a good smack in the jaw.

GRUMIO. Are you or aren't you going to give me somethin' to feed the cows?

[TRANIO *threatens him, and he jumps back.*]

All right, go on the way you've started: get drunk, live like Greeks, eat, stuff yourselves, carve up the fatted calf.

TRANIO. Shut up and go back to the farm. I'm off to Piraeus to select a fish for my dinner. I'll send someone with your fodder tomorrow. Well, what are you scowling about now, jailbait?

GRUMIO. Jailbait? By gorry, that's goin' to be *your* name pretty soon.

TRANIO. As long as things are as they are, I should worry about "pretty soon."

GRUMIO. All well and good. But don't forget that what you don't want runs a lot faster than what you do want.

TRANIO. Oh, stop pestering me and get back to the farm. By heavens, I
won't be held up by you any longer.
[*He runs down the street in the direction of the harbor.*]

GRUMIO. So there he goes, and didn't care a straw for what I said. Oh,
immortal gods, have mercy on us. Bring back our Old Master—three
years he's been gone—before everything goes to pot: farm, fireside and
all. If he stays away, there's only a few months' livings left. But now I'll
get back to the farm. I see there's the master's son, a wretched mess
made out of a boy of promise.
[*He goes off in the opposite direction.*]

[*Enter* PHILOLACHES, *a handsome young man, just tipsy enough to be full
of philosophy and remorse. He steadies himself against* SIMO'S *house, and
declaims like a schoolboy taking part in a commencement exercise.*]

PHILOLACHES. I've wondered much and pondered long,
    And argued back and forth with myself;
    Turned over this problem and debated it
    In my mind—if I've *got* a mind:—
    What thing is a man like when he is born,
    What's he resemble, what's his analogue?
      And this is the image I've found.
    Mr. Chairman and Friends:
    A man when he's born is like a new house.
    Wait, let me produce my proof,
    And however unlikely the simile seems
      I'll make you believe that it's sound.
    I'll convince you at once that it's just as I say
    And you folks afterwards, I know, will agree
    That it's just as I say when you've heard what I say;
      Then you'll say what I say.
    Attend to my reasoning upon this point;
    I want you . . . be enlightened like me.
    —Here's a house just finished according to plan
      All shiny and new and gay.
You praise building and builder, and want one yourself
You'll build one just like it, spare no labor or pelf.
    And then, in moves some lazy bum
    With a family that's filthy and feckless,
And the house becomes run-down, a good thing neglected.
    First thing you know, along comes a squall
    And rips off the roof tiles, the gutters, and all.
    The owner's too lazy to tend to his topping,
    So the rains slop the walls till they're lit'rally sopping.
    Beams rotted—all lost is the artisan's care.
    In conclusion, the house is the worser for wear.
Now don' blame the builder, but the lazy householder:

Though for trifling cost could his house be protected,
To repairing the old one he turned a cold shoulder,
Till naught can be done but a new one erected.

Now you're edified 'bout ed'fices; I will then
Explain metaphorically how houses are men.
The parents are builders of children, *in primis*,
To lay firm foundations their 'ndeavor supreme is.
The walls they erect must be solid and tight,
Be useful to others and pleasing to sight.
So nex'-best, secon'-rate mater-i-al *won'* do,
No expense too expensive, no skimping.—*Secundo:*
They put on refinements, the finishing touches,
Letters and morals and other like suches.
Spend money and labor in portions most ample
That all may admire their child as Example.

[*He pauses, thinks, and prepares for a fresh attack.*]
Then comes time for army service, and they put the boys in the hands
of some relative to guide them. And so the sons leave the builders'
hands.

And when they return from a campaign's burn-out
You can plainly see signs how the "building" will turn out.
I was steady and honest in composition
When the builder was still in control of my thinking.
But after I moved into my own disposition
I ruined the builder's work in a winking.
It began with a squall that let in the rain,
A tempest of idleness beat on my brain,
My modesty, virtue, sailed off in the air,
And I was too lazy for any repair.
And love, which when younger I'd held in abhorrence,
Seeped into my breast, drowned my heart in its torrents.
Now my cash and my credit are goodness knows where,
And just like the house, I am worser for wear.
All rotted my timbers, and crumbling the floor,
And no one to help me repair them once more.
It breaks my heart to see
The difference between the before and after me.
Then, my studies won acclaim,
Then, I took prizes in every kind of game:
Discus, spear, catch, fencing, sprint, *manège*,
In all I held the edge.
A model of the strict and simple life, you see,
And all the other fellows tried to copy me.
And now that my house is ruined, I've at last discovered the spirit

that's haunted it—me.

[PHILOLACHES *sniffles quietly as* PHILEMATIUM *and her old maidservant,* SCAPHA, *enter from the house of* THEOPROPIDES. *Two slaves are with them, carrying a dressing table, with a cosmetic chest, some gowns, and a bench. The women do not notice* PHILOLACHES.]

PHILEMATIUM. My gracious, it's been a long time since I've enjoyed a cold bath so much. Oh Scapha, I've never felt so completely clean.

SCAPHA. All outcomes have causes; no great harvest without a great spring.

PHILEMATIUM. What has a harvest to do with my bath?

SCAPHA. Nothing more than what your bath has to do with a harvest.

PHILOLACHES [*seeing them*]. O lovable Love, here is the windstorm that ripped off the roof of modesty that covered me, that let Desire and Cupid flood into my breast, until it was too late to repair it. The walls of my heart are saturated, the house is a ruin.

PHILEMATIUM [*whirling around*]. Dear Scapha, do you think this dress is becoming? I want to please Philolaches, my sweetheart, my protector.

SCAPHA. Why not wear just pretty ways, since you're so pretty? It's not the *stuff* the lover loves, it's the *stuffing.*

PHILOLACHES [*eavesdropping*]. So help me, Scapha's a pretty one herself. She knows a bag of tricks. It's pretty tricky to know so well what lovers think about.

PHILEMATIUM. Well then?

SCAPHA. Well what?

PHILEMATIUM [*holding up another dress*]. See if you think this one is becoming.

SCAPHA. With that figure anything you put on is becoming.

PHILOLACHES. There! For those words, Scapha, this very day I shall give you—something. Who praises one who pleases me'll never go unrewarded.

PHILEMATIUM. I'm not asking you for flattery.

SCAPHA. Don't be a silly girl. Would you rather be criticized falsely than praised truthfully? For me, I'd rather have a thousand false compliments than a single honest criticism, or to be laughed at for my looks.

PHILEMATIUM. I love the truth, I want to be told the truth. I detest lies.

SCAPHA. As you love me, as your Philolaches loves you, I swear the dress is becoming.

PHILOLACHES [*changing his tune*]. What's that, you old devil? What kind of an oath is that? "As your Philolaches loves you!" What about her love for me; why wasn't that added? I take back my gift. You're sunk; whatever gift I was going to give you, you've lost.

SCAPHA. I really am surprised that such a shrewd, intelligent, well-trained girl should turn so silly.

PHILEMATIUM. I'd be glad for your advice, when I make a mistake.

SCAPHA. Well, by the gods, you're certainly making a mistake when you sit around waiting for that one man, practically worshiping him and ignoring all the others. To be tied down to one lover is for wives, not courtesans.

PHILOLACHES [*barely holding himself back*]. By God! What evil spirit is loose in my house? May all the gods and goddesses torment me with the worst of torments if I don't torment that old hag with thirst and hunger and cold.

PHILEMATIUM. Scapha, I won't listen to any bad advice from you.

SCAPHA. You're a simple fool if you think he'll be loving and kind forever. I give you fair warning, he'll leave you when you're dated and he's sated.

PHILEMATIUM. I hope that will never happen.

SCAPHA. Unhoped for things happen more often than you hope. Here,— if none of my words can persuade you that you ought to believe my words, learn from the facts. You know what I look like now, and what I used to be. I used to be just as pretty as you are now, and had just as many suitors. I devoted myself to just one of them, and, by the gods, when age began to change the color of my head, he walked out and left me flat. I think it'll be the same in your case.

PHILOLACHES [*clenching his fists*]. I can hardly keep from tearing the eyes out of that antique mischief-maker.

PHILEMATIUM. He set me free with his own money—me only, for himself only. I think I'm right in keeping myself only for him only.

PHILOLACHES. Immortal gods, a pretty girl with a sense of honor! I did the right thing, and I rejoice that I went broke for her sake.

SCAPHA. You're being just plain silly.

PHILEMATIUM. Why?

SCAPHA. Because you care about whether he loves you.

PHILEMATIUM. But my goodness, why shouldn't I care?

SCAPHA. You're a free woman now. What you were after, you've got. But he'll lose all the principal he paid to free you, unless he keeps up his interest in your love.

PHILOLACHES. May Hercules squash me, if I don't torture her with endless torment. She's poisoning my girl with the evil advice of a bawd.

PHILEMATIUM. I will never be able to give him the gratitude he deserves from me. Scapha, you can never persuade me to lower my estimation of him.

SCAPHA. But just consider this one fact: if you bind yourself just to him while you are still so young, you'll be sorry when you're older.

PHILOLACHES [*hopping with rage*]. Oh, if I could change myself into a quinsy and lodge in the old witch's throat I'd strangle the mischief-maker.

PHILEMATIUM. I must feel the same affection, now that I'm free, as I did when I used to caress him before I won it.

PHILOLACHES. For that speech, may the gods do what they will to me, if I don't set you free all over again, and scatter Scapha all over the street.

SCAPHA. If you have a guarantee that he'll foot your bills from now on, and be "Yours Truly" for the rest of your life, I suppose you should keep yourself for him alone, and put your hair up.[1]

PHILEMATIUM. If a person has a good reputation, she doesn't usually have to worry about money. If I keep my good name, I'll be rich enough.

PHILOLACHES. By God, if it comes to that I'll sell my own father before you shall beg or starve as long as I'm alive.

SCAPHA. What's to happen to all the others who are in love with you?

PHILEMATIUM. They'll love me all the more when they see that I keep my favors for the most deserving.

PHILOLACHES. I wish news of my father's death had just been announced. I'd disinherit myself of everything and make her my heir.

SCAPHA. Anyway, all he's got will be gone soon: day and night, eating and drinking, and nobody considering the expense. Living like lords.

PHILOLACHES [with determination]. By God I'll begin considering the expense, and I'll begin with you. You'll eat nothing and you'll drink nothing at my house for the next ten days.

PHILEMATIUM. If you've anything nice to say about him, you have my permission to speak. But if you go on talking improperly, I'll have you whipped.

PHILOLACHES [to the audience]. By golly, if I had bought an ox to sacrifice to Jove with the money I gave for her freedom, it would never have been as well invested. You can see she really loves me. Oh, a clever man am I: when I needed someone to plead my cause, I liberated a lawyer!

SCAPHA. Since I see you don't value any man more than Philolaches, I will agree with you rather than be whipped—if you have a guarantee he'll be "Yours Truly" for the rest of your life.

PHILEMATIUM. Give me my looking glass and jewel box, quick, Scapha. I want to be all prettied up when he gets here, Philolaches, my sweetie.

SCAPHA. A woman who worries about her age, she's the one who needs a looking glass. What good is a looking glass to you? You can outglass any glass.

PHILOLACHES [seeming to relent]. Ah, Scapha, not for nothing did you speak that speech so trippingly. This very day I will certainly give something to—you, my sweet Philematium.

PHILEMATIUM. Please look, Scapha. Does my hair look right?

SCAPHA. If you look right, you needn't worry about your hair.

PHILOLACHES. Ph! Do you ever remember anything worse than that woman? The old devil is now a Yes-woman, a minute ago she was a No-woman.

PHILEMATIUM. May I have the rouge?

SCAPHA. What do you want rouge for?

PHILEMATIUM. To put on my cheeks.

SCAPHA. That's the same as whitening ivory with shoe-blacking.

---

[1] The mark of a married woman.

PHILOLACHES. A neat phrase: Ivory with shoeblacking! Hurray! Good for Scapha!

PHILEMATIUM. Well, then, give me the eye-shadow.

SCAPHA. I will not. You've got some sense. Would adding more paint to a brand new picture make it more charming? At your age you shouldn't touch cosmetics: rouge, beauty-clay, or any other stuff.

PHILEMATIUM. Here then, hold the mirror.

[SCAPHA holds the mirror and PHILEMATIUM, overcome by what she sees, touches it with her lips.]

PHILOLACHES. Damn it, she's kissed the mirror. If I had a stone, I'd break that mirror's face.

SCAPHA. Take this towel and wipe your hands.

PHILEMATIUM. For heaven's sakes, why?

SCAPHA. Because you were holding the mirror, and I'm afraid your hands may smell of silver. Philolaches must never suspect that you've been receiving silver.

PHILOLACHES. I don't think I've ever seen a more experienced old bawd. Very neat that business about the mirror, the old hag.

PHILEMATIUM. What do you think about a little perfume?

SCAPHA. Of course not.

PHILEMATIUM. Why not?

SCAPHA. Gracious, a woman always smells best when she smells of nothing. Why those old hags who drench with scent, who, youthless and toothless, try to hide wrinkles with paint, as soon as their sweat and their perfume combine they smell like the kitchen when a cook has poured all his sauces into one pot. You don't know what the smell is, but you know this: it ain't good.

PHILOLACHES. A learned bawd! She wrote the book. [To the audience.] It's true, isn't it: you fellows all know it very well, particularly the ones whose wives are old and who bought you with their dowries.

PHILEMATIUM. Now Scapha, look over my jewelry and my dress; do they suit me?

SCAPHA. That's not for me to say.

PHILEMATIUM. For goodness' sake, who is, then?

SCAPHA. That's easy: Philolaches. He shouldn't buy you anything he doesn't think will suit you. Anyway, what's the point in displaying something he doesn't really want? Fancy dress is to cover up old age, fancy jewels offset ugliness. A pretty girl without clothes is prettier than one dressed up. And ornament doesn't do much good if natural charm is lacking. Women who are unattractive only spoil beautiful clothing. And if they're beautiful they need no ornament.

PHILOLACHES. I've kept my hands out of this long enough.

[Moves over to the women.]

What have you been doing for so long?

PHILEMATIUM. I've been dressing myself up to please you.

PHILOLACHES. You're dressed up enough. [*To* SCAPHA *and the slaves.*] You, go in and take this stuff away. Now, Philematium, my sweet, I'd love to have some wine with you.

PHILEMATIUM. O my! And I with you. Whatever you want, I want, sweetheart.

PHILOLACHES. Ah, that word is cheap at twenty minas.[2]

PHILEMATIUM. Well, give me ten, dear; I want to sell that name to you at bargain prices.

PHILOLACHES. Then you still owe me ten. Add it up if you like. I gave thirty minas to buy your freedom.

PHILEMATIUM. Why do you blame me—

PHILOLACHES [*interrupting*]. Blame *you*? I love to have *myself* "blamed" for that. Indeed, I haven't made such a good investment in a long, long time.

PHILEMATIUM. And in loving you, I couldn't have chosen a better line.

PHILOLACHES. Our credit and debits thus balance precisely:
        Your love and my love pair off very nicely.
[*To the audience sentimentally.*] May those who are happy about this be utterly happy forever. May those who are envious never have anything to make anyone envious of them.

PHILEMATIUM [*moves over to the bench*]. Come and sit down. [*To a slave.*] Boy, fetch some water for our hands and put the little table over here. Go, see where the dice are. [*To* PHILOLACHES.] Would you like some cologne?

PHILOLACHES. What for? I'm sitting by attar of roses. [*Looking down the street.*] But isn't that my pal prancing along with his girl friend? It is, Callidamates on parade with his mistress! Hurray, my sweet! The reg'ment's assembling, *hup!* Prepare to portion the plunder.
[*Enter* CALLIDAMATES, *very drunk, leaning on* DELPHIUM, *a courtesan.*]

CALLIDAMATES [*speaking over his shoulder, to an offstage servant*]. I want you to fetch me at Philolaches', early. Hear? Thass an order.
    Why, that place where I was, I ducked out of the doors I got so damn sick of the comp'ny 'n' the talk. Now I'll go to Philolaches' house for a feshampcdder,[3] where we'll get a warm welcome and a hot time.
    Shay, do I sheem mememem-mellow?

DELPHIUM. You're about as usual and fated to be late.

CALLIDAMATES. Why not I hug you and you hug me, huh?

DELPHIUM. If your heart's set on it, all right.

CALLIDAMATES. You're sweet. Lead on, sweetheart.

DELPHIUM. Careful not to fall—stand up!

CALLIDAMATES. Ll-light of my life—you're my pet, my hon.

DELPHIUM. Careful not to fall down in the street before we get to lie down on the couch over there.

---

[2] Mina, a coin roughly equivalent to $20.00.
[3] i.e., *fête champêtre* (picnic).

CALLIDAMATES. O lemme, lemme fall.

DELPHIUM. Then fall.

[*He falls, and pulls her down with him.*]

CALLIDAMATES [*clutching her*]. Wha's'is in my hands?

DELPHIUM. If you fall, you can't fall without me.

CALLIDAMATES [*cheerfully*]. Someone'll find us lying here and pick us up, after a while.

DELPHIUM. The man is plastered.

CALLIDAMATES. Did you say I'm ppplastered?

DELPHIUM [*getting up*]. Take my hand, I don't want you to get wrecked.

CALLIDAMATES. Well, take it.

DELPHIUM. Come, go along.

CALLIDAMATES. Come where?

DELPHIUM. Forgotten already?

CALLIDAMATES. I know; it just came into my head: going home to a party. [*Starts off.*]

DELPHIUM. Not that way, this.

CALLIDAMATES. I remember absolutely.

PHILOLACHES. You don't mind if I go to meet them, darling? He's my closest friend, after all. Back in a minute.

PHILEMATIUM. That minute will be an hour to me.

CALLIDAMATES [*approaching* PHILOLACHES]. Anyone at home?

PHILOLACHES. Certainly is.

CALLIDAMATES. Well, Philolaches! Greetings, bestest frien' in all the world.

PHILOLACHES. The gods protect you. Sit down, Callidamates. Where've you been?

CALLIDAMATES. Anywhere you can get drunk.

PHILEMATIUM. Dear Delphium, won't you sit here? [*To a slave.*] Get him a drink.

CALLIDAMATES. Now I'm going to sleep.

PHILOLACHES. What's new and different about that?

DELPHIUM. What'll I do with him *now?*

PHILEMATIUM. Dear, leave him be. Quick boy, pass the tankard. Delphium first.

ACT TWO

[*While the party continues,* TRANIO *enters from the harbor, loaded with packages. He stops at a distance from the others and soliloquizes, in a burlesque tragedy strain.*]

TRANIO. The mightiest God with might and main to hell
     Philolaches and me, his man, would drag.
     Hope is dead and Confidence decamped;

Salvation couldn't save us if She would.
A mountain-mass of misery and misfortune
Is at the pier. My master's disembarked
And Tranio's goose is cooked.
[*To the audience.*] Anyone like to make a little money
By being a stand-in at a crucifixion?
Where are the bullies with rhinoceros hides,
Or those who lead the charge against the foe
For two bits a day and all the spears your body can hold?
A talent[4] to the first to take my cross—
Provided his legs and arms are nailed on double.
When the job is done, just come collect the cash.
But I—I'm a fool not to run right home.
[*He moves toward the others.*]

PHILOLACHES [*seeing him*]. At last, here's the food. Here's Tranio back from the harbor.

TRANIO. Philolaches—

PHILOLACHES. What's up?

TRANIO. You and I—

PHILOLACHES. What about you and I?

TRANIO. We're sunk.

PHILOLACHES. How so?

TRANIO. Your father's home.

PHILOLACHES. What did I hear you say?

TRANIO. We're goners. I said your father's back.

PHILOLACHES. Damn it, *where* is he?

TRANIO. *Where* is he? He's *here*.

PHILOLACHES. Who said so? Who saw him?

TRANIO. I tell you I saw him myself.

PHILOLACHES. Oh boy! Now what do I do?

TRANIO. You ask me what you're doing? You're lying on the couch.

PHILOLACHES. You saw him yourself?

TRANIO. My very own self.

PHILOLACHES. You're sure?

TRANIO. Sure.

PHILOLACHES. I'm as good as dead if your story is true.

TRANIO. And what good would it do me to lie?

PHILOLACHES. Now what do I do?

TRANIO [*pointing to the wine and the benches*]. Have all this stuff taken away. Who's the sleeping beauty?

PHILOLACHES. Callidamates. Delphium, wake him up.

DELPHIUM [*shakes him*]. Callidamates! Callidamates, wake up!

CALLIDAMATES. I'm 'wake. Let's have a drink. [*Nods.*]

---

[4] Talent: a silver coin roughly equivalent to $500.00.

DELPHIUM [*shakes him again*]. Wake up. Philolaches' father's come back.

CALLIDAMATES. A health t' thee, father. [*Snores.*]

PHILOLACHES. Healthy father! [*Shaking* CALLIDAMATES.] I'm the one who's dead and gone.

CALLIDAMATES. Dead *and* gone? How can you die twice?

PHILOLACHES. For heaven's sake, get up; Father's coming.

CALLIDAMATES. Father's coming? Tell him to go 'way. Why's he want to come back here for? [*Snores.*]

PHILOLACHES. What shall I do? Father'll come and find me drunk here, with the house full of drunks and women. It's stupid to wait until you're dying of thirst to start digging a well. Just like me: Father's back and I'm just beginning to wonder what to do.

[CALLIDAMATES *snores.*]

TRANIO. Look at him. He's tucked in his head and gone to sleep. Get him up.

PHILOLACHES [*trying to haul* CALLIDAMATES *to his feet*]. Wake up, will you? I've been trying to tell you my father's coming here.

CALLIDAMATES [*sitting on the edge of the couch*]. D'you say your father? Gimme boots, gimme weapons! Cripes, I'll kill your father.

PHILOLACHES [*pushing him down*]. You'll just make everything worse.

DELPHIUM. Shut up, dearie.

PHILOLACHES [*to the* SLAVES]. Pick him up and carry him inside.

CALLIDAMATES [*as the* SLAVES *fling his arms over their shoulders*]. Boys, I'm going to use you for a chamber pot unless you get me to one.

[*The* SLAVES *drag him into* THEOPROPIDES' *house in a hurry.*]

PHILOLACHES [*drops on the couch*]. I'm sunk!

TRANIO. Don't be downhearted. I've got just the medicine for you.

PHILOLACHES. I'm as good as dead.

TRANIO. Quiet. I'll concoct a sedative for your nerves. How if I fix it so that, when your father arrives, he not only won't go in the house; he'll actually run away from it? [PHILOLACHES *looks doubtful.*] You get inside and take all this stuff with you, quick!

PHILOLACHES. Where'll I be?

TRANIO. Wherever you want to be most: you'll be with her, [DELPHIUM], or her [PHILEMATIUM].

DELPHIUM [*apprehensive*]. Shouldn't we be going?

TRANIO. Not a step, Delphium. And when you're inside don't drink a drop less because of this.

PHILOLACHES. Uh-uh, it makes me sweat to think what your fancy talk may lead to.

TRANIO. Control yourself and do as I say.

PHILOLACHES. I can try.

TRANIO. First of all, Philematium, you go inside, and you too, Delphium.

DELPHIUM [*mocking*]. We are yours to command.

TRANIO [*with a leer*]. I wish to God you were!

[*The girls go into the house.* TRANIO *turns to* PHILOLACHES.]
Now listen carefully while I tell you what I want you to do. First of all,
have them shut the house up tight, and nobody utter a sound—
PHILOLACHES. I'll see to that.
TRANIO. As if there wasn't a mother's son living in the house.
PHILOLACHES. I understand.
TRANIO. And nobody is to answer when the Old Man knocks on the door.
PHILOLACHES [*nodding*]. Anything else?
TRANIO. Have the front door key brought out to me. I want to lock the
place up from the outside.
PHILOLACHES [*as he goes into the house*]. I'm putting myself and my future
into your hands, Tranio.
TRANIO. There's not a hair's difference whether the better man is patron
or client.
[*He sings.*]
> A timid man when under stress
> Of good or bad will make a mess.
> To avert a sure catastrophe
> 's a job for a man of wit like me.
> —*Like* me? It *is* me!
> The storm I've raised, I'll turn to quiet
> And no one will be bothered by it.
> —Watch me, you'll see!

[*Enter* SPHAERIO, *from the house of* THEOPROPIDES.]
What are you coming out here for, Sphaerio? Oh, yes. You've carried
out my orders precisely.
SPHAERIO. Master ordered me to beg you earnestly to scare his father anyway you can, so he won't go in and find him.
TRANIO. Give your master this communiqué: I'll fix it so his father won't
dare look at the house; he'll hide his head and run off in holy terror.
[*Holds out his hand.*] Give me the key. [SPHAERIO *does so.*] Go inside and
shut the door. I'll lock from this side.
[SPHAERIO *goes in and the door is shut.* TRANIO *turns the key and tucks it
in his clothing.*]
Now, let him come. I'll give the Old Man a greater send-off while he's
alive than he'll ever get when he dies. I'll get away from the door, over
here where I can see better, and load the Old Man with a pack of lies
when he gets here.
[TRANIO *hides in the alleyway as* THEOPROPIDES, *the Old Man, enters. He
is an irrascible, astute businessman, but stupid and naïve in human affairs.
There are two slaves with him, bearing luggage. He, too, speaks in the vein
of burlesque tragedy.*]
THEOPROPIDES. O Neptune, hearty thanks I give to thee:
> You sent me home again almost alive.
> But if you ever catch me after this

With one toe on the water, go ahead
And finish what you started on this trip.
But as of now, be gone, be gone from me.
No further trust I'll ever put in you.

TRANIO. By heaven, Neptune made a big mistake
In letting that fine fat prize get away.

THEOPROPIDES. [*Crossing toward his house. The porters follow.*] After three years in Egypt, here I am back home. I'm sure everyone'll be glad to see me.

TRANIO. Not so glad, I'll bet, as someone who came to say that you were dead.

THEOPROPIDES [*at the door*]. But how's this? The door locked in the day-time? I'll knock. [*He does so.*] Hey, there, anyone inside? Open up the door. [*Pounds on it.*]

TRANIO [*stepping out of the alleyway*]. My god, who's that going right up to our house?

THEOPROPIDES [*turning*]. This fellow's my servant Tranio.

TRANIO [*runs to him*]. Oh, Theopropides, master, greetings! I rejoice in your safe return. Have you been in good health?

THEOPROPIDES. Right along, as you see.

TRANIO. My congratulations.

THEOPROPIDES. But what's the matter, are you all crazy?

TRANIO. Why?

THEOPROPIDES. Why! Here you are lolling about outdoors, not a mother's son taking care of the house, or opening the door, or answering it. I almost broke the door down, pounding it.

TRANIO [*drawing back in affected horror*]. Good lord! You didn't touch the building?

THEOPROPIDES. Why shouldn't I touch it? I told you I almost broke the door down with pounding.

TRANIO [*incredulous*]. You *touched* it?

THEOPROPIDES. I touched it, I tell you—I banged it.

TRANIO [*turning away, sadly*]. Ah, too bad.

THEOPROPIDES. What's the matter?

TRANIO. You've done it now.

THEOPROPIDES [*anxiously*]. What's this all about?

TRANIO. I haven't words to describe what a terrible, dreadful thing you've done.

THEOPROPIDES. What is it?

TRANIO [*retreating to the alleyway*]. Beat it, for God's sake. Get away from the house. Run over here, run closer to me. [THEOPROPIDES *moves closer to him.*] You touched the door?

THEOPROPIDES. How could I knock on it, if I didn't touch it?

TRANIO. Lord, you've killed—

THEOPROPIDES. Killed who?

TRANIO. —All your family.

THEOPROPIDES. May all the gods and goddesses confound you and your superstitions.

TRANIO. I'm afraid you can never purify yourself and those fellows [*the porters*].

THEOPROPIDES. Why should I? And what is all this strange business about my door?

TRANIO. Please tell those two to get away from there.

THEOPROPIDES [*going up to the porters, at the door*]. Go away. [*They move off.*]

TRANIO. Don't touch the house.

  [THEOPROPIDES *returns, center.*]

  You'd better touch the ground, too.

THEOPROPIDES. For heaven's sake, tell me what's up.

TRANIO. For seven months no one has put a foot into this house, since we moved out.

THEOPROPIDES. Keep talking—why?

TRANIO. Look around. Can anyone hear us?

THEOPROPIDES [*looks right and left*]. All's clear.

TRANIO. Look some more.

THEOPROPIDES [*obeys*]. There's nobody. Now, speak up.

TRANIO. A terrible crime has been committed.

THEOPROPIDES. What? I don't understand.

TRANIO. I tell you a crime was committed, long ago,—once upon a time.

THEOPROPIDES [*what he doesn't understand, he repeats*]. Once upon a time?

TRANIO. We've only just now uncovered the facts.

THEOPROPIDES [*with a kind of stumbling eagerness*]. What was the crime and who did it? Tell me.

TRANIO. The master of this house seized a guest and murdered him. I think he's the very man who sold you the house.

THEOPROPIDES [*one idea behind*]. Murdered him?

TRANIO. He stole all his guest's money, and then buried his guest under the house.

THEOPROPIDES. Just how did you discover anything like that?

TRANIO. I'll tell you. Now listen carefully. One night, your son was eating out, and when he got home from the dinner, we all went to bed. We all went sound asleep. By chance, I forgot to put out the light. And all of a sudden he let out a loud yell.

THEOPROPIDES. Who did? My son?

TRANIO. Sh! Quiet! Listen. He said that in his sleep a dead man had come to him.

THEOPROPIDES. Oh, it was just in his sleep?

TRANIO. Sure. But listen: he said the dead man spoke to him like this—

THEOPROPIDES. In his sleep?

TRANIO. D'you expect him to speak to him when he was awake, after being dead for sixty years? Sometimes you're a little slow. . . .

THEOPROPIDES. I'll be quiet.

TRANIO. But listen to what he told him *in his sleep*: "I am Diapontius, a guest from overseas. Here I abide for this is my appointed abiding place. For Orcus has refused to admit me to Acheron, since I lost my life before my time. By my own faith I was deceived. My host murdered me and buried me secretly here in the house without any funeral rites, the wretch, to get my money. Now, you move out of here. This is a house accursed, the abode of evil." It would take a year to tell all the strange things that have happened here.

THEOPROPIDES [*suddenly*]. Sh, Sh!

TRANIO. For heaven's sake, what's the matter?

THEOPROPIDES. The door—it creaked. [*He quakes.*]

TRANIO [*pretending fright, he looks heavenward and points at* THEOPROPIDES]. *This* is the one who knocked.

THEOPROPIDES. My blood is turning to water. The dead are going to take me to Acheron while I'm alive.

TRANIO [*to the audience*]. Damn it! Those people in there are going to spoil the whole show. I'm scared he'll catch me red-handed.

THEOPROPIDES. What are you talking to yourself for?

TRANIO. Get away from that door. Quick, for God's sake!

THEOPROPIDES. Where'll I go? You go first.

TRANIO. I'm safe. I have made peace with the dead.

VOICE WITHIN. Hey, Tranio!

TRANIO. You won't call me if you know what you're doing. I had no part in the knocking at your door.

VOICE. I want to know—

TRANIO [*close to the door*]. Careful. Not another word.

THEOPROPIDES. What's the matter, Tranio? Who're you talking to?

TRANIO [*turns toward his master*]. Oh, was it you that called to me? As God is my witness, I thought it was the dead man complaining because you knocked on his door. But are you still here? Won't you do what I say?

THEOPROPIDES. What shall I do?

TRANIO [*pointing off stage*]. Don't look back. Get away fast. Cover your head.[5]

THEOPROPIDES. Why aren't *you* going?

TRANIO. I am at peace with the dead.

THEOPROPIDES. I see. But what about a minute ago? Why were you so scared?

TRANIO. Just you don't worry about me, master; I can take care of myself. But you better take yourself off as fast as you can run, and pray for help from Hercules.

---

[5] A ritual gesture for protection from spirits.

THEOPROPIDES [*as he rushes off the stage*]. I call upon thee Hercules, O
Hercules—
TRANIO. And so do I—to bring you today, Old Man, a mess of mischief.
Immortal gods preserve us all! What a fine crooked deal I've got on the
fire.

ACT THREE

[*Enter* MISARGYRIDES, *the moneylender, mumbling to himself. He does not,
of course, see* TRANIO.]
MISARGYRIDES. I've never seen a worse year in the moneylending business
than this one. I spend the hours from dawn to dusk at my bank in the
forum, with never a nibble for a loan. [*He mumbles on, as he stands
counting on his fingers.*]
TRANIO. Oh boy, now I'm really fixed, good and proper. Here comes the
loanshark who let us have the money to buy the girl and run the house.
The jig is up unless I get to him before the Old Man finds out. I'll
intercept him.
[*He looks over his shoulder and sees* THEOPROPIDES *coming back on the
stage.*]
But what on earth is *he* coming back to the house so soon for? I'm afraid
somebody's been whispering about this business. I'll go speak to him.
[*Starts, then stops.*]
Oh misery, I'm frightened. Nothing's more miserable than a man with a
bad conscience, and that's me. Well, whatever he may have found out
about it, I'll stir things up some more. That's what the doctor ordered.
[*Crosses to* THEOPROPIDES.]
Where've you been?
THEOPROPIDES. Where I met the man I bought the house from.
TRANIO. You didn't tell him what I told you?
THEOPROPIDES. I absolutely did, every bit of it.
TRANIO [*aside*]. Ouch! I guess my plan is finished.
THEOPROPIDES. What did you say?
TRANIO. Nothing at all. But look here, did you really tell him?
THEOPROPIDES. Everything, from start to finish.
TRANIO. And he confessed about the guest?
THEOPROPIDES. Denied the whole thing.
TRANIO. The villain! Denied it?
THEOPROPIDES. That's what I said: he denied it.
TRANIO. Think now, are you sure he didn't confess, a teeny bit?
THEOPROPIDES. I'd tell you if he confessed. What do you think ought to
be done?
TRANIO. What do I think? For heaven's sake, drag him with you before a

judge. [*Aside.*] Only see you take him before a judge who will believe me [*aloud*] and you'll win as easily as a bear eats honey. [*He turns toward the moneylender.*]

MISARGYRIDES. Hey, there's Philolaches' servant, Tranio. They haven't paid me principal or interest.

THEOPROPIDES. Where're you going?

TRANIO. I wasn't going anywhere special. Don't I have the accursèd luck! Born when all the gods were feeling dyspeptic. While that one's [MISARGYRIDES] here, he [THEOPROPIDES] has to arrive. I'm in a terrible spot, because this way or that way my plans are revealed. But I'll take him on first.

[*Scampers to* MISARGYRIDES.]

MISARGYRIDES. He's actually coming to meet me. I'm saved! There's hope for my money.

TRANIO. He's smiling; he's fooling himself. A very good day to you, Misargyrides.

MISARGYRIDES. Hello. Where's the money?

TRANIO. Take yourself off, you brute. I'm hardly in range before you've opened fire.

MISARGYRIDES [*to the audience, pointing to* TRANIO]. This fellow's purse is full of nothing.

TRANIO [*to the audience, pointing at* MISARGYRIDES]. My God, the man can see through clothing.

MISARGYRIDES [*noticing* TRANIO'S *mimicry*]. Why not stop the nonsense!

TRANIO. Why? What do you want me to do?

MISARGYRIDES. Where is Philolaches?

TRANIO. You couldn't possibly have come at a more opportune moment.

MISARGYRIDES. Now what?

TRANIO [*tries to drag him further from* THEOPROPIDES]. Step over here.

MISARGYRIDES [*demanding loudly*]. Why don't I get my interest?

TRANIO. I know you've got good lungs. You don't need to shout.

MISARGYRIDES. I will too shout, by God!

TRANIO. Look, just do as I ask.

MISARGYRIDES. What do you ask me to do?

TRANIO [*pushing him toward the exit*]. Go away, go back to your house.

MISARGYRIDES. Go back?

TRANIO. And come back here around noon.

MISARGYRIDES. To get my interest?

TRANIO. You'll get it; now go on.

[*Pushes him.*]

MISARGYRIDES [*returning*]. Why run back here and spend all that energy—or waste it? Better I stay right here till noon.

TRANIO [*pushing*]. Go back to your house; I'm telling the truth; only go back.

MISARGYRIDES [*returning*]. Why don't you give me my interest? Why this trifling?

TRANIO. By Hercules, you—listen to me, go away.

MISARGYRIDES. No sir, I'm going to call for Philolaches.

TRANIO. Good and loud. You're only happy when calling.

MISARGYRIDES. I want what's coming to me. For days now you've been fooling me like this. If I bother you, give me my money: I go away. Just say the word and you're free of me.

TRANIO. Take the principal.

MISARGYRIDES. Unh-unh, the interest. I want that first.

TRANIO. What do you say, you nasty old man? Did you come here to see how far you could push us? Go as far as you like. He'll give you nothing, he owes you nothing.

MISARGYRIDES. Owes me nothing?

TRANIO. You can't get a shred out of him. You're not afraid he'll skip the country to avoid paying your interest, when he's ready to hand over the principal here and now?

MISARGYRIDES. But I'm not asking for the principal; first I want the interest that's coming to me.

TRANIO. Stop bothering me. Nobody's going to pay you, no matter what you do. I guess you think you're the only shark in the business?

MISARGYRIDES. I want my interest. Give me my interest. Both of you give me my interest. Are you going to give me my interest right now? Am I to get my interest?

TRANIO. Interest here, interest there. He doesn't know any other word to say but interest. Be off! I don't think I ever saw a lousier beast than you.

MISARGYRIDES. By heavens, you can't scare me away with that kind of talk.

THEOPROPIDES [*who has been watching with interested puzzlement*]. A hot argument; even this far away, it burns me. [*Talks to* TRANIO.] What is this interest, for goodness' sake, that he's looking for?

TRANIO. See, there's his father who just got back from a long journey. He'll give you your interest *and* your principal. Don't try to involve us further in your debts. You'll see he won't keep you waiting.

MISARGYRIDES. Well, I'll take it, if he gives it.

THEOPROPIDES. Answer me!

TRANIO [*crossing to Theopropides*]. What do you want to know?

THEOPROPIDES. Who is that? What's he after? Why was he yelling for my boy, Philolaches? Why was he quarreling with you? What's owing him?

TRANIO [*turning back to* MISARGYRIDES]. Heavens, order us to throw the money at his greedy snout.

THEOPROPIDES. Order you—?

TRANIO. Command us to pound his face with money.

MISARGYRIDES [*advancing eagerly*]. I'm prepared to endure it, if it's really in pounds.

THEOPROPIDES. What's this about money?

TRANIO. It's just—well, Philolaches owes him a little.

THEOPROPIDES. How little?

TRANIO. Well—forty minas; surely you don't think that's very much?

MISARGYRIDES. And that's all I want.

TRANIO. Hear that? Isn't he the typical moneylender, by God, the rottenest race in the world?

THEOPROPIDES. I don't care who he is, or what he is, or where he's from. There's just one thing I want to be told, one thing I'm interested in knowing about: I hear there's some interest owing on this principal?

TRANIO. We owe him forty-four minas. Say you'll pay and he'll go away.

THEOPROPIDES. Tell him I'll pay.

TRANIO. You tell him.

THEOPROPIDES. Me?

TRANIO. You yourself. Take my advice and tell him. Come on, give him your word. I tell you it's all right.

THEOPROPIDES. Tell me, what was the money used for?

TRANIO [thinking hard]. It's quite safe.

THEOPROPIDES. If it's so safe, you can safely pay it back.

TRANIO [an inspiration]. Your son bought a house.

THEOPROPIDES [stupidly]. A house?

TRANIO. A house.

THEOPROPIDES [delighted]. Hurray! Philolaches is a chip off the old block; he's turned into a businessman. You did say, a house?

TRANIO. I said a house. But do you know what kind of a house?

THEOPROPIDES. How could I know that?

TRANIO [whistles!].

THEOPROPIDES. What sort is it?

TRANIO. Don't ask me.

THEOPROPIDES. Why not?

TRANIO. Even a mirror would be dazzled by it. They don't come any better.

THEOPROPIDES. Well done, by God! How much is it costing him?

TRANIO. Oh, a cool talent, times you and me.[6] He gave the forty minas for an option. Borrowed money from him for a down payment. Understand now? After your house turned out as I told you, your son immediately went out and bought the other house.

THEOPROPIDES. Well done, by God!

MISARGYRIDES. Hey, it's twelve o'clock already.

TRANIO. Won't you give him what he wants? He'll make us both sick. He's owed forty-four minas, principal and interest.

MISARGYRIDES. That's the total. I'm not looking for a penny more.

TRANIO [aside, his palm itching]. By God, I wish you would ask for a leetle more.

THEOPROPIDES. Young man, you'll do business with me.

[6] i.e., two talents.

MISARGYRIDES. You mean I get my money from you?

THEOPROPIDES. Ask me for it tomorrow.

MISARGYRIDES [*promptly*]. I'm off—and tomorrow I'll be better off.
[*Hastens away.*]

TRANIO. Damn you tomorrow. He almost made a royal mess of my plan.
By God, there's no class more rotten or more dishonest than the moneylenders.

THEOPROPIDES. Where is this house my son bought?

TRANIO. Oh—oh, more trouble.

THEOPROPIDES. Will you answer my question?

TRANIO. Yes. But—I'm trying to think of the owner's name.

THEOPROPIDES. Well, think of it then.

TRANIO [*to the audience*]. Now, what do I do? Unless I tell him that his son
bought the house of his next-door neighbor? I've always heard that the
best lie is one that's boiling hot. Whatever the Gods inspire me with I'll
pass on to him as gospel.

THEOPROPIDES. Come now. Thought of the fellow's name yet?

TRANIO. Damn this fellow. Your son bought the house of your next-door
neighbor.

THEOPROPIDES. Honestly?
[*Turns to look at* SIMO'S *house.*]

TRANIO. If you pay the money, then it's honest. If you don't, it isn't.

THEOPROPIDES. He picked a good location.

TRANIO. Never a better.

THEOPROPIDES. I'm dying to take a look at the house. Knock on the door
and see if you can call someone out, Tranio.

TRANIO. Here we go again! Now I don't know what to say. Once again I'm
stuck on the same old rock.

THEOPROPIDES. What's the matter now?

TRANIO. Gods, what can I think of now? I'm caught good and proper.

THEOPROPIDES. Call someone out and ask to be shown around.

TRANIO. But sir, there are ladies living here. We must find out first whether
they'd permit it or not.

THEOPROPIDES. That's a very good point. You go and get permission. Meantime I'll wait over here till you get back.
[*He watches for a moment, then slowly falls into a doze.*]

TRANIO [*crossing the stage*]. Old Man, may all the gods and goddesses rip
you up by the roots. Every plan I get, you undermine.
[*Notices* SIMO'S *door beginning to open.*]
Say, this is good—here's Simo, the owner of the house, just coming
out.
[TRANIO *ducks into the alleyway.*]
I'll step in here while I call my wits into emergency session. When I've
hit on a plan, I'll attack.
[SIMO, *who is about* THEOPROPIDES' *age, but a ladies' man rather than a*

*businessman, comes out and closes the door behind him. He is chuckling
with pleasure.*]

SIMO. Though a married man's days are mostly of grief
   This one for a change was a pleasant relief.
   My wife served lunch right off the fire—
   And then proposed that we retire.
   My wife thought if I were well-fed
   She then could trick me into bed.
   Said I (her purpose I'd a hunch on):
   "It's bad to sleep right after luncheon."
   And secretly I slipped outside—
   In there, my wife's fit to be tied.

TRANIO [*aside*]. I see bad things for him ahead,
   Unpleasantries in board and bed.

SIMO. A husband's days are never sunny
   Whose wife is rich in years and money.
   She never gives in to the sandman
   He's just a payment-on-demand-man.
   In part, I share her feelings, as a
   Matter of fact, I'm bound for the Plaza.
   Your wife's like mine? Then let me mention:
   The Forum beds have no contention.
   The past is bad, as I have stated,
   But worse, I'm sure, for me is fated.

TRANIO [*aside*]. Your escapade has got you into trouble, old man.
   Blame not the gods in this particular,
   But enterprize ex*tra*-cubicular.

But now it's time for me to speak to the old boy. Here goes for the *coup
de grace!* I've found a way to fix Theopropides, to cut him down
and save my own skin. I'll go to meet him. The gods be gracious to you,
Simo.

SIMO. The same, Tranio.

TRANIO. How're you feeling?

SIMO. Not bad. How are you?

TRANIO. I'm shaking hands with the best fellow in the world.

SIMO. Kind of you to say such nice things.

TRANIO. The least I could say.

SIMO. Right. And I'm shaking hands with a good—[*aside*]—for nothing—
servant.

THEOPROPIDES. Hey, you scoundrel! Come here.

TRANIO. Be with you directly.

SIMO. Well now. How much longer—?

TRANIO. What?

SIMO. What usually goes on in there? [*Pointing to* THEOPROPIDES' *house.*]

TRANIO. What do you mean?

SIMO. You know perfectly well what I'm talking about. But you're right: Look out for number one, and remember how short life is.

TRANIO. What? Oh, I see. I didn't quite understand you were talking about our affairs.

SIMO. By God, you live the life of joy. You know what's good, wine and food, the finest fish; you live on nothing but the best.

TRANIO. Well, we *did* live on nothing but the best, Simo, but now everything has been ruined.

SIMO. How so?

TRANIO. We're singly and summarily sunk, Simo.

SIMO. You don't say? Everything was going your way prosperously enough up to now.

TRANIO. I don't deny that you speak the truth. We certainly had the best of everything we wanted. But Simo, now the wind has been taken out of our sails.

SIMO. Yes? How'd that happen?

TRANIO. The worst way.

SIMO. How could anything happen to a ship tied up on shore?

TRANIO. Alas!

SIMO. What's the matter?

TRANIO. Damn me, I'm sunk!

SIMO. Why?

TRANO. Because a ship has come to ram us broadside.

SIMO. I'd like to wish as you wish, Tranio. But what's the business?

TRANIO. I'll tell you; master's back from his trip.

SIMO. Then you'll be whipped, chained, and crucified.

TRANIO. By your knees, I beg you not to give evidence against me.

SIMO. Don't be afraid, he'll learn nothing from me.

TRANIO. Thank you, my patron.

SIMO. Hah! I'll keep my patronage to myself.

TRANIO. Now, here's what the old man sent me to speak to you about.

SIMO. First, I want an answer to this question: what does your master know about your carryings-on?

TRANIO. Not a thing.

SIMO. Hasn't given the boy a bawling out?

TRANIO. Everything's quiet, just like a lake on a cloudless day. Now here's what he told me to ask you particularly, whether you'll permit him to inspect your house.

SIMO. It's not for sale.

TRANIO. I know that. But the old boy wants to add a lady's parlor, and a bathroom, and a walk and a portico to his own house.

SIMO. Where did he dream that up?

TRANIO. I'll explain. He wants to find his son a wife as soon as possible: that's why he wants a new lady's parlor. And he says that some architect, I forget who, praised yours for being terribly well-planned. So he wants to take this as a model, unless you object. Even more he wants to take yours as a model because he's heard it's remarkably well-shaded in the summer, all day long even under the hottest sky.

SIMO. Well, he's wrong there. When every place else is shady the sun shines down on me from dawn to dusk. It hangs around my door like a bill collector. There isn't a bit of shade here anywhere, unless maybe at the bottom of the well.

TRANIO. Oh? Why not get a shady lady?

SIMO. No joke. I'm telling you the facts.

TRANIO. Well anyway, he wants to have a look.

SIMO. He can look if he likes. If there's anything that strikes his fancy, he can build after my model.

TRANIO. May I go and call him?

SIMO. Sure, go ahead.

TRANIO [*as he crosses to the center*]. Alexander the Great and Agathocles, they say, were two doers of mighty deeds. Shouldn't I be the third for committing immortal outrages all by myself? He's [SIMO] carrying one of my bags, and the other old man another. I've started a new business, and a pretty good one. Muleteers have mules to carry their packs, but I've got a packtrain of men. And these can carry a great load; whatever you pile on 'em, they carry. Now, I don't know whether to speak to him. I'll go over to him.

[*Crosses.*]

Oh, Theopropides!

THEOPROPIDES [*startled*]. Huh? Who's calling me?

TRANIO. My master's ever-faithful slave.

THEOPROPIDES. Where've you been?

TRANIO. Where you sent me to ask—it's all set.

THEOPROPIDES. For heaven's sake, why did it take you so long?

TRANIO. The old man was busy. I had to wait for him.

THEOPROPIDES. Still the same old Tranio—always late.

TRANIO. Aw, sir! Just remember the old saying, you can't push and pull all at once. I could hardly be here and there at the same time.

THEOPROPIDES. What next?

TRANIO. Go and see it. Look it over as much as you want to.

THEOPROPIDES. Let's go then. You lead the way.

[TRANIO *skips away*, THEOPROPIDES *hobbling after*.]

TRANIO [*over his shoulder*]. I'm not keeping you, am I?

THEOPROPIDES. Right behind you.

TRANIO [*pauses while* THEOPROPIDES *catches up*]. See, the old man himself is waiting for you by the door. He feels sorry he sold it.

THEOPROPIDES. How do you know?

TRANIO. He asked me to persuade Philolaches to sell it back.

THEOPROPIDES. I should think not. Every man reaps his own fields. If we had got the worst of the deal, he'd never let us back out of it. Whatever you win is yours to carry home. A man should only be softhearted with himself.

TRANIO. Now, by God, you're the one who's making us late. Follow me.

THEOPROPIDES. Right. Lead on.

TRANIO. There's the old boy. [*To* SIMO.] Sir, I've brought this man to meet you.

SIMO. Glad to see you safely home from your trip, Theopropides.

THEOPROPIDES. God bless you.

SIMO. Tranio says you want to have a look at my house.

THEOPROPIDES. If it's not inconvenient for you.

SIMO. No inconvenience. Walk in and look around.

THEOPROPIDES. Yes, but the women—

SIMO. Don't worry your head about the women. Go anywhere in the house you like, just as if it was yours.

THEOPROPIDES. "Just as if?"

TRANIO [*quickly, aside to* THEOPROPIDES]. Ah, don't throw up to him that you bought the house, now that he's so sorry. Don't you see how sad the old man's face is?

THEOPROPIDES. I see.

TRANIO. So don't seem to laugh at him or gloat over him: don't mention that you bought the place.

THEOPROPIDES. I understand, and I think that's good advice. You are very considerate. Now what?

SIMO. Why don't you go inside and look all around, much as you like?

THEOPROPIDES. I think this is very kind and considerate of you.

SIMO. I hope I have been, indeed.

TRANIO [*beckoning* THEOPROPIDES *to the front door*]. Come look at this porch, and the promenade in front.

THEOPROPIDES. Indeed, they're splendid.

TRANIO. Now take a look at the door-posts.

[*The two old men are standing by the door.* TRANIO *winks at the audience.*] See how solid they are and—how thick!

THEOPROPIDES. I've never seen finer posts.

SIMO. Well, I paid plenty for them once.

TRANIO [*to* THEOPROPIDES]. Hear that "once"? He can hardly hold back the tears.

THEOPROPIDES. How much did you pay for these?

SIMO. I paid three minas for the pair, plus freight.

THEOPROPIDES [*looking closely*]. Say, they're in worse condition than I thought at first.

TRANIO. How's that?

THEOPROPIDES [*bending over and pointing, presenting his rear to the audience*; SIMO *does likewise*]. Well, look—there's a wormhole at the bottom of each of them.

TRANIO [*with another wink at the audience*]. I think they were cut out of

season; that's what wrong with them. They'd be all right even now, if
you smeared them with pitch. No garlic-eating immigrant carpenter did
this work. And look at the joints.

THEOPROPIDES. I am.

TRANIO. See how weak they are.

THEOPROPIDES. Weak?

TRANIO. Yes—I meant to say, how *slick* they are. Get my point?

THEOPROPIDES. The more I look at it, the better I like it.

TRANIO [*pointing vaguely within*]. Do you see the picture, there, of a magpie
teasing the two old vultures?

THEOPROPIDES [*peers about*]. No, I don't see it anywhere.

TRANIO [*steps between the old men*]. Oh, I can see it: the magpie is in
between the two old vultures, and he's pulling feathers out of both of
them. If you look toward me, you can see the magpie. See it?

THEOPROPIDES. No, I don't see any magpie anywhere.

TRANIO. Well, look toward yourselves then, if you can't see the magpie.
Maybe you'll see the two old vultures.

THEOPROPIDES. Oh, give it up. I don't see any picture of any birds.

TRANIO. All right, I understand: your eyes aren't as sharp as they used
to be.

THEOPROPIDES. But everything that I can see is positively splendid.

SIMO. It'll be worth your while to look around some more.

THEOPROPIDES. Very good idea indeed.

SIMO [*calling to a slave inside*]. Boy, you there, boy! Take this gentleman
around the house, into all the apartments. I'd take you in myself, but I
have some important business in the forum.

THEOPROPIDES. Never mind taking me in; I'm not used to it. I'd rather make
my own mistakes than be taken in by someone else. [*A feeble joke, but
he relishes it.*]

SIMO. I mean, the house.

THEOPROPIDES. So, I'll go in without being taken in.

SIMO. As you please.

THEOPROPIDES. I'll go in then.

TRANIO [*grabs his arm*]. Hold a minute—I'll see whether the dog—

THEOPROPIDES. Yes, go look.

TRANIO [*sticks his head in the door*]. Sssssic, go way, dog! *Sssssssssicum!*
Get out of there! Get the hellandgone out of there! Are you still there?
Sssssicum, Sicum! Git!

SIMO. There's no danger, go right ahead. The dog's as quiet as a lamb. You
can go in as if you owned the place. I'm going to the forum.

THEOPROPIDES. You've been very considerate. Have a nice walk.

[SIMO *goes down the street.*]

Tranio, go and have someone take that dog away from the door, harmless or not.

TRANIO. But just look and see how quietly it's lying there, unless you want
    to look like a nuisance or a coward.
THEOPROPIDES. All right, then. But you come along too.
TRANIO. Right behind you, never fear!
[*They go into the house.*]

ACT FOUR

[PHANISCUS *comes along the street towards* THEOPROPIDES' *house. He is
looking for his master,* CALLIDAMATES.]
PHANISCUS. Slaves who worry about whippings even though they are
       viceless
     To their owners are the most priceless.
     For those who fear nothing after they have done something
       punishable, take thought:
     They train for sprinting, and off they go; but if they are caught
     They collect no cash but a lash—
     They begin with a trifle and end with a smash.
     But my plan of life is, the whip to eschew
     Until I've done something that makes it my due.
     So to date I've conducted myself to keep my hide unmarred
     And lashings I've debarred.
     If I stick to this rule, I will have a sound roof.
     If trouble rains in on others, it will leave me aloof.
     For, as the slaves desire the master to be, he is, right enough;
     If they're good, so's he; if dishonest, he's tough.
     Right now in our house there's a rare crew of clip-crows,
     All blowing their tips but getting lots of whipblows.
     If you tell one of them, "Go fetch master to the house."
     "I'm not going," he'll say. "Why bother with the old souse?
     I know what you want; to cotton up to the boss; you bet, you
       old pig, you want to swill at the trough."
     That's the prize I got from them for good service. So I came off.
     I'm the only one of all of these
     To go fetch Callidamates.
     Tomorrow when master comes to and is wiser
     He'll fix them with his tannic exorciser.
     I value their backs less than my own, I hope.
     They'll be in for a hiding long before I'm dancing on a rope.
[PINACIUM, *another of* CALLIDAMATES' *slaves, comes running on stage.*]
PINACIUM. Wait up there, right where you are! Phaniscus, look back here!
PHANISCUS. You're nothing but a pest to me.

PINACIUM. Look at the choosey monkey. Will you stop a minute, you greedy parasite?

PHANISCUS. What do you mean, I'm a parasite?

PINACIUM. I'll tell you why; you'd go anywhere for a meal.

PHANISCUS. That's my business; eating is fun. What's it to you?

PINACIUM. You're very snooty, because the master likes you.

PHANISCUS. Ouch! My eyes are smarting.

PINACIUM. Why?

PHANISCUS. Too much gas in the air.

PINACIUM. Shut up, fakir, you coiner of counterfeit quips.

PHANISCUS. By God, you can't force me to curse you. Master knows all about me.

PINACIUM. Well, he certainly ought to know his own sleeping bag.

PHANISCUS. If you were sober, you wouldn't talk libel.

PINACIUM. I should be nice to you, when you won't be nice to me? Well, come along with me to meet him, stinky.

PHANISCUS. All right. But for heaven's sake will you stop bringing up— that subject?

PINACIUM. Sure, and I'll knock on the door.

[*He pounds on* THEOPROPIDES' *door.*]

Isn't anybody coming to defend this beaten portal?
To open up the door before its injuries are mortal?
A crowd of drunken sots alone such banging would not answer;
Oh, Callidamates! (*thump! thump!*) It's Pinacium, your man, sir!
I'd better think of something else, and cease to knock so madly,
Or one of them will come out here and beat us just as badly.

[THEOPROPIDES, *followed by* TRANIO, *comes out of* SIMO'S *house.*]

TRANIO. Well, how does the bargain look to you?

THEOPROPIDES. I'm delighted, delighted.

TRANIO. You don't think we paid too much?

THEOPROPIDES. By God, I've never known a house to go so cheap.

TRANIO. Everything's satisfactory?

THEOPROPIDES. You ask me if everything's satisfactory? It's much, much more than satisfactory, by Heaven.

TRANIO. How about the ladies' parlor? The portico?

THEOPROPIDES. Absolutely splendid. I don't think there's a bigger one on the plaza.

TRANIO. Well, I myself and Philolaches measured all the porticos on the plaza.

THEOPROPIDES. And you found—?

TRANIO. This is the longest by a long shot.

THEOPROPIDES. Immortal gods! A delicious bargain! By heaven, if he offered me six talents of solid silver for it, I wouldn't take them.

TRANIO. Believe me, if you dreamed of taking it, I'd never let you.

THEOPROPIDES. Our money's well invested in this bargain.

TRANIO. Now, frankly admit I was the one who accomplished this by needling and wheedling. I got young master to go to the moneylender for the money we gave for the option.

THEOPROPIDES. You saved the whole ship. Now we owe him eighty minas?

TRANIO. Not a smidgeon more.

THEOPROPIDES. He shall have them today.

TRANIO. Good idea. There'll be no chance of his backing out. Or pay the money to me, and I'll see it paid in turn to him.

THEOPROPIDES. There must be no double-dealing, if I give it to you.

TRANIO. Would I dare to trick you in word or deed, even as a joke?

THEOPROPIDES. Would I dare to be off guard if I ever trusted you with anything?

TRANIO. Have I ever deceived you in anything since I've been yours?

THEOPROPIDES. Hah! I've been too careful; I thank the gods and my own character. I'm wise enough to keep a watchful eye on you.

TRANIO [aside]. Smartest thing you ever did!

THEOPROPIDES. Now go out to the farm, and tell my son I'm back.

TRANIO. I shall do as you wish.

THEOPROPIDES. Tell him to get back to the city with you, in a hurry.

TRANIO. All right.

[He moves away.]

Now I'll slip through the back door and join the fun. I'll tell them how things have quieted down, and how I've taken care of him.

[He disappears down the alleyway.]

PHANISCUS [listening at THEOPROPIDES' door]. Strange. I don't hear any of the usual party noises in there, no flute-girl playing and singing or anything.

THEOPROPIDES [noticing the two SLAVES]. Now what's this? What do those fellows want in front of my house? What are they doing? What are they looking for?

PHANISCUS. I'll try knocking again.

[He pounds and calls.]

Hey, unlock! Hey, Tranio, will you open up?

THEOPROPIDES. What kind of a performance is this?

PHANISCUS [knocking]. Will you open up? We've come to fetch our master, Callidamates.

THEOPROPIDES [crossing the stage to the slaves]. Here, you boys, what are you doing? Why are you pounding the house down?

PINACIUM [impertinent]. Here, you old man, why are you asking about something that's none of your business?

THEOPROPIDES. None of my business?

PINACIUM. Unless you've just been made sanitary inspector to snoop and pry, and peer and eavesdrop, in other people's business.

THEOPROPIDES. That's my house you're at.

PINACIUM. What are you talking about? Has Philolaches sold his house? Or is the old boy playing some kind of game?

THEOPROPIDES. I'm telling the truth. But what's your business here?

PHANISCUS. If you must know, our master's having a few drinks here.

THEOPROPIDES [*repetition is his forte*]. Your master's having a few drinks here?

PHANISCUS. You heard me.

THEOPROPIDES. Boy, you're fooling.

PINACIUM. We've come to fetch him.

THEOPROPIDES. Him? What him?

PINACIUM. Our master. Say, how many times do we have to tell you?

THEOPROPIDES. Boy, nobody lives there. Still, you seem straightforward enough to me.

PHANISCUS. Doesn't young Philolaches live in this house here?

THEOPROPIDES. He did live here, but he moved out quite a while ago.

PHANISCUS [*to* PINACIUM]. The old boy needs a doctor. I'm sure you're wrong, sir. Because unless he moved out today, or yesterday, I know perfectly well he lives here.

THEOPROPIDES. No one has lived here for six months.

PINACIUM. You're dreaming.

THEOPROPIDES. I am?

PINACIUM. You.

THEOPROPIDES. No more of your foolishness. I'll talk to that boy.

[*Tries* PHANISCUS]

There's no one living here.

PHANISCUS. He certainly does live here, because yesterday and the day before, and the day before that, and the day before that, and the day before that,—indeed, since his father went on his voyage, there hasn't been a three-day stretch without a party.

THEOPROPIDES. What are you talking about?

PHANISCUS. Not one three-day period without dining and wining, nuzzling and guzzling, with flute-girls and lute-girls.

THEOPROPIDES. Who was doing all this?

PHANISCUS. Philolaches.

THEOPROPIDES. What Philolaches?

PHANISCUS. His father is called Theopropides, if I remember right.

THEOPROPIDES [*aside*]. A-i-i-i-y! I'm sunk, if he remembers right. I must check him further.

[*To* PHANISCUS.]

You say that this Philolaches, whoever he is, regularly has your master for a drinking companion?

PHANISCUS. And I say it again.

THEOPROPIDES. Boy, you're stupider than you look. Now think: didn't you stop off for a bite to eat somewhere *en route* and, maybe, drink a little more than you can hold?

PHANISCUS. What's that?

THEOPROPIDES. I mean, so that you came to the wrong house, by mistake?

PHANSICUS. I know where I meant to go and I know the place I've come to. This is where Philolaches lives, the son of Theopropides. And after his father went off on a business trip, he bought a flute-girl and set her free.

THEOPROPIDES. Philolaches did that?

PHANISCUS. He did. A girl named Philematium.

THEOPROPIDES. For how much?

PHANISCUS. Thirty —

THEOPROPIDES [*expecting the worst*]. Talents?

PHANISCUS. *Mon dieu*, no! Minas.

THEOPROPIDES. He set her free.

PHANISCUS. Indeed he freed her, for thirty minas.

THEOPROPIDES. Are you telling me it cost thirty minas to get Philolaches a woman—?

PHANISCUS. That's what I said.

THEOPROPIDES. And, after his father set out on a business trip, he devoted himself to drinking, along with your master?

PHANISCUS. That's what I said.

THEOPROPIDES. What? Did he buy this house next door?

PHANISCUS. That's what I *didn't* say.

THEOPROPIDES. He gave the owner forty minas as a down payment?

PHANISCUS. I didn't say that, either.

THEOPROPIDES. Oh! You're ruining me.

PHANISCUS. Oh no! He's ruining his father.

THEOPROPIDES. O, true prophesying!

PHANISCUS. I wish I was lying. You seem to be a friend of his father's.

THEOPROPIDES. By heaven, your words prophesy great sorrow for the father.

PHANISCUS. Oh, that's nothing, the thirty minas, beside all that he spends on banquets and other things.

THEOPROPIDES. He's destroyed his father.

PHANISCUS. One of his slaves is a very devil—Tranio: he could eat his way through the riches of Croesus. By heaven, I pity his poor father. When he finds out what's happened, he'll turn to ashes from heartburn.

THEOPROPIDES. If all these things are true.

PHANISCUS. Now what good would it do me to lie about this?

PINACIUM [*pounding on the door again*]. Hey, you inside, will somebody open up?

PHANISCUS. Why keep knocking if nobody's inside? They must have gone off some where together. Let's go along—

THEOPROPIDES. Boys—

PHANISCUS. —and see if we can find them. Come on.

[*Starts down the street.*]

PINACIUM. Coming.

[*Follows him.*]

THEOPROPIDES. Boy, are you leaving so soon?

PHANISCUS. You've got your freedom to wrap yourself up in. Me, unless I
  obey my master and serve him well, I've got nothing to cover my
  carcass.

[*The* SLAVES *exeunt.*]

THEOPROPIDES [*in tragic tones*]. Damned, damned, forever lost. No words
              Can total up my ruin and despair.
              I thought my journey just to Egypt lay—
              Hah! I find I have been taken for a ride
              To lands so distant, shores so remote,
              I know not where I am.

[SIMO *comes on stage, somewhat disgruntled.*]

  But I'll know soon, for there's the man my son bought the house from.
  What are you doing?

SIMO. Coming home from the forum.

THEOPROPIDES. Anything new at the forum today?

SIMO. Sure.

THEOPROPIDES. Well, what?

SIMO. I saw a corpse carried out.

THEOPROPIDES. Hem! [*Spits on the palm of his hand, and jabs his forefinger
  in it, for luck.*]

SIMO. They said he'd been alive just a minute before.

THEOPROPIDES. The hell with it.

SIMO. Why are you hanging around asking for news?

THEOPROPIDES. Well, after all, I just got back from my trip today.

SIMO. I'm invited out, you mustn't expect me to invite you to dinner.

THEOPROPIDES. It never crossed my mind.

SIMO. Maybe tomorrow. Unless someone else asks me, I'll dine with you
  —at your house.

THEOPROPIDES. That never crossed my mind either. But unless you've got
  something else to do, listen to me.

SIMO. A pleasure.

THEOPROPIDES. As I understand it, you received forty minas from Philolaches.

SIMO. As I understand it, not a nickel.

THEOPROPIDES. Well then, from his slave, Tranio.

SIMO. Even less from him.

THEOPROPIDES. I mean the money for the down payment.

SIMO. Where did you dream this up?

THEOPROPIDES. Me dream? You're dreaming if you think you can get out
  of a business deal by this kind of pretending.

SIMO. Out of what deal?

THEOPROPIDES. The one my son negotiated with you while I was away.

SIMO. He made a deal with me while you were away? What deal? What date?

THEOPROPIDES. I owe you eighty silver minas.

SIMO [*quickly*]. Not to me you don't. [*Then reconsidering.*] Well, if you owe it, I'll take it. Promises must be lived up to; no repudiating.

THEOPROPIDES. I certainly don't repudiate the debt, and I intend to pay. But you better not deny that he's already given forty minas.

SIMO. Now see here, look me right in the eye and tell me why you owe me these eighty minas.

THEOPROPIDES. I tell you he bought your house from you, gave you a down payment and owes you the rest.

SIMO. He did? He bought this house from me?

THEOPROPIDES. That's what Tranio told me.

SIMO. Well, Tranio told *me* you wanted your son to get married and so you wanted to build an addition to your house over there.

THEOPROPIDES. I wanted to build an addition?

SIMO. That's what he told me.

THEOPROPIDES. That does it! Words fail me! Friend, I'm doomed and done for!

SIMO. Has Tranio been stirring up a mess?

THEOPROPIDES. He's made a mess of me. He made an absolute fool of me today.

SIMO. What do you mean?

THEOPROPIDES. I mean exactly what I said: he made an everlasting fool of me today. Now, for heaven's sake, be a good fellow and help me out.

SIMO. What can I do?

THEOPROPIDES. Come over here a minute, will you? [*Moving to* SIMO'S *house.*]

SIMO. Sure thing.

THEOPROPIDES. Let me have the use of a couple of slaves and a horse-whip.

SIMO. They're yours.

THEOPROPIDES. While we're getting set, I'll tell you the whole story of how today I was turned into the greatest fool on earth.

[*They go into the house.*]

ACT FIVE

[TRANIO *returns down the alleyway.*]

TRANIO. The man who gets scared when the future is unpredictable, to
    my way of thinking isn't worth a continental—
      I'm not sure what that is, except whatever it is,
        it isn't complimental.

Now, after master sent me to summon his son from
   his country estate
I tiptoed down the alleyway here till I came to
   our backyard gate.
I opened the door and led out my troops, men and
   women alike, and the siege was ended.
Then I summoned a special session of the senate, to
   explain to my troops what I intended.
But as soon as I called the meeting to order, they
   crowded me out of the chair.
Hardly fair!
When I saw that I was being shoved out of my own
   preserves
I did what lots of others do when the situation seems
   desperate: I called for my reserves.
My reserves of ingenuity, I mean, to create a stupendous
   befoggery
And put an end to ambitious demagoguery.

Now I see there's no way to keep what we've done secret from the old
man. So I'll get there first, before they come, and make a treaty. I'm
wasting time. But what is this creaking of our next door neighbor's gate?
It's my master. I'll sample what he's talking about.

[THEOPROPIDES *comes through* SIMO'S *door, speaking to the* SLAVES *he has
stationed within.*]

THEOPROPIDES. Stand there, inside the door, so when I give the signal, you
can jump right out. Snap the manacles on quick. I'll stand by the house
and be ready for my master of the revels, whose hide I will ravel to bits,
if I live.

TRANIO. The jig is up! Now you better see what you can do, Tranio.

THEOPROPIDES [*to the audience*]. When my fish comes, I must play him with
craft and skill. I won't show him the hook right away, I'll pay out the
line bit by bit. I'll pretend not to know anything about anything.

TRANIO. O, wicked wight! I declare there isn't a wilier old coot in Athens. It
won't be possible to fool him with words anymore than you could—a
rock. However, I'll go over and start the conversation.

THEOPROPIDES. I wish he were here now.

TRANIO [*approaching him*]. If by he you mean me, I'm here face to face.

THEOPROPIDES. Hu-uh! Tranio, how are things?

TRANIO. The farmers come from the farm. Philolaches is on his way.

THEOPROPIDES. By heaven, you've got here just in time. I think our neighbor
has a lot of nerve. He can't be trusted.

TRANIO. Why's that?

THEOPROPIDES. Because he says he doesn't know you—

TRANIO. He doesn't?
   [*Steps back.*]

THEOPROPIDES [*following him*]. —and that you never ever gave him any money at all.

TRANIO. Go on, you're fooling. I can't believe he denies it.

THEOPROPIDES. What now?

TRANIO. I know you're joking about it. He couldn't deny it.

[*Moves away.*]

THEOPROPIDES. By heaven, he certainly does deny everything, especially that he sold this house to Philolaches.

[*Follows* TRANIO.]

TRANIO. He really denies that any money was given to him?

THEOPROPIDES. He even promised to swear an oath, if I wanted him to.

TRANIO [*dodging*]. That he hadn't sold the house or received any money?

THEOPROPIDES. That's what we were talking about.

[*Tries to get close to* TRANIO.]

TRANIO. And what did he say?

THEOPROPIDES. He promised to give me his slaves for cross-examination.

TRANIO. That's a joke!

[*Backs off.*]

He wouldn't go through with it.

THEOPROPIDES. He'll do it all right.

[*Moves closer.*]

TRANIO. Very well, take him into court.

[*Starts to leave.*]

THEOPROPIDES. Stay here, I think I'll try the slaves, first.

[*Turns to* SIMO'S *door.*]

TRANIO. You "think?" You've already made up your mind. Leave him to me.

[*Runs to the altar.*]

THEOPROPIDES [*gestures toward* SIMO'S *house*]. Suppose I were to call for his slaves?

TRANIO. You should have done it long ago. Or tell Philolaches to attach the property.

[*Leans casually against the altar.*]

THEOPROPIDES. No, first I want to bring out his slaves for cross-examination.

TRANIO. I think that's a good idea.

[*Gets a firm grip on the altar.*]

Meanwhile I'll take possession of the altar.

THEOPROPIDES. What for?

TRANIO. Don't you get the point? So the slaves he gives you for questioning can't take refuge here. While I'm on guard here for you, the cross-examination can't break down.

[*He sits down on the altar.*]

THEOPROPIDES. Oh, get up.

TRANIO. No, thanks.

THEOPROPIDES. Please, don't hog the altar.

TRANIO. Why not?

THEOPROPIDES. I'll explain. [*Thinking as fast as he can.*] I'm really very anxious to have them take refuge at the altar. I want them to: then it will be all the easier for me to sue for damages in court.

TRANIO. If that's what you want, go to it. But why plant more trouble for yourself? Don't you know what a prickly thing it is to sue in court?

THEOPROPIDES. Get up and come over here. I want your advice about something.

TRANIO. I'll give you my advice from here. I'm never smarter than when I'm sitting down. And you get more reliable advice from holy places. [*Pretending to be a sybil.*]

THEOPROPIDES. Stop this foolishness and get up. Look me in the eye.

TRANIO. I already have.

THEOPROPIDES. Do you see—

TRANIO. I see, all right. If a third person stepped in here, he'd die of hunger.

THEOPROPIDES. Why so?

TRANIO. There'd be no pickings for him. We're both so damn smart.

THEOPROPIDES. Oh, dammit!
[*He gives up the pretence.*]

TRANIO. What's the matter with you?

THEOPROPIDES. Foiled again!

TRANIO. How?

THEOPROPIDES. You cleaned me out.

TRANIO. Look and see if I did a good job: ears clean?

THEOPROPIDES. Ears! You cleaned out all the brains from my head. I've found out about your dirty tricks from the very bottom; not just from the bottom, by God, but from beneath the bottom.

TRANIO. Believe me, I'll never leave here until I'm ready.

THEOPROPIDES. I'll order you surrounded with faggots and fire, you hangman!

TRANIO. Don't do that, I taste much better boiled than roasted.

THEOPROPIDES. By God, I'll make an example of you.

TRANIO. Set me up as an example, because I please you so much?

THEOPROPIDES. Tell me, when I went away, what kind of a son did I leave behind me?

TRANIO. One with feet, hands (with fingers to 'em), ears. eyes, and lips.

THEOPROPIDES. I asked a different question.

TRANIO. I give you a different answer. But there, I see your boy's friend, Callidamates, coming along. If you want anything from me, do it in his presence.

[CALLIDAMATES, *sober at last, comes down the alleyway.*]

CALLIDAMATES. After I slept off my sleep and got over my jag, Philolaches told me his father was back from his trip and how his servant had pulled his leg at his homecoming. Philolaches said he was afraid to go and meet his father. So I'm elected sole representative of our tribe to smoke a peacepipe with pater. [*Spies* THEOPROPIDES.] Good! There he is. Greetings, Theopropides, I'm glad to see you safely back from your journey. Have dinner today with us, won't you?

THEOPROPIDES [*formally*]. Bless you, Callidamates. And for the invitation, thanks just the same.

CALLIDAMATES. Will you come?

TRANIO [*snugly on the altar*]. Accept. I'll go in your place, if you don't want to.

THEOPROPIDES. Blast you! Still making jokes?

TRANIO. Because I offer to go to dinner in your place?

THEOPROPIDES. Well, you won't go. I'll have you carried—to the cross as you deserve.

CALLIDAMATES. Forget about all that. Come dine with me—

TRANIO. Tell him you'll come. Why the silence?

CALLIDAMATES [*notices* TRANIO]. But why have you taken refuge on the altar?

TRANIO. A dumb fool came along and scared me.
[*To* THEOPROPIDES.]
Tell what I've done. Now we have a judge for both sides: present your case.

THEOPROPIDES. I accuse you of corrupting my son.

TRANIO [*to "Judge"* CALLIDAMATES]. Now, listen to my side. I admit Philolaches has done wrong, set his sweetheart free while you were away, borrowed money at interest—which I also admit he got rid of fast. But has he done anything more than the sons of our very best families?

THEOPROPIDES. I'll have to watch out for you all right, you're a fast talker.

CALLIDAMATES [*to* TRANIO]. I'm supposed to be the judge here. Get up, and let me sit down.

THEOPROPIDES. By all means, take the case and decide the damages.

TRANIO. There's a catch here, somewhere. Promise I have nothing to worry about and that you'll do some worrying in exchange.

THEOPROPIDES. The worst of it is the way he made a fool of me.

TRANIO. I did a good job, by heaven, and I'm glad I did. A man your age ought to have some sense under those white hairs.

THEOPROPIDES. What shall I do now?

TRANIO. If you happen to know Plautus, the playwright, you might tell him how your servant made a fool of you. You'll give him some marvelous gulling scenes for his comedies.

CALLIDAMATES. Now be quiet a minute! Let me have my turn. Hear this!

THEOPROPIDES. Go ahead.

CALLIDAMATES. You know that I am closest to your son of all his friends. He turned to me because he was afraid to come to you, knowing that you know about all the things he did. Now I beg you, forgive him for

being foolish and for being young. He's your son. And you know that
at his age they're full of fun and games. And whatever he did, we did
with him; we're all delinquents. As for the interest, the principal, and all
the money paid for the girl, we'll make an arrangement and pay it out
of our own pockets, not yours.

THEOPROPIDES [*immediately pleased*]. There couldn't be a more powerful
persuader than you. I'm not angry with him anymore. Why, in my
presence even, let him love and drink and do what he likes. I am completely satisfied if he feels a sense of shame—for having spent all that
money, I mean.

CALLIDAMATES. He's abject.

TRANIO. So he gets forgiven—what do I get?

THEOPROPIDES. Scum of the earth, whipping and hanging!

TRANIO. Even if I'm ashamed?

THEOPROPIDES. I'll see you dead as sure as I'm alive.

CALLIDAMATES. Make it a general pardon. Forgive Tranio's trickery for
my sake.

THEOPROPIDES. There's nothing you could ask I wouldn't rather do than
let this fellow get away with his diabolical diddling.
[TRANIO *thumbs his nose.*]

CALLIDAMATES. Come on, forgive him.

THEOPROPIDES. Do you see what that jailbait is doing?

CALLIDAMATES. Tranio, be quiet, if you've got any brains in your head.

THEOPROPIDES. And you be quiet about your request. And I'll quiet him
down with a horsewhip.

TRANIO. Unnecessary expenditure of energy.

CALLIDAMATES. Come on, do as I ask.

THEOPROPIDES. I don't want you to ask.

CALLIDAMATES. But I ask just the same.

THEOPROPIDES. I said I don't want you to ask it.

CALLIDAMATES. Whether you want it or not. Just this one offense, this one—
please for my sake.

TRANIO. Why trouble yourself? As if I shouldn't be committing another
offense tomorrow. Then you can settle the whole account at once—
today's offense and tomorrow's.

CALLIDAMATES. Permit me to persuade you.

THEOPROPIDES. All right, take yourself off unpunished. But there's the man
to thank. Spectators, the play is finished. Give us your applause.

SHUDRAKA

THE TOY CART

THE MIRROR

ONE OF THE BY-PRODUCTS of the invention and development
of dramatic art is, inevitably, the birth of dramatic criticism. The
first problem of the critic is to define his subject. The theater of
Greece, having produced its Aeschylus and Sophocles and
Euripides, next faced its critic, Aristotle; the theater of Rome,
having produced Plautus and Terence, faced its critic, Cicero.
And from these two aestheticians came two definitions that have
been at least the starting point of most subsequent discussions of
the art.

"Tragedy," said Aristotle (384–322 B.C.), "is an imitation of a
worthy or illustrious and complete action, possessing magnitude,
in pleasing language, using separately the several kinds of imitation
in its parts, by men acting, and not through narration, through
pity and fear effecting a purification from such like passions."* It
will be seen that the Greek philosopher stresses the elements of
imitation and performance, the elements discussed in the prefaces
to *The Bacchae* and *Antigone* as impersonation and *enthousiasm*.
His statement of the purpose of playing, to purify the spectator of
the emotions of pity and fear, is equally dogmatic, but the implications or the limitations of the dogma have been the subject of
still-continuing critical argument.

Aristotle, of course, was speaking for his own time and his own
theater, and with his own understanding of human psychology.
To point out that just as times change, so do theaters and concepts
of human psychology, is perhaps to labor the obvious; yet it is a
principle that any student of the drama must keep constantly in

* Translated by Theodore Buckley, emended.

130

his awareness, if he is to experience the full pleasure and profit of the art.

A Roman restatement of Aristotle's precept is less specific, less limited, and therefore a more serviceable companion. In response to the question "What is a play?" Cicero (106–43 B.C.) is credited with saying "*Est imitatio vitae, speculum consuetudinis, imago veritatis* (It is an imitation of life, a mirror of custom, an image of truth)." The effective word here is *speculum*, mirror, which caught the fancy of players, playgoers, and critics ever after. Most memorably, it appealed to the imagination of that royal amateur of the theater, Hamlet, Prince of Denmark, who lectured a troupe of traveling actors on their art: "The purpose of playing . . . both at the first and now, was and is, to hold, as 'twere, the mirror up to nature; to show virtue her own feature, scorn her own image, and the very age and body of the time his form and pressure."

The concept of the stage as a mirror is useful in two ways: it recognizes the essential relationship between the dramatic fiction and the daily experience of the spectator, but more important, it insists on the condition of the mirror: it reflects what is placed before it; the same mirror may reflect vastly different subjects.

Consider briefly the first three plays in this volume as mirrors of their audiences. Both *The Bacchae* and *Antigone* in their actions present an image of finality: what's done cannot be undone, there can be no evasion of the consequences of decisions taken and actions performed. The world of Pentheus and Creon is circumscribed, controlled by inexorable law. The spectator is invited to watch the protagonists as they try to contravene the law, to struggle against the decrees of the gods, and to go down in defeat, forever destroyed. Those who survive, chiefly the members of the chorus, are those who comply, who walk the middle way with caution, too unimaginative (perhaps) to dare a fall with the gods, too timid (perhaps) to be laggard in their small responsibilities.

The final moments of the two tragedies create powerful visual emblems of this world-view: the mother clutching the dismembered head of her own son, the tyrant cradling the corpse of his son and heir. These emblems exemplify the Aristotelian precept that an action must be complete; there can be no sequel to *The Bacchae*, no sequel to *Antigone*. This is the essence of the tragic view of man's life as reflected in the mirror of the Greek stage.

The comic mirror, of course, presents only a temporary finality. The ending of *Mostellaria* is a compromise effected by the necessity of bringing about some kind of conclusion. Not all comedy, as we shall see, comes to its point in such helter-skelter fashion, but the Plautine mirror is generally expected to display folly-in-action. The spectator is not to observe with awe and wonder the extremes to which passionate conviction can drive the protagonist, but to laugh at the ease with which a common man obsessed (for example) with a mania for money can be gulled. The comic mirror of the Greco-Roman world avoids images of finality by avoiding the subjects which both playwright and playgoer knew would only result in those images: matters of state and religion.

Yet this same mirror, the stage, can reflect with equal precision and fullness other world-views, other concepts of the condition of man. *The Toy Cart* (second century A.D.) is a classic of the Hindu theater, a romantic comedy totally inconceivable in the theaters of Athens or Rome, almost wholly at variance with the precepts of Aristotle, while conforming to Cicero's *speculum consuetudinis, imago veritatis*.

In many ways *The Toy Cart* is a mirror before which the modern reader or spectator can sit with greater ease than before the mirrors of fifth-century Greece. The action, vastly more complex than the single-minded economic plotting of Sophocles, is displayed in careful detail from inciting incident through every hazard and obstacle confronting the characters to its fortunate conclusion. Its chief concern is to bring about the union of two exemplary lovers. In its ten acts a variety of moral and philosophical issues are raised and disposed of, principally by aphorism; no large moral problem dominates the action. In place of the unity of tone, the high seriousness of Greek tragedy, there is sufficient room in the Hindu play for broad farce, domestic realism, comedy of manners, lyric romance, fantasy, and some moments that approach tragedy. Further, no rank or profession in society is excluded: the persons of the drama include a merchant, a monk, a cowherd, a masseur, a courtesan, gamblers, courtiers; the action moves indoors and outdoors, in houses and courtrooms, on streets, and in a garden. The dramatic structure is not unlike that of a contemporary motion picture in its freedom to move in time and place.

In actual performance, however, one familiar aspect of the film is missing. The Hindu theater, like the Greek, grew out of religious practices, and temples or temple courtyards were the first playing places. There is no evidence that these playing places made any attempt at a realistic presentation of *locale*. The platform on which the actors performed was bare of scenery, though it may have had some kind of formal decor. The audience knew the scene was in a garden from the descriptive comments of the actors, and playwrights relied heavily on a conventional system of gesture and pantomime to convey to the spectator that the actor was going through a door, mounting a horse, or picking flowers. To gratify the desire for visual splendor there were costumes and such properties as jewel chests and bullock carts. But the audience was expected to bring an active imagination to the performances.

If we examine the attempts of Hindu aestheticians to define and explain dramatic art, we will find another striking similarity between the plays of the classic Sanskrit theater and the modern movie. The Hindu Aristotle, a perhaps legendary sage named Bharata, replaces the theory of the dramatic experience as a purification of certain emotions with the theory of *rasa*, aesthetic pleasure. There are, he is reputed to have written, two kinds of emotions: the deep mainsprings of action like love and pathos, and the transitory, evanescent ones like anxiety or anger which contribute to the development of those more profound. Emotions are manifested by grimace and gesture: quickly moving eyebrows, sidelong glances. "Through an harmonious blending of deeper and lesser emotions and their representation in facial expression and pantomime, there arises in the audience a certain climax of emotion, invariably accompanied by a thrill or sense of joy: i.e. *rasa*, or aesthetic pleasure."

The Hindu audience was not asked to evaluate, but to experience. The playwright, choosing his subject, responds to it emotionally. He endeavors to transfer his emotion to the spectator through the dramatic structure he contrives, by means of the characters he creates. In their love of classification, the Sanskrit aestheticians codified the kinds of *rasa* proper to drama: love, humor, pathos, wrath, heroism, terror, disgust, awe, serene bliss. Each play will incorporate all nine *rasas*, but one will dominate. The spectator will thus experience a variety of emotions, but, through the predominance of one, will also have the satisfaction of a sense of unity. So, in the movie, the filmic devices of close-up, crosscutting, moving camera (and the more eccentric experiments of Third-Dimension and Cinerama) bring the spectator "into the picture," allow him to share the emotional experiences of the characters, while at the same time the script adheres to the conventions of a type (love story, western, gangster, horror) for overall unity of tone.

The most striking difference between the drama of the Greeks and the drama of the Hindus is that there is no Hindu tragedy. And in the explanation of this difference the world reflected in the mirror is of supreme importance. It is a world without the finality essential to a tragic view. Death is the prelude to rebirth, and while the social structure of the world was rigid, death was the gateway to a different status *in this world* as well as in the world of supernature. By successive rebirths man is capable of attaining higher and higher rank on earth, and at last in heaven; according to the Brahminic code, each man is governed by a fate which he himself determines and selects through his own deeds. The ancient Greek heroes inherited curses, or were born to predetermined fates. The Hindu heroes have in their own possession the remedy against their misfortunes and the gods, if they chance to meddle in the action at all, look out for the heroes.

Consequently, where Greek tragedy was a selection and arrangement of incidents leading to a recognition and reversal of the hero's fortunes, Hindu drama is a collection and arrangement of obstacles whose surmountability is a foregone conclusion. The total action, the plot, thus becomes a secondary concern, otherwise the audience might be directed to philosophical or intellectual rather than emotional matters. Singing and dancing add to the aesthetic pleasure of the dramatic experience, and there is a free use of the marvelous if it will create an additional pleasurable situation.

The Toy Cart with its fantasy, its farce, its romance represents
the reality of Hindu life as the audience conceived it. If the path
of true love does not run smooth, the worst devices of an oafish
and highly-placed villain cannot prevent a happy ending.
Chārudatta represents the highest ideal for his caste, a man whose
generosity cannot be corrupted by poverty. His choice of
Vasantasenā as his second wife is further evidence of his sense of
honor as well as his good taste. Although a courtesan, she must
be thought of as comparable to the Greek hetaera rather than a
common prostitute—she is witty, talented, even learned (of the
women in the play she alone speaks Sanskrit), and is anxious to
escape from her profession into marriage. The minor characters,
too, are portrayed with deft and revealing strokes, the gambler
who cannot pay his debts, the Buddhist monk who cannot touch
a woman even when she is at the point of death, the five adven-
turers equally ready to steal a jewel box or a throne, the small boy
grumbling over his playthings.

On the authority of the prologue *The Toy Cart* is supposed to
have been written by King Shudraka. The prologue is, of course, a
later addition to the text and the assignment of authorship has
not been unquestioned. King or not, the author was a man of
delicacy and invention and his play is a full and lively reflection
of a society, centuries away in time and half-a-world in space,
but with its many *rasas* ready to be shared with all who look into
the dramatic mirror.

Characters

THE PRELUDE

MANAGER

ACTRESS

THE PLAY

Men

CHĀRUDATTA
*a Brahman of a wealthy and respectable family,
reduced to poverty by his munificence,
beloved by* VASANTASENĀ

ROHASENA
the son of CHĀRUDATTA, *a boy*

MAITREYA
a Brahman, the friend and companion of CHĀRUDATTA,
*a character of mixed shrewdness and simplicity,
with an affectionate disposition*

VARDHAMĀNA
the servant of CHĀRUDATTA

SAMSTHĀNAKA
*the brother-in-law of the King,
an ignorant, frivolous and cruel coxcomb*

VITA
the attendant, tutor, or parasite of the preceding

STHĀVARAKA
the servant of the prince

ĀRYAKA
a cowherd and insurgent, finally successful

SHARVILAKA
*a dissipated Brahman, the friend of the preceding,
in love with* MADANIKĀ

SAMVĀHAKA, or MASSEUR,
who becomes a Buddhist MONK

MĀTHURA
the keeper of a gaming-house

DARDURAKA
a gambler

ANOTHER GAMBLER

KARNAPURAKA
VASANTASENĀ'S *servant*

JUDGE

PROVOST

RECORDER

CHANDANAKA
VĪRAKA
captains of the Town Guard

VITA
or parasite attendant of VASANTASENĀ

KUMBHILAKA
a servant of VASANTASENĀ

TWO PUBLIC EXECUTIONERS

OFFICERS OF THE COURT

Women

WIFE
of CHĀRUDATTA

VASANTASENĀ
a courtesan, in love with CHĀRUDATTA, *and beloved by him:*
the object also of SAMSTHĀNAKA'S *addresses*

MOTHER
of VASANTASENĀ

MADANIKĀ
the attendant of VASANTASENĀ, *beloved by* SHARVILAKA

RADANIKĀ
the servant of CHĀRUDATTA'S *house*

PASSERS-BY, ATTENDANTS, GUARDS, ETC.

SCENE: *Ujjayin, the city and the suburbs.* TIME: *four days.*

THE TOY CART

Shudraka

Translated by Horace Hayman Wilson

ACT ONE

PRELUDE

BENEDICTION.

I. May that profound meditation of Shiva[1] protect you! which is intent on
Brahman, the absorbing end of every effort of abstract vision; as he
contemplates with the eye of wisdom, spirit, in himself, detached from all
material instruments; his senses being restrained by holy knowledge, as
he sits ruminating with suspended breath, whilst his serpents coil with the
folds of his vesture round his bended knees.

II. May the neck of Shiva, which resembles a dark cloud in hue, and which
is decorated by the entwining arms of Gaurī,[2] as brilliant as the lightning,
be ever your protection.

[*Enter* MANAGER.]

MANAGER. Enough: delay not longer to gratify the curiosity of this assembly.
Saluting, therefore, this gentle audience, I apprise them that we are
prepared to enact the drama entitled *The Toy Cart*.

There was a celebrated poet whose gait was that of an elephant, whose
eyes resembled those of the partridge, whose countenance was like
the full moon, and who was of stately person and profound veracity;
chiefest of the Kshattriya race and distinguished by the appellation of
Shudraka: he was well versed in the *Rig-* and *Sāma-Vedas*, in mathematical sciences, in the elegant arts, and the management of elephants.
By the favor of Shiva he enjoyed eyes uninvaded by darkness, and
beheld his son seated on the throne: after performing the exalted horse-
sacrifice, having attained the age of a hundred years and ten days, he

[1] One of the three chief gods of the Hindu pantheon: one of his concerns was
with the theater and the arts generally.
[2] Wife of Shiva.

entered the fatal fire. Valiant was he in war, and ready to encounter
with his single arm the elephant of his adversary; yet he was void of
wrath, eminent amongst those skilled in the *Vedas*, and affluent in piety:
a prince was Shudraka. In this drama, written by him, it is thus related.

In Avantī lived a young Brahman of distinguished rank, but of exceeding poverty; his name was Chārudatta. Of the many excellences of
Chārudatta, a courtesan, Vasantasenā by name, became enamored, and
the story of their loves is the subject of King Shudraka's drama, which
exhibits the infamy of wickedness, the villainy of law, the efficacy of
virtue, and the triumph of faithful love.

[*Walks round the stage.*]

Hey! the boards are deserted: where can all the actors have vanished?
Ah, I understand. Empty is the house of the childless—empty is the heart
of one that has no friends; the universe is a blank to the blockhead, and
all is desolate to the poor. I have been chanting and reciting until my
eyes ache, the pupils twinkling with hunger, like the seeds of the lotus
shriveled in the hot weather by the rays of a scorching sun. I will call
one of my wenches, and see if there be anything in the house for breakfast. What ho there—Here am I! But I had better talk to them in a
language they can understand.[3]—What ho—I say! What with long
fasting and loud shouting my limbs are shriveled like dry lotus stalks.
It is high time to take myself home, and see what is prepared for my
coming. This is my mansion—I will go in.

[*Enters and looks around.*]

Hey day!—Some new frolic is going on in this mansion of mine. The
ground, like a young damsel fresh from her toilet, wears a beauty-mark
smeared with the discolored water of the rice that has been boiled in the
iron kettle, and is perfumed with most savory smells. Verily, my hunger
increaseth. What, in the name of wonder, have my people found a
treasure—or from the promptings of my appetite do I fancy everything
smacks of boiled rice? If there be no breakfast for me at home, this
hunger will be the death of me. Yet everything puts on a new face: one
hussy is grinding perfumes, another is stringing flowers: the meaning of
all this must be inquired into. Come hither one of you.

[*Enter ACTRESS.*]

ACTRESS. Here am I; sir.

MANAGER. Welcome, welcome.

ACTRESS. What are your commands?

MANAGER. Hark ye, girl, I have been bawling myself both hoarse and
hungry: is there anything in the house for me to eat?

---

[3] Hindu classic plays employ two languages, Sanskrit for male characters in
general, particularly the upper castes, and Prakrit for the lower castes and for all
women. The manager here switches from Sanskrit to Prakrit to address the house-
maids.

ACTRESS. There is everything, sir.

MANAGER. Indeed; and what is there?

ACTRESS. For example—there is rice, dressed or undressed, sugar, curds; in short, there is sustenance for a century—so may the gods comply with all your desires.

MANAGER. Hark ye, my girl, is all this in my house, or do you jest?

ACTRESS [apart]. Oh, as he doubts, I will have a laugh at him. [Aloud.] Indeed and indeed, sir, there is all that I have mentioned—in the market.

MANAGER. Ah, you hussy! May you be so disappointed. The deuce take you—you have hoisted me up like a ball on a turret top, that I might tumble down again.

ACTRESS. Patience, sir, patience, I did but jest.

MANAGER. Then what is the meaning of all this unusual preparation; this grinding of perfumes and stringing of chaplets? The ground is strewed with offerings of flowers of every dye.

ACTRESS. We hold a solemn fast today.

MANAGER. A fast, for what?

ACTRESS. That we may have a desirable master.

MANAGER. In this world, or the next?

ACTRESS. Ah, in the next, to be sure.

MANAGER. Here, gentles, [to the audience] here is pretty usage: these damsels would engage a new manager in another world at my expense in this!

ACTRESS. Be appeased, sir. I have observed the fast, in order that I might have you again for my master in a future birth.

MANAGER. That alters the case. But, pray, who directed you to hold this fast?

ACTRESS. Your particular friend, Chūrnavriddha.

MANAGER. Oh, you son of a slave, I shall see you, Chūrnavriddha, some day or other, fast bound by King Pālaka, like the perfumed tresses of a new-married girl.

ACTRESS. Pardon us, dear sir; this fast was observed to secure the future felicity of our worthy Manager.
[Falls at his feet.]

MANAGER. Rise; enough. We must now consider by whom this fast is to be completed.

ACTRESS. We must invite some Brahman of our own degree.

MANAGER. Well, go, finish your preparations: I will seek the Brahman.

ACTRESS. I obey.
[Exit.]

MANAGER. Alas! in such a flourishing city as Ujjayin, where am I to find a Brahman who is not of a superior rank to mine? [Looking out.] Yonder comes Maitreya, the friend of Chārudatta. I will ask him; he is poor enough. What, ho! Maitreya; condescend to be the first to eat in my house today.

MAITREYA [*behind the scenes*]. Call some other Brahman; I am particularly
  engaged.

MANAGER. Food is provided; no enemy is in the way, and you shall have a
  present into the bargain.

MAITREYA [*behind*]. I have already given you an answer. It is useless to
  disturb me.

MANAGER. I shall not prevail upon him, and must therefore set off in quest
  of some other Brahman.
  [*Exit.*]

ACT ONE

*The scene is supposed to represent a street on one side, and on the other
the first court of* CHĀRUDATTA'S *house: the outside of the house is also
seen in the part next to the street.*

[MAITREYA *enters the court with a piece of cloth in his hand.*]

MAITREYA. Truly, Maitreya, your condition is sad enough, and well
  qualified to subject you to be picked up in the street and fed by strangers.
  In the days of Chārudatta's prosperity, I was accustomed to stuff
  myself till I could eat no more, on scented dishes, until I breathed
  perfume; and sat lolling at yonder gateway, dyeing my fingers like a
  painter's, by dabbling amongst the colored comfits, or chewing the cud
  at leisure like a high-fed city bull. Now, in the season of his poverty,
  I wander about from house to house, like a tame pigeon, to pick up
  such crumbs as I can get. I am now sent by his dear friend Chūrnavriddha,
  with this garment that has lain amongst jasmine flowers till it is quite
  scented by them: it is for Chārudatta's wearing, when he has finished
  his devotions.—Oh, here he comes, he is presenting the oblation to the
  household gods.

[*Enter* CHĀRUDATTA *and* RADANIKĀ.]

CHĀRUDATTA [*with a sigh*]. Alas! how changed; the offering to the gods,
        That swans and stately storks, in better time
        About my threshold flocking, bore away,
        Now a scant tribute to the insect tribe,
        Falls 'midst rank grass, by worms to be devoured.
  [*Sits down.*]

MAITREYA. I will approach the respectable Chārudatta. Health to you;
  may you prosper.

CHĀRUDATTA. Maitreya, friend of all seasons, welcome; sit you down.

MAITREYA. As you command. [*Sits down.*] This garment, perfumed by the
  jasmines it has lain amongst, is sent to you by your friend Chūrnavriddha,
  to be worn by you at the close of your devotions.

[CHĀRUDATTA *takes it and appears thoughtful.*]

MAITREYA. On what do you meditate?

CHĀRUDATTA. My friend—

> The happiness that follows close on sorrow,
> Shows like a lamp that breaks upon the night:
> But he that falls from affluence to poverty,
> May wear the human semblance, but exists
> A lifeless form alone.

MAITREYA. What think you preferable then, death or poverty?

CHĀRUDATTA. Had I the choice,
> Death, and not poverty, were my election:
> To die is transient suffering; to be poor,
> Interminable anguish.

MAITREYA. Nay, never heed. The loss of your wealth, lavished upon your kind friends, only enhances your merits; as the moon looks most lovely when reduced to the slender fragment that the draughts of the gods for half a month have left it.

CHĀRUDATTA. I do not, trust me, grieve for my lost wealth:
> But that the guest no longer seeks the dwelling,
> Whence wealth has vanished, does, I own, afflict me.
> Like the ungrateful bees, who wanton fly
> The elephant's broad front when thick congeals
> The dried-up dew,[4] they visit me no more.

MAITREYA. The sons of slaves! your guest is ever ready to make a morning meal of a fortune: he is like the cattle-boy, who, as if afraid of a gadfly, drives his herds from place to place in the thicket, and sets them to feed always in fresh pasture.

CHĀRUDATTA. 'Tis true.—I think not of my wasted fortune.
> As fate decrees, so riches come and vanish.
> But I lament to find the love of friends
> Hangs all unstrung because a man is poor.
> And then with poverty comes disrespect;
> From disrespect does self-dependence fail,
> Then scorn and sorrow, following, overwhelm
> The intellect; and when the judgment fails
> The being perishes; and thus from poverty
> Each ill that pains humanity proceeds.

MAITREYA. Ah well, it is but waste of thought to send it after the wealth hunters; we have had enough of this subject.

CHĀRUDATTA. But poverty is aye the curse of thought.
> It is our enemy's reproach; the theme
> Of scorn to our best friends and dearest kin.
> I had abjured the world and sought the hermitage,
> But that my wife had shared in my distress.

---

[4] During the mating season, a fragrant liquor exudes from the forehead of the elephant. Of this liquor bees are very fond. (Note from Arthur William Ryder (trans.), *The Little Clay Cart*, Harvard University Press, 1905.)

Alas, the fires of sorrow in the heart
Glow impotent; they pain but burn not.
My friend, I have already made oblation
Unto the household gods—Go you to where
The four roads meet, and there present it
To the Great Mothers.

MAITREYA. Not I, indeed.

CHĀRUDATTA. Why not?

MAITREYA. Of what use is it? You have worshiped the gods: what have they done for you? it is labor in vain to bestow upon them adoration.

CHĀRUDATTA. Speak not profanely. It is our duty.

And the gods
Undoubtedly are pleased with what is offered
In lowliness of spirit and with reverence,
In thought, and deed, and pious self-denial:
Go therefore and present the offering.

MAITREYA. I will not go, indeed; send somebody else. With me every part of the ritual is apt to get out of its place, and, as in the reflection of a mirror, the right becomes left and the left right. At this time of the evening, too, the royal road is crowded with loose persons, with cutthroats, courtiers, and courtesans: amongst such a set I shall fare like the unhappy mouse, that fell into the clutches of the snake which was lying in ambush for the frog. I cannot go, indeed. Why not go yourself? You have nothing to do but to sit here.

CHĀRUDATTA. Well, well—attend then whilst I tell my beads.

[*They retire.*]

VOICE BEHIND THE SCENE. Stop, Vasantasenā, stop!

[*Enter* VASANTASENĀ *pursued by* SAMSTHĀNAKA, *the king's brother-in-law, the* VITA,[5] *and his own* SERVANT.]

VITA. Stop, Vasantasenā, stop! Why, losing your gentleness in your fears, do you ply those feet so fast, that should be nimble only in the dance? You run along like the timid deer from the pursuing hunter, casting tremulous glances fearfully around.

SAMSTHĀNAKA. Shtop, Vashantashenā, shtop! Why do you thush scamper away, shtumbling at every step? Be pacified, you are in no danger. With love alone is my poor heart inflamed; it is burnt to a cinder, like a piece of meat upon the blazing coals.

SERVANT. Stop, lady, stop! Why, sister, do you fly? She runs along like a peahen in summer with a tail in full feather, whilst my master follows her like the young hound that chases the bird through the thicket.

VITA. Stop, Vasantasenā, stop! You tremble like the young plantain tree,

[5] A conventional figure, somewhat akin to the parasite of Roman comedy. He is the companion and minister of pleasures to one of the major characters (in this case, Samsthānaka), and seems to have been a private tutor in the arts and social graces as well as an entertainer. Samsthānaka, it will be obvious, was a poor pupil.

whilst the ends of your red vesture wanton on the wind. The seeds of the red lotus are put to shame by your glowing eyes, and the vein of red arsenic, when first penetrated by the axe, is rivaled by the complexion of your cheeks.

SAMSTHĀNAKA. Shtop, Vashantashenā, shtop! Why do you thush fly from a liking, a love, a passion which you inflame? My nights you deprive of resht, and you avoid me by day. It is unavailing: you will trip and tumble into my hands as Kuntī fell into those of Rāvana.[6]

VITA. Why, Vasantasenā, do you grace my steps by leaving traces for them to obliterate? Like a snake from the monarch of the birds, you glide away from me, but vain is your flight. I could outstrip the wind in such a chase, and shall I not overtake so delicate a fugitive?

SAMSTHĀNAKA. Mosht worthy shir, I have invoked her by ten names. I have called her the taper lash of that filcher of broad pieces, Kāma[7]; the fish-eater, the dancer, the pug-nosed untamable shrew. I have termed her Love's dining-dish—the gulf of the poor man's shubstance— the walking frippery—the harlot—the hushy—the baggage—the wanton. I have addressed her by all theshe pretty names, and yet she will have nothing to shay to me.

VITA. Why, Vasantasenā, do you fly us? The trembling pendants of your ears toss agitated against your cheeks, and make such music as the lute to a master's touch. You fly like the female crane that starts away from the sound of thunder.

SAMSTHĀNAKA. Your ornaments jingle to your paces ash you run from ush, ash Draupadī fled from Rāma. But I shall have you; I will dart upon you like Hanumat upon Subhadrā, the lovely shishter of Viswāvasu.

SERVANT. Relent, relent, be gracious to the prince's friend; accept the flesh and the fish. When they can get fish and flesh, the dogs prey not upon carrion.

VITA. What should have so strangely alarmed you? Believe me, you look like the guardian goddess of the city, as round your slender waist sparkles with starlike gems that tinkling girdle, and your countenance is pale with terror.

SAMSTHĀNAKA. Ash the female jackal is hunted by the dogs, sho run you, and sho we follow: you run along with your prey, and bear off from me both heart and pericardium.

VASANTASENĀ [calling for her female attendants]. What ho! Pallavā, Parabhritikā.

SAMSTHĀNAKA [in alarm to the VITA]. Eh, shir, shir! men, men!

[6] Here as elsewhere, Samsthānaka's mythology is wildly confused. To a Hindu the effect must be ludicrous enough: but the humor is necessarily lost in a translation. It therefore seems hardly worthwhile to explain his mythological vagaries in detail. (Note from Arthur William Ryder (trans.), *The Little Clay Cart*, Harvard University Press, 1905.)

[7] i.e., Cupid.

VITA. Never fear.

VASANTASENĀ. Mādhavikā, what ho!

VITA. Blockhead; she is calling her servants.

SAMSTHĀNAKA. What, her women?

VITA. To be sure.

SAMSTHĀNAKA. Who is afraid? I am a hero—a match for a hundred of them.

VASANTASENĀ. Alas, alas! my people are not within hail: I must trust to myself alone for my escape.

VITA. Search about, search about.

SAMSTHĀNAKA. Vasantashenā, what is the ushe of your bawling there for bud and blossom, or all shpring together! Who is to presherve you when I purshue? What could Bhīmasena do for you, or the shon of Jamadagni, or the shon of Kuntī, or Dasakandhara himshelf? I would take them, like Duhsāsana, by their hair, and, as you shall shee, with one touch of my well-sharpened shword off goes your head. Come, come, we have had enough of your running away. One who is deshirous of dying cannot be shaid to live.

VASANTASENĀ. Good sir, I am only a weak woman.

VITA. True, therefore you may live.

SAMSTHĀNAKA. True, you shall not die.

VASANTASENĀ [apart]. His very courtesy appals me. I will try this. [Aloud.] Pray, sirs, why do you thus pursue me, or why address such language to me? Do you seek my jewels?

VITA. Fie, fie, what have we to do with your ornaments? Who plucks the blossoms of the creeper?

VASANTASENĀ. What is it, then, you require?

SAMSTHĀNAKA. That I, who am a pershon of celestial nature, a mortal Vāsudeva, obtain your affections.

VASANTASENĀ. Get you gone; you talk idly.

SAMSTHĀNAKA [claps his hands and laughs]. What think you of that, shir? Hear how this gentle damshel regards me: she bids me go and resht myshelf, no doubt, after my fatigue in running after her; but I shwear by your head and my feet, that I have gone ashtray neither in town nor village, but have kept closhe to your heels all the way, by the which I am wearied.

VITA [apart]. The blockhead! he misapprehends the whole. [Aloud.] Why, Vasantasenā, you act quite out of character: the dwelling of a harlot is the free resort of youth: a courtesan is like a creeper that grows by the roadside—her person is an article for sale, her love a thing that money will buy, and her welcome is equally bestowed upon the amiable and disgusting. The sage and the idiot, the Brahman and the outcast, all bathe in the same stream, and the crow and the peacock perch upon the branches of the same creeper. The Brahman, the Kshattriya, the Vaisya, and all of every caste are ferried over in the same boat; and like the boat, the creeper, and the stream, the courtesan is equally accessible to all.

VASANTASENĀ. What you say may be just, but, believe me, merit alone, not brutal violence, inspires love.

SAMSTHĀNAKA. Shir, shir, the truth is, that the baggage has had the perversheness to fall in love with a misherable wretch, one Chārudatta, whom she met in the garden of Kāmadeva's temple: he lives closhe by here on our left, so take care she does not shlip through our fingers.

VITA [aside]. Confound the fool, he lets out everything he ought to conceal. In love with Chārudatta—humph! no wonder; it is truly said, pearls string with pearls: well, let it be so, never mind this simpleton. [Aloud.] What say you, is the house of Chārudatta on our left? the deuce it is.

SAMSTHĀNAKA. Very true, I assure you.

VASANTASENĀ [aside]. Indeed! the house of Chārudatta so near! These wretches have unintentionally befriended me, and promoted a meeting with my beloved.

SAMSTHĀNAKA. Shir, shir, Vasantashenā is no longer vishible; she is losht in the dark, like an ink-cake in a pile of black beans.

VITA. It is very dark, indeed! The gloom cheats my eyesight of its faculty; my eyes open only to be closed by it; such obscurity envelops everything, as if the heavens rained lamp-black: sight is as unavailing as the service of a worthless man.

SAMSTHĀNAKA. I must shearch for Vasantashenā.

VITA. Indeed! [Aloud.] Is there not anything by which you may trace her?

SAMSTHĀNAKA. What should there be?

VITA. The tinkling of her ornaments, the odor of her perfumes, and the fragrance of her garland.

SAMSTHĀNAKA. Very true; I can hear with my noshtrils the shent of her garland shpreading through the darkness, but I do not shee the shound of her ornaments.

VITA [apart, in the direction of VASANTASENĀ]. Very well, Vasantasenā. True, you are hidden by the gloom of the evening, like the lightning between gathering clouds, but the fragrance of your chaplet, the music of your anklets, will betray you,—do you hear?

VASANTASENĀ [to herself]. I hear and comprehend.

[Takes off her garland and the rings from her ankles.]

If I am not mistaken, the private entrance is in this direction: by running my hands along the wall—[feels for the door]—ah, it is shut.

CHĀRUDATTA. [within the court]. My prayer is finished; now, Maitreya, go, present the offering to the Divine Mothers.

MAITREYA. I tell you I will not go.

CHĀRUDATTA. Alas it does embitter poverty

    That then our friends grow deaf to our desires,
    And lend a keener anguish to our sorrows.
    The poor man's truth is scorned: the tender light
    Of each mild virtue languishes; suspicion
    Stamps him the perpetrator of each crime

That others are the authors of: no man seeks
To form acquaintance with him, nor exchange
Familiar greeting or respectful courtesy.
If e'er he find a place in rich men's dwellings
At solemn festivals, the wealthier guests
Survey him with disdainful wonder; and
Whene'er by chance he meets upon the road
With state and wealth, he sneaks into a corner,
Ashamed of his scant covering, till they pass,
Rejoicing to be overlooked. Believe me,
He who incurs the guilt of poverty
Adds a sixth sin to those we term most heinous.[8]
In truth, I mourn e'en poverty for thee,
Whose cherished dwelling is this wasting frame,
And oft I sadly wonder what asylum,
When this shall be no more, shall then receive thee.

MAITREYA. Ah! well, if I must go, I must; but let your maid Radanikā go along with me.

CHĀRUDATTA. Radanikā, follow Maitreya.

RADANIKĀ. As you command, sir.

MAITREYA. Here, Radanikā, do you take the offerings and the lamp, while I open the back door. [*Opens the door.*]

VASANTASENĀ [*on the outside*]. Luckily for me, the door is opened: I shall now get in. Ah the lamp.
[*Brushes it out with her scarf, and enters.*]

CHĀRUDATTA. What was that?

MAITREYA. Opening the door let in a gust of wind, which has blown the lamp out: never mind—go on, Radanikā. I will just step into the house and relight the lamp, and will be with you again immediately.

SAMSTHĀNAKA [*on the outside*]. What can have become of Vashantasenā!

VITA. Search, search.

SAMSTHĀNAKA. So I do, but cannot find her—I have her. [*Lays hold of the* VITA.]

VITA. Blockhead, you've caught me.

SAMSTHĀNAKA. Shtand out of the way then. [*Lays hold of the* SERVANT.] Now then I have caught her.

SERVANT. No, your honor has caught me.

SAMSTHĀNAKA. Here then, thish way, thish way, here, mashter, shervant, shervant, mashter, here, here, shtand here.
[*Lays hold of* RADANIKĀ *by the hair as she comes out.*]
Ha, ha! now I have her indeed. I detected her endeavoring to escape by

---

[8] The five great crimes of the Hindu code are; stealing gold, drinking alcoholic liquors, murder of a Brahman, adultery with the wife of a spiritual teacher, and association with a person guilty of any of these crimes.

the shent of the garland. I have her fasht by the hair, as Chānakya caught
Draupadī.

VITA. Very well, young lady, very pretty; running after honest men's sons,
in the pride of youth, with your head full dressed with flowers; you are
caught in the fact.

SAMSTHĀNAKA. You are the young girl, I believe, that wash caught by the
hair of the head: now call, and cry, and shcream, and cursh, and abuse
Shiva, Shambhu, Shankara, and Ishwara[9].

RADANIKĀ [in alarm]. Bless me, gentlemen, what do you mean?

VITA. How now! the voice is that of another person.

SAMSTHĀNAKA. Oh, shir, your female can change her voice when she will,
as the cat mewsh in a different key when she attempts to shteal cream.

VITA. Such a difference can scarcely be, and yet it is possible. Yes, it may be
she has been taught to disguise her voice in the way of her profession,
both for the purposes of deception and the performance of music.

[Enter MAITREYA.]

MAITREYA. How funnily the lamp burns: it goes flutter, flutter, in the evening
breeze, like the heart of a goat just caught in a snare. [Seeing RADANIKĀ
and the rest.] Hey, Radanikā!

SAMSTHĀNAKA. Holloa, mashter—a man.

MAITREYA. What is all this?—it is not right; not right at all—although Chārudatta be poor, yet strangers are not to come into his house without leave.

RADANIKĀ. See here; Maitreya, here's disrespect to me.

MAITREYA. Not you merely, but all of us. To me as well as you.

RADANIKĀ. You, indeed—how can that be?

MAITREYA. Why, have they been rude to you?

RADANIKĀ. Rude indeed—to be sure, rude enough.

MAITREYA. No, really.

RADANIKĀ. Yes, really.

MAITREYA [in wrath and taking up a stick]. Then I will do for them: this is
quite unbearable—every dog will bark in his own kennel, and why not a
Brahman? With this dry bamboo staff, as crooked as our fortunes, will
I batter that head of thine, thou abominable villain.

VITA. Patience, patience! worthy Brahman.

MAITREYA [to him]. Eh! this cannot be the offender. [Turns to SAMSTHĀNAKA.]
Oh! here he is. Oh, you king's brother-in-law! you abominable miscreant!
have you no decency? Do not you know that, notwithstanding the worthy
Chārudatta be poor, he is an ornament to Ujjayin, and how dare you
think of forcing your way into his house and maltreating his people?
There is no disgrace in an untoward fate; disgrace is in misconduct; a
worthless man of wealth is contemptible.

VITA. Worthy Brahman, pardon us, we mistook the person: we intended
no affront, but looking for a female—

[9] These are all names of Shiva, who is said to have ten thousand.

MAITREYA. For her? [*Pointing to* RADANIKĀ.]

VITA. Heaven forbid!—No, no, for a girl her own mistress, who has run away. Searching for her, we lighted upon this damsel, and committed an unintentional indecorum. We beg your pardon, and submit ourselves to whatever you may please to ordain.

[*Gives his sword and falls at* MAITREYA'S *feet.*]

MAITREYA. You are a man of sense; arise. I knew not your quality when I addressed you so roughly; now I am aware of it, I shall treat you with proper politeness.

VITA. You are entitled to our respect. I will only rise on one condition.

MAITREYA. Declare it.

VITA. That you will say nothing to Chārudatta of what has chanced.

MAITREYA. I will not say anything to him on the subject.

VITA. I will place your kindness, Brahman, on my head; armed with every excellence, you are invincible by arms.

SAMSTHĀNAKA. What do you mean, my friend, by putting your hands together and falling at the feet of shuch a contemptible fellow?

VITA. I am afraid.

SAMSTHĀNAKA. Of what?

VITA. Of the eminent virtues of Chārudatta.

SAMSTHĀNAKA. Very eminent, indeed, when they cannot afford hish visitors a dinner.

VITA. Never mind that; he has become impoverished by his liberality: like the lake in the summer which is exhausted by relieving the thirst of the travelers; in his prosperity he was kind to all, and never treated any one with disrespect.

SAMSTHĀNAKA. Who is this shlave, the shon of a shlave? Is he a warrior, a hero? Is he Pāndu, Swetaketu, the shon of Rādhā, Rāvana, or Indradatta? Was he begotten on Kuntī, by Rāma, or is he Aswatthāman, Dharmaputra, or Jatāyu?

VITA. No, you wiscacre, I will tell you who he is: he is Chārudatta, the tree of plenty to the poor, bowed down by its abundant fruit. He is the cherisher of the good, the mirror of the wise, a touchstone of piety, an ocean of decorum, the doer of good to all, of evil to none, a treasure of manly virtues, intelligent, liberal, and upright; in a word, he only is worthy of admiration: in the plenitude of his merits he may be said to live indeed; other men merely breathe. So come, we had better depart.

SAMSTHĀNAKA. What, without Vasantasenā?

VITA. Vasantasenā is lost.

SAMSTHĀNAKA. How losht?

VITA. Like the sight of the blind, the health of the sick, the wisdom of the fool, and the prosperity of the sluggard; like the learning of the dull and dissipated, and the friendship of foes.

SAMSTHĀNAKA. Well, I will not go hensh until I recover her.

VITA. You may as well. Have you never heard the saying:

An elephant may be held by a chain,
A steed be curbed by his rider's art;
But even go hang, if you cannot gain
The only bond woman obeys—her heart.
You may as well, therefore, come away.

SAMSTHĀNAKA. Go, if you pleash; I shall shtay where I am.

VITA. Very well, I leave you.

[*Exit.*]

SAMSTHĀNAKA. Let him go; who cares? [*To* MAITREYA.] Now, you crowfoot pated pupil of mendicity, down with you.

MAITREYA. We are cast down already.

SAMSTHĀNAKA. By whom?

MAITREYA. By destiny.

SAMSTHĀNAKA. Get up then.

MAITREYA. So we will.

SAMSTHĀNAKA. When?

MAITREYA. When fortune smiles.

SAMSTHĀNAKA. Weep, weep.

MAITREYA. So we do.

SAMSTHĀNAKA. What for?

MAITREYA. Our misfortunes.

SAMSTHĀNAKA. Laugh, blockhead, laugh!

MAITREYA. So we shall.

SAMSTHĀNAKA. When?

MAITREYA. When Chārudatta is again in prosperity.

SAMSTHĀNAKA. Hark ye, fellow; do you carry a messhage from me to the beggar Chārudatta. Shay to him thush from me: a common wanton, called Vashantasenā, covered with gold upon gold, like the chief of a troop of comedians about to act a new play, shaw you in the garden of Kāmadeva's temple, and took a fancy to you. Having put ush to the trouble of ushing violence to shecure her, she fled, and hash taken refuge in your houshe. If you will give her up, and put her yourshelf into my hands without any litigation, her delivery shall be rewarded with my most particular regard; but if you will not put her forth, depend upon my eternal and exterminating enmity. Conshider that a presherved pumpkin, a dried potherb, fried flesh, and boiled rice that has stood for a night in the cold weather, shtink when kept too long. Let him then not loshe this opportunity. You shpeak well and dishtinctly; you musht, therefore, shpeak my messhage so that I may hear you, as I shit in the upper terrace of my houshe, here adjoining. If you do not shay what I have told you, I shall grind your head between my teeth, ash I would a nut beneath my door.

MAITREYA. I will deliver your message.

SAMSTHĀNAKA. Ish the worthy Vita really gone? [*To the* SERVANT.]

SERVANT. He is, sir.

SAMSTHĀNAKA. Then, let us follow him quick.

SERVANT. Please to take your sword.

SAMSTHĀNAKA. No, carry it after me.

SERVANT. This is your honor's sword.

SAMSTHĀNAKA. Ah, very well, give it me. [*Takes it by the wrong end.*] I bear it on my shoulder, shleeping in its pink sheath; and thus go I home as a jackal retires to his lair, followed by the yell of all the dogs and bitches of the village.

[*Exit, with his* SERVANT.]

MAITREYA. My good Radanikā, say nothing to Chārudatta about your having been insulted in this currish place, by that king's brother-in-law: he frets already about his affairs, and this business, I am sure, would double his vexation.

RADANIKĀ. I am only Radanikā, Maitreya; I can hold my tongue.

MAITREYA. So be it then.

[*They retire.*]

CHĀRUDATTA [*within the house, to* VASANTASENĀ]. Radanikā, my boy Rohasena must have enjoyed the breeze long enough; he will be chilled by the evening dews; take him in, and cover him with this cloth.

VASANTASENĀ [*apart*]. He mistakes me for one of the servants.

[*Takes the cloth and smells it.*]

Scented with jasmine flowers! Ha, then, he is not all philosopher.

[*Retires.*]

CHĀRUDATTA. Radanikā, carry Rohasena to the inner apartments.

VASANTASENĀ [*apart*]. Alas! my fortune gives me no admission to them.

CHĀRUDATTA. What! No reply, Radanikā?—Alas! when a man has been unfortunate enough to have outlived his means, his best friends lose their regard, and old attachments change into dislike.

[*Enter* MAITREYA *and* RADANIKĀ.]

MAITREYA. Here, sir, is Radanikā.

CHĀRUDATTA. Here—then who is this? Not knowing her, I have degraded her by the touch of my vestment.

VASANTASENĀ [*apart*]. Degraded; no, exalted.

CHĀRUDATTA. She looks like the waning moon, half hidden by autumnal clouds; fie, fie, another's wife; this is not a meet object for my regards.

MAITREYA [*recognizing* VASANTASENĀ]. A wife indeed, a pretty wife! Why, sir, this is Vasantasenā, a lady, who, having had the felicity of seeing you in the gardens of Kāmadeva's temple, has taken it into her head to honor you with her affection.

CHĀRUDATTA [*apart*]. Indeed; is this Vasantasenā
    What now avails it to return her love
    In my declining fortunes; let it sink
    Suppressed in silence, as a coward checks
    The wrath he dares not utter.

MAITREYA. I have a message, too, from the king's brother-in-law.

CHĀRUDATTA. What?

MAITREYA. Thus he says: "A common wanton, Vashantasenā, covered with gold upon gold, like the chief of a troop of comedians about to act a new play, shaw you in the garden of Kāmadeva's temple, and took a fancy to you. Having put ush to the trouble of violence to shecure her"—

VASANTASENĀ. "Violence to secure her!" Oh, I am honored by such words.

MAITREYA. "She fled, and hash taken refuge in your houshe. If you will give her up, and put her yourshelf into my hands without litigation, her delivery shall be rewarded with my mosht particular regard; but if you will not put her forth, depend upon my eternal and exterminating enmity."

CHĀRUDATTA [with disdain]. He is a fool.

　　[To himself.] She would become a shrine—
　　The pride of wealth
　　Presents no charm to her, and she disdains
　　The palace she is roughly bid to enter;
　　Nor makes she harsh reply, but silent leaves
　　The man she scorns, to waste his idle words.
　　Lady—I knew you not, and thus unwittingly
　　Mistaking you for my attendant, offered you
　　Unmeet indignity, I bend my head,
　　In hope of your forgiveness.

VASANTASENĀ. Nay, sir, I am the offender, by intruding into a place of which I am unworthy; it is my head that must be humbled in reverence and supplication.

MAITREYA. Very pretty on both sides; and whilst you two stand there, nodding your heads to each other like a field of long grass, permit me to bend mine, although in the style of a young camel's stiff knees, and request that you will be pleased to hold yourselves upright again.

CHĀRUDATTA. Be it so; no further ceremony.

VASANTASENĀ [aside]. How kind his manner, how pleasing his expression! But it is not proper for me to remain longer: let me think. It shall be so. [Aloud.] Sir, respected sir, if truly I have found favor in your sight, permit me to leave these ornaments in your house; it was to rob me of them, that the villains I fled from pursued me.

CHĀRUDATTA. This house, lady, is unsuited to such a trust.

VASANTASENĀ. Nay, worthy sir, you do not speak me true. Men, and not houses, are the things we trust to.

CHĀRUDATTA. Maitreya, take the jewels.

VASANTASENĀ. You have obliged me.

MAITREYA. Much obliged to your ladyship.
　　[Taking them.]

CHĀRUDATTA. Blockhead, this is but a trust.

MAITREYA [to him apart]. What if they should be stolen?

CHĀRUDATTA. They will be here but a short time.

MAITREYA. What she has given us is ours.

CHĀRUDATTA. I shall send you about your business.

VASANTASENĀ. Worthy sir, I could wish to have the safeguard of this your
friend's company to return home.

CHĀRUDATTA. Maitreya, attend the lady.

MAITREYA. Go yourself; you are the properest person; attending her graceful
form as the stately swan upon his mate. I am but a poor Brahman, and
should as soon be demolished by these libertines as a meat offering in
the marketplace by the dogs.

CHĀRUDATTA. Well, well, I will attend her, and for further security on the
road let the torches be prepared.

MAITREYA. What ho! Vardhamāna—

[*Enter* SERVANT.]

—light the torches.

VARDHAMĀNA. You dunderhead, how are they to be lighted without oil?

MAITREYA [*apart to* CHĀRUDATTA]. To say the truth, sir, our torches are
like harlots; they shine not in poor men's houses.

CHĀRUDATTA. Never heed; we shall not need a torch.
> Pale as the maiden's cheek who pines with love,
> The moon is up, with all its starry train—
> And lights the royal road with lamps divine,
> Whilst through the gloom its milk-white rays descend,
> Like streamlets winding o'er the miry plain.

[*They proceed.*]

This, lady, is your dwelling.

[VASANTASENĀ *makes an obeisance, and exits.*]
> Come, my friend, let us return—
> The road is solitary, save where the watch
> Performs his wonted round: the silent night—
> Fit season only for dishonest acts—
> Should find us not abroad.
> As to this casket, let it be your charge
> By night, by day it shall be Vardhamāna's.

MAITREYA. As you command.

[*Exeunt.*]

ACT TWO

VASANTASENĀ'S *house.*

[*Enter a* FEMALE ATTENDANT.]

ATTENDANT. I am sent to Vasantasenā with a message from her mother,
I will therefore enter and deliver it to her. Ah, there she sits. She seems
uneasy, I must approach her.

[VASANTASENĀ *discovered seated,* MADANIKĀ *attending.*]

VASANTASENĀ. Well, girl, you must then—

MADANIKĀ. Then—when—madam? You have given me no orders.

VASANTASENĀ. What said I?

MADANIKĀ. You said, girl, you must then—

VASANTASENĀ. True.

ATTENDANT [*approaches*]. Madam, your mother desires that you will perform your ablutions and come to worship.

VASANTASENĀ. Tell my lady mother, child, that I shall not attend today; let the Brahman complete the ceremony.

ATTENDANT. As you command.

[*Exit.*]

MADANIKĀ. Dear madam, affection, not malice, compels me to ask what you meant to say?

VASANTASENA. Why, Madanikā, what think you of me?

MADANIKĀ. I should guess from your being so absent that you are in love.

VASANTASENĀ. Well said, Madanikā; you are a judge of hearts, it should seem.

MADANIKĀ. Excuse me, but Love is a resistless god, and holds his holiday in the breast of youth: so tell me, what prince or courtier does my lady serve?

VASANTASENĀ. I pretend, Madanikā, to be a mistress, not a slave.

MADANIKĀ. What young and learned Brahman, then, is it that you love?

VASANTASENĀ. A Brahman is to be venerated, not loved.

MADANIKĀ. It must be a merchant then, rich with the collected wealth of the many countries he has visited.

VASANTASENĀ. Nay, Madanikā, it were very ill advised to fix my affections on a trader to foreign lands. His repeated absence would subject me to a life of incessant grief.

MADANIKĀ. Neither a prince nor a courtier, a Brahman nor a merchant; who then can he possibly be?

VASANTASENĀ. Madanikā, you were with me in the garden of Kāmadeva's temple.

MADANIKĀ. I was, madam.

VASANTASENĀ. Then why do you ask me, as if you knew nothing?

MADANIKĀ. Ah! now I know—he in whose house you told me you had taken refuge.

VASANTASENĀ. How is he called?

MADANIKĀ. He lives near the Exchange.

VASANTASENĀ. I asked you his name.

MADANIKĀ. His well-selected name is Chārudatta.

VASANTASENĀ. Right, Madanikā; right, girl, now you know all.

MADANIKĀ [*aside*]. Is it so! But, lady, it is said that he is very poor.

VASANTASENĀ. I love him, nevertheless. No longer let the world believe that a courtesan is insensible to a poor man's merit.

MADANIKĀ. Yet, lady, do the bees swarm in the mango-tree after it has shed its blossoms.

VASANTASENĀ. Therefore are they called maybes.

MADANIKĀ. Well, if he is the object of your affections, why not contrive an interview?

VASANTASENĀ. I have provided for it: the scheme must succeed; and although it is not easy to get access to him, yet it may be managed.

MADANIKĀ. I suppose it was with this view that your ornaments were deposited in his hands?

VASANTASENĀ. You have a shrewd guess, wench.

[*They retire.*]

A street, with an open temple; voice behind.

Halloa, sirs, halloa! Yon gambler has lost ten gold-pieces, and is running off without paying—stop him! stop him! Ah, I see you, there you go—stop! stop!

[*Enter the* MASSEUR *hastily, talking to himself.*]

Curse on my gambling propensities; I am kicked by an ass, as it were by a she-ass just broke away from her first halter; I am picked up by a pike; no sooner did I see the master of the table intent upon the score, than I started. Now I have got away from them, where can I conceal myself? The gamester and the master are at my heels. Here is an empty temple; I will walk backward into it, and take my stand as its deity.

[*Enters the temple.*]

[*Enter* MĀTHURA, *the keeper of the gaming-house, and the* GAMBLER.]

MĀTHURA. Halloa, sirs! stop him, stop him.

GAMBLER. Though you hide in hell, or take shelter with Indra, you shall not escape: Rudra himself cannot protect you. The keeper of the gaming-house is your only chance.

MĀTHURA. Whither, you deceiver of a courteous publican, have you flown? You are shaking with fear, every limb of you; I know it by your irregular footmarks, as your feet have slipped and stumbled over the ground, blackening your family and fame.

GAMBLER. So far he has run, but here the track is lost.

MĀTHURA. Hey, the footmarks are all reversed. This temple had no image in it. Oh, the villain, he has walked backward into it.

GAMBLER. Let us after him.

MĀTHURA. Agreed.

[*They enter the temple, and signify in dumb show to each other the discovery of the* MASSEUR.]

GAMBLER. Is this image, think you, of wood?

MĀTHURA. No, it appears to me to be of stone.

[*They shake and pinch the* MASSEUR.]

Never mind it, let us sit down and play out our game.

[*They gamble.*]

MASSEUR [*who gradually expresses an interest in watching the game*]. The rattling of the dice are as tantalizing to a man without a penny, as the sound of a drum to a king without a kingdom. I shall not play, I know. Gambling is as bad as being pitched from the top of Mount Meru: and yet, like the nightingale's song, the sound of the dice is really bewitching.

GAMBLER. The throw is mine.

MĀTHURA. No, no, it is mine.

MASSEUR [*forgetting himself and jumping off the pedestal*]. No, no, it is mine.

GAMBLER. The man is taken.

MĀTHURA [*seizing the* MASSEUR]. Now, you scoundrel, we have you; where are the ten gold-pieces?

MASSEUR. I will pay them in the course of the day.

MĀTHURA. Pay them now.

MASSEUR. Have patience, and you shall be paid.

MĀTHURA. I must be paid immediately.

MASSEUR. Oh, dear, oh, lord, my head.

[*Falls down as in a swoon. They beat him.*]

MĀTHURA. You are fast now in the gaming ring.

MASSEUR [*rising and expressing pain*]. It is very hard that you will not give me a little time; where am I to get the money?

MĀTHURA. Give me a pledge then.

MASSEUR. Very well. [*Taking the* GAMESTER *aside.*] I tell you what, I will pay you half the money if you will forgive the rest.

GAMBLER. Agreed.

MASSEUR [*to* MĀTHURA, *aside*]. I will give you security for half the debt, if you cry quits for the other half.

MĀTHURA. Agreed.

MASSEUR [*to the* GAMESTER *aloud*]. You let me off half the debt?

GAMBLER. I do.

MASSEUR. And you give up half? [*To* MĀTHURA.]

MĀTHURA. Yes, I do.

MASSEUR. Then, good morning to you, gentlemen. [*Going.*]

MĀTHURA. Halloa, not so fast, where are you going?

MASSEUR. See here, my masters—one has forgiven me one-half, and the other has let me off another half; is it not clear that I am quits for the whole?

MĀTHURA. Hark ye, my friend, my name is Māthura. I know a thing or two, and am not to be done in this way: so down directly with the whole sum.

MASSEUR. Where am I to get it?

MĀTHURA. Sell your father.

MASSEUR. Where is my father?

MĀTHURA. Sell your mother.

MASSEUR. Where is she?

MĀTHURA. Sell yourself.

MASSEUR. Well, well, be pacified, take me upon the highway.

MĀTHURA. Come along. [*They proceed.*] What ho, good worthy friends; pray, some one buy me of this gambler for ten gold-pieces.

PASSER-BY. What noise is that?

MASSEUR. I will be your servant, your slave. Gone, and no reply—well, try again: who buys, who buys; will no one buy me of this gambler for ten gold-pieces? He has passed and not said a syllable! Ah, luckless me, ever since the noble Chārudatta came to poverty, I prosper only in misfortunes.

MĀTHURA. Come, come—give me the money.

MASSEUR. How should I give it?

[*Falls and is dragged along by* MĀTHURA.] Murder, murder! help—protect me.

[*Enter* DARDURAKA.]

DARDURAKA. Gambling is to the gamester an empire without a throne; he never anticipates defeat, but levies tribute from all, and liberally disburses what he obtains; he enjoys the revenues of a prince, and counts the opulent amongst his servants; money, wife, friends, all are to be won at the gaming-table, and all is gained, all possessed, and all lost at play. Let me see: *Tray* carried off everything; *Deuce* set my skin crawling; *Ace* settled the point, and *Doublets* dished me completely. Ha! here's my acquaintance, the keeper of the gaming-house, Māthura: I cannot avoid him, so I will wrap myself up so as not to be known. Eh! this vest is rather threadbare; it is embellished with sundry holes. It makes but a sorry covering, and looks best folded up.

[*Folds up his uppercloth after examining it, and puts it under his arm.*]

Never mind him; what can he do to me? I can stand with one foot on the ground, and the other in the air,[10] as long as the sun is in the heavens.

MĀTHURA. Come, come; your money.

MASSEUR. Whence is it to be got?

DARDURAKA. What is going on here?

PASSER-BY. This gambler is getting a thrashing from the gambling-master, and nobody will take his part.

DARDURAKA. Indeed! then I must interfere, I see. [*Approaches.*] Make way here; heigh, sirs: Māthura, that rogue, and the Masseur; the wretch, whose head is hanging below his heels at sunset, whose back is variegated with stripes and bruises, and whose legs are daily nibbled by the dogs; what has he, with his lank emaciated carcass, to do with gambling? I must appease Māthura. Good day, Māthura.

MĀTHURA. Good day, good day.

DARDURAKA. What are you at here?

MĀTHURA. This fellow owes me ten gold-pieces.

---

[10] A comic reference to the practice of the Hindu ascetics.

DARDURAKA. A trifle, a trifle.

MĀTHURA [*snatching* DARDURAKA'S *ragged cloth from him*]. See here, my
masters; here is a pretty fellow, in a ragged robe, to call ten gold-pieces a
trifle.

DARDURAKA. Why, you blockhead, how often do I stake ten gold-pieces
on a throw? What is a man to do with his money? Carry it in his
waistband? But you; you are villain enough, for the sake of ten gold-
pieces, to demolish the five senses of a man.

MĀTHURA. Keep your gold-pieces for your morning meal, if you like: this
is my property.

DARDURAKA. Very well; hear me! Give him other ten gold-pieces, and let
him play you for the whole.

MĀTHURA. How so?

DARDURAKA. If he wins, he shall pay you the money.

MĀTHURA. And if he lose?

DARDURAKA. Then, he shall not pay.

MĀTHURA. Go to; you talk nonsense. Will you give it? My name's Māthura;
I am a cheat, and win other men's money unfairly: what then? I am not
to be bullied by such a blackguard as you.

DARDURAKA. Whom do you call a blackguard?

MĀTHURA. You are a blackguard.

DARDURAKA. Your father was a blackguard.

[*Makes signs to the* MASSEUR *to escape.*]

MĀTHURA. You son of a slave! Are you not a gambler yourself?

DARDURAKA. Me? Do you call me a gambler?

MĀTHURA. Enough, enough. [*To the* MASSEUR.] Come, do you pay the ten
gold-pieces.

MASSEUR. I will pay them today.

[MĀTHURA *drags him along.*]

DARDURAKA. You villain! no one shall maltreat the poor in my presence.

[MĀTHURA *gives the* MASSEUR *a blow on the nose; it bleeds; the* MASSEUR,
on seeing his blood, faints and falls on the ground. DARDURAKA *approaches,
gets between him and* MĀTHURA, *and a scuffle ensues: they pause.*]

MĀTHURA. You villain! you son of a slave! you shall suffer for this.

DARDURAKA. You fool! you have assaulted me on the king's highway;
you shall see tomorrow, in court, whether you are to beat people in this
manner.

MĀTHURA. Ah, ha! yes, yes, I shall see; depend upon it.

DARDURAKA. How so! how will you see?

MĀTHURA. How! why, so, to be sure. [*Thrusting his face forward.*]

[DARDURAKA *throws a handful of dust into his eyes!* MĀTHURA *cries out
with pain and falls; the* MASSEUR *recovers, and according to* DARDURAKA'S
gesticulations makes his escape.]

DARDURAKA. Māthura is a man of some weight here, that's certain; I had
better therefore take myself off. My friend Sharvilaka told me that a

cunning man has prophesied to a cowherd named Āryaka, that he shall be king, and people like myself are flocking to him accordingly: my plan is to join him with the rest.
[*Exit.*]

VASANTASENĀ'S *house* (*outside and inside*).

[*Enter the* MASSEUR, *wandering about.*]
MASSEUR [*interior*]. The door of this house is open; I will enter it.
[*Enters and sees* VASANTASENĀ.]
Lady, I seek protection.
VASANTASENĀ. It is offered you; fear nothing. Madanikā, shut the door. What do you fly from?
MASSEUR. A creditor.
VASANTASENĀ. Secure the door. [*To* MADANIKĀ.]
MASSEUR [*to himself*]. She seems to be as much afraid of a creditor as myself; so much the better; he that takes a burden suited to his strength will not slip by the way, nor perish in the thicket. My situation is duly known here, it seems.
[*Enter* (*outside of the house*) MĀTHURA *and the* GAMBLER.]
MĀTHURA [*rubbing his eyes*]. The money, I say; I will have the money.
GAMBLER. Sir, whilst we were struggling with Darduraka, the other rogue has run off.
MĀTHURA. The villain! but I have flattened his nose for him; we shall track him by the blood.
GAMBLER. He has entered here. [*Stops at* VASANTASENĀ'S *door.*]
MĀTHURA. The ten gold-pieces are gone.
GAMBLER. Let us complain to the prince.
MĀTHURA. In the meantime the scoundrel will come forth and escape. No; let us wait here; we shall have him yet.
[*Inside of the house* VASANTASENĀ *makes signs to* MADANIKĀ].
MADANIKĀ [*to the* MASSEUR]. My mistress, sir, wishes to know whence you are; who you are; what you are; and what you are afraid of.
MASSEUR. I will tell you. I was born, lady, at Pātāliputra; I am the son of a householder, and follow the profession of a Masseur.
VASANTASENĀ. Were you trained to this effeminate occupation?
MASSEUR. I learned the practice, lady, to get a livelihood.
MADANIKĀ. So far so good. Proceed.
MASSEUR. Whilst living in my father's house, I heard travelers talk of distant countries, and felt curious to visit them myself. Accordingly, I came to Ujjayin, where I entered into the service of a distinguished person, whose like for an engaging figure and courteous speech never yet acknowledged kindness or forgot offense—enough said; he only values his consequence as it enables him to do good and cherish all who seek his protection.

MADANIKĀ. Who is this that so graces Ujjayin, having stolen the good qualities my lady loves?

VASANTASENĀ. Right, Madanikā, my heart suggests to me the same inquiry.

MADANIKĀ. Proceed.

MASSEUR. This gentleman having by his munificent bounty—

VASANTASENĀ. Lavished all his wealth.

MASSEUR. How should your ladyship know? I have not yet told you this.

VASANTASENĀ. I need no telling: worth and wealth are rarely found together. The pool is full to the brim, whose water is unfit for drinking.

MADANIKĀ. Oblige us with his name.

MASSEUR. To whom is the appellation of that earthly moon unknown, entitled to universal eulogium? His habitation is near the Exchange; his name is Chārudatta.

VASANTASENĀ [springs from her seat]. Girl, girl, a seat. This house is yours, sir; pray be seated. A fan! wench—quick; our worthy guest is fatigued.

MASSEUR [to himself]. Such respect from the simple utterance of Chārudatta's name! Bravo! excellent Chārudatta! you in this world live; other men only breathe.
[Falls at VASANTASENĀ's feet.]
Pray, lady, resume your seat.

VASANTASENĀ [sitting down]. Where is your wealthy dun?

MASSEUR. He is truly wealthy, who is rich in good acts, although he own not perishable riches. He who knows how to honor others, knows how his honor may be best deserved.

VASANTASENĀ. Proceed.

MASSEUR. I was made by that gentleman one of his personal attendants; but in his reduced circumstances being necessarily discharged, I took to play, and by a run of ill-luck have lost ten gold-pieces.

MĀTHURA [without]. I am robbed! I am plundered!

MASSEUR. Hear, lady, hear; those two gamblers are lying wait for me; what is your ladyship's will?

VASANTASENĀ. Madanikā, the birds are fluttering about and rustling in the leaves of the adjoining tree; go to this poor fellow's pursuers, and say to them that he sends them this jewel in payment.

MADANIKĀ. As you command.
[Exit.]
[Outside of the house.]

MĀTHURA. I am robbed!
[MADANIKĀ enters by the side door unobserved.]

MADANIKĀ. These two, by their casting such anxious looks up to the house, their agitation, their close conference, and the diligence with which they watch the door, must be the gambler and the keeper of the gaming-house. I salute you, sir.

MĀTHURA. Joy be with you, wench.

MADANIKĀ. Which of you two is the master of the gaming-house?

MĀTHURA. He, my graceful damsel, whom you now address with pouting lip, soft speech, and wicked eye; but get you gone; I have nothing for you.

MADANIKĀ. If you talk thus, you are no gambler. What! have you no one in your debt?

MĀTHURA. Yes, there is a fellow owes me ten gold-pieces: what of him?

MADANIKĀ. On his behalf, my mistress sends—nay, I mistake—he sends you this bracelet.

MĀTHURA. Ha, ha! tell him I take this as a pledge, and that he may come and have his revenge when he will.

[*Exeunt severally.*]

Inside of the house.

[*Enter* MADANIKĀ.]

MADANIKĀ. They have gone away, madam, quite pleased.

VASANTASENĀ. Now, my friend, depart, and relieve the anxiety of your family.

MASSEUR. If there be anything, lady, in which I can be of use to you, employ me.

VASANTASENĀ. There is a higher claim upon your service; you should still be ready to minister to him by whom you were once employed, and on whose account your skill was acquired.

MASSUER. The lady discards me; how shall I requite her kindness! [*Aloud.*] Lady, as I find my profession only begets disgrace, I will become a Buddhist monk; I tell you my design, and beg you will keep it in your recollection.

VASANTASENĀ. Nay, friend, do nothing rashly.

MASSEUR. I am determined, lady. [*Going.*] In bidding adieu to gambling, the hands of men are no longer armed against me: I can now hold up my head boldly as I go along the public road. [*A noise behind the scenes.*] What is the matter now?

VOICE BEHIND THE SCENE. Vasantasenā's hunting elephant has broken loose.

MASSEUR. I must go and see this furious beast;—yet why should I, as I purpose a pious life?

[*Exit.*]

[*A continued clamor without till* KARNAPŪRAKA *enters hastily.*]

KARNAPŪRAKA. Where is my lady?

MADANIKĀ. You unmannerly fellow! what ails you? Cannot you see your mistress and address her fittingly?

KARNAPŪRAKA. Lady, I salute you.

VASANTASENĀ. Karnapūraka, you seem highly pleased with something; what is it?

KARNAPŪRAKA. You have lost a great deal today in not witnessing your humble servant's achievement.

VASANTASENĀ. What achievement?

KARNAPŪRAKA. Only hear. Your ladyship's fierce elephant Khunthamoraka killed his keeper and broke his chain; he then scoured off along the high road, making a terrible confusion. The people shouted and screamed, "Carry off the children, get up the trees, climb the walls, the elephant is coming!" Away went girdles and anklets; and pearls and diamonds were scattering about in all directions. There he was, plunging about in Ujjayin, and tearing everything to pieces with his trunk, his feet, and his tusks, as if the city had been a large tank full of lotus flowers. A Buddhist monk[11] came in his way; the elephant broke his staff, water-pot, and platter, sprinkled him with water from his trunk, and held him up between his tusks; all cried out, "The holy man will be killed."

VASANTASENĀ. Alas! alas!

KARNAPŪRAKA. Don't be alarmed; only hear. Seeing him thus at large, and handling the holy man so roughly, I, Karnapūraka, my lady's humblest slave, determined to rescue the monk and punish my gentleman; so I quickly snatched up an iron bar, and approaching him sidelong, made a desperate blow at the animal.

VASANTASENĀ. Go on.

KARNAPŪRAKA. Big as he was, like the peaks of Vindhya, I brought him down and saved the monk.

VASANTASENĀ. You have done well.

KARNAPŪRAKA. So everybody said, "Well done, Karnapūraka, well done!" for all Ujjayin, in a panic, like a boat ill-laden, was heaped on one spot, and one person, who had no great matter of dress to boast of himself, turning his eyes upward, and fetching a deep sigh, threw his garment over me.

VASANTASENĀ. Does it smell of jasmines?

KARNAPŪRAKA. The smell of the elephant's frontal moisture is still in my nostrils; so I cannot tell how the garment smells.

VASANTASENĀ. Is there any name on it? see, see!

KARNAPŪRAKA. Here are letters; your ladyship will best be able to read them.

VASANTASENĀ [reads]. Chārudatta!

[Throws the cloth round her with delight.]

MADANIKĀ. How well the garment becomes our mistress, does it not?

KARNAPŪRAKA [sulkily]. Yes, it becomes her well enough.

VASANTASENĀ. Karnapūraka, be this your recompense.

[Gives him an ornament.]

KARNAPŪRAKA [puts it to his head and bows]. Now indeed the garment is becoming.

VASANTASENĀ. Where did you leave Chārudatta?

[11] i.e., the ex-masseur.

KARNAPŪRAKA. Going home, I believe, along this road.

VASANTASENĀ [to MADANIKĀ]. Quick, girl, quick; up on this terrace, and we may yet catch a glimpse of him.

[Exeunt.]

ACT THREE

CHĀRUDATTA'S *house* (*outside and inside*).

[*Enter* VARDHAMĀNA (*inside*).]

VARDHAMĀNA. A worthy kind master, even though he be poor, is the delight of his servants; whilst a morose haughty fellow, who has only his wealth to boast of, is a constant vexation. There is no changing nature; nothing can keep an ox out of a field of corn, nor stop a man who covets another's wife. There is no parting a gamester from the dice, and there is no remedy for an innate defect.[12] My excellent master has gone to a concert. It is not quite midnight, I suppose. I need not expect his return yet awhile; I shall therefore take a nap in the hall. [*Sleeps.*]

[*Enter* (*outside*) CHĀRUDATTA *and* MAITREYA.]

CHĀRUDATTA. Excellent, excellent indeed; Rebhila sang most exquisitely.

Although not ocean-born, the tuneful lute
Is most assuredly a gem of heaven—
Like a dear friend, it cheers the lonely heart,
And lends new luster to the social meeting.
It lulls the pain that absent lovers feel,
And adds fresh impulse to the glow of passion.

MAITREYA. Come, sir, let us get home.

CHĀRUDATTA. In truth, brave Rebhila, 'twas deftly sung.

MAITREYA. Now, to me, there are two things at which I cannot choose but laugh, a woman reading Sanskrit, and a man singing a song: the woman snuffles like a young cow when the rope is first passed through her nostrils; and the man wheezes like an old Pandit[13] who has been repeating his bead-roll till the flowers of his chaplet are as dry as his throat: to my seeming it is vastly ridiculous.

CHĀRUDATTA. What, my good friend, were you not pleased tonight with Rebhila's fine execution ?—

Smooth were the tones, articulate and flowing
With graceful modulation, sweet and pleasing,
And fraught with warm and passionate expression;
So that I often thought the dulcet sounds
Some female, stationed covertly, must utter.
Still echoes in my ears the soothing strain,

12 Chārudatta's open-handedness.
13 Priest.

And as I pace along, methinks I hear
The liquid cadence and melodious utterance.
The lute's sweet notes, now gently undulating,
Now swelling high, now dying to a close—
Sporting awhile in desultory descant,
And still recurring to the tasteful theme.

MAITREYA. Come, my friend, the very dogs in the high road through the marketplace are fast asleep; let us go home. See, see, the moon descends from his mansion in the skies, making his way through the darkness.

CHĀRUDATTA. True have you said. From his high palace bowed,
And hastening to his setting, scantly gleams
The waning moon, amidst the gathering gloom;
In slender crescent, like the tusk's fine point,
That peers above the darkening wave, where bathes
The forest elephant.

MAITREYA. Here we are at home. Holloa! Vardhamāna, arise and open the door.

VARDHAMĀNA [within]. Hark, I hear Maitreya's voice: Chārudatta is returned; I must let him in. [Opens the door.] Sir, I salute you; you also Maitreya. Here are the couches ready spread; please you to repose. [They enter and sit.]

MAITREYA. Vardhamāna, tell Radanikā to bring water for the feet.

CHĀRUDATTA. Nay, nay, disturb not those who are asleep.

VARDHAMĀNA. I will bring water, and Maitreya here can wash your feet.

MAITREYA. Do you hear, my friend, the son of a slave? he is to hold the water, and he sets me, who am a Brahman, to wash your feet.

CHĀRUDATTA. Do you, Maitreya, hold the water; Vardhamāna can perform the rest.

VARDHAMĀNA. Come then, worthy Maitreya, pour out the water.
[VARDHAMĀNA washes CHĀRUDATTA's feet, and is going.]

CHĀRUDATTA. Nay, Vardhamāna, wash the feet of the Brahman.

MAITREYA. Never mind; it is of little use; I must soon go tramping over the ground again, like a jackass.

VARDHAMĀNA. Most worthy Maitreya, you are a Brahman, are you?

MAITREYA. To be sure I am; like the boa amongst serpents, so am I, a Brahman amongst Brahmans.

VARDHAMĀNA. I cry you mercy: that being the case, I will wash your feet. [Does so.] Now, Maitreya, this gold casket, of which I have had the charge by day, it is your turn to take care of. [Gives it to him, and exits.]

MAITREYA. So; it is safe through the day. What! have we no thieves in Ujjayin, that no one could have carried off this vile pilferer of my rest: pray let me carry it into the courtyard.

CHĀRUDATTA. Impossible, it has been left in trust;
And is not to be parted with to any

But the right owner; Brahman, take heed to it. [*Lies down.*]
Still do I hear the soothing strain.

MAITREYA. Pray, sir, is it your intention to go to sleep?

CHĀRUDATTA. Assuredly.

I feel the drowsy deity invade
My forehead, and descend upon my eyelids.
Sleep, like decay, viewless and variable,
Grows stronger in its triumph o'er our strength.

MAITREYA. Very true, so let us go to sleep. [*They sleep.*]

[*Enter* SHARVILAKA (*outside*). *He soliloquizes:*][14]

Creeping along the ground, like a snake crawling out of his old skin, I effect with slight and strength a passage for my cowering frame. [*Looking up.*] The sovereign of the skies is in his decline: 'tis well. Night, like a tender mother, shrouds with her protecting darkness those of her children whose prowess assails the dwellings of mankind, and shrinks from an encounter with the servants of the king. I have made a breach in the garden wall, and have got into the midst of the garden. Now for the house. Men call this practice infamous, whose chief success is gained from the sleep of others, and whose booty is won by craft. If not heroism, it is at least independence, and preferable to the homage paid by slaves. As to nocturnal attacks, did not Aswatthāman[15] long ago overpower in a night-onset his slumbering foes? Where shall I make the breach? What part is softened by recent damp? Where is it likely that no noise will be made by the falling fragments? Where is a wide opening most practicable which will not be afterwards visible? In what part of the wall are the bricks old, and corroded by saline exudations? Where can I penetrate without encountering women? And where am I likely to light upon my booty?

[*Feels the wall.*]

The ground here is softened by continual sprinkling with water and exposure to the sun, and is crusted with salt. Here is a rat-hole. The prize is sure: this is the first omen of success the sons of Skanda[16] have laid down. Let me see: how shall I proceed? The god of the golden spear teaches four modes of breaching a house: picking out burned bricks, cutting through unbaked ones, throwing water on a mud wall, and boring through one of wood. This wall is of baked bricks: they must be picked out, but I must give them a sample of my skill. Shall the breach be the shape of a lotus blossom, the full sun or the new moon, the lake, the swastika, or the water-jar? It must be something to astonish the natives. The water-jar looks best in a brick wall;—that shall be the

[14] This scene satirizes the Hindu love of system and classification. (Note from Arthur William Ryder (trans.), *The Little Clay Cart*, Harvard University Press, 1905.)

[15] A character in the Sanskrit epic, *The Mahabharata*.

[16] "The god of the golden spear," patron saint of thieves.

shape. In other walls that I have breached by night, the neighbors have had occasion both to censure and approve my talents. Reverence to the Prince Skanda, the giver of all good; reverence to the god of the golden spear; to Brāhmanya, the celestial champion of the celestials; the son of fire. Reverence to the teacher of magic, whose chief scholar I am, and by whom well pleased was the magic unguent conferred upon me, anointed with which, no eye beholds nor weapon harms me. Shame on me! I have forgotten my measuring-line,—never mind, my Brahmanical cord will answer the purpose. This cord is a most useful appendage to a Brahman, especially one of my complexion: it serves to measure the depth and height of walls, and to withdraw ornaments from their position; it opens a latch in a door as well as a key, and is an excellent tourniquet for the bite of a snake. Let us take measure, and go to work: so, so—

[*Extracting the bricks.*]

—one brick alone remains. Ha! hang it; I am bitten by a snake—

[*Ties the finger with the cord.*]

— tis well again,—I must get on. [*Looks in.*] How! a lamp alight! the golden ray streaming through the opening in the wall shows amidst the exterior darkness, like the yellow streak of pure metal on the touch-stone. The breach is perfect; now to enter. There is no one. Reverence to Skanda.

[*Enters.*]

Here are two men asleep; let me set the outer door open to get off easily if there should be occasion; how it creaks! it is stiff with age; a little water will be of use.

[*Sprinkles the floor.*]

Nay, not so, it makes too much noise pattering on the ground.

[*Supports the door with his back, and opens it.*]

So far, so well. Now, are these true sleepers or only counterfeits?

[*He tries them.*]

They are sound: the breathing is regular and not fluttered; the eye is fast and firmly shut; the body is all relaxed; the joints are loose, and the limbs protrude beyond the limits of the bed. If shamming sleep, they will not bear the gleam of the lamp upon their faces.

[*Passes the lamp over their faces.*]

All is safe. What have we here? A drum, a tabor, a lute, pipes; and here are books. Why, zounds, I have got into the house of a dancer or a poet. I took it for the dwelling of some man of consequence, or I should have let it alone. Is this poverty, or only the show of poverty? Fear of thieves, or dread of the king? Are the effects hid underground? Whatever is underground is my property. Let us scatter the seed, whose sowing leaves nothing undiscernible.

[*Throws about seeds.*]

The man is an absolute pauper, and so I leave him.

[*Going.*]

MAITREYA [*dreaming*]. Master, they are breaking into the house. I see the thief. Here, here! do you take care of the gold casket.

SHARVILAKA. How! does he perceive me? does he mock me with his poverty? He dies. [*Approaching*.] Haply he dreams. [*Looking at* MAITREYA.] Eh! sure enough, there is in the light of the lamp something like a casket wrapped up in a ragged bathing-gown; that must be mine. No, no; it is cruel to ruin a worthy man, so miserably reduced already. I will even let it alone.

MAITREYA [*dreaming*]. My friend, if you do not take the casket, may you incur the guilt of disappointing a cow, and of deceiving a Brahman.

SHARVILAKA. These invocations are irresistible: take it I must. Softly: the light will betray me. I have a special moth to put it out. I must cast it into the lamp. [*Takes out the insect*.] Place and time requiring, let this insect fly. It hovers round the wick—with the wind of its wings the flame is extinguished. Shame on this total darkness, or rather shame on the darkness with which I have obscured the luster of my race! how well it suits that Sharvilaka, a Brahman, the son of a Brahman, learnèd in the four *Vedas*, and above receiving donations from others, should now be engaged in such unworthy courses! And why? For the sake of a harlot, for the sake of Madanikā. Ah, well! I must even go on, and acknowledge the courtesy of this Brahman.

MAITREYA [*half-awake*]. Eh, my good friend, how cold your hand is!

SHARVILAKA. Blockhead! I had forgotten, I have chilled my hand by the water I touched; I will put it to my side.

[*Chafes his left hand on his side and takes the casket with it*.]

MAITREYA [*still only half-awake*]. Have you got it?

SHARVILAKA. The civility of this Brahman is exceeding! I have it.

MAITREYA. Now like a pedlar that has sold all his wares, I shall go soundly to sleep. [*Sleeps*.]

SHARVILAKA. Sleep, illustrious Brahman! May you sleep a hundred years! Fie on this love! for whose dear sake I thus bring trouble on a Brahman's dwelling—nay, rather call down shame upon myself; and fie! and fie! upon this unmanning poverty, that urges me to acts which I must needs condemn. Now to Vasantasenā to redeem my beloved Madanikā with this night's booty. I hear footsteps; should it be the watch—what then?— shall I stand here like a post?—no, let Sharvilaka be his own protection. Am I not a cat in climbing, a deer in running, a snake in twisting, a hawk in darting upon the prey, a dog in baying man, whether asleep or awake? In assuming various forms am I not Illusion herself, and Goddess of Speech in the gift of tongues? A lamp in the night, a mule in a defile, a horse by land, a boat by water, a snake in motion, and a rock in stability? In hovering about I compete with the king of birds, and in an eye to the ground, am keener than the hare. Am I not like a wolf in seizing, and like a lion in strength?

[*Enter* RADANIKĀ.]

RADANIKĀ. Bless me! what has become of Vardhamāna? He was asleep at the hall door, but is there no longer. I must wake Maitreya. [*Approaches.*]

SHARVILAKA [*going to stab her*]. Ha! a woman! she is safe, and I may depart. [*Exit.*]

RADANIKĀ. Oh, dear me! a thief has broken into the house, and there he goes out at the door. Why, Maitreya! Maitreya! up, up, I say. A thief has broken into the house, and has just made his escape.

MAITREYA. Eh, what do you say, you foolish toad? A thief made his escape?

RADANIKĀ. Nay, this is no joke—see here.

MAITREYA. What say you, hey, the outer door opened! Chārudatta, friend, awake! a thief has been in the house and has just made his escape.

CHĀRUDATTA. This is not an hour to jest.

MAITREYA. It is true enough, as you may satisfy yourself.

CHĀRUDATTA. Where did he get in?

MAITREYA. Look here. [*Discovers the breach.*]

CHĀRUDATTA. Upon my word, a not unseemly fissure; the bricks are taken out above and below; the head is small, the body large: there is really talent in this thief.

MAITREYA. The opening must have been made by one of two persons; by a novice, merely to try his hand, or by a stranger to this city; for who in Ujjayin is ignorant of the poverty of our mansion?

CHĀRUDATTA. No doubt, by a stranger—one who did not know the condition of my affairs, and forgot that those only sleep soundly who have little to lose. Trusting to the external semblance of this mansion, erected in more prosperous times, he entered full of hope, and has gone away disappointed. What will the poor fellow have to tell his comrades? "I have broken into the house of the son of the chief of a corporation, and found nothing."

MAITREYA. Really, I am very much concerned for the luckless rogue. Ah, ha! thought he, here is a fine house; now for jewels, for caskets. [*Recollecting.*] By the by, where is the casket? oh yes, I remember. Ha, ha! my friend, you are apt to say of me, that blockhead Maitreya! that dunderhead Maitreya! but it was a wise trick of mine to give the casket to you: had I not done so, the villain would have walked off with it.

CHĀRUDATTA. Come, come, this jesting is misplaced.

MAITREYA. Jesting—no, no; blockhead though I be, I know when a joke is out of season.

CHĀRUDATTA. When did you give the casket to me?

MAITREYA. When I called out to you, "How cold your hand is!"

CHĀRUDATTA. It must be so. [*Looking about.*] My good friend, I am much obliged by your kindness.

MAITREYA. Why: is not the casket stolen?

CHĀRUDATTA. It is stolen.

MAITREYA. Then what have you to thank me for?

CHĀRUDATTA. That the poor rogue has not gone away empty-handed.

MAITREYA. He has carried off what was left in trust.

CHĀRUDATTA. How! in trust, alas!

[*Faints.*]

MAITREYA. Revive, revive, sir! though the thief has stolen the deposit, why should it so seriously affect you?

CHĀRUDATTA. Alas! my friend, who will believe it stolen?

> A general ordeal waits me. In this world
> Cold poverty is doomed to wake suspicion.
> Alas! till now, my fortune only felt
> The enmity of fate; but now its venom
> Sheds a foul blight upon my dearer fame.

MAITREYA. I tell you what. I will maintain that the casket was never entrusted to us. Who gave it, pray? Who took it? Where are your witnesses?

CHĀRUDATTA. Think you I can sanction thus a falsity?

> No, no; I will beg alms, and so obtain
> The value of the pledge, and quit its owner;
> But cannot condescend to shame my soul
> By utterance of a lie.

[*Exit.*]

RADANIKĀ. I will go and tell my mistress what has happened.

[*Exit.*]

Another room.

[*Enter the* WIFE *of* CHĀRUDATTA *and* RADANIKĀ.]

WIFE. But indeed is my lord unhurt? Is he safe, and his friend Maitreya?

RADANIKĀ. Both safe, madam, I assure you, but the ornaments left by the courtesan are stolen.

WIFE. Alas, girl! what say you? My husband's person is unharmed: that glads me. Yet better had his person come to harm than his fair fame incur disparagement. The people of Ujjayin will now be ready to suspect that indigence has impelled him to an unworthy act. Destiny, thou potent deity, thou sportest with the fortunes of mankind, and renderest them as tremulous as the watery drop that quivers on the lotus leaves. This string of jewels was given me in my maternal mansion: it is all that is left to us, and I know my husband, in the loftiness of his spirit, will not accept it from me. Girl, go call the worthy Maitreya hither.

[*Exit.*]

[RADANIKĀ *returns with* MAITREYA.]

MAITREYA. Health to you, respected lady.

WIFE. I salute you, sir. Oblige me by facing the east.

MAITREYA. You are obeyed.

WIFE. I pray you accept this.

MAITREYA. Nay, not so.

WIFE. I fasted on the Ceremony of the Gems, when, as you know, wealth must be given to a Brahman. My Brahman had been provided elsewhere, and I beg therefore that, in his stead, you will accept this string of jewels.

MAITREYA. Very well; I will go and state the matter to my friend.

WIFE. Thanks, Maitreya; but take heed, do not put me to shame.

[*Exit.*]

The hall. CHĀRUDATTA *discovered.*

CHĀRUDATTA. Maitreya tarries long; in his distress I hope he does not purpose aught unfitting.

[*Enter* MAITREYA.]

MAITREYA. Here am I, sir, and bring you this. [*Gives the string of jewels.*]

CHĀRUDATTA. What is this?

MAITREYA. The fruit borne by the excellence of a wife worthy of her husband.

CHĀRUDATTA. Is this the kindness of the Brahman's wife?

> Out on it!—that I should be reduced so low
> As, when my own has disappeared, to need
> Assistance from a woman's wealth. So true
> It is, our very natures are transformed
> By opulence: the poor man helpless grows,
> And woman wealthy acts with manly vigor.—
> 'Tis false; I am not poor:—a wife whose love
> Outlives my fortune; a true friend who shares
> My sorrows and my joy; and honesty
> Unwarped by indigence, these still are mine.
> Maitreya, hie thee to Vasantasenā,
> Tell her the casket, heedlessly impledged,
> Was lost by me at play, but in its stead
> I do beseech her to accept these jewels.

MAITREYA. I will do no such thing. What! are we to part with these gems, the quintessence of the four oceans, for a thing carried off by thieves, and which we have neither eaten nor drank, nor touched a penny for?

CHĀRUDATTA. Not so; to me, confiding in my care

> And honesty, the casket was entrusted;
> And for that faith, which cannot be o'ervalued,
> A price of high amount must be repaid.
> Touching my breast, I therefore supplicate,
> You will not hence, this charge not undertaken.
> You, Vardhamāna, gather up these bricks
> To fill the chasm again; we'll leave no trace
> To catch the idle censure of men's tongues.
> Come, come, Maitreya, rouse a liberal feeling,
> Nor act in this a despicable niggard.

MAITREYA. How can a pauper be a niggard? He has nothing to part with.

CHĀRUDATTA. I am not poor, I tell thee, but retain
    Treasures I prize beyond whate'er is lost.
    Go then, discharge this office, and meanwhile
    I hail the dawn with its accustomed rites.
    [*Exit.*]

ACT FOUR

VASANTASENĀ'S *house.*

[*Enter* FEMALE ATTENDANT.]

ATTENDANT. I am sent to the lady Vasantasenā by her mother: oh, here she is, looking on a picture, and engaged in conversation with Madanikā.
[*Enter* VASANTASENĀ *and* MADANIKA.]

VASANTASENĀ. But, Madanikā, is this a good likeness of Chārudatta?

MADANIKĀ. Very good.

VASANTASENĀ. How do you know?

MADANIKĀ. I conclude so, madam, from the affectionate looks which you bestow upon it.

VASANTASENĀ. How, wench, do you say this in the language of our profession?

MADANIKĀ. Nay, madam, surely even one of us is not incapable of speaking truth.

VASANTASENĀ. The woman, wench, that admits the love of many men is false to them all.

MADANIKĀ. Yet, madam, when the eyes and thoughts are intent but on one object, it is very unnecessary to inquire the cause.

VASANTASENĀ. But tell me, girl, do I not seem ridiculous to my friends?

MADANIKĀ. Nay, not so, madam; a woman is secure of the sympathy of her companions.

[ATTENDANT *advances.*]

ATTENDANT. Madam, your mother desires you to ascend your litter and repair to the private apartments.

VASANTASENĀ. To meet my Chārudatta.

ATTENDANT. The person, madam, who has sent the chariot has sent very costly ornaments.

VASANTASENĀ. Who is he?

ATTENDANT. Samsthānaka, the King's brother-in-law.

VASANTASENĀ. Begone, let me not hear him named.

ATTENDANT. Forgive me, madam; I but deliver my message.

VASANTASENĀ. The message is odious.

ATTENDANT. What reply am I to convey to your lady mother?

VASANTASENĀ. Tell her, if she would not have me dead, she must send me no more such messages.

ATTENDANT. I shall obey.
  [*Exit.*]

The outside of the house—a garden.

  [*Enter* SHARVILAKA (*below*).]
SHARVILAKA. My course is like the moon's, and with the dawn
      Declines its fading beams: my deeds have shamed
      The lazy night, have triumphed over sleep,
      And mocked the baffled vigilance of the watch.
      Yet I am scant secure, and view with terror
      Him who appears to track my rapid steps,
      Or seems to hasten where I rest my flight.—
      Thus guilty conscience makes me fear, for man
      Is ever frightened by his own offenses.
      'Tis for Madanikā's dear sake alone
      I perpetrate this violence, as I shun
      The leader and his train, avoid the mansion
      A woman sole inhabits, or I stand
      Still as the doorpost, while the town-guard passes,
      And with a hundred tricks thus make the night
      As full of action as the busy day.
VASANTASENĀ [*within*]. Here, girl, take the picture, lay it on my couch; and
  here, bring me my fan.
MADANIKĀ. I obey.
  [*Exit* MADANIKĀ.]
SHARVILAKA. This is the dwelling of Vasantasenā.
  [*Enters.*]
  Where can Madanikā be found?
  [MADANIKĀ *enters with the fan.*]
SHARVILAKA. Ah, here she comes, as graceful as the bride
      Of love, and soothing to my burning heart
      As sandal to the fevered flesh. Madanikā!
MADANIKĀ. Eh! Sharvilaka? health to you. Whence do you come?
SHARVILAKA. I will tell you.
  [*Enter* VASANTASENĀ (*above*).]
VASANTASENĀ [*above*]. Madanikā tarries long; where can she be? [*Looks
  from the window.*] How! she is engaged in conversation with a man: her
  eyes are fixed intently upon him, and seem to quaff overflowing drafts
  of love; they appear to understand each other. He woos her probably
  to be his companion: well, be it so; never be genuine affection thwarted.
  I will wait her leisure.
MADANIKĀ. Well, Sharvilaka, proceed.
  [*He looks cautiously round.*]
  Why do you thus examine the place? You seem alarmed.

SHARVILAKA. I have a secret to entrust you with; are we alone?
MADANIKĀ. Quite.
VASANTASENĀ. A secret! then I must not listen longer.
SHARVILAKA. Tell me, Madanikā, what cost procures
　　Your manumission of Vasantasenā?
VASANTASENĀ. He names me; the secret then regards me, and I must be a
　　party in it; behind this window I can overhear him unobserved.
MADANIKĀ. My lady has often declared, Sharvilaka, that she would liberate
　　us all without price if she were her own mistress; but where is the wealth
　　with which you are to purchase my freedom?
SHARVILAKA. To tell you sooth, my poverty and love
　　Have urged me to an act of violence.
VASANTASENĀ. How has this act transformed his otherwise goodly
　　appearance!
MADANIKĀ. Ah! Sharvilaka, for a transitory enjoyment you have en-
　　dangered two valuable things.
SHARVILAKA. And what are they?
MADANIKĀ. Your person and your reputation.
SHARVILAKA. Silly girl! fortune favors force.
MADANIKĀ [*ironically*]. Your conduct is without blame; the violence you
　　have committed on my account is no doubt quite proper.
SHARVILAKA. It may be venial, for I have not plundered
　　A lovely woman graced with glittering gems,
　　The blossoms of a creeper. I have not filched
　　A Brahman's gold, for purposes of piety
　　Collected, nor from the heedless nurse
　　Have I borne off the innocent babe for hire.
　　I have well weighed whate'er I have committed.
　　Apprise your mistress, then, these gems are hers,
　　That seem as they were made on purpose for her,
　　If she will yield you up, but let her keep them
　　Carefully concealed.
MADANIKĀ. An ornament that must never be worn is but ill suited to my
　　mistress. But come, let me see these trinkets.
SHARVILAKA. Behold them.
MADANIKĀ. I have certainly seen them before: where did you get them?
SHARVILAKA. That concerns not you; ask no questions, but take them.
MADANIKĀ [*angrily*]. If you can place no confidence in me, why seek to
　　make me yours?
SHARVILAKA. I was informed, then, that near the Bazaar resided the chief
　　of his tribe, one Chārudatta.
　　[VASANTASENĀ *and* MADANIKĀ *both faint.*]
SHARVILAKA. Madanikā, revive! what ails the wench?
　　Her limbs are all unstrung, her looks are wild.
　　Why, girl, is this your love? is then so terrible

The thought to share your destiny with mine?

MADANIKĀ. Avoid me, wretch! Yet stay, I dread to ask. Was no one hurt
or murdered in that mansion?

SHARVILAKA. I touch not one who trembles or who sleeps.
Unharmed by me were all in that abode.

MADANIKĀ. In truth?

SHARVILAKA. In very truth.

VASANTASENĀ. Do I yet live?

MADANIKĀ. This is indeed a blessing.

SHARVILAKA [*with jealous warmth*].

You seem to take strange interest in this business.
'Twas love of you that urged me to the act—
Me, sprung of virtuous and of pure descent.
Spurred by my passion, I have offered you
A life of credit and a faithful heart;
And this is my reward—to be reviled,
And find your cares devoted to another.
In vain the lofty tree of flowering youth
Bears goodly fruit, the prey of harlot birds.
Wealth, manhood, all we value, are consumed
By passion's fierce ungovernable fire.
Ah! what a fool is man, to place his trust
In woman or in fortune, fickle both
As serpent-nymphs! Be woman's love unwooed,
For humble love she pays with scorn. Let her
First proffer tenderness, and whilst it lasts
Be kind, but leave her as her fondness cools.
'Tis wisely said, for money woman weeps
And smiles at will, and of his confidence,
The man she trusts not, craftily beguiles.
Let then the youth of merit and of birth
Beware the wanton's charms, that baleful blow
Like flowers on charnel ground; the ocean waves
Are less unsteady, and the varying tints
Of eve less fleeting than a woman's fondness.
Wealth is her aim; as soon as man is drained
Of all his goods, like a squeezed color bag,
She casts him off. Brief as the lightning's flash
Is woman's love. Nay, she can look devotion
To one man whilst another rules her heart,
And even whilst she holds in fond embrace
One lover, for his rival breathes her sighs.
But why expect what nature has withheld?
The lotus blooms not on the mountain's brow,
Nor bears the mule the burden of the horse;

The grain of barley buds not into rice,
Nor dwells one virtue in the breast of woman.
Fool that I was, to let that wretch escape;
'Tis not too late, and Chārudatta dies. [*Going.*]

MADANIKĀ [*catching hold of him*]. You have talked a great deal of stuff, and are 'angry without rhyme or reason.

SHARVILAKA. How, without reason?

MADANIKĀ. These ornaments are in truth the property of Vasantasenā.

SHARVILAKA. Indeed!

MADANIKĀ. And were left by her in deposit with Chārudatta.

SHARVILAKA. For what purpose?

MADANIKĀ. I will tell you. [*Whispers.*]

SHARVILAKA. I am overcome with shame. The friendly branch
That gave me shadow when oppressed with heat,
My heedless hand has shorn of its bright leaves.

VASANTASENĀ. I am glad that he repents: he has acted without reflection.

SHARVILAKA. What is to be done?

MADANIKĀ. You are the best judge.

SHARVILAKA. Nay, not so.
Nature is woman's teacher, and she learns
More sense than man, the pedant, gleans from books.

MADANIKĀ. I should advise you then, go and return these ornaments to Chārudatta.

SHARVILAKA. And what if he deliver me up to justice?

MADANIKĀ. There is no heat from the moon.

SHARVILAKA. I heed not of his gentleness, and brave
Unshrinkingly the consequence of all
I dare to do—but this, this act I blush for;
And of such petty scoundrels as myself
How must the prince dispose? No—no,
We must devise some other means.

MADANIKĀ. I have.

VASANTASENĀ. What can she suggest?

MADANIKĀ. You shall pass yourself off as a messenger from Chārudatta, sent to restore these trinkets to my lady.

SHARVILAKA. And what results?

MADANIKĀ. You will be no thief; Chārudatta will sustain no loss, and my lady recover her own property.

SHARVILAKA. This is downright robbery, carrying off my booty.

MADANIKĀ. If you do not relinquish it, that will be much more like robbery.

VASANTASENĀ. Well said, Madanikā; you advise as a faithful friend.

SHARVILAKA. I have gained much by asking your advice.
When there is no moon at night, 'tis difficult
To get a guide that may be safely followed.

MADANIKĀ. Stay here, whilst I give notice to my mistress.

SHARVILAKA. Be it so.

MADANIKĀ [*approaches* VASANTASENĀ]. Lady, a Brahman attends you from Chārudatta.

VASANTASENĀ. How do you know his mission?

MADANIKĀ. Do I not know my own affairs?

VASANTASENĀ [*smiling*]. Very true; let him advance, Madanikā.

[*She descends, and brings* SHARVILAKA *forward as* VASANTASENĀ *enters below.*]

SHARVILAKA. Lady, I salute you; peace be with you.

VASANTASENĀ. I salute you. Pray be seated. [*Sits.*]

SHARVILAKA. The respected Chārudatta informs you, that as his house is very insecure, he is apprehensive this casket may be lost, and therefore begs you will take it back again.

[*Gives it to* MADANIKĀ *and is going.*]

VASANTASENĀ. Stay; I have a favor to request. Let me trouble you to convey to the worthy sender something from me.

SHARVILAKA [*aside*]. Who the deuce is to give it to him? [*Aloud.*] What am I to take?

VASANTASENĀ. Madanikā.

SHARVILAKA. I understand you not.

VASANTASENĀ. I understand myself.

SHARVILAKA. What mean you?

VASANTASENĀ. The truth is, it was agreed between Chārudatta and me, that the person by whom he should send back these jewels should receive Madanikā as a present from me on his account: you are therefore to take this damsel, and thank Chārudatta for her. You understand me now.

SHARVILAKA [*apart*]. She knows the truth; that is clear. No matter. [*Aloud.*]

      May all prosperity bless Chārudatta.
      'Tis politic in man to nurture merit,
      For poverty with worth is richer far
      Than majesty without all real excellence.
      Nought is beyond its reach; the radiant moon
      Won by its worth a seat on Shiva's brow.

VASANTASENĀ. Who waits? bring forth the bullock cart.

SHARVILAKA. It attends. [*The carriage comes on.*]

VASANTASENĀ. My dear girl, Madanikā, ascend the litter; I have given you away: look at me well; do not forget me.

MADANIKĀ [*weeping*]. I am discarded by my mistress.

[*Falls at her feet.*]

VASANTASENĀ. Nay, wench, rise, it is now my place to stoop to you; go take your seat, and keep me ever in your recollection.

SHARVILAKA. Lady, may every good attend you! Madanikā, with grateful looks survey your bounteous benefactress; bow your head in gratitude to her to whom you owe the unexpected dignity that waits upon the title and the state of wife.

[*They salute* VASANTASENĀ *as she departs, and ascend the car.*]

VOICE BEHIND THE SCENE. Who hears? who hears? the Governor commands. In consequence of a reported prophecy, that the son of a cowherd, named Āryaka, shall ascend the throne, his majesty Pālaka has deemed it expedient to apprehend him, and detain him in confinement. Let all men therefore remain quietly in their houses, and entertain no alarm.

SHARVILAKA. How! the king has seized my dear friend Āryaka, and I am thinking of a wife!

>This world presents two things most dear to all men;
>A friend and mistress; but the friend is prized
>Above a hundred beauties. I must hence,
>And try to liberate him. [*Alights.*]

MADANIKĀ. Stay but a while, my dearest lord; consign me first to reputable friends, then leave me, if it must be so.

SHARVILAKA. You speak my thoughts, love. Hark ye. [*To the servant.*]

>Know you the residence of Rebhila,
>The chief of the musicians?

SERVANT. I do, sir.

SHARVILAKA. Convey my lady thither.

SERVANT. As you command.

MADANIKĀ. I obey. Farewell. For my sake, be not rash. [*Exit.*]

SHARVILAKA. Now then to rouse the friends of Āryaka,

>Our kindred and associates—all who deem
>The king has wronged their will, and all who trust
>The prowess of their arms. We will redeem
>Our chief from bonds, as by his faithful minister
>Udayana[17] was rescued.
>This seizure is unjust, it is the deed
>Of a most cowardly and treacherous foe;
>But we shall soon release him from such grasp,
>Like the fair moon from Rāhu's jaws set free.[18]
>[*Exit.*]

VASANTASENĀ'S *dwelling* (*inside*).

[*Enter a* FEMALE ATTENDANT, *meeting* VASANTASENĀ.]

ATTENDANT. Lady, you are fortunate, a Brahman from Chārudatta.

VASANTASENĀ. This is indeed a lucky day. Receive him with all respect; request him to enter, and call the Chamberlain to attend him.

ATTENDANT. As you command. [*Exit.*]

[17] A Hindu prince captured by a usurper, but liberated by the usurper's minister and his daughter.

[18] According to Hindu astronomy, eclipses of the moon were caused by the dragon Rahu who would from time to time seize it in his jaws.

Outside of the house.

[*Enter* MAITREYA *and the* ATTENDANT.]

MAITREYA. Here's honor! The king of demons, Rāvana, travels in the Car of Blossoms, obtained by the force of his devotions; but I, who am a poor Brahman, and no saint, yet I am conveyed about by lovely damsels.

ATTENDANT. This is the outer door, sir.

MAITREYA. A very pretty entrance, indeed. The threshold is very neatly colored, well swept and watered; the floor is beautified with strings of sweet flowers; the top of the gate is lofty and gives one the pleasure of looking up to the clouds, whilst the jasmine festoon hangs tremblingly down, as if it were now tossing on the trunk of the celestial elephant. Over the doorway is a lofty arch of ivory; above it again wave flags dyed with safflower, their fringes curling in the wind, like fingers that beckon me, "come hither." On either side, the capitals of the doorposts support elegant crystal flowerpots, in which young mango trees are springing up. The door panels are of gold, stuck, like the stout breast of a demon, with studs of adamant. The whole cries "away" to a poor man, whilst its splendor catches the eye of the wisest.

ATTENDANT. This leads to the first court. Enter, sir, enter.

[*They enter the first court.*]

MAITREYA. Bless me! why here is a line of palaces, as white as the moon, as the conch, as the stalk of the water lily—the stucco has been laid on here by handfuls; golden steps, embellished with various stones, lead to the upper apartments, whence the crystal windows, festooned with pearls, and bright as the eyes of a moon-faced maid, look down upon Ujjayin. The porter dozes on an easy-chair as stately as a Brahman deep in the *Vedas*; and the very crows, crammed with rice and curds, disdain the fragments of the sacrifice, as if they were no more than scattered plaster. Proceed.

ATTENDANT. That is the second court. Enter.

[*They enter the second court.*]

MAITREYA. Oh, here are the stables; the carriage oxen are in good case, pampered with fodder I declare; and straw and oil-cakes are ready for them; their horns are bright with grease. Here we have a buffalo snorting indignantly, like a Brahman of high caste whom somebody has affronted; here the ram stands to have his neck well rubbed, like a wrestler after a match; here they dress the manes of the horses; here is a monkey tied as fast a thief; and here the mahouts are plying the elephants with balls of rice and ghee.[19] Proceed.

ATTENDANT. This sir, is the third gateway.

[*They enter the third court.*]

MAITREYA. Oh, this is the public court, where the young bucks of Ujjayin

---

[19] Butter reduced to oil by boiling.

assemble; these are their seats, I suppose—the half-read book lies on the gaming-table, the dice of which are made of jewels. Oh, yonder are some old hangers-on, lounging about with many-colored pictures in their hands, and skilled in the peace and war of love. What next?

ATTENDANT. This is the entrance to the fourth court.

[*They enter the fourth court.*]

MAITREYA. Oh, ho! this is a very gay scene: here the drums, whilst beaten by taper fingers, emit, like clouds, a murmuring tone; there the cymbals beating time, flash as they descend like the unlucky stars that fall from heaven. The flute here breathes the soft hum of the bee, whilst here a damsel holds the lute in her lap, and frets its wires with her finger nails, like some wild minx that sets her mark on the face of her offending swain: some damsels are singing, like so many bees intoxicated with flowery nectar; others are practicing the graceful dance, and others are employed in reading plays and poems. The place is hung with water-jars, suspended to catch the cooling breeze. What comes next?

ATTENDANT. This is the gate of the fifth court.

[*They enter the fifth court.*]

MAITREYA. Ah, how my mouth waters! what a savory scent of oil and asafetida! The kitchen sighs softly forth its fragrant and abundant smoke—the odors are delicious—they fill me with rapture. The butcher's boy is washing the skin of an animal just slain, like so much foul linen; the cook is surrounded with dishes; the sweetmeats are mixing; the cakes are baking. [*Apart.*] Oh that I could meet with someone to do me a friendly turn; one who would wash my feet, and say, eat, sir, eat. [*Aloud.*] This is certainly Indra's heaven; the damsels are Apsarasas,[20] the Chamberlains are Gandharbas.[21] Pray, why do they call you bastards?

ATTENDANT. We inhabit the dwellings of others and eat the bread of the stranger: we are the offspring of parents whom no tie connects: we exercise our indescribable merits in gaining men's money, and we sport through life as free and unrestrained as the cubs of the elephant.

MAITREYA. What do we come to next?

ATTENDANT. This is the sixth entry.

[*They enter.*]

MAITREYA. The arched gateway is of gold and many-colored gems on a ground of sapphire, and looks like the rainbow in an azure sky. What is going forward here so busily? It is the jeweler's court: skillful artists are examining pearls, topazes, sapphires, emeralds, rubies, the lapis lazuli, coral, and other jewels; some set rubies in gold, some work gold ornaments on colored thread, some string pearls, some grind the lapis lazuli, some pierce shells, and some cut coral. Here we have perfumers drying the saffron bags, shaking the musk bags, pressing the sandal juice

---

[20] Heavenly choristers.
[21] Heavenly nymphs.

and compounding essences. Whom have we here? fair damsels and their
gallants, laughing, talking, chewing musk and betel, and drinking wine.
Here are the male and female attendants, and here are miserable hangers-
on—men that neglected their own families and spent their all upon the
harlot, and are now glad to quaff the drainings of her wine-cup.

ATTENDANT. This is the seventh court. Enter.

[*They enter the seventh court.*]

MAITREYA. This is the aviary—very handsome indeed! The doves bill and
coo in comfort; the pampered parrot croaks like a Brahman pandit,
stuffed with curds and rice, chanting a hymn from the *Vedas*; the
thrush chatters as glibly as a housemaid issuing her mistress's command
to her fellow-servants, while the cuckoo, crammed with juicy fruit,
whines like a water carrier. The quails fight; the partridges cry; the
domestic peacock dances about delighted, and fans the palace with his
gem-emblazoned tail, as if to cool its heated walls; the swans, like balls
of moonlight, roll about in pairs, and follow each graceful maid, as if to
learn to imitate her walk, whilst the long-legged cranes stalk about the
court, like eunuchs on guard. I declare the lady lives here amongst the
winged race as if she tenanted Indra's garden. Well, where do you go
now?

ATTENDANT. Enter, sir, the eighth court.

[*They enter.*]

MAITREYA. Pray, who is that gentleman dressed in silken raiment, glittering
with rich ornaments, and rolling about as if his limbs were out of joint?

ATTENDANT. That, sir, is my lady's brother.

MAITREYA. Humph—what course of pious austerity in his last life made him
Vasantasenā's brother? Nay, not so; for after all, though smooth, bright,
and fragrant, the champa tree that grows on funeral ground is not to be
approached. And pray, who is that lady dressed in flowered muslin?—a
goodly person truly; her feet shining with oil thrust into a pair of slippers:
she sits in state, high on a gorgeous throne.

ATTENDANT. That is my lady's mother.

MAITREYA. A portly old hag, indeed: how did she contrive to get in here?
Oh, I suppose she was first set up here, as they do with an unwieldy idol,
and then the walls were built round her.

ATTENDANT. How now, slave? What! do you make a jest of our lady,
affected, too, as she is with a quartan ague?

MAITREYA. A what? O mighty Fever, be pleased to afflict me with a quartan,
if such are its symptoms!

ATTENDANT. You will die, slave.

MAITREYA. No, hussy; better that this bloated porpoise, swelled up with
wine and years, die; there will then be a dinner for a thousand jackals.
But no matter; what do you know about it? I had heard of Vasantasenā's
wealth, and now I find it true; it seems to me that the treasures of the
three worlds are collected in this mansion. I am in doubt whether to

regard it as the dwelling of a courtesan or the palace of Kuvera.[22]
Where is your lady?

ATTENDANT. She's in the arbor. Enter.

[*They enter the garden.*]

MAITREYA. A very lovely scene! the numerous trees are bowed down by
delicious fruit, and between them are silken swings constructed for the
light form of youthful beauty: the yellow jasmine, the graceful mālatī,
the full-blossomed mallikā, the blue clitoria, spontaneous shed their
flowers, and strew the ground with a carpet more lovely than any in the
groves of Indra; the reservoir glows with the red lotus blossoms, like the
dawn with the fiery beams of the rising sun; and here the ashoka tree,
with its rich crimson blossoms, shines like a young warrior bathed with
the sanguine shower of the furious fight. Where is your lady?

ATTENDANT. Look lower, and you will see her.

MAITREYA [*approaching* VASANTASENĀ]. Health to you, lady.

VASANTASENĀ [*rising and speaking in Sanskrit*]. Welcome, Maitreya; take
a seat.

MAITREYA. Pray, keep you yours. [*They sit.*]

VASANTASENĀ. I hope all is well with the son of the merchant.

MAITREYA. Is all well with your ladyship?

VASANTASENĀ. Undoubtedly, Maitreya; the birds of affection gladly nestle
in the tree, which, fruitful in excellence, puts forth the flowers of magnanimity and the leaves of merit, and rises with the trunk of modesty from
the root of honor.

MAITREYA [*apart*]. Figurative indeed. [*Aloud.*] What else?

VASANTASENĀ. What brings you hither?

MAITREYA. I will tell you:—Chārudatta presents his respects to you.

VASANTASENĀ. With respect I receive his commands.

MAITREYA. He desires me to say, that he has lost your golden casket; it
was impledged by him at play, and the keeper of the tables, a servant of
the prince, is gone, no one knows whither.

ATTENDANT. Lady, you are in luck; the grave Chārudatta turned gambler.

VASANTASENĀ [*apart*]. How? the casket has been stolen, and he says it was
lost at play. Yet even in this I love him.

MAITREYA. As the accident cannot now be helped, he requests, in lieu of the
casket, you will accept this string of diamonds.

VASANTASENĀ [*apart*]. Shall I show him the ornaments? [*Considering.*] No,
not so.

MAITREYA. Will you not receive this equivalent?

VASANTASENĀ [*smiling*]. Why not, Maitreya?

[*Takes and puts it to her heart.*]

But how is this? Do drops of nectar fall from the mango-tree after it has
shed its blossoms? My good friend, tell that sad gambler, Chārudatta,

[22] God of wealth.

that I shall call upon him in the evening.

MAITREYA [*apart*]. So, so; she intends to get more out of him, I suppose. [*Aloud.*] I shall so inform him, madam. [*Apart.*] I wish he was rid of this precious acquaintance.

[*Exit.*]

VASANTASENĀ. Here, girl, take the jewels and attend me to Chārudatta.

ATTENDANT. But look, madam, look! a sudden storm is gathering.

VASANTASENĀ. No matter.

> Let the clouds gather and dark night descend,
> And heavy fall unintermitted showers;
> I heed them not, wench, when I haste to seek
> His presence, whose loved image warms my heart.—
> Take charge of these, and lightly trip along.

[*Exit.*]

ACT FIVE

CHĀRUDATTA'S *garden*.

[*Enter* CHĀRUDATTA (*looking up*).]

CHĀRUDATTA. A heavy storm impends: the gathering gloom
> Delights the peacock and distracts the swan,
> Not yet prepared for periodic flight;
> And these deep shades contract with sad despondence
> The heart that pines in absence. Through the air,
> A rival Vishnu[23] the purple cloud
> Rolls stately on, girt by the golden lightning,
> As by his yellow garb, and bearing high
> The long white line of storks, God's trumpeters:
> From the dark womb, in rapid fall descend
> The silvery drops, and glittering in the gleam,
> Shot from the lightning, bright and fitful, sparkle
> Like a rich fringe rent from the robe of heaven.
> The firmament is filled with scattered clouds,
> And, as they fly before the wind, their forms,
> As in a picture, image various shapes,
> The semblances of storks and soaring swans,
> Of dolphins and the monsters of the deep,
> Of dragons vast, and pinnacles, and towers.
> The spreading shade, methinks, is like the host
> Of Dhritarāshtra shouting loud in thunder.
> Yon strutting peacock welcomes its advance,
> Like proud Duryodhan, vaunting of his might:

[23] One of the epithets of Vishnu was "The Black." Vishnu, Shiva, and Brahma were the three chief Hindu gods.

From its dread enmity, the cuckoo flies,
Like luckless Yudhishthira, by the dice
Bereaved of power, and scatter wild the swans,
Like the proscribed and houseless Pāndavas,
Wandering from home and every comfort far,
Through paths untrod, till then, and realms unknown.
Maitreya long delays. Will not today
Apprise me of the issue of his visit?
[*Retires.*]

[*Enter* MAITREYA.]

MAITREYA. What a rapacious, mean wretch is this harlot! Scarcely a word did she say, but, without any ceremony, pounced upon the necklace. With all her pomp and parade, she could not say to me, my good friend, Maitreya, take a little refreshment; not even so much as to offer me a draught of water—her wealth is positively all thrown away upon her. It is very true, there is no lotus that has not a stalk; no trader that is not a cheat; there is not a goldsmith that is not a thief; there never was a village meeting without a quarrel; and there never will be a harlot without rapacity: these are things that always go together. I shall therefore dissuade my worthy friend from his infatuation. Ha! yonder I see him in the garden. Health and prosperity to Chārudatta!

CHĀRUDATTA [*comes forward*]. Welcome, my good friend; Maitreya, sit down.

MAITREYA. I am seated. [*Sits.*]

CHĀRUDATTA. Now, my friend, your news?

MAITREYA. It is all over.

CHĀRUDATTA. How so? does she refuse the proffered gems?

MAITREYA. We have no such luck; she put her soft hands to her forehead, and then laid hold of the necklace.

CHĀRUDATTA. Then, why do you complain?

MAITREYA. Why? reason enough. We have made a pretty job of it; to lose a necklace worth the four seas, for a thing of little value, and one we neither ate, nor drank, and which a thief carried off.

CHĀRUDATTA. You reason idly.

The pledge was here deposited in trust,
And for that trust a costly price was due.

MAITREYA. I have another cause of complaint. She made signs to her damsels, and they covered their faces with their veils and made me their merriment. I beg, therefore, that you will desist from such unbecoming intercourse. A courtesan is like a thorn that has run into your foot; you cannot even get rid of it without pain; and it is indisputably true, that wherever a harlot, an elephant, a scribe, a mendicant, a spy, or a jackass, find admission, they are sure to do mischief.

CHĀRUDATTA. Enough of this unmerited reviling.

My fallen fortunes are a sure protection.

The fiery steed bounds fleetly o'er the plain
Till fading breath retards his lagging course;
So man's desires first urge his heedless path,
But soon exhausted shrink into his bosom.
Believe me, friend, a female of this order,
A true wealth-hunter, troubles not the poor:
[*Apart.*] She, she, alone, bestows her love on merit.
[*Aloud.*] We are by wealth abandoned, and by her.

MAITREYA [*apart*]. This love is the devil: he turns up his eyes and sighs from the very bottom of his heart. I see plainly my advice to him to conquer his passion only serves to confirm it. [*Aloud.*] She desired me to say, she intends paying you a visit this evening. I suspect she is not satisfied with the necklace, and intends to demand something more valuable.

CHĀRUDATTA. Well, let her come; she shall depart contented.

[*Enter* KUMBHILAKA, VASANTASENĀ'S *servant.*]

KUMBHILAKA. I wish every one to take notice, that the harder it rains the more thoroughly do I get ducked, and the colder the wind that blows down my back, the more do my limbs shiver. A pretty situation for a man of my talents; for one who can play the flute with seven holes, the lute with seven strings, can sing like a jackass, and who acknowledges no musical superior, except perhaps the gods. Vasantasenā sends me to Chārudatta's house. [*Advances.*] There is Chārudatta in the garden, and that dunderhead Maitreya with him. I must throw out a signal to him.

[*Throws a clod of earth at* MAITREYA.]

MAITREYA. Holloa! who pelts me with a pellet, like an apple tree in an orchard?

CHĀRUDATTA. It was probably thrown down in their sport by the pigeons that tenant the top of the garden wall.

MAITREYA. Wait a while, you saucy son of a slave, and with this stick I will knock you off the wall, like a ripe mango from the tree.

CHĀRUDATTA. Sit down, sit down; fright not the gentle bird, nor chase him from his mate.

KUMBHILAKA. The blockhead! he sees the pigeons and cannot see me. I must give him another salutation.

[*Throws another clod.*]

MAITREYA. Hey, again! [*Looks up.*] O Kumbhilaka! is it you? Wait a while, and I will come to you.

[*Goes to the door.*]

Come in; how fares it?

KUMBHILAKA. I salute you, sir.

MAITREYA. And what brings you here in such foul weather?

KUMBHILAKA. She sent me.

MAITREYA. And who is she?

KUMBHILAKA. She. See? She.

MAITREYA. She—she—she! What are you sputtering about, like an old miser when things are dear? Who—who—who?

KUMBHILAKA. Hoo—hoo—hoo! What are you too-whooing about, like an owl that has been scared from a sacrifice?

MAITREYA. Speak out, man, intelligibly.

KUMBHILAKA. I will; but first I'll give you something to guess.

MAITREYA. I shall give you a box of the ears, I believe.

KUMBHILAKA. Never mind that. In which season, pray, does the mango blossom?

MAITREYA. In summer to be sure, you blockhead!

KUMBHILAKA. Blockhead yourself! it does no such thing.

MAITREYA. Hey, how is that? I must ask my friend. Stop a moment.

[*Goes to* CHĀRUDATTA.]

Pray, sir, in which season does the mango blossom?

CHĀRUDATTA. Why, you simpleton, in Vasanta, in the spring.

MAITREYA [*to* KUMBHILAKA]. Why, you simpleton, the mango blossoms in Vasanta.

KUMBHILAKA. Very well. Now answer me one more question: Who guards wealthy towns?

MAITREYA. Why, the town guard, to be sure.

KUMBHILAKA. No; that is not it.

MAITREYA. No? Let me see. [*Aside.*] I must consult Chārudatta. Pray, sir, who guards wealthy towns?

CHĀRUDATTA. The army undoubtedly, the Senā.

MAITREYA [*to* KUMBHILAKA]. The Senā undoubtedly.

KUMBHILAKA. Very well; now put your answers together; quick, quick!

MAITREYA. Ha, I have it! Vasantasenā.

KUMBHILAKA. She is here.

MAITREYA. I must apprise my friend. Sir, we have a creditor here.

CHĀRUDATTA. Here? A creditor in my house?

MAITREYA. I do not know anything about the house, but there is one at the door. Vasantasenā is arrived.

CHĀRUDATTA. Nay, now you jest?

MAITREYA. If you do not believe me, ask this fellow. Here, you Kumbhilaka!

KUMBHILAKA [*advancing*]. Sir, I salute you.

CHĀRUDATTA. You are welcome; tell me, is Vasantasenā here?

KUMBHILAKA. She is, sir.

CHĀRUDATTA. Never be good news unrewarded; this for your pains. [*Gives him his garment.*]

KUMBHILAKA [*bows*]. I shall inform my mistress.

[*Exit.*]

MAITREYA. Now, I hope you are satisfied. To come out in such weather; you can have no doubt what brings her.

CHĀRUDATTA. I do not feel quite confident.

MAITREYA. Depend upon it, I am right; the casket was worth more than the necklace, and she comes for the difference.

CHĀRUDATTA [*apart*]. She shall be gratified.
[*They retire.*]

Outside of the garden.

[*Enter* VASANTASENĀ *splendidly dressed, attended by her* VITA, *a* FEMALE SERVANT, *and one carrying a large umbrella.*]

SERVANT. Lady, upon the mountain's brow, the clouds
    Hang dark and drooping, as the aching heart
    Of her who sorrows for her absent lord;
    Their thunders rouse the peacocks, and the sky
    Is agitated by their wings, as fanned
    By thousand fans with costly gems inchased.
    The chattering frog quaffs the pellucid drops
    That cleanse his miry jaws. The peahen shrieks
    With transport, and the Nipa freshly blooms.
    The moon is blotted by the driving scud,
    As is the saintly character by those
    Who wear its garb to veil their abject lives;
    And like the damsel whose fair fame is lost
    In ever-changing loves, the lightning, true
    To no one quarter, flits along the skies.
VASANTASENĀ [*in Sanskrit*]. You speak it well, my friend: to me it seems—
    The jealous night, as with the gloom she wantons,
    Looks on me as a rival bride, and dreading
    I may disturb her pleasures, stops my path
    And bids me angrily my steps retrace.
SERVANT. Reply with courage, chide her to submission.
VASANTASENĀ. Reviling is the weakness of our sex,
    And but of small avail,—I heed her not.
    Let the clouds fall in torrents, thunder roar,
    And heaven's red bolt dash fiery to the ground,
    The dauntless damsel faithful love inspires,
    Treads boldly on, nor dreads the maddening storm.
VITA. Like an invading prince, who holds his court
    Within the city of his humbled foe,
    Yon mighty cloud, advancing with the wind,
    With store of arrowy shower, with thundering drums,
    And blazing streamers, marches to assail
    In his own heavens the monarch of the night.
VASANTASENĀ. Nay, nay, not so; I rather read it thus:
    The clouds, that like unwieldly elephants
    Roll their inflated masses grumbling on,
    Or whiten with the migratory troop

Of hovering cranes, teach anguish to the bosom.
The stork's shrill cry sounds like the plaintive tabor
To her who, while she wanders o'er its parchment,
Is lost in musings of her lord's return,
And every tone that hails the rainy season,
Falls on her heart like brine upon a wound.

VITA. Behold, where yonder ponderous cloud assumes
The stature of the elephant, the storks
Entwine a fillet for his front, and waves
The lightning, like a streamer o'er his head.

VASANTASENĀ. Observe, my friend, the day is swallowed up
By these deep shades, dark as the dripping leaf
Of the tamāla tree, and, like an elephant
That cowering shuns the battle's arrowy sleet,
So shrinks the scattering ant hill from the shower.
The fickle lightning darts such brilliant rays,
As gleam from golden lamps in temples hung,
Whilst, like the consort of an humble lord,
The timid moonlight peeps amidst the clouds.

VITA. There, like a string of elephants, the clouds
In regular file, by lightning fillets bound,
Move slowly at their potent god's commands.
The heavens let down a silver chain to earth.
The earth, that shines with buds and sheds sweet odors,
Is pierced with showers, like diamond-shafted darts
Launched from the rolling mass of deepest blue,
Which heaves before the breeze and foams with flame;
Like ocean's dark waves by the tempest driven,
And tossing high their flashing surge to shore.

VASANTASENĀ. Hailed by the peacocks with their shrillest cries,
By the pleased storks delightedly caressed,
And by the provident swans with anxious eye
Regarded, yonder rests one threatening cloud
Involving all the atmosphere in gloom.

VITA. The countenance of heaven is close concealed,
By shades the lightning scant irradiates.
The day and night confusedly intermix,
And all the lotus eyes of either close,
The world is lulled to slumber by the sound
Of falling waters, sheltered by the clouds
That countless crowd the chambers of the sky.

VASANTASENĀ. The stars are all extinct, as fades the memory
Of kindness in a bad man's heart. The heavens
Are shorn of all their radiance, as the wife
Her glory loses in her husband's absence.

In sooth, I think the firmament dissolves:
Melted by Indra's scorching bolt it falls
In unexhausted torrents. Now the cloud
Ascends—now stoops—now roars aloud in thunder—
Now sheds its streams—now frowns with deeper gloom,
Full of fantastic change, like one new raised
By fortune's fickle favors.

VITA.   Now the sky
With lightning flames, now laughs with whitening storks—
Now glows with Indra's painted bow, that hurls
Its hundred shafts—now rattles with his bolt—
Now loud it chafes with rushing winds, and now
With clustering clouds that roll their spiry folds
Like sable snakes along—it thickens dark,
As if 'twere clothed with vapors, such as spread
When incense soars in curling wreaths to heaven.

VASANTASENĀ. Shame on thee, cloud, that seekest to affright me
With thy loud threats, and with thy watery shafts
Wouldst stay my progress, hastening to my love.
Indra! I violate no vows to thee,
That thou shouldst thunder angrily reproof;
It ill becomes thee to obstruct my path.
Draw off thy clouds in pity to my passion,
If ever thou wert conscious of affection,
And for Ahalyā[24] wore a husband's form.
Or be it so—rage on—still pour thy deluge,
And launch thy hundred-shafted bolt, in vain.
Thou canst not stop the faithful maid that flies
To lose her terrors in a lover's arms.
If the clouds roar—e'en be it so—it is
Their nature—all of man is ever savage.
But gentle lightning, how canst thou not know
The cares that agitate the female bosom?

VITA. Enough—she now befriends us, like a lamp
That glows in Indra's palace, like a banner,
Whose white folds wave upon a mountain's brow,
Or like the gold cord on Airāvat's[25] breast,
She gleams and shows you where your lord resides.

VASANTASENĀ. Is this the mansion?

VITA. It is; I will anounce your coming.

[24] The story of Indra and Ahalyā is similar to the classical myth of Amphytrion.
The wife of the sage Gautama, Ahalyā refused the advances of the god until he
assumed the shape of her husband. Indra may be equated with the Greek Zeus,
also the god of thunder.
[25] The elephant of Indra.

Ho there! inform the worthy Chārudatta,
A lady at his door awaits; her locks
Are drenched with rain, her gentle nerves are shaken
By angry tempests, and her delicate feet
By cumbering mire and massy anklets wearied,
She pauses to refresh with cooling streams.

CHĀRUDATTA [to MAITREYA]. Hear you, my friend?

MAITREYA. As you command. [Opens the door.]
Health to you, lady.

VASANTASENĀ. Sir, I salute you. [To the VITA.] Here, let the umbrella-bearer wait upon you.

VITA [apart]. A hint for me, I take it, to withdraw. I shall obey you.
[Exit.]

VASANTASENĀ. Now, good Maitreya, where is our gambler?

MAITREYA [apart]. Gambler indeed! my friend is much honored by the appellation. There he sits, madam, in the arbor.

VASANTASENĀ. In the arbor—is it dry?

MAITREYA. Quite; there is nothing to eat or drink in it: enter, enter.

VASANTASENĀ [to her SERVANT]. What shall I say?

SERVANT. Gambler, good evening to you.

VASANTASENĀ. Shall I be able?

SERVANT. Opportunity will give you courage.

MAITREYA. Enter, lady, enter.

VASANTASENĀ [enters, and approaching CHĀRUDATTA, throws flowers at him]. Gambler, good evening to you.

CHĀRUDATTA [rising]. Vasantasenā!
Lady, believe me, every day has passed
Most heavily, and sleepless dragged my nights,
But now your charms appear my cares are over,
And this glad evening terminates my sorrows.
Then welcome, welcome to my bower—be seated.

MAITREYA. Take a seat, madam. [They sit.]

CHĀRUDATTA. Maitreya, from the flowers that grace her ear
Surcharged with rain, the drops have trickled down
And bathed her bosom, like a young prince
A sharing partner of imperial honors. Haste and bring
A vest of finest texture to replace
This chilling robe.

ATTENDANT. Stop, Maitreya, I will assist my mistress if you please. [Does so.]

MAITREYA [to CHĀRUDATTA]. Now sir, shall I inquire the object of this visitation?

CHĀRUDATTA. Do so.

MAITREYA. And now, madam, may I ask what has brought you out, on such a vile, dark, rainy evening?

ATTENDANT. Lady, here's a smart Brahman!

VASANTASENĀ. Nay, an able one, so call him.

ATTENDANT. My mistress, sir, wished to be informed of the real value of the necklace that you brought her.

MAITREYA. There, I said so. [*To* CHĀRUDATTA.]

ATTENDANT. The reason why she wishes to know is that she has pledged it at play, and the keeper of the tables, being a servant of the prince's, is gone on some duty, and is not to be found.

MAITREYA. Umph, tit for tat.

ATTENDANT. Until he can be heard of, and the necklace be redeemed, be pleased to accept in lieu of it this golden casket.

[*Gives him the casket stolen by* SHARVILAKA. MAITREYA *examines it.*]

You examine it very closely; one would suppose you had seen it before.

MAITREYA. It is very curious: the cunning of the workman beguiles my eyes.

ATTENDANT. No, your eyesight is defective, it is the very same.

MAITREYA. Indeed! my worthy friend, here is the gold casket again that was stolen from our house.

CHĀRUDATTA. No, no, it is but a requital
    Of our attempt to substitute a change
    Of that entrusted to us; this is the truth,
    Howe'er the casket may appear the same.

MAITREYA. It is the same! I swear it, as I am a Brahman.

CHĀRUDATTA. I am glad of it.

MAITREYA. Shall I ask how they came by it?

CHĀRUDATTA. Why not?

MAITREYA [*whispers to the* ATTENDANT]. Is it so indeed?

ATTENDANT [*whispers to* MAITREYA]. It is indeed.

CHĀRUDATTA. What is?—why leave us out?

MAITREYA [*whispers to* CHĀRUDATTA]. This it is indeed.

CHĀRUDATTA [*to the* ATTENDANT]. Is this indeed, my girl, the golden casket?

ATTENDANT. It is the same, sir.

CHĀRUDATTA. A pleasing speech with me should never go
    Without fit recompense,—accept this ring.
    [*Looks at his hand; finds he has no ring; expresses shame*]

VASANTASENĀ. How well he merits wealth.

CHĀRUDATTA [*apart*]. How can that man be said to live, who lives
    A pauper, and whose gratitude and wrath
    Are barren both. The bird whose wings are clipped—
    The leafless tree—the desiccated pool—
    The desolate mansion, and the toothless snake—
    Are all meet emblems of the hapless wretch
    Whose festive hours no fond associates grace,
    And brightest moments yield no fruit to others.

MAITREYA [*to him*]. Enough, enough, there is no good in fretting. [*Aloud.*]
    But, lady, I shall thank you to restore me my bathing-gown, in which

the casket was wrapped at the time it was stolen.

VASANTASENĀ. And now, worthy Chārudatta, believe me, when the casket
was stolen, it was quite unnecessary to send me this equivalent.

CHĀRUDATTA. Had I not sent it, lady, who had trusted me?—
I and my wealth in most men's eyes are equal,
And poverty will ever be suspected.

MAITREYA. A word, damsel; do you mean to take up your abode here?

ATTENDANT. Fie, Maitreya, how you talk!

MAITREYA. My good friend, the clouds are collecting again, and the heavy
drops drive us from our easy seats.

CHĀRUDATTA. 'Tis true, they penetrate the yielding clouds
As sinks the lotus stalk into its bed
Of plashy mire, and now again they fall
Like tears celestial from the weeping sky
That wails the absent moon.
The clouds, like Baladeva's vesture, dark
Profusely shed a shower of precious pearls
From Indra's treasury—the drops descend
Rapid and rattling, like the angry shafts
From Arjun's quiver, and of like purity
As are the hearts of holy men.
See, lady, how the firmament, anointed
With unguent of the black tamāla's hue,
And fanned by fragrant and refreshing gales,
Is by the lightning tenderly embraced,
As the loved lord whom fearlessly she flies to.

[VASANTASENĀ *gesticulates affection, and falls into* CHĀRUDATTA'S
arms.]

CHĀRUDATTA [*embracing her*]. Louder and louder still roar on, ye clouds!
To me the sound is music, by your aid
My love is blessed, my heart expands with hope.

MAITREYA [*as to the cloud*]. You foul-faced rascal, you are a worthless
reprobate, to have so scared her ladyship by your lightnings.

CHĀRUDATTA. Reprove it not, for let the rain descend,
The heavens still lour, and wide the lightnings launch
A hundred flames; they have befriended me,
And given me her for whom I sighed in vain.
Happy, thrice happy, they whose walls enshrine
The fair they worship, and whose arms enfold
Her shivering beauties in their warm embrace.
Look, love, the bow of Indra arches heaven;
Like outspread arms, extended with fatigue,
It stretches forth; the yawning sky displays
Its lightning tongue—its chin of clouds hangs low—
All woo us to repose—let us retire: the drops

Fall musical, and pattering on the leaves
Of the tall palm, or on the pebbly ground,
Or in the brook, emit such harmony
As sweetly wakens from the voice and lute.
[*Exit.*]

ACT SIX

CHĀRUDATTA'S *house, inside and outside as before.*

[*Inside. Enter* FEMALE SERVANT.]

SERVANT. Hey-day! does not my lady mean to rise this morning? I shall make bold to call her. Madam!

[*Enter* VASANTASENĀ.]

Look, madam, it is day.

VASANTASENĀ. How! why the morning dawns as darkling as if it still were night.

SERVANT. It is morning to us, though it may be night to you, madam.

VASANTASENĀ. Where is your gambler?

SERVANT. Chārudatta, madam, having given his orders to Vardhamāna, is gone to the old flower garden of Pushpakaranda.

VASANTASENĀ. What orders gave he?

SERVANT. To get your litter ready.

VASANTASENĀ. Whither am I to go?

SERVANT. Whither Chārudatta is gone.

VASANTASENĀ. Very well, girl, I have scarcely yet beheld him; today will gratify me with his sight. What! did I find my way into the inner apartments?

SERVANT. Not only that, madam, but into every one's heart.

VASANTASENĀ. I fear me his family are vexed.

SERVANT. They will be vexed then only when—

VASANTASENĀ. When?

SERVANT. When you depart.

VASANTASENĀ. Then is it my place first to be afflicted. Here, girl, take this necklace to my respected sister, his good wife, and say from me, I am Chārudatta's handmaid and your slave, then be this necklace again the ornament of that neck to which it of right belongs.

SERVANT. But, lady, Chārudatta will be displeased.

VASANTASENĀ. Go, do as I bid you; he will not be offended.

SERVANT. As you command.

[*Exit, and returns presently.*]

Madam, thus says the lady: "You are favored by the son of my lord; it is not proper for me to accept this necklace. Know that the only ornament I value is my husband."

[*Enter* RADANIKĀ *and* CHĀRUDATTA'S CHILD.]

RADANIKĀ. Come along, my child, let us ride in your cart.

CHILD. I do not want this cart; it is only of clay—I want one of
gold.

RADANIKĀ. And where are we to get the gold, my little man? Wait till your
father is rich again, and then he will buy you one: now this will do. Come,
let us go and see Vasantasenā. Lady, I salute you.

VASANTASENĀ. Welcome Radanikā. Whose charming boy is this? Although
so ill-attired, his lovely face quite fascinates me.

RADANIKĀ. This is Rohasena, the son of Chārudatta.

VASANTASENĀ [*stretching out her arms*]. Come here, my little dear, and kiss
me.

[*Takes him on her lap.*]

How like his father!

RADANIKĀ. He is like him too in disposition. Chārudatta dotes on him.

VASANTASENĀ. Why does he weep?

RADANIKĀ. The child of our neighbor had a golden cart, which this little
fellow saw and wanted. I made him this of clay, but he is not pleased with
it, and is crying for the other.

VASANTASENĀ. Alas, alas, this little creature is already mortified by another's
prosperity. O fate! thou sportest with the fortunes of mankind, like
drops of water trembling on the lotus leaf. Don't cry, my good boy,
and you shall have a gold cart.

CHILD. Radanikā, who is this?

VASANTASENĀ. A handmaid purchased by your father's merits.

RADANIKĀ. This is your lady mother, child.

CHILD. You tell me untruth, Radanikā; how can this be my mother when
she wears such fine things?

VASANTASENĀ. How piteous a speech for so soft a tongue!

[*Takes off her ornaments in tears.*]

Now I am your mother. Here, take this trinket and go buy a gold
cart.

CHILD. Away, I will not take it, you cry at parting with it.

VASANTASENĀ [*wiping her eyes*]. I weep no more, Go, love, and play.

[*Fills his cart with her jewels.*]

There go, get you a golden cart.

[*Exit* RADANIKĀ *with* CHILD.]

[*Outside. Enter* VARDHAMĀNA *with the bullock cart.*]

VASANTASENĀ. Radanikā, let the lady know the carriage waits for her at
the private door.

[*Inside. Enter* RADANIKĀ.]

RADANIKĀ. Lady, the covered litter attends you at the back door.

VASANTASENĀ. Stay a moment whilst I prepare myself.

RADANIKĀ. Stay a moment, Vardhamāna, the lady is not quite ready.

VARDHAMĀNA. And I have forgotten the cushions of the carriage. Wait till I bring them. These oxen are not steady enough to be left; I will drive back and return presently.

[*Exit with the car.*]

VASANTASENĀ [*inside*]. Bring me my things, girl, I can put them on myself. [*Dressing.*]

[*Outside. Enter* STHĀVARAKA, *the* SERVANT *of* SAMSTHĀNAKA, *with a carriage.*]

STHĀVARAKA. I am ordered by the king's brother-in-law, my master, to take this vehicle with all speed to the old flower-garden, Pushpakaranda. Come up, come up. [*Looking.*] Why, the road is blocked with country carts. Holloa there! get out of the way. What says he, whose carriage is it? Samsthānaka's, the king's brother-in-law; quick, quick! clear the road. [*Drives on.*] Who should that be, that looked at me so curiously, and then stole off down another road, like an unlucky gambler that runs away from the table-keeper? No matter; I must get on. Holloa you! out of the way there! What! Come and give you a turn of the wheel: it sticks, does it! It is very likely that the king's brother-in-law's man shall assist you to a twist of the wheel. Oh, it is a poor miserable rustic, and alone too. Well, I will lend you a hand. This is Chārudatta's postern door. I can leave the carriage here in the meantime so, stop there, I will be with you.

[*Exit, leaving the carriage at the door.*]

SERVANT [*inside*]. I hear the wheels: the carriage is returned, madam.

VASANTASENĀ. Quick, quick! I feel strangely flurried;—open the door.

SERVANT. 'Tis done.

VASANTASENĀ. Go you to rest.

SERVANT. As you command.

[*Exit.*]

VASANTASENĀ [*goes forth and ascends* SAMSTHĀNAKA'S *carriage*]. My right eye twitches;[26] never mind, meeting Chārudatta will prove it causeless. [*Draws the curtains.*]

[*Reenter* STHĀVARAKA.]

STHĀVARAKA. I have helped him, and now have a clear road.

[*Mounts and proceeds.*]

Why, the vehicle is heavier than it was, or it appears so to me, because I am tired with helping yonder cart. No matter, I must proceed;—come up.

VOICE BEHIND THE SCENE. Who ho, there, guards! look to it; be vigilant—sleep not at your posts; the cowherd Āryaka has burst his bonds, slain his gaoler, and broken from his prison; he is now in flight—seize him! seize him!

STHĀVARAKA. Here's a precious uproar! I had better get clear of it.

[*Exit with the car.*]

[*Enter* ĀRYAKA *as in flight.*]

---

[26] A bad omen for a woman.

ĀRYAKA. I have swam thus far to shore, and from the wave
    Of fell captivity the tyrant Pālaka
    Had plunged me into once more have escaped.
    Like a tame elephant from his stall broke loose,
    I drag along with me my ruptured chain.
    Sharvilaka, my friend, to thee I owe
    My freedom and my life. Condemned to pine
    In the dark dungeon, where the monarch's fears,
    Awakened by the sage's prophecies,
    Cast me to die, dragged from my humble home. [*Weeps.*]
    What crime have I committed, to be sought
    Thus like a venomous snake, to be destroyed!
    If such my destiny, as is foretold,
    In what consists my guilt? be fate accused—
    Fate is a power resistless, and a king
    Alike demands our homage. Who contends
    With force superior? mine is to submit.
    Yet for my life I fly—ah! whither now
    Shall I find refuge? See, yon door invites me!
    Some good man's gate is open, and like me
    Its withered fortunes, for the bolt is broken,
    And the broad valves are shattered and decayed:
    It calls me kinsman, and it proves my friend.
VARDHAMĀNA [*returning with* CHĀRUDATTA'S *carriage* (*without*)]. Come up,
    come up!
ĀRYAKA [*listening*]. A carriage, and it comes this way.
    If it should be a village car, not freighted
    With passengers uncourteous, or a vehicle
    For women, but its fair load not received,
    Or be it traveling from the town, and fit
    For decent occupancy—be it but empty
    And unattended, and my fate befriends me.
  [*Enter* VARDHAMĀNA *with the carriage.*]
VARDHAMĀNA. What ho! Radanikā, I have got the cushions, and the car is
  ready: so inform the lady Vasantasenā; tell her to ascend, that I may
  set off for Pushpakarandaka.
ĀRYAKA. It is a courtesan's, and traveling outward;
      'Tis fortunate—I mount. [*Advances.*]
VARDHAMĀNA [*listening and hearing the ringing of* ĀRYAKA'S *chain*]. I hear
  the sound of the anklets, she is here. Get up quick, lady; get up behind;
  the cattle are impatient, I must not leave them.
  [ĀRYAKA *ascends.*]
VARDHAMĀNA. The sound has ceased, and the carriage is heavier than it
  was: her ladyship must be seated, so here goes.
  [*Exit with the car.*]

Another street.

[*Enter* VĪRAKA, *Captain of the Watch, attended.*]

VĪRAKA. Halloa! Jaya, Jayamāna, Chandanaka, Mangala, Pushpabhadra, and the rest, follow quick, and we shall catch the villain, though he has broken his prison and the king's slumbers. Here, fall in; go you to the east gate, you to the west, you to the south, you to the north: on this pile of broken bricks, Chandanaka and I will stop and look about us. What ho, Chandanaka!

[*Enter* CHANDANAKA *attended, in a bustle.*]

CHANDANAKA. What ho! Vīraka, Visalya, Bhīmāngada, Dandakala, Dandashura, quick, quick! never let the king's fortune move off into another family: away with you, search the streets, the roads, the gardens, the houses, the stalls, the markets, and let no suspicious corner pass unexamined;—away!

[*Exeunt guard.*]

Well, Vīraka, what say you? will any one convey this runaway cowherd out of peril? Verily, whoever dares to carry him off whilst Chandanaka lives, had better have had at his birth the Sun in the eighth mansion, the Moon in the fourth, Venus in the sixth, Mars in the fifth, Jupiter in the sixth, and Saturn in the ninth.[27]

VĪRAKA. He must have had assistance, no doubt, valiant Chandanaka; but, by your heart, I swear that he escaped before dawn.

[*Enter* VARDHAMĀNA *with the car and* ĀRYAKA *concealed.*]

CHANDANAKA. What ho, there! see, see, a covered litter passes along the high road; inquire whose it is and whither going.

VĪRAKA. What ho, driver! stop and answer. Whose vehicle is this; who is inside; and where are you going?

VARDHAMĀNA. The carriage belongs, sir, to the worthy Chārudatta; the lady Vasantasenā is inside, and I am carrying her to the old flower-garden to meet Chārudatta there.

CHANDANAKA. Let him pass.

VĪRAKA. Without inspection?

CHANDANAKA. Undoubtedly.

VĪRAKA. On what surety?

CHANDANAKA. Chārudatta's.

VĪRAKA. And who is Chārudatta, or who is Vasantasenā, that the carriage is to pass free?

CHANDANAKA. Do you not know who they are? If you know not Chārudatta and Vasantasenā, you know not the moon and moonlight when you see them together in the skies. Who is there that is not acquainted with that moon of mildness, that lotus of merit, that liberator from sorrow, that

---

[27] Astrological signs foreboding various kinds of physical and mental distress.

pearl, the essence of the four oceans, Chārudatta? Both are of the
highest respectability, the boast and pride of the city, the lovely
Vasantasenā and virtuous Chārudatta.

vīraka. Phoo, phoo! I know them well enough, but in the discharge of my
duty my own father must be a stranger.

āryaka [*in the car*]. Yon Vīraka has ever been my foe,
    Chandanaka my friend; the two are ill
    Associated in a common duty.
    One fire the marriage ceremony asks,
    Another serves to light the funeral pile.

chandanaka. Well, careful captain, high in the king's confidence, do you
    then look into the carriage, I will look to the cattle.

vīraka. Nay, you are in command and confidence as well as I am; do you
    inspect it.

chandanaka. What I see is in fact seen by you.

vīraka. Not only by me, but by the king himself.

chandanaka. Holloa, you! stop the car.

āryaka. Unfortunately, I am discovered; I have no sword;
    Like Bhīma then I must employ my hands;
    Better to die than be again a captive.
    Yet, hold, it is not yet despair.

[chandanaka *looks into the car.*]

āryaka. Protection:—I am at your mercy.

chandanaka. Fear not, who seeks protection will obtain it.

āryaka. Fortune forsakes, tribe, family, and friends
    Discard, and all men scorn the coward slave
    Who fears to grant protection to the wretched.

chandanaka. How! Āryaka!
    Like the poor bird that, flying from the hawk,
    Falls in the fowler's net, art thou my prize,
    And, luckless wretch, appliest to me for aid?
    He is in Chārudatta's car, his crime
    Is none; Sharvilaka, to whom I owe
    My own life, is his friend; but then—
    My duty to the prince. What's to be done?
    E'en be it so—I told him not to fear;
    The words have passed my lips. I must befriend him,
    Come on't what will: the succor once assured,
    Must be extended, though the end be ruin.

[*Returning.*] I have seen—Ārya—Āryā Vasantasenā, and she says right;
    it is indecorous to detain her on the road when she has an appointment
    with Chārudatta.

vīraka. Excuse me, Chandanaka; I have some doubts in the matter.

chandanaka. How so?

VĪRAKA. You seem flurried, and it was with some indistinctness you call
out first Ārya, then corrected yourself, and said Āryā Vasantasenā.[28]
I have some strange misgivings.

CHANDANAKA. Misgivings, indeed! why, you know, we of the South are
not very nice in our articulation, and are apt to confound sounds. Being
accustomed to speak the dialects of a number of barbarous and other
outcast tribes, it would be all the same to us, whether it was Ārya or
Āryā, masculine, feminine, or neuter.

VĪRAKA. Ah, well—I shall take a look myself: such are the prince's orders—
he knows he can trust me.

CHANDANAKA. And am I not trusted by him?

VĪRAKA. True, but I must obey his orders.

CHANDANAKA [apart]. If it is known that the cowherd was seized in
Chārudatta's carriage, he will be involved in the punishment. I must give
my friend here a specimen of Carnatic eloquence. [Aloud.] Hark ye,
Vīraka, I have already inspected the carriage; why are you to inspect it
again? who the deuce are you, I should like to know?

VĪRAKA. And who are you, pray?

CHANDANAKA. I'll tell you: one entitled to your most profound respect:
you should recollect your caste.

VĪRAKA. My caste, what is it then?

CHANDANAKA. Oh, I do not wish to say.

VĪRAKA. Say, say if you like, and if you don't like it, leave it alone.

CHANDANAKA. I do not wish to shame you: let it be; it is not worthwhile
to break a rotten apple.

VĪRAKA. Nay, I insist.

[CHANDANAKA intimates by signs that VĪRAKA is a Chamār, or worker in
leather.]

VĪRAKA. It is false—I deny it.

CHANDANAKA. You were wont to carry a dead jackal in your hand to
replace dislocated joints, and to flourish a pair of shears; and you are
now a general. A very pretty general!

VĪRAKA. You are a most high and mighty hero, no doubt, far above your
real origin.

CHANDANAKA. What was my origin?

VĪRAKA. Excuse me.

CHANDANAKA. I defy you,—my caste is as pure as the moon.

VĪRAKA. No doubt; vastly pure, when your mother was a tabor, your father
a kettle drum, and your brother a tamborine; but you—you are a general.

CHANDANAKA. I a Chamār, I Chandanaka, a Chamār; mighty well, mighty

---

[28] This sentence involves an untranslatable play on words. *Ārya* is the Sanskrit
word for "The Respected," but Chandanaka, through a slip of the tongue, uses the
masculine form (Ārya—the respected gentleman) before correcting himself with
the feminine (Āryā—the respected lady).

well! Look, by all means.

VĪRAKA. Ho, driver! Stay till I inspect the car.

[VĪRAKA *approaches it;* CHANDANAKA *seizes him by the hair, drags him back, throws him down and kicks him.*]

VĪRAKA [*rising*]. What do you mean by this treatment of me?—but I will have vengeance. If I have not your head severed from your body, and your limbs quartered and exposed in the public place, I am not Vīraka. [*Exit.*]

CHANDANAKA. Away to the palace, or the court. Complain; I care not. Who will heed such a dog as you? [*To* VARDHAMĀNA.] Quick, and if any one stops you, say the carriage has been inspected by Vīraka and Chandanaka. Lady Vasantasenā, I give you this as a passport. [*Gives* ĀRYAKA *a sword.*]

ĀRYAKA. My right arm throbs as I receive the weapon.
Fortune is friendly to me. I am safe.

CHANDANAKA. The Arya will remember Chandana.
I ask not this for favor, but in love.

ĀRYAKA. Fate has this day made Chandana my friend.
If the saint's prophecy should be fulfilled,
I will remember well how much I owe him.

CHANDANAKA. May every deity befriend your cause;
And may your enemies before you fall,
Like Sumbha and Nisumbha by the wrath
Of the resentful goddess. Drive on.
[*Exit* VARDHAMĀNA *with car.*]

CHANDANAKA [*looking after it*]. Ha! yonder I see my friend Sharvilaka follows the carriage. Well, may they prosper. Vīraka will now to the prince and tell how he has been handled: I must collect my friends and relatives, and follow him without delay.
[*Exit.*]

ACT SEVEN

The garden Pushpakaranda.

[*Enter* CHĀRUDATTA *and* MAITREYA.]

MAITREYA. How bravely the old garden looks.

CHĀRUDATTA. 'Tis true; like wealthy merchants are the trees
Who spread in clustering flowers the choicest wares;
Amongst them busily the bees are straying
To gather tribute for the royal hive.

MAITREYA. Here is a fine block of stone; sit down on it.

CHĀRUDATTA [*seated*]. Vardhamāna tarries long.

MAITREYA. I told him to make all possible haste.

CHĀRUDATTA. Then why so tardy? Or the car rolls heavily;
  Or it has broken down upon the way;
  Or the old traces have been snapped; or lies
  A tree across their path; or have they strayed
  Another road, or are the beasts untractable
  Or have—oh, here he comes.
  [*Enter* VARDHAMĀNA *with the car*.]
  Come up.
ĀRYAKA [*in the car*]. Fled from the monarch's myrmidons, and cramped
  By this vile fetter round my foot, I owe
  My safety to this vehicle—where, like the cuckoo
  Nursed in a stranger nest, I find concealment.
  Now, far beyond the city, I am safe.
  Shall I alight, and seek to gain a refuge
  Amidst the dark recesses of these groves,
  Or shall I dare encounter with the owner
  Of this befriending car? 'Twere far more grateful
  To meet with Chārudatta, than to hear
  His pity only as I darkling lurk
  Among these shades. My new acquired liberty
  Will yield him pleasure, and my wasted form
  Will grow once more to vigor from the interview.
VARDHAMĀNA. This is the place:—what ho! Maitreya.
MAITREYA. Welcome, Vardhamāna; I have been looking out for you.
VARDHAMĀNA. Well, here I am; and so is Vasantasenā.
MAITREYA. But, you son of a slave, what has detained you so long?
VARDHAMĀNA. Do not be angry, Maitreya. I was obliged to go back to find
 the cushions which I had at first forgot.
CHĀRUDATTA. Well, well.—Maitreya, assist Vasantasenā to alight.
MAITREYA. What! has she got fetters on her feet, that she cannot come down
 by herself?
 [*Goes to the car and looks in*.]
 Holloa! what have we here? This is not Vasantasenā—it is Mr. Vasan-
 tasena, I suppose.
CHĀRUDATTA. Refrain your mirth, my friend; love ill-sustains
  The least delay. I help her to alight. [*Rises*.]
ĀRYAKA. Here comes the worthy Chārudatta;
  Cheering his voice, and gentle is his aspect:
  I need not fear.
CHĀRUDATTA [*looking in*]. How! who is this?
  His arms are like the elephant's vast tusks—
  His breasts, his shoulders, brawny as the lion's—
  His eyes are coppery-red and roll in anger—
  How should a person of such goodly presence
  Bear fetters on his limbs? Who art thou, say?

ĀRYAKA. My name is Āryaka: to tend the herds
       The duty I was born to; and to thee
       I hither come, a suppliant for protection.
CHĀRUDATTA. Art thou that Āryaka, our prince's fears
       Dragged from his humble station to a prison?
ĀRYAKA. The same.
CHĀRUDATTA. Fate, that has brought thee hither, is thy friend.
       My life I may resign, but cannot turn
       Away from one who sues to me for refuge.
       Vardhamāna, remove those fetters.
VARDHAMĀNA [obeys]. The chains are off, sir.
ĀRYAKA [to CHĀRUDATTA]. And chains more lasting by this aid imposed.
MAITREYA. Then now pray take yourself off too. Come, my good friend,
now this gentleman is at large, I think we had better get home as quick
as we can.
CHĀRUDATTA. Fie on thy speech! what need of haste?
ĀRYAKA. Excuse me, Chārudatta, that I mounted,
       Nor sought permission first, into this car.
CHĀRUDATTA. You have graced me by such courtesy.
ĀRYAKA. Have I your leave to leave you?
CHĀRUDATTA. It is yours.
ĀRYAKA. I will descend.
CHĀRUDATTA. Nay, friend, not so.
       Your steps still labor from the weighty bond
       So recently removed: besides, the car
       Will unsuspected bear you on your way
       Beyond our boundaries—pray keep your seat.
ĀRYAKA. As you direct.
CHĀRUDATTA. Auspicious be your way
       To join your friends.
ĀRYAKA. I hope I leave one here.
CHĀRUDATTA. 'Tis one who hopes to be remembered by you
       In other times.
ĀRYAKA. Can I forget myself?
CHĀRUDATTA. The gods protect your path.
ĀRYAKA. It is to you
       I owe my safety.
CHĀRUDATTA. Not so, you owe it
       To your bright fortunes.
ĀRYAKA. Of the which, indeed,
       I hold you as the cause.
CHĀRUDATTA. But Pālaka
       Must still be heeded; and around he sends
       A numerous guard, who may detain your steps.
       Use no delay; but with all speed depart.

ĀRYAKA. To meet again.
    [*Exit.*]
CHĀRUDATTA. The deed that I have done will little please
    The king, should it be known; and kings behold
    Their subjects' actions by their spies. 'Twere well
    To leave this spot at once. Maitreya, cast
    The fetters deep into this ancient well. [*His eyes throbbing.*]
    'Tis sad to miss a meeting with my love—
    But that such chance today at least is hopeless
    My left eye indicates; and without cause
    A sudden languor creeps into my heart.
    Let us leave this. [*Going.*] Ha, an evil omen!
    A Buddhist monk approaches us. [*Stops.*] Yet—hold—
    Let him advance—we'll take another path.
    [*Exit.*]

ACT EIGHT

Scene the same.

[*Enter the* SHRAMANAKA, *the Buddhist monk,*[29] *with a wet garment in his hand.*]

SHRAMANAKA [*sings*]. Be virtue, friends, your only store,
    And restless appetite restrain,
    Beat meditation's drum, and sore
    Your watch against each sense maintain;
    The thief that still in ambush lies,
    To make devotion's wealth his prize.

    Cast the five senses all away,
    That triumph o'er the virtuous will;
    The pride of self-importance slay,
    And ignorance remorseless kill:
    So shall you safe the body guard,
    And Heaven shall be your last reward.

    Why shave the head and mow the chin
    Whilst bristling follies choke the breast?
    Apply the knife to parts within,
    And heed not how deformed the rest:
    The heart of pride and passion weed,
    And then the man is pure indeed.

[29] This is the Masseur of Act II.

My cloth is heavy with the yet moist dye. I will enter this garden belonging
to the king's brother-in-law, and wash it in the pool, and then I shall
proceed more lightly. [*Does so.*]

VOICE BEHIND THE SCENE. What, ho! you rashcally Shramanaka, what are
you doing there

SHRAMANAKA. Alas, alas! here he is, Samsthānaka himself. He has been
affronted by one monk, and whenever he meets another he sends him
off with his nose slit like an ox. Where shall I fly to?—the lord Buddha
be my refuge.

[*Enter* SAMSTHĀNAKA *with the* VITA, *his sword drawn.*]

SAMSTHĀNAKA. Shtop, you vile vagabond, or off I take that head of thine,
as they shnap off the top of a red radish in a dram-shop.

[*Beats him.*]

VITA. Nay, nay, hold! beat not the poor wretch thus clad in the colored
garment of humility. This garden was intended by your excellency to
be the seat of delight, and these trees were destined to afford shade and
relief to the unsheltered; but now they are disappointed of their objects;
they fail their promise, like the no longer hidden villainy of a scoundrel,
and are only to be enjoyed at the risk of peril, like a new sovereignty
disposed of before it is yet subdued.

SHRĀMANAKA. Mercy, sir; be my protector, my savior.

SAMSTHĀNAKA. Hear him, the shcoundrel, how he abuses me.

VITA. How so?

SAMSTHĀNAKA. He calls me a shaver.

VITA. Not so, he entreats you humbly.

SAMSTHĀNAKA. And what are you doing here?

SHRAMANAKA. I was about to cleanse my garment in this pond.

SAMSTHĀNAKA. Villain, was this shuperlative garden given to me by my
shishter's hushband, the king, for such a base purpose? Dogs drink
here by day, and jackals by night: exalted in rank ash I am, I do not
bathe here, and shall you preshume here to wash your foul and fetid
rags;—but I shall make short work with you.

VITA. In that case I suspect he will not have long followed the profession.

SAMSTHĀNAKA. How sho?

VITA. Observe: his head shines as if it had only been lately shaven; and his
garment has been so little worn that there are no scars on his shoulder.
The ochry dye has not yet fully stained the cloth, and the open web,
yet fresh and flaccid, hangs loosely over his arms.

SHRAMANAKA. I do not deny it, worthy sir; it is true I have but lately
adopted the profession of a beggar.

SAMSTHĀNAKA. And why sho? why did you not become a beggar ash
shoon ash you were born, you shcoundrel? [*Beats him.*]

SHRAMANAKA. Glory to Buddha.

VITA. Enough, enough! now let him go. [*To the* SHRAMANAKA.] Away with
you.

SAMSTHĀNAKA. Shtop, shtop! I must first ashk leave.

VITA. From whom?

SAMSTHĀNAKA. My own mind.

VITA. Well, he is not gone.

SAMSTHĀNAKA. My life, my heart, my chick, my child, shall this fellow go or shtay? Very well, my mind shays—

VITA. What?

SAMSTHĀNAKA. He shall neither go, nor shtay, nor move, nor breathe—let him fall down and be put to death.

SHRAMANAKA. Glory to Buddha! mercy, mercy!

VITA. Oh, let him go.

SAMSTHĀNAKA. On one condition.

VITA. What is that?

SAMSTHĀNAKA. He shall take all the clay of this pool out without muddying the water; or he shall make a pile of clean water and throw the mud ashide.

VITA. Absurd! You might as well ask for skins of stone, and meat from trees. This world is sadly burdened with fools.

[SHRAMANAKA *gesticulates imprecations.*]

SAMSTHĀNAKA. What does he mean?

VITA. He blesses you.

SAMSTHĀNAKA. Shpeak my blessings.

SHRAMANAKA. Be as prosperous as you are pious.

SAMSTHĀNAKA. Begone!

[*Exit* SHRAMANAKA.]

VITA. Come, come, to other thoughts direct your mind;

Look round the garden; mark these stately trees,
Which duly, by the king's command attended,
Put forth abundantly their fruits and flowers,
And clasped by twining creepers, they resemble
The manly husband and the tender wife.

SAMSTHĀNAKA. The ground is quite a picture, shtrewed with many-tinted flowers; the trees are bowed down with bloshoms; the graceful creepers completely shurmount even their tops; and the monkeys are shporting about like sho many breadfruits.

VITA. Here let us take our seat.

SAMSTHĀNAKA. I am sheated. And now, my good friend, trusht me, I cannot help thinking of Vashantashenā: she holds her place in my heart, and rankles like the abuse of a blackguard.

VITA [*aside*]. To little purpose are these thoughts indulged:

So true it is—
The scorn of woman in ignoble breasts,
But adds fresh fuel to the scorching flame.
The manly heart disdain with scorn repays,
And soon subdues its unrequited passion.

SAMSTHĀNAKA. What hour is it? That fellow Sthāvaraka wash ordered to
be here early; what can be the reashon he does not make his appearance?
It is almosht noon; I feel hungry, and it is imposhible to think of walking
at thish time of day. The shun is now in mid-heaven, and looks ash fierce
ash an angry ape; and the ground is ash dry and shriveled as Gāndhārī
looked when her hundred shons were shlain.

VITA. 'Tis true: the cattle dozing in the shade
    Let fall the unchamped fodder from their mouths;
    The lively ape with slow and languid pace
    Creeps to the pool to slake his parching thirst
    In its now tepid waters; not a creature
    Is seen upon the public road, nor braves
    One solitary passenger the sun.
    Perhaps the carriage from the heated track
    Has turned aside, and waits a cooler hour.

SAMSTHĀNAKA. Very likely, and I am left here to furnish a lodgment in
my brains for the rays of the shun. The birds have all shlunk into shelter
amongst the branches, and pashengers panting and breathing flame, are
glad to mount the umbrella even in the shade. That fellow will not be
here today; come let us amuse ourshelves: I will give you a shong.
[He sings.]
There, shir, what shay you to that?

VITA. Say? That you are verily a Gandharba.

SAMSTHĀNAKA. How should I fail being so; I make a practice of taking
ashafetida, cummin-seed, orrish-root, treacle and ginger; my voice
musht necesharily be very *shweet*. I will give you another shpecimen.
[Sings.]
There, what think you now?

VITA. That you are a very Gandharba.

SAMSTHĀNAKA. I knew you would think sho; but I take care to train
myself shuitably. I always feed upon meat preshented to me by shome
of my shlaves, and I have it fried in oil and ghee, and seasoned
well with ashafetida and black pepper; that is your only diet for a
shweet voice. Oh, that shcoundrel, he will never arrive!

VITA. Have patience: he will soon be here. [They retire.]
[Enter STHĀVARAKA with the car in which VASANTASENĀ is.]

STHĀVARAKA. I am in a terrible fright; it is near noon; my master will be
in a violent rage. Come up.

VASANTASENĀ [in the car]. Alas! alas! that is not Vardhamāna's voice.
Who can it be? Whose vehicle is this? Has Chārudatta sent another car
and servant to spare his own? Ha! my right eye throbs, my heart
flutters, my sight is dim, everything forebodes misfortunes.

SAMSTHĀNAKA Mashter, the car is here.

VITA. How do you know?

SAMSTHĀNAKA. Do you not hear a shnorting like an old hog's?

VITA. You are right; here it is.

SAMSTHĀNAKA. How, my good fellow, Sthāvaraka, are you come at lasht?

STHĀVARAKA. Yes, sir.

SAMSTHĀNAKA. And the car?

STHĀVARAKA. Here it is, sir.

SAMSTHĀNAKA. And the oxen?

STHĀVARAKA. Here they are.

SAMSTHĀNAKA. And yourshelf?

STHĀVARAKA. We are all together, your honor.

SAMSTHĀNAKA. Then drive in.

STHĀVARKA. Which way, sir?

SAMSTHĀNAKA. Here, where the wall is broken.

STHĀVARAKA. It is impossible, sir: it will kill the beasts, smash the car, and I shall get my neck broken into the bargain.

SAMSTHĀNAKA. Do you recollect, shirrah, that I am the king's brother-in-law: be the cattle killed, I can buy others; let the car shmash, I can have another made; and if you break your neck, I musht hire another driver.

STHĀVARAKA. That is very true, your honor; the loss will be mine; I shall not be able to replace myself.

SAMSTHĀNAKA. I care not; drive in here, over the broken walls.

STHĀVARAKA. Very well, sir, here goes. Break the car, go to pieces you and your driver; others are to be had, and I must report your fate to your master. [*Drives.*] How, all safe! There, sir, the carriage has come in.

SAMSTHĀNAKA. You shee what a lying rogue you are, and no mischief.

STHĀVARAKA. Very true, sir.

SAMSTHĀNAKA. Come, my friend, let us go to the car. You are my ever honored teacher and mashter, precede: I know what is due to your dignity, ashcend.

VITA. I comply.

SAMSTHĀNAKA. Shtop! shtop! Did you make the carriage, pray? I am the owner of it, and shall therefore get in the first.

VITA. I did as you desired.

SAMSTHĀNAKA. Very poshibly; but you erred in not requeshting me to precede.

VITA. Will your excellency be pleased to enter?

SAMSTHĀNAKA. That is right. I shall ashend.

[*Getting up, returns hastily, and lays hold of the* VITA *in alarm.*]

Oh dear! I am a losht man; there's a thief or a she-devil in the carriage! If a devil, we shall be robbed; if a thief, we shall be devoured alive!

VITA. Fear not; how should a she-devil get into a bullock carriage? It was nothing but the shadow of Sthāvaraka, I dare say, which, your eyes having been dazzled with the glare, you saw indistinctly, and mistook for a living figure.

SAMSTHĀNAKA. My poor Sthāvaraka, are you alive?

STHĀVARAKA. I rather think so, your honor.

SAMSTHĀNAKA. There shertainly is a woman in the car,—look yourshelf.
[*To the* VITA.]
VITA. A woman! ha, ha!
> Afraid to gaze upon the man of birth,
> Who prides himself on my companionship,
> They walk with downcast eyes, like shrinking cattle
> That hang their heads against the driving rain.

VASANTASENĀ. Alas, that odious wretch, the king's brother!
> What will become of me—unhappy girl!
> A luckless seed my coming hither sows
> In the parched soil of my disastrous fate.

SAMSTHĀNAKA. That vile shlave, not to have examined the carriage!—
Come, mashter, look.
VITA. I am going.
SAMSTHĀNAKA. Do jackals fly or crows run? Do men eat with their eyes
and shee with their teeth? Sho surely will I not shtay here.
VITA [*looking in*]. How! can it be?
> What brings the doe into the tiger's den?
> Or does the cygnet fly the distant mate,
> Though bright as autumn's moon, to wed the crow!
> It is not well; or has your mother's will,
> On gain intent, compelled you to come hither
> To earn reluctant presents late despised?
> You arc by nature false, your fickle tribe,
> I told you truly, ever are prepared
> To yield their blandishments to those they scorn.

VASANTASENĀ. Believe it not of me—I was deceived,
> Mistook the vehicle, and the fatal error
> Has brought me hither. Oh, befriend—protect me!

VITA. I will befriend you; banish every fear.
> I will beguile this blockhead. [*Descends.*]
> There is indeed a devil in the car.

SAMSTHĀNAKA. Indeed! how happens it she hash not run off with you?
If a thief, how ish it she has not eaten you up?
VITA. Never mind.
> Hence to Ujjayin a line of groves affords
> Unbroken shade; let us walk there, 'twere better.

SAMSTHĀNAKA. How sho?
VITA. 'Twill yield us healthy exercise, and spare
> The jaded cattle.

SAMSTHĀNAKA. Sho be it. Come, Sthāvaraka, follow us with the carriage.—
No shtop; I go on foot only before gods and Brahmans—I cannot walk
along the road; I musht get into the car, and then as I pash, the citizens
will shay to each other, There, that is he, his exshellency the prinsh's
most noble brother-in-law.

VITA [*apart*]. What is to be done? the case is critical,—
  The remedy not obvious: yes, this were best.
  [*Aloud to the prince.*] I did but jest. There is no female fiend.
  Vasantasenā has come here to meet you.
VASANTASENĀ. Ah me!
SAMSTHĀNAKA. Am I not, mashter, a fine fellow, another Vāsudeva?
VITA. Undoubtedly.
SAMSTHĀNAKA. It is therefore that thish unparalleled goddesh waits upon
  me. I lately dishpleashed her; I will now go and casht myshelf at her feet.
VITA. Well devised.
SAMSTHĀNAKA. I go. [*Kneels to* VASANTASENĀ.] Celeshtial Mother, lishten
  to my prayers; behold me with thoshe lotush eyes thush lowly at thy
  feet, and mark my hands uplifted thush to thy heavenly countenance.
  Forgive, most grasheful nymph, the faults that love hash urged me to
  commit, and acshept me for thy shervant and thy shlave.
VASANTASENĀ. Away! your regard is my abhorrence.
  [*Spurns him with her foot.*]
SAMSTHĀNAKA [*rising in great wrath*]. What! shall thish head that bows not
  to the gods, thish head that my mother careshed be humbled to the
  ground, to be treated like a dead carcash by the jackals in a thicket?
  What ho! Sthāvaraka, where did you pick up thish woman?
STHĀVARAKA. Why, sir, to tell you the truth, some village carts blocked up
  the road near Chārudatta's garden; I got down to clear the way, and in
  the meantime left the carriage at his gate; I fancy she then came out of
  his house and ascended the car, mistaking it for another.
SAMSTHĀNAKA. A mishtake! Oh, then, she did not come here to sheek me.
  Come down, madam, thish carriage is mine. You come, I shuppose, to
  meet that beggar's brat, the shon of a merchant, and you take advantage
  of my cattle,—but turn out directly, I say.
VASANTASENĀ. That which you make my blame I make my boast;
  As for the rest, whatever must be may be.
SAMSTHĀNAKA. With theshe fair hands, armed with ten nails, and dexteroush
  in inflicting punishment, I drag you from the carriage by the hair of your
  head, as Jatāyu seized upon the wife of Bāli.
VITA. Forbear, forbear, nor rudely thus invade
  These graceful tresses. What destructive hand
  Would roughly rend the creeper from the tree,
  Or tear the blossom from the slender stem
  Leave her to me, I'll bring her from the car.
  [*Goes and hands* VASANTASENĀ *down.*]
SAMSTHĀNAKA [*aside*]. The wrath that her dishdainful treatment jushtly
  kindled ish now more violent than ever: a blow! a kick! to be shpurned!
  I am resholved,—she dies. [*Aloud.*] Mashter, if you have any relish for a
  mantle with a broad border and a hundred tashels, or have any curioshity
  to tashte a bit of delicate flesh, now is your time.

VITA. What mean you?

SAMSTHĀNAKA. Will you oblige me?

VITA. In anything not unreasonable.

SAMSTHĀNAKA. There is no more flavor of unreashonableness than of she-devils in it.

VITA. Well, speak on.

SAMSTHĀNAKA. Put Vashantashenā to death.

VITA [*stopping his ears*]. Murder a young and unoffending female,
Of courteous manners and unrivaled beauty,
The pride of all Ujjayin! Where shall I find,
Believe you, a fit raft to waft my soul
Safe o'er the river of futurity?

SAMSTHĀNAKA. I will have one made for you. Come, come, what have you to fear? In this lowly plashe, who shall shee you?

VITA. All nature—the surrounding realms of space;
The genii of these groves, the moon, the sun,
The winds, the vault of heaven, the firm-set earth,
Hell's awful ruler, and the conscious soul—
These all bear witness to the good or ill
That men perform, and these will see the deed.

SAMSTHĀNAKA. Throw a cloth over her then, and hide her.

VITA. Fool! you are crazed.

SAMSTHĀNAKA. And you are an old good-for-nothing dashtardly jackal. Very well, I shall find shome one elsh. Sthāvaraka shall do it. Here, Sthāvaraka, my lad, I will give you gold brashelets.

STHĀVARAKA. Thank your honor, I will wear them.

SAMSTHĀNAKA. You shall have a gold sheat.

STHAVARAKA. I will sit upon it.

SAMSTHĀNAKA. You shall have every dainty dish from my table.

STHĀVARAKA. I will eat it; never fear me.

SAMSTHĀNAKA. You shall be head over all my shlaves.

STHĀVARAKA. I shall be a very great man.

SAMSTHĀNAKA. But attend to what I order.

STHĀVARAKA. Depend upon me, in everything that may be done.

SAMSTHĀNAKA. It may be done well enough.

STHĀVARAKA. Say on, sir.

SAMSTHĀNAKA. Kill this Vashantashenā.

STHĀVARAKA. Excuse me, sir, I brought her here.

SAMSTHĀNAKA. Why, you villain, am I not your mashter?

STHĀVARAKA. You are, sir; my body is yours, but not my innocence: I dare not obey you.

SAMSTHĀNAKA. Of whom are you, my shervant, to be afraid?

STHĀVARAKA. Futurity.

SAMSTHĀNAKA. And who is Mr. Futurity, pray?

STHĀVARAKA. The requiter of our good and evil deeds.

SAMSTHĀNAKA. And what is the return for good?

STHĀVARAKA. Wealth and power like your honor's.

SAMSTHĀNAKA. And what for evil?

STHĀVARAKA. Eating, as I do, the bread of slavery; I will not do, therefore, what ought not to be done.

SAMSTHĀNAKA. You will not obey me? [Beats him.]

STHĀVARAKA. Beat me if you will, kill me if you will, I cannot do what ought not to be done. Fate has already punished me with servitude for the misdeeds of a former life, and I will not incur the penalty of being born again a slave.

VASANTASENĀ. Oh, sir, protect me. [To the VITA.]

VITA. Come, come, be pacified. [To the prince.]

> Sthāvaraka is right; revolving fate
> Has doomed him to a low and servile station,
> From which he wisely hopes a life of virtue
> Hereafter sets him free. Do you too think,
> Though degradation wait not close on crime,
> And many, obstinately foes to virtue,
> Suffer not here the punishment they merit,
> Yet destiny not blindly works. Though now
> Her will gives servitude to him, to you
> A master's sway; yet in a future being,
> Your affluence may his portion be assigned,
> And yours, to do submissively his bidding.

SAMSTHĀNAKA [apart]. The old dashtard, and thish fool of a shlave, are both afraid of futurity; but what shall I fear? I, who am the brother of a prinsh, and a man of courage as well ash rank? [To STHĀVARAKA.] Begone, shlave; retire into the garden, and wait apart.

STHĀVARAKA. I obey, sir. [To VASANTASENĀ.] Lady, fear not me.
   [Exit.]

SAMSTHĀNAKA [tightening his girdle]. Now, Vashantashenā, die.
   [Goes to seize her; the VITA stops him.]

VITA. In my presence!
   [Throws him down.]

SAMSTHĀNAKA. Ah, villain! would you kill your prinsh? [Faints.] Ah, you who have sho long fed at my cosht, do you now become my foe? [Rising; apart.] Let me think; thish will do. I shaw the old shcoundrel give a shignal. I musht get him out of the way and then deshpatch her. [Aloud.] My good friend, how could you so mishtake what I shaid? How could you shupposhe that I, born of sho high a race, should sheriously purposh shuch an unworthy action? I merely ushed thoshe menaces to terrify her into compliance.

VITA. Believe me, sir, it is of little import
> To boast of noble birth, unless accord
> The manners with the rank:—ungrateful thorns

Are most offensive in a goodly soil.

SAMSTHĀNAKA. The truth of the matter ish, that Vashantashenā ish bashful in your preshence: leave ush by ourshelves a little. That fellow Sthāvaraka, too, I am sure, intends to run away; go, bring him back, and I dare shay when we are alone a little she will relent.

VITA [apart]. It may be true that, valiant in my presence,
Vasantasenā may continue still
To drive this fool to madness by denial.
Passion in privacy gains confidence.
I will consent to leave them for a while.
[Aloud.] I shall retire and obey your orders.

VASANTASENĀ [laying hold of his garment]. Oh, leave me not! I have no hope but you.

VITA. You have no cause for terror. Hear me, sir:
I leave Vasantasenā as a pledge,
And safe expect her from your hands again.

SAMSTHĀNAKA. Be ashured of it, she shall be sho acshepted.

VITA. In truth?

SAMSTHĀNAKA. In truth.

VITA [apart]. He may deceive me. I'll at first retire;
But so, that unobserved I may behold
His acts, and satisfy me of his purpose.

SAMSTHĀNAKA. He ish gone, and now she dies. But hold:—perhaps he juggles with me, the shly old fox, and now lies watch to shee what I am doing: he shall meet his match; the deceiver be deceived.
[He gathers flowers and decorates himself.]
Come, Vashantashenā, child, why so pettish? come, come.

VITA. I see his love revives; I now may leave them. [Departs.]

SAMSTHĀNAKA. I will give you gold, I will treat you tenderly, I will lay head and turban at your feet. Oh, if you shtill dishdain me, and will not accept me ash your shlave, what have I to do longer with mankind?

VASANTASENĀ. Why should I hesitate? I spurn you;
Nor can you tempt me, abject wretch, with gold.
Though soiled the leaves, the bees fly not the lotus,
Nor shall my heart prove traitor to the homage
It pays to merit, though its lord be poor.
To love such excellence exalts my life,
And sheds a luster on my humble lot.
And why should I forgo it? Can I leave
The mango's stately stem to twine around
The low and worthless locust?

SAMSTHĀNAKA. What! dare you compare the beggar Chārudatta to a mango-tree, and me to the locusht! Ish it thush you treat me and cherish the recollection of Chārudatta?

VASANTASENĀ. How can I cease to think of one who dwells for ever in my heart?

SAMSTHĀNAKA. We'll shoon try that, and cut short your recollections and yourself together. Shtop, you inamorata of a beggarly Brahman.

VASANTASENĀ. Delightful words! proceed, you speak my praise.

SAMSTHĀNAKA. Let him defend you if he can.

VASANTASENĀ. Defend me! I were safe if he were here!

SAMSTHĀNAKA. What! is he shakra, or the shon of Bāli—Mahendra, or the shon of Rambhā—Kālanemi, or Shubhandu—Rudra or the shon of Drona—Jatāyu—Chānakya—Dhundhumāra or Trishanku? If he were all theshe together, he could not aid you. As Shītā wash shlain by Chānakya, ash Draupadī by Jatāyu, sho art thou by me. [*Seizes her.*]

VASANTASENĀ. Oh, my dear mother! Oh, my loved Chārudatta!

> Too short and too imperfect are our loves—
> Too soon I perish. I will cry for succor—
> What! shall Vasantasenā's voice be heard
> Abroad? Oh, that were infamy! No more
> But this. Bless, bless my Chārudatta.

SAMSTHĀNAKA. Shtill do you repeat that name! Once more, now. [*Seizing her by the throat.*]

VASANTASENĀ [*in a struggling tone*]. Bless my Chārudatta.

SAMSTHĀNAKA. Die, harlot, die.

[*Strangles her with his hands.*]

'Tish done, she ish no more. Thish bundle of vishe, thish manshion of cruelty, hash met her fate, inshtead of him whom she came in her love to meet. To what shall I compare the prowess of thish arm? Deshtroyed in the fulnesh of her hopes, she hash fallen like Shītā in the Bhārata. Deaf to my deshires, she perishes in my reshentment. The garden ish empty; I may drag her away unpersheived. My father and my mother, ash well ash my brothers, may regret that they did not shee the valiant actions of my mother's shon. The old jackal will be here again preshently. I will withdraw and obsherve him.

[*Enter the* VITA *and* STHĀVARAKA.]

VITA. I have brought back Sthāvaraka. Where is he? Here are footmarks,— these are woman's!

SAMSTHĀNAKA [*advances*]. Welcome, mashter: you are well returned, Sthāvaraka.

VITA. Now render back my pledge.

SAMSTHĀNAKA. What wash that?

VITA. Vasantasenā.

SAMSTHĀNAKA. Oh, she ish gone.

VITA. Whither?

SAMSTHĀNAKA. After you.

VITA. She came not in that direction.

SAMSTHĀNAKA. Which way went you?

VITA. To the east.

SAMSTHĀNAKA. Ah, that accounts for it; she turned off to the shouth.

VITA. I went south too.

SAMSTHĀNAKA. Then, I shuppose, she went north.

VITA. What mean you? I comprehend you not. Speak out.

SAMSTHĀNAKA. I shwear by your head and my feet, that you may make
   yourself perfectly eashy. Dishmish all alarm; I have killed her.

VITA. Killed her!

SAMSTHĀNAKA. What! you do not believe me? Then look here, shee thish
   firsht proof of my prowesh. [*Shows the body.*]

VITA. Alas, I die! [*Faints.*]

SAMSTHĀNAKA. Hey-dey! ish it all over with him?

STHĀVARAKA. Revive, sir; it is I who am to blame: my inconsiderately
   bringing her hither has caused her death.

VITA [*reviving*]. Alas! Vasantasenā,
         The stream of tenderness is now dried up,
         And beauty flies us for her native sphere.
         Adorned with every grace, of lovely aspect,
         Radiant with playfulness, alas! poor wench,
         River of gentle feeling, isle of mirth,
         And friendly refuge for all such as I am;
         Alas! love's richest store, a mart exhaustless
         Of exquisite delights, is here broke open.
         This crime will amply be avenged. A deed
         Done by such hands, in such a place committed,
         Will bring down infamy upon the state,
         And drive our guardian goddess from our city.
         Let me reflect;—this villain may involve
         Me in the crime—I will depart from hence.
         [*The prince lays hold of him.*]
         Detain me not; I have already been
         Too long your follower and friend.

SAMSTHĀNAKA. Very likely, indeed. You have murdered Vashantashenā,
   and sheek to accushe me of the crime. Do you imagine I am without
   friends?

VITA. You are a wretch.

SAMSTHĀNAKA. Come, come, I will give you money, a hundred gold-pieces,
   clothes, a turban. The conshequence of abushe is common to all men.

VITA. Keep your gifts.

STHĀVARAKA. Shame! shame!

SAMSTHĀNAKA. Ha, ha, ha! [*Laughing.*]

VITA. Restrain your mirth. Let there be hate between us.
         That friendship that confers alone disgrace
         Is not for me; it must no more unite us.
         I cast it from me, as a snapped

And stringless bow.

SAMSTHĀNAKA. Come, good mashter, be appeashed. Let ush go bathe.

VITA. Whilst you were free from crime you might exact
My duty, but obedience to you now
Would but proclaim myself alike unworthy.
I cannot wait on guilt, nor, though I know
My innocence, have courage to encounter
Those speaking glances every female eye
Will cast abhorrent upon one who holds
Communion with a woman's murderer.
Poor, poor Vasantasenā! may thy virtues
Win thee in after-life a happier portion;
And may the days of shame, and death of violence
That thou hast suffered in existence past,
Ensure thee honored birth, the world's regard,
And wealth and happiness, in that to come. [*Going.*]

SAMSTHĀNAKA. Where would you fly? In thish, my garden, you have murdered a female; come along with me, and defend yourshelf before my brother-in-law. [*Seizes him.*]

VITA. Away, fool. [*Draws his sword.*]

SAMSTHĀNAKA [*falls back*]. Oh, very well, if you are afraid, you may depart.

VITA. I am in danger here; yes, I will join
Sharvilaka and Chandana, and with them sheek
The band that Ārya has assembled.
[*Exit.*]

SAMSTHĀNAKA. Go, fool, to death. Well, Sthāvaraka, my lad, what think you of this bushiness?

STHĀVARAKA. That it is most horrible.

SAMSTHĀNAKA. How, shlave, do you condemn me? With all my heart, be it sho. Here, take theshe.

[*Gives him his ornaments.*]

I make you a preshent of them, that when I am full dreshed, you may be shuitably equipped to attend me: it ish my command.

STHĀVARAKA. These are too costly,—what am I to do with them, sir?

SAMSTHĀNAKA. Take them, take them, and away with you. Conduct the carriage to the porch of my palash, and there wait my coming.

STHĀVARAKA. I obey, sir.
[*Exit.*]

SAMSTHĀNAKA. My worthy preshceptor hash taken himshelf off in alarm. Ash to the shlave, ash shoon ash I return I will put him in confinement; sho my shecret is shafe, and I may depart without apprehension. Hold! let me be sure,—ish she dead, or musht I kill her again? no, she ish shafe. I will cover the body with my mantle. Shtop! it bears my name, and will dishcover me. Well thought of,—the wind hash shcattered about a quantity of dry leaves; I will cover her over with them.

[*Collects the leaves and piles them over* VASANTASENĀ.]

Now to the court, where I will enter an accushation againsht Chārudatta of having murdered Vashantashenā for her wealth. Ingenioushly devished! Chārudatta will be ruined; the virtuous shity cannot tolerate even the death of an animal. Now to my work. [*Going.*] Here comes that rashcally monk again, and by the very road I wash about to take; he owes me a grudge for threatening to shlit his noshe, and should he shee me here, he will out of revenge come forward and tax me with thish murder. How shall I avoid him? I can leap the broken wall here. Thus I fly, ash the monkey Mahendra leaped through heaven, over earth and hell, from Hanumat Peak to Lankā. [*Jumps down.*]

[*Enter the monk.*]

SHRAMANAKA. I have washed my mantle, and will hang it on these boughs to dry. No, here are a number of monkeys; I'll spread it on the ground. No, there is too much dust. Ha! yonder the wind has blown together a pile of dry leaves; that will answer exactly; I'll spread it upon them.

[*Spreads his wrapper over* VASANTASENĀ *and sits down.*]

Glory to Buddha!

[*Repeats the moral stanzas at the beginning of Act Eight.*]

But enough of this. I covet not the other world, until in this I may make some return for the lady Vasantasenā's charity. On the day she liberated me from the gamester's clutches she made me her slave for ever. Holloa! something sighed amidst yon leaves! or perhaps it was only their crackling, scorched by the sun, and moistened by my damp garment. Bless me, they spread out like the wings of a bird. [*One of* VASANTASENĀ's *hands appears.*] A woman's hand, as I live, with rich ornaments—and another; surely I have seen that hand before. It is, it is— it is the hand that once was stretched forth to save me. What should this mean!

[*Throws off the wrapper and leaves, and sees* VASANTASENĀ.]

It is the lady Vasantasenā; the devoted worshiper of Buddha.

[VASANTASENĀ *expresses by signs the want of water.*]

She wants water: the pool is far away; what's to be done? Ha! my wet garment.

[*Applies it to her face and mouth and fans her.*]

VASANTASENĀ [*reviving*]. Thanks, thanks, my friend; who art thou?

SHRAMANAKA. Do you not recollect me, lady? You once redeemed me with ten gold-pieces.

VASANTASENĀ. I remember *you*; aught else I have forgotten. I have suffered since.

SHRAMANAKĀ. How, lady?

VASANTASENĀ. As my fate deserved.

SHRAMANAKA. Rise, lady, rise; drag yourself to this tree: here, hold by this creeper.[30]

[30] A monk may not touch a woman.

[*Bends it down to her; she lays hold of it and rises.*]
In a neighboring convent dwells a holy sister; rest a while with her,
lady, and recover your spirits: gently, lady, gently.
[*They proceed.*]
Stand aside, good friends, stand aside; make way for a young female
and a poor monk. It is my duty to restrain the hands and mouth, and
keep the passions in subjection. What should such a man care for kingdoms? His is the world to come.
[*Exit.*]

ACT NINE

The Hall of Justice. (Exterior and Interior.)

[*Enter* OFFICER.]
OFFICER. I am commanded to prepare the benches in this hall for the judges.
[*Arranges them.*] All is ready for their reception, the floor is swept, and
the seats are placed, and I have only now to inform them all is ready.
[*Going.*] Ha! here comes the king's brother-in-law, a worthless fellow;
I will get out of his way.
[*Retires.*]
[*Enter* SAMSTHĀNAKA, *splendidly dressed.*]
SAMSTHĀNAKA. I have bathed in limpid water and shat in a shady grove,
pashing my time like a sheleshtial chorishter of elegant form, amidsht
an attendant train of lovely damshels, now tying my hair, then twishting
it into a braid, then opening it in flowing treshes, and again gathering
it into a graceful knot. Oh! I am a mosht accomplished and ashtonishing
young prinsh, and yet I feel a vacanshy, an interior chashm; such ash
ish shought for by the fatal worm that works its darkling way through the
human entrails. How shall I fill it up?—on whom shall I shatiate my
craving? Ha! I recollect; it ish deshigned for the misherable Chārudatta.
Sho be it. I will repair to the court, and caushe an accushation to be
registhered againsht him of the death of Vashantashenā, asherting that
he hash robbed and murdered her. The court ish open, I shee.
[*Enters.*]
How! the sheats are ready for the arrival of the judges. I shall wait their
coming on thish grash plot.
DOORKEEPER. Here comes the Court; I must attend.
[*Enter the* JUDGE, *with the* PROVOST *and* RECORDER *and others.*]
CRIER. Hear, all men, the judge's commands.
JUDGE. Amidst the conflicting details of parties engaged in legal con-
troversy, it is difficult for the judge to ascertain what is really in their
hearts. Men accuse others of secret crimes, and even though the charge
be disproved, they acknowledge not their fault, but, blinded by passion,

persevere; and whilst their friends conceal their errors, and their foes
exaggerate them, the character of the prince is assailed. Reproach indeed
is easy, discrimination of but rare occurrence, and the quality of a
judge is readily the subject of censure. A judge should be learned,
sagacious, eloquent, dispassionate, impartial; he should pronounce
judgment only after due deliberation and inquiry; he should be a
guardian to the weak, a terror to the wicked; his heart should covet
nothing, his mind be intent on nothing but equity and truth, and he
should keep aloof the anger of the king.

PROVOST and RECORDER. The character of your worship is as free from
censure as the moon is from the imputation of obscurity.

JUDGE. Officers, lead the way to the seat of judgment.

OFFICER. As your worship commands. [*They sit.*]

JUDGE. Now go forth, and see who comes to demand justice.

OFFICER. By command of his honor the judge, I ask, who waits to demand
justice?

SAMSTHĀNAKA [*advancing*]. Oh, oh! the judges are sheated. I demand
jushtice; I, a man of rank, a Vāsudeva, and brother-in-law of the King;—
I have a plaint to enter.

OFFICER. Have the goodness to wait a moment, your excellency, whilst I
apprise the Court.
[*Returns.*]
So please your worship, the first plaintiff is his Majesty's brother-in-law.

JUDGE. The King's brother-in-law to proffer a plaint? An eclipse of the
rising sun foreruns the downfall of some illustrious character: but there
are other matters before us. Return and tell him his cause cannot come
on today.
[*Officer returns to* SAMSTHĀNAKA.]

OFFICER. I am desired to inform your honor that your cause cannot be
tried today.

SAMSTHĀNAKA. How! not today? Then I shall apply to the king, my
shishter's hushband. I shall apply to my shishter, and to my mother,
and have this judge dishmissed, and another appointed immediately.
[*Going.*]

OFFICER. Stay one moment, your honor, and I will carry your message to
the Court. [*Goes to the* JUDGE.] Please your worship, his excellency is
very angry; and declares if you do not try his suit today, he will complain
to the royal family, and procure your worship's dismissal.

JUDGE. The blockhead has it in his power, it is true. Well, call him hither:
his plaint shall be heard.

OFFICER [*to* SAMSTHĀNAKA]. Will your excellency be pleased to enter; your
plaint will be heard.

SAMSTHĀNAKA. Oh, oh! firsht it could not be tried; now it will be heard;
very well, the judges fear me: they will do what I deshire.
[*Enters.*]

I am well pleashed, gentlemen; you may therefore be sho too, for it ish in my hands to dishtribute or withhold shatishfaction.

JUDGE [*apart*]. Very like the language of a complainant this! [*Aloud.*] Be seated.

SAMSTHĀNAKA. Ashuredly. This plashe ish mine, and I shall shit where I pleashe. [*To the* PROVOST.] I will shit here; no [*to the* RECORDER], I will shit here; no, no, [*puts his hands on the* JUDGE's *head, and then sits down by his side*]. I will even shit here.

JUDGE. Your excellency has a complaint?

SAMSTHĀNAKA. To be sure I have.

JUDGE. Prefer it.

SAMSTHĀNAKA. I will, in good time; but remember, I am born in a dishtinguished family. My father ish the king's father-in-law; the king ish my father's shon-in-law; I am the king's brother; and the king ish my shishter's hushband.

JUDGE. We know all this; but why dwell on family honors? Personal excellence is more important; there are always thorn bushes in the fairest forests: declare therefore your suit.

SAMSTHĀNAKA. Thish it ish; but it involves no fault of mine. My noble brother-in-law, in his good pleashure, preshented me, for my eashe and recreation, the besht of the royal gardens, the ancient Pushpakarandaka. It is my practish to vishit it daily, and shee it well shwept and weeded, and kept in order; and having, ash my wont, gone thish day thither, what should I behold, but—I could shcarshely believe my eyes—the dead body of a female!

JUDGE. Did you know the person?

SAMSTHĀNAKA. Alash! too well. She wash once our shity's greatesht pride. Her rich attire musht have tempted shome execrable wretch to beguile her into the lonely garden; and there, for the shake of her jewels, was the lovely Vashantashenā shtrangled by his hands, not by me. [*Stops himself.*]

JUDGE. What neglect in the police! You heard the plaint, gentlemen; let it be recorded, including the words "not by me."

RECORDER [*writes it*]. It is done.

SAMSTHĀNAKA [*apart*]. Vile careleshness! My heedleshness hash plunged me into peril, like a man croshing a narrow bridge preshipitately, who tumbles into the shtream: it cannot now be helped. [*Aloud.*] Well, shagacious adminishtrators of justish, you make a mighty fush about a trifle. I was going to obsherve, not by me was the deed beheld.

[*Puts his foot on the record, and wipes out the last part.*]

JUDGE. How, then, do you know the truth of what you have stated, that for the sake of her ornaments she was strangled by some person's hands?

SAMSTHĀNAKA. I conclude sho, for the neck was bare and shwollen, and her dresh rifled of its ornaments.

PROVOST. The case is likely enough.

SAMSTHĀNAKA [*apart*]. Good; I am alive again.

PROVOST. Whom else do we require in this suit?

JUDGE. The case is twofold, and must be investigated both in relation to assertion and facts; the verbal investigation relates to plaintiff and respondent, that of facts depends upon the judge.

PROVOST. The cause then requires the evidence of Vasantasenā's mother.

JUDGE. Undoubtedly. Officers, go and civilly call Vasantasenā's mother into court.

[*Exit Officer, and returns with the old woman.*]

OFFICER. Come along, dame.

MOTHER. My daughter is gone to a friend's house. This old fellow comes and says to me: "Come along; his honor the judge has sent for you." I am ready to faint, and my heart flutters so.—Very well, sir, very well, sir, lead me to the court.

OFFICER. Here we are;—enter.

[*They enter.*]

MOTHER. Health and happiness to your worships!

JUDGE. You are welcome;—sit down. [*She sits.*]

SAMSTHĀNAKA. Oh, old procuresh, you are there, are you?

JUDGE. You are the mother of Vasantasenā?

MOTHER. I am.

JUDGE. Where is your daughter?

MOTHER. At a friend's house.

JUDGE. The name of that friend?

MOTHER [*apart*]. Oh dear me, this is very awkward. [*Aloud.*] Surely, your worship, this is not a fit question for your worship to ask.

JUDGE. No hesitation;—the law asks the question.

PROVOST and RECORDER. Speak out; the law asks the question; there is no impropriety in answering.

MOTHER. Why then, gentlemen, to say the truth, she is at the house of a very nice gentleman:—the son of Sāgardatta, grandson of the Provost Vinayadatta, whose own name is Chārudatta; he lives near the Exchange: my daughter is with him.

SAMSTHĀNAKA. You hear, judges;—let this be registered. I accushe Chārudatta.

PROVOST. Chārudatta, her friend! he cannot be criminal.

JUDGE. The cause, however, requires his presence.

PROVOST. Certainly.

JUDGE [*to the* RECORDER]. Dhanadatta, write down that Vasantasenā last went to Chārudatta's residence: this is the first step. Let me consider; how can Chārudatta be summoned hither? However, the law must be enforced. Officer, repair to Chārudatta, and say to him, the magistrate, with all due respect, requests to see him at his perfect convenience.

[OFFICER *goes out, and reenters with* CHĀRUDATTA.]

OFFICER. This way, sir.

CHĀRUDATTA. The prince well knows my rank and character,
      And yet thus calls me to his public court.
      Haply he may have heard my cart conveyed
      The fugitive he feared beyond his reach,
      Borne to his ear by some unfriendly spy.
      Or haply—but away with fancies; soon
      I learn the truth, arrived at the tribunal.
OFFICER. This way, this way, sir.
CHĀRUDATTA. What should this mean? his harshest note, yon crow
      Responsive utters to his fellow's call,
      With croak repeated. Ha! my left eye throbs;
      What new misfortunes threaten?
OFFICER. Proceed, sir, never fear.
CHĀRUDATTA. Facing the sun, on yonder blighted tree,
      The bird of evil augury is perched;
      Ha! on my path, the black snake sleeping lies.
      Roused from his slumber, he unfolds in wrath
      His spiry length, and threatening beats the ground
      With bulk inflated, as he turns on me
      His angry eyes, and from between his fangs
      Protrudes his hissing tongue. I slip, yet here
      No plashy mire betrays my heedless feet.—
      Still throbs my left eye, and my left arm trembles;
      And still that bird in flight sinistral cries,
      To warn me of impending ill. Yes, death—
      Terrible death awaits me. Be it so—
      It is not mine to murmur against destiny,
      Nor doubt that righteous which the gods ordain.
OFFICER. This is the court, sir, enter.
CHĀRUDATTA [*entering and looking round*]. The prospect is but little
            pleasing.
      The court looks like a sea;—its councilors
      Are deep engulfed in thought; its tossing waves
      Are wrangling advocates; its brood of monsters
      Are these wild animals—death's ministers—
      Attorneys skim like wily snakes the surface—
      Spies are the shellfish cowering 'midst its weeds,
      And vile informers, like the hovering curlew,
      Hang fluttering o'er, then pounce upon their prey:
      The beach, that should be justice, is unsafe,
      Rough, rude, and broken by oppression's storms.
      [*As he advances he knocks his head against the door-frame.*]
      More inauspicious omens! they attend
      Each step I take; fate multiplies its favors.
JUDGE. Chārudatta approaches. Observe him;—that face and form never

gave shelter to causeless crime. Appearance is a test of character; and
not only in man, but in elephants, horses and kine, the disposition never
deviates from the perfect shape.

CHĀRUDATTA. Hail to the court; prosperity attend
    The delegated ministers of justice.

JUDGE. Sir, you are welcome; officer, bring a seat.

OFFICER. It is here; be seated, sir. [*To* CHĀRUDATTA; *he sits.*]

SAMSTHĀNAKĀ. Sho, Mr. Woman-killer, you are here: very decoroush
    thish, indeed, to treat shuch a fellow with sho much shivility; but never
    mind.

JUDGE. Worthy Chārudatta, allow me to ask if any intimacy or connection
    has ever subsisted between you and this woman's daughter?

CHĀRUDATTA. What woman?

JUDGE. This. [*Showing Vasantasenā's* MOTHER.]

CHĀRUDATTA [*rising*]. Lady, I salute you.

MOTHER. Son, long may you live! [*Apart.*] This is Chārudatta, then; really
    my daughter has made a good choice.

JUDGE. Tell us, Chārudatta, were you ever acquainted with that courtesan?
    [CHĀRUDATTA *ashamed, hesitates.*]

SAMSTHĀNAKA. Ah! he pretends to be vashtly modesht, or very much
    alarmed; it is merely a pretext to evade confeshing his vicious courshes:
    but that he murdered the woman for her wealth, the prinsh shall shoon
    make manifesht.

PROVOST. Away with this hesitation, Chārudatta: there is a charge against
    you.

CHĀRUDATTA. Well, sirs, what shall I say? What if she were
    A friend of mine? be youth accused, not habit.

JUDGE. Let me beg—no evasion, banish all reserve, speak the truth and
    act ingenuously: remember it is the law that calls upon you.

CHĀRUDATTA. First tell me who is my accuser?

SAMSTHĀNAKA. I am—I.

CHĀRUDATTA. Thou! a mighty matter truly.

SAMSTHĀNAKA. Indeed, you woman-killer! What! are you to murder shuch
    a woman as Vashantashenā, and rob her of her jewels, and to think
    it will not be known?

CHĀRUDATTA. Thou art crazed.

JUDGE. Enough of this; declare the truth: was the courtesan your friend?

CHĀRUDATTA. She was, she was.

JUDGE. And where is Vasantasenā now?

CHĀRUDATTA. Gone.

PROVOST. Gone! how, whither, and how attended?

CHĀRUDATTA [*apart*]. Shall I say she went privately? [*Aloud.*] She went to
    her own dwelling: what more can I say?

SAMSTHĀNAKA. What more? Why, did you not accompany her to my
    prinshely garden; and did you not there, for the shake of her jewels,

shtrangle her, with your own hands? How then can you shay she is gone home?

CHĀRUDATTA. Foul calumniator.
> No rain from heaven upon thy face descends,
> Dark as the jay's unmoistened wing in showers.
> These falsehoods parch thy lips, as wintry winds
> Despoil the shriveled lotus of its beauty.

JUDGE [*apart*]. I see it were as easy to weigh Himālaya, ford the ocean, or grasp the wind, as fix a stain on Chārudatta's reputation. [*Aloud.*] It cannot be that this worthy man is guilty.

SAMSTHĀNAKA. What have you to do with his defensh?—Let the cashe be tried.

JUDGE. Away, fool, is it not thus?—If you expound the Vedas will not your tongue be cut out? If you gaze upon the midday sun, will you not lose your eyesight? If you plunge your hand into flame, will it not be burned? and think you that if you revile Chārudatta, the earth will not open and swallow you? This is Chārudatta—how can such a man have committed such a crime? He has exhausted in lavish munificence the ocean of his disregarded wealth, and is it possible that he, who was best among the best, and who has ever shown the most princely liberality, should have been guilty of a deed most hateful to a noble mind, for the sake of plunder?

SAMSTHĀNAKA. I shay again, it ish not your provinsh to undertake his defensh; you are to try the caushe.

MOTHER. I say the accusation is false. When in his distress my daughter entrusted a casket of jewels to his care, and it was stolen from him; even then he replaced it with a necklace of still greater value; and can he now, for the sake of wealth, have turned murderer? Oh, never! Alas! would that my daughter were here! [*Weeps.*]

JUDGE. Inform us, Chārudatta, how did she leave you—on foot or in a carriage?

CHĀRUDATTA. I did not see her depart, and know not.

[*Enter* VĪRAKA *in haste.*]

VĪRAKA. Now go I to the Court, to tell them how I have been maltreated, kicked, and abused for keeping a good lookout after the runaway. Hail to your worships!

JUDGE. Ha! here is Vīraka, the captain of the watch: what brings you hither, Vīraka?

VĪRAKA. Hear me, your honor. Whilst engaged last night in quest of Āryaka, who had broke loose, we stopped a covered carriage: the captain, Chandanaka, looked into it, and I was going to do so too, when he prevented me, pulled me back, and cuffed and kicked me. I beg your honors will take proper notice of this business.

JUDGE. We will. Whose was the carriage, do you know?

VĪRAKA. The driver said it belonged to this gentleman, Chārudatta; and that it carried Vasantasenā to meet him in Pushpakarandaka.

SAMSTHĀNAKA. You hear, shirs!

JUDGE. Truly this spotless moon is threatened by the demon of eclipse; the limpid stream is sullied by the falling of the banks. We will inquire into your complaint, Vīraka; in the meantime mount one of the messenger's horses at the gate; go to Pushpakarandaka with all speed, and bring us word whether the body of a murdered woman lies there.

VĪRAKA. I shall.

[*Goes out, and presently returns.*]

I have been to the garden, and have ascertained that a female body has been carried off by the beasts of prey.

JUDGE. How know you it was a female?

VĪRAKA. By the remains of the hair, and the marks of the hands and feet.

JUDGE. How difficult it is to discover the truth: the more one investigates, the greater is the perplexity. The points of law are sufficiently clear here, but the understanding still labors like a cow in a quagmire.

CHĀRUDATTA [*apart*]. When first the flower unfolds, as flock the bees
     To drink the honeyed dew, so mischiefs crowd
     The entrance opened by man's falling fortune.

JUDGE. Come, Chārudatta, speak the truth.

CHĀRUDATTA. The wretch that sickens at another's merits,
     The mind, by passion blinded, bent to ruin
     The object of its malice, do not claim
     Reply, nor any heed to what they utter,
     Which from their very nature must be falsehood.
     For me—you know me—would I pluck a flower,
     I draw the tender creeper gently to me,
     Nor rudely rob it of its clustering beauty.
     How think you then?—could I with violent hands
     Tear from their lovely seat those jetty locks,
     More glossy than the black bee's wing, or how
     So wrong my nature, and betray my love,
     As with remorseless heart to blast in death
     The weeping charms that vainly sued for mercy?

SAMSTHĀNAKA. I tell you, judges, you will be held as the defendant's friends and abettors, if you allow him longer to remain sheated in your preshence.

JUDGE. Officer, remove him from his seat. [OFFICER *obeys*.]

CHĀRUDATTA. Ministers of justice, yet reflect. [*Sits on the ground*.]

SAMSTHĀNAKA [*apart*]. Ha, ha! my deeds are now shafely deposhited on another's head; I will go and shit near Chārudatta. [*Does so*.] Come, Chārudatta, look at me: confess; shay honeshtly, "I killed Vashanta-shenā."

CHĀRUDATTA. Vile wretch, away! Alas! my humble friend,

My good Maitreya, what will be thy grief
To hear of my disgrace? and thine, dear wife,
The daughter of a pure and pious race?
Alas! my boy, amidst thy youthful sports
How little think'st thou of thy father's shame!
Where can Maitreya tarry? I had sent him
To seek Vasantasenā, and restore
The costly gems her lavish love bestowed
Upon my child—where can he thus delay?

Outside.

[*Enter* MAITREYA *with* VASANTASENĀ'S *jewels.*]

MAITREYA. I am to return these trinkets to Vasantasenā; the child took
them to his mother; I must restore them, and, on no account, consent
to take them back again. [*Speaking to someone behind the scenes.*] Ha!
Rebhila; how now Rebhila, what is the matter? You seem agitated,
what has chanced? [*Listening.*] Hey! what say you, my dear friend?
summoned to the court? this is very alarming. Let me think:— I must
go to him, and see what it means; I can go to Vasantasenā afterward.
Oh, here is the court.

[*Enters.*]

Salutation to your worships! where is my friend?

JUDGE. There.

MAITREYA. My dear friend, all happiness—

CHĀRUDATTA. Will be hereafter.

MAITREYA. Patience.

CHĀRUDATTA. That I have.

MAITREYA. But why so downcast? what are you brought here for?

CHĀRUDATTA. I am a murderer—reckless of futurity—
          Repaying woman's tender love with blood—
          What else, let him declare.

MAITREYA. What!

CHĀRUDATTA [*whispers to him*]. Even so.

MAITREYA. Who says so?

CHĀRUDATTA [*to the king's brother-in-law*]. Yon miserable man, the
          instrument.
          That destiny employs to work my fall.

MAITREYA. Why not say she is gone home?

CHĀRUDATTA. It recks not what I say; my humble state
          Is not to be believed.

MAITREYA. How, sirs! what is all this? Can he who has beautified our city
with its chief ornaments, who has filled Ujjayin with gardens, and gates,
and convents, and temples, and wells, and fountains,—can he, an utter
reprobate, for the object of a few beggarly ornaments, have done such

an iniquitous act? [*In anger.*] And you—you wretch, you king's brother-in-law, Samsthānaka,—you who stop at nothing, and are a stuffed vessel of everything offensive to mankind,—you monkey, tricked out with golden toys: say again before me, that my friend, who never plucked a flower roughly in his life, who never pulled more than one at a time, and always left the young buds untouched;—say that he has been guilty of a crime detestable in both worlds, and I will break thy head into a thousand pieces with this staff, as knotty and crooked as thy own heart.

SAMSTHĀNAKA. Hear him, my mashters. What hash thish crowfootpated hypocritical fellow to do with the caush between me and Chārudatta, that he ish to break my head? Attempt it, if you dare, you hypocritical shcoundrel.

[MAITREYA *strikes him; a struggle ensues, in which* VASANTASENĀ'S *jewels fall from his girdle.* SAMSTHĀNAKA *picks them up.*]

Shee here, shirs! here,—here are the poor wench's jewels, for the shake of which yon villain murdered her.

[*The judges hang down their heads.*]

CHĀRUDATTA [*to* MAITREYA]. In an ill hour these jewels spring to light.
  Such is my fate, their fall will lead to mine.

MAITREYA. Why not explain?

CHĀRUDATTA. The regal eye is feeble to discern
  The truth amidst perplexity and doubt.
  I can but urge—I have not done the deed,
  And poverty like mine must hope to gain
  Unwilling credence; shameful death awaits me.

JUDGE. Alas! Mars is obstructed and Jupiter obscured, and a new planet like a comet wanders in their orbits.

PROVOST. Come hither, lady [*to Vasantasenā's* MOTHER]; look at this casket; was it your daughter's?

MOTHER. It is very like, but not the same.

SAMSTHĀNAKA. Oh, you old baggage! your eyes tell one shtory and your tongue another.

MOTHER. Away, slanderer!

PROVOST. Be careful of what you say: is it your daughter's, or is it not?

MOTHER. Why, your worship, the skill of the workman makes it difficult to trust one's eyes; but this is not my daughter's.

JUDGE. Do you know these ornaments?

MOTHER. Have I not said? They may be different, though like: I cannot say more; they may be imitations made by some skillful artist.

JUDGE. It is true. Provost, examine them: they may be different, though like; the dexterity of the artists is no doubt very great, and they readily fabricate imitations of ornaments they have once seen, in such a manner, that the difference shall scarcely be discernible.

PROVOST. Are these ornaments your property, Chārudatta?

CHĀRUDATTA. They are not.

PROVOST. Whose then?

CHĀRUDATTA. This lady's daughter's.

PROVOST. How come they out of the owner's possession?

CHĀRUDATTA. She parted with them.

PROVOST. Consider, Chārudatta, you must speak the truth. Truth alone is internal satisfaction; not to declare the truth is a crime; the truth is readily told; seek not to conceal it by a lie.

CHĀRUDATTA. I do not know the ornaments; but this I know, they are now brought from my house.

SAMSTHĀNAKA. You killed her in my garden firsht, and sho obtained them; thish prevarication is only to hide the truth.

JUDGE. Chārudatta, own the truth, or it must be my pleasure that heavy lashes fall upon that delicate frame.

CHĀRUDATTA. Sprung from a race incapable of crime,
    I have not shamed my sires—if you confound
    The innocent with the guilty, I must suffer.
    [Apart.] If I have lost indeed Vasantasenā,
    Life is a burden to me. [Aloud.] What avails it
    To proffer further plea? be it acknowledged.
    I have abandoned virtue, and deserved
    Abhorrence here and punishment hereafter.
    Let me be called a murderer, or what else
    It pleases him [to SAMSTHĀNAKA] to declare.

SAMSTHĀNAKA. She ish killed: shay at once, I killed her.

CHĀRUDATTA. You have said.

SAMSTHĀNAKA. You hear him: he confeshes it; all doubt ish removed by hish own words: let him be punished. Poor Chārudatta!

JUDGE. Officer, obey the prince—secure the malefactor.

MOTHER. Yet, good gentlemen, hear me. I am sure the charge is false. If my dear daughter be slain, let him live, who is my life. Who are the parties in this cause? I make no complaint, and why then is he to be detained? Oh! set him at liberty.

SAMSTHĀNAKA. Shilence, you old fool! what have you to do with him?

JUDGE. Withdraw, lady. Officer, lead her forth.

MOTHER. My son, my dear son! [Is forced out.]

SAMSTHĀNAKA. I have done the bushness worthy of myshelf, and shall now depart.
    [Exit.]

JUDGE. Chārudatta, the business of proof it was ours to effect, the sentence rests with the prince. Officer, apprise the royal Pālaka, that the convicted culprit being a Brahman, he cannot according to Manu[31] be put to death, but he may be banished from the kingdom with his property untouched.

---

[31] Author of the Hindu code of laws.

OFFICER. I obey.

[*Goes out and returns.*]

I have been, and the king thus commands. Let the ornaments of Vasanta-senā be suspended to the neck of the criminal; let him be conducted by beat of drum to the southern cemetery, and there let him be impaled; that, by the severity of this punishment, men may be in future deterred from the commission of such atrocious acts.

CHĀRUDATTA. Unjust and inconsiderate monarch.

> 'Tis thus that evil councilors impel
> The heedless prince into the scorching flames
> Of fierce iniquity and foul disgrace;
> And countless victims perish by the guilt
> Of treacherous ministers, who thus involve
> Both prince and people in promiscuous ruin!
> My friend Maitreya, I bequeath to you
> My helpless family; befriend my wife,
> And be a second parent to my child.

MAITREYA. Alas! when the root is destroyed, how can the tree remain?

CHĀRUDATTA. Not so; a father lives beyond his death

> And in his son survives; 'tis meet my boy
> Enjoy that friendship which thou show'dst his sire.

MAITREYA. You have ever been most dear to me, most excellent Chārudatta; I cannot cherish life deprived of you.

CHĀRUDATTA. Bring my boy to me.

MAITREYA. That shall be done.

JUDGE. Officer, lead him forth. Who waits there? Let the executioners be called.

[*Exit with Court.*]

OFFICER. This way.

CHĀRUDATTA. Alas, my poor friend!

> Had due investigation been allowed me,
> Or any test proposed—water or poison,
> The scales or scorching fire, and I had failed
> The proof, then might the law have been fulfilled,
> And I deservedly received my doom.
> But this will be avenged: and for the sentence
> That dooms a Brahman's death on the mere charge
> Of a malicious foe, the bitter portion
> That waits for thee, and all thy line, O king,
> Is hell. Proceed—I am prepared.

[*Exeunt.*]

ACT TEN

The Road to the Place of Execution.

[*Enter* CHĀRUDATTA *with two* EXECUTIONERS.]

FIRST EXECUTIONER. Out of the way, sirs! out of the way! room for Chārudatta. Adorned with the oleander garland, and attended by his dexterous
executioners, he approaches his end like a lamp ill-fed with oil.

CHĀRUDATTA. Sepulchral blossoms decorate my limbs,
  Covered with dust, and watered by my tears,
  And round me harshly croak the carrion birds,
  Impatient to enjoy their promised prey.

SECOND EXECUTIONER. Out of the way, sirs! what do you stare at? A good
man whose head is to be chopped off by the axe of destiny? A tree that
gave shelter to gentle birds to be cut down? Come on, Chārudatta.

CHĀRUDATTA. Who can foresee the strange vicissitudes
  Of man's sad destiny?—I little thought
  That such a fate would ever be my portion,
  Nor could have credited I should live to be
  Dragged like a beast to public sacrifice,
  Stained with the ruddy sandal spots and smeared
  With meal—a victim to the sable goddess.
  Yet as I pass along, my fellow-citizens
  Console me with their tears, and execrate
  The cruel sentence that decrees my death.
  Unable to preserve my life, they pray
  That heaven await me, and reward my sufferings.

FIRST EXECUTIONER. Stand out of the way—what crowd you to see? There
are four things not to be looked at: Indra carried forth,[32] the birth of a
calf, the transit of a star, and the misfortune of a good man. Look,
brother Ahinta; the whole city is under sentence!—What! does the sky
weep, or the thunderbolt fall without a cloud?

SECOND EXECUTIONER. No, brother Goha, not so; the shower falls from
yonder cloud of women; yet though all the people weep, yet such is the
throng, that their tears cannot lay the dust.

CHĀRUDATTA. From every window lovely faces shed
  The kindly drops, and bathe me with their tears.

FIRST EXECUTIONER. Here stop! strike the drum, and cry the sentence.—
Hear ye, hear ye! This is Chārudatta, son of Sāgaradatta, son of Provost
Vinayadatta, by whom the courtesan Vasantasenā has been robbed
and murdered; he has been convicted and condemned, and we are
ordered by King Pālaka to put him to death: so will his majesty ever

---

[32] i.e., lightning.

punish those that commit such crimes as both worlds abhor.

CHĀRUDATTA. Dreadful reverse—to hear such wretches herald
    My death, and blacken thus with lies my fame:
    Not so, my sires—for them the frequent shout
    Has filled the sacred temple, where the crowd
    Of holy Brahmans to the gods proclaimed
    The costly rite accomplished: and shall I,
    Alas! Vasantasenā, who have drunk
    Thy nectared tones from lips whose ruby glow
    Disgraced the coral, and displayed the charms
    Of teeth more pearly than the moon's chaste light,
    Profane my ears with such envenomed draughts
    Of infamy whilst yet my soul is free?

[*Puts his hands to his ears.*]

FIRST EXECUTIONER. Stand apart there—make way!

CHĀRUDATTA. My friends avoid me as I pass, and, hiding
    Their faces with their raiment, turn away.
    Whilst fortune smiles each stranger is a friend,
    But friends are strangers in adversity.

FIRST EXECUTIONER. The road is now tolerably clear,—bring along the culprit.

VOICE BEHIND THE SCENE. Father! father!
    My friend! my friend!

CHĀRUDATTA. My worthy friends, grant me this one indulgence.

FIRST EXECUTIONER. What! will you condescend to take anything of us?

CHĀRUDATTA. Disdain not my request. Though basely born,
    You are not cruel, and a gentle nature
    Ranks you above your sovereign. I implore you,
    By all your future hopes, oh once permit me
    To view my son, ere I depart to death!

FIRST EXECUTIONER. Let him come.—Men, stand back, and let the child approach: here, this way.

[*Enter* MAITREYA *with* ROHASENA.]

MAITREYA. Here we have him, boy, once more; your dear father, who is going to be murdered.

ROHASENA. Father! father!

CHĀRUDATTA. Come hither, my dear child.

[*Embraces him and takes his hands.*]

    These little hands will ill-suffice to sprinkle
    The last sad drops upon my funeral pyre.
    Scant will my spirit sip thy love, and then
    A long and painful thirst in heaven succeeds.
    What sad memorial shall I leave thee, boy,
    To speak to thee hereafter of thy father?
    This sacred cord, whilst yet 'tis mine, I give thee.

The Brahman's proudest decoration, boy,
Is not of gold nor gems; but this by which
He ministers to sages and to gods.
This grace my child when I shall be no more.
[*Takes off his Brahmanical cord and puts it round his son's neck.*]

FIRST EXECUTIONER. Come, you Chārudatta, come along.

SECOND EXECUTIONER. More respect, my master; recollect, by night or day, in adversity or prosperity, fate holds its course, and puts men to trial. Come, sir; complaints are unavailing; and it is not to be expected that men will honor the moon when Rahu, the dragon, has hold of him.

ROHASENA. Where do you lead my father, vile executioner?

CHĀRUDATTA. I go to death, my child; the fatal chaplet
Of oleander hangs around my neck;
The stake upon my shoulder rests, my heart
Is burdened with despair, as, like a victim
Dressed for the sacrifice, I meet my fate.

FIRST EXECUTIONER. Hark ye, my boy: they who are born executioners are not the only ones; they who oppress the virtuous are executioners too.

ROHASENA. Why, then, want to kill my father?

FIRST EXECUTIONER. The king orders us; it is his fault, not ours.

ROHASENA. Take and kill me; let my father go.

FIRST EXECUTIONER. My brave little fellow, long life to you!

CHĀRUDATTA [*embracing him*]. This is the truest wealth; love equal
            smiles
On poor and rich; the bosom's precious balm
Is not the fragrant herb, nor costly unguent—
But nature's breath, affection's holy perfume.

MAITREYA. Come now, my good fellows, let my worthy friend escape: you only want a body,—mine is at your disposal.

CHĀRUDATTA. Forbear, forbear!

FIRST EXECUTIONER. Come on! stand off! what do you throng to see? a good man who has lost his all and fallen into despair, like a gold bucket whose rope breaks and it tumbles into the well.

SECOND EXECUTIONER. Here stop: beat the drum, and proclaim the sentence.
[*The* FIRST EXECUTIONER *does so.*]

CHĀRUDATTA. This is the heaviest pang of all; to think
Such bitter fruit attends my closing life.
And oh! what anguish, love, to hear the calumny,
Thus noised abroad, that thou wast slain by me!
[*Exeunt.*]

A room in the Palace.

[STHĀVARAKA *discovered above, bound, listening to the drum and proclamation.*]

STHĀVARAKA. How! the innocent Chārudatta to be executed, and I in chains still! I may be heard. What ho there! friends, hear me:—it was I, sinner that I am, who drove Vasantasenā to the royal garden. There my master met us, and finding her deaf to his wishes, with his own hands strangled her. He is the murderer, not this worthy man.—They cannot hear me: I am too far off. Cannot I leap down?—it shall be so; better any chance than that Chārudatta should suffer. I can get out of this window and spring from the balcony: better I perish than Chārudatta, and if I die, heaven is my reward. [*Jumps down.*] I am not hurt, and fortunately my chain has snapped. Now, whence comes the cry of the executioners:—ha! yonder,—I will overtake them. What ho there, stop! [*Exit.*]

The road.

[*Enter* CHĀRUDATTA *as before—to them* STHĀVARAKA.]

STHĀVARAKA. What ho, stop!

FIRST EXECUTIONER. Who calls to us to stop?

STHĀVARAKA. Hear me; Chārudatta is innocent. I took Vasantasenā to the garden, where my master strangled her with his own hands.

CHĀRUDATTA. Who comes rejoicing thus my latest hours,
　　To snatch me from the galling bonds of fate?
　　Like the full cloud, distent with friendly showers,
　　That timely hangs to save the dropping grain?
　　Heard you the words?—my fame again is clear.
　　My death I heeded not, I feared disgrace.
　　Death without shame is welcome as the babe
　　New-born. I perish now by hate
　　I ne'er provoked; by ignorance and malice—
　　I fall the mark of arrows dipped in venom,
　　And aimed at me by infamy and guilt.

FIRST EXECUTIONER. Hark ye, Sthāvaraka,—do you speak the truth?

STHĀVARAKA. I do; and would have ere now proclaimed it: for fear of that I was chained, and shut up in one of the rooms of the palace.

[*Enter* SAMSTHĀNAKA (*above*).]

SAMSTHĀNAKA. I have had a mosht shumptuous regale in the palashe here: rishe, with ashid shauce, and meat, and fish, and vegetables, and shweetmeats. What shounds were thoshe I heard? The Executioner's voishe, ash harsh ash a cracked bell, and the beat of the death-drum; the beggar Chārudatta is going to execution. The deshtruction of an enemy ish a banquet to the heart. I have heard, too, that whoever looks upon the death of an advershary will never have bad eyes in his next birth. I will ashcend the terrace of my palashe and contemplate my triumph. [*Ascends.*] What a crowd hash collected to shee the execution of this misherable wretch! If sho many flock to shee him; what a concourshe there would be to behold a great man like myshelf put to death!

He is dreshed like a young shteer. They are taking him to the shouth.
What brings them thish way, and why sheases the noishe? [*Looks into
the chamber.*] Hey! where is the shlave Sthāvaraka? He hash made his
eshcape!—all my schemes will be ruined!—I must sheek him. [*Descends.*]

STHĀVARAKA. Here comes my master.

FIRST EXECUTIONER. Out of the way there! make room! Here he comes,
like a mad ox, butting with the sharp horn of arrogance.

SAMSTHĀNAKA. Room, room here! My boy Sthāvaraka, come you along
with me.

STHĀVARAKA. What, sir! are you not satisfied with having murdered
Vasantasenā, that you now endeavor to compass the death of the
excellent Chārudatta?

SAMSTHĀNAKA. I,—I,—a veshel of rich jewels, I murder a woman!

CROWD. Yes, yes, you murdered her; not Chārudatta.

SAMSTHĀNAKA. Who says so?

CROWD. This honest man.

SAMSTHĀNAKA. Sthāvaraka, my shervant. [*Apart.*] He ish the only witnesh
of my guilt. I have ill-shecured him. It shall be sho. [*Aloud.*] Hear ye,
my masters: this is my shlave; he ish a thief, and for theft I punished
and confined him: he owes me a grudge for thish, and hash made up
thish shtory to be revenged. Confesh [*to* STHĀVARAKA], ish it not so?
[*Approaches and in an undertone.*] Take thish; [*offers him a bracelet*] it
is yours;—recall your words.

STHĀVARAKA [*takes the bracelet and holds it up*]. See here, my friends,
he bribes me even now, to silence!

SAMSTHĀNAKA [*snatches the bracelet*]. Thish ish it; the very ornament I
punished him for shtealing; look here, Executioners: for pilfering from
my treasury, which was under his charge, I had him whipped; if you
doubt me, look at his back.

FIRST EXECUTIONER. It is very true; and a scorched slave will set anything
on fire.

STHĀVARAKA. Alas! this is the curse of slavery, to be disbelieved even
when we speak the truth. Worthy Chārudatta, I can do no more. [*Falls
at his feet.*]

CHĀRUDATTA. Rise, thou who feelest for a good man's fall,
And com'st a virtuous friend to the afflicted.
Grieve not thy cares are vain. Whilst destiny
Forbids my liberation, all attempts
Like thine will profit nothing.

FIRST EXECUTIONER. As your honor has already chastised this slave, you
should let him go.

SAMSTHĀNAKA. Come, come. What ish thish delay, why do you not dishpatch
thish fellow?

FIRST EXECUTIONER. If you are in such haste, sir, you had better do it yourself.

ROHASENA. Kill me and let my father live.

SAMSTHĀNAKA. Kill both; father and shon perish together.

CHĀRUDATTA. All answers to his wish. Return, my child,
    Go to thy mother, and with her repair
    To some asylum, where thy father's fate
    Shall leave no stain on thee. My friend, conduct them
    Hence without delay.

MAITREYA. Think not, my dear friend, that I intend to survive you.

CHĀRUDATTA. My good Maitreya, the vital spirit owes not
    Obedience to our mortal will: beware
    How you presume to cast that life away:
    It is not thine to give or to abandon.

MAITREYA [apart]. It may not be right, but I cannot bear to live when he is
gone. I will take the boy to the Brahman's wife, and then follow my
friend. [Aloud.] Well, I obey; this task is easy.

[Falls at his feet, and rising, takes the child in his arms.]

SAMSTHĀNAKA. Holloa! did I not order you to put the boy to death along
with his father? [CHĀRUDATTA expresses alarm.]

FIRST EXECUTIONER. We have no such orders from the King—away, boy,
away.

[Forces off MAITREYA and ROHASENA.]

This is the third station, beat the drum, and proclaim the sentence.

[They proclaim the sentence again.]

SAMSTHĀNAKA [apart]. The people seem to dishbelieve the charge. [Aloud.]
Why, Chārudatta, the townshmen doubt all thish; be honesht; shay at
once, "I killed Vashantashenā." [CHĀRUDATTA continues silent.] Ho!
Executioner, this vile shinner ish dumb; make him shpeak: lay your
cane acrosh his back.

SECOND EXECUTIONER. Speak, Chārudatta. [Strikes him.]

CHĀRUDATTA. Strike! I fear not blows; in sorrow plunged,
    Think you such lesser ills can shake my bosom?
    Alone I feel the flame of men's reports,
    The foul assertion that I slew my love.

SAMSTHĀNAKA. Confesh, confesh!

CHĀRUDATTA. My friends and fellow-citizens, ye know me.

SAMSTHĀNAKA. She is murdered.

CHĀRUDATTA. Be it so.

FIRST EXECUTIONER. Come; the execution is your duty.

SECOND EXECUTIONER. No; it is yours.

FIRST EXECUTIONER. Let us reckon. [They count.][33] Now, if it be my turn,
    I shall delay it as long as I can.

SECOND EXECUTIONER. Why?

---

[33] The stage direction in the Sanskrit text indicates that they write or make
marks for a long time before speaking.

FIRST EXECUTIONER. I will tell you:— my father, when about to depart to
heaven, said to me, "Son, whenever you have a culprit to execute,
proceed deliberately; never do your work in a hurry; for, perhaps,
some worthy character may purchase the criminal's liberation; perhaps
a son may be born to the King, and a general pardon be proclaimed;
perhaps an elephant may break loose and the prisoner escape in the
confusion; or, perhaps, a change of rulers may take place, and every one
in bondage be set at large."

SAMSTHĀNAKA [apart]. A change of rulers!

FIRST EXECUTIONER. Come, let us finish our reckoning.

SAMSTHĀNAKA. Be quick, be quick! get rid of your prishoner.
[Retires.]

FIRST EXECUTIONER. Worthy Chārudatta, we but discharge our duty; the
king is culpable, not we, who must obey his orders: consider—have you
anything to say?

CHĀRUDATTA. If virtue yet prevail, may she who dwells
    Amongst the blest above, or breathes on earth,
    Clear my fair fame from the disastrous spots
    Unfriendly fate and man's accusing tongue
    Have fixed upon me—whither do you lead me?

FIRST EXECUTIONER. Behold the place, the southern cemetery, where
criminals quickly get rid of life. See, where jackals feast upon one half
of the mangled body, whilst the other yet grins ghastly on the pointed
stake!

CHĀRUDATTA. Alas, my fate! [Sits down.]

SAMSTHĀNAKA. I shall not go till I have sheen his death. How—sheated!

FIRST EXECUTIONER. What! are you afraid, Chārudatta?

CHĀRUDATTA [rising]. Of infamy I am, but not of death.

FIRST EXECUTIONER. Worthy sir, in heaven itself the sun and moon are not
free from change and suffering: how should we, poor weak mortals,
hope to escape them in this lower world: one man rises but to fall,
another falls to rise again; and the vesture of the carcass is at one time
laid aside, and at another resumed: think of these things, and be firm.
This is the fourth station: proclaim the sentence. [Proclamation as before.]
[Enter the MONK and VASANTASENĀ.]

MONK. Bless me, what shall I do? Thus leading Vasantasenā, am I acting
conformably to the laws of my order? Lady, whither shall I conduct
you?

VASANTASENĀ. To the house of Chārudatta, my good friend;
    His sight will bring me back to life, as the bright moon
    Revives the leaflets of the drooping flower.

MONK. Let us get into the high road: here it is. Hey! what noise is this?

VASANTASENĀ. And what a crowd is here!—inquire the cause;
    For all Ujjayin is gathered on one spot,
    And earth is off its balance with the load.

FIRST EXECUTIONER. This is the last station: proclaim the sentence. [*Proclamation as before.*] Now, Chārudatta, forgive us; all will soon be over.

CHĀRUDATTA. The gods are mighty.

MONK. Lady! lady! they say here you have been murdered by Chārudatta, and they are therefore going to put him to death.

VASANTASENĀ. Unhappy wretch! that I should be the cause
Of so much danger to my Chārudatta.
Quick! lead me to him.

MONK. Quick, lady; worthy servant of Buddha, hasten to save Chārudatta. Room, good friends; make way.

VASANTASENĀ. Room! room! [*Pressing through the crowd.*]

FIRST EXECUTIONER. Remember, worthy Chārudatta, we but obey the king's commands; the sin is his, not ours.

CHĀRUDATTA. Enough! perform your office.

FIRST EXECUTIONER [*draws his sword*]. Stand straight, your face upward, and one blow sends you to heaven.

[CHĀRUDATTA *obeys, the* FIRST EXECUTIONER *goes to strike, and drops his sword.*]
How? I held the hilt firmly in my grasp! Yet the sword, as unerring as a thunderbolt, has fallen on the ground! Chārudatta will escape; it is a sure sign. Goddess of the Sahya hills, be pleased to hear me! If Chārudatta be yet set free, the greatest favor will be conferred upon the whole caste of Executioners.

SECOND EXECUTIONER. Come, let us do as we are ordered.

FIRST EXECUTIONER. Be it so.

[*They are leading* CHĀRUDATTA *to the stake, when* VASANTASENĀ *rushes through the crowd.*]

VASANTASENĀ. Forbear, forbear! in me behold the wretch
For whom he dies!

FIRST EXECUTIONER. Hey! who is this that with disheveled locks and uplifted arms calls us to forbear?

VASANTASENĀ. Is it not true, dear, dearest Chārudatta? [*Throws herself on his bosom.*]

MONK. Is it not true, respected Chārudatta? [*Falls at his feet.*]

FIRST EXECUTIONER. Vasantasenā! The innocent must not perish by our hands.

MONK. He lives! Chārudatta lives!

FIRST EXECUTIONER. May he live a hundred years!

VASANTASENĀ. I revive.

FIRST EXECUTIONER. Away! bear the news to the king; he is at the public place of sacrifice.

[*Some go out.*]

SAMSTHĀNAKA [*seeing* VASANTASENĀ]. Alive shtill! Who hash done thish? I am not shafe here, and musht fly.

[*Exit.*]

FIRST EXECUTIONER [*to the other*]. Hark ye, brother, we were ordered to
  put to death the murderer of Vasantasenā: we had better therefore
  secure the king's brother-in-law.
SECOND EXECUTIONER. Agreed; let's follow him.
  [*Exeunt.*]
CHĀRUDATTA. Who thus, like showers to dying grain, has come
      To snatch me from the uplifted sword and face
      Of present death? Vasantasenā,
      Can this be she? or has another form
      Like hers from heaven descended to my succor?
      Am I awake, or do my senses wander—
      Is my Vasantasenā still alive?
      Speeds she from spheres divine, in earthly charms
      Arrayed again, to save the life she loved,
      Or comes some goddess in her beauteous likeness?
VASANTASENĀ [*falls at his feet*]. You see herself, the guilty cause that
          brought
      This sad reverse upon thy honored course.
CHĀRUDATTA [*taking her up and looking at her*]. My love, Vasantasenā,
      is it thou?
VASANTASENĀ. That ill-starred wretch.
CHĀRUDATTA. Vasantasenā—can it— can it be?
      And why these starting tears?—Away with grief!
      Didst thou not come, and like the wondrous spell
      That brings back life to its deserted source,
      Redeem triumphant from the grasp of death
      This frame to be henceforward all thine own?
      Such is the force of love omnipotent,
      Who calls the very dead to life again!
      Behold, my sweet, these emblems, that so late
      Denoted shame and death, shall now proclaim
      A different tale, and speak our nuptial joy—
      This crimson vesture be the bridegroom's garb,
      This garland be the bride's delightful present,
      And this brisk drum shall change its mournful sounds
      To cheerful tones of marriage celebration.
VASANTASENĀ. Ingenious ever is my lord's device.
CHĀRUDATTA. Thy plotted death, dear girl, was my sad doing.
      The king's brother has been long my foe;
      And in his hate, which future doom will punish,
      He sought, and partly worked his will, my fall.
VASANTASENĀ. Forbear, nor utter such ill-omened words.
      By him, and him alone, my death was purposed.
CHĀRUDATTA. And who is this?
VASANTASENĀ. To him I owe my life:

His seasonable aid preserved me.

CHĀRUDATTA. Who art thou, friend?

MONK. Your honor does not recollect me. I was employed as your personal servant: afterward becoming connected with gamblers, and unfortunate, I should have been reduced to slavery, had not this lady redeemed me. I have since then adopted the life of a monk; and coming in my wanderings to the king's garden, was fortunately enabled to assist my former benefactress.

VOICES BEHIND THE SCENE. Victory to Shiva, the despoiler of Daksha's sacrifice! Glory to the six-faced scatterer of armies, the foe of Krauncha! Victory to Āryaka, the subjugator of his adversaries, and triumphant monarch of the widespread mountain-bannered earth!

[*Enter* SHARVILAKA.]

SHARVILAKA. This hand has slain the king, and on the throne
    Of Pālaka ascends our valiant chief,
    Resistless Āryaka, in haste anointed.
    Now to obey his first commands, and raise
    The worthy Chārudatta far above
    Calamity and fear. All is achieved—
    Of valor and of conduct destitute
    The foe has fallen— the citizens behold
    Well pleased the change, and thus has noble daring
    Wrested an empire from its ancient lords,
    And won a sway as absolute on earth
    As that which Indra proudly holds in heaven.
    This is the spot;—he must be near at hand
    By this assemblage of the people. Well begins
    The reign of Āryaka, if his first cares
    Reap the rich fruit of Chārudatta's life.
    Give way, and let me pass; 'tis he!—he lives!—
    Vasantasenā too!—my monarch's wish
    Is all accomplished. Long this generous Brahman
    Has mourned his sullied brightness like the moon
    That labors in eclipse, but now he bounds
    Again to honor and to happiness,
    Borne safely o'er a boundless sea of troubles
    By firm affection's bark, and favoring fate.
    How shall I, sinner as I am, approach
    Such lofty merit; yet the honest purpose
    Is everywhere a passport. Chārudatta,
    Hail, most worthy sir!

[*Joins his hands and raises them to his forehead.*]

CHĀRUDATTA. Who thus addresses me?

SHARVILAKA. In me behold
    The plunderer, that desperate forced his way

By night into your mansion, and bore off
The pledge entrusted to your care: I come
To own my fault and throw me on your mercy.
CHĀRUDATTA. Not so, my friend, you may demand my thanks.
[*Embraces him.*]
SHARVILAKA. And further I inform you, that the king,
The unjust Pālaka, has fallen a victim,
Here in the place of sacrifice, to one
Who has avenged his wrongs and thine; to Āryaka,
Who ready homage pays to birth and virtue.
CHĀRUDATTA. How say you?
SHARVILAKA. That the fugitive,
Whom late your car conveyed in safety hence,
Has now returned, and in the place of offering
Slain Pālaka as a victim.
CHĀRUDATTA. I rejoice
In his success—it was to you he owed
Escape from his confinement.
SHARVILAKA. But to you
Escape from death; and to requite his debt
He gives to your authority in Ujjayin,
Along the Venā's banks, Kusāvatī—
A proof of his esteem and gratitude.
VOICES BEHIND THE SCENE. Bring him along! bring him along! the king's
villainous brother-in-law.
[SAMSTHĀNAKA, *his arms tied behind him, dragged on by the mob.*]
SAMSTHĀNAKA. Alas, alas! how am I maltreated: bound and dragged along
ash if I were a reshtive ash, or a dog, or any brute beasht. I am beshet
by the enemies of the shtate; whom can I fly to for protection?—yesh,
I will have recourshe to him.
[*Approaches* CHĀRUDATTA.]
Presherve me. [*Falls at his feet.*]
VOICES BEHIND THE SCENE. Let him alone, Chārudatta; leave him to us;
we'll dispatch him.
SAMSTHĀNAKA. Oh, pray Chārudatta! I am helplesh, I have no hope but
you.
CHĀRUDATTA. Banish your terror: they that sue for mercy
Have nothing from their foes to dread.
SHARVILAKA. Hence with the wretch!
Drag him from Chārudatta. Worthy sir,
Why spare this villain? Bind him, do you hear,
And cast him to the dogs; saw him asunder;
Or hoist him on the stake: dispatch, away.
CHĀRUDATTA. Hold, hold! may I be heard?
SHARVILAKA. Assuredly.

SAMSTHĀNAKA. Mosht excellent Chārudatta, I have flown to you for refuge; oh, protect me! shpare me now, I will never sheek your harm any more.

VOICES BEHIND THE SCENE. Kill him, kill him! why should such a wretch be suffered to live?

[VASANTASENĀ *takes the garland off* CHĀRUDATTA'S *neck, and throws it round* SAMSTHĀNAKA'S.]

SAMSTHĀNAKA. Gentle daughter of a courtesan, have pity upon me: I will never kill you again, never, never!

SHARVILAKA. Give your commands, sirs, that he may be removed, and how we shall dispose of him.

CHĀRUDATTA. Will you obey in what I shall enjoin?

SHARVILAKA. Be sure of it.

CHĀRUDATTA. In truth?

SHARVILAKA. In very truth.

CHĀRUDATTA. Then for the prisoner—

SHARVILAKA. Kill him.

CHĀRUDATTA. Set him free.

SHARVILAKA. Why so?

CHĀRUDATTA. An humbled foe, who prostrate at your feet
Solicits quarter, must not feel your sword.

SHARVILAKA. Admit the law, then give him to the dogs.

CHĀRUDATTA. Not so!
His punishment be mercy.

SHARVILAKA. You move my wonder, but shall be obeyed.
What is your pleasure?

CHĀRUDATTA. Loose him, and let him go.

SHARVILAKA. He is at liberty. [*Unties him.*]

SAMSTHĀNAKA. Huzza! I am again alive.

VOICES BEHIND THE SCENE. Alas, alas! the noble wife of Chārudatta, with her child vainly clinging to her raiment, seeks to enter the fatal fire, in spite of the entreaties of the weeping crowd.

[*Enter* CHANDANAKA.]

SHARVILAKA. How now, Chandanaka, what has chanced?

CHANDANAKA. Does not your excellency see yon crowd collected on the south of the royal palace? There the wife of Chārudatta is about to commit herself to the flames; I delayed the deed by assuring her that Chārudatta was safe;—but who in the agonies of despair is susceptible of consolation or confidence?

CHĀRUDATTA. Alas! my love, what frantic thought is this!
Although thy widowed virtues might disdain
The abject earth, yet, when to heaven transported,
What happiness canst thou enjoy, whilst yet
The husband's presence fails his faithful bride. [*Faints.*]

SHARVILAKA. Out on this folly! we should fly to save

The dame, and he is senseless—all conspires
To snatch from our exertions this reward.

VASANTASENĀ. Dear Chārudatta, rouse thy fainting soul;
Haste to preserve her; want not firmness now,
Or all is unavailing.

CHĀRUDATTA. Where is she?
Speak love! where art thou?—answer to my call.

CHANDANAKA. This way, this way!

[Exeunt.]

Chārudatta's house (exterior).

[Enter the WIFE of Chārudatta, ROHASENA holding her garment,
MAITREYA and RADANIKĀ.—The fire kindled.]

WIFE. Loose me, my child! oppose not my desires,
I cannot live and hear my lord defamed.

ROHASENA. Hold! my dear mother; think of me your child;
How shall I learn to live, deprived of you?

MAITREYA. Lady, forbear! your purpose is a crime:—our holy laws declare
it sinful for a Brahman's wife to mount a separate pile.

WIFE. Better I sin than hear my husband's shame—
Remove my boy; he keeps me from the flames.

RADANIKĀ. Nay, madam; I would rather give him help.

MAITREYA. Excuse me: if you determine to perish, you must give me
precedence; it is a Brahman's duty to consecrate a funeral fire.

WIFE. What! neither listen to me! My dear child,
Remain to offer to your helpless parents
The sacred rites they claim from filial duty.
Alas! you know no more a father's care.

CHĀRUDATTA [coming forward and taking his child in his arms]. His father
still will guard him.

WIFE. His voice! his form!—it is my lord, my love!

ROHASENA. My father holds me in his arms again! Now, mother, you are
happy.

CHĀRUDATTA [embraces his WIFE]. My dearest love, what frenzy drove
thy mind
To seek destruction whilst thy lord survived?
Whilst yet the sun rides bright along the sky
The lotus closes not its amorous leaves.

WIFE. True, my loved lord; but then his glowing kisses
Give her glad consciousness her love is present.

MAITREYA. And do these eyes really see my dear friend once more?
The wonderful effect of a virtuous wife! Her purpose of entering the fire
has reunited her with her lord. Long life to Chārudatta.

CHĀRUDATTA. My dear, my faithful friend. [Embraces him.]

RADANIKĀ. Sir, I salute you. [*Falls at his feet.*]
CHĀRUDATTA. Rise, good Radanikā. [*Puts his hand upon her shoulder.*]
WIFE [*to* VASANTASENĀ]. Welcome, happy sister!
VASANTASENĀ. I now indeed am happy. [*They embrace.*]
SHARVILAKA. You are fortunate in your friends.
CHĀRUDATTA. To you I owe them.
SHARVILAKA. Lady Vasantasenā, with your worth
  The new king is well acquainted, and requests
  To hold you as his kinswoman.
VASANTASENĀ. Sir, I am grateful.
  [SHARVILAKA *throws a veil over her.*]34
SHARVILAKA. What shall we do for this good monk?
CHĀRUDATTA. Speak, Shramanaka, your wishes.
MONK. To follow still the path I have selected,
  For all I see is full of care and change.
CHĀRUDATTA. Since such is his resolve, let him be made
  Chief of the monasteries of the Buddhists.
SHARVILAKA. It shall be so.
MONK. It likes me well.
SHARVILAKA. Sthāvaraka remains to be rewarded.
CHĀRUDATTA. Let him be made a free man;—slave no more.
  For these Executioners let them be appointed
  Heads of their tribe; and to Chandanaka
  The power the king's brother-in-law abused
  To his own purposes, be now assigned.
SHARVILAKA. As you direct: is there ought else?—command.
CHĀRUDATTA. Nought but this.
  Since Āryaka enjoys the sovereign sway,
  And holds me as his friend;—since all my foes
  Are now destroyed, save one poor wretch released,
  To learn repentance for his former faults,
  Since my fair fame again is clear, and this
  Dear girl, my wife, and all I cherish most,
  Are mine once more, I have no further suit
  That asks for your indulgence, and no wish
  That is not gratified. Fate views the world
  A scene of mutual and perpetual struggle,
  And sports with life as if it were the wheel
  That draws the limpid waters from the well.
  For some are raised to affluence, some depressed
  In want, and some are borne a while aloft,
  And some hurled down to wretchedness and woe.

34 A token of honorable marriage. (Note from Arthur William Ryder (trans.),
The Little Clay Cart, Harvard University Press, 1905.)

Then let us all thus limit our desires:
Full-uddered be the kine; the soil be fertile;
May copious showers descend, and balmy gales
Breathe health and happiness on all mankind;
From pain be every living creature free,
And reverence on the pious Brahman wait;
And may all monarchs, prosperous and just,
Humble their foes and guard the world in peace.
[*Exeunt omnes.*]

ANONYMOUS

EVERYMAN

THE GREAT WORLD
THEATER

IN SHAKESPEARE'S *As You Like It*, a philosophical courtier sums up the state of man in a famous extended metaphor which begins:

> All the world's a stage
> And all the men and women merely players;
> They have their exits and their entrances;
> And one man in his time plays many parts.

The comparison recurs frequently in Shakespeare's works, not unexpectedly in a poet who gave his whole life to the theater. But it is a comparison that was widely used and antedates Shakespeare by some centuries. Indeed, the opening lines of the courtier's speech are but an English version of a Roman aphorism: *Totus mundus agit histrionem.* The idea that the world was a theater, or conversely that the theater was the world in little, is but an extension of the earlier concept of the dramatic action as a mirror of nature.

The fullest dramatic statement of the metaphor was made by the Spanish playwright, Calderón, in 1642. His *The Great World Theater* begins with a scene in which the Author (God) summons the World to him and announces his intention of staging a pageant which will display God's power and glory: "Know that Man's life is but a play from cradle to grave. Prepare, therefore, to perform the Play of Life, whose spectator shall be heaven. Thou, World, shall set the stage, I will the play direct, and men and women . . . shall be the actors in it."* The actors are then called and assigned

* Translated by M. H. Singleton.

244

their roles: Rich Man, Beggar, King, Husbandman, Beauty, Discretion, Infant. Not all the actors are content with their parts, and the Author attempts to mollify them. To the beggar he explains:

> Nor because more pain is laid
> Upon thee who beggar art
> Is the King's a better part
> Than the beggar's, if well played.
> One and other shall be paid
> Freely all their salary,
> When it once deserved shall be;
> And with any part it can
> Be so earned, the life of man
> Being all one comedy.*

The name of the play to be performed is *Act your Best, For God is God,* and the actors are cautioned that there can be no rehearsal, that they must take their cues from the Author, constantly bearing in mind that "life is only drama, the signs and symbols and reflections of some other life to come."

Preparations for the performance continue as the World gives to each actor the costume appropriate for his role.

KING. Crown and purple I demand.
WORLD. Why must crown and robe be thine?
KING. Even because this part is mine. [*He shows the page containing his speeches to the* WORLD.]
WORLD. 'Tis already furnished here. [*Gives the* KING *his costume.*]

The costume, that is, manifests the character, his status, his profession, his attitude. But the player—and the spectator—is reminded that the costume (and what it implies) so readily given and accepted can be as easily taken away.

The action of the little play is a series of moral and ethical debates conducted by paired opposites, King and Husbandman, Rich Man and Peasant, Beauty and Discretion. The Beggar tries to get alms from his fellow players but each, totally immersed in his character and concerns, spurns him. Then one by one they are summoned for their exits (deaths). The World begins collecting

* Translated by R. C. Trench.

the properties and costumes as the actors return to see if the World remembers their performances, but he replies: "World little heeds nor long remembers who men were." Rejected by the World, the actors turn to the Author who invites the entire company, except the Rich Man, to a banquet. The Rich Man is cast down into eternal fire, and the World addresses the audience in the actual theater:

> The World's a stage, and you have seen Life's play;
> Now with applauding hands, our fears allay.

The image of the world as a theater was peculiarly appropriate for a Christian audience, an audience constantly reminded of the transitory nature of the things of this earth, place, possessions, even personality, constantly admonished to look to the next world, and instructed that birth and death are but entrance and exit in a scene which is a prologue to the omen coming on (the phrase is the scholarly Horatio's in *Hamlet*). Only in Calderón is the idea developed so explicitly and extensively; but it would be difficult to find a play from the great repertory of the European Renaissance in which the metaphor was not at least implicit. The governor is "robed in a little brief authority," the villain must "act the part" of innocence, the seeker after justice must "play the antic." The earth is a "great stage of fools," an "insubstantial pageant." And from observing the player-kings and player-fools in this microcosm, this model of the great world, the spectator would come away enlightened about his own condition. In 1566 an English editor attempted to explain to his readers the function of the theater. A theater, he wrote, is a place

in which [the spectator] may contemplate and be advised of his infirmity and misery, and not withdrawn from himself, to this end that in making a view and review of all the parts of his life, he may thereby be moved to detest and abhor his vile nature.*

The primary function of the theatrical repertory which grew up in the Western world after 1000 A.D. was moral instruction. Entertainment, purification of emotions became secondary, and the spectator is constantly reminded by the dramatic experience that he should consider his own end.

* J. Alday, *The Theater or Rule of the World.*

Calderón achieves his purpose by the way of *allegory*, a dramatic pattern in which the moral meaning is uppermost. It is quite possible for the spectator to attend a performance, of *The Toy Cart* for instance, which excites and gives pleasure without demanding constant conscious appraisal on his part. Allegory, however, requires the spectator to be instantly and continuously aware of the abstract idea being bodied forth by the actors and their action. It is a form similar to the parable, the fable, the political cartoon where the stated moral or clarifying labels are essential in carrying the work to completion. Because the roles are played by dimensional human beings the abstract qualities (Beauty, Discretion) in Calderón's play may evoke the same sympathetic response as Chārudatta and Vasantasenā, but the playwright is interested in their quality rather than in their concrete personality.

For instance, in the mid-section of *The Great World Theater*, Beauty and Discretion enter, arguing. We may imagine the one as a young girl brightly dressed, the other an ascetic monklike young man. But their argument is wholly moral. Beauty tries to persuade her companion to sport in the meadow, but Discretion holds back:

> I abandon not my cloister,
> Having this religion chose
> To entomb my life, and thus
> That I am Discretion show.
> BEAUTY. I that am Beauty, while
> To be seen and see I go. [*They part.*]

Whereupon World comments that Beauty and Discretion have never maintained a stable relationship.

Allegory, in so pure a state, is rather out of fashion in the twentieth century, but it has provided a medium for writers as diverse as Dante and John Bunyan, and in the decades when the modern drama was developing out of the Biblical playlets of the medieval church, it created a unique and widely influential theatrical form generally called the *morality play*.

The name is doubly significant. First, it proclaims that the playwright's purpose is didactic. In an age when the plurality of the audience was illiterate, drama was considered a medium of instruction, and the Morality was particularly effective because it presented abstract principles in human guise. More important, it revealed the possibility of *creating* a dramatic action, not, as hitherto, dramatizing a historical or Biblical event. The playwright was given a way to invent a hero and an opponent for the hero and to set them in a locale and an action which would have the same sense of truth as subjects taken from well-known stories. If we are not attracted by the direct statement of the allegorical method, we must not forget that it made possible the works of Marlowe, Shakespeare, Webster, and that it still underlies most of the dramatic repertory of the contemporary world.

Everyman (1475) is deservedly the most familiar of the morality plays. It exists both in Dutch and English, and no conclusive evidence has been found for the priority of either version. This in itself suggests the universality of the little play: it represents what was, for its time, truly a world-view. Indeed it would not be surprising if a German version were to be discovered.

The allegory in *Everyman* is arrived at by the simple device of equating the Last Judgment with an earthly trial. Divested of its religious metaphor the action is the realistic story of a steward who is commanded to appear before his master to give an account of his stewardship; he seeks character-witnesses and counselors, but finally realizes that the ultimate judgment upon him must be based on the records in his ledgers. The story ends as he throws himself on the mercy of the court.

It is, perhaps, not a very exciting or even illuminating story. However if the playwright calls the master God, the bailiff or summoner Death, and the hero Everyman, he is at least attempting to indicate the pertinence of his action to each individual playgoer. The refusal of Fellowship and Cousin to appear as character-witnesses, the retreat of Beauty, Strength, and Five-Wits, the counselors, as they come near the court, are actions intended to suggest to the playgoer that he should inquire into the conduct of his own life. When only Good-Deeds will pass through the door of the courthouse with Everyman, the lesson is finally completed: *Respice finem*, look upon thy end.

The morality play is a dramatized sermon, generally introduced and summed up by a "Doctor," that is to say, someone in holy orders. But, curiously enough, the morality play does not seem to have been performed in a church (*Everyman* is a possible exception). In the fifteenth and sixteenth centuries, the period of its greatest flourishing, the morality was the more or less exclusive property of touring professional actors, who played not for the glory of God, but for money. The fact is worth noting, for it requires us to acknowledge that allegory was a highly popular medium and the morality a widely successful popular form. Moral instruction disguised as common human experience had great appeal, possibly because it seemed to confirm in action what had been taught in principle. This, at least, was the element of the allegorical morality on which the great structure of Elizabethan drama was to be erected.

Characters

MESSENGER

EVERYMAN

GOD

DEATH

FELLOWSHIP

COUSIN

KINDRED

GOODS

GOOD-DEEDS

STRENGTH

DISCRETION

FIVE-WITS

BEAUTY

KNOWLEDGE

CONFESSION

ANGEL

DOCTOR

EVERYMAN

Anonymous

Here beginneth a treatise how the high father of Heaven sendeth death to summon every creature to come and give account of their lives in this world and is in manner of a moral play.

MESSENGER. I pray you all give your audience,
  And hear this matter with reverence,
  By figure a moral play—
  The *Summoning of Everyman* called it is,
  That of our lives and ending shows
  How transitory we be all day.
  This matter is wondrous precious,
  But the intent of it is more gracious,
  And sweet to bear away.
  The story saith,—Man, in the beginning,   10
  Look well, and take good heed to the ending,
  Be you never so gay!
  Ye think sin in the beginning full sweet,
  Which in the end causeth thy soul to weep,
  When the body lieth in clay.
  Here shall you see how Fellowship and Jollity,
  Both Strength, Pleasure, and Beauty,
  Will fade from thee as flowers in May.
  For ye shall hear, how our Heaven King
  Calleth Everyman to a general reckoning: 20
  Give audience, and hear what he doth say.
GOD. I perceive here in my majesty,
  How that all creatures be to me unkind,
  Living without dread in worldly prosperity:
  Of ghostly sight the people be so blind,
  Drowned in sin, they know me not for their God;
  In worldly riches is all their mind,
  They fear not my rightwiseness, the sharp rod;
  My law that I showed, when I for them died,
  They forget clean, and shedding of my blood red;   30

I hanged between two, it cannot be denied;
To get them life I suffered to be dead;
I healed their feet, with thorns hurt was my head:
I could do no more than I did truly,
And now I see the people do clean forsake me.
They use the seven deadly sins damnable;
As pride, covetize, wrath, and lechery,
Now in the world be made commendable;
And thus they leave of angels the heavenly company;
Everyman liveth so after his own pleasure,   10
And yet of their life they be nothing sure:
I see the more that I them forbear
The worse they be from year to year;
All that liveth appeareth fast,
Therefore I will in all the haste
Have a reckoning of Everyman's person
For and I leave the people thus alone
In their life and wicked tempests,
Verily they will become much worse than beasts;
For now one would by envy another up eat;   20
Charity they all do clean forget.
I hoped well that Everyman
In my glory should make his mansion,
And thereto I had them all elect;
But now I see, like traitors deject,
They thank me not for the pleasure that I to them meant,
Nor yet for their being that I them have lent;
I proffered the people great multitude of mercy,
And few there be that asketh it heartily;
They be so cumbered with worldly riches,   30
That needs on them I must do justice,
On Everyman living without fear.
Where art thou, Death, thou mighty messenger?

DEATH. Almighty God, I am here at your will,
          Your commandment to fulfil.

GOD. Go thou to Everyman,
          And show him in my name
          A pilgrimage he must on him take,
          Which he in no wise may escape;
          And that he bring with him a sure reckoning   40
          Without delay or any tarrying.

DEATH. Lord, I will in the world go run over all,
          And cruelly outsearch both great and small;
          Every man will I beset that liveth beastly
          Out of God's laws, and dreadeth not folly:

He that loveth riches I will strike with my dart,
His sight to blind, and from heaven to depart,
Except that alms be his good friend,
In hell for to dwell, world without end.
Lo, yonder I see Everyman walking;
Full little he thinketh on my coming;
His mind is on fleshly lusts and his treasure,
And great pain it shall cause him to endure
Before the Lord Heaven King.
Everyman, stand still; whither art thou going   10
Thus gaily? Hast thou thy Maker forgot?

EVERYMAN. Why askest thou?
Wouldest thou wot?

DEATH. Yea, sir, I will show you;
In great haste I am sent to thee
From God out of his majesty.

EVERYMAN. What, sent to me?

DEATH. Yea, certainly.
Though thou have forgot him here,
He thinketh on thee in the heavenly sphere,   20
As, or we depart, thou shalt know.

EVERYMAN. What desireth God of me?

DEATH. That shall I show thee;
A reckoning he will needs have
Without any longer respite.

EVERYMAN. To give a reckoning longer leisure I crave;
This blind matter troubleth my wit.

DEATH. On thee thou must take a long journey:
Therefore thy book of count with thee thou bring;
For turn again thou can not by no way,   30
And look thou be sure of thy reckoning:
For before God thou shalt answer, and show
Thy many bad deeds and good but a few;
How thou hast spent thy life, and in what wise,
Before the chief lord of paradise.
Have ado that we were in that way,
For, wote thou well, thou shalt make none attorney.

EVERYMAN. Full unready I am such reckoning to give.
I know thee not: what messenger art thou?

DEATH. I am Death, that no man dreadeth.   40
For every man I rest and no man spareth;
For it is God's commandment
That all to me should be obedient.

EVERYMAN. O Death, thou comest when I had thee least in mind;
In thy power it lieth me to save,

Yet of my good will I give thee, if ye will be kind,
Yea, a thousand pound shalt thou have,
And defer this matter till another day.
DEATH. Everyman, it may not be by no way;
    I set not by gold, silver, nor riches,
    Nor by pope, emperor, king, duke, nor princes.
    For and I would receive gifts great,
    All the world I might get;
    But my custom is clean contrary.
    I give thee no respite: come hence, and not tarry.   10
EVERYMAN. Alas, shall I have no longer respite?
    I may say Death giveth no warning:
    To think on thee, it maketh my heart sick,
    For all unready is my book of reckoning.
    But twelve year and I might have abiding,
    My counting book I would make so clear,
    That my reckoning I should not need to fear.
    Wherefore, Death, I pray thee, for God's mercy,
    Spare me till I be provided of remedy.
DEATH. Thee availeth not to cry, weep, and pray: 20
    But haste thee lightly that you were gone the journey,
    And prove thy friends if thou can.
    For, wot thou well, the tide abideth no man,
    And in the world each living creature
    For Adam's sin must die of nature.
EVERYMAN. Death, if I should this pilgrimage take,
    And my reckoning surely make,
    Show me, for Saint Charity,
    Should I not come again shortly?
DEATH. No, Everyman; and thou be once there,   30
    Thou mayest never come here,
    Trust me verily.
EVERYMAN. O gracious God, in the high seat celestial,
    Have mercy on me in this most need;
    Shall I have no company from this vale terrestrial
    Of mine acquaintance that way me to lead?
DEATH. Yea, if any be so hardy,
    That would go with thee and bear thee company.
    Hie thee that you were gone to God's magnificence,
    Thy reckoning to give before his presence.   40
    What, weenest thou thy life is given thee,
    And thy world goods also?
EVERYMAN. I had wend so, verily.
DEATH. Nay, nay; it was but lent thee;
    For as soon as thou art gone,

Another awhile shall have it, and then go therefrom
Even as thou hast done.
Everyman, thou art mad; thou hast thy wits five,
And here on earth will not amend thy life,
For suddenly I do come.

EVERYMAN. O wretched caitiff, whither shall I flee,
That I might scape this endless sorrow!
Now, gentle Death, spare me till tomorrow,
That I may amend me
With good advisement.   10

DEATH. Nay, thereto I will not consent,
Nor no man will I respite,
But to the heart suddenly I shall smite
Without any advisement.
And now out of thy sight I will me hie;
See thou make thee ready shortly,
For thou mayest say this is the day
That no man living may scape away.

EVERYMAN. Alas, I may well weep with sighs deep;
Now have I no manner of company   20
To help me in my journey, and me to keep;
And also my writing is full unready.
How shall I do now for to excuse me?
I would to God I had never been begot
To my soul a full great profit it had be;
For now I fear pains huge and great.
Time passeth; Lord, help that all wrought;
For though I mourn it availeth nought.
The day passeth, and is almost a-go;
I wot not well what for to do.   30
To whom were I best my complaint to make?
What and I to Fellowship thereof spake,
And showed him of this sudden chance?
For in him is all mine affiance;
We have in the world so many a day
Been good friends in sport and play.
I see him yonder, certainly;
I trust that he will bear me company;
Therefore to him will I speak to ease my sorrow.
Well met, good Fellowship, and good morrow!   40

FELLOWSHIP [speaketh]. Everyman, good morrow by this day.
Sir, why lookest thou so piteously?
If anything be amiss, I pray thee, me say,
That I may help to remedy.

EVERYMAN. Yea, good Fellowship, yea.

I am in great jeopardy.

FELLOWSHIP. My true friend, show to me your mind;
  I will not forsake thee, unto my life's end,
  In the way of good company.

EVERYMAN. That was well spoken, and lovingly.

FELLOWSHIP. Sir, I must needs know your heaviness;
  I have pity to see you in any distress;
  If any have you wronged ye shall revenged be,
  Though I on the ground be slain for thee,—
  Though that I know before that I should die.   10

EVERYMAN. Verily, Fellowship, gramercy.

FELLOWSHIP. Tush! by thy thanks I set not a straw.
  Show me your grief, and say no more.

EVERYMAN. If I my heart should to you break,
  And then you to turn your mind from me,
  And would not me comfort, when you hear me speak,
  Then should I ten times sorrier be.

FELLOWSHIP. Sir, I say as I will do in deed.

EVERYMAN. Then be you a good friend in need;
  I have found you true here before.   20

FELLOWSHIP. And so ye shall evermore;
  For, in faith, and thou go to Hell,
  I will not forsake thee by the way!

EVERYMAN. Ye speak like a good friend; I believe you well;
  I shall deserve it, and I may.

FELLOWSHIP. I speak of no deserving, by this day.
  For he that will say and nothing do
  Is not worthy with good company to go;
  Therefore show me the grief of your mind,
  As to your friend most loving and kind.   30

EVERYMAN. I shall show you how it is;
  Commanded I am to go a journey,
  A long way, hard and dangerous,
  And give a strait account without delay
  Before the high judge Adonai.
  Wherefore I pray you, bear me company,
  As ye have promised in, this journey.

FELLOWSHIP. That is matter indeed!
  Promise is duty,
  But, and I should take such a voyage on me,   40
  I know it well, it should be to my pain:
  Also it make me afeard, certain.
  But let us take counsel here as well as we can,
  For your words would fear a strong man.

EVERYMAN. Why, ye said, if I had need,

> Ye would me never forsake, quick nor dead,
> Though it were to hell truly.

FELLOWSHIP. So I said, certainly,
> But such pleasures be set aside, thee sooth to say:
> And also, if we took such a journey,
> When should we come again?

EVERYMAN. Nay, never again till the day of doom.

FELLOWSHIP. In faith, then will not I come there!
> Who hath you these tidings brought?

EVERYMAN. Indeed, Death was with me here.   10

FELLOWSHIP. Now, by God that all hath bought,
> If Death were the messenger,
> For no man that is living today
> I will not go that loath journey—
> Not for the father that begat me!

EVERYMAN. Ye promised other wise, pardie.

FELLOWSHIP. I wot well I said so truly;
> And yet if thou wilt eat, and drink, and make good cheer,
> Or haunt to women, the lusty company,
> I would not forsake you, while the day is clear,   20
> Trust me verily!

EVERYMAN. Yea, thereto ye would be ready;
> To go to mirth, solace, and play,
> Your mind will sooner apply
> Than to bear me company in my long journey.

FELLOWSHIP. Now, in good faith, I will not that way.
> But and thou wilt murder, or any man kill,
> In that I will help thee with a good will!

EVERYMAN. O that is a simple advice indeed!
> Gentle fellow, help me in my necessity;   30
> We have loved long, and now I need,
> And now, gentle Fellowship, remember me.

FELLOWSHIP. Whether ye have loved me or no,
> By Saint John, I will not with thee go.

EVERYMAN. Yet I pray thee, take the labor, and do so much for me
> To bring me forward, for Saint Charity,
> And comfort me till I come without the town.

FELLOWSHIP. Nay, and thou would give me a new gown,
> I will not a foot with thee go;
> But and you had tarried I would not have left thee so.   40
> And as now, God speed thee in thy journey,
> For from thee I will depart as fast as I may.

EVERYMAN. Whither away, Fellowship? will you forsake me?

FELLOWSHIP. Yea, by my fay, to God I betake thee.

EVERYMAN. Farewell, good Fellowship; for thee my heart is sore;

Adieu for ever, I shall see thee no more.
FELLOWSHIP. In faith, Everyman, farewell now at the end;
    For you I will remember that parting is mourning.
    [*Exit.*]
EVERYMAN. Alack! shall we thus depart indeed?
    Our Lady, help, without any more comfort,
    Lo, Fellowship forsaketh me in my most need:
    For help in this world whither shall I resort?
    Fellowship herebefore with me would merry make;
    And now little sorrow for me doth he take.
    It is said, in prosperity men friends may find,   10
    Which in adversity be full unkind.
    Now whither for succor shall I flee,
    Sith that Fellowship hath forsaken me?
    To my kinsmen I will truly,
    Praying them to help me in my necessity;
    I believe that they will do so,
    For kind will creep where it may not go.
    I will go say, for yonder I see them go.
    Where be ye now, my friends and kinsmen?
KINDRED. Here be we now at your commandment.   20
    Cousin, I pray you show us your intent
    In any wise, and not spare.
COUSIN. Yea, Everyman, and to us declare
    If ye be disposed to go any whither,
    For wot you well, we will live and die together.
KINDRED. In wealth and woe we will with you hold,
    For over his kin a man may be bold.
EVERYMAN. Gramercy, my friends and kinsmen kind.
    Now shall I show you the grief of my mind:
    I was commanded by a messenger,   30
    That is an high king's chief officer;
    He bade me go a pilgrimage to my pain,
    And I know well I shall never come again;
    Also I must give a reckoning straight,
    For I have a great enemy, that hath me in wait,
    Which intendeth me for to hinder.
KINDRED. What account is that which ye must render?
    That would I know.
EVERYMAN. Of all my works I must show
    How I have lived and my days spent;   40
    Also of ill deeds, that I have used
    In my time, sith life was me lent;
    And of all virtues that I have refused.
    Therefore I pray you go thither with me,

To help to make mine account, for Saint Charity.
COUSIN. What, to go thither? Is that the matter?
    Nay, Everyman, I had liefer fast bread and water
    All this five year and more.
EVERYMAN. Alas, that ever I was bore!
    For now shall I never be merry
    If that you forsake me.
KINDRED. Ah sir; what, ye be a merry man!
    Take good heart to you, and make no moan.
    But one thing I warn you, by Saint Anne,   10
    As for me, ye shall go alone.
EVERYMAN. My Cousin, will you not with me go?
COUSIN. No, by our Lady; I have the cramp in my toe.
    Trust not to me, for, so God me speed,
    I will deceive you in your most need.
KINDRED. It availeth not us to entice.
    Ye shall have my maid with all my heart;
    She loveth to go to feasts, there to be nice,
    And to dance, and abroad to start:
    I will give her leave to help you in that journey,   20
    If that you and she may agree.
EVERYMAN. Now show me the very effect of your mind.
    Will you go with me, or abide behind?
KINDRED. Abide behind? yea, that I will and I may!
    Therefore farewell until another day.
    [*Exit.*]
EVERYMAN. How should I be merry or glad?
    For fair promises men to me make,
    But when I have most need, they me forsake.
    I am deceived; that maketh me sad.
COUSIN. Cousin Everyman, farewell now,   30
    For verily I will not go with you;
    Also of mine own an unready reckoning
    I have to account; therefore I make tarrying.
    Now, God keep thee, for now I go.
    [*Exit.*]
EVERYMAN. Ah Jesus, is all come hereto?
    Lo, fair words maketh fools feign;
    They promise and nothing will do certain.
    My kinsmen promised me faithfully
    For to abide with me steadfastly,
    And now fast away do they flee.   40
    Even so Fellowship promised me.
    What friend were best me of to provide?
    I lose my time here longer to abide.

Yet in my mind a thing there is;—
All my life I have loved riches;
If that my Good now help me might,
He would make my heart full light.
I will speak to him in this distress.—
Where art thou, my Goods and riches?

GOODS. Who calleth me? Everyman? what haste thou hast!
I lie here in corners, trussed and piled so high,
And in chests I am locked so fast,
Also sacked in bags, thou mayest see with thine eye,   10
I cannot stir; in packs low I lie.
What would ye have, lightly me say.

EVERYMAN. Come hither, Goods, in all the haste thou may,
For of counsel I must desire thee.

GOODS. Sir, and ye in the world have trouble or adversity,
That can I help you to remedy shortly.

EVERYMAN. It is another disease that grieveth me;
In this world it is not, I tell thee so.
I am sent for another way to go,
To give a straight account general   20
Before the highest Jupiter of all;
And all my life I have had joy and pleasure in thee.
Therefore I pray thee go with me,
For, peradventure, thou mayest before God Almighty
My reckoning help to clean and purify;
For it is said ever among,
That money maketh all right that is wrong.

GOODS. Nay, Everyman, I sing another song,
I follow no man in such voyages;
For and I went with thee   30
Thou shouldst fare much the worse for me;
For because on me thou did set thy mind,
Thy reckoning I have made blotted and blind,
That thine account thou can not make truly;
And that hast thou for the love of me.

EVERYMAN. That would grieve me full sore,
When I should come to that fearful answer.
Up, let us go thither together.

GOODS. Nay, not so, I am too brittle, I may not endure;
I will follow no man one foot, be ye sure.   40

EVERYMAN. Alas, I have thee loved, and had great pleasure
All my life-days on goods and treasure.

GOODS. That is to thy damnation without lesing,
For my love is contrary to the love everlasting.
But if thou had me loved moderately during,

As, to the poor give part of me,
Then shouldst thou not in this dolor be,
Nor in this great sorrow and care.

EVERYMAN. Lo, now was I deceived ere I was aware,
And all I may blame on my spending of time.

GOODS. What, weenest thou that I am thine?

EVERYMAN. I had thought so.

GOODS. Nay, Everyman, I say no;
As for a while I was lent thee,
A season thou hast had me in prosperity;   10
My condition is man's soul to kill;
If I save one, a thousand I do spill;
Weenest thou that I will follow thee?
Nay, from this world, not verily.

EVERYMAN. I had thought otherwise.

GOODS. Therefore to thy soul Goods is a thief;
For when thou art dead, this is my guise
Another to deceive in the same wise
As I have done thee, and all to his soul's grief.

EVERYMAN. O false Goods, cursed thou be!   20
Thou traitor to God, that hast deceived me,
And caught me in thy snare.

GOODS. Marry, thou brought thyself in care,
Whereof I am glad,
I must needs laugh, I cannot be sad.

EVERYMAN. Ah Goods, thou hast had long my heartly love;
I gave thee that which should be the Lord's above.
But wilt thou not go with me in deed?
I pray thee truth to say.

GOODS. No, so God me speed,   30
Therefore farewell, and have good day.
[*Exit.*]

EVERYMAN. O, to whom shall I make my moan
For to go with me in that heavy journey?
First Fellowship said he would with me go;
His words were very pleasant and gay,
But afterward he left me alone.
Then spake I to my kinsmen all in despair,
And also they gave me words fair,
They lacked no fair speaking,
But all forsake me in the ending.   40
Then went I to my Goods that I loved best,
In hope to have comfort, but there had I least;
For my Goods sharply did me tell
That he bringeth many into hell.

Then of myself I was ashamed,
And so I am worthy to be blamed;
Thus may I well myself hate.
Of whom shall I now counsel take?
I think that I shall never speed
Till that I got to my Good-Deeds,
But alas, she is so weak,
That she can neither go nor speak;
Yet will I venture on her now.—
My Good-Deeds, where be you?   10
GOOD-DEEDS. Here I lie cold in the ground;
      Thy sins hath me sore bound,
      That I cannot stir.
EVERYMAN. O, Good-Deeds, I stand in fear;
      I must you pray of counsel,
      For help now should come right well.
GOOD-DEEDS. Everyman, I have understanding
      That ye be summoned account to make
      Before Messias, of Jerusalem King;
      And you do seek me that journey with you will I take.   20
EVERYMAN. Therefore I come to you, my moan to make;
      I pray you, that ye will go with me.
GOOD-DEEDS. I would full fain, but I cannot stand verily.
EVERYMAN. Why, is there anything on you fall?
GOOD-DEEDS. Yea, sir, I may thank you of all;
      If ye had perfectly cheered me,
      Your book of account now full ready had be.
      Look, the books of your works and deeds eke;
      Oh, see how they lie under the feet,
      To your soul's heaviness.   30
EVERYMAN. Our Lord Jesus, help me!
      For one letter here I can not see.
GOOD-DEEDS. There is a blind reckoning in time of distress!
EVERYMAN. Good-Deeds, I pray you, help me in this need,
      Or else I am for ever damned indeed;
      Therefore help me to make reckoning
      Before the redeemer of all thing,
      That king is, and was, and ever shall.
GOOD-DEEDS. Everyman, I am sorry of your fall,
      And fain would I help you, and I were able.   40
EVERYMAN. Good-Deeds, your counsel I pray you give me.
GOOD-DEEDS. That shall I do verily;
      Though that on my feet I may not go,
      I have a sister, that shall with you also,
      Called Knowledge, which shall with you abide,

To help you to make that dreadful reckoning.
KNOWLEDGE. Everyman, I will go with thee, and be thy guide,
    In thy most need to go by thy side.
EVERYMAN. In good condition I am now in everything,
    And am wholly content with this good thing;
    Thanked be God my Creator.
GOOD-DEEDS. And when he hath brought thee there,
    Where thou shalt heal thee of thy smart,
    Then go you with your reckoning and your Good-Deeds together,
    For to make you joyful at heart   10
    Before the blessed Trinity.
EVERYMAN. My Good-Deeds, gramercy;
    I am well content, certainly,
    With your words sweet.
KNOWLEDGE. Now go we together lovingly,
    To Confession, that cleansing river.
EVERYMAN. For joy I weep; I would we were there;
    But, I pray you, give me cognition
    Where dwelleth that holy man, Confession.
KNOWLEDGE. In the house of salvation: 20
    We shall find him in that place,
    That shall us comfort by God's grace.
    Lo, this is Confession; kneel down and ask mercy,
    For he is in good conceit with God almighty.
EVERYMAN. O glorious fountain that all uncleanness doth clarify,
    Wash from me the spots of vices unclean,
    That on me no sin may be seen;
    I come with Knowledge for my redemption,
    Repent with hearty and full contrition;
    For I am commanded a pilgrimage to take,   30
    And great accounts before God to make.
    Now, I pray you, Shrift, mother of salvation,
    Help my good deeds for my piteous exclamation.
CONFESSION. I know your sorrow well, Everyman;
    Because with Knowledge ye come to me,
    I will you comfort as well as I can,
    And a precious jewel I will give thee,
    Called penance, wise voider of adversity;
    Therewith shall your body chastised be,
    With abstinence and perseverance in God's service: 40
    Here shall you receive that scourge of me,
    Which is penance strong, that ye must endure,
    To remember thy Savior was scourged for thee
    With sharp scourges, and suffered it patiently;
    So must thou, ere thou scape that painful pilgrimage;

Knowledge, keep him in this voyage,
And by that time Good-Deeds will be with thee.
But in any wise, be sure of mercy,
For your time draweth fast, and ye will saved be;
Ask God mercy, and He will grant truly.
When with the scourge of penance man doth him bind,
The oil of forgiveness then shall he find.

EVERYMAN. Thanked be God for his gracious work!
For now I will my penance begin;
This hath rejoiced and lighted my heart,   10
Though the knots be painful and hard within.

KNOWLEDGE. Everyman, look your penance that ye fulfil,
What pain that ever it to you be,
And Knowledge shall give you counsel at will,
How your accounts ye shall make clearly.

EVERYMAN. O eternal God, O heavenly figure,
O way of rightwiseness, O goodly vision,
Which descended down in a virgin pure
Because he would Everyman redeem,
Which Adam forfeited by his disobedience: 20
O blessed Godhead, elect and high-divine,
Forgive my grievous offence;
Here I cry thee mercy in this presence.
O ghostly treasure, O ransomer and redeemer
Of all the world, hope and conductor,
Mirror of joy, and founder of mercy,
Which illumineth heaven and earth thereby,
Hear my clamorous complaint, though it late be;
Receive my prayers; unworthy in this heavy life
Though I be, a sinner most abominable,   30
Yet let my name be written in Moses' table;
O Mary, pray to the Maker of all thing,
Me for to help at my ending,
And save me from the power of my enemy,
For death assaileth me strongly;
And, Lady, that I may by means of thy prayer
Of your Son's glory to be partaker,
By the means of his passion I it crave,
I beseech you, help my soul to save.—
Knowledge, give me the scourge of penance;   40
My flesh therewith shall give a quittance:
I will now begin, if God give me grace.

KNOWLEDGE. Everyman, God give you time and space:
Thus I bequeath you in the hands of our Savior,
Now may you make your reckoning sure.

EVERYMAN. In the name of the Holy Trinity,
  My body sore punished shall be:
  Take this body for the sin of the flesh;
  Also thou delightest to go gay and fresh,
  And in the way of damnation thou did me bring;
  Therefore suffer now strokes and punishing.
  Now of penance I will wade the water clear,
  To save me from purgatory, that sharp fire.
GOOD-DEEDS. I thank God, now I can walk and go;
  And am delivered of my sickness and woe.   10
  Therefore with Everyman I will go, and not spare;
  His good works I will help him to declare.
KNOWLEDGE. Now, Everyman, be merry and glad;
  Your Good-Deeds cometh now; ye may not be sad;
  Now is your Good-Deeds whole and sound,
  Going upright upon the ground.
EVERYMAN. My heart is light, and shall be evermore;
  Now will I smite faster than I did before.
GOOD-DEEDS. Everyman, pilgrim, my special friend,
  Blessed be thou without end;   20
  For thee is prepared the eternal glory.
  Ye have me made whole and sound,
  Therefore I will bide by thee in every stand.
EVERYMAN. Welcome, my Good-Deeds; now I hear thy voice,
  I weep for very sweetness of love.
KNOWLEDGE. Be no more sad, but ever rejoice,
  God seeth thy living in his throne above.
  Put on this garment to thy behove,
  Which is wet with your tears,
  Or else before God you may it miss,   30
  When you to your journey's end come shall.
EVERYMAN. Gentle Knowledge, what do you it call?
KNOWLEDGE. It is a garment of sorrow:
  From pain it will you borrow;
  Contrition it is,
  That getteth forgiveness;
  It pleaseth God passing well.
GOOD-DEEDS. Everyman, will you wear it for your heal?
EVERYMAN. Now blessed be Jesu, Mary's Son!
  For now have I on true contrition.   40
  And let us go now without tarrying;
  Good-Deeds, have we clear our reckoning?
GOOD-DEEDS. Yea, indeed I have it here.
EVERYMAN. Then I trust we need not fear;
  Now, friends, let us not part in twain.

KNOWLEDGE. Nay, Everyman, that will we not, certain.
GOOD-DEEDS. Yet must thou lead with thee
    Three persons of great might.
EVERYMAN. Who should they be?
GOOD-DEEDS. Discretion and Strength they hight,
    And thy Beauty may not abide behind.
KNOWLEDGE. Also ye must call to mind
    Your Five-Wits as for your counselors.
GOOD-DEEDS. You must have them ready at all hours.
EVERYMAN. How shall I get them hither?   10
KNOWLEDGE. You must call them all together,
    And they will hear you incontinent.
EVERYMAN. My friends, come hither and be present,
    Discretion, Strength, my Five-Wits, and Beauty.
BEAUTY. Here at your will we be already.
    What will ye that we should do?
GOOD-DEEDS. That ye would with Everyman go,
    And help him in his pilgrimage,
    Advise you, will ye with him or not in that voyage?
STRENGTH. We will bring him all thither,   20
    To his help and comfort, ye may believe me.
DISCRETION. So will we go with him all together.
EVERYMAN. Almighty God, loved thou be,
    I give thee laud that I have hither brought
    Strength, Discretion, Beauty, and Five-Wits; lack I nought;
    And my Good-Deeds, with Knowledge clear,
    All be in my company at my will here;
    I desire no more to my business.
STRENGTH. And I, Strength, will by you stand in distress,
    Though thou would in battle fight on the ground.   30
FIVE-WITS. And though it were through the world round,
    We will not depart for sweet nor sour.
BEAUTY. No more will I unto death's hour,
    Whatsoever thereof befall.
DISCRETION. Everyman, advise you first of all;
    Go with a good advisement and deliberation;
    We all give you virtuous monition
    That all shall be well.
EVERYMAN. My friends, hearken what I will tell:
    I pray God reward you in his heavenly sphere.   40
    Now hearken, all that be here,
    For I will make my testament
    Here before you all present.
    In alms half my good I will give with my hands twain
    In the way of charity, with good intent,

  And the other half still shall remain
  In quiet to be returned there it ought to be.
  This I do in despite of the fiend of hell
  To go quite out of his peril
  Ever after and this day.
KNOWLEDGE. Everyman, hearken what I say;
  Go to priesthood, I you advise,
  And receive of him in any wise
  The holy sacrament and ointment together;
  Then shortly see ye turn again hither;   10
  We will all abide you here.
FIVE-WITS. Yea, Everyman, hie you that ye ready were,
  There is no emperor, king, duke, nor baron,
  That of God hath commission,
  As hath the least priest in the world being;
  For of the blessed sacraments pure and benign,
  He beareth the keys and thereof hath the cure
  For man's redemption, it is ever sure;
  Which God for our soul's medicine
  Gave us out of his heart with great pain;   20
  Here in this transitory life, for thee and me
  The blessed sacraments seven there be,
  Baptism, confirmation, with priesthood good,
  And the sacrament of God's precious flesh and blood,
  Marriage, the holy extreme unction, and penance;
  These seven be good to have in remembrance,
  Gracious sacraments of high divinity.
EVERYMAN. Fain would I receive that holy body
  And meekly to my ghostly father I will go.
FIVE-WITS. Everyman, that is the best that ye can do: 30
  God will you to salvation bring,
  For priesthood exceedeth all other thing;
  To us Holy Scripture they do teach,
  And converteth man from sin heaven to reach;
  God hath to them more power given,
  Than to any angel that is in heaven;
  With five words he may consecrate
  God's body in flesh and blood to make,
  And handleth his Maker between his hands;
  The priest bindeth and unbindeth all bands,   40
  Both in earth and in heaven;
  Thou ministers all the sacraments seven;
  Though we kissed thy feet thou wert worthy;
  Thou art surgeon that cureth sin deadly:
  No remedy we find under God

But all only priesthood.
Everyman, God gave priests that dignity,
And setteth them in his stead among us to be;
Thus be they above angels in degree.
KNOWLEDGE. If priests be good it is so surely;
But when Jesus hanged on the cross with great smart
There he gave, out of his blessed heart,
The same sacrament in great torment:
He sold them not to us, that Lord Omnipotent.
Therefore Saint Peter the apostle doth say   10
That Jesu's curse hath all they
Which God their Savior do buy or sell,
Or they for any money do take or tell.
Sinful priests giveth the sinners example bad;
Their children sitteth by other men's fires, I have heard;
And some haunteth women's company,
With unclean life, as lusts of lechery.
These be with sin made blind.
FIVE-WITS. I trust to God no such may we find;
Therefore let us priesthood honor,   20
And follow their doctrine for our soul's succor;
We be their sheep, and they shepherds be
By whom we all be kept in surety.
Peace, for yonder I see Everyman come,
Which hath made true satisfaction.
GOOD-DEEDS. Methinketh it is he indeed.
EVERYMAN. Now Jesu be your alder speed.
I have received the sacrament for my redemption,
And then mine extreme unction:
Blessed be all they that counseled me to take it!   30
And now, friends, let us go without longer respite;
I thank God that ye have tarried so long.
Now set each of you on this rod your hand,
And shortly follow me:
I go before, there I would be; God be our guide.
STRENGTH. Everyman, we will not from you go,
Till ye have gone this voyage long.
DISCRETION. I, Discretion, will bide by you also.
KNOWLEDGE. And though this pilgrimage be never so strong,
I will never part you fro: 40
Everyman, I will be as sure by thee
As ever I did by Judas Maccabee.
EVERYMAN. Alas, I am so faint I may not stand.
My limbs under me do fold;
Friends, let us not turn again to this land,

Not for all the world's gold.
For into this cave must I creep
And turn to the earth and there to sleep.
BEAUTY. What, into this grave? alas!
EVERYMAN. Yea, there shall you consume more and less.
BEAUTY. And what, should I smother here?
EVERYMAN. Yea, by my faith, and never more appear.
    In this world live no more we shall,
    But in heaven before the highest Lord of all.
BEAUTY. I cross out all this; adieu by Saint John;   10
    I take my cap in my lap and am gone.
EVERYMAN. What, Beauty, whither will ye?
BEAUTY. Peace, I am deaf; I look not behind me,
    Not and thou would give me all the gold in thy chest.
    [*Exit.*]
EVERYMAN. Alas, whereto may I trust?
    Beauty goeth fast away hie;
    She promised with me to live and die.
STRENGTH. Everyman, I will thee also forsake and deny;
    Thy game liketh me not at all.
EVERYMAN. Why, then ye will forsake me all.   20
    Sweet Strength, tarry a little space.
STRENGTH. Nay, sir, by the rood of grace
    I will hie me from thee fast,
    Though thou weep till thy heart burst.
EVERYMAN. Ye would ever bide by me, ye said.
STRENGTH. Yea, I have you far enough conveyed;
    Ye be old enough, I understand,
    Your pilgrimage to take on hand;
    I repent me that I hither came.
EVERYMAN. Strength, you to displease I am to blame;   30
    Will you break promise that is debt?
STRENGTH. In faith, I care not;
    Thou art but a fool to complain,
    You spend your speech and waste your brain;
    Go thrust thee into the ground.
    [*Exit.*]
EVERYMAN. I had thought surer I should you have found.
    He that trusteth in his Strength
    She him deceiveth at the length.
    Both Strength and Beauty forsaketh me,
    Yet they promised me fair and lovingly.   40
DISCRETION. Everyman, I will after Strength be gone,
    As for me, I will leave you alone.
EVERYMAN. Why, Discretion, will ye forsake me?

DISCRETION. Yea, in faith, I will go from thee,
    For when Strength goeth before
    I follow after evermore.
EVERYMAN. Yet, I pray thee, for the love of the Trinity,
    Look in my grave once piteously.
DISCRETION. Nay, so nigh will I not come.
    Farewell, every one!
    [*Exit.*]
EVERYMAN. O all thing faileth, save God alone;
    Beauty, Strength, and Discretion;
    For when Death bloweth his blast,   10
    They all run from me full fast.
FIVE-WITS. Everyman, my leave now of thee I take;
    I will follow the other, for here I thee forsake.
EVERYMAN. Alas! then may I wail and weep,
    For I took you for my best friend.
FIVE-WITS. I will no longer thee keep;
    Now farewell, and there an end.
    [*Exit.*]
EVERYMAN. O Jesu, help, all hath forsaken me!
GOOD-DEEDS. Nay, Everyman, I will bide with thee,
    I will not forsake thee indeed;   20
    Thou shalt find me a good friend at need.
EVERYMAN. Gramercy, Good-Deeds; now may I true friends see;
    They have forsaken me every one;
    I loved them better than my Good-Deeds alone.
    Knowledge, will ye forsake me also?
KNOWLEDGE. Yea, Everyman, when ye to death do go:
    But not yet for no manner of danger.
EVERYMAN. Gramercy, Knowledge, with all my heart.
KNOWLEDGE. Nay, yet I will not from hence depart,
    Till I see where ye shall be come.   30
EVERYMAN. Methinketh, alas, that I must be gone,
    To make my reckoning and my debts pay,
    For I see my time is nigh spent away.
    Take example, all ye that this do hear or see,
    How they that I loved best do forsake me,
    Except my Good-Deeds that bideth truly.
GOOD-DEEDS. All earthly things is but vanity:
    Beauty, Strength, and Discretion, do man forsake,
    Foolish friends and kinsmen, that fair spake,
    All fleeth save Good-Deeds, and that am I.   40
EVERYMAN. Have mercy on me, God most mighty;
    And stand by me, thou Mother and Maid, holy Mary.
GOOD-DEEDS. Fear not, I will speak for thee.

EVERYMAN. Here I cry God mercy.
GOOD-DEEDS. Short our end, and diminish our pain;
    Let us go and never come again.
EVERYMAN. Into thy hands, Lord, my soul I commend;
    Receive it, Lord, that it be not lost;
    As thou me boughtest, so me defend,
    And save me from the fiend's boast,
    That I may appear with that blessed host
    That shall be saved at the day of doom.
    In manus tuas—of might's most   10
    For ever—*commendo spiritum meum.**
    [EVERYMAN *and* GOOD-DEEDS *enter the grave.*]
KNOWLEDGE. Now hath he suffered that we all shall endure;
    The Good-Deeds shall make all sure.
    Now hath he made ending;
    Methinketh that I hear angels sing
    And make great joy and melody,
    Where Everyman's soul received shall be.
ANGEL. Come, excellent elect spouse to Jesu:
    Hereabove thou shalt go
    Because of thy singular virtue.   20
    Now the soul is taken the body fro;
    Thy reckoning is crystal-clear.
    Now shalt thou into the heavenly sphere,
    Unto the which all ye shall come
    That liveth well before the day of doom.
DOCTOR. This moral men may have in mind;
    Ye hearers, take it of worth, old and young,
    And forsake Pride, for he deceiveth you in the end,
    And remember Beauty, Five-Wits, Strength and Discretion,
    They all at the last do Everyman forsake,   30
    Save his Good-Deeds, there doth he take.
    But beware, and they be small
    Before God, he hath no help at all.
    None excuse may be there for Everyman:
    Alas, how shall he do then?
    For after death amends may no man make,
    For then mercy and pity do him forsake.
    If his reckoning be not clear when he do come,
    God will say—*ite maledicti in ignem aeternum.***
    And he that hath his account whole and sound,   40
    High in heaven he shall be crowned;
    Unto which place God bring us all thither

* Into Thy hands, I commend my spirit.
** Go, cursed ones, into eternal fire.

That we may live body and soul together.
Thereto help the Trinity,
Amen, say ye, for Saint Charity.
   Thus endeth this moral play of Everyman.

JOHN WEBSTER

THE DUCHESS OF
MALFI

THE WORLD AS IDEA

FROM "EVERYMAN" (1475) to *The Duchess of Malfi* (1613) is a giant step in dramaturgy as well as in time. In the Bibliography at the end of this book will be found references to several scholars who have painstakingly picked out the path of the dramatist from morality to tragedy on the English stage: how the morality turned its attention from sacred to secular subjects, allegorizing on matters of government or social relations; how schoolmasters seized upon it as a vehicle for teaching everything from grammar to astronomy; how ambitious playwrights, fresh from the universities, fused the morality pattern with historical materials; how the allegorical or moral element became increasingly sublimated until it was possible to look upon a dramatic character as if he had a biography and not merely a quality.

Juxtaposing *Everyman* and *The Duchess*, however, may assist in the understanding of Webster's work and may provide the proper angle for viewing. For sublimated though the allegorical elements may be, the contemporary audience continued to be aware of them. In Ben Jonson's *The Staple of News* (1626) a group of play-goers are talking about the performance they are watching. The conversation turns to the Vice, a popular character-type, generally an agent of the devil, of the older morality.

MIRTH. How liked you the Vice in the play?
EXPECTATION. Which is he?
MIRTH. Three or four: old Covetousness, the sordid Pennyboy, the Moneybawd . . . .
TATTLE. But here is never a fiend to carry him away. Besides he has never a wooden dagger! I'd not give a rush for a Vice that has not a dagger to snap at everyone he meets.

MIRTH. That was the old way, gossip, when Iniquity came in like Hokus-Pokus in a juggler's jerkin, with false skirts like the Knave of Clubs. But now they are attired like men and women of the time, the vices male and female.

Mirth's last speech, which compresses a hundred years of dramatic history into a sentence, is the clue to the response expected by the playwright of his audience: under realistic clothing were figures whose theatrical function was still allegorical. In the words of an earlier dramatist, the characters of the play "plainly represent . . . the manners of men and fashion of the world nowadays,"* while connoting something broader, more abstract, more universal by their apparently representational action.

Unless this principle is clearly understood any of the major works of the great period of English drama generally called Elizabethan is going to look to the modern reader like a huge patchwork: two or more actions (each with sufficient magnitude for a play in its own right) unfolding simultaneously; a stage crowded with actors; scenes of the highest seriousness juxtaposed with scenes of wild and apparently irrelevant farce. The typical Elizabethan play, in fact, is not unlike the conventional drama of the Hindus, with the major difference that the Elizabethan mirror could reflect a final tragic view of human experience.

The Duchess of Malfi is another instance of how carefully the playwright constructs a theatrical world to reproduce in little the world in which his spectators exist. Not, of course, in the physical sense: the Elizabethan stage was a bare platform without scenery, and the sense of place could only be conveyed by the actors, their costumes, and their expository speeches. No famous landmarks or architectural monuments could be used to localize the action as taking place in Italy, or as moving from Amalfi to Ancona to Rome. Even the dialogue, on which we must rely for our sense of place, is reticent with details. That the scene is Italy we may infer from the names of the characters, from the opening comparison with the court of France, from a few "directorial" remarks. We soon become aware that, as in the case of the characters, Italy is only the representational name covering a broader, more universal idea of the world.

* T. Lupton, *All for Money*, c. 1570.

Malfi is a gloomy world, a shadow, and a deep pit of darkness,
in the poetry of the play together with its dramatic counterpart:
most of the major situations—Bosola's discovery of the Duchess's
child, the beginning of her persecution—transpire in the night-
time, always symbolized for the audience by the use of dark
lanterns. Bosola, again, is not only appealing to a familiar
Renaissance concept but also to the world of the play as created
by Webster, as he begs the dying Duchess to

> Return, fair soul, from darkness, and lead mine
> Out of this sensible hell.

The very word hell occurs at least fifteen times in the play, and
much of the imagery is governed by it; when Ferdinand offers
money to his tool, Bosola replies

>   Take your devils,
> Which hell calls angels; . . .
> And should I take these, they'd take me to hell.

Ferdinand's response is equally relevant to the iterated image:

> Sir, I'll take nothing from you that I have given,

for in this particular hell, Ferdinand is a major devil. Malateste
describes him, indeed, as the devil's child, and when Bosola has
agreed to become his creature, Bosola assumes the character of a
lesser devil—after a few sententious remarks, he comments

> Sometimes the devil doth preach.

Indeed the word *devil*, like the word *hell*, is constantly on the lips
of the actors; and never as a mere expletive, but always with the
intention of developing the picture of a hellish world. There are
few classical references in the play, but the most notable ones are
to Charon and Tantalus.

This image of a gloomy, evil world is intensified by its flora and
fauna: it is filled with blackbirds, crows, pies, caterpillars, moths,
toads, horse-leeches, spiders in foul black cobwebs, lice, grave-
worms, snakes, owls, hyenas, foxes, tigers, and most significantly,
wolves. The disease of the body is named from it, the ulcerous
wolf; the dead children are young wolves; the wolf will uncover
the grave of the Duchess; and at the end of the play, Ferdinand,

who has been most often described as a wolf, goes mad and his madness takes the form of lycanthropy; he becomes a werewolf, which is realization of the poetic image with a vengeance.

The people of this world of Malfi are an appropriate collection. There are a number of minor characters in the play—politicians and nobles—whom we see only briefly. At greater length we meet an Old Lady and Castruchio, who have little to do with the action, but who give Bosola a chance to describe the behavior of a typical courtier and the contents of a lady's cosmetic kit, suggesting in each case that foulness has been covered with even more obscene artifice. Antonio's officers play him false, beauty is mere leprosy, and the few words spent on the minor lords generally display them as unmanly cowards.

The world is a pathless wilderness, filled with tempests, plagues, and earthquakes; mandrakes shriek in it, and apples are grafted onto crabs, and plums on hawthorns. Bosola's corruption grows out of horse-dung, and horse-dung ripens the apricots which give away the Duchess's secret. In such a world the events of the play cease to be melodramatic. Adultery, excommunication, murder, betrayal, revenge, torture, madmen, dead hands, poisoned books, strangling, and disguise are its normal components.

It is a world, in short, to tempt the virtuous man to despair, the ultimate sin for which there is no forgiveness. One of the constant themes of Christian drama from its medieval origins was the assurance that the grace of God awaited any repentant sinner. Again, this doctrine could have led to a conventional dramatic action like that of the Hindu theater, to which the finality of tragedy was denied by the doctrine of rebirth. However, Christian theology recognized a particular manifestation of human pride, or presumptuousness; there were men, so far captive to their own wills, that they could not conceive of mercy or of grace. Unable to forgive those who had offended them, they refused to acknowledge that God might forgive them. In other words, they equated themselves with God, and fell into the sin of despair.

These ideas were as familiar to Webster's audience as they were to the playwright, and it must be insisted upon that the play was not written as propaganda, nor was it written to explicate a religious or moral system. Exactly the reverse is true; the moral system makes possible the creation of an appropriate dramatic world; permits the author to people it with characters whose actions will be consistent, significant, and capable of evaluation; serves as a vehicle for a tragic vision.

The world of the Duchess of Malfi is a kind of purgatory, a "suburb of hell," controlled (if only partially created) by her evil brothers. And the abstract ideas bodied forth in the representational action are of purgation and damnation. The Duchess is purged of her sin, and the Duke is damned for his. The damnation of the Cardinal, too, is presented in a series of actions as he rejects Bosola, makes love to another man's wife (who is in turn presented as the basest of women, insatiate in lust), "bears himself much too cruel" to his sister, and is finally trapped by his own conniving. Ferdinand and the Cardinal are, of course, symbolic in another way. Their *costumes* indicate that they represent the Church and the State, the ruling power in the world of the play, the power which Bosola aspires to serve. The *action* of the play *demonstrates* to Bosola the corruption of the world in which he has willingly and blindly involved himself. By the action, his eyes are opened and the recognition leads to action as he dies the death of a true tragic hero.

The horrors of *The Duchess of Malfi* are perhaps the major obstacle for the modern reader, even while acknowledging the truth of Charles Lamb's statement: "The tragic auditory wants blood." Corpses in the theater are subject to the law of diminishing returns, and Webster's unending flow of human gore may swamp the play for the uninstructed reader. But this kind of literal-mindedness is out of its element in understanding the dramatic experience intended by the Elizabethan playwright. To refuse to recognize the underlying allegory, or the overriding symbolic level of action is to see only half the play. However, to see symbolism or allegory as ends in themselves is equally myopic. Like every other tool or device available to the dramatist they are but means to a greater end, an ordering of an imaginary world with such form and completeness that the spectator may leave the theater with an increased awareness of the world outside the magic doors.

Characters

FERDINAND
Duke of Calabria

THE CARDINAL
his brother

ANTONIO BOLOGNA
steward of the household to the DUCHESS

DELIO
his friend

DANÌEL DE BOSOLA
gentleman of the horse to the DUCHESS

CASTRUCHIO

MARQUIS OF PESCARA

COUNT MALATESTE

SILVIO *a Lord, of Milan*
RODERIGO
gentlemen attending on the DUCHESS

GRISOLAN

DOCTOR

**SEVERAL MADMEN, PILGRIMS, EXECUTIONERS,
OFFICERS, ATTENDANTS,** ETC.

DUCHESS OF MALFI
sister of FERDINAND *and the* CARDINAL

CARIOLA
her woman

JULIA
CASTRUCHIO'S *wife, and the* CARDINAL'S *mistress*

OLD LADY, LADIES and CHILDREN

SCENE: *Amalfi, Rome, and Milan.*

THE DUCHESS OF MALFI

John Webster

ACT ONE

Scene One

Amalfi. The presence-chamber in the Duchess's palace.

[*Enter* ANTONIO *and* DELIO.]

DELIO. You are welcome to your country, dear Antonio;
  You have been long in France, and you return
  A very formal Frenchman in your habit:
  How do you like the French court?

ANTONIO.   I admire it:
  In seeking to reduce both state and people
  To a fixed order, their judicious king
  Begins at home; quits[1] first his royal palace
  Of flattering sycophants, of dissolute
  And infamous persons,—which he sweetly terms   10
  His master's masterpiece, the work of Heaven;
  Considering duly that a prince's court
  Is like a common fountain, whence should flow
  Pure silver drops in general, but if it chance
  Some cursed example poison it near the head,
  Death and diseases through the whole land spread.
  And what is it makes this blessed government
  But a most provident council, who dare freely
  Inform him the corruption of the times?
  Though some of the court hold it presumption   20
  To instruct princes what they ought to do,
  It is a noble duty to inform them
  What they ought to foresee.—Here comes Bosola,
  The only court-gall; yet I observe his railing
  Is not for simple love of piety:

---

[1] Purges.

Indeed, he rails at those things which he wants;
Would be as lecherous, covetous, or proud,
Bloody, or envious, as any man,
If he had means to be so.—Here's the Cardinal.
[*Enter the* CARDINAL *and* BOSOLA.]

BOSOLA. I do haunt you still.

CARDINAL. So.

BOSOLA. I have done you better service than to be slighted thus.
Miserable age, where only the reward of doing well is the doing
of it!

CARDINAL. You enforce your merit too much.   10

BOSOLA. I fell into the galleys in your service; where, for two years
together, I wore two towels instead of a shirt, with the knot on the
shoulder, after the fashion of a Roman mantle. Slighted thus? I
will thrive some way: blackbirds fatten best in hard weather; why
not I in these dog-days?

CARDINAL. Would you could become honest!

BOSOLA. With all your divinity do but direct me the way to it. I have
known many travel far for it, and yet return as arrant knaves as
they went forth, because they carried themselves always along with
them.   20

[*Exit* CARDINAL.]

Are you gone? Some fellows, they say, are possessed with the
devil, but this great fellow were able to possess the greatest devil,
and make him worse.

ANTONIO. He hath denied thee some suit?

BOSOLA. He and his brother are like plum-trees that grow crooked
over standing-pools; they are rich and over-laden with fruit, but
none but crows, pies, and caterpillars feed on them. Could I be
one of their flattering panders, I would hang on their ears like a
horseleech, till I were full, and then drop off. I pray, leave me.
Who would rely upon these miserable dependencies, in expecta-   30
tion to be advanced tomorrow? What creature ever fed worse than
hoping Tantalus? Nor ever died any man more fearfully than he
that hoped for a pardon. There are rewards for hawks and dogs
when they have done us serivce; but for a soldier that hazards his
limbs in a battle, nothing but a kind of geometry in his last sup-
portation.

DELIO. Geometry?

BOSOLA. Aye, to hang in a fair pair of slings, take his latter swing
in the world upon an honorable pair of crutches, from hospital to
hospital. Fare ye well, sir: and yet do not you scorn us; for places 40
in the court are but like beds in the hospital, where this man's head
lies at that man's foot, and so lower and lower.

[*Exit.*]

DELIO. I knew this fellow seven years in the galleys
    For a notorious murder; and 'twas thought
    The Cardinal suborned it: he was released
    By the French general, Gaston de Foix,
    When he recovered Naples.
ANTONIO.   'Tis great pity
    He should be thus neglected: I have heard
    He's very valiant. This foul melancholy
    Will poison all his goodness; for, I'll tell you,
    If too immoderate sleep be truly said   10
    To be an inward rust unto the soul,
    It then doth follow want of action
    Breeds all black malcontents; and their close rearing,
    Like moths in cloth, do hurt for want of wearing.
DELIO. The presence 'gins to fill: you promised me
    To make me the partaker of the natures
    Of some of your great courtiers.
ANTONIO.   The lord Cardinal's,
    And other strangers' that are now in court?
    I shall.—Here comes the great Calabrian duke.   20
    [*Enter* FERDINAND, CASTRUCHIO, SILVIO, RODERIGO, GRISO-
    LAN, *and* ATTENDANTS.]
FERDINAND. Who took the ring oftenest?[2]
SILVIO. Antonio Bologna, my lord.
FERDINAND. Our sister duchess's great-master of her household?
    give him the jewel.—When shall we leave this sportive action,
    and fall to action indeed?
CASTRUCHIO. Methinks, my lord, you should not desire to go to war
    in person.
FERDINAND. Now for some gravity:—why, my lord?
CASTRUCHIO. It is fitting a soldier arise to be a Prince, but not
    necessary a prince descend to be a captain.   30
FERDINAND. No?
CASTRUCHIO. No, my lord; he were far better do it by a deputy.
FERDINAND. Why should he not as well sleep or eat by a deputy?
    this might take idle, offensive, and base office from him, where
    as the other deprives him of honor.
CASTRUCHIO. Believe my experience, that realm is never long in quiet
    where the ruler is a soldier.
FERDINAND. Thou toldest me thy wife could not endure fighting.
CASTRUCHIO. True, my lord.
FERDINAND. And of a jest she broke of a captain she met full of   40
    wounds: I have forgot it.

[2] In a tilting competition.

CASTRUCHIO. She told him, my lord, he was a pitiful fellow, to lie, like the children of Ismael, all in tents.[3]

FERDINAND. Why, there's a wit were able to undo all the surgeons of the city; for although gallants should quarrel, and had drawn their weapons, and were ready to go to it, yet her persuasions would make them put up.

CASTRUCHIO. That she would, my lord.

FERDINAND. How do you like my Spanish gennet?[4]

RODERIGO. He is all fire.

FERDINAND. I am of Pliny's opinion, I think he was begot by the   10
wind; he runs as if he were ballasted with quicksilver.

SILVIO. True, my lord, he reels from the tilt often.

RODERIGO and GRISOLAN. Ha, ha, ha!

FERDINAND. Why do you laugh? methinks you that are courtiers should be my touchwood, take fire when I give fire; that is, laugh but when I laugh, were the subject never so witty.

CASTRUCHIO. True, my lord: I myself have heard a very good jest, and have scorned to seem to have so silly a wit as to understand it.

FERDINAND. But I can laugh at your fool, my lord.   20

CASTRUCHIO. He cannot speak, you know, but he makes faces: my lady cannot abid him.

FERDINAND. No?

CASTRUCHIO. Nor endure to be in merry company; for she says too much laughing, and too much company, fills her too full of the wrinkle.

FERDINAND. I would, then, have a mathematical instrument made for her face, that she might not laugh out of compass.— I shall shortly visit you at Milan, Lord Silvio.

SILVIO. Your grace shall arrive most welcome.   30

FERDINAND. You are a good horseman, Antonio: you have excellent riders in France: what do you think of good horsemanship?

ANTONIO. Nobly, my lord: as out of the Grecian horse issued many famous princes, so out of brave horsemanship arise the first sparks of growing resolution, that raise the mind to noble action.

FERDINAND. You have bespoke it worthily.

SILVIO. Your brother, the lord Cardinal, and sister duchess.

[*Reenter* CARDINAL, *with* DUCHESS, CARIOLA, *and* JULIA.]

CARDINAL. Are the galleys come about?

GRISOLAN.   They are, my lord.

FERDINAND. Here's the Lord Silvio is come to take his leave.   40

DELIO [*aside to* ANTONIO]. Now, sir, your promise; what's that Cardinal?

[3] Bandages.
[4] Jennet, a small horse.

        I mean his temper? they say he's a brave fellow,
        Will play his five thousand crowns at tennis, dance,
        Court ladies, and one that hath fought single combats.

ANTONIO. Some such flashes superficially hang on him for form;
but observe his inward character: he is a melancholy churchman;
the spring in his face is nothing but the engendering of toads;
where he is jealous of any man, he lays worse plots for them than
ever was imposed on Hercules, for he strews in his way flatterers,
panders, intelligencers, atheists, and a thousand such political
monsters. He should have been Pope; but instead of coming to   10
it by the primitive decency of the Church, he did bestow bribes
so largely and so impudently as if he would have carried it away
without Heaven's knowledge. Some good he hath done—

DELIO. You have given too much of him. What's his brother?

ANTONIO. The duke there? a most perverse and turbulent nature:
        What appears in him mirth is merely outside;
        If he laughs heartily, it is to laugh
        All honesty out of fashion.

DELIO.   Twins?

ANTONIO.   In quality.   20
        He speaks with others' tongues, and hears men's suits
        With others' ears; will seem to sleep on the bench
        Only to entrap offenders in their answers;
        Dooms men to death by information;
        Rewards by hearsay.

DELIO.   Then the law to him
        Is like a foul black cobweb to a spider,—
        He makes of it his dwelling and a prison
        To entangle those shall feed him.

ANTONIO.   Most true: 30
        He never pays debts unless they be shrewd turns,
        And those he will confess that he doth owe.
        Last, for his brother there, the Cardinal,
        They that do flatter him most say oracles
        Hang at his lips; and verily I believe them,
        For the devil speaks in them.
        But for their sister, the right noble duchess,
        You never fixed your eye on three fair medals
        Cast in one figure, of so different temper.
        For her discourse, it is so full of rapture,   40
        You only will begin then to be sorry
        When she doth end her speech, and wish, in wonder,
        She held it less vainglory to talk much,
        Than your penance to hear her: whilst she speaks,
        She throws upon a man so sweet a look,

That it were able to raise one to a galliard[5]
That lay in a dead palsy, and to dote
On that sweet countenance; but in that look
There speaketh so divine a continence
As cuts off all lascivious and vain hope.
Her days are practiced in such noble virtue,
That sure her nights, nay, more, her very sleeps,
Are more in heaven than other ladies' shrifts.
Let all sweet ladies break their flattering glasses,
And dress themselves in her.   10

DELIO.   Fie, Antonio,
You play the wire-drawer[6] with her commendations.

ANTONIO. I'll case the picture up: only thus much;
All her particular worth grows to this sum,—
She stains the time past, lights the time to come.

CARIOLA. You must attend my lady in the gallery,
Some half an hour hence.

ANTONIO.   I shall.
[*Exeunt* ANTONIO *and* DELIO.]

FERDINAND. Sister, I have a suit to you.

DUCHESS.   To me, sir?   20

FERDINAND. A gentleman here, Daniel de Bosola,
One that was in the galleys—

DUCHESS.   Yes, I know him.

FERDINAND. A worthy fellow he is: pray, let me entreat for
The provisorship of your horse.

DUCHESS.   Your knowledge of him
Commends him and prefers him.

FERDINAND.   Call him hither.
[*Exit* ATTENDANT.]
We are now upon parting. Good Lord Silvio,
Do us commend to all our noble friends   30
At the leaguer.[7]

SILVIO.   Sir, I shall.

DUCHESS.   You are for Milan?

SILVIO. I am.

DUCHESS.   Bring the caroches. We'll bring you down
To the haven.
[*Exeunt all but* FERDINAND *and the* CARDINAL.]

CARDINAL. Be sure you entertain[8] that Bosola

---

[5] A quick dance.
[6] i.e., one who spins out finely and at length.
[7] Camp.
[8] Employ.

For your intelligence: I would not be seen in it;
And therefore many times I have slighted him
When he did court our furtherance, as this morning.
FERDINAND. Antonio, the great-master of her household,
    Had been far fitter.
CARDINAL.   You are deceived in him:
    His nature is too honest for such business.—
    He comes: I'll leave you.
    [*Exit.*]
    [*Reenter* BOSOLA.]
BOSOLA.   I was lured to you.
FERDINAND. My brother, here, the Cardinal could never   10
    Abide you.
BOSOLA. Never since he was in my debt.
FERDINAND. Maybe some oblique character in your face
    Made him suspect you.
BOSOLA.   Doth he study physiognomy?
    There's no more credit to be given to the face
    Than to a sick man's urine, which some call
    The physician's whore because she cozens him.
    He did suspect me wrongfully.
FERDINAND.   For that   20
    You must give great men leave to take their times.
    Distrust doth cause us seldom be deceived:
    You see the oft shaking of the cedar-tree
    Fastens it more at root.
BOSOLA.   Yet, take heed;
    For to suspect a friend unworthily
    Instructs him the next way to suspect you,
    And prompts him to deceive you.
FERDINAND [*giving him money*]. There's gold.
BOSOLA.   So: 30
    What follows? never rained such showers as these
    Without thunderbolts in the tail of them: whose throat must
    I cut?
FERDINAND. Your inclination to shed blood rides post
    Before my occasion to use you. I give you that
    To live in the court here, and observe the duchess;
    To note all the particulars of her 'havior,
    What suitors do solicit her for marriage,
    And whom she best affects. She's a young widow:
    I would not have her marry again.   40
BOSOLA.   No, sir?
FERDINAND. Do not you ask the reason; but be satisfied
    I say I would not.

BOSOLA.   It seems you would create me
    One of your familiars.
FERDINAND.   Familiar? what's that?
BOSOLA. Why, a very quaint invisible devil in flesh,
    An intelligencer.
FERDINAND.   Such a kind of thriving thing
    I would wish thee; and ere long thou mayest arrive
    At a higher place by it.
BOSOLA.   Take your devils,
    Which hell calls angels; these cursed gifts would make   10
    You a corrupter, me an impudent traitor;
    And should I take these, they'd take me to hell.
FERDINAND. Sir, I'll take nothing from you that I have given:
    There is a place that I procured for you
    This morning, the provisorship of the horse;
    Have you heard on it?
BOSOLA.   No.
FERDINAND. 'Tis yours: is it not worth thanks?
BOSOLA. I would have you curse yourself now, that your bounty,
    Which makes men truly noble, e'er should make me   20
    A villain. Oh, that to avoid ingratitude
    For the good deed you have done me, I must do
    All the ill man can invent! Thus the devil
    Candies[9] all sins o'er; and what heaven terms vile,
    That names he complimental.
FERDINAND.   Be yourself;
    Keep your old garb of melancholy; 'twill express
    You envy those that stand above your reach,
    Yet strive not to come near 'em: this will gain
    Access to private lodgings, where yourself   30
    May, like a politic dormouse—
BOSOLA.   As I have seen some
    Feed in a lord's dish, half asleep, not seeming
    To listen to any talk; and yet these rogues
    Have cut his throat in a dream. What's my place?
    The provisorship of the horse? say, then, my corruption
    Grew out of horse-dung: I am your creature.
FERDINAND.   Away!
    [*Exit.*]
BOSOLA. Let good men, for good deeds, covet good fame,
    Since place and riches oft are bribes of shame: 40
    Sometimes the devil doth preach.
    [*Exit.*]

   [9] Sugarcoats.

Scene Two

A gallery in the DUCHESS'S *palace.*

[*Enter* FERDINAND, DUCHESS, CARDINAL, *and* CARIOLA.]
CARDINAL. We are to part from you; and your own discretion
    Must now be your director.
FERDINAND.   You are a widow:
    You know already what man is; and therefore
    Let not youth, high promotion, eloquence—
CARDINAL.   No,
    Nor anything without the addition, honor,
    Sway your high blood.
FERDINAND. Marry! they are most luxurious[10]
    Will wed twice.   10
CARDINAL.   Oh, fie!
FERDINAND.   Their livers are more spotted
    Than Laban's sheep.[11]
DUCHESS.   Diamonds are of most value,
    They say, that have passed through most jewelers' hands.
FERDINAND. Whores by that rule are precious.
DUCHESS.   Will you hear me?
    I'll never marry.
CARDINAL.   So most widows say;
    But commonly that motion lasts no longer   20
    Than the turning of an hourglass: the funeral sermon
    And it end both together.
FERDINAND.   Now hear me:
    You live in a rank pasture, here, in the court;
    There is a kind of honey-dew that's deadly;
    'Twill poison your fame; look to it: be not cunning;
    For they whose faces do belie their hearts
    Are witches ere they arrive at twenty years,
    Aye, and give the devil suck.
DUCHESS.   This is terrible good counsel.   30
FERDINAND. Hypocrisy is woven of a fine small thread,
    Subtler than Vulcan's engine[12]: yet, believe it,
    Your darkest actions, nay, your privatest thoughts,
    Will come to light.

[10] Lustful.
[11] *cf*. Genesis 30: 37–39.
[12] The trap by which Vulcan caught his wife Venus with her lover.

CARDINAL.   You may flatter yourself,
        And take your own choice; privately be married
        Under the eaves of night—
FERDINAND.   Thinkest the best voyage
        That e'er you made; like the irregular crab,
        Which, though it goes backward, thinks that it goes right
        Because it goes its own way; but observe,
        Such weddings may more properly be said
        To be executed than celebrated.
CARDINAL.   The marriage night   10
        Is the entrance into some prison.
FERDINAND.   And those joys,
        Those lustful pleasures, are like heavy sleeps
        Which do forerun man's mischief.
CARDINAL.   Fare you well.
        Wisdom begins at the end: remember it.
        [*Exit.*]
DUCHESS. I think this speech between you both was studied,
        It came so roundly off.
FERDINAND.   You are my sister;
        This was my father's poniard, do you see?   20
        I'd be loth to see it look rusty, because 'twas his.
        I would have you to give over these chargeable revels:
        A visor and a mask are whispering-rooms
        That were never built for goodness;—fare ye well;—
        And women like that part which, like the lamprey,
        Hath never a bone in it.
DUCHESS.   Fie, sir!
FERDINAND.   Nay,
        I mean the tongue; variety of courtship:
        What cannot a neat knave with a smooth tale   30
        Make a woman believe? Farewell, lusty widow.
        [*Exit.*]
DUCHESS. Shall this move me? If all my royal kindred
        Lay in my way unto this marriage,
        I'd make them my low footsteps: and even now,
        Even in this hate, as men in some great battles,
        By apprehending danger, have achieved
        Almost impossible actions (I have heard soldiers say so),
        So I through frights and threatenings will assay
        This dangerous venture. Let old wives report
        I winked and chose a husband.—Cariola,   40
        To thy known secrecy I have given up
        More than my life—my fame.[13]

[13] Reputation.

CARIOLA.   Both shall be safe;
    For I'll conceal this secret from the world
    As warily as those that trade in poison
    Keep poison from their children.
DUCHESS.   Thy protestation
    Is ingenious and hearty: I believe it.
    Is Antonio come?
CARIOLA.   He attends you.
DUCHESS.   Good dear soul,
    Leave me; but place thyself behind the arras,[14]   10
    Where thou mayst overhear us. Wish me good speed;
    For I am going into a wilderness
    Where I shall find nor path nor friendly clue
    To be my guide.
    [CARIOLA *goes behind the arras.*]
    [*Enter* ANTONIO.]
                 I sent for you: sit down;
    Take pen and ink, and write: are you ready?
ANTONIO.   Yes.
DUCHESS. What did I say?
ANTONIO. That I should write somewhat.
DUCHESS.   Oh, I remember.   20
    After these triumphs and this large expense,
    It's fit, like thrifty husbands,[15] we inquire
    What's laid up for tomorrow.
ANTONIO. So please your beauteous excellence.
DUCHESS.   Beauteous?
    Indeed, I thank you: I look young for your sake;
    You have taken my cares upon you.
ANTONIO.   I'll fetch your grace
    The particulars of your revenue and expense.
DUCHESS. Oh, you are an upright treasurer: but you mistook;   30
    For when I said I meant to make inquiry
    What's laid up for tomorrow, I did mean
    What's laid up yonder for me.
ANTONIO.   Where?
DUCHESS.   In heaven.
    I am making my will (as 'tis fit princes should,
    In perfect memory), and, I pray, sir, tell me,
    Were not one better make it smiling, thus,
    Than in deep groans and terrible ghastly looks,
    As if the gifts we parted with procured   40
    That violent distraction?

[14] Tapestry curtain.
[15] Husbandmen, careful providers.

ANTONIO.   Oh, much better.
DUCHESS. If I had a husband now, this care were quit:
    But I intend to make you overseer.
    What good deed shall we first remember? say.
ANTONIO. Begin with that first good deed began in the world
    After man's creation, the sacrament of marriage:
    I'd have you first provide for a good husband;
    Give him all.
DUCHESS.   All?
ANTONIO.   Yes, your excellent self.   10
DUCHESS. In a winding-sheet?[16]
ANTONIO.   In a couple.
DUCHESS.   Saint Winfred,
    That were a strange will!
ANTONIO. 'Twere stranger if there were no will in you
    To marry again.
DUCHESS.   What do you think of marriage?
ANTONIO. I take it, as those that deny purgatory;
    It locally contains or Heaven or hell;
    There's no third place in it.   20
DUCHESS.   How do you affect it?
ANTONIO. My banishment, feeling my melancholy,
    Would often reason thus.
DUCHESS.   Pray, let's hear it.
ANTONIO. Say a man never marry, nor have children,
    What takes that from him? only the bare name
    Of being a father, or the weak delight
    To see the little wanton ride a-cock-horse
    Upon a painted stick, or hear him chatter
    Like a taught starling.   30
DUCHESS.   Fie, fie, what's all this?
    One of your eyes is bloodshot; use my ring to it,
    They say 'tis very sovereign: 'twas my wedding-ring,
    And I did vow never to part with it
    But to my second husband.
ANTONIO.   You have parted with it now.
DUCHESS. Yes, to help your eyesight.
ANTONIO.   You have made me stark blind.
DUCHESS.   How?
ANTONIO. There is a saucy and ambitious devil   40
    Is dancing in this circle.
DUCHESS.   Remove him.
ANTONIO.   How?

[16] Shroud.

DUCHESS. There needs small conjuration, when your finger
    May do it: this; is it fit?
    [*She puts the ring upon his finger: he kneels.*]
ANTONIO.   What said you?
DUCHESS.   Sir,
    This goodly roof of yours is too low built;
    I cannot stand upright in it nor discourse,
    Without I raise it higher: raise yourself;
    Or, if you please, my hand to help you: so.
    [*Raises him.*]
ANTONIO. Ambition, madam, is a great man's madness,
    That is not kept in chains and close-pent rooms,   10
    But in fair lightsome lodgings, and is girt
    With the wild noise of prattling visitants,
    Which makes it lunatic beyond all cure.
    Conceive not I am so stupid but I aim[17]
    Whereto your favors tend: but he's a fool
    That, being a-cold, would thrust his hands in the fire
    To warm them.
DUCHESS.   So, now the ground's broke,
    You may discover what a wealthy mine
    I make you lord of.   20
ANTONIO.   O my unworthiness!
DUCHESS. You were ill to sell yourself:
    This darkening of your worth is not like that
    Which tradesmen use in the city, their false lights
    Are to rid bad wares off: and I must tell you,
    If you will know where breathes a complete man
    (I speak it without flattery), turn your eyes,
    And progress through yourself.
ANTONIO.   Were there nor heaven
    Nor hell, I should be honest: I have long served virtue,   30
    And never taken wages of her.
DUCHESS.   Now she pays it.
    The misery of us that are born great!
    We are forced to woo, because none dare woo us;
    And as a tyrant doubles with his words,
    And fearfully equivocates, so we
    Are forced to express our violent passions
    In riddles and in dreams, and leave the path
    Of simple virtue, which was never made
    To seem the thing it is not. Go, go brag   40
    You have left me heartless; mine is in your bosom:

[17] Understand.

I hope 'twill multiply love there. You do tremble:
Make not your heart so dead a piece of flesh,
To fear more than to love me. Sir, be confident:
What is it distracts you? This is flesh and blood, sir;
'Tis not the figure cut in alabaster
Kneels at my husband's tomb. Awake, awake, man!
I do here put off all vain ceremony,
And only do appear to you a young widow
That claims you for her husband, and, like a widow,
I use but half a blush in it.   10

ANTONIO.   Truth speak for me;
I will remain the constant sanctuary
Of your good name.

DUCHESS.   I thank you, gentle love:
And 'cause you shall not come to me in debt,
Being now my steward, here upon your lips
I sign your *Quietus est*:[18] This you should have begged now:
I have seen children oft eat sweetmeats thus,
As fearful to devour them too soon.

ANTONIO.   But for your brothers?   20

DUCHESS.   Do not think of them:
All discord without this circumference
Is only to be pitied, and not feared:
Yet, should they know it, time will easily
Scatter the tempest.

ANTONIO.   These words should be mine,
And all the parts you have spoke, if some part of it
Would not have savored flattery.

DUCHESS.   Kneel.
[CARIOLA *comes from behind the arras.*]

ANTONIO.   Ha!   30

DUCHESS. Be not amazed; this woman's of my counsel:
I have heard lawyers say, a contract in a chamber
Per verba de presenti[19] is absolute marriage.
[*She and* ANTONIO *kneel.*]
Bless, heaven, this sacred gordian,[20] which let violence
Never untwine!

ANTONIO. And may our sweet affections, like the spheres,
Be still in motion!

DUCHESS.   Quickening, and make
The like soft music!

---

[18] Finishing stroke.
[19] i.e., in the presence of a witness.
[20] Knot.

ANTONIO. That we may imitate the loving palms,
    Best emblem of a peaceful marriage, that ne'er
    Bore fruit, divided!
DUCHESS.   What can the Church force more?
ANTONIO. That fortune may not know an accident,
    Either of joy or sorrow, to divide
    Our fixèd wishes!
DUCHESS.   How can the Church build faster?
    We now are man and wife, and 'tis the Church
    That must but echo this.—Maid, stand apart: 10
    I am now blind.
ANTONIO.   What's your conceit in this?
DUCHESS. I would have you lead your fortune by the hand
    Unto your marriage bed:
    (You speak in me this, for we now are one:)
    We'll only lie, and talk together, and plot
    To appease my humorous kindred; and if you please,
    Like the old tale in "Alexander and Lodowick,"
    Lay a naked sword between us, keep us chaste.
    Oh, let me shroud my blushes in your bosom,   20
    Since 'tis the treasury of all my secrets!
    [*Exeunt* DUCHESS *and* ANTONIO.]
CARIOLA. Whether the spirit of greatness or of woman
    Reign most in her, I know not; but it shows
    A fearful madness: I owe her much of pity.
    [*Exit.*]

ACT TWO

Scene One

A room in the palace of the DUCHESS.

[*Enter* BOSOLA *and* CASTRUCHIO.]
BOSOLA. You say you would fain be taken for an eminent courtier?
CASTRUCHIO. 'Tis the very main of my ambition.
BOSOLA. Let me see: you have a reasonable good face for it already,
    and your nightcap expresses your ears sufficient largely. I would
    have you learn to twirl the strings of your band with a good grace,
    and in a set speech, at the end of every sentence, to hum three or   30
    four times, or blow your nose till it smart again, to recover
    your memory. When you come to be a president in criminal causes,
    if you smile upon a prisoner, hang him, but if you frown upon
    him and threaten him, let him be sure to escape the gallows.

CASTRUCHIO. I would be a very merry president.

BOSOLA. Do not sup of night; 'twill beget you an admirable wit.

CASTRUCHIO. Rather it would make me have a good stomach to quarrel; for they say, your roaring boys eat meat seldom, and that makes them so valiant. But how shall I know whether the people take me for an eminent fellow?

BOSOLA. I will teach a trick to know it: give out you lie a-dying, and if you hear the common people curse you, be sure you are taken for one of the prime nightcaps.[21]

[*Enter an* OLD LADY.]

You come from painting now.   10

OLD LADY. From what?

BOSOLA. Why, from your scurvy face-physic. To behold thee not painted inclines somewhat near a miracle; these in thy face here were deep ruts and foul sloughs the last progress.[22] There was a lady in France that, having had the smallpox, flayed the skin off her face to make it more level; and whereas before she looked like a nutmeg-grater, after she resembled an abortive hedgehog.

OLD LADY. Do you call this painting?

BOSOLA. No, no, but you call it careening of an old morphewed lady, to make her disembogue again: there's rough-cast phrase to   20
your plastic.

OLD LADY. It seems you are well acquainted with my closet.

BOSOLA. One would suspect it for a shop of witchcraft, to find in it the fat of seprents, spawn of snakes, Jew's spittle, and their young children's ordure; and all these for the face. I would sooner eat a dead pigeon taken from the soles of the feet of one sick of the plague than kiss one of you fasting. Here are two of you, whose sin of your youth is the very patrimony of the physician; makes him renew his foot-cloth with the spring, and change his high-priced courtesan with the fall of the leaf. I do wonder you do not   30
loathe yourselves. Observe my meditation now.

> What thing is in this outward form of man
> To be beloved? We account it ominous,
> If nature do produce a colt, or lamb,
> A fawn, or goat, in any limb resembling
> A man, and fly from it as a prodigy:
> Man stands amazed to see his deformity
> In any other creature but himself.
> But in our own flesh, though we bear diseases
> Which have their true names only taken from beasts,—   40
> As the most ulcerous wolf and swinish measle,—

[21] *cf.*, "nightowl."
[22] Procession of state; court ceremony.

Though we are eaten up of lice and worms,
And though continually we bear about us
A rotten and dead body, we delight
To hide it in rich tissue: all our fear
Nay, all our terror, is lest our physician
Should put us in the ground to be made sweet.—
Your wife's gone to Rome: you two couple, and get you
To the wells at Lucca to recover your aches.
I have other work on foot.
[*Exeunt* CASTRUCHIO *and* OLD LADY.]
                             I observe our duchess   10
Is sick a-days, she pukes, her stomach seethes,
The fins of her eyelids look most teeming blue,
She wanes in the cheek, and waxes fat in the flank,
And, contrary to our Italian fashion,
Wears a loose-bodied gown: there's somewhat in it.
I have a trick may chance discover it,
A pretty one; I have brought some apricots,
The first our spring yields.
[*Enter* ANTONIO *and* DELIO, *talking together apart.*]
DELIO.   And so long since married?
You amaze me.   20
ANTONIO.   Let me seal your lips for ever:
For, did I think that anything but the air
Could carry these words from you, I should wish
You had no breath at all.—Now, sir, in your contemplation?
You are studying to become a great wise fellow?
BOSOLA. Oh, sir, the opinion of wisdom is a foul tetter[23] that runs
all over a man's body: if simplicity direct us to have no evil, it
directs us to a happy being; for the subtlest folly proceeds from
the subtlest wisdom: let me be simply honest.   30
ANTONIO. I do understand your inside.
BOSOLA.   Do you so?
ANTONIO. Because you would not seem to appear to the world
     Puffed up with your preferment, you continue
     This out-of-fashion melancholy: leave it, leave it.
BOSOLA. Give me leave to be honest in any phrase, in any compliment whatsoever. Shall I confess myself to you? I look no
higher than I can reach: they are the gods that must ride on
winged horses. A lawyer's mule of a slow pace will both suit my
disposition and business; for, mark me, when a man's mind rides   40
faster than his horse can gallop, they quickly both tire.
ANTONIO. You would look up to heaven, but I think
     The devil, that rules in the air, stands in your light.
[23] Eczema.

BOSOLA. Oh, sir, you are lord of the ascendant, chief man with the
  duchess; a duke was your cousin-german removed. Say you were
  lineally descended from King Pepin, or he himself, what of this?
  Search the heads of the greatest rivers in the world, you shall find
  them but bubbles of water. Some would think the souls of princes
  were brought forth by some more weighty cause than those of
  meaner persons: they are deceived, there's the same hand to them;
  the like passions sway them; the same reason that makes a vicar
  go to law for a tithe-pig, and undo his neighbors, makes them
  spoil a whole province, and batter down goodly cities with the   10
  cannon.
        [*Enter* DUCHESS *and* LADIES.]
DUCHESS. Your arm, Antonio: do I not grow fat?
        I am exceeding short-winded.—Bosola,
        I would have you, sir, provide for me a litter;
        Such a one as the Duchess of Florence rode in.
BOSOLA. The duchess used one when she was great with child.
DUCHESS. I think she did.—Come hither, mend my ruff;
        Here, when?
        Thou art such a tedious lady; and thy breath smells
        Of lemon-peels; would thou hadst done! Shall I swoon   20
        Under thy fingers! I am so troubled
        With the mother![24]
BOSOLA [*aside*]. I fear too much.
DUCHESS.   I have heard you say
        That the French courtiers wear their hats on 'fore
        The king.
ANTONIO. I have seen it.
DUCHESS.   In the presence?
ANTONIO.   Yes.
DUCHESS. Why should not we bring up that fashion? 'Tis   30
        Ceremony more than duty that consists
        In the removing of a piece of felt:
        Be you the example to the rest of the court;
        Put on your hat first.
ANTONIO.   You must pardon me:
        I have seen, in colder countries than in France,
        Nobles stand bare to the prince; and the distinction
        Methought showed reverently.
BOSOLA. I have a present for your grace.
DUCHESS.   For me, sir?   40
BOSOLA. Apricots, madam.
DUCHESS.   O, sir, where are they?
        I have heard of none to-year.

[24] Hysteria.

BOSOLA [*aside*].   Good; her color rises.
DUCHESS. Indeed, I thank you: they are wondrous fair ones.
    What an unskillful fellow is our gardener!
    We shall have none this month.
BOSOLA.   Will not your grace pare them?
DUCHESS. No: they taste of musk, methinks; indeed they do.
BOSOLA. I know not: yet I wish your grace had pared them.
DUCHESS. Why?
BOSOLA.   I forgot to tell you, the knave gardener.
    Only to raise his profit by them the sooner,   10
    Did ripen them in horse-dung.
DUCHESS.   O, you jest.—
    You shall judge: pray taste one.
ANTONIO.   Indeed, madam,
    I do not love the fruit.
DUCHESS.   Sir, you are loath
    To rob us of our dainties: 'tis a delicate fruit;
    They say they are restorative.
BOSOLA.   'Tis a pretty art,
    This grafting.   20
DUCHESS.   'Tis so; a bettering of nature.
BOSOLA. To make a pippin grow upon a crab,
    A damson on a blackthorn.—[*Aside.*] How greedily she
      eats them!
    A whirlwind strike off these bawd farthingales!
    For, but for that and the loose-bodied gown,
    I should have discovered apparently
    The young springal[25] cutting a caper in her belly.
DUCHESS. I thank you, Bosola: they were right good ones,
    If they do not make me sick.   30
ANTONIO.   Now now, madam?
DUCHESS. This green fruit and my stomach are not friends:
    How they swell me!
BOSOLA [*aside*]. Nay, you are too much swelled already.
DUCHESS. Oh, I am in an extreme cold sweat!
BOSOLA.   I am very sorry.
DUCHESS. Lights to my chamber!—O good Antonio,
    I fear I am undone!
DELIO.   Lights there, lights!
    [*Exeunt* DUCHESS *and* LADIES. *Exit, on the other side,* BOSOLA.]
ANTONIO. O my most trusty Delio, we are lost!   40
    I fear she's fallen in labor; and there's left
    No time for her remove.

[25] Stripling.

DELIO.   Have you prepared
　　Those ladies to attend her? and procured
　　That politic safe conveyance for the midwife
　　Your duchess plotted?
ANTONIO. I have.
DELIO.   Make use, then, of this forced occasion:
　　Give out that Bosola hath poisoned her
　　With these apricots; that will give some color
　　For her keeping close.
ANTONIO.   Fie, fie, the physicians   10
　　Will then flock to her.
DELIO.   For that you may pretend
　　She'll use some prepared antidote of her own,
　　Lest the physicians should repoison her.
ANTONIO. I am lost in amazement: I know not what to think on it.
　　[*Exeunt*]

Scene Two

A hall in the same palace.

[*Enter* BOSOLA.]
BOSOLA. So, so, there's no question but her tetchiness and most
　　vulturous eating of the apricots are apparent signs of breeding.
　　[*Enter an* OLD LADY.]
　　Now?
OLD LADY. I am in haste, sir.
BOSOLA. There was a young waiting-woman had a monstrous desire   20
　　to see the glass-house[26]—
OLD LADY. Nay, pray let me go.
BOSOLA. And it was only to know what strange instrument it was
　　should swell up a glass to the fashion of a woman's belly.
OLD LADY. I will hear no more of the glass-house. You are still
　　abusing women?
BOSOLA. Who, I? no; only, by the way now and then, mention
　　your frailties. The orange-tree bears ripe and green fruit and
　　blossoms all together; and some of you give entertainment for
　　pure love, but more for more precious reward. The lusty spring   30
　　smells well; but drooping autumn tastes well. If we have the same
　　golden showers that rained in the time of Jupiter the thunderer,
　　you have the same Danaës still, to hold up their laps to receive
　　them. Didst thou never study the mathematics?
OLD LADY. What's that, sir?

　　[26] Factory for glass-making.

BOSOLA. Why, to know the trick how to make a-many lines meet in
   one center. Go, go, give your foster-daughters good counsel:
   tell them, that the devil takes delight to hang at a woman's girdle,
   like a false rusty watch, that she cannot discern how the time
   passes.
   [*Exit* OLD LADY.]
   [*Enter* ANTONIO, DELIO, RODERIGO, *and* GRISOLAN.]
ANTONIO. Shut up the court-gates.
RODERIGO.   Why, sir? what's the danger?
ANTONIO. Shut up the posterns presently, and call
   All the officers of the court.
GRISOLAN.   I shall instantly.   10
   [*Exit.*]
ANTONIO. Who keeps the key of the park gate?
RODERIGO.   Forobosco.
ANTONIO. Let him bring it presently.
   [*Reenter* GRISOLAN *with* SERVANTS.]
FIRST SERVANT. O, gentlemen of the court, the foulest treason!
BOSOLA [*aside*]. If that these apricots should be poisoned now,
       Without my knowledge!
FIRST SERVANT.   There was taken even now
   A Switzer in the duchess's bed-chamber—
SECOND SERVANT.   A Switzer?
FIRST SERVANT. With a pistol in his great codpiece.   20
BOSOLA.   Ha, ha, ha!
FIRST SERVANT. The codpiece was the case for it.
SECOND SERVANT.   There was
   A cunning traitor: who would have searched his codpiece?
FIRST SERVANT. True, if he had kept out of the ladies' chambers:
   And all the molds of his buttons were leaden bullets.
SECOND SERVANT. O wicked cannibal!
   A fire-lock in his codpiece!
FIRST SERVANT.   'Twas a French plot,
   Upon my life.   30
SECOND SERVANT.   To see what the devil can do!
ANTONIO. Are all the officers here?
SERVANTS.   We are.
ANTONIO.   Gentlemen,
   We have lost much plate you know; and but this evening
   Jewels, to the value of four thousand ducats,
   Are missing in the duchess's cabinet.
   Are the gates shut?
SERVANTS.   Yes.
ANTONIO.   'Tis the duchess's pleasure   40
   Each officer be locked into his chamber

Till the sunrising; and to send the keys
Of all their chests and of their outward doors
Into her bed-chamber. She is very sick.

RODERIGO. At her pleasure.

ANTONIO.   She entreats you take it not ill:
The innocent shall be the more approved by it.

BOSOLA. Gentleman of the wood-yard, where's your Switzer now?

FIRST SERVANT. By this hand, 'twas credibly reported by one of the
    black guard.

    [*Exeunt all except* ANTONIO *and* DELIO.]

DELIO. How fares it with the duchess?   10

ANTONIO.   She's exposed
Unto the worst of torture, pain and fear.

DELIO. Speak to her all happy comfort.

ANTONIO. How I do play the fool with mine own danger!
You are this night, dear friend, to post to Rome:
My life lies in your service.

DELIO.   Do not doubt me.

ANTONIO. Oh, 'tis far from me: and yet fear presents me
Somewhat that looks like danger.

DELIO.   Believe it,   20
'Tis but the shadow of your fear, no more;
How superstitiously we mind our evils!
The throwing down salt, or crossing of a hare,
Bleeding at nose, the stumbling of a horse,
Or singing of a cricket, are of power
To daunt whole man in us. Sir, fare you well:
I wish you all the joys of a blessèd father:
And, for my faith, lay this unto your breast,—
Old friends, like old swords, still are trusted best.

    [*Exit.*]

    [*Enter* CARIOLA.]

CARIOLA. Sir, you are the happy father of a son: 30
Your wife commends him to you.

ANTONIO.   Blessèd comfort!—
For Heaven's sake tend her well: I'll presently
Go set a figure for his nativity.

    [*Exeunt.*]

Scene Three

The courtyard of the same palace.

[*Enter* BOSOLA, *with a dark lantern.*]

BOSOLA. Sure I did hear a woman shriek: list, ha!
 And the sound came, if I received it right,
 From the duchess's lodgings. There's some stratagem
 In the confining all our courtiers
 To their several wards: I must have part of it;
 My intelligence will freeze else. List, again!
 It may be 'twas the melancholy bird,
 Best friend of silence and of solitariness,
 The owl, that screamed so.—Ha! Antonio?
 [*Enter* ANTONIO *with a candle, his sword drawn.*]

ANTONIO. I heard some noise.—Who's there? what art thou? speak. 10

BOSOLA. Antonio? put not your face nor body
 To such a forced expression of fear:
 I am Bosola, your friend.

ANTONIO.   Bosola!—
 [*Aside.*] This mole does undermine me.—Heard you not
 A noise even now?

BOSOLA.   From whence?

ANTONIO.   From the duchess's lodging.

BOSOLA. Not I: did you?

ANTONIO.   I did, or else I dreamed. 20

BOSOLA. Let's walk toward it.

ANTONIO.   No: it may be 'twas
 But the rising of the wind.

BOSOLA.   Very likely.
 Methinks 'tis very cold, and yet you sweat:
 You look wildly.

ANTONIO.   I have been setting a figure
 For the duchess's jewels.

BOSOLA.   Ah, and how falls your question?
 Do you find it radical?[27]   30

ANTONIO.   What's that to you?
 'Tis rather to be questioned what design,
 When all men were commanded to their lodgings,
 Makes you a night-walker.

BOSOLA.   In sooth, I'll tell you:

27 Answerable.

                   Now all the court's asleep, I thought the devil
                   Had least to do here; I came to say my prayers;
                   And if it do offend you I do so,
                   You are a fine courtier.
ANTONIO [*aside*]. This fellow will undo me.—
                   You gave the duchess apricots today:
                   Pray Heaven they were not poisoned!
BOSOLA.   Poisoned? A Spanish fig
                   For the imputation!
ANTONIO.   Tràitors are ever confident   10
                   Till they are discovered. There were jewels stolen too:
                   In my conceit, none are to be suspected
                   More than yourself.
BOSOLA.   You are a false steward.
ANTONIO. Saucy slave, I'll pull thee up by the roots.
BOSOLA. Maybe the ruin will crush you to pieces.
ANTONIO. You are an impudent snake indeed, sir:
                   Are you scarce warm, and do you show your sting?
                   You libel well, sir.
BOSOLA.   No, sir: copy it out.   20
                   And I will set my hand to it.
ANTONIO [*aside*].   My nose bleeds.
                   One that were superstitious would count
                   This ominous, when it merely comes by chance:
                   Two letters, that are wrought here for my name,
                   Are drowned in blood!
                   Mere accident.—For you, sir, I'll take order
                   In the morn you shall be safe:—[*aside*] 'tis that must color
                   Her lying-in:—sir, this door you pass not:
                   I do not hold it fit that you come near   30
                   The duchess's lodgings, till you have quit yourself.—
                   [*Aside*.] The great are like the base, nay, they are the same,
                   When they seek shameful ways to avoid shame.
                   [*Exit*.]
BOSOLA. Antonio hereabout did drop a paper:—
                   Some of your help, false friend: [*Opening his lantern*.]—
                   Oh, here it is.
                   What's here? a child's nativity calculated?
                   [*Reads*.]
"The duchess was delivered of a son, 'tween the hours twelve
and one in the night, *Anno Domini* 1504,"—that's this year—
"*decimo nono Decembris*,"—that's this night,—"taken according   40
to the meridian of Malfi,"—that's our duchess: happy discovery!
—"The lord of the first house being combust in the ascendant,
signifies short life; and Mars being in a human sign, joined to

the tail of the Dragon, in the eighth house, doth threaten a violent
death. *Caetera non scrutantur.*[28]
      Why, now 'tis most apparent: this precise fellow
Is the duchess's bawd:—I have it to my wish!
This is a parcel of intelligency
Our courtiers were cased up for: it needs must follow
That I must be committed on pretense
Of poisoning her; which I'll endure, and laugh at.
If one could find the father now! but that
Time will discover. Old Castruchio   10
In the morning posts to Rome: by him I'll send
A letter that shall make her brothers' galls
O'erflow their livers. This was a thrifty way.
Though lust do mask in ne'er so strange disguise,
She's oft found witty, but is never wise.
[*Exit.*]

Scene Four

A room in the palace of the Cardinal at Rome.

[*Enter* CARDINAL *and* JULIA.]
CARDINAL. Sit: thou art my best of wishes. Prithee, tell me
    What trick didst thou invent to come to Rome
    Without thy husband.
JULIA.   Why, my lord, I told him
    I came to visit an old anchorite   20
    Here for devotion.
CARDINAL.   Thou art a witty false one—
    I mean, to him.
JULIA.   You have prevailed with me
    Beyond my strongest thoughts! I would not now
    Find you inconstant.
CARDINAL.   Do not put thyself
    To such a voluntary torture, which proceeds
    Out of your own guilt.
JULIA.   How, my lord?   30
CARDINAL.   You fear
    My constancy, because you have approved
    Those giddy and wild turnings in yourself.
JULIA. Did you e'er find them?
CARDINAL.   Sooth, generally for women;

---

[28] "The rest was not examined."

        A man might strive to make glass malleable,
        Ere he should make them fixed.

JULIA.   So, my lord.

CARDINAL. We had need go borrow that fantastic glass
        Invented by Galileo the Florentine
        To view another spacious world in the moon,
        And look to find a constant woman there.

JULIA. This is very well, my lord.

CARDINAL.   Why do you weep?
        Are tears your justification? the self-same tears   10
        Will fall into your husband's bosom, lady,
        With a loud protestation that you love him
        Above the world. Come, I'll love you wisely,
        That's jealously; since I am very certain
        You cannot make me cuckold.

JULIA.   I'll go home
        To my husband.

CARDINAL.   You may thank me, lady,
        I have taken you off your melancholy perch,
        Bore you upon my fist, and showed you game,   20
        And let you fly at it.—I pray thee, kiss me.—
        When thou wast with thy husband, thou wast watched
        Like a tame elephant:—still you are to thank me:—
        Thou hadst only kisses from him and high feeding;
        But what delight was that? 'twas just like one
        That hath a little fingering on the lute,
        Yet cannot tune it:—still you are to thank me.

JULIA. You told me of a piteous wound in the heart
        And a sick liver, when you wooed me first,
        And spake like one in physic.   30

CARDINAL.   Who's that?—
        [*Enter* SERVANT.]
        Rest firm, for my affection to thee,
        Lightning moves slow to it.

SERVANT.   Madam, a gentleman,
        That's come post from Malfi, desires to see you.

CARDINAL. Let him enter: I'll withdraw.
        [*Exit.*]

SERVANT.   He says
        Your husband, old Castruchio, is come to Rome,
        Most pitifully tired with riding post.
        [*Exit.*]
        [*Enter* DELIO.]

JULIA. Signor Delio! [*Aside.*] 'Tis one of my old suitors.   40

DELIO. I was bold to come and see you.

JULIA.   Sir, you are welcome.
DELIO. Do you lie here?
JULIA.   Sure, your own experience
     Will satisfy you no: our Roman prelates
     Do not keep lodging for ladies.
DELIO.   Very well:
     I have brought you no commendations from your husband,
     For I know none by him.
JULIA.   I hear he's come to Rome.
DELIO. I never knew man and beast, or a horse and a knight,   10
     So weary of each other: if he had had a good back,
     He would have undertook to have borne his horse,
     His breech was so pitifully sore.
JULIA.   Your laughter
     Is my pity.
DELIO.   Lady, I know not whether
     You want money, but I have brought you some.
JULIA. From my husband?
DELIO.   No, from mine own allowance.
JULIA. I must hear the condition, ere I be bound to take it.   20
DELIO. Look on it, 'tis gold: hath it not a fine color?
JULIA. I have a bird more beautiful.
DELIO. Try the sound on it.
JULIA.   A lute-string far exceeds it:
     It hath no smell, like cassia or civet;
     Nor is it physical, though some fond doctors
     Persuade us seethe it in cullises. I'll tell you,
     This is a creature bred by—
     [*Reenter* SERVANT.]
SERVANT.   Your husband's come.
     Hath delivered a letter to the Duke of Calabria   30
     That, to my thinking, hath put him out of his wits.
     [*Exit.*]
JULIA. Sir, you hear:
     Pray, let me know your business and your suit
     As briefly as can be.
DELIO. With good speed: I would wish you,
     At such time as you are non-resident
     With your husband, my mistress.
JULIA. Sir, I'll go ask my husband if I shall,
     And straight return your answer.
     [*Exit.*]
DELIO   Very fine!   40
     Is this her wit, or honesty, that speaks thus?
     I heard one say the duke was highly moved

With a letter sent from Malfi. I do fear
Antonio is betrayed: how fearfully
Shows his ambition now! unfortunate fortune!
They pass through whirlpools, and deep woes do shun,
Who the event weigh ere the action's done.
[*Exit.*]

Scene Five

Another room in the same palace.

[*Enter* CARDINAL, *and* FERDINAND *with a letter.*]
FERDINAND. I have this night digged up a mandrake.[29]
CARDINAL.   Say you?
FERDINAND. And I am grown mad with it.
CARDINAL.   What's the prodigy?
FERDINAND. Read there,—a sister damned: she's loose in the hilts;   10
   Grown a notorious strumpet.
CARDINAL.   Speak lower.
FERDINAND.   Lower?
   Rogues do not whisper it now, but seek to publish it
   (As servants do the bounty of their lords)
   Aloud; and with a covetous searching eye,
   To mark who note them. O, confusion seize her!
   She hath had most cunning bawds to serve her turn,
   And more secure conveyances for lust
   Than towns of garrison for service.   20
CARDINAL.   Is it possible?
   Can this be certain?
FERDINAND.   Rhubarb, oh, for rhubarb
   To purge this choler! here's the cursèd day
   To prompt my memory; and here it shall stick
   Till of her bleeding heart I made a sponge
   To wipe it out.
CARDINAL.   Why do you make yourself
   So wild a tempest?
FERDINAND.   Would I could be one,   30
   That I might toss her palace 'bout her ears,
   Root up her goodly forests, blast her meads,
   And lay her general territory as waste
   As she hath done her honors.

---

[29] A root whose screams when pulled from the earth were fabled to drive men mad.

CARDINAL.   Shall our blood,
    The royal blood of Arragon and Castile,
    Be thus attainted?
FERDINAND.   Apply desperate physic:
    We must not now use balsamum, but fire,
    The smarting cupping-glass, for that is the mean
    To purge infected blood, such blood as hers.
    There is a kind of pity in mine eye,—
    I'll give it to my handkercher; and now 'tis here,
    I'll bequeath this to her bastard.   10
CARDINAL.   What to do?
FERDINAND. Why, to make soft lint for his mother's wounds,
    When I have hewed her to pieces.
CARDINAL.   Cursed creature!
    Unequal nature, to place women's hearts
    So far upon the left side!
FERDINAND.   Foolish men,
    That e'er will trust their honor in a bark
    Made of so slight weak bulrush as is woman,
    Apt every minute to sink it!   20
CARDINAL. Thus ignorance, when it hath purchased honor,
    It cannot wield it.
FERDINAND.   Methinks I see her laughing—
    Excellent hyena! Talk to me somewhat, quickly,
    Or my imagination will carry me
    To see her in the shameful act of sin.
CARDINAL. With whom?
FERDINAND. Happily[30] with some strong-thighed bargeman,
    Or one of the woodyard that can quoit the sledge[31]
    Or toss the bar, or else some lovely squire   30
    That carries coals up to her privy lodgings.
CARDINAL. You fly beyond your reason.
FERDINAND.   Go to, mistress!
    'Tis not your whore's milk that shall quench my wild fire,
    But your whore's blood.
CARDINAL. How idly shows this rage, which carries you,
    As men conveyed by witches through the air,
    On violent whirlwinds! this intemperate noise
    Fitly resembles deaf men's shrill discourse,
    Who talk aloud, thinking all other men   40
    To have their imperfection.
FERDINAND.   Have not you
    My palsy?

[30] Possibly.
[31] Throw the hammer.

CARDINAL.   Yes, I can be angry, but
          Without this rupture: there is not in nature
          A thing that makes man so deformed, so beastly,
          As doth intemperate anger. Chide yourself.
          You have divers men who never yet expressed
          Their strong desire of rest but by unrest,
          By vexing of themselves. Come, put yourself
          In tune.
FERDINAND.   So; I will only study to seem
          The thing I am not. I could kill her now,   10
          In you, or in myself; for I do think
          It is some sin in us heaven doth revenge
          By her.
CARDINAL. Are you stark mad?
FERDINAND.   I would have their bodies
          Burnt in a coal-pit with the ventage stopped,
          That their cursed smoke might not ascend to heaven;
          Or dip the sheets they lie in in pitch or sulphur,
          Wrap them in it, and then light them like a match;
          Or else to boil their bastard to a cullis,[32]   20
          And give it his lecherous father to renew
          The sin of his back.
CARDINAL.   I'll leave you.
FERDINAND.   Nay, I have done.
          I am confident, had I been damned in hell,
          And should have heard of this, it would have put me
          Into a cold sweat. In, in; I'll go sleep.
          Till I know who leaps my sister, I'll not stir:
          That known, I'll find scorpions to string my whips,
          And fix her in a general eclipse.   30
          [*Exeunt.*]

ACT THREE

Scene One

A room in the palace of the DUCHESS.

          [*Enter* ANTONIO *and* DELIO.]
ANTONIO. Our noble friend, my most beloved Delio!
          Oh, you have been a stranger long at court;
          Came you along with the Lord Ferdinand?

          [32] A broth for invalids.

DELIO. I did, sir: and how fares your noble duchess?
ANTONIO. Right fortunately well: she's an excellent
   Feeder of pedigrees; since you last saw her,
   She hath had two children more, a son and daughter.
DELIO. Methinks 'twas yesterday: let me but wink,
   And not behold your face, which to mine eye
   Is somewhat leaner, verily I should dream
   It were within this half-hour.
ANTONIO. You have not been in law, friend Delio,
   Nor in prison, nor a suitor at the court,   10
   Nor begged the reversion of some great man's place,
   Nor troubled with an old wife, which doth make
   Your time so insensibly hasten.
DELIO.   Pray, sir, tell me,
   Hath not this news arrived yet to the ear
   Of the lord cardinal?
ANTONIO.   I fear it hath:
   The Lord Ferdinand, that is newly come to court,
   Doth bear himself right dangerously.
DELIO.   Pray, why?   20
ANTONIO. He is so quiet that he seems to sleep
   The tempest out, as dormice do in winter:
   Those houses that are haunted are most still
   Till the devil be up.
DELIO.   What say the common people?
ANTONIO. The common rabble do directly say
   She is a strumpet.
DELIO.   And your graver heads
   Which would be politic, what censure they?
ANTONIO. They do observe I grow to infinite purchase,[33]   30
   The left hand way, and all suppose the duchess
   Would amend it, if she could; for, say they,
   Great princes, though they grudge their officers
   Should have such large and unconfinèd means
   To get wealth under them, will not complain,
   Lest thereby they should make them odious
   Unto the people; for other obligation
   Of love or marriage between her and me
   They never dream of.
DELIO.   The Lord Ferdinand 40
   Is going to bed.
   [*Enter* DUCHESS, FERDINAND, *and* BOSOLA.]
FERDINAND. I'll instantly to bed,

---

[33] Estate, possessions.

For I am weary.—I am to bespeak
A husband for you.

DUCHESS.   For me, sir? pray, who is it?

FERDINAND. The great Count Malateste.

DUCHESS.   Fie upon him!
A count? he's a mere stick of sugar-candy;
You may look quite through him. When I choose
A husband, I will marry for your honor.

FERDINAND. You shall do well in it.—How is it, worthy Antonio?

DUCHESS. But, sir, I am to have private conference with you   10
About a scandalous report is spread
Touching mine honor.

FERDINAND.   Let me be ever deaf to it:
One of Pasquil's[34] paper bullets, court-calumny,
A pestilent air, which princes' palaces
Are seldom purged of. Yet, say that it were true,
I pour it in your bosom, my fixèd love
Would strongly excuse, extenuate, nay, deny
Faults, were they apparent in you. Go, be safe
In your own innocency.   20

DUCHESS [aside].   O blessed comfort!
This deadly air is purged.

[Exeunt DUCHESS, ANTONIO, and DELIO.]

FERDINAND.   Her guilt treads on
Hot-burning coulters.—Now, Bosola,
How thrives our intelligence?

BOSOLA.   Sir, uncertainly
'Tis rumored she hath had three bastards, but
By whom we may go read in the stars.

FERDINAND.   Why, some
Hold opinion all things are written there.   30

BOSOLA. Yes, if we could find spectacles to read them.
I do suspect there hath been some sorcery
Used on the duchess.

FERDINAND.   Sorcery? to what purpose?

BOSOLA. To make her dote on some desertless fellow
She shames to acknowledge.

FERDINAND.   Can your faith give way
To think there is power in potions or in charms,
To make us love whether we will or no?

BOSOLA. Most certainly.   40

FERDINAND. Away! these are mere gulleries, horrid things,
Invented by some cheating mountebanks

[34] Common name for a satirist.

To abuse us. Do you think that herbs or charms
Can force the will? Some trials have been made
In this foolish practice, but the ingredients
Were lenitive poisons, such as are of force
To make the patient mad; and straight the witch
Swears by equivocation they are in love.
The witchcraft lies in her rank blood. This night
I will force confession from her. You told me
You had got, within these two days, a false key
Into her bed-chamber.   10

BOSOLA.   I have.

FERDINAND.   As I would wish.

BOSOLA. What do you intend to do?

FERDINAND.   Can you guess?

BOSOLA.   No.

FERDINAND. Do not ask, then:
He that can compass me, and know my drifts,
May say he hath put a girdle 'bout the world,
And sounded all her quicksands.

BOSOLA.   I do not   20
Think so.

FERDINAND. What do you think, then, pray?

BOSOLA.   That you
Are your own chronicle too much, and grossly
Flatter yourself.

FERDINAND. Give me thy hand; I thank thee:
I never gave pension but to flatterers,
Till I entertained thee. Farewell.
That friend a great man's ruin strongly checks,
Who rails into his belief all his defects.   30
[Exeunt.]

Scene Two

The bed-chamber of the DUCHESS.

[Enter DUCHESS, ANTONIO, and CARIOLA.]

DUCHESS. Bring me the casket hither, and the glass.—
You get no lodging here tonight, my lord.

ANTONIO. Indeed, I must persuade one.

DUCHESS.   Very good:
I hope in time 'twill grow into a custom,
That noblemen shall come with cap and knee
To purchase a night's lodging of their wives.

ANTONIO. I must lie here.

DUCHESS.   Must! you are a lord of misrule.

ANTONIO. Indeed, my rule is only in the night.

DUCHESS. To what use will you put me?

ANTONIO.   We'll sleep together.

DUCHESS. Alas,
 What pleasure can two lovers find in sleep!

CARIOLA. My lord, I lie with her often; and I know
 She'll much disquiet you.

ANTONIO.   See, you are complained of.   10

CARIOLA. For she's the sprawlingest bedfellow.

ANTONIO.   I shall like her
 The better for that.

CARIOLA.   Sir, shall I ask you a question?

ANTONIO. Oh, I pray thee, Cariola.

CARIOLA.   Wherefore still, when you lie
 With my lady, do you rise so early?

ANTONIO.   Laboring men
 Count the clock oftenest, Cariola, are glad
 When their task is ended.   20

DUCHESS.   I'll stop your mouth.
 [*Kisses him.*]

ANTONIO. Nay, that's but one; Venus had two soft doves
 To draw her chariot; I must have another—
 [*She kisses him again.*]
 When wilt thou marry, Cariola?

CARIOLA.   Never, my lord.

ANTONIO. Oh, fie upon this single life! forgo it.
 We read how Daphne, for her peevish flight,
 Became a fruitless bay-tree; Syrinx turned
 To the pale empty reed; Anaxarete
 Was frozen into marble: whereas those   30
 Which married, or proved kind unto their friends,[35]
 Were by a gracious influence transhaped
 Into the olive, pomegranate, mulberry,
 Became flowers, precious stones, or eminent stars.

CARIOLA. This is a vain poetry: but I pray you tell me,
 If there were proposed me, wisdom, riches, and beauty,
 In three several young men, which should I choose?

ANTONIO. 'Tis a hard question: this was Paris' case,
 And he was blind in it, and there was great cause;
 For how was it possible he could judge right,   40
 Having three amorous goddesses in view.

[35] Lovers.

And they stark naked? 'twas a motion
Were able to benight the apprehension
Of the severest counselor of Europe.
Now I look on both your faces so well formed,
It puts me in mind of a question I would ask.

CARIOLA. What is it?

ANTONIO.   I do wonder why hard-favored ladies,
For the most part, keep worse-favored waiting-women
To attend them, and cannot endure fair ones.

DUCHESS. Oh, that's soon answered.   10
Did you ever in your life know an ill painter
Desire to have his dwelling next door to the shop
Of an excellent picture-maker? 'twould disgrace
His face-making, and undo him. I prithee,
When were we so merry?—My hair tangles.

ANTONIO. Pray thee, Cariola, let's steal forth the room,
And let her talk to herself: I have divers times
Served her the like, when she hath chafed extremely.
I love to see her angry. Softly, Cariola.
[Exeunt ANTONIO and CARIOLA.]

DUCHESS. Doth not the color of my hair begin to change?   20
When I wax grey, I shall have all the court
Powder their hair with arras,³⁶ to be like me.
You have cause to love me; I entered you into my heart
Before you would vouchsafe to call for the keys.
[Enter FERDINAND behind.]
We shall one day have my brother take you napping;
Methinks his presence, being now in court,
Should make you keep your own bed; but you'll say
Love mixed with fear is sweetest. I'll assure you,
You shall get no more children till my brothers
Consent to be your gossips.³⁷ Have you lost your tongue?   30
'Tis welcome:
For know, whether I am doomed to live or die,
I can do both like a prince.

FERDINAND.   Die, then, quickly!
[Giving her a poniard.]
Virtue, where art thou hid? what hideous thing
Is it that doth eclipse thee?

DUCHESS.   Pray, sir, hear me.

FERDINAND. Or is it true thou art but a bare name,
And no essential thing?

³⁶ Orris, a white powder.
³⁷ Godparents (to your children).

DUCHESS.   Sir,—
FERDINAND.   Do not speak.
DUCHESS. No, sir: I will plant my soul in mine ears, to hear you.
FERDINAND. O most imperfect light of human reason,
    That makest us so unhappy to foresee
    What we can least prevent! Pursue thy wishes,
    And glory in them: there is in shame no comfort
    But to be past all bounds and sense of shame.
DUCHESS. I pray, sir, hear me: I am married.
FERDINAND.   So!   10
DUCHESS. Happily, not to your liking: but for that,
    Alas, your shears do come untimely now
    To clip the bird's wings that is already flown!
    Will you see my husband?
FERDINAND.   Yes, if I could change
    Eyes with a basilisk.
DUCHESS.   Sure, you came hither
    By his confederacy.
FERDINAND.   The howling of a wolf
    Is music to thee, screech-owl: prithee, peace.—   20
    Whate'er thou art that hast enjoyed my sister,
    For I am sure thou hearest me, for thine own sake
    Let me not know thee. I came hither prepared
    To work thy discovery; yet am now persuaded
    It would beget such violent effects
    As would damn us both. I would not for ten millions
    I had beheld thee: therefore use all means
    I never may have knowledge of thy name;
    Enjoy thy lust still, and a wretched life,
    On that condition.—And for thee, vile woman,   30
    If thou do wish thy lecher may grow old
    In thy embracements, I would have thee build
    Such a room for him as our anchorites
    To holier use inhabit. Let not the sun
    Shine on him till he's dead; let dogs and monkeys
    Only converse with him, and such dumb things
    To whom nature denies use to sound his name;
    Do not keep a paraquito, lest she learn it;
    If thou do love him, cut out thine own tongue,
    Lest it betray him.   40
DUCHESS.   Why might not I marry?
    I have not gone about in this to create
    Any new world or custom.
FERDINAND.   Thou art undone:
    And thou hast taken that massy sheet of lead

That hid thy husband's bones, and folded it
About my heart.
DUCHESS.   Mine bleeds for it.
FERDINAND.   Thine? thy heart?
What should I name it unless a hollow bullet
Filled with unquenchable wildfire?
DUCHESS.   You are in this
Too strict; and were you not my princely brother,
I would say, too willful: my reputation
Is safe.   10
FERDINAND.   Dost thou know what reputation is?
I'll tell thee,—to small purpose, since the instruction
Comes now too late.
Upon a time Reputation, Love, and Death,
Would travel o'er the world; and it was concluded
That they should part, and take three several ways.
Death told them, they should find him in great battles,
Or cities plagued with plagues: Love gives them counsel
To inquire for him 'mongst unambitious shepherds,
Where dowries were not talked of, and sometimes   20
'Mongst quiet kindred that had nothing left
By their dead parents: "Stay," quoth Reputation,
"Do not forsake me; for it is my nature,
If once I part from any man I meet,
I am never found again." And so for you:
You have shook hands with Reputation,
And made him invisible. So, fare you well:
I will never see you more.
DUCHESS.   Why should only I,
Of all the other princes of the world,   30
Be cased up, like a holy relic? I have youth
And a little beauty.
FERDINAND.   So you have some virgins
That are witches. I will never see thee more.
[*Exit.*]
[*Reenter* ANTONIO *with a pistol, and* CARIOLA.]
DUCHESS. You saw this apparition?
ANTONIO.   Yes: we are
Betrayed. How came he hither?—I should turn
This to thee, for that.
[*Pointing the pistol at* CARIOLA.]
CARIOLA.   Pray, sir, do; and when
That you have cleft my heart, you shall read there   40
Mine innocence.
DUCHESS.   That gallery gave him entrance.

ANTONIO. I would this terrible thing would come again,
    That, standing on my guard, I might relate
    My warrantable love.—
    [*She shows the poniard.*]
                              Ha! what means this?
DUCHESS. He left this with me.
ANTONIO.   And it seems did wish
    You would use it on yourself.
DUCHESS.   His action seemed
    To intend so much.
ANTONIO.   This hath a handle to it,   10
    As well as a point: turn it toward him, and
    So fasten the keen edge in his rank gall.
    [*Knocking within.*]
    How now! who knocks? more earthquakes?
DUCHESS.   I stand
    As if a mine beneath my feet were ready
    To be blown up.
CARIOLA.   'Tis Bosola.
DUCHESS.   Away!
    O misery! methinks unjust actions
    Should wear these masks and curtains, and not we.   20
    You must instantly part hence: I have fashioned it
    Already.
    [*Exit* ANTONIO.]
    [*Enter* BOSOLA.]
BOSOLA. The duke your brother is taken up in a whirlwind,
    Hath took horse, and is rid post to Rome.
DUCHESS.   So late?
BOSOLA. He told me, as he mounted into the saddle,
    You were undone.
DUCHESS. Indeed, I am very near it.
BOSOLA.   What is the matter?
DUCHESS. Antonio, the master of our household,   30
    Hath dealt so falsely with me in his accounts:
    My brother stood engaged with me for money
    Taken up of certain Neapolitan Jews,
    And Antonio lets the bonds be forfeit.
BOSOLA. Strange!—[*Aside.*] This is cunning.
DUCHESS.   And hereupon
    My brother's bills at Naples are protested
    Against.—Call up our officers.
BOSOLA.   I shall.
    [*Exit.*]
    [*Reenter* ANTONIO.]

DUCHESS. The place that you must fly to is Ancona:
    Hire a house there; I'll send after you
    My treasure and my jewels. Our weak safety
    Runs upon enginous[38] wheels: short syllables
    Must stand for periods. I must now accuse you
    Of such a feignèd crime as Tasso calls
    Magnanima menzogna, a noble lie,
    'Cause it must shield our honors.—Hark! they are coming.
    [*Reenter* BOSOLA *and* OFFICERS.]
ANTONIO. Will your grace hear me?
DUCHESS. I have got well by you; you have yielded me   10
    A million of loss: I am like to inherit
    The people's curses for your stewardship.
    You had the trick in audit-time to be sick,
    Till I had signed your *quietus;* and that cured you
    Without help of a doctor.—Gentlemen,
    I would have this man be an example to you all;
    So shall you hold my favor; I pray, let him;
    For he has done that, alas, you would not think of,
    And, because I intend to be rid of him,
    I mean not to publish.—Use your fortune elsewhere.   20
ANTONIO. I am strongly armed to brook my overthrow;
    As commonly men bear with a hard year,
    I will not blame the cause on it; but do think
    The necessity of my malevolent star
    Procures this, not her humour. Oh, the inconstant
    And rotten ground of service! you may see,
    'Tis even like him, that in a winter night,
    Takes a long slumber o'er a dying fire,
    A-loth to part from it; yet parts thence as cold
    As when he first sat down.   30
DUCHESS.   We do confiscate,
    Toward the satisfying of your accounts,
    All that you have.
ANTONIO.   I am all yours; and 'tis very fit
    All mine should be so.
DUCHESS.   So, sir, you have your pass.
ANTONIO. You may see, gentlemen, what 'tis to serve
    A prince with body and soul.
    [*Exit.*]
BOSOLA. Here's an example for extortion: what moisture is drawn
  out of the sea, when foul weather comes, pours down, and runs   40
  into the sea again.

---

[38] Devised, but not very secure.

DUCHESS. I would know what are your opinions of this Antonio.

SECOND OFFICER. He could not abide to see a pig's head gaping:
I thought your grace would find him a Jew.

THIRD OFFICER. I would you had been his officer, for your own
sake.

FOURTH OFFICER. You would have had more money.

FIRST OFFICER. He stopped his ears with black wool, and to those
came to him for money said he was thick of hearing.

SECOND OFFICER. Some said he was an hermaphrodite, for he could
not abide a woman.   10

FOURTH OFFICER. How scurvy proud he would look when the treasury
was full! Well, let him go!

FIRST OFFICER. Yes, and the chippings of the buttery fly after him,
to scour his gold chain!

DUCHESS. Leave us.

[*Exeunt* OFFICERS.]
What do you think of these?

BOSOLA. That these are rogues that in his prosperity, but to have
waited on his fortune, could have wished his dirty stirrup riveted
through their noses, and followed after his mule, like a bear in
a ring; would have prostituted their daughters to his lust; made   20
their first-born intelligencers; thought none happy but such as
were born under his blessed planet, and wore his livery: and do
these lice drop off now? Well, never look to have the like again:
he hath left a sort of flattering rogues behind him; their doom
must follow. Princes pay flatterers in their own money: flatterers
dissemble their vices, and they dissemble their lies; that is justice.
Alas, poor gentleman!

DUCHESS. Poor? he hath amply filled his coffers.

BOSOLA. Sure, he was too honest. Pluto,[39] the god of riches, when
he is sent by Jupiter to any man, he goes limping, to signify that 30
wealth that comes on God's name comes slowly; but when he is
sent on the devil's errand, he rides post and comes in by scuttles. Let
me show you what a most unvalued jewel you have in a wanton
humour thrown away, to bless the man shall find him. He was an
excellent courtier and most faithful; a soldier that thought it as
beastly to know his own value too little as devilish to acknowledge
it too much. Both his virtue and form deserved a far better fortune:
his discourse rather delighted to judge itself than show itself: his
breast was filled with all perfection, and yet it seemed a private
whispering-room, it made so little noise of it.   40

DUCHESS. But he was basely descended.

BOSOLA. Will you make yourself a mercenary herald, rather to exam-

---

[39] Actually the god of hell (perhaps a deliberate double-meaning).

ine men's pedigrees than virtues? You shall want him: for know, an honest statesman to a prince is like a cedar planted by a spring; the spring bathes the tree's root, the grateful tree rewards it with his shadow: you have not done so. I would sooner swim to the Bermoothes on two politicians' rotten bladders, tied together with an intelligencer's heartstring, than depend on so changeable a prince's favor. Fare thee well, Antonio! since the malice of the world would needs down with thee, it cannot be said yet that any ill happened unto thee, considering thy fall was accompanied with virtue.   10

DUCHESS. Oh, you render me excellent music!

BOSOLA.   Say you?

DUCHESS. This good one that you speak of is my husband.

BOSOLA. Do I not dream? can this ambitious age
   Have so much goodness in it as to prefer
   A man merely for worth, without these shadows
   Of wealth and painted honors? possible?

DUCHESS. I have had three children by him.

BOSOLA.   Fortunate lady!
   For you have made your private nuptial bed   20
   The humble and fair seminary of peace.
   No question but many an unbeneficed scholar
   Shall pray for you for this deed, and rejoice
   That some preferment in the world can yet
   Arise from merit. The virgins of your land
   That have no dowries shall hope your example
   Will raise them to rich husbands. Should you want
   Soldiers, 'twould make the very Turks and Moors
   Turn Christians, and serve you for this act.
   Last, the neglected poets of your time,   30
   In honor of this trophy of a man,
   Raised by that curious engine, your white hand,
   Shall thank you, in your grave, for it; and make that
   More reverend than all the cabinets
   Of living princes. For Antonio,
   His fame shall likewise flow from many a pen,
   When heralds shall want coats to sell to men.

DUCHESS. As I taste comfort in this friendly speech,
   So would I find concealment.

BOSOLA. Oh, the secret of my prince,   40
   Which I will wear on the inside of my heart!

DUCHESS. You shall take charge of all my coin and jewels,
   And follow him; for he retires himself
   To Ancona.

BOSOLA.   So.

DUCHESS.   Whither, within few days,
    I mean to follow thee.
BOSOLA.   Let me think:
    I would wish your grace to feign a pilgrimage
    To our Lady of Loretto, scarce seven leagues
    From fair Ancona; so may you depart
    Your country with more honor, and your flight
    Will seem a princely progress, retaining
    Your usual train about you.
DUCHESS.   Sir, your direction   10
    Shall lead me by the hand.
CARIOLA.   In my opinion,
    She were better progress to the baths at Lucca,
    Or go visit the Spa in Germany;
    For, if you will believe me, I do not like
    This jesting with religion, this feigned
    Pilgrimage.
DUCHESS. Thou art a superstitious fool:
    Prepare us instantly for our departure.
    Past sorrows, let us moderately lament them;   20
    For those to come, seek wisely to prevent them.
    [*Exeunt* DUCHESS *and* CARIOLA.]
BOSOLA. A politician is the devil's quilted anvil;
    He fashions all sins on him, and the blows
    Are never heard: he may work in a lady's chamber,
    As here for proof. What rests but I reveal
    All to my lord? Oh, this base quality
    Of intelligencer! why, every quality in the world
    Prefers but gain or commendation:
    Now for this act I am certain to be raised,
    And men that paint weeds to the life are praised.   30
    [*Exit.*]

Scene Three

A room in the CARDINAL'*s palace at Rome.*

[*Enter* CARDINAL, FERDINAND, MALATESTE, PESCARA, SILVIO,
and DELIO.]
CARDINAL. Must we turn soldier, then?
MALATESTE.   The emperor,
    Hearing your worth that way, ere you attained
    This reverend garment, joins you in commission
    With the right fortunate soldier the Marquis of Pescara,
    And the famous Lannoy.

CARDINAL.   He that had the honor
    Of taking the French king prisoner?
MALATESTE.   The same.
    Here's a plot drawn for a new fortification
    At Naples.
    [*They talk apart.*]
FERDINAND. This great Count Malateste, I perceive,
    Hath got employment?
DELIO.   No employment, my lord;
    A marginal note in the muster-book, that he is
    A voluntary lord.   10
FERDINAND.   He's no soldier?
DELIO. He has worn gunpowder in his hollow tooth for the toothache.
SILVIO. He comes to the leaguer with a full intent
    To eat fresh beef and garlic, means to stay
    Till the scent be gone, and straight return to court.
DELIO. He hath read all the late service as the city chronicle relates it;
    and keeps two pewterers going, only to express battles in model.
SILVIO. Then he'll fight by the book.
DELIO. By the almanac, I think, to choose good days and shun the
    critical; that's his mistress's scarf.   20
SILVIO. Yes, he protests he would do much for that taffeta.
DELIO. I think he would run away from a battle, to save it from
    taking prisoner.
SILVIO. He is horribly afraid gunpower will spoil the perfume on it.
DELIO. I saw a Dutchman break his pate once for calling him pot-gun;
    he made his head have a bore in it like a musket.
SILVIO. I would he had made a touchhole to it. He is indeed a guarded
    sumpter-cloth,[40] only for the remove of the court.
    [*Enter* BOSOLA *and speaks to* FERDINAND *and the* CARDINAL.]
PESCARA. Bosola arrived? what should be the business?
    Some falling-out amongst the cardinals.   30
    These factions amongst great men, they are like
    Foxes; when their heads are divided,
    They carry fire in their tails, and all the country
    About them goes to wrack for it.
SILVIO.   What is that Bosola?
DELIO. I knew him in Padua—a fantastical scholar, like such who
    study to know how many knots was in Hercules' club, of what
    color Achilles' beard was, or whether Hector were not troubled
    with the toothache. He hath studied himself half blear-eyed to
    know the true symmetry of Caesar's nose by a shoeing-horn;   40
    and this he did to gain the name of a speculative man.

---

[40] Horse-blanket.

PESCARA. Mark Prince Ferdinand:
        A very salamander lives in his eye,
        To mock the eager violence of fire.
SILVIO. That Cardinal hath made more bad faces with his oppression
  than ever Michelangelo made good ones: he lifts up his nose, like
  a foul porpoise before a storm.
PESCARA. The Lord Ferdinand laughs.
DELIO.   Like a deadly cannon that lightens
        Ere it smokes.
PESCARA. These are your true pangs of death,   10
        The pangs of life, that struggle with great statesmen.
DELIO. In such a deformed silence witches whisper
        Their charms.
CARDINAL. Doth she make religion her riding-hood
        To keep her from the sun and tempest?
FERDINAND.   That,
        That damns her. Methinks her fault and beauty,
        Blended together, show like leprosy,
        The whiter, the fouler. I make it a question
        Whether her beggarly brats were ever christened.   20
CARDINAL. I will instantly solicit the state of Ancona
        To have them banished.
FERDINAND.   You are for Loretto?
        I shall not be at your ceremony; fare you well.—
        Write to the Duke of Malfi, my young nephew
        She had by her first husband, and acquaint him
        With his mother's honesty.
BOSOLA.   I will.
FERDINAND.   Antonio!
        A slave that only smelled of ink and counters,[41]   30
        And never in his life looked like a gentleman,
        But in the audit-time.—Go, go presently,
        Draw me out an hundred and fifty of our horse,
        And meet me at the fort-bridge.
        [*Exeunt.*]

Scene Four

The shrine of Our Lady of Loretto.

[*Enter* TWO PILGRIMS.]
FIRST PILGRIM. I have not seen a goodlier shrine than this;
        Yet I have visited many.

[41] Money.

SECOND PILGRIM.   The Cardinal of Arragon
    Is this day to resign his cardinal's hat:
    His sister duchess likewise is arrived
    To pay her vow of pilgrimage. I expect
    A noble ceremony.
FIRST PILGRIM.   No question.
    —They come.

[*Here the ceremony of the* CARDINAL'S *instalment, in the habit of
a soldier, is performed in delivering up his cross, hat, robes, and ring,
at the shrine, and investing him with sword, helmet, shield, and
spurs; then* ANTONIO, *the* DUCHESS, *and their children, having presented themselves at the shrine, are, by a form of banishment in
dumb-show expressed toward them by the* CARDINAL *and the state
of Ancona, banished: during all which ceremony, this ditty is sung,
to very solemn music, by diverse churchmen.*]

    Arms and honors deck thy story,
    To thy fame's eternal glory!
    Adverse fortune ever fly thee;   10
    No disastrous fate come nigh thee!

    I alone will sing thy praises,
    Whom to honor virtue raises;
    And thy study, that divine is,
    Bent to martial discipline is.
    Lay aside all those robes lie by thee;
    Crown thy arts with arms, they'll beautify thee.

    O worthy of worthiest name, adorned in this manner,
    Lead bravely thy forces on under war's warlike banner!
    Oh, mayst thou prove fortunate in all martial courses!   20
    Guide thou still by skill in arts and forces!
    Victory attend thee nigh, whilst fame sings loud thy powers;
    Triumphant conquest crown thy head, and blessings pour
        down showers!
[*Exeunt all except the* TWO PILGRIMS.]
FIRST PILGRIM. Here's a strange turn of state! who would have
      thought
    So great a lady would have matched herself
    Unto so mean a person? yet the Cardinal
    Bears himself much too cruel.
SECOND PILGRIM.   They are banished.   30
FIRST PILGRIM. But I would ask what power hath this state
    Of Ancona to determine of a free prince?
SECOND PILGRIM. They are a free state, sir, and her brother showed
    How that the Pope, fore-hearing of her looseness,

Hath seized into the protection of the Church
The dukedom which she held as dowager.
FIRST PILGRIM. But by what justice?
SECOND PILGRIM.   Sure, I think by none,
Only her brother's instigation.
FIRST PILGRIM. What was it with such violence he took
Off from her finger?
SECOND PILGRIM.   'Twas her wedding-ring;
Which he vowed shortly he would sacrifice
To his revenge.   10
FIRST PILGRIM. Alas, Antonio!
If that a man be thrust into a well,
No matter who sets hands to it, his own weight
Will bring him sooner to the bottom. Come, let's hence.
Fortune makes this conclusion general,
All things do help the unhappy man to fall.
[*Exeunt.*]

Scene Five

Near Loretto.

[*Enter* DUCHESS, ANTONIO, CHILDREN, CARIOLA, *and* SERVANTS.]
DUCHESS. Banished Ancona?
ANTONIO.   Yes, you see what power
Lightens in great men's breath.
DUCHESS.   Is all our train   20
Shrunk to this poor remainder?
ANTONIO.   These poor men,
Which have got little in your service, vow
To take your fortune: but your wiser buntings,
Now they are fledged, are gone.
DUCHESS.   They have done wisely.
This puts me in mind of death: physicians thus,
With their hands full of money, use to give o'er
Their patients.
ANTONIO.   Right the fashion of the world: 30
From decayed fortunes every flatterer shrinks;
Men cease to build where the foundation sinks.
DUCHESS. I had a very strange dream tonight.
ANTONIO.   What was it?
DUCHESS. Methought I wore my coronet of state,
And on a sudden all the diamonds
Were changed to pearls.
ANTONIO.   My interpretation

Is, you'll weep shortly; for to me the pearls
Do signify your tears.

DUCHESS.   The birds that live
In the field on the wild benefit of nature
Live happier than we; for they may choose their mates,
And carol their sweet pleasures to the spring.

[*Enter* BOSOLA *with a letter.*]

BOSOLA. You are happily o'ertaken.

DUCHESS.   From my brother?

BOSOLA. Yes, from the Lord Ferdinand your brother
All love and safety.   10

DUCHESS.   Thou dost blanch mischief,
Wouldst make it white. See, see, like to calm weather
At sea before a tempest, false hearts speak fair
To those they intend most mischief.

[*Reads.*]

"Send Antonio to me; I want his head in a business."
A politic equivocation!
He doth not want your counsel, but your head;
That is, he cannot sleep till you be dead.
And here's another pitfall that's strewed o'er
With roses: mark it, 'tis a cunning one: 20

[*Reads.*]

"I stand engaged for your husband for several debts at Naples:
let not that trouble him; I had rather have his heart than his money:"
And I believe so too.

BOSOLA.   What do you believe?

DUCHESS. That he so much distrusts my husband's love,
He will by no means believe his heart is with him
Until he see it: the devil is not cunning
Enough to circumvent us in riddles.

BOSOLA. Will you reject that noble and free league
Of amity and love which I present you?   30

DUCHESS. Their league is like that of some politic kings,
Only to make themselves of strength and power
To be our after-ruin: tell them so.

BOSOLA. And what from you?

ANTONIO.   Thus tell him; I will not come.

BOSOLA. And what of this?

[*Pointing to the letter.*]

ANTONIO.   My brothers have dispersed
Blood-hounds abroad; which till I hear are muzzled,
No truce, though hatched with ne'er such politic skill,
Is safe, that hangs upon our enemies' will.   40
I'll not come at them.

BOSOLA.   This proclaims your breeding:
Every small thing draws a base mind to fear,
As the adamant draws iron. Fare you well, sir
You shall shortly hear from us.
[*Exit.*]
DUCHESS.   I suspect some ambush:
Therefore by all my love I do conjure you
To take your eldest son, and fly toward Milan.
Let us not venture all this poor remainder
In one unlucky bottom.
ANTONIO.   You counsel safely.   10
Best of my life, farewell. Since we must part,
Heaven hath a hand in it; but no otherwise
Than as some curious artist takes in sunder
A clock or watch, when it is out of frame,
To bring it in better order.
DUCHESS.   I know not
Which is best, to see you dead, or part with you.
—Farewell, boy:
Thou art happy that thou hast not understanding
To know thy misery; for all our wit   20
And reading brings us to a truer sense
Of sorrow.—In the eternal church, sir,
I do hope we shall not part thus.
ANTONIO.   Oh, be of comfort!
Make patience a noble fortitude,
And think not how unkindly we are used:
Man, like to cassia, is proved best being bruised.
DUCHESS. Must I, like to a slave-born Russian,
Account it praise to suffer tyranny?
And yet, O heaven, thy heavy hand is in it!   30
I have seen my little boy oft scourge his top,
And compared myself to it: naught made me e'er
Go right but heaven's scourge-stick.
ANTONIO.   Do not weep:
Heaven fashioned us of nothing, and we strive
To bring ourselves to nothing.—Farewell, Cariola,
And thy sweet armful.—If I do never see thee more,
Be a good mother to your little ones,
And save them from the tiger: fare you well.
DUCHESS. Let me look upon you once more; for that speech   40
Came from a dying father.—Your kiss is colder
Than that I have seen an holy anchorite
Give to a dead man's skull.
ANTONIO. My heart is turned to a heavy lump of lead,

With which I sound my danger: fare you well.
[*Exeunt* ANTONIO *and his* SON.]
DUCHESS. My laurel is all withered.
CARIOLA. Look, madam, what a troop of armèd men
      Make toward us.
DUCHESS.   Oh, they are very welcome:
      When Fortune's wheel is over-charged with princes,
      The weight makes it move swift: I would have my ruin
      Be sudden.
      [*Reenter* BOSOLA *visarded*,[42] *with a* GUARD.]
                           I am your adventure, am I not?
BOSOLA. You are: you must see your husband no more.   10
DUCHESS. What devil art thou that counterfeits heaven's thunder?
BOSOLA. Is that terrible? I would have you tell me whether
      Is that note worse that frights the silly birds
      Out of the corn, or that which doth allure them
      To the nets? you have hearkened to the last too much.
DUCHESS. Oh, misery! like to a rusty o'ercharged cannon,
      Shall I never fly in pieces? Come, to what prison?
BOSOLA. To none.
DUCHESS.   Whither, then?
BOSOLA.   To your palace.   20
DUCHESS.   I have heard
      That Charon's[43] boat serves to convey all o'er
      The dismal lake, but brings none back again.
BOSOLA. Your brothers mean you safety and pity.
DUCHESS.   Pity!
      With such a pity men preserve alive
      Pheasants and quails, when they are not fat enough
      To be eaten.
BOSOLA. These are your children?
DUCHESS.   Yes.   30
BOSOLA.   Can they prattle?
DUCHESS.   No;
      But I intend, since they were born accursed,
      Curses shall be their first language.
BOSOLA.   Fie, madam!
      Forget this base, low fellow—
DUCHESS.   Were I a man
      I'd beat that counterfeit face into thy other.
BOSOLA. One of no birth.
DUCHESS.   Say that he was born mean,   40

---

[42] Masked.
[43] Pilot of the boat that carried condemned souls to hell.

        Man is most happy when his own actions
        Be arguments and examples of his virtue.
BOSOLA. A barren, beggarly virtue!
DUCHESS. I prithee, who is greatest? can you tell?
        Sad tales befit my woe: I'll tell you one.
        A salmon, as she swam unto the sea,
        Met with a dogfish, who encounters her
        With this rough language: "Why art thou so bold
        To mix thyself with our high state of floods,
        Being no eminent courtier, but one   10
        That for the calmest and fresh time of the year
        Dost live in shallow rivers, rankest thyself
        With silly smelts and shrimps? and darest thou
        Pass by our dog-ship without reverence?"
        "Oh," quoth the salmon, "sister, be at peace:
        Thank Jupiter we both have passed the net!
        Our value never can be truly known,
        Till in the fisher's basket we be shown:
        In the market then my price may be the higher,
        Even when I am nearest to the cook and fire."   20
        So to great men the moral may be stretchèd;
        Men oft are valued high, when they're most wretched.—
        But come, whither you please. I am armed 'gainst misery;
        Bent to all sways of the oppressor's will:
        There's no deep valley but near some great hill.
        [*Exeunt.*]

ACT FOUR

Scene One

A room in the DUCHESS'*s palace at Malfi.*

[*Enter* FERDINAND *and* BOSOLA.]
FERDINAND. How doth our sister duchess bear herself
        In her imprisonment?
BOSOLA.   Nobly: I'll describe her.
        She is sad as one long used to it, and she seems
        Rather to welcome the end of misery   30
        Than shun it; a behavior so noble
        As gives a majesty to adversity:
        You may discern the shape of loveliness
        More perfect in her tears than in her smiles:
        She will muse four hours together; and her silence,
        Methinks, expresseth more than if she spake.

FERDINAND. Her melancholy seems to be fortified
    With a strange disdain.
BOSOLA.   'Tis so; and this restraint,
    Like English mastiffs that grow fierce with tying,
    Makes her too passionately apprehend
    Those pleasures she is kept from.
FERDINAND.   Curse upon her!
    I will no longer study in the book
    Of another's heart. Inform her what I told you.
    [*Exit.*]
    [*Enter* DUCHESS.]
BOSOLA. All comfort to your grace!   10
DUCHESS.   I will have none.
    Pray thee, why doest thou wrap thy poisoned pills
    In gold and sugar?
BOSOLA. Your elder brother, the Lord Ferdinand,
    Is come to visit you, and sends you word,
    'Cause once he rashly made a solemn vow
    Never to see you more, he comes in the night;
    And prays you gently neither torch nor taper
    Shine in your chamber: he will kiss your hand,
    And reconcile himself; but for his vow   20
    He dares not see you.
DUCHESS.   At his pleasure.—Take hence
    the lights.—
    He is come.
    [*Enter* FERDINAND.]
FERDINAND. Where are you?
DUCHESS.   Here sir.
FERDINAND.   This darkness suits you well.
DUCHESS. I would ask you pardon.
FERDINAND.   You have it; for I account it
    The honorablest revenge, where I may kill   30
    To pardon.—Where are your cubs?
DUCHESS.   Whom?
FERDINAND.   Call them your children;
    For though our national law distinguish bastards
    From true legitimate issue, compassionate nature
    Makes them all equal.
DUCHESS.   Do you visit me for this?
    You violate a sacrament of the Church
    Shall make you howl in hell for it.
FERDINAND.   It had been well   40
    Could you have lived thus always; for, indeed,
    You were too much in the light:—but no more;

I come to seal my peace with you. Here's a hand
[*gives her a dead man's hand*]
To which you have vowed much love; the ring upon it
You gave.

DUCHESS. I affectionately kiss it.

FERDINAND. Pray, do, and bury the print of it in your heart.
I will leave this ring with you for a love-token;
And the hand as sure as the ring; and do not doubt
But you shall have the heart too: when you need a friend,
Send it to him that owned it; you shall see
Whether he can aid you.   10

DUCHESS.   You are very cold:
I fear you are not well after your travel.—
Ha! lights!——Oh, horrible!

FERDINAND.   Let her have lights enough.
[*Exit.*]

DUCHESS. What witchcraft doth he practice, that he hath left
A dead man's hand here?

[*Here is discovered, behind a traverse,*[44] *the artificial figures of*
ANTONIO *and his* CHILDREN, *appearing as if they were dead.*]

BOSOLA. Look you, here's the piece from which 'twas taken.
He doth present you this sad spectacle,
That, now you know directly they are dead,
Hereafter you may wisely cease to grieve   20
For that which cannot be recovered.

DUCHESS. There is not between heaven and earth one wish
I stay for after this: it wastes me more
Than were it my picture, fashioned out of wax,
Stuck with a magical needle, and then buried
In some foul dunghill; and yond is an excellent property
For a tyrant, which I would account mercy.

BOSOLA.   What is that?

DUCHESS. If they would bind me to that lifeless trunk,
And let me freeze to death.   30

BOSOLA.   Come, you must live.

DUCHESS. That is the greatest torture souls feel in hell,
In hell, that they must live, and cannot die.
Portia,[45] I'll new kindle thy coals again,
And revive the rare and almost dead example
Of a loving wife.

BOSOLA.   Oh, fie! despair? remember
You are a Christian.

---

[44] A curtain drawn across a closet or cabinet.
[45] Daughter of Cato, married to Brutus, and the archetype of noble Wifehood.

DUCHESS.   The Church enjoins fasting:
        I'll starve myself to death.
BOSOLA.   Leave this vain sorrow.
        Things being at the worst begin to mend: the bee
        When he hath shot his sting into your hand, may then
        Play with your eyelid.
DUCHESS.   Good comfortable fellow,
        Persuade a wretch that is broke upon the wheel
        To have all his bones new set; entreat him live
        To be executed again. Who must dispatch me?   10
        I account this world a tedious theater,
        For I do play a part in it 'gainst my will.
BOSOLA. Come, be of comfort; I will save your life.
DUCHESS.   Indeed,
        I have not leisure to tend so small a business.
BOSOLA. Now, by my life, I pity you.
DUCHESS.   Thou art a fool, then,
        To waste thy pity on a thing so wretched
        As cannot pity itself. I am full of daggers.
        Puff, let me blow these vipers from me.   20
        [Enter SERVANT.]
        What are you?
SERVANT.   One that wishes you long life.
DUCHESS. I would thou wert hanged for the horrible curse
        Thou hast given me: I shall shortly grow one
        Of the miracles of pity. I'll go pray;—
        No, I'll go curse.
BOSOLA.   Oh, fie!
DUCHESS.   I could curse the stars—
BOSOLA. Oh, fearful!
DUCHESS. And those three smiling seasons of the year   30
        Into a Russian winter: nay, the world
        To its first chaos.
BOSOLA. Look you, the stars shine still.
DUCHESS.   Oh, but you must
        Remember, my curse hath a great way to go.—
        Plagues, that make lanes through largest families,
        Consume them!—
BOSOLA. Fie, lady!
DUCHESS.   Let them, like tyrants,
        Never be remembered but for the ill they have done;   40
        Let all the zealous prayers of mortified
        Churchmen forget them!—
BOSOLA.   Oh, uncharitable!
DUCHESS. Let Heaven a little while cease crowning martyrs,

To punish them!—
Go, howl them this, and say, I long to bleed:
It is some mercy when men kill with speed.
[*Exeunt* DUCHESS *and* SERVANT.]
[*Reenter* FERDINAND.]

FERDINAND. Excellent, as I would wish; she's plagued in art:
These presentations are but framed in wax
By the curious master in that quality,
Vincentio Lauriola, and she takes them
For true substantial bodies.

BOSOLA.   Why do you do this?

FERDINAND. To bring her to despair.   10

BOSOLA.   'Faith, end here,
And go no farther in your cruelty:
Send her a penitential garment to put on
Next to her delicate skin, and furnish her
With beads and prayer-books.

FERDINAND.   Damn her! that body of hers,
While that my blood ran pure in it, was more worth
Than that which thou wouldst comfort, called a soul.
I will send her masks of common courtesans,
Have her meat served up by bawds and ruffians,   20
And, 'cause she'll needs be mad, I am resolved
To remove forth the common hospital
All the mad-folk, and place them near her lodging;
There let them practice together, sing and dance,
And act their gambols to the full of the moon:
If she can sleep the better for it, let her.
Your work is almost ended.

BOSOLA.   Must I see her again?

FERDINAND. Yes.

BOSOLA.   Never.   30

FERDINAND.   You must.

BOSOLA.   Never in mine own shape;
That is forfeited by my intelligence
And this last cruel lie: when you send me next,
The business shall be comfort.

FERDINAND.   Very likely:
Thy pity is nothing of kin to thee. Antonio
Lurks about Milan: thou shalt shortly thither
To feed a fire as great as my revenge,
Which ne'er will slack till it have spent his fuel: 40
Intemperate agues make physicians cruel.
[*Exeunt.*]

Scene Two

Another room in the DUCHESS'*s lodging.*

[*Enter* DUCHESS *and* CARIOLA.]

DUCHESS. What hideous noise was that?

CARIOLA.   'Tis the wild consort[46]
Of madmen, lady, which your tyrant brother
Hath placed about your lodging: this tyranny,
I think, was never practiced till this hour.

DUCHESS. Indeed, I thank him: nothing but noise and folly
Can keep me in my right wits; whereas reason
And silence make me stark mad. Sit down;
Discourse to me some dismal tragedy.

CARIOLA. Oh, 'twill increase your melancholy.   10

DUCHESS.   Thou art deceived:
To hear of greater grief would lessen mine.
This is a prison?

CARIOLA.   Yes, but you shall live
To shake this durance off.

DUCHESS.   Thou art a fool:
The robin-redbreast and the nightingale
Never live long in cages.

CARIOLA.   Pray, dry your eyes.
What think you of, madam?   20

DUCHESS.   Of nothing; when I muse thus,
I sleep.

CARIOLA.   Like a madman, with your eyes open?

DUCHESS. Dost thou think we shall know one another in the other
  world?

CARIOLA. Yes, out of question.

DUCHESS.   Oh, that it were possible
We might but hold some two days' conference
With the dead! From them I should learn somewhat, I
  am sure   30
I shall never know here. I'll tell thee a miracle;
I am not mad yet, to my cause of sorrow:
The heaven o'er my head seems made of molten brass,
The earth of flaming sulphur, yet I am not mad.
I am acquainted with sad misery
As the tanned galley-slave is with his oar;
Necessity makes me suffer constantly,

[46] Group of musicians.

And custom makes it easy. Who do I look like now?
CARIOLA. Like to your picture in the gallery,
    A deal of life in show, but none in practice;
    Or rather like some reverend monument
    Whose ruins are even pitied.
DUCHESS.   Very proper;
    And Fortune seems only to have her eyesight
    To behold my tragedy.—
    How now! what noise is that?
    [*Enter* SERVANT.]
SERVANT.   I am come to tell you   10
    Your brother hath intended you some sport.
    A great physician, when the Pope was sick
    Of a deep melancholy, presented him
    With several sorts of madmen, which wild object
    Being full of change and sport, forced him to laugh,
    And so the imposthume broke: the self-same cure
    The duke intends on you.
DUCHESS.   Let them come in.
SERVANT. There's a mad lawyer; and a secular priest;
    A doctor that hath forfeited his wits   20
    By jealousy; an astrologian
    That in his works said such a day of the month
    Should be the day of doom, and, failing of it,
    Ran mad; an English tailor crazed in the brain
    With the study of new fashions; a gentleman-usher
    Quite beside himself with care to keep in mind
    The number of his lady's salutations
    Or "How do you's" she employed him in each morning;
    A farmer, too, an excellent knave in grain,
    Mad 'cause he was hindered transportation: 30
    And let one broker that is mad loose to these,
    You'd think the devil were among them.
DUCHESS. Sit, Cariola.—Let them loose when you please,
    For I am chained to endure all your tyranny.
    [*Enter* MADMEN.]
    [*Here this song is sung by a* MADMAN *to a dismal kind of music.*]
    Oh, let us howl some heavy note,
    Some deadly doggèd howl,
    Sounding as from the threatening throat
    Of beasts and fatal fowl!
    As ravens, screech-owls, bulls, and bears,
    We'll bell, and bawl our parts,   40
    Till irksome noise have cloyed your ears
    And corrosived your hearts.

> At last, whenas our choir wants breath,
> Our bodies being blest,
> We'll sing, like swans, to welcome death,
> And die in love and rest.

FIRST MADMAN. Doomsday not come yet? I'll draw it nearer by a perspective, or make a glass that shall set all the world on fire upon an instant. I cannot sleep; my pillow is stuffed with a litter of porcupines.

SECOND MADMAN. Hell is a mere glass-house, where the devils are continually blowing up women's souls on hollow irons, and the fire never goes out.   10

THIRD MADMAN. I will lie with every woman in my parish the tenth night; I will tithe them over like haycocks.

FOURTH MADMAN. Shall my pothecary out-go me because I am a cuckold? I have found out his roguery; he makes alum of his wife's urine, and sells it to Puritans that have sore throats with overstraining.

FIRST MADMAN. I have skill in heraldry.

SECOND MADMAN. Hast?

FIRST MADMAN. You do give for your crest a woodcock's head with   20
the brains picked out on it; you are a very ancient gentleman.

THIRD MADMAN. Greek is turned Turk: we are only to be saved by the Helvetian translation.[47]

FIRST MADMAN. Come on, sir, I will lay the law to you.

SECOND MADMAN. Oh, rather lay a corrosive: the law will eat to the bone.

THIRD MADMAN. He that drinks but to satisfy nature is damned.

FOURTH MADMAN. If I had my glass here, I would show a sight should make all the women here call me mad doctor.

FIRST MADMAN. What's he? a rope-maker?   30

SECOND MADMAN. No, no, no, a snuffling knave that, while he shows the tombs, will have his hand in a wench's placket.

THIRD MADMAN. Woe to the caroche that brought home my wife from the masque at three o'clock in the morning! it had a large feather-bed in it.

FOURTH MADMAN. I have pared the devil's nails forty times, roasted them in raven's eggs, and cured agues with them.

THIRD MADMAN. Get me three hundred milchbats, to make possets to procure sleep.

FOURTH MADMAN. All the college may throw their caps at me: I have   40
made a soap-boiler costive; it was my masterpiece.

[*Here the dance, consisting of* EIGHT MADMEN, *with music answerable thereunto; after which* BOSOLA, *like an old man, enters.*]

---

[47] The Geneva Bible, published 1560.

DUCHESS. Is he mad too?

SERVANT.   Pray, question him. I'll leave you.

[*Exeunt* SERVANT *and* MADMEN.]

BOSOLA. I am come to make thy tomb.

DUCHESS.   Ha! my tomb?
    Thou speakest as if I lay upon my deathbed,
    Gasping for breath: dost thou perceive me sick?

BOSOLA. Yes, and the more dangerously, since thy sickness
    Is insensible.

DUCHESS. Thou art not mad, sure: dost know me?

BOSOLA. Yes.   10

DUCHESS.   Who am I?

BOSOLA. Thou art a box of worm-seed, at best but a salvatory[48] of
green mummy. What's this flesh? a little crudded milk, fantastical
puffpaste. Our bodies are weaker than those paper-prisons boys
use to keep flies in; more contemptible, since ours is to preserve
earthworms. Didst thou ever see a lark in a cage? Such is the soul
in the body; this world is like her little turf of grass, and the heaven
o'er our heads, like her looking-glass, only gives us a miserable
knowledge of the small compass of our prison.

DUCHESS. Am not I thy duchess?   20

BOSOLA. Thou art some great woman, sure, for riot begins to sit on
thy forehead (clad in grey hairs) twenty years sooner than on a
merry milkmaid's. Thou sleepest worse than if a mouse should be
forced to take up her lodging in a cat's ear: a little infant that
breeds its teeth, should it lie with thee, would cry out, as if thou
wert the more unquiet bedfellow.

DUCHESS. I am Duchess of Malfi still.

BOSOLA. That makes thy sleeps so broken:
    Glories, like glowworms, afar off shine bright,
    But looked to near, have neither heat nor light.   30

DUCHESS. Thou art very plain.

BOSOLA. My trade is to flatter the dead, not the living; I am a tomb-
maker.

DUCHESS. And thou comest to make my tomb?

BOSOLA. Yes.

DUCHESS. Let me be a little merry:—of what stuff wilt thou
make it?

BOSOLA. Nay, resolve me first, of what fashion?

DUCHESS. Why, do we grow fantastical in our deathbed? do we affect
fashion in the grave?

BOSOLA. Mosy ambitiously. Princes' images on their tombs do not lie,   40
as they were wont, seeming to pray up to heaven; but with their
hands under their cheeks, as if they died of the toothache: they are

---

[48] A box for salve or ointment.

not carved with their eyes fixed upon the stars; but as their minds
were wholly bent upon the world, the self-same way they seem to
turn their faces.

DUCHESS. Let me know fully therefore the effect
   Of this thy dismal preparation,
   This talk fit for a charnel.

BOSOLA.   Now I shall:—
   [*Enter* EXECUTIONERS, *with a coffin, cords, and a bell.*]
   Here is a present from your princely brothers;
   And may it arrive welcome, for it brings
   Last benefit, last sorrow.   10

DUCHESS.   Let me see it:
   I have so much obedience in my blood,
   I wish it in their veins to do them good.

BOSOLA. This is your last presence-chamber.

CARIOLA.   O my sweet lady!

DUCHESS. Peace; it affrights not me.

BOSOLA.   I am the common bellman,
   That usually is sent to condemned persons
   The night before they suffer.

DUCHESS.   Even now   20
   Thou saidest thou wast a tomb-maker.

BOSOLA.   'Twas to bring you
   By degrees to mortification. Listen.
   Hark, now every thing is still
   The screech-owl and the whistler shrill
   Call upon our dame aloud,
   And bid her quickly don her shroud!
   Much you had of land and rent:
   Your length is clay's now competent:
   A long war disturbed your mind;   30
   Here your perfect peace is signed.
   Of what is it fools make such vain keeping:
   Sin their conception, their birth weeping,
   Their life a general mist of error,
   Their death a hideous storm of terror.
   Strew your hair with powders sweet,
   Don clean linen, bathe your feet,
   And (the foul fiend more to check)
   A crucifix let bless your neck:
   'Tis now full tide 'tween night and day; 40
   End your groan, and come away.

CARIOLA. Hence, villains, tyrants, murderers! alas!
   What will you do with my lady?—Call for help.

DUCHESS. To whom? to our next neighbors? they are madfolks.

BOSOLA. Remove that noise.

DUCHESS.   Farewell, Cariola.
    In my last will I have not much to give:
    A many hungry guests have fed upon me;
    Thine will be a poor reversion.
CARIOLA.   I will die with her.
DUCHESS. I pray thee, look thou givest my little boy
    Some syrup for his cold, and let the girl
    Say her prayers ere she sleep.
    [CARIOLA *is forced out by the* EXECUTIONERS.]
                    Now what you please:
    What death?   10
BOSOLA. Strangling;
    Here are your executioners.
DUCHESS.   I forgive them:
    The apoplexy, catarrh, or cough of the lungs,
    Would do as much as they do.
BOSOLA. Doth not death fright you?
DUCHESS.   Who would be afraid on it,
    Knowing to meet such excellent company
    In the other world?
BOSOLA.   Yet, methinks,   20
    The manner of your death should much afflict you:
    This cord should terrify you.
DUCHESS.   Not a whit:
    What would it pleasure me to have my throat cut
    With diamonds? or to be smothered
    With cassia? or to be shot to death with pearls?
    I know death hath ten thousand several doors
    For men to take their exits; and 'tis found
    They go on such strange geometrical hinges,
    You may open them both ways.—Any way, for heaven   30
       sake,
    So I were out of your whispering. Tell my brothers
    That I perceive death, now I am well awake,
    Best gift is they can give or I can take.
    I would fain put off my last woman's fault,
    I'd not be tedious to you.
FIRST EXECUTIONER. We are ready.
DUCHESS. Dispose my breath how please you; but my body
    Bestow upon my women, will you?
FIRST EXECUTIONER.   Yes.   40
DUCHESS. Pull, and pull strongly, for your able strength
    Must pull down heaven upon me:—
    Yet stay; heaven-gates are not so highly arched
    As princes' palaces; they that enter there

Must go upon their knees. [*Kneels.*]—Come, violent death,
Serve for mandragora to make me sleep!—
Go tell my brothers, when I am laid out,
They then may feed in quiet.
[*They strangle her.*]

BOSOLA. Where's the waiting woman? Fetch her: some other
Strangle the children.
[*Exeunt* EXECUTIONERS, *some of whom return with* CARIOLA.]
Look you, there sleeps your mistress.

CARIOLA.   Oh, you are damned
Perpetually for this! My turn is next,
Is it not so ordered?   10

BOSOLA.   Yes, and I am glad
You are so well prepared for it.

CARIOLA.   You are deceived, sir,
I am not prepared for it, I will not die;
I will first come to my answer, and know
How I have offended.

BOSOLA.   Come, dispatch her —
You kept her counsel; now you shall keep ours.

CARIOLA. I will not die, I must not; I am contracted
To a young gentleman.   20

FIRST EXECUTIONER. Here's your wedding-ring.

CARIOLA. Let me but speak with the duke; I'll discover
Treason to his person.   Delays:—throttle her.

BOSOLA.

FIRST EXECUTIONER. She bites and scratches.

CARIOLA.   If you kill me now,
I am damned; I have not been at confession
This two years.

BOSOLA [*to* EXECUTIONERS]. When?

CARIOLA.   I am quick with child   30

BOSOLA.   Why, then
Your credit[49] is saved.
[*They strangle* CARIOLA.]
                          Bear her into the next room;
Let this lie still.
[*Exeunt the* EXECUTIONERS *with the body of* CARIOLA.]
[*Enter* FERDINAND.]

FERDINAND. Is she dead?

BOSOLA.   She is what
You'd have her. But here begin your pity:
[*Shows the* CHILDREN *strangled.*]
Alas, how have these offended?

[49] Reputation.

FERDINAND.   The death
    Of young wolves is never to be pitied.
BOSOLA.   Fix
    Your eye here.
FERDINAND. Constantly.
BOSOLA.   Do you not weep?
    Other sins only speak; murder shrieks out:
    The element of water moistens the earth,
    But blood flies upward and bedews the heavens.
FERDINAND. Cover her face; mine eyes dazzle: she died young.   10
BOSOLA. I think not so; her infelicity
    Seemed to have years too many.
FERDINAND.   She and I were twins;
    And should I die this instant, I had lived
    Her time to a minute.
BOSOLA.   It seems she was born first:
    You have bloodily approved the ancient truth,
    That kindred commonly do worse agree
    Than remote strangers.
FERDINAND.   Let me see her face   20
    Again. Why didst not thou pity her? What
    An excellent honest man mightst thou have been,
    If thou hadst borne her to some sanctuary!
    Or, bold in a good cause, opposed thyself,
    With thy advancèd sword above thy head,
    Between her innocence and my revenge!
    I bade thee, when I was distracted of my wits,
    Go kill my dearest friend, and thou hast done it.
    For let me but examine well the cause:
    What was the meanness of her match to me?   30
    Only I must confess I had a hope,
    Had she continued widow, to have gained
    An infinite mass of treasure by her death:
    And that was the main cause; her marriage,
    That drew a stream of gall quite through my heart.
    For thee, as we observe in tragedies
    That a good actor many times is cursed
    For playing a villain's part, I hate thee for it,
    And, for my sake, say thou hast done much ill well.
BOSOLA. Let me quicken your memory, for I perceive   40
    You are falling into ingratitude: I challenge
    The reward due to my service.
FERDINAND.   I'll tell thee
    What I'll give thee.
BOSOLA.   Do.

FERDINAND.   I'll give thee a pardon
    For this murder.
BOSOLA.   Ha!
FERDINAND.   Yes, and 'tis
    The largest bounty I can study to do thee.
    By what authority didst thou execute
    This bloody sentence?
BOSOLA.   By yours.
FERDINAND.   Mine? was I her judge?
    Did any ceremonial form of law   10
    Doom her to not-being? did a complete jury
    Deliver her conviction up in the court?
    Where shalt thou find this judgment registered,
    Unless in hell? See, like a bloody fool,
    Thou forfeited thy life, and thou shalt die for it.
BOSOLA.   The office of justice is perverted quite
    When one thief hangs another. Who shall dare
    To reveal this?
FERDINAND.   Oh, I'll tell thee;
    The wolf shall find her grave, and scrape it up,   20
    Not to devour the corpse, but to discover
    The horrid murder.
BOSOLA.   You, not I, shall quake for it.
FERDINAND. Leave me.
BOSOLA.   I will first receive my pension.
FERDINAND. You are a villain.
BOSOLA.   When your ingratitude
    Is judge, I am so.
FERDINAND.   Oh, horror, that not the fear
    Of him which binds the devils can prescribe man   30
    Obedience!—Never look upon me more.
BOSOLA. Why, fare thee well.
    Your brother and yourself are worthy men:
    You have a pair of hearts are hollow graves,
    Rotten, and rotting others; and your vengeance,
    Like two chained bullets, still goes arm in arm:
    You may be brothers; for treason, like the plague,
    Doth take much in a blood. I stand like one
    That long hath taken a sweet and golden dream:
    I am angry with myself, now that I wake.   40
FERDINAND. Get thee into some unknown part of the world,
    That I may never see thee.
BOSOLA.   Let me know
    Wherefore I should be thus neglected. Sir,
    I served your tyranny, and rather strove

To satisfy yourself than all the world:
And though I loathed the evil, yet I loved
You that did counsel it; and rather sought
To appear a true servant than an honest man.
FERDINAND. I'll go hunt the badger by owl-light:
'Tis a deed of darkness.
[*Exit.*]
BOSOLA. He's much distracted. Off, my painted honor!
While with vain hopes our faculties we tire,
We seem to sweat in ice and freeze in fire.
What would I do, were this to do again?   10
I would not change my peace of conscience
For all the wealth of Europe.—She stirs; here's life:—
Return, fair soul, from darkness, and lead mine
Out of this sensible hell:—she's warm, she breathes:—
Upon thy pale lips I will melt my heart,
To store them with fresh color.—Who's there!
Some cordial drink!—Alas! I dare not call:
So pity would destroy pity.—Her eye opes,
And heaven in it seems to ope, that late was shut,
To take me up to mercy.   20
DUCHESS. Antonio!
BOSOLA.   Yes, madam, he is living;
The dead bodies you saw were but feigned statues:
He's reconciled to your brothers: the Pope hath wrought
The atonement.
DUCHESS.   Mercy!
[*Dies.*]
BOSOLA. Oh, she's gone again! there the cords of life broke.
Oh, sacred innocence, that sweetly sleeps
On turtles' feathers,[50] whilst a guilty conscience
Is a black register wherein is writ   30
All our good deeds and bad, a perspective
That shows us hell! That we cannot be suffered
To do good when we have a mind to it!
This is manly sorrow; these tears, I am very certain,
Never grew in my mother's milk: my estate
Is sunk below the degree of fear: where were
These penitent fountains while she was living?
Oh, they were frozen up! Here is a sight
As direful to my soul as is the sword
Unto a wretch hath slain his father. Come, I'll bear thee   40
Hence, and execute thy last will; that's deliver

---

[50] i.e., turtle-doves' feathers.

Thy body to the reverend dispose
Of some good women: that the cruel tyrant
Shall not deny me. Then I'll post to Milan,
Where somewhat I will speedily enact
Worth my dejection.
[*Exit with the body.*]

ACT FIVE

Scene One

A public place in Milan.

[*Enter* ANTONIO *and* DELIO.]

ANTONIO. What think you of my hope of reconcilement
    To the Arragonian brethren?

DELIO.   I misdoubt it;
    For though they have sent their letters of safe-conduct
    For your repair to Milan, they appear   10
    But nets to entrap you. The Marquis of Pescara,
    Under whom you hold certain land in cheat,[51]
    Much 'gainst his noble nature hath been moved
    To seize those lands; and some of his dependants
    Are at this instant making it their suit
    To be invested in your revenues.
    I cannot think they mean well to your life
    That do deprive you of your means of life,
    Your living.

ANTONIO. You are still an heretic   20
    To any safety I can shape myself.

DELIO. Here comes the marquis: I will make myself
    Petitioner for some part of your land,
    To know whither it is flying.

ANTONIO.   I pray do.
    [*Withdraws to back.*]
    [*Enter* PESCARA.]

DELIO. Sir, I have a suit to you.

PESCARA.   To me?

DELIO.   An easy one:
    There is the citadel of Saint Bennet,
    With some demesnes, of late in the possession   30
    Of Antonio Bologna—please you bestow them on me.

---

[51] Escheat; to be taken away from the tenant upon his failure to meet certain conditions.

PESCARA. You are my friend; but this is such a suit,
    Nor fit for me to give, nor you to take.
DELIO. No, sir?
PESCARA.   I will give you ample reason for it
    Soon in private:—here's the Cardinal's mistress.
    [*Enter* JULIA.]
JULIA. My lord, I am grown your poor petitioner,
    And should be an ill beggar, had I not
    A great man's letter here, the Cardinal's,
    To court you in my favor.
    [*Gives a letter.*]
PESCARO.   He entreats for you   10
    The citadel of Saint Bennet, that belonged
    To the banished Bologna.
JULIA.   Yes.
PESCARA.   I could not
    Have thought of a friend I could rather pleasure with it:
    'Tis yours.
JULIA. Sir, I thank you; and he shall know
    How doubly I am engaged both in your gift,
    And speediness of giving, which makes your grant
    The greater.   20
    [*Exit.*]
ANTONIO [*aside*]. How they fortify themselves
    With my ruin!
DELIO.   Sir, I am little bound to you.
PESCARA.   Why?
DELIO. Because you denied this suit to me, and gave it
    To such a creature.
PESCARA.   Do you know what it was?
    It was Antonio's land; not forfeited
    By course of law, but ravished from his throat
    By the Cardinal's entreaty: it were not fit   30
    I should bestow so main a piece of wrong
    Upon my friend; 'tis a gratification
    Only due to a strumpet, for it is injustice.
    Shall I sprinkle the pure blood of innocents
    To make those followers I call my friends
    Look ruddier upon me? I am glad
    This land, taken from the owner by such wrong,
    Returns again unto so foul an use
    As salary for his lust. Learn, good Delio,
    To ask noble things of me, and you shall find   40
    I'll be a noble giver.
DELIO.   You instruct me well.

ANTONIO [*aside*]. Why, here's a man who would fright impudence
        From sauciest beggars.
PESCARA.   Prince Ferdinand's come to Milan,
        Sick, as they give out, of an apoplexy;
        But some say 'tis a frenzy: I am going
        To visit him.
        [*Exit.*]
ANTONIO. 'Tis a noble old fellow.
DELIO. What course do you mean to take, Antonio?
ANTONIO. This night I mean to venture all my fortune,
        Which is no more than a poor lingering life,   10
        To the Cardinal's worst of malice: I have got
        Private access to his chamber; and intend
        To visit him about the mid of night,
        As once his brother did our noble duchess.
        It may be that the sudden apprehension
        Of danger—for I'll go in mine own shape—
        When he shall see it fraught with love and duty,
        May draw the poison out of him, and work
        A friendly reconcilement: if it fail,
        Yet it shall rid me of this infamous calling;   20
        For better fall once than be ever falling.
DELIO. I'll second you in all danger; and, howe'er,
        My life keeps rank with yours.
ANTONIO.   You are still my loved
        And best friend.
        [*Exeunt.*]

Scene Two

A gallery in the CARDINAL'*s palace at Milan.*

[*Enter* PESCARA *and* DOCTOR.]
PESCARA. Now, doctor, may I visit your patient?
DOCTOR. If it please your lordship: but he's instantly
        To take the air here in the gallery
        By my direction.
PESCARA.   Pray thee, what's his disease?   30
DOCTOR. A very pestilent disease, my lord,
        They call it lycanthropia.
PESCARA.   What's that?
        I need a dictionary to it.
DOCTOR.   I'll tell you.
        In those that are possessed with it there o'erflows
        Such melancholy humour they imagine
        Themselves to be transformed into wolves;

Steal forth to churchyards in the dead of night,
And dig dead bodies up: as two nights since
One met the duke 'bout midnight in a lane
Behind Saint Mark's Church, with the leg of a man
Upon his shoulder; and he howled fearfully;
Said he was a wolf, only the difference
Was, a wolf's skin was hairy on the outside,
His on the inside; bade them take their swords,
Rip up his flesh, and try: straight I was sent for,
And, having ministered to him, found his grace   10
Very well recovered.

PESCARA. I am glad on it.

DOCTOR.   Yet not without some fear
Of a relapse. If he grow to his fit again,
I'll go a nearer way to work with him
Than ever Paracelsus[52] dreamed of; if
They'll give me leave, I'll buffet his madness
Out of him. Stand aside; he comes.

[*Enter* FERDINAND, CARDINAL, MALATESTE, *and* BOSOLA.]

FERDINAND.   Leave me.

MALATESTE. Why doth your lordship love this solitariness?   20

FERDINAND. Eagles commonly fly alone: they are crows, daws, and
    starlings that flock together. Look, what's that follows me?

MALATESTE. Nothing, my lord.

FERDINAND. Yes.

MALATESTE. 'Tis your shadow.

FERDINAND. Stay it; let it not haunt me.

MALATESTE. Impossible, if you move, and the sun shine.

FERDINAND. I will throttle it.

[*Throws himself on the ground.*]

MALATESTE. O, my lord, you are angry with nothing.

FERDINAND. You are a fool: how is it possible I should catch my   30
    shadow, unless I fall upon it? When I go to hell, I mean to carry
    a bribe; for, look you, good gifts evermore make way for the
    worst persons.

PESCARA. Rise, good my lord.

FERDINAND. I am studying the art of patience.

PESCARA. 'Tis a noble virtue.

FERDINAND. To drive six snails before me from this town to Mos-
    cow; neither use goad nor whip to them, but let them take their
    own time;—the patientest man in the world match me for an
    experiment:—and I'll crawl after like a sheep-biter.   40

CARDINAL. Force him up.

[*They raise him.*]

[52] Swiss-German physician.

FERDINAND. Use me well, you were best. What I have done, I have
done: I'll confess nothing.

DOCTOR. Now let me come to him.—Are you mad, my lord? are you
out of your princely wits?

FERDINAND. What's he?

PESCARA. Your doctor.

FERDINAND. Let me have his beard sawed off, and his eyebrows filed
more civil.

DOCTOR. I must do mad tricks with him, for that's the only way on
it.—I have brought your grace a salamander's skin to keep you   10
from sunburning.

FERDINAND. I have cruel sore eyes.

DOCTOR. The white of a cockatrix's[53] egg is present remedy.

FERDINAND. Let it be a new laid one, you were best.—Hide
me from him: physicians are like kings,—they brook no contradiction.

DOCTOR. Now he begins to fear me: now let me alone with him.

CARDINAL. How now? put off your gown?

DOCTOR. Let me have some forty urinals filled with rosewater; he and
I'll go pelt one another with them.—Now he begins to fear me.—   20
Can you fetch a frisk, sir?—Let him go, let him go, upon my
peril: I find by his eye he stands in awe of me; I'll make him as tame
as a dormouse.

FERDINAND. Can you fetch your frisks, sir?—I will stamp him into
a cullis, flay off his skin, to cover one of the anatomies this rogue
hath set in the cold yonder in Barber-Surgeon's hall.—Hence,
hence! you are all of you like beasts for sacrifice: there's nothing
left of you but tongue and belly, flattery and lechery.
[*Exit.*]

PESCARA. Doctor, he did not fear you throughly.

DOCTOR.   True;   30
I was somewhat too forward.

BOSOLA.   Mercy upon me,
What a fatal judgment hath fallen upon this Ferdinand!

PESCARA. Knows your grace what accident hath brought
Unto the prince this strange distraction?

CARDINAL [*aside*]. I must feign somewhat.—Thus they say it grew.
You have heard it rumored, for these many years
None of our family dies but there is seen
The shape of an old woman, which is given
By tradition to us to have been murdered   40
By her nephews for her riches. Such a figure
One night, as the prince sat up late at his book,
Appeared to him; when crying out for help,

[53] A fabled serpent with a deadly glance.

The gentlemen of his chamber found his grace
All on a cold sweat, altered much in face
And language: since which apparition,
He hath grown worse and worse, and I much fear
He cannot live.

BOSOLA. Sir, I would speak with you.

PESCARA.   We'll leave your grace,
Wishing to the sick prince, our noble lord,
All health of mind and body.

CARDINAL.   You are most welcome.   10
[*Exeunt* PESCARA, MALATESTE, *and* DOCTOR.]
Are you come? so.—[*Aside*.] This fellow must not know
By any means I had intelligence
In our duchess's death; for, though I counseled it,
The full of all the engagement seemed to grow
From Ferdinand.—Now, sir, how fares our sister?
I do not think but sorrow makes her look
Like to an oft-dyed garment: she shall now
Taste comfort from me. Why do you look so wildly?
Oh, the fortune of your master here the prince   20
Dejects you; but be you of happy comfort:
If you'll do one thing for me I'll entreat,
Though he had a cold tombstone o'er his bones,
I'd make you what you would be.

BOSOLA.   Anything;
Give it me in a breath, and let me fly to it:
They that think long small expedition win,
For musing much on the end cannot begin.
[*Enter* JULIA.]

JULIA. Sir, will you come in to supper?

CARDINAL.   I am busy;   30
Leave me.

JULIA [*aside*]. What an excellent shape hath that fellow!
[*Exit*.]

CARDINAL. 'Tis thus. Antonio lurks here in Milan:
Inquire him out, and kill him. While he lives,
Our sister cannot marry; and I have thought
Of an excellent match for her. Do this, and style me
Thy advancement.

BOSOLA.   But by what means shall I find him out?

CARDINAL. There is a gentleman called Delio
Here in the camp, that hath been long approved   40
His loyal friend. Set eye upon the fellow;
Follow him to mass; maybe Antonio,
Although he do account religion

But a school-name, for fashion of the world
May accompany him; or else go inquire out
Delio's confessor, and see if you can bribe
Him to reveal it. There are a thousand ways
A man might find to trace him; as to know
What fellows haunt the Jews for taking up
Great sums of money, for sure he is in want;
Or else to go to the picture-makers, and learn
Who bought her picture lately: some of these
Happily may take.   10

BOSOLA.   Well, I'll not freeze in the business:
I would see that wretched thing, Antonio,
Above all sights in the world.

CARDINAL.   Do, and be happy.
    [Exit.]

BOSOLA. This fellow doth breed basilisks in his eyes,
He's nothing else but murder; yet he seems
Not to have notice of the duchess's death.
'Tis his cunning: I must follow his example;
There cannot be a surer way to trace
Than that of an old fox.   20
    [Reenter JULIA, with a pistol.]

JULIA.   So, sir, you are well met.

BOSOLA. How now?

JULIA.   Nay, the doors are fast enough: Now, sir,
I will make you confess your treachery.

BOSOLA.   Treachery?

JULIA.   Yes,
Confess to me which of my women 'twas
You hired to put love-powder into my drink?

BOSOLA. Love-powder?

JULIA.   Yes, when I was at Malfi.   30
Why should I fall in love with such a face else?
I have already suffered for thee so much pain,
The only remedy to do me good
Is to kill my longing.

BOSOLA.   Sure, your pistol holds
Nothing but perfumes or kissing-comfits.[54]
Excellent lady! You have a pretty way on it
To discover your longing. Come, come, I'll disarm you,
And arm you thus: yet this is wondrous strange.

JULIA. Compare thy form and my eyes together, you'll find 40
My love no such great miracle. Now you'll say

[54] Pastiles to sweeten the breath.

I am wanton: this nice modesty in ladies
Is but a troublesome familiar that haunts them.

BOSOLA. Know you me, I am a blunt soldier.

JULIA.   The better:
Sure, there wants fire where there are no lively sparks
Of roughness.

BOSOLA.   And I want compliment.

JULIA.   Why, ignorance
In courtship cannot make you do amiss,
If you have a heart to do well.   10

BOSOLA.   You are very fair.

JULIA. Nay, if you lay beauty to my charge,
I must plead unguilty.

BOSOLA.   Your bright eyes carry
A quiver of darts in them sharper than sunbeams.

JULIA. You will mar me with commendation,
Put yourself to the charge of courting me,
Whereas now I woo you.

BOSOLA [aside]. I have it, I will work upon this creature.—
Let us grow most amorously familiar: 20
If the great Cardinal now should see me thus,
Would he not count me a villain?

JULIA.   No, he might
Count me a wanton, not lay a scruple
Of offense on you; for if I see and steal
A diamond, the fault is not in the stone,
But in me the thief that purloins it. I am sudden
With you: we that are great women of pleasure
Use to cut off these uncertain wishes
And unquiet longings, and in an instant join   30
The sweet delight and the pretty excuse together.
Had you been in the street, under my chamber-window,
Even there I should have courted you.

BOSOLA.   Oh, you are
An excellent lady!

JULIA.   Bid me do somewhat for you
Presently to express I love you.

BOSOLA.   I will;
And if you love me, fail not to effect it.
The Cardinal is grown wondrous melancholy;   40
Demand the cause, let him not put you off
With feigned excuse; discover the main ground on it.

JULIA. Why would you know this?

BOSOLA.   I have depended on him,
And I hear that he is fallen in some disgrace

With the emperor: if he be, like the mice
That forsake falling houses, I would shift
To other dependence.

JULIA.   You shall not need
Follow the wars: I'll be your maintenance.

BOSOLA. And I your loyal servant: but I cannot
Leave my calling.

JULIA.   Not leave an ungrateful
General for the love of a sweet lady?
You are like some cannot sleep in featherbeds,   10
But must have blocks for their pillows.

BOSOLA.   Will you do this?

JULIA. Cunningly.

BOSOLA. Tomorrow I'll expect the intelligence.

JULIA. Tomorrow? get you into my cabinet;[55]
You shall have it with you. Do not delay me,
No more than I do you: I am like one
That is condemned; I have my pardon promised,
But I would see it sealed. Go, get you in:
You shall see me wind my tongue about his heart   20
Like a skein of silk.

[*Exit* BOSOLA.]
[*Reenter* CARDINAL.]

CARDINAL.   Where are you?

[*Enter* SERVANTS.]

SERVANTS.   Here.

CARDINAL. Let none, upon your lives, have conference
With the Prince Ferdinand, unless I know it.—
[*Aside.*] In this distraction he may reveal
The murder.

[*Exeunt* SERVANTS.]

                         Yond's my lingering consumption:
I am weary of her, and by any means
Would be quit of.   30

JULIA.   How now, my lord? what ails you?

CARDINAL. Nothing.

JULIA.   Oh, you are much altered: come, I must be
Your secretary, and remove this lead
From off your bosom: what's the matter?

CARDINAL.   I may not
Tell you.

JULIA. Are you so far in love with sorrow

---

[55] Private room.

You cannot part with part of it? or think you
I cannot love your grace when you are sad
As well as merry? or do you suspect
I, that have been a secret to your heart
These many winters, cannot be the same
Unto your tongue?

CARDINAL.   Satisfy thy longing—
The only way to make thee keep my counsel
Is, not to tell thee.

JULIA.   Tell your echo this,   10
Or flatterers, that like echoes still report
What they hear though most imperfect, and not me;
For if that you be true unto yourself,
I'll know.

CARDINAL. Will you rack me?

JULIA.   No, judgment shall
Draw it from you: it is an equal fault,
To tell one's secrets unto all or none.

CARDINAL. The first argues folly.

JULIA.   But the last tyranny.   20

CARDINAL. Very well: why, imagine I have committed
Some secret deed which I desire the world
May never hear of.

JULIA.   Therefore may not I know it?
You have concealed for me as great a sin
As adultery. Sir, never was occasion
For perfect trial of my constancy
Till now: sir, I beseech you——

CARDINAL.   You'll repent it.

JULIA. Never.   30

CARDINAL. It hurries thee to ruin: I'll not tell thee.
Be well advised, and think what danger 'tis
To receive a prince's secrets: they that do,
Had need have their breasts hooped with adamant
To contain them. I pray thee, yet be satisfied;
Examine thine own frailty; 'tis more easy
To tie knots than unloose them: 'tis a secret
That, like a lingering poison, may chance lie
Spread in thy veins, and kill thee seven year hence.

JULIA. Now you dally with me.   40

CARDINAL.   No more; thou shalt know it.
By my appointment the great Duchess of Malfi
And two of her young children, four nights since,
Were strangled.

JULIA.   O Heaven, sir! what have you done!

CARDINAL. How now! how settles this? think you your bosom
    Will be a grave dark and obscure enough
    For such a secret?
JULIA.   You have undone yourself, sir.
CARDINAL. Why?
JULIA.   It lies not in me to conceal it.
CARDINAL.   No?
    Come, I will swear you to it upon this book.
JULIA. Most religiously.
CARDINAL.   Kiss it.   10
    [*She kisses the book.*]
                         Now you shall
    Never utter it; thy curiosity
    Hath undone thee: thou art poisoned with that book;
    Because I knew thou couldst not keep my counsel,
    I have bound thee to it by death.
    [*Reenter* BOSOLA.]
BOSOLA.   For pity sake,
    Hold!
CARDINAL.   Ha! Bosola?
JULIA.   I forgive you
    This equal piece of justice you have done;   20
    For I betrayed your counsel to that fellow:
    He overheard it; that was the cause I said
    It lay not in me to conceal it.
BOSOLA.   O foolish woman,
    Couldst not thou have poisoned him?
JULIA.   'Tis weakness,
    Too much to think what should have been done. I go,
    I know not whither.
    [*Dies.*]
CARDINAL.   Wherefore comest thou hither?
BOSOLA. That I might find a great man like yourself,   30
    Not out of his wits as the Lord Ferdinand,
    To remember my service.
CARDINAL.   I'll have thee hewed in pieces.
BOSOLA. Make not yourself such a promise of that life
    Which is not yours to dispose of.
CARDINAL.   Who placed thee there?
BOSOLA. Her lust, as she intended.
CARDINAL.   Very well:
    Now you know me for your fellow-murderer.
BOSOLA. And wherefore should you lay fair marble colors   40
    Upon your rotten purposes to me?
    Unless you imitate some that do plot great treasons,

And when they have done, go hide themselves in the graves
Of those were actors in it?
CARDINAL.   No more; there is
A fortune attends thee.
BOSOLA.   Shall I go sue
To Fortune any longer? 'Tis the fool's
Pilgrimage.
CARDINAL. I have honors in store for thee.
BOSOLA. There are a-many ways that conduct to seeming
Honor, and some of them very dirty ones.   10
CARDINAL.   Throw
To the devil thy melancholy.   The fire burns well:
What need we keep a-stirring of it, and make
A greater smother? Thou wilt kill Antonio?
BOSOLA. Yes.
CARDINAL.   Take up that body.
BOSOLA.   I think I shall
Shortly grow the common bearer for churchyards.
CARDINAL. I will allow thee some dozen of attendants
To aid thee in the murder.   20
BOSOLA. Oh, by no means. Physicians that apply horse-leeches to any
rank swelling use to cut off their tails, that the blood may run
through them the faster: let me have no train when I go to shed
blood, lest it make me have a greater when I ride to the gallows.
CARDINAL. Come to me after midnight, to help to remove
That body to her own lodging: I'll give out
She died of the plague; 'twill breed the less inquiry
After her death.
BOSOLA.   Where's Castruchio, her husband?   30
CARDINAL. He's rode to Naples, to take possession
Of Antonio's citadel.
BOSOLA.   Believe me, you have done
A very happy turn.
CARDINAL.   Fail not to come:
There is the master-key of our lodgings; and by that
You may conceive what trust I plant in you.
BOSOLA. You shall find me ready.
      [*Exit* CARDINAL.]
                                        O poor Antonio,
Though nothing be so needful to thy estate   40
As pity, yet I find nothing so dangerous;
I must look to my footing:
In such slippery ice-pavements men had need
To be frost-nailed well, they may break their necks else;

The precedent's here afore me. How this man
Bears up in blood! seems fearless! Why, 'tis well:
Security some men call the suburbs of hell,
Only a dead wall between. Well, good Antonio,
I'll seek thee out; and all my care shall be
To put thee into safety from the reach
Of these most cruel biters that have got
Some of thy blood already. It may be,
I'll join with thee in a most just revenge:
The weakest arm is strong enough that strikes   10
With the sword of justice. Still methinks the duchess
Haunts me.—There, there, 'tis nothing but my melancholy.
O Penitence, let me truly taste thy cup,
That throws men down only to raise them up!
[*Exit.*]

Scene Three

A fortification at Milan.

[*Enter* ANTONIO *and* DELIO.]
DELIO. Yond's the Cardinal's window. This fortification
Grew from the ruins of an ancient abbey;
And to yond side of the river lies a wall,
Piece of a cloister, which in my opinion
Gives the best echo that you ever heard,
So hollow and so dismal, and withal   20
So plain in the distinction of our words,
That many have supposed it is a spirit
That answers.
ANTONIO.   I do love these ancient ruins.
We never tread upon them but we set
Our foot upon some reverend history:
And, questionless, here in this open court,
Which now lies naked to the injuries
Of stormy weather, some men lie interred
Loved the church so well, and gave so largely to it,   30
They thought it should have canopied their bones
Till doomsday; but all things have their end:
Churches and cities, which have diseases
Like to men, must have like death that we have.
ECHO. "Like death that we have."
DELIO. Now the echo hath caught you.

ANTONIO.   It groaned, methought, and gave
          A very deadly accent.
ECHO.   "Deadly accent."
DELIO. I told you 'twas a pretty one: you may make it
          A huntsman, or a falconer, a musician,
          Or a thing of sorrow.
ECHO.   "A thing of sorrow."
ANTONIO. Aye, sure, that suits it best.
ECHO.   "That suits it best."
ANTONIO. 'Tis very like my wife's voice.   10
ECHO.   "Aye, wife's voice."
DELIO. Come, let's walk further from it. I would not have you
          Go to the Cardinal's tonight: do not.
ECHO.   "Do not."
DELIO. Wisdom doth not more moderate wasting sorrow
          Than time: take time for it; be mindful of thy safety.
ECHO. "Be mindful of thy safety."
ANTONIO.   Necessity compels me:
          Make scrutiny throughout the passes of
          Your own life, you'll find it impossible   20
          To fly your fate.
ECHO.   "Oh, fly your fate."
DELIO.   Hark!
          The dead stones seem to have pity on you, and give you
          Good counsel.
ANTONIO.   Echo, I will not talk with thee,
          For thou art a dead thing.
ECHO.   "Thou art a dead thing."
ANTONIO. My duchess is asleep now,
          And her little ones, I hope sweetly: O Heaven,   30
          Shall I never see her more?
ECHO.   "Never see her more."
ANTONIO. I marked not one repetition of the echo
          But that; and on the sudden a clear light
          Presented me a face folded in sorrow.
DELIO. Your fancy merely.
ANTONIO.   Come, I'll be out of this ague,
          For to live thus is not indeed to live;
          It is a mockery and abuse of life:
          I will not henceforth save myself by halves;   40
          Lose all, or nothing.
DELIO.   Your own virtue save you!
          I'll fetch your eldest son, and second you:
          It may be that the sight of his own blood
          Spread in so sweet a figure may beget

The more compassion. However, fare you well.
Though in our miseries Fortune have a part,
Yet in our noble sufferings she hath none:
Contempt of pain, that we may call our own.
[*Exeunt.*]

Scene Four

A room in the CARDINAL'*s palace.*

[*Enter* CARDINAL, PESCARA, MALATESTE, RODERIGO, *and*
GRISOLAN.]
CARDINAL. You shall not watch tonight by the sick prince;
    His grace is very well recovered.
MALATESTE. Good my lord, suffer us.
CARDINAL.   Oh, by no means;
    The noise, and change of object in his eye,
    Doth more distract him: I pray, all to bed;   10
    And though you hear him in his violent fit,
    Do not rise, I entreat you.
PESCARA.   So, sir; we shall not.
CARDINAL. Nay, I must have you promise upon your honors,
    For I was enjoined to it by himself; and he seemed
    To urge it sensibly.
PESCARA.   Let our honors bind
    This trifle.
CARDINAL. Nor any of your followers.
MALATESTE.   Neither.   20
CARDINAL. It may be, to make trial of your promise,
    When he's asleep, myself will rise and feign
    Some of his mad tricks, and cry out for help,
    And feign myself in danger.
MALATESTE.   If your throat were cutting,
    I'd not come at you, now I have protested against it.
CARDINAL. Why, I thank you.
GRISOLAN.   'Twas a foul storm tonight.
RODERIGO. The Lord Ferdinand's chamber shook like an osier.
MALATESTE. 'Twas nothing but pure kindness in the devil,   30
    To rock his own child.
    [*Exeunt all except the* CARDINAL.]
CARDINAL. The reason why I would not suffer these
    About my brother, is, because at midnight
    I may with better privacy convey
    Julia's body to her own lodging. Oh, my conscience!

I would pray now; but the devil takes away my heart
For having any confidence in prayer.
About this hour I appointed Bosola
To fetch the body: when he hath served my turn,
He dies.
[*Exit.*]
[*Enter* BOSOLA.]

BOSOLA. Ha! 'twas the Cardinal's voice; I heard him name
    Bosola and my death. Listen; I hear
    One's footing.
    [*Enter* FERDINAND.]

FERDINAND. Strangling is a very quiet death.

BOSOLA [*aside*]. Nay, then, I see I must stand upon my guard.   10

FERDINAND. What say to that? whisper softly; do you agree to it?
  So; it must be done in the dark: the Cardinal would not for a
  thousand pounds the doctor should see it.

BOSOLA. My death is plotted; here is the consequence of murder.
    We value not desert nor Christian breath,
    When we know black deeds must be cured with death.
    [*Enter* ANTONIO *and* SERVANT.]

SERVANT. Here stay, sir, and be confident, I pray:
    I'll fetch you a dark lantern.
    [*Exit.*]

ANTONIO.   Could I take him
    At his prayers, there were hope of pardon.   20

BOSOLA.   Fall right, my sword!—
    [*Stabs him.*]
    I'll not give thee so much leisure as to pray.

ANTONIO. Oh, I am gone! Thou hast ended a long suit
    In a minute.

BOSOLA.   What art thou?

ANTONIO.   A most wretched thing,
    That only have thy benefit in death,
    To appear myself.
    [*Reenter* SERVANT *with a lantern.*]

SERVANT.   Where are you, sir?

ANTONIO.   Very near my home.—Bosola?   30

SERVANT.   Oh, misfortune!

BOSOLA. Smother thy pity, thou art dead else.—Antonio?
    The man I would have saved 'bove mine own life!
    We are merely the stars' tennis-balls, struck and bandied
    Which way please them.—O good Antonio,
    I'll whisper one thing in thy dying ear
    Shall make thy heart break quickly! thy fair duchess
    And two sweet children——

ANTONIO.   Their very names
    Kindle a little life in me.
BOSOLA.   Are murdered.
ANTONIO. Some men have wished to die
    At the hearing of sad tidings; I am glad
    That I shall do it in sadness: I would not now
    Wish my wounds balmed nor healed, for I have no use
    To put my life to. In all our quest of greatness,
    Like wanton boys, whose pastime is their care,
    We follow after bubbles blown in the air.   10
    Pleasure of life, what is it? only the good
    Hours of an ague; merely a preparative
    To rest, to endure vexation. I do not ask
    The process of my death; only commend me
    To Delio.
BOSOLA.   Break, heart!
ANTONIO.   And let my son
    Fly the courts of princes.
    [*Dies.*]
BOSOLA.   Thou seemest
    To have loved Antonio?   20
SERVANT.   I brought him hither,
    To have reconciled him to the Cardinal.
BOSOLA. I do not ask thee that.
    Take him up, if thou tender thine own life,
    And bear him where the lady Julia
    Was wont to lodge.—Oh, my fate moves swift;
    I have this Cardinal in the forge already;
    Now I'll bring him to the hammer. O direful misprision!
    I will not imitate things glorious,
    No more than base; I'll be mine own example.—   30
    On, on, and look thou represent, for silence,
    The thing thou bearest.
    [*Exeunt.*]

Scene Five

Another room in the same.

[*Enter* CARDINAL, *with a book.*]
CARDINAL. I am puzzled in a question about hell:
    He says, in hell there is one material fire,
    And yet it shall not burn all men alike.
    Lay him by. How tedious is a guilty conscience!
    When I look into the fish-ponds in my garden,

Methinks I see a thing armed with a rake,
That seems to strike at me.
[*Enter* BOSOLA, *and* SERVANT *bearing* ANTONIO'S *body.*]
                                    Now, art thou come?
Thou lookest ghastly:
There sits in thy face some great determination
Mixed with some fear.

BOSOLA.   Thus it lightens into action:
I am come to kill thee.

CARDINAL.   Ha!—Help! our guard!

BOSOLA. Thou art deceived; they are out of thy howling.   10

CARDINAL. Hold; and I will faithfully divide
Revenues with thee.

BOSOLA.   Thy prayers and proffers
Are both unseasonable.

CARDINAL.   Raise the watch!
We are betrayed!

BOSOLA.   I have confined your flight:
I'll suffer your retreat to Julia's chamber,
But no further.

CARDINAL. Help! we are betrayed!   20
[*Enter, above,* PESCARA, MALATESTE, RODERIGO, *and* GRISOLAN].

MALATESTE. Listen.

CARDINAL.   My dukedom for rescue!

RODERIGO.   Fie upon
His counterfeiting!

MALATESTE.   Why, 'tis not the Cardinal.

RODERIGO. Yes, yes, 'tis he: but I'll see him hanged
Ere I'll go down to him.

CARDINAL.   Here is a plot upon me;
I am assaulted! I am lost, unless some rescue.

GRISOLAN. He doth this pretty well; but it will not serve   30
To laugh me out of mine honor.

CARDINAL.   The sword is at my throat!

RODERIGO. You would not bawl so loud then.

MALATESTE.   Come, come,
Let's go to bed: he told us thus much aforehand.

PESCARA. He wished you should not come at him; but, believe it,
The accent of the voice sounds not in jest:
I'll down to him, howsoever, and with engines
Force ope the doors.
[*Exit above.*]

RODERIGO.   Let's follow him aloof,   40
And note how the Cardinal will laugh at him.
[*Exeunt, above,* MALATESTE, RODERIGO, *and* GRISOLAN.]

BOSOLA. There's for first,
> [*Kills the* SERVANT.]
> 'Cause you shall not unbarricade the door
> To let in rescue.
CARDINAL. What cause hast thou to pursue my life?
BOSOLA.   Look there.
CARDINAL. Antonio?
BOSOLA.   Slain by my hand unwittingly.
> Pray, and be sudden: when thou killedest thy sister,
> Thou tookest from Justice her most equal balance,
> And left her naught but her sword.   10
CARDINAL.   Oh, mercy!
BOSOLA. Now, it seems thy greatness was only outward;
> For thou fallest faster of thyself than calamity
> Can drive thee. I'll not waste longer time; there!
> [*Stabs him.*]
CARDINAL. Thou hast hurt me.
BOSOLA.   Again!
> [*Stabs him again.*]
CARDINAL.   Shall I die like a leveret,
> Without any resistance?—Help, help, help!
> I am slain!
> [*Enter* FERDINAND.]
FERDINAND. The alarum? give me a fresh horse;   20
> Rally the vaunt-guard, or the day is lost.
> Yield, yield! I give you the honor of arms,
> Shake my sword over you; will you yield?
CARDINAL.   Help me;
> I am your brother!
FERDINAND.   The devil! My brother fight
> Upon the adverse party?
> [*He wounds the* CARDINAL, *and, in the scuffle, gives* BOSOLA
> *his death-wound.*]
>   There flies your ransom.
CARDINAL. O justice!
> I suffer now for what hath former been: 30
> Sorrow is held the eldest child of sin.
FERDINAND. Now you're brave fellows. Caesar's fortune was harder
than Pompey's; Caesar died in the arms of prosperity, Pompey at
the feet of disgrace. You both died in the field. The pain is nothing:
pain many times is taken away with the apprehension of greater,
as the toothache with the sight of a barber that comes to pull it
out: there's philosophy for you.
BOSOLA. Now my revenge is perfect.—Sink, thou main cause
> [*Kills* FERDINAND.]

    Of my undoing!—The last part of my life
    Hath done me best service.
FERDINAND. Give me some wet hay; I am broken-winded. I do account
    this world but a dog-kennel: I will vault credit[56] and affect high
    pleasures beyond death.
BOSOLA. He seems to come to himself, now he is so near
    The bottom.
FERDINAND. My sister, O my sister! there is the cause on it.
    Whether we fall by ambition, blood, or lust,
    Like diamonds we are cut with our own dust.   10
    [*Dies.*]
CARDINAL. Thou hast thy payment too.
BOSOLA. Yes, I hold my weary soul in my teeth.
    'Tis ready to part from me. I do glory
    That thou, which stoodest like a huge pyramid
    Begun upon a large and ample base,
    Shalt end in a little point, a kind of nothing.
    [*Enter, below*, PESCARA, MALATESTE, RODERIGO, *and* GRISOLAN.]
PESCARA. How now, my lord?
MALATESTE.   O sad disaster!
RODERIGO.   How
    Comes this?   20
BOSOLA. Revenge for the Duchess of Malfi murdered
    By the Arragonian brethren; for Antonio
    Slain by this hand; for lustful Julia
    Poisoned by this man; and lastly for myself,
    That was an actor in the main of all,
    Much 'gainst mine own good nature, yet in the end
    Neglected.
PESCARA. How now, my lord?
CARDINAL. Look to my brother: he gave us these large wounds
    As we were struggling here in the rushes. And now,   30
    I pray, let me be laid by and never thought of.
    [*Dies.*]
PESCARA. How fatally, it seems, he did withstand
    His own rescue!
MALATESTE.   Thou wretched thing of blood,
    How came Antonio by his death?
BOSOLA.   In a mist;
    I know not how: such a mistake as I
    Have often seen in a play. Oh, I am gone!
    We are only like dead walls or vaulted graves,
    That, ruined, yield no echo. Fare you well.   40
    It may be pain, but no harm, to me to die

---

[56] Do things beyond belief.

In so good a quarrel. Oh, this gloomy world!
In what a shadow, or deep pit of darkness,
Doth, womanish and fearful, mankind live!
Let worthy minds ne'er stagger in distrust
To suffer death or shame for what is just:
Mine is another voyage.
[*Dies.*]

PESCARO. The noble Delio, as I came to the palace,
Told me of Antonio's being here, and showed me
A pretty gentleman, his son and heir.
[*Enter* DELIO *and* ANTONIO'S SON.]

MALATESTE. O sir,   10
You come too late!

DELIO.   I heard so, and was armed for it
Ere I came. Let us make noble use
Of this great ruin; and join all our force
To establish this young hopeful gentleman
In his mother's right. These wretched eminent things
Leave no more fame behind them, than should one
Fall in a frost, and leave his print in snow;
As soon as the sun shines, it ever melts,
Both form and matter. I have ever thought   20
Nature doth nothing so great for great men
As when she is pleased to make them lords of truth:
Integrity of life is fame's best friend,
Which nobly, beyond death, shall crown the end.
[*Exeunt.*]

MOLIÈRE

THE MISANTHROPE

THE COMEDY OF MASKS

THE PLAYS SO FAR CONSIDERED in this collection represent
mirrors of a world the audience conceived as true or ideal, the
concept based on a widely understood relationship between man
and the gods. Only Plautus, by looking in other directions, restricted himself to the relations between man and other men; he
was not, of course, unique: comedy was generally recognized as
a mirror of man in society. In comedy it was not necessary for the
playwright to investigate the larger ethical or moral issues but to
"observe with precision the avarice or the prudence of old men,
the loves and passions of youths, the wiles and clever tricks of
their mistresses, the lies and deceits of pandars ... the bravado
and vainglory of military veterans, the industriousness of nurses,
and the indulgence of mothers."*

In its origin and early development, comedy was more concerned
with character and situation than with a carefully manipulated
complete action; its significance for the audience was in scenes of
folly and gulling, not in the slow process of self-discovery which
was so often the purpose of serious dramaturgy. Indeed, Aristotle
commented on the primacy of action in determining the tragic
view: the sight of a madwoman carrying a man's head on a pole may
be horrible, but the very power of horror lies in its meaningless-
ness. Agave becomes a tragic character only when placed in the
context of the total action of *The Bacchae*. On the other hand, it is
common experience that a comic response, laughter, can be
aroused by a single moment in the life of an otherwise unknown
character: a pail of garbage dumped from an upper window on

* Peletier de Mans, *Art Poétique*, 1555.

the head of a passing policeman, an archbishop in full regalia slipping on a patch of ice, a bemedaled general pursued by a yapping cur.

It will be noticed that these comic figures are not altogether unknown: their costumes identify them as representatives of some kind of authority and the fun arises from the undermining of the authority represented rather than from the personality to whom the event occurs. But comedy is not restricted to characters who wear some identifiable official regalia; the categories quoted above include a miser, a pandar, a mother. To make possible the immediate identification necessary for comedy, playwrights resorted to the mask.

The mask is inseparable from the drama of all cultures and periods. In ancient Greece it was a covering of linen, supposedly invented by Thespis, to make the actor's face more readily visible in the vast reaches of the *alfresco* theater. In the orient, it was a system of face-painting in which stylized patterns of color and line indicated status and attitude. In the Middle Ages, "heads" were used to represent God and his angels. In the classical comic theater, a conventional, codified set of masks was employed to reveal age, status, attitude and function: one stereotyped facial pattern indicated the benevolent old man, another the avaricious, another the lecherous, and so on. A glance would give the spectator the whole history of a character, insofar as it had a relation to the comic situations he was about to enjoy; a glance would take the place of the four episodes which revealed the true nature of the tragic protagonist. The mask was a kind of shorthand employed by the playwright to permit him to get to his business, the enjoyment of folly.

The purest example of this concept of comic drama found influential expression first in northern Italy in the sixteenth century. Here groups of actors, protesting against the intrusion of literary and academic amateurs into their art, formed themselves into companies to protect their interests and exercise their profession. They called their performances *commedia dell' arte* (professional plays), and they acted *ex tempore*, without a formal, completely written text. This was possible because each member of the company had an assigned comic "mask" or character, whose attitudes and status he would know, and hence would be expected to react predictably in any situation thrust upon him. One actor was always the old man, the *pantalone*, another the clever servant, the *harlequin*, a third the pert servant-maid, the *colombine*, a fourth the learned imposter, the doctor, and a fifth the braggart warrior, the *capitano*. Given a scenario, an outline of the plot and an indication of the situation to be developed, a *commedia* troupe went before its spectators with the assurance of professionals who knew, without the help of an author, how to create laughter at the expense of their own or their fellow-actors' masks. The *commedia* was immediately popular, and companies followed the reports of their success throughout Europe, to England, France, Scandinavia, even to Russia. Thus the tradition of pure comedy was revitalized for the modern world, a tradition that was to survive the centuries and to manifest itself in the famous short-films of Charlie Chaplin, in the television routines of countless comedians, even to appear in almost its original state in the contemporary Peacock Theater of the Tivoli Gardens in Copenhagen.

Pure comedy is not interested in drawing conclusions. It does not exist to explain the mask, but to exploit it. Sophoclean action is often a series of debates: what is the truth of the character in his situation, why is it true? Pure comic action is not debate but display: this is how Pantalone, or Charlie, behaves when he finds himself in such-and-such circumstances. There is no occasion for debate because there are no questions to be raised; particularly there is no question of the identity of the comic braggart, the comic old man, the comic shrew. They may more often than not play the fool, but they do not fool the spectator. The audience is delighted by the anticipated devices with which the braggart warrior evades combat; it would not be at all pleased if he were unexpectedly to stand and deliver. The comic mask is the theatrical equivalent of the historical present in grammar: it represents a condition permanently true.

The comic mask, whether it be miser, or hypochondriac, lover, or parasite, is the eternal re-expression of human self-interest, the whole hearted, ardent preoccupation with oneself that makes life tolerable, eccentricity combined with egocentricity. In observing the mask in action, the spectator is required only to recognize the egocentricity of everybody else (what fools my fellow mortals be) without wincing at the discovery of his own braggadocio, or greed. So the comic mask permitted the actor an open revelation of truths that would be unwelcome in a more serious action, and pure comedy itself is a kind of larger mask for the playwright, permitting his vision of the truth about human experience to take the air in public without fear, assured of favor.

Jean-Baptiste Poquelin, called Molière (1622–1673), encountered *commedia* troupes and their pure comedy early in his career as a strolling player. Disappointed in his own aspirations to fill heroic roles, he recognized the appeal of the improvised comic action and the mask of demonic egocentricity. Settled in Paris, he at once established his own success with a series of short comedies about old guardians who hoped to marry young wards for their fortunes, fantastically ignorant quack-doctors, female pretenders to virtue or taste. When accused of aiming his comic shafts at recognizable Parisians, he replied that nothing annoyed him so much as to be accused of hitting off a particular individual in his comic types; that his purpose was to depict manners in general rather than personal foibles.* One of his characters, discussing a play, suggests the proper reaction to these pure comedies: "They are public mirrors, and we should never admit that we see ourselves in them; and if we take offense at reproof, we are making a public confession of our faults."**

Pure comedy is hard to justify as art simply because it does not seem to be saying anything: it does not say that this man is a fool and *must be* punished for his folly; that this man is a quack and *must be* exposed; that society is in need of common sense, either of the good old days or of the brave new world. Actually, where it seems to be saying nothing, pure comedy says nearly everything. And what it says, over and over again is, "What *fun* these mortals be." The theme is precious, the intent is gracious, and in the hands of a master, the reward is great.

Molière is sometimes described as a satirist or a writer of

* See his *Impromptu at Versailles.*
** *Critique of L'Ecole des Femmes.*

comedies of manners, but both of these media involve certain elements which are not emphasized in such a play as *The Misanthrope*. The chief masks in satirical or manners comedy are without compensatory virtues; the chief mask in pure comedy generally exaggerates a quality (thrift, for example) which might be a virtue in moderation. The action of satirical or manners comedy is frequently intended to demonstrate why the wearer of the mask is unworthy of a place in the social group, if not in the human race. Pure comedy addresses itself to depicting what happens to a world (society in general, or a family in particular) in which the egocentricity of the chief mask is an active, probably dominant, force. Pure comedy is concerned with what happens; satire or manners with what happens and what ought to happen. Moral comedy proceeds to a destruction of the mask through surrender or exposure; in pure comedy the chief character exits still clinging to his mask; he is exhibited, not punished.

In locating Molière on the scale of comedy, it is thus important to observe the focus of the entire play. The satirist focuses on the agent who dupes or betrays, and who must be exposed; Molière focuses on the victim, who victimizes himself, by intent, against reason. Blind to the situation, he is deaf to those who can see.

For another standard mask in pure comedy is the man of reason, fluent with loud advice. It is common to call him a chorus character, the man "who speaks for the author." In Molière's works, at any rate, he does not. The character of reason speaks for the play, which is a vastly different matter. It would be unscholarly, unwise, uncritical, and untrue to assume that Molière was a man of reason. It would be true to hazard a guess that, since he chose to interpret on the stage the main characters he created with his pen, the author's voice may be heard in the opinions and the joyous self-delusions of these egocentrics.

The Misanthrope is, for many critics, Molière's masterpiece, mingling a chief mask whose egocentricity is so bitter as to verge upon mania, social and literary satire, and an ending that approaches tragedy as closely as comedy might dare to do. But to stop with such comments is to risk misunderstanding Molière, to lose the appetite for pure comedy while sitting at its richest banquet.

Full understanding begins with seeing the chief mask in its theatrical context. Molière's hero is a Quixote mad with morality, who insists upon strict honesty, plain-speaking, and no-compromise in every situation he confronts. And Molière requires him to confront situation after situation in which one grain of common sense tempering his honesty would allow him to escape with dignity. But he lashes out at all and sundry, bowling over a Sunday poet with energy that would have wiped out the complete works of Horace, rounding upon a couple of silly courtiers as if their hands were stained with the blood of Louis XIV, and then falling in love with a very lovable girl who delights in gossip, enjoys whispering behind her fan, and doubtless is not above encouraging poetasters. After four acts of misanthropic Alexandrines the hero storms from the stage, giving up the arts, his friend, his society, and the woman he loves to seek "some lonely cranny of the earth/Where a man is free to be a man of honor." To be sure the elements of French society displayed are sufficiently unreasonable to invite attack, to be sure the hero has a friend always at hand to beg him to moderate his excessive demands. But the questions implicit in satire or comedy of manners—"How shall a man behave in society? Should he be honest at all costs, or reasonable?"—are never asked, and need not be inferred except by those who cannot see the true wisdom of pure comedy.

To see the hero of *The Misanthrope*, not as near-tragic or as satirized, but as purely comic is to bring his whole play into proper focus, to recognize that excess is a continuing part of the human situation along with pretension, and vanity, and ambition, and right reason. The typical comic action ends in a compromise, and the typical experience of comedy in theater is the understanding on the part of the spectator that whatever is typical will probably continue to be, and in the perspective of the comic view cannot only be endured, but enjoyed.

Characters

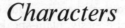

ALCESTE
PHILINTE
ORONTE
ACASTE
CLITANDRE
gentlemen of the Court

CÉLIMÈNE
ÉLIANTE, CÉLIMÈNE'S *cousin*
ARSINOÉ
ladies of the Court

BASQUE
CÉLIMÈNE'S *footman*

AN OFFICER
of the Court of Honor

DU BOIS
ALCESTE'S *manservant*

The scene throughout is a salon in the Paris house of CÉLIMÈNE.

THE MISANTHROPE

Molière

Translated by Morris Bishop

ACT ONE

[*Enter* ALCESTE *rapidly, followed by* PHILINTE.]

PHILINTE. What is the matter with you?

ALCESTE.   Let me alone!

PHILINTE. But wait! Tell me what crazy idea possessed you—

ALCESTE. Let me alone, I say! Go hide your face!

PHILINTE. But you can listen, at least, and not get angry?

ALCESTE. I want to be angry! I don't want to listen!

PHILINTE. I'm baffled by your sudden sulky fits.
Good friends as we are, nevertheless I feel—

ALCESTE. Your friend, am I? Don't be so sure of that!
Certainly I've declared it, up to now;   10
But your behavior has enlightened me.
I tell you frankly, I'm your friend no longer.
I want no place in a corrupted heart.

PHILANTE. And so, Alceste, you judge me very guilty?

ALCESTE. Why, you should go and die out of pure shame!
There can be no excuse for such an action!
A man of honor should be scandalized!
I watch you load a man with compliments,
With protests of the tenderest affection;
You put your arm around him, uttering vows   20
Of aid and comfort and profound esteem;
And when I ask you afterwards who he is,
You're hardly able to recall his name—
You tell me he's a man of no importance.

        Good God! I call it infamous, outrageous,
        To stoop to the betrayal of one's self;
        And if by some misfortune I had done so,
        I think remorse would make me hang myself.
PHILINTE. I hope that hanging's not imperative;
        And I will ask you for your kind indulgence
        To let me plead an appeal from your decision.
        Please don't insist that I go hang myself.
ALCESTE. I don't think the occasion calls for humor.
PHILINTE. But seriously, what should a person do?   10
ALCESTE. A man should be sincere; and in all honor
        He shouldn't say a word his heart disclaims.
PHILINTE. When a man greets you warmly, joyfully,
        You naturally respond in the same way.
        You meet his cordiality with your own,
        And match his offers and return his vows.
ALCESTE. No, I can't stand that mean, unworthy fashion
        Which you society people now affect.
        There's nothing I detest like the contortions
        Of all these great dispensers of lip service,   20
        Spreading their arms for insincere embraces,
        Overflowing with useless courtesies,
        Trying to win a war of compliments,
        Treating alike the gentleman and the fool.
        What does it mean if a man pats and pets you,
        Swears to his friendship, constancy, regard,
        Extols your shining merits to the skies,
        Then does the same to the next nobody?
        A man who has some self-respect despises
        The expression of such prostituted homage.   30
        One's vanity is easily satisfied
        By having a share in universal honors.
        But true esteem is based on preference;
        Esteeming everyone, you esteem nothing.
        Since you accept the vices of our time,
        Morbleu, Philinte, you're not the man for me!
        And I reject a love so comprehensive
        That it can see no difference in merit.
        I want a special love; to put it frankly,
        The friend of the human race is not my friend.   40
PHILINTE. Well, in society you have to express
        The usual formulas of polite behavior.
ALCESTE. But I say no! I say you should denounce
        This shameful game of imitation friendship!
        A man should be a man, and dare to show

The substance of his spirit in his words.
A man's true self should speak, and never mask
His genuine feelings in vain compliments.
PHILINTE. Still, there are many times when utter frankness
    Would be ridiculous and out of place.
    Sometimes, with all respect to your high honor,
    It's a good thing to hide what's in one's heart.
    Would it be suitable to tell to people
    Everything that you really think about them?
    Dealing with someone whom you much dislike   10
    Or really hate, ought you to tell him so?
ALCESTE. Yes.
PHILINTE.   What! And so you'd tell old Émilie
    It's time to lay aside her claims to beauty,
    Say her enameled face is really an outrage?
ALCESTE. Surely.
PHILINTE.   Tell Dorilas that he's a bore,
    That he has deafened every ear at court
    With his nobility and gallant deeds?
ALCESTE. Assuredly.   20
PHILINTE.   You're joking!
ALCESTE.   Not at all.
I'm going to tell the truth, and spare no man.
I've seen enough. The life of court and town
Presents a picture which revolts my soul.
I'm filled with loathing, I am nauseated
To see how men behave with one another.
All I see everywhere is flattery,
Injustice, treason, selfishness, deceit.
It makes me furious; I cannot stand it;   30
I will defy the entire human race.
PHILINTE. Your spleen is philosophic, but excessive.
    In fact, your evil humor makes me laugh.
    We two, with the same background, make me think
    Of the brothers in Molière's *The School for Husbands*,
    Wherein—
ALCESTE.   Oh, that comparison's too silly.
PHILINTE. Now seriously, give up these violent fits.
    The world won't change for anything you do.
    And since you think that frankness is so charming,   40
    I will be frank, and say that your obsession
    Amuses people, everywhere you go;
    And your high fury against current customs
    Makes you ridiculous in the eyes of many.
ALCESTE. Splendid, *morbleu!* Splendid! That's what I want!

An excellent sign! I am delighted at it!
Men have become so odious to me
I'd hate to have them think me sensible!
PHILINTE. You certainly have it in for human nature.
ALCESTE. Yes, I have learned to hate it thoroughly.
PHILINTE. And all poor mortal men, without exception,
Will be the objects of your disapproval?
I see a number, as I look about me—
ALCESTE. My hate is general; I detest all men;
Some because they are wicked and do evil,   10
Others because they tolerate the wicked,
Refusing them the active, vigorous scorn
Which vice should stimulate in virtuous minds.
Why, only see their toleration toward
The arrant rogue who's gone to law with me!
Behind his mask the scoundrel's visible.
Here everybody knows his character;
And his protesting eyes, his honeyed tongue,
Impose on no one but a casual stranger.
And that contemptible boor notoriously   20
Has made his way in the world by dirty means,
So that his present splendid situation
Makes merit grumble and makes virtue blush.
Whatever eminence he may have gained,
There's no one to respect his reputation.
Call him an infamous swindler, filthy sneak,
You hear no contradiction; all agree.
And yet his fawning face is widely welcomed,
He crawls in everywhere, he is accepted;
And if intrigue can gain some precedence,   30
You see him win, over the worthiest man.
Damnation! How it wounds me to the heart
To see how tactful people are with vice!
And sometimes I am seized by a wild impulse
To flee from human beings to some desert.
PHILINTE. Don't take so seriously our social habits,
And be more merciful to human nature.
Don't treat it with such rigorous principle,
And look a little kindly on its errors.
Virtue should be indulgent, in our world;   40
A man who is overwise may be at fault.
The soundest judgment flees extremities,
Urging that we be sober in our wisdom.
The rigid virtue of the ancient sages
Is out of key with present usages;

It asks too much perfection of mankind.
A man should bend to the prevailing mood;
And it's assuredly a signal folly
To try to reform and cure society.
Like you, I notice a hundred things a day
Which might be better if they were different;
But when these matters do present themselves,
I don't fly into a fury, as you do.
I just take men serenely as they are,
And train myself to suffer what they do.   10
I think that both at court and in the city
My calm is philosophic as your spleen.

ALCESTE. But, sir, this calm, which reasons so astutely,
Cannot this calm be stirred by anything?
And if it chances that a friend betrays you,
And baits a trap to get your property,
Or if he spreads slanderous tales about,
You'll see all that without becoming angry?

PHILINTE. Why, yes; I see these faults which you complain of
As vices which are part of human nature.   20
In short, my spirit is no more offended
To observe a selfish, unjust, rascally man
Than to see vultures upon their prey,
Or mischievous monkeys, or ferocious wolves.

ALCESTE. And I should see myself betrayed and robbed,
And I should not—*Morbleu!* I shan't reply.
Your argument is far too idiotic.

PHILINTE. In fact, you would do well to hold your peace.
Don't rage so much against your adversary,
And pay some more attention to your case.   30

ALCESTE. I won't pay any at all, and that is that.

PHILINTE. But who will make solicitation for you?

ALCESTE. Who? Reason, my just right, and equity.

PHILINTE. You won't have anyone call upon the judge?

ALCESTE. By no means. Is my case unjust or doubtful?

PHILINTE. Certainly not. But schemers can make trouble,
And—

ALCESTE.   No, I've resolved I will not take a step.
I'm right or I'm wrong.

PHILINTE.   I wouldn't trust to that.   40

ALCESTE. I will not move an inch.

PHILINTE.   Your enemy's strong;
He has his gang—

ALCESTE.   It makes no difference.

PHILINTE. You'll suffer for it.

ALCESTE.   I want to see what happens.
PHILINTE. But—
ALCESTE.   Then to lose the case will be my pleasure.
PHILINTE. However—
ALCESTE.   In this lawsuit I will learn
    If men will have enough effrontery,
    If they'll be wicked and rascally enough
    To do injustice in the sight of the world.
PHILINTE. What a man!
ALCESTE.   Yes, no matter what it costs,   10
    I'd like to lose the case, for the beauty of it.
PHILINTE. People would really laugh at you, Alceste,
    If they should hear you talking in this way.
ALCESTE. Then let them laugh.
PHILINTE.   But these high principles
    Which you expect to be exactly followed,
    And this uprightness of your character,
    Can they be matched in the lady whom you love?
    Frankly, I am surprised that you, who seem
    To be the enemy of the human race,   20
    Have chosen, from odious humanity,
    A representative who charms your eyes.
    And what astonishes me even more
    Is that you've picked on this particular person.
    Éliante the sincere has a liking for you,
    The prim Arsinoé looks kindly on you,
    And yet you seem unconscious of their fondness,
    While Célimène holds you in servitude—
    She whose coquettish humor and sharp tongue
    Are so consistent with the current fashion.   30
    And since you hate this fashion so intensely,
    How can you bear the lady's pleasure in it?
    Do the faults vanish in so sweet a creature?
    Do you excuse the faults? Or don't you see them?
ALCESTE. The love I feel for the lady, widowed so young,
    Can hardly blind me to her obvious faults.
    I am the first to see them and condemn them,
    Despite the affection she inspires in me.
    Nevertheless, whatever I may do,
    I grant my weakness, recognize her power.   40
    And though I see her faults and blame them in her,
    It is too much for me, she makes me love her.
    Her charm subdues me; but certainly my love
    Will cure her of these fashionable vices.
PHILINTE. If you do that, you will be doing something.

And so you're sure she loves you?
ALCESTE.   Yes, *parbleu!*
   I shouldn't love her if I didn't think so.
PHILINTE. But if her preference is evident,
   Why are you so disturbed about your rivals?
ALCESTE. A total love demands a total love;
   And I came here with only this in mind:
   To tell her what I feel and what I ask.
PHILINTE. If I were free to follow my impulses,
   Her cousin Éliante would be my choice.   10
   She has an upright spirit, she esteems you;
   She would be much more suitable for you.
ALCESTE. It's true, my reason often tells me so;
   But reason's not the governor of love.
PHILINTE. I don't feel easy for you; and your hopes
   Might well . . .
   [*Enter* ORONTE. *During the following speech* ALCESTE,
   dreaming, seems unaware that he is addressed.]
ORONTE.   I learned downstairs that Célimène
   And her cousin Éliante have gone out shopping;
   But when I was informed that you were here,
   I came right up to tell you I've conceived   20
   Almost incredible regard for you.
   And my regard has stimulated me
   To a passionate desire to be your friend.
   I recognize true merit, I applaud it.
   I long for brotherhood with its possessor.
   I think a true friend, of my noble rank,
   Is not to be too casually rejected.
   . . . It is to you, sir, that my words are addressed.
ALCESTE. To me, sir?
ORONTE.   Yes. I hope you aren't offended.   30
ALCESTE. Oh, no, indeed; but I am much surprised.
   I didn't expect the honor that you do me.
ORONTE. You shouldn't be surprised by my regard;
   You might well claim it from the universe.
ALCESTE. Monsieur—
ORONTE.   The country has no parallel
   For the lofty virtues I discern in you.
ALCESTE. Monsieur—
ORONTE.   I hold that you're superior
   To the most eminent of all our nation.   40
ALCESTE. Monsieur—
ORONTE.   May heaven blast me if I lie!
   In evidence of my sincerity,

Permit me to embrace you lovingly,
Asking to be admitted to your friendship.
Your hand, sir, if you please. You'll promise me
To be my friend?

ALCESTE.   Monsieur—
ORONTE.   What! You resist?
ALCESTE. Monsieur, it's too much honor that you do me.
But friendship asks a little mystery;
And we profane its name, assuredly,
By making it too easy to attain.   10
This union should be circumspectly formed,
And first, we ought to know each other better.
We might turn out to have such characters
That we would both be sorry for our bargain.

ORONTE. *Parbleu!* You speak like the wise man that you are,
And I esteem you all the more for it!
Let us then trust to time to do its work,
And meanwhile, let me offer my devotion.
If you should need some influence at court,
I'm on an excellent footing with the King.   20
He listens to my counsel; no one, in fact,
Could be more decent than His Majesty.
In short, consider me quite at your service.
And as I prize your judgment and your taste,
I'll make my first appeal to your good will
By showing you a sonnet I have written,
And asking whether I should make it public.

ALCESTE. Sir, I am ill equipped to be a judge,
So please excuse me.

ORONTE.   Why?   30
ALCESTE.   I have the fault
Of being far too frank in such a case.

ORONTE. That's what I want! And I should be offended
If, when I ask for your sincere opinion,
You should betray me, holding something back.

ALCESTE. Well, I am willing, sir, since you insist.

ORONTE. [*At each pause, he looks at* ALCESTE.]
"Sonnet." It is a sonnet. "Hope—" A lady
Had flattered my devotion, offering hope.
"Hope—" It is not your pompous, high-flown verse,
But rather gentle, tender, languorous.   40

ALCESTE. We'll soon see.

ORONTE.   "Hope—" I don't know if the style
Will seem to you sufficiently clear and smooth,
If you'll be satisfied with the choice of words.

ALCESTE. We'll see, monsieur.
ORONTE.   Anyway, you must know
    I dashed it off in a quarter of an hour.
ALCESTE. The time one takes doesn't affect the product.
ORONTE. Hope, it is true, relieves us,
    By hope our woe's disguised;
    But, Phyllis, hope deceives us
    If never realized!
PHILINTE. I am already charmed by the dainty verse.
ALCESTE [to PHILINTE]. You have the cheek to say that that is good?   10
ORONTE. And hope you offered freely
    In pity for my moan;
    Ah, you were heartless, really,
    To offer hope alone!
PHILINTE. An elegant and happy choice of words!
ALCESTE [to PHILINTE]. *Morbleu*, bootlicker, you can praise this
        nonsense?
ORONTE. If I must wait forever,
    While torment quits me never,
    To Death I shall repair!   20
    Restrain me not! For clearly
    Perpetual hope is merely
    Perpetual despair!
PHILINTE. Why, what a sweet, seductive dying fall!
ALCESTE [to PHILINTE]. The devil take the fall, you poisoner!
    I wish you'd take one which would break your skull!
PHILINTE. I've never heard such deftly rendered lines.
ALCESTE. *Morbleu!*
ORONTE.   You flatter me! Perhaps you think—
PHILINTE. No, I'm not flattering.   30
ALCESTE [to PHILINTE].   What *are* you doing?
ORONTE [to ALCESTE]. But, sir, you know what our agreement is,
    So tell me, please, in all sincerity.
ALCESTE. Sir, this affair is always delicate;
    We always like to hear our wit commended.
    But once a friend of mine, I won't say who,
    Showed me some poetry he'd just composed.
    I said a gentleman should never yield
    Too readily to the itch of authorship;
    He ought to hold in check his urgent wish   40
    To publicly display his private pleasures.
    I said our eagerness to show our works
    Leads us to play an inadvisable role.
ORONTE. And are you trying to tell me by these words
    That I am wrong to wish—

ALCESTE.   I don't say that.
    I told my friend to avoid all tepid writing,
    Which is enough to bring a man discredit,
    For though we have good qualities aplenty,
    We're commonly judged according to our faults.
ORONTE. You have some criticism of my sonnet?
ALCESTE. I don't say that. But, to discourage him,
    I hinted that this mania for writing
    Has injured many well-considered men.
ORONTE. Do I write badly? I resemble them?   10
ALCESTE. I don't say that. But anyway, I asked him:
    "What is your pressing need to rhyme? And why
    For God's sake must you get yourself in print?
    The only excuse for a bad book's publication
    Is that some needy hack has written it.
    Take my advice and fight against temptation,
    And hide your occupations from the public,
    And don't let folk persuade you to exchange
    Your reputation as a man of sense
    For that, conferred by a mercenary printer,   20
    Of a ridiculous and wretched author."
    That's what I tried to make him comprehend.
ORONTE. Oh, very good. I think I understand you.
    But may I not discover how my sonnet—
ALCESTE. Frankly, it's only fit to be pigeonholed.
    You've taken bad examples as your models,
    And your expressions are not natural.
    What do you mean—"By hope our woe's disguised"?
    And did you moan for pity audibly?
    And is your torment driving you to death?   30
    Was Phyllis really heartless, offering hope?
    Do you believe perpetual hope is merely
    Perpetual despair? Is that a fact?
    This sickly imagery that's now the rage
    Is false to human nature and to truth;
    It's only word play, it's pure affectation,
    And that is not the way that Nature talks.
    The bad taste of our time is terrifying;
    That of our rude forefathers was much better.
    I think much less of what is now admired   40
    Than of an old song which I'll sing to you:
        If the King should offer me
           Paris, his great city,
        If he said the price would be
           That I'd leave my pretty,

          I would tell the King Henri:
          Keep your Paris, leave me be,
          I prefer my pretty sweet,
             I prefer my pretty.
   The rhyme is obvious and the style is old,
   But don't you see that that's a better poem
   Than all these trumpery things that flout good sense,
   For there emotion's talking her true language.
          If the King should offer me
             Paris, his great city,   10
          If he said the price would be
             That I'd leave my pretty,
          I would tell the King Henri:
          Keep your Paris, leave me be,
          I prefer my pretty sweet,
             I prefer my pretty.
   That's what a man in love might really say.
   [*To* PHILINTE.]
   Yes, you may laugh; despite your intellectuals,
   I prize that more than all the affectation
   Of the gimcrack poetry of the current mode.   20
ORONTE. And I maintain my poem's excellent.
ALCESTE. You have your reasons to esteem it so;
       But you'll permit me to have other reasons
       Which will dispense me from accepting yours.
ORONTE. Since others praise it, that's enough for me.
ALCESTE. They have the art of feigning; I have not.
ORONTE. You think then all the wit in the world is yours?
ALCESTE. I would need more, in order to praise your poem.
ORONTE. I can do very well without your approval.
ALCESTE. I fear that you will have to do without it.   30
ORONTE. I should just like to see you write a poem
       On the same subject and in your own style.
ALCESTE. I could write one, unhappily, just as bad,
       But I'd be certain not to show it around.
ORONTE. This is high talk! You're very sure of yourself—
ALCESTE. If you want incense, go find someone else.
ORONTE. My little man, don't take this lofty tone!
ALCESTE. Why, my big man, I take the tone I like.
PHILINTE [*interposing*]. Gentlemen, calm yourselves! Enough of this!
ORONTE. All my profound regrets. I take my leave.   40
       I am, monsieur, your very humble servant.
ALCESTE. And I, sir, most obsequiously yours.
       [*Exit* ORONTE.]
PHILINTE. Well, you can see; by being too sincere

      You've got a nasty business on your hands.
      Now clearly Oronte, in order to be flattered—
ALCESTE. Don't talk to me!
PHILINTE.   But look—
ALCESTE.   And leave me alone.
PHILINTE. Why, really—
ALCESTE.   On your way!
PHILINTE.   If I—
ALCESTE.   No talk!
PHILINTE. What?   10
ALCESTE.   I won't listen.
PHILINTE.   But—
ALCESTE.   Enough!
PHILINTE.   Now wait—
ALCESTE. This is too much, *parbleu!* Don't follow me!
PHILINTE. Say what you please, I shall stay right beside you.
      [*Exeunt.*]

ACT TWO

      [*Enter* ALCESTE, *giving his hand to* CÉLIMÈNE.]
ALCESTE. Madame, you wish me to speak all my thought?
      I am offended by the way you act,
      And your behavior wounds me to the heart.
      I fear that we may come to an outright breach.   20
      If I spoke otherwise I should deceive you;
      Sooner or later we shall have to quarrel.
      Though I should promise you the contrary
      A thousand times, I could not keep my word.
CÉLIMÈNE. And so it was to scold me, evidently,
      That you entreated so to bring me home?
ALCESTE. I am not scolding; but your attitude
      Is far too cordial to the casual stranger.
      You have too many suitors always about you,
      And that's a thing I find it hard to stomach.   30
CÉLIMÈNE. Is it my fault if people choose to court me?
      How can I help it if I seem attractive?
      When people take some pains to visit me,
      You want me to seize a stick and drive them out?
ALCESTE. No, madame, no; it's not a stick you need,
      Rather a heart less welcoming to their vows.
      I know that you are always beautiful;
      Your charm attracts men, then your manner holds them.
      Your gracious disposition toward your captives

Completes the work your loveliness began.
You kindle in them overconfidence,
Which makes them persevere in their attentions.
A somewhat less promiscuous affability
Would soon drive off this multitude of suitors.
Tell me at least, madame, by what enchantment
Clitandre is so fortunate as to please you?
Upon what fund of merit and of virtue
Do you bestow the honor of your regard?
Is it his lengthy little fingernail   10
That has established him in your esteem?
Have you surrendered, with society,
To the excellence of his bright yellow wig?
Is it his great knee ruffles which have won you?
Or the profusion of his dangling ribbons?
Did his wide German breeches cast a spell,
When he professed himself to be your slave?
Perhaps it is his high falsetto snigger
Which found the way to captivate your heart?
CÉLIMÈNE. You take offense at him too readily.   20
You must know, surely, why I humor him—
Because he's promised to engage his friends
To help me in the lawsuit on my hands.
ALCESTE. Then lose your case, madame, with fortitude,
Rather than humor my offensive rival.
CÉLIMÈNE. You're getting jealous of the entire world!
ALCESTE. Because you give the entire world your welcome.
CÉLIMÈNE. But this should reassure your sensitive soul:
That I act pleasantly to all alike.
You would have much more cause to be offended   30
If I distinguished one particular man.
ALCESTE.   But I, whom you accuse of jealousy,
What do I have, madame, that they have not?
CÉLIMÈNE. The happiness of knowing that I love you.
ALCESTE. And what grounds do you give me to believe it?
CÉLIMÈNE. I think that since I venture to admit it,
My statement should be quite enough for you.
ALCESTE. And what assures me that you are not making
A similar statement to the other men?
CÉLIMÈNE. Now that's a pretty compliment from a lover!   40
What a sweet character you give to me!
I will relieve you, since you're so distressed,
And take back everything I've just been saying.
No one can now deceive you but yourself,
And so be happy.

ALCESTE.   God! Why must I love you!
         Why, if my heart is mine again, I'll bless
         Heaven for granting me its kindly favor!
         I won't disguise the fact, I do my best
         To kill the infatuation of my heart;
         But all my utmost efforts are in vain.
         It must be for my sins I love you so.
CÉLIMÈNE. Your love—it is remarkable, at least.
ALCESTE. Why, yes, it is indeed. It's like no other.
         It is beyond conception; and I grant   10
         No one has ever loved, madame, as I do.
CÉLIMÈNE. In fact, the manner has its novelty.
         You love a lady only to abuse her,
         Stating your passion with a string of insults.
         Such an ill-tempered love is something new.
ALCESTE. But it is in your power to change its humor,
         So let us have no more disputes, I beg you.
         Let us speak frankly, find a way to check—
         [*Enter* BASQUE.]
BASQUE. Monsieur Acaste is here.
CÉLIMÈNE. Well, send him up.   20
         [*Exit* BASQUE.]
ALCESTE. What! I can never speak to you alone?
         I always find you ready to welcome guests?
         You never can make up your mind to say
         To visitors that you cannot receive them?
CÉLIMÈNE. So I should have a falling-out with him?
ALCESTE. But your civilities I find excessive.
CÉLIMÈNE. He is a man who never would forgive me
         If he should learn I did not welcome him.
ALCESTE. And why should that disturb you in the least?
CÉLIMÈNE. Why, the good will of men like him is useful.   30
         They have acquired at court, I don't know how,
         The privilege of being listened to.
         They have a share in every conversation.
         They may not help you, but they *can* do harm.
         No matter what protection one may have,
         One shouldn't quarrel with these windy ranters.
ALCESTE. And so, whatever one may say or argue,
         You justify receiving everybody,
         And all your actions rest upon precaution—
         [*Enter* BASQUE.]
BASQUE. Monsieur Clitandre's here, madame.   40
ALCESTE.   Exactly.
         [*Exit* BASQUE. ALCESTE *makes a move to leave.*]

CÉLIMÈNE. Where are you going?
ALCESTE.   Away.
CÉLIMÈNE.   No, wait!
ALCESTE.   And why?
CÉLIMÈNE. Please wait!
ALCESTE.   I can't.
CÉLIMÈNE.   I want you to.
ALCESTE.   No use.
      These conversations merely bore me stiff,
      And it's too much to try to make me bear them.   10
CÉLIMÈNE. I want you to.
ALCESTE.   No, it's impossible.
CÉLIMÈNE. All right, then; go away. I won't prevent you.
      [ALCESTE *retires. Enter* BASQUE, ÉLIANTE, PHILINTE.]
ÉLIANTE. The marquises were coming up with us.
      Were they announced?
CÉLIMÈNE.   Yes. Basque, some chairs!
      [BASQUE *arranges chairs and exits;* ALCESTE *comes forward.*]
      [*To* ALCESTE.]
      Still here?
ALCESTE.   Quite so. I want you to make clear
      Whether your preference is for them or me.
CÉLIMÈNE. Be quiet!   20
ALCESTE.   You will explain yourself today.
CÉLIMÈNE. You're crazy!
ALCESTE.   No. You will declare yourself.
CÉLIMÈNE. Ah!
ALCESTE.   You'll make up your mind.
CÉLIMÈNE.   I think you're joking.
ALCESTE. No, you will choose. I've borne this long enough.
      [*Enter* CLITANDRE *and* ACASTE. *Exaggerated salutations.*
      All take seats.]
CLITANDRE. Madame, I've just come from the King's levee—
      And how ridiculous Cléonte appeared!
      Has he no charitable friend who might   30
      Give him some good advice about his manners?
CÉLIMÈNE. It's true he plays the fool in society,
      And at first glimpse he strikes you as peculiar.
      But after you've not seen him for a while,
      You meet him again—he's even more peculiar.
ACASTE. *Parbleu!* And, speaking of peculiar people,
      I've just escaped from one of the prime examples:
      Damon the man of words. He kept me standing
      An hour in the sun, with a foot in my sedan chair.
CÉLIMÈNE. He's perfect in his way. He has learned the art   40

Of saying all and signifying nothing.
Since he achieves a total lack of meaning,
His words are properly a social noise.
ÉLIANTE [*to* PHILINTE]. A good beginning! And it promises
A nice annihilation of our neighbors.
CLITANDRE. And Timante too, madame, is a curious type.
CÉLIMÈNE. He's the embodiment of mystery.
He casts at you a frantic, furtive glance,
And he is always busy—about nothing.
How he contorts his face to tell you something,   10
And how he wearies you with his affectations!
He draws you out of a pleasant conversation
To tell you a secret—which you know already.
He makes a marvel of every commonplace,
And even "Good morning!" he whispers in your ear.
ACASTE. And how about Géralde?
CÉLIMÈNE.   The snob reporter!
His single subject is the high nobility,
He has no intimates without a title,
And only quotes a princess, prince, or duke.   20
He's mad about gentility; all his talk
Is horses, hounds, and hunting ceremonies.
He always uses first names for the great;
"Monsieur" is dropped from his vocabulary.
CLITANDRE. They say he's very friendly with Bélise.
CÉLIMÈNE. Well, she is dull enough, poor thing, to match him.
It is a torture to receive her call.
You struggle for a theme within her grasp,
And then her helplessness in finding words
Keeps conversation at the point of death.   30
In vain, to rouse her from her sodden silence,
You try to startle her with platitudes.
But even rain and sunshine, cold and heat,
Are subjects soon exhausted in her presence.
And still her appalling visit lasts and lasts,
Until it seems to approach infinity.
You look at the clock, you yawn a dozen times,
But she's immovable as a block of wood.
ACASTE. How do you like Adraste?
CÉLIMÈNE.   The man of pride,   40
Inflated with affection for himself!
His virtue's most dissatisfied with the court;
He rails against its actions every day.
Every appointment that the court announces
He takes as a personal insult to his merit.

CLITANDRE. And popular young Cléon, who receives
    All the best people, what do you think of him?
CÉLIMÈNE. His most outstanding merit is his cook,
    So people call upon his dinner table.
ÉLIANTE. It's true he serves very delicious food.
CÉLIMÈNE. But I could wish he did not serve himself.
    His foolish person is unappetizing,
    And spoils the savors of his splendid dinners.
PHILINTE. His uncle Damis is well spoken of.
    How do you like him?   10
CÉLIMÈNE.   He's a friend of mine.
PHILINTE. I find him a worthy man, intelligent.
CÉLIMÈNE. Yes, but he's too intelligent for me.
    He tries too hard; and when he holds the floor,
    You hear the grinding of his witticisms.
    Since he's become an intellectual,
    Nothing can please his taste, he's so refined.
    He sees the faults in all our literature,
    And thinks that clever men should never applaud,
    That criticism shows your scholarship,   20
    That only idiots admire and laugh,
    And that one proves superiority
    By disapproving all contemporaries.
    He even looks askance at conversation;
    He cannot stoop to deal with commonplaces.
    Crossing his arms, he looks with pity down
    From his intellectual summit on the babblers.
ACASTE. Damme if that is not his perfect portrait!
CLITANDRE. How marvelous your character sketches are!
ALCESTE. Now thrust and stab, my worthy courtly friends!   30
    No one is spared, everyone has his turn.
    And yet if one of them should show himself,
    We'd see you all hurry to welcome him,
    Hold out your hands and take him in your arms,
    Swearing you are his very humble servants.
CLITANDRE. Why attack *us*? If you don't like this talk,
    You should address your scoldings to Madame.
ALCESTE. No, no! To you, *morbleu!* Your fawning laughter
    Impels her to produce these cynical slurs!
    And you encourage her satiric humor   40
    By the cajolement of your flatteries.
    She would be less inclined to mock and sneer,
    If she observed that you did not applaud her.
    And so the flatterers are most to blame
    For the common vices of humanity.

PHILINTE. Why do you take such interest in the victims?
    You would condemn in them what she condemns.
CÉLIMÈNE. The gentleman is forced to contradict.
    You don't expect that he would condescend
    To common judgments, failing to display
    His native character of opposition?
    He never likes what other people like,
    And his opinion's always the contrary.
    He thinks he'd seem an ordinary man,
    If he should ever agree with anyone.   10
    He likes so much the honor of contradicting,
    He often starts an argument with himself.
    He battles against his own sincere convictions
    As soon as he hears another man express them.
ALCESTE. Madame, you have the laughters on your side,
    And you can satirize me as you please.
PHILINTE. Still, it's a fact that you are always ready
    To shout defiance to every utterance.
    The peevish humor you yourself confess
    Takes issue with both praise and criticism.   20
ALCESTE. *Morbleu!* The fact is, men are always wrong,
    And peevishness against them's always proper.
    I note in every circumstance they're either
    Untimely applauders or unblushing critics.
CÉLIMÈNE. But—
ALCESTE.   No, madame, I'll say it though it kills me.
    You have amusements which I can't endure;
    And one does wrong to encourage an inclination
    For the very faults which privately one condemns.
CLITANDRE. Well, I can testify I've always thought   30
    That Célimène possessed no fault at all.
ACASTE. And I can well discern her charms and graces;
    But faults? They are invisible to me.
ALCESTE. They're visible to me; I don't disguise them;
    And she knows well how I reproach her for them.
    The more you love, the less you ought to flatter;
    And true love is incapable of pardon.
    If I were she, I'd banish all admirers
    Submissive to my slightest sentiment,
    Fawning upon me with their cheap applause   40
    For even my most extreme extravagances.
CÉLIMÈNE. In short, according to your laws for lovers,
    You would forbid all pretty compliments;
    And the supreme ideal of perfect love
    Is to insult and vilify one's darling.

ÉLIANTE. Love doesn't fit with such high principles.
　　　　Lovers are always sure they've chosen well.
　　　　They can't see qualities to criticize,
　　　　For in the loved one all is lovable.
　　　　And so defects take on the air of virtues,
　　　　And love provides its own vocabulary.
　　　　The pale girl is as pure and white as jasmine,
　　　　The swarthy one's a smoldering brunette,
　　　　The thin young lady's willowy and svelte,
　　　　The fat girl has a fine majestic carriage,　　　　　　　10
　　　　The sloppy and untidy miss becomes
　　　　A wild and carefree harum-scarum beauty:
　　　　The giantess takes on a goddess air,
　　　　The dwarf is dainty and too cute for words,
　　　　The vain girl has a dignity serene,
　　　　The sly girl's smart, the dull girl's sweet and simple,
　　　　The chatterbox has an engaging humor,
　　　　The silent one has dark, mysterious depths.
　　　　And thus a truly smitten lover loves
　　　　Even the faults of his inamorata.　　　　　　　　　　20
ALCESTE. For my part, I maintain—
CÉLIMÈNE.　　　　　　　　　　　　Enough of this.
　　　　Come, let us take a walk in the gallery.
　　　　. . . Gentlemen, you're not going?
CLITANDRE *and* ACASTE:　　　　　　　　　No, madame.
ALCESTE [*to* CÉLIMÈNE]. You are obsessed with fear of their
　　　　　　departure.
　　　　. . . Leave when you like, messieurs! I give you warning
　　　　That I won't go till after you have left!
ACASTE. Unless Madame should find my call excessive,　　　30
　　　　I have no reason to leave for the rest of the day.
CLITANDRE. Provided I'm present at the King's retirement,
　　　　I've no engagements of significance.
CÉLIMÈNE [*to* ALCESTE]. You're joking, surely.
ALCESTE.　　　　　　　　　　　　Not by any means.
　　　　We'll see if I'm the one you ask to leave.
　　　　[*Enter* BASQUE.]
BASQUE [*to* ALCESTE]. Monsieur, a gentleman would like to see
　　　　　　you
　　　　About a matter which, he says, is urgent.
ALCESTE. Tell him there's no such thing as an urgent matter.　　40
BASQUE. He wears a uniform with a swallow-tail,
　　　　And gold all over!
CÉLIMÈNE.　　　　　　　Go and see what it is,
　　　　Or have him enter.

ALCESTE [*speaking into wings*]. What do you want with me?
         Come in, come in.
         [*Enter* OFFICER. *Exit* BASQUE.]
OFFICER.   Sir, I've a message for you.
ALCESTE. Speak up, sir; there's no need for secrecy.
OFFICER. The Court of Honor, of which I am the agent,
         Commands, sir, your immediate appearance.
ALCESTE. Who, me, monsieur?
OFFICER.   Yourself, sir.
ALCESTE.   And what for?
PHILINTE. It's that ridiculous business with Oronte.   10
CÉLIMÈNE. What's that?
PHILINTE.   Oronte and he have had a quarrel
         About some poetry he didn't approve.
         The court desires to pacify the affair.
ALCESTE. I'll never make a base capitulation.
PHILINTE. You must obey the order; make up your mind.
ALCESTE. What do they want as reconciliation?
         Will the decision of the court condemn me
         To find the poetry in question good?
         I won't unsay a single thing I've said.   20
         The poem's bad.
PHILINTE.   If you'll just take it easy—
ALCESTE. I won't retract. The poem's terrible.
PHILINTE. You'll have to act in a reasonable manner.
         Come on!
ALCESTE.   All right, I'll go; but nothing will force me
         To take my words back.
PHILINTE.   Come; we'll answer the summons.
ALCESTE. Unless a special order from the King
         Orders me to approve the poem in question,   30
         I will maintain forever it is bad,
         And that the man who wrote it should be hanged!
         [CLITANDRE *and* ACASTE *laugh*.]
         Zounds, gentlemen, I didn't realize
         I was so funny!
CÉLIMÈNE.   Hurry, make your appearance
          Before the court!
ALCESTE.   Madame, I'll do so; then
          I'll come back here to finish our discussion.
         [*Exeunt*.]

ACT THREE

[*Enter* CLITANDRE *and* ACASTE.]

CLITANDRE. My dear Marquis, you're looking very cheerful!
　　　　Nothing upsets your equanimity!
　　　　Is it your own imagination merely,
　　　　Or is there reason for your satisfaction?
ACASTE. *Parbleu!* If I review my situation,
　　　　I see no reason to afflict myself.
　　　　I'm young and well-to-do; my family
　　　　Is noble, there's no argument about it.
　　　　And I am qualified by birth to hold
　　　　Almost any appointment at the court.   10
　　　　And as for bravery, which the world esteems,
　　　　I think I've given satisfactory proofs:
　　　　For I took on a little affair of honor,
　　　　And carried it decently to its conclusion.
　　　　Surely I have sufficient wit and taste
　　　　To treat all subjects with authority,
　　　　And at first nights, to take a seat on the stage,
　　　　And prove to the public I'm a connoisseur,
　　　　And clap my hands to indicate excellence,
　　　　And mark the good lines with "Oho! Aha!"   20
　　　　I've a good figure, an engaging manner;
　　　　I'm quick and deft; my teeth are really fine.
　　　　And as for taste in clothes, I shouldn't boast,
　　　　But how can one dispute the evidence?
　　　　It's clear I'm well regarded everywhere;
　　　　The ladies like me, and the King does too.
　　　　And so, my dear Marquis, it seems to me
　　　　I have some reason for self-satisfaction.
CLITANDRE. But you can make many an easy conquest,
　　　　So why come here, to utter sighs in vain?   30
ACASTE. In vain? *Parbleu*, I'm not the kind of person
　　　　To endure the chilly blasts of a frozen beauty!
　　　　We'll let the common fellows, the out-of-fashion,
　　　　Display their constancy for a cruel belle,
　　　　Languish before her, obey her harsh commands,
　　　　And do the best they can with sighs and tears,
　　　　And try to obtain by long fidelity
　　　　What they can hardly gain by their own merits.
　　　　People like me, Marquis, are not the kind
　　　　To pay the costs of love on speculation.   40

The ladies may be very admirable,
But after all, we are worth something too;
And if they hold a heart like mine in thrall,
It isn't right that they should have it free.
And if you look at the matter fairly and squarely,
The advances should be made on equal terms.

CLITANDRE. Your standing here would seem to be excellent.

ACASTE. Indeed, Marquis, I have some grounds to think so.

CLITANDRE. I think, my friend, you are in total error.
    I think you're blindly flattering yourself.   10

ACASTE. That's true, I'm blindly flattering myself!

CLITANDRE. What makes you sure that you're so fortunate?

ACASTE. I'm flattering myself!

CLITANDRE.   What basis have you?

ACASTE. I'm blind!

CLITANDRE.   But have you any kind of proof?

ACASTE. Oh, I must be mistaken!

CLITANDRE.   Célimène,
    Has she made any admission of her feelings?

ACASTE. No, she is brutal to me!   20

CLITANDRE.   Won't answer you?

ACASTE. Nothing but snubs!

CLITANDRE.   Let's drop the comedy;
    Tell me what hope she may have given you.

ACASTE. I'm the unhappy one, and you are favored;
    She actually has a loathing for my person.
    One of these days I'll have to hang myself.

CLITANDRE. Marquis, to simplify our competition,
    Suppose we both agree about one thing.
    If one of us obtains clear indication   30
    Of preference in Célimène's affections,
    The other will yield the palm to the evident victor,
    And free him from an annoying rivalry.

ACASTE. *Parbleu!* I like the idea very well.
    I'll be extremely glad to make the deal.
    But hush!
        [*Enter* CÉLIMÈNE.]

CÉLIMÈNE.   Still here?

CLITANDRE.   It's love that holds us spellbound.

CÉLIMÈNE. I heard a carriage entering the court.
    You don't know who—   40

CLITANDRE.   Oh, no.
        [*Enter* BASQUE.]

BASQUE.   Madame, madame
    Arsinoé is here.

CÉLIMÈNE.   What does she want?
BASQUE. Madame Éliante is talking to her now.
        [*Exit* BASQUE.]
CÉLIMÈNE. I wonder what inspired her to come here.
ACASTE. She passes as the epitome of the prude.
        Her ardent piety—
CÉLIMÈNE.   It's all a sham.
        Her heart is still in the social world; she's trying
        Forever to catch a man, without success.
        She can see only with an envious eye
        The avowed admirers of her lady friends.   10
        Her poor attractions having lost their power,
        She angrily attacks the oblivious world.
        She tries to cover with a prudish veil
        The fact that never a suitor sighs for her.
        She treats as criminal all physical charm,
        To vindicate the absence of her own.
        And yet she'd find a lover very welcome;
        She even has a weakness for Alceste.
        She takes to heart his courtesies to me;
        She thinks that I am thieving them from her.   20
        Her jealous spite, which she can hardly hide,
        She's always manifesting against me.
        It is the silliest thing I've ever seen;
        She really is outrageously indecent.
        And—
        [*Enter* ARSINOÉ.]
            Oh, what a lucky chance has brought you here!
        Madame, to tell the truth, I've missed you sadly.
ARSINOÉ. I've come, from duty, to bring you information.
CÉLIMÈNE. Heavens, my dear, how happy I am to see you!
        [ACASTE *and* CLITANDRE *laugh, bow, and exit.*]
ARSINOÉ. They leave, in fact, at a convenient moment.   30
CÉLIMÈNE. Shall we sit down?
ARSINOÉ.   It isn't necessary,
        Madame. True friendship ought to show itself
        In matters that are really of importance.
        And as no matters can be more important
        Than those which touch one's standing in society,
        I'll prove my friendship by informing you
        Of something which affects your reputation.
        Yesterday, at a most distinguished house,
        The conversation chanced to turn on you.   40
        Your—shall I say?—conspicuous behavior
        Had the misfortune not to be approved.

The swarm of visitors whom you receive
And your coquettishness, as it was termed,
Aroused, I fear, excessive criticism,
Which was so harsh it caused me real distress.
You can imagine how I spoke to that;
In your defense I said all that I could,
And I insisted on your good intentions,
And vouched for your character's integrity.
And yet you know that some things in this life
Are hard to excuse, no matter how you wish to;   10
And so I found myself obliged to agree
Your way of life reflects a little on you.
It looks peculiar to the social world,
And stimulates some most regrettable stories.
In short, you might well alter your behavior
To give less cause for hostile criticism.
Not that I think there's anything really wrong—
Heaven preserve me from the very thought!—
But even the shadow of evil makes presumptions;
One cannot live sufficient to oneself.   20
Madame, I'm sure you're sensible enough
To take this good advice in the way it's meant,
And recognize that it is prompted only
By my concern for your best interests.
CÉLIMÈNE. Madame, I'm very deeply grateful to you.
I cannot take such information ill.
I can repay it only by telling you
Something which touches your own reputation.
And as you show your friendship by revealing
The tales in circulation about me,   30
I want to follow your excellent example
By warning you what people say of you.
I was just calling at a certain house
Where a most estimable group was gathered.
The conversation turning on the rules
For the good life, your name, madame, was mentioned.
Your prudery and your excessive zeal
Were not regarded as the best of models.
Your affectation of a serious manner,
Your everlasting talk of good behavior,   40
Your screams at any hint of the indecent
Contained within a perfectly innocent word,
The high regard you evidence for yourself,
The pitying air you manifest to others,
Your frequent and embittered criticism

Of things which seem entirely chaste and pure—
All this, madame, if I may be so frank,
Was, by the general consent, condemned.
They said: "Her sage, demure, and modest manner,
Makes a strange contrast with the way she acts.
While she is most punctilious in her prayers,
She beats her servants, and she doesn't pay them.
She goes to church to show her piety,
But why does she have to paint her face so much?
She covers up the nudities of pictures,   10
But has a liking for the realities."
I came to your defense against them all;
It was all ugly slander, I maintained;
But everybody took the contrary view,
And their conclusion was, you would do well
To bother less with other people's actions
And make a closer scrutiny of your own.
One ought to make a self-examination
Before one ventures to admonish others.
Only a blameless life can authorize   20
One who assumes the post of general censor;
And still, that task might better be confided
To those whom Heaven has chosen for the purpose.
I think you too are sensible enough
To take this good advice in the way it's meant,
And recognize that it is prompted only
By my concern for your best interests.
ARSINOÉ. To give advice, I know, is dangerous;
And yet I am surprised by your reply.
Your acrid tone, madame, makes evident   30
That my sincerity has wounded you.
CÉLIMÈNE. Why, not at all, madame! If we were wise,
We'd make a practice of such mutual aid;
And thus, by frankness, we would put an end
To our sad ignorance about ourselves.
It rests with you whether we shall continue
To put this excellent device to service,
And make a point of telling all we know,
You about me, I about you, madame.
ARSINOÉ. Oh, about you, I can hear nothing, surely;   40
I am the one who should be criticized.
CÉLIMÈNE. Why, everything deserves both praise and blame,
And everyone is right—for his age and type.
There is a season for the game of love,
Another for the game of prudishness,

Which we may choose to play deliberately,
When once the natural bloom of youth is gone.
To hedge against unlucky accidents,
Some day, perhaps, I'll follow your example.
The years bring everything. And yet, madame,
Twenty is not the age to play the prude.

ARSINOÉ. How proud you are of a very small advantage!
You are unduly smug about your age!
I am not older by so many years
That one need make such a to-do about it!   10
I don't know why you seem to be impelled,
Madame, to make this strange assault upon me.

CÉLIMÈNE. And as for me, madame, I don't know why
You should attack me everywhere in public.
Why do you blame me for your own distresses?
If gentlemen don't court you, can I help it?
If I have something which makes people love me,
And if they come to offer me addresses
Which you may long to see eliminated,
It's not my fault; there's nothing I can do.   20
The field is open; and I don't prevent you
From having charms sufficient to allure.

ARSINOÉ. And do you think that I'm at all concerned
By the great swarm of suitors you're so proud of?
And do you think I don't know what's required
To keep them persevering, nowadays?
And do you think you can convince the world
That it's your merit which attracts that throng?
And that their love for you is honorable,
And that it is your virtues they are wooing?   30
The world is not so easily taken in;
We're not so stupid. There are plenty of women
With every quality to arouse affection,
But who discourage amorous young men.
From that I think we fairly may conclude
That one can't fish for lovers without bait,
And that it's not our beautiful eyes they sigh for,
And that one has to pay for their devotion.
You needn't be puffed up with vanity
For conquests hardly worthy of remark.   40
Your charms are not so mighty that you need
To treat the world with superciliousness.
Why, if we really envied you your victims,
I'm sure that we could imitate your system:
Let ourselves go. And thus we'd demonstrate

That if one wishes lovers, one can have them.
CÉLIMÈNE. By all means have some lovers, then, madame.
You know the secret of allurement, so—
ARSINOÉ. This conversation has gone far enough.
We might say things we should be sorry for.
Indeed, I should have taken leave long since,
Had not my carriage been delayed, it seems.
CÉLIMÈNE. Why, you may stop as long as you desire,
Madame; don't be in any hurry at all.
[ALCESTE *appears at door*.]
So, without making needless ceremony,   10
I'm going to give you better company.
This gentleman, whom happy chance has brought,
Will be a better host to you than I.
Alceste, excuse me; I must write a letter
Which cannot be delayed another minute.
Stay with Madame; and she will be so kind
As to excuse my incivility.
[*Exit* CÉLIMÈNE.]
ARSINOÉ. You see, she wants me to converse with you
For a moment or two, until my carriage comes.
In point of fact, she couldn't offer me   20
An opportunity I'd find more welcome.
Really exceptional people must attract
The affectionate regard of everyone;
And your own quality is such, it moves me
To sympathize with all your purposes.
I wish the court would pay you more attention
And better appreciate your genuine merit.
You're badly treated, sir. It makes me angry
To see you have no adequate reward.
ALCESTE. Reward? What should I be rewarded for?   30
What service have I rendered to the state?
What are my brilliant deeds, to justify
Complaints about the court's ingratitude?
ARSINOÉ. The people who enjoy the royal favor
Have often rendered no particular service.
Ability must find some circumstance
To show itself; and your most evident merit
Should really—
ALCESTE.   Please, let's drop this talk of merit!
How can the court concern itself with that?   40
It certainly would be busy if it had to
Discover and reveal the merit of men!
ARSINOÉ. Exceptional merit must reveal itself,

And yours is much esteemed by many people.
Why, only yesterday, in two great houses,
I heard you praised by people of importance.

ALCESTE. Today, madame, one praises everybody.
The present age has no distinctions left.
With merit all are equally endowed,
So it's no honor to be the subject of praise.
Now everyone is smothered in compliments;
Even my footman's in the society news.

ARSINOÉ. I wish your qualities were made more public,   10
And that a court appointment might attract you.
If you would manifest some interest,
One might well pull the necessary strings.
I have some friends whom I can put to work;
They'll readily remove all difficulties.

ALCESTE. What would you have me do in such a post?
I'm out of humor with the entire system.
Madame, the character that I was born with
Makes me unfit for the court's etiquette.
I haven't got the necessary virtues   20
To play its games and to succeed in them.
My greatest talent is to be sincere;
I don't know how to win by double talk.
A man who can't dissemble what he thinks
Cannot last long in this society.
Away from court, you won't get much support,
You won't get any honorary titles,
You won't achieve so much; but you won't have
The consciousness you're acting like a fool.
You needn't bear its spurns and insolence,   30
You needn't praise fine gentlemen's poetry,
Burn incense under a great lady's nose,
And laugh at our little lordlings' witticisms.

ARSINOÉ. Please, let us drop this matter of the court.
I want to say I'm sorry about your courtship.
To be entirely frank, I could have wished
You'd found another object of affection.
Certainly you deserve much better treatment.
Your charmer is not worthy of your love.

ALCESTE. When you say that, madame, do you remember,   40
I wonder, that the lady is your friend?

ARSINOÉ. Yes; but my conscience tells me to protest
Against the indecent treatment you receive.
I suffer deeply, seeing your situation;
And I must tell you that your love's betrayed.

ALCESTE. Why, this is very kind of you, madame.
  A lover's much indebted for such news.
ARSINOÉ. Though she's my friend, I'm certain she is hardly
  Fit to possess an honorable heart.
  All her affection for you is a sham.
ALCESTE. That well may be; one cannot look in hearts.
  And yet you might have had the charity
  Not to put this suspicion in my own.
ARSINOÉ. Of course, if you don't want to know the facts,
  It's easy enough not to say anything.   10
ALCESTE. No matter what one says on such a theme,
  It's doubt which is the most distressing thing.
  I wish that people would inform me only
  Of things that they can definitely prove.
ARSINOÉ. Certainly, if you wish. You will receive
  Considerable light upon the subject.
  I want you to inspect the evidence.
  If you will just conduct me to my home,
  I will provide you with convincing proof
  Of the disloyalty of your fair lady.   20
  And if your heart can turn to other objects,
  I'm sure that it will find its consolation.
  [*Exeunt.*]

ACT FOUR

[*Enter* PHILINTE *and* ÉLIANTE.]
PHILINTE. You never saw a man so hard to manage,
  Or so much trouble in an arbitration!
  Everyone tried in vain to work on him;
  They couldn't make him alter his opinion.
  I think it was the most peculiar quarrel
  The Court of Honor ever had to settle.
  "No, sirs," he said, "I won't take back a word.
  I'll yield on everything except this point.   30
  Why does he feel insulted anyway?
  There's nothing shameful in not writing well.
  What difference does my opinion make?
  One can be virtuous and a wretched poet;
  That's not a matter to affect one's honor.
  I think him an accomplished gentleman,
  A man of rank, merit, and character,
  Whatever you like; but he's a dreadful author.
  I'll praise his lavish getup if you like,

His horsemanship, his fencing, or his dancing,
But for his poetry, you must excuse me.
If that's the very best a man can do,
He ought to give up writing verse, unless
He's forced to, under penalty of death."
And finally, the only compromise
That he could force his principles to make
Was to express this handsome qualification:
"Sir, I'm distressed to be so difficult;
Out of regard for you, most heartily   10
I wish I could have found your sonnet better."
And so the case concluded; and the two
Principals were commanded to embrace.
ÉLIANTE. He's very singular in all his actions;
But I admit I think most highly of him.
In that sincerity that he's so proud of
There's something rather noble and heroic.
That's not a common virtue nowadays;
I'd like to see some more of it around.
PHILINTE. Well, as for me, the thing that seems most strange   20
Is the infatuation of his heart.
Considering his cast of character,
I don't know how he came to fall in love,
And even more I cannot understand
How it's your cousin that he fell in love with.
ÉLIANTE. That seems to indicate that love is not
Always affinity of character.
Let people talk of hidden sympathies;
Here's an example on the opposite side.
PHILINTE. But, from the look of things, you think she loves him?   30
ÉLIANTE. That's not an easy matter to decide.
How can you settle if she really loves him?
Her heart is not quite sure of its own feelings.
A heart may love, denying that it loves,
Or think it loves, in ignorance of the truth.
PHILINTE. I think our friend, by fixing on your cousin,
Is building up more troubles than he knows.
And if he shared my feelings, the fact is
That he would look in a different direction,
And he'd have wit enough to take advantage   40
Of all your kindliness to him, madame.
ÉLIANTE. Well, I'll be frank about it; I believe
One ought to tell the truth about these matters.
I don't oppose his love for Célimène;
Indeed, I give it all encouragement.

If the affair were under my control,
I would unite him to the one he loves.
But if his love for her should run afoul
Of circumstances, as so well may happen,
If it falls out that she should wed another,
I should be ready to accept his suit.
I should not be offended by the fact
That he had been rejected by another.

PHILINTE. And for my part, madame, I have no quarrel
    With all the kindness which you show to him.   10
    And he can tell you, if he wishes to,
    How I have counseled him upon the matter.
    But if he were united with his loved one,
    And thus debarred from paying you his suit,
    I should attempt to capture for my own
    That blissful favor which you show to him;
    And if his heart can disregard it, I
    Shall be most happy if it falls to me.

ÉLIANTE. My dear Philinte, you're joking.

PHILINTE.   No, madame.   20
    I speak sincerely; and I long to have
    Freedom to make to you a formal offer,
    And thus fulfill my uttermost desires.

    [*Enter* ALCESTE.]

ALCESTE. Help me, madame, to get me vengeance for
    An insult which has robbed me of my strength!

ÉLIANTE. What is it that has so excited you?

ALCESTE. Why, it's a matter that it's death to think of!
    And the convulsion of all nature could
    Not overwhelm me like this circumstance.
    I'm done for. And my love—no, I can't speak!   30

ÉLIANTE. Alceste—do try to collect your wits a little.

ALCESTE. Heaven! How can such charm and grace be joined
    To the odious vices of the meanest souls!

ÉLIANTE. Once more, what is it—

ALCESTE.   Oh, it's all destroyed!
    I am betrayed, I am assassinated!
    For Célimène—is it believable?—
    She has deceived me, she is a faithless creature!

ÉLIANTE. Have you good reason for believing this?

PHILINTE. Perhaps you form a fanciful suspicion;   40
    Sometimes your jealousy imagines things.

ALCESTE. *Morbleu*, monsieur! Please mind your own affairs!
    I have the best proof of her treachery
    Here in my pocket, written by her own hand.

Yes, madame, yes! A letter to Oronte
Has shown me my misfortune and her shame!
Oronte! I thought that she avoided him.
I feared him less than any of my rivals.
PHILINTE. A letter often gives a false impression.
It may not be as guilty as it seems.
ALCESTE. Monsieur, again I ask you, leave me alone.
Busy yourself with matters that concern you.
ÉLIANTE. You should control this outburst of ill temper—
ALCESTE. Madame, I put that task into your hands.   10
It is to you my heart now has recourse
To free itself from unendurable torment.
Avenge me on your graceless, faithless cousin,
Who basely cheats my ardent constancy.
Avenge me for her despicable action!
ÉLIANTE. Avenge you? How do you mean?
ALCESTE.   Accept my heart,
Madame: accept it; take the ingrate's place,
And thus I'll have my vengeance on the creature.
I'll punish her by the sincere engagement,   20
The genuine love and the respectful care,
The earnest regard, and the assiduous service
Which I am ready to consecrate to you.
ÉLIANTE. Surely, I sympathize with all you suffer;
I do not scorn the heart you offer me.
And yet perhaps the evil's not so great.
You may renounce your eagerness for vengeance.
When it's a charming person who offends us,
We make a lot of plans we don't fulfill.
Whatever reasons we may have for rupture,   30
A guilty dear one soon becomes innocent,
And all our rancor promptly dissipates.
We know well what a lover's anger is.
ALCESTE. No, no, madame. The offense is a deadly one,
And definitely we've come to the final break.
Nothing can change the purpose in my mind;
Never again can I give her my respect.
But here she is. It drives me mad to see her.
I shall reproach her for her villainous deed,
I shall expose her utterly, and then   40
Bring you a heart freed from her domination.
[Enter CÉLIMÈNE. Exit ÉLIANTE and PHILINTE.]
God! Can I keep my righteous wrath in check?
CÉLIMÈNE. Dear me! You look as though you were upset!
What do you mean by your tremendous sighs?

What are you scowling at so frightfully?
ALCESTE. I mean that the worst sins of the human mind
Can't be compared with your disloyalty;
That fate and angry heaven and all the demons
Never produced your match in wickedness!
CÉLIMÈNE. These are some novel compliments indeed!
ALCESTE. Please don't be funny; this is no time to laugh.
Rather, you ought to blush; you've reason to.
I have sure testimony of your treason!
There were forebodings in my troubled mind;   10
My love with excellent reason took alarm.
And by my dark suspicions, which seemed shocking,
I sought the affliction which is now my lot.
In spite of all your care, your skill in feigning,
My star forewarned me what I had to fear.
But don't presume that I am going to suffer
This rude indignity without revenge!
I know one has no power over impulsions,
That love is free, rejecting all controls,
That not by main force can one take a heart,   20
That every soul elects its conqueror.
Thus I would have no reason to complain
If you had spoken openly to me,
Rejecting my advances from the first;
Then I would have only my fate to blame.
But to entice my love with false avowals
Is treachery, it's a perfidious act
Deserving the extremest punishment,
And I can give free rein to my resentment.
You are in danger, after such an outrage;   30
I am enraged, I can't restrain myself.
Since you have struck me with a mortal blow,
My senses are no longer ruled by reason.
I yield to the impulses of my anger;
I'm not responsible for what I do.
CÉLIMÈNE. Tell me, what is the reason for this frenzy?
Have you perhaps gone totally insane?
ALCESTE. Yes, I am crazy, since the day I took
The drug you offered me, to my misfortune.
I thought that there was some sincerity   40
Lodged in the beauty that enraptured me.
CÉLIMÈNE. What is this treachery that you complain of?
ALCESTE. Oh, double heart that well knows how to feign!
But I have means to put it to the test!
Just look at this, and recognize your hand!

This letter alone suffices to confound you;
There is no answer to this testimony.
CÉLIMÈNE. So that's the thing that has upset your wits!
ALCESTE. You do not blush to see these written words?
CÉLIMÈNE. Is there some reason why I ought to blush?
ALCESTE. So! You are brazen in duplicity!
Since there's no signature, you disavow it?
CÉLIMÈNE. Why disavow a letter I have written?
ALCESTE. And you can see it and not be confounded
To recognize the crime which it reveals?   10
CÉLIMÈNE. The fact is, you are really too absurd.
ALCESTE. What! You defy conclusive evidence
Which shows your inclination for Oronte?
Doesn't this outrage me and prove your shame?
CÉLIMÈNE. Oronte? You think the letter was for him?
ALCESTE. That's what the person who gave it to me says.
But never mind, suppose it's for another,
I have as good a reason to reproach you,
You're just as guilty and as false to me.
CÉLIMÈNE. But if the letter's written to a woman,   20
What's guilty in it? How does it offend you?
ALCESTE. Oh, that's a splendid shift, a fine excuse!
I grant you that I hadn't thought of that,
So now you think I'm perfectly convinced!
How do you dare employ such shabby tricks?
And do you think that people are so stupid?
I'm looking forward to the arguments
You'll use to bolster up a downright lie.
I want to see you fit to a woman friend
All of the phrases of this ardent letter.   30
Explain, to cover up your breach of faith,
What I'm about to read—
CÉLIMÈNE.   No, I don't want to.
You have no business to be so high and mighty,
And dare to talk to me as you've been doing.
ALCESTE. Now, don't get angry; but just undertake
To justify to me these phrases here.
CÉLIMÈNE. I shall do nothing of the sort. Whatever
You choose to think concerns me not at all.
ALCESTE. Now please, just show me, I'll be satisfied,   40
How you explain this letter as to a woman.
CÉLIMÈNE. It's for Oronte; I want to have you think so.
I welcome his attentions with delight,
I love his talk, I think he's wonderful,
And I'll agree with anything you please.

So choose your course of action, go ahead,
And stop your shouting and don't bother me.
ALCESTE. God! Is there greater cruelty than this?
Was ever a lover treated in this way?
And I complain, and I'm the one who's scolded!
My pain, and my suspicions, are encouraged;
She leaves me to my doubt, and glories in it!
And yet my heart is still too cowardly
To rise and break the chains which fetter it,
To arm itself with a high-hearted scorn   10
Against the ingrate whom it loves too much!
How well you know, my faithless one, the way
To use against myself my utter weakness!
And turn to your advantage the excess
Of fatal love which you yourself inspired!
Make your defense at least against my charge,
And stop pretending that you're guilty toward me.
Prove, if you can, this letter innocent;
My love will even struggle to assist you.
If you endeavor only to seem true,   20
I shall endeavor to believe you so.
CÉLIMÈNE. Why, you are crazy in your jealous fits;
You don't deserve to have a person love you.
I wonder what could force me to descend,
For your sake, to the meanness of pretending,
And why, if I should take another fancy,
I shouldn't tell it with all sincerity!
Doesn't the fact that I have given assurance
Of my affection answer your suspicions?
And is my word not of some weight against them?   30
In heeding them, aren't you insulting me?
And since a woman's heart must make an effort
When it resolves to make an avowal of love,
And since our honor is love's enemy,
And always is averse to such admissions,
The lover who sees this obstacle surmounted
Cannot with safety doubt his revelation.
Is he not guilty if he does not trust
What's only spoken after an inner conflict?
Oh, such suspicions well deserve my anger;   40
You are not worthy of my consideration.
I am a fool; I'm sorry I'm so simple
As still to preserve some charity for you.
I should transfer my favor to another,
And give you a proper reason for complaint.

ALCESTE. Faithless! How strange it is I love you still!
　　　　No doubt you cheat me with these easy words.
　　　　No matter; I must follow my destiny.
　　　　I have committed my spirit to your faith.
　　　　I must still watch to see what your heart's made of,
　　　　Whether it is so black it will betray me.
CÉLIMÈNE. You do not love me as a man should love.
ALCESTE. My love is too extreme for comparisons,
　　　　And in its eagerness to show itself, -
　　　　It even imagines fantasies to your hurt.   10
　　　　Yes, I could wish that no one found you charming,
　　　　That you were reduced to some most wretched state,
　　　　That heaven had given you nothing at your birth,
　　　　Not rank, gentility, or property,
　　　　So that the public offering of my heart
　　　　Might then repair the injustice of your lot,
　　　　That I might have the glory and the joy
　　　　Of making you owe everything to my love.
CÉLIMÈNE. That's a peculiar way to wish me well!
　　　　May heaven preserve me from the chance occurring!   20
　　　　... But here's your man Du Bois! How odd he looks!
　　　　[*Enter* DU BOIS, *dressed in traveling costume, with high boots.*]
ALCESTE. What does this outfit mean? This frightened look?
　　　　What's wrong?
DU BOIS.　　　　　Monsieur—
ALCESTE.　　　　　　　　　Well?
DU BOIS.　　　　　　　　　　　　Many mysteries!
ALCESTE. What is it?
DU BOIS.　　　　　We're in a nasty situation!
ALCESTE. What?
DU BOIS.　　　Shall I tell all?   30
ALCESTE.　　　　　　　　　　　Yes, and be quick about it.
DU BOIS. Isn't there someone here—
ALCESTE.　　　　　　　　　　Oh, hurry up!
　　　　Speak up!
DU BOIS.　　　　　Monsieur, we'll have to sound retreat!
ALCESTE. How's that?
DU BOIS.　　　　　We must decamp, give ground, dislodge.
ALCESTE. And why?
DU BOIS.　　　　　We must abandon our position.
ALCESTE. What for?   40
DU BOIS.　　　　　We'll take the leave denoted French.
ALCESTE. But tell me why you're giving this opinion.
DU BOIS. Because, sir, we must fall back and re-form.
ALCESTE. Oh I will break your head in certainly,

Unless you tell me what you mean, you rascal.

DU BOIS. A man most dark, in costume and in manner,
Came to our house and left on the kitchen table
A paper couched in very barbarous style,
Beyond the power of mortal man to fathom.
It has to do, assuredly, with your lawsuit;
But the devil himself could hardly understand it.

ALCESTE. Villain, what has this paper got to do
With the departure you've been talking of?

DU BOIS. I mean to say, sir, a bare hour afterwards,   10
A man who often pays his calls on you
Came to inquire for you most urgently.
And when he didn't find you, he ordered me,
Knowing that I'm your very faithful servant,
To give you a message—wait now, what's his name?

ALCESTE. What did he tell you? Never mind his name.

DU BOIS. Well, anyway, he's one of your good friends.
He said that you're in danger, you must flee,
And there's a chance that you may be arrested.

ALCESTE. Didn't he tell you anything specific?   20

DU BOIS. No, he just asked to have some paper and ink,
And wrote you a little note, which will reveal,
As I suppose, the clue to the mystery.

ALCESTE. Then give it to me!

CÉLIMÈNE.   What's at the bottom of this?

ALCESTE. I don't know yet; I hope to before long.
Why can't you hurry, you damnable idiot?

DU BOIS [after a long search in his pockets]. Good faith, monsieur, I left
it on your table.

ALCESTE. Why I don't hit you—   30

CÉLIMÈNE.   Alceste, don't get angry.
Hurry and find out what the trouble is.

ALCESTE. It seems that fate, in spite of my best efforts,
Has sworn to interrupt our conversation.
I won't be beaten; so, madame, permit me
To see you again before the day is over.
[Exeunt.]

ACT FIVE

[Enter ALCESTE and PHILINTE.]

ALCESTE. I tell you I have quite made up my mind.

PHILINTE. However hard the blow may be, it needn't—

ALCESTE. There's no use talking, no use arguing;

Nothing can turn me from my resolution.
There's too much wickedness in the world today;
I'm going to quit human society.
What! Honor, justice, decency, and the law
Are all arrayed against my adversary,
And everyone proclaims my cause is just,
And I'm at ease, in confidence of my rights—
And yet I see myself betrayed by the outcome!
Justice is on my side—I lose my case!
A scoundrel, whose scandalous record is well known,   10
Triumphs, by means of filthy perjuries!
Thus honesty must yield to treachery!
He wins his victory by slaying me!
His false and grinning face he puts in the scales
To outweigh justice, upset equity!
He gets his crimes upheld by a court injunction!
And as if he hadn't done me harm enough,
There's a revolting book in circulation,
Which ought to be prohibited by law,
A book which deserves a pitiless punishment—   20
And he has the face to say that I'm the author!
And then we see Oronte nodding his head
And trying to substantiate the fraud!
Oronte, who plays the gentleman at court!
His only grievance is my sincerity.
He forced himself upon me, against my will,
To ask my judgment on his poetry;
And just because I use him honestly,
Unwilling to betray him, or truth either,
He helps to charge me with an imagined crime!   30
Now he's become my greatest enemy,
And never can I hope to have his pardon,
Because I would not call his sonnet good!
So that, *morbleu*, is the character of men!
These are the deeds their vanity inspires!
This is the virtue, the fidelity,
The justice and the honor of mankind!
I've suffered disillusion long enough;
It's time to leave this den of thieves and cutthroats.
Since men make here a society of wolves,   40
I shall not spend the rest of my life among them.
PHILINTE. Your verdict seems to me a little hasty;
The evil's not so great as you assume.
The imputations of your adversary
Have not availed to compass your arrest.

His perjury may well be undermined;
Perhaps this time he's overreached himself.
ALCESTE. Oh, he doesn't mind publicity for his tricks!
Roguery is his regular stock in trade,
And this adventure, far from injuring him,
Tomorrow will put him in a better posture.
PHILINTE. Anyway, people clearly don't much credit
The story he's maliciously invented.
You needn't be alarmed in that regard.
As for the lawsuit, you may properly grumble,   10
But you have legal grounds for an appeal
Against the judgment—
ALCESTE.   No, I want to accept it.
Although the verdict does me injury,
I've no intention of getting it reversed.
It's a pure case of justice's miscarriage;
I want to leave it to posterity
To be a famous mark and testimony
To the scoundrelism of the present day.
It may well cost me twenty thousand francs,   20
But twenty thousand francs will give me the right
To curse the iniquity of human nature,
And cherish an unfailing hate for it.
PHILINTE. But after all—
ALCESTE.   But after all, don't bother.
There's nothing on this theme that you can tell me.
You wouldn't go so far as to excuse
The horrors of the present situation?
PHILINTE. No, I'll agree with everything you please.
The world is run by selfish interest,   30
And trickery and graft are in the saddle,
And man should be a different kind of creature.
But is his guiltiness sufficient reason
To drive us out of his society?
These human failings furnish us with means
Of exercising our philosophy,
And that's the best employment for our virtue.
If truth and rectitude were universal,
If every heart were frank and reasonable,
Most of the virtues would be meaningless,   40
Because they enable us to bear serenely
The injustice of others, when our cause is just.
And even as an honorable heart—
ALCESTE. I know that you're a very brilliant talker;
You always have most wonderful arguments.

But now you're wasting both your talk and time.
It would be prudent for me to retire.
I cannot properly control my tongue.
I dare not answer for my spoken words;
I'd have a dozen squabbles on my hands.
Let me, without more talk, see Célimène.
She must consent to what I have in mind.
I shall discover if she really loves me;
This is the moment which will prove the case.

PHILINTE. We'd better wait in Éliante's apartment.   10

ALCESTE. No, I am too disquieted in mind.
　　　　You go and see her; leave me here alone
　　　　In this dark corner with my gloomy heart.
　　　　[*He sits in a shadowed corner of the room.*]

PHILINTE. That's no companion for your solitude.
　　　　I'll beg of Éliante that she come down.
　　　　[*Exit* PHILINTE. *Enter* CÉLIMÈNE *and* ORONTE.]

ORONTE. Madame, the choice is yours: to bind me to you
　　　　In love's delicious bonds, if that's your will.
　　　　But I must have assurance of your spirit;
　　　　A lover cannot bear uncertainty.
　　　　If I have moved you by my fervent passion,   20
　　　　You should not hesitate to let me know it.
　　　　And here's the evidence I ask of you:
　　　　No longer to permit Alceste to court you,
　　　　To sacrifice him to my love, madame,
　　　　And forthwith to forbid his presence here.

CÉLIMÈNE. But what's the reason for your irritation?
　　　　I've heard you talk so often of his merits.

ORONTE. Madame, it's not the time for explanations.
　　　　The essential thing to know is, what are your feelings?
　　　　So please decide to keep one man or the other;   30
　　　　For on your resolution mine depends.

ALCESTE [*emerging from his retreat*]. The gentleman is right; you'll
　　　　　　have to choose.
　　　　For his request and my desire agree.
　　　　My love, like his, demands an explanation;
　　　　My love requires an evidence of yours.
　　　　Things cannot drag on longer in this manner.
　　　　The time has come for you to declare yourself.

ORONTE. I do not wish, sir, by my urgencies
　　　　To bring disturbance to your happiness.   40

ALCESTE. I do not wish, sir, whether jealous or not,
　　　　To make division of her heart with you.

ORONTE. If she prefers your courtship to my own—

ALCESTE. If she has even a slight regard for you—
ORONTE. I swear that I shall make no claim upon her.
ALCESTE. I swear that I shall never see her again.
ORONTE. Madame, you're free to speak without reserve.
ALCESTE. Madame, explain yourself without a qualm.
ORONTE. You only need to say who has your heart.
ALCESTE. You only need to choose between us two.
ORONTE. What! The decision seems to embarrass you?
ALCESTE. What! You are wavering and disconcerted?
CÉLIMÈNE. But this insistence is quite out of place,   10
  And both of you are most unreasonable!
  Of course I know what my own preference is;
  It's not my heart that's wavering, undecided.
  It isn't balancing between you two,
  And I could make my choice immediately.
  But really, I am tortured at the thought
  Of uttering such admissions to your face.
  Such words as these are bound to be unpleasant;
  They shouldn't be spoken in another's presence.
  I think we show our feelings clearly enough   20
  Without being forced to such crude revelations.
  There are more kindly ways to break the news
  To a lover that his addresses are unwelcome.
ORONTE. No, I am not afraid of a frank admission.
  For my part, I consent.
ALCESTE.   And I insist.
  And what I ask for is an open statement;
  I don't want any feelings to be spared.
  You're too concerned with holding everyone.
  So now, no more delay and uncertainty!   30
  You must explain yourself upon this matter,
  Or I shall take a refusal as a verdict;
  Your silence I shall understand to mean
  The confirmation of my worst suspicions.
ORONTE. I am obliged, sir, for your angry words.
  I put to her the same request that you do.
CÉLIMÈNE. Oh, how you bore me with this freak of yours!
  Can there be any sense in your demand?
  Didn't I tell the motive which restrains me?
  But here is Éliante; let her be judge.   40
  [Enter ÉLIANTE and PHILINTE.]
  Cousin, I'm being persecuted here
  By a pair of gentlemen with a fixed idea.
  They both insist, with an excessive heat,
  That I declare my preference between them,

That I forbid, by a public declaration,
One of the two to pay me courtesies.
Have people ever acted in this way?
ÉLIANTE. You needn't appeal to me upon the subject.
You might find my decision most unwelcome.
I am in favor of saying what one thinks.
ORONTE. Madame, you are defending yourself in vain.
ALCESTE. Your shifts and dodges get no countenance here.
ORONTE. You must declare yourself; stop paltering.
ALCESTE. If you persist in keeping silence, of course—   10
ORONTE. A single word's enough to settle things.
ALCESTE. Even without a word, I'll get my answer.
[*Enter* ACASTE, CLITANDRE, *and* ARSINOÉ.]
ACASTE [*to* CÉLIMÈNE]. Madame, we two have come, if you don't mind,
To get some light upon a little matter.
CLITANDRE. And gentlemen, your presence is convenient,
For you too are concerned in the affair.
ARSINOÉ. Madame, you'll be surprised to see me here,
But these two gentlemen are responsible.
They came to see me and they made a complaint
About a circumstance I couldn't believe.   20
For I esteem too much your character
To think you capable of such a misdeed.
I wouldn't credit the evidence they showed me;
My friendship disregards our little quarrel.
So I consented to accompany them,
To see you clear yourself of this calumny.
ACASTE. Let us be calm, madame, and let us see
How you will go about explaining this.
Here is a letter which you wrote Clitandre.
CLITANDRE. And here is a tender note you wrote Acaste.   30
ACASTE. Gentlemen, you must recognize this writing.
I do not doubt that she's been kind enough
To give you all examples of her hand.
But this is really worth being read aloud:
"You're a strange fellow, Clitandre, to complain of my cheerful-
ness and to reproach me because I'm never so happy as when I
am not with you. Nothing could be more unjust; and if you don't
come soon to ask my pardon for this offense, I won't forgive you
as long as I live. Our big gawky vicomte—" He really should be
here! "Our big gawky vicomte, whom you complain about, is a   40
man I could never like; and since the time I watched him, for a
good three quarters of an hour, spitting into a well to make rings,
I have never been able to hold a good opinion of him. As for the
little marquis—" If I may say so without vanity, that's me. "As

for the little marquis, who held my hand so long yesterday while
escorting me, I think he's about as insignificant as it is possible
to be; all his merit lies in his cloak and sword. As for the man
with the green ribbons—"

[*To* ALCESTE.] Now it's your turn, sir. "As for the man with the
green ribbons, he sometimes amuses me with his bluntness and
his sour humours; but there are many times when I find him
most irritating. And as for the man with the short coat—"

[*To* ORONTE.] Here's your present. "As for the man with the short
coat, who is going in for intellect and wants to be an author in
spite of everybody, I can't take the trouble to listen to what he
says, and I find his prose as tiresome as his verse. So please understand that I don't always have as good a time as you think, and
that I miss you sorely in all the parties I am dragged to, and that
the presence of people one is really fond of is the best seasoning
for social amusements."

CLITANDRE. And now here I am.

"Your Clitandre, whom you mention, with his cooing manner,
is the last man I could really care for. It is absurd for you to
imagine that one could be fond of him, and you are absurd to
think that one is not fond of you. To be reasonable, just reverse
your opinions; and see me as much as you can, to help me to
bear the distress of being bored by him."

    So there's a noble character depicted.
    You know the common name of it, madame?
    Enough. We'll go together to pay some calls,
    And show the glorious portrait of your heart.

ACASTE. There's plenty of subject here for my reproaches,
    But I don't think you're worthy of my anger.
    I'll show you that the little marquises
    Can find more honest hearts for their consolation.
    [*Exit* ACASTE *and* CLITANDRE.]

ORONTE. So this is the way I find myself traduced,
    Despite the gulling words you've written me!
    Your heart, displaying the tinsel shams of love,
    Offers itself to the whole human race!
    I was a dupe; I shall be dupe no more.
    You do me a service by this revelation.
    I gain my heart, which you return to me,
    And in your loss of it my vengeance lies.
    [*To* ALCESTE.]
    Sir, I remove an obstacle from your path.
    You may conclude your business with Madame.
    [*Exit* ORONTE.]

ARSINOÉ. Really, I'm shocked by this unhappy business!

It makes me furious; I can't hold back.
Has anyone ever seen such strange behavior?
Disregarding the other gentlemen,
Alceste, whom your good fortune drew to you,
A gentleman of merit and of honor,
A gentleman who simply idolized you,
Did he deserve—

ALCESTE.   Permit me, please, madame,
To handle my own interests in the case.
You needn't assume unnecessary burdens.   10
However much you may espouse my cause,
I can't repay your zeal with any affection;
And if in vengeance I should seek a heart
As substitute, the heart would not be yours.

ARSINOÉ. Ho! Do you think, sir, that I had that thought?
That one could be so eager to possess you?
I think you're overfull of vanity,
If you have flattered yourself with that belief!
The cast-offs of Madame are articles
With which no sensible woman could be pleased.   20
Open your eyes, don't be so high and mighty;
I'm not the sort of person that you need.
You will do better to dangle after her;
I'm looking forward to that glorious match!
[*Exit* ARSINOÉ.]

ALCESTE. Well, in despite of all, I have kept silence,
And I've allowed everyone else to speak.
Have I controlled myself sufficiently,
And may I now—

CÉLIMÈNE.   Yes, you may say it all.
You have the right to make complaint of me,   30
And to reproach me for—whatever you wish.
I'm wrong, and I admit it. I'm confused.
I shall not try to find some vain excuse.
I can despise the anger of the others;
I must admit I have mistreated you.
Your bitterness is only reasonable;
I know too well how guilty I must seem,
How everything proclaims my treachery,
How, finally, you have good cause to hate me.
Hate me, then; I submit.   40

ALCESTE.   Oh, faithless, can I?
Can I thus triumph over all my love?
However eagerly I wish to hate you,
Have I a heart that's ready to obey?

[*To* ÉLIANTE *and* PHILINTE.]
You see the power of an unworthy love;
I make you both witnesses of my weakness.
But that's not all my weakness, I'm afraid;
You'll see me carry it to exaggeration,
And show how far from reasonable men are,
For man's essential frailty hides in the heart.
[*To* CÉLIMÈNE.]
Yes, I will willingly forget your offenses
And find excuses for them in my mind,
I'll call them merely the infirmities
Which the conventions of our time encourage,   10
Provided you sincerely join with me
In my design, to flee society,
Provided you agree forthwith to share
My solitude, where I have vowed to live.
That is the only way you can repair
The hurt your words have done your reputation.
Thus, after this abominable scene,
My heart will have the right to love you still.
CÉLIMÈNE. What, leave society before I'm old,
And go and bury myself in your solitude?   20
ALCESTE. Why, if your passion corresponds with mine,
What do you care for all the rest of the world?
And can you not be satisfied with me?
CÉLIMÈNE. I'm only twenty; solitude terrifies me.
I fear that I am just not strong enough
To take upon myself so high a purpose.
But if our union can be recompense,
I can determine to accept its bonds;
And marriage—
ALCESTE.   No. Now I have learned to hate you.   30
This is your one unpardonable deed.
Since you acknowledge that you cannot find
Your all in me, as I find all in you,
I shall not marry you. This last offense
Frees me forever from my long subjection.
[CÉLIMÈNE *goes upstage;* ALCESTE *turns his back on her. She turns,
curtsies, awaits a word from him, then snaps open her fan resolutely,
and exits. To* ÉLIANTE.]
Madame, you're virtuous and beautiful;
I recognize your frank sincerity.
Long have I honored and respected you.
Let my esteem remain the same, unaltered.
Suffer that in my manifold afflictions   40

I make no offering of my troubled heart.
I am not worthy. I begin to know
That heaven did not destine me for wedlock.
A heart refused by your inferior
Would be for you a most unworthy homage.
ÉLIANTE. Why, you may follow this thought to its conclusion;
And I may grant my favors where I will.
I might perchance find someone like our friend here
Who would accept my hand, if I should ask him.
PHILINTE. Madame, this honor is my sole desire;   10
I'd sacrifice my life, my blood, for it.
ALCESTE. May you forever keep this way of feeling
One for the other, and gain true happiness.
While I, betrayed, and loaded with injustice,
Flee from this dunghill home of every vice,
And seek some lonely cranny of the earth
Where a man is free to be a man of honor.
[*Exit* ALCESTE.]
PHILINTE. Madame, come, let us employ ourselves
To thwart the purpose of his unruly heart.
[*Exeunt.*]

OLIVER GOLDSMITH

SHE STOOPS TO
CONQUER

DR. GOLDSMITH'S
PRESCRIPTION

ALTHOUGH A DRAMATIC FORM is in a more or less constant
state of evolution, it is sometimes useful for dramatists to look
back to the beginnings. Both tragedy and comedy are susceptible
to the kind of adulteration and corruption which increases
theatrical impact at the expense of dramatic experience.

It is understandable, for example, that a playwright, seeking to
attract spectators, could forget that the catastrophic finale of
tragedy was secondary to the deepened understanding of man's
fate intended by Sophocles. The true horror of the fifth episode of
Antigone is the perception by the spectator that not even a king is
exempt from the unforeseeable consequences of his decisions, even
from decisions arrived at with the most honorable purpose. But
soon the horror becomes more important theatrically than the
truth; violence resulting from unreason or blindness is
replaced by the violence resulting from passion or madness. Instead of Oedipus blinding himself and going into lifelong exile,
Medea slaughters her children and escapes the consequences in a
magic chariot. Or, consider the tragedy of frustrated love:
Shakespeare's Romeo and Juliet are kept apart by a family feud.
In an attempt to circumvent parental disapproval they wed in
secret and set off a chain of consequences that results in their
double suicide. A theatrical generation later, John Ford took up
the subject in *'Tis Pity She's a Whore* (1633). This time the lovers
are brother and sister and as a consequence of their incest the
brother murders his sister and presents the audience with the sight
of her heart impaled on his dagger before being himself killed
by bandits. It is no giant step from tragedy—

> When we our betters see bearing our woes
> We scarcely think our miseries our foes.
> Who alone suffers suffers most i' th' mind,
> Leaving free things and happy shows behind;
> But then the mind much sufferance doth o'erskip
> When grief hath mates, and bearing fellowship.
>
> (*King Lear*, III, 6)

—to melodrama:

> These violent delights have violent ends.
>
> (*Romeo and Juliet*, II, 6)

Comedy is equally subject to corruption. If it, in its origin, was given to the exhibition of folly and excess, just as tragedy was, it was dedicated to the principle that the consequences of unreason could be circumvented, endured, or (even) enjoyed. Lovers kept apart by stern parents or social custom had at their command the power of attaining a happy union. The self-deluded, the egocentric, might have the capacity to create temporary disorder, but ultimately they could be contained, if not reformed. The necessary conclusion of comedy was "the happy ending" as the necessary conclusion of tragedy was catastrophe. But, just as violence eventually became a kind of end in itself and tempted the tragic writer into melodrama, so the spirit of the happy ending, sweetness and light, could become pervasive in the total action of comedy.

A pertinent instance of the adulteration of the comic point of view can be found in the English theater of the eighteenth century. This century had inherited the comic repertory of the Restoration, the plays of George Etherege, William Wycherley, William Congreve, comedies of manners reflecting and laughing at the absurdities and eccentricities of the courtiers and city folk who made up their audiences. The world of these plays is a world of gentlemen's dressing rooms, chocolate houses, and heavily planted parks; the characters are lecherous old men and women, cast mistresses who will not take no for an answer, pretenders to wit and position, fortune-seeking bachelors and the witty heiresses who outsmart them. In observing this world and its inhabitants the reader is reminded of two famous epigrams by Oscar Wilde: "In matters of grave importance, style not sincerity is the vital thing," and "The truth is rarely pure and never simple."

With the coming of the eighteenth century, however, there was a radical shift in the playgoing population and an equally radical compensatory shift in the comic mirror. The increasing wealth, and hence political and social power, of the middle classes made them year by year a more considerable element in the theatrical audience, and it became necessary year by year to pay greater attention to their tastes and preferences. The tradesman, who appeared in the world of the Restoration hero only to be cheated, becomes himself the hero of *The London Merchant* (1731). The witty fortune-hunter becomes the industrious apprentice, Lady Wishfort becomes Lady Bountiful, the coy mistress becomes "my nown true-love." Comedy of manners, in sum, becomes sentimental comedy.

The eighteenth-century audience wished not to laugh at folly but to applaud virtue, and preferred moralization to epigram. The Restoration hero could be sure of sympathy when he declared:

> A fellow that lives in a windmill has not a more whimsical dwelling than the heart of a man that is lodg'd in a woman;

the eighteenth-century lover was applauded for another sort of vow:

> If ever I marry, it must be a staid, sober, considerate damsel, with blood in her veins as cold as a turtle's; quick of scent as a vulture, when danger's in the wind; wary and sharp-sighted as a hawk, when treachery is on foot: with such a companion at my elbow, forever whispering in my ear, "Have a care of this man, he's a cheat . . . overhead there's a scaffold, underfoot there's a well;" oh sir! such a woman might lead me up and down this great city without difficulty or danger.
>
> *(The West-Indian,* III, 1)

The good heart replaced the quicksilver mind, and Sir Richard Steele dogmatically wrote that the purpose of the new comedy was "to moralize the stage."

If wit, humor, and satire did not wholly abdicate from eighteenth-century comedy, they found themselves demoted by an emphasis on scenes and situations exploiting the distresses of impoverished heroes or unjustly maligned heroines. Racial stereotypes (Irishmen, Jews) that had been sources of instant laughter now reeked of magnanimity. The darkness of tragedy and the glitter of comedy were merged into the widely diffused greyness of a genre without a name. As a contemporary critic protested:

> It will continue as a kind of *mulish* production, with all the defects of its opposite parents, and marked with sterility. If we are permitted to make comedy weep, we have an equal right to make tragedy laugh, and to set down in blank verse the jests and repartees of all the attendants in a funeral procession . . . .
> Humor at present seems to be departing from the stage, and it will soon happen that our comic players will have nothing left for it but a fine coat and a song.

The protesting critic was Oliver Goldsmith (1728–1774), a doctor of medicine, man of letters, and intimate friend of Samuel Johnson and of David Garrick, the chief actor of the century. Like Anton Chekhov, another man of medicine and of letters, Goldsmith not only criticized but created. His "Comparison between Laughing and Sentimental Comedy," from which the above quotation is excerpted, appeared in 1772; in the next year he presented the theater with *She Stoops to Conquer*.

The stage-history of his comedy is the best justification of his critical views. Of the hundreds of sentimental plays which brought tears to contemporary eyes, none now holds the stage; *She Stoops to Conquer* outlived its original audience and continues today to delight audiences in the living theater. Sentiments are fashions while follies are eternal. Sentimental dramas are, in Goldsmith's word. *mulish*; laughing comedy can have generations without number.

Laughing comedy, of course, does not mean farce, the comic analogue of melodrama. Farce relies almost entirely on situation to entertain, comedy insists on a relation between character and situation from which the audience will recognize (and perhaps forgive) its own excesses. Mother-love, for example, is a human characteristic often sentimentalized out of human proportions; the behavior of Mrs. Hardcastle restores perspective. The ambivalent reactions of young Marlow mock the irrationality of romantic love without denying its sweetness. And Tony Lumpkin is not the cloddish rustic his name suggests, but a shrewdly observed adolescent escaping from the domestic smother. Although the time is the era of the American Revolution, and transportation is by coach and innkeepers were still "hosts" and not officials of international hotel-chains, the basic conditions of the characters are permanently true. And in this truth is the continuing vitality of *She Stoops to Conquer*.

The play did not banish sentimental comedy from the eighteenth-century theater; the mulish form was too pleasing to the audience. In varying degrees and with varying popularity, sentimental comedies continued to be written in succeeding centuries, and became the staple fare of the movies, radio, and television. There is, therefore, a valid present caution in the concluding sentences of Goldsmith's essay:

> It depends upon the audience whether they will actually drive those poor merry creatures from the stage, or sit at a play as gloomy as at the Tabernacle. It is not easy to recover an art when once lost; and it will be but a just punishment, that when, by our being too fastidious, we have banished humor from the stage, we should ourselves be deprived of the art of laughing.

Characters

Men

SIR CHARLES MARLOW

YOUNG MARLOW
his son

HARDCASTLE

HASTINGS

TONY LUMPKIN

DIGGORY

Women

MRS. HARDCASTLE

MISS HARDCASTLE

MISS NEVILLE

MAID

LANDLORDS, SERVANTS, ETC.

SHE STOOPS TO CONQUER
OR, THE MISTAKES OF A NIGHT

Oliver Goldsmith

PROLOGUE
By David Garrick, Esq.[1]

[*Enter* MR. WOODWARD,[2] *dressed in black, and holding a handker-chief to his eyes.*]
Excuse me, sirs, I pray—I can't yet speak—
I'm crying now—and have been all the week!
'Tis not alone this mourning suit, good masters;
I've that within—for which there are no plasters!
Pray would you know the reason why I'm crying?
The Comic Muse, long sick, is now a dying!
And if she goes, my tears will never stop;
For as a player, I can't squeeze out one drop:
I am undone, that's all—shall lose my bread—
I'd rather, but that's nothing—lose my head.
When the sweet maid is laid upon the bier,
Shuter[3] and *I* shall be chief mourners here.
To *her* a mawkish drab of spurious breed,
Who deals in *sentimentals* will succeed!
Poor *Ned* and *I* are dead to all intents,
We can as soon speak *Greek* as *sentiments!*
Both nervous grown, to keep our spirits up,
We now and then take down a hearty cup.
What shall we do?—If Comedy forsake us!
They'll turn us out, and no one else will take us;
But why can't I be moral?—Let me try—
My heart thus pressing—fixed my face and eye—
With a sententious look, that nothing means,
(Faces are blocks in sentimental scenes),

---

[1] The leading actor-manager of the English stage in the eighteenth century.
[2] Henry Woodward, a favorite *comic* actor.
[3] Edward (Ned) Shuter, another comic actor. He created the role of Hardcastle.

429

Thus I begin—*All is not gold that glitters,*
Pleasure seems sweet, but proves a glass of bitters.
When ignorance enters, folly is at hand;
Learning is better far than house and land.
Let not your virtue trip, who trips may stumble,
And virtue is not virtue, if she tumble.
    I give it up—morals won't do for me;
To make you laugh I must play tragedy.
One hope remains—hearing the maid was ill,
A *doctor* comes this night to show his skill.
To cheer her heart, and give your muscles motion,
He in *five draughts* prepared, presents a potion:
A kind of magic charm—for be assured,
If you will *swallow* it, the maid is cured.
But desperate the Doctor, and her case is,
If you reject the dose, and make wry faces!
This truth he boasts, will boast it while he lives,
No *poisonous drugs* are mixed in what he gives;
Should he succeed, you'll give him his degree;
If not, within he will receive no fee!
The college *you*, must his pretensions back,
Pronounce him *regular*, or dub him *quack*.

ACT ONE

Scene One

A chamber in an old-fashioned house.

[*Enter* MRS. HARDCASTLE *and* MR. HARDCASTLE.]

MRS. HARDCASTLE. I vow, Mr. Hardcastle, you're very particular. Is there a creature in the whole country but ourselves that does not take a trip to town now and then, to rub off the rust a little? There's the two Miss Hoggs, and our neighbor, Mrs. Grigsby, go to take a month's polishing every winter.

HARDCASTLE. Aye, and bring back vanity and affectation to last them the whole year. I wonder why London cannot keep its own fools at home. In my time, the follies of the town crept slowly among us, but now they travel faster than a stagecoach. Its fopperies come down, not only as inside passengers, but in the very basket.

MRS. HARDCASTLE. Aye, *your* times were fine times, indeed; you have been telling us of *them* for many a long year. Here we live in an old rumbling mansion, that looks for all the world like an inn, but that we never see company. Our best visitors are old Mrs. Oddfish, the curate's wife, and little Cripplegate, the lame dancing-master: and all our entertainment your old stories of Prince Eugene and the Duke of Marlborough. I hate such old-fashioned trumpery.

HARDCASTLE. And I love it. I love every thing that's old: old friends, old times, old manners, old books, old wine; and, I believe, Dorothy [*taking her hand*], you'll own I have been pretty fond of an old wife.

MRS. HARDCASTLE. Lord, Mr. Hardcastle, you're for ever at your Dorothy's and your old wife's. You may be a Darby, but I'll be no Joan, I promise you. I'm not so old as you'd make me by more than one good year. Add twenty to twenty, and make money of that.

HARDCASTLE. Let me see; twenty added to twenty—makes just fifty and seven!

MRS. HARDCASTLE. It's false, Mr. Hardcastle: I was but twenty when I was brought to bed of Tony, that I had by Mr. Lumpkin, my first husband; and he's not come to years of discretion yet.

HARDCASTLE. Nor ever will, I dare answer for him. Aye, you have taught *him* finely!

MRS. HARDCASTLE. No matter, Tony Lumpkin has a good fortune. My son is not to live by his learning. I don't think a boy wants much learning to spend fifteen hundred a year.

HARDCASTLE. Learning, quotha! A mere composition of tricks and mischief!

MRS. HARDCASTLE. Humour, my dear: nothing but humour. Come, Mr. Hardcastle, you must allow the boy a little humour.

HARDCASTLE. I'd sooner allow him a horse-pond! If burning the footmen's shoes, frighting the maids, and worrying the kittens, be humour, he has it. It was but yesterday he fastened my wig to the back of my chair, and when I went to make a bow, I popped my bald head in Mrs. Frizzle's face!

MRS. HARDCASTLE. And am I to blame? The poor boy was always too sickly to do any good. A school would be his death. When he comes to be a little stronger, who knows what a year or two's Latin may do for him?

HARDCASTLE. Latin for him! A cat and fiddle! No, no, the ale-house and the stable are the only schools he'll ever go to.

MRS. HARDCASTLE. Well, we must not snub the poor boy now, for I believe we shan't have him long among us. Any body that looks in his face may see he's consumptive.

HARDCASTLE. Aye, if growing too fat be one of the symptoms.

MRS. HARDCASTLE. He coughs sometimes.

HARDCASTLE. Yes, when his liquor goes the wrong way.

MRS. HARDCASTLE. I'm actually afraid of his lungs.

HARDCASTLE. And truly, so am I; for he sometimes whoops like a speaking trumpet—[TONY *hallooing behind the scenes*]—O, there he goes—A very consumptive figure, truly!

[*Enter* TONY, *crossing the stage.*]

MRS. HARDCASTLE. Tony, where are you going, my charmer? Won't you
give papa and I a little of your company, lovee?

TONY. I'm in haste, mother, I cannot stay.

MRS. HARDCASTLE. You shan't venture out this raw evening, my dear: you
look most shockingly.

TONY. I can't stay, I tell you. *The Three Pigeons* expects me down every
moment. There's some fun going forward.

HARDCASTLE. Aye; the alehouse, the old place: I thought so.

MRS. HARDCASTLE. A low, paltry set of fellows.

TONY. Not so low, neither. There's Dick Muggins, the exciseman; Jack
Slang, the horse doctor; Little Aminadab, that grinds the music box;
and Tom Twist, that spins the pewter platter.

MRS. HARDCASTLE. Pray, my dear, disappoint them for one night, at
least.

TONY. As for disappointing *them*, I should not so much mind; but I can't
abide to disappoint *myself*.

MRS. HARDCASTLE [*detaining him*]. You shan't go.

TONY. I will, I tell you.

MRS. HARDCASTLE. I say you shan't.

TONY. We'll see which is strongest, you or I.
[*Exit, hauling her out.*]
[HARDCASTLE, *solus.*]

HARDCASTLE. Aye, there goes a pair that only spoil each other. But is not
the whole age in a combination to drive sense and discretion out of
doors? There's my pretty darling, Kate; the fashions of the times have
almost infected her too. By living a year or two in town, she is as fond
of gauze and French frippery as the best of them.
[*Enter* MISS HARDCASTLE.]

HARDCASTLE. Blessings on my pretty innocence! Dressed out as usual, my
Kate! Goodness! What a quantity of superfluous silk hast thou got about
thee, girl! I could never teach the fools of this age that the indigent world
could be clothed out of the trimmings of the vain.

MISS HARDCASTLE. You know our agreement, sir. You allow me the morning
to receive and pay visits, and to dress in my own manner; and in the
evening, I put on my housewife's dress, to please you.

HARDCASTLE. Well, remember, I insist on the terms of our agreement; and,
by-the-bye, I believe I shall have occasion to try your obedience this very
evening.

MISS HARDCASTLE. I protest, sir, I don't comprehend your meaning.

HARDCASTLE. Then, to be plain with you, Kate, I expect the young gentleman I have chosen to be your husband from town this very day. I have
his father's letter, in which he informs me his son is set out, and that he
intends to follow himself shortly after.

MISS HARDCASTLE. Indeed! I wish I had known something of this before.
Bless me, how shall I behave? It's a thousand to one I shan't like him;

our meeting will be so formal, and so like a thing of business that I shall find no room for friendship or esteem.

HARDCASTLE. Depend upon it, child, I'll never control your choice; but Mr. Marlow, whom I have pitched upon, is the son of my old friend, Sir Charles Marlow, of whom you have heard me talk so often. The young gentleman has been bred a scholar, and is designed for an employment in the service of his country. I am told he's a man of an excellent understanding.

MISS HARDCASTLE. Is he?

HARDCASTLE. Very generous.

MISS HARDCASTLE. I believe I shall like him.

HARDCASTLE. Young and brave.

MISS HARDCASTLE. I'm sure I shall like him.

HARDCASTLE. And very handsome.

MISS HARDCASTLE. My dear papa, say no more [*kissing his hand*], he's mine, I'll have him!

HARDCASTLE. And, to crown all, Kate, he's one of the most bashful and reserved young fellows in all the world.

MISS HARDCASTLE. Eh! you have frozen me to death again. That word *reserved* has undone all the rest of his accomplishments. A reserved lover, it is said, always makes a suspicious husband.

HARDCASTLE. On the contrary, modesty seldom resides in a breast that is not enriched with nobler virtues. It was the very feature in his character that first struck me.

MISS HARDCASTLE. He must have more striking features to catch me, I promise you. However, if he be so young, so handsome, and so everything, as you mention, I believe he'll do still. I think I'll have him.

HARDCASTLE. Aye, Kate, but there is still an obstacle. It's more than an even wager, he may not have *you*.

MISS HARDCASTLE. My dear papa, why will you mortify one so?—Well, if he refuses, instead of breaking my heart at his indifference, I'll only break my glass for its flattery, set my cap to some newer fashion, and look out for some less difficult admirer.

HARDCASTLE. Bravely resolved! In the meantime, I'll go prepare the servants for his reception; as we seldom see company, they want as much training as a company of recruits the first day's muster.

[*Exit.*]

[MISS HARDCASTLE, *sola.*]

MISS HARDCASTLE. Lud, this news of papa's puts me all in a flutter. *Young, handsome*; these he put last; but I put them foremost. *Sensible, good-natured*; I like all that. But then *reserved*, and *sheepish*, that's much against him. Yet, can't he be cured of his timidity by being taught to be proud of his wife? Yes, and can't I—But I vow I'm disposing of the husband before I have secured the lover!

[*Enter* MISS NEVILLE.]

MISS HARDCASTLE. I'm glad you're come, Neville, my dear. Tell me, Constance, how do I look this evening? Is there anything whimsical about me? Is it one of my well looking days, child? Am I in face today?

MISS NEVLLE. Perfectly, my dear. Yet, now I look again—bless me!— surely no accident has happened among the canary birds or the goldfishes? Has your brother or the cat been meddling? Or has the last novel been too moving?

MISS HARDCASTLE. No; nothing of all this. I have been threatened—I can scarce get it out—I have been threatened with a lover!

MISS NEVILLE. And his name—

MISS HARDCASTLE. Is Marlow.

MISS NEVILLE. Indeed!

MISS HARDCASTLE. The son of Sir Charles Marlow.

MISS NEVILLE. As I live, the most intimate friend of Mr. Hastings, *my* admirer. They are never asunder. I believe you must have seen him when we lived in town.

MISS HARDCASTLE. Never.

MISS NEVILLE. He's a very singular character, I assure you. Among women of reputation and virtue, he is the modestest man alive; but his acquaintance give him a very different character among creatures of another stamp: you understand me.

MISS HARDCASTLE. An odd character, indeed! I shall never be able to manage him. What shall I do? Pshaw, think no more of him, but trust to occurrences for success. But how goes on your own affair, my dear? Has my mother been courting you for my brother Tony, as usual?

MISS NEVILLE. I have just come from one of our agreeable *tête-à-têtes*. She has been saying a hundred tender things, and setting off her pretty monster as the very pink of perfection.

MISS HARDCASTLE. And her partiality is such that she actually thinks him so. A fortune like yours is no small temptation. Besides, as she has the sole management of it, I'm not surprised to see her unwilling to let it go out of the family.

MISS NEVILLE. A fortune like mine, which chiefly consists in jewels, is no such mighty temptation. But at any rate, if my dear Hastings be but constant, I make no doubt to be too hard for her at last. However, I let her suppose that I am in love with her son, and she never once dreams that my affections are fixed upon another.

MISS HARDCASTLE. My good brother holds out stoutly. I could almost love him for hating you so.

MISS NEVILLE. It is a good natured creature at bottom, and I'm sure would wish to see me married to anybody but himself. But my aunt's bell rings for our afternoon's walk round the improvements. *Allons.* Courage is necessary, as our affairs are critical.

MISS HARDCASTLE. Would it were bedtime and all were well.[4]
[*Exeunt.*]

Scene Two

An alehouse room. Several shabby fellows, with punch and tobacco. TONY
at the head of the table, a little higher than the rest: a mallet in his hand.
OMNES. Hurrah, hurrah, hurrah, bravo!
FIRST FELLOW. Now, gentlemen, silence for a song. The 'Squire is going to
knock himself down for a song.
OMNES. Aye, a song, a song.
TONY. Then I'll sing you, gentlemen, a song I made upon this alehouse,
The Three Pigeons.

SONG

Let schoolmasters puzzle their brain,
With grammar, and nonsense, and learning;
Good liquor, I stoutly maintain,
Gives genus *a better discerning,*
Let them brag of their Heathenish Gods,
Their Lethes, their Styxes, and Stygians;
Their Quis, and their Quæs, and their Quods,
They're all but a parcel of Pigeons.

Toroddle, toroddle, toroll!

When Methodist preachers come down,
A-preaching that drinking is sinful,
I'll wager the rascals a crown,
They always preach best with a skinful.
But when you come down with your pence,
For a slice of their scurvy religion,
I'll leave it to all men of sense,
But you, my good friend, are the pigeon.

Toroddle, toroddle, toroll!

Then come, put the jorum about,
And let us be merry and clever,
Our hearts and our liquors are stout,
Here's the Three Jolly Pigeons for ever.
Let some cry up woodcock or hare,
Your bustards, your ducks, and your widgeons;
But of all the birds in the air,
Here's a health to the Three Jolly Pigeons.

Toroddle, toroddle, toroll!

OMNES. Bravo, bravo!

[4] One of the many Shakespearean allusions in the play. Miss Hardcastle
remembers Falstaff parting from Prince Hal on the battlefield (I *Henry IV*, V, 1).

FIRST FELLOW. The 'Squire has got spunk in him.

SECOND FELLOW. I loves to hear him sing, bekeays he never gives us nothing that's *low*.

THIRD FELLOW. O damn anything that's *low*, I cannot bear it!

FOURTH FELLOW. The genteel thing is the genteel thing at any time. If so be that a gentleman bees in a concatenation accordingly.

THIRD FELLOW. I like the maxum of it, Master Muggins. What, tho' I am obligated to dance a bear, a man may be a gentleman for all that. May this be my poison if my bear ever dances but to the very genteelest of tunes. *Water Parted*, or the minuet in *Ariadne*.[5]

SECOND FELLOW. What a pity it is the 'Squire is not come to his own. It would be well for all the publicans within ten miles round of him.

TONY. Ecod, and so it would, Master Slang. I'd then show what it was to keep choice of company.

SECOND FELLOW. O, he takes after his own father for that. To be sure, old 'Squire Lumpkin was the finest gentleman I ever set my eyes on. For winding the straight horn, or beating a thicket for a hare, or a wench, he never had his fellow. It was a saying in the place that he kept the best horses, dogs, and girls in the whole county.

TONY. Ecod, and when I'm of age, I'll be no bastard, I promise you. I have been thinking of Bett Bouncer and the miller's grey mare to begin with. But come, my boys, drink about and be merry, for you pay no reckoning. Well, Stingo, what's the matter?

[*Enter* LANDLORD.]

LANDLORD. There be two gentlemen in a post-chaise at the door. They have lost their way upon the forest; and they are talking something about Mr. Hardcastle.

TONY. As sure as can be, one of them must be the gentleman that's coming down to court my sister. Do they seem to be Londoners?

LANDLORD. I believe they may. They look woundily like Frenchmen.

TONY. Then desire them to step this way, and I'll set them right in a twinkling. [*Exit* LANDLORD.] Gentlemen, as they mayn't be good enough company for you, step down for a moment, and I'll be with you in the squeezing of a lemon.

[*Exeunt* MOB.]

[TONY *solus*.]

TONY. Father-in-law[6] has been calling me whelp and hound, this half year. Now, if I pleased, I could be so revenged upon the old grumbletonian. But then I'm afraid—afraid of what? I shall soon be worth fifteen hundred a year, and let him frighten me out of *that* if he can!

[*Enter* LANDLORD, *conducting* MARLOW *and* HASTINGS.]

---

[5] "Water parted from the sea" is an aria from the opera of *Artaxerxes* by Thomas Arne: *Ariadne* is an opera by Handel.

[6] i.e., stepfather.

MARLOW. What a tedious, uncomfortable day have we had of it! We were told it was but forty miles across the country, and we have come above threescore!

HASTINGS. And all, Marlow, from that unaccountable reserve of yours, that would not let us inquire more frequently on the way.

MARLOW. I own, Hastings, I am unwilling to lay myself under an obligation to every one I meet; and often stand the chance of an unmannerly answer.

HASTINGS. At present, however, we are not likely to receive any answer.

TONY. No offense, gentlemen. But I'm told you have been inquiring for one Mr. Hardcastle, in these parts. Do you know what part of the country you are in?

HASTINGS. Not in the least, sir, but should thank you for information.

TONY. Nor the way you came?

HASTINGS. No, sir; but if you can inform us—

TONY. Why, gentlemen, if you know neither the road you are going, nor where you are, nor the road you came, the first thing I have to inform you is, that—you have lost your way.

MARLOW. We wanted no ghost to tell us that.[7]

TONY. Pray, gentlemen, may I be so bold as to ask the place from whence you came?

MARLOW. That's not necessary toward directing us where we are to go.

TONY. No offense; but question for question is all fair, you know. Pray, gentlemen, is not this same Hardcastle a cross-grained, old-fashioned, whimsical fellow with an ugly face, a daughter, and a pretty son?

HASTINGS. We have not seen the gentleman, but he has the family you mention.

TONY. The daughter, a tall, trapesing, trolloping, talkative maypole— The son, a pretty, well-bred, agreeable youth, that everybody is fond of!

MARLOW. Our information differs in this. The daughter is said to be well-bred and beautiful; the son, an awkward booby, reared up and spoiled at his mother's apron-string.

TONY. He-he-hem—then, gentlemen, all I have to tell you is, that you won't reach Mr. Hardcastle's house this night, I believe.

HASTINGS. Unfortunate!

TONY. It's a damned long, dark, boggy, dirty, dangerous way. Stingo, tell the gentlemen the way to Mr. Hardcastle's;—[winking upon the LAND-LORD] Mr. Hardcastle's of Quagmire Marsh, you understand me.

LANDLORD. Master Hardcastle's! Lack-a-daisy, my masters, you're come a deadly deal wrong! When you came to the bottom of the hill, you should have crossed down Squash-lane.

MARLOW. Cross down Squash-lane!

LANDLORD. Then you were to keep straight forward till you came to four roads.

[7] See *Hamlet*, I, 5.

MARLOW. Come to where four roads meet!

TONY. Aye, but you must be sure to take only one of them.

MARLOW. O, sir, you're facetious.

TONY. Then, keeping to the right, you are to go sideways till you come upon Crack-skull Common: there you must look sharp for the track of the wheel, and go forward till you come to Farmer Murrain's barn. Coming to the farmer's barn, you are to turn to the right, and then to the left, and then to the right about again, till you find out the old mill—

MARLOW. Zounds, man, we could as soon find out the longitude!

HASTINGS. What's to be done, Marlow?

MARLOW. This house promises but a poor reception; though, perhaps, the landlord can accommodate us.

LANDLORD. Alack, master, we have but one spare bed in the whole house.

TONY. And to my knowledge, that's taken up by three lodgers already. [*After a pause in which the rest seem disconcerted.*] I have hit it. Don't you think, Stingo, our landlady could accommodate the gentlemen, by the fireside, with—three chairs and a bolster?

HASTINGS. I hate sleeping by the fireside.

MARLOW. And I detest your three chairs and a bolster.

TONY. You do, do you?—then let me see—what—if you go on a mile further, to the Buck's Head; the old Buck's Head on the hill, one of the best inns in the whole county?

HASTINGS. O ho! so we have escaped an adventure for this night, however.

LANDLORD [*apart to* TONY]. Sure, you ben't sending them to your father's as an inn, be you?

TONY. Mum, you fool, you. Let *them* find that out. [*To them.*] You have only to keep on straight forward till you come to a large old house by the roadside. You'll see a pair of large horns over the door. That's the sign. Drive up the yard, and call stoutly about you.

HASTINGS. Sir, we are obliged to you. The servants can't miss the way?

TONY. No, no; but I tell you, though, the landlord is rich, and going to leave off business; so he wants to be thought a gentleman, saving your presence, he! he! he! He'll be for giving you his company, and, ecod, if you mind him, he'll persuade you that his mother was an alderman, and his aunt a justice of peace!

LANDLORD. A troublesome old blade, to be sure; but a keeps as good wines and beds as any in the whole country.

MARLOW. Well, if he supplies us with these, we shall want no further connection. We are to turn to the right, did you say?

TONY. No, no; straight forward. I'll just step myself and show you a piece of the way. [*To the* LANDLORD.] Mum.

LANDLORD. Ah, bless your heart, for a sweet, pleasant—damned mischievous son of a whore.

[*Exeunt.*]

ACT TWO

An old-fashioned house.

[*Enter* HARDCASTLE, *followed by three or four awkward* SERVANTS.]

HARDCASTLE. Well, I hope you're perfect in the table exercise I have been teaching you these three days. You all know your posts and your places, and can show that you have been used to good company without ever stirring from home.

OMNES. Aye, aye.

HARDCASTLE. When company comes, you are not to pop out and stare, and then run in again, like frighted rabbits in a warren.

OMNES. No, no.

HARDCASTLE. You, Diggory, whom I have taken from the barn, are to make a show at the side-table; and you, Roger, whom I have advanced from the plough, are to place yourself behind *my* chair. But you're not to stand so, with your hands in your pockets. Take your hands from your pockets, Roger; and from your head, you blockhead, you. See how Diggory carries his hands. They're a little too stiff, indeed, but that's no great matter.

DIGGORY. Aye, mind how I hold them. I learned to hold my hands this way, when I was upon drill for the militia. And so being upon drill—

HARDCASTLE. You must not be so talkative, Diggory. You must be all attention to the guests. You must hear us talk, and not think of talking; you must see us drink, and not think of drinking; you must see us eat, and not think of eating.

DIGGORY. By the laws, your worship, that's perfectly unpossible. Whenever Diggory sees yeating going forward, ecod, he's always wishing for a mouthful himself.

HARDCASTLE. Blockhead! Is not a belly-full in the kitchen as good as a belly-full in the parlor? Stay your stomach with that reflection.

DIGGORY. Ecod, I thank your worship, I'll make a shift to stay my stomach with a slice of cold beef in the pantry.

HARDCASTLE. Diggory, you are too talkative. Then, if I happen to say a good thing, or tell a good story at table, you must not all burst out a-laughing, as if you made part of the company.

DIGGORY. Then, ecod, your worship must not tell the story of Old Grouse in the gun room: I can't help laughing at that—he! he! he!—for the soul of me! We have laughed at that these twenty years—ha! ha! ha!

HARDCASTLE. Ha! ha! ha! The story is a good one. Well, honest Diggory, you may laugh at that—but still remember to be attentive. Suppose one of the company should call for a glass of wine, how will you behave? A glass of wine, sir, if you please [*to* DIGGORY]—Eh, why don't you move?

DIGGORY. Ecod, your worship, I never have courage till I see the eatables and drinkables brought upon the table, and then I'm as bold as a lion.

HARDCASTLE. What, will nobody move?

FIRST SERVANT. I'm not to leave this place.

SECOND SERVANT. I'm sure it's no place of mine.

THIRD SERVANT. Nor mine, for certain.

DIGGORY. Wounds, and I'm sure it can't be mine.

HARDCASTLE. You numbskulls! and so, while, like your betters, you are quarreling for places, the guests must be starved. O you dunces! I find I must begin all over again—but don't I hear a coach drive into the yard? To your posts, you blockheads! I'll go in the meantime and give my old friend's son a hearty reception at the gate.

[*Exit* HARDCASTLE.]

DIGGORY. By the elevens, my place is gone quite out of my head!

ROGER. I know that my place is to be everywhere!

FIRST SERVANT. Where the devil is mine?

SECOND SERVANT. My place is to be nowhere at all; and so Ize go about my business!

[*Exeunt* SERVANTS, *running about as if frighted, different ways.*]

[*Enter* SERVANT *with candles, showing in* MARLOW *and* HASTINGS.]

SERVANT. Welcome, gentlemen, very welcome. This way.

HASTINGS. After the disappointments of the day, welcome once more, Charles, to the comforts of a clean room and a good fire. Upon my word, a very well-looking house; antique but creditable.

MARLOW. The usual fate of a large mansion. Having first ruined the master by good housekeeping, it at last comes to levy contributions as an inn.

HASTINGS. As you say, we passengers are to be taxed to pay all these fineries. I have often seen a good sideboard, or a marble chimney-piece, tho' not actually put in the bill, inflame a reckoning confoundedly.

MARLOW. Travelers, George, must pay in all places. The only difference is that in good inns you pay dearly for luxuries; in bad inns you are fleeced and starved.

HASTINGS. You have lived pretty much among them. In truth, I have been often surprised that you who have seen so such of the world, with your natural good sense, and your many opportunities, could never yet acquire a requisite share of assurance.

MARLOW. The Englishman's malady. But tell me, George, where could I have learned that assurance you talk of? My life has been chiefly spent in a college, or an inn, in seclusion from that lovely part of the creation that chiefly teach men confidence. I don't know that I was ever familiarly acquainted with a single modest woman—except my mother—But among females of another class, you know—

HASTINGS. Aye, among them you are impudent enough of all conscience!

MARLOW. They are of *us*, you know.

HASTINGS. But in the company of women of reputation I never saw such an idiot, such a trembler; you look for all the world as if you wanted an opportunity of stealing out of the room.

MARLOW. Why, man, that's because I *do* want to steal out of the room. Faith, I have often formed a resolution to break the ice, and rattle away at any rate. But I don't know how, a single glance from a pair of fine eyes has totally overset my resolutions. An impudent fellow may counterfeit modesty, but I'll be hanged if a modest man can ever counterfeit impudence.

HASTINGS. If you could but say half the fine things to them that I have heard you lavish upon the barmaid of an inn, or even a college bedmaker—

MARLOW. Why, George, I can't say fine things to them. They freeze, they petrify me. They may talk of a comet, or a burning mountain, or some such bagatelle. But to me, a modest woman, dressed out in all her finery, is the most tremendous object of the whole creation.

HASTINGS. Ha! ha! ha! At this rate, man, how can you ever expect to marry!

MARLOW. Never, unless, as among kings and princes, my bride were to be courted by proxy. If, indeed, like an Eastern bridegroom, one were to be introduced to a wife he never saw before, it might be endured. But to go through all the terrors of a formal courtship, together with the episode of aunts, grandmothers and cousins, and at last to blurt out the broad, staring question of, *Madam, will you marry me?* No, no, that's a strain much above me, I assure you!

HASTINGS. I pity you. But how do you intend behaving to the lady you are come down to visit at the request of your father?

MARLOW. As I behave to all other ladies. Bow very low. Answer yes, or no, to all her demands—But for the rest, I don't think I shall venture to look in her face till I see my father's again.

HASTINGS. I'm surprised that one who is so warm a friend can be so cool a lover.

MARLOW. To be explicit, my dear Hastings, my chief inducement down was to be instrumental in forwarding your happiness, not my own. Miss Neville loves you, the family don't know you, as my friend you are sure of a reception, and let honor do the rest.

HASTINGS. My dear Marlow! But I'll suppress the emotion. Were I a wretch, meanly seeking to carry off a fortune, you should be the last man in the world I would apply to for assistance. But Miss Neville's person is all I ask, and that is mine, both from her deceased father's consent and her own inclination.

MARLOW. Happy man! You have talents and art to captivate any woman. I'm doomed to adore the sex, and yet to converse with the only part of it I despise. This stammer in my address, and this awkward, unprepossessing visage of mine, can never permit me to soar above the reach of a

milliner's 'prentice, or one of the duchesses of Drury-lane.[8] Pshaw, this
fellow here to interrupt us!

[*Enter* HARDCASTLE.]

HARDCASTLE. Gentlemen, once more you are heartily welcome. Which is
Mr. Marlow? Sir, you're heartily welcome. It's not my way, you see, to
receive my friends with my back to the fire. I like to give them a hearty
reception, in the old style, at my gate. I like to see their horses and
trunks taken care of.

MARLOW [*aside*]. He has got our names from the servants already. [*To him.*]
We approve your caution and hospitality, sir. [*To* HASTINGS.] I have been
thinking, George, of changing our traveling dresses in the morning. I am
grown confoundedly ashamed of mine.

HARDCASTLE. I beg, Mr. Marlow, you'll use no ceremony in this house.

HASTINGS. I fancy, George, you're right: the first blow is half the battle. I
intend opening the campaign with the white and gold.

HARDCASTLE. Mr. Marlow—Mr. Hastings—gentlemen—pray be under no
constraint in this house. This is Liberty-hall, gentlemen. You may do
just as you please here.

MARLOW. Yet, George, if we open the campaign too fiercely at first, we may
want ammunition before it is over. I think to reserve the embroidery to
secure a retreat.

HARDCASTLE. Your talking of a retreat, Mr. Marlow, puts me in mind of
the Duke of Marlborough, when we went to besiege Denain. He first
summoned the garrison—

MARLOW. Don't you think the *ventre d'or* waistcoat will do with the plain
brown?

HARDCASTLE. He first summoned the garrison, which might consist of about
five thousand men—

HASTINGS. I think not: brown and yellow mix but very poorly.

HARDCASTLE. I say, gentlemen, as I was telling you, he summoned the
garrison, which might consist of about five thousand men—

MARLOW. The girls like finery.

HARDCASTLE. Which might consist of about five thousand men, well
appointed with stores, ammunition, and other implements of war.
"Now," says the Duke of Marlborough to George Brooks, that stood
next to him—you must have heard of George Brooks; "I'll pawn my
dukedom," says he, "but I take that garrison without spilling a drop of
blood!" So—

MARLOW. What, my good friend, if you gave us a glass of punch in the
meantime; it would help us to carry on the siege with vigor.

HARDCASTLE [*aside*]. Punch, sir!—This is the most unaccountable kind of
modesty I ever met with!

MARLOW. Yes, sir, punch! A glass of warm punch, after our journey, will
be comfortable. This is Liberty-hall, you know.

[8] i.e., prostitute.

HARDCASTLE. Here's cup, sir.

MARLOW [*aside*]. So this fellow, in his Liberty-hall, will only let us have just what he pleases.

HARDCASTLE [*taking the cup*]. I hope you'll find it to your mind. I have prepared it with my own hands, and I believe you'll own the ingredients are tolerable. Will you be so good as to pledge me, sir? Here, Mr. Marlow, here is to our better acquaintance!
[*Drinks.*]

MARLOW [*aside*]. A very impudent fellow this! But he's a character, and I'll humor him a little.—Sir, my service to you.
[*Drinks.*]

HASTINGS [*aside*]. I see this fellow wants to give us his company, and forgets that he's an innkeeper before he has learned to be a gentleman.

MARLOW. From the excellence of your cup, my old friend, I suppose you have a good deal of business in this part of the country. Warm work, now and then, at elections, I suppose?

HARDCASTLE. No, sir, I have long given that work over. Since our betters have hit upon the expedient of electing each other, there's no business *for us that sell ale.*[9]

HASTINGS. So, then you have no turn for politics, I find.

HARDCASTLE. Not in the least. There was a time, indeed, I fretted myself about the mistakes of government, like other people; but, finding myself every day grow more angry, and the government growing no better, I left it mend itself. Since that, I no more trouble my head about *Hyder Ally*, or *Ally Cawn*, than about *Ally Croaker*.[10] Sir, my service to you.

HASTINGS. So that, with eating above stairs, and drinking below, with receiving your friends within, and amusing them without, you lead a good, pleasant, bustling life of it.

HARDCASTLE. I do stir about a great deal, that's certain. Half the differences of the parish are adjusted in this very parlor.

MARLOW [*after drinking*]. And you have an argument in your cup, old gentleman, better than any in Westminster-hall.

HARDCASTLE. Aye, young gentleman, that, and a little philosophy.

MARLOW [*aside*]. Well, this is the first time I ever heard of an innkeeper's philosophy.

HASTINGS. So then, like an experienced general, you attack them on every quarter. If you find their reason manageable, you attack it with your philosophy; if you find they have no reason, you attack them with this. Here's your health, my philosopher.
[*Drinks.*]

HARDCASTLE. Good, very good, thank you; ha! ha! Your generalship puts

[9] A popular expression of the time. It was common practice to bribe voters with free ale.

[10] Hyder Ali was the Sultan of Mysore, Ali Khan the Subah of Bengal; "Ally Croaker," on the other hand, is a popular Irish tune.

me in mind of Prince Eugene, when he fought the Turks at the battle of Belgrade. You shall hear—

MARLOW. Instead of the battle of Belgrade, I believe it's almost time to talk about supper. What has your philosophy got in the house for supper?

HARDCASTLE [aside]. For supper, sir!—Was ever such a request to a man in his own house!

MARLOW. Yes, sir, supper, sir; I begin to feel an appetite. I shall make devilish work tonight in the larder, I promise you.

HARDCASTLE [aside]. Such a brazen dog, sure, never my eyes beheld. [To him.] Why, really, sir, as for supper I can't well tell. My Dorothy, and the cook maid, settle these things between them. I leave these kind of things entirely to them.

MARLOW. You do, do you?

HARDCASTLE. Entirely. By-the-bye, I believe they are in actual consultation upon what's for supper this moment in the kitchen.

MARLOW. Then I beg they'll admit me as one of their privy council. It's a way I have got. When I travel, I always choose to regulate my own supper. Let the cook be called. No offense, I hope, sir.

HARDCASTLE. O, no, sir, none in the least; yet, I don't know how: our Bridget, the cook maid, is not very communicative upon these occasions. Should we send for her, she might scold us all out of the house.

HASTINGS. Let's see your list of the larder, then. I ask it as a favor. I always match my appetite to my bill of fare.

MARLOW [to HARDCASTLE, who looks at them with surprise]. Sir, he's very right, and it's my way too.

HARDCASTLE. Sir, you have a right to command here. Here, Roger, bring us the bill of fare for tonight's supper. I believe it's drawn out. [Exit ROGER.] Your manner, Mr. Hastings, puts me in mind of my uncle, Colonel Wallop. It was a saying of his that no man was sure of his supper till he had eaten it.

HASTINGS [aside]. All upon the high ropes! His uncle a colonel! We shall soon hear of his mother being a justice of peace. [Re-enter ROGER.] But let's hear the bill of fare.

MARLOW [perusing]. What's here? For the first course; for the second course; for the desert. The devil, sir, do you think we have brought down the whole Joiners Company, or the Corporation of Bedford, to eat up such a supper? Two or three little things, clean and comfortable, will do.

HASTINGS. But let's hear it.

MARLOW [reading]. For the first course, at the top, a pig, and prune sauce.

HASTINGS. Damn your pig, I say!

MARLOW. And damn your prune sauce, say I!

HARDCASTLE. And yet, gentlemen, to men that are hungry pig with prune sauce is very good eating.

MARLOW. At the bottom, a calf's tongue and brains.

HASTINGS. Let your brains be knocked out, my good sir; I don't like them.

MARLOW. Or you may clap them on a plate by themselves. I do.

HARDCASTLE [aside]. Their impudence confounds me. [To them.] Gentlemen, you are my guests, make what alterations you please. Is there anything else you wish to retrench or alter, gentlemen?

MARLOW. Item: a pork pie, a boiled rabbit and sausages, a florentine, a shaking pudding, and a dish of [stammering] tiff—taff—taffety cream!

HASTINGS. Confound your made dishes! I shall be as much at a loss in this house as at a green and yellow dinner at the French Ambassador's table. I'm for plain eating.

HARDCASTLE. I'm sorry, gentlemen, that I have nothing you like, but if there be anything you have a particular fancy to—

MARLOW. Why, really, sir, your bill of fare is so exquisite that any one part of it is full as good as another. Send us what you please. So much for supper. And now to see that our beds are aired and properly taken care of.

HARDCASTLE. I entreat you'll leave all that to me. You shall not stir a step.

MARLOW. Leave that to you! I protest, sir, you must excuse me, I always look to these things myself.

HARDCASTLE. I must insist, sir, you'll make yourself easy on that head.

MARLOW [aside]. You see I'm resolved on it.—A very troublesome fellow this, as ever I met with.

HARDCASTLE [aside]. Well, sir, I'm resolved at least to attend you. This may be modern modesty, but I never saw any thing look so like old-fashioned impudence.

[Exeunt MARLOW and HARDCASTLE.]

[HASTINGS, solus.]

HASTINGS. So I find this fellow's civilities begin to grow troublesome. But who can be angry at those assiduities which are meant to please him? Ha! what do I see? Miss Neville, by all that's happy!

[Enter MISS NEVILLE.]

MISS NEVILLE. My dear Hastings! To what unexpected good fortune, to what accident, am I to ascribe this happy meeting?

HASTINGS. Rather let me ask the same question, as I could never have hoped to meet my dearest Constance at an inn.

MISS NEVILLE. An inn! Sure you mistake! My aunt, my guardian, lives here. What could induce you to think this house an inn?

HASTINGS. My friend, Mr. Marlow, with whom I came down, and I, have been sent here as to an inn, I assure you. A young fellow whom we accidentally met at a house hard by directed us hither.

MISS NEVILLE. Certainly it must be one of my hopeful cousin's tricks, of whom you have heard me talk so often, ha! ha! ha! ha!

HASTINGS. He whom your aunt intends for you? He of whom I have such just apprehensions?

MISS NEVILLE. You have nothing to fear from him, I assure you. You'd adore him if you knew how heartily he despises me. My aunt knows it too, and has undertaken to court me for him, and actually begins to think she has made a conquest.

HASTINGS. Thou dear dissembler! You must know, my Constance, I have just seized this happy opportunity of my friend's visit here to get admittance into the family. The horses that carried us down are now fatigued with their journey, but they'll soon be refreshed; and then, if my dearest girl will trust in her faithful Hastings, we shall soon be landed in France, where even among slaves the laws of marriage are respected.

MISS NEVILLE. I have often told you, that though ready to obey you, I yet should leave my little fortune behind with reluctance. The greatest part of it was left me by my uncle, the India Director, and chiefly consists in jewels. I have been for some time persuading my aunt to let me wear them. I fancy I'm very near succeeding. The instant they are put into my possession you shall find me ready to make them and myself yours.

HASTINGS. Perish the baubles! Your person is all I desire. In the meantime, my friend Marlow must not be let into his mistake. I know the strange reserve of his temper is such that, if abruptly informed of it, he would instantly quit the house before our plan was ripe for execution.

MISS NEVILLE. But how shall we keep him in the deception? Miss Hardcastle is just returned from walking; what if we still continue to deceive him?— This, this way—

[*They confer.*]

[*Enter* MARLOW.]

MARLOW. The assiduities of these good people tease me beyond bearing. My host seems to think it ill manners to leave me alone, and so he claps not only himself but his old-fashioned wife on my back. They talk of coming to sup with us, too; and then, I suppose, we are to run the gauntlet thro' all the rest of the family—What have we got here!—

HASTINGS. My dear Charles! Let me congratulate you!—The most fortunate accident! Who do you think is just alighted?

MARLOW. Cannot guess.

HASTINGS. Our mistresses, boy, Miss Hardcastle and Miss Neville. Give me leave to introduce Miss Constance Neville to your acquaintance. Happening to dine in the neighborhood, they called, on their return, to take fresh horses, here. Miss Hardcastle has just stepped into the next room, and will be back in an instant. Wasn't it lucky? eh!

MARLOW [*aside*]. I have just been mortified enough of all conscience, and here comes something to complete my embarrassment.

HASTINGS. Well! but wasn't it the most fortunate thing in the world?

MARLOW. Oh, yes! Very fortunate—a most joyful encounter—But our dresses, George, you know, are in disorder—What if we should postpone the happiness till tomorrow?—Tomorrow at her own house—It will be

every bit as convenient—And rather more respectful—Tomorrow let
it be.
[*Offering to go.*]

MISS NEVILLE. By no means, sir. Your ceremony will displease her. The
disorder of your dress will show the ardor of your impatience. Besides,
she knows you are in the house, and will permit you to see her.

MARLOW.˙ O, the devil! how shall I support it? Hem! hem! Hastings, you
must not go. You are to assist me, you know. I shall be confoundedly
ridiculous. Yet, hang it, I'll take courage! Hem!

HASTINGS. Pshaw, man, it's but the first plunge, and all's over! She's but a
woman, you know.

MARLOW. And of all women she that I dread most to encounter!

[*Enter* MISS HARDCASTLE, *as returned from walking, a bonnet, etc.*[11]]

HASTINGS [*introducing them*]. Miss Hardcastle, Mr. Marlow; I'm proud of
bringing two persons of such merit together, that only want to know, to
esteem each other.

MISS HARDCASTLE [*aside*]. Now for meeting my modest gentleman with a
demure face, and quite in his own manner. [*After a pause, in which he
appears very uneasy and disconcerted.*] I'm glad of your safe arrival, sir—
I'm told you had some accidents by the way.

MARLOW. Only a few, madam. Yes, we had some. Yes, madam, a good
many accidents, but should be sorry—madam—or rather glad of any
accidents—that are so agreeably concluded. Hem!

HASTINGS [*to him*]. You never spoke better in your whole life. Keep it up,
and I'll insure you the victory.

MISS HARDCASTLE. I'm afraid you flatter, sir. You that have seen so much
of the finest company can find little entertainment in an obscure corner
of the country.

MARLOW [*gathering courage*]. I have lived, indeed, in the world, madam;
but I have kept very little company. I have been but an observer upon
life, madam, while others were enjoying it.

MISS NEVILLE. But that, I am told, is the way to enjoy it at last.

HASTINGS [*to him*]. Cicero never spoke better. Once more, and you are
confirmed in assurance for ever.

MARLOW [*to him*]. Hem! Stand by me, then, and when I'm down, throw in
a word or two to set me up again.

MISS HARDCASTLE. An observer, like you, upon life, were, I fear, disagreeably
employed, since you must have had much more to censure than to
approve.

MARLOW. Pardon me, madam. I was always willing to be amused. The folly
of most people is rather an object of mirth than uneasiness.

HASTINGS [*to him*]. Bravo, bravo. Never spoke so well in your whole life.
Well, Miss Hardcastle, I see that you and Mr. Marlow are going to be

---

[11] At this time it was fashionable to wear a huge bonnet which effectively hid
the face from view.

very good company. I believe our being here will but embarrass the interview.

MARLOW. Not in the least, Mr. Hastings. We like your company of all things. [*To him.*] Zounds, George! sure you won't go? How can you leave us?

HASTINGS. Our presence will but spoil conversation, so we'll retire to the next room. [*To him.*] You don't consider, man, that we are to manage a little *tête-à-tête* of our own.

[*Exeunt* HASTINGS *with* MISS NEVILLE.]

MISS HARDCASTLE [*after a pause*]. But you have not been wholly an observer, I presume, sir. The ladies, I should hope, have employed some part of your addresses.

MARLOW [*relapsing into timidity*]. Pardon me, madam, I—I—I—as yet have studied—only—to—deserve them.

MISS HARDCASTLE. And that, some say, is the very worst way to obtain them.

MARLOW. Perhaps so, madam. But I love to converse only with the more grave and sensible part of the sex—But I'm afraid I grow tiresome.

MISS HARDCASTLE. Not at all, sir; there is nothing I like so much as grave conversation myself: I could hear it for ever. Indeed, I have often been surprised how a man of *sentiment* could ever admire those light, airy pleasures, where nothing reaches the heart.

MARLOW. It's—a disease—of the mind, madam. In the variety of tastes there must be some who, wanting a relish for—um-a-um.

MISS HARDCASTLE. I understand you, sir. There must be some, who, wanting a relish for refined pleasures, pretend to despise what they are incapable of tasting.

MARLOW. My meaning, madam, but infinitely better expressed. And I can't help observing—a—

MISS HARDCASTLE [*aside*]. Who could ever suppose this fellow impudent upon some occasions. [*To him.*] You were going to observe, sir—

MARLOW. I was observing, madam—I protest, madam, I forget what I was going to observe.

MISS HARDCASTLE [*aside*]. I vow and so do I. [*To him.*] You were observing, sir, that in this age of hypocrisy—something about hypocrisy, sir.

MARLOW. Yes, madam. In this age of hypocrisy, there are few who upon strict enquiry do not—a—a—a—

MISS HARDCASTLE. I understand you perfectly, sir.

MARLOW [*aside*]. Egad, and that's more than I do myself!

MISS HARDCASTLE. You mean that in this hypocritical age there are few that do not condemn in public what they practice in private, and think they pay every debt to virtue when they praise it.

MARLOW. True, madam; those who have most virtue in their mouths have least of it in their bosoms. But I'm sure I tire you, madam.

MISS HARDCASTLE. Not in the least, sir; there's something so agreeable and spirited in your manner, such life and force—pray, sir, go on.

MARLOW. Yes, madam. I was saying—that there are some occasions—when a total want of courage, madam, destroys all the—and puts us—upon a—a—a—

MISS HARDCASTLE. I agree with you entirely: a want of courage upon some occasions assumes the appearance of ignorance, and betrays us when we most want to excel. I beg you'll proceed.

MARLOW. Yes, madam. Morally speaking, madam—but I see Miss Neville expecting us in the next room. I would not intrude for the world.

MISS HARDCASTLE. I protest, sir, I never was more agreeably entertained in all my life. Pray, go on.

MARLOW. Yes, madam. I was—but she beckons us to join her. Madam, shall I do myself the honor to attend you?

MISS HARDCASTLE. Well, then, I'll follow.

MARLOW [aside]. This pretty smooth dialogue has done for me.

[Exit.]

[MISS HARDCASTLE, sola.]

MISS HARDCASTLE. Ha! ha! ha! Was there ever such a sober, sentimental interview? I'm certain he scarce looked in my face the whole time. Yet the fellow, but for his unaccountable bashfulness, is pretty well too. He has good sense, but then so buried in his fears that it fatigues one more than ignorance. If I could teach him a little confidence, it would be doing somebody that I know of a piece of service. But who is that somebody?— that, faith, is a question I can scarce answer.

[Exit.]

[Enter TONY and MISS NEVILLE, followed by MRS. HARDCASTLE and HASTINGS.]

TONY. What do you follow me for, Cousin Con? I wonder you're not ashamed to be so very engaging.

MISS NEVILLE. I hope, cousin, one may speak to one's own relations, and not be to blame.

TONY. Aye, but I know what sort of a relation you want to make me, though; but it won't do. I tell you, Cousin Con, it won't do; so I beg you'll keep your distance. I want no nearer relationship.

[She follows, coqueting him, to the back scene.]

MRS. HARDCASTLE. Well! I vow, Mr. Hastings, you are very entertaining. There's nothing in the world I love to talk of so much as London, and the fashions, though I was never there myself.

HASTINGS. Never there! You amaze me! From your air and manner, I concluded you had been bred all your life either at Ranelagh, St. James's, or Tower Wharf.

MRS. HARDCASTLE. O, sir! you're only pleased to say so. We country persons can have no manner at all. I'm in love with the town, and that serves to raise me above some of our neighboring rustics; but who can have a manner that has never seen the Pantheon, the Grotto Gardens, the Borough, and such places where the nobility chiefly resort? All I can do is to enjoy London at second-hand. I take care to know every *tête-à-tête* from the *Scandalous Magazine*, and have all the fashions as they come out, in a letter from the two Miss Rickets of Crooked-lane. Pray how do you like this head,[12] Mr. Hastings?

HASTINGS. Extremely elegant and *degagée*, upon my word, madam. Your friseur is a Frenchman, I suppose?

MRS. HARDCASTLE. I protest, I dressed it myself from a print in the *Ladies Memorandum-book* for the last year.

HASTINGS. Indeed. Such a head in a side-box, at the Play-house, would draw as many gazers as my Lady Mayoress at a City Ball.

MRS. HARDCASTLE. I vow, since inoculation began, there is no such thing to be seen as a plain woman; so one must dress a little particular or one may escape in the crowd.

HASTINGS. But that can never be your case, madam, in any dress! [*Bowing.*]

MRS. HARDCASTLE. Yet, what signifies *my* dressing when I have such a piece of antiquity by my side as Mr. Hardcastle: all I can say will never argue down a single button from his clothes. I have often wanted him to throw off his great flaxen wig, and where he was bald, to plaster it over, like my Lord Pately, with powder.

HASTINGS. You are right, madam: for, as among the ladies there are none ugly, so among the men there are none old.

MRS. HARDCASTLE. But what do you think his answer was? Why, with his usual Gothic vivacity, he said I only wanted him to throw off his wig to convert it into a *tête* for my own wearing!

HASTINGS. Intolerable! At your age you may wear what you please, and it must become you.

MRS. HARDCASTLE. Pray, Mr. Hastings, what do you take to be the most fashionable age about town?

HASTINGS. Some time ago forty was all the mode; but I'm told the ladies intend to bring up fifty for the ensuing winter.

MRS. HARDCASTLE. Seriously? Then I shall be too young for the fashion!

HASTINGS. No lady begins now to put on jewels till she's past forty. For instance, miss there, in a polite circle, would be considered as a child, as a mere maker of samplers.

MRS. HARDCASTLE. And yet Mrs. Niece thinks herself as much a woman, and is as fond of jewels as the oldest of us all.

HASTINGS. Your niece, is she? And that young gentleman,—a brother of yours, I should presume?

MRS. HARDCASTLE. My son, sir. They are contracted to each other. Observe their little sports. They fall in and out ten times a day, as if they were man and wife already. [*To them.*] Well, Tony, child, what soft things are you saying to your Cousin Constance, this evening?

TONY. I have been saying no soft things; but that it's very hard to be

---

[12] Style of dressing the hair.

followed about so. Ecod! I've not a place in the house now that's left
to myself but the stable.

MRS. HARDCASTLE. Never mind him, Con, my dear. He's in another story
behind your back.

MISS NEVILLE. There's something generous in my cousin's manner. He falls
out before faces to be forgiven in private.

TONY. That's a damned confounded—crack.

MRS. HARDCASTLE. Ah, he's a sly one! Don't you think they're like each
other about the mouth, Mr. Hastings? The Blenkinsop mouth to a T.
They're of a size too. Back to back, my pretties, that Mr. Hastings may
see you. Come, Tony.

TONY. You had as good not make me, I tell you.
[*Measuring.*]

MISS NEVILLE. O lud! he has almost cracked my head.

MRS. HARDCASTLE. O, the monster! For shame, Tony. You a man, and
behave so!

TONY. If I'm a man, let me have my fortune. Ecod! I'll not be made a fool
of no longer.

MRS. HARDCASTLE. Is this, ungrateful boy, all that I'm to get for the pains
I have taken in your education? I that have rocked you in your cradle,
and fed that pretty mouth with a spoon! Did not I work that waistcoat
to make you genteel? Did not I prescribe for you every day, and weep
while the receipt was operating?

TONY. Ecod! you had reason to weep, for you have been dosing me ever
since I was born. I have gone through every receipt in the complete
huswife[13] ten times over; and you have thoughts of coursing me through
Quincy next spring. But, ecod! I tell you, I'll not be made a fool of no
longer.

MRS. HARDCASTLE. Wasn't it all for your good, viper? Wasn't it all for
your good?

TONY. I wish you'd let me and my good alone, then. Snubbing this way
when I'm in spirits. If I'm to have any good, let it come of itself; not to
keep dinging it, dinging it into one so.

MRS. HARDCASTLE. That's false; I never see you when you're in spirits.
No, Tony, you then go the alehouse or kennel. I'm never to be delighted
with your agreeable wild notes, unfeeling monster.

TONY. Ecod, Mamma, your own notes are the wildest of the two!

MRS. HARDCASTLE. Was ever the like? But I see he wants to break my heart,
I see he does.

HASTINGS. Dear madam, permit me to lecture the young gentleman a little.
I'm certain I can persuade him to his duty.

MRS. HARDCASTLE. Well! I must retire. Come Constance, my love. You see,

---

[13] A manual of hints for homemakers containing, among other things,
remedies for common ailments.

Mr. Hastings, the wretchedness of my situation. Was ever poor woman so plagued with a dear, sweet, pretty, provoking, undutiful boy.

[*Exeunt* MRS. HARDCASTLE *and* MISS NEVILLE.]

TONY [*singing*]. *There was a young man riding by, and fain would have his will. Rang do didlo dee.* Don't mind her. Let her cry. It's the comfort of her heart. I have seen her and sister cry over a book for an hour together, and they said they liked the book the better the more it made them cry.

HASTINGS. Then you're no friend to the ladies, I find, my pretty young gentleman?

TONY. That's as I find 'um.

HASTINGS. Not to her of your mother's choosing, I dare answer? And yet she appears to me a pretty, well-tempered girl.

TONY. That's because you don't know her as well as I. Ecod! I know every inch about her; and there's not a more bitter, cantankerous toad in all Christendom!

HASTINGS [*aside*]. Pretty encouragement, this, for a lover!

TONY. I have seen her since the height of that. She has as many tricks as a hare in a thicket, or a colt the first day's breaking.

HASTINGS. To me she appears sensible and silent!

TONY. Aye, before company. But when she's with her playmates, she's as loud as a hog in a gate.

HASTINGS. But there is a meek modesty about her that charms me.

TONY. Yes, but curb her never so little, she kicks up, and you're flung in a ditch.

HASTINGS. Well, but you must allow her a little beauty.—Yes, you must allow her some beauty.

TONY. Bandbox! She's all a made up thing, mun. Ah! could you but see Bet Bouncer of these parts, you might then talk of beauty. Ecod, she has two eyes as black as sloes, and cheeks as broad and red as a pulpit cushion. She'd make two of she.

HASTINGS. Well, what say you to a friend that would take this bitter bargain off your hands?

TONY. Anon.

HASTINGS. Would you thank him that would take Miss Neville, and leave you to happiness and your dear Betsy?

TONY. Aye; but where is there such a friend, for who would take *her?*

HASTINGS. I am he. If you but assist me, I'll engage to whip her off to France, and you shall never hear more of her.

TONY. Assist you! Ecod, I will, to the last drop of my blood. I'll clap a pair of horses to your chaise that shall trundle you off in a twinkling, and maybe get you a part of her fortune besides, in jewels, that you little dream of.

HASTINGS. My dear Squire, this looks like a lad of spirit.

TONY. Come along then, and you shall see more of my spirit before you have done with me.

[*Singing.*]
> We are the boys
> That fears no noise
> Where the thundering cannons roar.

[*Exeunt.*]

ACT THREE

The house.

[*Enter* HARDCASTLE, *solus.*]

HARDCASTLE. What could my old friend Sir Charles mean by recommending his son as the modestest young man in town? To me he appears the most impudent piece of brass that ever spoke with a tongue. He has taken possession of the easy chair by the fireside already. He took off his boots in the parlor, and desired me to see them taken care of. I'm desirous to know how his impudence affects my daughter.—She will certainly be shocked at it.

[*Enter* MISS HARDCASTLE, *plainly dressed.*]

HARDCASTLE. Well, my Kate, I see you have changed your dress as I bid you; and yet, I believe, there was no great occasion.

MISS HARDCASTLE. I find such a pleasure, sir, in obeying your commands, that I take care to observe them without ever debating their propriety.

HARDCASTLE. And yet, Kate, I sometimes give you some cause, particularly when I recommended my *modest* gentleman to you as a lover today.

MISS HARDCASTLE. You taught me to expect something extraordinary, and I find the original exceeds the description!

HARDCASTLE. I was never so surprised in my life! He has quite confounded all my faculties!

MISS HARDCASTLE. I never saw any thing like it! And a man of the world, too!

HARDCASTLE. Aye, he learned it all abroad,—what a fool was I, to think a young man could learn modesty by traveling. He might as soon learn wit at a masquerade.

MISS HARDCASTLE. It seems all natural to him.

HARDCASTLE. A good deal assisted by bad company and a French dancing-master!

MISS HARDCASTLE. Sure, you mistake, papa! a French dancing-master could never have taught him that timid look,—that awkward address,—that bashful manner—

HARDCASTLE. Whose look, whose manner, child?

MISS HARDCASTLE. Mr. Marlow's: his *mauvaise honte*, his timidity struck me at the first sight.

HARDCASTLE. Then your first sight deceived you; for I think him one of the most brazen first sights that ever astonished my senses!

MISS HARDCASTLE. Sure, sir, you rally! I never saw any one so modest.

HARDCASTLE. And can you be serious! I never saw such a bouncing, swaggering puppy since I was born. Bully Dawson was but a fool to him.

MISS HARDCASTLE. Surprising! He met me with a respectful bow, a stammering voice, and a look fixed on the ground.

HARDCASTLE. He met me with a loud voice, a lordly air, and a familiarity that made my blood freeze again.

MISS HARDCASTLE. He treated me with diffidence and respect; censured the manners of the age; admired the prudence of girls that never laughed; tired me with apologies for being tiresome; then left the room with a bow, and, "Madam, I would not for the world detain you."

HARDCASTLE. He spoke to me as if he knew me all his life before. Asked twenty questions, and never waited for an answer. Interrupted my best remarks with some silly pun, and when I was in my best story of the Duke of Marlborough and Prince Eugene, he asked if I had not a good hand at making punch. Yes, Kate, he asked your father if he was a maker of punch!

MISS HARDCASTLE. One of us must certainly be mistaken.

HARDCASTLE. If he be what he has shown himself, I'm determined he shall never have my consent.

MISS HARDCASTLE. And if he be the sullen thing I take him, he shall never have mine.

HARDCASTLE. In one thing then we are agreed—to reject him.

MISS HARDCASTLE. Yes. But upon conditions. For if you should find him less impudent, and I more presuming; if you find him more respectful, and I more importunate—I don't know—the fellow is well enough for a man—Certainly we don't meet many such at a horse race in the country.

HARDCASTLE. If we should find him so—But that's impossible. The first appearance has done my business. I'm seldom deceived in that.

MISS HARDCASTLE. And yet there may be many good qualities under that first appearance.

HARDCASTLE. Aye, when a girl finds a fellow's outside to her taste, she then sets about guessing the rest of his furniture. With her, a smooth face stands for good sense, and a genteel figure for every virtue.

MISS HARDCASTLE. I hope, sir, a conversation begun with a compliment to my good sense won't end with a sneer at my understanding?

HARDCASTLE. Pardon me, Kate. But if young Mr. Brazen can find the art of reconciling contradictions, he may please us both, perhaps.

MISS HARDCASTLE. And as one of us must be mistaken, what if we go to make further discoveries?

HARDCASTLE. Agreed. But depend on it I'm in the right.

MISS HARDCASTLE. And depend on it I'm not much in the wrong.

[*Exeunt.*]

[*Enter* TONY, *running in with a casket.*]

TONY. Ecod! I have got them. Here they are. My Cousin Con's necklaces, bobs and all. My mother shan't cheat the poor souls out of their fortune neither. O, my genus! is that you?

[*Enter* HASTINGS.]

HASTINGS. My dear friend, how have you managed with your mother? I hope you have amused her with pretending love for your cousin, and that you are willing to be reconciled at last? Our horses will be refreshed in a short time, and we shall soon be ready to set off.

TONY. And here's something to bear your charges by the way,–[*giving the casket*] your sweetheart's jewels. Keep them, and hang those, I say, that would rob you of one of them!

HASTINGS. But how have you procured them from your mother?

TONY. Ask me no questions, and I'll tell you no fibs. I procured them by the rule of thumb. If I had not a key to every drawer in mother's bureau, how could I go to the alehouse so often as I do? An honest man may rob himself of his own at any time.

HASTINGS. Thousands do it every day. But to be plain with you; Miss Neville is endeavoring to procure them from her aunt this very instant. If she succeeds, it will be the most delicate way at least of obtaining them.

TONY. Well, keep them, till you know how it will be. But I know how it will be well enough; she'd as soon part with the only sound tooth in her head!

HASTINGS. But I dread the effects of her resentment when she finds she has lost them.

TONY. Never you mind her resentment, leave *me* to manage that. I don't value her resentment the bounce of a cracker. Zounds! here they are! Morrice, Prance!

[*Exit* HASTINGS.]

[*Enter* MRS. HARDCASTLE *and* MISS NEVILLE.]

MRS. HARDCASTLE. Indeed, Constance, you amaze me. Such a girl as you want jewels? It will be time enough for jewels, my dear, twenty years hence, when your beauty begins to want repairs.

MISS NEVILLE. But what will repair beauty at forty will certainly improve it at twenty, madam.

MRS. HARDCASTLE. Yours, my dear, can admit of none. That natural blush is beyond a thousand ornaments. Besides, child, jewels are quite out at present. Don't you see half the ladies of our acquaintance, my Lady Kill-daylight, and Mrs. Crump, and the rest of them, carry their jewels to town, and bring nothing but paste and marcasites back?

MISS NEVILLE. But who knows, madam, but somebody that shall be nameless would like me best with all my little finery about me?

MRS. HARDCASTLE. Consult your glass, my dear, and then see, if with such a pair of eyes, you want any better sparklers. What do you think, Tony, my dear, does your Cousin Con want any jewels, in your eyes, to set off her beauty?

TONY. That's as thereafter may be.

MISS NEVILLE. My dear aunt, if you knew how it would oblige me.

MRS. HARDCASTLE. A parcel of old-fashioned rose and table-cut things. They would make you look like the court of King Solomon at a puppet-show. Besides, I believe I can't readily come at them. They may be missing, for aught I know to the contrary.

TONY [*apart to* MRS. HARDCASTLE]. Then why don't you tell her so at once, as she's so longing for them. Tell her they're lost. It's the only way to quiet her. Say they're lost, and call me to bear witness.

MRS. HARDCASTLE [*apart to* TONY]. You know, my dear, I'm only keeping them for you. So if I say they're gone, you'll bear me witness, will you? He! he! he!

TONY [*apart to* MRS. HARDCASTLE]. Never fear me. Ecod! I'll say I saw them taken out with my own eyes.

MISS NEVILLE. I desire them but for a day, madam. Just to be permitted to show them as relics, and then they may be locked up again.

MRS. HARDCASTLE. To be plain with you, my dear Constance, if I could find them, you should have them. They're missing, I assure you. Lost, for aught I know; but we must have patience wherever they are.

MISS NEVILLE. I'll not believe it; this is but a shallow pretence to deny me. I know they're too valuable to be so slightly kept, and as you are to answer for the loss.

MRS. HARDCASTLE. Don't be alarmed, Constance. If they be lost, I must restore an equivalent. But my son knows they are missing, and not to be found.

TONY. That I can bear witness to. They are missing, and not to be found, I'll take my oath on it.

MRS. HARDCASTLE. You must learn resignation, my dear; for tho' we lose our fortune, yet we should not lose our patience. See me, how calm I am.

MISS NEVILLE. Aye, people are generally calm at the misfortunes of others.

MRS. HARDCASTLE. Now, I wonder a girl of your good sense should waste a thought upon such trumpery. We shall soon find them; and, in the meantime, you shall make use of my garnets till your jewels be found.

MISS NEVILLE. I detest garnets!

MRS. HARDCASTLE. The most becoming things in the world to set off a clear complexion. You have often seen how well they look upon me. You *shall* have them.

[*Exit.*]

MISS NEVILLE. I dislike them of all things. You shan't stir.—Was ever anything so provoking,—to mislay my own jewels, and force me to wear her trumpery.

TONY. Don't be a fool. If she gives you the garnets, take what you can get. The jewels are your own already. I have stolen them out of her bureau, and she does not know it. Fly to your spark, he'll tell you more of the matter. Leave me to manage *her*.

MISS NEVILLE. My dear cousin!

TONY. Vanish. She's here, and has missed them already. [*Exit* MISS

NEVILLE.] Zounds! how she fidgets and spits about like a Catherine wheel.
[*Enter* MRS. HARDCASTLE.]

MRS. HARDCASTLE. Confusion! thieves! robbers! We are cheated, plundered, broke open, undone!

TONY. What's the matter, what's the matter, mamma? I hope nothing has happened to any of the good family!

MRS. HARDCASTLE. We are robbed. My bureau has been broke open, the jewels taken out, and I'm undone!

TONY. Oh! is that all? Ha! ha! ha! By the laws, I never saw it better acted in my life. Ecod, I thought you was ruined in earnest, ha, ha, ha!

MRS. HARDCASTLE. Why, boy, I *am* ruined in earnest. My bureau has been broke open, and all taken away.

TONY. Stick to that; ha, ha, ha! stick to that. I'll bear witness, you know, call me to bear witness.

MRS. HARDCASTLE. I tell you, Tony, by all that's precious, the jewels are gone, and I shall be ruined for ever.

TONY. Sure I know they're gone, and I am to say so.

MRS. HARDCASTLE. My dearest Tony, but hear me. They're gone, I say.

TONY. By the laws, mamma, you make me for to laugh, ha! ha! I know who took them well enough, ha! ha! ha!

MRS. HARDCASTLE. Was there ever such a blockhead, that can't tell the difference between jest and earnest. I tell you I'm not in jest, booby!

TONY. That's right, that's right! You must be in a bitter passion, and then nobody will suspect either of us. I'll bear witness that they are gone.

MRS. HARDCASTLE. Was there ever such a cross-grained brute, that won't hear me! Can you bear witness that you're no better than a fool? Was ever poor woman so beset with fools on one hand, and thieves on the other?

TONY. I can bear witness to that.

MRS. HARDCASTLE. Bear witness again, you blockhead, you, and I'll turn you out of the room directly. My poor niece, what will become of *her*! Do you laugh, you unfeeling brute, as if you enjoyed my distress?

TONY. I can bear witness to that.

MRS. HARDCASTLE. Do you insult me, monster? I'll teach you to vex your mother, I will!

TONY. I can bear witness to that.
[*He runs off; she follows him.*]
[*Enter* MISS HARDCASTLE *and* MAID.]

MISS HARDCASTLE. What an unaccountable creature is that brother of mine, to send them to the house as an inn, ha! ha! I don't wonder at his impudence.

MAID. But what is more, madam, the young gentleman as you passed by in your present dress, asked me if you were the barmaid? He mistook you for the barmaid, madam!

MISS HARDCASTLE. Did he? Then as I live I'm resolved to keep up the delusion. Tell me, Pimple, how do you like my present dress? Don't you think I look something like Cherry in the *Beaux' Stratagem*?[14]

MAID. It's the dress, madam, that every lady wears in the country, but when she visits or receives company.

MISS HARDCASTLE. And are you sure he does not remember my face or person?

MAID. Certain of it!

MISS HARDCASTLE. I vow, I thought so; for though we spoke for some time together, yet his fears were such that he never once looked up during the interview. Indeed, if he had, my bonnet would have kept him from seeing me.

MAID. But what do you hope from keeping him in his mistake?

MISS HARDCASTLE. In the first place, I shall be *seen*, and that is no small advantage to a girl who brings her face to market. Then I shall perhaps make an acquaintance, and that's no small victory gained over one who never addresses any but the wildest of her sex. But my chief aim is to take my gentleman off his guard, and like an invisible champion of romance examine the giant's force before I offer to combat.

MAID. But are you sure you can act your part, and disguise your voice, so that he may mistake that, as he has already mistaken your person?

MISS HARDCASTLE. Never fear me. I think I have got the true bar cant.—Did your honor call?—Attend the Lion there.—Pipes and tobacco for the Angel.—The Lamb[15] has been outrageous this half hour!

MAID. It will do, madam. But he's here.

[*Exit* MAID.]

[*Enter* MARLOW.]

MARLOW. What a bawling in every part of the house; I have scarce a moment's repose. If I go to the best room, there I find my host and his story. If I fly to the gallery, there we have my hostess with her courtesy down to the ground. I have at last got a moment to myself, and now for recollection.

[*Walks and muses.*]

MISS HARDCASTLE. Did you call, sir? Did your honor call?

MARLOW [*musing*]. As for Miss Hardcastle, she's too grave and sentimental for me.

MISS HARDCASTLE. Did your honor call?

[*She still places herself before him, he turning away.*]

MARLOW. No, child! [*Musing.*] Besides, from the glimpse I had of her, I think she squints.

MISS HARDCASTLE. I'm sure, sir, I heard the bell ring.

MARLOW. No, no! [*Musing.*] I have pleased my father, however, by coming down, and I'll tomorrow please myself by returning.

[*Taking out his tablets, and perusing.*]

14 In Farquhar's comedy (1707), Cherry is an innkeeper's daughter
15 It was the custom to give names to inn-rooms, hence Lion, Angel, and Lamb.

MISS HARDCASTLE. Perhaps the other gentleman called, sir?

MARLOW. I tell you no.

MISS HARDCASTLE. I should be glad to know, sir. We have such a parcel of servants.

MARLOW. No, no, I tell you. [*Looks full in her face.*] Yes, child, I think I did call. I wanted—I wanted—I vow, child, you are vastly handsome!

MISS HARDCASTLE. O la, sir, you'll make one ashamed.

MARLOW. Never saw a more sprightly, malicious eye. Yes, yes, my dear, I did call. Have you got any of your—a—what d'ye call it in the house?

MISS HARDCASTLE. No, sir, we have been out of that these ten days.

MARLOW. One may call in this house, I find, to very little purpose. Suppose I should call for a taste, just by way of trial, of the nectar of your lips; perhaps I might be disappointed in that, too?

MISS HARDCASTLE. Nectar? nectar? that's a liquor there's no call for in these parts. French, I suppose. We keep no French wines here, sir.

MARLOW. Of true English growth, I assure you.

MISS HARDCASTLE. Then it's odd I should not know it. We brew all sorts of wines in this house, and I have lived here these eighteen years.

MARLOW. Eighteen years! Why one would think, child, you kept the bar before you were born. How old are you?

MISS HARDCASTLE. O! sir, I must not tell my age. They say women and music should never be dated.

MARLOW. To guess at this distance, you can't be much above forty. [*Approaching.*] Yet nearer, I don't think so much. [*Approaching.*] By coming close to some women, they look younger still; but when we come very close indeed—

[*Attempting to kiss her.*]

MISS HARDCASTLE. Pray, sir, keep your distance. One would think you wanted to know one's age as they do horses, by mark of mouth.

MARLOW. I protest, child, you use me extremely ill. If you keep me at this distance, how is it possible you and I can be ever acquainted?

MISS HARDCASTLE. And who wants to be acquainted with you? I want no such acquaintance, not I. I'm sure you did not treat Miss Hardcastle that was here awhile ago in this obstropalous manner. I'll warrant me, before her you looked dashed, and kept bowing to the ground, and talked, for all the world, as if you was before a justice of peace.

MARLOW [*aside*]. Egad! she has hit it, sure enough. [*To her.*] In awe of her, child? Ha! ha! ha! A mere awkward, squinting thing! No, no! I find you don't know me. I laughed, and rallied her a little; but I was unwilling to be too severe. No, I could not be too severe, curse me!

MISS HARDCASTLE. O! then, sir, you are a favorite, I find, among the ladies?

MARLOW. Yes, my dear, a great favorite. And yet, hang me, I don't see what they find in me to follow. At the Ladies Club in town I'm called their agreeable Rattle. Rattle, child, is not my real name, but one I'm

known by. My name is Solomons. Mr. Solomons, my dear, at your service.
[*Offering to salute her.*]
MISS HARDCASTLE. Hold, sir; you were introducing me to your club, not to yourself. And you're so great a favorite there you say?
MARLOW. Yes, my dear. There's Mrs. Mantrap, Lady Betty Blackleg, the Countess of Sligo, Mrs. Longhorns, old Miss Biddy Buckskin, and your humble servant, keep up the spirit of the place.
MISS HARDCASTLE. Then it's a very merry place, I suppose.
MARLOW. Yes, as merry as cards, suppers, wine, and old women can make us.
MISS HARDCASTLE. And their agreeable Rattle, ha! ha! ha!
MARLOW [*aside*]. Egad! I don't quite like this chit. She looks knowing, methinks. You laugh, child!
MISS HARDCASTLE. I can't but laugh to think what time they all have for minding their work or their family.
MARLOW [*aside*]. All's well, she don't laugh at me. [*To her.*] Do *you* ever work, child?
MISS HARDCASTLE. Aye, sure. There's not a screen or a quilt in the whole house but what can bear witness to that.
MARLOW. Odso! Then you must show me your embroidery. I embroider and draw patterns myself a little. If you want a judge of your work you must apply to me.
[*Seizing her hand.*]
[*Enter* HARDCASTLE, *who stands in surprise.*]
MISS HARDCASTLE. Aye, but the colors don't look well by candlelight. You shall see all in the morning.
[*Struggling.*]
MARLOW. And why not now, my angel? Such beauty fires beyond the power of resistance.—Pshaw! the father here! My old luck: I never nicked seven[16] that I did not throw ames-ace[17] three times following.
[*Exit* MARLOW.]
HARDCASTLE. So, madam! So I find *this* is your *modest* lover. This is your humble admirer that kept his eyes fixed on the ground, and only adored at humble distance. Kate, Kate, art thou not ashamed to deceive your father so?
MISS HARDCASTLE. Never trust me, dear papa, but he's still the modest man I first took him for; you'll be convinced of it as well as I.
HARDCASTLE. By the hand of my body, I believe his impudence is infectious! Didn't I see him seize your hand? Didn't I see him haul you about like a milkmaid? And now you talk of his respect and his modesty, forsooth!
MISS HARDCASTLE. But if I shortly convince you of his modesty, that he has

---

16 i.e., throw a "lucky seven" in dicing.
17 "Snake-eyes," the lowest possible throw of the dice.

only the faults that will pass off with time, and the virtues that will improve with age, I hope you'll forgive him.

HARDCASTLE. The girl would actually make one run mad! I tell you I'll not be convinced. I am convinced. He has scarcely been three hours in the house, and he has already encroached on all my prerogatives. You may like his impudence, and call it modesty. But my son-in-law, madam, must have very different qualifications.

MISS HARDCASTLE. Sir, I ask but this night to convince you.

HARDCASTLE. You shall not have half the time, for I have thoughts of turning him out this very hour.

MISS HARDCASTLE. Give me that hour then, and I hope to satisfy you.

HARDCASTLE. Well, an hour let it be then. But I'll have no trifling with your father. All fair and open, do you mind me?

MISS HARDCASTLE. I hope, sir, you have ever found that I considered your commands as my pride; for your kindness is such that my duty as yet has been inclination.

[*Exeunt.*]

ACT FOUR

The house.

[*Enter* HASTINGS *and* MISS NEVILLE.]

HASTINGS. You surprise me! Sir Charles Marlow expected here this night? Where have you had your information?

MISS NEVILLE. You may depend upon it. I just saw his letter to Mr. Hardcastle, in which he tells him he intends setting out a few hours after his son.

HASTINGS. Then, my Constance, all must be completed before he arrives. He knows me; and should he find me here, would discover my name, and perhaps my designs, to the rest of the family.

MISS NEVILLE. The jewels, I hope, are safe.

HASTINGS. Yes, yes. I have sent them to Marlow, who keeps the keys of our baggage. In the meantime, I'll go to prepare matters for our elopement. I have had the Squire's promise of a fresh pair of horses; and, if I should not see him again, will write him further directions.

[*Exit.*]

MISS NEVILLE. Well, success attend you! In the meantime, I'll go amuse my aunt with the old pretense of a violent passion for my cousin.

[*Exit.*]

[*Enter* MARLOW, *followed by a* SERVANT.]

MARLOW. I wonder what Hastings could mean by sending me so valuable a thing as a casket to keep for him, when he knows the only place I have is the seat of a post-coach at an inn-door. Have you deposited the casket with the landlady, as I ordered you? Have you put it into her own hands?

SERVANT. Yes, your honor.

MARLOW. She said she'd keep it safe, did she?

SERVANT. Yes, she said she'd keep it safe enough; she asked me how I came by it, and she said she had a great mind to make me give an account of myself.

[*Exit* SERVANT.]

MARLOW. Ha! Ha! Ha! They're safe, however. What an unaccountable set of beings have we got amongst! This little barmaid, though, runs in my head most strangely, and drives out the absurdities of all the rest of the family. She's mine, she must be mine, or I'm greatly mistaken!

[*Enter* HASTINGS.]

HASTINGS. Bless me! I quite forgot to tell her that I intended to prepare at the bottom of the garden. Marlow here, and in spirits too!

MARLOW. Give me joy, George! Crown me, shadow me with laurels! Well, George, after all, we modest fellows don't want for success among the women.

HASTINGS. Some women, you mean. But what success has your honor's modesty been crowned with now that it grows so insolent upon us?

MARLOW. Didn't you see the tempting, brisk, lovely little thing that runs about the house with a bunch of keys to its girdle?

HASTINGS. Well! and what then?

MARLOW. She's mine, you rogue, you. Such fire, such motion, such eyes. such lips—but egad! she would not let me kiss them though.

HASTINGS. But are you sure, so very sure of her?

MARLOW. Why, man, she talked of showing me her work above-stairs, and I am to improve the pattern.

HASTINGS. But how can *you*, Charles, go about to rob a woman of her honor?

MARLOW. Pshaw! pshaw! we all know the honor of the barmaid of an inn. I don't intend to *rob* her, take my word for it; there's nothing in this house, I shan't honestly *pay* for!

HASTINGS. I believe the girl has virtue.

MARLOW. And if she has, I should be the last man in the world that would attempt to corrupt it.

HASTINGS. You have taken care, I hope, of the casket I sent you to lock up? It's in safety?

MARLOW. Yes, yes. It's safe enough. I have taken care of it. But how could you think the seat of a post-coach at an inn-door a place of safety? Ah! numbskull! I have taken better precautions for you than you did for yourself.—I have—

HASTINGS. What!

MARLOW. I have sent it to the landlady to keep for you.

HASTINGS. To the landlady!

MARLOW. The landlady.

HASTINGS. You did!

MARLOW. I did. She's to be answerable for its forthcoming, you know.

HASTINGS. Yes, she'll bring it forth with a witness.

MARLOW. Wasn't I right? I believe you'll allow that I acted prudently upon this occasion?

HASTINGS [aside]. He must not see my uneasiness.

MARLOW. You seem a little disconcerted, though, methinks. Sure nothing has happened?

HASTINGS. No, nothing. Never was in better spirits in all my life. And so you left it with the landlady, who, no doubt, very readily undertook the charge?

MARLOW. Rather too readily. For she not only kept the casket, but, thro' her great precaution, was going to keep the messenger too. Ha! ha! ha!

HASTINGS. He! he! he! They're safe, however.

MARLOW. As a guinea in a miser's purse.

HASTINGS [aside]. So now all hopes of fortune are at an end, and we must set off without it. [To him.] Well, Charles, I'll leave you to your meditations on the pretty barmaid, and, he! he! he! may you be as successful for yourself as you have been for me.
[Exit.]

MARLOW. Thank ye, George! I ask no more. Ha! ha! ha!
[Enter HARDCASTLE.]

HARDCASTLE. I no longer know my own house. It's turned all topsy-turvy. His servants have got drunk already. I'll bear it no longer,—and yet, from my respect for his father, I'll be calm. [To him.] Mr. Marlow, your servant. I'm your very humble servant.
[Bowing low.]

MARLOW. Sir, your humble servant. [Aside.] What's to be the wonder now?

HARDCASTLE. I believe, sir, you must be sensible, sir, that no man alive ought to be more welcome than your father's son, sir. I hope you think so?

MARLOW. I do, from my soul, sir. I don't want much entreaty. I generally make my father's son welcome wherever he goes.

HARDCASTLE. I believe you do, from my soul, sir. But tho' I say nothing to your own conduct, that of your servants is insufferable. Their manner of drinking is setting a very bad example in this house, I assure you.

MARLOW. I protest, my very good sir, that's no fault of mine. If they don't drink as they ought, *they* are to blame. I ordered them not to spare the cellar; I did, I assure you. [To the side scene.] Here let one of my servants come up. [To him.] My positive directions were, that as I did not drink myself, they should make up for my deficiencies below.

HARDCASTLE. Then they had your orders for what they do! I'm satisfied!

MARLOW. They had, I assure you. You shall hear from one of themselves.
[Enter SERVANT, drunk.]

MARLOW. You, Jeremy! Come forward, sirrah! What were my orders? Were you not told to drink freely, and call for what you thought fit, for the good of the house?

HARDCASTLE [*aside*]. I begin to lose my patience.

JEREMY. Please your honor, liberty and Fleet-street forever! Tho' I'm but a servant, I'm as good as another man. I'll drink for no man before supper, sir, dammy! Good liquor will sit upon a good supper, but a good supper will not sit upon—hiccup—upon my conscience, sir. [*Exit* JEREMY.]

MARLOW. You see, my old friend, the fellow is as drunk as he can possibly be. I don't know what you'd have more, unless you'd have the poor devil soused in a beer-barrel.

HARDCASTLE. Zounds! He'll drive me distracted if I contain myself any longer. Mr. Marlow. Sir; I have submitted to your insolence for more than four hours, and I see no likelihood of its coming to an end. I'm now resolved to be master here, sir, and I desire that you and your drunken pack may leave my house directly.

MARLOW. Leave your house!—Sure, you jest, my good friend! What, when I'm doing what I can to please you!

HARDCASTLE. I tell you, sir, you don't please me; so I desire you'll leave my house.

MARLOW. Sure, you cannot be serious! At this time of night, and such a night! You only mean to banter me?

HARDCASTLE. I tell you, sir, I'm serious; and, now that my passions are roused, I say this house is mine, sir; this house is mine, and I command you to leave it directly.

MARLOW. Ha! ha! ha! A puddle in a storm. I shan't stir a step, I assure you. [*In a serious tone.*] This your house, fellow! It's my house. This is my house. Mine, while I choose to stay. What right have you to bid me leave this house, sir? I never met with such impudence, curse me, never in my whole life before!

HARDCASTLE. Nor I, confound me if ever I did! To come to my house, to call for what he likes, to turn me out of my own chair, to insult the family, to order his servants to get drunk, and then to tell me,—*This house is mine, sir*. But all that's impudent, it makes me laugh. Ha! ha! ha! Pray, sir, [*bantering*] as you take the house, what think you of taking the rest of the furniture? There's a pair of silver candlesticks, and there's a fire screen, and here's a pair of brazen-nosed bellows, perhaps you may take a fancy to them?

MARLOW. Bring me your bill, sir, bring me your bill, and let's make no more words about it.

HARDCASTLE. There are a set of prints too. What think you of the *Rake's Progress* for your own apartment?

MARLOW. Bring me your bill, I say; and I'll leave you and your infernal house directly.

HARDCASTLE. Then there's a mahogany table, that you may see your face in.

MARLOW. My bill, I say.

HARDCASTLE. I had forgot the great chair, for your own particular slumbers, after a hearty meal.

MARLOW. Zounds! Bring me my bill, I say, and let's hear no more on it.

HARDCASTLE. Young man, young man, from your father's letter to me, I was taught to expect a well-bred, modest man as a visitor here, but now I find him no better than a coxcomb and a bully; but he will be down here presently, and shall hear more of it.

[*Exit.*]

MARLOW. How's this! Sure, I have not mistaken the house? Every thing looks like an inn. The servants cry "Coming." The attendance is awkward; the barmaid, too, to attend us. But she's here, and will further inform me.

[*Enter* MISS HARDCASTLE.]

MARLOW. Whither so fast, child? A word with you.

MISS HARDCASTLE. Let it be short, then. I'm in a hurry.—[*Aside.*] I believe he begins to find out his mistake, but it's too soon quite to undeceive him.

MARLOW. Pray, child, answer me one question. What are you, and what may your business in this house be?

MISS HARDCASTLE. A relation of the family, sir.

MARLOW. What! A poor relation?

MISS HARDCASTLE. Yes, sir. A poor relation appointed to keep the keys, and to see that the guests want nothing in my power to give them.

MARLOW. That is, you act as the barmaid of this inn.

MISS HARDCASTLE. Inn! O law!—What brought that in your head? One of the best families in the county keep an inn! Ha, ha, ha, old Mr. Hardcastle's house an inn!

MARLOW. Mr. Hardcastle's house! Is this house Mr. Hardcastle's house, child?

MISS HARDCASTLE. Aye, sure. Whose else should it be?

MARLOW. So then all's out, and I have been damnably imposed on. O, confound my stupid head, I shall be laughed at over the whole town. I shall be stuck up in caricatura in all the printshops. The Dullissimo Maccaroni.[18] To mistake this house of all others for an inn, and my father's old friend for an innkeeper! What a swaggering puppy must he take me for! What a silly puppy do I find myself! There again, may I be hanged, my dear, but I mistook you for the barmaid!

MISS HARDCASTLE. Dear me! dear me! I'm sure there's nothing in my *behavior* to put me upon a level with one of that stamp.

MARLOW. Nothing, my dear, nothing. But I was in for a list of blunders, and could not help making you a subscriber. My stupidity saw every thing the wrong way. I mistook your assiduity for assurance, and your simplicity for allurement. But it's over—this house I no more show *my* face in!

MISS HARDCASTLE. I hope, sir, I have done nothing to disoblige you. I'm

18 In current slang, a macaroni was a fop or dandy.

sure I should be sorry to affront any gentleman who has been so polite, and said so many civil things to me. I'm sure I should be sorry [*pretending to cry*] if he left the family upon my account. I'm sure I should be sorry people said anything amiss, since I have no fortune but my character.

MARLOW [*aside*]. By heaven, she weeps! This is the first mark of tenderness I ever had from a modest woman, and it touches me. [*To her.*] Excuse me, my lovely girl, you are the only part of the family I leave with reluctance. But to be plain with you, the difference of our birth, fortune and education, make an honorable connection impossible; and I can never harbor a thought of seducing simplicity that trusted in my honor, or bring ruin upon one whose only fault was being too lovely.

MISS HARDCASTLE [*aside*]. Generous man! I now begin to admire him. [*To him.*] But I'm sure my family is as good as Miss Hardcastle's, and though I'm poor, that's no great misfortune to a contented mind, and, until this moment, I never thought that it was bad to want[19] fortune.

MARLOW. And why now, my pretty simplicity?

MISS HARDCASTLE. Because it puts me at a distance from one that if I had a thousand pound I would give it all to.

MARLOW [*aside*]. This simplicity bewitches me, so that if I stay I'm undone. I must make one bold effort, and leave her. [*To her.*] Your partiality in my favor, my dear, touches me most sensibly, and were I to live for myself alone, I could easily fix my choice. But I owe too much to the opinion of the world, too much to the authority of a father, so that—I can scarcely speak of it—it affects me! Farewell!
[*Exit.*]

MISS HARDCASTLE. I never knew half his merit till now. He shall not go, if I have power or art to detain him. I'll still preserve the character in which I stooped to conquer, but will undeceive my papa, who, perhaps, may laugh him out of his resolution.
[*Exit.*]
[*Enter* TONY, MISS NEVILLE.]

TONY. Aye, you may steal for yourselves the next time. I have done my duty. She has got the jewels again, that's a sure thing; but she believes it was all a mistake of the servants.

MISS NEVILLE. But, my dear cousin, sure you won't forsake us in this distress. If she in the least suspects that I am going off, I shall certainly be locked up, or sent to my Aunt Pedigree's, which is ten times worse.

TONY. To be sure, aunts of all kinds are damned bad things. But what can I do? I have got you a pair of horses that will fly like Whistlejacket, and I'm sure you can't say but I have courted you nicely before her face. Here she comes; we must court a bit or two more, for fear she should suspect us. [*They retire, and seem to fondle.*]
[*Enter* MRS. HARDCASTLE.]

[19] i.e., lack.

MRS. HARDCASTLE. Well, I was greatly fluttered, to be sure. But my son tells me it was all a mistake of the servants. I shan't be easy, however, till they are fairly married, and then let her keep her own fortune. But what do I see! Fondling together, as I'm alive! I never saw Tony so sprightly before. Ah, have I caught you, my pretty doves? What, billing, exchanging stolen glances, and broken murmurs! Ah!

TONY. As for murmurs, mother, we grumble a little now and then, to be sure. But there's no love lost between us.

MRS. HARDCASTLE. A mere sprinkling, Tony, upon the flame, only to make it burn brighter.

MISS NEVILLE. Cousin Tony promises to give us more of his company at home. Indeed, he shan't leave us any more. It won't leave us, Cousin Tony, will it?

TONY. O, it's a pretty creature! No, I'd sooner leave my horse in a pound than leave you when you smile upon one so. Your laugh makes you so becoming.

MISS NEVILLE. Agreeable cousin! Who can help admiring that natural humor, that pleasant, broad, red, thoughtless, [*patting his cheek*]—ah, it's a bold face!

MRS. HARDCASTLE. Pretty innocence!

TONY. I'm sure I always loved Cousin Con's hazel eyes, and her pretty long fingers, that she twists this way and that over the haspicholls, like a parcel of bobbins.

MRS. HARDCASTLE. Ah, he would charm the bird from the tree. I was never so happy before. My boy takes after his father, Mr. Lumpkin, exactly. The jewels, my dear Con, shall be yours incontinently. You shall have them. Isn't he a sweet boy, my dear? You shall be married tomorrow, and we'll put off the rest of his education, like Dr. Drowsy's sermons, to a fitter opportunity.

[*Enter* DIGGORY.]

DIGGORY. Where's the 'Squire? I have got a letter for your worship.

TONY. Give it to my mamma. She reads all my letters first.

DIGGORY. I had orders to deliver it into your own hands.

TONY. Who does it come from?

DIGGORY. Your worship mun ask that of the letter itself.

[*Exit* DIGGORY.]

TONY. I could wish to know, tho'.

[*Turning the letter, and gazing on it.*]

MISS NEVILLE [*aside*]. Undone, undone! A letter to him from Hastings. I know the hand. If my aunt sees it, we are ruined for ever. I'll keep her employed a little if I can. [*To* MRS. HARDCASTLE.] But I have not told you, madam, of my cousin's smart answer just now to Mr. Marlow. We so laughed—You must know, madam—this way a little, for he must not hear us.

[*They confer.*]

TONY [*still gazing*]. A damned cramp piece of penmanship as ever I saw in
my life. I can read your print-hand very well. But here there are such
handles, and shanks, and dashes that one can scarce tell the head from
the tail. *To Anthony Lumpkin, Esquire.* It's very odd, I can read the outside
of my letters, where my own name is, well enough. But when I come to
open it, it's all—buzz. That's hard, very hard; for the inside of the letter
is always the cream of the correspondence.

MRS. HARDCASTLE. Ha! ha! ha! Very well, very well. And so my son was
too hard for the philosopher.

MISS NEVILLE. Yes, madam; but you must hear the rest, madam. A little
more this way, or he may hear us. You'll hear how he puzzled him again.

MRS. HARDCASTLE. He seems strangely puzzled now himself, methinks.

TONY [*still gazing*]. A damned up and down hand, as if it was disguised in
liquor. [*Reading*] *Dear Sir.* Aye that's that. Then there's an *M*, and a
T, and an *S*, but whether the next be an izzard or an *R*, confound me, I
cannot tell!

MRS. HARDCASTLE. What's that, my dear? Can I give you any assistance?

MISS NEVILLE. Pray, aunt, let me read it. No body reads a cramp hand better
than I. [*Twitching the letter from her.*] Do you know who it is from?

TONY. Can't tell, except from Dick Ginger the feeder.

MISS NEVILLE. Aye, so it is. [*Pretending to read.*]
"Dear 'Squire,
"Hoping that you're in health, as I am at this present. The gentlemen
of the Shake-bag club has cut the gentlemen of Goose-green quite out
of feather. The odds—um—odd battle—um—long fighting—um, here,
here, it's all about cocks, and fighting; it's of no consequence; here, put
it up, put it up.
[*Thrusting the crumpled letter upon him.*]

TONY. But, I tell you, miss, it's of all the consequence in the world! I
would not lose the rest of it for a guinea! Here, mother, do you make it
out. Of no consequence!
[*Giving* MRS. HARDCASTLE *the letter.*]

MRS. HARDCASTLE. How's this! [*Reads.*] "Dear 'Squire, I'm now waiting
for Miss Neville, with a post-chaise and pair, at the bottom of the
garden, but I find my horses yet unable to perform the journey. I
expect you'll assist us with a pair of fresh horses, as you promised.
Dispatch is necessary, as the *hag*, (aye, the hag) your mother, will otherwise suspect us. Yours, Hastings." Grant me patience. I shall run
distracted! My rage chokes me!

MISS NEVILLE. I hope, madam, you'll suspend your resentment for a few
moments, and not impute to me any impertinence or sinister design that
belongs to another.

MRS. HARDCASTLE [*curtesying very low*]. Fine spoken, madam; you are
most miraculously polite and engaging, and quite the very pink of
courtesy and circumspection, madam. [*Changing her tone.*] And you, you

great ill-fashioned oaf, with scarce sense enough to keep your mouth shut. Were you, too, joined against me? But I'll defeat all your plots in a moment. As for you, madam, since you have got a pair of fresh horses ready, it would be cruel to disappoint them. So, if you please, instead of running away with your spark, prepare, this very moment, to run off with *me*. Your old Aunt Pedigree will keep you secure, I'll warrant me. You too, sir, may mount your horse, and guard us upon the way. Here, Thomas, Roger, Diggory! I'll show you that I wish you better than you do yourselves.

[*Exit.*]

MISS NEVILLE. So now I'm completely ruined.

TONY. Aye, that's a sure thing.

MISS NEVILLE. What better could be expected from being connected with such a stupid fool,—and after all the nods and signs I made him!

TONY. By the laws, miss, it was your own cleverness, and not my stupidity, that did your business. You were so nice and so busy with your Shake-bags and Goose-greens that I thought you could never be making believe.

[*Enter* HASTINGS.]

HASTINGS. So, sir, I find by my servant that you have shown my letter and betrayed us. Was this well done, young gentleman?

TONY. Here's another. Ask miss there who betrayed you. Ecod, it was her doing; not mine.

[*Enter* MARLOW.]

MARLOW. So I have been finely used here among you. Rendered contemptible, driven into ill manners, insulted, laughed at.

TONY. Here's another. We shall have old Bedlam[20] broke loose presently.

MISS NEVILLE. And there, sir, is the gentleman to whom we all owe every obligation.

MARLOW. What can I say to him, a mere boy, an idiot, whose ignorance and age are a protection.

HASTINGS. A poor contemptible booby that would but disgrace correction.

MISS NEVILLE. Yet with cunning and malice enough to make himself merry with all our embarrassments.

HASTINGS. An insensible cub.

MARLOW. Replete with tricks and mischief.

TONY. Baw! damme, but I'll fight you both one after the other,—with baskets!

MARLOW. As for him, he's below resentment. But your conduct, Mr. Hastings, requires an explanation. You knew of my mistakes, yet would not undeceive me.

HASTINGS. Tortured as I am with my own disappointments, is this a time for explanations? It is not friendly, Mr. Marlow.

[20] Bethlehem Hospital, an asylum for madmen.

MARLOW. But, sir—

MISS NEVILLE. Mr. Marlow, we never kept on your mistake, till it was too late to undeceive you. Be pacified.

[*Enter* SERVANT.]

SERVANT. My mistress desires you'll get ready immediately, madam. The horses are putting to. Your hat and things are in the next room. We are to go thirty miles before morning.

[*Exit* SERVANT.]

MISS NEVILLE. Well, well; I'll come presently.

MARLOW [*to* HASTINGS]. Was it well done, sir, to assist in rendering me ridiculous? To hang me out for the scorn of all my acquaintance? Depend upon it, sir, I shall expect an explanation.

HASTINGS. Was it well done, sir, if you're upon that subject, to deliver what I entrusted to yourself to the care of another, sir?

MISS NEVILLE. Mr. Hastings. Mr. Marlow. Why will you increase my distress by this groundless dispute? I implore you—I entreat you—

[*Enter* SERVANT.]

SERVANT. Your cloak, madam. My mistress is impatient.

MISS NEVILLE. I come. [*Exit* SERVANT.] Pray be pacified. If I leave you thus, I shall die with apprehension!

[*Enter* SERVANT.]

SERVANT. Your fan, muff, and gloves, madam. The horses are waiting.

MISS NEVILLE. O, Mr. Marlow! if you knew what a scene of constraint and ill-nature lies before me, I'm sure it would convert your resentment into pity.

MARLOW. I'm so distracted with a variety of passions that I don't know what I do. Forgive me, madam. George, forgive me. You know my hasty temper, and should not exasperate it.

HASTINGS. The torture of my situation is my only excuse.

MISS NEVILLE. Well, my dear Hastings, if you have that esteem for me that I think, that I am sure you have, your constancy for three years will but increase the happiness of our future connection. If—

MRS. HARDCASTLE [*within*]. Miss Neville! Constance, why, Constance, I say.

MISS NEVILLE. I'm coming. Well, constancy. Remember, constancy is the word.

[*Exit, followed by the* SERVANT.]

HASTINGS. My heart! How can I support this! To be so near happiness, and such happiness!

MARLOW [*to* TONY]. You see now, young gentleman, the effects of your folly. What might be amusement to you is here disappointment, and even distress.

TONY [*from a reverie*]. Ecod, I have hit it. It's here. Your hands. Your and yours, my poor Sulky. My boots there, ho! Meet me two hours hence at the bottom of the garden; and if you don't find Tony Lumpkin a more good-natured fellow than you thought for, I'll give you leave to take my best horse, and Bet Bouncer into the bargain! Come along. My boots, ho!

[*Exeunt.*]

ACT FIVE

Scene One

Continues.

[*Enter* HASTINGS *and* SERVANT.]

HASTINGS. You saw the old lady and Miss Neville drive off, you say?

SERVANT. Yes, your honor. They went off in a post-coach, and the young 'Squire went on horseback. They're thirty miles off by this time.

HASTINGS. Then all my hopes are over.

SERVANT. Yes, sir. Old Sir Charles is arrived. He and the old gentleman of the house have been laughing at Mr. Marlow's mistake this half hour. They are coming this way.

HASTINGS. Then I must not be seen. So now to my fruitless appointment at the bottom of the garden. This is about the time.

[*Exit.*]

[*Enter* SIR CHARLES *and* HARDCASTLE.]

HARDCASTLE. Ha! ha! ha! The peremptory tone in which he sent forth his sublime commands.

SIR CHARLES. And the reserve with which I suppose he treated all your advances.

HARDCASTLE. And yet he might have seen something in me above a common innkeeper too.

SIR CHARLES. Yes, Dick, but he mistook you for an uncommon innkeeper, ha! ha! ha!

HARDCASTLE. Well, I'm in too good spirits to think of any thing but joy. Yes, my dear friend, this union of our families will make our personal friendships hereditary: and tho' my daughter's fortune is but small—

SIR CHARLES. Why, Dick, will you talk of fortune to *me?* My son is possessed of more than a competence already, and can want nothing but a good and virtuous girl to share his happiness and increase it. If they like each other, as you say they do—

HARDCASTLE. *If*, man! I tell you they *do* like each other. My daughter as good as told me so.

SIR CHARLES. But girls are apt to flatter themselves, you know.

HARDCASTLE. I saw him grasp her hand in the warmest manner myself; and here he comes to put you out of your *ifs*, I warrant him.

[*Enter* MARLOW.]

MARLOW. I come, sir, once more, to ask pardon for my strange conduct. I can scarce reflect on my insolence without confusion.

HARDCASTLE. Tut, boy, a trifle. You take it too gravely. An hour or two's laughing with my daughter will set all to rights again. She'll never like you the worse for it.

MARLOW. Sir, I shall be always proud of her approbation.

HARDCASTLE. Approbation is but a cold word, Mr. Marlow; if I am not deceived, you have something more than approbation thereabouts. You take me.

MARLOW. Really, sir, I have not that happiness.

HARDCASTLE. Come, boy, I'm an old fellow, and know what's what as well as you that are younger. I know what has passed between you; but mum.

MARLOW. Sure, sir, nothing has passed between us but the most profound respect on my side, and the most distant reserve on hers. You don't think, sir, that my impudence has been passed upon all the rest of the family?

HARDCASTLE. Impudence! No, I don't say that—Not quite impudence—Though girls like to be played with, and rumpled a little, too, sometimes. But she has told no tales, I assure you.

MARLOW. I never gave her the slightest cause.

HARDCASTLE. Well, well, I like modesty in its place well enough. But this is over-acting, young gentleman. You may be open. Your father and I will like you the better for it.

MARLOW. May I die, sir, if I ever—

HARDCASTLE. I tell you, she don't dislike you; and as I'm sure you like her—

MARLOW. Dear sir—I protest, sir—

HARDCASTLE. I see no reason why you should not be joined as fast as the parson can tie you.

MARLOW. But hear me, sir—

HARDCASTLE. Your father approves the match, I admire it, every moment's delay will be doing mischief, so—

MARLOW. But why won't you hear me? By all that's just and true, I never gave Miss Hardcastle the slightest mark of my attachment, or even the most distant hint to suspect me of affection. We had but one interview, and that was formal, modest, and uninteresting.

HARDCASTLE [aside]. This fellow's formal, modest impudence is beyond bearing.

SIR CHARLES. And you never grasped her hand, or made any protestations!

MARLOW. As Heaven is my witness, I came down in obedience to your commands. I saw the lady without emotion, and parted without reluctance. I hope you'll exact no further proofs of my duty, nor prevent me from leaving a house in which I suffer so many mortifications.

[Exit.]

SIR CHARLES. I'm astonished at the air of sincerity with which he parted.

HARDCASTLE. And I'm astonished at the deliberate intrepidity of his assurance.

SIR CHARLES. I dare pledge my life and honor upon his truth.

HARDCASTLE. Here comes my daughter, and I would stake my happiness upon her veracity.

[*Enter* MISS HARDCASTLE.]

HARDCASTLE. Kate, come hither, child. Answer us sincerely, and without reserve; has Mr. Marlow made you any professions of love and affection?

MISS HARDCASTLE. The question is very abrupt, sir! But since you require unreserved sincerity, I think he has.

HARDCASTLE [*to* SIR CHARLES]. You see.

SIR CHARLES. And pray, madam, have you and my son had more than one interview?

MISS HARDCASTLE. Yes, sir, several.

HARDCASTLE [*to* SIR CHARLES]. You see.

SIR CHARLES. But did he profess any attachment?

MISS HARDCASTLE. A lasting one.

SIR CHARLES. Did he talk of love?

MISS HARDCASTLE. Much, sir.

SIR CHARLES. Amazing. And all this formally?

MISS HARDCASTLE. Formally.

HARDCASTLE. Now, my friend, I hope you are satisfied.

SIR CHARLES. And how did he behave, madam?

MISS HARDCASTLE. As most professed admirers do. Said some civil things of my face, talked much of his want of merit, and the greatness of mine; mentioned his heart, gave a short tragedy speech, and ended with pretended rapture.

SIR CHARLES. Now I'm perfectly convinced, indeed. I know his conversation among women to be modest and submissive. This forward, canting, ranting manner by no means describes him, and I am confident he never sat for the picture.

MISS HARDCASTLE. Then what, sir, if I should convince you to your face of my sincerity? If you and my papa, in about half an hour, will place yourselves behind that screen, you shall hear him declare his passion to me in person.

SIR CHARLES. Agreed. And if I find him what you describe, all my happiness in him must have an end.

[*Exit.*]

MISS HARDCASTLE. And if you don't find him what I describe—I fear my happiness must never have a beginning.

[*Exeunt.*]

Scene Two

Changes to the back of the garden.

[*Enter* HASTINGS.]

HASTINGS. What an idiot am I, to wait here for a fellow who probably takes a delight in mortifying me. He never intended to be punctual and I'll wait no longer. What do I see? It is he, and perhaps with news of my Constance.

[*Enter* TONY, *booted and spattered.*]

HASTINGS. My honest 'Squire! I now find you a man of your word. This looks like friendship.

TONY. Aye, I'm your friend, and the best friend you have in the world, if you knew but all. This riding by night, by-the-bye, is cursedly tiresome. It has shook me worse than the basket of a stagecoach.

HASTINGS. But how? Where did you leave your fellow travelers? Are they in safety? Are they housed?

TONY. Five and twenty miles in two hours and a half is no such bad driving. The poor beasts have smoked for it: rabbit me,[21] but I'd rather ride forty miles after a fox than ten with such *varmint*.

HASTINGS. Well, but where have you left the ladies? I die with impatience.

TONY. Left them? Why, where should I leave them but where I found them?

HASTINGS. This is a riddle.

TONY. Riddle me this, then. What's that goes round the house, and round the house, and never touches the house?

HASTINGS. I'm still astray.

TONY. Why, that's it, mon. I have led them astray. By jingo, there's not a pond or slough within five miles of the place but they can tell the taste of.

HASTINGS. Ha, ha, ha, I understand; you took them in a round while they supposed themselves going forward. And so you have at last brought them home again.

TONY. You shall hear. I first took them down Featherbed-lane, where we stuck fast in the mud. I then rattled them crack over the stones of Up-and-down Hill—I then introduced them to the gibbet on Heavy-tree Heath, and from that, with a circumbendibus, I fairly lodged them in the horse-pond at the bottom of the garden.

HASTINGS. But no accident, I hope.

TONY. No, no. Only mother is confoundedly frightened. She thinks herself forty miles off. She's sick of the journey, and the cattle can scarce crawl. So, if your own horses be ready, you may whip off with Cousin, and I'll be bound that no soul here can budge a foot to follow you.

HASTINGS. My dear friend, how can I be grateful?

TONY. Aye, now its "dear friend," "noble 'Squire." Just now, it was all

[21] Literally, humble me.

"idiot," "cub," and run me through the guts. Damn *your* way of fighting, I say. After we take a knock in this part of the country, we kiss and be friends. But if you had run me through the guts, then I should be dead, and you might go kiss the hangman.

HASTINGS. The rebuke is just. But I must hasten to relieve Miss Neville; if you keep the old lady employed, I promise to take care of the young one.

TONY. Never fear me. Here she comes. Vanish. [*Exit* HASTINGS.] She's got from the pond, and draggled up to the waist like a mermaid.

[*Enter* MRS. HARDCASTLE.]

MRS. HARDCASTLE. Oh, Tony, I'm killed. Shook. Battered to death. I shall never survive it. That last jolt that laid us against the quickset hedge has done my business.

TONY. Alack, mama, it was all your own fault. You would be for running away by night, without knowing one inch of the way.

MRS. HARDCASTLE. I wish we were at home again. I never met so many accidents in so short a journey. Drenched in the mud, overturned in a ditch, stuck fast in a slough, jolted to a jelly, and at last to lose our way! Whereabouts do you think we are, Tony?

TONY. By my guess we should be upon Crackskull Common, about forty miles from home.

MRS. HARDCASTLE. O lud! O lud! the most notorious spot in all the country. We only want a robbery to make a complete night on it.

TONY. Don't be afraid, mama, don't be afraid. Two of the five that kept here are hanged, and the other three may not find us. Don't be afraid. Is that a man that's galloping behind us? No; it's only a tree. Don't be afraid.

MRS. HARDCASTLE. The fright will certainly kill me.

TONY. Do you see anything like a black hat moving behind the thicket?

MRS. HARDCASTLE. Oh death!

TONY. No, it's only a cow. Don't be afraid, mama, don't be afraid.

MRS. HARDCASTLE. As I'm alive, Tony, I see a man coming toward us. Ah! I'm sure on it. If he perceives us, we are undone.

TONY [*aside*]. Father in law, by all that's unlucky, come to take one of his night walks. [*To her.*] Ah, it's a highwayman, with pistols as long as my arm. A damned ill-looking fellow.

MRS. HARDCASTLE. Good Heaven defend us! He approaches.

TONY. Do you hide yourself in that thicket, and leave me to manage him. If there be any danger, I'll cough and cry hem. When I cough be sure to keep close.

[MRS. HARDCASTLE *hides behind a tree in the back scene.*]

[*Enter* HARDCASTLE.]

HARDCASTLE. I'm mistaken, or I heard voices of people in want of help. Oh, Tony, is that you? I did not expect you so soon back. Are your mother and her charge in safety?

TONY. Very safe, sir, at my Aunt Pedigree's. Hem.

MRS. HARDCASTLE [*from behind*]. Ah, death! I find there's danger.

HARDCASTLE. Forty miles in three hours; sure that's too much, my youngster.

TONY. Stout horses and willing minds make short journies, as they say. Hem.

MRS. HARDCASTLE [*from behind*]. Sure he'll do the dear boy no harm.

HARDCASTLE. But I heard a voice here; I should be glad to know from whence it came?

TONY. It was I, sir, talking to myself, sir. I was saying that forty miles in four hours was very good going. Hem. As to be sure it was. Hem. I have got a sort of cold by being out in the air. We'll go in, if you please. Hem.

HARDCASTLE. But if you talked to yourself, you did not answer yourself. I am certain I heard two voices, and am resolved [*raising his voice*] to find the other out.

MRS. HARDCASTLE [*from behind*]. Oh, he's coming to find me out! Oh!

TONY. What need you go, sir, if I tell you? Hem. I'll lay down my life for the truth—hem—I'll tell you all, sir.
[*Detaining him.*]

HARDCASTLE. I tell you I will not be detained. I insist on seeing. It's in vain to expect I'll believe you.

MRS. HARDCASTLE [*running forward from behind*]. O lud, he'll murder my poor boy, my darling. Here, good gentleman, whet your rage upon me. Take my money, my life, but spare that young gentleman, spare my child, if you have any mercy.

HARDCASTLE. My wife, as I'm a Christian! From whence can she come, or what does she mean?

MRS. HARDCASTLE [*kneeling*]. Take compassion on us, good Mr. Highwayman. Take our money, our watches, all we have, but spare our lives. We will never bring you to justice, indeed we won't, good Mr. Highwayman.

HARDCASTLE. I believe the woman's out of her senses. What, Dorothy don't you know *me?*

MRS. HARDCASTLE. Mr. Hardcastle, as I'm alive! My fears blinded me. But, who, my dear, could have expected to meet you here, in this frightful place, so far from home. What has brought you to follow us?

HARDCASTLE. Sure, Dorothy, you have not lost your wits! So far from home, when you are within forty yards of your own door! [*To him.*] This is one of your old tricks, you graceless rogue, you! [*To her.*] Don't you know the gate, and the mulberry-tree; and don't you remember the horse-pond, my dear?

MRS. HARDCASTLE. Yes, I shall remember the horse-pond as long as I live; I have caught my death in it. [*To* TONY.] And is it to you, you graceless varlet, I owe all this? I'll teach you to abuse your mother, I will.

TONY. Ecod, mother, all the parish says you spoiled me, and so you may take the fruits on it.

MRS. HARDCASTLE. I'll spoil you, I will.
[*Follows him off the stage. Exit.*]

HARDCASTLE. There's morality, however, in his reply.

[*Exit.*]

[*Enter* HASTINGS *and* MISS NEVILLE.]

HASTINGS. My dear Constance, why will you deliberate thus? If we delay a moment, all is lost for ever. Pluck up a little resolution, and we shall soon be out of the reach of her malignity.

MISS NEVILLE. I find it impossible. My spirits are so sunk with the agitations I have suffered that I am unable to face any new danger. Two or three years patience will at last crown us with happiness.

HASTINGS. Such a tedious delay is worse than inconstancy. Let us fly, my charmer. Let us date our happiness from this very moment. Perish fortune. Love and content will increase what we possess beyond a monarch's revenue. Let me prevail.

MISS NEVILLE. No, Mr. Hastings, no. Prudence once more comes to my relief, and I will obey its dictates. In the moment of passion, fortune may be despised, but it ever produces a lasting repentance. I'm resolved to apply to Mr. Hardcastle's compassion and justice for redress.

HASTINGS. But tho' he had had the will, he has not the power to relieve you.

MISS NEVILLE. But he has influence, and upon that I am resolved to rely.

HASTINGS. I have no hopes. But since you persist, I must reluctantly obey you.

[*Exeunt.*]

Scene Three

Changes to a room at MR. HARDCASTLE'S.

[*Enter* SIR CHARLES *and* MISS HARDCASTLE.]

SIR CHARLES. What a situation am I in! If what you say appears, I shall then find a guilty son. If what he says be true, I shall then lose one that, of all others, I most wished for a daughter.

MISS HARDCASTLE. I am proud of your approbation; and, to show I merit it, if you place yourselves as I directed, you shall hear his explicit declaration. But he comes.

SIR CHARLES. I'll to your father, and keep him to the appointment.

[*Exit* SIR CHARLES.]

[*Enter* MARLOW.]

MARLOW. Tho' prepared for setting out, I come once more to take leave, nor did I, till this moment, know the pain I feel in the separation.

MISS HARDCASTLE [*in her own natural manner*]. I believe these sufferings cannot be very great, sir, which you can so easily remove. A day or two longer, perhaps, might lessen your uneasiness, by showing the little value of what you now think proper to regret.

MARLOW [*aside*]. This girl every moment improves upon me. [*To her.*] It must not be, madam. I have already trifled too long with my heart. My very pride begins to submit to my passion. The disparity of education and fortune, the anger of a parent, and the contempt of my equals begin to lose their weight, and nothing can restore me to myself but this painful effort of resolution.

MISS HARDCASTLE. Then go, sir. I'll urge nothing more to detain you. Tho' my family be as good as hers you came down to visit, and my education, I hope, not inferior, what are these advantages without equal affluence? I must remain contented with the slight approbation of imputed merit; I must have only the mockery of your addresses, while all your serious aims are fixed on fortune.

[*Enter* HARDCASTLE *and* SIR CHARLES *from behind.*]

SIR CHARLES. Here, behind this screen.

HARDCASTLE. Aye, aye, make no noise. I'll engage my Kate covers him with confusion at last.

MARLOW. By heavens, madam, fortune was ever my smallest consideration. Your beauty at first caught my eye; for who could see that without emotion? But every moment that I converse with you steals in some new grace, heightens the picture, and gives it stronger expression. What at first seemed rustic plainness, now appears refined simplicity. What seemed forward assurance, now strikes me as the result of courageous innocence and conscious virtue.

SIR CHARLES. What can it mean? He amazes me!

HARDCASTLE. I told you how it would be. Hush!

MARLOW. I am now determined to stay, madam, and I have too good an opinion of my father's discernment, when he sees you, to doubt his approbation.

MISS HARDCASTLE. No, Mr. Marlow, I will not, cannot detain you. Do you think I could suffer a connection in which there is the smallest room for repentance? Do you think I would take the mean advantage of a transient passion to load you with confusion? Do you think I could ever relish that happiness which was acquired by lessening yours?

MARLOW. By all that's good, I can have no happiness but what's in your power to grant me. Nor shall I ever feel repentance but in not having seen your merits before. I will stay, even contrary to your wishes; and tho' you should persist to shun me, I will make my respectful assiduities atone for the levity of my past conduct.

MISS HARDCASTLE. Sir, I must entreat you'll desist. As our acquaintance began, so let it end, in indifference. I might have given an hour or two to levity; but, seriously, Mr. Marlow, do you think I could ever submit to a connection where *I* must appear mercenary and *you* imprudent? Do you think I could ever catch at the confident addresses of a secure admirer?

MARLOW [*kneeling*]. Does this look like security? Does this look like confidence? No, madam, every moment that shows me your merit only serves to increase my diffidence and confusion. Here let me continue—

SIR CHARLES. I can hold it no longer. Charles, Charles, how hast thou deceived me! Is this your indifference, your uninteresting conversation!

HARDCASTLE. Your cold contempt! your formal interview! What have you to say now?

MARLOW. That I'm all amazement? What can it mean?

HARDCASTLE. It means that you can say and unsay things at pleasure. That you can address a lady in private, and deny it in public; that you have one story for us, and another for my daughter!

MARLOW. Daughter!—this lady, your daughter!

HARDCASTLE. Yes, sir, my only daughter. My Kate, whose else should she be?

MARLOW. Oh, the devil!

MISS HARDCASTLE. Yes, sir, that very identical tall, squinting lady you were pleased to take me for. [*Curtesying*.] She that you addressed as the mild, modest, sentimental man of gravity, and the bold, forward, agreeable Rattle of the Ladies Club; ha, ha, ha!

MARLOW. Zounds, there's no bearing this; it's worse than death!

MISS HARDCASTLE. In which of your characters, sir, will you give us leave to address you? As the faltering gentleman, with looks on the ground, that speaks just to be heard, and hates hypocrisy: or the loud, confident creature that keeps it up with Mrs. Mantrap and old Miss Biddy Buckskin till three in the morning; ha, ha, ha!

MARLOW. O, curse on my noisy head. I never attempted to be impudent yet that I was not taken down. I must be gone.

HARDCASTLE. By the hand of my body, but you shall not. I see it was all a mistake, and I am rejoiced to find it. You shall not, sir, I tell you. I know she'll forgive you. Won't you forgive him, Kate? We'll all forgive you. Take courage, man.

[*They retire, she tormenting him, to the back scene.*]

[*Enter* MRS. HARDCASTLE *and* TONY.]

MRS. HARDCASTLE. So, so, they're gone off. Let them go. I care not.

HARDCASTLE. Who gone?

MRS. HARDCASTLE. My dutiful niece and her gentleman, Mr. Hastings, from town. He who came down with our modest visitor, here.

SIR CHARLES. Who, my honest George Hastings? As worthy a fellow as lives, and the girl could not have made a more prudent choice.

HARDCASTLE. Then, by the hand of my body, I'm proud of the connection.

MRS. HARDCASTLE. Well, if he has taken away the lady, he has not taken her fortune; that remains in this family to console us for her loss.

HARDCASTLE. Sure, Dorothy, you would not be so mercenary?

MRS. HARDCASTLE. Aye, that's my affair, not yours.

HARDCASTLE. But, you know, if your son, when of age, refuses to marry his cousin, her whole fortune is then at her own disposal.

MRS. HARDCASTLE. Aye, but he's not of age, and she has not thought proper to wait for his refusal.

[*Enter* HASTINGS *and* MISS NEVILLE.]

MRS. HARDCASTLE [*aside*]. What! returned so soon? I begin not to like it.

HASTINGS [*to* HARDCASTLE]. For my late attempt to fly off with your niece, let my present confusion be my punishment. We are now come back, to appeal from your justice to your humanity. By her father's consent, I first paid her my addresses, and our passions were first founded in duty.

MISS NEVILLE. Since his death, I have been obliged to stoop to dissimulation to avoid oppression. In an hour of levity, I was ready even to give up my fortune to secure my choice. But I'm now recovered from the delusion, and hope from your tenderness what is denied me from a nearer connection.

MRS. HARDCASTLE. Pshaw, pshaw, this is all but the whining end of a modern novel!

HARDCASTLE. Be it what it will, I'm glad they're come back to reclaim their due. Come hither, Tony, boy. Do you refuse this lady's hand whom I now offer you?

TONY. What signifies my refusing? You know I can't refuse her till I'm of age, father.

HARDCASTLE. While I thought concealing your age, boy, was likely to conduce to your improvement, I concurred with your mother's desire to keep it secret. But since I find she turns it to a wrong use, I must now declare, you have been of age these three months.

TONY. Of age! Am I of age, father?

HARDCASTLE. Above three months.

TONY. Then you'll see the first use I'll make of my liberty. [*Taking* MISS NEVILLE'S *hand*.) Witness all men by these presents, that I, Anthony Lumpkin, Esquire, of BLANK place, refuse you, Constantia Neville, spinster, of no place at all, for my true and lawful wife. So Constance Neville may marry whom she pleases, and Tony Lumpkin is his own man again!

SIR CHARLES. O brave 'Squire!

HASTINGS. My worthy friend!

MRS. HARDCASTLE. My undutiful offspring!

MARLOW. Joy, my dear George, I give you joy sincerely. And could I prevail upon my little tyrant here to be less arbitrary, I should be the happiest man alive, if you would return me the favor.

HASTINGS [*to* MISS HARDCASTLE]. Come, madam, you are now driven to the very last scene of all your contrivances. I know you like him, I'm sure he loves you, and you must and shall have him.

HARDCASTLE [*joining their hands*]. And I say so too. And Mr. Marlow, if she makes as good a wife as she has a daughter, I don't believe you'll ever repent your bargain. So now to supper; tomorrow we shall gather all the poor of the parish about us, and the Mistakes of the Night shall

be crowned with a merry morning; so boy, take her; and as you have
been mistaken in the mistress, my wish is that you may never be mistaken
in the wife.

EPILOGUE

Spoken by Miss Hardcastle

By Dr. Goldsmith

WELL, having stooped to conquer with success,
And gained a husband without aid from dress,
Still as a barmaid, I could wish it, too,
As I have conquered him to conquer you:
And let me say, for all your resolution,
That pretty barmaids have done execution.
Our life is all a play, composed to please,
"We have our exits and our entrances."[22]
The first act shows the simple country maid,
Harmless and young, of every thing afraid,
Blushes when hired, and with unmeaning action,
I hopes as how to give you satisfaction.
Her second act displays a livelier scene,—
The unblushing barmaid of a country inn.
Who whisks about the house, at market caters,
Talks loud, coquets the guests, and scolds the waiters.
Next the scene shifts to town, and there she soars,
The chophouse toast of ogling connoisseurs.
On 'Squires and Cits she there displays her arts,
And on the gridiron broils her lovers' hearts—
And as she smiles, her triumphs to complete,
Even Common Councilmen forget to eat.
The fourth act shows her wedded to the 'Squire,
And Madam now begins to hold it higher;
Pretends to taste, at Operas cries *caro*,
And quits her *Nancy Dawson*, for *Che Faro*.[23]
Dotes upon dancing, and in all her pride,
Swims round the room, the *Heinel*[24] of Cheapside:
Ogles and leers with artificial skill,
Till having lost in age the power to kill,

---

[22] Quoting Jaques in *As You Like It*, II, 7.
[23] i.e., giving up popular songs for operatic arias.
[24] A ballet dancer.

She sits all night at cards, and ogles at spadille.
Such, thro' our lives, the eventful history—
The fifth and last act still remains for me.
The barmaid now for your protection prays,
Turns female barrister, and pleads for Bayes.[25]

[25] A traditional cognomen for a poet or playwright.

HENRIK IBSEN

SOLNESS,
THE MASTER BUILDER

THE DESCRIPTION OF MAN

THE TWENTIETH-CENTURY READER approaches Ibsen with a variety of preconceptions: he is the father of the modern drama, a realistic writer, a naturalistic writer, a writer of problem plays, a social critic, the dramatist of eternal night. None of these preconceptions is completely true, none is entirely wrong, except the last, an epithet attached to Ibsen by one of the last stars of the romantic theater. Correctly, both the actor and Ibsen would maintain that their artistic attitudes represented the truth about life in nineteenth-century Europe, but a century has two ends and the actor was, apparently, unaware of the great revolution that lay between the beginning of the nineteenth century and its last years.

The revolution expressed itself in many ways: in one instance it was the industrial revolution, the beginning of the machine age; again, it was the agrarian revolt, the beginning of the age of cities. It was the scientific revolution, the search for evidence that the history of life, of the earth, of the cosmos was a chain of causes and effects, that the universe was a process of change. It was a political revolution, the attempts to overthrow established orders, to found republics, to unite small states with larger. It was a social revolution, dedicated to advancing the rights of man, the emancipation of women, the reformation of economic inequities. A revolution so many-faceted, so universal could scarcely fail to find reflection in the theater.

But, for the first time perhaps, the audience is not preconditioned to recognize the truth of the reflection. The little world on stage does not necessarily represent the great world outside the theater to every spectator. Some (like the romantic actor) will cling to an older ideal world, some will demand the new. One measure of this condition is the record of audience riots in the theatrical history of the nineteenth century. Audiences had been unruly in the past, of course, principally because they resented an actor's performance or an increase in admission prices. But now there are riots in Berlin, New York, Paris, and expressions of disagreement in London: not so much because of the subject matter of the plays, as because of the author's attitudes toward the subject matter. Although the dramatists under attack—Ibsen, Chekhov, Synge, Shaw—would eventually become the accepted classic writers of the modern theater once audiences accepted the revolutionary positions they represented, revolution itself did not cease. Once set off balance, the orderly world never found more than temporary stasis, the theater could never again be the universal mirror of fixed social and moral attitudes.

The theatrical career of Henrik Ibsen (1828–1906) is itself a mirror of the nineteenth century's revolutions. Born in Skien, Norway, he spent his adolescent years in frustrated attempts to find a place in a profession, as scholar, lawyer, painter, poet. He associated himself with groups of young intellectuals and thus early became aware of advanced ideas in European science and politics which had not yet touched the larger public of a country that had been for centuries a cultural backwater of the continent. His first play, *Catalina* (1850), while a melodrama, sees its hero as a fighter in the ranks of the dispossessed and hence accurately predicts the course of its author's development. In 1851 Ibsen was appointed a director of the National Theater in Bergen and immediately became an influential figure, both through the plays he chose to present and those that came from his own pen. At first his subjects were those of the romantic drama to which the early nineteenth century was devoted, plays of bustling panoramic action, mingling the heroic and the comic, and generally set in a remote time. Then, in response to new developments in the continental theater, particularly in France, he experimented with contemporary subject matter, current social and domestic problems, in the form of the well-made play [see below]. These plays, *A Doll's House* (1879), *Ghosts* (1881), *An Enemy of the People* (1882), found a wide audience in the theaters outside Norway and were largely responsible, not just for Ibsen's reputation, but for his acceptance as an influence and model by his contemporaries and successors. Yet even in these plays it is possible to see Ibsen's concern with ideas deeper and more universal than the daily problems of Norwegian society. And in the last period of his career, commencing with *The Wild Duck* (1883) and including *The Master Builder* (1891), he created an enduring picture of the position of man in a world forever unstable.

Not the least of the problems confronting an artist in a rapidly changing world is to find a form which can express his sense of that world without itself becoming chaotic. Ibsen had two tools ready to his hand. The first was theatrical, for in the last century play-production had become increasingly illusionistic. The bare acting areas available to the Greeks or the Hindus or the Elizabethans had been replaced first by painted settings and later by constructed settings intended to convey a precise notion of the locale of the action. As these settings became more detailed, more realistic, in the early nineteenth century they posed a problem for both producer and playwright. It was no longer possible to shift the locale with a descriptive phrase or by the simple raising or lowering of a drop: a constructed set must be dismantled before another could be put in its place. Economically and artistically, the better part of reason was to limit the number of locales represented: the new theater imposed a unity of place on the playwright nearly as strict as that practiced by the Greeks.

The second tool was a dramatic structure commonly called *the well-made play*. This too was a device for economy; the luxuriously plotted, character-filled action of post-Elizabethan drama was replaced by a tight, limited action that insisted on keeping foremost the logic of the pattern of events, to make the audience aware of the sequence of cause and effect. No situation could be employed whose cause was not carefully presented. Cause-and-effect was, of course, also the major tenet of the scientific thinking of the century, so the well-made play (which was never intended for more than entertainment) became the vehicle for the expression of the most profound convictions of the century. It was not merely that events had causes, but that given certain situations future events were absolutely predictable. If an architect died in a plunge from a steeple, it was the result of an identifiable chain of happenings in his past; but also, observing that past in detail, his mortal fall could be foreseen. The nineteenth-century dramatist, Ibsen in particular, discovered in the heredity and environment of his heroes an analogue to the fate of the Greek world or the divinely imposed moral order of the post-medieval world.

Thus the story of Master-Builder Solness, lived wholly in the society of his times, without oracles, without the direction of supernatural forces, has the unity and finality of Greek tragedy, the inevitability of that Christian drama in which the world order is breached. Solness is a man of pride, like Pentheus, like Ferdinand, but he is not punished for his pride because he has insulted the gods or the laws of God. Solness's pride has caused him to sin against his fellow-men, his wife, his children, old Brovik, Kaia. But he has also sinned against himself, against his talent: from the builder of churches he descends to the building of homes, hoping for gratitude from those whose lives he would improve. The multiple ironies of the play emphasize the sense of the inevitability of retribution: the girl who comes to "save" the artist, kills him; for descending from his place as a creative artist, he gets not gratitude but complaint; when he thinks he has set youth against youth, he has really set youth beside youth in opposition to his own age; the "new home" which he has built, with its three nurseries, is in effect a tomb; the success which he has achieved is a dead life, because the joy of living is not in it.

To this sense of inevitability the structure of the play, the selection and arrangement of incidents, makes a major contribution. The spectator does not follow Solness from his early success as a self-taught artist through the successive stages of his career to his final defeat. The spectator meets him, as the witches did Macbeth, in the day of his success, and in less than twelve hours his life is over. The forward action of the play is accompanied by revelations of past events at those moments in the present when the significance of the past will have clearest relevance. By such structure the past becomes something more than the foundation of the story acted on the stage; in a sense, it *is* the story. The exposition, that is, is not something the audience must know to understand the present, the play itself is something that must be known to understand the past. Seeing the present, the audience learns more of the past that created it, until there is no escape for Solness from the environment and heredity that have determined and continue to determine his actions.

Yet the play is not simply a scientific analysis of an artist's career, a kind of case history. Ibsen universalizes his story by the free use of symbols. Many of these are conventional enough to need little explanation: the tower which is first an image of aspiration, later of challenge; the fire out of which Solness's fortunes, phoenix-like, arise though his marriage and his wife remain in the ashes; the dolls with which Mrs. Solness solaces herself for the realization that has been denied her. But there are larger symbols, more of the theater, and hence difficult to realize from a reading of the play. It has been noted above that in the theater of realistic illusion it was impractical to shift scenery unless the play could not otherwise be presented. Solness's life is acted out in three different locales, his office, his parlor, his veranda. In performance the effect of the change of locale is dynamic: in the office the audience sees the public front, the mask, of the Master Builder; in the intimacy of the family parlor, the audience looks more closely into his true nature; the veranda, the exposed "room" of his house, is the special stage on which he himself is exposed and from which his destruction is observed.

Solness himself thus becomes something more than a man, and his actions something more than an individual biography. The play exemplifies the forces unleashed in the unstable world, suggests that the life of modern man is as uncompromisingly tragic as that of ages that conceived of themselves as stable. If there are no Olympian gods to be wary of, no inflexible omnipotent moral codes, there are human values which men ignore at their peril. And if political order crumbles overnight, if the scientific observer can only go on peering after the unknown, the artist remains as the observer and enlightener. Ibsen refused to think of himself as a reformer or commentator on specific problems. His task, he once declared, was the description of man. Such a statement is the continuing justification for the existence of the artist in the modern world.

Characters

HALVARD SOLNESS
Master Builder

ALINE SOLNESS
his wife

DOCTOR HERDAL
physician

KNUT BROVIK
formerly an architect, now in SOLNESS'S *employment*

RAGNAR BROVIK
his son, draughtsman

KAIA FOSLI
his niece, bookkeeper

MISS HILDA WANGEL

SOME LADIES

A CROWD IN THE STREET

The action passes in and about SOLNESS'S *house.*

SOLNESS,
THE MASTER BUILDER

Henrik Ibsen

Translated by William Archer

ACT ONE

A plainly furnished workroom in the house of HALVARD SOLNESS. *Folding doors on the left lead out to the hall. On the right is the door leading to the inner rooms of the house. At the back is an open door into the draughts-men's office. In front, on the left, a desk with books, papers, and writing materials. Further back than the folding door, a stove. In the right-hand corner, a sofa, a table, and one or two chairs. On the table a water-bottle and glass. A smaller table, with a rocking chair and armchair, in front on the right. Lighted lamps, with shades, on the table in the draughtsmen's office, on the table in the corner, and on the desk.*

In the draughtsmen's office sit KNUT BROVIK *and his son* RAGNAR, *occupied with plans and calculations. At the desk in the outer office stands* KAIA FOSLI, *writing in the ledger.* KNUT BROVIK *is a spare old man with white hair and beard. He wears a rather threadbare but well-brushed black coat, spectacles, and a somewhat discolored white neckcloth.* RAGNAR BROVIK *is a well-dressed, light-haired man in his thirties, with a slight stoop.* KAIA FOSLI *is a slightly built girl, a little over twenty, carefully dressed, and delicate-looking. She has a green shade over her eyes.—All three go on working for some time in silence.*

KNUT BROVIK [*rises suddenly, as if in distress, from the table; breathes heavily and laboriously as he comes forward into the doorway*]. No, I can't bear it much longer!

KAIA [*going up to him*]. You are feeling very ill this evening, are you not, uncle?

BROVIK. Oh, I seem to get worse every day.

RAGNAR [*has risen and advances*]. You ought to go home, father. Try to get a little sleep—

491

BROVIK [*impatiently*]. Go to bed, I suppose? Would you have me stifled outright?

KAIA. Then take a little walk.

RAGNAR. Yes, do. I will come with you.

BROVIK [*with warmth*]. I will not go till he comes! I am determined to have it out this evening with—[*in a tone of suppressed bitterness*]—with him—with the chief.

KAIA [*anxiously*]. Oh no, uncle,—do wait awhile before doing that!

RAGNAR. Yes, better wait, father!

BROVIK [*draws his breath laboriously*]. Ha—ha—! *I* haven't much time for waiting.

KAIA [*listening*]. Hush! I hear him on the stairs.

[*All three go back to their work. A short silence.*

HALVARD SOLNESS *comes in through the hall door. He is a man no longer young, but healthy and vigorous, with close-cut curly hair, dark moustache and dark thick eyebrows. He wears a greyish-green buttoned jacket with an upstanding collar and broad lapels. On his head he wears a soft grey felt hat, and he has one or two light portfolios under his arm.*]

SOLNESS [*near the door, points towards the draughtsmen's office, and asks in a whisper:*]. Are they gone?

KAIA [*softly, shaking her head*]. No. [*She takes the shade off her eyes.*

SOLNESS *crosses the room, throws his hat on a chair, places the portfolios on the table by the sofa, and approaches the desk again.* KAIA *goes on writing without intermission, but seems nervous and uneasy.*]

SOLNESS [*aloud*]. What is that you are entering, Miss Fosli?

KAIA [*starts*]. Oh, it is only something that—

SOLNESS. Let me look at it, Miss Fosli.

[*Bends over her, pretends to be looking into the ledger, and whispers:*] Kaia!

KAIA [*softly, still writing*]. Well?

SOLNESS. Why do you always take that shade off when I come?

KAIA [*as before*]. I look so ugly with it on.

SOLNESS [*smiling*]. Then you don't like to look ugly, Kaia?

KAIA [*half glancing up at him*]. Not for all the world. Not in your eyes.

SOLNESS [*strokes her hair gently*]. Poor, poor little Kaia—

KAIA [*bending her head*]. Hush—they can hear you!

[SOLNESS *strolls across the room to the right, turns and pauses at the door of the draughtsmen's office.*]

SOLNESS. Has any one been here for me?

RAGNAR [*rising*]. Yes, the young couple who want a villa built, out at Lövstrand.

SOLNESS [*growling*]. Oh, those two! They must wait. I am not quite clear about the plans yet.

RAGNAR [*advancing, with some hesitation*]. They were very anxious to have the drawings at once.

SOLNESS [*as before*]. Yes, of course—so they all are.

BROVIK [*looks up*]. They say they are longing so to get into a house of their own.

SOLNESS. Yes, yes—we know all that! And so they are content to take whatever is offered them. They get a—a roof over their heads—an address—but nothing to call a home. No thank you! In that case, let them apply to somebody else. Tell them *that*, the next time they call.

BROVIK [*pushes his glasses up on to his forehead and looks in astonishment at him*]. To somebody else? Are you prepared to give up the commission?

SOLNESS [*impatiently*]. Yes, yes, yes, devil take it! If that is to be the way of it—. Rather that, than build away at random. [*Vehemently.*] Besides, I know very little about these people as yet.

BROVIK. The people are safe enough. Ragnar knows them. He is a friend of the family. Perfectly safe people.

SOLNESS. Oh, safe—safe enough! That is not at all what I mean. Good lord—don't you understand me either? [*Angrily.*] I won't have anything to do with these strangers. They may apply to whom they please, so far as I am concerned.

BROVIK [*rising*]. Do you really mean that?

SOLNESS [*sulkily*]. Yes I do.—For once in a way.

[*He comes forward.*]

[BROVIK *exchanges a glance with* RAGNAR, *who makes a warning gesture. Then* BROVIK *comes into the front room.*]

BROVIK. May I have a few words with you?

SOLNESS. Certainly.

BROVIK [*to* KAIA]. Just go in there for a moment, Kaia.

KAIA [*uneasily*]. Oh, but uncle—

BROVIK. Do as I say, child. And shut the door after you.

[KAIA *goes reluctantly into the draughtsmen's office, glances anxiously and imploringly at* SOLNESS, *and shuts the door.*]

BROVIK [*lowering his voice a little*]. I don't want the poor children to know how ill I am.

SOLNESS. Yes, you have been looking very poorly of late.

BROVIK. It will soon be all over with me. My strength is ebbing—from day to day.

SOLNESS. Won't you sit down?

BROVIK. Thanks—may I?

SOLNESS [*placing the armchair more conveniently*]. Here—take this chair.— And now?

BROVIK [*has seated himself with difficulty*]. Well, you see, it's about Ragnar. That is what weighs most upon me. What is to become of him?

SOLNESS. Of course your son will stay with me as long as ever he likes.

BROVIK. But that is just what he does not like. He feels that he cannot stay here any longer.

SOLNESS. Why, I should say he was very well off here. But if he wants more money, I should not mind—

BROVIK. No, no! It is not that. [*Impatiently.*] But sooner or later he, too, must have a chance of doing something on his own account.

SOLNESS [*without looking at him*]. Do you think that Ragnar has quite talent enough to stand alone?

BROVIK. No, that is just the heartbreaking part of it—I have begun to have my doubts about the boy. For you have never said so much as—as one encouraging word about him. And yet I cannot but think there must be something in him—he can't be without talent.

SOLNESS. Well, but he has learnt nothing—nothing thoroughly, I mean. Except, of course, to draw.

BROVIK [*looks at him with covert hatred, and says hoarsely*]. You had learned little enough of the business when you were in my employment. But that did not prevent you from setting to work—[*breathing with difficulty*]—and pushing your way up, and taking the wind out of my sails—mine, and so many other people's.

SOLNESS. Yes, you see—circumstances favored me.

BROVIK. You are right there. Everything favored you. But then how can you have the heart to let me go to my grave—without having seen what Ragnar is fit for? And of course I am anxious to see them married, too—before I go.

SOLNESS [*sharply*]. Is it she who wishes it?

BROVIK. Not Kaia so much as Ragnar—he talks about it every day. [*Appealingly.*] You must—you *must* help him to get some independent work now! I must see something that the lad has done. Do you hear?

SOLNESS [*peevishly*]. Hang it, man, you can't expect me to drag commissions down from the moon for him!

BROVIK. He has the chance of a capital commission at this very moment. A big bit of work.

SOLNESS [*uneasily, startled*]. Has he?

BROVIK. If you would give your consent.

SOLNESS. What sort of work do you mean?

BROVIK [*with some hesitation*]. He can have the building of that villa out at Lövstrand.

SOLNESS. That! Why I am going to build that myself.

BROVIK. Oh you don't much care about doing it.

SOLNESS [*flaring up*]. Don't care! I! Who dares to say that?

BROVIK. You said so yourself just now.

SOLNESS. Oh, never mind what I say.—Would they give Ragnar the building of that villa?

BROVIK. Yes. You see, he knows the family. And then—just for the fun of the thing—he has made drawings and estimates and so forth—

SOLNESS. Are they pleased with the drawings? The people who will have to live in the house?

BROVIK. Yes. If you would only look through them and approve of them—

SOLNESS. Then they would let Ragnar build their home for them?

BROVIK. They were immensely pleased with his idea. They thought it exceedingly original, they said.

SOLNESS. Oho! Original! Not the old-fashioned stuff that *I* am in the habit of turning out!

BROVIK. It seemed to them different.

SOLNESS [*with suppressed irritation*]. So it was to see Ragnar that they came here—whilst I was out!

BROVIK. They came to call upon you—and at the same time to ask whether you would mind retiring—

SOLNESS [*angrily*]. Retire? I?

BROVIK. In case you thought that Ragnar's drawings—

SOLNESS. I! Retire in favor of your son!

BROVIK. Retire from the agreement, they meant.

SOLNESS. Oh, it comes to the same thing. [*Laughs angrily.*] So that is it, is it? Halvard Solness is to see about retiring now! To make room for younger men! For the very youngest, perhaps! He must make room! Room! Room!

BROVIK. Why, good heavens! there is surely room for more than one single man—

SOLNESS. Oh, there's not so very much room to spare either. But, be that as it may—I will never retire! I will never give way to anybody! Never of my own free will. Never in this world will I do that!

BROVIK [*rises with difficulty*]. Then I am to pass out of life without any certainty? Without a gleam of happiness? Without any faith or trust in Ragnar? Without having seen a single piece of work of his doing? Is that to be the way of it?

SOLNESS [*turns half aside, and mutters*]. H'm—don't ask more just now.

BROVIK. I must have an answer to this one question. Am I to pass out of life in such utter poverty?

SOLNESS [*seems to struggle with himself; finally he says, in a low but firm voice*]. You must pass out of life as best you can.

BROVIK. Then be it so.

[*He goes up the room.*]

SOLNESS [*following him, half in desperation*]. Don't you understand that I cannot help it? I am what I am, and I cannot change my nature!

BROVIK. No, no; I suppose you can't.

[*Reels and supports himself against the sofa-table.*]

May I have a glass of water?

SOLNESS. By all means.

[*Fills a glass and hands it to him.*]

BROVIK. Thanks.

[*Drinks and puts the glass down again.* SOLNESS *goes up and opens the door of the draughtsmen's office.*]

SOLNESS. Ragnar—you must come and take your father home.

[RAGNAR *rises quickly. He and* KAIA *come into the workroom.*]

RAGNAR. What is the matter, father?

BROVIK. Give me your arm. Now let us go.

RAGNAR. Very well. You had better put your things on, too, Kaia.

SOLNESS. Miss Fosli must stay—just for a moment. There is a letter I want written.

BROVIK [*looks at* SOLNESS]. Good night. Sleep well—if you can.

SOLNESS. Good night.

[BROVIK *and* RAGNAR *go out by the hall door.* KAIA *goes to the desk.* SOLNESS *stands with bent head, to the right, by the armchair.*]

KAIA [*dubiously*]. Is there any letter—?

SOLNESS [*curtly*]. No, of course not. [*Looks sternly at her.*] Kaia!

KAIA [*anxiously, in a low voice*]. Yes!

SOLNESS [*points imperatively to a spot on the floor*]. Come here! At once!

KAIA [*hesitatingly*]. Yes.

SOLNESS [*as before*]. Nearer!

KAIA [*obeying*]. What do you want with me?

SOLNESS [*looks at her for a while*]. Is it you I have to thank for all this?

KAIA. No, no, don't think that!

SOLNESS. But confess now—you want to get married!

KAIA [*softly*]. Ragnar and I have been engaged for four or five years, and so—

SOLNESS. And so you think it time there were an end of it. Is not that so?

KAIA. Ragnar and Uncle say I *must*. So I suppose I shall have to give in.

SOLNESS [*more gently*]. Kaia, don't you really care a little bit for Ragnar, too?

KAIA. I cared very much for Ragnar once—before I came here to you.

SOLNESS. But you don't now? Not in the least?

KAIA [*passionately, clasping her hands and holding them out towards him*]. Oh, you know very well there is only one person I care for now! One, and one only, in all the world! I shall never care for anyone else.

SOLNESS. Yes, you say that. And yet you go away from me—leave me alone here with everything on my hands.

KAIA. But could I not stay with you, even if Ragnar—?

SOLNESS [*repudiating the idea*]. No, no, that is quite impossible. If Ragnar leaves me and starts work on his own account, then of course he will need you himself.

KAIA [*wringing her hands*]. Oh, I feel as if I *could* not be separated from you! It's quite, quite impossible!

SOLNESS. Then be sure you get those foolish notions out of Ragnar's head. Marry him as much as you please—[*Alters his tone.*] I mean—don't let him throw up his good situation with me. For then I can keep you too, my dear Kaia.

KAIA. Oh yes, how lovely that would be, if it could only be managed!

SOLNESS [*clasps her head with his two hands and whispers*]. For I cannot get on without you, you see. I must have you with me every single day.

KAIA [*in nervous exaltation*]. My God! My God!

SOLNESS [*kisses her hair*]. Kaia—Kaia!

KAIA [*sinks down before him*]. Oh, how good you are to me! How unspeakably good you are!

SOLNESS [*vehemently*]. Get up! For goodness' sake get up! I think I hear some one!

[*He helps her to rise. She staggers over to the desk.* MRS. SOLNESS *enters by the door on the right. She looks thin and wasted with grief, but shows traces of bygone beauty. Blonde ringlets. Dressed with good taste, wholly in black. Speaks somewhat slowly and in a plaintive voice.*]

MRS. SOLNESS [*in the doorway*]. Halvard!

SOLNESS [*turns*]. Oh, are you there, my dear—?

MRS. SOLNESS [*with a glance at* KAIA]. I am afraid I am disturbing you.

SOLNESS. Not in the least. Miss Fosli has only a short letter to write.

MRS. SOLNESS. Yes, so I see.

SOLNESS. What do you want with me, Aline?

MRS. SOLNESS. I merely wanted to tell you that Dr. Herdal is in the drawing-room. Won't you come and see him, Halvard?

SOLNESS [*looks suspiciously at her*]. H'm—is the doctor so very anxious to talk to me?

MRS. SOLNESS. Well, not exactly anxious. He really came to see me; but he would like to say how-do-you-do to you at the same time.

SOLNESS [*laughs to himself*]. Yes, I daresay. Well, you must ask him to wait a little.

MRS. SOLNESS. Then you will come in presently?

SOLNESS. Perhaps I will. Presently, presently, dear. In a little while.

MRS. SOLNESS [*glancing again at* KAIA]. Well now, don't forget, Halvard.

[*Withdraws and closes the door behind her.*]

KAIA [*softly*]. Oh dear, oh dear—I am sure Mrs. Solness thinks ill of me in some way!

SOLNESS. Oh, not in the least. Not more than usual at any rate. But all the same, you had better go now, Kaia.

KAIA. Yes, yes, now I must go.

SOLNESS [*severely*]. And mind you get that matter settled for me. Do you hear?

KAIA. Oh, if it only depended on me—

SOLNESS. I will have it settled, I say! And tomorrow too—not a day later!

KAIA [*terrified*]. If there's nothing else for it, I am quite willing to break off the engagement.

SOLNESS [*angrily*]. Break it off? Are you mad? Would you think of breaking it off?

KAIA [*distracted*]. Yes, if necessary. For I must—I must stay here with you! I can't leave you! That is utterly—utterly impossible!

SOLNESS [*with a sudden outburst*]. But deuce take it—how about Ragnar then! It's Ragnar that I—

KAIA [*looks at him with terrified eyes*]. It is chiefly on Ragnar's account, that—that you—?

SOLNESS [*collecting himself*]. No, no, of course not! You don't understand me either. [*Gently and softly.*] Of course it is you I want to keep—you above everything, Kaia. But for that very reason, you must prevent Ragnar, too, from throwing up his situation. There, there,—now go home.

KAIA. Yes, yes—goodnight, then.

SOLNESS. Goodnight. [*As she is going.*] Oh, stop a moment! Are Ragnar's drawings in there?

KAIA. I did not see him take them with him.

SOLNESS. Then just go and find them for me. I might perhaps glance over them, after all.

KAIA [*happily*]. Oh yes, please do!

SOLNESS. For your sake, Kaia dear. Now, let me have them at once, please.

[KAIA *hurries into the draughtsmen's office, searches anxiously in the table drawer, finds a portfolio and brings it with her.*]

KAIA. Here are all the drawings.

SOLNESS. Good. Put them down there on the table.

KAIA [*putting down the portfolio*]. Goodnight, then. [*Beseechingly.*] And please, please think kindly of me.

SOLNESS. Oh, that I always do. Goodnight, my dear little Kaia. [*Glances to the right.*] Go, go now!

[MRS. SOLNESS *and* DR. HERDAL *enter by the door on the right. He is a stoutish, elderly man, with a round, good-humored face, clean-shaven, with thin, light hair, and gold spectacles.*]

MRS. SOLNESS [*still in the doorway*]. Halvard, I cannot keep the doctor any longer.

SOLNESS. Well then, come in here.

MRS. SOLNESS [*to* KAIA, *who is turning down the desk-lamp*]. Have you finished the letter already, Miss Fosli?

KAIA [*in confusion*]. The letter—?

SOLNESS. Yes, it was quite a short one.

MRS. SOLNESS. It must have been very short.

SOLNESS. You may go now, Miss Fosli. And please come in good time tomorrow morning.

KAIA. I will be sure to. Goodnight, Mrs. Solness.

[*She goes out by the hall door.*]

MRS. SOLNESS. She must be quite an acquisition to you, Halvard, this Miss Fosli.

SOLNESS. Yes, indeed. She is useful in all sorts of ways.

MRS. SOLNESS. So it seems.

DR. HERDAL. Is she good at bookkeeping too?

SOLNESS. Well—of course she has had a good deal of practice during these two years. And then she is so nice and willing to do whatever one asks of her.

MRS. SOLNESS. Yes, that must be very delightful—

SOLNESS. It is. Especially when one is not too much accustomed to that sort of thing.

MRS. SOLNESS [*in a tone of gentle remonstrance*]. Can you say that, Halvard?

SOLNESS. Oh, no, no, my dear Aline; I beg your pardon.

MRS. SOLNESS. There's no occasion.—Well then, doctor, you will come back later on, and have a cup of tea with us?

DR. HERDAL. I have only that one patient to see, and then I'll come back.

MRS. SOLNESS. Thank you.

[*She goes out by the door on the right.*]

SOLNESS. Are you in a hurry, doctor?

DR. HERDAL. No, not at all.

SOLNESS. May I have a little chat with you?

DR. HERDAL. With the greatest of pleasure.

SOLNESS. Then let us sit down.

[*He motions the doctor to take the rocking chair, and sits down himself in the armchair. Looks searchingly at him.*] Tell me—did you notice anything odd about Aline?

DR. HERDAL. Do you mean just now, when she was here?

SOLNESS. Yes, in her manner to me. Did you notice anything?

DR. HERDAL [*smiling*]. Well, I admit—one couldn't well avoid noticing that your wife—h'm—

SOLNESS. Well?

DR. HERDAL.—that your wife is not particularly fond of this Miss Fosli.

SOLNESS. Is that all? I have noticed that myself.

DR. HERDAL. And I must say I am scarcely surprised at it.

SOLNESS. At what?

DR. HERDAL. That she should not exactly approve of your seeing so much of another woman, all day and every day.

SOLNESS. No, no, I suppose you are right there—and Aline too. But it's impossible to make any change.

DR. HERDAL. Could you not engage a clerk?

SOLNESS. The first man that came to hand? No, thank you—that would never do for me.

DR. HERDAL. But now, if your wife—? Suppose, with her delicate health, all this tries her too much?

SOLNESS. Even then—I might almost say—it can make no difference. I must keep Kaia Fosli. No one else could fill her place.

DR. HERDAL. No one else?

SOLNESS [*curtly*]. No, no one.

DR. HERDAL [*drawing his chair closer*]. Now listen to me, my dear Mr. Solness. May I ask you a question, quite between ourselves?

SOLNESS. By all means.

DR. HERDAL. Women, you see—in certain matters, they have a deucedly keen intuition—

SOLNESS. They have, indeed. There is not the least doubt of that. But—?

DR. HERDAL. Well, tell me now—if your wife can't endure this Kaia Fosli—?

SOLNESS. Well, what then?

DR. HERDAL.—may she not have just—just the least little bit of reason for this instinctive dislike?

SOLNESS [*looks at him and rises*]. Oho!

DR. HERDAL. Now don't be offended—but hasn't she?

SOLNESS [*with curt decision*]. No.

DR. HERDAL. No reason of any sort?

SOLNESS. No other reason than her own suspicious nature.

DR. HERDAL. I know you have known a good many women in your time.

SOLNESS. Yes, I have.

DR. HERDAL. And have been a good deal taken with some of them, too.

SOLNESS. Oh yes, I don't deny it.

DR. HERDAL. But as regards Miss Fosli, then? There is nothing of that sort in the case?

SOLNESS. No; nothing at all—on my side.

DR. HERDAL. But on her side?

SOLNESS. I don't think you have any right to ask that question, doctor.

DR. HERDAL. Well, you know, we were discussing your wife's intuition.

SOLNESS. So we were. And for that matter—[*lowers his voice*]—Aline's intuition, as you call it—in a certain sense, it has not been so far astray.

DR. HERDAL. Aha! there we have it!

SOLNESS [*sits down*]. Doctor Herdal—I am going to tell you a strange story—if you care to listen to it.

DR. HERDAL. I like listening to strange stories.

SOLNESS. Very well then. I daresay you recollect that I took Knut Brovik and his son into my employment—after the old man's business had gone to the dogs.

DR. HERDAL. Yes, so I have understood.

SOLNESS. You see, they really are clever fellows, these two. Each of them has talent in his own way. But then the son took it into his head to get engaged; and the next thing, of course, was that he wanted to get married —and begin to build on his own account. That is the way with all these young people.

DR. HERDAL [*laughing*]. Yes, they have a bad habit of wanting to marry.

SOLNESS. Just so. But of course that did not suit my plans; for I needed Ragnar myself—and the old man too. He is exceedingly good at calculating bearing-strains and cubic contents—and all that sort of deviltry, you know.

DR. HERDAL. Oh yes, no doubt that's indispensable.

SOLNESS. Yes, it is. But Ragnar was absolutely bent on setting to work for himself. He would hear of nothing else.

DR. HERDAL. But he has stayed with you all the same.

SOLNESS. Yes, I'll tell you how that came about. One day this girl, Kaia Fosli, came to see them on some errand or other. She had never been here before. And when I saw how utterly infatuated they were with each other, the thought occurred to me: if I could only get her into the office here, then perhaps Ragnar too would stay where he is.

DR. HERDAL. That was not at all a bad idea.

SOLNESS. Yes, but at the time I did not breathe a word of what was in my mind. I merely stood and looked at her—and kept on wishing intently that I could have her here. Then I talked to her a little, in a friendly way —about one thing and another. And then she went away.

DR. HERDAL. Well?

SOLNESS. Well then, next day, pretty late in the evening, when old Brovik and Ragnar had gone home, she came here again, and behaved as if I had made an arrangement with her.

DR. HERDAL. An arrangement? What about?

SOLNESS. About the very thing my mind had been fixed on. But I hadn't said one single word about it.

DR. HERDAL. That was most extraordinary.

SOLNESS. Yes, was it not? And now she wanted to know what she was to do here—whether she could begin the very next morning, and so forth.

DR. HERDAL. Don't you think she did it in order to be with her sweetheart?

SOLNESS. That was what occurred to me at first. But no, that was not it. She seemed to drift quite away from him—when once she had come here to me.

DR. HERDAL. She drifted over to you, then?

SOLNESS. Yes, entirely. If I happen to look at her when her back is turned, I can tell that she feels it. She quivers and trembles the moment I come near her. What do you think of that?

DR. HERDAL. H'm—that's not very hard to explain.

SOLNESS. Well, but what about the other thing? That she believed I had said to her what I had only wished and willed—silently—inwardly— to myself? What do you say to that? Can you explain that, Dr. Herdal?

DR. HERDAL. No, I won't undertake to do that.

SOLNESS. I felt sure you would not; and so I have never cared to talk about it till now.—But it's a cursed nuisance to me in the long run, you understand. Here have I got to go on day after day pretending—. And it's a shame to treat her so, too, poor girl. [*Vehemently.*] But I cannot do anything else. For if she runs away from me—then Ragnar will be off too.

DR. HERDAL. And you have not told your wife the rights of the story?

SOLNESS. No.

DR. HERDAL. Then why on earth don't you?

SOLNESS [*looks fixedly at him, and says in a low voice*]. Because I seem to find a sort of—of salutary self-torture in allowing Aline to do me an injustice.

DR. HERDAL [*shakes his head*]. I don't in the least understand what you mean.

SOLNESS. Well, you see—it is like paying off a little bit of a huge, immeasurable debt—

DR. HERDAL. To your wife?

SOLNESS. Yes; and that always helps to relieve one's mind a little. One can breathe more freely for a while, you understand.

DR. HERDAL. No, goodness knows, I don't understand at all—

SOLNESS [*breaking off, rises again*]. Well, well, well—then we won't talk any more about it.

[*He saunters across the room, returns, and stops beside the table. Looks at the doctor with a sly smile.*]

I suppose you think you have drawn me out nicely now, doctor?

DR. HERDAL [*with some irritation*]. Drawn you out? Again I have not the faintest notion what you mean, Mr. Solness.

SOLNESS. Oh come, out with it; I have seen it quite clearly, you know.

DR. HERDAL. What have you seen?

SOLNESS [*in a low voice, slowly*]. That you have been quietly keeping an eye upon me.

DR. HERDAL. That *I* have! And why in all the world should I do that?

SOLNESS. Because you think that I— [*Passionately.*] Well, devil take it— you think the same of me as Aline does.

DR. HERDAL. And what does she think about you?

SOLNESS [*having recovered his self-control*]. She has begun to think that I am—that I am—ill.

DR. HERDAL. Ill! You! She has never hinted such a thing to me. Why, what can she think is the matter with you?

SOLNESS [*leans over the back of the chair and whispers*]. Aline has made up her mind that I am mad. That is what she thinks.

DR. HERDAL [*rising*]. Why, my dear good fellow—!

SOLNESS. Yes, on my soul she does! I tell you it is so. And she has got you to think the same! Oh, I can assure you, doctor, I see it in your face as clearly as possible. You don't take me in so easily, I can tell you.

DR. HERDAL [*looks at him in amazement*]. Never, Mr. Solness—never has such a thought entered my mind.

SOLNESS [*with an incredulous smile*]. Really? Has it not?

DR. HERDAL. No, never! Nor your wife's mind either, I am convinced. I could almost swear to that.

SOLNESS. Well, I wouldn't advise you to. For, in a certain sense, you see, perhaps—perhaps she is not so far wrong in thinking something of the kind.

DR. HERDAL. Come now, I really must say—

SOLNESS [*interrupting, with a sweep of his hand*]. Well, well, my dear doctor
—don't let us discuss this any further. We had better agree to differ.
[*Changes to a tone of quiet amusement.*] But look here now, doctor—
h'm—

DR. HERDAL. Well?

SOLNESS. Since you don't believe that I am—ill—and crazy—and mad, and
so forth—

DR. HERDAL. What then?

SOLNESS. Then I daresay you fancy that I am an extremely happy man.

DR. HERDAL. Is that mere fancy?

SOLNESS [*laughs*]. No, no—of course not! Heaven forbid! Only think—
to be Solness the master builder! Halvard Solness! What could be more
delightful?

DR. HERDAL. Yes, I must say it seems to me you have had the luck on your
side to an astounding degree.

SOLNESS [*suppresses a gloomy smile*]. So I have. I can't complain on that
score.

DR. HERDAL. First of all that grim old robbers' castle was burnt down for
you. And that was certainly a great piece of luck.

SOLNESS [*seriously*]. It was the home of Aline's family. Remember that.

DR. HERDAL. Yes, it must have been a great grief to her.

SOLNESS. She has not got over it to this day—not in all these twelve or
thirteen years.

DR. HERDAL. Ah, but what followed must have been the worst blow for her.

SOLNESS. The one thing with the other.

DR. HERDAL. But you—yourself—you rose upon the ruins. You began as a
poor boy from a country village—and now you are at the head of your
profession. Ah, yes, Mr. Solness, you have undoubtedly had the luck
on your side.

SOLNESS [*looking at him with embarrassment*]. Yes, but that is just what
makes me so horribly afraid.

DR. HERDAL. Afraid? Because you have the luck on your side!

SOLNESS. It terrifies me—terrifies me every hour of the day. For sooner or
later the luck must turn, you see.

DR. HERDAL. Oh nonsense! What should make the luck turn?

SOLNESS [*with firm assurance*]. The younger generation.

DR. HERDAL. Pooh! The younger generation! You are not laid on the shelf
yet, I should hope. Oh no—your position here is probably firmer now
than it has ever been.

SOLNESS. The luck will turn. I know it—I feel the day approaching. Some
one or other will take it into his head to say: Give me a chance! And then
all the rest will come clamoring after him, and shake their fists at me and
shout: Make room—make room—make room! Yes, just you see,
doctor—presently the younger generation will come knocking at my
door—

DR. HERDAL [*laughing*]. Well, and what if they do?

SOLNESS. What if they do? Then there's an end of Halvard Solness.

[*There is a knock at the door on the left.*]

SOLNESS [*starts*]. What's that? Did you not hear something?

DR. HERDAL. Someone is knocking at the door.

SOLNESS [*loudly*]. Come in.

[HILDA WANGEL *enters by the hall door. She is of middle height, supple, and delicately built. Somewhat sunburned. Dressed in a tourist costume, with skirt caught up for walking, a sailor's collar open at the throat, and a small sailor hat on her head. Knapsack on back, plaid in strap, and alpenstock.*]

HILDA [*goes straight up to* SOLNESS, *her eyes sparkling with happiness*]. Good evening!

SOLNESS [*looks doubtfully at her*]. Good evening!

HILDA [*laughs*]. I almost believe you don't recognize me!

SOLNESS. No—I must admit that—just for the moment—

DR. HERDAL [*approaching*]. But *I* recognize you, my dear young lady—

HILDA [*pleased*]. Oh, is it you that—

DR. HERDAL. Of course it is. [*To* SOLNESS.] We met at one of the mountain stations this summer. [*To* HILDA.] What became of the other ladies?

HILDA. Oh, they went westward.

DR. HERDAL. They didn't much like all the fun we used to have in the evenings.

HILDA. No, I believe they didn't.

DR. HERDAL [*holds up his finger at her*]. And I am afraid it can't be denied that you flirted a little with us.

HILDA. Well, that was better fun than to sit there knitting stockings with all those old women.

DR. HERDAL [*laughs*]. There I entirely agree with you!

SOLNESS. Have you come to town this evening?

HILDA. Yes, I have just arrived.

DR. HERDAL. Quite alone, Miss Wangel?

HILDA. Oh yes!

SOLNESS. Wangel? Is your name Wangel?

HILDA [*looks in amused surprise at him*]. Yes, of course it is.

SOLNESS. Then you must be a daughter of the district doctor up at Lysanger?

HILDA [*as before*]. Yes, who else's daughter should I be?

SOLNESS. Oh, then I suppose we met up there, that summer when I was building a tower on the old church.

HILDA [*more seriously*]. Yes, of course it was then we met.

SOLNESS. Well, that is a long time ago.

HILDA [*looks hard at him*]. It is exactly the ten years.

SOLNESS. You must have been a mere child then, I should think.

HILDA [*carelessly*]. Well, I was twelve or thirteen.

DR. HERDAL. Is this the first time you have ever been up to town, Miss Wangel?

HILDA. Yes, it is indeed.

SOLNESS. And don't you know any one here?

HILDA. Nobody but you. And of course, your wife.

SOLNESS. So you know her, too?

HILDA. Only a little. We spent a few days together at the sanatorium.

SOLNESS. Ah, up there?

HILDA. She said I might come and pay her a visit if ever I came up to town. [*Smiles.*] Not that that was necessary.

SOLNESS. Odd that she should never have mentioned it.

[HILDA *puts her stick down by the stove, takes off the knapsack and lays it and the plaid on the sofa.* DR. HERDAL *offers to help her.* SOLNESS *stands and gazes at her.*]

HILDA [*going toward him*]. Well, now I must ask you to let me stay the night here.

SOLNESS. I am sure there will be no difficulty about that.

HILDA. For I have no other clothes than those I stand in, except a change of linen in my knapsack. And that has to go to the wash, for it's very dirty.

SOLNESS. Oh yes, that can be managed. Now I'll just let my wife know—

DR. HERDAL. Meanwhile I will go and see my patient.

SOLNESS. Yes, do; and come again later on.

DR. HERDAL [*playfully, with a glance at* HILDA]. Oh that I will, you may be very certain! [*Laughs.*] So your prediction has come true, Mr. Solness!

SOLNESS. How so?

DR. HERDAL. The younger generation did come knocking at your door.

SOLNESS [*cheerfully*] Yes, but in a very different way from what I meant.

DR. HERDAL. Very different, yes. That's undeniable.

[*He goes out by the hall door.* SOLNESS *opens the door on the right and speaks into the side room.*]

SOLNESS. Aline! Will you come in here, please. Here is a friend of yours— Miss Wangel.

MRS. SOLNESS [*appears in the doorway*]. Who do you say it is? [*Sees* HILDA.] Oh, is it you, Miss Wangel?

[*Goes up to her and offers her hand.*]

So you have come to town after all.

SOLNESS. Miss Wangel has this moment arrived; and she would like to stay the night here.

MRS. SOLNESS. Here with us? Oh yes, certainly.

SOLNESS. Till she can get her things a little in order, you know.

MRS. SOLNESS. I will do the best I can for you. It's no more than my duty. I suppose your trunk is coming on later?

HILDA. I have no trunk.

MRS. SOLNESS. Well, it will be all right, I daresay. In the meantime, you must excuse my leaving you here with my husband, until I can get a room made a little comfortable for you.

SOLNESS. Can we not give her one of the nurseries? They are all ready as it is.

MRS. SOLNESS. Oh yes. There we have room and to spare. [*To* HILDA.] Sit down now, and rest a little.

[*She goes out to the right.* HILDA, *with her hands behind her back, strolls about the room and looks at various objects.* SOLNESS *stands in front, beside the table, also with his hands behind his back, and follows her with his eyes.*]

HILDA [*stops and looks at him*]. Have you several nurseries?

SOLNESS. There are three nurseries in the house.

HILDA. That's a lot. Then I suppose you have a great many children?

SOLNESS. No. We have no child. But now you can be the child here, for the time being.

HILDA. For tonight, yes. I shall not cry. I mean to sleep as sound as a stone.

SOLNESS. Yes, you must be very tired, I should think.

HILDA. Oh no! But all the same—. It's so delicious to lie and dream.

SOLNESS. Do you dream much of nights?

HILDA. Oh yes! Almost always.

SOLNESS. What do you dream about most?

HILDA. I sha'n't tell you tonight. Another time, perhaps.

[*She again strolls about the room, stops at the desk and turns over the books and papers a little.*]

SOLNESS [*approaching*]. Are you searching for anything?

HILDA. No, I am merely looking at all these things. [*Turns.*] Perhaps I mustn't?

SOLNESS. Oh, by all means.

HILDA. Is it you that write in this great ledger?

SOLNESS. No, it's my bookkeeper.

HILDA. Is it a woman?

SOLNESS [*smiles*]. Yes.

HILDA. One you employ here, in your office?

SOLNESS. Yes.

HILDA. Is she married?

SOLNESS. No, she is single.

HILDA. Oh, indeed!

SOLNESS. But I believe she is soon going to be married.

HILDA. That's a good thing for her.

SOLNESS. But not such a good thing for me. For then I shall have nobody to help me.

HILDA. Can't you get hold of someone else who will do just as well?

SOLNESS. Perhaps you would stay here and—and write in the ledger?

HILDA [*measures him with a glance*]. Yes, I daresay! No, thank you— nothing of that sort for me.

[*She again strolls across the room, and sits down in the rocking chair.* SOLNESS *too goes to the table.*]

HILDA [*continuing*]. For there must surely be plenty of other things to be done here. [*Looks smilingly at him.*] Don't you think so, too?

SOLNESS. Of course. First of all, I suppose, you want to make a round of the shops, and get yourself up in the height of fashion.

HILDA [*amused*]. No, I think I shall let that alone!

SOLNESS. Indeed?

HILDA. For you must know I have run through all my money.

SOLNESS [*laughs*]. Neither trunk nor money, then!

HILDA. Neither one nor the other. But never mind—it doesn't matter now.

SOLNESS. Come now, I like you for that.

HILDA. Only for that?

SOLNESS. For that among other things.

[*Sits in the armchair.*]

Is your father alive still?

HILDA. Yes, father's alive.

SOLNESS. Perhaps you are thinking of studying here?

HILDA. No, that hadn't occurred to me.

SOLNESS. But I suppose you will be staying for some time?

HILDA. That must depend upon circumstances.

[*She sits awhile rocking herself and looking at him, half seriously, half with a suppressed smile. Then she takes off her hat and puts it on the table in front of her.*]

Mr. Solness!

SOLNESS. Well?

HILDA. Have you a very bad memory?

SOLNESS. A bad memory? No, not that I am aware of.

HILDA. Then have you nothing to say to me about what happened up there?

SOLNESS [*in momentary surprise*]. Up at Lysanger? [*Indifferently.*] Why, it was nothing much to talk about, it seems to me.

HILDA [*looks reproachfully at him*]. How can you sit there and say such things?

SOLNESS. Well, then, you talk to me about it.

HILDA. When the tower was finished, we had grand doings in the town.

SOLNESS. Yes, I shall not easily forget that day.

HILDA [*smiles*]. Will you not? That comes well from you.

SOLNESS. Comes well?

HILDA. There was music in the churchyard—and many, many hundreds of people. We schoolgirls were dressed in white; and we all carried flags.

SOLNESS. Ah yes, those flags—I can tell you I remember them!

HILDA. Then you climbed right up the scaffolding, straight to the very top; and you had a great wreath with you; and you hung that wreath right away up on the weather vane.

SOLNESS [*curtly interrupting*]. I always did that in those days. It is an old custom.

HILDA. It was so wonderfully thrilling to stand below and look up at you. Fancy, if he should fall over! He—the master builder himself!

SOLNESS [*as if to divert her from the subject*]. Yes, yes, yes, that might very well have happened, too. For one of those white-frocked little devils— she went on in such a way, and screamed up at me so—

HILDA [*sparkling with pleasure*]. "Hurrah for Master-Builder Solness!" Yes!

SOLNESS.—and waved and flourished with her flag, so that I—so that it almost made me giddy to look at it.

HILDA [*in a lower voice, seriously*]. That little devil—that was *I*.

SOLNESS [*fixes his eyes steadily upon her*]. I am sure of that now. It must have been you.

HILDA [*lively again*]. Oh, it was so gloriously thrilling! I could not have believed there was a builder in the whole world that could build such a tremendously high tower. And then, that you yourself should stand at the very top of it, as large as life! And that you should not be the least bit dizzy! It was that above everything that made one—made one dizzy to think of.

SOLNESS. How could you be so certain that I was not—?

HILDA [*scouting the idea*]. No indeed! Oh no! I knew that instinctively. For if you had been, you could never have stood up there and sung.

SOLNESS [*looks at her in astonishment*]. Sung? Did *I* sing?

HILDA. Yes, I should think you did.

SOLNESS [*shakes his head*]. I have never sung a note in my life.

HILDA. Yes indeed, you sang then. It sounded like harps in the air.

SOLNESS [*thoughtfully*]. This is very strange—all this.

HILDA [*is silent awhile, looks at him and says in a low voice*]. But then,— it was after that—that the real thing happened.

SOLNESS. The real thing?

HILDA [*sparkling with vivacity*]. Yes, I surely don't need to remind you of that?

SOLNESS. Oh yes, do remind me a little of that, too.

HILDA. Don't you remember that a great dinner was given in your honor at the Club?

SOLNESS. Yes, to be sure. It must have been the same afternoon, for I left the place next morning.

HILDA. And from the Club you were invited to come round to our house to supper.

SOLNESS. Quite right, Miss Wangel. It is wonderful how all these trifles have impressed themselves on your mind.

HILDA. Trifles! I like that! Perhaps it was a trifle, too, that I was alone in the room when you came in?

SOLNESS. Were you alone?

HILDA [*without answering him*]. You didn't call me a little devil then?

SOLNESS. No, I suppose I did not.

HILDA. You said I was lovely in my white dress, and that I looked like a little princess.

SOLNESS. I have no doubt you did, Miss Wangel.—And besides—I was feeling so buoyant and free that day—

HILDA. And then you said that when I grew up I should be your princess.

SOLNESS [*laughing a little*]. Dear, dear—did I say that too?

HILDA. Yes, you did. And when I asked how long I should have to wait, you said that you would come again in ten years—like a troll—and carry me off—to Spain or some such place. And you promised you would buy me a kingdom there.

SOLNESS [*as before*]. Yes, after a good dinner one doesn't haggle about the halfpence. But did I really say all that?

HILDA [*laughs to herself*]. Yes. And you told me, too, what the kingdom was to be called.

SOLNESS. Well, what was it?

HILDA. It was to be called the kingdom of Orangia, you said.

SOLNESS. Well, that was an appetizing name.

HILDA. No, I didn't like it a bit; for it seemed as though you wanted to make game of me.

SOLNESS. I am sure that cannot have been my intention.

HILDA. No, I should hope not—considering what you did next—

SOLNESS. What in the world did I do next?

HILDA. Well, that's the finishing touch, if you have forgotten that too. I should have thought no one could help remembering such a thing as that.

SOLNESS. Yes, yes, just give me a hint, and then perhaps—Well?

HILDA [*looks fixedly at him*]. You came and kissed me, Mr. Solness.

SOLNESS [*open-mouthed, rising from his chair*]. *I* did!

HILDA. Yes, indeed you did. You took me in both your arms, and bent my head back, and kissed me—many times.

SOLNESS. Now really, my dear Miss Wangel—!

HILDA [*rises*]. You surely cannot mean to deny it?

SOLNESS. Yes, I do. I deny it altogether!

HILDA [*looks scornfully at him*]. Oh, indeed!

[*She turns and goes slowly close up to the stove, where she remains standing motionless, her face averted from him, her hands behind her back. Short pause.*]

SOLNESS [*goes cautiously up behind her*]. Miss Wangel—!

[HILDA *is silent and does not move.*]

SOLNESS. Don't stand there like a statue. You must have dreamed all this. [*Lays his hand on her arm.*] Now just listen—

[HILDA *makes an impatient movement with her arm.*]

SOLNESS [*as a thought flashes upon him*]. Or—! Wait a moment! There is something under all this, you may depend!

[HILDA *does not move.*]

SOLNESS [*in a low voice, but with emphasis*]. I must have thought all that. I must have wished it—have willed it—have longed to do it. And then— May not that be the explanation?

[HILDA *is still silent.*]

SOLNESS [*impatiently*]. Oh very well, deuce take it all—then I did do it, I suppose.

HILDA [*turns her head a little, but without looking at him*]. Then you admit it now?

SOLNESS. Yes—whatever you like.

HILDA. You came and put your arms round me?

SOLNESS. Oh yes!

HILDA. And bent my head back?

SOLNESS. Very far back.

HILDA. And kissed me?

SOLNESS. Yes, I did.

HILDA. Many times?

SOLNESS. As many as ever you like.

HILDA [*turns quickly toward him and has once more the sparkling expression of gladness in her eyes*]. Well, you see, I got it out of you at last!

SOLNESS [*with a slight smile*]. Yes,—just think of my forgetting such a thing as that.

HILDA [*again a little sulky, retreats from him*]. Oh, you have kissed so many people in your time, I suppose.

SOLNESS. No, you mustn't think that of me.

[HILDA *seats herself in the armchair.* SOLNESS *stands and leans against the rocking chair. Looks observantly at her.*]

Miss Wangel!

HILDA. Yes!

SOLNESS. How was it now? What came of all this—between us two?

HILDA. Why, nothing more came of it. You know that quite well. For then the other guests came in, and then—bah!

SOLNESS. Quite so! The others came in. To think of my forgetting that too!

HILDA. Oh, you haven't really forgotten anything: you are only a little ashamed of it all. I am sure one doesn't forget things of that kind.

SOLNESS. No, one would suppose not.

HILDA [*lively again, looks at him*]. Perhaps you have even forgotten what day it was?

SOLNESS. What day—?

HILDA. Yes, on what day did you hang the wreath on the tower? Well? Tell me at once!

SOLNESS. H'm—I confess I have forgotten the particular day. I only know it was ten years ago. Some time in the autumn.

HILDA [*nods her head slowly several times*]. It was ten years ago—on the 19th of September.

SOLNESS. Yes, it must have been about that time. Fancy your remembering that too! [*Stops.*] But wait a moment—! Yes—it's the 19th of September today.

HILDA. Yes, it is; and the ten years are gone. And you didn't come—as you had promised me.

SOLNESS. Promised you? Threatened, I suppose you mean?

HILDA. I don't think there was any sort of threat in that.

SOLNESS. Well then, a little bit of fun.

HILDA. Was that all you wanted? To make fun of me?

SOLNESS. Well, or to have a little joke with you. Upon my soul, I don't recollect. But it must have been something of that kind; for you were a mere child then.

HILDA. Oh, perhaps I wasn't quite such a child either. Not such a mere chit as you imagine.

SOLNESS [*looks searchingly at her*]. Did you really and seriously expect me to come again?

HILDA [*conceals a half-teasing smile*]. Yes, indeed! I did expect that of you.

SOLNESS. That I should come back to your home, and take you away with me?

HILDA. Just like a troll—yes.

SOLNESS. And make a princess of you?

HILDA. That's what you promised.

SOLNESS. And give you a kingdom as well?

HILDA [*looks up at the ceiling*]. Why not? Of course it need not have been an actual, everyday sort of a kingdom.

SOLNESS. But something else just as good?

HILDA. Yes, at least as good. [*Looks at him a moment.*] I thought, if you could build the highest church-towers in the world, you could surely manage to raise a kingdom of one sort or another as well.

SOLNESS [*shakes his head*]. I can't quite make you out, Miss Wangel.

HILDA. Can you not? To me it seems all so simple.

SOLNESS. No, I can't make up my mind whether you mean all you say, or are simply having a joke with me.

HILDA [*smiles*]. Making fun of you, perhaps? I too?

SOLNESS. Yes, exactly. Making fun—of both of us. [*Looks at her.*] Is it long since you found out that I was married?

HILDA. I have known it all along. Why do you ask me that?

SOLNESS [*lightly*]. Oh, well, it just occurred to me.
[*Looks earnestly at her, and says in a low voice.*]
What have you come for?

HILDA. I want my kingdom. The time is up.

SOLNESS [*laughs involuntarily*]. What a girl you are!

HILDA [*gaily*]. Out with my kingdom, Mr. Solness! [*Raps with her fingers.*] The kingdom on the table!

SOLNESS [*pushing the rocking chair nearer and sitting down*]. Now, seriously

speaking—what have you come for? What do you really want to do
here?

HILDA. Oh, first of all, I want to go round and look at all the things that
you have built.

SOLNESS. That will give you plenty of exercise.

HILDA. Yes, I know you have built a tremendous lot.

SOLNESS. I have indeed—especially of late years.

HILDA. Many church-towers among the rest? Immensely high ones?

SOLNESS. No. I build no more church-towers now. Nor churches either.

HILDA. What do you build then?

SOLNESS. Homes for human beings.

HILDA [*reflectively*]. Couldn't you build a little—a little bit of a church-
tower over these homes as well?

SOLNESS [*starting*]. What do you mean by that?

HILDA. I mean—something that points—points up into the free air. With
the vane at a dizzy height.

SOLNESS [*pondering a little*]. Strange that you should say that—for that is
just what I am most anxious to do.

HILDA [*impatiently*]. Why don't you do it, then?

SOLNESS [*shakes his head*]. No, the people will not have it.

HILDA. Fancy their not wanting it!

SOLNESS [*more lightly*]. But now I am building a new home for myself—
just opposite here.

HILDA. For yourself?

SOLNESS. Yes. It is almost finished. And on that there is a tower.

HILDA. A high tower?

SOLNESS. Yes.

HILDA. Very high?

SOLNESS. No doubt people will say it is too high—too high for a dwelling
house.

HILDA. I'll go out and look at that tower the first thing tomorrow morning.

SOLNESS [*sits resting his cheek on his hand, and gazes at her*]. Tell me,
Miss Wangel—what is your name? Your Christian name, I mean?

HILDA. Why, Hilda, of course.

SOLNESS [*as before*]. Hilda? Indeed?

HILDA. Don't you remember that? You called me Hilda yourself—that
day when you misbehaved.

SOLNESS. Did I really?

HILDA. But then you said "little Hilda"; and I didn't like that.

SOLNESS. Oh, you didn't like that, Miss Hilda?

HILDA. No, not at such a time as that. But—"Princess Hilda"—that will
sound very well, I think.

SOLNESS. Very well indeed. Princess Hilda of—of—what was to be the name
of the kingdom?

HILDA. Pooh! I won't have anything to do with that stupid kingdom. I have set my heart upon quite a different one!

SOLNESS [*has leaned back in the chair, still gazing at her*]. Isn't it strange—? The more I think of it now, the more it seems to me as though I had gone about all these years torturing myself with—h'm—

HILDA. With what?

SOLNESS. With the effort to recover something—some experience, which I seemed to have forgotten. But I never had the least inkling of what it could be.

HILDA. You should have tied a knot in your pocket-handkerchief, Mr. Solness.

SOLNESS. In that case, I should simply have had to go racking my brains to discover what the knot could mean.

HILDA. Oh yes, I suppose there are trolls of that kind in the world, too.

SOLNESS [*rises slowly*]. What a good thing it is that you have come to me now.

HILDA [*looks deeply into his eyes*]. Is it a good thing!

SOLNESS. For I have been so lonely here. I have been gazing so helplessly at it all. [*In a lower voice.*] I must tell you—I have begun to be so afraid—so terribly afraid of the younger generation.

HILDA [*with a little snort of contempt*]. Pooh—is the younger generation a thing to be afraid of?

SOLNESS. It is indeed. And that is why I have locked and barred myself in. [*Mysteriously.*] I tell you the younger generation will one day come and thunder at my door! They will break in upon me!

HILDA. Then I should say you ought to go out and open the door to the younger generation.

SOLNESS. Open the door?

HILDA. Yes. Let them come in to you on friendly terms, as it were.

SOLNESS. No, no, no! The younger generation—it means retribution, you see. It comes, as if under a new banner, heralding the turn of fortune.

HILDA [*rises, looks at him, and says with a quivering twitch of her lips*]. Can *I* be of any use to you, Mr. Solness?

SOLNESS. Yes, you can indeed! For you, too, come—under a new banner, it seems to me. Youth marshaled against youth—!

[DR. HERDAL *comes in by the hall door.*]

DR. HERDAL. What—you and Miss Wangel here still?

SOLNESS. Yes. We have had no end of things to talk about.

HILDA. Both old and new.

DR. HERDAL. Have you really?

HILDA. Oh, it has been the greatest fun. For Mr. Solness—he has such a miraculous memory. All the least little details he remembers instantly. [MRS. SOLNESS *enters by the door on the right.*]

MRS. SOLNESS. Well, Miss Wangel, your room is quite ready for you now.

HILDA. Oh, how kind you are to me!

SOLNESS [*to* MRS. SOLNESS]. The nursery?

MRS. SOLNESS. Yes, the middle one. But first let us go in to supper.

SOLNESS [*nods to* HILDA]. Hilda shall sleep in the nursery, she shall.

MRS. SOLNESS [*looks at him*]. Hilda?

SOLNESS. Yes, Miss Wangel's name is Hilda. I knew her when she was a child.

MRS. SOLNESS. Did you really, Halvard? Well, shall we go? Supper is on the table.

[*She takes* DR. HERDAL'S *arm and goes out with him to the right.* HILDA *has meanwhile been collecting her traveling things.*]

HILDA [*softly and rapidly to* SOLNESS]. Is it true, what you said? Can I be of use to you?

SOLNESS [*takes the things from her*]. You are the very being I have needed most.

HILDA [*looks at him with happy, wondering eyes and clasps her hands*]. But then, great heavens—!

SOLNESS [*eagerly*]. What—?

HILDA. Then I have my kingdom!

SOLNESS [*involuntarily*]. Hilda—!

HILDA [*again with the quivering twitch of her lips*]. Almost—I was going to say.

[*She goes out to the right,* SOLNESS *follows her.*]

ACT TWO

A prettily furnished small drawing room in SOLNESS'S *house. In the back, a glass door leading out to the veranda and garden. The right-hand corner is cut off transversely by a large bay window, in which are flower-stands. The left-hand corner is similarly cut off by a transverse wall, in which is a small door papered like the wall. On each side, an ordinary door. In front, on the right, a console table with a large mirror over it. Well-filled stands of plants and flowers. In front, on the left, a sofa with a table and chairs. Further back, a bookcase. Well forward in the room, before the bay window, a small table and some chairs. It is early in the day.*

SOLNESS *sits by the little table with* RAGNAR BROVIK'S *portfolio open in front of him. He is turning the drawings over and closely examining some of them.* MRS. SOLNESS *moves about noiselessly with a small watering-pot, attending to her flowers. She is dressed in black as before. Her hat, cloak and parasol lie on a chair near the mirror. Unobserved by her,* SOLNESS *now and again follows her with his eyes. Neither of them speaks.*

[KAIA FOSLI *enters quietly by the door on the left.*]

SOLNESS [*turns his head, and says in an off-hand tone of indifference*]. Well, is that you?

KAIA. I merely wished to let you know that I have come.

SOLNESS. Yes, yes, that's all right. Hasn't Ragnar come too?

KAIA. No, not yet. He had to wait a little while to see the doctor. But he is coming presently to hear—

SOLNESS. How is the old man today?

KAIA. Not well. He begs you to excuse him; he is obliged to keep his bed today.

SOLNESS. Why, of course; by all means let him rest. But now, get to your work.

KAIA. Yes. [*Pauses at the door.*] Do you wish to speak to Ragnar when he comes?

SOLNESS. No—I don't know that I have anything particular to say to him.

[KAIA *goes out again to the left.* SOLNESS *remains seated, turning over the drawings.*]

MRS. SOLNESS [*over beside the plants*]. I wonder if he isn't going to die now, as well?

SOLNESS [*looks up at her*]. As well as who?

MRS. SOLNESS [*without answering*]. Yes, yes—depend upon it, Halvard, old Brovik is going to die too. You'll see that he will.

SOLNESS. My dear Aline, ought you not to go out for a little walk?

MRS. SOLNESS. Yes, I suppose I ought to.

[*She continues to attend to the flowers.*]

SOLNESS [*bending over the drawings*]. Is she still asleep?

MRS. SOLNESS [*looking at him*]. Is it Miss Wangel you are sitting there thinking about?

SOLNESS [*indifferently*]. I just happened to recollect her.

MRS. SOLNESS. Miss Wangel was up long ago.

SOLNESS. Oh, was she?

MRS. SOLNESS. When I went in to see her, she was busy putting her things in order

[*She goes in front of the mirror and slowly begins to put on her hat.*]

SOLNESS [*after a short pause*]. So we have found a use for one of our nurseries after all, Aline.

MRS. SOLNESS. Yes, we have.

SOLNESS. That seems to me better than to have them all standing empty.

MRS. SOLNESS. That emptiness is dreadful; you are right there.

SOLNESS [*closes the portfolio, rises and approaches her*]. You will find that we shall get on far better after this, Aline. Things will be more comfortable. Life will be easier—especially for you.

MRS. SOLNESS [*looks at him*]. After this?

SOLNESS. Yes, believe me, Aline—

MRS. SOLNESS. Do you mean—because she has come here?

SOLNESS [*checking himself*]. I mean, of course—when once we have moved into the new house.

MRS. SOLNESS [*takes her cloak*]. Ah, do you think so, Halvard? Will it be better then?

SOLNESS. I can't think otherwise. And surely you think so too?

MRS. SOLNESS. I think nothing at all about the new house.

SOLNESS [*cast down*]. It's hard for me to hear you say that; for you know it is mainly for your sake that I have built it.

[*He offers to help her on with her cloak.*]

MRS. SOLNESS [*evades him*]. The fact is, you do far too much for my sake.

SOLNESS [*with a certain vehemence*]. No, no, you really mustn't say that, Aline! I cannot bear to hear you say such things!

MRS. SOLNESS. Very well, then I won't say it, Halvard.

SOLNESS. But I stick to what *I* said. You'll see that things will be easier for you in the new place.

MRS. SOLNESS. Oh Heavens—easier for me—!

SOLNESS [*eagerly*]. Yes, indeed they will! You may be quite sure of that! For you see—there will be so very, very much there that will remind you of your own home—

MRS. SOLNESS. The home that used to be father's and mother's—and that was burnt to the ground—

SOLNESS [*in a low voice*]. Yes, yes, my poor Aline. That was a terrible blow for you.

MRS. SOLNESS [*breaking out in lamentation*]. You may build as much as ever you like, Halvard—you can never build up again a real home for me!

SOLNESS [*crosses the room*]. Well, in Heaven's name, let us talk no more about it then.

MRS. SOLNESS. We are not in the habit of talking about it. For you always put the thought away from you—

SOLNESS [*stops suddenly and looks at her*]. Do I? And why should I do that? Put the thought away from me?

MRS. SOLNESS. Oh yes, Halvard, I understand you very well. You are so anxious to spare me—and to find excuses for me too—as much as ever you can.

SOLNESS [*with astonishment in his eyes*]. You! Is it you—yourself, that you are talking about, Aline?

MRS. SOLNESS. Yes, who else should it be but myself?

SOLNESS [*involuntarily to himself*]. That too!

MRS. SOLNESS. As for the old house, I wouldn't mind so much about that. When once misfortune was in the air—why—

SOLNESS. Ah, you are right there. Misfortune will have its way—as the saying goes.

MRS. SOLNESS. But it's what came of the fire—the dreadful thing that followed—! That is the thing! That, that, that!

SOLNESS [*vehemently*]. Don't think about that, Aline!

MRS. SOLNESS. Ah, that is exactly what I cannot help thinking about. And now, at last, I must speak about it too; for I don't seem able to bear it any longer. And then never to be able to forgive myself—

SOLNESS [*exclaiming*]. Yourself—!

MRS. SOLNESS. Yes, for I had duties on both sides—both toward you and toward the little ones. I ought to have hardened myself—not to have let the horror take such hold upon me—nor the grief for the burning of my home. [*Wrings her hands.*] Oh, Halvard, if I had only had the strength!

SOLNESS [*softly, much moved, comes closer*]. Aline—you must promise me never to think these thoughts any more.—Promise me that, dear!

MRS. SOLNESS. Oh, promise, promise! One can promise anything.

SOLNESS [*clenches his hands and crosses the room*]. Oh, but this is hopeless, hopeless! Never a ray of sunlight! Not so much as a gleam of brightness to light up our home!

MRS. SOLNESS. This is no home, Halvard.

SOLNESS. Oh no, you may well say that. [*Gloomily.*] And God knows whether you are not right in saying that it will be no better for us in the new house, either.

MRS. SOLNESS. It will never be any better. Just as empty—just as desolate—there as here.

SOLNESS [*vehemently*]. Why in all the world have we built it then? Can you tell me that?

MRS. SOLNESS. No; you must answer that question for yourself.

SOLNESS [*glances suspiciously at her*]. What do you mean by that, Aline?

MRS. SOLNESS. What do I mean?

SOLNESS. Yes, in the devil's name! You said it so strangely—as if you had some hidden meaning in it.

MRS. SOLNESS. No, indeed, I assure you—

SOLNESS [*comes closer*]. Oh, come now—I know what I know. I have both my eyes and my ears about me, Aline—you may depend upon that!

MRS. SOLNESS. Why, what are you talking about? What is it?

SOLNESS [*places himself in front of her*]. Do you mean to say you don't find a kind of lurking, hidden meaning in the most innocent word I happen to say?

MRS. SOLNESS. *I*, do you say? *I* do that?

SOLNESS [*laughs*]. Ho-ho-ho! It's natural enough, Aline! When you have a sick man on your hands—

MRS. SOLNESS [*anxiously*]. Sick? Are you ill, Halvard?

SOLNESS [*violently*]. A half-mad man then! A crazy man! Call me what you will.

MRS. SOLNESS [*feels blindly for a chair and sits down*]. Halvard—for God's sake—

SOLNESS. But you are wrong, both you and the doctor. I am not in the state you imagine.

[*He walks up and down the room.* MRS. SOLNESS *follows him anxiously with her eyes. Finally he goes up to her.*]

SOLNESS [*calmly*]. In reality there is nothing whatever the matter with me.

MRS. SOLNESS. No, there isn't, is there? But then what is it that troubles you so?

SOLNESS. Why this, that I often feel ready to sink under this terrible burden of debt—

MRS. SOLNESS. Debt, do you say? But you owe no one anything, Halvard!

SOLNESS [*softly, with emotion*]. I owe a boundless debt to you—to you—to you, Aline.

MRS. SOLNESS [*rises slowly*]. What is behind all this? You may just as well tell me at once.

SOLNESS. But there is nothing behind it! I have never done you any wrong—not wittingly and wilfully, at any rate. And yet—and yet it seems as though a crushing debt rested upon me and weighed me down.

MRS. SOLNESS. A debt to me?

SOLNESS. Chiefly to you.

MRS. SOLNESS. Then you are—ill after all, Halvard.

SOLNESS [*gloomily*]. I suppose I must be—or not far from it. [*Looks toward the door to the right, which is opened at this moment.*] Ah! now it grows lighter.

[HILDA WANGEL *comes in. She has made some alteration in her dress, and let down her skirt.*]

HILDA. Good morning, Mr. Solness!

SOLNESS [*nods*]. Slept well?

HILDA. Quite deliciously! Like a child in a cradle. Oh—I lay and stretched myself like—like a princess!

SOLNESS [*smiles a little*]. You were thoroughly comfortable then?

HILDA. I should think so.

SOLNESS. And no doubt you dreamed, too.

HILDA. Yes, I did. But that was horrid.

SOLNESS. Was it?

HILDA. Yes, for I dreamed I was falling over a frightfully high, sheer precipice. Do you never have that kind of dream?

SOLNESS. Oh yes—now and then—

HILDA. It's tremendously thrilling—when you fall and fall—

SOLNESS. It seems to make one's blood run cold.

HILDA. Do you draw your legs up under you while you are falling?

SOLNESS. Yes, as high as ever I can.

HILDA. So do I.

MRS. SOLNESS [*takes her parasol*]. I must go into town now, Halvard. [*To* HILDA.] And I'll try to get one or two things that you may require.

HILDA [*making a motion to throw her arms round her neck*]. Oh, you dear, sweet Mrs. Solness! You are really much too kind to me! Frightfully kind—

MRS. SOLNESS [*deprecatingly, freeing herself*]. Oh, not at all. It's only my duty, so I am very glad to do it.

HILDA [*offended, pouts*]. But really, I think I am quite fit to be seen in the streets—now that I've put my dress to rights. Or do you think I am not?

MRS. SOLNESS. To tell you the truth, I think people would stare at you a little.

HILDA [*contemptuously*]. Pooh! Iş that all? That only amuses me.

SOLNESS [*with suppressed ill-humor*]. Yes, but people might take it into their heads that you were mad too, you see.

HILDA. Mad? Are there so many mad people here in town, then?

SOLNESS [*points to his own forehead*]. Here you see one at all events.

HILDA. You—Mr. Solness!

MRS. SOLNESS. Oh, don't talk like that, my dear Halvard!

SOLNESS. Have you not noticed that yet?

HILDA. No, I certainly have not.

[*Reflects and laughs a little.*]

And yet—perhaps in one single thing.

SOLNESS. Ah, do you hear that, Aline?

MRS. SOLNESS. What is that one single thing, Miss Wangel?

HILDA. No, I won't say.

SOLNESS. Oh yes, do!

HILDA. No thank you—I am not so mad as that.

MRS. SOLNESS. When you and Miss Wangel are alone, I daresay she will tell you, Halvard.

SOLNESS. Ah—you think she will?

MRS. SOLNESS. Oh yes, certainly. For you have known her so well in the past. Ever since she was a child—you tell me.

[*She goes out by the door on the left.*]

HILDA [*after a little while*]. Does you wife dislike me very much?

SOLNESS. Did you think you noticed anything of the kind?

HILDA. Did you not notice it yourself?

SOLNESS [*evasively*]. Aline has become exceedingly shy with strangers of late years.

HILDA. Has she really?

SOLNESS. But if only you could get to know her thoroughly—! Ah, she is so good—so kind—so excellent a creature—

HILDA [*impatiently*]. But if she is all that—what made her say that about her duty?

SOLNESS. Her duty?

HILDA. She said that she would go out and buy something for me, because it was her duty. Oh I can't bear that ugly, horrid word!

SOLNESS. Why not?

HILDA. It sounds so cold, and sharp, and stinging. Duty—duty—duty. Don't you think so, too? Doesn't it seem to sting you?

SOLNESS. H'm—haven't thought much about it.

HILDA. Yes, it does. And if she is so good—as you say she is—why should she talk in that way?

SOLNESS. But, good Lord, what would you have had her say, then?

HILDA. She might have said she would do it because she had taken a tremendous fancy to me. She might have said something like that—something really warm and cordial, you understand.

SOLNESS [*looks at her*]. Is that how you would like to have it?

HILDA. Yes, precisely.

[*She wanders about the room, stops at the bookcase and looks at the books.*]

What a lot of books you have.

SOLNESS. Yes, I have got together a good many.

HILDA. Do you read them all, too?

SOLNESS. I used to try to. Do you read much?

HILDA. No, never! I have given it up. For it all seems so irrelevant.

SOLNESS. That is just my feeling.

[HILDA *wanders about a little, stops at the small table, opens the portfolio and turns over the contents.*]

HILDA. Are all these drawings yours?

SOLNESS. No, they are drawn by a young man whom I employ to help me.

HILDA. Someone you have taught?

SOLNESS. Oh yes, no doubt he has learned something from me, too.

HILDA [*sits down*]. Then I suppose he is very clever. [*Looks at a drawing.*] Isn't he?

SOLNESS. Oh, he might be worse. For my purpose—

HILDA. Oh yes—I'm sure he is frightfully clever.

SOLNESS. Do you think you can see that in the drawings?

HILDA. Pooh—these scrawlings! But if he has been learning from you—

SOLNESS. Oh, so far as that goes—there are plenty of people here that have learnt from me, and have come to little enough for all that.

HILDA [*looks at him and shakes her head*]. No, I can't for the life of me understand how you can be so stupid.

SOLNESS. Stupid? Do you think I am so very stupid?

HILDA. Yes, I do indeed. If you are content to go about here teaching all these people—

SOLNESS [*with a slight start*]. Well, and why not?

HILDA [*rises, half serious, half laughing*]. No indeed, Mr. Solness! What can be the good of that? No one but you should be allowed to build. You should stand quite alone—do it all yourself. Now you know it.

SOLNESS [*involuntarily*]. Hilda—!

HILDA. Well!

SOLNESS. How in the world did that come into your head?

HILDA. Do you think I am so very far wrong then?

SOLNESS. No, that's not what I mean. But now I'll tell you something.

HILDA. Well?

SOLNESS. I keep on—incessantly—in silence and alone—brooding on that very thought.

HILDA. Yes, that seems to me perfectly natural.

SOLNESS [*looks somewhat searchingly at her*]. Perhaps you have noticed it already?

HILDA. No, indeed I haven't.

SOLNESS. But just now—when you said you thought I was—off my balance? In one thing, you said—

HILDA. Oh, I was thinking of something quite different.

SOLNESS. What was it?

HILDA. I am not going to tell you.

SOLNESS [*crosses the room*]. Well, well—as you please.

[*Stops at the bay window.*]

Come here, and I will show you something.

HILDA [*approaching*]. What is it?

SOLNESS. Do you see—over there in the garden—?

HILDA. Yes?

SOLNESS [*points*]. Right above the great quarry—?

HILDA. That new house, you mean?

SOLNESS. The one that is being built, yes. Almost finished.

HILDA. It seems to have a very high tower.

SOLNESS. The scaffolding is still up.

HILDA. Is that your new house?

SOLNESS. Yes.

HILDA. The house you are soon going to move into?

SOLNESS. Yes.

HILDA [*looks at him*]. Are there nurseries in that house, too?

SOLNESS. Three, as there are here.

HILDA. And no child.

SOLNESS. And there never will be one.

HILDA [*with a half-smile*]. Well, isn't it just as I said—?

SOLNESS. That—?

HILDA. That you are a little—a little mad after all.

SOLNESS. Was that what you were thinking of?

HILDA. Yes, of all the empty nurseries I slept in.

SOLNESS [*lowers his voice*]. We have had children—Aline and I.

HILDA [*looks eagerly at him*]. Have you—?

SOLNESS. Two little boys. They were of the same age.

HILDA. Twins, then.

SOLNESS. Yes, twins. It's eleven or twelve years ago now.

HILDA [*cautiously*]. And so both of them—? You have lost both the twins, then?

SOLNESS [*with quiet emotion*]. We kept them only about three weeks. Or scarcely so much. [*Bursts forth.*] Oh, Hilda, I can't tell you what a good

thing it is for me that you have come! For now at last I have someone
I can talk to!

HILDA. Can you not talk to—her, too?

SOLNESS. Not about this. Not as I want to talk and must talk. [*Gloomily*.]
And not about so many other things, either.

HILDA [*in a subdued voice*]. Was that all you meant when you said you
needed me?

SOLNESS. That was mainly what I meant—at all events, yesterday. For
today I am not so sure—[*Breaking off*.] Come here and let us sit down,
Hilda. Sit there on the sofa—so that you can look into the garden.
[HILDA *seats herself in the corner of the sofa.* SOLNESS *brings a chair closer*.]
Should you like to hear about it?

HILDA. Yes, I shall love to sit and listen to you.

SOLNESS [*sits down*]. Then I will tell you all about it.

HILDA. Now I can see both the garden and you, Mr. Solness. So now,
tell away! Begin!

SOLNESS [*points toward the bay window*]. Out there on the rising ground—
where you see the new house—

HILDA. Yes?

SOLNESS. Aline and I lived there in the first years of our married life. There
was an old house up there that had belonged to her mother; and we
inherited it, and the whole of the great garden with it.

HILDA. Was there a tower on that house, too?

SOLNESS. No, nothing of the kind. From the outside it looked like a great,
dark, ugly wooden box; but all the same, it was snug and comfortable
enough inside.

HILDA. Then did you pull down the ramshackle old place?

SOLNESS. No, it was burned down.

HILDA. The whole of it?

SOLNESS. Yes.

HILDA. Was that a great misfortune for you?

SOLNESS. That depends on how you look at it. As a builder, the fire was the
making of me—

HILDA. Well, but—?

SOLNESS. It was just after the birth of the two little boys—

HILDA. The poor little twins, yes.

SOLNESS. They came healthy and bonny into the world. And they were
growing too—you could see the difference from day to day.

HILDA. Little children do grow quickly at first.

SOLNESS. It was the prettiest sight in the world to see Aline lying with the
two of them in her arms.—But then came the night of the fire—

HILDA [*excitedly*]. What happened? Do tell me! Was anyone burned?

SOLNESS. No, not that. Everyone got safe and sound out of the house—

HILDA. Well, and what then—?

SOLNESS. The fright had shaken Aline terribly. The alarm—the escape—

the breakneck hurry—and then the ice-cold night air—for they had to be carried out just as they lay—both she and the little ones.

HILDA. Was it too much for them?

SOLNESS. Oh no, they stood it well enough. But Aline fell into a fever, and it affected her milk. She would insist on nursing them herself; because it was her duty, she said. And both our little boys, they—[*clenching his hands*]—they—oh!

HILDA. They did not get over that?

SOLNESS. No, that they did not get over. That was how we lost them.

HILDA. It must have been terribly hard for you.

SOLNESS. Hard enough for me: but ten times harder for Aline. [*Clenching his hands in suppressed fury.*] Oh, that such things should be allowed to happen here in the world! [*Shortly and firmly.*] From the day I lost them, I had no heart for building churches.

HILDA. Did you not like building the church-tower in our town?

SOLNESS. I didn't like it. I know how free and happy I felt when that tower was finished.

HILDA. *I* know that, too.

SOLNESS. And now I shall never—never build anything of that sort again! Neither churches nor church-towers.

HILDA [*nods slowly*]. Nothing but houses for people to live in.

SOLNESS. Homes for human beings, Hilda.

HILDA. But homes with high towers and pinnacles upon them.

SOLNESS. If possible. [*Adopts a lighter tone.*] But, as I said before, that fire was the making of me—as a builder, I mean.

HILDA. Why don't you call yourself an architect, like the others?

SOLNESS. I have not been systematically enough taught for that. Most of what I know I have found out for myself.

HILDA. But you succeeded all the same.

SOLNESS. Yes, thanks to the fire. I laid out almost the whole of the garden in villa lots; and there I was able to build after my own heart. So I came to the front with a rush.

HILDA [*looks keenly at him*]. You must surely be a very happy man, as matters stand with you.

SOLNESS [*gloomily*]. Happy? Do you say that, too—like all the rest of them?

HILDA. Yes, I should say you must be. If you could only cease thinking about the two little children—

SOLNESS [*slowly*]. The two little children—they are not so easy to forget, Hilda.

HILDA [*somewhat uncertainly*]. Do you still feel their loss so much—after all these years?

SOLNESS [*looks fixedly at her, without replying*]. A happy man you said—

HILDA. Well, now, are you not happy—in other respects?

SOLNESS [*continues to look at her*]. When I told you all this about the fire —h'm—

HILDA. Well?

SOLNESS. Was there not one special thought that you—that you seized upon?

HILDA [*reflects in vain*]. No. What thought should that be?

SOLNESS [*with subdued emphasis*]. It was simply and solely by that fire that I was enabled to build homes for human beings. Cozy, comfortable, bright homes, where father and mother and the whole troop of children can live in safety and gladness, feeling what a happy thing it is to be alive in the world—and most of all to belong to each other—in great things and in small.

HILDA [*ardently*]. Well, and is it not a great happiness for you to be able to build such beautiful homes?

SOLNESS. The price, Hilda! The terrible price I had to pay for the opportunity!

HILDA. But can you never get over that?

SOLNESS. No. That I might build homes for others, I had to forgo—to forgo for all time—the home that might have been my own. I mean a home for a troop of children—and for father and mother, too.

HILDA [*cautiously*]. But need you have done that? For all time, you say?

SOLNESS [*nods slowly*]. That was the price of this happiness that people talk about. [*Breathes heavily.*] This happiness—h'm—this happiness was not to be bought any cheaper, Hilda.

HILDA [*as before*]. But may it not come right even yet?

SOLNESS. Never in this world—never. That is another consequence of the fire—and of Aline's illness afterwards.

HILDA [*looks at him with an indefinable expression*]. And yet you build all these nurseries?

SOLNESS [*seriously*]. Have you never noticed, Hilda, how the impossible—how it seems to beckon and cry aloud to one?

HILDA [*reflecting*]. The impossible? [*With animation.*] Yes, indeed! Is that how you feel too?

SOLNESS. Yes, I do.

HILDA. Then there must be—a little of the troll in you too.

SOLNESS. Why of the troll?

HILDA. What would you call it, then?

SOLNESS [*rises*]. Well, well, perhaps you are right. [*Vehemently.*] But how can I help turning into a troll, when this is how it always goes with me in everything—in everything!

HILDA. How do you mean?

SOLNESS [*speaking low, with inward emotion*]. Mark what I say to you, Hilda. All that I have succeeded in doing, building, creating—all the beauty, security, cheerful comfort—ay, and magnificence too—[*Clenches his hands.*] Oh, is it not terrible even to think of—!

HILDA. What is so terrible?

SOLNESS. That all this I have to make up for, to pay for—not in money, but in human happiness. And not with my own happiness only, but with other people's too. Yes, yes, do you see that, Hilda? That is the price which my position as an artist has cost me—and others. And every single day I have to look on while the price is paid for me anew. Over again, and over again—and over again for ever!

HILDA [*rises and looks steadily at him*]. Now I can see that you are thinking of—of her.

SOLNESS. Yes, mainly of Aline. For Aline—she, too, had her vocation in life, just as much as I had mine. [*His voice quivers.*] But her vocation has had to be stunted, and crushed, and shattered—in order that mine might force its way to—to a sort of great victory. For you must know that Aline—she, too, had a talent for building.

HILDA. She! For building?

SOLNESS [*shakes his head*]. Not houses and towers, and spires—not such things as I work away at—

HILDA. Well, but what then?

SOLNESS [*softly, with emotion*]. For building up the souls of little children, Hilda. For building up children's souls in perfect balance, and in noble and beautiful forms. For enabling them to soar up into erect and full-grown human souls. That was Aline's talent. And there it all lies now—unused and unusable for ever—of no earthly service to any one—just like the ruins left by a fire.

HILDA. Yes, but even if this were so—?

SOLNESS. It is so! It is so! I know it!

HILDA. Well, but in any case it is not your fault.

SOLNESS [*fixes his eyes on her, and nods slowly*]. Ah, that is the great, the terrible question. That is the doubt that is gnawing me—night and day.

HILDA. That?

SOLNESS. Yes. Suppose the fault was mine—in a certain sense.

HILDA. Your fault! The fire!

SOLNESS. All of it; the whole thing. And yet, perhaps—I may not have had anything to do with it.

HILDA [*looks at him with a troubled expression*]. Oh, Mr. Solness—If you can talk like that, I am afraid you must be—ill, after all.

SOLNESS H'm—I don't think I shall ever be of quite sound mind on that point.

[RAGNAR BROVIK *cautiously opens the little door in the left-hand corner.* HILDA *comes forward.*]

RAGNAR [*when he sees* HILDA]. Oh. I beg pardon, Mr. Solness—

[*He makes a movement to withdraw.*]

SOLNESS. No, no, don't go. Let us get it over.

RAGNAR. Oh, yes—if only we could.

SOLNESS. I hear your father is no better?

RAGNAR. Father is fast growing weaker—and therefore I beg and implore you to write a few kind words for me on one of the plans! Something for father to read before he—

SOLNESS [*vehemently*]. I won't hear anything more about those drawings of yours!

RAGNAR. Have you looked at them?

SOLNESS. Yes—I have.

RAGNAR. And they are good for nothing? And *I* am good for nothing, too?

SOLNESS [*evasively*]. Stay here with me, Ragnar. You shall have everything your own way. And then you can marry Kaia, and live at your ease— and happily too, who knows? Only don't think of building on your own account.

RAGNAR. Well, well, then I must go home and tell father what you say— I promised I would.—Is this what I am to tell father—before he dies?

SOLNESS [*with a groan*]. Oh tell him—tell him what you will, for me. Best to say nothing at all to him! [*With a sudden outburst.*] I cannot do anything else, Ragnar!

RAGNAR. May I have the drawings to take with me?

SOLNESS. Yes, take them—take them by all means! They are lying there on the table.

RAGNAR [*goes to the table*]. Thanks.

HILDA [*puts her hand on the portfolio*]. No, no; leave them here.

SOLNESS. Why?

HILDA. Because I want to look at them, too.

SOLNESS. But you have been— [*To* RAGNAR.] Well, leave them here, then.

RAGNAR. Very well.

SOLNESS. And go home at once to your father.

RAGNAR. Yes, I suppose I must.

SOLNESS [*as if in desperation*]. Ragnar—you must not ask me to do what is beyond my power! Do you hear, Ragnar? You must not!

RAGNAR. No, no. I beg your pardon—

[*He bows, and goes out by the corner door.* HILDA *goes over and sits down on a chair near the mirror.*]

HILDA [*looks angrily at* SOLNESS]. That was a very ugly thing to do.

SOLNESS. Do you think so, too?

HILDA. Yes, it was horribly ugly—and hard and bad and cruel as well.

SOLNESS. Oh, you don't understand my position.

HILDA. No matter—. I say you ought not to be like that.

SOLNESS. You said yourself, only just now, that no one but *I* ought to be allowed to build.

HILDA. *I* may say such things—but you must not.

SOLNESS. I most of all, surely, who have paid so dear for my position.

HILDA. Oh yes—with what you call domestic comfort—and that sort of thing.

SOLNESS. And with my peace of soul into the bargain.

HILDA [*rising*]. Peace of soul! [*With feeling.*] Yes, yes, you are right in that! Poor Mrs. Solness—you fancy that—

SOLNESS [*with a quiet, chuckling laugh*]. Just sit down again, Hilda, and I'll tell you something funny.

HILDA [*sits down; with intent interest*]. Well?

SOLNESS. It sounds such a ludicrous little thing; for, you see, the whole story turns upon nothing but a crack in a chimney.

HILDA. No more than that?

SOLNESS. No, not to begin with.

[*He moves a chair nearer to* HILDA *and sits down.*]

HILDA [*impatiently, taps on her knee*]. Well, now for the crack in the chimney!

SOLNESS. I had noticed the split in the flue long, long before the fire. Every time I went up into the attic, I looked to see if it was still there.

HILDA. And it was?

SOLNESS. Yes; for no one else knew about it.

HILDA. And you said nothing?

SOLNESS. Nothing.

HILDA. And did not think of repairing the flue either?

SOLNESS. Oh yes, I thought about it—but never got any further. Every time I intended to set to work, it seemed just as if a hand held me back. Not today, I thought—tomorrow; and nothing ever came of it.

HILDA. But why did you keep putting it off like that?

SOLNESS. Because I was revolving something in my mind. [*Slowly, and in a low voice.*] Through that little black crack in the chimney, I might, perhaps, force my way upward—as a builder.

HILDA [*looking straight in front of her*]. That must have been thrilling.

SOLNESS. Almost irresistible—quite irresistible. For at that time it appeared to me a perfectly simple and straightforward matter. I would have had it happen in the winter-time—a little before midday. I was to be out driving Aline in the sleigh. The servants at home would have made huge fires in the stoves.

HILDA. For, of course, it was to be bitterly cold that day?

SOLNESS. Rather biting, yes—and they would want Aline to find it thoroughly snug and warm when she came home.

HILDA. I suppose she is very chilly by nature?

SOLNESS. She is. And as we drove home, we were to see the smoke.

HILDA. Only the smoke?

SOLNESS. The smoke first. But when we came up to the garden gate, the whole of the old timber-box was to be a rolling mass of flames.—That is how I wanted it to be, you see.

HILDA. Oh why, why could it not have happened so!

SOLNESS. You may well say that, Hilda.

HILDA. Well, but now listen, Mr. Solness. Are you perfectly certain that the fire was caused by that little crack in the chimney!

SOLNESS. No, on the contrary—I am perfectly certain that the crack in the chimney had nothing whatever to do with the fire.

HILDA. What!

SOLNESS. It has been clearly ascertained that the fire broke out in a clothes-cupboard—in a totally different part of the house.

HILDA. Then what is all this nonsense you are talking about the crack in the chimney!

SOLNESS. May I go on talking to you a little, Hilda?

HILDA. Yes, if you'll only talk sensibly—

SOLNESS. I will try to.

[*He moves his chair nearer.*]

HILDA. Out with it, then, Mr. Solness.

SOLNESS [*confidentially*]. Don't you agree with me, Hilda, that there exist special, chosen people who have been endowed with the power and faculty of desiring a thing, craving for a thing, willing a thing—so persistently and so—so inexorably—that at last it has to happen? Don't you believe that?

HILDA [*with an indefinable expression in her eyes*]. If that is so, we shall see, one of these days, whether *I* am one of the chosen.

SOLNESS. It is not one's self alone that can do such great things. Oh, no— the helpers and the servers—they must do their part too, if it is to be of any good. But they never come of themselves. One has to call upon them very persistently—inwardly, you understand.

HILDA. What are these helpers and servers?

SOLNESS. Oh, we can talk about that some other time. For the present, let us keep to this business of the fire.

HILDA. Don't you think that fire would have happened all the same— even without your wishing for it?

SOLNESS. If the house had been old Knut Brovik's it would never have burnt down so conveniently for him. I am sure of that; for he does not know how to call for the helpers—no, nor for the servers, either. [*Rises in unrest.*] So you see, Hilda—it is my fault, after all, that the lives of the two little boys had to be sacrificed. And do you think it is not my fault, too, that Aline has never been the woman she should and might have been—and that she most longed to be?

HILDA. Yes, but if it is all the work of those helpers and servers—?

SOLNESS. Who called for the helpers and servers? It was I! And they came and obeyed my will. [*In increasing excitement.*] That is what people call having the luck on your side; but I must tell you what this sort of luck feels like! It feels like a great raw place here on my breast. And the helpers and servers keep on flaying pieces of skin off other people in order to close my sore! —But still the sore is not healed—never, never! Oh, if you knew how it can sometimes gnaw and burn!

HILDA [*looks attentively at him*]. You are ill, Mr. Solness. Very ill, I almost think.

SOLNESS. Say mad; for that is what you mean.

HILDA. No, I don't think there is much amiss with your intellect.

SOLNESS. With what then? Out with it!

HILDA. I wonder whether you were not sent into the world with a sickly conscience.

SOLNESS. A sickly conscience? What deviltry is that?

HILDA. I mean that your conscience is feeble—too delicately built, as it were—hasn't strength to take a grip of things—to lift and bear what is heavy.

SOLNESS [*growls*]. H'm! May I ask, then, what sort of a conscience one ought to have?

HILDA. I should like your conscience to be—to be thoroughly robust.

SOLNESS. Indeed? Robust, eh? Is your own conscience robust, may I ask?

HILDA. Yes, I think it is. I have never noticed that it wasn't.

SOLNESS. It has not been put very severely to the test, I should think.

HILDA [*with a quivering of the lips*]. Oh, it was no such simple matter to leave father—I am so awfully fond of him.

SOLNESS. Dear me! for a month or two—

IIILDA. I think I shall never go home again.

SOLNESS. Never? Then why did you leave him?

HILDA [*half-seriously, half-banteringly*]. Have you forgotten again that the ten years are up?

SOLNESS. Oh nonsense. Was anything wrong at home? Eh?

HILDA [*quite seriously*]. It was this impulse within me that urged and goaded me to come—and lured and drew me on, as well.

SOLNESS [*eagerly*]. There we have it! There we have it, Hilda! There is a troll in you too, as in me. For it's the troll in one, you see—it is *that* that calls to the powers outside us. And then you must give in—whether you will or no.

HILDA. I almost think you are right, Mr. Solness.

SOLNESS [*walks around the room*]. Oh, there are devils innumerable abroad in the world, Hilda, that one never sees!

HILDA. Devils, too?

SOLNESS [*stops*]. Good devils and bad devils; light-haired devils and black-haired devils. If only you could always tell whether it is the light or dark ones that have got hold of you! [*Paces about.*] Ho-ho! Then it would be simple enough!

HILDA [*follows him with her eyes*]. Or if one had a really vigorous, radiantly healthy conscience—so that one dared to do what one would.

SOLNESS [*stops beside the console table*]. I believe, now, that most people are just as puny creatures as I am in that respect.

HILDA. I shouldn't wonder.

SOLNESS [*leaning against the table*]. In the sagas—. Have you read any of the old sagas?

HILDA. Oh yes! When I used to read books, I—

SOLNESS. In the sagas you read about vikings, who sailed to foreign lands, and plundered and burned and killed men—

HILDA. And carried off women—

SOLNESS.—and kept them in captivity—

HILDA.—took them home in their ships—

SOLNESS.—and behaved to them like—like the very worst of trolls.

HILDA [*looks straight before her, with a half-veiled look*]. I think that must have been thrilling.

SOLNESS [*with a short, deep laugh*]. To carry off women, eh?

HILDA. To be carried off.

SOLNESS [*looks at her a moment*]. Oh, indeed.

HILDA [*as if breaking the thread of the conversation*]. But what made you speak of these vikings, Mr. Solness?

SOLNESS. Why, those fellows must have had robust consciences, if you like! When they got home again, they could eat and drink, and be as happy as children. And the women, too! They often would not leave them on any account. Can you understand that, Hilda?

HILDA. Those women I can understand exceedingly well.

SOLNESS. Oho! Perhaps you could do the same yourself?

HILDA. Why not?

SOLNESS. Live—of your own free will—with a ruffian like that?

HILDA. If it was a ruffian I had come to love—

SOLNESS. Could you come to love a man like that?

HILDA. Good heavens, you know very well one can't choose whom one is going to love.

SOLNESS [*looks meditatively at her*]. Oh no, I suppose it is the troll within one that's responsible for that.

HILDA [*half-laughingly*]. And all those blessèd devils, that you know so well—both the light-haired and the dark-haired ones.

SOLNESS [*quietly and warmly*]. Then I hope with all my heart that the devils will choose carefully for you, Hilda.

HILDA. For me they have chosen already—once and for all.

SOLNESS [*looks earnestly at her*]. Hilda—you are like a wild bird of the woods.

HILDA. Far from it. I don't hide myself away under the bushes.

SOLNESS No, no. There is rather something of the bird of prey in you.

HILDA. That is nearer it—perhaps. [*Very vehemently.*] And why not a bird of prey? Why should not *I* go a-hunting—I, as well as the rest? Carry off the prey I want—if only I can get my claws into it, and do with it as I will.

SOLNESS. Hilda—do you know what you are?

HILDA. Yes, I suppose I am a strange sort of bird.

SOLNESS. No. You are like a dawning day. When I look at you—I seem to be looking toward the sunrise.

HILDA. Tell me, Mr. Solness—are you certain that you have never called me to you? Inwardly, you know?

SOLNESS [*softly and slowly*]. I almost think I must have.

HILDA. What did you want with me?

SOLNESS. You are the younger generation, Hilda.

HILDA [*smiles*]. That younger generation that you are so afraid of?

SOLNESS [*nods slowly*]. And which, in my heart, I yearn toward so deeply.
[HILDA *rises, goes to the little table, and fetches* RAGNAR BROVIK'S *portfolio.*]

HILDA [*holds out the portfolio to him*]. We were talking of these drawings—

SOLNESS [*shortly, waving them away*]. Put those things away! I have seen enough of them.

HILDA. Yes, but you have to write your approval on them.

SOLNESS. Write my approval on them? Never!

HILDA. But the poor old man is lying at death's door! Can't you give him and his son this pleasure before they are parted? And perhaps he might get the commission to carry them out, too.

SOLNESS. Yes, that is just what he would get. He has made sure of that—has my fine gentleman!

HILDA. Then, good heavens—if that is so—can't you tell the least little bit of a lie for once in a way?

SOLNESS. A lie? [*Raging.*] Hilda—take those devil's drawings out of my sight!

HILDA [*draws the portfolio a little nearer to herself*]. Well, well, well—don't bite me.—You talk of trolls—but I think you go on like a troll yourself. [*Looks round.*] Where do you keep your pen and ink?

SOLNESS. There is nothing of the sort in here.

HILDA [*goes toward the door*]. But in the office where that young lady is—

SOLNESS. Stay where you are, Hilda!—I ought to tell a lie, you say. Oh yes, for the sake of his old father I might well do that—for in my time I have crushed him, trodden him under foot—

HILDA. Him, too?

SOLNESS. I needed room for myself. But this Ragnar—he must on no account be allowed to come to the front.

HILDA. Poor fellow, there is surely no fear of that. If he has nothing in him—

SOLNESS [*comes closer, looks at her, and whispers*]. If Ragnar Brovik gets his chance, he will strike me to the earth. Crush me—as I crushed his father.

HILDA. Crush you? Has he the ability for that?

SOLNESS. Yes, you may depend upon it he has the ability! He is the younger generation that stands ready to knock at my door—to make an end of Halvard Solness.

HILDA [*looks at him with quiet reproach*]. And yet you would bar him out. Fie, Mr. Solness!

SOLNESS. The fight I have been fighting has cost heart's blood enough.—And I am afraid, too, that the helpers and servers will not obey me any longer.

HILDA. Then you must go ahead without them. There is nothing else for it.

SOLNESS. It is hopeless, Hilda. The luck is bound to turn. A little sooner or a little later. Retribution is inexorable.

HILDA [*in distress, putting her hands over her ears*]. Don't talk like that! Do you want to kill me? To take from me what is more than my life?

SOLNESS. And what is that?

HILDA. The longing to see you great. To see you, with a wreath in your hand, high, high up upon a church-tower. [*Calm again.*] Come, out with your pencil now. You must have a pencil about you?

SOLNESS [*takes out his pocketbook*]. I have one here.

HILDA [*lays the portfolio on the sofa-table*]. Very well. Now let us two sit down here, Mr. Solness.

[SOLNESS *seats himself at the table.* HILDA *stands behind him, leaning over the back of the chair.*]

And now we will write on the drawings. We must write very, very nicely and cordially—for this horrid Ruar—or whatever his name is.

SOLNESS [*writes a few words, turns his head and looks at her*]. Tell me one thing, Hilda.

HILDA. Yes!

SOLNESS. If you have been waiting for me all these ten years—

HILDA. What then?

SOLNESS. Why have you never written to me? Then I could have answered you.

HILDA [*hastily*]. No, no, no! That was just what I did not want.

SOLNESS. Why not?

HILDA. I was afraid the whole thing might fall to pieces.—But we were going to write on the drawings, Mr. Solness.

SOLNESS. So we were.

HILDA [*bends forward and looks over his shoulder while he writes*]. Mind now, kindly and cordially! Oh how I hate—how I hate this Ruald—

SOLNESS [*writing*]. Have you never really cared for anyone, Hilda?

HILDA [*harshly*]. What do you say?

SOLNESS. Have you never cared for anyone?

HILDA. For anyone else, I suppose you mean?

SOLNESS [*looks up at her*]. For anyone else, yes. Have you never? In all these ten years? Never?

HILDA. Oh yes, now and then. When I was perfectly furious with you for not coming.

SOLNESS. Then you did take an interest in other people, too?

HILDA. A little bit—for a week or so. Good heavens, Mr. Solness, you surely know how such things come about.

SOLNESS. Hilda—what is it you have come for?

HILDA. Don't waste time talking. The poor old man might go and die in the meantime.

SOLNESS. Answer me, Hilda. What do you want of me?

HILDA. I want my kingdom.

SOLNESS. H'm—

[*He gives a rapid glance toward the door on the left, and then goes on writing on the drawings. At the same moment* MRS. SOLNESS *enters; she has some packages in her hand.*]

MRS. SOLNESS. Here are a few things I have got for you, Miss Wangel. The large parcels will be sent later on.

HILDA. Oh, how very, very kind of you!

MRS. SOLNESS. Only my simple duty. Nothing more than that.

SOLNESS [*reading over what he has written*]. Aline!

MRS. SOLNESS. Yes?

SOLNESS. Did you notice whether the—the bookkeeper was out there?

MRS. SOLNESS. Yes, of course, she was there.

SOLNESS [*puts the drawings in the portfolio*]. H'm—

MRS. SOLNESS. She was standing at the desk, as she always is—when *I* go through the room.

SOLNESS [*rises*]. Then I'll give this to her, and tell her that—

HILDA [*takes the portfolio from him*]. Oh, no, let me have the pleasure of doing that!

[*Goes to the door, but turns.*]

What is her name?

SOLNESS. Her name is Miss Fosli.

HILDA. Pooh, that sounds so cold! Her Christian name, I mean?

SOLNESS. Kaia—I believe.

HILDA [*opens the door and calls out*]. Kaia, come in here! Make haste! Mr. Solness wants to speak to you.

[KAIA FOSLI *appears at the door.*]

KAIA [*looking at him in alarm*]. Here I am—?

HILDA [*handing her the portfolio*]. See here, Kaia! You can take this home; Mr. Solness has written on them now.

KAIA. Oh, at last!

SOLNESS. Give them to the old man as soon as you can.

KAIA. I will go straight home with them.

SOLNESS. Yes, do. Now Ragnar will have a chance of building for himself.

KAIA. Oh, may he come and thank you for all—?

SOLNESS [*harshly*]. I won't have any thanks! Tell him that from me.

KAIA. Yes, I will—

SOLNESS. And tell him at the same time that henceforward I do not require his services—nor yours either.

KAIA [*softly and quiveringly*]. Not mine either?

SOLNESS. You will have other things to think of now, and to attend to; and that is a very good thing for you. Well, go home with the drawings now, Miss Fosli. At once! Do you hear?

KAIA [*as before*]. Yes, Mr. Solness.

[*She goes out.*]

MRS. SOLNESS. Heavens! what deceitful eyes she has.

SOLNESS. She? That poor little creature?

MRS. SOLNESS. Oh—I can see what I can see, Halvard— Are you really dismissing them?

SOLNESS. Yes.

MRS. SOLNESS. Her as well?

SOLNESS. Was not that what you wished?

MRS. SOLNESS. But how can you get on without her—? Oh well, no doubt you have some one else in reserve, Halvard.

HILDA [*playfully*]. Well, *I* for one am not the person to stand at that desk.

SOLNESS. Never mind, never mind—it will be all right, Aline. Now all you have to do is to think about moving into our new home—as quickly as you can. This evening we will hang up the wreath—[*turns to* HILDA]—right on the very pinnacle of the tower. What do you say to that, Miss Hilda?

HILDA [*looks at him with sparkling eyes*]. It will be splendid to see you so high up once more.

SOLNESS. Me!

MRS. SOLNESS. For heaven's sake, Miss Wangel, don't imagine such a thing! My husband!—when he always gets so dizzy!

HILDA. He get dizzy! No, I know quite well he does not!

MRS. SOLNESS. Oh yes, indeed he does.

HILDA. But I have seen him with my own eyes right up at the top of a high church-tower!

MRS. SOLNESS. Yes, I hear people talk of that; but it is utterly impossible—

SOLNESS [*vehemently*]. Impossible—impossible, yes! But there I stood all the same!

MRS. SOLNESS. Oh, how can you say so, Halvard? Why, you can't even bear to go out on the second-story balcony here. You have always been like that.

SOLNESS. You may perhaps see something different this evening.

MRS. SOLNESS [*in alarm*]. No, no, no! Please God I shall never see that. I will write at once to the doctor—and I am sure he won't let you do it.

SOLNESS. Why, Aline—!

MRS. SOLNESS. Oh, you know you're ill, Halvard. This proves it! Oh God— Oh God!

[*She goes out hastily to the right.*]

HILDA [*looks intently at him*]. Is it so, or is it not?

SOLNESS. That I turn dizzy?

HILDA. That my master builder dares not—*cannot*—climb as high as he builds?

SOLNESS. Is that the way you look at it?

HILDA. Yes.

SOLNESS. I believe there is scarcely a corner in me that is safe from you.

HILDA [*looks toward the bay window*]. Up there, then. Right up there—

SOLNESS [*approaches her*]. You might have the topmost room in the tower, Hilda—there you might live like a princess.

HILDA [*indefinably, between earnest and jest*]. Yes, that is what you promised me.

SOLNESS. *Did* I really?

HILDA. Fie, Mr. Solness! You said I should be a princess, and that you would give me a kingdom. And then you went and—Well!

SOLNESS [*cautiously*]. Are you quite certain that this is not a dream—a fancy, that has fixed itself in your mind?

HILDA [*sharply*]. Do you mean that you did not do it?

SOLNESS. I scarcely know myself. [*More softly.*] But now I know so much for certain, that I—

HILDA. That you—? Say it at once!

SOLNESS.—that I ought to have done it.

HILDA [*exclaims with animation*]. Don't tell me you can ever be dizzy!

SOLNESS. This evening, then, we will hang up the wreath—Princess Hilda.

HILDA [*with a bitter curve of the lips*]. Over your new home, yes.

SOLNESS. Over the new house, which will never be a home for me.

[*He goes out through the garden door.*]

HILDA [*looks straight in front of her with a far-away expression and whispers to herself. The only words audible are:*] —frightfully thrilling—

ACT THREE

The large, broad veranda of SOLNESS'S *dwelling-house. Part of the house, with outer door leading to the veranda, is seen to the left. A railing along the veranda to the right. At the back, from the end of the veranda, a flight of steps leads down to the garden below. Tall old trees in the garden spread their branches over the veranda and toward the house. Far to the right, in among the trees, a glimpse is caught of the lower part of the new villa, with scaffolding round so much as is seen of the tower. In the background the garden is bounded by an old wooden fence. Outside the fence, a street with low, tumbledown cottages.*

Evening sky with sunlit clouds.

On the veranda, a garden bench stands along the wall of the house, and in front of the bench a long table. On the other side of the table, an armchair and some stools. All the furniture is of wickerwork.

MRS. SOLNESS, *wrapped in a large white crêpe shawl, sits resting in the armchair and gazes over to the right. Shortly after,* HILDA WANGEL *comes up the flight of steps from the garden. She is dressed as in the last act, and wears her hat. She has in her bodice a little nosegay of small common flowers.*

MRS. SOLNESS [*turning her head a little*]. Have you been round the garden, Miss Wangel?

HILDA. Yes, I have been taking a look at it.

MRS. SOLNESS. And found some flowers too, I see.

HILDA. Yes, indeed! There are such heaps of them in among the bushes.

MRS. SOLNESS. Are there really? Still? You see I scarcely ever go there.

HILDA [*closer*]. What! Don't you take a run down into the garden every day, then?

MRS. SOLNESS [*with a faint smile*]. I don't "run" anywhere, nowadays.

HILDA. Well, but do you not go down now and then to look at all the lovely things there?

MRS. SOLNESS. It has all become so strange to me. I am almost afraid to see it again.

HILDA. Your own garden!

MRS. SOLNESS. I don't feel that it is mine any longer.

HILDA. What do you mean—?

MRS. SOLNESS. No, no, it is not—not as it was in my mother's and father's time. They have taken away so much—so much of the garden, Miss Wangel. Fancy—they have parcelled it out—and built houses for strangers—people that I don't know. And they can sit and look in upon me from their windows.

HILDA [*with a bright expression*]. Mrs. Solness!

MRS. SOLNESS. Yes!

HILDA. May I stay here with you a little?

MRS. SOLNESS. Yes, by all means, if you care to.

[HILDA *moves a stool close to the armchair and sits down.*]

HILDA. Ah—here one can sit and sun oneself like a cat.

MRS. SOLNESS [*lays her hand softly on* HILDA'S *neck*]. It is nice of you to be willing to sit with me. I thought you wanted to go in to my husband.

HILDA. What should I want with him?

MRS. SOLNESS. To help him, I thought.

HILDA. No, thank you. And besides, he is not in. He is over there with his workmen. But he looked so fierce that I did not dare to talk to him.

MRS. SOLNESS. He is so kind and gentle in reality.

HILDA. He!

MRS. SOLNESS. You do not really know him yet, Miss Wangel.

HILDA [*looks affectionately at her*]. Are you pleased at the thought of moving over to the new house?

MRS. SOLNESS. I ought to be pleased; for it is what Halvard wants—

HILDA. Oh, not just on that account, surely.

MRS. SOLNESS. Yes, yes, Miss Wangel; for it is only my duty to submit myself to him. But very often it is dreadfully difficult to force one's mind to obedience.

HILDA. Yes, that must be difficult indeed.

MRS. SOLNESS. I can tell you it is—when one has so many faults as I have—

HILDA. When one has gone through so much trouble as you have—

MRS. SOLNESS. How do you know about that?

HILDA. Your husband told me.

MRS. SOLNESS. To me he very seldom mentions these things.—Yes, I can tell you I have gone through more than enough trouble in my life, Miss Wangel.

HILDA [*looks sympathetically at her and nods slowly*]. Poor Mrs. Solness. First of all there was the fire—

MRS. SOLNESS [*with a sigh*]. Yes, everything that was mine was burned.

HILDA. And then came what was worse.

MRS. SOLNESS [*looking inquiringly at her*]. Worse?

HILDA. The worst of all.

MRS. SOLNESS. What do you mean?

HILDA [*softly*]. You lost the two little boys.

MRS. SOLNESS. Oh yes, the boys. But, you see, that was a thing apart. That was a dispensation of Providence; and in such things one can only bow in submission—yes, and be thankful, too.

HILDA. Then you are so?

MRS. SOLNESS. Not always, I am sorry to say. I know well enough that it is my duty—but all the same I cannot.

HILDA. No, no, I think that is only natural.

MRS. SOLNESS. And often and often I have to remind myself that it was a righteous punishment for me—

HILDA. Why?

MRS. SOLNESS. Because I had not fortitude enough in misfortune.

HILDA. But I don't see that—

MRS. SOLNESS. Oh, no, no, Miss Wangel—do not talk to me anymore about the two little boys. We ought to feel nothing but joy in thinking of them; for they are so happy—so happy now. No, it is the small losses in life that cut one to the heart—the loss of all that other people look upon as almost nothing.

HILDA [*lays her arms on* MRS. SOLNESS's *knees, and looks up at her affectionately*]. Dear Mrs. Solness—tell me what things you mean!

MRS. SOLNESS. As I say, only little things. All the old portraits were burned on the walls. And all the old silk dresses were burned, that had belonged to the family for generations and generations. And all mother's and grandmother's lace—that was burned too. And only think—the jewels, too! [*Sadly.*] And then all the dolls.

HILDA. The dolls?

MRS. SOLNESS [*choking with tears*]. I had nine lovely dolls.

HILDA. And they were burned too?

MRS. SOLNESS. All of them. Oh, it was hard—so hard for me.

HILDA. Had you put by all these dolls, then? Ever since you were little?

MRS. SOLNESS. I had not put them by. The dolls and I had gone on living together.

HILDA. After you were grown up?

MRS. SOLNESS. Yes, long after that.

HILDA. After you were married, too?

MRS. SOLNESS. Oh yes, indeed. So long as he did not see it—. But they were all burned up, poor things. No one thought of saving them. Oh, it is so miserable to think of. You mustn't laugh at me, Miss Wangel.

HILDA. I am not laughing in the least.

MRS. SOLNESS. For you see, in a certain sense, there was life in them, too. I carried them under my heart—like little unborn children.

[DR. HERDAL, *with his hat in his hand, comes out through the door, and observes* MRS. SOLNESS *and* HILDA.]

DR. HERDAL. Well, Mrs. Solness, so you are sitting out here catching cold?

MRS. SOLNESS. I find it so pleasant and warm here today.

DR. HERDAL. Yes, yes. But is there anything going on here? I got a note from you.

MRS. SOLNESS [*rises*]. Yes, there is something I must talk to you about.

DR. HERDAL. Very well; then perhaps we had better go in. [*To* HILDA.] Still in your mountaineering dress, Miss Wangel?

HILDA [*gaily, rising*]. Yes—in full uniform! But today I am not going climbing and breaking my neck. We two will stop quietly below and look on, doctor.

DR. HERDAL. What are we to look on at?

MRS. SOLNESS [*softly, in alarm, to* HILDA]. Hush, hush—for God's sake! He is coming! Try to get that idea out of his head. And let us be friends, Miss Wangel. Don't you think we can?

HILDA [*throws her arms impetuously round* MRS. SOLNESS's *neck*]. Oh, if we only could!

MRS. SOLNESS [*gently disengages herself*]. There, there, there! There he comes, doctor. Let me have a word with you.

DR. HERDAL. Is it about him!

MRS. SOLNESS. Yes, to be sure it's about him. Do come in.

[*She and the doctor enter the house. Next moment* SOLNESS *comes up from the garden by the flight of steps. A serious look comes over* HILDA's *face.*]

SOLNESS [*glances at the house-door, which is closed cautiously from within*]. Have you noticed, Hilda, that as soon as I come, she goes?

HILDA. I have noticed that as soon as you come, you make her go.

SOLNESS. Perhaps so. But I cannot help it. [*Looks observantly at her.*] Are you cold, Hilda? I think you look cold.

HILDA. I have just come up out of a tomb.

SOLNESS. What do you mean by that?

HILDA. That I have got chilled through and through, Mr. Solness.

SOLNESS [*slowly*]. I believe I understand—

HILDA. What brings you up here just now?

SOLNESS. I caught sight of you from over there.

HILDA. But then you must have seen her too?

SOLNESS. I knew she would go at once if I came.

HILDA. Is it very painful for you that she should avoid you in this way?

SOLNESS. In one sense, it's a relief as well.

HILDA. Not to have her before your eyes?

SOLNESS. Yes.

HILDA. Not to be always seeing how heavily the loss of the little boys weighs upon her?

SOLNESS. Yes. Chiefly that.

[HILDA *drifts across the veranda with her hands behind her back, stops at the railing and looks out over the garden.*]

SOLNESS [*after a short pause*]. Did you have a long talk with her?

[HILDA *stands motionless and does not answer.*]

SOLNESS. Had you a long talk, I asked?

[HILDA *is silent as before.*]

SOLNESS. What was she talking about, Hilda?

[HILDA *continues silent.*]

SOLNESS. Poor Aline! I suppose it was about the little boys.

[*A nervous shudder runs through* HILDA; *then she nods hurriedly once or twice.*]

SOLNESS. She will never get over it—never in this world.

[*Approaches her.*]

Now you are standing there again like a statue; just as you stood last night.

HILDA [*turns and looks at him, with great serious eyes*]. I am going away.

SOLNESS [*sharply*]. Going away!

HILDA. Yes.

SOLNESS. But I won't allow you to!

HILDA. What am I to do here now?

SOLNESS. Simply to be here, Hilda!

HILDA [*measures him with a look*]. Oh, thank you. You know it wouldn't end there.

SOLNESS [*heedlessly*]. So much the better!

HILDA [*vehemently*]. I cannot do any harm to one whom I know! I can't take away anything that belongs to her.

SOLNESS. Who wants you to do that?

HILDA [*continuing*]. A stranger, yes! for that is quite a different thing! A person I have never set eyes on. But one that I have come into close contact with—! Oh no! Oh no! Ugh!

SOLNESS. Yes, but I never proposed you should.

HILDA. Oh, Mr. Solness, you know quite well what the end of it would be. And that is why I am going away.

SOLNESS. And what is to become of me when you are gone? What shall I have to live for then?—After that?

HILDA [*with the indefinable look in her eyes*]. It is surely not so hard for you.

You have your duties to her. Live for those duties.

SOLNESS. Too late. These powers—these—these—

HILDA.—devils—

SOLNESS. Yes, these devils! And the troll within me as well—they have drawn all the life-blood out of her. [*Laughs in desperation.*] They did it for my happiness! Yes, yes! [*Sadly.*] And now she is dead—for my sake. And I am chained alive to a dead woman. [*In wild anguish.*] I—I who cannot live without joy in life!

[HILDA *moves round the table and seats herself on the bench, with her elbows on the table, and her head supported by her hands.*]

HILDA [*sits and looks at him awhile*]. What will you build next?

SOLNESS [*shakes his head*]. I don't believe I shall build much more.

HILDA. Not those cozy, happy homes for mother and father, and for the troop of children?

SOLNESS. I wonder whether there will be any use for such homes in the coming time.

HILDA. Poor Mr. Solness! And you have gone all these ten years—and staked your whole life—on that alone.

SOLNESS. Yes, you may well say so, Hilda.

HILDA [*with an outburst*]. Oh, it all seems to me so foolish—so foolish!

SOLNESS. All what?

HILDA. Not to be able to grasp at your own happiness—at your own life! Merely because someone you know happens to stand in the way!

SOLNESS. One whom you have no right to set aside.

HILDA. I wonder whether one really has not the right! And yet, and yet— Oh! if one could only sleep the whole thing away!

[*She lays her arms flat down on the table, rests the left side of her head on her hands, and shuts her eyes.*]

SOLNESS [*turns the armchair and sits down at the table*]. Had you a cozy, happy home—up there with your father, Hilda?

HILDA [*without stirring, answers as if half asleep*]. I had only a cage.

SOLNESS. And you are determined not to go back to it?

HILDA [*as before*]. The wild bird never wants to go into the cage.

SOLNESS. Rather range through the free air—

HILDA [*still as before*]. The bird of prey loves to range—

SOLNESS [*lets his eyes rest on her*]. If only one had the viking-spirit in life—

HILDA [*in her usual voice; opens her eyes but does not move*]. And the other thing? Say what that was!

SOLNESS. A robust conscience.

[HILDA *sits erect on the bench, with animation. Her eyes have once more the sparkling expression of gladness.*]

HILDA [*nods to him*]. I know what you are going to build next!

SOLNESS. Then you know more than I do, Hilda.

HILDA. Yes, builders are such stupid people.

SOLNESS. What is it to be then?

HILDA [*nods again*]. The castle.

SOLNESS. What castle?

HILDA. *My* castle, of course.

SOLNESS. Do you want a castle now?

HILDA. Don't you owe me a kingdom, I should like to know?

SOLNESS. You say I do.

HILDA. Well—you admit you owe me this kingdom. And you can't have a kingdom without a royal castle, I should think!

SOLNESS [*more and more animated*]. Yes, they usually go together.

HILDA. Good! Then build it for me! This moment!

SOLNESS [*laughing*]. Must you have that on the instant, too?

HILDA. Yes, to be sure! For the ten years are up now, and I am not going to wait any longer. So—out with the castle, Mr. Solness!

SOLNESS. It's no light matter to owe you anything, Hilda.

HILDA. You should have thought of that before. It is too late now! So— [*tapping the table*]—the castle on the table! It is my castle! I will have it at once!

SOLNESS [*more seriously, leans over toward her, with his arms on the table*]. What sort of castle have you imagined, Hilda?

[*Her expression becomes more and more veiled. She seems gazing inward at herself.*]

HILDA [*slowly*]. My castle shall stand on a height—on a very great height—with a clear outlook on all sides, so that I can see far—far around.

SOLNESS. And no doubt it is to have a high tower!

HILDA. A tremendously high tower. And at the very top of the tower there shall be a balcony. And I will stand out upon it—

SOLNESS [*involuntarily clutches at his forehead*]. How can you like to stand at such a dizzy height—?

HILDA. Yes, I will! Right up there will I stand and look down on the other people—on those that are building churches, and homes for mother and father and the troop of children. And you may come up and look on at it, too.

SOLNESS [*in a low tone*]. Is the builder to be allowed to come up beside the princess?

HILDA. If the builder will.

SOLNESS [*more softly*]. Then I think the builder will come.

HILDA [*nods*]. The builder—he will come.

SOLNESS. But he will never be able to build any more. Poor builder!

HILDA [*animated*]. Oh yes, he will! We two will set to work together. And then we will build the loveliest—the very loveliest—thing in all the world.

SOLNESS [*intently*]. Hilda—tell me what that is!

HILDA [*looks smilingly at him, shakes her head a little, pouts, and speaks as if to a child*]. Builders—they are such very—very stupid people.

SOLNESS. Yes, no doubt they are stupid. But now tell me what it is—the loveliest thing in the world—that we two are to build together?

HILDA [*is silent a little while, then says with an indefinable expression in her eyes*]. Castles in the air.

SOLNESS. Castles in the air?

HILDA [*nods*]. Castles in the air, yes! Do you know what sort of thing a castle in the air is?

SOLNESS. It is the loveliest thing in the world, you say.

HILDA [*rises with vehemence, and makes a gesture of repulsion with her hand*]. Yes, to be sure it is! Castles in the air—they are so easy to take refuge in. And so easy to build, too—[*looks scornfully at him*]—especially for the builders who have a—a dizzy conscience.

SOLNESS [*rises*]. After this day we two will build together, Hilda.

HILDA [*with a half-dubious smile*]. A real castle in the air?

SOLNESS. Yes. One with a firm foundation under it.

[RAGNAR BROVIK *comes out from the house. He is carrying a large, green wreath with flowers and silk ribbons.*]

HILDA [*with an outburst of pleasure*]. The wreath! Oh, that will be glorious!

SOLNESS [*in surprise*]. Have you brought the wreath, Ragnar?

RAGNAR. I promised the foreman I would.

SOLNESS [*relieved*]. Ah, then I suppose your father is better?

RAGNAR. No.

SOLNESS. Was he not cheered by what I wrote?

RAGNAR. It came too late.

SOLNESS. Too late!

RAGNAR. When she came with it he was unconscious. He had had a stroke.

SOLNESS. Why, then, you must go home to him! You must attend to your father!

RAGNAR. He does not need me any more.

SOLNESS. But surely you ought to be with him.

RAGNAR. She is sitting by his bed.

SOLNESS [*rather uncertainly*]. Kaia?

RAGNAR [*looking darkly at him*]. Yes—Kaia.

SOLNESS. Go home, Ragnar—both to him and to her. Give me the wreath.

RAGNAR [*suppresses a mocking smile*]. You don't mean that you yourself—?

SOLNESS. I will take it down to them myself. [*Takes the wreath from him.*] And now you go home; we don't require you today.

RAGNAR. I know you do not require me any more; but today I shall remain.

SOLNESS. Well, remain then, since you are bent upon it.

HILDA [*at the railing*]. Mr. Solness, I will stand here and look on at you.

SOLNESS. At me!

HILDA. It will be fearfully thrilling.

SOLNESS [*in a low tone*]. We will talk about that presently, Hilda.
[*He goes down the flight of steps with the wreath, and away through the garden.*]

HILDA [*looks after him, then turns to* RAGNAR]. I think you might at least have thanked him.

RAGNAR. Thanked him? Ought I to have thanked him?

HILDA. Yes, of course you ought!

RAGNAR. I think it is rather you I ought to thank.

HILDA. How can you say such a thing?

RAGNAR [*without answering her*]. But I advise you to take care, Miss Wangel! For you don't know him rightly yet.

HILDA [*ardently*]. Oh, no one knows him as I do!

RAGNAR [*laughs in exasperation*]. Thank him, when he has held me down year after year! When he made father disbelieve in me—made me disbelieve in myself! And all merely that he might—!

HILDA [*as if divining something*]. That he might—? Tell me at once!

RAGNAR. That he might keep her with him.

HILDA [*with a start toward him*]. The girl at the desk.

RAGNAR. Yes.

HILDA [*threateningly, clenching her hands*]. That is not true! You are telling falsehoods about him!

RAGNAR. I would not believe it either until today—when she said so herself.

HILDA [*as if beside herself*]. What did she say? I will know! At once! at once!

RAGNAR. She said that he had taken possession of her mind—her whole mind—centered all her thoughts upon himself alone. She says that she can never leave him—that she will remain here, where he is—

HILDA [*with flashing eyes*]. She will not be allowed to!

RAGNAR [*as if feeling his way*]. Who will not allow her?

HILDA [*rapidly*]. He will not either!

RAGNAR. Oh no—I understand the whole thing now. After this, she would merely be—in the way.

HILDA. You understand nothing—since you can talk like that! No, *I* will tell you why he kept hold of her.

RAGNAR. Well then, why?

HILDA. In order to keep hold of you.

RAGNAR. Has he told you so?

HILDA. No, but it is so. It must be so! [*Wildly.*] I will—I will have it so!

RAGNAR. And at the very moment when you came—he let her go.

HILDA. It was you—you that he let go! What do you suppose he cares about strange women like her?

RAGNAR [*reflects*]. Is it possible that all this time he has been afraid of me?

HILDA. He afraid! I would not be so conceited if I were you.

RAGNAR. Oh, he must have seen long ago that I had something in me too. Besides—cowardly—that is just what he is, you see.

HILDA. He! Oh yes, I am likely to believe that!

RAGNAR. In a certain sense he is cowardly—he, the great master builder. He is not afraid of robbing others of their life's happiness—as he has done both for my father and for me. But when it comes to climbing up a paltry bit of scaffolding—he will do anything rather than that.

HILDA. Oh, you should just have seen him high, high up—at the dizzy height where I once saw him.

RAGNAR. Did you see that?

HILDA. Yes, indeed I did. How free and great he looked as he stood and fastened the wreath to the church vane!

RAGNAR. I know that he ventured that, once in his life—one solitary time. It is a legend among us younger men. But no power on earth would induce him to do it again.

HILDA. Today he will do it again!

RAGNAR [*scornfully*]. Yes, I daresay!

HILDA. We shall see it!

RAGNAR. That neither you nor I will see.

HILDA [*with uncontrollable vehemence*]. I will see it! I will and I must see it!

RAGNAR. But he will not do it. He simply dare not do it. For you see he cannot get over this infirmity—master builder though he be.

[MRS. SOLNESS *comes from the house onto the veranda.*]

MRS. SOLNESS [*looks around*]. Is he not here? Where has he gone to?

RAGNAR. Mr. Solness is down with the men.

HILDA. He took the wreath with him.

MRS. SOLNESS [*terrified*]. Took the wreath with him! Oh God! oh God! Brovik—you must go down to him! Get him to come back here!

RAGNAR. Shall I say you want to speak to him, Mrs. Solness?

MRS. SOLNESS. Oh yes, do!—No, no—don't say that *I* want anything! You can say that somebody is here, and that he must come at once.

RAGNAR. Good. I will do so, Mrs. Solness.

[*He goes down the flight of steps and away through the garden.*]

MRS. SOLNESS. Oh, Miss Wangel, you can't think how anxious I feel about him.

HILDA. Is there anything in this to be so terribly frightened about?

MRS. SOLNESS. Oh yes; surely you can understand. Just think, if he were really to do it! If he should take it into his head to climb up the scaffolding!

HILDA [*eagerly*]. Do you think he will?

MRS. SOLNESS. Oh, one can never tell what he might take into his head. I am afraid there is nothing he mightn't think of doing.

HILDA. Aha! Perhaps you too think that he is—well—?

MRS. SOLNESS. Oh, I don't know what to think about him now. The Doctor has been telling me all sorts of things; and putting it all together with several things I have heard him say—

[DR. HERDAL *looks out, at the door.*]

DR. HERDAL. Is he not coming soon?

MRS. SOLNESS. Yes, I think so. I have sent for him at any rate.

DR. HERDAL [*advancing*]. I am afraid you will have to go in, my dear lady—

MRS. SOLNESS. Oh no! Oh no! I shall stay out here and wait for Halvard.

DR. HERDAL. But some ladies have just come to call on you—

MRS. SOLNESS. Good heavens, that too! And just at this moment!

DR. HERDAL. They say they positively must see the ceremony.

MRS. SOLNESS. Well, well, I suppose I must go to them after all. It is my duty.

HILDA. Can't you ask the ladies to go away?

MRS. SOLNESS. No, that would never do. Now that they are here, it is my duty to see them. But do you stay out here in the meantime—and receive him when he comes.

DR. HERDAL. And try to occupy his attention as long as possible—

MRS. SOLNESS. Yes, do, dear Miss Wangel. Keep as firm hold of him as ever you can.

HILDA. Would it not be best for you to do that?

MRS. SOLNESS. Yes; God knows that is my duty. But when one has duties in so many directions—

DR. HERDAL [*looks toward the garden*]. There he is coming.

MRS. SOLNESS. And I have to go in!

DR. HERDAL [*to* HILDA]. Don't say anything about my being here.

HILDA. Oh no! I daresay I shall find something else to talk to Mr. Solness about.

MRS. SOLNESS. And be sure you keep firm hold of him. I believe you can do it best.

[MRS. SOLNESS *and* DR. HERDAL *go into the house.* HILDA *remains standing on the veranda.* SOLNESS *comes from the garden, up the flight of steps.*]

SOLNESS. Somebody wants me, I hear.

HILDA. Yes; it is I, Mr. Solness.

SOLNESS. Oh, is it you, Hilda? I was afraid it might be Aline or the Doctor.

HILDA. You are very easily frightened, it seems!

SOLNESS. Do you think so?

HILDA. Yes; people say that you are afraid to climb about—on the scaffoldings, you know.

SOLNESS. Well, that is quite a special thing.

HILDA. Then it is true that you are afraid to do it?

SOLNESS. Yes, I am.

HILDA. Afraid of falling down and killing yourself?

SOLNESS. No, not of that.

HILDA. Of what, then?

SOLNESS. I am afraid of retribution, Hilda.

HILDA. Of retribution? [*Shakes her head.*] I don't understand that.

SOLNESS. Sit down, and I will tell you something.

HILDA. Yes, do! At once!

[*She sits on a stool by the railing, and looks expectantly at him.*]

SOLNESS [*throws his hat on the table*]. You know that I began by building churches.

HILDA [*nods*]. I know that well.

SOLNESS. For, you see, I came as a boy from a pious home in the country; and so it seemed to me that this church-building was the noblest task I could set myself.

HILDA. Yes, yes.

SOLNESS. And I venture to say that I built those poor little churches with such honest and warm and heartfelt devotion that—that—

HILDA. That—? Well?

SOLNESS. Well, that I think that he ought to have been pleased with me.

HILDA. He? What he?

SOLNESS. He who was to have the churches, of course! He to whose honor and glory they were dedicated.

HILDA. Oh, indeed! But are you certain, then, that—that he was not—pleased with you?

SOLNESS [*scornfully*]. He pleased with me! How can you talk so, Hilda? He who gave the troll in me leave to lord it just as it pleased. He who bade them be at hand to serve me, both day and night—all these—all these—

HILDA. Devils—

SOLNESS. Yes, of both kinds. Oh no, he made me feel clearly enough that he was not pleased with me. [*Mysteriously.*] You see, that was really the reason why he made the old house burn down.

HILDA. Was that why?

SOLNESS. Yes, don't you understand? He wanted to give me the chance of becoming an accomplished master in my own sphere—so that I might build all the more glorious churches for him. At first I did not understand what he was driving at; but all of a sudden it flashed upon me.

HILDA. When was that?

SOLNESS. It was when I was building the church-tower up at Lysanger.

HILDA. I thought so.

SOLNESS. For you see, Hilda—up there, amidst those new surroundings, I used to go about musing and pondering within myself. Then I saw plainly why he had taken my little children from me. It was that I should have nothing else to attach myself to. No such thing as love and happiness, you understand. I was to be only a master builder—nothing else. And all my life long I was to go on building for him. [*Laughs.*] But I can tell you nothing came of that!

HILDA. What did you do, then?

SOLNESS. First of all, I searched and tried my own heart—

HILDA. And then?

SOLNESS. Then I did the impossible—I no less than he.

HILDA. The impossible?

SOLNESS. I had never before been able to climb up to a great, free height. But that day I did it.

HILDA [*leaping up*]. Yes, yes, you did!

SOLNESS. And when I stood there, high over everything, and was hanging the wreath over the vane, I said to him: Hear me now, thou Mighty One! From this day forward I will be a free builder—I too, in my sphere— just as thou in thine. I will never more build churches for thee—only homes for human beings.

HILDA [*with great sparkling eyes*]. That was the song that I heard through the air!

SOLNESS. But afterward his turn came.

HILDA. What do you mean by that?

SOLNESS [*looks despondently at her*]. Building homes for human beings— is not worth a rap, Hilda.

HILDA. Do you say that now?

SOLNESS. Yes, for now I see it. Men have no use for these homes of theirs— to be happy in. And I should not have had any use for such a home, if I had had one. [*With a quiet, bitter laugh.*] See, that is the upshot of the whole affair, however far back I look. Nothing really built; nor anything sacrificed for the chance of building. Nothing, nothing! the whole is nothing!

HILDA. Then you will never build anything more?

SOLNESS [*with animation*]. On the contrary, I am just going to begin!

HILDA. What, then? What will you build? Tell me at once!

SOLNESS. I believe there is only one possible dwelling-place for human happiness—and that is what I am going to build now.

HILDA [*looks fixedly at him.*] Mr. Solness—you mean our castles in the air.

SOLNESS. The castles in the air—yes.

HILDA. I am afraid you would turn dizzy before we got halfway up.

SOLNESS. Not if I can mount hand in hand with you, Hilda.

HILDA [*with an expression of suppressed resentment*]. Only with me? Will to there be no others of the party?

SOLNESS. Who else should there be?

HILDA. Oh—that girl—that Kaia at the desk. Poor thing—don't you want to take her with you too?

SOLNESS. Oho! Was it about her that Aline was talking to you?

HILDA. Is it so—or is it not?

SOLNESS [*vehemently*]. I will not answer such a question. You must believe in me, wholly and entirely!

HILDA. All these ten years I have believed in you so utterly—so utterly.

SOLNESS. You must go on believing in me!

HILDA. Then let me see you stand free and high up!

SOLNESS [*sadly*]. Oh Hilda—it is not every day that I can do that.

HILDA [*passionately*]. I will have you do it! I will have it! [*Imploringly.*] Just once more, Mr. Solness! Do the impossible once again!

SOLNESS [*stands and looks deep into her eyes*]. If I try it, Hilda, I will stand up there and talk to him as I did that time before.

HILDA [*in rising excitement*]. What will you say to him?

SOLNESS. I will say to him: Hear me, Mighty Lord—thou mayest judge me as seems best to thee. But hereafter I will build nothing but the loveliest thing in the world—

HILDA [*carried away*]. Yes—yes—yes!

SOLNESS.—build it together with a princess, whom I love—

HILDA. Yes, tell him that! Tell him that!

SOLNESS. Yes. And then I will say to him: Now I shall go down and throw my arms round her and kiss her—

HILDA.—many times! Say that!

SOLNESS.—many, many times, I will say!

HILDA. And then—?

SOLNESS. Then I will wave my hat—and come down to the earth—and do as I said to him.

HILDA [*with outstretched arms*]. Now I see you again as I did when there was song in the air!

SOLNESS [*looks at her with his head bowed*]. How have you become what you are, Hilda?

HILDA. How have you made me what I am?

SOLNESS [*shortly and firmly*]. The princess shall have her castle.

HILDA [*jubilant, clapping her hands*]. Oh, Mr. Solness—! My lovely, lovely castle. Our castle in the air!

SOLNESS. On a firm foundation.

[*In the street a crowd of people has assembled, vaguely seen through the trees. Music of wind-instruments is heard far away behind the new house.* MRS. SOLNESS, *with a fur collar round her neck,* DOCTOR HERDAL *with her white shawl on his arm, and some ladies, come out on the veranda.* RAGNAR BROVIK *comes at the same time up from the garden.*]

MRS. SOLNESS [*to* RAGNAR]. Are we to have music, too?

RAGNAR. Yes. It's the band of the Mason's Union. [*To* SOLNESS.] The foreman asked me to tell you that he is ready now to go up with the wreath.

SOLNESS [*takes his hat*]. Good. I will go down to him myself.

MRS. SOLNESS [*anxiously*]. What have you to do down there, Halvard?

SOLNESS [*curtly*]. I must be down below with the men.

MRS. SOLNESS. Yes, down below—only down below.

SOLNESS. That is where I always stand—on everyday occasions. [*He goes down the flight of steps and away through the garden.*]

MRS. SOLNESS [*calls after him over the railing*]. But do beg the man to be careful when he goes up! Promise me that, Halvard!

DR. HERDAL [*to* MRS. SOLNESS]. Don't you see that I was right? He has given up all thought of that folly.

MRS. SOLNESS. Oh, what a relief! Twice workmen have fallen, and each time they were killed on the spot. [*Turns to* HILDA.] Thank you, Miss Wangel, for having kept such a firm hold upon him. I should never have been able to manage him.

DR. HERDAL [*playfully*]. Yes, yes, Miss Wangel, you know how to keep firm hold on a man, when you give your mind to it.

[MRS. SOLNESS *and* DR. HERDAL *go up to the ladies, who are standing nearer to the steps and looking over the garden.* HILDA *remains standing beside the railing in the foreground.* RAGNAR *goes up to her.*]

RAGNAR [*with suppressed laughter, half whispering*]. Miss Wangel—do you see all those young fellows down in the street?

HILDA. Yes.

RAGNAR. They are my fellow students, come to look at the master.

HILDA. What do they want to look at him for?

RAGNAR. They want to see how he daren't climb to the top of his own house.

HILDA. Oh, that is what those boys want, is it?

RAGNAR [*spitefully and scornfully*]. He has kept us down so long—now we are going to see him keep quietly down below himself.

HILDA. You will not see that—not this time.

RAGNAR [*smiles*]. Indeed! Then where shall we see him?

HILDA. High—high up by the vane! That is where you will see him!

RAGNAR [*laughs*]. Him! Oh yes, I daresay!

HILDA. His will is to reach the top—so at the top you shall see him.

RAGNAR. His will, yes; that I can easily believe. But he simply cannot do it. His head would swim round, long, long before he got halfway. He would have to crawl down again on his hands and knees.

DR. HERDAL [*points across*]. Look! There goes the foreman up the ladders.

MRS. SOLNESS. And of course he has the wreath to carry too. Oh, I do hope he will be careful!

RAGNAR [*stares incredulously and shouts*]. Why, but it's—

HILDA [*breaking out in jubilation*]. It is the master builder himself?

MRS. SOLNESS [*screams with terror*]. Yes, it is Halvard! Oh my great God—! Halvard! Halvard!

DR. HERDAL. Hush! Don't shout to him!

MRS. SOLNESS [*half beside herself*]. I must go to him! I must get him to come down again!

DR. HERDAL [*holds her*]. Don't move, any of you! Not a sound!

HILDA [*immovable, follows* SOLNESS *with her eyes*]. He climbs and climbs. Higher and higher! Higher and higher! Look! Just look!

RAGNAR [*breathless*]. He must turn now. He can't possibly help it.

HILDA. He climbs and climbs. He will soon be at the top now.

MRS. SOLNESS. Oh, I shall die of terror. I cannot bear to see it.

DR. HERDAL. Then don't look up at him.

HILDA. There he is standing on the topmost planks. Right at the top!

DR. HERDAL. Nobody must move! Do you hear?

HILDA [*exulting, with quiet intensity*]. At last! At last! Now I see him great and free again!

RAGNAR [*almost voiceless*]. But this is im—

HILDA. So I have seen him all through these ten years. How secure he stands! Frightfully thrilling all the same. Look at him! Now he is hanging the wreath round the vane!

RAGNAR. I feel as if I were looking at something utterly impossible.

HILDA. Yes, it is the impossible that he is doing now! [*With the indefinable expression in her eyes.*] Can you see anyone else up there with him?

RAGNAR. There is no one else.

HILDA. Yes, there is one he is striving with.

RAGNAR. You are mistaken.

HILDA. Then do you hear no song in the air, either?

RAGNAR. It must be the wind in the tree-tops.

HILDA. *I* hear a song—a mighty song! [*Shouts in wild jubilation and glee.*] Look, look! Now he is waving his hat! He is waving it to us down here! Oh, wave, wave back to him! For now it is finished!

[*Snatches the white shawl from the* DOCTOR, *waves it, and shouts up to* SOLNESS.] Hurrah for Master-Builder Solness!

DR. HERDAL. Stop! Stop! For God's sake—!

[*The ladies on the veranda wave their pocket-handkerchiefs, and the shouts of "Hurrah" are taken up in the street below. Then they are suddenly silenced, and the crowd bursts out into a shriek of horror. A human body with planks and fragments of wood, is vaguely perceived crashing down behind the trees.*]

MRS. SOLNESS AND THE LADIES [*at the same time*]. He is falling! He is falling!

[MRS. SOLNESS *totters, falls backward, swooning, and is caught, amid cries and confusion, by the* LADIES. *The crowd in the street breaks down the fence and storms into the garden. At the same time* DR. HERDAL, *too, rushes down thither. A short pause.*]

HILDA [*stares fixedly upward and says, as if petrified*]. My Master Builder!

RAGNAR [*supports himself, trembling, against the railing*]. He must be dashed to pieces—killed on the spot.

ONE OF THE LADIES [*as* MRS. SOLNESS *is carried into the house*]. Run down for the Doctor—

RAGNAR. I can't stir a foot—

ANOTHER LADY. Then call to someone!

RAGNAR [*tries to call out*]. How is it? Is he alive?

A VOICE [*below in the garden*]. Mr. Solness is dead!

OTHER VOICES [*nearer*]. The head is all crushed.—He fell right into the quarry.

HILDA [*turns to* RAGNAR, *and says quietly*]. I can't see him up there now!

RAGNAR. This is terrible. So, after all, he could not do it.

HILDA [*as if in quiet spellbound triumph*]. But he mounted right to the top! And I heard harps in the air.

[*Waves her shawl in the air, and shrieks with wild intensity.*]

My—my Master Builder!

ANTON CHEKHOV

THREE SISTERS

THE NEW VERISIMILITUDE

AFTER SEEING "THE WILD DUCK," Anton Chekhov (1860–1904) is reported to have announced, "Ibsen does not know life; in life it does not happen like that." It is dangerous to interpret the aphoristic pronouncements of one artist upon another, yet a comparison of *The Master Builder* and *Three Sisters* suggests that the Russian was placing himself in the ranks of naturalism, a literary creed that firmly rejected the well-made play as a false mirror of experience.

Naturalism was an artistic manifestation of the scientific theory of evolution set forth by Darwin, the most familiar catch-phrase of which is "the survival of the fittest." Darwin posited that the changes that may occur in a species over the ages are determined by environment and heredity, but always by accident, as opposed to plan or purpose. Ibsen's plays, it is clear, are written from the author's deep commitment to naturalistic principles: he is meticulous in presenting the hereditary and environmental causes that determine the personality and actions of his characters.

But Ibsen also was compelled to seek a form as a vehicle for his naturalistic attitude and he found it in the well-made play, whose tidiness, logic, almost mathematical precision, did not sufficiently project the naturalist's dogmatic insistence on accident. Émile Zola, the French novelist who assumed the responsibility of formulating the doctrine of naturalism, attacked the well-made play as a "heap of clever tricks." In a play truly verisimilar, truly reflective of human experience, there would be no formal structure, no planned action, only a presentation of the twofold life of character in its environment. Zola had little difficulty in demonstrating his principle in a series of highly successful novels; in the theater, however, he met comparative failure. As a naturalist he perhaps should have remembered that a plan to change a species cannot be effective if hereditary characteristics are stubborn or if the environment is not favorable. The playwright is only one of the forces that must combine to bring about a change in the theater. Actors, designers, directors, even spectators must share in the revolutionary movement.

Fortunately for the naturalists the ground was being prepared. The theater of the nineteenth century became over the years increasingly responsive to a public interest in accuracy. Where, in the early years, it had been content with haphazard staging and painted settings frequently unrelated to the exact milieu of the action, by mid-century a new sense of history and an enthusiasm for the past led first to almost pedantic attempts to reproduce historical settings and later to an enthusiasm for realistic illusion irrespective of period. Melodrama, in which actual boats, or tenements, or railroad trains were as important as the characters in providing the audience with thrilling situations, contributed to experiments in realistic production, though completely unconcerned with "reality" in plotting or characterization. Slowly a theory of production evolved which considered setting, not as background for the action, but as the *home* of the action: settings did not simply reproduce locales, they intended to reflect attitude and tone. It was not enough to supply actors with the precise number of chairs demanded by their stage business; the chairs must be chosen with an eye to reminding the audience that the characters were frugal bourgeois, or newly rich aspirants to social status.

Once the setting had been adjusted to the particular play, a new concept of acting was required; the actors must learn to behave in the setting as well as act on the stage. André Antoine, one of the pioneers of the new staging technique, pointed out that

> Plays founded on observation should not be acted in the same way as the classical repertory. To understand these modern people, one must leave behind all old conventions; the characters in these plays are people like us, living not in spacious halls with the dimensions of cathedrals, but in rooms like our own, by their fireplaces, under the lamps, around the table and not—as in the old repertory—close to the prompter's box. They have voices like ours, their language

is that of ordinary life, with its contractions, its familiar tricks of speech, and not the rhetoric and lofty style of our classics.

And so, over a period of decades, the seedbed for naturalistic playwriting was prepared, and the audience, at the same time, became accustomed to the modifications in staging and acting necessary for their acceptance of a different kind of reflection in the theatrical mirror.

Anton Chekhov was by profession a doctor of medicine and his scientific training no doubt conditioned him to accept the theories of naturalism when he turned to literature and the drama. At any rate he described the contemporary Russian theater as "an eruption, a nasty disease of the cities," and declared that writers, as children of their age, ought to surrender to the external conditions of their age. In an era of scientific thinking it was wrong to perpetuate romantic conventions; the writer must be as objective as a chemist.

To read or to see any one of Chekhov's plays is to be at once aware of their apparent objectivity, their apparent photographic accuracy. Although a great deal is going on within the setting, nothing seems to be happening in the conventional dramatic sense; the plot does not progress smoothly as a conflict is established and developed in intensity to a climax and resolution. Instead—and the *Three Sisters* is typical of the Chekhovian structure—the curtain rises on a family or an established social group into which a stranger, or an alien force is introduced. This was a familiar device of the well-made play, permitting the exposition of the situation with some semblance of realism. But in Chekhov it is the center of the entire action: the story begins with the arrival of the stranger and ends with his departure; what the audience is invited to observe is his catalytic power in revealing the inner nature of the characters of the established group.

Such a dramatic situation permits an ostensibly aimless, verisimilar structure. There seems to be little logic (as in life) in the succession of scenes, one event does not prepare for that which immediately follows. The sense of life in Chekhov's comedies derives from structure by juxtaposition. No situation is permitted to develop to its resolution, every situation is broken or interrupted by another designedly inconsequential. If the relationship of the characters on stage is working toward pathos or emotionalism there is sure to be an intrusion of the trivial or the absurd. Conversely, a moment of comedy will be brushed aside by the unexpected entrance of serious matter. Thus the unpredictability or instability of experience is suggested, while at the same time retaining the artist's strict control of his materials.

To increase the verisimilitude of his plays, Chekhov laid great importance on physical details. He was insistent on accuracy of costume, that the character appear on stage exactly as he had seen him in his mind's eye. He once said to the leading actor after a performance, "You acted splendidly, but not my character. I did not write that." The actor, distressed, asked how he had misrepresented his part, and the playwright replied, "He has striped trousers and boots out-at-heel. He wears striped trousers and smokes a cigar, *this* way." To the naturalist, all details are unalterable. Clothing does not type a character, as in the older theater; instead, his choice of trousers, the condition of his boots, his manner of smoking are means of presenting his individuality, his uniqueness.

Ready to Chekhov's hand was a theatrical troupe prepared to share his enthusiasm for naturalism, to produce his work with the attention to detail he desired. This was the Moscow Theater of Art, established in 1898 by Constantin Stanislavsky and Vladimir Nemirovich-Danchenko. Stanislavsky's theory of acting, his so-called "Method," is widely known, but it is only one aspect of a total theory of production which insists on the setting as the environment representing the characters and governing their behavior. Chekhov once shook his head over the extravagance with which the company wasted time, energy, and money in the interest of psychological and architectural truth, but he was nonetheless fortunate to have found such collaborators.

No detail was too small, too unimportant to be ignored. The third act of the *Three Sisters* is played against a fire burning somewhere in a provincial town; it is an unseen fire, never a part of the action on stage. Yet the author joined with the sound-effects man at the theater for long hours of experimentation to get the precise sound of a firebell that had been in his mind as he conceived the scene. His interest, of course, was not simply documentary truth:

the sound of a firebell in the darkness of a small town has its own quality of terror. More than authenticating locale, the sound added to the texture, the intensity, of the accompanying action. So a concertina or the chirping of crickets may define a mood by underlining or contrast, so a military band fading into the distance may summarize and give finality to an action that can have no climactic resolution if it is to remain true to the sense of life.

"In life it does not happen like that," said Chekhov of *The Wild Duck*; the thread of cause and effect does not reveal itself so readily, death and catastrophe do not occur at appropriate moments. It is perhaps proper to inquire why such a declaration had not been made earlier, perhaps by Aristotle or by one of his successors who were so concerned with decorum, propriety in characterization and action. Possibly even Ibsen, subscribing to nineteenth-century scientism, should have been aware of his failure to comply with its artistic manifesto.

Here, once again, the critic must look not just to the mirror but to the world. The classical age had found stature and finality in the conflicts between heroes and gods; the Renaissance dreamed of the extension of man and his powers in a brave new world; Ibsen was alert to the potential benefits of the great revolutions of this century. But the Russian world at the end of the century was ably anatomized by Bernard Shaw in the preface to *Heartbreak House*:

> [The] utter enervation and futilization in that overheated drawing-room atmosphere . . . The nice people could read, some of them could write . . . They wished to realize their favorite fictions and poems in their own lives; and, when they could, they lived without scruple on incomes which they did nothing to earn. They took the only part of our society in which there was leisure for high culture and made it an economic, political, and, as far as possible, a moral vacuum; and as Nature, abhorring the vacuum, immediately filled it up with sex and with all sorts of refined pleasures, it was a very delightful place at its best for moments of relaxation. In other moments it was disastrous.

Chekhov's plays mirror a world in which positive action seems an impossibility. His characters, like the people they reflect, have reached a point of stasis in their evolutionary development. They can yearn for another life, another world, but they are fixed by their own hopelessness. "In two or three hundred years life on earth will be unimaginably beautiful, marvelous." says Vershinin, but the individual can do nothing about the mass of darkness surrounding him. Chekhov's characters have not the power of taking arms against a sea of troubles; even if they are intellectually aware of the changes beginning to appear in the great world, they cannot associate themselves with a new way of life. The three sisters who cannot get to Moscow represent a whole society and its concerns. Yet they escape from being representations of a vanished past, they continue to live in the theater of the twentieth century. Shaw pointed out that Chekhov's Russians were typical of the inhabitants of country houses all over Europe before the First World War. But they are not merely Russian, not merely European, and they did not vanish from the earth with the early decades of this century.

Characters

ANDREY SERGEYEVITCH PROZOROV

NATALYA IVANOVNA
(*also called* NATASHA)
his fiancée, afterward his wife

OLGA
MASHA
IRINA
his sisters

FYODOR ILYITCH KULIGIN
a high-school teacher, husband of MASHA

LIEUTENANT-COLONEL ALEXANDR IGNATYEVITCH
VERSHININ
Battery-Commander

BARON NIKOLAY LVOVITCH TUSENBACH
Lieutenant

VASSILY VASSILYEVITCH SOLYONY
Captain

IVAN ROMANITCH TCHEBUTYKIN
army doctor

ALEXEY PETROVITCH FEDOTIK
Second Lieutenant

VLADIMIR KARLOVITCH RODDEY
Second Lieutenant

FERAPONT
an old porter from the Rural Board

ANFISA
the nurse, an old woman of eighty

The action takes place in a provincial town.

THREE SISTERS

Anton Chekhov

Translated by Constance Garnett

ACT ONE

In the house of the PROZOROVS. *A drawing room with columns beyond which a large room is visible. Midday; it is bright and sunny. The table in the farther room is being laid for lunch.*

OLGA, *in the dark-blue uniform of a high-school teacher, is correcting exercise books, at times standing still and then walking up and down;* MASHA, *in a black dress, with her hat on her knee, is reading a book;* IRINA, *in a white dress, is standing plunged in thought.*

OLGA. Father died just a year ago, on this very day—the fifth of May, your name-day, Irina. It was very cold, snow was falling. I felt as though I should not live through it; you lay fainting as though you were dead. But now a year has passed and we can think of it calmly; you are already in a white dress, your face is radiant. [*The clock strikes twelve.*] The clock was striking then too. [*A pause.*] I remember the band playing and the firing at the cemetery as they carried the coffin. Though he was a general in command of a brigade, yet there weren't many people there. It was raining, though. Heavy rain and snow.

IRINA. Why recall it!

[BARON TUSENBACH, TCHEBUTYKIN, *and* SOLYONY *appear near the table in the dining room, beyond the columns.*]

OLGA. It is warm today, we can have the windows open, but the birches are not in leaf yet. Father was given his brigade and came here with us from Moscow eleven years ago and I remember distinctly that in Moscow at this time, at the beginning of May, everything was already in flower; it was warm, and everything was bathed in sunshine. It's eleven years ago, and yet I remember it all as though we had left it yesterday. Oh, dear! I woke up this morning, I saw a blaze of sunshine. I saw the spring, and joy stirred in my heart. I had a passionate longing to be back at home again!

Reprinted from *The Plays of Chekov*, translated by Constance Garnett, Modern Library, 1930.

TCHEBUTYKIN. The devil it is!

TUSENBACH. Of course, it's nonsense.

[MASHA, *brooding over a book, softly whistles a song.*]

OLGA. Don't whistle, Masha. How can you! [*A pause.*] Being all day in
school and then at my lessons till the evening gives me a perpetual headache and thoughts as gloomy as though I were old. And really these four
years that I have been at the high-school I have felt my strength and my
youth oozing away from me every day. And only one yearning grows
stronger and stronger. . . .

IRINA. To go back to Moscow. To sell the house, to make an end of everything here, and off to Moscow. . . .

OLGA. Yes! To Moscow, and quickly.

[TCHEBUTYKIN *and* TUSENBACH *laugh.*]

IRINA. Andrey will probably be a professor, he will not live here anyhow.
The only difficulty is poor Masha.

OLGA. Masha will come and spend the whole summer in Moscow every year.

[MASHA *softly whistles a tune.*]

IRINA. Please God it will all be managed. [*Looking out of window.*] How fine
it is today. I don't know why I feel so lighthearted! I remembered this
morning that it was my name-day and at once I felt joyful and thought
of my childhood when mother was living. And I was thrilled by such
wonderful thoughts, such thoughts!

OLGA. You are radiant today and looking lovelier than usual. And Masha
is lovely too. Andrey would be nice-looking, but he has grown too fat
and that does not suit him. And I have grown older and ever so much
thinner. I suppose it's because I get so cross with the girls at school.
Today now I am free, I am at home, and my head doesn't ache, and I
feel younger than yesterday. I am only twenty-eight. . . . It's all quite
right, it's all from God, but it seems to me that if I were married and
sitting at home all day, it would be better. [*A pause.*] I should be fond
of my husband.

TUSENBACH [*to* SOLYONY]. You talk such nonsense, I am tired of listening to
you. [*Coming into the drawing room.*] I forgot to tell you, you will receive
a visit today from Vershinin, the new commander of our battery. [*Sits
down to the piano.*]

OLGA. Well, I shall be delighted.

IRINA. Is he old?

TUSENBACH. No, nothing to speak of. Forty or forty-five at the most.
[*Softly plays the piano.*] He seems to be a nice fellow. He is not stupid,
that's certain. Only he talks a lot.

IRINA. Is he interesting?

TUSENBACH. Yes, he is all right, only he has a wife, a mother-in-law and
two little girls. And it's his second wife too. He is paying calls and telling
everyone that he has a wife and two little girls. He'll tell you so too. His
wife seems a bit crazy, with her hair in a long plait like a girl's, always

talks in a high-flown style, makes philosophical reflections and frequently attempts to commit suicide, evidently to annoy her husband. I should
have left a woman like that years ago, but he puts up with her and merely
complains.

SOLYONY [*coming into the drawing room with* TCHEBUTYKIN]. With one hand
I can only lift up half a hundredweight, but with both hands I can lift up a
hundredweight and a half or even a hundredweight and three-quarters.
From that I conclude that two men are not only twice but three times as
strong as one man, or even more. . . .

TCHEBUTYKIN [*reading the newspaper as he comes in*]. For hair falling out
. . . two ounces of naphthaline in half a bottle of spirit . . . to be dissolved
and used daily . . . [*Puts it down in his notebook.*] Let's make a note of it!
No, I don't want it . . . [*Scratches it out.*] It doesn't matter.

IRINA. Ivan Romanitch, dear Ivan Romanitch!

TCHEBUTYKIN. What is it, my child, my joy?

IRINA. Tell me, why is it I am so happy today? As though I were sailing
with the great blue sky above me and big white birds flying over it. Why
is it? Why?

TCHEBUTYKIN [*kissing both her hands, tenderly*]. My white bird. . . .

IRINA. When I woke up this morning, got up and washed, it suddenly
seemed to me as though everything in the world was clear to me and that
I knew how one ought to live. Dear Ivan Romanitch, I know all about it.
A man ought to work, to toil in the sweat of his brow, whoever he may
be, and all the purpose and meaning of his life, his happiness, his ecstasies lie in that alone. How delightful to be a workman who gets up before
dawn and breaks stones on the road, or a shepherd, or a schoolmaster
teaching children, or an engine-driver. . . . Oh, dear! to say nothing of
human beings, it would be better to be an ox, better to be a humble
horse and work, than a young woman who wakes at twelve o'clock, then
has coffee in bed, then spends two hours dressing. . . . Oh, how awful
that is! Just as one has a craving for water in hot weather I have a craving
for work. And if I don't get up early and work, give me up as a friend,
Ivan Romanitch.

TCHEBUTYKIN [*tenderly*]. I'll give you up, I'll give you up. . . .

OLGA. Father trained us to get up at seven o'clock. Now Irina wakes at
seven and lies in bed at least till nine thinking. And she looks so serious!
[*Laughs.*]

IRINA. You are used to thinking of me as a child and are suprised when I
look serious. I am twenty!

TUSENBACH. The yearning for work, oh dear, how well I understand it! I
have never worked in my life. I was born in cold, idle Petersburg, in a
family that had known nothing of work or cares of any kind. I remember,
when I came home from the school of cadets, a footman used to pull off
my boots. I used to be troublesome, but my mother looked at me with
reverential awe, and was surprised when other people did not do the

same. I was guarded from work. But I doubt if they have succeeded in guarding me completely, I doubt it! The time is at hand, an avalanche is moving down upon us, a mighty clearing storm which is coming, is already near and will soon blow the laziness, the indifference, the distaste for work, the rotten boredom out of our society. I shall work, and in another twenty-five or thirty years everyone will have to work. Everyone!

TCHEBUTYKIN. I am not going to work.

TUSENBACH. You don't count.

SOLYONY. In another twenty-five years you won't be here, thank God. In two or three years you will kick the bucket, or I shall lose my temper and put a bullet through your head, my angel.

[*Pulls a scent-bottle out of his pocket and sprinkles his chest and hands.*]

TCHEBUTYKIN [*laughs*]. And I really have never done anything at all. I haven't done a stroke of work since I left the University, I have never read a book, I read nothing but newspapers . . . . [*Takes another newspaper out of his pocket.*] Here . . . I know, for instance, from the newspapers that there was such a person as Dobrolyubov, but what he wrote, I can't say. . . . Goodness only knows. . . .

[*A knock is heard on the floor from the story below.*]

There . . . they are calling me downstairs, someone has come for me. I'll be back directly. . . . Wait a minute . . . . [*Goes out hurriedly, combing his beard.*]

IRINA. He's got something up his sleeve.

TUSENBACH. Yes, he went out with a solemn face, evidently he is just going to bring you a present.

IRINA. What a nuisance!

OLGA. Yes, it's awful. He is always doing something silly.

MASHA. By the sea-strand an oak-tree green . . . upon that oak a chain of gold . . . upon that oak a chain of gold. [*Gets up, humming softly.*]

OLGA. You are not very cheerful today, Masha.

[MASHA, *humming, puts on her hat.*]

OLGA. Where are you going?

MASHA. Home.

IRINA. How queer! . . .

TUSENBACH. To go away from a name-day party!

MASHA. Never mind. . . . I'll come in the evening. Good-bye, my darling . . . . [*Kisses* IRINA.] Once again I wish you, be well and happy. In old days, when father was alive, we always had thirty or forty officers here on name-days; it was noisy, but today there is only a man and a half, and it is as still as the desert. . . . I'll go. . . . I am in the blues today, I am feeling glum, so don't you mind what I say. [*Laughing through her tears.*] We'll talk some other time, and so for now good-bye, darling, I am going. . . .

IRINA [*discontentedly*]. Oh, how tiresome you are. . . .

OLGA [*with tears*]. I understand you, Masha.

SOLYONY. If a man philosophises, there will be philosophy or sophistry, anyway, but if a woman philosophises, or two do it, then you may just snap your fingers!

MASHA. What do you mean to say by that, you terrible person?

SOLYONY. Nothing. He had not time to say "alack," before the bear was on his back. [*A pause.*]

MASHA [*to* OLGA, *angrily*]. Don't blubber!

[*Enter* ANFISA *and* FERAPONT *carrying a cake.*]

ANFISA. This way, my good man. Come in, your boots are clean. [*To* IRINA.] From the Rural Board, from Mihail Ivanitch Protopopov. . . . A cake.

IRINA. Thanks. Thank him. [*Takes the cake.*]

FERAPONT. What?

IRINA [*more loudly*]. Thank him from me!

OLGA. Nurse dear, give him some pie. Ferapont, go along, they will give you some pie.

FERAPONT. Eh?

ANFISA. Come along, Ferapont Spiridonitch, my good soul, come along . . . [*Goes out with* FERAPONT.]

MASHA. I don't like that Protopopov, that Mihail Potapitch or Ivanitch. He ought not to be invited.

IRINA. I did not invite him.

MASHA. That's a good thing.

[*Enter* TCHEBUTYKIN, *followed by an orderly with a silver samovar; a hum of surprise and displeasure.*]

OLGA [*putting her hands over her face*]. A samovar! How awful! [*Goes out to the table in the dining room.*]

IRINA. My dear Ivan Romanitch, what are you thinking about!

TUSENBACH [*laughs*]. I warned you!

MASHA. Ivan Romanitch, you really have no conscience!

TCHEBUTYKIN. My dear girls, my darlings, you are all that I have, you are the most precious treasures I have on earth. I shall soon be sixty, I am an old man, alone in the world, a useless old man. . . . There is nothing good in me, except my love for you, and if it were not for you, I should have been dead long ago. . . . [*To* IRINA.] My dear, my little girl, I've known you from a baby . . . I've carried you in my arms. . . . I loved your dear mother. . . .

IRINA. But why such expensive presents?

TCHEBUTYKIN [*angry and tearful*]. Expensive presents. . . . Get along with you! [*To the orderly.*] Take the samovar in there . . . [*Mimicking.*] Expensive presents . . . .

[*The orderly carries the samovar into the dining room.*]

ANFISA [*crossing the room*]. My dears, a colonel is here, a stranger. . . . He has taken off his greatcoat, children, he is coming in here. Irinushka, you must be nice and polite, dear ... [*As she goes out.*] And it's time for lunch already ... mercy on us. ...

TUSENBACH. Vershinin, I suppose.

[*Enter* VERSHININ.]

TUSENBACH. Colonel Vershinin.

VERSHININ [*to* MASHA *and* IRINA]. I have the honor to introduce myself, my name is Vershinin. I am very, very glad to be in your house at last. How you have grown up! Aie-aie!

IRINA. Please sit down. We are delighted to see you.

VERSHININ [*with animation*]. How glad I am, how glad I am! But there are three of you sisters. I remember—three little girls. I don't remember your faces, but that your father, Colonel Prozorov, had three little girls I remember perfectly, and saw them with my own eyes. How time passes! Hey-ho, how it passes!

TUSENBACH. Alexandr Ignatyevitch has come from Moscow.

IRINA. From Moscow? You have come from Moscow?

VERSHININ. Yes. Your father was in command of a battery there, and I was an officer in the same brigade. [*To* MASHA.] Your face, now, I seem to remember.

MASHA. I don't remember you.

IRINA. Olya! Olya! [*Calls into the dining room.*] Olya, come!

[OLGA *comes out of the dining room into the drawing room.*]

IRINA. Colonel Vershinin is from Moscow, it appears.

VERSHININ. So you are Olga Sergeyevna, the eldest.... And you are Marya.... And you are Irina, the youngest. ...

OLGA. You come from Moscow?

VERSHININ. Yes. I studied in Moscow. I began my service there, I served there for years, and at last I have been given a battery here—I have come here as you see. I don't remember you exactly, I only remember you were three sisters. I remember your father. If I shut my eyes, I can see him as though he were living. I used to visit you in Moscow. ...

OLGA. I thought I remembered everyone, and now all at once ...

VERSHININ. My name is Alexandr Ignatyevitch.

IRINA. Alexandr Ignatyevitch, you have come from Moscow. ... What a surprise!

OLGA. We are going to move there, you know.

IRINA. We are hoping to be there by the autumn. It's our native town, we were born there. ... In Old Basmanny Street ... [*Both laugh with delight.*]

MASHA. To see someone from our own town unexpectedly! [*Eagerly.*] Now I remember! Do you remember, Olya, they used to talk of the "love-sick major?" You were a lieutenant at that time and were in love, and for some reason everyone called you "major" to tease you. ...

VERSHININ [*laughs*]. Yes, yes. ... The love-sick major, that was it.

MASHA. You only had a moustache then.... Oh, how much older you look! [*Through tears.*] how much older!

VERSHININ. Yes, when I was called the love-sick major I was young, I was in love. Now it's very different.

OLGA. But you haven't a single grey hair. You have grown older but you are not old.

VERSHININ. I am in my forty-third year, though. Is it long since you left Moscow?

IRINA. Eleven years. But why are you crying, Masha, you queer girl? . . . [*Through her tears.*] I shall cry too. . . .

MASHA. I am all right. And in which street did you live?

VERSHININ. In Old Basmanny.

OLGA. And that's where we lived too. . . .

VERSHININ. At one time I lived in Nyemetsky Street. I used to go from there to the Red Barracks. There is a gloomy-looking bridge on the way, where the water makes a noise. It makes a lonely man feel melancholy. [*A pause.*] And here what a broad, splendid river! A marvelous river!

OLGA. Yes, but it is cold. It's cold here and there are gnats. . . .

VERSHININ. How can you! You've such a splendid healthy Russian climate here. Forest, river . . . and birches here too. Charming, modest birches, I love them better than any other trees. It's nice to live here. The only strange thing is that the railway station is fifteen miles away. . . . And no one knows why it is so.

SOLYONY. I know why it is. [*They all look at him.*] Because if the station had been near it would not have been so far, and if it is far, it's because it is not near.

[*An awkward silence.*]

TUSENBACH. He is fond of his joke, Vassily Vassilyevitch.

OLGA. Now I recall you, too. I remember.

VERSHININ. I knew your mother.

TCHEBUTYKIN. She was a fine woman, the Kingdom of Heaven be hers.

IRINA. Mother is buried in Moscow.

OLGA. In the Novo-Dyevitchy. . . .

MASHA. Would you believe it, I am already beginning to forget her face. So people will not remember us either . . . they will forget us.

VERSHININ. Yes. They will forget us. Such is our fate, there is no help for it. What seems to us serious, significant, very important, will one day be forgotten or will seem unimportant. [*A pause.*] And it's curious that we can't possibly tell what exactly will be considered great and important, and what will seem paltry and ridiculous. Did not the discoveries of Copernicus or Columbus, let us say, seem useless and ridiculous at first, while the nonsensical writings of some wiseacre seemed true? And it may be that our present life, which we accept so readily, will in time seem queer, uncomfortable, not sensible, not clean enough, perhaps even sinful. . . .

TUSENBACH. Who knows? Perhaps our age will be called a great one and remembered with respect. Now we have no torture-chamber, no executions, no invasions, but at the same time how much unhappiness there is!

SOLYONY [*in a high-pitched voice*]. Chook, chook, chook. . . . It's bread and meat to the baron to talk about ideas.

TUSENBACH. Vassily Vassilyevitch, I ask you to let me alone . . . [*Moves to another seat.*] It gets boring, at last.

SOLYONY [*in a high-pitched voice*]. Chook, chook, chook. . . .

TUSENBACH [*to* VERSHININ]. The unhappiness which one observes now— there is so much of it—does indicate, however, that society has reached a certain moral level.

VERSHININ. Yes, yes, of course.

TCHEBUTYKIN. You said just now, baron, that our age will be called great; but people are small all the same . . . [*Gets up.*] Look how small I am. [*A violin is played behind the scenes.*]

MASHA. That's Andrey playing, our brother.

IRINA. He is the learned one of the family. We expect him to become a professor. Father was a military man, but his son has gone in for a learned career.

MASHA. It was father's wish.

OLGA. We have been teasing him today. We think he is a little in love.

IRINA. With a young lady living here. She will come in today most likely.

MASHA. Oh, how she dresses! It's not that her clothes are merely ugly or out of fashion, they are simply pitiful. A queer gaudy yellowish skirt with some sort of vulgar fringe and a red blouse. And her cheeks scrubbed till they shine! Andrey is not in love with her—I won't admit that, he has some taste anyway—it's simply for fun, he is teasing us, playing the fool. I heard yesterday that she is going to be married to Protopopov, the chairman of our Rural Board. And a very good thing too. . . . [*At the side door.*] Andrey, come here, dear, for a minute! [*Enter* ANDREY.]

OLGA. This is my brother, Andrey Sergeyevitch.

VERSHININ. My name is Vershinin.

ANDREY. And mine is Prozorov. [*Mops his perspiring face.*] You are our new battery commander?

OLGA. Only fancy, Alexandr Ignatyevitch comes from Moscow.

ANDREY. Really? Well, then, I congratulate you. My sisters will let you have no peace.

VERSHININ. I have had time to bore your sisters already.

IRINA. See what a pretty picture-frame Andrey has given me today! [*Shows the frame.*] He made it himself.

VERSHININ [*looking at the frame and not knowing what to say*]. Yes . . . it is a thing. . . .

IRINA. And that frame above the piano, he made that too!

[ANDREY *waves his hand in despair and moves away.*]

OLGA. He is learned, and he plays the violin, and he makes all sorts of things with the fretsaw. In fact he is good all round. Andrey, don't go! That's a way he has—he always tries to make off! Come here!

[MASHA *and* IRINA *take him by the arms and, laughing, lead him back.*]

MASHA. Come, come!

ANDREY. Leave me alone, please!

MASHA. How absurd he is! Alexandr Ignatyevitch used to be called the love-sick major at one time, and he was not a bit offended.

VERSHININ. Not in the least!

MASHA. And I should like to call you the love-sick violinist!

IRINA. Or the love-sick professor!

OLGA. He is in love! Andryusha is in love!

IRINA [*claps her hands*]. Bravo, bravo! Encore! Andryusha is in love!

TCHEBUTYKIN [*comes up behind* ANDREY *and puts both arms round his waist*]. Nature our hearts for love created! [*Laughs, then sits down and reads the newspaper which he takes out of his pocket.*]

ANDREY. Come, that's enough, that's enough . . . [*Mops his face.*] I haven't slept all night and this morning I don't feel quite myself, as they say. I read till four o'clock and then went to bed, but it was no use. I thought of one thing and another, and then it gets light so early; the sun simply pours into my bedroom. I want while I am here during the summer to translate a book from the English. . . .

VERSHININ. You read English then?

ANDREY. Yes. Our father, the Kingdom of Heaven be his, oppressed us with education. It's absurd and silly, but it must be confessed I began to get fatter after his death, and I have grown too fat in one year, as though a weight had been taken off my body. Thanks to our father we all know English, French and German, and Irina knows Italian too. But what it cost us!

MASHA. In this town to know three languages is an unnecessary luxury! Not even a luxury, but an unnecessary encumbrance, like a sixth finger. We know a great deal that is unnecessary.

VERSHININ. What next! [*Laughs.*] You know a great deal that is unnecessary! I don't think there can be a town so dull and dismal that intelligent and educated people are unnecessary in it. Let us suppose that of the hundred thousand people living in this town, which is, of course, uncultured and behind the times, there are only three of your sort. It goes without saying that you cannot conquer the mass of darkness round you; little by little, as you go on living, you will be lost in the crowd. You will have to give in to it. Life will get the better of you, but still you will not disappear without a trace. After you there may appear perhaps six like you, then twelve and so on until such as you form a majority. In two or three hundred years life on earth will be unimaginably beautiful, marvelous. Man needs such a life and, though he hasn't it yet, he must have a presentiment of it, expect it, dream of it, prepare for it; for that he must see and know more than his father and grandfather. [*Laughs.*] And you complain of knowing a great deal that's unnecessary.

MASHA [*takes off her hat*]. I'll stay to lunch.

IRINA [*with a sigh*]. All that really ought to be written down. . . .

[ANDREY *has slipped away unobserved.*]

TUSENBACH. You say that after many years life on earth will be beautiful and marvelous. That's true. But in order to have any share, however far off, in it now one must be preparing for it, one must be working. . . .

VERSHININ [*gets up*]. Yes. What a lot of flowers you have! [*Looking round.*] And delightful rooms. I envy you! I've been knocking about all my life from one wretched lodging to another, always with two chairs and a sofa and stoves which smoke. What I have been lacking all my life is just such flowers . . . [*Rubs his hands.*] But there, it's no use thinking about it!

TUSENBACH. Yes, we must work. I'll be bound you think the German is getting sentimental. But on my honor I am Russian and I can't even speak German. My father belonged to the Orthodox Church . . . . [*A pause.*]

VERSHININ [*walks about the stage*]. I often think, what if one were to begin life over again, knowing what one is about! If one life, which has been already lived, were only a rough sketch so to say, and the second were the fair copy! Then, I fancy, every one of us would try before everything not to repeat himself, anyway he would create a different setting for his life; would have a house like this with plenty of light and masses of flowers. . . . I have a wife and two little girls, my wife is in delicate health and so on and so on, but if I were to begin life over again I would not marry. . . . No, no!

[*Enter* KULIGIN *in the uniform of a school-master.*]

KULIGIN [*goes up to* IRINA]. Dear sister, allow me to congratulate you on your name-day and with all my heart to wish you good health and everything else that one can desire for a girl of your age. And to offer you as a gift this little book. [*Gives her a book.*] The history of our high-school for fifty years, written by myself. An insignificant little book, written because I had nothing better to do, but still you can read it. Good morning, friends. [*To* VERSHININ.] My name is Kuligin, teacher in the high-school here. [*To* IRINA.] In that book you will find a list of all who have finished their studies in our high-school during the last fifty years. *Feci quod potui, faciant meliora potentes.*[1] [*Kisses* MASHA.]

IRINA. Why, but you gave me a copy of this book at Easter.

KULIGIN [*laughs*]. Impossible! If that's so, give it me back, or better still, give it to the Colonel. Please accept it, Colonel. Some day when you are bored you can read it.

VERSHININ. Thank you. [*Is about to take leave.*] I am extremely glad to have made your acquaintance. . . .

OLGA. You are going? No, no!

[1] I did what I could, let those who are able do better.

IRINA. You must stay to lunch with us. Please do.

OLGA. Pray do!

VERSHININ [*bows*]. I believe I have chanced on a name-day. Forgive me, I did not know and have not congratulated you . . . [*Walks away with* OLGA *into the dining room.*]

KULIGIN. Today, gentlemen, is Sunday, a day of rest. Let us all rest and enjoy ourselves each in accordance with our age and our position. The carpets should be taken up for the summer and put away till the winter . . . Persian powder or naphthaline. . . . The Romans were healthy because they knew how to work and they knew how to rest, they had *mens sana in corpore sano.*[2] Their life was molded into a certain framework. Our headmaster says that the most important thing in every life is its framework. . . . What loses its framework, comes to an end—and it's the same in our everyday life. [*Puts his arm round* MASHA'S *waist, laughing.*] Masha loves me. My wife loves me. And the window curtains, too, ought to be put away together with the carpets. . . . Today I feel cheerful and in the best of spirits. Masha, at four o'clock this afternoon we have to be at the headmaster's. An excursion has been arranged for the teachers and their families.

MASHA. I am not going.

KULIGIN [*grieved*]. Dear Masha, why not?

MASHA. We'll talk about it afterward . . . [*Angrily.*] Very well, I will go, only let me alone, please . . . [*Walks away.*]

KULIGIN. And then we shall spend the evening at the headmaster's. In spite of the delicate state of his health, that man tries before all things to be sociable. He is an excellent, noble personality. A splendid man. Yesterday, after the meeting, he said to me, "I am tired, Fyodor Ilyitch, I am tired." [*Looks at the clock, then at his watch.*] Your clock is seven minutes fast. "Yes," he said, "I am tired."

[*Sounds of a violin behind the scenes.*]

OLGA. Come to lunch, please. There's a pie!

KULIGIN. Ah, Olga, my dear Olga! Yesterday I was working from early morning till eleven o'clock at night and was tired out, and today I feel happy. [*Goes up to the table in the dining room.*] My dear. . . .

TCHEBUTYKIN [*puts the newspaper in his pocket and combs his beard*]. Pie? Splendid!

MASHA [*to* TCHEBUTYKIN, *sternly*]. Only mind you don't drink today! Do you hear? It's bad for you to drink.

TCHEBUTYKIN. Oh, come, that's a thing of the past. It's two years since I got drunk. [*Impatiently.*] But there, my good girl, what does it matter!

MASHA. Anyway, don't you dare to drink. Don't dare. [*Angrily, but so as not to be heard by her husband.*] Again, damnation take it, I am to be bored a whole evening at the headmaster's!

TUSENBACH. I wouldn't go if I were you. . . . It's very simple.

2 "A sound mind in a sound body."

TCHEBUTYKIN. Don't go, my love.

MASHA. Oh, yes, don't go! . . . . It's a damnable life, insufferable . . . . [*Goes to the dining room.*]

TCHEBUTYKIN [*following her*]. Come, come. . . .

SOLYONY [*going to the dining room*]. Chook, chook, chook. . . .

TUSENBACH. Enough, Vassily Vassilyevitch! Leave off!

SOLYONY. Chook, chook, chook. . . .

KULIGIN [*gaily*]. Your health, Colonel! I am a school-master and one of the family here, Masha's husband. . . . She is very kind, really, very kind. . . .

VERSHININ. I'll have some of this dark-colored vodka . . . . [*Drinks.*] To your health! [*To* OLGA.] I feel so happy with all of you!

[*No one is left in the drawing room but* IRINA *and* TUSENBACH.]

IRINA. Masha is in low spirits today. She was married at eighteen, when she thought him the cleverest of men. But now it's not the same. He is the kindest of men, but he is not the cleverest.

OLGA [*impatiently*]. Andrey, do come!

ANDREY [*behind the scenes*]. I am coming. [*Comes in and goes to the table.*]

TUSENBACH. What are you thinking about?

IRINA. Nothing. I don't like that Solyony of yours, I am afraid of him. He keeps on saying such stupid things. . . .

TUSENBACH. He is a queer man. I am sorry for him and annoyed by him, but more sorry. I think he is shy. . . . When one is alone with him he is very intelligent and friendly, but in company he is rude, a bully. Don't go yet, let them sit down to the table. Let me be by you. What are you thinking of? [*A pause.*] You are twenty, I am not yet thirty. How many years have we got before us, a long, long chain of days full of my love for you. . . .

IRINA. Nikolay Lvovitch, don't talk to me about love.

TUSENBACH [*not listening*]. I have a passionate craving for life, for struggle, for work, and that craving is mingled in my soul with my love for you, Irina, and just because you are beautiful it seems to me that life too is beautiful! What are you thinking of?

IRINA. You say life is beautiful. . . . Yes, but what if it only seems so! Life for us three sisters has not been beautiful yet, we have been stifled by it as plants are choked by weeds. . . . I am shedding tears. . . . I mustn't do that. [*Hurriedly wipes her eyes and smiles.*] I must work, I must work. The reason we are depressed and take such a gloomy view of life is that we know nothing of work. We come of people who despised work. . . .

[*Enter* NATALYA IVANOVNA; *she is wearing a pink dress with a green sash.*]

NATASHA. They are sitting down to lunch already. . . . I am late . . . [*Steals a glance at herself in the glass and sets herself to rights.*] I think my hair is all right. [*Seeing* IRINA.] Dear Irina Sergeyevna, I congratulate you! [*Gives her a vigorous and prolonged kiss.*] You have a lot of visitors, I really feel shy. . . . Good day, Baron!

OLGA [*coming into the drawing room*]. Well, here is Natalya Ivanovna! How are you, my dear? [*Kisses her.*]

NATASHA. Congratulations on the name-day. You have such a big party and I feel awfully shy. . . .

OLGA. Nonsense, we have only our own people. [*In an undertone, in alarm.*] You've got on a green sash! My dear, that's not nice!

NATASHA. Why, is that a bad omen?

OLGA. No, it's only that it doesn't go with your dress . . . and it looks queer. . . .

NATASHA [*in a tearful voice*]. Really? But you know it's not green exactly, it's more a dead color. [*Follows* OLGA *into the dining room.*]

[*In the dining room they are all sitting down to lunch; there is no one in the drawing room.*]

KULIGIN. I wish you a good husband, Irina. It's time for you to think of getting married.

TCHEBUTYKIN. Natalya Ivanovna, I hope we may hear of your engagement, too.

KULIGIN. Natalya Ivanovna has got a suitor already.

MASHA [*strikes her plate with her fork*]. Ladies and gentlemen, I want to make a speech!

KULIGIN. You deserve three bad marks for conduct.

VERSHININ. How nice this cordial is! What is it made of?

SOLYONY. Beetles.

IRINA [*in a tearful voice*]. Ugh, ugh! How disgusting.

OLGA. We are going to have roast turkey and apple pie for supper. Thank God I am at home all day and shall be at home in the evening. . . . Friends, won't you come this evening?

VERSHININ. Allow me to come too.

IRINA. Please do.

NATASHA. They don't stand on ceremony.

TCHEBUTYKIN. Nature our hearts for love created! [*Laughs.*]

ANDREY [*angrily*]. Do leave off, I wonder you are not tired of it!

[FEDOTIK *and* RODDEY *come in with a big basket of flowers.*]

FEDOTIK. I say, they are at lunch already.

RODDEY [*speaking loudly, with a lisp*]. At lunch? Yes, they are at lunch already. . . .

FEDOTIK. Wait a minute. [*Takes a snapshot.*] One! Wait another minute . . . . [*Takes another snapshot.*] Two! Now it's ready.

[*They take the basket and walk into the dining room, where they are greeted noisily.*]

RODDEY [*loudly*]. My congratulations! I wish you everything, everything! The weather is delightful, perfectly magnificent. I've been out all the morning for a walk with the high-school boys. I teach them gymnastics.

FEDOTIK. You may move, Irina Sergeyevna, you may move. [*Taking a photograph.*] You look charming today. [*Taking a top out of his pocket.*] Here is a top, by the way. . . . It has a wonderful note. . . .

IRINA. How lovely!

MASHA. By the seashore an oak-tree green. . . . Upon that oak a chain of gold . . . [*Complainingly.*] Why do I keep saying that? That phrase has been haunting me all day. . . .

KULIGIN. Thirteen at table!

RODDEY [*loudly*]. Surely you do not attach importance to such superstitions? [*Laughter.*]

KULIGIN. If there are thirteen at table, it means that someone present is in love. It's not you, Ivan Romanovitch, by any chance? [*Laughter.*]

TCHEBUTYKIN. I am an old sinner, but why Natalya Ivanovna is overcome, I can't imagine . . .

[*Loud laughter;* NATASHA *runs out from the dining room into the drawing room followed by* ANDREY.]

ANDREY. Come, don't take any notice! Wait a minute . . . stop, I entreat you. . . .

NATASHA. I am ashamed. . . . I don't know what's the matter with me and they make fun of me. I know it's improper for me to leave the table like this, but I can't help it. . . . I can't . . . [*Covers her face with her hands.*]

ANDREY. My dear girl, I entreat you, I implore you, don't be upset. I assure you they are only joking, they do it in all kindness. My dear, my sweet, they are all kind, warmhearted people and they are fond of me and of you. Come here to the window, here they can't see us . . . [*Looks round.*]

NATASHA. I am so unaccustomed to society! . . .

ANDREY. Oh youth, lovely, marvelous youth! My dear, my sweet, don't be so distressed! Believe me, believe me. . . . I feel so happy, my soul is full of love and rapture. . . . Oh, they can't see us, they can't see us! Why, why, I love you, when I first loved you—oh, I don't know. My dear, my sweet, pure one, be my wife! I love you, I love you . . . as I have never loved anyone . . . [*A kiss.*]

[*Two officers come in and, seeing the pair kissing, stop in amazement.*]

ACT TWO

The same scene as in Act I. Eight o'clock in the evening. Behind the scenes in the street there is the faintly audible sound of a concertina. There is no light. NATALYA IVANOVNA *enters in a dressing gown, carrying a candle; she comes in and stops at the door leading to* ANDREY'S *room.*

NATASHA. What are you doing, Andryusha? Reading? Never mind, I only just asked . . .

[*Goes and opens another door and, peeping into it, shuts it again.*] Is there a light?

ANDREY [*enters with a book in his hand*]. What is it, Natasha?

NATASHA. I was looking to see whether there was a light. . . . It's Carnival, the servants are not themselves; one has always to be on the lookout for fear something goes wrong. Last night at twelve o'clock I passed through the dining room, and there was a candle left burning. I couldn't find out who had lighted it. [*Puts down the candle.*] What's the time?

ANDREY [*looking at his watch*]. A quarter past eight.

NATASHA. And Olga and Irina aren't in yet. They haven't come in. Still at work, poor dears! Olga is at the teachers' council and Irina at the telegraph office . . . . [*Sighs.*] I was saying to your sister this morning, "Take care of yourself, Irina darling," said I. But she won't listen. A quarter past eight, you say? I am afraid our Bobik is not at all well. Why is he so cold? Yesterday he was feverish and today he is cold all over. . . . I am so anxious!

ANDREY. It's all right, Natasha. The boy is quite well.

NATASHA. We had better be careful about his food, anyway. I am anxious. And I am told that the mummers are going to be here for the Carnival at nine o'clock this evening. It would be better for them not to come, Andryusha.

ANDREY. I really don't know. They've been invited, you know.

NATASHA. Baby woke up this morning, looked at me, and all at once he gave a smile; so he knew me. "Good morning, Bobik!" said I. "Good morning, darling!" And he laughed. Children understand; they understand very well. So I shall tell them, Andryusha, not to let the carnival party come in.

ANDREY [*irresolutely*]. That's for my sisters to say. It's for them to give orders.

NATASHA. Yes, for them too; I will speak to them. They are so kind . . . . [*Is going.*] I've ordered junket for supper. The doctor says you must eat nothing but junket, or you will never get thinner. [*Stops.*] Bobik is cold. I am afraid his room is chilly, perhaps. We ought to put him in a different room till the warm weather comes, anyway. Irina's room, for instance, is just right for a nursery: it's dry and the sun shines there all day. I must tell her; she might share Olga's room for the time. . . . She is never at home, anyway, except for the night . . . . [*A pause.*] Andryushantchik, why don't you speak?

ANDREY. Nothing. I was thinking. . . . Besides, I have nothing to say.

NATASHA. Yes . . . what was it I meant to tell you? . . . Oh, yes; Ferapont has come from the Rural Board, and is asking for you.

ANDREY [*yawns*]. Send him in.

[NATASHA *goes out*; ANDREY, *bending down to the candle which she has left behind, reads. Enter* FERAPONT; *he wears an old shabby overcoat, with the collar turned up, and has a scarf over his ears.*]

ANDREY. Good evening, my good man. What is it?

FERAPONT. The chairman has sent a book and a paper of some sort here ... [*Gives the book and an envelope.*]

ANDREY. Thanks. Very good. But why have you come so late? It is past eight.

FERAPONT. Eh?

ANDREY [*louder*]. I say, you have come late. It is eight o'clock.

FERAPONT. Just so. I came before it was dark, but they wouldn't let me see you. The master is busy, they told me. Well, of course, if you are busy, I am in no hurry. [*Thinking that* ANDREY *has asked him a question.*] Eh?

ANDREY. Nothing. [*Examines the book.*] Tomorrow is Friday. We haven't a sitting, but I'll come all the same ... and do my work. It's dull at home .... [*A pause.*] Dear old man, how strangely life changes and deceives one! Today I was so bored and had nothing to do, so I picked up this book—old university lectures—and I laughed. ... Good heavens! I am the secretary of the Rural Board of which Protopopov is the chairman. I am the secretary, and the most I can hope for is to become a member of the Board! Me, a member of the local Rural Board, while I dream every night I am professor of the University of Moscow—a distinguished man, of whom all Russia is proud!

FERAPONT. I can't say, sir. ... I don't hear well. ...

ANDREY. If you did hear well, perhaps I should not talk to you. I must talk to somebody, and my wife does not understand me. My sisters I am somehow afraid of—I'm afraid they will laugh at me and make me ashamed. ... I don't drink, I am not fond of restaurants, but how I should enjoy sitting at Tyestov's in Moscow at this moment, dear old chap!

FERAPONT. A contractor was saying at the Board the other day that there were some merchants in Moscow eating pancakes; one who ate forty, it seems, died. It was either forty or fifty, I don't remember.

ANDREY. In Moscow you sit in a huge room at a restaurant; you know no one and no one knows you, and at the same time you don't feel a stranger. ... But here you know everyone and everyone knows you, and yet you are a stranger—a stranger. ... A stranger, and lonely. ...

FERAPONT. Eh? [*A pause.*] And the same contractor says—maybe it's not true—that there's a rope stretched right across Moscow.

ANDREY. What for?

FERAPONT. I can't say, sir. The contractor said so.

ANDREY. Nonsense. [*Reads.*] Have you ever been in Moscow?

FERAPONT [*after a pause*]. No, never. It was not God's will I should. [*A pause.*] Am I to go?

ANDREY. You can go. Good-bye.

[FERAPONT *goes out.*]

Good-bye. [*Reading.*] Come tomorrow morning and take some papers

here.... Go.... [*A pause.*] He has gone. [*A ring.*] Yes, it is a business
... [*Stretches and goes slowly into his own room.*]
[*Behind the scenes a* NURSE *is singing, rocking a baby to sleep. Enter*
MASHA *and* VERSHININ. *While they are talking a maidservant is lighting a*
lamp and candles in the dining room.]

MASHA. I don't know. [*A pause.*] I don't know. Of course habit does a great
deal. After father's death, for instance, it was a long time before we
could get used to having no orderlies in the house. But apart from habit,
I think it's a feeling of justice makes me say so. Perhaps it is not so in
other places, but in our town the most decent, honorable, and well-bred
people are all in the army.

VERSHININ. I am thirsty. I should like some tea.

MASHA [*glancing at the clock*]. They will soon be bringing it. I was married
when I was eighteen, and I was afraid of my husband because he was a
teacher, and I had only just left school. In those days I thought him an
awfully learned, clever, and important person. And now it is not the
same, unfortunately....

VERSHININ. Yes.... I see....

MASHA. I am not speaking of my husband—I am used to him; but among
civilians generally there are so many rude, ill-mannered, badly brought-
up people. Rudeness upsets and distresses me: I am unhappy when I see
that a man is not refined, not gentle, not polite enough. When I have to
be among the teachers, my husband's colleagues, it makes me quite
miserable.

VERSHININ. Yes.... But, to my mind, it makes no difference whether
they are civilians or military men—they are equally uninteresting, in this
town anyway. It's all the same! If one listens to a man of the educated
class here, civilian or military, he is worried to death by his wife, worried
to death by his house, worried to death by his estate, worried to
death by his horses.... A Russian is peculiarly given to exalted ideas,
but why is it he always falls so short in life? Why?

MASHA. Why?

VERSHININ. Why is he worried to death by his children and by his wife?
And why are his wife and children worried to death by him?

MASHA. You are rather depressed this evening.

VERSHININ. Perhaps.... I've had no dinner today, and had nothing to eat
since the morning. My daughter is not quite well, and when my little
girls are ill I am consumed by anxiety; my conscience reproaches me for
having given them such a mother. Oh, if you had seen her today! She is
a wretched creature! We began quarreling at seven o'clock in the morning, and at nine I slammed the door and went away. [*A pause.*] I never
talk about it. Strange, it's only to you I complain. [*Kisses her hand.*]
Don't be angry with me. ... Except for you I have no one—no
one ....
[*A pause.*]

MASHA. What a noise in the stove! Before father died there was howling in the chimney. There, just like that.

VERSHININ. Are you superstitious?

MASHA. Yes.

VERSHININ. That's strange. [*Kisses her hand.*] You are a splendid, wonderful woman. Splendid! Wonderful! It's dark, but I see the light in your eyes.

MASHA [*moves to another chair*]. It's lighter here.

VERSHININ. I love you—love, love. . . . I love your eyes, your movements, I see them in my dreams. . . . Splendid, wonderful woman!

MASHA [*laughing softly*]. When you talk to me like that, for some reason I laugh, though I am frightened. . . . Please don't do it again . . . [*In an undertone.*] You may say it, though; I don't mind . . . [*Covers her face with her hands.*] I don't mind. . . . Someone is coming. Talk of something else.

[IRINA *and* TUSENBACH *come in through the dining room.*]

TUSENBACH. I've got a three-barreled name. My name is Baron Tusenbach-Krone-Altschauer, but I belong to the Orthodox Church and am just as Russian as you. There is very little of the German left in me—nothing, perhaps, but the patience and perseverance with which I bore you. I see you home every evening.

IRINA. How tired I am!

TUSENBACH. And every day I will come to the telegraph office and see you home. I'll do it for ten years, for twenty years, till you drive me away . . . [*Seeing* MASHA *and* VERSHININ, *delightedly.*] Oh, it's you! How are you?

IRINA. Well, I am home at last. [*To* MASHA.] A lady came just now to telegraph to her brother in Saratov that her son died today, and she could not think of the address. So she sent it without an address—simply to Saratov. She was crying. And I was rude to her for no sort of reason. Told her I had no time to waste. It was so stupid. Are the Carnival people coming tonight?

MASHA. Yes.

IRINA [*sits down in an armchair*]. I must rest. I am tired.

TUSENBACH [*with a smile*]. When you come from the office you seem so young, so forlorn . . . [*A pause.*]

IRINA. I am tired, No, I don't like telegraph work, I don't like it.

MASHA. You've grown thinner . . . [*Whistles.*] And you look younger, rather like a boy in the face.

TUSENBACH. That's the way she does her hair.

IRINA. I must find some other job, this does not suit me. What I so longed for, what I dreamed of, is the very thing that it's lacking in. . . . It is work without poetry, without meaning. . . . [*A knock on the floor.*] There's the doctor knocking. . . . [*To* TUSENBACH.] Do knock, dear. . . . I can't. . . . I am tired.

[TUSENBACH *knocks on the floor.*]

IRINA. He will come directly. We ought to do something about it. The doctor and our Andrey were at the Club yesterday and they lost again. I am told Andrey lost two hundred roubles.

MASHA [*indifferently*]. Well, it can't be helped now.

IRINA. A fortnight ago he lost money, in December he lost money. I wish he'd make haste and lose everything, then perhaps we should go away from this town. My God, every night I dream of Moscow, it's perfect madness. [*Laughs.*] We'll move there in June and there is still left February, March, April, May . . . almost half a year.

MASHA. The only thing is Natasha must not hear of his losses.

IRINA. I don't suppose she cares.

[TCHEBUTYKIN, *who has only just got off his bed—he has been resting after dinner—comes into the dining room combing his beard, then sits down to the table and takes a newspaper out of his pocket.*]

MASHA. Here he is . . . has he paid his rent?

IRINA [*laughs*]. No. Not a kopek for eight months. Evidently he has forgotten.

MASHA [*laughs*]. How gravely he sits. [*They all laugh; a pause.*]

IRINA. Why are you so quiet, Alexandr Ignatyevitch?

VERSHININ. I don't know. I am longing for tea. I'd give half my life for a glass of tea. I have had nothing to eat since the morning.

TCHEBUTYKIN. Irina Sergeyevna!

IRINA. What is it?

TCHEBUTYKIN. Come here. *Venez ici.*

[IRINA *goes and sits down at the table.*] I can't do without you. [IRINA *lays out the cards for patience.*]

VERSHININ. Well, if they won't bring tea, let us discuss something.

TUSENBACH. By all means. What?

VERSHININ. What? Let us dream . . . for instance of the life that will come after us, in two or three hundred years.

TUSENBACH. Well? When we are dead, men will fly in balloons, change the fashion of their coats, will discover a sixth sense, perhaps, and develop it, but life will remain just the same, difficult, full of mysteries and happiness. In a thousand years man will sigh just the same, "Ah, how hard life is," and yet just as now he will be afraid of death and not want it.

VERSHININ [*after a moment's thought*]. Well, I don't know. . . . It seems to me that everything on earth is bound to change by degrees and is already changing before our eyes. In two or three hundred, perhaps in a thousand years—the time does not matter—a new, happy life will come. We shall have no share in that life, of course, but we are living for it, we are working, well, yes, and suffering for it, we are creating it—and that alone is the purpose of our existence, and is our happiness, if you like.

[MASHA *laughs softly.*]

TUSENBACH. What is it?

MASHA. I don't know. I've been laughing all day.

VERSHININ. I was at the same school as you were, I did not go to the

Military Academy; I read a great deal, but I do not know how to choose my books, and very likely I read quite the wrong things, and yet the longer I live the more I want to know. My hair is turning grey, I am almost an old man, but I know so little, oh so little! But all the same I fancy that I do know and thoroughly grasp what is essential and matters most. And how I should like to make you see that there is no happiness for us, that there ought not to be and will not be. . . . We must work and work, and happiness is the portion of our remote descendants. [*A pause.*] If it is not for me, at least it is for the descendants of my descendants. . . .

[FEDOTIK *and* RODDEY *appear in the dining room; they sit down and sing softly, playing the guitar.*]

TUSENBACH. You think it's no use even dreaming of happiness! But what if I am happy?

VERSHININ. No.

TUSENBACH [*flinging up his hands and laughing*]. It is clear we don't understand each other. Well, how am I to convince you?

[MASHA *laughs softly.*]

TUSENBACH [*holds up a finger to her*]. Laugh! [*To* VERSHININ.] Not only in two or three hundred years but in a million years life will be just the same; it does not change, it remains stationary, following its own laws which we have nothing to do with or which, anyway, we shall never find out. Migratory birds, cranes for instance, fly backward and forward, and whatever ideas, great or small, stray through their minds, they will still go on flying just the same without knowing where or why. They fly and will continue to fly, however philosophic they may become; and it doesn't matter how philosophical they are so long as they go on flying. . . .

MASHA. But still there is a meaning?

TUSENBACH. Meaning. . . . Here it is snowing. What meaning is there in that? [*A pause.*]

MASHA. I think man ought to have faith or ought to seek a faith, or else his life is empty, empty. . . . To live and not to understand why cranes fly; why children are born; why there are stars in the sky. . . . One must know what one is living for or else it is all nonsense and waste. [*A pause.*]

VERSHININ. And yet one is sorry that youth is over. . . .

MASHA. Gogol[3] says: it's dull living in this world, friends!

TUSENBACH. And I say: it is difficult to argue with you, my friends, God bless you. . . .

TCHEBUTYKIN [*reading the newspaper*]. Balzac[4] was married at Berditchev. [IRINA *hums softly.*]

TCHEBUTYKIN. I really must put that down in my book. [*Writes.*] Balzac was married at Berditchev. [*Reads the paper.*]

---

[3] Nikolai Gogol, novelist and playwright.
[4] Honoré de Balzac, French novelist.

IRINA [*lays out the cards for patience, dreamily*]. Balzac was married at Berditchev.

TUSENBACH. The die is cast. You know, Marya Sergeyevna, I've resigned my commission.

MASHA. So I hear. And I see nothing good in that. I don't like civilians.

TUSENBACH. Never mind . . . [*Gets up.*] I am not good-looking enough for a soldier. But that does not matter, though . . . I am going to work. If only for one day in my life, to work so that I come home at night tired out and fall asleep as soon as I get into bed . . . [*Going into the dining room.*] Workmen must sleep soundly!

FEDOTIK [*to* IRINA]. I bought these chalks for you just now as I passed the shop. . . . And this penknife. . . .

IRINA. You've got into the way of treating me as though I were little, but I am grown up, you know . . . [*Takes the chalks and the penknife, joyfully.*] How lovely!

FEDOTIK. And I bought a knife for myself . . . look . . . one blade, and another blade, a third, and this is for the ears, and here are scissors, and that's for cleaning the nails. . . .

RODDEY [*loudly*]. Doctor, how old are you?

TCHEBUTYKIN. I? Thirty-two. [*Laughter.*]

FEDOTIK. I'll show you another patience . . . [*Lays out the cards.*]

[*The samovar is brought in;* ANFISA *is at the samovar; a little later* NATASHA *comes in and is also busy at the table;* SOLYONY *comes in, and after greeting the others sits down at the table.*]

VERSHININ. What a wind there is!

MASHA. Yes. I am sick of the winter. I've forgotten what summer is like.

IRINA. It's coming out right, I see. We shall go to Moscow.

FEDOTIK. No, it's not coming out. You see, the eight is over the two of spades. [*Laughs.*] So that means you won't go to Moscow.

TCHEBUTYKIN [*reads from the newspaper*]. Tsi-tsi-kar. Smallpox is raging here.

ANFISA [*going up to* MASHA]. Masha, come to tea, my dear. [*To* VERSHININ.] Come, your honor . . . excuse me, sir, I have forgotten your name. . . .

MASHA. Bring it here, nurse, I am not going there.

IRINA. Nurse!

ANFISA. I am coming!

NATASHA [*to* SOLYONY]. Little babies understand very well. "Good morning Bobik, good morning, darling," I said. He looked at me in quite a special way. You think I say that because I am a mother, but no, I assure you! He is an extraordinary child.

SOLYONY. If that child were mine, I'd fry him in a frying-pan and eat him.

[*Takes his glass, comes into the drawing room and sits down in a corner.*]

NATASHA [*covers her face with her hands*]. Rude, ill-bred man!

MASHA. Happy people don't notice whether it is winter or summer. I fancy if I lived in Moscow I should not mind what the weather was like. . . .

VERSHININ. The other day I was reading the diary of a French minister written in prison. The minister was condemned for the Panama affair. With what enthusiasm and delight he describes the birds he sees from the prison window, which he never noticed before when he was a minister. Now that he is released, of course he notices birds no more than he did before. In the same way, you won't notice Moscow when you live in it. We have no happiness and never do have, we only long for it.

TUSENBACH [*takes a box from the table*]. What has become of the sweets?

IRINA. Solyony has eaten them.

TUSENBACH. All?

ANFISA [*handing tea*]. There's a letter for you, sir.

VERSHININ. For me? [*Takes the letter.*] From my daughter. [*Reads.*] Yes, of course. . . . Excuse me, Marya Sergeyevna, I'll slip away. I won't have tea. [*Gets up in agitation.*] Always these upsets. . . .

MASHA. What is it? Not a secret?

VERSHININ [*in a low voice*]. My wife has taken poison again. I must go. I'll slip off unnoticed. Horribly unpleasant it all is. [*Kisses* MASHA'S *hand.*] My fine, dear, splendid woman. . . . I'll go this way without being seen . . . [*Goes out.*]

ANFISA. Where is he off to? I've just given him his tea. . . . What a man.

MASHA [*getting angry*]. Leave off! Don't pester, you give one no peace . . . [*Goes with her cup to the table.*] You bother me, old lady.

ANFISA. Why are you so huffy? Darling!

[ANDREY'S *voice:* "Anfisa!"]

ANFISA [*mimicking*]. Anfisa! he sits there. . . . [*Goes out.*]

MASHA [*by the table in the dining room, angrily*]. Let me sit down! [*Mixes the cards on the table.*] You take up all the table with your cards. Drink your tea!

IRINA. How cross you are, Masha!

MASHA. If I'm cross, don't talk to me. Don't interfere with me.

TECHEBUTYKIN [*laughing*]. Don't touch her, don't touch her!

MASHA. You are sixty, but you talk rot like a schoolboy.

NATASHA [*sighs*]. Dear Masha, why make use of such expressions in conversation? With your attractive appearance I tell you straight out, you would be simply fascinating in a well-bred social circle if it were not for the things you say. *Je vous prie, pardonnez-moi, Marie, mais vous avez des manières un peu grossières.*[5]

TUSENBACH [*suppressing a laugh*]. Give me . . . give me . . . I think there is some brandy there.

NATASHA. *Il paraît que mon Bobik déjà ne dort pas,*[6] he is awake. He is not well today. I must go to him, excuse me. . . . [*Goes out.*]

---

[5] "I beg you, excuse me, Marie, but you have rather vulgar manners."
[6] "Apparently my Bobik is not still asleep."

IRINA. Where has Alexandr Ignatyevitch gone?

MASHA. Home. Something queer with his wife again.

TUSENBACH [*goes up to* SOLYONY *with a decanter of brandy in his hand*]. You always sit alone, thinking, and there's no making out what you think about. Come, let us make it up. Let us have a drink of brandy. [*They drink.*] I shall have to play the piano all night, I suppose, play all sorts of trash. . . . Here goes!

SOLYONY. Why make it up? I haven't quarreled with you.

TUSENBACH. You always make me feel as though something had gone wrong between us. You are a queer character, there's no denying that.

SOLYONY [*declaims*]. I am strange, who is not strange! Be not wroth, Aleko!

TUSENBACH. I don't see what Aleko has got to do with it. . . .

SOLYONY. When I am *tête-à-tête* with somebody, I am all right, just like anyone else, but in company I am depressed, ill at ease and . . . . say all sorts of idiotic things, but at the same time I am more conscientious and straightforward than many. And I can prove it. . . .

TUSENBACH. I often feel angry with you, you are always attacking me when we are in company, and yet I somehow like you. Here goes, I am going to drink a lot today. Let's drink!

SOLYONY. Let us. [*Drinks.*] I have never had anything against you, Baron. But I have the temperament of Lermontov.[7] [*In a low voice.*] In fact I am rather like Lermontov to look at . . . so I am told. [*Takes out scent-bottle and sprinkles scent on his hands.*]

TUSENBACH. I have sent in my papers. I've had enough of it! I have been thinking of it for five years and at last I have come up to the scratch. I am going to work.

SOLYONY [*declaims*]. Be not wroth, Aleko. . . . Forget, forget thy dreams. . . . [*While they are talking* ANDREY *comes in quietly with a book and sits down by a candle.*]

TUSENBACH. I am going to work.

TCHEBUTYKIN [*coming into the drawing room with* IRINA]. And the food too was real Caucasian stuff: onion soup and for the meat course *tchehart-ma*. . . .

SOLYONY. *Tcheremsha* is not meat at all, it's a plant rather like our onion.

TCHEBUTYKIN. No, my dear soul, it's not onion, but mutton roasted in a special way.

SOLYONY. But I tell you that *tcheremsha* is an onion.

TCHEBUTYKIN. And I tell you that *tchehartma* is mutton.

SOLYONY. And I tell you that *tcheremsha* is an onion.

TCHEBUTYKIN. What's the use of my arguing with you? You have never been to the Caucasus or eaten *tchehartma*.

SOLYONY. I haven't eaten it because I can't bear it. *Tcheremsha* smells like garlic.

7 Mikhail Lermontov, romantic poet and novelist.

ANDREY [*imploringly*]. That's enough! Please!

TUSENBACH. When are the Carnival party coming?

IRINA. They promised to come at nine, so they will be here directly.

TUSENBACH [*embraces* ANDREY *and sings*]. "Oh my porch, oh my new porch . . ."

ANDREY [*dances and sings*]. "With posts of maple wood. . . ."

TCHEBUTYKIN [*dances*]. "And lattice work complete . . ." [*Laughter.*]

TUSENBACH [*kisses* ANDREY]. Hang it all, let us have a drink. Andryusha, let us drink to our everlasting friendship. I'll go to the University when you do, Andryusha.

SOLYONY. Which? There are two universities in Moscow.

ANDREY. There is only one university in Moscow.

SOLYONY. I tell you there are two.

ANDREY. There may be three for aught I care. So much the better.

SOLYONY. There are two universities in Moscow! [*A murmur and hisses.*] There are two universities in Moscow: the old one and the new one. And if you don't care to hear, if what I say irritates you, I can keep quiet. I can even go into another room. [*Goes out at one of the doors.*]

TUSENBACH. Bravo, bravo! [*Laughs.*] Friends, begin, I'll sit down and play! Funny fellow that Solyony. . . . [*Sits down to the piano and plays a waltz.*]

MASHA [*dances a waltz alone*]. The baron is drunk, the baron is drunk, the baron is drunk.

[*Enter* NATASHA.]

NATASHA [*to* TCHEBUTYKIN]. Ivan Romanitch!

[*Says something to* TCHEBUTYKIN, *then goes out softly.* TCHEBUTYKIN *touches* TUSENBACH *on the shoulder and whispers something to him.*]

IRINA. What is it?

TCHEBUTYKIN. It's time we were going. Good night.

TUSENBACH. Good night. It's time to be going.

IRINA. But I say . . . what about the Carnival party?

ANDREY [*with embarrassment*]. They won't be coming. You see, dear, Natasha says Bobik is not well, and so . . . In fact I know nothing about it, and don't care either.

IRINA [*shrugs her shoulders*]. Bobik is not well!

MASHA. Well, it's not the first time we've had to lump it! If we are turned out, we must go. [*To* IRINA.] It's not Bobik that is ill, but she is a bit . . . [*Taps her forehead with her finger.*] Petty, vulgar creature!

[ANDREY *goes by door on right to his own room,* TCHEBUTYKIN *following him; they are saying good-bye in the dining room.*]

FEDOTIK. What a pity! I was meaning to spend the evening, but of course if the child is ill . . . I'll bring him a toy tomorrow.

RODDEY [*loudly*]. I had a nap today after dinner on purpose, I thought I would be dancing all night. . . . Why, it's only nine o'clock.

MASHA. Let us go into the street; there we can talk. We'll decide what to do. [*Sounds of* "Good-bye! Good night!" *The good-humored laugh of*

TUSENBACH *is heard. All go out.* ANFISA *and the maidservant clear the table and put out the light. There is the sound of the nurse singing.* ANDREY *in his hat and coat, and* TCHEBUTYKIN *come in quietly.*]

TCHEBUTYKIN. I never had time to get married, because life has flashed by like lightning and because I was passionately in love with your mother, who was married.

ANDREY. One shouldn't get married. One shouldn't, because it's boring.

TCHEBUTYKIN. That's all very well, but what about loneliness? Say what you like, it's a dreadful thing to be lonely, my dear boy.... But no matter, though!

ANDREY. Let's make haste and go.

TCHEBUTYKIN. What's the hurry? We have plenty of time.

ANDREY. I am afraid my wife may stop me.

TCHEBUTYKIN. Oh!

ANDREY. I am not going to play today, I shall just sit and look on. I don't feel well. . . . What am I to do, Ivan Romanitch, I am so short of breath?

TCHEBUTYKIN. It's no use asking me! I don't remember, dear boy.... I don't know. . . .

ANDREY. Let us go through the kitchen. [*They go out.*]

[*A ring, then another ring; there is a sound of voices and laughter.*]

IRINA [*enters*]. What is it?

ANFISA [*in a whisper*]. The mummers, all dressed up. [*A ring.*]

IRINA. Nurse, dear, say there is no one at home. They must excuse us.

[ANFISA *goes out.* IRINA *walks about the room in hesitation; she is excited. Enter* SOLYONY.]

SOLYONY [*in perplexity*]. No one here. . . . Where are they all?

IRINA. They have gone home.

SOLYONY. How queer. Are you alone here?

IRINA. Yes. [*A pause.*] Good night.

SOLYONY. I behaved tactlessly, without sufficient restraint just now. But you are not like other people, you are pure and lofty, you see the truth. You alone can understand me. I love you, I love you deeply, infinitely.

IRINA. Good night! You must go.

SOLYONY. I can't live without you. [*Following her.*] Oh, my bliss! [*Through his tears.*] Oh, happiness! Those glorious, exquisite, marvelous eyes such as I have never seen in any other woman.

IRINA [*coldly*]. Don't, Vassily Vassilyitch!

SOLYONY. For the first time I am speaking of love to you, and I feel as though I were not on earth but on another planet. [*Rubs his forehead.*] But there, it does not matter. There is no forcing kindness, of course. . . . But there must be no happy rivals. . . . There must not. . . . I swear by all that is sacred I will kill any rival. . . . O exquisite being!

[NATASHA *passes with a candle.*]

NATASHA. [*Peeps in at one door, then at another and passes by the door that leads to her husband's room.*] Andrey is there. Let him read. Excuse me, Vassily Vassilyitch, I did not know you were here, and I am in my dressing gown. . . .

SOLYONY. I don't care. Good-bye! [*Goes out.*]

NATASHA. You are tired, my poor, dear little girl! [*Kisses* IRINA.] You ought to go to bed earlier. . . .

IRINA. Is Bobik asleep?

NATASHA. He is asleep, but not sleeping quietly. By the way, dear, I keep meaning to speak to you, but either you are out or else I haven't the time. . . . I think Bobik's nursery is cold and damp. And your room is so nice for a baby. My sweet, my dear, you might move for a time into Olya's room!

IRINA [*not understanding*]. Where?

[*The sound of a three-horse sledge with bells driving up to the door.*]

NATASHA. You would be in the same room with Olya, and Bobik in your room. He is such a poppet. I said to him today, "Bobik, you are mine, you are mine!" and he looked at me with his funny little eyes. [*A ring.*] That must be Olya. How late she is!

[*The maid comes up to* NATASHA *and whispers in her ear.*]

NATASHA. Protopopov? What a queer fellow he is! Protopopov has come, and asks me to go out with him in his sledge. [*Laughs.*] How strange men are! . . . [*A ring.*] Somebody has come. I might go for a quarter of an hour. . . . [*To the maid.*] Tell him I'll come directly. [*A ring.*] You hear . . . it must be Olya. [*Goes out.*]

[*The maid runs out;* IRINA *sits lost in thought;* KULIGIN, OLGA *and* VERSHININ *come in.*]

KULIGIN. Well, this is a surprise! They said they were going to have an evening party.

VERSHININ. Strange! And when I went away half an hour ago they were expecting the Carnival people. . . .

IRINA. They have all gone.

KULIGIN. Has Masha gone too? Where has she gone? And why is Protopopov waiting below with his sledge? Whom is he waiting for?

IRINA. Don't ask questions. . . . I am tired.

KULIGIN. Oh, you little cross-patch. . . .

OLGA. The meeting is only just over. I am tired out. Our headmistress is ill and I have to take her place. Oh, my head, my head does ache; oh, my head! [*Sits down.*] Andrey lost two hundred roubles yesterday at cards. . . . The whole town is talking about it. . . .

KULIGIN. Yes, I am tired out by the meeting too. [*Sits down.*]

VERSHININ. My wife took it into her head to give me a fright, she nearly poisoned herself. It's all right now, and I'm glad, it's a relief. . . . So we are to go away? Very well, then, I will say good night. Fyodor Ilyitch, let us go somewhere together! I can't stay at home, I absolutely can't. . . . Come along!

KULIGIN. I am tired. I am not coming. [*Gets up.*] I am tired. Has my wife gone home?

IRINA. I expect so.

KULIGIN [*kisses* IRINA's *hand*]. Good-bye! I have all day tomorrow and next day to rest. Good night! [*Going.*] I do want some tea. I was reckoning on spending the evening in pleasant company. . . . *O fallacem hominum spem!*[8] . . . Accusative of exclamation.

VERSHININ. Well, then, I must go alone. [*Goes out with* KULIGIN, *whistling.*]

OLGA. My head aches, oh, how my head aches. . . . Andrey has lost at cards. . . . The whole town is talking about it. . . . I'll go and lie down. [*Is going.*] Tomorrow I shall be free. . . . Oh, goodness, how nice that is! Tomorrow I am free, and the day after I am free. . . . My head does ache, oh, my head . . . [*Goes out.*]

IRINA [*alone*]. They have all gone away. There is no one left.

[*A concertina plays in the street, the nurse sings.*]

NATASHA [*in a fur cap and coat crosses the dining room, followed by the maid*]. I shall be back in half an hour. I shall only go a little way. [*Goes out.*]

IRINA [*left alone, in dejection*]. Oh, to go to Moscow, to Moscow!

ACT THREE

The bedroom of OLGA *and* IRINA. *On left and right beds with screens round them. Past two o'clock in the night. Behind the scenes a bell is ringing on account of a fire in the town, which has been going on for some time. It can be seen that no one in the house has gone to bed yet. On the sofa* MASHA *is lying, dressed as usual in black.*

[*Enter* OLGA *and* ANFISA.]

ANFISA. They are sitting below, under the stairs. . . . I said to them, "Come upstairs; why, you mustn't stay there"—they only cried. "We don't know where father is," they said. "What if he is burned!" What an idea! And the poor souls in the yard . . . they are all undressed too.

OLGA [*taking clothes out of the cupboard*]. Take this grey dress . . . and this one . . . and the blouse too . . . and that skirt, nurse. . . . Oh, dear, what a dreadful thing! Kirsanov Street is burned to the ground, it seems. . . . Take this . . . take this . . . [*Throws clothes into her arms.*] The Vershinins have had a fright, poor things. . . . Their house was very nearly burned. Let them stay the night here . . . we can't let them go home. . . . Poor Fedotik has had everything burned, he has not a thing left. . . .

[8] "Alas, the falseness of men's hope."

ANFISA. You had better call Ferapont, Olya darling, I can't carry it all.

OLGA [rings]. No one will answer the bell. [At the door.] Come here, whoever is there!

[Through the open door can be seen a window red with fire; the fire brigade
is heard passing the house.]

How awful it is! And how sickening!

[Enter FERAPONT.]

OLGA. Here take these, carry them downstairs. . . . The Kolotilin young
ladies are downstairs . . . give it to them . . . and give this too.

FERAPONT. Yes, miss. In 1812 Moscow was burned too. . . . Mercy on us!
The French marveled.

OLGA. You can go now.

FERAPONT. Yes, miss. [Goes out.]

OLGA. Nurse darling, give them everything. We don't want anything, give
it all to them. . . . I am tired, I can hardly stand on my feet. . . . We
mustn't let the Vershinins go home. . . . The little girls can sleep in the
drawing room, and Alexandr Ignatyevitch down below at the baron's.
. . . Fedotik can go to the baron's, too, or sleep in our dining room. . . .
As ill-luck will have it, the doctor is drunk, frightfully drunk, and no one
can be put in his room. And Vershinin's wife can be in the drawing
room too.

ANFISA [wearily]. Olya darling, don't send me away; don't send me away!

OLGA. That's nonsense, nurse. No one is sending you away.

ANFISA [lays her head on OLGA's shoulder]. My own, my treasure, I work,
I do my best. . . . I'm getting weak, everyone will say "Be off!" And
where am I to go? Where? I am eighty. Eighty-one.

OLGA. Sit down, nurse darling. . . . You are tired, poor thing . . . [Makes
her sit down.] Rest, dear good nurse. . . . How pale you are!

[Enter NATASHA.]

NATASHA. They are saying we must form a committee at once for the assistance of those whose houses have been burned. Well, that's a good idea.
Indeed, one ought always to be ready to help the poor, it's the duty of
the rich. Bobik and baby Sophie are both asleep, sleeping as though
nothing were happening. There are such a lot of people everywhere,
wherever one goes, the house is full. There is influenza in the town now;
I am so afraid the children may get it.

OLGA [not listening]. In this room one does not see the fire, it's quiet here.

NATASHA. Yes . . . my hair must be untidy. [In front of the looking glass.]
They say I have grown fatter . . . but it's not true! Not a bit! Masha is
asleep, she is tired out, poor dear. . . . [To ANFISA coldly.] Don't dare to
sit down in my presence! Get up! Go out of the room! [ANFISA goes out;
a pause.] Why you keep that old woman, I can't understand!

OLGA [taken aback]. Excuse me, I don't understand either. . . .

NATASHA. She is no use here. She is a peasant; she ought to be in the
country. . . . You spoil people! I like order in the house! There ought to

be no useless servants in the house. [*Strokes her cheek.*] You are tired, poor darling. Our headmistress is tired! When baby Sophie is a big girl and goes to the high-school, I shall be afraid of you.

OLGA. I shan't be headmistress.

NATASHA. You will be elected, Olya. That's a settled thing.

OLGA. I shall refuse. I can't. . . . It's too much for me . . . [*Drinks water.*] You were so rude to nurse just now. . . . Excuse me, I can't endure it. . . . It makes me feel faint.

NATASHA [*perturbed*]. Forgive me, Olya; forgive me. . . . I did not mean to hurt your feelings.

[MASHA *gets up, takes her pillow, and goes out in a rage.*]

OLGA. You must understand, my dear, it may be that we have been strangely brought up, but I can't endure it. . . . Such an attitude oppresses me, it makes me ill. . . . I feel simply unnerved by it. . . .

NATASHA. Forgive me; forgive me . . . [*Kisses her.*]

OLGA. The very slightest rudeness, a tactless word, upsets me. . . .

NATASHA. I often say too much, that's true, but you must admit, dear, that she might just as well be in the country.

OLGA. She has been thirty years with us.

NATASHA. But now she can't work! Either I don't understand, or you won't understand me. She is not fit for work. She does nothing but sleep or sit still.

OLGA. Well, let her sit still.

NATASHA [*surprised*]. How, sit still? Why, she is a servant. [*Through tears.*] I don't understand you, Olya. I have a nurse to look after the children as well as a wet nurse for baby, and we have a housemaid and a cook, what do we want that old woman for? What's the use of her?

[*The alarm bell rings behind the scenes.*]

OLGA. This night has made me ten years older.

NATASHA. We must come to an understanding, Olya. You are at the high-school, I am at home; you are teaching while I look after the house, and if I say anything about the servants, I know what I'm talking about; I do know what I am talking about. . . . And that old thief, that old hag . . . [*stamps*] that old witch shall clear out of the house tomorrow! . . . I won't have people annoy me! I won't have it! [*Feeling that she has gone too far.*] Really, if you don't move downstairs, we shall always be quarreling. It's awful.

[*Enter* KULIGIN.]

KULIGIN. Where is Masha? It's time to be going home. The fire is dying down, so they say. [*Stretches.*] Only one part of the town has been burned, and yet there was a wind; it seemed at first as though the whole town would be destroyed. [*Sits down.*] I am exhausted. Olya, my dear . . . I often think if it had not been for Masha I should have married you. You are so good. . . . I am tired out. [*Listens.*]

OLGA. What is it?

KULIGIN. It is unfortunate the doctor should have a drinking bout just now; he is helplessly drunk. Most unfortunate. [*Gets up.*] Here he comes, I do believe. . . . Do you hear? Yes, he is coming this way . . . [*Laughs.*] What a man he is, really. . . . I shall hide. [*Goes to the cupboard and stands in the corner.*] Isn't he a ruffian!

OLGA. He has not drunk for two years and now he has gone and done it . . . [*Walks away with* NATASHA *to the back of the room.*]

[TCHEBUTYKIN *comes in; walking as though sober without staggering, he walks across the room, stops, looks round; then goes up to the washing-stand and begins to wash his hands.*]

TCHEBUTYKIN [*morosely*]. The devil take them all . . . damn them all. They think I am a doctor, that I can treat all sorts of complaints, and I really know nothing about it, I have forgotten all I did know, I remember nothing, absolutely nothing.

[OLGA *and* NATASHA *go out unnoticed by him.*]

The devil take them. Last Wednesday I treated a woman at Zasyp—she died, and it's my fault that she died. Yes . . . I did know something twenty-five years ago, but now I remember nothing, nothing. Perhaps I am not a man at all but only pretend to have arms and legs and head; perhaps I don't exist at all and only fancy that I walk about, eat and sleep. [*Weeps.*] Oh, if only I did not exist! [*Leaves off weeping, morosely.*] I don't care! I don't care a scrap! [*A pause.*] Goodness knows. . . . The day before yesterday there was a conversation at the club: they talked about Shakespeare, Voltaire. . . . I have read nothing, nothing at all, but I looked as though I had read them. And the others did the same as I did. The vulgarity! The meanness! And that woman I killed on Wednesday came back to my mind . . . and it all came back to my mind and everything seemed nasty, disgusting and all awry in my soul. . . . I went and got drunk. . . .

[*Enter* IRINA, VERSHININ *and* TUSENBACH; TUSENBACH *is wearing a fashionable new civilian suit.*]

IRINA. Let us sit here. No one will come here.

VERSHININ. If it had not been for the soldiers, the whole town would have been burned down. Splendid fellows! [*Rubs his hands with pleasure.*] They are first-rate men! Splendid fellows!

KULIGIN [*going up to them*]. What time is it?

TUSENBACH. It's past three. It's getting light already.

IRINA. They are all sitting in the dining-room. No one seems to think of going. And that Solyony of yours is sitting there too. . . . [*To* TCHEBUTY-KIN.] You had better go to bed, doctor.

TCHEBUTYKIN. It's all right. . . . Thank you! [*Combs his beard.*]

KULIGIN [*laughs*]. You are a bit fuddled, Ivan Romanitch! [*Slaps him on the shoulder.*] Bravo! *In vino veritas,*[9] the ancients used to say.

---

[9] "There's truth in wine."

TUSENBACH. Everyone is asking me to get up a concert for the benefit of the families whose houses have been burned down.

IRINA. Why, who is there? . . .

TUSENBACH. We could get it up, if we wanted to. Marya Sergeyevna plays the piano splendidly, to my thinking.

KULIGIN. Yes, she plays splendidly.

IRINA. She has forgotten. She has not played for three . . . or four years.

TUSENBACH. There is absolutely no one who understands music in this town, not one soul, but I do understand and on my honor I assure you that Marya Sergeyevna plays magnificently, almost with genius.

KULIGIN. You are right, Baron. I am very fond of her; Masha, I mean. She is a good sort.

TUSENBACH. To be able to play so gloriously and to know that no one understands you!

KULIGIN [sighs]. Yes. . . . But would it be suitable for her to take part in a concert? [A pause.] I know nothing about it, my friends. Perhaps it would be all right. There is no denying that our director is a fine man, indeed a very fine man, very intelligent, but he has such views. . . . Of course it is not his business, still if you like I'll speak to him about it.

[TCHEBUTYKIN takes up a china clock and examines it.]

VERSHININ. I got dirty all over at the fire. I am a sight. [A pause.] I heard a word dropped yesterday about our brigade being transferred ever so far away. Some say to Poland, and others to Tchita.

TUSENBACH. I've heard something about it too. Well! The town will be a wilderness then.

IRINA. We shall go away too.

TCHEBUTYKIN [drops the clock, which smashes]. To smithereens!

KULIGIN [picking up the pieces]. To smash such a valuable thing—oh, Ivan Romanitch, Ivan Romanitch! I should give you minus zero for conduct!

IRINA. That was mother's clock.

TCHEBUTYKIN. Perhaps. . . . Well, if it was hers, it was. Perhaps I did not smash it, but it only seems as though I had. Perhaps it only seems to us that we exist, but really we are not here at all. I don't know anything—nobody knows anything. [By the door.] What are you staring at? Natasha has got a little affair with Protopopov, and you don't see it. . . . You sit here and see nothing, while Natasha has a little affair with Protopopov . . . [Sings.] May I offer you this date? . . . [Goes out.]

VERSHININ. Yes . . . [Laughs.] How very queer it all is, really! [A pause.] When the fire began I ran home as fast as I could. I went up and saw our house was safe and sound and out of danger, but my little girls were standing in the doorway in their nightgowns; their mother was nowhere to be seen, people were bustling about, horses and dogs were running about, and my children's faces were full of alarm, horror, entreaty, and I don't know what; it wrung my heart to see their faces. My God, I thought, what more have these children to go through in the long years to come! I took their hands and ran along with them, and could think of nothing else but what more they would have to go through in this world! [*A pause*.] When I came to your house I found their mother here, screaming, angry.

[MASHA *comes in with the pillow and sits down on the sofa*.]

VERSHININ. And while my little girls were standing in the doorway in their nightgowns and the street was red with the fire, and there was a fearful noise, I thought that something like it used to happen years ago when the enemy would suddenly make a raid and begin plundering and burning. ... And yet, in reality, what a difference there is between what is now and has been in the past! And when a little more time has passed— another two or three hundred years—people will look at our present manner of life with horror and derision, and everything of today will seem awkward and heavy, and very strange and uncomfortable. Oh, what a wonderful life that will be—what a wonderful life! [*Laughs*.] Forgive me, here I am airing my theories again! Allow me to go on. I have such a desire to talk about the future. I am in the mood. [*A pause*.] It's as though everyone were asleep. And so, I say, what a wonderful life it will be! Can you only imagine? ... There are only three of your sort in the town now, but in generations to come there will be more and more and more; and the time will come when everything will be changed and be as you would have it; they will live in your way, and later on you too will be out of date—people will be born who will be better than you. ... [*Laughs*.] I am in such a strange state of mind today. I have a fiendish longing for life ... [*Sings*.] Young and old are bound by love, and precious are its pangs ... [*Laughs*.]

MASHA. Tram-tam-tam!

VERSHININ. Tam-tam!

MASHA. Tra-ra-ra?

VERSHININ. Tra-ta-ta! [*Laughs*.]

[*Enter* FEDOTIK.]

FEDOTIK [*dances*]. Burned to ashes! Burned to ashes! Everything I had in the world. [*Laughter*.]

IRINA. A queer thing to joke about. Is everything burned?

FEDOTIK [*laughs*]. Everything I had in the world. Nothing is left. My guitar is burned, and the camera and all my letters. ... And the notebook I meant to give you—that's burned too.

[*Enter* SOLYONY.]

IRINA. No; please go, Vassily Vassilyitch. You can't stay here.

SOLYONY. How is it the baron can be here and I can't?

VERSHININ. We must be going, really. How is the fire?

SOLYONY. They say it is dying down. No, I really can't understand why the baron may be here and not I. [*Takes out a bottle of scent and sprinkles himself.*]

VERSHININ. Tram-tam-tam!

MASHA. Tram-tam!

VERSHININ [*laughs, to* SOLYONY]. Let us go into the dining room.

SOLYONY. Very well; we'll make a note of it. I might explain my meaning further, but fear I may provoke the geese . . . . [*Looking at* TUSENBACH.] Chook, chook, chook! . . . [*Goes out with* VERSHININ *and* FEDOTIK.]

IRINA. How that horrid Solyony has made the room smell of tobacco! . . . [*In surprise.*] The baron is asleep! Baron, baron!

TUSENBACH [*waking up*]. I am tired, though. . . . The brickyard. I am not talking in my sleep. I really am going to the brickyard directly, to begin work. . . . It's nearly settled. [*To* IRINA, *tenderly.*] You are so pale and lovely and fascinating. . . . It seems to me as though your paleness sheds a light through the dark air. . . . You are melancholy; you are dissatisfied with life. . . . Ah, come with me; let us go and work together!

MASHA. Nikolay Lvovitch, do go!

TUSENBACH [*laughing*]. Are you here? I didn't see you . . . [*Kisses* IRINA'S *hand.*] Good-bye, I am going. . . . I look at you now, and I remember as though it were long ago how on your name-day you talked of the joy of work, and were so gay and confident. . . . And what a happy life I was dreaming of then! What has become of it? [*Kisses her hand.*] There are tears in your eyes. Go to bed, it's getting light . . . it is nearly morning. . . . If it were granted to me to give my life for you!

MASHA. Nikolay Lvovitch, do go! Come, really. . . .

TUSENBACH. I am going. [*Goes out.*]

MASHA [*lying down*]. Are you asleep, Fyodor?

KULIGIN. Eh?

MASHA. You had better go home.

KULIGIN. My darling Masha, my precious girl! . . .

IRINA. She is tired out. Let her rest, Fedya.

KULIGIN. I'll go at once. . . . My dear, charming wife! . . . I love you, my only one! . . .

MASHA [*angrily*]. Amo, amas, amat; amamus, amatis, amant.

KULIGIN [*laughs*]. Yes, really she is wonderful. You have been my wife for seven years, and it seems to me as though we were only married yesterday. Honor bright! Yes, really you are a wonderful woman! I am content, I am content, I am content!

MASHA. I am bored, I am bored, I am bored! . . . [*Gets up and speaks, sitting down.*] And there's something I can't get out of my head. . . . . It's simply revolting. It sticks in my head like a nail; I must speak of it. I mean about Andrey. . . . He has mortgaged this house in the bank and his wife has grabbed all the money, and you know the house does not belong to him alone, but to us four! He ought to know that, if he is a decent man.

KULIGIN. Why do you want to bother about it, Masha? What is it to you? Andryusha is in debt all round, so there it is.

MASHA. It's revolting, anyway. [*Lies down.*]

KULIGIN. We are not poor. I work—I go to the high-school, and then I give private lessons. . . . I do my duty. . . . There's no nonsense about me. *Omnia mea mecum porto*,[10] as the saying is.

MASHA. I want nothing, but it's the injustice that revolts me. [*A pause.*] Go, Fyodor.

KULIGIN [*kisses her*]. You are tired, rest for half an hour, and I'll sit and wait for you. . . . Sleep . . . [*Goes.*] I am content, I am content, I am content. [*Goes out.*]

IRINA. Yes, how petty our Andrey has grown, how dull and old he has become beside that woman! At one time he was working to get a professorship and yesterday he was boasting of having succeeded at last in becoming a member of the Rural Board. He is a member, and Protopopov is chairman. . . . The whole town is laughing and talking of it and he is the only one who sees and knows nothing. . . . And here everyone has been running to the fire while he sits still in his room and takes no notice. He does nothing but play his violin . . . . [*Nervously.*] Oh, it's awful, awful, awful! [*Weeps.*] I can't bear it anymore, I can't! I can't, I can't! [OLGA *comes in and begins tidying up her table.*]

IRINA [*sobs loudly*]. Turn me out, turn me out, I can't bear it any more!

OLGA [*alarmed*]. What is it? What is it, darling?

IRINA [*sobbing*]. Where? Where has it all gone? Where is it? Oh, my God, my God! I have forgotten everything, everything . . . everything is in a tangle in my mind. . . . I don't remember the Italian for window or ceiling . . . I am forgetting everything; every day I forget something more and life is slipping away and will never come back, we shall never, never go to Moscow. . . . I see that we shan't go. . . .

OLGA. Darling, darling. . . .

IRINA [*restraining herself*]. Oh, I am wretched. . . . I can't work, I am not going to work. I have had enough of it, enough of it! I have been a telegraph clerk and now I have a job in the town council and I hate and despise every bit of the work they give me. . . . I am nearly twenty-four, I have been working for years, my brains are drying up, I am getting thin and old and ugly and there is nothing, nothing, not the slightest satisfaction, and time is passing and one feels that one is moving away from a real, fine life, moving farther and farther away and being drawn into the depths. I am in despair and I don't know how it is I am alive and have not killed myself yet. . . .

OLGA. Don't cry, my child, don't cry. It makes me miserable.

IRINA. I am not crying, I am not crying. . . . It's over. . . . There, I am not crying now. I won't . . . I won't.

OLGA. Darling, I am speaking to you as a sister, as a friend, if you care for my advice, marry the baron!

[IRINA *weeps.*]

[10] I carry all my things with me.

OLGA [*softly*]. You know you respect him, you think highly of him. . . . It's true he is ugly, but he is such a thoroughly nice man, so good. . . . One doesn't marry for love, but to do one's duty. . . . That's what I think, anyway, and I would marry without love. Whoever proposed to me I would marry him, if only he were a good man. . . . I would even marry an old man. . . .

IRINA. I kept expecting we should move to Moscow and there I should meet my real one. I've been dreaming of him, loving him. . . . But it seems that was all nonsense, nonsense. . . .

OLGA [*puts her arms round her sister*]. My darling, lovely sister, I understand it all; when the baron left the army and came to us in a plain coat, I thought he looked so ugly that it positively made me cry. . . . He asked me, "Why are you crying?" How could I tell him! But if God brought you together I should be happy. That's a different thing, you know, quite different.

[NATASHA *with a candle in her hand walks across the stage from door on right to door on left without speaking.*]

MASHA [*sits up*]. She walks about as though it were she had set fire to the town.

OLGA. Masha, you are silly. The very silliest of the family, that's you. Please forgive me. [*A pause.*]

MASHA. I want to confess my sins, dear sisters. My soul is yearning. I am going to confess to you and never again to anyone. . . . I'll tell you this minute. [*Softly.*] It's my secret, but you must know everything. . . . I can't be silent . . . . [*A pause.*] I am in love, I am in love. . . . I love that man. . . . You have just seen him. . . . Well, I may as well say it straight out. I love Vershinin.

OLGA [*going behind her screen*]. Leave off. I don't hear anyway.

MASHA. But what am I to do? [*Clutches her head.*] At first I thought him queer . . . then I was sorry for him . . . then I came to love him . . . to love him with his voice, his words, his misfortunes, his two little girls. . . .

OLGA [*behind the screen*]. I don't hear you anyway. Whatever silly things you say I shan't hear them.

MASHA. Oh, Olya, you are silly. I love him—so that's my fate. It means that that's my lot. . . . And he loves me. . . . It's all dreadful. Yes? Is it wrong? [*Takes* IRINA *by the hand and draws her to herself.*] Oh, my darling. . . . How are we going to live our lives, what will become of us? . . When one reads a novel it all seems stale and easy to understand, but when you are in love yourself you see that no one knows anything and we all have to settle things for ourselves. . . . My darling, my sister. . . . I have confessed it to you, now I'll hold my tongue. . . . I'll be like Gogol's madman . . . silence . . . silence. . . .

[*Enter* ANDREY *and after him* FERAPONT.]

ANDREY [*angrily*]. What do you want? I can't make it out.

FERAPONT [*in the doorway, impatiently*]. I've told you ten times already, Andrey Sergeyevitch.

ANDREY. In the first place I am not Andrey Sergeyevitch, but your honor, to you!

FERAPONT. The firemen ask leave, your honor, to go through the garden on their way to the river. Or else they have to go round and round, an awful nuisance for them.

ANDREY. Very good. Tell them, very good. [FERAPONT *goes out.*] I am sick of them. Where is Olga?

[OLGA *comes from behind the screen.*] I've come to ask you for the key of the cupboard, I have lost mine. You've got one, it's a little key.

[OLGA *gives him the key in silence;* IRINA *goes behind her screen; a pause.*]

ANDREY. What a tremendous fire! Now it's begun to die down. Hang it all, that Ferapont made me so cross I said something silly to him. Your honor . . . . [*A pause.*] Why don't you speak, Olya? [*A pause.*] It's time to drop this foolishness and sulking all about nothing. . . . You are here, Masha, and you too, Irina—very well, then, let us have things out thoroughly, once for all. What have you against me? What is it?

OLGA. Leave off, Andryusha. Let us talk tomorrow. [*Nervously.*] What an agonizing night!

ANDREY [*greatly confused*]. Don't excite yourself. I ask you quite coolly, what have you against me? Tell me straight out.

[VERSHININ'S *voice:* "Tram-tam-tam!"]

MASHA [*standing up, loudly*]. Tra-ta-ta! [*To* OLGA.] Good night, Olya, God bless you . . . .

[*Goes behind the screen and kisses* IRINA.]

Sleep well. . . . Good night, Andrey. You'd better leave them now, they are tired out . . . you can go into things tomorrow. [*Goes out.*]

OLGA. Yes, really, Andryusha, let us put it off till tomorrow . . . [*Goes behind her screen.*] It's time we were in bed.

ANDREY. I'll say what I have to say and then go. Directly. . . . First, you have something against Natasha, my wife, and I've noticed that from the very day of my marriage. Natasha is a splendid woman, conscientious, straightforward and honorable—that's my opinion! I love and respect my wife, do you understand? I respect her, and I insist on other people respecting her too. I repeat, she is a conscientious, honorable woman, and all your disagreements are simply caprice, or rather the whims of old maids. Old maids never like and never have liked their sisters-in-law—that's the rule. [*A pause.*] Secondly, you seem to be cross with me for not being a professor, not working at something learned. But I am in the service of the Zemstvo,[11] I am a member of the Rural Board, and I consider this service just as sacred and elevated as the service of learning. I am a member of the Rural Board and I am proud

---

[11] County council.

of it, if you care to know .... [*A pause.*] Thirdly ... there's something
else I have to say. ... I have mortgaged the house without asking your
permission. ... For that I am to blame, yes, and I ask your pardon for
it. I was driven to it by my debts ... thirty-five thousand. ... I am not
gambling now—I gave up cards long ago; but the chief thing I can say
in self-defense is that you are, so to say, of the privileged sex—you get a
pension ... while I had not ... my wages, so to speak .... [*A pause.*]

KULIGIN [*at the door*]. Isn't Masha here? [*Perturbed.*] Where is she? It's
strange ... [*Goes out.*]

ANDREY. They won't listen. Natasha is an excellent, conscientious woman.
[*Paces up and down the stage in silence, then stops.*] When I married her,
I thought we should be happy ... happy, all of us. ... But, my God!
[*Weeps.*] Dear sisters, darling sisters, you must not believe what I say,
you mustn't believe it ... [*Goes out.*]

KULIGIN [*at the door, uneasily*]. Where is Masha? Isn't Masha here? How
strange! [*Goes out.*]

[*The firebell rings in the street. The stage is empty.*]

IRINA [*behind the screen*]. Olya! Who is that knocking on the floor?

OLGA. It's the doctor, Ivan Romanitch. He is drunk.

IRINA. What a troubled night! [*A pause.*] Olya! [*Peeps out from behind the
screen.*] Have you heard? The brigade is going to be taken away; they are
being transferred to some place very far off.

OLGA. That's only a rumor.

IRINA. Then we shall be alone. ... Olya!

OLGA. Well?

IRINA. My dear, my darling, I respect the baron, I think highly of him, he
is a fine man—I will marry him, I consent, only let us go to Moscow! I
entreat you, do let us go! There's nothing in the world better than
Moscow! Let us go, Olya! Let us go!

ACT FOUR

Old garden of the PROZOROVS' *house. A long avenue of fir trees, at the end
of which is a view of the river. On the farther side of the river there is a
wood. On the right the veranda of the house; on the table in it are bottles
and glasses; evidently they have just been drinking champagne. It is
twelve o'clock noon. People pass occasionally from the street across the
garden to the river; five soldiers pass rapidly.*

TCHEBUTYKIN, *in an affable mood, which persists throughout the act, is
sitting in an easy chair in the garden, waiting to be summoned; he is
wearing a military cap and has a stick.* IRINA, KULIGIN *with a decoration
on his breast and with no moustache, and* TUSENBACH, *standing on the*

veranda, are saying good-bye to FEDOTIK *and* RODDEY, *who are going down the steps; both officers are in marching uniform.*

TUSENBACH [*kissing* FEDOTIK]. You are a good fellow; we've got on so happily together. [*Kisses* RODDEY.] Once more. . . . Good-bye, my dear boy. . . .

IRINA. Till we meet again!

FEDOTIK. No, it's good-bye for good; we shall never meet again.

KULIGIN. Who knows! [*Wipes his eyes, smiles.*] Here I am crying too.

IRINA. We shall meet some day.

FEDOTIK. In ten years, or fifteen perhaps? But then we shall scarcely recognize each other—we shall greet each other coldly . . . [*Takes a snapshot.*] Stand still. . . . Once more, for the last time.

RODDEY [*embraces* TUSENBACH]. We shall not see each other again. . . . [*Kisses* IRINA's *hand.*] Thank you for everything, everything. . . .

FEDOTIK [*with vexation*]. Oh, do wait!

TUSENBACH. Please God we shall meet again. Write to us. Be sure to write to us.

RODDEY [*taking a long look at the garden*]. Good-bye, trees! [*Shouts.*] Halloo! [*A pause.*] Good-bye, echo!

KULIGIN. I shouldn't wonder if you get married in Poland. . . . Your Polish wife will clasp you in her arms and call you *kochany!* [*Laughs.*]

FEDOTIK [*looking at his watch*]. We have less than an hour. Of our battery only Solyony is going on the barge; we are going with the rank and file. Three divisions of the battery are going today and three more tomorrow —and peace and quiet will descend upon the town.

TUSENBACH. And dreadful boredom too.

RODDEY. And where is Marya Sergeyevna?

KULIGIN. Masha is in the garden.

FEDOTIK. We must say good-bye to her.

RODDEY. Good-bye. We must go, or I shall begin to cry . . . . [*Hurriedly embraces* TUSENBACH *and* KULIGIN *and kisses* IRINA'S *hand.*] We've had a splendid time here.

FEDOTIK [*to* KULIGIN]. This is a little souvenir for you . . . a notebook with a pencil. . . . We'll go down here to the river . . . [*As they go away both look back.*]

RODDEY [*shouts*]. Halloo-oo!

KULIGIN [*shouts*]. Good-bye!

[RODDEY *and* FEDOTIK *meet* MASHA *in the background and say good-bye to her; she walks away with them.*]

IRINA. They've gone . . . [*Sits down on the bottom step of the veranda.*]

TCHEBUTYKIN. They have forgotten to say good-bye to me.

IRINA. And what were you thinking about?

TCHEBUTYKIN. Why, I somehow forget, too. But I shall see them again soon, I am setting off tomorrow. Yes . . . I have one day more. In a year

I shall be on the retired list. Then I shall come here again and shall spend the rest of my life near you. . . . There is only one year now before I get my pension. [*Puts a newspaper into his pocket and takes out another.*] I shall come here to you and arrange my life quite differently. . . . I shall become such a quiet . . . God-fearing . . . well-behaved person.

IRINA. Well, you do need to arrange your life differently, dear Ivan Romanitch. You certainly ought to somehow.

TCHEBUTYKIN. Yes, I feel it. [*Softly hums.*] "Tarara-boom-dee-ay—Tararaboom-dee-ay."[12]

KULIGIN. Ivan Romanitch is incorrigible! Incorrigible!

TCHEBUTYKIN. You ought to take me in hand. Then I should reform.

IRINA. Fyodor has shaved off his moustache. I can't bear to look at him!

KULIGIN. Why, what's wrong?

TCHEBUTYKIN. I might tell you what your countenance looks like now, but I really can't.

KULIGIN. Well! It's the thing now, *modus vivendi*. Our headmaster is cleanshaven and now I am second to him I have taken to shaving too. Nobody likes it, but I don't care. I am content. With moustache or without moustache I am equally content. [*Sits down.*]

[*In the background* ANDREY *is wheeling a baby asleep in a perambulator.*]

IRINA. Ivan Romanitch, darling, I am dreadfully uneasy. You were on the boulevard yesterday, tell me what was it that happened?

TCHEBUTYKIN. What happened? Nothing. Nothing much. [*Reads the newspaper.*] It doesn't matter!

KULIGIN. The story is that Solyony and the baron met yesterday on the boulevard near the theater. . . .

TUSENBACH. Oh, stop it! Really . . . [*With a wave of his hand walks away into the house.*]

KULIGIN. Near the theater. . . . Solyony began pestering the baron and he couldn't keep his temper and said something offensive. . . .

TCHEBUTYKIN. I don't know. It's all nonsense.

KULIGIN. A teacher at a divinity school wrote "nonsense" at the bottom of an essay and the pupil puzzled over it thinking it was a Latin word . . . [*Laughs.*] It was fearfully funny. . . . They say Solyony is in love with Irina and hates the baron. . . . That's natural. Irina is a very nice girl.

[*From the background behind the scenes,* "Aa-oo! Halloo!"]

IRINA [*starts*]. Everything frightens me somehow today. [*A pause.*] All my things are ready, after dinner I shall send off my luggage. The baron and I are to be married tomorrow, tomorrow we go to the brickyard and the day after that I shall be in the school. A new life is beginning. God will help me! How will it fare with me? When I passed my exam as a teacher I felt so happy, so blissful, that I cried . . . . [*A pause.*] The cart will soon be coming for my things. . . .

[12] Refrain of a popular English and American song.

KULIGIN. That's all very well, but it does not seem serious. It's all nothing but ideas and very little that is serious. However, I wish you success with all my heart.

TCHEBUTYKIN [*moved to tenderness*]. My good, delightful darling. . . . My heart of gold. . . .

KULIGIN. Well, today the officers will be gone and everything will go on in the old way. Whatever people may say, Masha is a true, good woman. I love her dearly and am thankful for my lot! . . . People have different lots in life. . . . There is a man called Kozyrev serving in the Excise here. He was at school with me, but he was expelled from the fifth form because he could never understand *ut consecutivum.*[13] Now he is frightfully poor and ill, and when I meet him I say, "How are you, *ut consecutivum?*" "Yes," he says, "just so—*consecutivum*" . . . and then he coughs. . . . Now I have always been successful, I am fortunate, I have even got the order of the Stanislav of the second degree and I am teaching others that *ut consecutivum*. Of course I am clever, cleverer than very many people, but happiness does not lie in that . . . . [*A pause.*]

[*In the house the* "*Maiden's Prayer*" *is played on the piano.*]

IRINA. Tomorrow evening I shall not be hearing that "Maiden's Prayer," I shan't be meeting Protopopov . . . . [*A pause.*] Protopopov is sitting there in the drawing room; he has come again today. . . .

KULIGIN. The headmistress has not come yet?

IRINA. No. They have sent for her. If only you knew how hard it is for me to live here alone, without Olya. . . . Now that she is headmistress and lives at the high-school and is busy all day long, I am alone, I am bored, I have nothing to do, and I hate the room I live in. . . . I have made up my mind, since I am not fated to be in Moscow, that so it must be. It must be destiny. There is no help for it. . . . It's all in God's hands, that's the truth. When Nikolay Lvovitch made me an offer again . . . I thought it over and made up my mind. . . . He is a good man, it's wonderful really how good he is. . . . And I suddenly felt as though my soul had grown wings, my heart felt so light and again I longed for work, work. . . . Only something happened yesterday, there is some mystery hanging over me.

TCHEBUTYKIN. Nonsense.

NATASHA [*at the window*]. Our headmistress!

KULIGIN. The headmistress has come. Let us go in. [*Goes into the house with* IRINA.]

TCHEBUTYKIN [*reads the newspaper, humming softly*]. "Tarara-boom-dee-ay."

[MASHA *approaches; in the background* ANDREY *is pushing the perambulator.*]

MASHA. Here he sits, snug and settled.

---

[13] A rhetorical principle.

TCHEBUTYKIN. Well, what then?

MASHA [*sits down*]. Nothing. . . . [*A pause.*] Did you love my mother?

TCHEBUTYKIN. Very much.

MASHA. And did she love you?

TCHEBUTYKIN [*after a pause*]. That I don't remember.

MASHA. Is my man here? It's just like our cook Marfa used to say about her policeman: is my man here?

TCHEBUTYKIN. Not yet.

MASHA. When you get happiness by snatches, by little bits, and then lose it, as I am losing it, by degrees one grows coarse and spiteful . . . [*Points to her bosom.*] I'm boiling here inside . . . [*Looking at* ANDREY, *who is pushing the perambulator.*] Here is our Andrey. . . . All our hopes are shattered. Thousands of people raised the bell, a lot of money and of labor was spent on it, and it suddenly fell and smashed. All at once, for no reason whatever. That's just how it is with Andrey. . . .

ANDREY. When will they be quiet in the house? There is such a noise.

TCHEBUTYKIN. Soon. [*Looks at his watch.*] My watch is an old-fashioned one with a repeater . . . [*Winds his watch, it strikes.*] The first, the second, and the fifth batteries are going at one o'clock. [*A pause.*] And I am going tomorrow.

ANDREY. For good?

TCHEBUTYKIN. I don't know. Perhaps I shall come back in a year. Though goodness knows. . . . It doesn't matter one way or another.

[*There is the sound of a harp and violin being played far away in the street.*]

ANDREY. The town will be empty. It's as though one put an extinguisher over it. [*A pause.*] Something happened yesterday near the theater; everyone is talking of it, and I know nothing about it.

TCHEBUTYKIN. It was nothing. Foolishness. Solyony began annoying the baron and he lost his temper and insulted him, and it came in the end to Solyony's having to challenge him. [*Looks at his watch.*] It's time, I fancy. . . . It was to be at half-past twelve in the Crown forest that we can see from here beyond the river . . . Piff-paff! [*Laughs.*] Solyony imagines he is a Lermontov and even writes verses. Joking apart, this is his third duel.

MASHA. Whose?

TCHEBUTYKIN. Solyony's.

MASHA. And the baron's?

TCHEBUTYKIN. What about the baron? [*A pause.*]

MASHA. My thoughts are in a muddle. . . . Anyway, I tell you, you ought not to let them do it. He may wound the baron or even kill him.

TCHEBUTYKIN. The baron is a very good fellow, but one baron more or less in the world, what does it matter? Let them! It doesn't matter. [*Beyond the garden a shout of* "Aa-oo! Halloo!"] You can wait. That is Skvortsov, the second, shouting. He is in a boat. [*A pause.*]

ANDREY. In my opinion to take part in a duel, or to be present at it even in the capacity of a doctor, is simply immoral.

TCHEBUTYKIN. That only seems so. . . . We are not real, nothing in the world is real, we don't exist, but only seem to exist. . . . Nothing matters!

MASHA. How they keep on talking, talking all day long. [*Goes.*] To live in such a climate, it may snow any minute, and then all this talk on the top of it. [*Stops.*] I am not going indoors, I can't go in there. . . . When Vershinin comes, tell me . . . [*Goes down the avenue.*] And the birds are already flying south . . . [*Looks up.*] Swans or geese. . . . Darlings, happy things. . . . [*Goes out.*]

ANDREY. Our house will be empty. The officers are going, you are going, Irina is getting married, and I shall be left in the house alone.

TCHEBUTYKIN. What about your wife?

[*Enter* FERAPONT *with papers.*]

ANDREY. A wife is a wife. She is a straightforward, upright woman, good-natured, perhaps, but for all that there is something in her which makes her no better than some petty, blind, hairy animal. Anyway she is not a human being. I speak to you as to a friend, the one man to whom I can open my soul. I love Natasha, that is so, but sometimes she seems to me wonderfully vulgar, and then I don't know what to think, I can't account for my loving her or, anyway, having loved her.

TCHEBUTYKIN [*gets up*]. I am going away tomorrow, my boy, perhaps we shall never meet again, so this is my advice to you. Put on your cap, you know, take your stick and walk off . . . walk off and just go, go without looking back. And the farther you go, the better. [*A pause.*] But do as you like! It doesn't matter. . . .

[SOLYONY *crosses the stage in the background with two officers; seeing* TCHEBUTYKIN *he turns toward him; the officers walk on.*]

SOLYONY. Doctor, it's time! It's half-past twelve. [*Greets* ANDREY.]

TCHEBUTYKIN. Directly. I am sick of you all. [*To* ANDREY.] If anyone asks for me, Andryusha, say I'll be back directly . . . [*Sighs.*] Oho-ho-ho!

SOLYONY. He had not time to say alack before the bear was on his back. [*Walks away with the doctor.*] Why are you croaking, old chap?

TCHEBUTYKIN. Come!

SOLYONY. How do you feel?

TCHEBUTYKIN [*angrily*]. Like a pig in clover.

SOLYONY. The old chap need not excite himself. I won't do anything much, I'll only shoot him like a snipe. [*Takes out scent and sprinkles his hands.*] I've used a whole bottle today, and still they smell. My hands smell like a corpse. [*A pause.*] Yes. . . . Do you remember the poem? "And, restless, seeks the stormy ocean, as though in tempest there were peace." . . .

TCHEBUTYKIN. Yes. He had not time to say alack before the bear was on his back.

[*Goes out with* SOLYONY. *Shouts are heard:* "Halloo! Oo-oo!" ANDREY *and* FERAPONT *come in.*]

FERAPONT. Papers for you to sign. . . .

ANDREY [*nervously*]. Let me alone! Let me alone! I entreat you! [*Walks away with the perambulator.*]

FERAPONT. That's what the papers are for—to be signed. [*Retires into the background.*]

[*Enter* IRINA *and* TUSENBACH *wearing a straw hat;* KULIGIN *crosses the stage shouting* "Aa-oo, Masha,. aa-oo!"]

TUSENBACH. I believe that's the only man in the town who is glad that the officers are going away.

IRINA. That's very natural. [*A pause.*] Our town will be empty now.

TUSENBACH. Dear, I'll be back directly.

IRINA. Where are you going?

TUSENBACH. I must go into the town, and then . . . to see my comrades off.

IRINA. That's not true. . . . Nikolay, why are you so absentminded today? [*A pause.*] What happened yesterday near the theater?

TUSENBACH [*with a gesture of impatience*]. I'll be here in an hour and with you again. [*Kisses her hands.*] My beautiful one . . . [*Looks into her face.*] For five years now I have loved you and still I can't get used to it, and you seem to me more and more lovely. What wonderful, exquisite hair! What eyes! I shall carry you off tomorrow, we will work, we will be rich, my dreams will come true. You shall be happy. There is only one thing, one thing: you don't love me!

IRINA. That's not in my power! I'll be your wife and be faithful and obedient, but there is no love, I can't help it. [*Weeps.*] I've never been in love in my life! Oh, I have so dreamed of love, I've been dreaming of it for years, day and night, but my soul is like a wonderful piano of which the key has been lost. [*A pause.*] You look uneasy.

TUSENBACH. I have not slept all night. There has never been anything in my life so dreadful that it could frighten me, and only that lost key frets at my heart and won't let me sleep. . . . Say something to me . . . . [*A pause.*] Say something to me. . . .

IRINA. What? What am I to say to you? What?

TUSENBACH. Anything.

IRINA. There, there! [*A pause.*]

TUSENBACH. What trifles, what little things suddenly *à propos* of nothing acquire importance in life! One laughs at them as before, thinks them nonsense, but still one goes on and feels that one has not the power to stop. Don't let us talk about it! I am happy. I feel as though I were seeing these pines, these maples, these birch trees for the first time in my life, and they all seem to be looking at me with curiosity and waiting. What beautiful trees, and, really, how beautiful life ought to be under them! [*A shout of* "Halloo! Aa-oo!"] I must be off; it's time. . . . See, that tree is dead, but it waves in the wind with the others. And so it seems to me that if I die I shall still have part in life, one way or another. Good-bye, my darling . . . [*Kisses her hands.*] Those papers of yours you gave me are lying under the calendar on my table.

IRINA. I am coming with you.

TUSENBACH [*in alarm*]. No, no! [*Goes off quickly, stops in the avenue.*] Irina! IRINA. What is it?

TUSENBACH [*not knowing what to say*]. I didn't have any coffee this morning. Ask them to make me some. [*Goes out quickly.*]

[IRINA *stands lost in thought, then walks away into the background of the scene and sits down on the swing. Enter* ANDREY *with the perambulator, and* FERAPONT *comes into sight.*]

FERAPONT. Andrey Sergeyevitch, the papers aren't mine; they are Government papers. I didn't invent them.

ANDREY. Oh, where is it all gone? What has become of my past, when I was young, gay, and clever, when my dreams and thoughts were exquisite, when my present and my past were lighted up by hope? Why on the very threshold of life do we become dull, grey, uninteresting, lazy, indifferent, useless, unhappy? . . . Our town has been going on for two hundred years—there are a hundred thousand people living in it; and there is not one who is not like the rest, not one saint in the past, or the present, not one man of learning, not one artist, not one man in the least remarkable who could inspire envy or a passionate desire to imitate him. . . . They only eat, drink, sleep, and then die . . . others are born, and they also eat and drink and sleep, and not to be bored to stupefaction they vary their lives by nasty gossip, vodka, cards, litigation; and the wives deceive their husbands, and the husbands tell lies and pretend that they see and hear nothing, and an overwhelmingly vulgar influence weighs upon the children, and the divine spark is quenched in them and they become the same sort of pitiful, dead creatures, all exactly alike, as their fathers and mothers. . . . [*To* FERAPONT, *angrily.*] What do you want?

FERAPONT. Eh? There are papers to sign.

ANDREY. You bother me!

FERAPONT [*handing him the papers*]. The porter from the local treasury was saying just now that there was as much as two hundred degrees of frost in Petersburg this winter.

ANDREY. The present is hateful, but when I think of the future, it is so nice! I feel so lighthearted, so free. A light dawns in the distance, I see freedom. I see how I and my children will become free from sloth, from kvass,[14] from goose and cabbage, from sleeping after dinner, from mean, parasitic living. . . .

FERAPONT. He says that two thousand people were frozen to death. The people were terrified. It was either in Petersburg or Moscow, I don't remember.

[14] Beer.

ANDREY [*in a rush of tender feeling*]. My dear sisters, my wonderful sisters! [*Through tears.*] Masha, my sister!

NATASHA [*in the window*]. Who is talking so loud out there? Is that you, Andryusha? You will wake baby Sophie. *Il ne faut pas faire de bruit, la Sophie est dormée déjà. Vous êtes un ours.*[15] [*Getting angry.*] If you want to talk, give the perambulator with the baby to somebody else. Ferapont, take the perambulator from the master!

FERAPONT. Yes, ma'am. [*Takes the pram.*]

ANDREY [*in confusion*]. I am talking quietly.

NATASHA [*petting her child, inside the room*]. Bobik! Naughty Bobik! Little rascal!

ANDREY [*looking through the papers*]. Very well, I'll look through them and sign what wants signing, and then you can take them back to the Board . . .

[*Goes into the house reading the papers;* FERAPONT *pushes the pram farther into the garden.*]

NATASHA [*speaking indoors*]. Bobik, what is mamma's name? Darling, darling! And who is this? This is Auntie Olya. Say to Auntie, "Good morning, Olya!"

[*Two wandering musicians, a man and a girl, enter and play a violin and a harp; from the house enter* VERSHININ *with* OLGA *and* ANFISA, *and stand for a minute listening in silence;* IRINA *comes up.*]

OLGA. Our garden is like a public passage; they walk and ride through. Nurse, give those people something.

ANFISA [*gives money to the musicians*]. Go away, and God bless you, my dear souls!

[*The musicians bow and go away.*]

Poor things. People don't play if they have plenty to eat. [*To* IRINA.] Good morning, Irisha! [*Kisses her.*] Aye, aye, my little girl, I am having a time of it! Living in the high-school, in a government flat, with dear Olya— that's what the Lord has vouchsafed me in my old age! I have never lived so well in my life, sinful woman that I am. . . . It's a big flat, and I have a room to myself and a bedstead. All at the government expense. I wake up in the night and, O Lord, Mother of God, there is no one in the world happier than I!

VERSHININ [*looks at his watch*]. We are just going, Olga Sergeyevna. It's time to be off. [*A pause.*] I wish you everything, everything. . . . Where is Marya Sergeyevna?

IRINA. She is somewhere in the garden. . . . I'll go and look for her.

VERSHININ. Please be so good. I am in a hurry.

ANFISA. I'll go and look for her too. [*Shouts.*] Mashenka, aa-oo!

[*Goes with* IRINA *into the farther part of the garden.*]

Aa-oo! Aa-oo!

[15] "You mustn't be noisy, Sophie is still asleep. You're a bear."

VERSHININ. Everything comes to an end. Here we are parting. [*Looks at his watch.*] The town has given us something like a lunch; we have been drinking champagne, the mayor made a speech. I ate and listened, but my heart was here, with you all . . . [*Looks round the garden.*] I've grown used to you. . . .

OLGA. Shall we ever see each other again?

VERSHININ. Most likely not. [*A pause.*] My wife and two little girls will stay here for another two months; please, if anything happens, if they need anything . . .

OLGA. Yes, yes, of course. Set your mind at rest. [*A pause.*] By tomorrow there won't be a soldier in the town—it will all turn into a memory, and of course for us it will be like beginning a new life. . . . [*A pause.*] Nothing turns out as we would have it. I did not want to be a headmistress, and yet I am. It seems we are not to live in Moscow. . . .

VERSHININ. Well. . . . Thank you for everything. . . . Forgive me if anything was amiss. . . . I have talked a great deal: forgive me for that too—don't remember evil against me.

OLGA [*wipes her eyes*]. Why doesn't Masha come?

VERSHININ. What else am I to say to you at parting? What am I to theorize about? . . . [*Laughs.*] Life is hard. It seems to many of us blank and hopeless; but yet we must admit that it goes on getting clearer and easier, and it looks as though the time were not far off when it will be full of happiness. [*Looks at his watch.*] It's time for me to go! In old days men were absorbed in wars, filling all their existence with marches, raids, victories, but now all that is a thing of the past, leaving behind it a great void which there is so far nothing to fill: humanity is searching for it passionately, and of course will find it. Ah, if only it could be quickly! [*A pause.*] If, don't you know, industry were united with culture and culture with industry . . . [*Looks at his watch.*] But, I say, it's time for me to go. . . .

OLGA. Here she comes.

[MASHA *comes in.*]

VERSHININ. I have come to say good-bye. . . .

[OLGA *moves a little away to leave them free to say good-bye.*]

MASHA [*looking into his face*]. Good-bye . . . . [*A prolonged kiss.*]

OLGA. Come, come. . . .

[MASHA *sobs violently.*]

VERSHININ. Write to me. . . . Don't forget me! Let me go! . . . Time is up! . . . Olga Sergeyevna, take her, I must . . . go . . . I am late . . . [*Much moved, kisses* OLGA's *hands; then again embraces* MASHA *and quickly goes off.*]

OLGA. Come, Masha! Leave off, darling.

[*Enter* KULIGIN.]

KULIGIN [*embarrassed*]. Never mind, let her cry—let her. . . . My good Masha, my dear Masha! . . . You are my wife, and I am happy, anyway.

... I don't complain; I don't say a word of blame. ... Here Olya is my witness. ... We'll begin the old life again, and I won't say one word, not a hint. ...

MASHA [*restraining her sobs*]. By the sea-strand an oak-tree green. ... Upon that oak a chain of gold. ... Upon that oak a chain of gold. ... I am going mad. ... By the sea-strand ... an oak-tree green. ...

OLGA. Calm yourself, Masha. ... Calm yourself. ... Give her some water.

MASHA. I am not crying now. ...

KULIGIN. She is not crying now ... she is good. ...

[*The dim sound of a faraway shot.*]

MASHA. By the sea-strand an oak-tree green, upon that oak a chain of gold. ... The cat is green ... the oak is green. ... I am mixing it up ... [*Drinks water.*] My life is a failure. ... I want nothing now. ... I shall be calm directly. ... It doesn't matter. ... What does "strand" mean? Why do these words haunt me? My thoughts are in a tangle.

[*Enter* IRINA.]

OLGA. Calm yourself, Masha. Come, that's a good girl. Let us go indoors.

MASHA [*angrily*]. I am not going in. Let me alone! [*Sobs, but at once checks herself.*] I don't go into that house now and I won't.

IRINA. Let us sit together, even if we don't say anything. I am going away tomorrow, you know ... . [*A pause.*]

KULIGIN. I took a false beard and moustache from a boy in the third grade yesterday, just look ... [*Puts on the beard and moustache.*] I look like the German teacher ... [*Laughs.*] Don't I? Funny creatures, those boys.

MASHA. You really do look like the German teacher.

OLGA [*laughs*]. Yes.

[MASHA *weeps.*]

IRINA. There, Masha!

KULIGIN. Awfully like. ...

[*Enter* NATASHA.]

NATASHA [*to the maid*]. What? Mr. Protopopov will sit with Sophie, and let Andrey Sergeyitch wheel Bobik up and down. What a lot there is to do with children ... [*To* IRINA.] Irina, you are going away tomorrow, what a pity. Do stay just another week.

[*Seeing* KULIGIN *utters a shriek; the latter laughs and takes off the beard and moustache.*]

Well, what next, you gave me such a fright! [*To* IRINA.] I am used to you and do you suppose that I don't feel parting with you? I shall put Andrey with his violin into your room—let him saw away there!—and we will put baby Sophie in his room. Adorable, delightful baby! Isn't she a child! Today she looked at me with such eyes and said "Mamma"!

KULIGIN. A fine child, that's true.

NATASHA. So tomorrow I shall be all alone here. [*Sighs.*] First of all I shall have this avenue of fir trees cut down, and then that maple. ... It looks so ugly in the evening. ... [*To* IRINA.] My dear, that sash does not suit

you at all. . . . It's in bad taste. You want something light. And then I
shall have flowers, flowers planted everywhere, and there will be such a
scent. . . . [*Severely*.] Why is there a fork lying about on that seat?
[*Going into the house, to the maid*.] Why is there a fork lying about on
this seat. I ask you? [*Shouts*.] Hold your tongue!

KULIGIN. She is at it!

[*Behind the scenes the band plays a march; they all listen*.]

OLGA. They are going.

[*Enter* TCHEBUTYKIN.]

MASHA. Our people are going. Well . . . a happy journey to them! [*To her
husband*.] We must go home. . . . Where are my hat and cape?

KULIGIN. I took them into the house . . . I'll get them directly. . . .

OLGA. Yes, now we can go home, it's time.

TCHEBUTYKIN. Olga Sergeyevna!

OLGA. What is it? [*A pause*.] What?

TCHEBUTYKIN. Nothing. . . . I don't know how to tell you. [*Whispers in her
ear*.]

OLGA [*in alarm*]. It can't be!

TCHEBUTYKIN. Yes . . . such a business. . . . I am so worried and worn out,
I don't want to say another word. . . . [*With vexation*.] But there, it
doesn't matter!

MASHA. What has happened?

OLGA [*puts her arms round* IRINA]. This is a terrible day. . . . I don't know
how to tell you, my precious. . . .

IRINA. What is it? Tell me quickly, what is it? For God's sake! [*Cries*.]

TCHEBUTYKIN. The baron has just been killed in a duel.

IRINA [*weeping quietly*]. I knew, I knew. . . .

TCHEBUTYKIN [*in the background of the scene sits down on a garden seat*].
I am worn out . . . [*Takes a newspaper out of his pocket*.] Let them cry.
. . . [*Sings softly*.] "Tarara-boom-dee-ay" . . . It doesn't matter.

[*The three sisters stand with their arms round one another*.]

MASHA. Oh, listen to that band! They are going away from us; one has gone
altogether, gone forever. We are left alone to begin our life over again.
. . . We've got to live . . . we've got to live. . . .

IRINA [*lays her head on* OLGA'S *bosom*]. A time will come when everyone
will know what all this is for, why there is this misery; there will be no
mysteries and, meanwhile, we have got to live . . . we have got to work,
only to work! Tomorrow I shall go alone; I shall teach in the school,
and I will give all my life to those to whom it may be of use. Now it's
autumn; soon winter will come and cover us with snow, and I will work,
I will work.

OLGA [*embraces both her sisters*]. The music is so gay, so confident, and
one longs for life! O my God! Time will pass, and we shall go away for
ever, and we shall be forgotten, our faces will be forgotten, our voices,
and how many there were of us; but our sufferings will pass into joy for

those who will live after us, happiness and peace will be established upon earth, and they will remember kindly and bless those who have lived before. Oh, dear sisters, our life is not ended yet. We shall live! The music is so gay, so joyful, and it seems as though a little more and we shall know what we are living for, why we are suffering. . . . If we only knew—if we only knew!

[*The music grows more and more subdued*; KULIGIN, *cheerful and smiling, brings the hat and cape;* ANDREY *pushes the perambulator in which* BOBIK *is sitting.*]

TCHEBUTYKIN [*humming softly*]. "Tarara-boom-dee-ay!" [*Reads his paper.*] It doesn't matter, it doesn't matter.

OLGA. If we only knew, if we only knew!

JEAN GIRAUDOUX

TIGER AT THE GATES

THE PAST REVISITED

FROM THE BEGINNING of the history of drama the form of a play was rarely accidental. The shaping of the action may be determined by the structure of the theater (as in ancient Greece), or by a view of the human condition held in common by the playwright and the members of his audience (as in India or in Europe before the nineteenth century). However, in the discussions of Ibsen and Chekhov, it was pointed out that both dramatists had to discover or invent a form for their highly individual purposes, and this condition has continued to be a problem for their heirs. Modern drama is experimental not just in its subject matter and points of view, but in its form. The teasing cloudiness of symbolism, the purposeful fragmentation of expressionism, the mingling of realism and fantasy, the revival of older forms, these have been among the many experiments of artists in search of forms appropriate to the concept with which they happen to be engaged. And the artist in his career may try many forms in his quest for an ordering of the chaos of daily life.

The search for form has led to a widespread and artistically fruitful exploitation of ancient myth and legend. To be sure such stories have been retold many times by many playwrights, but their special usefulness in the modern theater was pointed out by T. S. Eliot in his famous review of James Joyce's *Ulysses*, a novel about a day in the life of a group of Dubliners:

> In using the myth, in manipulating a continuous parallel between contemporaneity and antiquity, Mr. Joyce is pursuing a method which others must pursue after him . . . . It is simply a way of controlling, of ordering, of giving a shape and a significance to the immense panorama of futility and anarchy which is contemporary history.

Joyce, of course, uses mythical inference. His story of Bloom and Dedalus is set in the contemporary world, his characters are insistently contemporary Dubliners. But their relationships, their actions are designed to recall constantly the wanderings of Ulysses in Homer. This is one approach to myth; another, and more common, is to display the ancient story in its own setting, but in such a manner as to remind the audience of its direct relevance to the world in which they live. The Joycean method was followed by Mr. Eliot himself in adapting Aeschylus' *Oresteia* for his *The Family Reunion* and by Eugene O'Neill in his trilogy, *Mourning Becomes Electra*. But, particularly in France, the rewriting of myth in the setting of its own time has been customary for playwrights as varied as Jean Cocteau, Jean Anouilh, André Gide, and Jean Giraudoux.

French playwrights have an advantage denied to those of the English-speaking world, for the classics of their repertory, constantly kept alive in state-supported theaters, are the works of Corneille and Racine, seventeenth-century dramatists who devoted themselves almost exclusively to the stories of Greece and Rome. The French audience thus had through playgoing experience almost as close a familiarity with the heroes and their histories as the audiences of Athens and Rome. That is to say, the French playwrights immediately benefited from the existence of true classic irony. The Greek spectator knew what the fated outcome was to be and watched the hero struggle against it. So the modern spectator—at least in France—knows that the Trojan War did take place, knows most of the characters involved in the war and their destinies. The playwright ignores the war itself and its familiar events in devising his action, but the audience must never be unaware of the ultimate end of Hector, Andromache, Hecuba, Helen. Giraudoux utilizes this knowledge on the part of his audience to make a very simple action yield a highly complex and disturbing theatrical experience.

The opening line of the play goes directly to the simple, single action, but hardly suggests the audacity of Giraudoux's purpose. "There's not going to be a Trojan War, Cassandra!" cries Andromache. The speaker is the heroic wife who, after the war, will become part of the victor's spoils. Her companion is the priestess of Apollo, destined for the bed of Agamemnon, leader of the Greek forces. Shortly we meet Hector, prince of Troy, and are reminded of his corpse dragged ignominiously around the walls of his besieged city. Among the other characters are Hecuba, consigned by legend to the despised Ulysses, and Polyxene, sacrificed on the tomb of Achilles. These figures take the stage with their intimations of catastrophe, and fall to debating the possibility of averting a war as if it were not at all inevitable.

Perhaps, at first, the audience may take it as a game, sporting with history, but not for long. The passion of the characters, the glow of their deepest feelings so magnificently expressed, begin to create a hope in the spectator that there will in fact be no Trojan War. The forthrightness of Hector's arguments, the reasonableness of most of those who must be won over, increasingly persuades the spectator that history must be wrong, that the war was a fiction of Greeks seeking national glory. Hector, in his efforts to persuade becomes the spokesman, not just for Troy, but for the modern world.

Everyone is most persuadable. The cause of the war is the rape of Helen, but Giraudoux presents the Paris-Helen *entente* as surprisingly unimpassioned, uncommitted. Paris is willing to leave the decision to Priam, Priam is willing to leave it to Helen, and Helen, indifferent to all things, agrees. Even Ulysses, the Greek ambassador who can out-argue Hector with ease, gives in for reasons of his own. The opposing forces are, of course, the forces of unreason: the sailors with their parodied sense of national honor, Demokos with his poet's inversion of the relationship between names and objects, the gods with their contradictory demands. Hector and his friends are so patently superior to the opposition in persuasiveness that their success becomes increasingly predictable as the play proceeds.

Tiger at the Gates, however, is a play and not a debate, and Giraudoux's inventive use of the tools of the theater is important in arriving at the nature of the experience he intended. Iris, the befuddled messenger of the gods, for example, is something more than comic relief. Her self-canceling messages remind the audience, not of the divinely dominated world in which the characters must pursue their appointed ends, but of the irresponsibility of supernatural forces of which Cassandra has spoken in the opening scene: the decisive actions, whatever they are to be, must be taken in Troy by the characters; the gods will play their own games. The *deus ex machina* so useful to Euripides and his characters in determining the outcome of their conflicts is revived by Giraudoux for a very different purpose.

Even so commonplace an element of the stage as the curtain behaves in a new way. As Hector overcomes obstacle after obstacle, as he controls his own wrath during the attempted violation of his wife, as Ulysses and his companion start for the ships, the curtain begins to descend on a triumphant repetition of the opening line of the play. At this familiar signal that the play has reached its conclusion, the audience can only share Hector's sense of elation: the impossible has been accomplished. But the curtain changes its mind, rises again, thus underlining the act of unreason which permits history to run its remembered course.

With words, another of the playwright's tools, Giraudoux is equally self-conscious. His characters argue and orate, they make love, and law, and poetry. But always the playwright is raising semantic questions: what do you mean when you say *love* or *honor*? What is the truth of metaphor? What is the relation between the effect of a poem and its content? It is a bitter irony that a man of letters should portray a poet as the most effective force of unreason, the ultimate cause of the meaningless war. Giraudoux here returns not to Aristotle, who saw the poet as psychiatrist and healer, but to Plato who would exclude poets— as liars—from his ideal state. And Cassandra's final prophecy resigns the reputation of the Trojans to the hands of Homer, the Greek poet and, by inference, liar.

A French critic of the original performance of *Tiger at the Gates* (1935) described it as a poem of despair. A production, actually in rehearsal, in New York was abandoned with the outbreak of the Second World War. And it is quite possible that the playwright, looking at the condition of France in 1935—a political, economic, and social chaos—might well have been moved to create an equally chaotic world to mirror his despair. But the later history of the play suggests that this interpretation is limited, shortsighted. As the liberating armies of the allies moved across Europe, as theaters were reopened, or purged of the usurping forces, *Tiger at the Gates* was one of the first plays to be restored to the repertory in country after country. A decade after its writing it had become not a poem of despair but a comedy of hope.

That it is at least in part a comedy must not be forgotten. There are moments of satire, there is the cynicism of Hecuba and Cassandra, but there are also scenes of wit, of broad farce, even of slapstick. And these comic scenes are not the equivalent of whistling in a graveyard; they are in the old tradition of Plautus or Molière, the joyous exploitation of the follies of man. They are meant to be laughed at, in the full knowledge that however true they may be of the particular, the individual, even the type, they are not cosmic truth: the particular will change, the individual will die, the cosmos will endure. War, however catastrophic, is never final.

Tiger at the Gates is a complex experience of irony. Its combination of comedy and seriousness, of extravaganza, burlesque, pathos, its manipulation of myth and the elements of theater, create an almost unique play. If there is despair in Hector's "The war will happen," the preceding action has clearly made the point that war is not inevitable if men are not misled by words, by thoughtlessness, by false pride, by refusal to face reality. The war is caused by small errors rather than large crimes. And yet a less didactic method of making a point can hardly be imagined. If this is a triumph of the theater, an entertainment which makes full use of the resources of the physical medium, it is also a triumph of the drama: idea, plot, structure, characters, all work to a common end, the exposition not merely of the futility of war, but of the cheerful stupidity of man, who will allow words, which are his invention and his servants, to become his masters.

Giraudoux' play exists in two different French versions, one published for the reading public, and a somewhat different version for the original production. Christopher Fry's translation is a faithful rendering of the acting version although the title has, on questionable grounds, been altered. The original title, announcing and enhancing the irony of the dramatic experience, should be translated as *The Trojan War Will Not Take Place*.

Characters

ANDROMACHE

CASSANDRA

LAUNDRESS

HECTOR

PARIS

PRIAM

DEMOKOS

HECUBA

MATHEMATICIAN

SERVANT

POLYXENE

HELEN

MESSENGER

TROILUS

ABNEOS

BUSIRIS

AJAX

ULYSSES

A TOPMAN

OLPIDES

SERVANT

SENATOR

SAILOR

PEACE, IRIS, FIRST OLD MAN, SECOND OLD MAN,
MESSENGERS, GUARDS, CROWD

TIGER AT THE GATES

Jean Giraudoux

Translated by Christopher Fry

ACT ONE

ANDROMACHE. There's not going to be a Trojan War, Cassandra!

CASSANDRA. I shall take that bet, Andromache.

ANDROMACHE. The Greeks are quite right to protest. We are going to receive their ambassador very civilly. We shall wrap up his little Helen and give her back to him.

CASSANDRA. We shall receive him atrociously. We shall refuse to give Helen back. And there *will* be a Trojan War.

ANDROMACHE. Yes, if Hector were not here. But he is here, Cassandra, he is home again. You can hear the trumpets. At this moment he is marching into the city, victorious. And Hector is certainly going to have something to say. When he left, three months ago, he promised me this war would be the last.

CASSANDRA. It is the last. The next is still ahead of him.

ANDROMACHE. Doesn't it ever tire you to see and prophesy only disasters?

CASSANDRA. I see nothing. I prophesy nothing. All I ever do is to take account of two great stupidities: the stupidity of men, and the wild stupidity of the elements.

ANDROMACHE. Why should there be a war? Paris and Helen don't care for each other any longer.

CASSANDRA. Do you think it will matter if Paris and Helen don't care for each other any longer? Has destiny ever been interested in whether things were still true or not?

ANDROMACHE. I don't know what destiny is.

CASSANDRA. I'll tell you. It is simply the relentless logic of each day we live.

ANDROMACHE. I don't understand abstractions.

CASSANDRA. Never mind. We can try a metaphor. Imagine a tiger. You can understand that? It's a nice, easy metaphor. A sleeping tiger.

ANDROMACHE. Let it sleep.

CASSANDRA. There's nothing I should like better. But certain cocksure statements have been prodding him out of his sleep. For some considerable time Troy has been full of them.

ANDROMACHE. Full of what?

CASSANDRA. Of cocksure statements, a confident belief that the world, and the supervision of the world, is the province of mankind in general, and Trojan men and women in particular.

ANDROMACHE. I don't follow you.

CASSANDRA. Hector at this very moment is marching into Troy?

ANDROMACHE. Yes. Hector at this very moment has come home to his wife.

CASSANDRA. And Hector's wife is going to have a child?

ANDROMACHE. Yes; I am going to have a child.

CASSANDRA. Don't you call these statements a little over-confident?

ANDROMACHE. Don't frighten me, Cassandra.

[*A* YOUNG LAUNDRESS *goes past with an armful of linen.*]

LAUNDRESS. What a beautiful day, miss!

CASSANDRA. Does it seem so, indeed?

LAUNDRESS. It's the most beautiful Spring day Troy has seen this year. [*Exit.*]

CASSANDRA. Even the laundrymaid is confident!

ANDROMACHE. And so she should be, Cassandra. How can you talk of a war on a day like this? Happiness is falling on us out of the sky.

CASSANDRA. Like a blanket of snow.

ANDROMACHE. And beauty, as well. Look at the sunshine. It is finding more mother-of-pearl on the rooftops of Troy than was ever dragged up from the bed of the sea. And do you hear the sound coming up from the fishermen's houses, and the movement of the trees, like the murmuring of sea shells? If ever there were a chance to see men finding a way to live in peace, it is today. To live in peace, in humility. And to be immortal.

CASSANDRA. Yes, I am sure those cripples who have been carried out to lie in their doorways feel how immortal they are.

ANDROMACHE. And to be good. Do you see that horseman, in the advance-guard, leaning from his saddle to stroke a cat on the battlements? Perhaps this is also going to be the first day of true fellowship between men and the animals.

CASSANDRA. You talk too much. Destiny, the tiger, is getting restive, Andromache!

ANDROMACHE. Restive, maybe, in young girls looking for husbands; but not otherwise.

CASSANDRA. You are wrong. Hector has come home in triumph to the wife he adores. The tiger begins to rouse, and opens one eye. The incurables lie out on their benches in the sun and feel immortal. The tiger stretches himself. Today is the chance for peace to enthrone herself over all the world. The tiger licks his lips. And Andromache is going to have a son! And the horsemen have started leaning from their saddles to stroke tom-cats on the battlements! The tiger starts to prowl.

ANDROMACHE. Be quiet!

CASSANDRA. He climbs noiselessly up the palace steps. He pushes open the doors with his snout. And here he is, here he is!

[HECTOR's *voice:* Andromache!]

ANDROMACHE. You are lying! It is Hector!

CASSANDRA. Whoever said it was not?

[*Enter* HECTOR.]

ANDROMACHE. Hector!

HECTOR. Andromache!

[THEY *embrace.*]

And good morning to you, too, Cassandra. Ask Paris to come to me, if you will. As soon as he can.

[CASSANDRA *lingers.*]

Have you something to tell me?

ANDROMACHE. Don't listen to her! Some catastrophe or other!

HECTOR. Tell me.

CASSANDRA. Your wife is going to have a child.

[*Exit* CASSANDRA.]

[HECTOR *takes* ANDROMACHE *in his arms, leads her to a stone bench, and sits beside her. A short pause.*]

HECTOR. Will it be a son or a daughter?

ANDROMACHE. Which did you want to create when you called it into life?

HECTOR. A thousand boys. A thousand girls.

ANDROMACHE. Why? Because it would give you a thousand women to hold in your arms? You are going to be disappointed. It will be a son, one single son.

HECTOR. That may very well be. Usually more boys are born than girls at the end of a war.

ANDROMACHE. And before a war? Which, before a war?

HECTOR. Forget wars, Andromache, even this war. It's over. It lost you a father and a brother, but it gave you back a husband.

ANDROMACHE. It has been too kind. It may think better of it presently.

HECTOR. Don't worry. We won't give it the chance. Directly I leave you I shall go into the square, and formally close the Gates of War. They will never open again.

ANDROMACHE. Close them, then. But they will open again.

HECTOR. You can even tell me the day, perhaps?

ANDROMACHE. I can even tell you the day: the day when the cornfields are heavy and golden, when the vines are stooping, ready for harvest, and every house is sheltering a contented couple.

HECTOR. And peace, no doubt, at its very height?

ANDROMACHE. Yes. And my son is strong and glowing with life.

[HECTOR *embraces her.*]

HECTOR. Perhaps your son will be a coward. That's one possible safe-guard.

ANDROMACHE. He won't be a coward. But perhaps I shall have cut off the index finger of his right hand.

HECTOR. If every mother cut off her son's right-hand index finger, the armies of the world would fight without index fingers. And if they cut off their sons' right legs, the armies would be one-legged. And if they put out their eyes, the armies would be blind, but there would still be armies: blind armies groping to find the fatal place in the enemy's groin, or to get at his throat.

ANDROMACHE. I would rather kill him.

HECTOR. There's a truly maternal solution to war!

ANDROMACHE. Don't laugh. I can still kill him before he is born.

HECTOR. Don't you want to see him at all, not even for a moment? After that, you would think again. Do you mean never to see your son?

ANDROMACHE. It is your son that interests me. Hector, it's because he is yours, because he is you, that I'm so afraid. You don't know how like you he is. Even in this no-man's-land where he is waiting, he already has everything, all those qualities you brought to this life we live together. He has your tenderness, your silences. If you love war, he will love it. Do you love war?

HECTOR. Why ask such a question?

ANDROMACHE. Admit, sometimes you love it.

HECTOR. If a man can love what takes away hope, and happiness, and all those nearest to his heart.

ANDROMACHE. And you know it can be so. Men do love it.

HECTOR. If they let themselves be fooled by that little burst of divinity the gods give them at the moment of attack.

ANDROMACHE. Ah, there, you see! At the moment of attack you feel like a god.

HECTOR. More often not as much as a man. But sometimes, on certain mornings, you get up from the ground feeling lighter, astonished, altered. Your whole body, and the armor on your back, have a different weight, they seem to be made of a different metal. You are invulnerable. A tenderness comes over you, submerging you, a kind of tenderness of battle: you are tender because you are pitiless; what, in fact, the tenderness of the gods must be. You advance toward the enemy slowly, almost absentmindedly, but lovingly. And you try not to crush a beetle crossing your path. You brush off the mosquito without hurting it. You never at any time had more respect for the life you meet on your way.

ANDROMACHE. And then the enemy comes?

HECTOR. Then the enemy comes, frothing at the mouth. You pity him; you can see him there, behind the swollen veins and the whites of his eyes, the helpless, willing little man of business, the well-meaning husband and son-in-law who likes to grow his own vegetables. You feel a sort of love for him. You love the wart on his cheek and the cast in his eye. You love him. But he comes on; he is insistent. Then you kill him.

ANDROMACHE. And you bend over the wretched corpse as though you are a god; but you are not a god; you can't give back his life again.

HECTOR. You don't wait to bend over him. There are too many more waiting for you, frothing at the mouth and howling hate. Too many more unassuming, law-abiding family men.

ANDROMACHE. Then you kill them.

HECTOR. You kill them. Such is war.

ANDROMACHE. All of them: you kill them all?

HECTOR. This time we killed them all. Quite deliberately. They belonged to an incorrigibly warlike race, the reason why wars go on and multiply in Asia. Only one of them escaped.

ANDROMACHE. In a thousand years time, there the warlike race will be again, descended from that one man. His escape made all that slaughter futile after all. My son is going to love war, just as you do.

HECTOR. I think, now that I've lost my love for it, I hate it.

ANDROMACHE. How do you come to hate what you once worshiped?

HECTOR. You know what it's like when you find out a friend is a liar? Whatever he says, after that, sounds false, however true it may be. And strangely enough, war used to promise me many kinds of virtue: goodness, generosity, and a contempt for anything base and mean. I felt I owed it all my strength and zest for life, even my private happiness, you, Andromache. And until this last campaign there was no enemy I haven't loved.

ANDROMACHE. Very soon you will say you only kill what you love.

HECTOR. It's hard to explain how all the sounds of war combined to make me think it was something noble. The galloping of horse in the night, the clatter of bowls and dishes where the cooks were moving in and out of the firelight, the brush of silk and metal against your tent as the night-patrol went past, and the cry of the falcon wheeling high above the sleeping army and their unsleeping captain: it all seemed then so right, marvelously right.

ANDROMACHE. But not this time: this time war had no music for you?

HECTOR. Why was that? Because I am older? Or was it just the kind of weariness with your job which, for instance, a carpenter will be suddenly seized by, with a table half finished, as I was seized one morning, standing over an adversary of my own age, about to put an end to him? Up to that time, a man I was going to kill had always seemed my direct opposite. This time I was kneeling on a mirror, the death I was going to give was a kind of suicide. I don't know what the carpenter does at such a time, whether he throws away his hammer and plane, or goes on with it. I went on with it. But after that nothing remained of the perfect trumpet note of war. The spear as it slid against my shield rang suddenly false; so did the shock of the killed against the ground, and, some hours later, the palace crumbling into ruin. And, moreover, war knew that I understood, and gave up any pretence of shame. The cries of the dying sounded false. I had come to that.

ANDROMACHE. But it all still sounded right for the rest of them.

HECTOR. The rest of them heard it as I did. The army I brought back hates war.

ANDROMACHE. An army with poor hearing.

HECTOR. No. When we first came in sight of Troy, an hour ago, you can't imagine how everything in that moment sounded true for them. There wasn't a regiment which didn't halt, racked to the heart by this sense of returning music. So much so, we were afraid to march boldly in through the gates: we broke up into groups outside the walls. It feels like the only job worthy of a good army, laying peaceful siege to the open cities of your own country.

ANDROMACHE. You haven't understood, this is where things are falser than anywhere. War is here, in Troy, Hector. That is what welcomed you at the gates.

HECTOR. What do you mean?

ANDROMACHE. You haven't heard that Paris has carried off Helen?

HECTOR. They told me so. What else?

ANDROMACHE. Did you know that the Greeks are demanding her back? And their ambassador arrives today? And if we don't give her up, it means war.

HECTOR. Why shouldn't we give her up? I shall give her back to them myself.

ANDROMACHE. Paris will never agree to it.

HECTOR. Paris will agree, and very soon. Cassandra is bringing him to me.

ANDROMACHE. But Paris can't agree. His honor, as you all call it, won't let him. Nor his love either, he may tell you.

HECTOR. Well, we shall see. Run and ask Priam if he will let me speak to him at once. And set your heart at rest. All the Trojans who have been fighting, or who can fight, are against a war.

ANDROMACHE. There are still the others, remember.

[*As* ANDROMACHE *goes,* CASSANDRA *enters with* PARIS.]

CASSANDRA. Here is Paris.

HECTOR. Congratulations, Paris. I hear you have been very well occupied while we were away.

PARIS. Not badly. Thank you.

HECTOR. What is this story they tell me about Helen?

PARIS. Helen is a very charming person. Isn't she, Cassandra?

CASSANDRA. Fairly charming.

PARIS. Why these reservations today? It was only yesterday you said you thought she was extremely pretty.

CASSANDRA. She is extremely pretty, and fairly charming.

PARIS. Hasn't she the ways of a young, gentle gazelle?

CASSANDRA. No.

PARIS. But you were the one who first said she was like a gazelle.

CASSANDRA. I made a mistake. Since then I have seen a gazelle again.

HECTOR. To hell with gazelles! Doesn't she look any more like a woman than that?

PARIS. She isn't the type of woman we know here, obviously.

CASSANDRA. What is the type of woman we know here?

PARIS. Your type, my dear sister. The fearfully unremote sort of woman.

CASSANDRA. When your Greek makes love she is a long way off, I suppose?

PARIS. You know perfectly well what I'm trying to say. I have had enough of Asiatic women. They hold you in their arms as though they were glued there, their kisses are like battering-rams, their words chew right into you. The more they undress the more elaborate they seem, until when they're naked they are more overdressed than ever. And they paint their faces to look as though they mean to imprint themselves on you. And they do imprint themselves on you. In short, you are definitely *with* them. But Helen is far away from me, even held in my arms.

HECTOR. Very interesting! But, one wonders, is it really worth a war, to allow Paris to make love at a distance?

CASSANDRA. With distance. He loves women to be distant but right under his nose.

PARIS. To have Helen with you not with you is worth anything in the world.

HECTOR. How did you fetch her away? Willingly, or did you compel her?

PARIS. Listen, Hector! You know women as well as I do. They are only willing when you compel them, but after that they're as enthusiastic as you are.

HECTOR. On horseback, in the usual style of seducers, leaving a heap of horse manure under the windows.

PARIS. Is this a court of enquiry?

HECTOR. Yes, it is. Try for once to answer precisely and accurately. Have you insulted her husband's house, or the Greek earth?

PARIS. The Greek water, a little. She was bathing.

CASSANDRA. She is born of the foam, is she? This cold one is born of the foam, like Venus.

HECTOR. You haven't disfigured the walls of the palace with offensive drawings, as you usually do? You didn't shout to the echoes any word which they would at once repeat to the betrayed husband?

PARIS. No. Menelaus was naked on the river bank, busy removing a crab from his big toe. He watched my boat sail past as if the wind were carrying his clothes away.

HECTOR. Looking furious?

PARIS. The face of a king being nipped by a crab isn't likely to look beatific.

HECTOR. No onlookers?

PARIS. My crew.

HECTOR. Perfect!

PARIS. Why perfect? What are you getting at?

HECTOR. I say perfect, because you have done nothing irrevocable. In other words: she was undressed, so neither her clothes nor her belongings have been insulted. Nothing except her body, which is negligible. I've enough acquaintance with the Greeks to know they will concoct a divine adventure out of it, to their own glory, the story of this little Greek queen who goes down into the sea, and quietly comes up again a few months later, with a look on her face of perfect innocence.

CASSANDRA. We can be quite sure of the look on her face.

PARIS. You think that I'm going to take Helen back to Menelaus?

HECTOR. We don't ask so much of you, or of her. The Greek ambassador will take care of it. He will put her back in the sea himself, like a gardener planting water-lilies, at a particular chosen spot. You will give her into his hands this evening.

PARIS. I don't know whether you are allowing yourself to notice how monstrous you are being, to suppose that a man who has the prospect of a night with Helen will agree to giving it up.

CASSANDRA. You still have an afternoon with Helen. Surely that's more Greek?

HECTOR. Don't be obstinate. We know you of old. This isn't the first separation you've accepted.

PARIS. My dear Hector, that's true enough. Up to now I have always accepted separations fairly cheerfully. Parting from a woman, however well you love her, induces a most pleasant state of mind, which I know how to value as well as anybody. You come out of her arms and take your first lonely walk through the town, and, the first little dressmaker you meet, you notice with a shock of surprise how fresh and unconcerned she looks, after that last sight you have had of the dear face you parted from, her nose red with weeping. Because you have come away from such broken, despairing farewells, the laundrygirls and the fruitsellers laughing their heads off, more than make up for whatever you've lost in the parting. By losing one person your life has become entirely repeopled. All the women in the world have been created for you afresh; they are all your own, in the liberty, honor, and peace of your conscience. Yes, you're quite right: when a love-affair is broken off it reaches its highest point of exaltation. Which is why I shall never be parted from Helen, because with Helen I feel as though I had broken with every other woman in the world, and that gives me the sensation of being free a thousand times over instead of once.

HECTOR. Because she doesn't love you. Everything you say proves it.

PARIS. If you like. But, if I had to choose one out of all the possible ways of passion, I would choose the way Helen doesn't love me.

HECTOR. I'm extremely sorry. But you will give her up.

PARIS. You are not the master here.

HECTOR. I am your elder brother, and the future master.

PARIS. Then order me about in the future. For the present, I obey my father.

HECTOR. That's all I want! You're willing that we should put this to Priam and accept his judgment?

PARIS. Perfectly willing.

HECTOR. On your solemn word? We both swear to accept that?

CASSANDRA. Mind what you're doing, Hector! Priam is mad for Helen. He would rather give up his daughters.

HECTOR. What nonsense is this?

PARIS. For once she is telling the truth about the present instead of the future.

CASSANDRA. And all our brothers, and all our uncles, and all our great-great uncles! Helen has a guard-of-honor which includes every old man in the city. Look there. It is time for her walk. Do you see, there's a fringe of white beards draped all along the battlements?

HECTOR. A beautiful sight. The beards are white, and the faces red.

CASSANDRA. Yes; it's the blood pressure. They should be waiting at the Scamander Gate, to welcome the victorious troops. But no; they are all at the Scaean Gate, waiting for Helen.

HECTOR. Look at them, all leaning forward as one man, like storks when they see a rat going by.

CASSANDRA. The rat is Helen.

PARIS. Is it?

CASSANDRA. There she is: on the second terrace, standing to adjust her sandal, and giving careful thought to the crossing of her legs.

HECTOR. Incredible. All the old men of Troy are there looking down at her.

CASSANDRA. Not all. There are certain crafty ones looking up at her.

[*Cries offstage:* Long live Beauty!]

HECTOR. What are they shouting?

PARIS. They're shouting "Long live Beauty!"

CASSANDRA. I quite agree with them, if they mean that they themselves should die as quickly as possible.

[*Cries offstage:* Long live Venus!]

HECTOR. And what now?

CASSANDRA. "Long live Venus." They are shouting only words without R's in them because of their lack of teeth. Long live Beauty, long live Venus, long live Helen. At least they imagine they're shouting, though, as you can hear, all they are doing is simply increasing a mumble to its highest power.

HECTOR. What has Venus to do with it?

CASSANDRA. They imagine it was Venus who gave us Helen. To show her gratitude to Paris for awarding her the apple on first sight.

HECTOR. That was another brilliant stroke of yours.

PARIS. Stop playing the elder brother!

[*Enter* TWO OLD MEN.]

FIRST OLD MAN. Down there we see her better.

SECOND OLD MAN. We had a very good view.

FIRST OLD MAN. But she can hear us better from up here. Come on. One, two, three!

BOTH. Long live Helen!

SECOND OLD MAN. It's a little tiring at our age, to have to climb up and down these impossible steps all the time, according to whether we want to look at her or to cheer her.

FIRST OLD MAN. Would you like us to alternate? One day we will cheer her? Another day we will look at her?

SECOND OLD MAN. You are mad! One day without looking at Helen, indeed! Goodness me, think what we've seen of her today! One, two, three!

BOTH. Long live Helen!

FIRST OLD MAN. And now down we go again!

[*They run off.*]

CASSANDRA. You see what they're like, Hector. I don't know how their poor lungs are going to stand it.

HECTOR. But our father can't be like this.

PARIS. Hector, before we have this out in front of my father, I suppose you wouldn't like to take just one look at Helen.

HECTOR. I don't care a fig about Helen. Ah: greetings to you, father!

[PRIAM *enters, with* HECUBA, ANDROMACHE, *the poet* DEMOKOS *and* ANOTHER OLD MAN. HECUBA *leads by the hand little* POLYXENE.]

PRIAM. What was it you said?

HECTOR. I said that we should make haste to shut the Gates of War, father, see them bolted and padlocked, so that not even a gnat can get between them.

PRIAM. I thought what you said was somewhat shorter.

DEMOKOS. He said he didn't care a fig about Helen.

PRIAM. Look over here.

[HECTOR *obeys.*]

Do you see her?

HECUBA. Indeed he sees her. Who, I ask myself, doesn't see her, or hasn't seen her? She takes the road which goes the whole way round the city.

DEMOKOS. It is Beauty's perfect circle.

PRIAM. Do you see her?

HECTOR. Yes, I see her. What of it?

DEMOKOS. Priam is asking you what you see.

HECTOR. I see a young woman adjusting her sandal.

CASSANDRA. She takes some time to adjust her sandal.

PARIS. I carried her off naked; she left her clothes in Greece. Those are your sandals, Cassandra. They're a bit big for her.

CASSANDRA. Anything's too big for these little women.

HECTOR. I see two charming buttocks.

HECUBA. He sees what all of you see.

PRIAM. I'm sorry for you!

HECTOR. Why?

PRIAM. I had no idea that the young men of Troy had come to this.

HECTOR. What have they come to?

PRIAM. To being impervious to beauty.

DEMOKOS. And, consequently, ignorant of love. And, consequently, unrealistic. To us who are poets reality is love or nothing.

HECTOR. But the old men, you think, can appreciate love and beauty?

HECUBA. But of course. If you make love, or if you are beautiful, you don't need to understand these things.

HECTOR. You come across beauty, father, at every street corner. I'm not alluding to Helen, though at the moment she condescends to walk our streets.

PRIAM. You are being unfair, Hector. Surely there have been occasions in your life when a woman has seemed to be more than merely herself, as though a radiance of thoughts and feelings glowed from her flesh, taking a special brilliance from it.

DEMOKOS. As a ruby represents blood.

HECTOR. Not to those who have seen blood. I have just come back from a close acquaintance with it.

DEMOKOS. A symbol, you understand. Soldier though you are, you have surely heard of symbolism? Surely you have come across women who as soon as you saw them seemed to you to personify intelligence, harmony, gentleness, whatever it might be?

HECTOR. It has happened.

DEMOKOS. And what did you do?

HECTOR. I went closer, and that was the end of it. And what does this we see here personify?

DEMOKOS. We have told you before: Beauty.

HECUBA. Then send her quickly back to the Greeks if you want her to personify that for long. Blonde beauty doesn't usually last for ever.

DEMOKOS. It's impossible to talk to these women!

HECUBA. Then don't talk *about* women. You're not showing much gallantry, I might say; nor patriotism either. All other races choose one of their own women as their symbol, even if they have flat noses and lips like two fishes on a plate. It's only you who have to go outside your own country to find it.

HECTOR. Listen, father: we are just back from a war, and we have come home exhausted. We have made quite certain of peace on our continent for ever. From now on we mean to live in happiness, and we mean our wives to be able to love us without anxiety, and to bear our children.

DEMOKOS. Wise principles, but war has never prevented wives from having children.

HECTOR. So explain to me why we have come back to find the city transformed, all because of Helen? Explain to me what you think she has given to us, worth a quarrel with the Greeks?

MATHEMATICIAN. Anybody will tell you! I can tell you myself!

HECUBA. Listen to the mathematician!

MATHEMATICIAN. Yes, listen to the mathematician! And don't think that mathematicians have no concern with women! We're the land-surveyors of your personal landscape. I can't tell you how we mathematicians suffer to see any slight disproportion of the flesh, on the chin or the thigh, any infringement of your geometical desirability. Well now, until this day mathematicians have never been satisfied with the countryside surrounding Troy. The line linking the plain with the hills seemed to us too slack: the line from the hills to the mountains too taut. Now, since Helen came, the country has taken on meaning and vigor. And, what is particularly evident to true mathematicians, space and volume have now found in Helen a common denominator. We can abolish all the instruments we have invented to reduce the universe to a manageable equation. There are no more feet and inches, ounces, pounds, milligrams or leagues. There is only the weight of Helen's footfall, the length of Helen's arm, the range of Helen's look or voice; and the movement of the air as she goes past is the measure of the winds. That is what the mathematicians will tell you.

HECUBA. The old fool is crying.

PRIAM. My dear son, you have only to look at this crowd, and you will understand what Helen is. She is a kind of absolution. To each one of these old men, whom you can see now like a frieze of grotesque heads all round the city walls: to the old swindler, the old thief, the old pandar, to all the old failures, she has shown they always had a secret longing to rediscover the beauty they had lost. If throughout their lives beauty had always been as close at hand as Helen is today, they would never have tricked their friends, or sold their daughters, or drunk away their inheritance. Helen is like a pardon to them: a new beginning for them, their whole future.

HECTOR. These old men's ancient futures are no concern of mine.

DEMOKOS. Hector, as a poet I approach things by the way of poetry. Imagine if beauty, never, at any time, touched our language. Imagine there being no such word as "delight."

HECTOR. We should get on well enough without it. I get on without it already. "Delight" is a word I use only when I'm absolutely driven to it.

DEMOKOS. Well, then, the word "desirable": you could get on without that as well, I suppose?

HECTOR. If it could be bought only at the cost of war, yes, I could get on without the word "desirable."

DEMOKOS. One of the most beautiful words there are was found only at the cost of war: the word "courage."

HECTOR. It has been well paid for.

HECUBA. And the word "cowardice" was inevitably found at the same time.

PRIAM. My son, why do you so deliberately not understand us?

HECTOR. I understand you very well. With the help of a quibble, by pretending to persuade us to fight for beauty you want to get us to fight for a woman.

PRIAM. Would you never go to war for any woman?

HECTOR. Certainly not!

HECUBA. And he would be unchivalrously right.

CASSANDRA. If there were only one woman, then perhaps he would go to war for her. But we have exceeded that number, quite extravagantly.

DEMOKOS. Wouldn't you go to war to rescue Andromache?

HECTOR. Andromache and I have already made our secret plans for escaping from any prison in the world, and finding our way back to each other again.

DEMOKOS. Even if there's no hope of it on earth?

HECTOR. Even then.

HECUBA. You have done well to unmask them, Hector. They want you to make war for the sake of a woman; it's the kind of lovemaking men believe in who are past making love in any other way.

DEMOKOS. And doesn't that make you all the more valuable?

HECUBA. Ah yes! You may say so!

DEMOKOS. Excuse me, but I can't agree with you. The sex which gave me my mother will always have my respect, even its least worthy representatives.

HECUBA. We know that. You have, as we know, shown your respect for instance to —

[*The* SERVANTS *who have stood by to hear the argument burst out laughing.*]

PRIAM. Hecuba! Daughters! What can this mean. Why on earth are you all so up in arms? The council are considering giving the city a public holiday in honor of one of your sex.

ANDROMACHE. I know of only one humiliation for a woman: injustice.

DEMOKOS. It's painful to say so, but there's no one knows less what a woman is than a woman.

[*The* YOUNG SERVANT, *passing:* Oh, dear! dear!]

HECUBA. We know perfectly well. I will tell you myself what a woman is.

DEMOKOS. Don't let them talk, Priam. You never know what they might say.

HECUBA. They might tell the truth.

PRIAM. I have only to think of one of you, my dears, to know what a woman is.

DEMOKOS. In the first place, she is the source of our energy. You know that, Hector. The soldiers who haven't a portrait of a woman in their kit aren't worth anything.

CASSANDRA. The source of your pride, yes, I agree.

HECUBA. Of your vices.

ANDROMACHE. She is a poor bundle of uncertainty, a poor mass of fears, who detests whatever is difficult, and adores whatever is vulgar and easy.

HECTOR. Dear Andromache!

HECUBA. It's very simple. I have been a woman for fifty years, and I've never yet been able to discover precisely what it is I am.

DEMOKOS. Secondly, whether she likes it or not, she's the only reward for courage. Ask any soldier. To kill a man is to merit a woman.

ANDROMACHE. She loves cowards and libertines. If Hector were a coward or a libertine I shouldn't love him less; I might even love him more.

PRIAM. Don't go too far, Andromache. You will prove the very opposite of what you want to prove.

POLYXENE. She is greedy. She tells lies.

DEMOKOS. So we're to say nothing of her fidelity, her purity: we are not to mention them?

THE SERVANT. Oh, dear! dear!

DEMOKOS. What did you say?

THE SERVANT. I said "Oh, dear! dear!" I say what I think.

POLYXENE. She breaks her toys. She puts them headfirst into boiling water.

HECUBA. The older we women grow, the more clearly we see what men really are: hypocrites, boasters, he-goats. The older men grow, the more they doll us up with every perfection. There isn't a slut you've hugged behind a wall who isn't transformed in your memories into a loved and lovely creature.

PRIAM. Have you ever deceived me, Hecuba?

HECUBA. Only with yourself; scores of time with yourself.

DEMOKOS. Has Andromache ever deceived Hector?

HECUBA. You can leave Andromache out of this. There is nothing she could recognize in the sad histories of erring women.

ANDROMACHE. But I know if Hector were not my husband, if he were a clubfooted, bandy-legged fisherman I should run after him and find him in his hovel, and lie down on the pile of oyster-shells and seaweed, and give him a son in adultery.

POLYXENE. She pretends to go to sleep at night, but she's really playing games in her head with her eyes shut.

HECUBA [to POLYXENE]. You may well say so! It's dreadful! You know how I scold you for it.

THE SERVANT. The only thing worse than a woman is a man; there are no words to describe him.

DEMOKOS. Then more's the pity if a woman deceives us! More's the pity if she scorns her own value and dignity! If she can't be true to a pattern of perfection which would save her from the ravages of conscience, we have to do it for her.

THE SERVANT. Oh, the kind guardian angel!

PARIS. One thing they've forgotten to say of themselves: they are never jealous.

PRIAM. My dear daughters, the fact that you're so furious is a proof in itself that we are right. I can't conceive of any greater unselfishness than the way you now fight for peace, when peace will give you idle, feeble, chicken-hearted husbands, and war would turn them into men.

DEMOKOS. Into heroes.

HECUBA. Yes, we know the jargon. In wartime a man is called a hero. It doesn't make him any braver, and he runs for his life. But at least it's a hero who is running away.

ANDROMACHE. Father, I must beg you to listen. If you have such a fondness for woman, listen to what they have to say to you, for I can promise I speak for all the women in the world. Let us keep our husbands as they are. The gods took care to see they were surrounded with enough obstacles and dangers to keep them brave and vigorous. Quite enough if they had nothing to cope with except floods and storms! Or only wild animals! The small game, foxes and hares and pheasants, which a woman can scarcely distinguish from the heather they hide in, prove a man's quickness of eye far better than this target you propose: the enemy's heart hiding in flesh and metal. Whenever I have seen a man kill a stag or an eagle, I have offered up thanks to them. I know they died for Hector. Why should you want me to owe Hector to the deaths of other men?

PRIAM. I don't want it, my dear child. But why do you think you are here now, all looking so beautiful, and valiantly demanding peace? Why: because your husbands and your fathers, and their fathers, and theirs, were fighting men. If they had been too lazy and self-indulgent to spring to arms, if they hadn't known how this dull and stupid business we call life suddenly leaps into flame and justifies itself through the scorn men have for it, you would find *you* were the cowards now, and you would be clamoring for war. A man has only one way of being immortal on this earth: he has to forget he is mortal.

ANDROMACHE. Why, exactly so, father: you're only too right. The brave men die in war. It takes great luck or judgment not to be killed. Once at least the head has to bow and the knee has to bend to danger. The soldiers who march back under the triumphal arches are death's deserters. How can a country increase in strength and honor by sending them both to their graves?

PRIAM. Daughter, the first sign of cowardice in a people is their first moment of decay.

ANDROMACHE. But which is the worse cowardice? To appear cowardly to others, and make sure of peace? Or to be cowardly in your own eyes, and let loose a war?

DEMOKOS. Cowardice is not to prefer death on every hand rather than the death of one's native land.

HECUBA. I was expecting poetry at this point. It never lets us down.

ANDROMACHE. Everyone always dies for his country. If you have lived in it, well and wisely and actively, you die for it too.

HECUBA. It would be better if only the old men fought the wars. Every country is the country of youth. When its youth dies it dies with them.

DEMOKOS. All this nonsense about youth! In thirty years time youth is nothing but these old men you talk about.

CASSANDRA. Wrong.

HECUBA. Wrong! When a grown man reaches forty we change him for an old one. He has completely disappeared. There's only the most superficial resemblance between the two of them. Nothing is handed on from one to the other.

DEMOKOS. I still take a serious concern in my fame as a poet.

HECUBA. Yes, that's quite true. And your rheumatism.

[*Another outburst of laughter from the* SERVANTS.]

HECTOR. And you can listen to all this without saying a word, Paris? Can you still not decide to give up an adventure to save us from years of unhappiness and massacre?

PARIS. What do you want me to say? My case is an international problem.

HECTOR. Are you really in love with Helen, Paris?

CASSANDRA. They've become now a kind of symbol of love's devotion. They don't still have to love each other.

PARIS. I worship Helen.

CASSANDRA [*at the rampart*]. Here she is.

HECTOR. If I persuade her to set sail, will you agree?

PARIS. Yes, I'll agree.

HECTOR. Father, if Helen is willing to go back to Greece, will you hold her here by force?

PRIAM. Why discuss the impossible?

HECTOR. Do you call it impossible? If women are a tenth of what you say they are, Helen will go of her own free will.

PARIS. Father, now *I'm* going to ask you to let him do what he wants. You have seen what it's like. As soon as the question of Helen cropped up, this whole tribe royal turned itself into a family conclave of all the poor girl's sisters-in-law, mother- and father-in-law, brother-in-law, worthy of the best middle-class tradition. I doubt if there's anything more humiliating than to be cast for the part of the seducer son in a large family. I've had quite enough of their insinuations. I accept Hector's challenge.

DEMOKOS. Helen's not only yours, Paris. She belongs to the city. She belongs to our country.

MATHEMATICIAN. She belongs to the landscape.

HECUBA. You be quiet, mathematician.

CASSANDRA. Here's Helen; here she is.

HECTOR. Father, I must ask you to let me handle this. Listen; they are calling us to go to the ceremony, to close the Gates of War. Leave this to me. I'll join you soon.

PRIAM. Do you really agree to this, Paris?

PARIS. I'm eager for it.

PRIAM. Very well, then; let it be so. Come along, the rest of you; we will see that the Gates of War are made ready.

CASSANDRA. Those poor gates. They need more oil to shut them than to open them.

[PARIS *and the rest withdraw.* DEMOKOS *stays.*]

HECTOR. What are you waiting for?

DEMOKOS. The visitation of my genius.

HECTOR. Say that again?

DEMOKOS. Every time Helen walks my way I am thrown into a transport of inspiration. I shake all over, break into sweat and improvise. Good heavens, here it is!

[*He declaims.*]

> Beautiful Helen, Helen of Sparta,
> Singular as the evening star,
> The gods forbid that we should part a
> Pair as fair as you and Paris are.

HECTOR. Your line-endings give me a headache.

DEMOKOS. It's an invention of mine. I can obtain effects even more surprising. Listen:

[*Declaims.*]

> Face the great Hector with no qualm,
> Troy's glory though he be, and the world's terror:
> He is the storm, and you the after-calm,
> Yours is the right, and his the boist'rous error.

HECTOR. Get out!

DEMOKOS. What are you glaring at? You look as though you have as little liking for poetry as you have for war.

HECTOR. They make a pretty couple! Now vanish.

[*Exit* DEMOKOS. *Enter* CASSANDRA.]

CASSANDRA. Helen!

[*Enter* HELEN *and* PARIS.]

PARIS. Here he is, Helen darling; this is Hector. He has a proposition to make to you, a perfectly simple proposition. He wants to hand you over to the Greeks, and prove to you that you don't love me. Tell me you do love me, before I leave you with him. Tell me in your own words.

HELEN. I adore you, my sweet.

PARIS. Tell me how beautiful the wave was which swept you away from Greece.

HELEN. Magnificent! A magnificent wave! Where did you see a wave? The sea was so calm.

PARIS. Tell me you hate Menelaus.

HELEN.   Menelaus? I hate him.

PARIS. You haven't finished yet. I shall never again return to Greece. Say that.

HELEN. You will never again return to Greece.

PARIS. No, no, this is about you, my darling.

HELEN. Oh, of course! How silly I am! I shall never again return to Greece.

PARIS. I didn't make her say it.—Now it's up to you.

   [*He goes off.*]

HECTOR. Is Greece a beautiful country?

HELEN. Paris found it ravishing.

HECTOR. I meant is Greece itself beautiful, apart from Helen?

HELEN. How very charming of you.

HECTOR. I was simply wondering what it is really like.

HELEN. Well, there are quite a great many kings, and a great many goats, dotted about on marble.

HECTOR. If the kings are in gold, and the goats angora, that would look pretty well when the sun was rising.

HELEN. I don't get up very early.

HECTOR. And a great many gods as well, I believe? Paris tells me the sky is crawling with them; he tells me you can see the legs of goddesses hanging down from the clouds.

HELEN. Paris always goes about with his nose in the air. He may have seen them.

HECTOR. But you haven't?

HELEN. I am not gifted that way. I will look out for them when I go back there again.

HECTOR. You were telling Paris you would never be going back there.

HELEN. He asked me to tell him so. I adore doing what Paris wants me to do.

HECTOR. I see. Is that also true of what you said about Menelaus? Do you not, after all, hate him?

HELEN. Why should I hate him?

HECTOR. For the one reason which might certainly make for hate. You have seen too much of him.

HELEN. Menelaus? Oh, no! I have never seen Menelaus. On the contrary.

HECTOR. You have never seen your husband?

HELEN. There are some things, and certain people, that stand out in bright colors for me. They are the ones I can see. I believe in them. I have never been able to see Menelaus.

HECTOR. Though I suppose he must have come very close to you sometimes.

HELEN. I have been able to touch him. But I can't honestly tell you I saw him.

HECTOR. They say he never left your side.

HELEN. Apparently. I must have walked across him a great many times without knowing it.

HECTOR. Whereas you have seen Paris.

HELEN. Vividly; in the clearest outline against the sky and the sun.

HECTOR. Does he still stand out as vividly as he did? Look down there: leaning against the rampart.

HELEN. Are you sure that's Paris, down there?

HECTOR. He is waiting for you.

HELEN. Good gracious! He's not nearly as clear as usual!

HECTOR. And yet the wall is freshly whitewashed. Look again: there he is in profile.

HELEN. It's odd how people waiting for you stand out far less clearly than people you are waiting for.

HECTOR. Are you sure that Paris loves you?

HELEN. I don't like knowing about other people's feelings. There is nothing more embarrassing. Just as when you play cards and you see your opponent's hand. You are sure to lose.

HECTOR. What about yourself? Do you love him?

HELEN. I don't much like knowing my own feelings either.

HECTOR. But, listen: when you make love with Paris, when he sleeps in your arms, when you are circled round with Paris, overwhelmed with Paris, haven't you any thoughts about it?

HELEN. My part is over. I leave any thinking to the universe. It does it much better than I do.

HECTOR. Have there been many others, before Paris?

HELEN. Some.

HECTOR. And there will be others after him, wouldn't you say, as long as they stand out in clear relief against the sky, or the wall, or the white sheets on the bed? It is just as I thought it was. You don't love Paris particularly, Helen; you love men.

HELEN. I don't dislike them. They're as pleasant as soap and a sponge and warm water; you feel cleansed and refreshed by them.

HECTOR. Cassandra! Cassandra!

CASSANDRA [*entering*]. What do you want?

HECTOR. Cassandra, Helen is going back this evening with the Greek ambassador.

HELEN. I? What makes you think so?

HECTOR. Weren't you telling me that you didn't love Paris particularly?

HELEN. That was your interpretation. Still, if you like.

HECTOR. I quote my authority. You have the same liking for men as you have for a cake of soap.

HELEN. Yes; or pumice stone perhaps is better. What about it?

HECTOR. Well, then, you're not going to hesitate in your choice between going back to Greece, which you don't mind, and a catastrophe as terrible as war?

HELEN. You don't understand me at all, Hector. Of course I'm not hesitating. It would be very easy to say "I will do this or that, so that this can happen or that can happen." You've discovered my weakness and you are overjoyed. The man who discovers a woman's weakness is like a huntsman in the heat of the day who finds a cool spring. He wallows in it. But you mustn't think, because you have convinced me, you've convinced the future, too. Merely by making children behave as you want them to, you don't alter the course of destiny.

HECTOR. I don't follow your Greek shades and subtleties.

HELEN. It's not a question of shades and subtleties. It's no less than a question of monsters and pyramids.

HECTOR. Do you choose to leave here, yes or no?

HELEN. Don't bully me. I choose what happens in the way I choose men, or anything else. I choose whatever is not indefinite and vague. I choose what I see.

HECTOR. I know, you said that: what you see in the brightest colors. And you don't see yourself returning to Menelaus in a few days' time?

HELEN. No. It's very difficult.

HECTOR. We could no doubt persuade your husband to dress with great brilliance for your return.

HELEN. All the purple dye from all the murex shells in the sea wouldn't make him visible to me.

HECTOR. Here you have a rival, Cassandra. Helen can read the future, too.

HELEN. No, I can't read the future. But when I imagine the future some of the pictures I see are colored, and some are dull and drab. And up to now it has always been the colored scenes which have happened in the end.

HECTOR. We are going to give you back to the Greeks at high noon, on the blinding sand, between the violet sea and the ocher-colored wall. We shall all be in golden armor with red skirts; and my sisters, dressed in green and standing between my white stallion and Priam's black mare, will return you to the Greek ambassador, over whose silver helmet I can imagine tall purple plumes. You see that, I think?

HELEN. No, none of it. It is all quite somber.

HECTOR. You are mocking me, aren't you?

HELEN. Why should I mock you? Very well, then. Let us go, if you like! Let us go and get ready to return me to the Greeks. We shall see what happens.

HECTOR. Do you realize how you insult humanity, or is it unconscious?

HELEN. I don't know what you mean.

HECTOR. You realize that your colored picture-book is holding the world up to ridicule? While we are all battling and making sacrifices to bring about a time we can call our own, there are you, looking at your pictures which nothing in all eternity can alter. What's wrong? Which one has made you stop and stare at it with those blind eyes? I don't doubt it's the one where you are standing here on the ramparts, watching the battle going on below. Is it the battle you see?

HELEN. Yes.

HECTOR. And the city is in ruins or burning, isn't that so?

HELEN. Yes. It's a vivid red.

HECTOR. And what about Paris? You are seeing his body dragged behind a chariot?

HELEN. Oh, do you think that is Paris? I see what looks like a flash of sunlight rolling in the dust. A diamond sparkling on his hand. Yes, it is! Often I don't recognize faces, but I always recognize the jewelry. It's his ring, I'm quite certain.

HECTOR. Exactly. Do I dare to ask you about Andromache, and myself, the scene of Andromache and Hector? You are looking at us. Don't deny it. How do you see us? Happy, grown old, bathed in light?

HELEN. I am not trying to see it.

HECTOR. The scene of Andromache weeping over the body of Hector, does that shine clearer?

HELEN. You seem to know. But sometimes I see things shining, brilliantly shining, and they never happen. No one is infallible.

HECTOR. You needn't go on. I understand. There is a son between the weeping mother and the father stretched on the ground?

HELEN. Yes. He is playing with his father's tangled hair. He is a sweet boy.

HECTOR. And these scenes are there in your eyes, down in the depths of them. Could I see them there?

HELEN. I don't know. Look.

HECTOR. Nothing. Nothing except the ashes of all those fires, the gold and the emerald in dust. How innocent it is, this crystal where the future is waiting. But there should be tears bathing it, and where are they? Would you cry, Helen, if you were going to be killed?

HELEN. I don't know. But I should scream. And I feel I shall scream if you go on at me like this, Hector. I am going to scream.

HECTOR. You will leave for Greece this evening, Helen, otherwise I shall kill you.

HELEN. But I want to leave! I'm prepared to leave. All that I'm trying to tell is that I simply can't manage to distinguish the ship that is going to carry me there. Nothing is shining in the least, neither the metal on the mast, nor the ring in the captain's nose, nor the cabin-boy's eyes, nor anything.

HECTOR. You will go back on a grey sea under a grey sun. But we must have peace.

HELEN. I cannot see peace.

HECTOR. Ask Cassandra to make her appear for you. Cassandra is a sorceress. She can summon up shapes and spirits.

A MESSENGER [entering]. Hector, Priam is asking for you. The priests are opposed to our shutting the Gates of War. They say the gods will consider it an insult.

HECTOR. It is curious how the gods can never speak for themselves in these difficult matters.

MESSENGER. They have spoken for themselves. A thunderbolt has fallen on the temple, several men have been killed, the entrails of the victims have been consulted, and they are unanimously against Helen's return to Greece.

HECTOR. I would give a good deal to be able to consult the entrails of the priests . . . I'll follow you.

[*The* MESSENGER *goes.*]

Well, now, Helen, do we agree about this?

HELEN. Yes.

HECTOR. From now on you will say what I tell you to say? You will do what I tell you to do?

HELEN. Yes.

HECTOR. When we come in front of Ulysses you won't contradict me, you will bear out everything I say?

HELEN. Yes.

HECTOR. Do you hear this, Cassandra? Listen to this solid wall of negation which says Yes! They have all given in to me. Paris has given in to me, Priam has given in to me, Helen has given in to me. And yet I can't help feeling that in each of these apparent victories I have been defeated. You set out, thinking you are going to have to wrestle with giants; you brace yourself to conquer them, and you find yourself wrestling with something inflexible reflected in a woman's eye. You have said yes beautifully, Helen, and you're brimful of a stubborn determination to defy me!

HELEN. That's possible. But how can I help it? It isn't my own determination.

HECTOR. By what peculiar vagary did the world choose to place its mirror in this obtuse head?

HELEN. It's most regrettable, obviously. But can you see any way of defeating the obstinacy of a mirror?

HECTOR. Yes, I've been considering that for the past several minutes.

ANOTHER MESSENGER [*entering*]. Hector, make haste. They are in a turmoil of revolt down on the beach. The Greek ships have been sighted, and they have hoisted their flag not masthead but hatchway. The honor of our navy is at stake. Priam is afraid the ambassador may be murdered as soon as he lands.

HECTOR. I leave you in charge of Helen, Cassandra. I must go and give my orders.

HELEN. If you break the mirror, will what is reflected in it cease to exist?

HECTOR. That is the whole question.

[*Exit* HECTOR.]

CASSANDRA. I never see anything at all, you know, either colored or not.

But I can feel the weight on me of every person who comes toward me. I know what is in store for them by the sensation of suffering which flows into my veins.

HELEN. Is it true that you are a sorceress? Could you really make Peace take shape and appear for us?

CASSANDRA. Peace? Very easily. She is always standing in her beggarly way on every threshold. Wait . . . you will see her now.

[PEACE *appears*.]

HELEN. Oh, how pretty she is!

PEACE. Come to my rescue, Helen: help me!

HELEN. But how pale and wan she is.

PEACE. Pale and wan? What do you mean? Don't you see the gold shining in my hair?

HELEN. Gold? Well, perhaps a golden grey. It's very original.

PEACE. Golden grey? Is my gold now grey?

[*She disappears.*]

CASSANDRA. I think she means to make herself clearer.

[PEACE *reappears, outrageously painted.*]

PEACE. Is that better now?

HELEN. I don't see her as well as I did before.

PEACE. Is that better?

CASSANDRA. Helen doesn't see you as well as she did.

PEACE. But you can see me: you are speaking to me.

CASSANDRA. It's my speciality to speak to the invisible.

PEACE. What is going on, then? Why are all the men in the city and along the beach making such a pandemonium?

CASSANDRA. Apparently their gods are insulted, and their honor is at stake.

PEACE. Their gods! Their honor!

CASSANDRA. Yes . . . You are ill!

CURTAIN

ACT TWO

A palace enclosure. At each corner a view of the sea. In the middle a monument, the Gates of War. They are wide open.

[HELEN. *The young* TROILUS.]

HELEN. You, you, hey! You down there! Yes, it's you I'm calling. Come here.

TROILUS. No.

HELEN. What is your name?

TROILUS. Troilus.

HELEN. Come here.

TROILUS. No.

HELEN. Come here, Troilus!

[TROILUS *draws near.*]

That's the way. You obey when you're called by your name: you are still very like a puppy. It's rather beguiling. Do you know you have made me call out to a man for the first time in my life. They keep so close to my side I have only usually to move my lips. I have called out to sea gulls, to dogs, to the echoes, but never before to a man. You will pay for that. What's the matter? Are you trembling?

TROILUS. No, I'm not.

HELEN. You tremble, Troilus.

TROILUS. Yes, I do.

HELEN. Why are you always just behind me? If I walk with my back to the sun and suddenly stop, the head of your shadow stubs itself against my feet. That doesn't matter, as long as it doesn't overshoot them. Tell me what you want.

TROILUS. I don't want anything.

HELEN. Tell me what you want, Troilus!

TROILUS. Everything! I want everything!

HELEN. You want everything. The moon?

TROILUS. Everything! Everything and more!

HELEN. You're beginning to talk like a real man already; you want to kiss me!

TROILUS. No!

HELEN. You want to kiss me, isn't that it, Troilus?

TROILUS. I would kill myself directly afterward!

HELEN. Come nearer. How old are you?

TROILUS. Fifteen. Alas!

HELEN. Bravo that alas. Have you kissed girls of your own age?

TROILUS. I hate them.

HELEN. But you have kissed them?

TROILUS. Well, yes, you're bound to kiss them, you kiss them all. I would give my life not to have kissed any of them.

HELEN. You seem prepared to get rid of quite a number of lives. Why haven't you said to me frankly: Helen, I want to kiss you! I don't see anything wrong in your kissing me. Kiss me.

TROILUS. Never.

HELEN. And then, when the day came to an end, you would have come quietly to where I was sitting on the battlements watching the sun go down over the islands, and you would have turned my head toward you with your hands—from golden it would have become dark, only shadow now, you would hardly have been able to see me—and you would have kissed me, and I should have been very happy. Why this is Troilus, I should have said to myself: young Troilus is kissing me! Kiss me.

TROILUS. Never.

HELEN. I see. You think, once you have kissed me, you would hate me?

TROILUS. Oh! older men have all the luck, knowing how to say what they want to!

HELEN. You say it well enough.

[*Enter* PARIS.]

PARIS. Take care Helen, Troilus is a dangerous fellow.

HELEN. On the contrary. He wants to kiss me.

PARIS. Troilus, you know that if you kiss Helen, I shall kill you?

HELEN. Dying means nothing to him; no matter how often.

PARIS. What's the matter with him? Is he crouching to spring? Is he going to take a leap at you? He's too nice a boy. Kiss Helen, Troilus. I'll let you.

HELEN. If you can make up his mind to it you're cleverer than I am.

[TROILUS *who was about to hurl himself on* HELEN *immediately draws back.*]

PARIS. Listen, Troilus! Here's a committee of our revered elders coming to shut the Gates of War. Kiss Helen in front of them; it will make you famous. You want to be famous, don't you, later on in life?

TROILUS. No. I want nobody to have heard of me.

PARIS. You don't want to be famous? You don't want to be rich and powerful?

TROILUS. No. Poor. Ugly.

PARIS. Let me finish! So that you can have all the women you want.

TROILUS. I don't want any, none at all, none.

PARIS. Here come the senators! Now you can choose: either you kiss Helen in front of them, or I shall kiss her in front of you. Would you rather I did it? All right! Look . . . Why, this was a new version of kiss you gave me, Helen. What was it?

HELEN. The kiss I had ready for Troilus.

PARIS. You don't know what you're missing, my boy! Are you leaving us? Good-bye, then.

HELEN. We shall kiss one another, Troilus. I'll answer for that.

[TROILUS *goes.*]

Troilus!

PARIS [*slightly unnerved*]. You called very loudly, Helen.

[*Enter* DEMOKOS.]

DEMOKOS. Helen, one moment! Look me full in the face. I've got here in my hand a magnificent bird which I'm going to set free. Are you looking? Here it is. Smooth back your hair, and smile a beautiful smile.

PARIS. I don't see how the bird will fly any better if Helen smooths her hair and gives a beautiful smile.

HELEN. It can't do me any harm, anyway.

DEMOKOS. Don't move. One! Two! Three! There! It's all over, you can go now.

HELEN. Where was the bird?

DEMOKOS. It's a bird who knows how to make himself invisible.

HELEN. Ask him next time to tell you how he does it.

[*She goes.*]

PARIS. What is this nonsense?

DEMOKOS. I am writing a song on the subject of Helen's face. I needed to look at it closely, to engrave it, smiling, on my memory.

[*Enter* HECUBA, POLYXENE, ABNEOS, *the* MATHEMATICIAN, *and some* OLD MEN.]

HECUBA. Well are you going to shut these Gates for us?

DEMOKOS. Certainly not. We might well have to open them again this very evening.

HECUBA. It is Hector's wish. And Hector will persuade Priam.

DEMOKOS. That is as we shall see. And what's more I have a surprise in store for Hector.

POLYXENE. Where do the Gates lead to, mama?

ABNEOS. To war, my child. When they are open it means there is war.

DEMOKOS. My friends . . .

HECUBA. War or not, it's an absurd symbolism, your Gateway, and those two great doors always left open look very unsightly. All the dogs stop there.

MATHEMATICIAN. This is no domestic matter. It concerns war and the gods.

HECUBA. Which is just as I said: the gods never remember to shut their doors.

POLYXENE. I remember to shut them very well, don't I, mama?

PARIS. And you even include your fingers in them, don't you, my pretty one?

DEMOKOS. May I ask for a moment of silence, Paris? Abneos, and you, Mathematician, and you, my friends: I asked you to meet here earlier than the time fixed for the ceremony so that we could hold our first council. And it promises well that this first council of war should be, not a council of generals, but a council of intellectuals. For it isn't enough in wartime to have our soldiers drilled, well-armed, and spectacular. It is absolutely necessary to bring their enthusiasm up to fever pitch. The physical intoxication which their officers will get from them by a generous allowance of cheap wine supplied at the right moment, will still be ineffective against the Greeks, unless it is reinforced by the spiritual and moral intoxication which the poets can pour into them. If we are too old to fight we can at least make sure that the fighting is savage. I see you have something to say on the subject, Abneos.

ABNEOS. Yes, We must make a war-song.

DEMOKOS. Very proper. A war requires a war-song.

PARIS. We have done without one up to now.

HECUBA. War itself sings quite loud enough.

ABNEOS. We have done without one because up to now we were fighting only barbarians. It was nothing more than a hunt, and the hunting horn was all we needed. But now with the Greeks we're entering a different region of war altogether.

DEMOKOS. Exactly so, Abneos. The Greeks don't fight with everybody.

PARIS. We already have a national anthem.

ABNEOS. Yes. But it's a song of peace.

PARIS. If you sing a song of peace with enough gestures and grimaces it becomes a war-song. What are the words we have already?

ABNEOS. You know them perfectly well. There's no spirit in them:
> "We cut and bind the harvest,
> We tread the vineyard's blood."

DEMOKOS. At the very most it's a war-song against farm produce. You won't frighten the Spartans by threatening a wheatfield.

PARIS. Sing it with a spear in your hand, and a dead body at your feet, you will be surprised.

HECUBA. It includes the word "blood," there's always that.

PARIS. The word "harvest" as well. War rather approves of the word "harvest."

ABNEOS. Why discuss it, when Demokos can invent an entirely new one in a couple of hours.

DEMOKOS. A couple of hours is rather short.

HECUBA. Don't be afraid; it's more than you need for it. And after the song will come the hymn, and after the hymn the cantata. As soon as war is declared it will be impossible to hold the poets back. Rhyme is still the most effective drum.

DEMOKOS. And the most useful, Hecuba: you don't know how wisely you speak. I know war. As long as war isn't with us, and the Gates are shut, each of us is free to insult it and execrate it as we will. But once war comes, its pride and autocracy is huge. You can gain its goodwill only by flattery and adoration. So the mission of those who understand how to speak and write is to compliment and praise war ceaselessly and indiscriminately, otherwise we shut ourselves out from his favor.

PARIS. Have you got an idea for your song already?

DEMOKOS. A marvelous idea, which no one will understand better than you. War must be tired of the mask we always give it, of Medusa's venomous hair and a Gorgon's lips. I have had the notion to compare War's face with Helen's. It will be enchanted by the comparison.

POLYXENE. What does War look like, mama?

HECUBA. Like your Aunt Helen.

POLYXENE. She is very pretty.

DEMOKOS. Then the discussion is closed. You can expect the war-song. Why are you looking worried, Mathematician?

MATHEMATICIAN. Because there are other things far more urgent than this war-song, far more urgent!

DEMOKOS. You think we should discuss the question of medals, false information, atrocity stories, and so on?

MATHEMATICIAN. I think we should discuss the insulting epithets.

HECUBA. The insulting epithets?

MATHEMATICIAN. Before they hurl their spears the Greek fighting-men hurl insults. You third cousin of a toad, they yell! You son of a sow!—They insult each other, like that! And they have a good reason for it. They know that the body is more vulnerable when self-respect has fled. Soldiers famous for their composure lose it immediately when they're treated as warts or maggots. We Trojans suffer from a grave shortage of insults.

DEMOKOS. The Mathematician is quite right. We are the only race in the world which doesn't insult its enemies before it kills them.

PARIS. You don't think it's enough that the civilians insult the enemy civilians?

MATHEMATICIAN. The armies have to show the same hatred the civilians do. You know what dissemblers armies can be in this way. Leave them to themselves and they spend their time admiring each other. Their front lines very soon become the only ranks of real brotherhood in the world. So naturally, when the theater of war is so full of mutual consideration, hatred is driven back on to the schools, the salons, the tradespeople. If our soldiers aren't at least equal to the Greeks in the fury of their epithets, they will lose all taste for insults and calumny, and as a natural consequence all taste for war.

DEMOKOS. Suggestion adopted! We will organize a cursing parade this evening.

PARIS. I should have thought they're big enough to find their own curses.

DEMOKOS. What a mistake! Could you, adroit as you are, find your own effective curses?

PARIS. I believe so.

DEMOKOS. You fool yourself. Come and stand face to face with Abneos and begin.

PARIS. Why Abneos?

DEMOKOS. Because he lends himself to this sort of thing, with his corpulence and one thing and another.

ABNEOS. Come on, then, speak up, you piece of pie-crust!

PARIS. No. Abneos doesn't inspire me. I'll start with you, if you don't mind.

DEMOKOS. With me? Certainly. You can let fly at ten paces. There we are. Begin.

HECUBA. Take a good look at him. You will be inspired.

PARIS. You old parasite! You filthy-footed iambic pentameter!

DEMOKOS. Just one second. To avoid any mistake you had better say who it is you're addressing.

PARIS. You're quite right! Demokos! Bloodshot bullock's eye! You fungus-ridden plum-tree.

DEMOKOS. Grammatically reasonable, but very naïve. What is there in a fungus-ridden plum-tree to make me rise up foaming at the lips?

HECUBA. He also called you a bloodshot bullock's eye.

DEMOKOS. Bloodshot bullock's eye is better. But you see how you flounder, Paris? Search for something that can strike home to me. What are my faults, in your opinion?

PARIS. You are cowardly: your breath smells, and you have no talent.

DEMOKOS. You're asking for trouble!

PARIS. I was trying to please you.

POLYXENE. Why are we scolding Uncle Demokos, mama?

HECUBA. Because he is a cuckoo, dearest!

DEMOKOS. What did you say, Hecuba?

HECUBA. I was saying that you're a cuckoo, Demokos. If cuckoos had the absurdity, the affectation, the ugliness and the stench of vultures, you would be a cuckoo.

DEMOKOS. Wait a bit, Paris! Your mother is better at this than you are. Model yourselves on her. One hour's exercise each day for each soldier, and Hecuba has given us the superiority in insults which we badly need. As for the war-song, I'm not sure it wouldn't be wiser to entrust that to her as well.

HECUBA. If you like. But if so, I shouldn't say that war looks like Helen.

DEMOKOS. What would you say it looks like, in your opinion?

HECUBA. I will tell you when the Gates have been shut.

[*Enter* PRIAM, HECTOR, ANDROMACHE, *and presently* HELEN. *During the closing of the gates,* ANDROMACHE *takes little* POLYXENE *aside and whispers a secret or an errand to her.*]

HECTOR. As they nearly are.

DEMOKOS. One moment, Hector!

HECTOR. Aren't we ready to begin the ceremony?

HECUBA. Surely? The hinges are swimming in oil.

HECTOR. Well, then.

PRIAM. What our friends want you to understand, Hector, is that war is ready, too. Consider carefully. They're not mistaken. If you shut these Gates, in a minute we may have to open them again.

HECUBA. Even one minute of peace is worth taking.

HECTOR. Father, you should know what peace means to men who have been fighting for months. It's like solid ground to someone who was drowning or sinking in the quicksands. Do let us get our feet on to a few inches of peace, touch it, if only with the tips of our toes.

PRIAM. Hector: consider: inflicting the word peace on to the city today is as ruthless as though you gave it poison. You will take her off her guard, undermine her iron determination, debase, with the word peace, the accepted values of memory, affection, and hope. The soldiers will rush to buy the bread of peace, to drink the wine of peace, to hold in their arms the woman of peace, and in an hour you will put them back to face a war.

HECTOR. The war will never take place!

[*The sound of clamor near the Gates.*]

DEMOKOS. No? Listen!

HECTOR. Shut the Gates. This is where we shall meet the Greeks. Conversation will be bitter enough as it is. We must receive them in peace.

PRIAM. My son, are we even sure we should let the Greeks disembark?

HECTOR. Disembark they shall. This meeting with Ulysses is our last chance of peace.

DEMOKOS. Disembark they shall not. Our honor is at stake. We shall be the laughingstock of the whole world.

HECTOR. And you're taking it upon yourself to recommend to the Senate an action which would certainly mean war?

DEMOKOS. Upon myself? No, not at all. Will you come forward now, Busiris. This is where your mission begins.

HECTOR. Who is this stranger?

DEMOKOS. He is the greatest living expert on the rights of nations. It's a lucky chance he should be passing through Troy today. You can't say that he's a biased witness. He is neutral. Our Senate is willing to abide by his decision, a decision which all other nations will agree with tomorrow.

HECTOR. And what is your opinion?

BUSIRIS. My opinion, Princes, based on my own observation and further enquiry, is that the Greeks, in relation to Troy, are guilty of three breaches of international law. If you give them permission to disembark you will have sacrificed your position as the aggrieved party, and so lost the universal sympathy which would certainly have been yours in the conflict to follow.

HECTOR. Explain yourself.

BUSIRIS. Firstly, they have hoisted their flag hatchway and not masthead. A ship of war, my dear Princes and colleagues, hoists its flag hatchway only when replying to a salute from a boat carrying cattle. Clearly, then, so to salute a city and a city's population is an insult. As it happens, we have a precedent. Last year the Greeks hoisted their flag hatchway when they were entering the port of Orphea. The reply was incisive. Orphea declared war.

HECTOR. And what happened?

BUSIRIS. Orphea was beaten. Orphea no longer exists, nor the Orpheans either.

HECUBA. Perfect.

BUSIRIS. But the annihilation of a people doesn't alter in the least their superior moral position.

HECTOR. Go on.

BUSIRIS. Secondly, on entering your territorial waters the Greeks adopted the formation known as frontal. At the last congress there was some talk of including this formation in the paragraph of measures called defensive-aggressive. I was very happy to be able to get it restored under its proper heading of aggressive-defensive: so without doubt it is now one of the subtle forms of naval manœuvre which is a disguised form of blockade: that is to say, it constitutes a fault of the first degree! We have a precedent for this, as well. Five years ago the Greek navy adopted the frontal formation when they anchored outside Magnesia. Magnesia at once declared war.

HECTOR. Did they win it?

BUSIRIS. They lost it. There's not one stone of Magnesia still standing on another. But my redraft of the paragraph is still standing.

HECUBA. I congratulate you. We were beginning to be anxious.

HECTOR. Go on.

BUSIRIS. The third fault is not so serious. One of the Greek triremes has crept close in to shore without permission. Its captain, Ajax, the most unruly and impossible man among the Greeks, is climbing up toward the city, shouting scandal and provocation, and swearing he would like to kill Paris. But this is a very minor matter, from the international point of view; because it isn't in any way, a formal breach of the law.

DEMOKOS. You have your information. The situation can only be resolved in one of two ways. To swallow an outrage, or return it. Choose.

HECTOR. Oneah, go and find Ajax. Head him off in this direction.

PARIS. I'm waiting here for him.

HECTOR. You will be good enough to stay in the palace until I call for you. As for you, Busiris, you must understand that our city has no intention of being insulted by the Greeks.

BUSIRIS. I am not surprised. Troy's incorruptible pride is a legend all the world over.

HECTOR. You are going to provide me, here and now, with an argument which will allow our Senate to say that there has been no fault on the part of our visitors, and with our pride untouched we welcome them here as our guests.

DEMOKOS. What nonsense is this?

BUSIRIS. It isn't in keeping with the facts, Hector.

HECTOR. My dear Busiris, all of us here know there's no better way of exercising the imagination than the study of law. No poet ever interpreted nature as freely as a lawyer interprets truth.

BUSIRIS. The Senate asked me for an opinion: I gave it.

HECTOR. And I ask you for an interpretation. An even subtler point of law.

BUSIRIS. It goes against my conscience.

HECTOR. Your conscience has seen Orphea destroyed, Magnesia destroyed: is it now contemplating, just as lightheartedly, the destruction of Troy?

HECUBA. Yes. He comes from Syracuse.

HECTOR. I do beg of you, Busiris. The lives of two countries depend on this. Help us.

BUSIRIS. Truth is the only help I can give you.

HECTOR. Precisely. Discover a truth which saves us. What is the use of justice if it doesn't hammer out a shield for innocent people? Forge us a truth. If you can't, there is one thing I can tell you, quite simply: we shall hold you here for as long as the war goes on.

BUSIRIS. What are you saying?

DEMOKOS. You're abusing your position, Hector!

HECUBA. During war we imprison the rights of man. There seems no reason why we shouldn't imprison a lawyer.

HECTOR. I mean what I say, Busiris. I've never failed yet to keep my promises, or my threats. And now either these guards are going to take you off to prison for a year or two, or else you leave here, this evening, heaped with gold. With this in mind, you can dispassionately examine the evidence once again.

BUSIRIS. Actually there are certain mitigating arguments.

HECTOR. I was sure there were.

BUSIRIS. In the case of the first fault, for instance, when the cattle-boat salute is given in certain seas where the shores are fertile, it could be interpreted as a salute from the sailors to the farmers.

HECTOR. That would be, in fact, the logical interpretation. The salute of the sea to the earth.

BUSIRIS. Not to mention that the cargo of cattle might easily be a cargo of bulls. In that case the homage would verge on flattery.

HECTOR. There you are. You've understood what I meant. We're arrived at our point of view.

BUSIRIS. And as to the frontal formation, that could as easily mean a promise as a provocation. Women wanting children give themselves not from the side but face to face.

HECTOR. Decisive argument.

BUSIRIS. Then, again, the Greek ships have huge carved nymphs for figureheads. A woman who comes toward you naked and open-armed is not a threat but an offer. An offer to talk, at any rate.

HECTOR. So there we have our honor safe and sound, Demokos. The next step is to make this consultation with Busiris public. Meanwhile, Minos, tell the port authorities to let Ulysses disembark without any loss of time.

DEMOKOS. It's no use even trying to discuss honor with these fighting men. They trade on the fact that you can't treat them as cowards.

MATHEMATICIAN. At any rate, Hector, deliver the Oration for the Dead. That will make you think again.

HECTOR. There's not going to be an Oration for the Dead.

PRIAM. But it's part of the ceremony. The victorious general must always speak in honor of the dead when the Gates are closed.

HECTOR. An Oration for the Dead of a war is a hypocritical speech in defense of the living, a plea for acquittal. I am not so sure of my innocence.

DEMOKOS. The High Command is not responsible.

HECTOR. Alas, no one is: nor the Gods either. Besides, I have given my oration for the dead already. I gave it to them in their last minute of life, when they were lying on the battlefield, on a little slope of olive-trees, while they could still attend me with what was left of their sight and hearing. I can tell you what I said to them. There was one, disemboweled, already turning up the whites of his eyes, and I said to him: "It's not so bad, you know, it's not so bad; you will do all right, old man." And one with his skull split in two; I said: "You look pretty comical with that broken nose." And my little equerry, with his left arm hanging useless and his last blood flowing out of him; and I said, "It's a good thing for you it's the left arm you've splintered." I am happy I gave them one final swig of life; it was all they asked for; they died drinking it. And there's nothing else to be said. Shut the Gates.

POLYXENE. Did the little equerry die, as well?

HECTOR. Yes, puss-cat. He died. He stretched out his right arm. Someone I couldn't see took him by his perfect hand. And then he died.

DEMOKOS. Our general seems to confuse remarks made to the dying with the Oration for the Dead.

PRIAM. Why must you be so stubborn, Hector?

HECTOR. Very well: you shall have the Oration. [*He takes a position below the gates.*]—You who cannot hear us, who cannot see us, listen to these words, look at those who come to honor you. We have won the war. I know that's of no moment to you. You are the victors, too. But we are victorious, and still live. That's where the difference is between us and why I'm ashamed. I don't know whether, among the crowd of the dead, any privilege is given to men who died victorious. But the living, whether victorious or not, have privilege enough. We have our eyes. We see the sun. We do what all men do under the sun. We eat. We drink. By the moon, we sleep with our wives. And with yours, now you have gone.

DEMOKOS. You insult the dead!

HECTOR. Do you think so?

DEMOKOS. Either the dead or the living.

HECTOR. There is a distinction.

PRIAM. Come to the peroration, Hector. The Greeks are coming ashore.

HECTOR. I will come to it now . . . Breathe in this incense, touch these offerings, you who can neither smell nor touch. And understand, since I speak to you sincerely, I haven't an equal tenderness and respect for all of you. Though all of you are the dead, with you as with us who survive there are men of courage and men of fear, and you can't make me confuse, for the sake of a ceremony, the dead I admire with those I can't admire. But what I have to say to you today is that war seems to me the most sordid, hypocritical way of making all men equal: and I accept death neither as a punishment or expiation for the coward, nor as a reward to the living. So, whatever you may be, absent, forgotten, purposeless, unresting, without existence, one thing is certain when we close these Gates: we must ask you to forgive us, we, the deserters who survive you, who feel we have stolen two great privileges, I hope the sound of their names will never reach you: the warmth of the living body, and the sky.

POLYXENE. The gates are shutting, mama!

HECUBA. Yes, darling.

POLYXENE. The dead men are pushing them shut.

HECUBA. They help, a little.

POLYXENE. They're helping quite a lot, especially over on the right.

HECTOR. Is it done? Are they shut?

GUARD. Tight as a clam.

HECTOR. We're at peace, father, we're at peace.

HECUBA. We're at peace!

POLYXENE. It feels much better, doesn't it, mama?

HECTOR. Indeed it does.

POLYXENE. I feel much better, anyway.

[*The sound of the Greeks' music.*]

A MESSENGER. The Greeks have landed, Priam!

DEMOKOS. What music! What frightful music! It's the most anti-Trojan music there could possibly be! Let's go and give them a welcome to match it.

HECTOR. Receive them royally, bring them here safely. You are responsible.

MATHEMATICIAN. At any rate we ought to counter with some Trojan music. Hector, if we can't be indignant any other way, you can authorize a battle of music.

CROWD. The Greeks! The Greeks!

MESSENGER. Ulysses is on the landing-stage, Priam. Where are we to take him?

PRIAM. Conduct him here. Send word to us in the palace when he comes. Keep with us, Paris. We don't want you too much in evidence just yet.

HECTOR. Let's go and prepare what we shall say to the Greeks, father.

DEMOKOS. You'd better prepare it somewhat better than your speech for the dead; you're likely to meet more contradiction.

[*Exeunt* PRIAM *and his* SONS.]

If you are going with them, tell us before you go, Hecuba, what it is you think war looks like.

HECUBA. You insist on knowing?

DEMOKOS. If you've seen what it looks like, tell us.

HECUBA. Like the bottom of a baboon. When the baboon is up in a tree, with its hind end facing us, there is the face of war exactly: scarlet, scaly, glazed, framed in a clotted, filthy wig.

DEMOKOS. So he has two faces: this you describe, and Helen's.

[*Exit.*]

ANDROMACHE. Here is Helen now. Polyxene, you remember what you have to say to her?

POLYXENE. Yes.

ANDROMACHE. Go to her, then.

[*Enter* HELEN.]

HELEN. Do you want to talk to me, darling?

POLYXENE. Yes, Aunt Helen.

HELEN. It must be important, you're so very tense.

POLYXENE. Yes, Aunt Helen.

HELEN. Is it something you can't tell me without standing so stiffly?

POLYXENE. No, Aunt Helen.

HELEN. Do tell me, then; you make me feel terrible when you stand there like a little stick.

POLYXENE. Aunt Helen, if you love anyone, please go away.

HELEN. Why should I go away, darling?

POLYXENE. Because of the war.

HELEN. Do you know about war already, then?

POLYXENE. I don't exactly know about it. I think it means we have to die.

HELEN. And do you know what dying is?

POLYXENE. I don't exactly. I think it means we don't feel anything any more.

HELEN. What exactly was it that Andromache told you to ask me?

POLYXENE. If you love us at all, please to go away.

HELEN. That doesn't seem to me very logical. If you loved someone you wouldn't leave them?

POLYXENE. Oh, no! Never!

HELEN. Which would you rather do: go right away from Hecuba, or never feel anything any more?

POLYXENE. Oh, never feel anything! I would rather stay, and never feel anything any more.

HELEN. You see how badly you put things to me. If I'm to leave you, I mustn't love you. Would you rather I didn't love you?

POLYXENE. Oh, no! I want you to love me.

HELEN. In other words, you didn't know what you were saying, did you?

POLYXENE. No.

HECUBA [*offstage*]. Polyxene!

[*Enter* HECUBA.]

Are you deaf, Polyxene? Why did you shut your eyes when you saw me? Are you playing at being a statue? Come with me.

HELEN. She is teaching herself not to feel anything. But she has no gift for it.

HECUBA. Can you hear me, Polyxene? And see me?

POLYXENE. Yes, I can hear you. I can see you, too.

HECUBA. Why are you crying? Don't you like to see and hear me?

POLYXENE. If I do, you will go away.

HECUBA. I think it would be better, Helen, if you left Polyxene alone. She is too sensitive to touch the insensitive, even through your beautiful dress and your beautiful voice.

HELEN. I quite agree with you. I advise Andromache to carry her own messages. Kiss me, Polyxene. I shall go away this evening, since that is what you would like.

POLYXENE. Don't go! Don't go!

HELEN. Bravo! You are quite loosened up again!

HECUBA. Are you coming with us, Andromache?

ANDROMACHE. No: I shall wait here.

[*Exeunt* HECUBA *and* POLYXENE.]

HELEN. You want an explanation?

ANDROMACHE. I believe it's necessary.

HELEN. Listen to the way they're shouting and arguing down below. Isn't that enough? Do you and I have to have explanations, too? And what explanations, since I'm leaving here anyway?

ANDROMACHE. Whether you go or stay isn't any longer the problem.

HELEN. Tell Hector that. You will make his day easier.

ANDROMACHE. Yes, Hector is obsessed by the thought of getting you away. All men are the same. They take no notice of the stag in the thicket because they're already chasing the hare. Perhaps men can hunt like that. But not the gods.

HELEN. If you have discovered what the gods are after in this affair, I congratulate you.

ANDROMACHE. I don't know that the gods are after anything. But there is something the universe is after. Ever since this morning, it seems to me, everything has begged and cried out for it, men, animals, even the leaves on the trees and my own child, not yet born.

HELEN. Cried out for what?

ANDROMACHE. That you should love Paris.

HELEN. If they know so certainly that I don't love Paris, they are better informed than I am.

ANDROMACHE. But you don't love him! You could love him, perhaps. But, at present, you are both living in a misunderstanding.

HELEN. I live with him happily, amicably, in complete agreement. We understand each other so well, I don't really see how this can be called a misunderstanding.

ANDROMACHE. Agreement is never reached in love. The life of a wife and husband who love each other is never at rest. Whether the marriage is true or false, the marriage portion is the same: elemental discord. Hector is my absolute opposite. He shares none of my tastes. We pass our days either getting the better of one another, or sacrificing ourselves. There is no tranquillity for lovers.

HELEN. And if I went pale whenever I saw Paris: and my eyes filled with tears, and the palms of my hands were moist, you think Menelaus would be delighted, and the Greeks pleased and quite satisfied?

ANDROMACHE. It wouldn't much matter then what the Greeks thought.

HELEN. And the war would never happen?

ANDROMACHE. Perhaps, indeed, it would never happen. Perhaps if you loved him, love would call to the rescue one of its own equals: generosity or intelligence. No one, not even destiny itself, attacks devotion lightheartedly. And even if the war did happen, why, I think even then,—

HELEN. Then it wouldn't be the same war, I suppose.

ANDROMACHE. Oh, no, Helen! You know what this struggle is going to be. Fate would never take so many precautions for an ordinary quarrel. It means to build the future on this war, the future of our countries and our peoples, and our ways of thinking. It won't be so bad if our thoughts and our future are built on the story of a man and a woman who truly love each other. But fate hasn't noticed yet that you are lovers only on paper, officially. To think that we're going to suffer and die only for a pair of theoretical lovers: and the splendor and calamity of the age to come will be founded on a trivial adventure between two people who don't love each other—that's what is so horrible.

HELEN. If everybody thinks that we love each other, it comes to the same thing.

ANDROMACHE. They don't think so. But no one will admit that he doesn't. Everyone, when there's war in the air, learns to live in a new element: falsehood. Everybody lies. Our old men don't worship beauty: they worship themselves, they worship ugliness. And this indignation the Greeks are showing us is a lie. God knows, they're amused enough at what you can do with Paris! Their boats, in the bay, with their patriotic anthems and their streamers flying, are a falsehood of the sea. And Hector's life and my son's life, too, are going to be played out in hypocrisy and pretense.

HELEN. So?

ANDROMACHE. I beg of you, Helen. You see how I'm pressed against you as though I were begging you to love me. Love Paris! Or tell me that I'm mistaken! Tell me that you would kill yourself if Paris were to die! Tell me that you would even let yourself be disfigured if it would keep him alive. Then the war will only be a scourge, not an injustice.

HELEN. You are being very difficult. I don't think my way of loving is as bad as all that. Certainly I don't get upset and ill when Paris leaves me to play bowls or go fishing for eels. But I do feel commanded by him, magnetically attracted. Magnetism is a kind of love, as much as devotion. And it's an old and fruitful passion in its own way, as desperate devotion and passionate weeping are in theirs. I'm as content in this love as a star in a constellation. It's my own center of gravity; I shine there; it's the way I breathe, and the way I take life in my arms. And it's easy to see what sons this love can produce: tall, clear-cut boys, of great distinction, with fine fingers and short noses. What will it all become if I fill it with jealousy, with emotion, and anxiety? The world is nervous enough already: look at yourself!

ANDROMACHE. Fill it with pity, Helen. That's the only help the world needs.

HELEN. There we are; I knew it would come; the word has been said.

ANDROMACHE. What word?

HELEN. The word "pity." You must talk to someone else. I'm afraid I'm not very good at pity.

ANDROMACHE. Because you don't know unhappiness.

HELEN. Maybe. It could also be that I think of unhappy people as my equals, I accept them, and I don't think of my health and my position and beauty as any better than their misery. It's a sense of brotherhood I have.

ANDROMACHE. You're blaspheming, Helen.

HELEN. I am sure people pity others to the same extent that they would pity themselves. Unhappiness and ugliness are mirrors they can't bear to look into. I haven't any pity for myself. You will see, if war breaks out. I'll put up with hunger and pain better than you will. And insults, too. Do you think I don't hear what the Trojan women say when I'm going past them? They treat me like a slut. They say that the morning light shows me up for what they think me. It may be true, or it may not be. It doesn't matter to me, one way or the other.

ANDROMACHE. Stop, Helen!

HELEN. And of course I can see, in what your husband called the colored picture-book in my head, pictures of Helen grown old, flabby, toothless, sitting hunched-up in the kitchen, sucking sweets. I can see the white enamel I've plastered over my wrinkles, and the bright colors the sweets are, very clearly. But it leaves me completely indifferent.

ANDROMACHE. I am lost.

HELEN. Why? If you're content with one perfect couple to make the war acceptable, there is always you and Hector, Andromache.

[*Enter* AJAX, *then* HECTOR.]

AJAX. Where is he? Where's he hiding himself? A coward! A typical Trojan!

HECTOR. Who are you looking for?

AJAX. I'm looking for Paris.

HECTOR. I am his brother.

AJAX. Beautiful family! I am Ajax! What's your name?

HECTOR. My name's Hector.

AJAX. It ought to be pimp!

HECTOR. I see that Greece has sent over her diplomats. What do you want?

AJAX. War.

HECTOR. Not a hope. Why do you want it?

AJAX. Your brother carried off Helen.

HECTOR. I am told she was willing.

AJAX. A Greek woman can do what she likes. She doesn't have to ask permission from you. He carried her off. It's a reason for war.

HECTOR. We can offer our apologies.

AJAX. What's a Trojan apology? We're not leaving here without your declaration of war.

HECTOR. Declare it yourselves.

AJAX. All right, we will. As from this evening.

HECTOR. That's a lie. You won't declare war. There isn't an island in the archipelago that will back you if we aren't in any way responsible. And we don't intend to be.

AJAX. Will you declare it yourself, personally, if I call you a coward?

HECTOR. That is a name I accept.

AJAX. I've never known such unmilitary reaction! Suppose I tell you what the people of Greece thinks of Troy, that Troy is a cess-pit of vice and stupidity?

HECTOR. Troy is obstinate. You won't get your war.

AJAX. Suppose I spit on her?

HECTOR. Spit.

AJAX. Suppose I strike you, you, one of her princes?

HECTOR. Try it.

AJAX. Suppose I slap your face, you disgusting example of Troy's conceit and her spurious honor?

HECTOR. Strike.

AJAX [*striking him*]. There. If this lady's your wife she must be proud of you.

HECTOR. I know her. She is proud.

[*Enter* DEMOKOS.]

DEMOKOS. What's all the noise about? What does this drunkard want, Hector?

HECTOR. He has got what he wants.

DEMOKOS. What is going on, Andromache?

ANDROMACHE. Nothing.

AJAX. Two times nothing. A Greek hits Hector, and Hector puts up with it.

DEMOKOS. Is this true, Hector?

HECTOR. Completely false, isn't it, Helen?

HELEN. The Greeks are great liars. Greek men, I mean.

AJAX. Is it natural for him to have one cheek redder than the other?

HECTOR. Yes. I am healthier on that side.

DEMOKOS. Tell the truth, Hector. Has he dared to raise his hand against you?

HECTOR. That is my concern.

DEMOKOS. It's the concern of war. You are the figurehead of Troy.

HECTOR. Exactly. No one is going to slap a figurehead.

DEMOKOS. Who are you, you brute? I am Demokos, second son of Achichaos!

AJAX. The second son of Achichaos? How do you do? Tell me: is it as serious to slap a second son of Achichaos as to strike Hector?

DEMOKOS. Quite as serious, you drunk. I am the head of the senate. If you want war, war to the death, you have only to try.

AJAX. All right, I'll try. [*He slaps* DEMOKOS.]

DEMOKOS. Trojans! Soldiers! To the rescue!

HECTOR. Be quiet, Demokos!

DEMOKOS. To arms! Troy's been insulted! Vengeance!

HECTOR. Be quiet, I tell you.

DEMOKOS. I *will* shout! I'll rouse the city!

HECTOR. Be quiet! If you won't, I shall hit you, too!

DEMOKOS. Priam! Anchises! Come and see the shame of Troy burning on Hector's face!

[HECTOR *strikes* DEMOKOS. AJAX *laughs. During the scene,* PRIAM *and his lords group themselves ready to receive* ULYSSES.]

PRIAM. What are you shouting for, Demokos?

DEMOKOS. I have been struck.

AJAX. Go and complain to Achichaos!

PRIAM. Who struck you?

DEMOKOS. Hector! Ajax! Ajax! Hector!

PARIS. What is he talking about? He's mad!

HECTOR. Nobody struck him, did they, Helen?

HELEN. I was watching most carefully, and I didn't notice anything.

AJAX. Both his cheeks are the same color.

PARIS. Poets often get upset for no reason. It's what they call their inspiration. We shall get a new national anthem out of it.

DEMOKOS. You will pay for this, Hector.

VOICES. Ulysses! Here is Ulysses!

[AJAX *goes amicably to* HECTOR.]

AJAX. Well done. Plenty of pluck. Noble adversary. A beautiful hit.

HECTOR. I did my best.

AJAX. Excellent method, too. Straight elbow. The wrist on an angle. Safe position for the carpus and metacarpus. Your slap must be stronger than mine is.

HECTOR. I doubt it.

AJAX. You must be able to throw a javelin magnificently with this iron forearm and this shoulder-bone for a pivot.

HECTOR. Eighty yards.

AJAX. My deepest respect! My dear Hector, forgive me. I withdraw my threats, I take back my slap. We have enemies in common, in the sons of Achichaos. I won't fight with anybody who shares with me an enmity for the sons of Achichaos. Not another mention of war. I don't know what Ulysses has got in mind, but count on me to arrange the whole thing.

[*He goes toward* ULYSSES *and comes back with him.*]

ANDROMACHE. I love you, Hector.

HECTOR [*showing his cheek*]. Yes; but don't kiss me just yet.

ANDROMACHE. You have won this round, as well. Be confident.

HECTOR. I win every round. But still with each victory the prize escapes me.

ULYSSES. Priam and Hector?

PRIAM. Yes. And behind us, Troy, and the suburbs of Troy, and the land of Troy, and the Hellespont.

ULYSSES. I am Ulysses.

PRIAM. This is Anchises.

ULYSSES. There are many people here for a diplomatic conversation.

PRIAM. And here is Helen.

ULYSSES. Good morning, my queen.

HELEN. I've grown younger here, Ulysses. I've become a princess again.

PRIAM. We are ready to listen to you.

AJAX. Ulysses, you speak to Priam. I will speak to Hector.

ULYSSES. Priam, we have come to take Helen home again.

AJAX. You do understand, don't you, Hector? We can't have things happening like this.

ULYSSES. Greece and Menelaus cry out for vengeance.

AJAX. If deceived husbands can't cry out for vengeance, what can they do?

ULYSSES. Deliver Helen over to us within an hour. Otherwise it means war.

HECTOR. But if we give Helen back to you give us your assurance there will be peace.

AJAX. Utter tranquillity.

HECTOR. If she goes on board within an hour, the matter is closed.

AJAX. And all is forgotten.

HECTOR. I think there's no doubt we can come to an understanding, can we not, Helen?

HELEN. Yes, no doubt.

ULYSSES. You don't mean to say that Helen is being given back to us?

HECTOR. Exactly that. She is ready.

AJAX. What about her baggage? She is sure to have more to take back than when she came.

HECTOR. We return her to you, bag and baggage, and you guarantee peace. No reprisals, no vengeance!

AJAX. A woman is lost, a woman is found, and we're back where we were. Perfect! Isn't it, Ulysses?

ULYSSES. Just wait a moment. I guarantee nothing. Before we say there are going to be no reprisals we have to be sure there has been no cause for reprisals. We have to make sure that Menelaus will find Helen exactly as she was when she was taken from him.

HECTOR. How is he going to discover any difference?

ULYSSES. A husband is very perceptive when a worldwide scandal has put him on his guard. Paris will have had to have respected Helen. And if that isn't so . . .

CROWD. Oh, no! It isn't so!

ONE VOICE. Not exactly!

HECTOR. And if it is so?

ULYSSES. Where is this leading us, Hector?

HECTOR. Paris has not touched Helen. They have both taken me into their confidence.

ULYSSES. What is this absurd story?

HECTOR. The true story, isn't it, Helen?

HELEN. Why does it seem to you so extraordinary?

A VOICE. It's terrible! It puts us to shame!

HECTOR. Why do you have to smile, Ulysses? Do you see the slightest indication in Helen that she has failed in her duty?

ULYSSES. I'm not looking for one. Water leaves less mark on a duck's back than dishonor does on a woman.

PARIS. You're speaking to a queen.

ULYSSES. Present queens excepted, naturally. So, Paris, you have carried off this queen, carried her off naked; and I imagine that you didn't go into the water wearing all your armor; and yet you weren't seized by any taste or desire for her?

PARIS. A naked queen is dressed in her dignity.

HELEN. She has only to remember to keep it on.

ULYSSES. Now long did the voyage last? I took three days with my ships, which are faster than yours.

VOICES. What are these intolerable insults to the Trojan navy?

A VOICE. Your winds are faster! Not your ships!

ULYSSES. Let us say three days, if you like. Where was the queen during those three days?

PARIS. Lying down on the deck.

ULYSSES. And Paris was where? In the crow's nest?

HELEN. Lying beside me.

ULYSSES. Was he reading as he lay beside you? Or fishing for goldfish?

HELEN. Sometimes he fanned me.

ULYSSES. Without ever touching you?

HELEN. One day, the second day, I think it was, he kissed my hand.

ULYSSES. Your hand! I see. An outbreak of the animal in him.

HELEN. I thought it was more dignified to take no notice.

ULYSSES. The rolling of the ship didn't throw you toward each other? I don't think it's an insult to the Trojan navy to suggest that its ships roll?

A VOICE. They roll much less than the Greek ships pitch!

AJAX. Pitch? Our Greek ships? If they seem to be pitching it's because of their high prows and their scooped-out sterns!

A VOICE. Oh, yes! The arrogant face and the flat behind, that's Greek all right.

ULYSSES. And what about the three nights you were sailing? The stars appeared and vanished again three times over the pair of you. Do you remember nothing of those three nights?

HELEN. I don't know. Oh, yes! I'd forgotten. I learned a lot more about the stars.

ULYSSES. While you were asleep, perhaps, he might have taken you . . .

HELEN. A mosquito can wake me.

HECTOR. They will both swear to you, if you like, by our goddess Aphrodite.

ULYSSES. We can do without that. I know what Aphrodite is. Her favorite oath is a perjury.—It's a curious story you're telling me: and it will certainly destroy the idea that the rest of the archipelago has always had of the Trojans.

PARIS. Why, what do they think of us in the archipelago?

ULYSSES. You're thought of as less accomplished at trading than we are, but handsome and irresistible. Go on with your story, Paris. It's an interesting contribution to the study of human behavior. What good reason could you have possibly had for respecting Helen when you had her at your mercy?

PARIS. I . . . I loved her.

HELEN. If you don't know what love is, Ulysses, I shouldn't venture on the subject.

ULYSSES. You must admit, Helen, you would never have followed him if you had known the Trojans were impotent.

VOICES. Shame! Muzzle him! Bring your women here, and you'll soon see! And your grandmother!

ULYSSES. I expressed myself badly. I meant that Paris, the handsome Paris, is impotent.

A VOICE. Why don't you say something, Paris? Are you going to make us the laughingstock of the world?

PARIS. Hector, you can see, this is a most unpleasant situation for me!

HECTOR. You have to put up with it only a few minutes longer. Good-bye, Helen. And I hope your virtue will become as proverbial as your frailty might have done.

HELEN. That doesn't worry me. The centuries always give us the recognition we deserve.

ULYSSES. Paris the impotent, that's a very good surname! If you care to, Helen, you can kiss him for once.

PARIS. Hector!

FIRST TOPMAN. Are you going to tolerate this farce, commander?

HECTOR. Be quiet! I am in charge here!

TOPMAN. And a rotten job you make of it! We've stood quite enough. We'll tell you, we, Paris's own seamen, we'll tell you what he did with your queen!

VOICES. Bravo! Tell him!

TOPMAN. He's sacrificing himself on his brother's orders. I was an officer on board his ship. I saw everything.

HECTOR. You were quite wrong.

TOPMAN. Do you think a Trojan sailor doesn't know what he sees? I can tell the sex of a sea gull thirty yards off. Come over here, Olpides. Olpides was up in the crow's nest. He saw everything from on top. I was standing on the stairs in the hatchway. My head was exactly on a level with them, like a cat on the end of a bed. Shall I tell him, Trojans?

HECTOR. Silence!

VOICES. Tell him! Go on and tell him!

TOPMAN. And they hadn't been on board more than two minutes, wasn't that true, Olpides?

OLPIDES. Only time enough for the queen to dry herself, being just come up out of the water, and to comb the parting into her hair again. I could see her parting, from her forehead over to the nape of her neck, from where I was.

TOPMAN. And he sent us all down into the hold, except the two of us who he couldn't see.

OLPIDES. And without a pilot, the ship drifted due north. There was no wind, and yet the sails were bellied out full.

TOPMAN. And when I looked out from where I was hiding, what I should have seen was the outline of one body, but what I did see was in the shape of two, like a wheaten loaf and rye bread, baking in the oven together.

OLPIDES. But from up where I was, I more often saw one body than two, but sometimes it was white, and sometimes it was golden brown.

TOPMAN. So much for impotence! And as for respectful, inexpressive love, and unspoken affection, you tell him, Olpides, what you heard from your ledge up there! Women's voices carry upward, men's voices stay on the ground. I shall tell you what Paris said.

OLPIDES. She call him her ladybird, her little ewe-lamb.

TOPMAN. And he called her his lion, his panther. They reversed the sexes. Because they were being so affectionate. It's not unusual.

OLPIDES. And then she said: "You are my darling oak-tree, I put my arms round you as if you were an oak-tree." When you're at sea you think about trees, I suppose.

TOPMAN. And he called her his birch-tree: "My trembling silver birch-tree!" I remember the word birch-tree very well. It's a Russian tree.

OLPIDES. And I had to stay up in the crow's nest all night. You don't half get thirsty up there, and hungry, and everything else.

TOPMAN. And when at last they got up from the deck to go to bed they swayed on their feet. And that's how your wife Penelope would have got on with Trojan impotence.

VOICES. Bravo! Bravo!

A WOMAN'S VOICE. All praise to Paris.

A JOVIAL MAN. Render to Paris what belongs to Paris!

HECTOR. This is a pack of lies, isn't it, Helen?

ULYSSES. Helen is listening enraptured.

HELEN. I forgot they were talking about me. They sound so wonderfully convincing.

ULYSSES. Do you dare to say they are lying, Paris?

PARIS. In some of the particulars, yes, I think they are.

TOPMAN. We're not lying, either in the general or the particular. Are we, Olpides? Do you deny the expressions of love you used? Do you deny the word panther?

PARIS. Not especially the word panther.

TOPMAN. Well, birch-tree, then? I see. It's the phrase "trembling silver birch-tree" that embarrasses you. Well, like it or not, you used it. I swear you used it, and anyway what is there to blush about in the word "birch-tree"? I have seen these silver birch-trees trembling against the snow in wintertime, by the shores of the Caspian, with their rings of black bark apparently separated by rings of space, so that you wondered what was carrying the branches. And I've seen them at the height of summer, beside the canal at Astrakhan, with their white rings like fresh mushrooms. And the leaves talked and made signs to me. To see them quivering, gold above and silver underneath, it makes your heart melt! I could have wept like a woman, isn't that true, Olpides? That's how I feel about the birch-tree.

CROWD. Bravo! Bravo!

ANOTHER SAILOR. And it wasn't only the topman and Olpides who saw them, Priam. The entire crew came wriggling up through the hatches and peering under the handrails. The whole ship was one great spyglass.

THIRD SAILOR. Spying out love.

ULYSSES. There you have it, Hector!

HECTOR. Be quiet, the lot of you.

TOPMAN. Well, keep this quiet, if you can!

[IRIS *appears in the sky.*]

PEOPLE. Iris! Iris.

PARIS. Has Aphrodite sent you?

IRIS. Yes, Aphrodite sent me, and told me that I should say to you that love is the world's chief law. Whatever strengthens love becomes in itself sacred, even falsehood, avarice, or luxury. She takes all lovers under her protection, from the king to the goatherd. And she forbids both of you, Hector and Ulysses, to separate Paris from Helen. Or else there will be war.

PARIS *and the* OLD MEN. Thank you, Iris.

HECTOR. Is there any message from Pallas Athene?

IRIS. Yes; Pallas Athene told me that I should say to you that reason is the chief law of the world. All who are lovers, she wishes me to say, are out of their minds. She would like you to tell her quite frankly what is more ridiculous than the mating of cocks with hens or flies with flies. And she orders both of you, Hector, and Ulysses, to separate Helen from this Paris of the curly hair. Or else there will be war.

HECTOR *and the* WOMEN. Thank you, Iris!

PRIAM. Oh, my son, it isn't Aphrodite nor Pallas Athene who rules the world. What is it Zeus commands us to do in this time of uncertainty?

IRIS. Zeus, the master of the gods, told me that I should say to you that those who see in the world nothing but love are as foolish as those who cannot see it at all. It is wise, Zeus, master of the gods informs you, it is wise sometimes to make love, and at other times not to make love. The decision he gives to Hector and Ulysses, is to separate Helen and Paris without separating them. He orders all the rest of you to go away and leave the negotiators to face each other. And let them so arrange matters that there will be no war. Or else—he swears to you: he swears there will be war.

[*Exit* IRIS.]

HECTOR. At your service, Ulysses!

ULYSSES. At your service.

[*All withdraw. A great rainbow is seen in the sky.*]

HELEN. How very like Iris to leave her scarf behind.

HECTOR. Now we come to the real tussle, Ulysses.

ULYSSES. Yes: out of which either war or peace is going to come.

HECTOR. Will war come of it?

ULYSSES. We shall know in five minutes time.

HECTOR. If it's to be a battle of words, my chances are small.

ULYSSES. I believe it will be more a battle of weight. It's as though we were one on each side of a pair of scales. How we weigh in the balance will be what counts in the end.

HECTOR. How we weigh in the balance? And what is my weight, Ulysses? My weight is a young man, a young woman, an unborn child. Joy of life, belief in life, a response to whatever's natural and good.

ULYSSES. And my weight is the mature man, the wife thirty-five years old, the son whose height I measure each month with notches against the doorpost of the palace. My weight is the pleasures of living, and a mistrust of life.

HECTOR. Hunting, courage, loyalty, love.

ULYSSES. Circumspection in the presence of the gods, of men, and everything else.

HECTOR. The Phrygian oak-tree, all the leafy, thickset oak-trees that grow on our hills with our curly-coated oxen.

ULYSSES. The power and wisdom of the olive-tree.

HECTOR. I weigh the hawk, I look straight into the sun.

ULYSSES. I weigh the owl.

HECTOR. I weigh the whole race of humble peasants, hard-working craftsmen, thousands of ploughs and looms, forges and anvils . . . Why is it, when I put all these in the scale in front of you, all at once they seem to me to weigh so light?

ULYSSES. I am the weight of this incorruptible, unpitying air of these coasts and islands.

HECTOR. Why go on? The scales have tipped.

ULYSSES. To my side? Yes, I think so.

HECTOR. And you want war?

ULYSSES. I don't want it. But I'm less sure whether war may not want us.

HECTOR. Our peoples have brought us together to prevent it. Our meeting itself shows that there is still some hope.

ULYSSES. You are young, Hector! It's usual on the eve of every war, for the two leaders of the peoples concerned to meet privately at some innocent village, on a terrace in a garden overlooking a lake. And they decide together that war is the world's worst scourge, and as they watch the rippling reflections in the water, with magnolia petals dropping on to their shoulders, they are both of them peace-loving, modest and friendly. They study one another. They look into each other's eyes. And, warmed by the sun and mellowed by the claret, they can't find anything in the other man's face to justify hatred, nothing, indeed, which doesn't inspire human affection, nothing incompatible in their languages anymore, or in their particular way of scratching the nose or drinking wine. They really are exuding peace, and the world's desire for peace. And when their meeting is over, they shake hands in a most sincere brotherly fashion, and turn to smile and wave as they drive away. And the next day war breaks out. And so it is with us both at this moment. Our peoples, who have drawn aside, saying nothing while we have this interview, are not expecting us to win a victory over the inevitable. They have merely given us full powers, isolated here together, to stand above the catastrophe and taste the essential brotherhood of enemies. Taste it. It's a rare dish. Savor it. But that is all. One of the privileges of the great is to witness catastrophes from a terrace.

HECTOR. Do you think this is a conversation between enemies we are having?

ULYSSES. I should say a duet before the full orchestra. Because we have been created sensible and courteous, we can talk to each other, an hour or so before the war, in the way we shall talk to each other long after it's over, like old antagonists. We are merely having our reconciliation before the struggle instead of after it. That may be unwise. If one day one of us should have to kill the other, it might be as well if it wasn't a friend's face we recognized as the body dropped to the ground. But, as the universe well knows, we are going to fight each other.

HECTOR. The universe might be mistaken. One way to recognize error is the fact that it's universal.

ULYSSES. Let's hope so. But when destiny has brought up two nations, as for years it has brought up yours and mine, to a future of similar invention and authority, and given to each a different scale of values (as you and I saw just now, when we weighed pleasure against pleasure, conscience against conscience, even nature itself against nature): when the nation's architects and poets and painters have created for them opposing kingdoms of sound, and form, and subtlety, when we have a Trojan tile roof, a Theban arch, Phrygian red, Greek blue: the universe knows that destiny wasn't preparing alternative ways for civilization to flower. It was contriving the dance of death, letting loose the brutality and human folly which is all that the gods are really contented by. It's a mean way to contrive things, I'agree. But we are Heads of State, you and I; we can say this between ourselves: it is Destiny's way of contriving things, inevitably.

HECTOR. And this time it has chosen to match Greece with Troy?

ULYSSES. This morning I was still in doubt. As soon as I stepped on to your landing stage I was certain of it.

HECTOR. You mean you felt yourself on enemy soil?

ULYSSES. Why will you always harp on the word enemy? Born enemies don't fight. Nations you would say were designed to go to war against each other—by their skins, their language, their smell: always jealous of each other, always hating each other—they're not the ones who fight. You will find the real antagonists in nations fate has groomed and made ready for the same war.

HECTOR. And you think we have been made ready for the Greek war?

ULYSSES. To an astonishing extent. Just as nature, when she foresees a struggle between two kinds of insects, equips them with weaknesses and weapons which correspond, so we, living well apart, unknown to ourselves, not even suspecting it, have both been gradually raised up to the level where war begins. All our weapons and habits correspond with each other and balance against each other like the beams of a gable. No other women in the word excite less brutality in us, or less desire, than your wives and daughters do; they give us a joy and an anguish of heart which is a sure sign of impending war between us. Doom has transfigured everything here with the color of storm: your grave buildings shaking with shadow and fire, the neighing horses, figures disappearing into the dark of a colonnade: the future has never impressed me before with such startling clarity. There is nothing to be done. You're already living in the light of the Greek war.

HECTOR. And do the rest of the Greeks think this?

ULYSSES. What they think is no more reassuring. The rest of the Greeks think Troy is wealthy, her warehouses bulging, her soil prolific. They think that they, on the other hand, are living cramped on a rock. And your golden temples and golden wheatfields flashed from your promontories a signal our ships will never forget. It isn't very wise to have such golden gods and vegetables.

HECTOR. This is more like the truth, at last. Greece has chosen Troy for her prey. Then why a declaration of war? It would have been simpler to have taken Troy by surprise when I was away with the army. You would have had her without striking a blow.

ULYSSES. There's a kind of permission for war which can be given only by the world's mood and atmosphere, the feel of its pulse. It would have been madness to undertake a war without that permission. We didn't have it.

HECTOR. But you have it now.

ULYSSES. I think we do.

HECTOR. But why against us? Troy is famous for her arts, her justice, her humanity.

ULYSSES. A nation doesn't put itself at odds with its destiny by its crimes, but by its faults. Its army may be strong, its treasury well filled, its poets at the height of inspiration. But one day, why it is no one knows, because of some simple event, such as the citizens wantonly cutting down the trees, or their prince wickedly making off with a woman, or the children getting out of hand, the nation is suddenly lost. Nations, like men, die by imperceptible disorders. We recognize a doomed people by the way they sneeze or pare their nails. There's no doubt you carried off Helen badly.

HECTOR. What fairness of proportion can you see between the rape of one woman, and the possible destruction of a whole people, yours or mine, in war?

ULYSSES. We are speaking of Helen. You and Paris have made a great mistake about Helen. I've known her fifteen years, and watched her carefully. There's no doubt about it: she is one of the rare creatures destiny puts on the earth for its own personal use. They're apparently quite unimportant. It might be not even a person, but a small town, or a village: a little queen, or a child; but if you lay hands on them, watch out! It's very hard to know how to recognize one of these hostages of fate among all the other people and places. You haven't recognized it. You could have laid hands with impunity on our great admirals or one of our kings. Paris could have let himself go with perfect safety in a Spartan bed, or a Theban bed, with generous returns twenty times over; but he chose the shallowest brain, the hardest heart, the narrowest understanding of sex. And so you are lost.

HECTOR. We are giving Helen back to you.

ULYSSES. The insult to destiny can't be taken back.

HECTOR. What are we discussing, then? I'm beginning to see what is really behind your words. Admit it. You want our wealth! You had Helen carried off to give you an honorable pretext for war! I blush for Greece. She will be responsible and ashamed for the rest of time.

ULYSSES. Responsible and ashamed? Do you think so? The two words hardly agree. Even if we believed we were responsible for the war, all our generation would have to do would be to deny it, and lie, to appease the conscience of future generations. And we shall lie. We'll make that sacrifice.

HECTOR. Ah, well, the die is cast, Ulysses. On with the war! The more I hate it, the more I find growing in me an irresistible need to kill. If you won't help me, it were better you should leave here.

ULYSSES. Understand me, Hector; you have my help. Don't ask me to interpret fate. All I have tried to do is to read the world's hand, in the great lines of desert caravans, the wake of ships, and the track of migrant birds and wandering peoples. Give me your hand. There are lines there, too. We won't search to see if their lesson tells the same story. We'll suppose that these three little lines at the base of Hector's hand contradict the waves, the wings, and the furrows. I am inquisitive by nature, and not easily frightened. I'm quite willing to join issue with fate. I accept your offer of Helen. I will take her back to Menelaus. I've more than enough eloquence to convince a husband of his wife's virtue. I will even persuade Helen to believe it herself. And I'll leave at once, to avoid any chance of disturbance. Once back on my ship perhaps we can take the risk of running war on to the rocks.

HECTOR. Is this part of Ulysses' cunning, or his greatness?

ULYSSES. In this particular instance, I'm using my cunning against destiny, not against you. It's my first attempt, so I deserve some credit for it. I am sincere, Hector. If I wanted war, I should have asked for a ransom more precious to you than Helen. I am going now. But I can't shake off the feeling that the road from here to my ship is a long way.

HECTOR. My guard will escort you.

ULYSSES. As long as the road of a visiting king, when he knows there has been a threat against his life. Where are the assassins hiding? We're lucky if it's not in the heavens themselves. And the distance from here to the corner of the palace is a long way. A long way, taking this first step. Where is it going to carry me among all these perils? Am I going to slip and kill myself? Will part of the cornice fall down on me? It's all new stonework here; at any moment a stone may be dislodged. But courage. Let us go. [*He takes a first step.*]

HECTOR. Thank you, Ulysses.

ULYSSES. The first step is safely over. How many more?

HECTOR. Four hundred and sixty.

ULYSSES. Now the second! You know what made me decide to go, Hector?

HECTOR. Yes. Your noble nature.

ULYSSES. Not precisely. Andromache's eyelashes dance as my wife Penelope's do.

[*Enter* ANDROMACHE *and* CASSANDRA.]

HECTOR. Were you there all the time, Andromache?

ANDROMACHE. Let me take your arm. I've no more strength.

HECTOR. Did you hear what we said?

ANDROMACHE. Yes. I am broken.

HECTOR. You see, we needn't despair.

ANDROMACHE. We needn't despair for ourselves, perhaps. But for the world, yes. That man is terrible. All the unhappiness of the world is in me.

HECTOR. A moment or two more, and Ulysses will be on board. You see how fast he is traveling. You can follow his progress from here. There he is, on a level with the fountains. What are you doing?

ANDROMACHE. I haven't the strength any longer to hear anymore. I am covering up my ears. I won't take my hands away until we know what our fate is to be.

HECTOR. Find Helen, Cassandra!

[AJAX *enters, more drunk than ever. He sees* ANDROMACHE. *Her back is toward him.*]

CASSANDRA. Ulysses is waiting for you down at the harbor, Ajax. Helen will be brought to you there.

AJAX. Helen! To hell with Helen! This is the one I want to get my arms around.

CASSANDRA. Go away, Ajax. That is Hector's wife.

AJAX. Hector's wife! Bravo! I've always liked my friends' wives, my best friends' wives!

CASSANDRA. Ulysses is already halfway there. Hurry.

AJAX. Don't worry, my dear. She's got her hands over her ears. I can say what I like, she can't hear me. If I touched her, now, if I kissed her, certainly! But words she can't hear, what's the matter with that?

CASSANDRA. Everything is the matter with that. Go away, Ajax!

[*While* CASSANDRA *tries to force* AJAX *away from* ANDROMACHE, HECTOR *slowly raises his javelin.*]

AJAX. Do you think so? Then I might as well touch her. Might as well kiss her. But chastely, always chastely, with your best friends' wives! What's the most chaste part of your wife, Hector, her neck? So much for her neck. Her ear has a pretty little look of chastity to me. So much for her ear. I'll tell you what I've always found the chastest thing about a woman . . . Let me alone, now; let me alone! She can't even hear when I kiss her . . . You're so cursed strong! All right, I'm going, I said I was going. Good-bye.

[*He goes.* HECTOR *imperceptibly lowers his javelin. At this moment* DEMOKOS *bursts in.*]

DEMOKOS. What's this cowardice? You're giving Helen back? Trojans, to arms! They've betrayed us. Fall in! And your war-song is ready! Listen to your war-song!

HECTOR [*striking him*]. Have that for your war-song!

DEMOKOS [*falling*]. He has killed me!

HECTOR. The war isn't going to happen, Andromache!

[*He tries to take* ANDROMACHE'S *hands from her ears: she resists, her eyes fixed on* DEMOKOS. *The curtain which had begun to fall is lifted little by little.*]

ABNEOS. They have killed Demokos! Who killed Demokos?

DEMOKOS. Who killed me? Ajax! Ajax! Kill him!

ABNEOS. Kill Ajax!

HECTOR. He's lying. I am the man who struck him.

DEMOKOS. No. It was Ajax.

ABNEOS. Ajax has killed Demokos. Catch him! Punish him!

HECTOR. I struck you, Demokos, admit it! Admit it, or I'll put an end
to you!

DEMOKOS. No, my dear Hector, my good dear Hector. It was Ajax. Kill
Ajax!

CASSANDRA. He is dying, just as he lived, croaking like a frog.

ABNEOS. There. They have taken Ajax. There. They have killed him!

HECTOR [*drawing* ANDROMACHE'S *hands away from her ears*]. The war will
happen.

[*The Gates of War slowly open, to show* HELEN *kissing* TROILUS.]

CASSANDRA. The Trojan poet is dead. And now the Grecian poet will have
his word.

THE CURTAIN FINALLY FALLS

THORNTON WILDER

THE SKIN OF OUR
TEETH

THE FREE THEATER

IT HAS BEEN SUGGESTED MANY TIMES in these introductions that the form as well as the subject matter and attitude of a play is ultimately determined by the world which it reflects, by the audience and its concepts of man, the state, the universe. Further, the older forms were the result of a steady evolution from primitive roots which, once arrived at a full and expressive unit, remained basically unchanged for decades. The Euripidean structure at the end of the great century of classical drama is not radically different from the Aeschylean at its beginning; the structure of Thomas Kyd's *Spanish Tragedy* of 1585 is not radically different from the structure of James Shirley's *The Cardinal* in 1642. In such ages the world, or the view of the world, changed slowly and the dramatic medium was agreeably stable.

It was also suggested that since the modern world recognized (if it did not welcome) change as the nature of things, the dramatist was confronted with the task of discovering or creating a form for his observations, deliberately to stabilize a medium whose function was to reflect at a time when a true reflection would have been highly unstable. The result was a paradox to which playwrights and critics responded in various ways, with wholehearted or grudging acceptance, with timid or bold rejection, with earnest attempts at compromise. As man projected his mind further and further into the cosmos, as he peered more and more deeply into his psyche, the restrictions of stabilized drama—primarily, the well-made play—became more and more oppressive. Even the freedom demanded by naturalism seemed limited as greater knowledge led to greater uncertainty about what causes would produce what effects.

The drama of the twentieth century thus became marked by experimentation: symbolism, expressionism, and various other efforts to break out of the conventions of representationalism briefly took the stage. The symbolic playwright in effect declared that the essential mystery of life could be only suggested, that definable characters were untrue, that logic either of action or character was unrelated to the new perceptions of life. The expressionist in effect declared that no man, no artist, could see life clearly and see it whole, that only in distorted fragments could the world be reflected in the dramatic mirror. But, no matter how convincing their arguments, their plays found limited audiences and the movements they sponsored soon faded from the scene.

In art, however, a freedom found, a technique learned, is seldom totally lost or forgotten. Contemporary writers of poetic drama, like T. S. Eliot, have found the ancient Greek chorus a useful device for creating mood and attitude. The mask has been revived to convey the insights of psychology. Asides and direct address to the audience, abandoned by the late nineteenth-century theater as destroying the illusion of actuality, have been resurrected in the hope of creating greater intimacy between actor and spectator. Realism, the logic of place and chronology, has become so interpenetrated with the techniques of the nonrealistic drama, that the spectator has come to accept almost any device that contributes to the full expression of the playwright's vision.

A particular case in point are the plays of Thornton Wilder (b. 1897) who has written that, although he felt drama to be the greatest of the arts, in the late 1920s he suddenly found himself bored by his theatergoing experiences. A man of wide cultural background he began looking more closely at the conventions of other theaters, other nations, and found the chief obstacle to be the proscenium arch which enclosed an illusionistic setting and thus cut the audience off from the full experience of the play. He looked with particular interest at the bare platform of the Elizabethans, jutting into the midst of the spectators, and establishing an inescapable intimacy between actor and observer, an intimacy that insured involvement for the playgoer as well as the player. Was it a coincidence that in other great theatrical repertories, the classic Greek, the Japanese, there was little attempt at representational production, but considerable opportunity for interplay between player and playgoer?

One of the results of his speculation was the writing of *Our Town* (1938) intended for a sceneryless, curtainless stage, on which the Stage Manager (a kind of master-of-ceremonies) spoke directly to the audience, summoned actors to perform scenes that would illustrate the points he wished to make, stepped into the scenes himself in minor roles, made time run fast or slow as suited his convenience, and shifted locales with a sentence or two of explanation. The point of the play, the wondrousness of nonheroic life, would have been shaded by the trifling detail of realistic production—without scenery or properties every action, every gesture, was magnified, every speech, however casual or commonplace, was heard with a new clarity. *Our Town* proved to be not just a new kind of mirror, but a mirror whose reflections struck the audience with a special sense of truth; its success was not only American but worldwide.

The Skin of our Teeth (1942) is equally concerned with basic (forgettable) truths, and is equally experimental, though vastly different from *Our Town*. Its action weaves together and freshly examines two widely accepted and perhaps contradictory dogmas: that history repeats itself, an expression of human cynicism, and that mankind has repeatedly escaped from threatened destruction by the skin of its teeth, an expression of human optimism. The time of its first production is perhaps important; in 1942 America was in the midst of the Second World War. But *The Skin of Our Teeth* is not a conventional war play; it is concerned, not with the victory of the allied forces, but with the survival of man.

The play begins with a parody of the old-fashioned dramaturgy that had so bored Mr. Wilder in the twenties. The curtain rises on a conventional middle-class interior setting which is being conventionally tidied by a maid as she delivers a conventional expository speech. But it is soon apparent that the suburban home in Excelsior, New Jersey, is something other than conventional. The audience hears of the coming ice age; Mr. Antrobus, head of the household, returns home with the wheel which he has just invented; Homer quotes in Greek from *The Iliad* and Moses in Hebrew from the Bible. But such elements do not merely establish the play as a parable whose moral is that history repeats itself. *The Skin of Our Teeth* is, rather, an allegory based on a theory of history that has recurred many times in the span of human existence. One of the most productive of its appearances was during the Middle Ages when artists, beginning with the concept that all things coexist in the mind of God, created those works which seem full of ignorant (amusing) anachronisms. To the original spectators, however, as well as to those who try to comprehend the medieval mind, they are full of wisdom, illumination, and profundity. James Joyce, in *Finnegan's Wake*, gives a modern expression to the same cyclical idea, and it is from Joyce, perhaps, that Mr. Wilder derived the inspiration for his form and technique, though not for his subject matter.

Although the Antrobus family, the family of man, makes many mistakes, the play is not concerned exclusively with error. Mr. Antrobus is vain and bad-tempered and mildly lecherous, but he is equally occupied with the preservation and advancement of knowledge, with the future of his children, with the maintenance of society. As the sheet of ice threatens the destruction of all life, he desperately drills his son in the multiplication table, sets his wife to teaching their daughter the beginnings of the Bible "on the chance she can use it." On the other hand, the more practical parlormaid begs the audience to start handing up their chairs to keep the home fires burning and save the human race from refrigeration. Life is coexistence and endurance is cooperation.

The early audiences of the play were somewhat disconcerted by the way actors kept stepping out of their roles, speaking directly to the spectator or complaining about the lines assigned to them. Disturbing too were the frequent interruptions of the Stage Manager making changes in the script, reading lines, or substituting understudies as emergencies arose. However several decades of experience with the "self-conscious stage" of such French playwrights as Giraudoux, and in particular the devices of the German Bertolt Brecht, have accustomed spectators to such breaches of illusion. Brecht, indeed, established to his own satisfaction the dramatic principle that the theater is at the highest peak of efficiency when the audience is "alienated" from the events enacted, when it no longer revels in the delights of vicarious experience. Wilder, however, is up to something quite different: he is not playing games, and he has no propagandistic line to sell. By bringing the audience directly into the action ("Pass up your chairs, everybody. Save the human race."), by giving the actors a chance to be themselves as well as their characters, he is adding to his time scheme: he deals with the ice age, and the flood, and the Greeks, and here-and-now.

The fundamentally simple device of stopping the action of the play to discuss the problems of play production removes the play from any historical moment, projects it into the timeless world of art where the great ideas of the human race meet with the ordinary playgoers of 1942 or 1964, a moving, inspiring, unforgettable encounter. Indeed the procession of the hours, with its Arnoldian "touchstones," is deliberately made the responsibility of the humblest members of the theatrical troupe to emphasize the good fortune of modern man in having available at all times such guides, philosophers, and friends.

Finally, it is apparent that Mr. Wilder, in exploiting the freedom of the contemporary playwright not only to abandon but to adopt any convention, has created a dramatic structure that restores the purity of truths easily overlooked in daily busyness. More than this, he has restated the enduring metaphor of the theater as the world, reminding the audience that parlormaids and understudies as well as poets and heroes are necessary contributors to the great play of human experience.

Characters
(*in the order of their appearance*)

ANNOUNCER

SABINA

MR. FITZPATRICK

MRS. ANTROBUS

DINOSAUR

MAMMOTH

TELEGRAPH BOY

GLADYS

HENRY

MR. ANTROBUS

DOCTOR

PROFESSOR

JUDGE

HOMER

MISS E. MUSE

MISS T. MUSE

MISS M. MUSE

TWO USHERS

TWO DRUM MAJORETTES

FORTUNE TELLER

TWO CHAIR-PUSHERS

SIX CONVEENERS

BROADCAST OFFICIAL

DEFEATED CANDIDATE

MR. TREMAYNE

HESTER

IVY

FRED BAILEY

ACT I *Home, Excelsior, New Jersey.*
ACT II *Atlantic City Boardwalk.*
ACT III *Home, Excelsior, New Jersey.*

THE SKIN OF OUR TEETH

Thornton Wilder

ACT ONE

[*A projection screen in the middle of the curtain. The first lantern slide: the name of the theater, and the words: NEWS EVENTS OF THE WORLD. An* ANNOUNCER'S *voice is heard.*]

ANNOUNCER. The management takes pleasure in bringing to you—The News Events of the World:

[*Slide of the sun appearing above the horizon.*]

Freeport, Long Island:

The sun rose this morning at 6:32 a.m. This gratifying event was first reported by Mrs. Dorothy Stetson of Freeport, Long Island, who promptly telephoned the Mayor.

The Society for Affirming the End of the World at once went into a special session and postponed the arrival of that event for TWENTY-FOUR HOURS.

All honor to Mrs. Stetson for her public spirit.

New York City: [*Slide of the front doors of the theater in which this play is playing; three cleaning* WOMEN *with mops and pails.*]

The X Theater. During the daily cleaning of this theater a number of lost objects were collected as usual by Mesdames Simpson, Pateslewski, and Moriarty.

Among these objects found today was a wedding ring, inscribed: To Eva from Adam. Genesis II: 18.

The ring will be restored to the owner or owners, if their credentials are satisfactory.

Tippehatchee, Vermont: [*Slide representing a glacier.*]

The unprecedented cold weather of this summer has produced a condition that has not yet been satisfactorily explained, There is a report that a wall of ice is moving southward across these counties. The disruption of communications by the cold wave now crossing the country has rendered exact information difficult, but little credence is given to the rumor that the ice had pushed the Cathedral of Montreal as far as St. Albans, Vermont.

For further information see your daily papers.

Excelsior, New Jersey: [*Slide of a modest suburban home.*]

The home of Mr. George Antrobus, the inventor of the wheel. The discovery of the wheel, following so closely on the discovery of the lever, has centered the attention of the country on Mr. Antrobus of this attractive suburban residence district. This is his home, a commodious seven-room house, conveniently situated near a public school, a Methodist church, and a firehouse; it is right handy to an A. and P. [*Slide of* MR. ANTROBUS *on his front steps, smiling and lifting his straw hat. He holds a wheel.*]

Mr. Antrobus, himself. He comes of very old stock and has made his way up from next to nothing.

It is reported that he was once a gardener, but left that situation under circumstances that have been variously reported.

Mr. Antrobus is a veteran of foreign wars, and bears a number of scars, front and back. [*Slide of* MRS. ANTROBUS, *holding some roses.*]

This is Mrs. Antrobus, the charming and gracious president of the Excelsior Mothers' Club.

Mrs. Antrobus is an excellent needlewoman; it is she who invented the apron on which so many interesting changes have been rung since. [*Slide of the family and* SABINA.]

Here we see the Antrobuses with their two children, Henry and Gladys, and friend. The friend in the rear, is Lily Sabina, the maid.

I know we all want to congratulate this typical American family on its enterprise. We all wish Mr. Antrobus a successful future. Now the management takes you to the interior of this home for a brief visit.

[*Curtain rises. Living room of a commuter's home.* SABINA—*straw-blonde, over-rouged—is standing by the window back center, a feather duster under her elbow.*]

SABINA. Oh, oh, oh! Six o'clock and the master not home yet.

Pray God nothing serious has happened to him crossing the Hudson River. If anything happened to him, we would certainly be inconsolable and have to move into a less desirable residence district.

The fact is I don't know what'll become of us. Here it is the middle of August and the coldest day of the year. It's simply freezing; the dogs are sticking to the sidewalks; can anybody explain that? No.

But I'm not surprised. The whole world's at sixes and sevens, and why the house hasn't fallen down about our ears long ago is a miracle to me.

[*A fragment of the right wall leans precariously over the stage.* SABINA *looks at it nervously and it slowly rights itself.*]

Every night this same anxiety as to whether the master will get home safely: whether he'll bring home anything to eat. In the midst of life we are in the midst of death, a truer word was never said.

[*The fragment of scenery flies up into the lofts.* SABINA *is struck dumb with surprise, shrugs her shoulders and starts dusting* MR. ANTROBUS' *chair, including the underside.*]

Of course, Mr. Antrobus is a very fine man, an excellent husband and father, a pillar of the church, and has all the best interests of the community at heart. Of course, every muscle goes tight every time he passes a policeman; but what I think is that there are certain charges that ought not to be made, and I think I may add, ought not to be allowed to be made; we're all human; who isn't?

[*She dusts* MRS. ANTROBUS' *rocking chair.*]

Mrs. Antrobus is as fine a woman as you could hope to see. She lives only for her children; and if it would be any benefit to her children she'd see the rest of us stretched out dead at her feet without turning a hair,—that's the truth. If you want to know anything more about Mrs. Antrobus, just go and look at a tigress, and look hard.

As to the children—

Well, Henry Antrobus is a real, clean-cut American boy. He'll graduate from high school one of these days, if they make the alphabet any easier.— Henry, when he has a stone in his hand, has a perfect aim; he can hit anything from a bird to an older brother—Oh! I didn't mean to say that!—but it certainly was an unfortunate accident, and it was very hard getting the police out of the house.

Mr. and Mrs. Antrobus' daughter is named Gladys. She'll make some good man a good wife some day, if he'll just come down off the movie screen and ask her.

So here we are!

We've managed to survive for some time now, catch as catch can, the fat and the lean, and if the dinosaurs don't trample us to death, and if the grasshoppers don't eat up our garden, we'll all live to see better days, knock on wood.

Each new child that's born to the Antrobuses seems to them to be sufficient reason for the whole universe's being set in motion; and each new child that dies seems to them to have been spared a whole world of sorrow, and what the end of it will be is still very much an open question.

We've rattled along, hot and cold, for some time now—[*A portion of the wall above the door, right, flies up into the air and disappears.*]—and my advice to you is not to inquire into why or whither, but just enjoy your ice cream while it's on your plate,—that's my philosophy.

Don't forget that a few years ago we came through the depression by the skin of our teeth! One more tight squeeze like that and where will we be? [*This is a cue line.* SABINA *looks angrily at the kitchen door and repeats:*] . . . we came through the depression by the skin of our teeth; one more tight squeeze like that and where will we be? [*Flustered, she looks through the opening in the right wall; then goes to the window and reopens the Act.*] Oh, oh, oh! Six o'clock and the master not home yet. Pray God nothing has happened to him crossing the Hudson. Here it is the middle of August and the coldest day of the year. It's simply freezing; the dogs are sticking. One more tight squeeze like that and where will we be?

VOICE [*offstage*]. Make up something! Invent something!

SABINA. Well . . . uh . . . this certainly is a fine American home . . . and— uh . . . everybody's very happy . . . and—uh . . .

[*Suddenly flings pretense to the winds and coming downstage says with indignation:*]

I can't invent any words for this play, and I'm glad I can't. I hate this play and every word in it.

As for me, I don't understand a single word of it, anyway,—all about the troubles the human race has gone through, there's a subject for you.

Besides, the author hasn't made up his silly mind as to whether we're all living back in caves or in New Jersey today, and that's the way it is all the way through.

Oh—why can't we have plays like we used to have—*Peg o' My Heart*, and *Smilin' Thru*, and *The Bat*—good entertainment with a message you can take home with you?

I took this hateful job because I had to. For two years I've sat up in my room living on a sandwich and a cup of tea a day, waiting for better times in the theater. And look at me now: I—I who've played *Rain* and *The Barretts of Wimpole Street* and *First Lady*—God in Heaven!

[*The* STAGE MANAGER *puts his head out from the hole in the scenery.*]

MR. FITZPATRICK. Miss Somerset! Miss Somerset!

SABINA. Oh! Anyway!—nothing matters! It'll all be the same in a hundred years. [*Loudly.*] We came through the depression by the skin of our teeth, —that's true!—one more tight squeeze like that and where will we be?

[*Enter* MRS. ANTROBUS, *a mother.*]

MRS. ANTROBUS. Sabina, you've let the fire go out.

SABINA [*in a lather*]. One-thing-and-another; don't-know-whether-my-wits-are-upside-or-down; might-as-well-be-dead-as-alive-in-a-house-all-sixes-and-sevens. . . .

MRS. ANTROBUS. You've let the fire go out. Here it is the coldest day of the year right in the middle of August, and you've let the fire go out.

SABINA. Mrs. Antrobus, I'd like to give my two weeks' notice, Mrs. Antrobus. A girl like I can get a situation in a home where they're rich enough to have a fire in every room, Mrs. Antrobus, and a girl don't have to carry the responsibility of the whole house on her two shoulders. And a home without children, Mrs. Antrobus, because children are a thing only a parent can stand, and a truer word was never said; and a home, Mrs. Antrobus, where the master of the house don't pinch decent, self-respecting girls when he meets them in a dark corridor. I mention no names and make no charges. So you have my notice, Mrs. Antrobus. I hope that's perfectly clear.

MRS. ANTROBUS. You've let the fire go out!—Have you milked the mammoth?

SABINA. I don't understand a word of this play.—Yes, I've milked the mammoth.

MRS. ANTROBUS. Until Mr. Antrobus comes home we have no food and we have no fire. You'd better go over to the neighbors and borrow some fire.

SABINA. Mrs. Antrobus! I can't! I'd die on the way, you know I would. It's worse than January. The dogs are sticking to the sidewalks. I'd die.

MRS. ANTROBUS. Very well, I'll go.

SABINA [*even more distraught, coming forward and sinking on her knees*]. You'd never come back alive; we'd all perish; if you weren't here, we'd just perish. How do we know Mr. Antrobus'll be back? We don't know. If you go out, I'll just kill myself.

MRS. ANTROBUS. Get up, Sabina.

SABINA. Every night it's the same thing. Will he come back safe, or won't he? Will we starve to death, or freeze to death, or boil to death or will we be killed by burglars? I don't know why we go on living. I don't know why we go on living at all. It's easier being dead.

[*She flings her arms on the table and buries her head in them. In each of the succeeding speeches she flings her head up—and sometimes her hands—then quickly buries her head again.*]

MRS. ANTROBUS. The same thing! Always throwing up the sponge, Sabina. Always announcing your own death. But give you a new hat—or a plate of ice cream—or a ticket to the movies, and you want to live forever.

SABINA. You don't care whether we live or die; all you care about is those children. If it would be any benefit to them you'd be glad to see us all stretched out dead.

MRS. ANTROBUS. Well, maybe I would.

SABINA. And what do they care about? Themselves—that's all they care about. [*Shrilly.*] They make fun of you behind your back. Don't tell me: they're ashamed of you. Half the time, they pretend they're someone else's children. Little thanks you get from them.

MRS. ANTROBUS. I'm not asking for any thanks.

SABINA. And Mr. Antrobus—you don't understand *him*. All that work he does—trying to discover the alphabet and the multiplication table. Whenever he tries to learn anything you fight against it.

MRS. ANTROBUS. Oh, Sabina, I know you.

When Mr. Antrobus raped you home from your Sabine hills, he did it to insult me.

He did it for your pretty face, and to insult me.

You were the new wife, weren't you?

For a year or two you lay on your bed all day and polished the nails on your hands and feet:

You made puff-balls of the combings of your hair and you blew them up to the ceiling.

And I washed your underclothes and I made you chicken broths.

I bore children and between my very groans I stirred the cream that you'd put on your face.

But I knew you wouldn't last.

You didn't last.

SABINA. But it was I who encouraged Mr. Antrobus to make the alphabet. I'm sorry to say it, Mrs. Antrobus, but you're not a beautiful woman, and you can never know what a man could do if he tried. It's girls like I who inspire the multiplication table.

I'm sorry to say it, but you're not a beautiful woman, Mrs. Antrobus, and that's the God's truth.

MRS. ANTROBUS. And you didn't last—you sank to the kitchen. And what do you do there? *You let the fire go out!*

No wonder to you it seems easier being dead.

Reading and writing and counting on your fingers is all very well in their way,—but I keep the home going.

MRS. ANTROBUS. —There's that dinosaur on the front lawn again.—Shoo! Go away. Go away.

[*The baby* DINOSAUR *puts his head in the window.*]

DINOSAUR. It's cold.

MRS. ANTROBUS. You go around to the back of the house where you belong.

DINOSAUR. It's cold.

[*The* DINOSAUR *disappears.* MRS. ANTROBUS *goes calmly out.* SABINA *slowly raises her head and speaks to the audience. The central portion of the center wall rises, pauses, and disappears into the loft.*]

SABINA. Now that you audience are listening to this, too, I understand it a little better.

I wish eleven o'clock were here: I don't want to be dragged through this whole play again.

[*The* TELEGRAPH BOY *is seen entering along the back wall of the stage from the right. She catches sight of him and calls:*]

Mrs. Antrobus! Mrs. Antrobus! Help! There's a strange man coming to the house. He's coming up the walk, help!

[*Enter* MRS. ANTROBUS *in alarm, but efficient.*]

MRS. ANTROBUS. Help me quick!

[*They barricade the door by piling the furniture against it.*]

Who is it? What do you want?

TELEGRAPH BOY. A telegram for Mrs. Antrobus from Mr. Antrobus in the city.

SABINA. Are you sure, are you sure? Maybe it's just a trap!

MRS. ANTROBUS. I know his voice, Sabina. We can open the door.

[*Enter the* TELEGRAPH BOY, *twelve years old, in uniform. The* DINOSAUR

and MAMMOTH *slip by him into the room and settle down front right.*]
I'm sorry we kept you waiting. We have to be careful, you know.
[*To the animals.*] Hm! . . . Will you be quiet? [*They nod.*] Have you had
your supper? [*They nod.*] Are you ready to come in? [*They nod.*] Young
man, have you any fire with you? Then light the grate, will you?
[*He nods, produces something like a briquet, and kneels by the imagined
fireplace, footlights center. Pause.*]
What are people saying about this cold weather?
[*He makes a doubtful shrug with his shoulders.*]
Sabina, take this stick and go and light the stove.

SABINA. Like I told you, Mrs. Antrobus; two weeks. That's the law. I hope
that's perfectly clear.
[*Exit.*]

MRS. ANTROBUS. What about this cold weather?

TELEGRAPH BOY [*lowered eyes*]. Of course, I don't know anything . . . but
they say there's a wall of ice moving down from the north, that's what
they say. We can't get Boston by telegraph, and they're burning pianos
in Hartford.
. . . It moves everything in front of it, churches and post offices and city
halls.
I live in Brooklyn myself.

MRS. ANTROBUS. What are people doing about it?

TELEGRAPH BOY. Well . . . uh . . . talking, mostly.
Or just what you'd do a day in February.
There are some that are trying to go south and the roads are crowded;
but you can't take old people and children very far in a cold like this.

MRS. ANTROBUS. —What's this telegram you have for me?

TELEGRAPH BOY [*fingertips to his forehead*]. If you wait just a minute; I've
got to remember it.
[*The animals have left their corner and are nosing him. Presently they take
places on either side of him, leaning against his hips, like heraldic beasts.*]
This telegram was flashed from Murray Hill to University Heights! And
then by puffs of smoke from University Heights to Staten Island.
And then by lantern from Staten Island to Plainfield, New Jersey. What
hath God wrought! [*He clears his throat.*]
"To Mrs. Antrobus, Excelsior, New Jersey:
"My dear wife, will be an hour late. Busy day at the office.
"Don't worry the children about the cold just keep them warm burn
everything except Shakespeare." [*Pause.*]

MRS. ANTROBUS. Men!—He knows I'd burn ten Shakespeares to prevent a
child of mine from having one cold in the head. What does it say next?
[*Enter* SABINA.]

TELEGRAPH BOY. "Have made great discoveries today have separated em
from en."

SABINA. I know what that is, that's the alphabet, yes it is. Mr. Antrobus is

just the cleverest man. Why, when the alphabet's finished, we'll be able
to tell the future and everything.

TELEGRAPH BOY. Then listen to this: "Ten tens make a hundred semicolon
consequences far-reaching." [*Watches for effect.*]

MRS. ANTROBUS. The earth's turning to ice, and all he can do is to make
up new numbers.

TELEGRAPH BOY. Well, Mrs. Antrobus, like the head man at our office said:
a few more discoveries like that and we'll be worth freezing.

MRS. ANTROBUS. What does he say next?

TELEGRAPH BOY. I . . . I can't do this last part very well. [*He clears his throat
and sings*] "Happy w'dding ann'vers'ry to you, Happy ann'vers'ry to
you—"

[*The animals begin to howl soulfully;* SABINA *screams with pleasure.*]

MRS. ANTROBUS. Dolly! Frederick! Be quiet.

TELEGRAPH BOY [*above the din*]. "Happy w'dding ann'vers'ry, dear Eva;
happy w'dding ann'vers'ry to you."

MRS. ANTROBUS. Is that in the telegram? Are they singing telegrams now?
[*He nods.*] The earth's getting so silly no wonder the sun turns cold.

SABINA. Mrs. Antrobus, I want to take back the notice I gave you. Mrs.
Antrobus, I don't want to leave a house that gets such interesting telegrams and I'm sorry for anything I said. I really am.

MRS. ANTROBUS. Young man, I'd like to give you something for all this
trouble; Mr. Antrobus isn't home yet and I have no money and no food
in the house—

TELEGRAPH BOY. Mrs. Antrobus . . . I don't like to . . . appear to . . . ask
for anything, but . . .

MRS. ANTROBUS. What is it you'd like?

TELEGRAPH BOY. Do you happen to have an old needle you could spare?
My wife just sits home all day thinking about needles.

SABINA [*shrilly*]. We only got two in the house. Mrs. Antrobus, you know
we only got two in the house.

MRS. ANTROBUS [*after a look at* SABINA *taking a needle from her collar*]. Why
yes, I can spare this.

TELEGRAPH BOY [*lowered eyes*]. Thank you, Mrs. Antrobus. Mrs. Antrobus,
can I ask you something else? I have two sons of my own; if the cold
gets worse, what should I do?

SABINA. I think we'll all perish, that's what I think. Cold like this in August
is just the end of the whole world. [*Silence.*]

MRS. ANTROBUS. I don't know. After all, what does one do about anything? Just keep as warm as you can. And don't let your wife and children
see that you're worried.

TELEGRAPH BOY. Yes. . . . Thank you, Mrs. Antrobus. Well, I'd better be
going.—Oh, I forgot! There's one more sentence in the telegram.
"Three cheers have invented the wheel."

MRS. ANTROBUS. A wheel? What's a wheel?

TELEGRAPH BOY. I don't know. That's what it said. The sign for it is like this. Well, goodbye.

[*The women see him to the door, with good-byes and injunctions to keep warm.*]

SABINA [*apron to her eyes, wailing*]. Mrs. Antrobus, it looks to me like all the nice men in the world are already married; I don't know why that is. [*Exit.*]

MRS. ANTROBUS [*thoughtful; to the animals*]. Do you ever remember hearing tell of any cold like this in August? [*The animals shake their heads.*] From your grandmothers or anyone? [*They shake their heads.*] Have you any suggestions?

[*They shake their heads. She pulls her shawl around, goes to the front door and opening it an inch calls.*]

HENRY. GLADYS. CHILDREN. Come right in and get warm. No, no, when mama says a thing she means it.

Henry! HENRY. Put down that stone. You know what happened last time. [*Shriek.*] HENRY! Put down that stone!

Gladys! Put down your dress!! Try and be a lady.

[*The children bound in and dash to the fire. They take off their winter things and leave them in heaps on the floor.*]

GLADYS. Mama, I'm hungry. Mama, why is it so cold?

HENRY [*at the same time*]. Mama, why doesn't it snow? Mama, when's supper ready? Maybe, it'll snow and we can make snowballs.

GLADYS. Mama, it's so cold that in one more minute I just couldn't of stood it.

MRS. ANTROBUS. Settle down, both of you, I want to talk to you.

[*She draws up a hassock and sits front center over the orchestra pit before the imaginary fire. The children stretch out on the floor, leaning against her lap. Tableau by Raphael. The animals edge up and complete the triangle.*]

It's just a cold spell of some kind. Now listen to what I'm saying:

When your father comes home I want you to be extra quiet. He's had a hard day at the office and I don't know but what he may have one of his moods.

I just got a telegram from him very happy and excited, and you know what that means. Your father's temper's uneven; I guess you know that.

[*Shriek.*] Henry! Henry!

Why—why can't you remember to keep your hair down over your forehead? You must keep that scar covered up. Don't you know that when your father sees it he loses all control over himself? He goes crazy. He wants to die.

[*After a moment's despair she collects herself decisively, wets the hem of her apron in her mouth and starts polishing his forehead vigorously.*]

Lift your head up. Stop squirming. Blessed me, sometimes I think that it's going away—and then there it is: just as red as ever.

HENRY. Mama, today at school two teachers forgot and called me by my old name. They forgot, Mama. You'd better write another letter to the principal, so that he'll tell them I've changed my name. Right out in class they called me: Cain.

MRS. ANTROBUS [*putting her hand on his mouth, too late; hoarsely*]. Don't say it. [*Polishing feverishly.*] If you're good they'll forget it. Henry, you didn't hit anyone . . . today, did you?

HENRY. Oh . . . no-o-o!

MRS. ANTROBUS [*still working, not looking at Gladys*]. And, Gladys, I want you to be especially nice to your father tonight. You know what he calls you when you're good—his little angel, his little star. Keep your dress down like a little lady. And keep your voice nice and low. Gladys Antrobus!! What's that red stuff you have on your face? [*Slaps her.*] You're a filthy detestable child! [*Rises in real, though temporary, repudiation and despair.*] Get away from me, both of you! I wish I'd never seen sight or sound of you. Let the cold come! I can't stand it. I don't want to go on. [*She walks away.*]

GLADYS [*weeping*]. All the girls at school do, Mama.

MRS. ANTROBUS [*shrieking*]. I'm through with you, that's all!—Sabina! Sabina!—Don't you know your father'd go crazy if he saw that paint on your face? Don't you know your father thinks you're perfect? Don't you know he couldn't live if he didn't think you were perfect?— Sabina!

[*Enter* SABINA.]

SABINA. Yes, Mrs. Antrobus!

MRS. ANTROBUS. Take this girl out into the kitchen and wash her face with the scrubbing brush.

MR. ANTROBUS [*outside, roaring*]. "I've been working on the railroad, all the livelong day . . . etc."

[*The animals start running around in circles, bellowing.* SABINA *rushes to the window.*]

MRS. ANTROBUS. Sabina, what's that noise outside?

SABINA. Oh, it's a drunken tramp. It's a giant, Mrs. Antrobus. We'll all be killed in our beds, I know it!

MRS. ANTROBUS. Help me quick. Quick. Everybody.

[*Again they stack all the furniture against the door.* MR. ANTROBUS *pounds and bellows.*]

Who is it? What do you want?—Sabina, have you any boiling water ready?—Who is it?

MR. ANTROBUS. Broken-down camel of a pig's snout, open this door.

MRS. ANTROBUS. God be praised! It's your father.—Just a minute, George! —Sabina, clear the door, quick. Gladys, come here while I clean your nasty face!

MR. ANTROBUS. She-bitch of a goat's gizzard, I'll break every bone in your body. Let me in or I'll tear the whole house down.

MRS. ANTROBUS. Just a minute, George, something's the matter with the lock.

MR. ANTROBUS. Open the door or I'll tear your livers out. I'll smash your brains on the ceiling, and Devil take the hindmost.

MRS. ANTROBUS. Now, you can open the door, Sabina. I'm ready.

[*The door is flung open. Silence.* MR. ANTROBUS—*face of a Keystone Comedy cop—stands there in fur cap and blanket. His arms are full of parcels, including a large stone wheel with a center in it. One hand carries a railroad man's lantern. Suddenly he bursts into joyous roar.*]

MR. ANTROBUS. Well, how's the whole crooked family?

[*Relief. Laughter. Tears. Jumping up and down. Animals cavorting.* ANTROBUS *throws the parcels on the ground. Hurls his cap and blanket after them. Heroic embraces. Melee of humans and animals,* SABINA *included.*] I'll be scalded and tarred if a man can't get a little welcome when he comes home. Well, Maggie, you old gunny-sack, how's the broken-down old weather hen?—Sabina, old fishbait, old skunkpot.—And the children,—how've the little smellers been?

GLADYS. Papa, Papa, Papa, Papa, Papa.

MR. ANTROBUS. How've they been, Maggie?

MRS. ANTROBUS. Well I must say, they've been as good as gold. I haven't had to raise my voice once. I don't know what's the matter with them.

ANTROBUS [*kneeling before* GLADYS]. Papa's little weasel, eh?—Sabina, there's some food for you.—Papa's little gopher?

GLADYS [*her arm around his neck*]. Papa, you're always teasing me.

ANTROBUS. And Henry? Nothing rash today, I hope. Nothing rash?

HENRY. No, Papa.

ANTROBUS [*roaring*]. Well that's good, that's good—I'll bet Sabina let the fire go out.

SABINA. Mr. Antrobus, I've given my notice. I'm leaving two weeks from today. I'm sorry, but I'm leaving.

ANTROBUS [*roar*]. Well, if you leave now you'll freeze to death, so go and cook the dinner.

SABINA. Two weeks, that's the law.

[*Exit.*]

ANTROBUS. Did you get my telegram?

MRS. ANTROBUS. Yes.—What's a wheel?

[*He indicates the wheel with a glance.* HENRY *is rolling it around the floor. Rapid, hoarse interchange.*]

MRS. ANTROBUS. What does this cold weather mean? It's below freezing.

ANTROBUS. Not before the children!

MRS. ANTROBUS. Shouldn't we do something about it?—start off, move?

ANTROBUS. Not before the children!!! [*He gives* HENRY *a sharp slap.*]

HENRY. Papa, you hit me!

ANTROBUS. Well, remember it. That's to make you remember today. Today. The day the alphabet's finished; and the day that we *saw* the hundred—

the hundred, the hundred, the hundred, the hundred, the hundred—there's no end to 'em.

I've had a day at the office!

Take a look at that wheel, Maggie—when I've got that to rights: you'll see a sight.

There's a reward there for all the walking you've done.

MRS. ANTROBUS. How do you mean?

ANTROBUS [*on the hassock looking into the fire; with awe*]. Maggie, we've reached the top of the wave. There's not much more to be done. We're there!

MRS. ANTROBUS [*cutting across his mood sharply*]. And the ice?

ANTROBUS. The ice!

HENRY [*playing with the wheel*]. Papa, you could put a chair on this.

ANTROBUS [*broodingly*]. Ye-e-s, any booby can fool with it now,—but I thought of it first.

MRS. ANTROBUS. Children, go out in the kitchen. I want to talk to your father alone.

[*The children go out.* ANTROBUS *has moved to his chair up left. He takes the goldfish bowl on his lap; pulls the canary cage down to the level of his face. Both the animals put their paws up on the arm of his chair.* MRS. ANTROBUS *faces him across the room, like a judge.*]

MRS. ANTROBUS. Well?

ANTROBUS [*shortly*]. It's cold.—How things been, eh? Keck, keck, keck.—And you, Millicent?

MRS. ANTROBUS. I know it's cold.

ANTROBUS [*to the canary*]. No spilling of sunflower seed, eh? No singing after lights-out, y'know what I mean?

MRS. ANTROBUS. You can try and prevent us freezing to death, can't you? You can do something? We can start moving. Or we can go on the animals' backs?

ANTROBUS. The best thing about animals is that they don't talk much.

MAMMOTH. It's cold.

ANTROBUS. Eh, eh, eh! Watch that!—

—By midnight we'd turn to ice. The roads are full of people now who can scarcely lift a foot from the ground. The grass out in front is like iron,—which reminds me, I have another needle for you.—The people up north—where are they?

Frozen . . . crushed. . . .

MRS. ANTROBUS. Is that what's going to happen to us?—Will you answer me?

ANTROBUS. I don't know. I don't know anything. Some say that the ice is going slower. Some say that it's stopped. The sun's growing cold. What can I do about that? Nothing we can do but burn everything in the house, and the fenceposts and the barn. Keep the fire going. When we have no more fire, we die.

MRS. ANTROBUS. Well, why didn't you say so in the first place?

[MRS. ANTROBUS *is about to march off when she catches sight of* TWO REFUGEES, *men, who have appeared against the back wall of the theater and who are soon joined by others.*]

REFUGEES. Mr. Antrobus! Mr. Antrobus! Mr. An-nn-tro-bus!

MRS. ANTROBUS. Who's that? Who's that calling you?

ANTROBUS [*clearing his throat guiltily*]. Hm—let me see. [TWO REFUGEES *come up to the window.*]

REFUGEE. Could we warm our hands for a moment, Mr. Antrobus. It's very cold, Mr. Antrobus.

ANOTHER REFUGEE. Mr. Antrobus, I wonder if you have a piece of bread or something that you could spare.

[*Silence. They wait humbly.* MRS. ANTROBUS *stands rooted to the spot. Suddenly a knock at the door, then another hand knocking in short rapid blows.*]

MRS. ANTROBUS. Who are these people? Why, they're all over the front yard. What have they come *here* for?

[*Enter* SABINA.]

SABINA. Mrs. Antrobus! There are some tramps knocking at the back door.

MRS. ANTROBUS. George, tell these people to go away. Tell them to move right along. I'll go and send them away from the back door. Sabina, come with me.

[*She goes out energetically.*]

ANTROBUS. Sabina! Stay here! I have something to say to you.

[*He goes to the door and opens it a crack and talks through it.*]

Ladies and gentlemen! I'll have to ask you to wait a few minutes longer. It'll be all right . . . while you're waiting you might each one pull up a stake of the fence. We'll need them all for the fireplace. There'll be coffee and sandwiches in a moment.

[SABINA *looks out door over his shoulder and suddenly extends her arm pointing, with a scream.*]

SABINA. Mr. Antrobus, what's that?? —that big white thing? Mr. Antrobus, it's ICE. It's ICE!!

ANTROBUS. Sabina, I want you to go in the kitchen and make a lot of coffee. Make a whole pail full.

SABINA. Pail full!!

ANTROBUS [*with gesture*]. And sandwiches . . . piles of them . . . like this.

SABINA. Mr. An . . . !!

[*Suddenly she drops the play, and says in her own person as* MISS SOMERSET, *with surprise.*]

Oh, *I* see what this part of the play means now! This means refugees.

[*She starts to cross to the proscenium.*] Oh, I don't like it. I don't like it.

[*She leans against the proscenium and bursts into tears.*]

ANTROBUS. Miss Somerset!

VOICE *of the* STAGE MANAGER. Miss Somerset!

SABINA [*energetically, to the audience*]. Ladies and gentlemen! Don't take this play serious. The world's not coming to an end. You know it's not. People exaggerate! Most people really have enough to eat and a roof over their heads. Nobody actually starves—you can always eat grass or something. That ice business—why, it was a long, long time ago. Besides they were only savages. Savages don't love their families—not like we do.

ANTROBUS *and* STAGE MANAGER. Miss Somerset!! [*There is renewed knocking at the door.*]

SABINA. All right. I'll say the lines, but I won't think about the play. [*Enter* MRS. ANTROBUS.]

SABINA [*parting thrust at the audience*]. And I advise *you* not to think about the play, either. [*Exit* SABINA.]

MRS. ANTROBUS. George, these tramps say that you asked them to come to the house. What does this mean? [*Knocking at the door.*]

ANTROBUS. Just . . . uh . . . There are a few friends, Maggie, I met on the road. Real nice, real useful people. . . .

MRS. ANTROBUS [*back to the door*]. Now, don't you ask them in!
George Antrobus, not another soul comes in here over my dead body.

ANTROBUS. Maggie, there's a doctor there. Never hurts to have a good doctor in the house. We've lost a peck of children, one way and another. You can never tell when a child's throat will get stopped up. What you and I have seen—!!! [*He puts his fingers on his throat, and imitates diphtheria.*]

MRS. ANTROBUS. Well, just one person then, the Doctor. The others can go right along the road.

ANTROBUS. Maggie, there's an old man, particular friend of mine—

MRS. ANTROBUS. I won't listen to you—

ANTROBUS. It was he that really started off the ABC's.

MRS. ANTROBUS. I don't care if he perishes. We can do without reading or writing. We can't do without food.

ANTROBUS. Then let the ice come!! Drink your coffee!! I don't want any coffee if I can't drink it with some good people.

MRS. ANTROBUS. Stop shouting. Who else is there trying to push us off the cliff?

ANTROBUS. Well, there's the man . . . who makes all the laws. Judge Moses!

MRS. ANTROBUS. Judges can't help us now.

ANTROBUS. And if the ice melts? . . . and if we pull through? Have you and I been able to bring up Henry? What have we done?

MRS. ANTROBUS. Who are those old women?

ANTROBUS [*coughs*]. Up in town there are nine sisters. There are three or four of them here. They're sort of music teachers . . . and one of them recites . . . and one of them—

MRS. ANTROBUS. That's the end. A singing troupe! Well, take your choice, live or die. Starve your own children before your face.

ANTROBUS [*gently*]. These people don't take much. They're used to starving. They'll sleep on the floor.

Besides, Maggie, listen: no, listen:

Who've we got in the house, but Sabina? Sabina's always afraid the worst will happen. Whose spirits can she keep up? Maggie, these people never give up. They think they'll live and work forever.

MRS. ANTROBUS [*walks slowly to the middle of the room*]. All right, let them in. Let them in. You're master here. [*Softly.*] —But these animals must go. Enough's enough. They'll soon be big enough to push the walls down, anyway. Take them away.

ANTROBUS [*sadly*]. All right. The dinosaur and mammoth—! Come on, baby, come on Frederick. Come for a walk. That's a good little fellow.

DINOSAUR. It's cold.

ANTROBUS. Yes, nice cold fresh air. Bracing.

[*He holds the door open and the animals go out. He beckons to his friends. The* REFUGEES *are typical elderly out-of-works from the streets of New York today.* JUDGE MOSES *wears a skull cap.* HOMER *is a blind beggar with a guitar. The seedy crowd shuffles in and waits humbly and expectantly.* ANTROBUS *introduces them to his wife who bows to each with a stately bend of her head.*]

Make yourself at home, Maggie, this the doctor . . . m . . . Coffee'll be here in a minute. . . . Professor, this is my wife. . . . And: . . . Judge . . . Maggie, you know the Judge. [*An old blind man with a guitar.*] Maggie, you know . . . you know Homer?—Come right in, Judge.— Miss Muse—are some of your sisters here? Come right in. . . . Miss E. Muse; Miss T. Muse, Miss M. Muse.

MRS. ANTROBUS. Pleased to meet you.

Just . . . make yourself comfortable. Supper'll be ready in a minute. [*She goes out, abruptly.*]

ANTROBUS. Make yourself at home, friends. I'll be right back.

[*He goes out. The* REFUGEES *stare about them in awe. Presently several voices start whispering* "*Homer! Homer!*" *All take it up.* HOMER *strikes a chord or two on his guitar, then starts to speak.*]

HOMER.

> Μῆνιν ἄειδε, θεὰ, Πηληϊάδεω 'Αχιλῆος,
> οὐλομένην, ἣ μυρί' 'Αχαιοῖς ἄλγε' ἔθηκεν,
> πολλὰς δ' ἰφθίμους ψυχὰς—[1]

[HOMER'S *face shows he is lost in thought and memory and the words die away on his lips. The* REFUGEES *likewise nod in dreamy recollection. Soon the whisper* "*Moses, Moses!*" *goes around. An aged Jew parts his beard and recites dramatically.*]

[1] The opening lines of *The Iliad*.

MOSES.

בְּרֵאשִׁית בָּרָא אֱלֹהִים אֵת הַשָּׁמַיִם וְאֵת הָאָרֶץ: וְהָאָרֶץ הָיְתָה תֹהוּ

וָבֹהוּ וְחֹשֶׁךְ עַל־פְּנֵי תְהוֹם וְרוּחַ אֱלֹהִים מְדַחֶפֶת עַל־פְּנֵי הַמָּיִם:²

[*The same dying away of the words takes place, and on the part of the* REFUGEES *the same retreat into recollection. Some of them murmur, " Yes, yes." The mood is broken by the abrupt entrance of* MR. *and* MRS. ANTROBUS *and* SABINA *bearing platters of sandwiches and a pail of coffee.* SABINA *stops and stares at the guests.*]

MR. ANTROBUS. Sabina, pass the sandwiches.

SABINA. I thought I was working in a respectable house that had respectable guests. I'm giving my notice, Mr. Antrobus: two weeks, that's the law.

MR. ANTROBUS. Sabina! Pass the sandwiches.

SABINA. Two weeks, that's the law.

MR. ANTROBUS. There's the law. That's Moses.

SABINA [*stares*]. The Ten Commandments—FAUGH!!—[*To audience.*] That's the worst line I've ever had to say on any stage.

ANTROBUS. I think the best thing to do is just not to stand on ceremony, but pass the sandwiches around from left to right.—Judge, help yourself to one of these.

MRS. ANTROBUS. The roads are crowded, I hear?

THE GUESTS [*all talking at once*]. Oh, ma'am, you can't imagine.... You can hardly put one foot before you ... people are trampling one another. [*Sudden silence.*]

MRS. ANTROBUS. Well, you know what I think it is,—I think it's sunspots!

THE GUESTS [*discreet hubbub*]. Oh, you're right, Mrs. Antrobus ... that's what it is.... That's what I was saying the other day. [*Sudden silence.*]

ANTROBUS. Well, I don't believe the whole world's going to turn to ice. [*All eyes are fixed on him, waiting.*] I can't believe it. Judge! Have we worked for nothing? Professor! Have we just failed in the whole thing?

MRS. ANTROBUS. It is certainly very strange—well fortunately on both sides of the family we come of very hearty stock.—Doctor, I want you to meet my children. They're eating their supper now. And of course I want them to meet you.

MISS M. MUSE. How many children have you, Mrs. Antrobus?

MRS. ANTROBUS. I have two,—a boy and a girl.

MOSES [*softly*]. I understood you had two sons, Mrs. Antrobus. [MRS. ANTROBUS *in blind suffering; she walks toward the footlights.*]

MRS. ANTROBUS [*in a low voice*]. Abel, Abel, my son, my son, Abel, my son, Abel, Abel, my son.

[*The* REFUGEES *move with few steps toward her as though in comfort*

² The opening lines of *Genesis*.

*murmuring words in Greek, Hebrew, German, etc. A piercing shriek from the kitchen,—*SABINA'S *voice. All heads turn.*]

ANTROBUS. What's that?

[SABINA *enters, bursting with indignation, pulling on her gloves.*]

SABINA. Mr. Antrobus—that son of yours, that boy Henry Antrobus—I don't stay in this house another moment!—He's not fit to live among respectable folks and that's a fact.

MRS. ANTROBUS. Don't say another word, Sabina. I'll be right back.

[*Without waiting for an answer she goes past her into the kitchen.*]

SABINA. Mr. Antrobus, Henry has thrown a stone again and if he hasn't killed the boy that lives next door, I'm very much mistaken. He finished his supper and went out to play; and I heard such a fight; and then I saw it. I saw it with my own eyes. And it looked to me like stark murder.

[MRS. ANTROBUS *appears at the kitchen door, shielding* HENRY *who follows her. When she steps aside, we see on* HENRY'S *forehead a large ocher and scarlet scar in the shape of a C.* MR. ANTROBUS *starts toward him. A pause.* HENRY *is heard saying under his breath:*]

HENRY. He was going to take the wheel away from me. He started to throw a stone at me first.

MRS. ANTROBUS. George, it was just a boyish impulse. Remember how young he is. [*Louder, in an urgent wail.*] George, he's only four thousand years old.

SABINA. And everything was going along so nicely! [*Silence.* ANTROBUS *goes back to the fireplace.*]

ANTROBUS. Put out the fire! Put out all the fires. [*Violently.*] No wonder the sun grows cold. [*He starts stamping on the fireplace.*]

MRS. ANTROBUS. Doctor! Judge! Help me!—George, have you lost your mind?

ANTROBUS. There is no mind. We'll not try to live. [*To the guests.*] Give it up. Give up trying. [MRS. ANTROBUS *seizes him.*]

SABINA. Mr. Antrobus! I'm downright ashamed of you.

MRS. ANTROBUS. George, have some more coffee.—Gladys! Where's Gladys gone? [GLADYS *steps in, frightened.*]

GLADYS. Here I am, Mama.

MRS. ANTROBUS. Go upstairs and bring your father's slippers. How could you forget a thing like that, when you know how tired he is?

[ANTROBUS *sits in his chair. He covers his face with his hands.* MRS. ANTROBUS *turns to the* REFUGEES.]

Can't some of you sing? It's your business in life to sing, isn't it? Sabina!

[*Several of the women clear their throats tentatively, and with frightened faces gather around* HOMER'S *guitar. He establishes a few chords. Almost inaudibly they start singing, led by* SABINA: *"Jingle Bells."* MRS. ANTROBUS *continues to* ANTROBUS *in a low voice, while taking off his shoes.*]

George, remember all the other times. When the volcanoes came right up in the front yard.

And the time the grasshoppers ate every single leaf and blade of grass, and all the grain and spinach you'd grown with your own hands. And the summer there were earthquakes every night.

ANTROBUS. Henry! Henry! [*Puts his hand on his forehead.*] Myself. All of us, we're covered with blood.

MRS. ANTROBUS. Then remember all the times you were pleased with him and when you were proud of yourself.—Henry! Henry! Come here and recite to your father the multiplication table that you do so nicely.

[HENRY *kneels on one knee beside his father and starts whispering the multiplication table.*]

HENRY [*finally*]. Two times six is twelve; three times six is eighteen—I don't think I know the sixes.

[*Enter* GLADYS *with the slippers.* MRS. ANTROBUS *makes stern gestures to her: Go in there and do your best. The guests are now singing "Tenting Tonight."*]

GLADYS [*putting slippers on his feet*]. Papa . . . papa . . . I was very good in school today. Miss Conover said right out in class that if all the girls had as good manners as Gladys Antrobus, that the world would be a very different place to live in.

MRS. ANTROBUS. You recited a piece at assembly, didn't you? Recite it to your father.

GLADYS. Papa, do you want to hear what I recited in class? [*Fierce directorial glance from her mother.*] "THE STAR" by Henry Wadsworth LONGFELLOW.

MRS. ANTROBUS. Wait!!! The fire's going out. There isn't enough wood! Henry, go upstairs and bring down the chairs and start breaking up the beds.

[*Exit* HENRY. *The singers return to "Jingle Bells," still very softly.*]

GLADYS. Look, Papa, here's my report card. Lookit. Conduct A! Look, Papa. Papa, do you want to hear the Star, by Henry Wadsworth Longfellow? Papa, you're not mad at me, are you?—I know it'll get warmer. Soon it'll be just like spring, and we can go to a picnic at the Hibernian picnic grounds like you always like to do, don't you remember? Papa, just look at me once.

[*Enter* HENRY *with some chairs.*]

ANTROBUS. You recited in assembly, did you? [*She nods eagerly.*] You didn't forget it?

GLADYS. No!!! I was perfect.

[*Pause. Then* ANTROBUS *rises, goes to the front door and opens it. The* REFUGEES *draw back timidly; the song stops; he peers out of the door, then closes it.*]

ANTROBUS [*with decision, suddenly*]. Build up the fire. It's cold. Build up the fire. We'll do what we can. Sabina, get some more wood. Come around the fire, everybody. At least the young ones may pull through. Henry, have you eaten something?

HENRY. Yes, papa.

ANTROBUS. Gladys, have you had some supper?

GLADYS. I ate in the kitchen, papa.

ANTROBUS. If you do come through this—what'll you be able to do? What do you know? Henry, did you take a good look at that wheel?

HENRY. Yes, papa.

ANTROBUS [*sitting down in his chair*]. Six times two are—

HENRY. —twelve; six times three are eighteen; six times four are—Papa, it's hot and cold. It makes my head all funny. It makes me sleepy.

ANTROBUS [*gives him a cuff*]. Wake up. I don't care if your head is sleepy. Six times four are twenty-four. Six times five are—

HENRY. Thirty. Papa!

ANTROBUS. Maggie, put something into Gladys' head on the chance she can use it.

MRS. ANTROBUS. What do you mean, George?

ANTROBUS. Six times six are thirty-six.

Teach her the beginning of the Bible.

GLADYS. But, Mama, it's so cold and close.

[HENRY *has all but drowsed off. His father slaps him sharply and the lesson goes on.*]

MRS. ANTROBUS. "In the beginning God created the heavens and the earth; and the earth was waste and void; and the darkness was upon the face of the deep—"

[*The singing starts up again louder.* SABINA *has returned with wood.*]

SABINA [*after placing wood on the fireplace comes down to the footlights and addresses the audience.*] Will you please start handing up your chairs? We'll need everything for this fire. Save the human race.—Ushers, will you pass the chairs up here? Thank you.

HENRY. Six times nine are fifty-four; six times ten are sixty.

[*In the back of the auditorium the sound of chairs being ripped up can be heard.* USHERS *rush down the aisles with chairs and hand them over.*]

GLADYS. "And God called the light Day and the darkness he called Night."

SABINA. Pass up your chairs, everybody. Save the human race.

[*Curtain*]

ACT TWO

[*Toward the end of the intermission, though with the houselights still up, lantern-slide projections begin to appear on the curtain. Timetables for trains leaving Pennsylvania Station for Atlantic City. Advertisements of Atlantic City hotels, drugstores, churches, rug merchants; fortune tellers, bingo parlors.*

When the houselights go down, the voice of an ANNOUNCER *is heard.*]
ANNOUNCER. The Management now brings you the News Events of the
World. Atlantic City, New Jersey: [*Projection of a chrome postcard
of the waterfront, trimmed in mica with the legend: FUN AT THE
BEACH,*]

This great convention city is playing host this week to the anniversary convocation of that great fraternal order,—the Ancient and Honorable Order of Mammals, Subdivision Humans. This great fraternal,
militant and burial society is celebrating on the Boardwalk, ladies and
gentlemen, its six hundred thousandth Annual Convention.

It has just elected its president for the ensuing term,—[*Projection of*
MR. *and* MRS. ANTROBUS *posed as they will be shown a few moments
later.*] Mr. George Antrobus of Excelsior, New Jersey. We show you
President Antrobus and his gracious and charming wife, every inch a
mammal. Mr. Antrobus has had a long and chequered career. Credit
has been paid to him for many useful enterprises including the introduction of the lever, of the wheel and the brewing of beer. Credit has
been also extended to President Antrobus's gracious and charming wife
for many practical suggestions, including the hem, the gore, and the
gusset; and the novelty of the year,—frying in oil. Before we show you
Mr. Antrobus accepting the nomination, we have an important an-
nouncement to make. As many of you know, this great celebration of
the Order of the Mammals has received delegations from the other
rival Orders,—or shall we say: esteemed concurrent Orders: the WINGS,
the FINS, the SHELLS, and so on. These Orders are holding their
conventions also, in various parts of the world, and have sent representatives to our own, two of a kind.

Later in the day we will show you President Antrobus broadcasting
his words of greeting and congratulation to the collected assemblies
of the whole natural world.

Ladies and Gentlemen! We give you President Antrobus!

[*The screen becomes a transparency.* MR. ANTROBUS *stands beside a
pedestal;* MRS. ANTROBUS *is seated wearing a corsage of orchids.* ANTROBUS
*wears an untidy Prince Albert; spats; from a red rosette in his buttonhole
hangs a fine long purple ribbon of honor. He wears a gay lodge hat,—
something between a fez and a legionnaire's cap.*]

ANTROBUS. Fellow-mammals, fellow-vertebrates, fellow-humans, I thank
you. Little did my dear parents think,—when they told me to stand on
my own two feet,—that I'd arrive at this place.

My friends, we have come a long way.

During this week of happy celebration it is perhaps not fitting that we
dwell on some of the difficult times we have been through. The dinosaur
is extinct—[*applause*]—the ice has retreated; and the common cold is
being pursued by every means within our power.

[MRS. ANTROBUS *sneezes, laughs prettily, and murmurs: "I beg your pardon.*"] In our memorial service yesterday we did honor to all our friends and relatives who are no longer with us, by reason of cold, earthquakes, plagues and . . . and . . . [*coughs*] differences of opinion.

As our Bishop so ably said . . . uh . . . so ably said . . .

MRS. ANTROBUS [*closed lips*]. Gone, but not forgotten.

ANTROBUS. "They are gone, but not forgotten."

I think I can say, I think I can prophesy with complete . . . uh . . . with complete . . .

MRS. ANTROBUS. Confidence.

ANTROBUS. Thank you, my dear,—With complete lack of confidence, that a new day of security is about to dawn.

The watchword of the closing year was: Work. I give you the watchword for the future: Enjoy Yourselves.

MRS. ANTROBUS. George, sit down!

ANTROBUS. Before I close, however, I wish to answer one of those unjust and malicious accusations that were brought against me during this last electoral campaign.

Ladies and gentlemen, the charge was made that at various points in my career I leaned toward joining some of the rival orders,—that's a lie.

As I told reporters of the *Atlantic City Herald*, I do not deny that a few months before my birth I hesitated between . . . uh . . . between pinfeathers and gill-breathing,—and so did many of us here,—but for the last million years I have been viviparous, hairy and diaphragmatic. [*Applause. Cries of "Good old Antrobus," "The Prince chap!" "Georgie," etc.*]

ANNOUNCER. Thank you. Thank you very much, Mr. Antrobus.

Now I know that our visitors will wish to hear a word from that gracious and charming mammal, Mrs. Antrobus, wife and mother,—Mrs. Antrobus! [MRS. ANTROBUS *rises, lays her program on her chair, bows and says:*]

MRS. ANTROBUS. Dear Friends, I don't really think I should say anything. After all, it was my husband who was elected and not I.

Perhaps, as president of the Women's Auxiliary Bed and Board Society, —I had some notes here, oh, yes, here they are:—I should give a short report from some of our committees that have been meeting in this beautiful city.

Perhaps it may interest you to know that it has at last been decided that the tomato is edible. Can you all hear me? The tomato *is* edible.

A delegate from across the sea reports that the thread woven by the silkworm gives a cloth . . . I have a sample of it here . . . can you see it? smooth, elastic. I should say that it's rather attractive,—though personally I prefer less shiny surfaces. Should the windows of a sleeping apartment be open or shut? I know all mothers will follow our debates on this matter with close interest. I am sorry to say that the most expert authorities have not yet decided. It does seem to me that the night air would be bound to be unhealthy for our children but there are many distinguished authorities on both sides. Well, I could go on talking forever,—as Shakespeare says: a woman's work is seldom done; but I think I'd better join my husband in saying thank you, and sit down. Thank you. [*She sits down.*]

ANNOUNCER. Oh, Mrs. Antrobus!

MRS. ANTROBUS. Yes?

ANNOUNCER. We understand that you are about to celebrate a wedding anniversary. I know our listeners would like to extend their felicitations and hear a few words from you on that subject.

MRS. ANTROBUS. I have been aksed by this kind gentleman . . . yes, my friends, this spring Mr. Antrobus and I will be celebrating our five-thousandth wedding anniversary.

I don't know if I speak for my husband, but I can say that, as for me, I regret every moment of it. [*Laughter of confusion.*] I beg your pardon. What I *mean* to say is that I do not regret one moment of it. I hope none of you catch my cold. We have two children. We've always had two children, though it hasn't always been the same two. But as I say, we have two fine children, and we're very grateful for that. Yes, Mr. Antrobus and I have been married five thousand years. Each wedding anniversary reminds me of the times when there were no weddings. We had to crusade for marriage. Perhaps there are some women within the sound of my voice who remember that crusade and those struggles; we fought for it, didn't we? We chained ourselves to lampposts and we made disturbances in the Senate,—anyway, at last we women got the ring.

A few men helped us, but I must say that most men blocked our way at every step: they said we were unfeminine.

I only bring up these unpleasant memories, because I see some signs of backsliding from that great victory.

Oh, my fellow mammals, keep hold of that.

My husband says that the watchword for the year is Enjoy Yourselves. I think that's very open to misunderstanding. My watch word for the year is: Save the Family. It's held together for over five thousand years: Save it! Thank you.

ANNOUNCER. Thank you, Mrs. Antrobus. [*The transparency disappears.*]

We had hoped to show you the beauty contest that took place here today.

President Antrobus, an experienced judge of pretty girls, gave the title of Miss Atlantic City 1942, to Miss Lily-Sabina Fairweather, charming hostess of our Boardwalk Bingo Parlor.

Unfortunately, however, our time is up, and I must take you to some views of the Convention City and conveeners,—enjoying themselves. [*A burst of music; the curtain rises.*

The Boardwalk. The audience is sitting in the ocean. A handrail of scarlet cord stretches across the front of the stage. A ramp—also with scarlet handrail—descends to the right corner of the orchestra pit where a great scarlet beach umbrella or a cabana stands. Front and right stage left are benches facing the sea; attached to each bench is a street-lamp.

The only scenery is two cardboard cut-outs six feet high, representing shops at the back of the stage. Reading from left to right they are: SALT WATER TAFFY; FORTUNE TELLER; then the blank space; BINGO PARLOR; TURKISH BATH. They have practical doors, that of the Fortune Teller's being hung with bright gypsy curtains.

By the left proscenium and rising from the orchestra pit is the weather signal; it is like the mast of a ship with cross bars. From time to time black discs are hung on it to indicate the storm and hurricane warnings. Three roller chairs, pushed by melancholy NEGROES *file by empty. Throughout the act they traverse the stage in both directions.*

From time to time, CONVEENERS, *dressed like* MR. ANTROBUS, *cross the stage. Some walk sedately by; others engage in inane horseplay. The old gypsy* FORTUNE TELLER *is seated at the door of her shop, smoking a corncob pipe.*

From the Bingo Parlor comes the voice of the CALLER.]

BINGO CALLER. A-Nine; A-Nine. C-Twenty-six; C-Twenty-six. A-Four; A-Four. B-Twelve.

CHORUS [*backstage*]. Bingo!!!

[*The front of the Bingo Parlor shudders, rises a few feet in the air and returns to the ground trembling.*]

FORTUNE TELLER [*mechanically, to the unconscious back of a passerby, pointing with her pipe*]. Bright's disease! Your partner's deceiving you in that Kansas City deal. You'll have six grandchildren. Avoid high places. [*She rises and shouts after another.*] Cirrhosis of the liver!

[SABINA *appears at the door of the Bingo Parlor. She hugs about her a blue raincoat that almost conceals her red bathing suit. She tries to catch the* FORTUNE TELLER'S *attention.*]

SABINA. Ssssst! Esmeralda! Ssssst!

FORTUNE TELLER. Keck!

SABINA. Has President Antrobus come along yet?

FORTUNE TELLER. No, no, no. Get back there. Hide yourself.

SABINA. I'm afraid I'll miss him. Oh, Esmeralda, if I fail in this, I'll die; I know I'll die. President Antrobus!!! And I'll be his wife! If it's the last thing I'll do, I'll be Mrs. George Antrobus.—Esmeralda, tell me my future.

FORTUNE TELLER. Keck!

SABINA. All right, I'll tell *you* my future. [*Laughing dreamily and tracing it out with one finger on the palm of her hand.*] I've won the Beauty Contest in Atlantic City,—well, I'll win the Beauty Contest of the whole world. I'll take President Antrobus away from that wife of his. Then I'll take every man away from his wife. I'll turn the whole earth upside down.

FORTUNE TELLER. Keck!

SABINA. When all those husbands just think about me they'll get dizzy.
They'll faint in the streets. They'll have to lean against lampposts.—
Esmeralda, who was Helen of Troy?

FORTUNE TELLER [*furiously*]. Shut your foolish mouth. When Mr. Antrobus
comes along you can see what you can do. Until then,—go away.

[SABINA *laughs. As she returns to the door of her Bingo Parlor a group of*
CONVEENERS *rush over and smother her with attentions.*]

CONVEENERS. Oh, Miss Lily, you know me. You've known me for years.

SABINA. Go away, boys, go away. I'm after bigger fry than you are.—Why,
Mr. Simpson!! How *dare* you!! I expect that even you nobodies must
have girls to amuse you; but where you find them and what you do with
them, is of absolutely no interest to me.

[*Exit. The* CONVEENERS *squeal with pleasure and stumble in after her. The*
FORTUNE TELLER *rises, puts her pipe down on the stool, unfurls her volu-
minous skirts, gives a sharp wrench to her bodice and strolls toward the
audience, swinging her hips like a young woman.*]

FORTUNE TELLER. I tell the future. Keck. Nothing easier. Everybody's
future is in their face. Nothing easier.

But who can tell your past,—eh? Nobody!

Your youth,—where did it go? It slipped away while you weren't looking.
While you were asleep. While you were drunk? Puh! You're like our
friends, Mr. and Mrs. Antrobus; you lie awake nights trying to know your
past. What did it mean? What was it trying to say to you?

Think! Think! Split your heads. I can't tell the past and neither can you.
If anybody tries to tell you the past, take my word for it, they're charlatans! Charlatans! But I can tell you the future. [*She suddenly barks at a
passing* CHAIR-PUSHER.] Apoplexy! [*She returns to the audience.*] Nobody
listens.—Keck! I see a face among you now—I won't embarrass him
by pointing him out, but, listen, it may be you: Next year the watch-
springs inside you will crumple up. Death by regret,—Type Y. It's in the
corners of your mouth. You'll decide that you should have lived for
pleasure, but that you missed it. Death by regret,—Type Y. . . . Avoid
mirrors. You'll try to be angry,—but no!—no anger. [*Far forward,
confidentially.*] And now what's the immediate future of our friends, the
Antrobuses? Oh, you've seen it as well as I have, keck,—that dizziness
of the head; that Great Man dizziness? The inventor of beer and gunpowder? The sudden fits of temper and then the long stretches of inertia?
"I'm a sultan; let my slave-girls fan me?"

You know as well as I do what's coming. Rain. Rain. Rain in floods.
The deluge. But first you'll see shameful things—shameful things. Some
of you will be saying: "Let him drown. He's not worth saving. Give the
whole thing up." I can see it in your faces. But you're wrong. Keep your
doubts and despairs to yourselves.

Again there'll be the narrow escape. The survival of a handful. From destruction,—total destruction. [*She points sweeping with her hand to the stage.*] Even of the animals, a few will be saved: two of a kind, male and female, two of a kind.

[*The heads of* CONVEENERS *appear about the stage and in the orchestra pit, jeering at her.*]

CONVEENERS. Charlatan! Madam Killjoy! Mrs. Jeremiah! Charlatan!

FORTUNE TELLER. And *you!* Mark my words before it's too late. Where'll *you* be?

CONVEENERS. The croaking raven. Old dust and ashes. Rags, bottles, sacks.

FORTUNE TELLER. Yes, stick out your tongues. You can't stick your tongues out far enough to lick the death-sweat from your foreheads. It's too late to work now—bail out the flood with your soup spoons. You've had your chance and you've lost.

CONVEENERS. Enjoy yourselves!!! [*They disappear. The* FORTUNE TELLER *looks off left and puts her finger on her lip.*]

FORTUNE TELLER. They're coming—the Antrobuses. Keck. Your hope. Your despair. Your selves.

[*Enter from the left,* MR. *and* MRS. ANTROBUS *and* GLADYS.]

MRS. ANTROBUS. Gladys Antrobus, stick your stummick in.

GLADYS. But it's easier this way.

MRS. ANTROBUS. Well, it's too bad the new president has such a clumsy daughter, that's all I can say. Try and be a lady.

FORTUNE TELLER. Aijah! That's been said a hundred billion times.

MRS. ANTROBUS. Goodness! Where's Henry? He was here just a minute ago. Henry!

[*Sudden violent stir. A roller-chair appears from the left. About it are dancing in great excitement* HENRY *and a* NEGRO CHAIR-PUSHER.]

HENRY [*slingshot in hand*]. I'll put your eye out. I'll make you yell, like you never yelled before.

NEGRO [*at the same time*]. Now, I warns you. I warns you. If you make me mad, you'll get hurt.

ANTROBUS. Henry! What is this? Put down that slingshot.

MRS. ANTROBUS [*at the same time*]. Henry! HENRY! Behave yourself.

FORTUNE TELLER. That's right, young man. There are too many people in the world as it is. Everybody's in the way, except one's self.

HENRY. All I wanted to do was—have some fun.

NEGRO. Nobody can't touch my chair, nobody, without I allow 'em to. You get clean away from me and you get away fast.

[*He pushes his chair off, muttering.*]

ANTROBUS. What were you doing, Henry?

HENRY. Everybody's always getting mad. Everybody's always trying to push you around. I'll make him sorry for this; I'll make him sorry.

ANTROBUS. Give me that slingshot.

HENRY. I won't. I'm sorry I came to this place. I wish I weren't here. I wish I weren't anywhere.

MRS. ANTROBUS. Now, Henry, don't get so excited about nothing. I declare I don't know what we're going to do with you. Put your slingshot in your pocket, and don't try to take hold of things that don't belong to you.

ANTROBUS. After this you can stay home. I wash my hands of you.

MRS. ANTROBUS. Come now, let's forget all about it. Everybody take a good breath of that sea air and calm down.

[*A passing* CONVEENER *bows to* ANTROBUS *who nods to him.*]

Who was that you spoke to, George?

ANTROBUS. Nobody, Maggie. Just the candidate who ran against me in the election.

MRS. ANTROBUS. The man who ran against you in the election!!

[*She turns and waves her umbrella after the disappearing* CONVEENER.]

My husband didn't speak to you and he never will speak to you.

ANTROBUS. Now, Maggie.

MRS. ANTROBUS. After those lies you told about him in your speeches! Lies, that's what they were.

GLADYS *and* HENRY. Mama, everybody's looking at you. Everybody's laughing at you.

MRS. ANTROBUS. If you must know, my husband's a SAINT, a downright SAINT, and you're not fit to speak to him on the street.

ANTROBUS. Now, Maggie, now, Maggie, that's enough of that.

MRS. ANTROBUS. George Antrobus, you're a perfect worm. If you won't stand up for yourself, I will.

GLADYS. Mama, you just act awful in public.

MRS. ANTROBUS [*laughing*]. Well, I must say I enjoyed it. I feel better. Wish his wife had been there to hear it. Children, what do you want to do?

GLADYS. Papa, can we ride in one of those chairs? Mama, I want to ride in one of those chairs.

MRS. ANTROBUS. No, sir. If you're tired you just sit where you are. We have no money to spend on foolishness.

ANTROBUS. I guess we have money enough for a thing like that. It's one of the things you do at Atlantic City.

MRS. ANTROBUS. Oh, we have? I tell you it's a miracle my children have shoes to stand up in. I didn't think I'd ever live to see them pushed around in chairs.

ANTROBUS. We're on a vacation, aren't we? We have a right to some treats, I guess. Maggie, some day you're going to drive me crazy.

MRS. ANTROBUS. All right, go. I'll just sit here and laugh at you. And you can give me my dollar right in my hand. Mark my words, a rainy day is coming. There's a rainy day ahead of us. I feel it in my bones. Go on, throw your money around. I can starve. I've starved before. I know how.

[*A* CONVEENER *puts his head through the Turkish Bath window, and says with raised eyebrows:*]

CONVEENER. Hello, George. How are ya? I see where you brought the WHOLE family along.

MRS. ANTROBUS. And what do you mean by that?

[CONVEENER *withdraws head and closes window.*]

ANTROBUS. Maggie, I tell you there's a limit to what I can stand. God's Heaven, haven't I worked *enough?* Don't I get *any* vacation? Can't I even give my children so much as a ride in a roller-chair?

MRS. ANTROBUS [*putting out her hand for raindrops*]. Anyway, it's going to rain very soon and you have your broadcast to make.

ANTROBUS. Now, Maggie, I warn you. A man can stand a family only just so long. I'm warning you.

[*Enter* SABINA *from the Bingo Parlor. She wears a flounced red silk bathing suit, 1905. Red stockings, shoes, parasol. She bows demurely to* ANTROBUS *and starts down the ramp.* ANTROBUS *and the children stare at her.* ANTROBUS *bows gallantly.*]

MRS. ANTROBUS. Why, George Antrobus, how can you say such a thing! You have the best family in the world.

ANTROBUS. Good morning, Miss Fairweather.

[SABINA *finally disappears behind the beach umbrella or in a cabana in the orchestra pit.*]

MRS. ANTROBUS. Who on earth was that you spoke to, George?

ANTROBUS [*complacent; mock-modest*]. Hm . . . m . . . just a . . . solambaka keray.

MRS. ANTROBUS. What? I can't understand you.

GLADYS. Mama, wasn't she beautiful?

HENRY. Papa, introduce her to me.

MRS. ANTROBUS. Children, will you be quiet while I ask your father a simple question?—Who did you say it was, George?

ANTROBUS. Why-uh . . . a friend of mine. Very nice refined girl.

MRS. ANTROBUS. I'm waiting.

ANTROBUS. Maggie, that's the girl I gave the prize to in the beauty contest, —that's Miss Atlantic City 1942.

MRS. ANTROBUS. Hm! She looked like Sabina to me.

HENRY [*at the railing*]. Mama, the lifeguard knows her, too. Mama, he knows her well.

ANTROBUS. Henry, come here.—She's a very nice girl in every way and the sole support of her aged mother.

MRS. ANTROBUS. So was Sabina, so was Sabina; and it took a wall of ice to open your eyes about Sabina.—Henry, come over and sit down on this bench.

ANTROBUS. She's a very different matter from Sabina. Miss Fairweather is a college graduate, Phi Beta Kappa.

MRS. ANTROBUS. Henry, you sit here by mama. Gladys—

ANTROBUS [*sitting*]. Reduced circumstances have required her taking a position as hostess in a bingo parlor; but there isn't a girl with higher principles in the country.

MRS. ANTROBUS. Well, let's not talk about it.—Henry, I haven't seen a whale yet.

ANTROBUS. She speaks seven languages and has more culture in her little finger than you've acquired in a lifetime.

MRS. ANTROBUS [*assuming amiability*]. All right, all right, George. I'm glad to know there are such superior girls in the bingo parlors.—Henry, what's that? [*Pointing at the storm signal, which has one black disk.*]

HENRY. What is it, Papa?

ANTROBUS. What? Oh, that's the storm signal. One of those black disks means bad weather; two means storm; three means hurricane; and four means the end of the world. [*As they watch it a second black disk rolls into place.*]

MRS. ANTROBUS. Goodness! I'm going this very minute to buy you all some raincoats.

GLADYS [*putting her cheek against her father's shoulder*]. Mama, don't go yet. I like sitting this way. And the ocean coming in and coming in. Papa, don't you like it?

MRS. ANTROBUS. Well, there's only one thing I lack to make me a perfectly happy woman: I'd like to see a whale.

HENRY. Mama, we saw two. Right out there. They're delegates to the convention. I'll find you one.

GLADYS. Papa, ask me something. Ask me a question.

ANTROBUS. Well . . . how big's the ocean?

GLADYS. Papa, you're teasing me. It's–three–hundred and sixty million square–miles–and–it–covers–three–fourths–of–the–earth's–surface– and–its–deepest–place–is–five–and–a–half–miles–deep–and–its–average– depth–is–twelve–thousand–feet. No, Papa, ask me something hard, real hard.

MRS. ANTROBUS [*rising*]. Now I'm going off to buy those raincoats. I think that bad weather's going to get worse and worse. I hope it doesn't come before your broadcast. I should think we have about an hour or so.

HENRY. I hope it comes and zzzzzz everything before it. I hope it—

MRS. ANTROBUS. Henry!—George, I think . . . maybe, it's one of those storms that are just as bad on land as on the sea. When you're just as safe and safer in a good stout boat.

HENRY. There's a boat out at the end of the pier.

MRS. ANTROBUS. Well, keep your eye on it. George, you shut your eyes and get a good rest before the broadcast.

ANTROBUS. Thundering Judas, do I have to be told when to open and shut my eyes? Go and buy your raincoats.

MRS. ANTROBUS. Now, children, you have ten minutes to walk around. Ten minutes. And, Henry: control yourself. Gladys, stick by your brother and don't get lost.

[*They run off.*]

MRS. ANTROBUS. Will you be all right, George?

[CONVEENERS *suddenly stick their heads out of the Bingo Parlor and Salt Water Taffy store, and voices rise from the orchestra pit.*]

CONVEENERS. George. Geo-r-r-rge! George! Leave the old hen-coop at home, George. Do-mes-ticated Georgie!

MRS. ANTROBUS [*shaking her umbrella*]. Low common oafs! That's what they are. Guess a man has a right to bring his wife to a convention, if he wants to. [*She starts off.*] What's the matter with a family, I'd like to know. What else have they got to offer?

[*Exit.* ANTROBUS *has closed his eyes. The* FORTUNE TELLER *comes out of her shop and goes over to the left proscenium. She leans against it watching* SABINA *quizzically.*]

FORTUNE TELLER. Heh! Here she comes!

SABINA [*loud whisper*]. What's he doing?

FORTUNE TELLER. Oh, he's ready for you. Bite your lips, dear, take a long breath and come on up.

SABINA. I'm nervous. My whole future depends on this. I'm nervous.

FORTUNE TELLER. Don't be a fool. What more could you want? He's forty-five. His head's a little dizzy. He's just been elected president. He's never known any other woman than his wife. Whenever he looks at her he realizes that she knows every foolish thing he's ever done.

SABINA [*still whispering*]. I don't know why it is, but every time I start one of these I'm nervous.

[*The* FORTUNE TELLER *stands in the center of the stage watching the following:*]

FORTUNE TELLER. You make me tired.

SABINA. First tell me my fortune.

[*The* FORTUNE TELLER *laughs drily and makes the gesture of brushing away a nonsensical question.* SABINA *coughs and says:*]

SABINA. Oh, Mr. Antrobus,—dare I speak to you for a moment?

ANTROBUS. What?—Oh, certainly, certainly, Miss Fairweather.

SABINA. Mr. Antrobus . . . I've been so unhappy. I've wanted . . . I've wanted to make sure that you don't think that I'm the kind of girl who goes out for beauty contests.

FORTUNE TELLER. That's the way!

ANTROBUS. Oh, I understand. I understand perfectly.

FORTUNE TELLER. Give it a little more. Lean on it.

SABINA. I knew you would. My mother said to me this morning: Lily, she said, that fine Mr. Antrobus gave you the prize because he saw at once that you weren't the kind of girl who'd go in for a thing like that. But, honestly, Mr. Antrobus, in this world, honestly, a good girl doesn't know where to turn.

FORTUNE TELLER. Now you've gone too far.

ANTROBUS. My dear Miss Fairweather!

SABINA. You wouldn't know how hard it is. With that lovely wife and daughter you have. Oh, I think Mrs. Antrobus is the finest woman I ever saw. I wish I were like her.

ANTROBUS. There, there. There's . . . uh . . . room for all kinds of people in the world, Miss Fairweather.

SABINA. How wonderful of you to say that. How generous!—Mr. Antrobus, have you a moment free? . . . I'm afraid I may be a little conspicuous here . . . could you come down, for just a moment, to my beach cabana . . . ?

ANTROBUS. Why-uh . . . yes, certainly . . . for a moment . . . just for a moment.

SABINA. There's a deck chair there. Because: you know you *do* look tired. Just this morning my mother said to me: Lily, she said, I hope Mr. Antrobus is getting a good rest. His fine strong face has deep deep lines in it. Now isn't it true, Mr. Antrobus: you work too hard?

FORTUNE TELLER. Bingo! [*She goes into her shop.*]

SABINA. Now you will just stretch out. No, I shan't say a word, not a word. I shall just sit there,—privileged. That's what I am.

ANTROBUS [*taking her hand*]. Miss Fairweather . . . you'll . . . spoil me.

SABINA. Just a moment. I have something I wish to say to the audience.— Ladies and gentlemen. I'm not going to play this particular scene tonight. It's just a short scene and we're going to skip it. But I'll tell you what takes place and then we can continue the play from there on. Now in this scene—

ANTROBUS [*between his teeth*]. But, Miss Somerset!

SABINA. I'm sorry. I'm sorry. But I have to skip it. In this scene, I talk to Mr. Antrobus, and at the end of it he decides to leave his wife, get a divorce at Reno and marry me. That's all.

ANTROBUS. Fitz!—Fitz!

SABINA. So that now I've told you we can jump to the end of it,—where you say: [*Enter in fury* MR. FITZPATRICK, *the Stage Manager.*]

MR. FITZPATRICK. Miss Somerset, we insist on your playing this scene.

SABINA. I'm sorry, Mr. Fitzpatrick, but I can't and I won't. I've told the audience all they need to know and now we can go on.

[*Other actors begin to appear on the stage, listening.*]

MR. FITZPATRICK. And *why* can't you play it?

SABINA. Because there are some lines in that scene that would hurt some people's feelings and I don't think the theater is a place where people's feelings ought to be hurt.

MR. FITZPATRICK. Miss Somerset, you can pack up your things and go home. I shall call the understudy and I shall report you to Equity.[3]

SABINA. I sent the understudy up to the corner for a cup of coffee and if

---

[3] The actors' union.

Equity tries to penalize me I'll drag the case right up to the Supreme Court. Now listen, everybody, there's no need to get excited.

MR. FITZPATRICK *and* ANTROBUS. Why can't you play it . . . what's the matter with the scene?

SABINA. Well, if you must know, I have a personal guest in the audience tonight. Her life hasn't been exactly a happy one. I wouldn't have my friend hear some of these lines for the whole world. I don't suppose it occurred to the author that some other women might have gone through the experience of losing their husbands like this. Wild horses wouldn't drag from me the details of my friend's life . . . well, they'd been married twenty years, and before he got rich, why, she'd done the washing and everything.

MR. FITZPATRICK. Miss Somerset, your friend will forgive you. We must play this scene.

SABINA. Nothing, nothing will make me say some of those lines . . . about "a man outgrows a wife every seven years" and . . . and that one about "the Mohammedans being the only people who looked the subject square in the face." Nothing.

MR. FITZPATRICK. Miss Somerset! Go to your dressing room. I'll *read* your lines.

SABINA. Now everybody's nerves are on edge.

MR. ANTROBUS. Skip the scene.

[MR. FITZPATRICK *and the other actors go off.*]

SABINA. Thank you. I knew you'd understand. We'll do just what I said. So Mr. Antrobus is going to divorce his wife and marry me. Mr. Antrobus, you say: "It won't be easy to lay all this before my wife."

[*The actors withdraw.* ANTROBUS *walks about, his hand to his forehead, muttering.*]

ANTROBUS. Wait a minute. I can't get back into it as easily as all that. "My wife is a very obstinate woman." Hm . . . then you say . . . hm . . . Miss Fairweather, I mean Lily, it won't be easy to lay all this before my wife. It'll hurt her feelings a little.

SABINA. Listen, George: *other* people haven't got feelings. Not in the same way that we have,—we who are presidents like you and prize-winners like me. Listen, other people haven't got feelings; they just imagine they have. Within two weeks they go back to playing bridge and going to the movies. Listen, dear: everybody in the world except a few people like you and me are just people of straw. Most people have no insides at all. Now that you're president you'll see that. Listen, darling, there's a kind of secret society at the top of the world,—like you and me,—that know this. The world was made for us. What's life anyway? Except for two things, pleasure and power, what is life? Boredom! Foolishness. You know it is. Except for those two things, life's nau-se-at-ing. So,—come here!

[*She moves close. They kiss.*]

So.

Now when your wife comes, it's really very simple; just tell her.

ANTROBUS. Lily, Lily: you're a wonderful woman.

SABINA. Of course I am.

[*They enter the cabana and it hides them from view. Distant roll of thunder. A third black disk appears on the weather signal. Distant thunder is heard.* MRS. ANTROBUS *appears carrying parcels. She looks about, seats herself on the bench left, and fans herself with her handkerchief. Enter* GLADYS *right, followed by two* CONVEENERS. *She is wearing red stockings.*]

MRS. ANTROBUS. Gladys!

GLADYS. Mama, here I am.

MRS. ANTROBUS. Gladys Antrobus!!! Where did you get those dreadful things?

GLADYS. Wha-a-t? Papa liked the color.

MRS. ANTROBUS. You go back to the hotel this minute!

GLADYS. I won't. I won't. Papa liked the color.

MRS. ANTROBUS. All right. All right. You stay here. I've a good mind to let your father see you that way. You stay right here.

GLADYS. I . . . I don't want to stay if . . . if you don't think he'd like it.

MRS. ANTROBUS. Oh . . . it's all one to me. I don't care what happens. I don't care if the biggest storm in the whole world comes. Let it come. [*She folds her hands.*] Where's your brother?

GLADYS [*in a small voice*]. He'll be here.

MRS. ANTROBUS. Will he? Well, let him get into trouble. I don't care. I don't know where your father is, I'm sure. [*Laughter from the cabana.*]

GLADYS [*leaning over the rail*]. I think he's . . . Mama, he's talking to the lady in the red dress.

MRS. ANTROBUS. Is that so? [*Pause.*] We'll wait till he's through. Sit down here beside me and stop fidgeting . . . what are you crying about?

[*Distant thunder. She covers* GLADYS' *stockings with a raincoat.*]

GLADYS. You don't like my stockings.

[TWO CONVEENERS *rush in with a microphone on a standard and various paraphernalia. The* FORTUNE TELLER *appears at the door of her shop. Other characters gradually gather.*]

BROADCAST OFFICIAL. Mrs. Antrobus! Thank God we've found you at last. Where's Mr. Antrobus? We've been hunting everywhere for him. It's about time for the broadcast to the conventions of the world.

MRS. ANTROBUS [*calm*]. I expect he'll be here in a minute.

BROADCAST OFFICIAL. Mrs. Antrobus, if he doesn't show up in time, I hope you will consent to broadcast in his place. It's the most important broadcast of the year.

[SABINA *enters from the cabana followed by* ANTROBUS.]

MRS. ANTROBUS. No, I shan't. I haven't one single thing to say.

BROADCAST OFFICIAL. Then won't you help us find him, Mrs. Antrobus? A storm's coming up. A hurricane. A deluge!

SECOND CONVEENER [*who has sighted* ANTROBUS *over the rail*]. Joe! Joe!
Here he is.

BROADCAST OFFICIAL. In the name of God, Mr. Antrobus, you're on the air
in five minutes. Will you kindly please come and test the instrument?
That's all we ask. If you just please begin the alphabet slowly.

[ANTROBUS, *with set face, comes ponderously up the ramp. He stops at the
point where his waist is level with the stage and speaks authoritatively to
the* OFFICIALS.]

ANTROBUS. I'll be ready when the time comes. Until then, move away. Go
away. I have something I wish to say to my wife.

BROADCAST OFFICIAL [*whimpering*]. Mr. Antrobus! *This is* the most important broadcast of the year.

[*The* OFFICIALS *withdraw to the edge of the stage.* SABINA *glides up the ramp
behind* ANTROBUS.]

SABINA [*whispering*]. Don't let her argue. Remember arguments have
nothing to do with it.

ANTROBUS. Maggie, I'm moving out of the hotel. In fact, I'm moving out
of everything. For good. I'm going to marry Miss Fairweather. I shall
provide generously for you and the children. In a few years you'll be able
to see that it's all for the best. That's all I have to say.

BROADCAST OFFICAL. Mr. Antrobus!
I hope you'll be ready. This is the
most important broadcast of the
year.

BINGO ANNOUNCER: A—nine; A—
nine. D—forty-two; D—forty-
two. C—thirty; C—thirty.
B—seventeen; B—seventeen. C—
forty; C—forty.

GLADYS. What did Papa say, Mama?
I didn't hear what Papa said.

BROADCAST OFFICIAL. Mr. Antrobus.
All we want to do is test your
voice with the alphabet.

CHORUS. Bingo!!

ANTROBUS. Go away. Clear out.

MRS. ANTROBUS [*composedly with lowered eyes*]. George, I can't talk to you
until you wipe those silly red marks off your face.

ANTROBUS. I think there's nothing to talk about. I've said what I have
to say.

SABINA. Splendid!!

ANTROBUS. You're a fine woman, Maggie, but . . . but a man has his own
life to lead in the world.

MRS. ANTROBUS. Well, after living with you for five thousand years I guess
I have a right to a word or two, haven't I?

ANTROBUS [*to* SABINA]. What can I answer to that?

SABINA. Tell her that conversation would only hurt her feelings. It's-kinder-
in-the-long-run-to-do-it-short-and-quick.

ANTROBUS. I want to spare your feelings in every way I can, Maggie.

BROADCAST OFFICIAL. Mr. Antrobus, the hurricane signal's gone up. We
could begin right now.

MRS. ANTROBUS [*calmly, almost dreamily*]. I didn't marry you because you were perfect. I didn't even marry you because I loved you. I married you because you gave me a promise. [*She takes off her ring and looks at it.*] That promise made up for your faults. And the promise I gave you made up for mine. Two imperfect people got married and it was the promise that made the marriage.

ANTROBUS. Maggie, . . . I was only nineteen.

MRS. ANTROBUS [*she puts her ring back on her finger*]. And when our children were growing up, it wasn't a house that protected them; and it wasn't our love, that protected them—it was that promise.

And when that promise is broken—this can happen!

[*With a sweep of the hand she removes the raincoat from* GLADYS' *stockings.*]

ANTROBUS [*stretches out his arm, apoplectic*]. Gladys!! Have you gone crazy? Has everyone gone crazy? [*Turning on* SABINA.] You did this. You gave them to her.

SABINA. I never said a word to her.

ANTROBUS [*to* GLADYS]. You go back to the hotel and take those horrible things off.

GLADYS [*pert*]. Before I go, I've got something to tell you,—it's about Henry.

MRS. ANTROBUS [*claps her hands peremptorily*]. Stop your noise,—I'm taking her back to the hotel, George. Before I go I have a letter. . . . I have a message to throw into the ocean. [*Fumbling in her handbag.*] Where is the plagued thing? Here it is.

[*She flings something—invisible to us—far over the heads of the audience to the back of the auditorium.*]

It's a bottle. And in the bottle's a letter. And in the letter is written all the things that a woman knows.

It's never been told to any man and it's never been told to any woman, and if it finds its destination, a new time will come. We're not what books and plays say we are. We're not what advertisements say we are. We're not in the movies and we're not on the radio.

We're not what you're all told and what you think we are: we're ourselves. And if any man can find one of us he'll learn why the whole universe was set in motion. And if any man harm any one of us, his soul —the only soul he's got—had better be at the bottom of that ocean,— and that's the only way to put it. Gladys, come here. We're going back to the hotel.

[*She drags* GLADYS *firmly off by the hand, but* GLADYS *breaks away and comes down to speak to her father.*]

SABINA. Such goings-on. Don't give it a minute's thought.

GLADYS. Anyway, I think you ought to know that Henry hit a man with a stone. He hit one of those colored men that push the chairs and the man's very sick. Henry ran away and hid and some policemen are looking for him very hard. And I don't care a bit if you don't want to have anything to do with mama and me, because I'll never like you again and I hope nobody ever likes you again,—so there!

[*She runs off.* ANTROBUS *starts after her.*]

ANTROBUS. I . . . I have to go and see what I can do about this.

SABINA. You stay right here. Don't you go now while you're excited. Gracious sakes, all these things will be forgotten in a hundred years. Come, now, you're on the air. Just say anything,—it doesn't matter what. Just a lot of birds and fishes and things.

BROADCAST OFFICIAL. Thank you, Miss Fairweather. Thank you very much. Ready, Mr. Antrobus.

ANTROBUS [*touching the microphone*]. What is it, what is it? Who am I talking to?

BROADCAST OFFICIAL. Why, Mr. Antrobus! To our order and to all the other orders.

ANTROBUS [*raising his head*]. What are all those birds doing?

BROADCAST OFFICIAL. Those are just a few of the birds. Those are the delegates to our convention,—two of a kind.

ANTROBUS [*pointing into the audience*]. Look at the water. Look at them all. Those fishes jumping. The children should see this!—There's Maggie's whales!! Here are your whales, Maggie!!

BROADCAST OFFICIAL. I hope you're ready, Mr. Antrobus.

ANTROBUS. And look on the beach! You didn't tell me these would be here!

SABINA. Yes, George. Those are the animals.

BROADCAST OFFICIAL [*busy with the apparatus*]. Yes, Mr. Antrobus, those are the vertebrates. We hope the lion will have a word to say when you're through. Step right up, Mr. Antrobus, we're ready. We'll just have time before the storm. [*Pause. In a hoarse whisper.*] They're wait-ing [*It has grown dark. Soon after he speaks a high whistling noise begins. Strange veering lights start whirling about the stage. The other characters disappear from the stage.*]

ANTROBUS. Friends. Cousins. Four score and ten billion years ago our forefather brought forth upon this planet the spark of life,—

[*He is drowned out by thunder. When the thunder stops the* FORTUNE TELLER *is seen standing beside him.*]

FORTUNE TELLER. Antrobus, there's not a minute to be lost. Don't you see the four disks on the weather signal? Take your family into that boat at the end of the pier.

ANTROBUS. My family? I have no family. Maggie! Maggie! They won't come.

FORTUNE TELLER. They'll come.—Antrobus! Take these animals into that boat with you. All of them,—two of each kind.

SABINA. George, what's the matter with you? This is just a storm like any other storm.

ANTROBUS. Maggie!

SABINA. Stay with me, we'll go . . . [*Losing conviction.*] This is just another thunderstorm,—isn't it? Isn't it?

ANTROBUS. Maggie!!!

[MRS. ANTROBUS *appears beside him with* GLADYS.]

MRS. ANTROBUS [*matter-of-fact*]. Here I am and here's Gladys.

ANTROBUS. Where've you been? Where have you been? Quick, we're going into that boat out there.

MRS. ANTROBUS. I know we are. But I haven't found Henry. [*She wanders off into the darkness calling "Henry!"*]

SABINA [*low urgent babbling, only occasionally raising her voice*]. I don't believe it. I don't believe it's anything at all. I've seen hundreds of storms like this.

FORTUNE TELLER. There's no time to lose. Go. Push the animals along before you. Start a new world. Begin again.

SABINA. Esmeralda! George! Tell me,—is it really serious?

ANTROBUS [*suddenly very busy*]. Elephants first. Gently, gently.—Look where you're going.

GLADYS [*leaning over the ramp and striking an animal on the back*]. Stop it or you'll be left behind!

ANTROBUS. Is the kangaroo there? *There* you are! Take those turtles in your pouch, will you? [*To some other animals, pointing to his shoulder.*] Here! You jump up here. You'll be trampled on.

GLADYS [*to her father, pointing below*]. Papa, look,—the snakes!

MRS. ANTROBUS. I can't find Henry. Hen-ry!

ANTROBUS. Go along. Go along. Climb on their backs.—Wolves! Jackals,— whatever you are,—tend to your own business!

GLADYS [*pointing, tenderly*]. Papa,—look.

SABINA. Mr. Antrobus—take me with you. Don't leave me here. I'll work. I'll help. I'll do anything.

[THREE CONVEENERS *cross the stage, marching with a banner.*]

CONVEENERS. George! What are you scared of?—George! Fellas, it looks like rain.—"Maggie, where's my umbrella?"—George, setting up for Barnum and Bailey.

ANTROBUS [*again catching his wife's hand*]. Come on now, Maggie,—the pier's going to break any minute.

MRS. ANTROBUS. I'm not going a step without Henry. Henry!

GLADYS [*on the ramp*]. Mama! Papa! Hurry. The pier's cracking, Mama. It's going to break.

MRS. ANTROBUS. Henry! Cain! CAIN!

[HENRY *dashes onto the stage and joins his mother.*]

HENRY. Here I am, Mama.

MRS. ANTROBUS. Thank God!—now come quick.

HENRY. I didn't think you wanted me.

MRS. ANTROBUS. Quick!

[*She pushes him down before her into the aisle.*]

SABINA [*all the* ANTROBUSES *are now in the theater aisle.* SABINA *stands at the top of the ramp.*] Mrs. Antrobus, take me. Don't you remember me? I'll work. I'll help. Don't leave me here!

MRS. ANTROBUS [*impatiently, but as though it were of no importance*]. Yes, yes. There's a lot of work to be done. Only hurry.

FORTUNE TELLER [*now dominating the stage, to* SABINA *with a grim smile*]. Yes, go—back to the kitchen with you.

SABINA [*half-down the ramp, to* FORTUNE TELLER]. I don't know why my life's always being interrupted—just when everything's going fine!!
[*She dashes up the aisle. Now the* CONVEENERS *emerge doing a serpentine dance on the stage. They jeer at the* FORTUNE TELLER.]

CONVEENERS. Get a canoe—there's not a minute to be lost! Tell me my future, Mrs. Croaker.

FORTUNE TELLER. Paddle in the water, boys—enjoy yourselves.

VOICE FROM THE BINGO PARLOR. A-nine; A-nine. C-Twenty-four. C-Twenty-four.

CONVEENERS. Rags, bottles, and sacks.

FORTUNE TELLER. Go back and climb on your roofs. Put rags in the cracks under your doors.—Nothing will keep out the flood. You've had your chance. You've had your day. You've failed. You've lost.

VOICE FROM THE BINGO PARLOR. B-fifteen. B-Fifteen.

FORTUNE TELLER [*shading her eyes and looking out to sea*]. They're safe. George Antrobus! Think it over! A new world to make.—Think it over!
[*Curtain.*]

ACT THREE

[*Just before the curtain rises, two sounds are heard from the stage: a cracked bugle call.*
The curtain rises on almost total darkness. Almost all the flats composing the walls of MR. ANTROBUS'S *house, as of Act One, are up, but they lean helter-skelter against one another, leaving irregular gaps. Among the flats missing are two in the back wall, leaving the frames of the window and door crazily out of line. Offstage, back right, some red Roman fire[4] is burning. The bugle call is repeated. Enter* SABINA *through the tilted door. She is dressed as a Napoleonic camp follower, "la fille du regiment," in begrimed reds and blues.*]

SABINA. Mrs. Antrobus! Gladys! Where are you?

---

[4] A device for simulating burning buildings.

The war's over. The war's over. You can come out. The peace treaty's
been signed.
Where are they?—Hmpf! Are they dead, too? Mrs. Annnntrobus!
Glaaaadus! Mr. Antrobus'll be here this afternoon. I just saw him
downtown. Hmmmurry and put things in order. He says that now that
the war's over we'll all have to settle down and be perfect.
[*Enter* MR. FITZPATRICK, *the Stage Manager, followed by the whole
company, who stand waiting at the edges of the stage.* MR. FITZPATRICK
tries to interrupt SABINA.]
MR. FITZPATRICK. Miss Somerset, we have to stop a moment.
SABINA. They may be hiding out in the back—
MR. FITZPATRICK. Miss Somerset! We have to stop a moment.
SABINA. What's the matter?
MR. FITZPATRICK. There's an explanation we have to make to the audience.
—Lights, please.
[*To the actor who plays* MR. ANTROBUS.] Will you explain the matter to the
audience?
[*The lights go up. We now see that a balcony or elevated runway has been
erected at the back of the stage, back of the wall of the Antrobus house.
From its extreme right and left ends ladderlike steps descend to the floor
of the stage.*]
ANTROBUS. Ladies and gentlemen, an unfortunate accident has taken place
backstage. Perhaps I should say *another* unfortunate accident.
SABINA. I'm sorry. I'm sorry.
ANTROBUS. The management feels, in fact, we all feel that you are due an
apology. And now we have to ask your indulgence for the most serious
mishap of all. Seven of our actors have . . . have been taken ill. Apparently, it was something they ate. I'm not exactly clear what happened.
[*All the actors start to talk at once.* ANTROBUS *raises his hand.*]
Now, now—not all at once. Fitz, do you know what it was?
MR. FITZPATRICK. Why, it's perfectly clear. These seven actors had dinner
together, and they ate something that disagreed with them.
SABINA. Disagreed with them!!! They have ptomaine poisoning. They're
in Bellevue Hospital this very minute in agony. They're having their
stomachs pumped out this very minute, in perfect agony.
ANTROBUS. Fortunately, we've just heard they'll all recover.
SABINA. It'll be a miracle if they do, a downright miracle. It was the lemon
meringue pie.
ACTORS. It was the fish . . . it was the canned tomatoes . . . it was the fish.
SABINA. It was the lemon meringue pie. I saw it with my own eyes; it had
blue mould all over the bottom of it.
ANTROBUS. Whatever it was, they're in no condition to take part in this
performance. Naturally, we haven't enough understudies to fill all those
roles; but we do have a number of splendid volunteers who have kindly
consented to help us out. These friends have watched our rehearsals, and

they assure me that they know the lines and the business very well. Let me introduce them to you—my dresser, Mr. Tremayne,—himself a distinguished Shakespearean actor for many years; our wardrobe mistress, Hester; Miss Somerset's maid, Ivy; and Fred Bailey, captain of the ushers in this theater.

[*These persons bow modestly.* IVY *and* HESTER *are colored girls.*]

Now this scene takes place near the end of the act. And I'm sorry to say we'll need a short rehearsal, just a short run-through. And as some of it takes place in the auditorium, we'll have to keep the curtain up. Those of you who wish can go out in the lobby and smoke some more. The rest of you can listen to us, or . . . or just talk quietly among yourselves, as you choose. Thank you. Now will you take it over, Mr. Fitzpatrick?

MR. FITZPATRICK. Thank you.—Now for those of you who are listening perhaps I should explain that at the end of this act, the men have come back from the War and the family's settled down in the house. And the author wants to show the hours of the night passing by over their heads, and the planets crossing the sky . . . uh . . . over their heads, and he says—this is hard to explain—that each of the hours of the night is a philosopher, or a great thinker. Eleven o'clock, for instance, is Aristotle. And nine o'clock is Spinoza. Like that. I don't suppose it means anything. It's just a kind of poetic effect.

SABINA. Not mean anything! Why, it certainly does. Twelve o'clock goes by saying those wonderful things. I think it means that when people are asleep they have all those lovely thoughts, much better than when they're awake.

IVY. Excuse me, I think it means,—excuse me, Mr. Fitzpatrick—

SABINA. What were you going to say, Ivy?

IVY. Mr. Fitzpatrick, you let my father come to a rehearsal; and my father's a Baptist minister, and he said that the author meant that—just like the hours and stars go by over our heads at night, in the same way the ideas and thoughts of the great men are in the air around us all the time and they're working on us, even when we don't know it.

MR. FITZPATRICK. Well, well, maybe that's it. Thank you, Ivy. Anyway,—the hours of the night are philosophers. My friends, are you ready? Ivy, can you be eleven o'clock? "This good estate of the mind possessing its object in energy we call divine." Aristotle.

IVY. Yes, sir. I know that and I know twelve o'clock and I know nine o'clock.

MR. FITZPATRICK. Twelve o'clock? Mr. Tremayne, the Bible.

TREMAYNE. Yes.

MR. FITZPATRICK. Ten o'clock? Hester,—Plato? [*She nods eagerly.*] Nine o'clock, Spinoza,—Fred?

BAILEY. Yes, *sir.*

[FRED BAILEY *picks up a great gilded cardboard numeral IX and starts up the steps of the platform.* MR. FITZPATRICK *strikes his forehead.*]

MR. FITZPATRICK. The planets!! We forgot all about the planets.

SABINA. O my God! The planets! Are they sick too? [*Actors nod.*]

MR. FITZPATRICK. Ladies and gentlemen, the planets are singers. Of course, we can't replace them, so you'll have to imagine them singing in this scene. Saturn sings from the orchestra pit down here. The Moon is way up there. And Mars with a red lantern in his hand, stands in the aisle over there—Tz-tz-tz. It's too bad; it all makes a very fine effect. However! Ready—nine o'clock: Spinoza.

BAILEY [*walking slowly across the balcony, left to right*]. "After experience had taught me that the common occurrences of daily life are vain and futile—"

MR. FITZPATRICK. Louder, Fred. "And I saw that all the objects of my desire and fear—"

BAILEY. "And I saw that all the objects of my desire and fear were in themselves nothing good nor bad save insofar as the mind was affected by them—"

MR. FITZPATRICK. Do you know the rest? All right. Ten o'clock. Hester. Plato.

HESTER. "Then tell me, O Critias, how will a man choose the ruler that shall rule over him? Will he not—"

MR. FITZPATRICK. Thank you. Skip to the end, Hester.

HESTER. ". . . can be multiplied a thousand fold in its effects among the citizens."

MR. FITZPATRICK. Thank you.—Aristotle, Ivy?

IVY. "This good estate of the mind possessing its object in energy we call divine. This we mortals have occasionally and it is this energy which is pleasantest and best. But God has it always. It is wonderful in us; but in Him how much more wonderful."

MR. FITZPATRICK. Midnight. Midnight, Mr. Tremayne. That's right,—you've done it before.—All right, everybody. You know what you have to do.—Lower the curtain. Houselights up. Act III of *The Skin of Our Teeth*. [*As the curtain descends he is heard saying:*] You volunteers, just wear what you have on. Don't try to put on the costumes today.

[*Houselights go down. The Act begins again. The bugle call. Curtain rises. Enter* SABINA.]

SABINA. Mrs. Antrobus! Gladys! Where are you? The war's over.—You've heard all this— [*She gabbles the main points.*] Where-are-they? Are-they-dead, too, etc. I-just-saw-Mr.-Antrobus-down town, etc.

[*Slowing up.*] He says that now that the war's over we'll all have to settle down and be perfect. They may be hiding out in the back somewhere. Mrs. An-tro-bus.

[*She wanders off. It has grown lighter. A trapdoor is cautiously raised and* MRS. ANTROBUS *emerges waist-high and listens. She is disheveled and worn; she wears a tattered dress and a shawl half covers her head. She talks down through the trapdoor.*]

MRS. ANTROBUS. It's getting light. There's still something burning over there—Newark, or Jersey City. What? Yes, I could swear I heard some-one moving about up here. But I can't see anybody. I say: I can't see anybody.

[*She starts to move about the stage.* GLADYS' *head appears at the trapdoor. She is holding a baby.*]

GLADYS. Oh, Mama. Be careful.

MRS. ANTROBUS. Now, Gladys, you stay out of sight.

GLADYS. Well, let me stay here just a minute. I want the baby to get some of this fresh air.

MRS. ANTROBUS. All right, but keep your eyes open. I'll see what I can find. I'll have a good hot plate of soup for you before you can say Jack Robinson. Gladys Antrobus! Do you know what I think I see? There's old Mr. Hawkins sweeping the sidewalk in front of his A. and P. store. Sweeping it with a broom. Why, he must have gone crazy, like the others! I see some other people moving about, too.

GLADYS. Mama, come back, come back.

[MRS. ANTROBUS *returns to the trapdoor and listens.*]

MRS. ANTROBUS. Gladys, there's something in the air. Everybody's move-ment's sort of different. I see some women walking right out in the middle of the street.

SABINA'S VOICE. Mrs. An-tro-bus!

MRS. ANTROBUS *and* GLADYS. What's that?!!

SABINA'S VOICE. Glaaaadys! Mrs. An-tro-bus!

[*Enter* SABINA.]

MRS. ANTROBUS. Gladys, that's Sabina's voice as sure as I live.—Sabina! Sabina!—Are you alive?!!

SABINA. Of course, I'm alive. How've you girls been?—*Don't* try and kiss me. I never want to kiss another human being as long as I live. Sh-sh, there's nothing to get emotional about. Pull yourself together, the war's over. Take a deep breath,—the war's over.

MRS. ANTROBUS. The war's over!! I don't believe you. I don't believe you. I can't believe you.

GLADYS. Mama!

SABINA. Who's that?

MRS. ANTROBUS. That's Gladys and her baby. I don't believe you. Gladys, Sabina says the war's over. Oh, Sabina.

SABINA [*leaning over the baby*]. Goodness! Are there any babies left in the world! Can it *see?* And can it cry and everything?

GLADYS. Yes, he can. He notices everything very well.

SABINA. Where on earth did you get it? Oh, I won't ask.—Lord, I've lived all these seven years around camp and I've forgotten how to behave.— Now we've got to think about the men coming home.—Mrs. Antrobus, go and wash your face, I'm ashamed of you. Put your best clothes on. Mr. Antrobus'll be here this afternoon. I just saw him downtown.

MRS. ANTROBUS *and* GLADYS. He's alive!! He'll be here!! Sabina, you're not joking?

MRS. ANTROBUS. And Henry?

SABINA [*dryly*]. Yes, Henry's alive, too, that's what they say. Now don't stop to talk. Get yourselves fixed up. Gladys, you look terrible. Have you any decent clothes? [SABINA *has pushed them toward the trapdoor.*]

MRS. ANTROBUS [*half down*]. Yes, I've something to wear just for this very day. But, Sabina,—who won the war?

SABINA. Don't stop now,—just wash your face. [*A whistle sounds in the distance.*] Oh, my God, what's that silly little noise?

MRS. ANTROBUS. Why, it sounds like . . . it sounds like what used to be the noon whistle at the shoe-polish factory.

[*Exit.*]

SABINA. That's what it is. Seems to me like peacetime's coming along pretty fast—shoe polish!

GLADYS [*half down*]. Sabina, how soon after peacetime begins does the milkman start coming to the door?

SABINA. As soon as he catches a cow. Give him time to catch a cow, dear.

[*Exit* GLADYS. SABINA *walks about a moment, thinking.*]

Shoe polish! My, I'd forgotten what peacetime was like.

[*She shakes her head, then sits down by the trapdoor and starts talking down the hole.*]

Mrs. Antrobus, guess what I saw Mr. Antrobus doing this morning at dawn. He was tacking up a piece of paper on the door of the Town Hall. You'll die when you hear: it was a recipe for grass soup, for a grass soup that doesn't give you the diarrhea. Mr. Antrobus is still thinking up new things.—He told me to give you his love. He's got all sorts of ideas for peacetime, he says. No more laziness and idiocy, he says. And oh, yes! Where are his books? What? Well, pass them up. The first thing he wants to see are his books. He says if you've burnt those books, or if the rats have eaten them, he says it isn't worthwhile starting over again. Everybody's going to be beautiful, he says, and diligent, and very intelligent. [*A hand reaches up with two volumes.*] What language is that? Pu-u-gh,—mold! And he's got such plans for you, Mrs. Antrobus. You're going to study history and algebra—and so are Gladys and I—and philosophy. You should hear him talk: [*Taking two more volumes.*] Well, these are in English, anyway.—To hear him talk, seems like he expects you to be a combination, Mrs. Antrobus, of a saint and a college professor, and a dancehall hostess, if you know what I mean. [*Two more volumes.*] Ugh. German! [*She is lying on the floor; one elbow bent, her cheek on her hand, meditatively.*] Yes, peace will be here before we know it. In a week or two we'll be asking the Perkinses in for a quiet evening of bridge. We'll turn on the radio and hear how to be big successes with a new toothpaste. We'll trot down to the movies and see how girls with

wax faces live—all *that* will begin again. Oh, Mrs. Antrobus, God forgive
me but I enjoyed the war. Everybody's at their best in wartime. I'm sorry
it's over. And, oh, I forgot! Mr. Antrobus sent you another message—
can you hear me?—

[*Enter* HENRY, *blackened and sullen. He is wearing torn overalls, but has
one gaudy admiral's epaulette hanging by a thread from his right shoulder,
and there are vestiges of gold and scarlet braid running down his left
trouser leg. He stands listening.*]

Listen! Henry's never to put foot in this house again, he says. He'll kill
Henry on sight, if he sees him.

You don't know about Henry??? Well, where have you been? What?
Well, Henry rose right to the top. Top of *what?* Listen, I'm telling you.
Henry rose from corporal to captain, to major, to general.—I don't
know how to say it, but the enemy is *Henry; Henry is* the enemy. Everybody knows that.

HENRY. He'll kill me, will he?

SABINA. Who are *you?* I'm not afraid of you. The war's over.

HENRY. I'll kill him so fast. I've spent seven years trying to find him; the
others I killed were just substitutes.

SABINA. Goodness! It's Henry!— [*He makes an angry gesture.*] Oh, I'm not
afraid of you. The war's over, Henry Antrobus, and you're not any more
important than any other unemployed. You go away and hide yourself,
until we calm your father down.

HENRY. The first thing to do is to burn up those old books; it's the ideas he
gets out of those old books that . . . that makes the whole world so you
can't live in it.

[*He reels forward and starts kicking the books about, but suddenly falls
down in a sitting position.*]

SABINA. You leave those books alone!! Mr. Antrobus is looking forward
to them a-special.—Gracious sakes, Henry, you're so tired you can't
stand up. Your mother and sister'll be here in a minute and we'll think
what to do about you.

HENRY. What did they ever care about me?

SABINA. There's that old whine again. All you people think you're not
loved enough, nobody loves you. Well, you start being lovable and we'll
love you.

HENRY [*outraged*]. I don't want anybody to love me.

SABINA. Then stop talking about it all the time.

HENRY. I *never* talk about it. The last thing I want is anybody to pay any
attention to me.

SABINA. I can hear it behind every word you say.

HENRY. I want everybody to hate me.

SABINA. Yes, you've decided that's second best, but it's still the same thing.
—Mrs. Antrobus! Henry's here. He's so tired he can't stand up.

[MRS. ANTROBUS *and* GLADYS, *with her baby, emerge. They are dressed as in Act I.* MRS. ANTROBUS *carries some objects in her apron, and* GLADYS *has a blanket over her shoulder.*]

MRS. ANTROBUS *and* GLADYS. Henry! Henry! Henry!

HENRY [*glaring at them*]. Have you anything to eat?

MRS. ANTROBUS. Yes, I have, Henry. I've been saving it for this very day,—two good baked potatoes. No! Henry! one of them's for your father. Henry!! Give me that other potato back this minute.

[SABINA *sidles up behind him and snatches the other potato away.*]

SABINA. He's so dog-tired he doesn't know what he's doing.

MRS. ANTROBUS. Now you just rest there, Henry, until I can get your room ready. Eat the potato good and slow, so you can get all the nourishment out of it.

HENRY. You all might as well know right now that I haven't come back here to live.

MRS. ANTROBUS. Sh. . . . I'll put this coat over you. Your room's hardly damaged at all. Your football trophies are a little tarnished, but Sabina and I will polish them up tomorrow.

HENRY. Did you hear me? I don't live here. I don't belong to anybody.

MRS. ANTROBUS. Why, how can you say a thing like that! You certainly do belong right here. Where else would you want to go? Your forehead's feverish, Henry, seems to me. You'd better give me that gun, Henry. You won't need that anymore.

GLADYS [*whispering*]. Look, he's fallen asleep already, with his potato half-chewed.

SABINA. Puh! The terror of the world.

MRS. ANTROBUS. Sabina, you mind your own business, and start putting the room to rights.

[HENRY *has turned his face to the back of the sofa.* MRS. ANTROBUS *gingerly puts the revolver in her apron pocket, then helps* SABINA. SABINA *has found a rope hanging from the ceiling. Grunting, she hangs all her weight on it, and as she pulls the walls begin to move into their right places.* MRS. ANTROBUS *brings the overturned tables, chairs and hassock into the positions of Act I.*]

SABINA. That's all we do—always beginning again! Over and over again. Always beginning again. [*She pulls on the rope and a part of the wall moves into place. She stops. Meditatively:*]

How do we know that it'll be any better than before? Why do we go on pretending? Someday the whole earth's going to have to turn cold anyway, and until that time all these other things'll be happening again: it will be more wars and more walls of ice and floods and earthquakes.

MRS. ANTROBUS. Sabina!! Stop arguing and go on with your work.

SABINA. All right. I'll go on just out of *habit*, but I won't believe in it.

MRS. ANTROBUS [*aroused*]. Now, Sabina. I've let you talk long enough. I don't want to hear any more of it. Do I have to explain to you what everybody knows,—everybody who keeps a home going? Do I have to say to you what nobody should ever *have* to say, because they can read it in each other's eyes?

Now listen to me: [MRS. ANTROBUS *takes hold of the rope.*] I could live for seventy years in a cellar and make soup out of grass and bark, without ever doubting that this world has a work to do and will do it. Do you hear me?

SABINA [*frightened*]. Yes, Mrs. Antrobus.

MRS. ANTROBUS. Sabina, do you see this house,—216 Cedar Street,—do you see it?

SABINA. Yes, Mrs. Antrobus.

MRS. ANTROBUS. Well, just to have known this house is to have seen the idea of what we can do someday if we keep our wits about us. Too many people have suffered and died for my children for us to start reneging now. So we'll start putting this house to rights. Now, Sabina, go and see what you can do in the kitchen.

SABINA. Kitchen! Why is it that however far I go away, I always find myself back in the kitchen?
[*Exit.*]

MRS. ANTROBUS [*still thinking over her last speech, relaxes and says with a reminiscent smile*]. Goodness gracious, wouldn't you know that my father was a parson? It was just like I heard his own voice speaking and he's been dead five thousand years. There! I've gone and almost waked Henry up.

HENRY [*talking in his sleep, indistinctly*]. Fellows . . . what have they done for us? . . . Blocked our way at every step. Kept everything in their own hands. And you've stood it. When are you going to wake up?

MRS. ANTROBUS. Sh, Henry. Go to sleep. Go to sleep. Go to sleep.—Well, that looks better. Now let's go and help Sabina.

GLADYS. Mama, I'm going out into the backyard and hold the baby right up in the air. And show him that we don't have to be afraid any more.
[*Exit* GLADYS *to the kitchen.* MRS. ANTROBUS *glances at* HENRY, *exits into kitchen.* HENRY *thrashes about in his sleep. Enter* ANTROBUS, *his arms full of bundles, chewing the end of a carrot. He has a slight limp. Over the suit of Act I he is wearing an overcoat too long for him, its skirts trailing on the ground. He lets his bundles fall and stands looking about. Presently his attention is fixed on* HENRY, *whose words grow clearer.*]

HENRY. All right! What have you got to lose? What have they done for us? That's right—nothing. Tear everything down. I don't care what you smash. We'll begin again and we'll show 'em.
[ANTROBUS *takes out his revolver and holds it pointing downwards. With his back towards the audience he moves toward the footlights.* HENRY'S *voice grows louder and he wakes with a start. They stare at one another. Then* HENRY *sits up quickly. Throughout the following scene* HENRY *is played, not as a misunderstood or misguided young man, but as a representation of strong unreconciled evil.*]

All right! Do something. [*Pause.*] Don't think I'm afraid of you, either. All right, do what you were going to do. Do it. [*Furiously.*] Shoot me, I tell you. You don't have to think I'm any relation of yours. I haven't got any father or any mother, or brothers or sisters. And I don't want any. And what's more I haven't got anybody over me; and I never will have. I'm alone, and that's all I want to be: alone. So you can shoot me.

ANTROBUS. You're the last person I wanted to see. The sight of you dries up all my plans and hopes. I wish I were back at war still, because it's easier to fight you than to live with you. War's a pleasure—do you hear me?—War's a pleasure compared to what faces us now: trying to build up a peacetime with you in the middle of it.

[ANTROBUS *walks up to the window.*]

HENRY. I'm not going to be a part of any peacetime of yours. I'm going a long way from here and make my own world that's fit for a man to live in. Where a man can be free, and have a chance, and do what he wants to do in his own way.

ANTROBUS [*his attention arrested; thoughtfully. He throws the gun out of the window and turns with hope.*] . . . Henry, let's try again.

HENRY. Try what? Living *here*?—Speaking polite downtown to all the old men like you? Standing like a sheep at the street corner until the red light turns to green? Being a good boy and a good sheep, like all the stinking ideas you get out of your books? Oh, no. I'll make a world, and I'll show you.

ANTROBUS [*hard*]. How can you make a world for people to live in, unless you've first put order in yourself? Mark my words: I shall continue fighting you until my last breath as long as you mix up your idea of liberty with your idea of hogging everything for yourself. I shall have no pity on you. I shall pursue you to the far corners of the earth. You and I want the same thing; but until you think of it as something that everyone has a right to, you are my deadly enemy and I will destroy you.—I hear your mother's voice in the kitchen. Have you seen her?

HENRY. I have no mother. Get it into your head. I don't belong here. I have nothing to do here. I have no home.

ANTROBUS. Then why did you come here? With the whole world to choose from, why did you come to this one place: 216 Cedar Street, Excelsior, New Jersey. . . . Well?

HENRY. What if I did? What if I wanted to look at it once more, to see if—

ANTROBUS. Oh, you're related, all right—When your mother comes in you must behave yourself. Do you hear me?

HENRY [*wildly*]. What is this?—*must behave* yourself. Don't you say *must* to me.

ANTROBUS. Quiet!

[*Enter* MRS. ANTROBUS *and* SABINA.]

HENRY. Nobody can say *must* to me. All my life everybody's been crossing me,—everybody, everything, all of you. I'm going to be free, even if I have to kill half the world for it. Right now, too. Let me get my hands on his throat. I'll show him.

[*He advances toward* ANTROBUS. *Suddenly,* SABINA *jumps between them and calls out in her own person:*]

SABINA. Stop! Stop! Don't play this scene. You know what happened last night. Stop the play.

[*The men fall back, panting.* HENRY *covers his face with his hands.*]

Last night you almost strangled him. You became a regular savage. Stop it!

HENRY. It's true. I'm sorry. I don't know what comes over me. I have nothing against him personally. I respect him very much ... I ... I admire him. But something comes over me. It's like I become fifteen years old again. I ... I ... listen: my own father used to whip me and lock me up every Saturday night. I never had enough to eat. He never let me have enough money to buy decent clothes. I was ashamed to go downtown. I never could go to the dances. My father and my uncle put rules in the way of everything I wanted to do. They tried to prevent my living at all.—I'm sorry. I'm sorry.

MRS. ANTROBUS [*quickly*]. No, go on. Finish what you were saying. Say it all.

HENRY. In this scene it's as though I were back in high school again. It's like I had some big emptiness inside me,—the emptiness of being hated and blocked at every turn. And the emptiness fills up with the one thought that you have to strike and fight and kill. Listen, it's as though you have to kill somebody else so as not to end up killing yourself.

SABINA. That's not true. I knew your father and your uncle and your mother. You imagined all that. Why, they did everything they could for you. How can you say things like that? They didn't lock you up.

HENRY. They did. They did. They wished I hadn't been born.

SABINA. That's not true.

ANTROBUS [*in his own person, with self-condemnation, but cold and proud*]. Wait a minute. I have something to say, too. It's not wholly his fault that he wants to strangle me in this scene. It's my fault, too. He wouldn't feel that way unless there were something in me that reminded him of all that. He talks about an emptiness. Well, there's an emptiness in me, too. Yes,—work, work, work,—that's all I do. I've ceased to *live*. No wonder he feels that anger coming over him.

MRS. ANTROBUS. There! At least you've said it.

SABINA. We're all just as wicked as we can be, and that's the God's truth.

MRS. ANTROBUS [*nods a moment, then comes forward; quietly*]. Come. Come and put your head under some cold water.

SABINA [*in a whisper*]. I'll go with him. I've known him a long while. You have to go on with the play. Come with me.

[HENRY *starts out with* SABINA, *but turns at the exit and says to* ANTROBUS:]

HENRY. Thanks. Thanks for what you said. I'll be all right tomorrow. I won't lose control in that place. I promise.

[*Exeunt* HENRY *and* SABINA. ANTROBUS *starts toward the front door, fastens it.* MRS. ANTROBUS *goes upstage and places the chair close to the table.*]

MRS. ANTROBUS. George, do I see you limping?

ANTROBUS, Yes, a little. My old wound from the other war started smarting again. I can manage.

MRS. ANTROBUS [*looking out of the window*]. Some lights are coming on,— the first in seven years. People are walking up and down looking at them. Over in Hawkins' open lot they've built a bonfire to celebrate the peace. They're dancing around it like scarecrows.

ANTROBUS. A bonfire! As though they hadn't seen enough things burning.— Maggie,—the dog died?

MRS. ANTROBUS. Oh, yes. Long ago. There are no dogs left in Excelsior.— You're back again! All these years. I gave up counting on letters. The few that arrived were anywhere from six months to a year late.

ANTROBUS. Yes, the ocean's full of letters, along with the other things.

MRS. ANTROBUS. George, sit down, you're tired.

ANTROBUS. No, you sit down. I'm tired but I'm restless. [*Suddenly, as she comes forward.*] Maggie! I've lost it. I've lost it.

MRS. ANTROBUS. What, George? What have you lost?

ANTROBUS. The most important thing of all: The desire to begin again, to start building.

MRS. ANTROBUS [*sitting in the chair right of the table*]. Well, it will come back.

ANTROBUS [*at the window*]. I've lost it. This minute I feel like all those people dancing around the bonfire—just relief. Just the desire to settle down; to slip into the old grooves and keep the neighbors from walking over my lawn.—Hm. But during the war,—in the middle of all that blood and dirt and hot and cold—every day and night, I'd have moments, Maggie, when I *saw* the things that we could do when it was over. When you're at war you think about a better life; when you're at peace you think about a more comfortable one. I've lost it. I feel sick and tired.

MRS. ANTROBUS. Listen! The baby's crying.

I hear Gladys talking. Probably she's quieting Henry again. George, while Gladys and I were living here—like moles, like rats, and when we were at our wits' end to save the baby's life—the only thought we clung to was that you were going to bring something good out of this suffering. In the night, in the dark, we'd whisper about it, starving and sick.—Oh, George, you'll have to get it back again. Think! What else kept us alive all these years? Even now, it's not comfort we want. We can suffer whatever's necessary; only give us back that promise.

[*Enter* SABINA *with a lighted lamp. She is dressed as in Act I.*]

SABINA. Mrs. Antrobus . . .

MRS. ANTROBUS. Yes, Sabina?

SABINA. Will you need me?

MRS. ANTROBUS. No, Sabina, you can go to bed.

SABINA. Mrs. Antrobus, if it's all right with you, I'd like to go to the bonfire and celebrate seeing the war's over. And, Mrs. Antrobus, they've
opened the Gem Movie Theater and they're giving away a hand-painted
soup tureen to every lady, and I thought one of us ought to go.

ANTROBUS. Well, Sabina, I haven't any money. I haven't seen any money
for quite a while.

SABINA. Oh, you don't need money. They're taking anything you can give
them. And I have some ... some ... Mrs. Antrobus, promise you
won't tell anyone. It's a little against the law. But I'll give you some, too.

ANTROBUS. What is it?

SABINA. I'll give you some, too. Yesterday I picked up a lot of ... of beef-
cubes!

[MRS. ANTROBUS *turns and says calmly:*]

MRS. ANTROBUS. But, Sabina, you know you ought to give that in to the
Center downtown. They know who needs them most.

SABINA [*outburst*]. Mrs. Antrobus, I didn't make this war. I didn't ask for
it. And, in my opinion, after anybody's gone through what we've gone
through, they have a right to grab what they can find. You're a very
nice man, Mr. Antrobus, but you'd have got on better in the world if
you'd realized that dog-eat-dog was the rule in the beginning and always
will be. And most of all now. [*In tears.*] Oh, the world's an awful place,
and you know it is. I used to think something could be done about it; but
I know better now. I hate it. I hate it.

[*She comes forward slowly and brings six cubes from the bag.*]
All right. All right. You can have them.

ANTROBUS. Thank you, Sabina.

SABINA. Can I have ... can I have one to go to the movies? [ANTROBUS *in
silence gives her one.*] Thank you.

ANTROBUS. Good night, Sabina.

SABINA. Mr. Antrobus, don't mind what I say. I'm just an ordinary girl, you
know what I mean, I'm just an ordinary girl. But you're a bright man,
you're a very bright man, and of course you invented the alphabet and
the wheel, and, my God, a lot of things ... and if you've got any other
plans, my God, don't let me upset them. Only every now and then I've
got to go to the movies. I mean my nerves can't stand it. But if you
have any ideas about improving the crazy old world, I'm really with
you. I really am. Because it's ... it's ... Good night.

[*She goes out.* ANTROBUS *starts laughing softly with exhilaration.*]

ANTROBUS. Now I remember what three things always went together when
I was able to see things most clearly: three things. Three things: [*He
points to where* SABINA *has gone out.*] The voice of the people in their confusion and their need. And the thought of you and the children and this
house.... And ... Maggie! I didn't dare ask you: my books! They
haven't been lost, have they?

MRS. ANTROBUS. No. There are some of them right here. Kind of tattered.

ANTROBUS. Yes.—Remember, Maggie, we almost lost them once before? And when we finally did collect a few torn copies out of old cellars they ran in everyone's head like a fever. They as good as rebuilt the world. [*Pauses, book in hand, and looks up.*] Oh, I've never forgotten for long at a time that living is struggle. I know that every good and excellent thing in the world stands moment by moment on the razor-edge of danger and must be fought for—whether it's a field, or a home, or a country. All I ask is the chance to build new worlds and God has always given us that. And has given us [*opening the book*] voices to guide us; and the memory of our mistakes to warn us. Maggie, you and I will remember in peacetime all the resolves that were so clear to us in the days of war. We've come a long ways. We've learned. We're learning. And the steps of our journey are marked for us here. [*He stands by the table turning the leaves of a book.*] Sometimes out there in the war,— standing all night on a hill—I'd try and remember some of the words in these books. Parts of them and phrases would come back to me. And after a while I used to give names to the hours of the night. [*He sits, hunting for a passage in the book.*] Nine o'clock I used to call Spinoza. Where is it: "After experience had taught me—"

[*The back wall has disappeared, revealing the platform.* FRED BAILEY *carrying his numeral has started from left to right.* MRS. ANTROBUS *sits by the table sewing.*]

BAILEY. "After experience had taught me that the common occurrences of daily life are vain and futile; and I saw that all the objects of my desire and fear were in themselves nothing good nor bad save insofar as the mind was affected by them; I at length determined to search out whether there was something truly good and communicable to man."

[*Almost without break* HESTER, *carrying a large Roman numeral ten, starts crossing the platform.* GLADYS *appears at the kitchen door and moves toward her mother's chair.*]

HESTER. "Then tell me, O Critias, how will a man choose the ruler that shall rule over him? Will he not choose a man who has first established order in himself, knowing that any decision that has its spring from anger or pride or vanity can be multiplied a thousand fold in its effects upon the citizens?"

[HESTER *disappears and* IVY, *as eleven o'clock starts speaking.*]

IVY. "This good estate of the mind possessing its object in energy we call divine. This we mortals have occasionally and it is this energy which is pleasantest and best. But God has it always. It is wonderful in us; but in Him how much more wonderful."

[*As* MR. TREMAYNE *starts to speak,* HENRY *appears at the edge of the scene, brooding and unreconciled, but present.*]

TREMAYNE. "In the beginning, God created the Heavens and the Earth; And the Earth was waste and void; And the darkness was upon the face of

the deep. And the Lord said let there be light and there was light."
[*Sudden blackout and silence, except for the last strokes of the midnight bell. Then just as suddenly the lights go up, and* SABINA *is standing at the window, as at the opening of the play.*]

SABINA. Oh, oh, oh. Six o'clock and the master not home yet. Pray God nothing serious has happened to him crossing the Hudson River. But I wouldn't be surprised. The whole world's at sixes and sevens, and why the house hasn't fallen down about our ears long ago is a miracle to me.
[*She comes down to the footlights.*]
This is where you came in. We have to go on for ages and ages yet.
You go home.
The end of this play isn't written yet.
Mr. and Mrs. Antrobus! Their heads are full of plans and they're as confident as the first day they began,—and they told me to tell you: good night.

ARTHUR MILLER

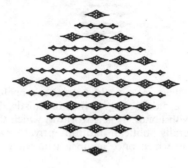

A VIEW FROM THE BRIDGE

TRAGEDY

Time is moving; there is a world to make, a civilization to create that will move toward the only goal the humanistic, democratic mind can ever accept with honor. It is a world in which the human being can live as a naturally political, naturally private, naturally engaged person, a world in which once again a true tragic victory may be scored.

With these words, in the Preface to *A View from the Bridge*, Arthur Miller (*b.* 1915) looks back to the origins of the drama and forward to a dramatic repertory designed to achieve the same ends as that of the ancient Greeks, to be concerned, in his words, with ultimate law, with the Grand Design. This was not, for Miller, a sudden shift or a change of direction; it was rather a final commitment to an element that has always been present in his works, a tragic vision overlaid sometimes by social criticism, sometimes by journalistic relevance.

His *Death of a Salesman* (1949), one of the most successful plays of the modern American theater, was principally an examination of what had happened to the American dream, the American sense of purpose, the American energy, as they became lost in the jungles of a commercial society. Yet the power of the play, its effect on its audiences, lay more in the character of Willy Loman, an archetypal portrait of the individual who necessarily sought to establish his individual identity without recognizing that the society in which he believed had no concern with individual identity. *The Crucible* (1953), an historical drama about the Salem witchcraft trials, inevitably seemed to be a direct commentary on the McCarthy era in Washington. Yet the play had its first great success in European theaters where audiences were indifferent to

732

news-stories from Washington, and was revived for a long run in New York when McCarthy was only a memory. Once again, the true strength of the play was in the hero's struggle against his society—a struggle which tested both the man and the society, "the ultimate law."

In the three-thousand-year history of the drama, tragedy as a term has acquired a special status; it describes the highest, most serious achievements. But an examination of the plays categorized as tragedies will reveal that the term has been affixed to a variety of attitudes, forms, purposes and points of view. In the Greek theater, the serious drama generally reached a conclusion of shuddering finality (like the fifth episode of *Antigone*); in the drama of the Renaissance the final action might result in the death of the hero, but often the audience was reminded that this was but the prelude to a greater life. In Greek drama the action is designed to bring the erring hero to an awareness of himself, the conventional recognition scene. In the modern theater (*Death of a Salesman*, for instance), it is more important that the audience be made aware.

One force, however, has made the creation of tragedy particularly difficult for the contemporary playwright. The widespread concern with psychology both among artists and spectators has frequently turned drama away from tragedy to case-history. The detailed analysis of the individual, discovering the inner forces or past accidental experiences that are responsible for his actions and reactions, has diminished the dramatic action and robbed it of its true function as a mirror of man. It is neither advisable nor useful to generalize upon the experiences of a neurotic.

It must not be forgotten that one of the greatest values of art, particularly of tragedy, is its generalizing power. Not in the arbitrary way of allegory: Everyman represents *you*; not in the sentimental way: there but for the grace of God go I. Tragic heroes were most frequently men so highly or peculiarly placed that either of those kinds of identification were denied their spectators. Rather, tragic action is designed to force the audience to judge, to evaluate, to understand what it has seen. By revealing a world and its inhabitants, tragedy invites the spectator to equate it with his own world. Having perceived the clarified world of the play, it is less easy for the spectator to shut his eyes to the world outside the theater; having understood the fictional hero of the world of the play, it is less easy for the spectator to shut his eyes to the men and women encountered in his daily life.

It is the restoration of the generalizing power of tragedy that Miller aims at in *A View from the Bridge.* If the classic dramatists chose a hero so highly placed that the audience was discouraged from "identifying" with him, Miller goes to the other extreme, choosing a central figure so lowly that theater audiences can rarely have encountered him. Like the hero defined by Aristotle, Miller's hero is essentially a man of virtue, only the particular circumstance in which he suddenly finds himself betrays his noblest characteristic (charity) as flawed. Had Eddie Carbone not willingly committed himself to a course of action governed by a kind of tribal law, there would have been no tragedy, no revelation for the audience. A flawed character alone is not the proper basis for tragedy, but for psychoanalysis; circumstance alone is not a proper basis for tragedy, but for melodrama.

Tragedy is a delicate and dangerous medium. Since it deals in high passions and violence, it constantly risks the simple titillation of its audiences. It requires, therefore, a means of maintaining balance, perspective, of keeping the end constantly in view. This, of course, was one of the functions of the Greek chorus, with its flatfooted interjections of moral commonplaces. In the later drama, playwrights have employed "chorus characters," whose tedious function is to be sure that no spectator lose his perspective. Neither the Greek chorus nor the conventionally minded chorus character was available in Miller's scheme: on the one hand the chorus suggested archaism, and on the other, to what common body of principles could the chorus character appeal?

The solution was the introduction of a lawyer who is at once central and peripheral to the action. As a professional man, the lawyer represents and interprets a code without necessarily acquiescing in it. If he speaks occasionally *for* the audience or some member of it, he speaks always in his professional capacity *to* the audience, reminding it both of the code by which it is able to "settle for half" and of the all-too-natural forces which the code is not always able to restrain. The scene in which Eddie Carbone, seeking a cure for a disease he does not understand, confronts the lawyer, who understands but can offer only the inflexible social code, is for Miller a tragic image as pertinent as the horrible awakening of Agave. After Eddie leaves him, the lawyer makes an explicit statement of an idea of tragedy:

> I knew where he was heading for;
> I knew where he was going to end.
> And I sat here many afternoons,
> Asking myself why, being an intelligent man,
> I was so powerless to stop it.

A View from the Bridge exists in two versions. Originally presented in one unbroken act, it was later revised and expanded into a two-act play. Both versions are equally effective in the theater; the one-act version is reprinted here for reasons best expressed by Miller himself in an Introductory Note to the play:

> *A View from the Bridge* is in one act because, quite simply, I did not know how to pull a curtain down anywhere before its end. While writing it, I kept looking for an act curtain, a point of pause, but none ever developed. Actually it is practically a full-length play in number of pages, needing only the addition of a little material to make it obvious as such.
>
> That little material, that further elaboration, is what seemed to me, however, exactly what it ought not to have. . . . This play has been in the back of my head for many years. And . . . I have been asking of it why it would not get any longer. The answer occurred finally that one ought to say on the stage as much as one knows, and this, quite simply, is what I know about [this subject].
>
> This is not to say that there is nothing more I could tell about any of the people involved. On the contrary, there is a great deal—several plays' worth, in fact. Furthermore, all the cues to great length of treatment are there in *A View from the Bridge*. It is wide open for a totally subjective treatment, involving, as it does, several elements which fashion has permitted us to consider down to the last detail. There are, after all, an incestuous motif, homosexuality, and, as I shall no doubt soon discover, eleven other neurotic patterns hidden within it, as well as the question of codes. It would be ripe for a slowly evolving drama through which the hero's antecedent life forces might, one by one, be brought to light until we know his relationships to his parents, his uncles, his grandmother, and the incident in his life which, when revealed toward the end of the second act, is clearly what drove him inevitably to his disaster.
>
> But as many times as I have been led backward into Eddie's life, "deeper" into the subjective forces that made him what he evidently

is, a counter-impulse drew me back. It was a sense of form, the shape of this work which I saw first sparely, as one sees a naked mast on the sea, or a barren cliff. What struck me first about this tale when I heard it one night in my neighborhood was how directly, with what breathtaking simplicity, it did evolve. It seemed to me, finally, that its very bareness, its absolutely unswerving path, its exposed skeleton, so to speak, was its wisdom and even its charm and must not be tampered with. In this instance to cleave to his story was to cleave to the man, for the naïveté with which Eddie Carbone attacked his apparent enemy, its very directness and suddenness, the kind of blatant confession he could make to a near-stranger, the clarity with which he saw a wrong course of action—these *qualities* of the events themselves, their texture, seemed to me more psychologically telling than a conventional investigation in width which would necessarily relax that clear, clean line of his catastrophe.

This play falls into a single act, also, because I saw the characters purely in terms of their action and because they are a kind of people who, when inactive, have no new significant definition as people. I use the word "significant" because I am tired of documentation which, while perfectly apt and evidently reasonable, does not add anything to our comprehension of the tale's essence. In so writing, I have made the assumption that the audience is like me and would like to see, for once, a fine, high, always visible arc of forces moving in full view to a single explosion.

There was, as well, another consideration that held ornamentation back. When I heard this tale first it seemed to me that I had heard it before, very long ago. After a time I thought that it must be some re-enactment of a Greek myth which was ringing a long-buried bell in my own subconscious mind. I have not been able to find such a myth and yet the conviction persists, and for that reason I wished not to interfere with the myth-like march of the tale. The thought has often occurred to me that the two "submarines," the immigrants who come to Eddie from Italy, set out, as it were, two thousand years ago. There was such an iron-bound purity in the autonomic egocentricity of the aims of each of the persons involved that the weaving together of their lives seemed almost the work of a fate. I have tried to press as far as my reason can go toward defining the objective and sub-jective elements that made that fate, but I must confess that in the end a mystery remains for me and I have not attempted to conceal that fact. I know a good many ways to explain this story, but none of them fills its outline completely. I wrote it in order to discover its meanings completely, and I have not got them all yet, for there is a wonder remaining for me even now, a kind of expectation that de-rives, I think, from a sense of having somehow stumbled upon a hallowed tale.

The form of this play, finally, had a special attraction for me because once the decision was made to tell it without an excess line, the play took a harder, more objective shape. In effect, the form announces in the first moments of the play that only that will be told which is cogent, and that this story is the only part of Eddie Carbone's life worth our notice and therefore no effort will be made to draw in elements of his life that are beneath these, the most tense and meaningful of his hours. The form is what it is because its aim is to recreate my own feeling toward this tale—namely, wonderment. It is not designed primarily to draw tears or laughter from an audience but to strike a particular note of astonishment at the way in which, and the reasons for which, a man will endanger and risk and lose his very life.

Characters

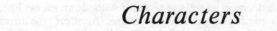

LOUIS

MIKE

ALFIERI

EDDIE

CATHERINE

BEATRICE

MARCO

TONY

RODOLPHO

FIRST IMMIGRATION OFFICER

SECOND IMMIGRATION OFFICER

MR. LIPARI

MRS. LIPARI

TWO "SUBMARINES"

A VIEW FROM THE BRIDGE

Arthur Miller

A tenement house and the street before it.

Like the play, the set is stripped of everything but its essential elements. The main acting area is Eddie Carbone's living-dining room, furnished with a round table, a few chairs, a rocker, and a phonograph.

This room is slightly elevated from the stage floor and is shaped in a free form designed to contain the acting space required, and that is all. At its back is an opaque wall-like shape, around whose right and left sides respectively entrances are made to an unseen kitchen and bedrooms.

Downstage, still in this room, and to the left, are two columnar shapes ending in air, and indicating the house front and entrance. Suspended over the entire front is an architectural element indicating a pediment over the columns, as well as the facing of a tenement building. Through this entrance a stairway is seen, beginning at floor level of the living-dining room, then curving upstage and around the back to the second-floor landing overhead.

Downstage center is the street. At the right, against the proscenium are a desk and chair belonging to Mr. Alfieri, whose office this is, and a coat hook or rack. Near the office, but separated from it, is a low iron railing such as might form a barrier on a street to guard a basement stair. Later in the play a coin telephone will appear against the proscenium at the left.

The intention is to make concrete the ancient element of this tale through the unmitigated forms of the commonest life of the big-city present, the one playing against the other to form a new world on the stage.

As the curtain rises, LOUIS *and* MIKE, *longshoremen, are pitching coins against the building at left.*

A distant foghorn blows.

Enter ALFIERI, *a lawyer in his fifties, turning gray, portly, good-humored, and thoughtful. The two pitchers nod to him as he passes; he crosses the stage to his desk and removes his hat and coat, hangs them, then turns to the audience.*

ALFIERI. I am smiling because they nod so uneasily to me.
That's because I am a lawyer, and in this neighborhood a lawyer's like
    a priest—
They only think of us when disaster comes. So we're unlucky.

Good evening. Welcome to the theater.
My name is Alfieri. I'll come directly to the point, even though I am a lawyer. I am getting on. And I share the weakness of so many of my profession—I believe I have had some amazingly interesting cases.
When one is still young the more improbable vagaries of life only make one impatient. One looks for logic.
But when one is old, facts become precious; in facts I find all the poetry, all the wonder, all the amazement of spring. And spring is especially beautiful after fifty-five. I love what happened, instead of what might or ought to have happened.
My wife has warned me, so have my friends: they tell me the people in this neighborhood lack elegance, glamor. After all, who have I dealt with in my life? Longshoremen and their wives and fathers and grand-fathers—compensation cases, evictions, family squabbles—the petty troubles of the poor—and yet . . .

When the tide is right,
And the wind blows the sea air against these houses,
I sit here in my office,
Thinking it is all so timeless here.
I think of Sicily, from where these people came,
The Roman rocks of Calabria,
Siracusa on the cliff, where Carthaginian and Greek
Fought such bloody fights. I think of Hannibal,
Who slew the fathers of these people; Caesar,
Whipping them on in Latin.

Which is all, of course, ridiculous.
Al Capone learned his trade on these pavements,
And Frankie Yale was cut in half
On the corner of Union Street and President,
Where so many were so justly shot,
By unjust men.

It's different now, of course.
I no longer keep a pistol in my filing cabinet;
We are quite American, quite civilized—
Now we settle for half. And I like it better.

And yet, when the tide is right,
And the green smell of the sea
Floats through my window,
I must look up at the circling pigeons of the poor,
And I see falcons there,
The hunting eagles of the olden time,
Fierce above Italian forests. . . .

This is Red Hook, a slum that faces the bay,
Seaward from Brooklyn Bridge.

[*Enter* EDDIE *along the street. He joins the penny-pitchers.*]
Once in every few years there is a case,
And as the parties tell me what the trouble is,
I see cobwebs tearing, Adriatic ruins rebuilding themselves; Calabria;
The eyes of the plaintiff seem sudddenly carved,
His voice booming toward me over many fallen stones.

This one's name was Eddie Carbone,
A longshoreman working the docks
From Brooklyn Bridge to the breakwater. . . .
[EDDIE *picks up the pennies.*]
EDDIE. Well, I'll see ya, fellas.
LOUIS. You workin' tomorrow?
EDDIE. Yeah, there's another day yet on that ship. See ya, Louis.
[EDDIE *goes into the house, climbs the stairs, as light rises in the apartment.*
EDDIE *is forty, a husky, slightly overweight longshoreman.*
CATHERINE, *his niece, is discovered standing at the window of the apart-
ment, waving down at* LOUIS, *who now sees her and waves back up. She
is seventeen and is now holding dishes in her hand, preparatory to laying
out the dinner on the table.*
EDDIE *enters, and she immediately proceeds to lay the table.*
The lights go out on* ALFIERI *and the street.*]
CATHERINE [*she has a suppressed excitement on her*]. Hi, Eddie.
EDDIE [*with a trace of wryness*]. What's the shoes for?
CATHERINE. I didn't go outside with them.
EDDIE [*removing his zipper jacket and hat*]. Do me a favor, heh?
CATHERINE. Why can't I wear them in the house?
EDDIE. Take them off, will you please?
You're beautiful enough without the shoes.

CATHERINE. I'm only trying them out.

EDDIE. When I'm home I'm not in the movies,
I don't wanna see young girls
Walking around in spike-heel shoes.

CATHERINE. Oh, brother.

[*Enter* BEATRICE, EDDIE'S *wife; she is his age.*]

BEATRICE. You find out anything?

EDDIE [*sitting in a rocker*]. The ship came in. They probably get off anytime now.

BEATRICE [*softly clapping her hands together, half in prayer, half in joy*]. Oh, boy. You find Tony?

EDDIE [*preoccupied*]. Yeah, I talked to him. They're gonna let the crew off tonight. So they'll be here any time, he says.

CATHERINE. Boy, they must be shakin'.

EDDIE. Naa, they'll get off all right. They got regular seamen papers; they walk off with the crew. [*To* BEATRICE.] I just hope they know where they're going to sleep, heh?

BEATRICE. I told them in the letter we got no room.

CATHERINE. You didn't meet them, though, heh? You didn't see them?

EDDIE. They're still on board. I only met Tony on the pier. What are you all hopped up about?

CATHERINE. I'm not hopped up.

BEATRICE [*in an ameliorative tone*]. It's something new in the house, she's excited.

EDDIE [*to* CATHERINE]. 'Cause they ain't comin' here for parties, they're only comin' here to work.

CATHERINE [*blushing, even enjoying his ribbing*]. Who's lookin' for parties?

EDDIE. Why don't you wear them nice shoes you got? [*He indicates her shoes*]. Those are for an actress. Go ahead.

CATHERINE. Don't tell nothin' till I come back. [*She hurries out, kicking off her shoes.*]

EDDIE [*as* BEATRICE *comes toward him*]. Why do you let her wear stuff like that? That ain't her type. [BEATRICE *bends and kisses his cheek.*] What's that for?

BEATRICE. For bein' so nice about it.

EDDIE. As long as they know we got nothin', B.; that's all I'm worried about.

BEATRICE. They're gonna pay for everything; I told them in the letter.

EDDIE. Because this ain't gonna end up with you on the floor, like when your mother's house burned down.

BEATRICE. Eddie, I told them in the letter we got no room.

[CATHERINE *enters in low-heeled shoes.*]

EDDIE. Because as soon as you see a relative I turn around you're on the floor.

BEATRICE [*half-amused, half-serious*]. All right, stop it already. You want a beer? The sauce is gotta cook a little more.

EDDIE [*to* BEATRICE]. No, it's too cold. [*To* CATHERINE.] You do your lessons today, Garbo?

CATHERINE. Yeah; I'm way ahead anyway. I just gotta practice from now on.

BEATRICE. She could take it down almost as fast you could talk already. She's terrific. Read something to her later, you'll be surprised.

EDDIE. That's the way, Katie. You're gonna be all right, kid, you'll see.

CATHERINE [*proudly*]. I could get a job right now, Eddie. I'm not even afraid.

EDDIE. You got time. Wait'll you're eighteen. We'll look up the ads—find a nice company, or maybe a lawyer's office or somethin' like that.

CATHERINE. Oh, boy! I could go to work now, my teacher said.

EDDIE. Be eighteen first. I want you to have a little more head on your shoulders. You're still dizzy yet. [*To* BEATRICE.] Where's the kids? They still outside?

BEATRICE. I put them with my mother for tonight. They'd never go to sleep otherwise. So what kinda cargo you have today?

EDDIE. Coffee. It was nice.

BEATRICE. I thought all day I smelled coffee here!

EDDIE. Yeah, Brazil. That's one time, boy, to be a longshoreman is a pleasure. The whole ship smelled from coffee. It was like flowers. We'll bust a bag tomorrow; I'll bring you some. Well, let's eat, heh?

BEATRICE. Two minutes. I want the sauce to cook a little more.

[EDDIE *goes to a bowl of grapes.*]

CATHERINE. How come he's not married, Beatrice, if he's so old? The younger one.

BEATRICE [*to* EDDIE]. Twenty-five is old!

EDDIE [*to* CATHERINE]. Is that all you got on your mind?

CATHERINE [*wryly*]. What else should I have on my mind?

EDDIE. There's plenty a things.

CATHERINE. Like what?

EDDIE. What the hell are you askin' me? I shoulda been struck by lightning when I promised your mother I would take care of you.

CATHERINE. You and me both.

EDDIE [*laughing*]. Boy, God bless you, you got a tongue in your mouth like the Devil's wife. You oughta be on the television.

CATHERINE. Oh, I wish!

EDDIE. You wish! You'd be scared to death.

CATHERINE. Yeah? Try me.

EDDIE. Listen, by the way, Garbo, what'd I tell you about wavin' from the window?

CATHERINE. I was wavin' to Louis!

EDDIE. Listen, I could tell you things about Louis which you wouldn't wave to him no more.

CATHERINE [*to* BEATRICE, *who is grinning*]. Boy, I wish I could find one guy that he couldn't tell me things about!

EDDIE [*going to her, cupping her cheek*]. Now look, Catherine, don't joke with me.

I'm responsible for you, kid.

I promised your mother on her deathbed.

So don't joke with me. I mean it.

I don't like the sound of them high heels on the sidewalk,

I don't like that clack, clack, clack,

I don't like the looks they're givin' you.

BEATRICE. How can she help it if they look at her?

EDDIE. She don't walk right. [*To* CATHERINE.] Don't walk so wavy like that.

[BEATRICE *goes out into the kitchen.*]

CATHERINE. Who's walkin' wavy?

EDDIE. Now don't aggravate me, Katie, you are walkin' wavy!

CATHERINE. Those guys look at all the girls, you know that.

EDDIE. They got mothers and fathers. You gotta be more careful.

[BEATRICE *enters with a tureen.*]

CATHERINE. Oh, Jesus! [*She goes out into the kitchen.*]

EDDIE [*calling after her*]. Hey, lay off the language, heh?

BEATRICE [*alone with him, loading the plates—she is riding lightly over a slightly sore issue*]. What do you want from her all the time?

EDDIE. Boy, she grew up! Your sister should see her now. I'm tellin' you, it's like a miracle—one day she's a baby; you turn around and she's— [*Enter* CATHERINE *with knives and forks.*] Y'know? When she sets a table she looks like a Madonna.

[BEATRICE *wipes a strand of hair off* CATHERINE'S *face. To* CATHERINE:] You're the Madonna type. That's why you shouldn't be flashy, Kate. For you it ain't beautiful. You're more the Madonna type. And anyway, it ain't nice in an office. They don't go for that in an office. [*He sits at the table.*]

BEATRICE [*sitting to eat*]. Sit down, Katie-baby. [CATHERINE *sits. They eat.*]

EDDIE. Geez, how quiet it is here without the kids!

CATHERINE. What happens? How they gonna find the house here?

EDDIE. Tony'll take them from the ship and bring them here.

BEATRICE. That Tony must be makin' a nice dollar off this.

EDDIE. Naa, the syndicate's takin' the heavy cream.

CATHERINE. What happens when the ship pulls out and they ain't on it though?

EDDIE. Don't worry; captain's pieced-off.

CATHERINE. Even the captain?

EDDIE. Why, the captain don't have to live? Captain gets a piece, maybe one of the mates, a piece for the guy in Italy who fixed the papers for them—[*To* BEATRICE.] They're gonna have to work six months for that syndicate before they keep a dime for theirselfs; they know that, I hope.

BEATRICE. Yeah, but Tony'll fix jobs for them, won't he?

EDDIE. Sure, as long as they owe him money he'll fix jobs; it's after the pay-off—they're gonna have to scramble like the rest of us. I just hope they know that.

BEATRICE. Oh, they must know. Boy, they must've been starvin' there. To go through all this just to make a couple a dollars. I'm tellin' ya, it could make you cry.

EDDIE. By the way, what are you going to tell the people in the house? If somebody asks what they're doin' here?

BEATRICE. Well, I'll tell 'em—Well, who's gonna ask? They probably know anyway.

EDDIE. What do you mean, they know? Listen, Beatrice, the Immigration Bureau's got stool pigeons all over the neighborhood.

BEATRICE. Yeah, but not in this house—?

EDDIE. How do you know, not in this house? Listen, both a yiz. If anybody asks you, they're your cousins visitin' here from Philadelphia.

CATHERINE. Yeah, but what would they know about Philadelphia? I mean if somebody asks them—

EDDIE. Well—they don't talk much, that's all. But don't get confidential with nobody, you hear me? Because there's a lotta guys do anything for a couple a dollars, and the Immigration pays good for that kinda news.

CATHERINE. I could teach them about Philadelphia.

EDDIE. Do me a favor, baby, will ya? Don't teach them, and don't mix in with them. Because with that blabbermouth the less you know the better off we're all gonna be. They're gonna work, and they're gonna come home here and go to sleep, and I don't want you payin' no attention to them. This is a serious business; this is the United States Government. So you don't know they're alive. I mean don't get dizzy with your friends about it. It's nobody's business. [*Slight pause.*] Where's the salt? [*Pause.*]

CATHERINE. It's gettin' dark.

EDDIE. Yeah, gonna snow tomorrow, I think. [*Pause*].

BEATRICE [*she is frightened*]. Geez, remember that Vinny Bolzano years ago? Remember him?

EDDIE. That funny? I was just thinkin' about him before.

CATHERINE. Who's he?

BEATRICE. You were a baby then. But there was a kid, Vinny, about sixteen. Lived over there on Sackett Street. And he snitched on somebody to the Immigration. He had five brothers, and the old man. And they grabbed him in the kitchen, and they pulled him down three flights, his head was bouncin' like a coconut—we lived in the next house. And they spit on him in the street, his own father and his brothers. It was so terrible.

CATHERINE. So what happened to him?

BEATRICE. He went away, I think. [*To* EDDIE.] Did you ever see him again?

EDDIE. Him? Naa, you'll never see him no more. A guy do a thing like that—how could he show his face again? There's too much salt in here.

BEATRICE. So what'd you put salt for?

[EDDIE *lays the spoon down, leaves the table.*]

EDDIE. Geez, I'm gettin' nervous, y'know?

BEATRICE. What's the difference; they'll only sleep here; you won't hardly see them. Go ahead, eat. [*He looks at her, disturbed.*] What could I do? They're my cousins. [*He returns to her and clasps her face admiringly as the lights fade on them and rise on* ALFIERI.]

ALFIERI. I only know that they had two children;
He was as good a man as he had to be
In a life that was hard and even.
He worked on the piers when there was work.
He brought home his pay, and he lived.
And toward ten o'clock of that night,
After they had eaten, the cousins came.

[*While he is speaking* EDDIE *goes to the window and looks out.* CATHERINE *and* BEATRICE *clear the dishes.* EDDIE *sits down and reads the paper.*

Enter TONY, *escorting* MARCO *and* RODOLPHO, *each with a valise.* TONY *halts, indicates the house. They stand for a moment, looking at it.*]

MARCO [*he is a square-built peasant of thirty-two, suspicious and quiet-voiced*]. Thank you.

TONY. You're on your own now. Just be careful, that's all. Ground floor.

MARCO. Thank you.

TONY. I'll see you on the pier tomorrow. You'll go to work.

[MARCO *nods.* TONY *continues on, walking down the street.*

RODOLPHO *is in his early twenties, an eager boy, one moment a gamin, the next a brooding adult. His hair is startlingly blond.*]

RODOLPHO. This will be the first house I ever walked into in America!

MARCO. Sssh! Come. [*They mount the stoop.*]

RODOLPHO. Imagine! She said they were poor!

MARCO. Ssh!

[*They pass between the columns. Light rises inside the apartment.* EDDIE, CATHERINE, BEATRICE *hear and raise their heads toward the door.* MARCO *knocks.* BEATRICE *and* CATHERINE *look to* EDDIE, *who rises and goes and opens the door. Enter* MARCO *and* RODOLPHO, *removing their caps.*]

EDDIE. You Marco?

[MARCO *nods, looks to the women, and fixes on* BEATRICE.]

MARCO. Are you my cousin?

BEATRICE [*touching her chest with her hand*]. Beatrice. This is my husband, Eddie. [*All nod.*] Catherine, my sister Nancy's daughter. [*The brothers nod.*]

MARCO [*indicating* RODOLPHO]. My brother. Rodolpho. [RODOLPHO *nods.*

MARCO *comes with a certain formal stiffness to* EDDIE.] I want to tell you now, Eddie—when you say go, we will go.

EDDIE. Oh, no—

MARCO. I see it's a small house, but soon, maybe, we can have our own house.

EDDIE. You're welcome, Marco, we got plenty of room here. Katie, give them supper, heh?

CATHERINE. Come here, sit down. I'll get you some soup.

[*They go to the table.*]

MARCO. We ate on the ship. Thank you. [*To* EDDIE.] Thank you.

BEATRICE. Get some coffee. We'll all have coffee. Come sit down.

CATHERINE. How come he's so dark and you're so light, Rodolpho?

RODOLPHO. I don't know. A thousand years ago, they say, the Danes invaded Sicily. [*He laughs.*]

CATHERINE [*to* BEATRICE]. He's practically blond!

EDDIE. How's the coffee doin'?

CATHERINE [*brought up short*]. I'm gettin' it. [*She hurries out.*]

EDDIE. Yiz have a nice trip?

MARCO. The ocean is always rough in the winter. But we are good sailors.

EDDIE. No trouble gettin' here?

MARCO. No. The man brought us. Very nice man.

RODOLPHO. He says we start to work tomorrow. Is he honest?

EDDIE. No. But as long as you owe them money they'll get you plenty of work. [*To* MARCO.] Yiz ever work on the piers in Italy?

MARCO. Piers? Ts! No.

RODOLPHO [*smiling at the smallness of his town*]. In our town there are no piers.

Only the beach, and little fishing boats.

BEATRICE. So what kinda work did yiz do?

MARCO [*shrugging shyly, even embarrassed*]. Whatever there is, anything.

RODOLPHO. Sometimes they build a house,

Or if they fix a bridge—

Marco is a mason,

And I bring him the cement.

[*He laughs.*]

In harvest time we work in the fields—

If there is work. Anything.

EDDIE. Still bad there, heh?

MARCO. Bad, yes.

RODOLPHO. It's terrible.

We stand around all day in the piazza,

Listening to the fountain like birds.

[*He laughs.*]

Everybody waits only for the train.

BEATRICE. What's on the train?

RODOLPHO. Nothing. But if there are many passengers
   And you're lucky you make a few lire
   To push the taxi up the hill.
   [*Enter* CATHERINE, *who sits, listens.*]
BEATRICE. You gotta push a taxi?
RODOLPHO [*with a laugh*]. Oh, sure! It's a feature in our town.
   The horses in our town are skinnier than goats.
   So if there are too many passengers
   We help to push the carriages up to the hotel.
   [*He laughs again.*]
   In our town the horses are only for the show.
CATHERINE. Why don't they have automobile taxis?
RODOLPHO. There is one—we push that too.
   [*They laugh.*]
   Everything in our town, you gotta push.
BEATRICE [*to* EDDIE, *sorrowfully*]. How do you like that—
EDDIE [*to* MARCO]. So what're you wanna do, you gonna stay here in this
   country or you wanna go back?
MARCO [*surprised*]. Go back?
EDDIE. Well, you're married, ain't you?
MARCO. Yes. I have three children.
BEATRICE. Three! I thought only one.
MARCO. Oh no. I have three now.
   Four years, five years, six years.
BEATRICE. Ah, I bet they're cryin' for you already, heh?
MARCO. What can I do?
   The older one is sick in his chest;
   My wife—she feeds them from her own mouth.
   I tell you the truth,
   If I stay there they will never grow up.
   They eat the sunshine.
BEATRICE. My God. So how long you want to stay?
MARCO. With your permission, we will stay maybe a—
EDDIE. She don't mean in this house, she means in the country.
MARCO. Oh. Maybe four, five, six years, I think.
RODOLPHO [*smiling*]. He trusts his wife.
BEATRICE. Yeah, but maybe you'll get enough,
   You'll be able to go back quicker.
MARCO. I hope. I don't know. [*To* EDDIE.] I understand it's not so good here
   either.
EDDIE. Oh, you guys'll be all right—till you pay them off, anyway. After
   that, you'll have to scramble, that's all. But you'll make better here than
   you could there.
RODOLPHO. How much? We hear all kinds of figures.
   How much can a man make? We work hard,

We'll work all day, all night . . .

EDDIE [*he is coming more and more to address* MARCO *only*]. On the average a whole year? Maybe—well, it's hard to say, see. Sometimes we lay off, there's no ships three-four weeks.

MARCO. Three, four weeks! Ts!

EDDIE. But I think you could probably—Thirty, forty a week over the whole twelve months of the year.

MARCO. Dollars.

EDDIE. Sure dollars.

MARCO [*looking happily at* RODOLPHO]. If we can stay here a few months, Beatrice—

BEATRICE. Listen, you're welcome, Marco—

MARCO. Because I could send them a little more if I stay here—

BEATRICE. As long as you want; we got plenty a room—

MARCO [*his eyes showing tears*]. My wife—my wife . . .

I want to send right away maybe twenty dollars.

EDDIE. You could send them something next week already.

MARCO [*near tears*]. Eduardo—

EDDIE. Don't thank me. Listen, what the hell, it's no skin off me.

[*To* CATHERINE.] What happened to the coffee?

CATHERINE. I got it on. [*To* RODOLPHO.] You married too? No.

RODOLPHO. Oh, no.

BEATRICE. I told you he—

CATHERINE [*to her*]. I know, I just thought maybe he got married recently.

RODOLPHO. I have no money to get married.

I have a nice face, but no money. [*He laughs*].

CATHERINE [*to* BEATRICE]. He's a real blond!

BEATRICE [*to* RODOLPHO]. You want to stay here too, heh? For good?

RODOLPHO. Me? Yes, forever! Me,

I want to be an American.

And then I want to go back to Italy

When I am rich. And I will buy a motorcycle. [*He smiles.*]

CATHERINE. A motorcycle!

RODOLPHO. With a motorcycle in Italy you will never starve anymore.

BEATRICE. I'll get you coffee. [*She exits.*]

EDDIE. What're you do with a motorcycle?

MARCO. He dreams, he dreams.

RODOLPHO. Why? Messages! The rich people in the hotel

Always need someone who will carry a message.

But quickly, and with a great noise.

With a blue motorcycle I would station myself

In the courtyard of the hotel,

And in a little while I would have messages.

MARCO. When you have no wife you have dreams.

EDDIE. Why can't you just walk, or take a trolley or sump'm?

[*Enter* BEATRICE *with coffee.*]

RODOLPHO. Oh, no, the machine, the machine is necessary.
A man comes into a great hotel and says,
"I am a messenger." Who is this man?
He disappears walking, there is no noise, nothing—
Maybe he will never come back,
Maybe he will never deliver the message.
But a man who rides up on a great machine,
This man is responsible, this man exists.
He will be given messages.
I am also a singer, though.

EDDIE. You mean a regular—?

RODOLPHO. Oh, yes. One night last year
Andreola got sick. Baritone.
And I took his place in the garden of the hotel.
Three arias I sang without a mistake;
Thousand-lire notes they threw from the tables,
Money was falling like a storm in the treasury;
It was magnificent.
We lived six months on that night, eh, Marco?
[MARCO *nods doubtfully.*]

MARCO. Two months.

BEATRICE. Can't you get a job in that place?

RODOLPHO. Andreola got better.
He's a baritone, very strong, otherwise I—

MARCO [*to* BEATRICE]. He sang too loud.

RODOLPHO. Why too loud!

MARCO. Too loud. The guests in that hotel are all Englishmen. They don't
like too loud.

RODOLPHO. Then why did they throw so much money?

MARCO. They pay for your courage. [*To* EDDIE.] The English like courage,
but once is enough.

RODOLPHO [*to all but* MARCO]. I never heard anybody say it was too loud.

CATHERINE. Did you ever hear of jazz?

RODOLPHO. Oh, sure! I sing jazz.

CATHERINE. You could sing jazz?

RODOLPHO. Oh, I sing Napolidan, jazz, bel canto—
I sing "Paper Doll"; you like "Paper Doll"?

CATHERINE. Oh, sure, I'm crazy for "Paper Doll." Go ahead, sing it.

RODOLPHO [*he takes his stance, and with a high tenor voice*].
"I'll tell you boys it's tough to be alone,
And it's tough to love a doll that's not your own.
I'm through with all of them,
I'll never fall again,
Hey, boy, what you gonna do—

I'm goin' to buy a paper doll that I can call my own,
A doll that other fellows cannot steal,
And then the flirty, flirty guys
With their flirty, flirty eyes
Will have to flirt with dollies that are real.
When I come home at night she will be waiting.
She'll be the truest doll in all this world—"

EDDIE [*he has been slowly moving in agitation*]. Hey, kid—hey, wait a minute—

CATHERINE [*enthralled*]. Leave him finish. It's beautiful! [*To* BEATRICE.] He's terrific! It's terrific, Rodolpho!

EDDIE. Look, kid; you don't want to be picked up, do ya?

MARCO. No-no!

EDDIE [*indicating the rest of the building*]. Because we never had no singers here—and all of a sudden there's a singer in the house, y'know what I mean?

MARCO. Yes, yes. You will be quiet, Rodolpho.

EDDIE [*flushed*]. They got guys all over the place, Marco. I mean.

MARCO. Yes. He will be quiet. [*To* RODOLPHO.] Quiet.

EDDIE [*with iron control, even a smile*]. You got the shoes again, Garbo?

CATHERINE. I figured for tonight—

EDDIE. Do me a favor, will you? [*He indicates the bedroom.*] Go ahead.

[*Embarrassed now, angered,* CATHERINE *goes out into the bedroom.* BEATRICE *watches her go and gets up, and, in passing, gives* EDDIE *a cold look, restrained only by the strangers, and goes to the table to pour coffee.*]

EDDIE [*to* MARCO, *but directed as much to* BEATRICE]. All actresses they want to be around here. [*He goes to draw a shade down.*]

RODOLPHO [*happy about it*]. In Italy too! All the girls.

EDDIE [*sizing up* RODOLPHO—*there is a concealed suspicion*]. Yeah, heh?

RODOLPHO. Yes! [*He laughs, indicating* CATHERINE *with his head—her bedroom*]. Especially when they are so beautiful!

[CATHERINE *emerges from the bedroom in low-heeled shoes, comes to the table.* RODOLPHO *is lifting a cup*].

CATHERINE. You like sugar?

RODOLPHO. Sugar? Yes! I like sugar very much!

[EDDIE *is downstage, watching, as she pours a spoonful of sugar into* RODOLPHO'S *cup.* EDDIE *turns and draws a shade, his face puffed with trouble, and the room dies. Light rises on* ALFIERI.]

ALFIERI. Who can ever know what will be discovered?

[*Sunlight rises on the street and house.*]

Eddie Carbone had never expected to have a destiny.

[EDDIE *comes slowly, ambling, down the stairs into the street.*]

A man works, raises his family, goes bowling,
Eats, gets old, and then he dies.
Now, as the weeks passed, there was a future,

There was a trouble that would not go away.

[BEATRICE *appears with a shopping bag. Seeing her,* EDDIE *meets her at the stoop.*]

EDDIE. It's after four.

BEATRICE. Well, it's a long show at the Paramount.

EDDIE. They must've seen every picture in Brooklyn by now.
He's supposed to stay in the house when he ain't workin'.
He ain't supposed to go advertising himself.

BEATRICE. So what am I gonna do?

EDDIE. Last night they went to the park.
You know that? Louis seen them in the park.

BEATRICE. She's goin' on eighteen, what's so terrible?

EDDIE. I'm responsible for her.

BEATRICE. I just wish once in a while you'd be responsible for me, you know that?

EDDIE. What're you beefin'?

BEATRICE. You don't know why I'm beefin'? [*He turns away, making as though to scan the street, his jaws clamped.*] What's eatin' you? You're gonna bust your teeth, you grind them so much in bed, you know that? It's like a factory all night. [*He doesn't answer, looks peeved.*] What's the matter, Eddie?

EDDIE. It's all right with you? You don't mind this?

BEATRICE. Well what you want, keep her in the house a little baby all her life? What do you want, Eddie?

EDDIE. That's what I brung her up for? For that character?

BEATRICE. Why? He's a nice fella. Hard-workin', he's a good-lookin' fella—

EDDIE. That's good-lookin'?

BEATRICE. He's handsome, for God's sake.

EDDIE. He gives me the heeby-jeebies. I don't like his whole way.

BEATRICE [*smiling*]. You're jealous, that's all.

EDDIE. Of *him*? Boy, you don't think much of me.

BEATRICE [*going to him*]. What are you worried about? She knows how to take care of herself.

EDDIE. She don't know nothin'. He's got her rollin'; you see the way she looks at him? The house could burn down she wouldn't know.

BEATRICE. Well, she's got a boyfriend finally, so she's excited. So?

EDDIE. He sings on the ships, didja know that?

BEATRICE [*mystified*]. What do you mean, he sings?

EDDIE. He sings. Right on the deck, all of a sudden—a whole song. They're callin' him Paper Doll, now. Canary. He's like a weird. Soon as he comes onto the pier it's a regular free show.

BEATRICE. Well, he's a kid; he don't know how to behave himself yet.

EDDIE. And with that wacky hair; he's like a chorus girl or sump'm.

BEATRICE. So he's blond, so—

EDDIE [*not looking at her*]. I just hope that's his regular hair, that's all I hope.

BEATRICE [*alarmed*]. You crazy or sump'm?

EDDIE [*only glancing at her*]. What's so crazy? You know what I heard them call him on Friday? I was on line for my check, somebody calls out, "Blondie!" I turn around, they're callin' *him!* Blondie now!

BEATRICE. You never seen a blond guy in your life? What about Whitey Balso?

EDDIE. Sure, but Whitey don't sing; he don't do like that on the ships—

BEATRICE. Well, maybe that's the way they do in Italy.

EDDIE. Then why don't his brother sing? Marco goes around like a man; nobody kids Marco. [*He shifts, with a glance at her.*] I don't like him, B. And I'm tellin' you now, I'm not gonna stand for it. For that character I didn't bring her up.

BEATRICE. All right—well, go tell her, then.

EDDIE. How am I gonna tell her? She won't listen to me, she can't even see me. I come home, she's in a dream. Look how thin she got, she could walk through a wall—

BEATRICE. All right, listen—

EDDIE. It's eatin' me out, B. I can't stand to look at his face. And what happened to the stenography? She don't practice no more, does she?

BEATRICE. All right, listen. I want you to lay off, you hear me? Don't work yourself up. You hear? This is her business.

EDDIE. B., he's takin' her for a ride!

BEATRICE. All right, that's her ride. It's time already; let her be somebody else's Madonna now. Come on, come in the house, you got your own to worry about. [*She glances around.*] She ain't gonna come any quicker if you stand on the street, Eddie. It ain't nice.

EDDIE. I'll be up right away. I want to take a walk. [*He walks away.*]

BEATRICE. Come on, look at the kids for once.

EDDIE. I'll be up right away. Go ahead.

BEATRICE [*with a shielded tone*]. Don't stand around, please. It ain't nice. I mean it.

[*She goes into the house. He reaches the upstage right extremity, stares at nothing for a moment; then, seeing someone coming, he goes to the railing downstage and sits, as* LOUIS *and* MIKE *enter and join him.*]

LOUIS. Wanna go bowlin' tonight?

EDDIE. I'm too tired. Goin' to sleep.

LOUIS. How's your two submarines?

EDDIE. They're okay.

LOUIS. I see they're gettin' work allatime.

EDDIE. Oh yeah, they're doin' all right.

MIKE. That's what we oughta do. We oughta leave the country and come in under the water. Then we get work.

EDDIE. You ain't kiddin'.

LOUIS. Well, what the hell. Y'know?

EDDIE. Sure.

LOUIS. Believe me, Eddie, you got a lotta credit comin' to you.

EDDIE. Aah, they don't bother me, don't cost me nutt'n.

MIKE. That older one, boy, he's a regular bull. I seen him the other day liftin' coffee bags over the Matson Line. They leave him alone he woulda load the whole ship by himself.

EDDIE. Yeah, he's a strong guy, that guy. My Frankie takes after him, I think. Their father was a regular giant, supposed to be.

LOUIS. Yeah, you could see. He's a regular slave.

MIKE. That blond one, though—[EDDIE *looks at him.*] He's got a sense a humor.

EDDIE [*searchingly*]. Yeah. He's funny—

MIKE [*laughing through his speech*]. Well, he ain't ezackly funny, but he's always like makin' remarks, like, y'know? He comes around, everybody's laughin'.

EDDIE [*uncomfortably*]. Yeah, well—he's got a sense a humor.

MIKE. Yeah, I mean, he's always makin' like remarks, like, y'know? [LOUIS *is quietly laughing with him.*]

EDDIE. Yeah, I know. But he's a kid yet, y'know? He—he's just a kid, that's all.

MIKE. I know. You take one look at him—everybody's happy. I worked one day with him last week over the Moore-MacCormack, I'm tellin' you they was all hysterical.

EDDIE. Why? What'd he do?

MIKE. I don't know—he was just humorous. You never can remember what he says, y'know? But it's the way he says it. I mean he gives you a look sometimes and you start laughin'!

EDDIE. Yeah. [*Troubled.*] He's got a sense a humor.

MIKE [*laughing*]. Yeah.

LOUIS. Well, we'll see ya, Eddie.

EDDIE. Take it easy.

LOUIS. Yeah. See ya.

MIKE. If you wanna come bowlin' later we're goin' Flatbush Avenue.

[*They go.* EDDIE, *in troubled thought, stares after them; they arrive at the left extremity, and their laughter, untroubled and friendly, rises as they see* RODOLPHO, *who is entering with* CATHERINE *on his arm. The longshoremen exit.* RODOLPHO *waves a greeting to them.*]

CATHERINE. Hey, Eddie, what a picture we saw! Did we laugh!

EDDIE [*he can't help smiling at sight of her*]. Where'd you go?

CATHERINE. Paramount. It was with those two guys, y'know? That—

EDDIE. Brooklyn Paramount?

CATHERINE [*with an edge of anger, embarrassed before* RODOLPHO]. Sure the Brooklyn Paramount. I told you we wasn't goin' to New York.

EDDIE [*retreating before the threat of her anger*]. All right, I only asked you.

[*To* RODOLPHO.] I just don't want her hangin' around Times Square, see; it's full of tramps over there.

RODOLPHO. I would like to go to Broadway once, Eddie.
I would like to walk with her once
Where the theaters are, and the opera;
Since I was a boy I see pictures of those lights—

EDDIE [*his little patience waning*]. I want to talk to her a minute, Rodolpho; go upstairs, will you?

RODOLPHO. Eddie, we only walk together in the streets,
She teaches me—

CATHERINE. You know what he can't get over?
That there's no fountains in Brooklyn!

EDDIE [*smiling unwillingly, to* RODOLPHO]. Fountains?
[RODOLPHO *smiles at his own naïveté.*]

CATHERINE. In Italy, he says, every town's got fountains,
And they meet there. And you know what?
They got oranges on the trees where he comes from,
And lemons. Imagine? On the trees?
I mean it's interesting. But he's crazy for New York!

RODOLPHO [*attempting familiarity*]. Eddie, why can't we go once to Broadway?

EDDIE. Look, I gotta tell her something—
[RODOLPHO *nods, goes to the stoop.*]

RODOLPHO. Maybe you can come too.
I want to see all those lights . . .
[*He sees no response in* EDDIE'S *face. He glances at* CATHERINE *and goes into the house.*]

CATHERINE. Why don't you talk to him, Eddie? He blesses you, and you don't talk to him hardly.

EDDIE [*enveloping her with his eyes*]. I bless you, and you don't talk to me.
[*He tries to smile.*]

CATHERINE. *I* don't talk to you? [*She hits his arm.*] What do you mean!

EDDIE. I don't see you no more. I come home you're runnin' around someplace—
[CATHERINE *takes his arm, and they walk a little.*]

CATHERINE. Well, he wants to see everything, that's all, so we go. You mad at me?

EDDIE. No. [*He is smiling sadly, almost moony.*] It's just I used to come home, you was always there. Now, I turn around, you're a big girl. I don't know how to talk to you.

CATHERINE. Why!

EDDIE. I don't know, you're runnin', you're runnin', Katie. I don't think you listening anymore to me.

CATHERINE. Ah, Eddie, sure I am. What's the matter? You don't like him?
[*Slight pause.*]

EDDIE. *You* like him, Katie?

CATHERINE [*with a blush, but holding her ground*]. Yeah, I like him.

EDDIE [*his smile goes*]. You like him.

CATHERINE [*looking down*]. Yeah. [*Now she looks at him for the consequences, smiling but tense. He looks at her like a lost boy.*] What're you got against him? I don't understand. He only blesses you.

EDDIE. He don't bless me, Katie.

CATHERINE. He does! You're like a father to him!

EDDIE. Katie.

CATHERINE. What, Eddie?

EDDIE. You gonna marry him?

CATHERINE. I don't know. We just been—goin' around, that's all.

EDDIE. He don't respect you, Katie.

CATHERINE. Why!

EDDIE. Katie, if you wasn't an orphan, wouldn't he ask your father's permission before he run around with you like this?

CATHERINE. Oh, well, he didn't think you'd mind.

EDDIE. He knows I mind, but it don't bother him if I mind, don't you see that?

CATHERINE. No, Eddie, he's got all kinds of respect for me. And you too! We walk across the street, he takes my arm—he almost bows to me! You got him all wrong, Eddie; I mean it, you—

EDDIE. Katie, he's only bowin' to his passport.

CATHERINE. His passport!

EDDIE. That's right. He marries you he's got the right to be an American citizen. That's what's goin' on here. [*She is puzzled and surprised.*] You understand what I'm tellin' you? The guy is lookin' for his break, that's all he's lookin' for.

CATHERINE [*pained*]. Oh, no, Eddie, I don't think so.

EDDIE. You don't think so! Katie, you're gonna make me cry here. Is that a workin' man? What does he do with his first money? A snappy new jacket he buys, records, a pointy pair new shoes, and his brother's kids are starvin' with tuberculosis over there? That's a hit-and-run guy, baby; he's got bright lights in his head, Broadway—them guys don't think of nobody but theirself! You marry him and the next time you see him it'll be for the divorce!

CATHERINE. Eddie, he never said a word about his papers or—

EDDIE. You mean he's supposed to tell you that?

CATHERINE. I don't think he's even thinking about it.

EDDIE. What's better for him to think about? He could be picked up any day here and he's back pushin' taxis up the hill!

CATHERINE. No, I don't believe it.

EDDIE [*grabbing her hand*]. Katie, don't break my heart, listen to me—

CATHERINE. I don't want to hear it. Lemme go.

EDDIE [*holding her*]. Katie, listen—

CATHERINE. He loves me!

EDDIE [*with deep alarm*]. Don't say that, for God's sake! This is the oldest racket in the country.

CATHERINE [*desperately, as though he had made his imprint*]. I don't believe it!

EDDIE. They been pullin' this since the immigration law was put in! They grab a green kid that don't know nothin' and they—

CATHERINE. I don't believe it and I wish to hell you'd stop it! [*She rushes, sobbing, into the house.*]

EDDIE. Katie!

[*He starts in after her, but halts as though realizing he has no force over her. From within, music is heard now, radio jazz. He glances up and down the street, then moves off, his chest beginning to rise and fall in anger. Light rises on* ALFIERI, *seated behind his desk.*]

ALFIERI. It was at this time that he first came to me.

I had represented his father in an accident case some years before,

And I was acquainted with the family in a casual way.

I remember him now as he walked through my doorway—

His eyes were like tunnels;

My first thought was that he had committed a crime,

[EDDIE *enters, sits beside the desk, cap in hand, looking out.*]

But soon I saw it was only a passion

That had moved into his body, like a stranger.

[ALFIERI *pauses, looks down at his desk, then to* EDDIE, *as though he were continuing a conversation with him.*]

I don't quite understand what I can do for you. Is there a question of law somewhere?

EDDIE. That's what I want to ask you.

ALFIERI. Because there's nothing illegal about a girl falling in love with an immigrant.

EDDIE. Yeah, but what about if the only reason for it is to get his papers?

ALFIERI. First of all, you don't know that—

EDDIE. I see it in his eyes; he's laughin' at her and he's laughin' at me.

ALFIERI. Eddie, I'm a lawyer; I can only deal in what's provable. You understand that, don't you? Can you prove that?

EDDIE. I know what's in his mind, Mr. Alfieri!

ALFIERI. Eddie, even if you could prove that—

EDDIE. Listen—Will you listen to me a minute? My father always said you was a smart man. I want you to listen to me.

ALFIERI. I'm only a lawyer, Eddie—

EDDIE. Will you listen a minute? I'm talkin' about the law. Lemme just bring out what I mean. A man, which he comes into the country illegal, don't it stand to reason he's gonna take every penny and put it in the sock? Because they don't know from one day to the other, right?

ALFIERI. All right.

EDDIE. He's spendin'. Records he buys now. Shoes. Jackets. Y'understand me? This guy ain't worried. This guy is *here*. So it must be that he's got it all laid out in his mind already—he's stayin'. Right?

ALFIERI. Well? What about it?

EDDIE. All right. [*He glances over his shoulder as though for intruders, then back to* ALFIERI, *then down to the floor*.] I'm talkin' to you confidential, ain't I?

ALFIERI. Certainly.

EDDIE. I mean it don't go no place but here. Because I don't like to say this about anybody. Even to my wife I didn't exactly say this.

ALFIERI. What is it?

EDDIE [*he takes a breath*]. The guy ain't right, Mr. Alfieri.

ALFIERI. What do you mean?

EDDIE [*glancing over his shoulder again*]. I mean he ain't right.

ALFIERI. I don't get you.

EDDIE. [*He shifts to another position in the chair*.] Dja ever get a look at him?

ALFIERI. Not that I know of, no.

EDDIE. He's a blond guy. Like—platinum. You know what I mean?

ALFIERI. No.

EDDIE. I mean if you close the paper fast—you could blow him over.

ALFIERI. Well, that doesn't mean—

EDDIE. Wait a minute, I'm tellin' you sump'm. He sings, see. Which is— I mean it's all right, but sometimes he hits a note, see. I turn around. I mean—high. You know what I mean?

ALFIERI. Well, that's a tenor.

EDDIE. I know a tenor, Mr. Alfieri. This ain't no tenor. I mean if you came in the house and you didn't know who was singin', you wouldn't be lookin' for him, you'd be lookin' for her.

ALFIERI. Yes, but that's not—

EDDIE. I'm tellin' you sump'm, wait a minute; please, Mr. Alfieri. I'm tryin' to bring out my thoughts here. Couple a nights ago my niece brings out a dress, which it's too small for her, because she shot up like a light this last year. He takes the dress, lays it on the table, he cuts it up; one-two-three, he makes a new dress. I mean he looked so sweet there, like an angel—you could kiss him he was so sweet.

ALFIERI. Now look, Eddie—

EDDIE. Mr. Alfieri, they're laughin' at him on the piers. I'm ashamed. Paper Doll, they call him. Blondie now. His brother thinks it's because he's got a sense a humor, see—which he's got—but that ain't what they're laughin'. Which they're not goin' to come out with it because they know he's my relative, which they have to see me if they make a crack, y'know? But I know what they're laughin' at, and when I think of that guy layin' his hands on her I could—I mean it's eatin' me out, Mr. Alfieri, because I struggled for that girl. And now he comes in my house—

ALFIERI. Eddie, look. I have my own children, I understand you. But the law is very specific. The law does not—

EDDIE [*with a fuller flow of indignation*]. You mean to tell me that there's no law that a guy which he ain't right can go to work and marry a girl and—?

ALFIERI. You have no recourse in the law, Eddie.

EDDIE. Yeah, but if he ain't right, Mr. Alfieri, you mean to tell me—

ALFIERI. There is nothing you can do, Eddie, believe me.

EDDIE. Nothin'.

ALFIERI. Nothing at all. There's only one legal question here.

EDDIE. What?

ALFIERI. The manner in which they entered the country. But I don't think you want to do anything about that, do you?

EDDIE. You mean—?

ALFIERI. Well, they entered illegally.

EDDIE. Oh, Jesus, no, I wouldn't do nothin' about that. I mean—

ALFIERI. All right, then, let me talk now, eh?

EDDIE. Mr. Alfieri, I can't believe what you tell me. I mean there must be some kinda law which—

ALFIERI. Eddie, I want you to listen to me.
[*Pause.*]
You know, sometimes God mixes up the people.
We all love somebody, the wife, the kids—
Every man's got somebody that he loves, heh?
But sometimes—there's too much. You know?
There's too much, and it goes where it mustn't.
A man works hard, he brings up a child,
Sometimes it's a niece, sometimes even a daughter,
And he never realizes it, but through the years—
There is too much love for the daughter,
There is too much love for the niece.
Do you understand what I'm saying to you?

EDDIE [*sardonically*]. What do you mean, I shouldn't look out for her good?

ALFIERI. Yes, but these things have to end, Eddie, that's all.
The child has to grow up and go away,
And the man has to learn how to forget.
Because after all, Eddie—
What other way can it end?
[*Pause.*]
Let her go. That's my advice. You did your job,
Now it's her life; wish her luck,
And let her go.
[*Pause.*]
Will you do that? Because there's no law, Eddie;
Make up your mind to it; the law is not interested in this.

EDDIE. You mean to tell me, even if he's a punk? If he's—

ALFIERI. There's nothing you can do.

[EDDIE *sits almost grinding his jaws. He stands, wipes one eye.*]

EDDIE. Well, all right, thanks. Thanks very much.

ALFIERI. What are you going to do?

EDDIE [*with a helpless but ironic gesture*]. What can I do? I'm a patsy, what can a patsy do? I worked like a dog twenty years so a punk could have her, so that's what I done. I mean, in the worst times, in the worst, when there wasn't a ship comin' in the harbor, I didn't stand around lookin' for relief—I hustled. When there was empty piers in Brooklyn I went to Hoboken, Staten Island, the West Side, Jersey, all over—because I made a promise. I took out of my own kids' mouths to give to her. I took out of my own mouth. I walked hungry plenty days in this city! [*It begins to break through.*] And now I gotta sit in my own house and look at a son-of-a-bitch punk like that!—which he came out of nowhere! I give him my house to sleep! I take the blankets off my bed for him, and he takes and puts his dirty filthy hands on her like a goddam thief!

ALFIERI. But Eddie, she's a woman now—

EDDIE. He's stealin' from me!

ALFIERI. She wants to get married, Eddie. She can't marry you, can she?

EDDIE [*furiously*]. What're you talkin' about, marry me! I don't know what the hell you're talkin' about!

[*Pause.*]

ALFIERI. I gave you my advice, Eddie. That's it.

[EDDIE *gathers himself. A pause.*]

EDDIE. Well, thanks. Thanks very much. It just—it's breakin' my heart, y'know. I—

ALFIERI. I understand. Put it out of your mind. Can you do that?

EDDIE. I'm— [*He feels the threat of sobs, and with a helpless wave.*] I'll see you around. [*He goes out.*]

ALFIERI. There are times when you want to spread an alarm,
But nothing has happened. I knew, I knew then and there—
I could have finished the whole story that afternoon.
It wasn't as though there were a mystery to unravel.
I could see every step coming, step after step,
Like a dark figure walking down a hall toward a certain door.
I knew where he was heading for;
I knew where he was going to end.
And I sat here many afternoons,
Asking myself why, being an intelligent man,
I was so powerless to stop it.
I even went to a certain old lady in the neighborhood,
A very wise old woman, and I told her,
And she only nodded, and said,
"Pray for him."

And so I—[*he sits*]—waited here.

[*As the light goes out on* ALFIERI *it rises in the apartment, where all are finishing dinner. There is silence, but for the clink of a dish. Now* CATHERINE *looks up.*]

CATHERINE. You know where they went?

BEATRICE. Where?

CATHERINE. They went to Africa once. On a fishing boat. [EDDIE *glances at her.*] It's true, Eddie.

EDDIE. I didn't say nothin'. [*He finishes his coffee and leaves the table.*]

CATHERINE. And I was never even in Staten Island.

EDDIE [*sitting with a paper in his rocker*]. You didn't miss nothin'. [*Pause.* CATHERINE *takes dishes out;* BEATRICE *and* RODOLPHO *stack the others.*] How long that take you, Marco—to get to Africa?

MARCO. Oh—two days, We go all over.

RODOLPHO. Once we went to Yugoslavia.

EDDIE [*to* MARCO]. They pay all right on them boats?

MARCO. If they catch fish they pay all right.

RODOLPHO. They're family boats, though. And nobody in our family owned one. So we only worked when one of the families was sick.

[CATHERINE *re-enters.*]

BEATRICE. Y'know, Marco, what I don't understand—there's an ocean full of fish and yiz are all starvin'.

EDDIE. They gotta have boats, nets, you need money.

BEATRICE. Yeah, but couldn't they like fish from the beach? You see them down Coney Island—

MARCO. Sardines.

EDDIE. Sure. How you gonna catch sardines on a hook?

BEATRICE. Oh, I didn't know they're sardines. [*To* CATHERINE.] They're sardines!

CATHERINE. Yeah, they follow them all over the ocean— Africa, Greece, Yugoslavia . . .

BEATRICE [*to* EDDIE]. It's funny, y'know? You never think of it, that sardines are swimming in the ocean!

CATHERINE. I know. It's like oranges and lemons on a tree. [*To* EDDIE.] I mean you ever think of oranges and lemons on a tree?

EDDIE. Yeah, I know. It's funny. [*To* MARCO.] I heard that they paint the oranges to make them look orange.

MARCO. Paint?

EDDIE. Yeah, I heard that they grow like green—

MARCO. No, in Italy the oranges are orange.

RODOLPHO. Lemons are green.

EDDIE [*resenting his instruction*]. I know lemons are green, for Christ's sake, you see them in the store they're green sometimes. I said oranges they paint, I didn't say nothin' about lemons.

BEATRICE [*diverting their attention*]. Your wife is gettin' the money all right, Marco?

MARCO. Oh, yes. She bought medicine for my boy.

BEATRICE. That's wonderful. You feel better, heh?

MARCO. Oh, yes! But I'm lonesome.

BEATRICE. I just hope you ain't gonna do like some of them around here. They're here twenty-five years, some men, and they didn't get enough together to go back twice.

MARCO. Oh, I know. We have many families in our town, the children never saw the father. But I will go home. Three, four years, I think.

BEATRICE. Maybe you should keep more here, no? Because maybe she thinks it comes so easy you'll never get ahead of yourself.

MARCO. Oh, no, she saves. I send everything. My wife is very lonesome. [*He smiles shyly.*]

BEATRICE. She must be nice. She pretty? I bet, heh?

MARCO [*blushing*]. No, but she understands everything.

RODOLPHO. Oh, he's got a clever wife!

EDDIE. I betcha there's plenty surprises sometimes when those guys get back there, heh?

MARCO. Surprises?

EDDIE. I mean, you know—they count the kids and there's a couple extra than when they left?

MARCO. No—no. The women wait, Eddie. Most. Most. Very few surprises.

RODOLPHO. It's more strict in our town. [EDDIE *looks at him now.*] It's not so free.

EDDIE. It ain't so free here either, Rodolpho, like you think. I seen greenhorns sometimes get in trouble that way—they think just because a girl don't go around with a shawl over her head that she ain't strict, y'know? Girl don't have to wear black dress to be strict. Know what I mean?

RODOLPHO. Well, I always have respect—

EDDIE. I know, but in your town you wouldn't just drag off some girl without permission, I mean. [*He turns.*] You know what I mean, Marco? It ain't that much different here.

MARCO [*cautiously*]. Yes.

EDDIE [*to* RODOLPHO]. I mean I seen some a yiz get the wrong idea sometimes. I mean it might be a little more free here but it's just as strict.

RODOLPHO. I have respect for her, Eddie. I do anything wrong?

EDDIE. Look, kid, I ain't her father, I'm only her uncle—

MARCO. No, Eddie, if he does wrong you must tell him. What does he do wrong?

EDDIE. Well, Marco, till he came here she was never out on the street twelve o'clock at night.

MARCO [*to* RODOLPHO]. You come home early now.

CATHERINE. Well, the movie ended late.

EDDIE. I'm just sayin'—he thinks you always stayed out like that. I mean he don't understand, honey, see?

MARCO. You come home early now, Rodolpho.

RODOLPHO [*embarrassed*]. All right, sure.

EDDIE. It's not only for her, Marco. [*To* CATHERINE.] I mean it, kid, he's gettin' careless. The more he runs around like that the more chance he's takin'. [*To* RODOLPHO.] I mean suppose you get hit by a car or sump'm, where's your papers, who are you? Know what I mean?

RODOLPHO. But I can't stay in the house all the time, I—

BEATRICE. Listen, he's gotta go out sometime—

EDDIE. Well, listen, it depends, Beatrice. If he's here to work, then he should work; if he's here for a good time, then he could fool around! [*To* MARCO.] But I understood, Marco, that you was both comin' to make a livin' for your family. You understand me, don't you, Marco?

MARCO [*he sees it nearly in the open now, and with reserve*]. I beg your pardon, Eddie.

EDDIE. I mean that's what I understood in the first place, see?

MARCO. Yes. That's why we came.

EDDIE. Well, that's all I'm askin'.

[*There is a pause, an awkwardness. Now* CATHERINE *gets up and puts a record on the phonograph. Music.*]

CATHERINE [*flushed with revolt*]. You wanna dance, Rodolpho?

RODOLPHO [*in deference to* EDDIE]. No, I—I'm tired.

CATHERINE. Ah, come on. He plays a beautiful piano, that guy. Come. [*She has taken his hand, and he stiffly rises, feeling* EDDIE's *eyes on his back, and they dance.*]

EDDIE [*to* CATHERINE]. What's that, a new record?

CATHERINE. It's the same one. We bought it the other day.

BEATRICE [*to* EDDIE]. They only bought three records. [*She watches them dance;* EDDIE *turns his head away.* MARCO *just sits there, waiting. Now* BEATRICE *turns to* EDDIE.] Must be nice to go all over in one of them fishin' boats. I would like that myself. See all them other countries?

EDDIE. Yeah.

BEATRICE [*to* MARCO]. But the women don't go along, I bet.

MARCO. No, not on the boats. Hard work.

BEATRICE. What're you got, a regular kitchen and everything?

MARCO. Yes, we eat very good on the boats—especially when Rodolpho comes along; everybody gets fat.

BEATRICE. Oh, he cooks?

MARCO. Sure, very good cook. Rice, pasta, fish, everything.

EDDIE. He's a cook too! [*He looks at* RODOLPHO.] He sings, he cooks . . . [RODOLPHO *smiles thankfully.*]

BEATRICE. Well, it's good; he could always make a living.

EDDIE. It's wonderful. He sings, he cooks, he could make dresses . . .

CATHERINE. They get some high pay, them guys. The head chefs in all the big hotels are men. You read about them.

EDDIE. That's what I'm sayin'.

[CATHERINE *and* RODOLPHO *continue dancing.*]

CATHERINE. Yeah, well, I mean.

EDDIE [*to* BEATRICE]. He's lucky, believe me. [*A slight pause; he looks away, then back to* BEATRICE.] That's why the waterfront is no place for him. I mean, like me—I can't cook, I can't sing, I can't make dresses, so I'm on the waterfront. But if I could cook, if I could sing, if I could make dresses, I wouldn't be on the waterfront. [*They are all regarding him now; he senses he is exposing the issue, but he is driven on.*] I would be some-place else. I would be like in a dress store. [*He suddenly gets up and pulls his pants up over his belly.*] What do you say, Marco, we go to the bouts next Saturday night? You never seen a fight, did you?

MARCO [*uneasily*]. Only in the moving pictures.

EDDIE. I'll treat yiz. What do you say, Danish? You wanna come along? I'll buy the tickets.

RODOLPHO. Sure, I like to go.

CATHERINE [*nervously happy now*]. I'll make some coffee, all right?

EDDIE. Go ahead, make some! [*He draws her near him.*] Make it nice and strong. [*Mystified, she smiles and goes out. He is weirdly elated; he is rubbing his fists into his palms.*] You wait, Marco, you see some real fights here. You ever do any boxing?

MARCO. No, I never.

EDDIE [*to* RODOLPHO]. Betcha you done some, heh?

RODOLPHO. No.

EDDIE. Well, get up, come on, I'll teach you.

BEATRICE. What's he got to learn that for?

EDDIE. Ya can't tell, one a these days somebody's liable to step on his foot, or sump'm. Come on, Rodolpho, I show you a couple a passes.

BEATRICE [*unwillingly, carefully*]. Go ahead, Rodolpho. He's a good boxer; he could teach you.

RODOLPHO [*embarrassed*]. Well, I don't know how to—

EDDIE. Just put your hands up. Like this, see? That's right. That's very good, keep your left up, because you lead with the left, see, like this. [*He gently moves his left into* RODOLPHO's *face.*] See? Now what you gotta do is you gotta block me, so when I come in like that you— [RODOLPHO *parries his left.*] Hey, that's very good! [RODOLPHO *laughs.*] All right, now come into me. Come on.

RODOLPHO. I don't want to hit you, Eddie.

EDDIE. Don't pity me, come on. Throw it; I'll show you how to block it. [RODOLPHO *jabs at him, laughing.*] 'At's it. Come on, again. For the jaw, right here. [RODOLPHO *jabs with more assurance.*] Very good!

BEATRICE [*to* MARCO]. He's very good!

EDDIE. Sure, he's great! Come on, kid, put sump'm behind it; you can't hurt me. [RODOLPHO, *more seriously, jabs at* EDDIE's *jaw and grazes it.*] Attaboy. Now I'm gonna hit you, so block me, see?

[CATHERINE *comes from the kitchen, watches.*]

CATHERINE [*with beginning alarm*]. What are they doin'?
[*They are lightly boxing now.*]

BEATRICE [*she senses only the comradeship in it now*]. He's teachin' him;
he's very good!

EDDIE. Sure, he's terrific! Look at him go! [RODOLPHO *lands a blow.*] 'At's
it! Now watch out, here I come, Danish! [*He feints with his left hand
and lands with his right. It mildly staggers* RODOLPHO.]

CATHERINE [*rushing to* RODOLPHO]. Eddie!

EDDIE. Why? I didn't hurt him. [*Going to help the dizzy* RODOLPHO.] Did I
hurt you, kid?

RODOLPHO. No, no, he didn't hurt me. [*To* EDDIE, *with a certain gleam and
a smile.*] I was only surprised.

BEATRICE. That's enough, Eddie; he did pretty good, though.

EDDIE. Yeah. [*He rubs his fists together.*] He could be very good, Marco.
I'll teach him again.

[MARCO *nods at him dubiously.*]

RODOLPHO [*as a new song comes on the radio, his voice betraying a new note
of command*]. Dance, Catherine. Come.

[RODOLPHO *takes her in his arms. They dance.* EDDIE, *in thought, sits in
his chair, and* MARCO *rises and comes downstage to a chair and looks down
at it.* BEATRICE *and* EDDIE *watch him.*]

MARCO. Can you lift this chair?

EDDIE. What do you mean?

MARCO. From here. [*He gets on one knee with one hand behind his back,
and grasps the bottom of one of the chair legs but does not raise it.*]

EDDIE. Sure, why not? [*He comes to the chair, kneels, grasps the leg, raises
the chair one inch, but it leans over to the floor.*] Gee, that's hard, I never
knew that. [*He tries again, and again fails.*] It's on an angle, that's why,
heh?

MARCO. Here. [*He kneels, grasps, and with strain slowly raises the chair
higher and higher, getting to his feet now.
And* RODOLPHO *and* CATHERINE *have stopped dancing as* MARCO *raises the
chair over his head.
He is face to face with* EDDIE, *a strained tension gripping his eyes and jaw,
his neck stiff, the chair raised like a weapon—and he transforms what
might appear like a glare of warning into a smile of triumph, and* EDDIE's
*grin vanishes as he absorbs the look; as the lights go down.
The stage remains dark for a moment. Ships' horns are heard. Light rises
on* ALFIERI *at his desk. He is discovered in dejection, his face bent to the
desk, on which his arms rest. Now he looks up and front.*]

ALFIERI. On the twenty-third of that December
A case of Scotch whisky slipped from a net
While being unloaded—as a case of Scotch whisky
Is inclined to do on the twenty-third of December
On Pier Forty-one. There was no snow, but it was cold.

His wife was out shopping.
Marco was still at work.
The boy had not been hired that day;
Catherine told me later that this was the first time
They had been alone together in the house.
[*Light is rising on* CATHERINE, *who is ironing in the apartment. Music is playing.* RODOLPHO *is in* EDDIE'S *rocker, his head leaning back. A piano jazz cadenza begins. Luxuriously he turns his head to her and smiles, and she smiles at him, then continues ironing. He comes to the table and sits beside her.*]

CATHERINE. You hungry?

RODOLPHO. Not for anything to eat. [*He leans his chin on the back of his hand on the table, watching her iron.*] I have nearly three hundred dollars. [*He looks up at her.*] Catherine?

CATHERINE. I heard you.

[RODOLPHO *reaches out and takes her hand and kisses it, then lets it go. She resumes ironing. He rests his head again on the back of his hand.*]

RODOLPHO. You don't like to talk about it anymore?

CATHERINE. Sure, I don't mind talkin' about it.

RODOLPHO. What worries you, Catherine?

[CATHERINE *continues ironing. He now reaches out and takes her hand off the iron, and she sits back in her chair, not looking directly at him.*]

CATHERINE. I been wantin' to ask you about something. Could I?

RODOLPHO. All the answers are in my eyes, Catherine. But you don't look in my eyes lately. You're full of secrets. [*She looks at him. He presses her hand against his cheek. She seems withdrawn.*] What is the question?

CATHERINE. Suppose I wanted to live in Italy.

RODOLPHO [*smiling at the incongruity*]. You going to marry somebody rich?

CATHERINE. No, I mean live there—you and me.

RODOLPHO [*his smile is vanishing*]. When?

CATHERINE. Well—when we get married.

RODOLPHO [*astonished*]. You want to be an Italian?

CATHERINE. No, but I could live there without being Italian. Americans live there.

RODOLPHO. Forever?

CATHERINE. Yeah.

RODOLPHO. You're fooling.

CATHERINE. No, I mean it.

RODOLPHO. Where do you get such an idea?

CATHERINE. Well, you're always saying it's so beautiful there, with the mountains and the ocean and all the—

RODOLPHO. You're fooling me.

CATHERINE. I mean it.

RODOLPHO. Catherine, if I ever brought you home.
With no money, no business, nothing,

They would call the priest and the doctor
And they would say Rodolpho is crazy.

CATHERINE. I know, but I think we would be happier there.

RODOLPHO. Happier! What would you eat? You can't cook the view!

CATHERINE. Maybe you could be a singer, like in Rome or—

RODOLPHO. Rome! Rome is full of singers.

CATHERINE. Well, I could work then.

RODOLPHO. Where?

CATHERINE. God, there must be jobs somewhere!

RODOLPHO. There's nothing! Nothing, nothing,
Nothing. Now tell me what you're talking about.
How can I bring you from a rich country
To suffer in a poor country?
What are you talking about?
[*She searches for words.*]
I would be a criminal stealing your face;
In two years you would have an old, hungry face.
When my brothers' babies cry they give them water,
Water that boiled a bone.
Don't you believe that?

CATHERINE [*quietly*]. I'm afraid of Eddie here.
[*A slight pause.*]

RODOLPHO. We wouldn't live here.
Once I am a citizen I could work anywhere.
And I would find better jobs,
And we would have a house, Catherine.
If I were not afraid to be arrested
I would start to be something wonderful here!

CATHERINE [*steeling herself*]. Tell me something. I mean just tell me, Rodolpho. Would you still want to do it if it turned out we had to go live
in Italy? I mean just if it turned out that way.

RODOLPHO. This is your question or his question?

CATHERINE. I would like to know, Rodolpho. I mean it.

RODOLPHO. To go there with nothing?

CATHERINE. Yeah.

RODOLPHO. No. [*She looks at him wide-eyed.*] No.

CATHERINE. You wouldn't?

RODOLPHO. No; I will not marry you to live in Italy.
I want you to be my wife
And I want to be a citizen.
Tell him that, or I will. Yes.
[*He moves about angrily.*]
And tell him also, and tell yourself, please,
That I am not a beggar,
And you are not a horse, a gift,

A favor for a poor immigrant.
CATHERINE. Well, don't get mad!
RODOLPHO. I am furious!
Do you think I am so desperate?
My brother is desperate, not me.
You think I would carry on my back
The rest of my life a woman I didn't love
Just to be an American? It's so wonderful?
You think we have no tall buildings in Italy?
Electric lights? No wide streets? No flags?
No automobiles? Only work we don't have.
I want to be an American so I can work,
That is the only wonder here—work!
How can you insult me, Catherine?
CATHERINE. I didn't mean that—
RODOLPHO. My heart dies to look at you.
Why are you so afraid of him?
CATHERINE [*near tears*]. I don't know!
[RODOLPHO *turns her to him.*]
RODOLPHO. Do you trust me, Catherine? You?
CATHERINE. It's only that I—
He was good to me, Rodolpho.
You don't know him; he was always the sweetest guy to me.
Good. He razzes me all the time,
But he don't mean it. I know.
I would—just feel ashamed if I made him sad.
'Cause I always dreamt that when I got married
He would be happy at the wedding, and laughin'.
And now he's—mad all the time, and nasty.
[*She is weeping.*]
Tell him you'd live in Italy—just tell him,
And maybe he would start to trust you a little, see?
Because I want him to be happy; I mean—
I like him, Rodolpho—and I can't stand it!
[*She weeps, and he holds her.*]
RODOLPHO. Catherine—oh, little girl—
CATHERINE. I love you, Rodolpho, I love you.
RODOLPHO. I think that's what you have to tell him, eh?
Can't you tell him?
CATHERINE. I'm scared, I'm so scared.
RODOLPHO. Ssssh. Listen, now. Tonight when he comes home
We will both sit down after supper
And we will tell him—you and I.
[*He sees her fear rising.*]
But you must believe me yourself, Catherine.

It's true—you have very much to give me;
A whole country! Sure, I hold America when I hold you.
But if you were not my love,
If every day I did not smile so many times
When I think of you,
I could never kiss you, not for a hundred Americas.
Tonight I'll tell him,
And you will not be frightened anymore, eh?
And then in two, three months I'll have enough,
We will go to the church, and we'll come back to our own—
[*He breaks off, seeing the conquered longing in her eyes, her smile.*]
Catherine—

CATHERINE. Now. There's nobody here.

RODOLPHO. Oh, my little girl. Oh God!

CATHERINE [*kissing his face*]. Now!

[*He turns her upstage. They walk embraced, her head on his shoulder, and he sings to her softly. They go into a bedroom.*
A pause. Ships' horns sound in the distance. EDDIE *enters on the street. He is unsteady, drunk. He mounts the stairs. The sounds continue. He enters the apartment, looks around, takes out a bottle from one pocket, puts it on the table; then another bottle from another pocket; and a third from an inside pocket. He sees the iron, goes over to it and touches it, pulls his hand quickly back, turns toward upstage.*]

EDDIE. Beatrice? [*He goes to the open kitchen door and looks in. He turns to a bedroom door.*] Beatrice? [*He starts for this door; it opens, and* CATHERINE *is standing there; under his gaze she adjusts her dress.*]

CATHERINE. You got home early.

EDDIE [*trying to unravel what he senses*]. Knocked off for Christmas early. [*She goes past him to the ironing board. Indicating the iron.*] You start a fire that way.

CATHERINE. I only left it for a minute.

[RODOLPHO *appears in the bedroom doorway.* EDDIE *sees him, and his arm jerks slightly in shock.* RODOLPHO *nods to him testingly.* EDDIE *looks to* CATHERINE, *who is looking down at the ironing as she works.*]

RODOLPHO. Beatrice went to buy shoes for the children.

EDDIE. Pack it up. Go ahead. Get your stuff and get outa here. [CATHERINE *puts down the iron and walks toward the bedroom, and* EDDIE *grabs her arm.*] Where you goin'?

CATHERINE. Don't bother me, Eddie. I'm goin' with him.

EDDIE. You goin' with him. You goin' with him, heh? [*He grabs her face in the vise of his two hands.*] You goin' with him!

[*He kisses her on the mouth as she pulls at his arms; he will not let go, keeps his face pressed against hers.* RODOLPHO *comes to them now.*]

RODOLPHO [*tentatively at first*]. Eddie! No, Eddie! [*He now pulls full force on Eddie's arms to break his grip.*] Don't! No!

[CATHERINE *breaks free, and* EDDIE *is spun around by* RODOLPHO's *force, to face him.*]

EDDIE. You want something?

RODOLPHO. She'll be my wife.

EDDIE. But what're you gonna be? That's what I wanna know! What're you gonna be!

RODOLPHO [*with tears of rage*]. Don't say that to me!

[RODOLPHO *flies at him in attack.* EDDIE *pins his arms, laughing, and suddenly kisses him.*]

CATHERINE. Eddie! Let go, ya hear me! I'll kill you! Leggo of him!

[*She tears at* EDDIE's *face, and* EDDIE *releases* RODOLPHO *and stands there, tears rolling down his face as he laughs mockingly at* RODOLPHO. *She is staring at him in horror, her breasts heaving.* RODOLPHO *is rigid; they are like animals that have torn at each other and broken up without a decision, each waiting for the other's mood.*]

EDDIE. I give you till tomorrow, kid. Get outa here. Alone. You hear me? Alone.

CATHERINE. I'm goin' with him, Eddie.

EDDIE [*indicating* RODOLPHO *with his head*]. Not with that. [*He sits, still panting for breath, and they watch him helplessly as he leans his head back on the chair and, striving to catch his breath, closes his eyes.*] Don't make me do nuttin', Catherine.

[*The lights go down on* EDDIE's *apartment and rise on* ALFIERI.]

ALFIERI. On December twenty-seventh I saw him next.
I normally go home well before six,
But that day I sat around,
Looking out my window at the bay,
And when I saw him walking through my doorway
I knew why I had waited.
And if I seem to tell this like a dream,
It was that way. Several moments arrived
In the course of the two talks we had
When it occurred to me how—almost transfixed
I had come to feel. I had lost my strength somewhere.

[EDDIE *enters, removing his cap, sits in the chair, looks thoughtfully out.*]

I looked in his eyes more than I listened—
In fact, I can hardly remember the conversation.
But I will never forget how dark the room became
When he looked at me; his eyes were like tunnels.
I kept wanting to call the police,
But nothing had happened.
Nothing at all had really happened.

[*He breaks off and looks down at the desk. Then he turns to* EDDIE.]

So in other words, he won't leave?

EDDIE. My wife is talkin' about renting a room upstairs for them. An old lady on the top floor is got an empty room.

ALFIERI. What does Marco say?

EDDIE. He just sits there. Marco don't say much.

ALFIERI. I guess they didn't tell him, heh? What happened?

EDDIE. I don't know; Marco don't say much.

ALFIERI. What does your wife say?

EDDIE [*unwilling to pursue this*]. Nobody's talkin' much in the house. So what about that?

ALFIERI. But you didn't prove anything about him.

EDDIE. Mr. Alfieri, I'm tellin' you—

ALFIERI. You're not telling me anything, Eddie;
It sounds like he just wasn't strong enough to break your grip.

EDDIE. I'm tellin' you I know—he ain't right.
Somebody that don't want it can break it.
Even a mouse, if you catch a teeny mouse
And you hold it in your hand, that mouse
Can give you the right kind of fight,
And he didn't give me the right kind of fight.
I know it, Mr. Alfieri, the guy ain't right.

ALFIERI. What did you do that for, Eddie?

EDDIE. To show her what he is! So she would see, once and for all! Her mother'll turn over in the grave! [*He gathers himself almost peremptorily.*] So what do I gotta do now? Tell me what to do.

ALFIERI. She actually said she's marrying him?

EDDIE. She told me, yeah. So what do I do?
[*A slight pause.*]

ALFIERI. This is my last word, Eddie,
Take it or not, that's your business.
Morally and legally you have no rights;
You cannot stop it; she is a free agent.

EDDIE [*angering*]. Didn't you hear what I told you?

ALFIERI [*with a tougher tone*]. I heard what you told me,
And I'm telling you what the answer is.
I'm not only telling you now, I'm warning you—
The law is nature.
The law is only a word for what has a right to happen.
When the law is wrong it's because it's unnatural,
But in this case it is natural,
And a river will drown you
If you buck it now.
Let her go. And bless her.
[*As he speaks, a phone begins to glow on the opposite side of the stage, a faint, lonely blue.* EDDIE *stands up, jaws clenched.*]
Somebody had to come for her, Eddie, sooner or later.

[EDDIE *starts to turn to go, and* ALFIERI *rises with new anxiety.*]
You won't have a friend in the world, Eddie!
Even those who understand will turn against you,
Even the ones who feel the same will despise you!
[EDDIE *moves off quickly.*]
Put it out of your mind! Eddie!
[*The light goes out on* ALFIERI. EDDIE *has at the same time appeared beside the phone, and he lifts it.*]

EDDIE. I want to report something. Illegal immigrants. Two of them. That's right. Four-forty-one Saxon Street, Brooklyn, yeah. Ground floor. Heh? [*With greater difficulty.*] I'm just around the neighborhood, that's all. Heh?
[*Evidently he is being questioned further, and he slowly hangs up. He comes out of the booth just as* LOUIS *and* MIKE *come down the street. They are privately laughing at some private joke.*]

LOUIS. Go bowlin', Eddie?

EDDIE. No, I'm due home.

LOUIS. Well, take it easy.

EDDIE. I'll see yiz.
[*They leave him, and he watches them go. They resume their evidently amusing conversation. He glances about, then goes up into the house, and, as he enters, the lights go on in the apartment.* BEATRICE *is seated, sewing a pair of child's pants.*]

BEATRICE. Where you been so late?

EDDIE. I took a walk, I told you. [*He gets out of his zipper jacket, picks up a paper that is lying in a chair, prepares to sit.*] Kids sleepin'?

BEATRICE. Yeah, they're all sleepin'.
[*Pause.* EDDIE *looks out the window.*]

EDDIE. Where's Marco?

BEATRICE. They decided to move upstairs with Mrs. Dondero.

EDDIE [*turning to her*]. They're up there now?

BEATRICE. They moved all their stuff. Catherine decided. It's better, Eddie, they'll be outa your way. They're happy and we'll be happy.

EDDIE. Catherine's up there too?

BEATRICE. She just went up to bring pillow cases. She'll be down right away.

EDDIE [*nodding*]. Well, they're better off up there; the whole house knows they were here anyway, so there's nothin' to hide no more.

BEATRICE. That's what I figured. And besides, with the other ones up there maybe it'll look like they're just boarders too, or sump'm. You want eat?

EDDIE. What other ones?

BEATRICE. The two guys she rented the other room to. She's rentin' two rooms. She bought beds and everything: I told you.

EDDIE. When'd you tell me?

BEATRICE. I don't know; I think we were talkin' about it last week, even. She's startin' like a little boarding house up there. Only she's got no pillow cases yet.

EDDIE. I didn't hear nothin' about no boarding house.

BEATRICE. Sure, I loaned her my big fryin' pan beginning of the week. I told you. [*She smiles and goes to him.*] You gotta come to yourself, kid; you're in another world all the time. [*He is silent, peering; she touches his head.*] I wanna tell you, Eddie; it was my fault, and I'm sorry. No kiddin'. I shoulda put them up there in the first place.

EDDIE. Dja ever see these guys?

BEATRICE. I see them on the stairs every couple a days. They're kinda young guys. You look terrible, y'know?

EDDIE. They longshoremen?

BEATRICE. I don't know; they never said only hello, and she don't say nothin', so I don't ask, but they look like nice guys. [EDDIE, *silent, stares.*] What's the matter? I thought you would like it.

EDDIE. I'm just wonderin'—where they come from? She's got no sign outside; she don't know nobody. How's she find boarders all of a sudden?

BEATRICE. What's the difference? She—

EDDIE. The difference is they could be cops, that's all.

BEATRICE. Oh, no, I don't think so.

EDDIE. It's all right with me, I don't care. Except for this kinda work they don't wear badges, y'know. I mean you gotta face it, they could be cops. And Rodolpho'll start to shoot his mouth off up there, and they got him.

BEATRICE. I don't think so. You want some coffee?

EDDIE. No. I don't want nothin'.

BEATRICE. You gettin sick or sump'm?'

EDDIE. Me—no, I'm all right. [*Mystified.*] When did you tell me she had boarders?

BEATRICE. Couple a times.

EDDIE. Geez, I don't even remember. I thought she had the one room. [*He touches his forehead, alarmed.*]

BEATRICE. Sure, we was all talkin' about it last week. I loaned her my big fryin' pan. I told you.

EDDIE. I must be dizzy or sump'm.

BEATRICE. I think you'll come to yourself now, Eddie. I mean it, we shoulda put them up there in the first place. You can never bring strangers in a house. [*Pause. They are seated.*] You know what?

EDDIE. What?

BEATRICE. Why don't you go to her and tell her it's all right—Katie? Give her a break. A wedding should be happy.

EDDIE. I don't care. Let her do what she wants to do.

BEATRICE. Why don't you tell her you'll go to the wedding? It's terrible, there wouldn't be no father there. She's brokenhearted.

EDDIE. They made up the date already?

BEATRICE. She wants him to have like six, seven hundred. I told her, I says, "If you start off with a little bit you never gonna get ahead of yourself," I says. So they're gonna wait yet. I think maybe the end of the summer. But if you would tell them you'll be at the wedding—I mean, it would be nice, they would both be happy. I mean live and let live, Eddie, I mean?

EDDIE [*as though he doesn't care*]. All right, I'll go to the wedding.

[CATHERINE *is descending the stairs from above.*]

BEATRICE [*darting a glance toward the sound*]. You want me to tell her?

EDDIE [*he thinks, then turns to her with a certain deliberativeness*]. If you want, go ahead.

[CATHERINE *enters, sees him, and starts for the bedroom door.*]

BEATRICE. Come here, Katie. [CATHERINE *looks doubtfully at her.*] Come here, honey. [CATHERINE *comes to her, and* BEATRICE *puts an arm around her.* EDDIE *looks off.*]

He's gonna come to the wedding.

CATHERINE. What do I care if he comes? [*She starts upstage, but* BEATRICE *holds her.*]

BEATRICE. Ah, Katie, don't be that way. I want you to make up with him; come on over here. You're his baby! [*She tries to draw* CATHERINE *near* EDDIE.]

CATHERINE. I got nothin' to make up with him, he's got somethin' to make up with me.

EDDIE. Leave her alone, Beatrice, she knows what she wants to do. [*Now, however, he turns for a second to* CATHERINE.] But if I was you I would watch out for those boarders up there.

BEATRICE. He's worried maybe they're cops.

CATHERINE. Oh, no, they ain't cops. Mr. Lipari from the butcher store— they're his nephews; they just come over last week.

EDDIE [*coming alive*]. They're submarines?

CATHERINE. Yeah, they come from around Bari. They ain't cops.

[*She walks to her bedroom.* EDDIE *tries to keep silent, and when he speaks it has an unwilling sharpness of anxiety.*]

EDDIE. Catherine. [*She turns to him. He is getting to his feet in a high but subdued terror.*] You think that's a good idea?

CATHERINE. What?

EDDIE. How do you know what enemies Lipari's got? Which they would love to stab him in the back? I mean you never do that, Catherine, put in two strange pairs like that together. They track one, they'll catch 'em all. I ain't tryin' to advise you, kid, but that ain't smart. Anybody tell you that. I mean you just takin' a double chance, y'understand?

CATHERINE. Well, what'll I do with them?

EDDIE. What do you mean? The neighborhood's full of rooms. Can't you stand to live a couple a blocks away from him? He's got a big family, Lipari—these guys get picked up he's liable to blame you or me, and we got his whole family on our head. That's no joke, kid. They got a temper, that family.

CATHERINE. Well, maybe tomorrow I'll find some other place—

EDDIE. Kid, I'm not tellin' you nothin' no more because I'm just an ignorant jerk. I know that; but if I was you I would get them outa this house tonight, see?

CATHERINE. How'm I gonna find a place tonight?

EDDIE [*his temper rising*]. Catherine, don't mix yourself with somebody else's family, Catherine.

[*Two men in overcoats and felt hats appear on the street, start into the house.*]

EDDIE. You want to do yourself a favor? Go up and get them out of the house, kid.

CATHERINE. Yeah, but they been in the house so long already—

EDDIE. You think I'm always tryin' to fool you or sump'm? What's the matter with you? Don't you believe I could think of your good? [*He is breaking into tears.*] Didn't I work like a horse keepin' you? You think I got no feelin's? I never told you nothin' in my life that wasn't for your good. Nothin'! And look at the way you talk to me! Like I was an enemy! Like I—[*There is a knock on the door. His head swerves. They all stand motionless. Another knock.* EDDIE *firmly draws* CATHERINE *to him. And, in a whisper, pointing upstage:*] Go out the back up the fire escape; get them out over the back fence.

FIRST OFFICER [*in the hall*]. Open up in there! Immigration!

EDDIE. Go, go. Hurry up! [*He suddenly pushes her upstage, and she stands a moment, staring at him in a realized horror.*] Well what're you lookin' at?

FIRST OFFICER. Open up!

EDDIE. Who's that there?

FIRST OFFICER. Immigration. Open up.

[*With a sob of fury and that glance,* CATHERINE *streaks into a bedroom.* EDDIE *looks at* BEATRICE, *who sinks into a chair, turning her face from him.*]

EDDIE. All right, take it easy, take it easy. [*He goes and opens the door. The officers step inside.*] What's all this?

FIRST OFFICER. Where are they?

EDDIE. Where's who?

FIRST OFFICER. Come on, come on, where are they?

EDDIE. Who? We got nobody here. [*The* FIRST OFFICER *opens the door and exits into a bedroom.* SECOND OFFICER *goes and opens the other bedroom door and exits through it.* BEATRICE *now turns her head to look at* EDDIE. *He goes to her, reaches for her, and involuntarily she withdraws herself. Then, pugnaciously, furious:*] What's the matter with *you?*

[*The* FIRST OFFICER *enters from the bedroom, calls quietly into the other bedroom.*]

FIRST OFFICER. Dominick?

[*Enter* SECOND OFFICER *from bedroom.*]

SECOND OFFICER. Maybe it's a different apartment.

FIRST OFFICER. There's only two more floors up there. I'll take the front, you go up the fire-escape. I'll let you in. Watch your step up there.

SECOND OFFICER. Okay, right, Charley. [*He re-enters the bedroom. The* FIRST OFFICER *goes to the apartment door, turns to* EDDIE.]

FIRST OFFICER. This is Four-Forty-one, isn't it?

EDDIE. That's right.

[*The officer goes out into the hall, closing the door, and climbs up out of sight.* BEATRICE *slowly sits at the table.* EDDIE *goes to the closed door and listens. Knocking is heard from above, voices.* EDDIE *turns to* BEATRICE. *She's look at him now and sees his terror, and weakened with fear, she leans her head on the table.*]

BEATRICE. Oh, Jesus, Eddie.

EDDIE. What's the matter with *you*? [*He starts toward her, but she swiftly rises, pressing her palms against her face, and walks away from him.*]

BEATRICE. Oh, my God, my God.

EDDIE. What're you, accusin' me?

BEATRICE [*her final thrust is to turn toward him instead of running from him*]. My God, what did you do!

[*Many steps on the outer stair draw his attention. We see the* FIRST OFFICER *descending with* MARCO, *behind him* RODOLPHO, *and* CATHERINE *and two strange men, followed by* SECOND OFFICER. BEATRICE *hurries and opens the door.*]

CATHERINE [*as they appear on the stairs*]. What do yiz want from them? They work, that's all. They're boarders upstairs, they work on the piers.

BEATRICE [*now appearing in the hall, to* FIRST OFFICER]. Ah, mister, what do you want from them? Who do they hurt?

CATHERINE [*pointing to* RODOLPHO]. They ain't no submarines; he was born in Philadelphia.

FIRST OFFICER. Step aside, lady.

CATHERINE. What do you mean? You can't just come in a house and—

FIRST OFFICER. All right, take it easy. [*To* RODOLPHO.] What street were you born in Philadelphia?

CATHERINE. What do you mean, what street? Could you tell me what street you were born?

FIRST OFFICER. Sure. Four blocks away, One-eleven Union Street. Let's go, fellas.

CATHERINE [*fending him off* RODOLPHO]. No, you can't! Now, get outa here!

FIRST OFFICER [*moving her into the apartment*]. Look, girlie, if they're all right they'll be back tomorrow. If they're illegal they go back where they came from. If you want, get yourself a lawyer, although I'm tellin' you now you're wasting your money. [*He goes back to the group in the hall.*] Let's get them in the car, Dom. [*To the men.*] Andiamo, andiamo, let's go.

[*The men start out toward the street—but* MARCO *hangs back, letting them pass.*]

BEATRICE. Who're they hurtin', for God's sake? What do you want from them? They're starvin' over there, what do you want?

[MARCO *suddenly breaks from the group and dashes into the room and faces* EDDIE, *and* BEATRICE *and the* FIRST OFFICER *rush in as* MARCO *spits into* EDDIE'S *face*. CATHERINE *has arrived at the door and sees it*. EDDIE, *with an enraged cry, lunges for* MARCO.]

EDDIE. Oh, you mother's—!

[*The* FIRST OFFICER *quickly intercedes and pushes* EDDIE *from* MARCO, *who stands there accusingly.*]

FIRST OFFICER [*pushing* EDDIE *from* MARCO]. Cut it out!

EDDIE [*over the* FIRST OFFICER'S *shoulder to* MARCO]. I'll kill you for that, you son of a bitch!

FIRST OFFICER. Hey! [*He shakes* EDDIE.] Stay in here now, don't come down, don't bother him. You hear me? Don't come down, fella.

[*For an instant there is silence. Then the* FIRST OFFICER *turns and takes* MARCO'S *arm and then gives a last, informative look at* EDDIE; *and as he and* MARCO *are going out into the hall* EDDIE *erupts.*]

EDDIE. I don't forget that, Marco! You hear what I'm sayin'?

[*Out in the hall, the* FIRST OFFICER *and* MARCO *go down the stairs*. CATHERINE *rushes out of the room and past them toward* RODOLPHO, *who, with the* SECOND OFFICER *and the two strange men, is emerging into the street. Now, in the street,* LOUIS, MIKE, *and several neighbors, including the butcher,* LIPARI, *a stout, intense, middle-aged man are gathering around the stoop.* EDDIE *follows* CATHERINE *and calls down after* MARCO. BEATRICE *watches him from within the room, her hands clasped together in fear and prayer.*]

EDDIE. That's the thanks I get? Which I took the blanket off my bed for yiz? [*He hurries down the stairs, shouting.* BEATRICE *descends behind him, ineffectually trying to hold him back.*] You gonna apologize to me, Marco! Marco!

[EDDIE *appears on the stoop and sees the little crowd looking up at him, and falls silent, expectant.* LIPARI, *the butcher, walks over to the two strange men, and he kisses them. His wife, keening, goes and kisses their hands.*]

FIRST OFFICER. All right, lady, let them go. Get in the car, fellas, it's right over there.

[*The* SECOND OFFICER *begins moving off with the two strange men and* RODOLPHO. CATHERINE *rushes to the* FIRST OFFICER, *who is drawing* MARCO *off now.*]

CATHERINE. He was born in Philadelphia! What do you want from him?

FIRST OFFICER. Step aside, lady, come on now—

MARCO [*suddenly, taking advantage of the* FIRST OFFICER'S *being occupied with* CATHERINE, *freeing himself and pointing up at* EDDIE]. That one!

I accuse that one!

FIRST OFFICER [*grabbing him and moving him quickly off*]. Come on!

MARCO [*as he is taken off, pointing back and up the stoop at* EDDIE]. That one! He killed my children! That one stole the food from my children! [MARCO *is gone. The crowd has turned to* EDDIE.]

EDDIE. He's crazy. I give them the blankets off my bed. Six months I kept them like my own brothers! [LIPARI, *the butcher, turns and starts off with his wife behind him.*] Lipari! [EDDIE *comes down and reaches* LIPARI *and turns him about.*] For Christ's sake, I kept them, I give them the blankets off my bed! [LIPARI *turns away in disgust and anger and walks off with his keening wife. The crowd is now moving away.* EDDIE *calls:*] Louis! [LOUIS *barely turns, then walks away with* MIKE.] LOUIS! [*Only* BEATRICE *is left on the stoop*—and CATHERINE *now returns, blank-eyed, from offstage and the car.* EDDIE *turns to* CATHERINE.] He's gonna take that back. He's gonna take that back or I'll kill him! [*He faces all the buildings, the street down which the crowd has vanished.*] You hear me? I'll kill him!

Blackout

[*There is a pause in darkness before the lights rise. On the left—opposite where the desk stands—is a backless wooden bench. Seated on it are* RODOLPHO *and* MARCO. *There are two wooden chairs. It is a room in the jail.* CATHERINE *and* ALFIERI *are seated on the chairs.*]

ALFIERI. I'm waiting, Marco. What do you say? [MARCO *glances at him, then shrugs.*] That's not enough; I want an answer from you.

RODOLPHO. Marco never hurt anybody.

ALFIERI. I can bail you out until your hearing comes up.
But I'm not going to do it—you understand me?—
Unless I have your promise. You're an honorable man,
I will believe your promise. Now what do you say?

MARCO. In my country he would be dead now.
He would not live this long.

ALFIERI. All right, Rodolpho, you come with me now. [*He rises.*]

RODOLPHO. No! Please, mister. Marco—
Promise the man. Please, I want you to watch the wedding.
How can I be married and you're in here?
Please, you're not going to do anything; you know you're not—
[MARCO *is silent.*]

CATHERINE. Marco, don't you understand? He can't bail you out if you're gonna do something bad. To hell with Eddie. Nobody is gonna talk to him again if he lives to a hundred. Everybody knows you spit in his face, that's enough, isn't it? Give me the satisfaction—I want you at the wedding. You got a wife and kids, Marco—you could be workin' till the hearing comes up, instead of layin' around here. You're just giving him satisfaction layin' here.

MARCO [*after a slight pause, to* ALFIERI]. How long you say before the hearing?

ALFIERI. I'll try to stretch it out, but it wouldn't be more than five or six weeks.

CATHERINE. So you could make a couple of dollars in the meantime, y'see?

MARCO [*to* ALFIERI]. I have no chance?

ALFIERI. No, Marco. You're going back. The hearing is a formality, that's all.

MARCO. But him? There is a chance, eh?

ALFIERI. When she marries him he can start to become an American. They permit that, if the wife is born here.

MARCO [*looking at* RODOLPHO]. Well—we did something. [*He lays a palm on* RODOLPHO's *cheek, then lowers his hand.*]

RODOLPHO. Marco, tell the man.

MARCO. What will I tell him? [*He looks at* ALFIERI.] He knows such a promise is dishonorable.

ALFIERI. To promise not to kill is not dishonorable.

MARCO. No?

ALFIERI. No.

MARCO [*gesturing with his head—this is a new idea*]. Then what is done with such a man?

ALFIERI. Nothing. If he obeys the law, he lives. That's all.

MARCO. The law? All the law is not in a book.

ALFIERI. Yes. In a book. There is no other law.

MARCO [*his anger rising*]. He degraded my brother—my blood. He robbed my children, he mocks my work. I work to come here, mister!

ALFIERI. I know, Marco—

MARCO. There is no law for that? Where is the law for that?

ALFIERI. There is none.

MARCO [*shaking his head*]. I don't understand this country. [*Pause. He stands staring in fury.*]

ALFIERI. Well? What is your answer? You have five or six weeks you could work. Or else you sit here. What do you say to me?

[MARCO *lowers his eyes. It almost seems he is ashamed.*]

MARCO. All right.

ALFIERI. You won't touch him. This is your promise.

[*Slight pause.*]

MARCO. Maybe he wants to apologize to me.

ALFIERI [*taking one of his hands*]. This is not God, Marco. You hear? Only God makes justice.

[MARCO *withdraws his hand and covers it with the other.*]

MARCO. All right.

ALFIERI. Is your uncle going to the wedding?

CATHERINE. No. But he wouldn't do nothin' anyway. He just keeps talkin' so people will think he's in the right, that's all. He talks. I'll take them to the church, and they could wait for me there.

ALFIERI. Why, where are you going?

CATHERINE. Well, I gotta get Beatrice.

ALFIERI. I'd rather you didn't go home.

CATHERINE. Oh, no, for my wedding I gotta get Beatrice. Don't worry, he just talks big, he ain't gonna do nothin', Mr. Alfieri. I could go home.

ALFIERI [*nodding, not with assurance*]. All right, then—let's go.

[MARCO *rises.* RODOLPHO *suddenly embraces him.* MARCO *pats him on the back, his mind engrossed.* RODOLPHO *goes to* CATHERINE, *kisses her hand. She pulls his head to her shoulder, and they go out.* MARCO *faces* ALFIERI.] Only God, Marco.

[MARCO *turns and walks out.* ALFIERI, *with a certain processional tread, leaves the stage. The lights dim out.*

Light rises in the apartment. EDDIE *is alone in the rocker, rocking back and forth in little surges. Pause. Now* BEATRICE *emerges from a bedroom, then* CATHERINE. *Both are in their best clothes, wearing hats.*]

BEATRICE [*with fear*]. I'll be back in about an hour, Eddie. All right?

EDDIE. What, have I been talkin' to myself?

BEATRICE. Eddie, for God's sake, it's her wedding.

EDDIE. Didn't you hear what I told you? You walk out that door to that wedding you ain't comin' back here, Beatrice.

BEATRICE. Why? What do you want?

EDDIE. I want respect. Didn't you ever hear of that? From my wife?

CATHERINE. It's after three; we're supposed to be there already, Beatrice. The priest won't wait.

BEATRICE. Eddie. It's her wedding. There'll be nobody there from her family. For my sister let me go. I'm goin' for my sister.

EDDIE. Look, I been arguin' with you all day already, Beatrice, and I said what I'm gonna say. He's gonna come here and apologize to me or nobody from this house is goin' to that church today. Now if that's more to you than I am, then go. But don't come back. You be on my side or on their side, that's all.

CATHERINE [*suddenly*]. Who the hell do you think you are?

BEATRICE. Sssh!

CATHERINE. You got no more right to tell nobody nothin! Nobody! The rest of your life, nobody!

BEATRICE. Shut up, Katie!

CATHERINE [*pulling* BEATRICE *by the arm*]. You're gonna come with me!

BEATRICE. I can't, Katie, I can't—

CATHERINE. How can you listen to him? This rat!

[EDDIE *gets up.*]

BEATRICE [*to* CATHERINE, *in terror at sight of his face*]. Go, go—I'm not goin'—

CATHERINE. What're you scared of? He's a rat! He belongs in the sewer!

In the garbage he belongs! [*She is addressing him.*] He's a rat from under the piers! He bites people when they sleep! He comes when nobody's lookin' and he poisons decent people!

[EDDIE *rushes at her with his hand raised, and* BEATRICE *struggles with him.* RODOLPHO *appears, hurrying along the street, and runs up the stairs.*]

BEATRICE [*screaming*]. Get out of here, Katie! [*To* EDDIE.] Please, Eddie, Eddie, please!

EDDIE [*trying to free himself of* BEATRICE]. Don't bother me!

[RODOLPHO *enters the apartment. A pause.*]

EDDIE. Get outa here.

RODOLPHO. Marco is coming, Eddie. [*Pause.* BEATRICE *raises her hands.*] He's praying in the church. You understand?

[*Pause.*]

BEATRICE [*in terror*]. Eddie. Eddie, get out.

EDDIE. What do you mean, get out?

BEATRICE. Eddie, you got kids, go 'way, go 'way from here! Get outa the house!

EDDIE. Me get outa the house? *Me* get outa the house?
What did I do that I gotta get outa the house?
That I wanted a girl not to turn into a tramp?
That I made a promise and I kept my promise
She should be sump'm in her life?

[CATHERINE *goes trembling to him.*]

CATHERINE. Eddie—

EDDIE. What do *you* want?

CATHERINE. Please, Eddie, go away. He's comin' for you.

EDDIE. What do you care? What do you care he's comin' for me?

CATHERINE [*weeping, she embraces him*]. I never meant to do nothin' bad to you in my life, Eddie!

EDDIE [*with tears in his eyes*]. Then who meant somethin' bad? How'd it get bad?

CATHERINE. I don't know, I don't know!

EDDIE [*pointing to* RODOLPHO *with the new confidence of the embrace*]. They made it bad! This one and his brother made it bad which they came like thieves to rob, to rob!

[*He grabs her arm and swings her behind him so that he is between her and* RODOLPHO, *who is alone at the door.*]

You go tell him to come and come quick.
You go tell him I'm waitin' here for him to apologize
For what he said to me in front of the neighborhood!
Now get goin'!

RODOLPHO [*starting round* EDDIE *toward* CATHERINE]. Come, Catherine, we—

EDDIE [*nearly throwing* RODOLPHO *out of the door*]. Get away from her!

RODOLPHO [*starting back in*]. Catherine!

EDDIE [*turning on* CATHERINE]. Tell him to get out! [*She stands paralyzed before him.*] Katie! I'll do somethin' if he don't get outa here!

BEATRICE [*rushing to him, her open hands pressed together before him as though in prayer*]. Eddie, it's her husband, it's her husband! Let her go, it's her husband!

[CATHERINE, *moaning, breaks for the door, and she and* RODOLPHO *start down the stairs;* EDDIE *lunges and catches her; he holds her, and she weeps up into his face. And he kisses her on the lips.*]

EDDIE [*like a lover, out of his madness*]. It's me, ain't it?

BEATRICE [*hitting his body*]. Eddie! God, Eddie!

EDDIE. Katie, it's me, ain't it? You know it's me!

CATHERINE. Please, please, Eddie, lemme go. Heh? Please?

[*She moves to go.* MARCO *appears on the street.*]

EDDIE [*to* RODOLPHO]. Punk! Tell her what you are! You know what you are, you punk!

CATHERINE [*pulling* RODOLPHO *out the doorway*]. Come on!

[EDDIE *rushes after them to the doorway.*]

EDDIE. Make him tell you what he is! Tell her, punk! [*He is on the stairway, calling down.*] Why don't he answer me! Punk, answer me! [*He rushes down the stairs,* BEATRICE *after him.*]

BEATRICE. Eddie, come back!

[*Outside,* RODOLPHO *sees* MARCO *and cries out, "No, Marco. Marco, go away, go away!" But* MARCO *nears the stoop, looking up at the descending* EDDIE.]

EDDIE [*emerging from the house*]. Punk, what are you gonna do with a girl! I'm waitin' for your answer, punk. Where's your—answer!

[*He sees* MARCO. *Two other neighbors appear on the street, stand and watch.* BEATRICE *now comes in front of him.*]

BEATRICE. Go in the house, Eddie!

EDDIE [*pushing her aside, coming out challengingly on the stoop, and glaring down at* MARCO]. What do you mean, go in the house?

Maybe he came to apologize to me.

[*To the people.*]

Which I took my blankets off my bed for them;

Which I brought up a girl, she wasn't even my daughter,

And I took from my own kids to give to her—

And they took her like you take from a stable,

Like you go in and rob from your own family!

And never a word to me!

And now accusations in the bargain?

Makin' my name like a dirty rag?

[*He faces* MARCO *now, and moves toward him.*]

You gonna take that back?

BEATRICE. Eddie! Eddie!

EDDIE. I want my good name, Marco! You took my name!

[BEATRICE *rushes past him to* MARCO *and tries to push him away.*]

BEATRICE. Go, go!

MARCO. Animal! You go on your knees to me!

[*He strikes* EDDIE *powerfully on the side of the head.* EDDIE *falls back and draws a knife.* MARCO *springs to a position of defense, both men circling each other.* EDDIE *lunges, and* MIKE, LOUIS, *and all the neighbors move in to stop them, and they fight up the steps of the stoop, and there is a wild scream*—BEATRICE'S—*and they all spread out, some of them running off.* MARCO *is standing over* EDDIE, *who is on his knees, a bleeding knife in his hands.* EDDIE *falls forward on his hands and knees, and he crawls a yard to* CATHERINE. *She raises her face away—but she does not move as he reaches over and grasps her leg, and, looking up at her, he seems puzzled, questioning, betrayed.*]

EDDIE. Catherine—why—?

[*He falls foward and dies.* CATHERINE *covers her face and weeps. She sinks down beside the weeping* BEATRICE. *The lights fade, and* ALFIERI *is illuminated in his office.*]

ALFIERI. Most of the time now we settle for half,
And I like it better.
And yet, when the tide is right
And the green smell of the sea
Floats in through my window,
The waves of this bay
Are the waves against Siracusa,
And I see a face that suddenly seems carved;
The eyes look like tunnels
Leading back toward some ancestral beach
Where all of us once lived.

And I wonder at those times
How much of all of us
Really lives there yet,
And when we will truly have moved on,
On and away from that dark place,
That world that has fallen to stones?

This is the end of the story. Good night.

LUIGI PIRANDELLO

SIX CHARACTERS IN SEARCH OF AN AUTHOR

THE ABSURD MICROCOSM

FROM THE BEGINNING OF TIME, as this collection of plays has tried to suggest, the stage has exercised a peculiar kind of fascination for its audiences. Originally they may have been drawn to the primitive orchestra for the purposes of ritual, to assist in the magic coercion of supernatural forces. As the art of the drama developed, another kind of magic supervened: ritual became revelation. Or it became an experience of laughter, a source of strength and occasionally wisdom. Later audiences might turn to the theater for widened horizons or sharper perspective, for intellectual stimulus, or emotional satisfaction. With a dozen varying immediate purposes, men of all races and cultures have for two millenia and a half been drawn by some basic instinct, some unconscious urge to assemble before this stage which is by turns a mirror and a microcosm.

Simultaneously a particular kind of men, throughout the ages, have been moved to assemble *on* the stage, to create the mirror or the microcosm. The separate world of theater folk is not just a creation of popular fiction. The performers in the plays of Aeschylus may have been amateurs, like the later performers of the medieval craft cycles, but they must have been aware that their function had originated in the priesthood: a century after the great age of Greek drama, actors were organized into a guild or craft-union with privileges denied ordinary citizens; the amateurs of the craft cycles were succeeded by professional actors, set apart from their fellow men by special legislation. The legislation, to be sure, was not intended to promote the profession but to be restrictive. From the earliest days of the Christian church, actors had been officially treated as pariahs, denied the sacraments, denied burial in a cemetery; such repression had the not unusual effect of creating a sort of secret society, a fraternity, a protective order against the world. In Renaissance England, where actors were legally cast with rogues and vagabonds as men without civil rights, they sought the sponsorship of noble lords and became liveried servants, thus achieving special status both by law and by the means they took to circumvent it. And, if the attitude has been redirected, it is by no means dead in our own day. The organs of publicity and promotion still trade heavily on the spectator's continuing belief that the actor is a person of mystery—glamor is the modern term—whose life is somehow exempt from the conventional demands of domesticity and commerce and who dwells in a Cloudcuckooland called Broadway or Hollywood or Television City. The belief is hardly rational, but it is firmly held by audiences and avidly encouraged by the people of the theater.

This is not to say that all the people of the theater themselves believe or wish to live in a world apart. They are unwilling to surrender their privileges and responsibilities as citizens, they despise the self-conscious disorderliness of bohemia, they draw some of their strength as artists from their sense of common humanity. They pay income taxes and make trips to the supermarket and sometimes run for Congress and take their children to the movies. And yet, willy-nilly, they are a special breed. The technique of acting, like the procedures of any profession, may be learned, but its basis—impersonation—does not come from study. Impersonation, in the theatrical sense, is not mimickry; the observant reproduction of surfaces is within the reach of children and monkeys. Impersonation is involved, rather, in the fate of Pentheus, in what the Greeks referred to as *enthousiasm*, becoming possessed by another being. *Enthousiasm* is the continuing mystery of the actor, the gift which enables him to create an imaginary world which the audience, in turn, will accept as truth.

Playwrights, as those represented in this collection have shown, take two attitudes toward the two worlds, theatrical and extra-theatrical, with which they must deal. One group considers the function of their art to be the selection of characters and incidents from the chaos of life outside the playhouse, and the arrangement of the selected material into a pattern which the audience will accept as verisimilar, an ordered commentary on general human experience. Another group boldly accepts the theater itself as a metaphor: the world is a stage and all the men and women merely players. Shakespeare, whose characters frequently comment on the roles they are forced to act, belongs with this group; Calderón, as we have seen, explores the metaphor allegorically in *The Great World Theater*; more recent writers, like Shaw, Giraudoux, Wilder, turn to it, confident of an understanding audience. Indeed as old creeds and social conventions have been overthrown, as man has become increasingly convinced of the complexity of the great world, the little world of the theater has become an almost conventional structural device. T. S. Eliot in *Murder in the Cathedral* and *The Family Reunion*, Jean Cocteau in *The Infernal Machine*, Eugene O'Neill in *The Great God Brown*, Maxwell Anderson in *Joan of Lorain*, Robert E. Sherwood in *Idiot's Delight*, Cole Porter in *Kiss Me Kate*, Ferenč Molnar in *The Play's The Thing*, such names and titles suggest how widespread the convention is and the various levels of seriousness at which it can be used.

Luigi Pirandello (1867–1936) was haunted throughout his career as a playwright by the metaphor of theater, most particularly by the concept of man as actor. He was not concerned, however, with the idea that all men were called upon to playact, but with the question of reality. What, he asks his audience to decide, is the truth about this character: is it his inner nature, is it the role he chooses to play, or is it, and here Pirandello adapts the metaphor to his own purposes, the way he appears to his wife, or his mistress, or his business partner? During his lifetime some critics and many spectators were content to see Pirandello as a jester, a great tease, who delighted in pulling the rug out from under any fixed conclusion or evaluation. Shakespeare's Iago will tell the audience quite frankly that he is not the man he pretends to be; Pirandello introduces a madman who believes himself to be King Henry IV and has persuaded his household to transform themselves into the courtiers and servants of a long-past regime, and then raises the question of who is mad, the hero or those who acquiesce in his mask? What is rational behavior in a world whose rationality is only a convenient illusion? As the twentieth century moved past the midpoint, as advanced literary circles caught up with the philosophers of existentialism, as science demonstrated that every quantity whose identity became known only led to a dozen unknown, and that the life of the mind was an electronic accident, the question that Pirandello had posed became a popular commonplace, widely used, if dimly comprehended, and hence a suitable theme for drama.

It became the theme for a small but significant school of contemporary playwrights—Beckett, Genet, Ionesco, Albee, who have been gathered under the not altogether appropriate title of the "Theater of the Absurd." The school did not spring fully formed from the waves, of course, like Venus on her shell. There are suggestions of it in the nineteenth century, in Strindberg and the later works of Ibsen, for example. When naturalism, with its firm belief in cause and effect, held possession of the Parisian theater before the First World War, avant-garde playwrights like Alfred Jarry were raucously mocking it in the little theaters. In Germany, expressionists like Georg Kaiser were affirming that the world could be perceived only in fragments through the multiple distortions of the private visions of various individuals. Even Bernard Shaw, the apostle of sanity in art, in such an extravaganza as *Too True to be Good*, abandons form and order, abandons that natural history scientifically observed for which he had been an advocate, and reveals a world of chance and circumstance in which it is not safe to predict or explain the nature of any character. The drama of the absurd had existed, in fact, throughout the century in a kind of theatrical underworld. It was not born with the astonishing world wide success of Beckett's *Waiting for Godot* in 1955; rather, audiences were prepared to recognize it.

Disregarding the appropriateness of the name and ignoring chronology (which is often deceiving in the history of art), it is clear that Pirandello not only anticipated the attitudes of these contemporary playwrights, but that in such a play as *Six Characters in Search of an Author* solved the problem of giving form and substance to subject matter intentionally insubstantial and without form. He achieved this by returning to the theater as metaphor.

The audience is first introduced to a group of actors who are about to rehearse a new play by Pirandello himself. This was a device employed by earlier dramatists (R. B. Sheridan in *The*

Critic) who wished to satirize the works of other authors, and indeed the director of the rehearsal has some rather uncomplimentary things to say about Pirandello's dramaturgy. But before the rehearsal gets under way, six figures, "characters" not people, intrude and try to persuade the Stage Manager that the drama of their lives is more interesting than the manuscript on which he is working; as a means of persuasion they act, or reenact, portions of that drama while the professional actors look on. This, too, is a conventional dramatic device, the "play within a play," most familiar from Shakespeare's *Hamlet*. In that tragedy, a group of traveling actors agrees to perform a specially rewritten version of a popular play in expectation that the King of Denmark, among the spectators, will be led "by the cunning of the scene" to betray his own villainy. Hamlet, the prince temporarily turned playwright, is interested only in discovering absolute evidence of the nature of the king.

Pirandello, as playwright, has quite other interests. The "Characters" as they perform are observed by the actors who will attempt to recreate their performance, and by the audience who see both the actuality and the artist's attitude toward actuality at the same time. In itself, this is an intriguing presentation of the nature of theater, and perhaps a comment on the familiar romantic concern with the conflict between reality and illusion. But this is only the surface of Pirandello's theme.

The plot for which the Characters were conceived is a domestic drama in the mode of French sensationalism, but the author has become disgusted with the trickery of the well-made play and has refused to write it down. The Manager, on the other hand, is eager to oblige the Characters by fitting them into a tight, well-organized action, to escape from the manuscript of Pirandello "where nobody understands anything, and the author plays the fool with us all." The Characters are, for the most part, willing to help by acting out scenes to be transcribed, but each scene degenerates into a debate about the nature of the participants. The Father, that is, acts according to his concept of his inner nature, the essence given him by the author, but he appears as three different persons to his wife, his daughter, his son; and the actor, who will later be assigned the Father's role, is observing him closely and, by instinct, transforming him to fit his own image of a man caught in a domestic conflict. The audience thus sees five interpretations of the character, any one of which can be stoutly defended by its interpreter as based on the truth of a particular situation. And Pirandello by the cunning of the scene intends to make it impossible for the spectator to leave the play with the conviction that he has solved its mystery.

Throughout the play the metaphor of theater is pervasive. During rehearsal, one of the professionals comments that the actor may often become possessed by his role, "the puppet of yourself," just as Pentheus had. Later, the Characters will be so caught up by the reality of the scene they have chosen to perform that they will be taken quite out of the theater; can anyone say with any security that the child at the end is acting? The Characters, who are figments of the imagination, are described in precise detail; the actors, who are real, are sketched with the broadest strokes. Each group must be presented in such a manner as to prevent the audience from distinguishing too mechanically between reality and illusion. After all, as the Characters point out to the self-important actors, they are but following the practice of the acting profession in giving life to fictional beings, less real but truer than actual men. That this reasonable aesthetic position is overwhelmed as the Characters relive their illusion only intensifies the Pirandellian theme.

It is not a theme that lends itself to simple statement; it is more to be experienced than codified. But the validity of the experience for an audience impressed by the increasingly insubstantial world outside the playhouse cannot be denied. In the age of Shakespeare, John Donne could declare that no man was an island, that every man was a piece of the continent. Today it would seem that the continent has disappeared, that the world is a scattering of archipelagoes, and that the passing bell tolls for each individual individually. Communication has become difficult and conscience is many-sided. It is this very up-to-date, fragmented world that is captured in Pirandello's metaphorical theater.

Historians might remind us that Pirandello and the playwrights of the absurd are merely giving a contemporary angle to the eternal condition of man. The theater has always kept the playgoer aware that life is enveloped by menace, not just death but some greater terror (unknowable, uncontrollable, absurd)—fate, fission, the day of wrath. At its greatest moments in the past, without denying or ignoring the menace, the dramatic experience has been a celebration of the dignity of the human spirit. Pirandello can write that "today's reality is tomorrow's illusion." Bernard Shaw declared that "every dream was a prophecy, every jest an earnest in the womb of time." The point of view the theater reflects will, of course, depend upon the audience which, since the time of Thespis, has been the third force with playwright and players in determining the nature of the dramatic experience.

Characters of the Comedy in the Making

THE FATHER

THE MOTHER

THE STEP-DAUGHTER

THE SON

THE BOY

THE CHILD
(*The last two do not speak.*)

MADAME PACE

Actors of the Company

THE MANAGER

LEADING LADY

LEADING MAN

SECOND LADY LEAD

L'INGÉNUE

JUVENILE LEAD

OTHER ACTORS AND ACTRESSES

PROPERTY MAN

PROMPTER

MACHINIST

MANAGER'S SECRETARY

DOORKEEPER

SCENE-SHIFTERS

Daytime. The stage of a theater.

N.B. *The comedy is without acts or scenes. The performance is interrupted once, without the curtain being lowered, when The Manager and the chief characters withdraw to arrange the scenario. A second interruption of the action takes place when, by mistake, the stage hands let the curtain down.*

SIX CHARACTERS IN SEARCH
OF AN AUTHOR

Luigi Pirandello

Translated by Edward Storer

ACT ONE

The spectators will find the curtain raised and the stage as it usually is during the daytime. It will be half dark, and empty, so that from the beginning the public may have the impression of an impromptu performance.
Prompter's box and a small table and chair for the manager.
Two other small tables and several chairs scattered about as during rehearsals.
The ACTORS *and* ACTRESSES *of the company enter from the back of the stage: first one, then another, then two together; nine or ten in all. They are about to rehearse a Pirandello play:* Mixing It Up.[1] *Some of the company move off toward their dressing rooms. The* PROMPTER *who has the "book" under his arm, is waiting for the manager in order to begin the rehearsal.*
The ACTORS *and* ACTRESSES, *some standing, some sitting, chat and smoke. One perhaps reads a paper; another cons his part.*
Finally, the MANAGER *enters and goes to the table prepared for him. His* SECRETARY *brings him his mail, through which he glances. The* PROMPTER *takes his seat, turns on a light, and opens the "book."*

THE MANAGER [*throwing a letter down on the table*]. I can't see. [*To* PROPERTY MAN.] Let's have a little light, please!
PROPERTY MAN. Yes sir, yes, at once. [*A light comes down onto the stage.*]

---

[1] i.e. *Il giuoco delle parti.* (Translator's note.)

THE MANAGER [*clapping his hands*]. Come along! Come along! Second act of *Mixing It Up*. [*Sits down.*]

[*The* ACTORS *and* ACTRESSES *go from the front of the stage to the wings, all except the three who are to begin the rehearsal.*]

THE PROMPTER [*reading the "book"*] "Leo Gala's house. A curious room serving as dining-room and study."

THE MANAGER [*to* PROPERTY MAN]. Fix up the old red room.

PROPERTY MAN [*noting it down*]. Red set. All right!

THE PROMPTER [*continuing to read from the "book"*]. "Table already laid and writing desk with books and papers. Bookshelves. Exit rear to Leo's bedroom. Exit left to kitchen. Principal exit to right."

THE MANAGER [*energetically*]. Well, you understand: The principal exit over there; here, the kitchen. [*Turning to actor who is to play the part of* SOCRATES.] You make your entrances and exits here. [*To* PROPERTY MAN.] The baize doors at the rear, and curtains.

PROPERTY MAN [*noting it down*]. Right!

PROMPTER [*reading as before*]. "When the curtain rises, Leo Gala, dressed in cook's cap and apron is busy beating an egg in a cup. Philip, also dressed as a cook, is beating another egg. Guido Venanzi is seated and listening."

LEADING MAN [*to* MANAGER]. Excuse me, but must I absolutely wear a cook's cap?

THE MANAGER [*annoyed*]. I imagine so. It says so there anyway. [*Pointing to the "book."*]

LEADING MAN. But it's ridiculous!

THE MANAGER [*jumping up in a rage*]. Ridiculous? Ridiculous? Is it my fault if France won't send us any more good comedies, and we are reduced to putting on Pirandello's works, where nobody understands anything, and where the author plays the fool with us all?

[*The* ACTORS *grin. The* MANAGER *goes to* LEADING MAN *and shouts.*]

Yes sir, you put on the cook's cap and beat eggs. Do you suppose that with all this egg-beating business you are on an ordinary stage? Get that out of your head. You represent the shell of the eggs you are beating! [*Laughter and comments among the* ACTORS.] Silence! and listen to my explanations, please! [*To* LEADING MAN.] "The empty form of reason without the fullness of instinct, which is blind."—You stand for reason, your wife is instinct. It's a mixing up of the parts, according to which you who act your own part become the puppet of yourself. Do you understand?

LEADING MAN. I'm hanged if I do.

THE MANAGER. Neither do I. But let's get on with it. It's sure to be a glorious failure anyway. [*Confidentially.*] But I say, please face three-quarters. Otherwise, what with the abstruseness of the dialogue, and the public that won't be able to hear you, the whole thing will go to hell. Come on! come on!

PROMPTER. Pardon sir, may I get into my box?[2] There's a bit of a draught.

THE MANAGER. Yes, yes, of course!

[*At this point, the* DOORKEEPER *has entered from the stage door and advances toward the manager's table, taking off his braided cap. During this maneuver, the* SIX CHARACTERS *enter, and stop by the door at back of stage, so that when the* DOORKEEPER *is about to announce their coming to the* MANAGER, *they are already on the stage. A tenuous light surrounds them, almost as if irradiated by them—the faint breath of their fantastic reality.*

This light will disappear when they come forward toward the ACTORS. *They preserve, however, something of the dream lightness in which they seem almost suspended; but this does not detract from the essential reality of their forms and expressions.*

He who is known as THE FATHER *is a man of about fifty: hair, reddish in color, thin at the temples; he is not bald, however; thick moustaches, falling over his still fresh mouth, which often opens in an empty and uncertain smile. He is fattish, pale; with an especially wide forehead. He has blue, oval-shaped eyes, very clear and piercing. Wears light trousers and a dark jacket. He is alternatively mellifluous and violent in his manner.*

THE MOTHER *seems crushed and terrified as if by an intolerable weight of shame and abasement. She is dressed in modest black and wears a thick widow's veil of crepe. When she lifts this, she reveals a waxlike face. She always keeps her eyes downcast.*

THE STEP-DAUGHTER *is dashing, almost impudent, beautiful. She wears mourning too, but with great elegance. She shows contempt for the timid half-frightened manner of the wretched* BOY (*fourteen years old, and also dressed in black*); *on the other hand, she displays a lively tenderness for her little sister,* THE CHILD (*about four*), *who is dressed in white, with a black silk sash at the waist.*

THE SON (*twenty-two*) *tall, severe in his attitude of contempt for* THE FATHER, *supercilious and indifferent to* THE MOTHER. *He looks as if he had come on the stage against his will.*]

DOORKEEPER [*cap in hand*]. Excuse me, sir . . .

THE MANAGER [*rudely*]. Eh? What is it?

DOORKEEPER [*timidly*]. These people are asking for you, sir.

THE MANAGER [*furious*]. I am rehearsing, and you know perfectly well no one's allowed to come in during rehearsals! [*Turning to the* CHARACTERS.] Who are you, please? What do you want?

THE FATHER [*coming forward a little, followed by the others who seem*

---

[2] The prompter's box is a small enclosure sunk into the stage near the footlights. In America it is customarily retained only in opera houses, but in Europe its hood, projecting above the lights at the center, is conventional equipment for repertory theaters.

embarrassed]. As a matter of fact . . . we have come here in search of an author . . .

THE MANAGER [*half-angry, half-amazed*]. An author? What author?

THE FATHER. Any author, sir.

THE MANAGER. But there's no author here. We are not rehearsing a new piece.

THE STEP-DAUGHTER [*vivaciously*]. So much the better, so much the better! We can be your new piece.

AN ACTOR [*coming forward from the others*]. Oh, do you hear that?

THE FATHER [*to* STEP-DAUGHTER]. Yes, but if the author isn't here . . . [*To* MANAGER.] unless you would be willing . . .

THE MANAGER. You are trying to be funny.

THE FATHER. No, for Heaven's sake, what are you saying? We bring you a drama, sir.

THE STEP-DAUGHTER. We may be your fortune.

THE MANAGER. Will you oblige me by going away? We haven't time to waste with mad people.

THE FATHER [*mellifluously*]. Oh sir, you know well that life is full of infinite absurdities, which, strangely enough, do not even need to appear plausible, since they are true.

THE MANAGER. What the devil is he talking about?

THE FATHER. I say that to reverse the ordinary process may well be considered a madness: that is, to create credible situations, in order that they may appear true. But permit me to observe that if this be madness, it is the sole *raison d'être* of your profession, gentlemen. [*The* ACTORS *look hurt and perplexed.*]

THE MANAGER [*getting up and looking at him*]. So our profession seems to you one worthy of madmen then?

THE FATHER. Well, to make seem true that which isn't true . . . without any need . . . for a joke as it were . . . Isn't that your mission, gentlemen: to give life to fantastic characters on the stage?

THE MANAGER [*interpreting the rising anger of the company*]. But I would beg you to believe, my dear sir, that the profession of the comedian is a noble one. If today, as things go, the playwrights give us stupid comedies to play and puppets to represent instead of men, remember we are proud to have given life to immortal works here on these very boards! [*The* ACTORS, *satisfied, applaud their* MANAGER.]

THE FATHER [*interrupting furiously*]. Exactly, perfectly, to living beings more alive than those who breathe and wear clothes: beings less real perhaps, but truer! I agree with you entirely. [*The* ACTORS *look at one another in amazement.*]

THE MANAGER. But what do you mean? Before, you said . . .

THE FATHER. No, excuse me, I meant it for you, sir, who were crying out that you had no time to lose with madmen, while no one better than yourself knows that nature uses the instrument of human fantasy in order to pursue her high creative purpose.

THE MANAGER. Very well,—but where does all this take us?

THE FATHER. Nowhere! It is merely to show you that one is born to life in many forms, in many shapes, as tree, or as stone, as water, as butterfly, or as woman. So one may also be born a character in a play.

THE MANAGER [*with feigned comic dismay*]. So you and these other friends of yours have been born characters?

THE FATHER. Exactly, and alive as you see! [MANAGER *and* ACTORS *burst out laughing.*]

THE FATHER [*hurt*]. I am sorry you laugh, because we carry in us a drama, as you can guess from this woman here veiled in black.

THE MANAGER [*losing patience at last and almost indignant*]. Oh, chuck it! Get away please! Clear out of here! [*To* PROPERTY MAN.] For Heaven's sake, turn them out!

THE FATHER [*resisting*]. No, no, look here, we . . .

THE MANAGER [*roaring*]. We come here to work, you know.

LEADING ACTOR. One cannot let oneself be made such a fool of.

THE FATHER [*determined, coming forward*]. I marvel at your incredulity, gentlemen. Are you not accustomed to see the characters created by an author spring to life in yourselves and face each other? Just because there is no "book" [*pointing to the* PROMPTER'S *box*] which contains us, you refuse to believe . . .

THE STEP-DAUGHTER [*advances toward* MANAGER, *smiling and coquettish*]. Believe me, we are really six most interesting characters, sir; sidetracked however.

THE FATHER. Yes, that is the word! [*To* MANAGER *all at once.*] In the sense, that is, that the author who created us alive no longer wished, or was no longer able, materially to put us into a work of art. And this was a real crime, sir; because he who has had the luck to be born a character can laugh even at death. He cannot die. The man, the writer, the instrument of the creation will die, but his creation does not die. And to live for ever, it does not need to have extraordinary gifts or to be able to work wonders. Who was Sancho Panza? Who was Don Abbondio?[3] Yet they live eternally because—live germs as they were—they had the fortune to find a fecundating matrix, a fantasy which could raise and nourish them: make them live for ever!

THE MANAGER. That is quite all right. But what do you want here, all of you?

THE FATHER. We want to live.

THE MANAGER [*ironically*]. For Eternity?

THE FATHER. No, sir, only for a moment . . . in you.

AN ACTOR. Just listen to him!

LEADING LADY. They want to live, in us . . . !

[3] Sancho Panza, the squire in Cervantes' *Don Quixote*: Don Abbondio, a comic character in Alessandro Manzoni's *I Promessi Sposi*.

JUVENILE LEAD [*pointing to the* STEP-DAUGHTER]. I've no objection, as far as that one is concerned!

THE FATHER. Look here! look here! The comedy has to be made. [*To the* MANAGER.] But if you and your actors are willing, we can soon concert it among ourselves.

THE MANAGER [*annoyed*]. But what do you want to concert? We don't go in for concerts here. Here we play dramas and comedies!

THE FATHER. Exactly! That is just why we have come to you.

THE MANAGER. And where is the "book"?

THE FATHER. It is in us! [*The* ACTORS *laugh*.] The drama is in us, and we are the drama. We are impatient to play it. Our inner passion drives us on to this.

THE STEP-DAUGHTER [*disdainful, alluring, treacherous, full of impudence*]. My passion, sir! Ah, if you only knew! My passion for him!

[*Points to the* FATHER *and makes a pretence of embracing him. Then she breaks out into a loud laugh.*]

THE FATHER [*angrily*]. Behave yourself! And please don't laugh in that fashion.

THE STEP-DAUGHTER. With your permission, gentlemen, I, who am a two months' orphan, will show you how I can dance and sing.

[*Sings and then dances* Prenez garde à Tchou-Tchin-Tchou.]

> Les chinois sont un peuple malin,
> De Shanghaï à Pékin,
> Ils ont mis des écriteaux partout:
> Prenez garde à Tchou-Tchin-Tchou.[4]

ACTORS *and* ACTRESSES. Bravo! Well done! Tip-top!

THE MANAGER. Silence! This isn't a café concert, you know! [*Turning to the* FATHER *in consternation*.] Is she mad?

THE FATHER. Mad? No, she's worse than mad.

THE STEP-DAUGHTER [*to* MANAGER]. Worse? Worse? Listen! Stage this drama for us at once! Then you will see that at a certain moment I . . . when this little darling here . . .

[*Takes the* CHILD *by the hand and leads her to the* MANAGER.]

Isn't she a dear?

[*Takes her up and kisses her.*]

Darling! Darling!

[*Puts her down again and adds feelingly:*]

Well, when God suddenly takes this dear little child away from that poor mother there; and this imbecile here [*seizing hold of the* BOY *roughly and pushing him forward*] does the stupidest things, like the fool he is, you will see me run away. Yes, gentlemen, I shall be off. But the moment hasn't arrived yet. After what has taken place between him and me

---

[4] "The Chinese are an evil folk: from Shanghai to Pekin they have put up notices: Watch out for Chu-Chin-Chu."

[*indicates the* FATHER *with a horrible wink*] I can't remain any longer in this society, to have to witness the anguish of this mother here for that fool . . . [*Indicates the* SON.] Look at him! Look at him! See how indifferent, how frigid he is, because he is the legitimate son. He despises me, despises him [*pointing to the* BOY], despises this baby here; because . . . we are bastards.
[*Goes to the* MOTHER *and embraces her.*]
And he doesn't want to recognize her as his mother—she who is the common mother of us all. He looks down upon her as if she were only the mother of us three bastards. Wretch! [*She says all this very rapidly, excitedly. At the word "bastards" she raises her voice, and almost spits out the final "Wretch!"*]

THE MOTHER [*to the* MANAGER, *in anguish*]. In the name of these two little children, I beg you . . .
[*She grows faint and is about to fall.*]
Oh God!

THE FATHER [*coming forward to support her as do some of the* ACTORS]. Quick, a chair, a chair for this poor widow!

THE ACTORS. Is it true? Has she really fainted?

THE MANAGER. Quick, a chair! Here!
[*One of the* ACTORS *brings a chair, the others proffer assistance. The* MOTHER *tries to prevent the* FATHER *from lifting the veil which covers her face.*]

THE FATHER. Look at her! Look at her!

THE MOTHER. No, no; stop it please!

THE FATHER [*raising her veil*]. Let them see you!

THE MOTHER [*rising and covering her face with her hands, in desperation*]. I beg you, sir, to prevent this man from carrying out his plan which is loathsome to me.

THE MANAGER [*dumbfounded*]. I don't understand at all. What is the situation? Is this lady your wife? [*To the* FATHER.]

THE FATHER. Yes, gentlemen; my wife!

THE MANAGER. But how can she be a widow if you are alive? [*The* ACTORS *find relief for their astonishment in a loud laugh.*]

THE FATHER. Don't laugh! Don't laugh like that, for Heaven's sake. Her drama lies just here in this: she has had a lover, a man who ought to be here.

THE MOTHER [*with a cry*]. No! No!

THE STEP-DAUGHTER. Fortunately for her, he is dead. Two months ago as I said. We are in mourning, as you see.

THE FATHER. He isn't here you see, not because he is dead. He isn't here— look at her a moment and you will understand—because her drama isn't a drama of the love of two men for whom she was incapable of feeling anything except possibly a little gratitude—gratitude not for me but for the other. She isn't a woman, she is a mother, and her drama—

powerful sir, I assure you—lies, as a matter of fact, all in these four children she has had by two men.

THE MOTHER. I had them? Have you got the courage to say that I wanted them? [*To the* COMPANY.] It was his doing. It was he who gave me that other man, who forced me to go away with him.

THE STEP-DAUGHTER. It isn't true.

THE MOTHER [*startled*]. Not true, isn't it?

THE STEP-DAUGHTER. No, it isn't true, it just isn't true.

THE MOTHER. And what can you know about it?

THE STEP-DAUGHTER. It isn't true. Don't believe it. [*To* MANAGER.] Do you know why she says so? For that fellow there. [*Indicates the* SON.] She tortures herself, destroys herself on account of the neglect of that son there; and she wants him to believe that if she abandoned him when he was only two years old, it was because he [*indicates the* FATHER] made her do so.

THE MOTHER [*vigorously*]. He forced me to it, and I call God to witness it. [*To the* MANAGER.] Ask him [*indicates* FATHER] if it isn't true. Let him speak. You [*to* DAUGHTER] are not in a position to know anything about it.

THE STEP-DAUGHTER. I know you lived in peace and happiness with my father while he lived. Can you deny it?

THE MOTHER. No, I don't deny it . . .

THE STEP-DAUGHTER. He was always full of affection and kindness for you. [*To the* BOY, *angrily*.] It's true, isn't it? Tell them! Why don't you speak, you little fool?

THE MOTHER. Leave the poor boy alone. Why do you want to make me appear ungrateful, daughter? I don't want to offend your father. I have answered him that I didn't abandon my house and my son through any fault of mine, nor from any willful passion.

THE FATHER. It is true. It was my doing.

LEADING MAN [*to the* COMPANY]. What a spectacle!

LEADING LADY. We are the audience this time.

JUVENILE LEAD. For once, in a way.

THE MANAGER [*beginning to get really interested*]. Let's hear them out. Listen!

THE SON. Oh yes, you're going to hear a fine bit now. He will talk to you of the Demon of Experiment.

THE FATHER. You are a cynical imbecile. I've told you so already a hundred times. [*To the* MANAGER.] He tries to make fun of me on account of this expression which I have found to excuse myself with.

THE SON [*with disgust*]. Yes, phrases! phrases!

THE FATHER. Phrases! Isn't everyone consoled when faced with a trouble or fact he doesn't understand, by a word, some simple word, which tells us nothing and yet calms us?

THE STEP-DAUGHTER. Even in the case of remorse. In fact, especially then.

THE FATHER. Remorse? No, that isn't true. I've done more than use words to quieten the remorse in me.

THE STEP-DAUGHTER. Yes, there was a bit of money too. Yes, yes, a bit of money. There were the hundred lire he was about to offer me in payment, gentlemen . . . [*Sensation of horror among the* ACTORS.]

THE SON [*to the* STEP-DAUGHTER]. This is vile.

THE STEP-DAUGHTER. Vile? There they were in a pale blue envelope on a little mahogany table in the back of Madame Pace's shop. You know Madame Pace—one of those ladies who attract poor girls of good family into their ateliers, under the pretext of their selling *robes et manteaux.*[5]

THE SON. And he thinks he has bought the right to tyrannize over us all with those hundred lire he was going to pay; but which, fortunately—note this, gentlemen—he had no chance of paying.

THE STEP-DAUGHTER. It was a near thing, though, you know! [*Laughs ironically.*]

THE MOTHER [*protesting*]. Shame, my daughter, shame!

THE STEP-DAUGHTER. Shame indeed! This is my revenge! I am dying to live that scene . . . The room . . . I see it . . . Here is the window with the mantles exposed, there the divan, the looking glass, a screen, there in front of the window the little mahogany table with the blue envelope containing one hundred lire. I see it. I see it. I could take hold of it . . . But you, gentlemen, you ought to turn your backs now: I am almost nude, you know. But I don't blush: I leave that to him. [*Indicating* FATHER.]

THE MANAGER. I don't understand this at all.

THE FATHER. Naturally enough. I would ask you, sir, to exercise your authority a little here, and let me speak before you believe all she is trying to blame me with. Let me explain.

THE STEP-DAUGHTER. Ah yes, explain it in your own way.

THE FATHER. But don't you see that the whole trouble lies here. In words, words. Each one of us has within him a whole world of things, each man of us his own special world. And how can we ever come to an understanding if I put in the words I utter the sense and value of things as I see them; while you who listen to me must inevitably translate them according to the conception of things each one of you has within himself. We think we understand each other, but we never really do. Look here! This woman [*indicating the* MOTHER] takes all my pity for her as a specially ferocious form of cruelty.

THE MOTHER. But you drove me away.

THE FATHER. Do you hear her? I drove her away! She believes I really sent her away.

THE MOTHER. You know how to talk, and I don't; but, believe me, sir [*to*

[5] Dresses and coats.

MANAGER], after he had married me . . . who knows why? . . . I was a poor insignificant woman . . .

THE FATHER. But, good Heavens! it was just for your humility that I married you. I loved this simplicity in you.

[*He stops when he sees she makes signs to contradict him, opens his arms wide in sign of desperation, seeing how hopeless it is to make himself understood.*]

You see she denies it. Her mental deafness, believe me, is phenomenal, the limit. [*Touches his forehead.*] Deaf, deaf, mentally deaf! She has plenty of feeling. Oh yes, a good heart for the children; but the brain—deaf, to the point of desperation—

THE STEP-DAUGHTER. Yes, but ask him how his intelligence has helped us.

THE FATHER. If we could see all the evil that may spring from good, what should we do?

[*At this point the* LEADING LADY *who is biting her lips with rage at seeing the* LEADING MAN *flirting with the* STEP-DAUGHTER, *comes forward and says to the* MANAGER:]

LEADING LADY. Excuse me, but are we going to rehearse today?

MANAGER. Of course, of course; but let's hear them out.

JUVENILE LEAD. This is something quite new.

L'INGÉNUE. Most interesting!

LEADING LADY. Yes, for the people who like that kind of thing. [*Casts a glance at* LEADING MAN.]

THE MANAGER [*to* FATHER]. You must please explain yourself quite clearly.

[*Sits down.*]

THE FATHER. Very well then: listen! I had in my service a poor man, a clerk, a secretary of mine, full of devotion, who became friends with her. [*Indicating the* MOTHER.] They understood one another, were kindred souls in fact, without, however, the least suspicion of any evil existing. They were incapable even of thinking of it.

THE STEP-DAUGHTER. So he thought of it—for them!

THE FATHER. That's not true. I meant to do good to them—and to myself, I confess, at the same time. Things had come to the point that I could not say a word to either of them without their making a mute appeal, one to the other, with their eyes. I could see them silently asking each other how I was to be kept in countenance, how I was to be kept quiet. And this, believe me, was just about enough of itself to keep me in a constant rage, to exasperate me beyond measure.

THE MANAGER. And why didn't you send him away then—this secretary of yours?

THE FATHER. Precisely what I did, sir. And then I had to watch this poor woman drifting forlornly about the house like an animal without a master, like an animal one has taken in out of pity.

THE MOTHER. Ah yes . . . !

THE FATHER [*suddenly turning to the* MOTHER]. It's true about the son any-way, isn't it?

THE MOTHER. He took my son away from me first of all.

THE FATHER. But not from cruelty. I did it so that he should grow up healthy and strong by living in the country.

THE STEP-DAUGHTER [*pointing to him ironically*]. As one can see.

THE FATHER [*quickly*]. Is it my fault if he has grown up like this? I sent him to a wet nurse in the country, a peasant, as *she* did not seem to me strong enough, though she is of humble origin. That was, anyway, the reason I married her. Unpleasant all this may be, but how can it be helped? My mistake possibly, but there we are! All my life I have had these con-founded aspirations toward a certain moral sanity. [*At this point the* STEP-DAUGHTER *bursts into a noisy laugh.*] Oh, stop it! Stop it! I can't stand it.

THE MANAGER. Yes, please stop it, for Heaven's sake.

THE STEP-DAUGHTER. But imagine moral sanity from him, if you please— the client of certain ateliers like that of Madame Pace!

THE FATHER. Fool! That is the proof that I am a man! This seeming con-tradiction, gentlemen, is the strongest proof that I stand here a live man before you. Why, it is just for this very incongruity in my nature that I have had to suffer what I have. I could not live by the side of that woman [*indicating the* MOTHER] any longer; but not so much for the boredom she inspired me with as for the pity I felt for her.

THE MOTHER. And so he turned me out—.

THE FATHER. —well provided for! Yes, I sent her to that man, gentlemen . . . to let her go free of me.

THE MOTHER. And to free himself.

THE FATHER. Yes, I admit it. It was also a liberation for me. But great evil has come of it. I meant well when I did it; and I did it more for her sake than mine. I swear it.

[*Crosses his arms on his chest; then turns suddenly to the* MOTHER.]

Did I ever lose sight of you until that other man carried you off to another town, like the angry fool he was? And on account of my pure interest in you . . . my pure interest, I repeat, that had no base motive in it . . . I watched with the tenderest concern the new family that grew up around her. She can bear witness to this. [*Points to the* STEP-DAUGHTER.]

THE STEP-DAUGHTER. Oh yes, that's true enough. When I was a kiddie, so so high, you know, with plaits over my shoulders and knickers longer than my skirts, I used to see him waiting outside the school for me to come out. He came to see how I was growing up.

THE FATHER. This is infamous, shameful!

THE STEP-DAUGHTER. No. Why?

THE FATHER. Infamous! infamous! [*Then excitedly to* MANAGER *explaining.*] After she [*indicating* MOTHER] went away, my house seemed suddenly empty. She was my incubus, but she filled my house. I was like a dazed fly alone in the empty rooms. This boy here [*indicating the* SON] was educated away from home, and when he came back, he seemed to me to be no more mine. With no mother to stand between him and me, he grew up entirely for himself, on his own, apart, with no tie of intellect or affection binding him to me. And then—strange but true—I was driven, by curiosity at first and then by some tender sentiment, toward her family, which had come into being through my will. The thought of her began gradually to fill up the emptiness I felt all around me. I wanted to know if she were happy in living out the simple daily duties of life. I wanted to think of her as fortunate and happy because far away from the complicated torments of my spirit. And so, to have proof of this, I used to watch that child coming out of school.

THE STEP-DAUGHTER. Yes, yes. True. He used to follow me in the street and smiled at me, waved his hand, like this. I would look at him with interest, wondering who he might be. I told my mother, who guessed at once. [*The* MOTHER *agrees with a nod.*] Then she didn't want to send me to school for some days; and when I finally went back, there he was again— looking so ridiculous—with a paper parcel in his hands. He came close to me, caressed me, and drew out a fine straw hat from the parcel, with a bouquet of flowers—all for me!

THE MANAGER. A bit discursive this, you know!

THE SON [*contemptuously*]. Literature! Literature!

THE FATHER. Literature indeed! This is life, this is passion!

THE MANAGER. It may be, but it won't act.

THE FATHER. I agree. This is only the part leading up. I don't suggest this should be staged. She [*pointing to the* STEP-DAUGHTER], as you see, is no longer the flapper with plaits down her back—.

THE STEP-DAUGHTER. —and the knickers showing below the skirt!

THE FATHER. The drama is coming now, sir; something new, complex, most interesting.

THE STEP-DAUGHTER. As soon as my father died . . .

THE FATHER. —there was absolute misery for them. They came back here, unknown to me. Through her stupidity! [*Pointing to the* MOTHER.] It is true she can barely write her own name; but she could anyhow have got her daughter to write to me that they were in need . . .

THE MOTHER. And how was I to divine all this sentiment in him?

THE FATHER. That is exactly your mistake, never to have guessed any of my sentiments.

THE MOTHER. After so many years apart, and all that had happened . . .

THE FATHER. Was it my fault if that fellow carried you away? It happened quite suddenly; for after he had obtained some job or other, I could find no trace of them; and so, not unnaturally, my interest in them dwindled. But the drama culminated unforeseen and violent on their return, when I was impelled by my miserable flesh that still lives . . . Ah!

what misery, what wretchedness is that of the man who is alone and disdains debasing *liaisons*! Not old enough to do without women, and not young enough to go and look for one without shame. Misery? It's worse than misery; it's a horror; for no woman can any longer give him love; and when a man feels this . . . One ought to do without, you say? Yes, yes, I know. Each of us when he appears before his fellows is clothed in a certain dignity. But every man knows what unconfessable things pass within the secrecy of his own heart. One gives way to the temptation, only to rise from it again, afterward, with a great eagerness to reestablish one's dignity, as if it were a tombstone to place on the grave of one's shame, and a monument to hide and sign the memory of our weaknesses. Everybody's in the same case. Some folks haven't the courage to say certain things, that's all!

THE STEP-DAUGHTER. All appear to have the courage to do them though.

THE FATHER. Yes, but in secret. Therefore, you want more courage to say these things. Let a man but speak these things out, and folks at once label him a cynic. But it isn't true. He is like all the others, better indeed, because he isn't afraid to reveal with the light of the intelligence the red shame of human bestiality on which most men close their eyes so as not to see it.

Woman—for example, look at her case! She turns tantalizing inviting glances on you. You seize her. No sooner does she feel herself in your grasp than she closes her eyes. It is the sign of her mission, the sign by which she says to man: "Blind yourself, for I am blind."

THE STEP-DAUGHTER. Sometimes she can close them no more: when she no longer feels the need of hiding her shame to herself, but dry-eyed and dispassionately, sees only that of the man who has blinded himself without love. Oh, all these intellectual complications make me sick, disgust me—all this philosophy that uncovers the beast in man, and then seeks to save him, excuse him . . . I can't stand it, sir. When a man seeks to "simplify" life bestially, throwing aside every relic of humanity, every chaste aspiration, every pure feeling, all sense of ideality, duty, modesty, shame . . . then nothing is more revolting and nauseous than a certain kind of remorse—crocodiles' tears, that's what it is.

THE MANAGER. Let's come to the point. This is only discussion.

THE FATHER. Very good, sir! But a fact is like a sack which won't stand up when it is empty. In order that it may stand up, one has to put into it the reason and sentiment which have caused it to exist. I couldn't possibly know that after the death of that man, they had decided to return here, that they were in misery, and that she [*pointing to the* MOTHER] had gone to work as a modiste, and at a shop of the type of that of Madame Pace.

THE STEP-DAUGHTER. A real high-class modiste, you must know, gentlemen. In appearance, she works for the leaders of the best society; but she arranges matters so that these elegant ladies serve her purpose . . . without prejudice to other ladies who are . . . well . . . only so-so.

THE MOTHER. You will believe me, gentlemen, that it never entered my mind that the old hag offered me work because she had her eye on my daughter.

THE STEP-DAUGHTER. Poor mamma! Do you know, sir, what that woman did when I brought her back the work my mother had finished? She would point out to me that I had torn one of my frocks, and she would give it back to my mother to mend. It was I who paid for it, always I; while this poor creature here believed she was sacrificing herself for me and these two children here, sitting up at night sewing Madame Pace's robes.

THE MANAGER. And one day you met there . . .

THE STEP-DAUGHTER. Him, him. Yes sir, an old client. There's a scene for you to play! Superb!

THE FATHER. She, the Mother arrived just then . . .

THE STEP-DAUGHTER [*treacherously*]. Almost in time!

THE FATHER [*crying out.*] No, in time! in time! Fortunately I recognized her . . . in time. And I took them back home with me to my house. You can imagine now her position and mine; she, as you see her; and I who cannot look her in the face.

THE STEP-DAUGHTER. Absurd! How can I possibly be expected—after that—to be a modest young miss, a fit person to go with his confounded aspirations for "a solid moral sanity"?

THE FATHER. For the drama lies all in this—in the conscience that I have, that each one of us has. We believe this conscience to be a single thing, but it is many-sided. There is one for this person, and another for that. Diverse consciences. So we have this illusion of being one person for all, of having a personality that is unique in all our acts. But it isn't true. We perceive this when, tragically perhaps, in something we do, we are as it were, suspended, caught up in the air on a kind of hook. Then we perceive that all of us was not in that act, and that it would be an atrocious injustice to judge us by that action alone, as if all our existence were summed up in that one deed. Now do you understand the perfidy of this girl? She surprised me in a place, where she ought not to have known me, just as I could not exist for her; and she now seeks to attach to me a reality such as I could never suppose I should have to assume for her in a shameful and fleeting moment of my life. I feel this above all else. And the drama, you will see, acquires a tremendous value from this point. Then there is the position of the others . . . his . . . [*Indicating the* SON.]

THE SON [*shrugging his shoulders scornfully*]. Leave me alone! I don't come into this.

THE FATHER. What? You don't come into this?

THE SON. I've got nothing to do with it, and don't want to have; because you know well enough I wasn't made to be mixed up in all this with the rest of you.

THE STEP-DAUGHTER. We are only vulgar folk! He is the fine gentleman. You may have noticed, Mr. Manager, that I fix him now and again with a look of scorn while he lowers his eyes—for he knows the evil he has done me.

THE SON [*scarcely looking at her*]. I?

THE STEP-DAUGHTER. You! you! I owe my life on the streets to you. Did you or did you not deny us, with your behavior, I won't say the intimacy of home, but even that mere hospitality which makes guests feel at their ease? We were intruders who had come to disturb the kingdom of your legitimacy. I should like to have you witness, Mr. Manager, certain scenes between him and me. He says I have tyrannized over everyone. But it was just his behavior which made me insist on the reason for which I had come into the house,—this reason he calls "vile"—into his house, with my mother who is his mother too. And I came as mistress of the house.

THE SON. It's easy for them to put me always in the wrong. But imagine, gentlemen, the position of a son, whose fate it is to see arrive one day at his home a young woman of impudent bearing, a young woman who inquires for his father, with whom who knows what business she has. This young man has then to witness her return bolder than ever, accompanied by that child there. He is obliged to watch her treat his father in an equivocal and confidential manner. She asks money of him in a way that lets one suppose he must give it her, *must*, do you understand, because he has every obligation to do so.

THE FATHER. But I have, as a matter of fact, this obligation. I owe it to your mother.

THE SON. How should I know? When had I ever seen or heard of her? One day there arrive with her [*indicating* STEP-DAUGHTER] that lad and this baby here. I am told: "This is *your* mother too, you know." I divine from her manner [*indicating* STEP-DAUGHTER *again*] why it is they have come home. I had rather not say what I feel and think about it. I shouldn't even care to confess to myself. No action can therefore be hoped for from me in this affair. Believe me, Mr. Manager, I am an "unrealized" character, dramatically speaking; and I find myself not at all at ease in their company. Leave me out of it, I beg you.

THE FATHER. What? It is just because you are so that . . .

THE SON. How do you know what I am like? When did you ever bother your head about me?

THE FATHER. I admit it. I admit it. But isn't that a situation in itself? This aloofness of yours which is so cruel to me and to your mother, who returns home and sees you almost for the first time grown up, who doesn't recognize you but knows you are her son . . . [*Pointing out the* MOTHER *to the* MANAGER.] See, she's crying!

THE STEP-DAUGHTER [*angrily, stamping her foot*]. Like a fool!

THE FATHER [*indicating* STEP-DAUGHTER]. She can't stand him you know.

[*Then referring again to the* SON.] He says he doesn't come into the affair, whereas he is really the hinge of the whole action. Look at that lad who is always clinging to his mother, frightened and humiliated. It is on account of this fellow here. Possibly his situation is the most painful of all. He feels himself a stranger more than the others. The poor little chap feels mortified, humiliated at being brought into a home out of charity as it were. [*In confidence.*] He is the image of his father. Hardly talks at all. Humble and quiet.

THE MANAGER. Oh, we'll cut him out. You've no notion what a nuisance boys are on the stage . . .

THE FATHER. He disappears soon, you know. And the baby too. She is the first to vanish from the scene. The drama consists finally in this: when that mother reenters my house, her family born outside of it, and shall we say superimposed on the original, ends with the death of the little girl, the tragedy of the boy and the flight of the elder daughter. It cannot go on, because it is foreign to its surroundings. So after much torment, we three remain: I, the mother, that son. Then, owing to the disappearance of that extraneous family, we too find ourselves strange to one another. We find we are living in an atmosphere of mortal desolation which is the revenge, as he [*indicating* SON] scornfully said of the Demon of Experiment, that unfortunately hides in me. Thus, sir, you see when faith is lacking, it becomes impossible to create certain states of happiness, for we lack the necessary humility. Vaingloriously, we try to substitute ourselves for this faith, creating thus for the rest of the world a reality which we believe after their fashion, while, actually, it doesn't exist. For each one of us has his own reality to be respected before God, even when it is harmful to one's very self.

THE MANAGER. There is something in what you say. I assure you all this interests me very much. I begin to think there's the stuff for a drama in all this, and not a bad drama either.

THE STEP-DAUGHTER [*coming forward*]. When you've got a character like me.

THE FATHER [*shutting her up, all excited to learn the decision of the* MANAGER]. You be quiet!

THE MANAGER [*reflecting, heedless of interruption*]. It's new . . . hem . . . yes . . .

THE FATHER. Absolutely new!

THE MANAGER. You've got a nerve though, I must say, to come here and fling it at me like this . . .

THE FATHER. You will understand, sir, born as we are for the stage . . .

THE MANAGER. Are you amateur actors then?

THE FATHER. No. I say born for the stage, because . . .

THE MANAGER. Oh, nonsense. You're an old hand, you know.

THE FATHER. No sir, no. We act that rôle for which we have been cast, that rôle which we are given in life. And in my own case, passion itself, as usually happens, becomes a trifle theatrical when it is exalted.

THE MANAGER. Well, well, that will do. But you see, without an author . . . I could give you the address of an author if you like . . .

THE FATHER. No, no. Look here! You must be the author.

THE MANAGER. I? What are you talking about?

THE FATHER. Yes, you, you! Why not? ˙

THE MANAGER. Because I have never been an author: that's why.

THE FATHER. Then why not turn author now? Everybody does it. You don't want any special qualities. Your task is made much easier by the fact that we are all here alive before you . . .

THE MANAGER. It won't do.

THE FATHER. What? When you see us live our drama . . .

THE MANAGER. Yes, that's all right. But you want someone to write it.

THE FATHER. No, no. Someone to take it down, possibly, while we play it, scene by scene! It will be enough to sketch it out at first, and then try it over.

THE MANAGER. Well . . . I am almost tempted. It's a bit of an idea. One might have a shot at it.

THE FATHER. Of course. You'll see what scenes will come out of it. I can give you one, at once . . .

THE MANAGER. By Jove, it tempts me. I'd like to have a go at it. Let's try it out. Come with me to my office. [Turning to the ACTORS.] You are at liberty for a bit, but don't step out of the theater for long. In a quarter of an hour, twenty minutes, all back here again! [To the FATHER.] We'll see what can be done. Who knows if we don't get something really extraordinary out of it?

THE FATHER. There's no doubt about it. They [indicating the CHARACTERS] had better come with us too, hadn't they?

THE MANAGER. Yes, yes. Come on! come on!

[Moves away and then turning to the ACTORS.]

Be punctual, please!

[MANAGER and the SIX CHARACTERS cross the stage and go off. The other ACTORS remain, looking at one another in astonishment.]

LEADING MAN. Is he serious? What the devil does he want to do?

JUVENILE LEAD. This is rank madness.

THIRD ACTOR. Does he expect to knock up a drama in five minutes?

JUVENILE LEAD. Like the improvisers!

LEADING LADY. If he thinks I'm going to take part in a joke like this . . .

JUVENILE LEAD. I'm out of it anyway.

FOURTH ACTOR. I should like to know who they are. [Alludes to CHARACTERS.]

THIRD ACTOR. What do you suppose? Madmen or rascals!

JUVENILE LEAD. And he takes them seriously!

L'INGÉNUE. Vanity! He fancies himself as an author now.

LEADING MAN. It's absolutely unheard of. If the stage has come to this . . . well I'm . . .

FIFTH ACTOR. It's rather a joke.

THIRD ACTOR. Well, we'll see what's going to happen next.

[*Thus talking, the* ACTORS *leave the stage; some going out by the little door at the back; others retiring to their dressing rooms.*
The curtain remains up.
The action of the play is suspended for twenty minutes.]

ACT TWO

The stage call-bells ring to warn the company that the play is about to begin again.
The STEP-DAUGHTER *comes out of the* MANAGER'S *office along with the* CHILD *and the* BOY. *As she comes out of the office, she cries:*

THE STEP-DAUGHTER. Nonsense! nonsense! Do it yourselves! I'm not going to mix myself up in this mess. [*Turning to the* CHILD *and coming quickly with her onto the stage.*] Come on, Rosetta, let's run!

[*The* BOY *follows them slowly, remaining a little behind and seeming perplexed.*]

THE STEP-DAUGHTER [*stops, bends over the* CHILD *and takes the latter's face between her hands*]. My little darling! You're frightened, aren't you? You don't know where we are, do you? [*Pretending to reply to a question of the* CHILD.] What is the stage? It's a place, baby, you know, where people play at being serious, a place where they act comedies. We've got to act a comedy now, dead serious, you know; and you're in it also, little one.

[*Embraces her, pressing the little head to her breast, and rocking the* CHILD *for a moment.*]

Oh darling, darling, what a horrid comedy you've got to play! What a wretched part they've found for you! A garden . . . a fountain . . . look . . . just suppose, kiddie, it's here. Where, you say? Why, right here in the middle. It's all pretence you know. That's the trouble, my pet: it's all make-believe here. It's better to imagine it though, because if they fix it up for you, it'll only be painted cardboard, painted cardboard for the rockery, the water, the plants . . . Ah, but I think a baby like this one would sooner have a make-believe fountain than a real one, so she could play with it. What a joke it'll be for the others! But for you, alas! not quite such a joke: you who are real, baby dear, and really play by a real fountain that is big and green and beautiful, with ever so many bamboos around it that are reflected in the water, and a whole lot of little ducks swimming about . . . No, Rosetta, no, your mother doesn't bother about you on account of that wretch of a son there. I'm in the devil of a temper, and as for that lad . . .

[*Seizes* BOY *by the arm to force him to take one of his hands out of his pockets.*]

What have you got there? What are you hiding?
[*Pulls his hand out of his pocket, looks into it and catches the glint of a revolver.*]
Ah! where did you get this? [*The* BOY, *very pale in the face, looks at her, but does not answer.*] Idiot! If I'd been in your place, instead of killing myself, I'd have shot one of those two, or both of them: father and son.
[*The* FATHER *enters from the office, all excited from his work. The* MANAGER *follows him.*]

THE FATHER. Come on, come on dear! Come here for a minute! We've arranged everything. It's all fixed up.

THE MANAGER [*also excited*]. If you please, young lady, there are one or two points to settle still. Will you come along?

THE STEP-DAUGHTER [*following him toward the office*]. Ouff! what's the good, if you've arranged everything.
[*The* FATHER, MANAGER *and* STEP-DAUGHTER *go back into the office again* (*off*) *for a moment. At the same time, the* SON, *followed by the* MOTHER, *comes out.*]

THE SON [*looking at the three entering office*]. Oh this is fine, fine! And to think I can't even get away!
[*The* MOTHER *attempts to look at him, but lowers her eyes immediately when he turns away from her. She then sits down. The* BOY *and the* CHILD *approach her. She casts a glance again at the* SON, *and speaks with humble tones, trying to draw him into conversation.*]

THE MOTHER. And isn't my punishment the worst of all? [*Then seeing from the* SON'S *manner that he will not bother himself about her.*] My God! Why are you so cruel? Isn't it enough for one person to support all this torment? Must you then insist on others seeing it also?

THE SON [*half to himself, meaning the* MOTHER *to hear, however*]. And they want to put it on the stage! If there was at least a reason for it! He thinks he has got at the meaning of it all. Just as if each one of us in every circumstance of life couldn't find his own explanation of it! [*Pauses.*] He complains he was discovered in a place where he ought not to have been seen, in a moment of his life which ought to have remained hidden and kept out of the reach of that convention which he has to maintain for other people. And what about my case? Haven't I had to reveal what no son ought ever to reveal: how father and mother live and are man and wife for themselves quite apart from that idea of father and mother which we give them? When this idea is revealed, our life is then linked at one point only to that man and that woman; and as such it should shame them, shouldn't it?
[*The* MOTHER *hides her face in her hands. From the dressing rooms and the little door at the back of the stage the* ACTORS *and* STAGE MANAGER *return, followed by the* PROPERTY MAN, *and the* PROMPTER. *At the same moment, the* MANAGER *comes out of his office, accompanied by the* FATHER *and the* STEP-DAUGHTER.*]

THE MANAGER. Come on, come on, ladies and gentlemen! Heh! you there, machinist!

MACHINIST. Yes sir?

THE MANAGER. Fix up the white parlor with the floral decorations. Two wings and a drop with a door will do. Hurry up!

[*The* MACHINIST *runs off at once to prepare the scene, and arranges it while the* MANAGER *talks with the* STAGE MANAGER, *the* PROPERTY MAN, *and the* PROMPTER *on matters of detail.*]

THE MANAGER [*to* PROPERTY MAN]. Just have a look, and see if there isn't a sofa or divan in the wardrobe . . .

PROPERTY MAN. There's the green one.

THE STEP-DAUGHTER. No no! Green won't do. It was yellow, ornamented with flowers—very large! and most comfortable!

PROPERTY MAN. There isn't one like that.

THE MANAGER. It doesn't matter. Use the one we've got.

THE STEP-DAUGHTER. Doesn't matter? It's most important!

THE MANAGER. We're only trying it now. Please don't interfere. [*To* PROPERTY MAN.] See if we've got a shop window—long and narrowish.

THE STEP-DAUGHTER. And the little table! The little mahogany table for the pale blue envelope!

PROPERTY MAN [*to* MANAGER]. There's that little gilt one.

THE MANAGER. That'll do fine.

THE FATHER. A mirror.

THE STEP-DAUGHTER. And the screen! We must have a screen. Otherwise how can I manage?

PROPERTY MAN. That's all right, Miss. We've got any amount of them.

THE MANAGER [*to the* STEP-DAUGHTER]. We want some clothes pegs too, don't we?

THE STEP-DAUGHTER. Yes, several, several!

THE MANAGER. See how many we've got and bring them all.

PROPERTY MAN. All right!

[*The* PROPERTY MAN *hurries off to obey his orders. While he is putting the things in their places, the* MANAGER *talks to the* PROMPTER *and then with the* CHARACTERS *and the* ACTORS.]

THE MANAGER [*to* PROMPTER]. Take your seat. Look here: this is the outline of the scenes, act by act. [*Hands him some sheets of paper.*] And now I'm going to ask you to do something out of the ordinary.

PROMPTER. Take it down in shorthand?

THE MANAGER [*pleasantly surprised*]. Exactly! Can you do shorthand?

PROMPTER. Yes, a little.

THE MANAGER. Good! [*Turning to a* STAGE HAND.] Go and get some paper from my office, plenty, as much as you can find.

[*The* STAGE HAND *goes off, and soon returns with a handful of paper which he gives to the* PROMPTER.]

THE MANAGER [*to* PROMPTER]. You follow the scenes as we play them, and try and get the points down, at any rate the most important ones. [*Then addressing the* ACTORS.] Clear the stage, ladies and gentlemen! Come over here [*pointing to the left*] and listen attentively.

LEADING LADY. But, excuse me, we . . .

THE MANAGER [*guessing her thought*]. Don't worry! You won't have to improvise.

LEADING MAN. What have we to do then?

THE MANAGER. Nothing. For the moment you just watch and listen. Everybody will get his part written out afterward. At present we're going to try the thing as best we can. They're going to act now.

THE FATHER [*as if fallen from the clouds into the confusion of the stage*]. We? What do you mean, if you please, by a rehearsal?

THE MANAGER. A rehearsal for them. [*Points to the* ACTORS.]

THE FATHER. But since we are the characters . . .

THE MANAGER. All right: "characters" then, if you insist on calling your-selves such. But here, my dear sir, the characters don't act. Here the actors do the acting. The characters are there, in the "book" [*pointing toward* PROMPTER'S *box*]— when there is a "book"!

THE FATHER. I won't contradict you; but excuse me, the actors aren't the characters. They want to be, they pretend to be, don't they? Now if these gentlemen here are fortunate enough to have us alive before them . . .

THE MANAGER. Oh this is grand! You want to come before the public yourselves then?

THE FATHER. As we are . . .

THE MANAGER. I can assure you it would be a magnificent spectacle!

LEADING MAN. What's the use of us here anyway then?

THE MANAGER. You're not going to pretend that you can act? It makes me laugh! [*The* ACTORS *laugh.*] There, you see, they are laughing at the notion. But, by the way, I must cast the parts. That won't be difficult. They cast themselves. [*To the* SECOND LADY LEAD.] You play the Mother. [*To the* FATHER.] We must find her a name.

THE FATHER. Amalia, sir.

THE MANAGER. But that is the real name of your wife. We don't want to call her by her real name.

THE FATHER. Why ever not, if it is her name? . . . Still, perhaps, if that lady must . . . [*Makes a slight motion of the hand to indicate the* SECOND LADY LEAD.] I see this woman here [*means the* MOTHER] as Amalia. But do as you like. [*Gets more and more confused.*] I don't know what to say to you. Already, I begin to hear my own words ring false, as if they had another sound . . .

THE MANAGER. Don't you worry about it. It'll be our job to find the right tones. And as for her name, if you want her Amalia, Amalia it shall be; and if you don't like it, we'll find another! For the moment though, we'll call the characters in this way: [*To* JUVENILE LEAD.] You are the Son.

[*To the* LEADING LADY.] You naturally are the Step-Daughter . . .

THE STEP-DAUGHTER [*excitedly*]. What? what? I, that woman there? [*Bursts out laughing.*]

THE MANAGER [*angry*]. What is there to laugh at?

LEADING LADY [*indignant*]. Nobody has ever dared to laugh at me. I insist on being treated with respect; otherwise I go away.

THE STEP-DAUGHTER. No, no, excuse me . . . I am not laughing at you . . .

THE MANAGER [*to* STEP-DAUGHTER]. You ought to feel honored to be played by . . .

LEADING LADY [*at once, contemptuously*]. "That woman there" . . .

THE STEP-DAUGHTER. But I wasn't speaking of you, you know. I was speaking of myself—whom I can't see at all in you! That is all. I don't know . . . but . . . you . . . aren't in the least like me . . .

THE FATHER. True. Here's the point. Look here, sir, our temperaments, our souls . . .

THE MANAGER. Temperament, soul, be hanged! Do you suppose the spirit of the piece is in you? Nothing of the kind!

THE FATHER. What, haven't we our own temperaments, our own souls?

THE MANAGER. Not at all. Your soul or whatever you like to call it takes shape here. The actors give body and form to it, voice and gesture. And my actors—I may tell you—have given expression to much more lofty material than this little drama of yours, which may or may not hold up on the stage. But if it does, the merit of it, believe me, will be due to my actors.

THE FATHER. I don't dare contradict you, sir; but, believe me, it is a terrible suffering for us who are as we are, with these bodies of ours, these features, to see . . .

THE MANAGER [*cutting him short and out of patience*]. Good heavens! The make-up will remedy all that, man, the make-up . . .

THE FATHER. Maybe. But the voice, the gestures . . .

THE MANAGER. Now, look here! On the stage, you as yourself cannot exist. The actor here acts you, and that's an end to it!

THE FATHER. I understand. And now I think I see why our author who conceived us as we are, all alive, didn't want to put us on the stage after all. I haven't the least desire to offend your actors. Far from it! But when I think that I am to be acted by . . . I don't know by whom . . .

LEADING MAN [*on his dignity*]. By me, if you've no objection!

THE FATHER [*humbly, mellifluously*]. Honored, I assure you, sir. [*Bows.*] Still, I must say that try as this gentleman may, with all his good will and wonderful art, to absorb me into himself . . .

LEADING MAN. Oh chuck it! "Wonderful art!" Withdraw that, please!

THE FATHER. The performance he will give, even doing his best with make-up to look like me . . .

LEADING MAN. It will certainly be a bit difficult! [*The* ACTORS *laugh.*]

THE FATHER. Exactly! It will be difficult to act me as I really am. The effect will be rather—apart from the make-up—according as to how he supposes I am, as he senses me—if he does sense me—and not as I inside of myself feel myself to be. It seems to me then that account should be taken of this by everyone whose duty it may become to criticize us . . .

THE MANAGER. Heavens! The man's starting to think about the critics now! Let them say what they like. It's up to us to put on the play if we can. [*Looking around.*] Come on! come on! Is the stage set? [*To the* ACTORS *and* CHARACTERS.] Stand back—stand back! Let me see, and don't let's lose any more time! [*To the* STEP-DAUGHTER.] Is it all right as it is now?

THE STEP-DAUGHTER. Well, to tell the truth, I don't recognize the scene.

THE MANAGER. My dear lady, you can't possibly suppose that we can construct that shop of Madame Pace piece by piece here? [*To the* FATHER.] You said a white room with flowered wallpaper, didn't you?

THE FATHER. Yes.

THE MANAGER. Well then. We've got the furniture right more or less. Bring that little table a bit further forward. [*The* STAGE HANDS *obey the order. To* PROPERTY MAN.] You go and find an envelope, if possible, a pale blue one; and give it to that gentleman. [*Indicates* FATHER.]

PROPERTY MAN. An ordinary envelope?

MANAGER *and* FATHER. Yes, yes, an ordinary envelope.

PROPERTY MAN. At once, sir.

[*Exit.*]

THE MANAGER. Ready, everyone! First scene—the Young Lady. [*The* LEADING LADY *comes forward.*] No, no, you must wait. I meant her [*indicating the* STEP-DAUGHTER]. You just watch—

THE STEP-DAUGHTER [*adding at once*]. How I shall play it, how I shall live it! . . .

LEADING LADY [*offended*]. I shall live it also, you may be sure, as soon as I begin!

THE MANAGER [*with his hands to his head*]. Ladies and gentlemen, if you please! No more useless discussions! Scene I: the young lady with Madame Pace: Oh! [*Looks around as if lost.*] And this Madame Pace, where is she?

THE FATHER. She isn't with us, sir.

THE MANAGER. Then what the devil's to be done?

THE FATHER. But she is alive too.

THE MANAGER. Yes, but where is she?

THE FATHER. One minute. Let me speak! [*Turning to the* ACTRESSES.] If these ladies would be so good as to give me their hats for a moment . . .

ACTRESSES [*half-surprised, half-laughing, in chorus*]. What?
Why?
Our hats?
What does he say?

THE MANAGER. What are you going to do with the ladies' hats? [*The* ACTORS *laugh.*]

THE FATHER. Oh nothing. I just want to put them on these pegs for a moment. And one of the ladies will be so kind as to take off her mantle ...

ACTORS. Oh, what d'you think of that?

Only the mantle?

He must be mad.

SOME ACTRESSES. But why?

Mantles as well?

THE FATHER. To hang them up here for a moment. Please be so kind, will you?

ACTRESSES [*taking off their hats, one or two also their cloaks, and going to hang them on the racks*]. After all, why not?

There you are!

This is really funny.

We've got to put them on show.

THE FATHER. Exactly; just like that, on show.

THE MANAGER. May we know why?

THE FATHER. I'll tell you. Who knows if, by arranging the stage for her, she does not come here herself, attracted by the very articles of her trade? [*Inviting the* ACTORS *to look toward the exit at back of stage.*] Look! Look!

[*The door at the back of stage opens and* MADAME PACE *enters and takes a few steps forward. She is a fat, oldish woman with puffy oxygenated[6] hair. She is rouged and powdered, dressed with a comical elegance in black silk. Round her waist is a long silver chain from which hangs a pair of scissors. The* STEP-DAUGHTER *runs over to her at once amid the stupor of the actors.*]

THE STEP-DAUGHTER [*turning toward her*]. There she is! There she is!

THE FATHER [*radiant*]. It's she! I said so, didn't I? There she is!

THE MANAGER [*conquering his surprise, and then becoming indignant*]. What sort of a trick is this?

LEADING MAN [*almost at the same time*]. What's going to happen next?

JUVENILE LEAD. Where does *she* come from?

L'INGÉNUE. They've been holding her in reserve, I guess.

LEADING LADY. A vulgar trick!

THE FATHER [*dominating the protests*]. Excuse me, all of you! Why are you so anxious to destroy in the name of a vulgar, commonplace sense of truth, this reality which comes to birth attracted and formed by the magic of the stage itself, which has indeed more right to live here than you, since it is much truer than you—if you don't mind my saying so? Which is the actress among you who is to play Madame Pace? Well, here is Madame Pace herself. And you will allow, I fancy, that the

---

[6] Bleached.

actress who acts her will be less true than this woman here, who is herself in person. You see my daughter recognized her and went over to her at once. Now you're going to witness the scene!

[*But the scene between the* STEP-DAUGHTER *and* MADAME PACE *has already begun despite the protest of the actors and the reply of the* FATHER. *It has begun quietly, naturally, in a manner impossible for the stage. So when the* ACTORS, *called to attention by the* FATHER, *turn round and see* MADAME PACE, *who has placed one hand under the* STEP-DAUGHTER'S *chin to raise her head, they observe her at first with great attention, but hearing her speak in an unintelligible manner their interest begins to wane.*]

THE MANAGER. Well? well?

LEADING MAN. What does she say?

LEADING LADY. One can't hear a word.

JUVENILE LEAD. Louder! Louder please!

THE STEP-DAUGHTER [*leaving* MADAME PACE, *who smiles a Sphinx-like smile, and advancing toward the* ACTORS]. Louder? Louder? What are you talking about? These aren't matters which can be shouted at the top of one's voice. If I have spoken them out loud, it was to shame him and have my revenge. [*Indicates* FATHER.] But for Madame it's quite a different matter.

THE MANAGER. Indeed? indeed? But here, you know, people have got to make themselves heard, my dear. Even we who are on the stage can't hear you. What will it be when the public's in the theater? And anyway, you can very well speak up now among yourselves, since we shan't be present to listen to you as we are now. You've got to pretend to be alone in a room at the back of a shop where no one can hear you.

[*The* STEP-DAUGHTER *coquettishly and with a touch of malice makes a sign of disagreement two or three times with her finger.*]

THE MANAGER. What do you mean by no?

THE STEP-DAUGHTER [*sotto voce, mysteriously*]. There's someone who will hear us if she [*indicating* MADAME PACE] speaks out loud.

THE MANAGER [*in consternation*]. What? Have you got someone else to spring on us now? [*The* ACTORS *burst out laughing.*]

THE FATHER. No, no sir. She is alluding to me. I've got to be here—there behind that door, in waiting; and Madame Pace knows it. In fact, if you will allow me, I'll go there at once, so I can be quite ready. [*Moves away.*]

THE MANAGER [*stopping him*]. No! Wait! wait! We must observe the conventions of the theater. Before you are ready . . .

THE STEP-DAUGHTER [*interrupting him*]. No, get on with it at once! I'm just dying, I tell you, to act this scene. If he's ready, I'm more than ready.

THE MANAGER [*shouting*]. But, my dear young lady, first of all, we must have the scene between you and this lady . . . [*Indicates* MADAME PACE.] Do you understand? . . .

THE STEP-DAUGHTER. Good Heavens! She's been telling me what you know already: that mamma's work is badly done again, that the material's ruined; and that if I want her to continue to help us in our misery I must be patient . . .

MADAME PACE [*coming forward with an air of great importance*]. Yes indeed, sir, I no wanta take advantage of her, I no wanta be hard . . .
[*Note.* MADAME PACE *is supposed to talk in a jargon half-Italian, half-English.*]

THE MANAGER [*alarmed*]. What? What? She talks like that? [*The* ACTORS *burst out laughing again.*]

THE STEP-DAUGHTER [*also laughing*]. Yes yes, that's the way she talks, half-English, half-Italian! Most comical it is!

MADAME PACE. Itta seem not verra polite gentlemen laugha atta me eef I trya best speaka English.

THE MANAGER. *Diamine!* Of course! Of course! Let her talk like that! Just what we want. Talk just like that, Madame, if you please! The effect will be certain. Exactly what was wanted to put a little comic relief into the crudity of the situation. Of course she talks like that! Magnificent!

THE STEP-DAUGHTER. Magnificent? Certainly! When certain suggestions are made to one in language of that kind, the effect is certain, since it seems almost a joke. One feels inclined to laugh when one hears her talk about an "old signore" "who wanta talka nicely with you." Nice old signore, eh, Madame?

MADAME PACE. Not so old my dear, not so old! And even if you no lika him, he won't make any scandal!

THE MOTHER [*jumping up amid the amazement and consternation of the* ACTORS *who had not been noticing her. They move to restrain her*]. You old devil! You murderess!

THE STEP-DAUGHTER [*running over to calm her* MOTHER]. Calm yourself, Mother, calm yourself! Please don't . . .

THE FATHER [*going to her also at the same time*]. Calm yourself! Don't get excited! Sit down now!

THE MOTHER. Well then, take that woman away out of my sight!

THE STEP-DAUGHTER [*to* MANAGER]. It is impossible for my mother to remain here.

THE FATHER [*to* MANAGER]. They can't be here together. And for this reason, you see: that woman there was not with us when we came . . . If they are on together, the whole thing is given away inevitably, as you see.

THE MANAGER. It doesn't matter. This is only a first rough sketch—just to get an idea of the various points of the scene, even confusedly . . .
[*Turning to the* MOTHER *and leading her to her chair.*] Come along, my dear lady, sit down now, and let's get on with the scene . . .
[*Meanwhile, the* STEP-DAUGHTER, *coming forward again, turns to* MADAME PACE.]

THE STEP-DAUGHTER. Come on, Madame, come on!

MADAME PACE [*offended*]. No, no, *grazie*. I not do anything witha your mother present.

THE STEP-DAUGHTER. Nonsense! Introduce this "old signore" who wants to talk nicely to me. [*Addressing the* COMPANY *imperiously.*] We've got to do this scene one way or another, haven't we? Come on! [*To* MADAME PACE.] You can go!

MADAME PACE. Ah yes! I go'way! I go'way! Certainly!

[*Exits furious.*]

THE STEP-DAUGHTER [*to the* FATHER]. Now you make your entry. No, you needn't go over here. Come here. Let's suppose you've already come in. Like that, yes! I'm here with bowed head, modest like. Come on! Out with your voice! Say "Good morning, Miss" in that peculiar tone, that special tone . . .

THE MANAGER. Excuse me, but are you the Manager, or am I? [*To the* FATHER, *who looks undecided and perplexed.*] Get on with it, man! Go down there to the back of the stage. You needn't go off. Then come right forward here.

[*The* FATHER *does as he is told, looking troubled and perplexed at first. But as soon as he begins to move, the reality of the action affects him, and he begins to smile and to be more natural. The* ACTORS *watch intently.*]

THE MANAGER [*sotto voce, quickly to the* PROMPTER *in his box*]. Ready! ready? Get ready to write now.

THE FATHER [*coming forward and speaking in a different tone*]. Good afternoon, Miss!

THE STEP-DAUGHTER [*head bowed down slightly, with restrained disgust*]. Good afternoon!

THE FATHER [*looks under her hat which partly covers her face. Perceiving she is very young, he makes an exclamation, partly of surprise, partly of fear lest he compromise himself in a risky adventure.*] Ah . . . but . . . ah . . . I say . . . this is not the first time that you have come here, is it?

THE STEP-DAUGHTER [*modestly*]. No sir.

THE FATHER. You've been here before, eh? [*Then seeing her nod agreement.*] More than once?

[*Waits for her to answer, looks under her hat, smiles, and then says:*] Well then, there's no need to be so shy, is there? May I take off your hat?

THE STEP-DAUGHTER [*anticipating him and with veiled disgust*]. No sir . . . I'll do it myself. [*Takes it off quickly.*]

[*The* MOTHER, *who watches the progress of the scene with the* SON *and the other two children who cling to her, is on thorns; and follows with varying expressions of sorrow, indignation, anxiety, and horror the words and actions of the other two. From time to time she hides her face in her hands and sobs.*]

THE MOTHER. Oh, my God, my God!

THE FATHER [*playing his part with a touch of gallantry*]. Give it to me! I'll put it down. [*Takes hat from her hands.*] But a dear little head like yours ought to have a smarter hat. Come and help me choose one from the stock, won't you?

L'INGÉNUE [*interrupting*]. I say . . . those are our hats you know.

THE MANAGER [*furious*]. Silence! silence! Don't try and be funny, if you please . . . We're playing the scene now I'd have you notice. [*To the* STEP-DAUGHTER.] Begin again, please!

THE STEP-DAUGHTER [*continuing*]. No thank you, sir.

THE FATHER. Oh, come now. Don't talk like that. You must take it. I shall be upset if you don't. There are some lovely little hats here; and then— Madame will be pleased. She expects it, anyway, you know.

THE STEP-DAUGHTER. No, no! I couldn't wear it!

THE FATHER. Oh, you're thinking about what they'd say at home if they saw you come in with a new hat? My dear girl, there's always a way round these little matters, you know.

THE STEP-DAUGHTER [*all keyed up*]. No, it's not that. I couldn't wear it because I am . . . as you see . . . you might have noticed . . . [*Showing her black dress.*]

THE FATHER. . . . in mourning! Of course: I beg your pardon: I'm frightfully sorry . . .

THE STEP-DAUGHTER [*forcing herself to conquer her indignation and nausea*]. Stop! Stop! It's I who must thank you. There's no need for you to feel mortified or specially sorry. Don't think any more of what I've said. [*Tries to smile.*] I must forget that I am dressed so . . .

THE MANAGER [*interrupting and turning to the* PROMPTER]. Stop a minute! Stop! Don't write that down. Cut out that last bit. [*Then to the* FATHER *and* STEP-DAUGHTER.] Fine! it's going fine! [*To the* FATHER *only.*] And now you can go on as we arranged. [*To the* ACTORS.] Pretty good that scene, where he offers her the hat, eh?

THE STEP-DAUGHTER. The best's coming now. Why can't we go on?

THE MANAGER. Have a little patience! [*To the* ACTORS.] Of course, it must be treated rather lightly.

LEADING MAN. Still, with a bit of go in it!

LEADING LADY. Of course! It's easy enough! [*To* LEADING MAN.] Shall you and I try it now?

LEADING MAN. Why, yes! I'll prepare my entrance.

[*Exit in order to make his entrance.*]

THE MANAGER [*to* LEADING LADY]. See here! The scene between you and Madame Pace is finished. I'll have it written out properly after. You remain here . . . oh, where are you going?

LEADING LADY. One minute. I want to put my hat on again.

[*Goes over to hat-rack and puts her hat on her head.*]

THE MANAGER. Good! You stay here with your head bowed down a bit.

THE STEP-DAUGHTER. But she isn't dressed in black.

LEADING LADY. But I shall be, and much more effectively than you.

THE MANAGER [*to* STEP-DAUGHTER]. Be quiet please, and watch! You'll be able to learn something. [*Clapping his hands.*] Come on! come on! Entrance, please!

[*The door at rear of stage opens, and the* LEADING MAN *enters with the lively manner of an old gallant. The rendering of the scene by the* ACTORS *from the very first words is seen to be quite a different thing, though it has not in any way the air of a parody. Naturally, the* STEP-DAUGHTER *and the* FATHER, *not being able to recognize themselves in the* LEADING LADY *and the* LEADING MAN, *who deliver their words in different tones and with a different psychology, express, sometimes with smiles, sometimes with gestures, the impression they receive.*]

LEADING MAN. Good afternoon, Miss . . .

THE FATHER [*at once unable to contain himself*]. No! no!

[*The* STEP-DAUGHTER *noticing the way the* LEADING MAN *enters, bursts out laughing.*]

THE MANAGER [*furious*]. Silence! And you please just stop that laughing. If we go on like this, we shall never finish.

THE STEP-DAUGHTER. Forgive me, sir, but it's natural enough. This lady [*indicating* LEADING LADY] stands there still; but if she is supposed to be me, I can assure you that if I heard anyone say "Good afternoon" in that manner and in that tone, I should burst out laughing as I did.

THE FATHER. Yes, yes, the manner, the tone . . .

THE MANAGER. Nonsense! Rubbish! Stand aside and let me see the action.

LEADING MAN. If I've got to represent an old fellow who's coming into a house of an equivocal character . . .

THE MANAGER. Don't listen to them, for Heaven's sake! Do it again! It goes fine. [*Waiting for the* ACTORS *to begin again.*] Well?

LEADING MAN. Good afternoon, Miss.

LEADING LADY. Good afternoon.

LEADING MAN [*imitating the gesture of the* FATHER *when he looked under the hat, and then expressing quite clearly first satisfaction and then fear*]. Ah, but . . . I say . . . this is not the first time that you have come here, is it?

THE MANAGER. Good, but not quite so heavily. Like this. [*Acts himself.*] "This isn't the first time that you have come here" . . . [*To* LEADING LADY.] And you say: "No, sir."

LEADING LADY. No sir.

LEADING MAN. You've been here before, more than once.

THE MANAGER. No, no, stop! Let her nod "yes" first. "You've been here before, eh?"

[*The* LEADING LADY *lifts up her head slightly and closes her eyes as though in disgust. Then she inclines her head twice.*]

THE STEP-DAUGHTER [*unable to contain herself*]. Oh my God! [*Puts a hand to her mouth to prevent herself from laughing.*]

THE MANAGER [*turning round*]. What's the matter?

THE STEP-DAUGHTER. Nothing, nothing!

THE MANAGER [*to* LEADING MAN]. Go on!

LEADING MAN. You've been here before, eh? Well then, there's no need to be so shy, is there? May I take off your hat?

[*The* LEADING MAN *says this last speech in such a tone and with such gestures that the* STEP-DAUGHTER, *though she has her hand to her mouth, cannot keep from laughing.*]

LEADING LADY [*indignant*]. I'm not going to stop here to be made a fool of by that woman there.

LEADING MAN. Neither am I! I'm through with it!

THE MANAGER [*shouting to* STEP-DAUGHTER]. Silence! for once and all, I tell you!

THE STEP-DAUGHTER. Forgive me! forgive me!

THE MANAGER. You haven't any manners: that's what it is! You go too far.

THE FATHER [*endeavoring to intervene*]. Yes, it's true, but excuse her . . .

THE MANAGER. Excuse what? It's absolutely disgusting.

THE FATHER. Yes, sir, but believe me, it has such a strange effect when . . .

THE MANAGER. Strange? Why strange? Where is it strange?

THE FATHER. No, sir; I admire your actors—this gentleman here, this lady; but they are certainly not us!

THE MANAGER. I should hope not. Evidently they cannot be you, if they are actors.

THE FATHER. Just so: actors! Both of them act our parts exceedingly well. But, believe me, it produces quite a different effect on us. They want to be us, but they aren't, all the same.

THE MANAGER. What is it then anyway?

THE FATHER. Something that is . . . that is theirs—and no longer ours . . .

THE MANAGER. But naturally, inevitably. I've told you so already.

THE FATHER. Yes, I understand . . . I understand . . .

THE MANAGER. Well then, let's have no more of it! [*Turning to the* ACTORS.] We'll have the rehearsals by ourselves, afterward, in the ordinary way. I never could stand rehearsing with the author present. He's never satisfied! [*Turning to* FATHER *and* STEP-DAUGHTER.] Come on! Let's get on with it again; and try and see if you can't keep from laughing.

THE STEP-DAUGHTER. Oh, I shan't laugh any more. There's a nice little bit coming for me now: you'll see.

THE MANAGER. Well then: when she says "Don't think any more of what I've said. I must forget, etc.," you [*addressing the* FATHER] come in sharp with "I understand, I understand;" and then you ask her . . .

THE STEP-DAUGHTER [*interrupting*]. What?

THE MANAGER. Why she is in mourning.

THE STEP-DAUGHTER. Not at all! See here: when I told him that it was useless for me to be thinking about my wearing mourning, do you know how he answered me? "Ah well," he said, "then let's take off this little frock."

THE MANAGER. Great! Just what we want, to make a riot in the theater!

THE STEP-DAUGHTER. But it's the truth!

THE MANAGER. What does that matter? Acting is our business here. Truth up to a certain point, but no further.

THE STEP-DAUGHTER. What do you want to do then?

THE MANAGER. You'll see, you'll see! Leave it to me.

THE STEP-DAUGHTER. No sir! What you want to do is to piece together a little romantic sentimental scene out of my disgust, out of all the reasons, each more cruel and viler than the other, why I am what I am. He is to ask me why I'm in mourning; and I'm to answer with tears in my eyes, that it is just two months since papa died. No sir, no! He's got to say to me; as he did say: "Well, let's take off this little dress at once." And I; with my two months' mourning in my heart, went there behind that screen, and with these fingers tingling with shame . . .

THE MANAGER [*running his hands through his hair*]. For Heaven's sake! What are you saying?

THE STEP-DAUGHTER [*crying out excitedly*]. The truth! The truth!

THE MANAGER. It may be. I don't deny it, and I can understand all your horror; but you must surely see that you can't have this kind of thing on the stage. It won't go.

THE STEP-DAUGHTER. Not possible, eh? Very well! I'm much obliged to you—but I'm off!

THE MANAGER. Now be reasonable! Don't lose your temper!

THE STEP-DAUGHTER. I won't stop here! I won't! I can see you've fixed it all up with him in your office. All this talk about what is possible for the stage . . . I understand! He wants to get at his complicated "cerebral drama," to have his famous remorses and torments acted; but I want to act my part, *my part!*

THE MANAGER [*annoyed, shaking his shoulders*]. Ah! Just *your* part! But, if you will pardon me, there are other parts than yours: His [*indicating the* FATHER] and hers! [*indicating the* MOTHER]. On the stage you can't have a character becoming too prominent and overshadowing all the others. The thing is to pack them all into a neat little framework and then act what is actable. I am aware of the fact that everyone has his own interior life which he wants very much to put forward. But the difficulty lies in this fact: to set out just so much as is necessary for the stage, taking the other characters into consideration, and at the same time hint at the unrevealed interior life of each. I am willing to admit, my dear young lady, that from your point of view it would be a fine idea if each character could tell the public all his troubles in a nice monologue or a regular one hour lecture. [*Good humoredly.*] You must restrain yourself, my dear, and in your own interest, too; because this fury of yours, this exaggerated disgust you show, may make a bad impression, you know. After you have confessed to me that there were others before him at Madame Pace's and more than once . . .

THE STEP-DAUGHTER [*bowing her head, impressed*]. It's true. But remember those others mean him for me all the same.

THE MANAGER [*not understanding*]. What? The others? What do you mean?

THE STEP-DAUGHTER. For one who has gone wrong, sir, he who was responsible for the first fault is responsible for all that follow. He is responsible for my faults, was, even before I was born. Look at him, and see if it isn't true!

THE MANAGER. Well, well! And does the weight of so much responsibility seem nothing to you? Give him a chance to act it, to get it over!

THE STEP-DAUGHTER. How? How can he act all his "noble remorses," all his "moral torments," if you want to spare him the horror of being discovered one day—after he had asked her what he did ask her—in the arms of her, that already fallen woman, that child, sir, that child he used to watch come out of school? [*She is moved.*]

[*The* MOTHER *at this point is overcome with emotion, and breaks out into a fit of crying. All are touched. A long pause.*]

THE STEP-DAUGHTER [*as soon as the* MOTHER *becomes a little quieter, adds resolutely and gravely*]. At present, we are unknown to the public. To-morrow, you will act us as you wish, treating us in your own manner. But do you really want to see drama, do you want to see it flash out as it really did?

THE MANAGER. Of course! That's just what I do want, so I can use as much of it as is possible.

THE STEP-DAUGHTER. Well then, ask that Mother there to leave us.

THE MOTHER [*changing her low plaint into a sharp cry*]. No! No! Don't permit it, sir, don't permit it!

THE MANAGER. But it's only to try it.

THE MOTHER. I can't bear it. I can't.

THE MANAGER. But since it has happened already . . . I don't understand!

THE MOTHER. It's taking place now. It happens all the time. My torment isn't a pretended one. I live and feel every minute of my torture. Those two children there—have you heard them speak? They can't speak anymore. They cling to me to keep up my torment actual and vivid for me. But for themselves, they do not exist, they aren't anymore. And she [*indicating the* STEP-DAUGHTER] has run away, she has left me, and is lost. If I now see her here before me, it is only to renew for me the tortures I have suffered for her too.

THE FATHER. The eternal moment! She [*indicating the* STEP-DAUGHTER] is here to catch me, fix me, and hold me eternally in the stocks for that one fleeting and shameful moment of my life. She can't give it up! And you sir, cannot either fairly spare me it.

THE MANAGER. I never said I didn't want to act it. It will form, as a matter of fact, the nucleus of the whole first act right up to her surprise. [*Indicates the* MOTHER.]

THE FATHER. Just so! This is my punishment: the passion in all of us that must culminate in her final cry.

THE STEP-DAUGHTER. I can hear it still in my ears. It's driven me mad, that cry!—You can put me on as you like; it doesn't matter. Fully dressed, if you like—provided I have at least the arm bare; because, standing like this [*she goes close to the* FATHER *and leans her head on his breast*] with my head so, and my arms round his neck, I saw a vein pulsing in my arm here; and then, as if that live vein had awakened disgust in me, I closed my eyes like this, and let my head sink on his breast. [*Turning to the* MOTHER.] Cry out mother! Cry out!

[*Buries head in* FATHER'S *breast, and with her shoulders raised as if to prevent her hearing the cry, adds in tones of intense emotion:*] Cry out as you did then!

THE MOTHER [*coming forward to separate them*]. No! My daughter, my daughter! [*And after having pulled her away from him.*] You brute! you brute! She is my daughter! Don't you see she's my daughter?

THE MANAGER [*walking backward toward footlights*]. Fine! fine! Damned good! And then, of course—curtain!

THE FATHER [*going toward him excitedly*]. Yes, of course, because that's the way it really happened.

THE MANAGER [*convinced and pleased*]. Oh, yes, no doubt about it. Curtain here, curtain!

[*At the reiterated cry of the* MANAGER, *the* MACHINIST *lets the curtain down, leaving the* MANAGER *and the* FATHER *in front of it before the footlights.*]

THE MANAGER. The darned idiot! I said "curtain" to show the act should end there, and he goes and lets it down in earnest. [*To the* FATHER, *while he pulls the curtain back to go on to the stage again.*] Yes, yes, it's all right. Effect certain! That's the right ending. I'll guarantee the first act at any rate.

ACT THREE

When the curtain goes up again, it is seen that the stage hands have shifted the bit of scenery used in the last part, and have rigged up instead at the back of the stage a drop, with some trees, and one or two wings. A portion of a fountain basin is visible. The MOTHER *is sitting on the right with the two children by her side. The* SON *is on the same side, but away from the others. He seems bored, angry, and full of shame. The* FATHER *and the* STEP-DAUGHTER *are also seated toward the right front. On the other side (left) are the* ACTORS, *much in the positions they occupied before the curtain was lowered. Only the* MANAGER *is standing up in the middle of the stage, with his hand closed over his mouth in the act of meditating.*

THE MANAGER [*shaking his shoulders after a brief pause*]. Ah yes: the second act! Leave it to me, leave it all to me as we arranged, and you'll see! It'll go fine!

THE STEP-DAUGHTER. Our entry into his house [*indicates* FATHER] in spite of him . . . [*Indicates the* SON.]

THE MANAGER [*out of patience*]. Leave it to me, I tell you!

THE STEP-DAUGHTER. Do let it be clear, at any rate, that it is in spite of my wishes.

THE MOTHER [*from her corner, shaking her head*]. For all the good that's come of it . . .

THE STEP-DAUGHTER [*turning toward her quickly*]. It doesn't matter. The more harm done us, the more remorse for him.

THE MANAGER [*impatiently*]. I understand! Good Heavens! I understand! I'm taking it into account.

THE MOTHER [*supplicatingly*]. I beg you, sir, to let it appear quite plain that for conscience' sake I did try in every way . . .

THE STEP-DAUGHTER [*interrupting indignantly and continuing for the* MOTHER]. . . . to pacify me, to dissuade me from spiting him. [*To* MANAGER.] Do as she wants: satisfy her, because it is true! I enjoy it immensely. Anyhow, as you can see, the meeker she is, the more she tries to get at his heart, the more distant and aloof does he become.

THE MANAGER. Are we going to begin this second act or not?

THE STEP-DAUGHTER. I'm not going to talk anymore now. But I must tell you this: you can't have the whole action take place in the garden, as you suggest. It isn't possible!

THE MANAGER. Why not?

THE STEP-DAUGHTER. Because he [*indicates the* SON *again*] is always shut up alone in his room. And then there's all the part of that poor dazed-looking boy there which takes place indoors.

THE MANAGER. Maybe! On the other hand, you will understand—we can't change scenes three or four times in one act.

LEADING MAN. They used to once.

THE MANAGER. Yes, when the public was up to the level of that child there.

LEADING LADY. It makes the illusion easier.

THE FATHER [*irritated*]. The illusion! For Heaven's sake, don't say illusion. Please don't use that word, which is particularly painful for us.

THE MANAGER [*astounded*]. And why, if you please?

THE FATHER. It's painful, cruel, really cruel; and you ought to understand that.

THE MANAGER. But why? What ought we to say then? The illusion, I tell you, sir, which we've got to create for the audience . . .

LEADING MAN. With our acting.

THE MANAGER. The illusion of a reality.

THE FATHER. I understand; but you, perhaps, do not understand us. Forgive me! You see . . . here for you and your actors, the thing is only—and rightly so . . . a kind of game . . .

LEADING LADY [*interrupting indignantly*]. A game! We're not children here, if you please! We are serious actors.

THE FATHER. I don't deny it. What I mean is the game, or play, of your art, which has to give, as the gentleman says, a perfect illusion of reality.

THE MANAGER. Precisely—!

THE FATHER. Now, if you consider the fact that we [*indicates himself and the other five* CHARACTERS], as we are, have no other reality outside of this illusion . . .

THE MANAGER [*astonished, looking at his* ACTORS, *who are also amazed*]. And what does that mean?

THE FATHER [*after watching them for a moment with a wan smile*]. As I say, sir, that which is a game of art for you is our sole reality.

[*Brief pause. He goes a step or two nearer the* MANAGER *and adds*:] But not only for us, you know, by the way. Just you think it over well. [*Looks him in the eyes.*] Can you tell me who you are?

THE MANAGER [*perplexed, half-smiling*]. What? Who am I? I am myself.

THE FATHER. And if I were to tell you that that isn't true, because you and I . . . ?

THE MANAGER. I should say you were mad—! [*The* ACTORS *laugh.*]

THE FATHER. You're quite right to laugh: because we are all making believe here. [*To* MANAGER.] And you can therefore object that it's only for a joke that that gentleman there [*indicates the* LEADING MAN], who naturally is himself, has to be me, who am on the contrary myself—this thing you see here. You see I've caught you in a trap! [*The* ACTORS *laugh.*]

THE MANAGER [*annoyed*]. But we've had all this over once before. Do you want to begin again?

THE FATHER. No, no! That wasn't my meaning! In fact, I should like to request you to abandon this game of art [*looking at the* LEADING LADY *as if anticipating her*] which you are accustomed to play here with your actors, and to ask you seriously once again: who are you?

THE MANAGER [*astonished and irritated, turning to his* ACTORS]. If this fellow here hasn't got a nerve! A man who calls himself a character comes and asks me who I am!

THE FATHER [*with dignity, but not offended*]. A character, sir, may always ask a man who he is. Because a character has really a life of his own, marked with his especial characteristics; for which reason he is always "somebody." But a man—I'm not speaking of you now—may very well be "nobody."

THE MANAGER. Yes, but you are asking these questions of me, the boss, the manager! Do you understand?

THE FATHER. But only in order to know if you, as you really are now, see yourself as you once were with all the illusions that were yours then, with all the things both inside and outside of you as they seemed to you— as they were then indeed for you. Well, sir, if you think of all those illusions that mean nothing to you now, of all those things which don't even *seem* to you to exist anymore, while once they *were* for you, don't you feel that—I won't say these boards—but the very earth under your feet is sinking away from you when you reflect that in the same way this *you* as you feel it today—all this present reality of yours—is fated to seem a mere illusion to you tomorrow?

THE MANAGER [*without having understood much, but astonished by the specious argument*]. Well, well! And where does all this take us anyway?

THE FATHER. Oh, nowhere! It's only to show you that if we [*indicating the* CHARACTERS] have no other reality beyond the illusion, you too must not count overmuch on your reality as you feel it today, since, like that of yesterday, it may prove an illusion for you tomorrow.

THE MANAGER [*determining to make fun of him*]. Ah, excellent! Then you'll be saying next that you, with this comedy of yours that you brought here to act, are truer and more real than I am.

THE FATHER [*with the greatest seriousness*]. But of course; without doubt!

THE MANAGER. Ah, really?

THE FATHER. Why, I thought you'd understand that from the beginning.

THE MANAGER. More real than I?

THE FATHER. If your reality can change from one day to another . . .

THE MANAGER. But everyone knows it can change. It is always changing, the same as anyone else's.

THE FATHER [*with a cry*]. No, sir, not ours! Look here! That is the very difference! Our reality doesn't change: it can't change! It can't be other than what it is, because it is already fixed for ever. It's terrible. Ours is an immutable reality which should make you shudder when you approach us if you are really conscious of the fact that your reality is a mere transitory and fleeting illusion, taking this form today and that tomorrow, according to the conditions, according to your will, your sentiments, which in turn are controlled by an intellect that shows them to you today in one manner and tomorrow . . . who knows how? . . . Illusions of reality represented in this fatuous comedy of life that never ends, nor can ever end! Because if tomorrow it were to end . . . then why, all would be finished.

THE MANAGER. Oh for God's sake, will you *at least* finish with this philosophizing and let us try and shape this comedy which you yourself have brought me here? You argue and philosophize a bit too much, my dear sir. You know you seem to me almost, almost . . . [*Stops and looks him over from head to foot.*] Ah, by the way, I think you introduced yourself to me as a—what shall . . . we say—a "character," created by an author who did not afterward care to make a drama of his own creations.

THE FATHER. It is the simple truth, sir.

THE MANAGER. Nonsense! Cut that out, please! None of us believes it, because it isn't a thing, as you must recognize yourself, which one can believe seriously. If you want to know, it seems to me you are trying to imitate the manner of a certain author whom I heartily detest—I warn you—although I have unfortunately bound myself to put on one of his works. As a matter of fact, I was just starting to rehearse it, when you arrived. [*Turning to the* ACTORS.] And this is what we've gained—out of the frying-pan into the fire!

THE FATHER. I don't know to what author you may be alluding, but believe me I feel what I think; and I seem to be philosophizing only for those who do not think what they feel, because they blind themselves with their own sentiment. I know that for many people this self-blinding seems much more "human"; but the contrary is really true. For man never reasons so much and becomes so introspective as when he suffers; since he is anxious to get at the cause of his sufferings, to learn who has produced them, and whether it is just or unjust that he should have to bear them. On the other hand, when he is happy, he takes his happiness as it comes and doesn't analyze it, just as if happiness were his right. The animals suffer without reasoning about their sufferings. But take the case of a man who suffers and begins to reason about it. Oh no! it can't be allowed! Let him suffer like an animal, and then—ah yet, he is "human"!

THE MANAGER. Look here! Look here! You're off again, philosophizing worse than ever.

THE FATHER. Because I suffer, sir! I'm not philosophizing: I'm crying aloud the reason of my sufferings.

THE MANAGER [*makes brusque movement as he is taken with a new idea*]. I should like to know if anyone has ever heard of a character who gets right out of his part and perorates and speechifies as you do. Have you ever heard of a case? I haven't.

THE FATHER. You have never met such a case, sir, because authors, as a rule, hide the labor of their creations. When the characters are really alive before their author, the latter does nothing but follow them in their action, in their words, in the situations which they suggest to him; and he has to will them the way they will themselves—for there's trouble if he doesn't. When a character is born, he acquires at once such an independence, even of his own author, that he can be imagined by everybody even in many other situations where the author never dreamed of placing him; and so he acquires for himself a meaning which the author never thought of giving him.

THE MANAGER. Yes, yes, I know this.

THE FATHER. What is there then to marvel at in us? Imagine such a misfortune for characters as I have described to you: to be born of an author's fantasy, and be denied life by him; and then answer me if these characters left alive, and yet without life, weren't right in doing what they did do and are doing now, after they have attempted everything in their power to persuade him to give them their stage life. We've all tried him in turn, I, she [*indicating the* STEP-DAUGHTER] and she [*indicating the* MOTHER].

THE STEP-DAUGHTER. It's true. I too have sought to tempt him, many, many times, when he has been sitting at his writing table, feeling a bit melancholy, at the twilight hour. He would sit in his armchair too lazy to switch on the light, and all the shadows that crept into his room were full of our presence coming to tempt him. [*As if she saw herself still there by the writing table, and was annoyed by the presence of the* ACTORS.] Oh. if you would only go away, go away and leave us alone—mother here with that son of hers—I with that Child—that Boy there always alone—and then I with him [*just hints at the* FATHER]—and then I alone, alone . . . in those shadows!

[*Makes a sudden movement as if in the vision she has of herself illuminating those shadows she wanted to seize hold of herself.*]

Ah! my life! my life! Oh, what scenes we proposed to him—and I tempted him more than any of the others!

THE FATHER. Maybe. But perhaps it was your fault that he refused to give us life: because you were too insistent, too troublesome.

THE STEP-DAUGHTER. Nonsense! Didn't he make me so himself?

[*Goes close to the* MANAGER *to tell him as if in confidence.*]

In my opinion he abandoned us in a fit of depression, of disgust for the ordinary theater as the public knows it and likes it.

THE SON. Exactly what it was, sir; exactly that!

THE FATHER. Not at all! Don't believe it for a minute. Listen to me! You'll be doing quite right to modify, as you suggest, the excesses both of this girl here, who wants to do too much, and of this young man, who won't do anything at all.

THE SON. No, nothing!

THE MANAGER. You too get over the mark occasionally, my dear sir, if I may say so.

THE FATHER. I? When? Where?

THE MANAGER. Always! Continuously! Then there's this insistence of yours in trying to make us believe you are a character. And then too, you must really argue and philosophize less, you know, much less.

THE FATHER. Well, if you want to take away from me the possibility of representing the torment of my spirit which never gives me peace, you will be suppressing me: that's all. Every true man, sir, who is a little above the level of the beasts and plants does not live for the sake of living, without knowing how to live; but he lives so as to give a meaning and a value of his own to life. For me this is *everything*. I cannot give up this, just to represent a mere fact as she [*indicating the* STEP-DAUGHTER] wants. It's all very well for her, since her "vendetta" lies in the "fact." I'm not going to do it. It destroys my *raison d'être*.

THE MANAGER. Your *raison d'être*! Oh, we're going ahead fine! First she starts off, and then you jump in. At this rate, we'll never finish.

THE FATHER. Now, don't be offended! Have it your own way—provided, however, that within the limits of the parts you assign us each one's sacrifice isn't too great.

THE MANAGER. You've got to understand that you can't go on arguing at your own pleasure. Drama is action, sir, action and not confounded philosophy.

THE FATHER. All right. I'll do just as much arguing and philosophizing as everybody does when he is considering his own torments.

THE MANAGER. If the drama permits! But for Heaven's sake, man, let's get along and come to the scene.

THE STEP-DAUGHTER. It seems to me we've got too much action with our coming into his house. [*Indicating* FATHER.] You said, before, you couldn't change the scene every five minutes.

THE MANAGER. Of course not. What we've got to do is to combine and group up all the facts in one simultaneous, close-knit, action. We can't have it as you want, with your little brother wandering like a ghost from room to room, hiding behind doors and meditating a project which— what did you say it did to him?

THE STEP-DAUGHTER. Consumes him, sir, wastes him away!

THE MANAGER. Well, it may be. And then at the same time, you want the little girl there to be playing in the garden . . . one in the house, and the other in the garden: isn't that it?

THE STEP-DAUGHTER. Yes, in the sun, in the sun! That is my only pleasure: to see her happy and careless in the garden after the misery and squalor of the horrible room where we all four slept together. And I had to sleep with her—I, do you understand?—with my vile contaminated body next to hers; with her folding me fast in her loving little arms. In the garden, whenever she spied me, she would run to take me by the hand. She didn't care for the big flowers, only the little ones; and she loved to show me them and pet me.

THE MANAGER. Well then, we'll have it in the garden. Everything shall happen in the garden; and we'll group the other scenes there. [*Calls a* STAGE HAND.] Here, a backcloth with trees and something to do as a fountain basin. [*Turning round to look at the·back of the stage.*] Ah, you've fixed it up. Good! [*To* STEP-DAUGHTER.] This is just to give an idea, of course. The Boy, instead of hiding behind the doors, will wander about here in the garden, hiding behind the trees. But it's going to be rather difficult to find a child to do that scene with you where she shows you the flowers. [*Turning to the* BOY.] Come forward a little, will you please? Let's try it now! Come along! come along! [*Then seeing him come shyly forward, full of fear and looking lost.*] It's a nice business, this lad here. What's the matter with him? We'll have to give him a word or two to say. [*Goes close to him, puts a hand on his shoulders, and leads him behind one of the trees.*] Come on! come on! Let me see you a little! Hide here . . . yes, like that. Try and show your head just a little as if you were looking for someone . . . [*Goes back to observe the effect, when the* BOY *at once goes through the action.*]

Excellent! fine! [*Turning to* STEP-DAUGHTER.] Suppose the little girl there were to surprise him as he looks round, and run over to him, so we could give him a word or two to say?

THE STEP-DAUGHTER. It's useless to hope he will speak, as long as that fellow there is here . . . [*Indicates the* SON.] You must send him away first.

THE SON [*jumping up*]. Delighted! Delighted! I don't ask for anything better. [*Begins to move away.*]

THE MANAGER [*at once stopping him*]. No! No! Where are you going? Wait a bit!

[*The* MOTHER *gets up alarmed and terrified at the thought that he is really about to go away. Instinctively she lifts her arms to prevent him, without, however, leaving her seat.*]

THE SON [*to* MANAGER *who stops him*]. I've got nothing to do with this affair. Let me go please! Let me go!

THE MANAGER. What do you mean by saying you've got nothing to do with this?

THE STEP-DAUGHTER [*calmly, with irony*]. Don't bother to stop him: he won't go away.

THE FATHER. He has to act the terrible scene in the garden with his mother.

THE SON [*suddenly resolute and with dignity*]. I shall act nothing at all. I've said so from the very beginning. [*To the* MANAGER.] Let me go!

THE STEP-DAUGHTER [*going over to the* MANAGER]. Allow me?

[*Puts down the* MANAGER'S *arm which is restraining the* SON.]

Well, go away then, if you want to!

[*The* SON *looks at her with contempt and hatred. She laughs and says:*]

You see, he can't, he can't go away! He is obliged to stay here, indissolubly bound to the chain. If I, who fly off when that happens which has to happen, because I can't bear him—if I am still here and support that face and expression of his, you can well imagine that he is unable to move. He has to remain here, has to stop with that nice father of his, and that mother whose only son he is. [*Turning to the* MOTHER.] Come on, mother, come along! [*Turning to* MANAGER *to indicate her.*] You see, she was getting up to keep him back. [*To the* MOTHER, *beckoning her with her hand.*] Come on! come on! [*Then to* MANAGER.] You can imagine how little she wants to show these actors of yours what she really feels; but so eager is she to get near him that . . . There, you see? She is willing to act her part.

[*And in fact, the* MOTHER *approaches him; and as soon as the* STEP-DAUGHTER *has finished speaking, opens her arms to signify that she consents.*]

THE SON [*suddenly*]. No! no! If I can't go away, then I'll stop here; but I repeat: I act nothing!

THE FATHER [*to* MANAGER *excitedly*]. You can force him, sir.

THE SON. Nobody can force me.

THE FATHER. I can.

THE STEP-DAUGHTER. Wait a minute, wait . . . First of all, the baby has to go to the fountain . . .

[*Runs to take the* CHILD *and leads her to the fountain.*]

THE MANAGER. Yes, yes of course; that's it. Both at the same time.

[*The* SECOND LADY LEAD *and the* JUVENILE LEAD *at this point separate themselves from the group of* ACTORS. *One watches the* MOTHER *attentively; the other moves about studying the movements and manner of the* SON *whom he will have to act.*]

THE SON [*to* MANAGER]. What do you mean by both at the same time? It isn't right. There was no scene between me and her. [*Indicates the* MOTHER.] Ask her how it was!

THE MOTHER. Yes, it's true. I had come into his room . . .

THE SON. Into my room, do you understand? Nothing to do with the garden.

THE MANAGER. It doesn't matter. Haven't I told you we've got to group the action?

THE SON [*observing the* JUVENILE LEAD *studying him*]. What do you want?

JUVENILE LEAD. Nothing! I was just looking at you.

THE SON [*turning toward the* SECOND LADY LEAD]. Ah! she's at it too: to re-act her part! [*Indicating the* MOTHER.]

THE MANAGER. Exactly! And it seems to me that you ought to be grateful to them for their interest.

THE SON. Yes, but haven't you yet perceived that it isn't possible to live in front of a mirror which not only freezes us with the image of ourselves, but throws our likeness back at us with a horrible grimace?

THE FATHER. That is true, absolutely true. You must see that.

THE MANAGER [*to* SECOND LADY LEAD *and* JUVENILE LEAD]. He's right! Move away from them!

THE SON. Do as you like. I'm out of this!

THE MANAGER. Be quiet, you, will you? And let me hear your mother! [*To* MOTHER.] You were saying you had entered . . .

THE MOTHER. Yes, into his room, because I couldn't stand it any longer. I went to empty my heart to him of all the anguish that tortures me . . . But as soon as he saw me come in . . .

THE SON. Nothing happened! There was no scene. I went away, that's all! I don't care for scenes!

THE MOTHER. It's true, true. That's how it was.

THE MANAGER. Well now, we've got to do this bit between you and him. It's indispensable.

THE MOTHER. I'm ready . . . when you are ready. If you could only find a chance for me to tell him what I feel here in my heart.

THE FATHER [*going to* SON *in a great rage*]. You'll do this for your mother, for your mother, do you understand?

THE SON [*quite determined*]. I do nothing!

THE FATHER [*taking hold of him and shaking him*]. For God's sake, do as I tell you! Don't you hear your mother asking you for a favor? Haven't you even got the guts to be a son?

THE SON [*taking hold of the* FATHER]. No! No! And for God's sake stop it, or else . . .

[*General agitation. The* MOTHER, *frightened, tries to separate them.*]

THE MOTHER [*pleading*]. Please! please!

THE FATHER [*not leaving hold of the* SON]. You've got to obey, do you hear?

THE SON [*almost crying from rage*]. What does it mean, this madness you've got? [*They separate.*] Have you no decency, that you insist on showing everyone our shame? I won't do it! I won't! And I stand for the will of our author in this. He didn't want to put us on the stage, after all!

THE MANAGER. Man alive! You came here . . .

THE SON [*indicating* FATHER]. *He* did! I didn't!

THE MANAGER. Aren't you here now?

THE SON. It was his wish, and he dragged us along with him. He's told you not only the things that did happen, but also things that have never happened at all.

THE MANAGER. Well, tell me then what did happen. You went out of your room without saying a word?

THE SON. Without a word, so as to avoid a scene!

THE MANAGER. And then what did you do?

THE SON. Nothing . . . walking in the garden . . . [*Hesitates for a moment with expression of gloom.*]

THE MANAGER [*coming closer to him, interested by his extraordinary reserve*]. Well, well . . . walking in the garden . . .

THE SON [*exasperated*]. Why on earth do you insist? It's horrible!

[*The* MOTHER *trembles, sobs, and looks toward the fountain.*]

THE MANAGER [*slowly observing the glance and turning toward the* SON *with increasing apprehension*]. The baby?

THE SON. There in the fountain . . .

THE FATHER [*pointing with tender pity to the* MOTHER]. She was following him at the moment . . .

THE MANAGER [*to the* SON *anxiously*]. And then you . . .

THE SON. I ran over to her; I was jumping in to drag her out when I saw something that froze my blood . . . the boy standing stock still, with eyes like a madman's, watching his little drowned sister, in the fountain! [*The* STEP-DAUGHTER *bends over the fountain to hide the* CHILD. *She sobs.*] Then . . . [*A revolver shot rings out behind the trees where the* BOY *is hidden.*]

THE MOTHER [*with a cry of terror runs over in that direction together with several of the* ACTORS *amid general confusion*]. My son! My son! [*Then amid the cries and exclamations one hears her voice.*] Help! Help!

THE MANAGER [*pushing the* ACTORS *aside while they lift up the* BOY *and carry him off*]. Is he really wounded?

SOME ACTORS. He's dead! dead!

OTHER ACTORS. No, no, it's only make believe, it's only pretence!

THE FATHER [*with a terrible cry*]. Pretence? Reality, sir, reality!

THE MANAGER. Pretence? Reality? To hell with it all! Never in my life has such a thing happened to me. I've lost a whole day over these people, a whole day!

APPENDIX

A GLOSSARY
OF DRAMATIC TERMS

by W. David Kay

Act. 1. The major division of modern plays. The action of Greek and Medieval drama was continuous. The division of plays into five acts was adopted by Renaissance dramatists, following a rule laid down by the Roman poet-critic, Horace. In England, act division did not become standard until the middle of the seventeenth century. Many Elizabethan plays, including Shakespeare's, were first carefully divided into acts by later editors. 2. To perform.

Action. 1. Physical movement performed by an actor on the stage. It may be either small or great—the filling of a pipe or the death of the hero—and it may represent a situation or reveal an attitude toward that situation. 2. The forward movement of the plot. 3. An episode or a limited portion of the plot.

Aesthetic distance (psychical distance). The separation between a dramatic work of art and the practical needs and emotions of the spectator. Aesthetic distance involves the recognition that the dramatic performance we experience is different from the pattern of relationships and experiences in which we normally participate. It permits us to experience drama both objectively and with an emotional response of a curious kind. A spectator may become involved in the fate of Othello, for example, without worrying about his own marriage. The term may also be applied to the artist's relationship to his material, in that he may dramatize personal experiences, but only when he is detached from the *purely* personal aspects of them.

Agon (Greek: "contest, struggle"). 1. The conflict between the opposing forces in a play. 2. One of the formal divisions of Old Comedy. See GREEK COMEDY.

Alarum. A call to battle (literally, "to arms"), heard offstage, and indicated by the sound of drums, trumpets, and weapons. It is usually joined with EXCURSIONS or the brief appearance of soldiers running or fighting on stage.

841

Alienation effect (German: *Verfremdungseffekt*). See EPIC DRAMA.

Allegory. A drama in which the actors, and sometimes the setting, represent moral qualities or general concepts. Allegorical action must be understood on two levels: the realistic and the symbolic. One of the most famous allegorical dramas is *Everyman*.

Anagnorisis (Greek: "recognition, disclosure"). 1. The sudden revelation of important information, such as the real identity of a character, which helps to resolve difficulties in the plot. 2. In tragedy, the protagonist's recognition of his faults. See TRAGEDY.

Antagonist. The principal character who opposes the protagonist.

Anticlimax. 1. A descent in the emotional pitch of the action after the tension of the climax, or 2. an event which causes that descent.

Antistrophe. See GREEK TRAGEDY.

Apron. The area of the stage in front of the proscenium arch. It was used as the principal acting area in the seventeenth and earlier eighteenth century.

Arras. The traverse curtain which screened the inner stage in the Elizabethan playhouse.

Aside. Words spoken by an actor which are intended to be heard by the audience but not by the other characters on the stage. Asides are frequently used to indicate irony. See DRAMATIC IRONY.

Backcloth (backdrop). A large flat canvas, suspended at the back of the scene to hide the backstage space. It is usually painted with a landscape or some other background and used in conjunction with wings.

Balcony. 1. Seats above the orchestra section at the rear of the auditorium. 2. The tarras or gallery at the front of the upper stage in the Elizabethan playhouse.

Border. A narrow strip of painted cloth suspended across the front of the stage behind the proscenium arch to hide the flies from the audience's sight.

Bourgeois drama (French: *drame bourgeois*). A type of drama which originated in France in the eighteenth century. Written for and about the middle class, it is serious drama which may end happily. Its primary purpose is moral and didactic, and it stresses the virtues of home life. See DOMESTIC TRAGEDY.

Box. A seating compartment, railed off from the other seating areas in the auditorium and containing chairs rather than fixed seats. Boxes are usually placed at the front of the first balcony or mezzanine.

Box set. An interior setting representing the three walls and the ceiling of a room by means of flats, generally containing workable doors and windows.

Braggart soldier (Latin: *miles gloriosus*). A comic type-character—the military man who boasts vainly of his prowess in battle only to be revealed as a coward in the subsequent action. The character originates with Plautus's memorable sketch of the vain and stupid Pyrgopolynices in *The Braggart Soldier*, and it frequently appears with variations in later drama, most notably as Falstaff in Shakespeare's *Henry IV*, Part I and as Bobadill in Jonson's *Every Man in his Humour*.

Built scenery. Three dimensional scenery such as stairs, elevated platforms, fireplaces, and columns, which are formed by light carpentry or papier-mâché.

Business. The minor physical movements of an actor, such as looking at a watch or powdering one's nose, introduced to add realistic effect to a performance.

Cast. 1. A list of actors and the roles they play. 2. To assign parts to actors.

Catastrophe. See DENOUEMENT.

Catharsis (Greek: *katharsis*). See TRAGEDY.

Cellar (cellarage). The area beneath the stage or acting area, in which the machinery for traps or other stage effects is located.

Character. 1. A personality in a play. 2. The true or inner nature of that personality; the "active essence" of his nature, which contributes to the movement of the plot and the development of the theme.

Choragos/choregos. See GREEK TRAGEDY.

Chorus. 1. In Greek drama, the group of performers who stood aside from the action and commented upon it in choral lyrics to which they danced. Aeschylus employed a chorus of twelve in his tragedy, but Sophocles later increased the number to fifteen. Choruses were originally composed of trained citizens, rather than professional performers, and many of the spectators at the Greek theater would therefore have been in choruses themselves at some time. 2. In Elizabethan and later drama, the speaker of the Prologue.

Chorus character. A character who participates in the action of the play and who comments on it, apparently from the author's point of view, in order to make the significance of the events clear.

Chronicle play. See HISTORY PLAY.

Climax. The point in a play or a scene at which emotional interest or tension is at its highest. This point frequently marks a turn in the protagonist's fortunes.

Clown. A comic character who may be either an amusing simpleton or a professional fool or jester.

Comedy. A dramatic work in which the outcome is favorable to the protagonist. The conflict is usually treated so as to arouse laughter, rather than deep concern, and the resolution of the conflict is generally attended by compromise between the conflicting parties following their recognition of delusion or folly. Although the tone of comedy is essentially lighthearted, it often deals seriously with the effects of such passions as love, anger, or jealousy and with such vices or follies as pride, greed, or prodigality. Aristotle, in his *Poetics*, distinguished between comedy and tragedy on the basis of their subject matter—comedy being concerned with characters of low stature; tragedy, with characters superior to average men—but later ages have not maintained this distinction. See COMEDY OF HUMOURS, COMEDY OF INTRIGUE, COMEDY OF MANNERS, GREEK COMEDY, ROMANTIC COMEDY, SENTIMENTAL COMEDY.

Comedy of Humours. Comedy whose characters are primarily humour characters. See HUMOUR CHARACTER.

Comedy of Intrigue. Comedy whose interest centers in the means by which the protagonist attempts to trick his opponent in order to gain some object, such as money or love. Most Roman comedy is intrigue comedy, and much seventeenth-century comedy, which is frequently indebted to Roman comedy, contains strong intrigue elements.

Comedy of Manners. Comedy which takes as its subject the fashionable life of its time. It depends for its effect on intrigue and witty dialogue, and it is frequently antiromantic.

Comic relief. Humorous scenes inserted into a serious play for the purpose of diminishing tension. In a good play, these are not merely extraneous elements, but contribute to the thematic development by providing illustrations or contrasts to the more serious action. See DRAMATIC METAPHOR.

Complication. 1. The rising action or section of the plot in which the protagonist is opposed. 2. A sudden change of events which presents a new problem for the protagonist.

Confidant (feminine: confidante). A character trusted by the protagonist, to whom the protagonist may reveal past action or future intention. The use of a confidant thus simplifies exposition, establishes standards against which action may be judged, or prepares for later events.

Conflict. The struggle with which the play is concerned between the protagonist and the forces opposing him. This opposition may be provided either by another character (the antagonist), by his own conflicting desires or needs, or by such impersonal forces as environment, fate, or God.

Convention. The tacit agreement between author and audience, based on usage, that certain stage actions correspond to the actual experience of the audience. Every period of the theater has its own conventions. In the Roman theater, one exit commonly led to the country, another to the harbor and forum. In the Elizabethan theater, entrance with a torch was enough to signify night. In the modern theater, we accept the raising and lowering of the curtain as indicative of the passing of time and the convention of the fourth wall. See FOURTH WALL.

Cosmic irony (irony of fate). The term used to denote a situation in which events seem to be manipulated by God, Fate, or some other supernatural being in order to frustrate or mock the protagonist.

Craft cycle. See MYSTERY PLAYS.

Cue. A signal, usually given by the last lines of a speech, which indicates when an actor should speak or act or when a stagehand should perform some duty.

Cup-and-saucer drama (drawing-room drama). Drama set in realistic, contemporary, domestic interior scenes and featuring many ordinary actions, such as serving tea or lighting a pipe, as part of the stage business in order to create an air of realism. It was introduced by the British dramatist, T. W. Robertson, in such plays as *Society* (1865) and *Caste* (1867).

Cyclorama. A curved wall or shell-shaped dome, built at the rear of the stage and used to create the illusion of infinite depth when properly lighted.

Denouement (French: "untieing"). The resolution of the plot, in which the various complications are unraveled and solved. The term catastrophe (Greek: "overturning") is occasionally used in place of denouement.

Deus ex machina. 1. A god lowered by a crane (*mēchanē;* Latin: *machina*) onto the acting area in Greek drama. 2. By extension, any device used to clear up a seemingly insoluble impasse in a plot.

Deuteragonist. See PROTAGONIST.

Dialogue. Lines written to be spoken by two or more actors on the stage.

Diction. 1. The style or manner employed by the actor to deliver his lines. 2. In poetic drama, the choice of words used by the poet.

Dionysos. The Greek god of wine and fertility whose death and sufferings were the subjects of the choral dithyrambs from which tragedy developed. All dramatic performances at Athens were held at two of the festivals in his honor: the Lenaea or Feast of the Wine-vats, which was celebrated about January; and the City Dionysia, which was celebrated in March or April. The first day of the festivals was devoted to a procession through the city streets. The dramatic contests were held on the three succeeding days, with tragic contests presented in the morning and comedies presented in the afternoon. The theater was located on the temple grounds and the priest of Dionysos sat in the seat of honor in the middle of the front row at each performance. See DITHYRAMB, GREEK COMEDY, GREEK TRAGEDY, SATYR-PLAY.

Direct address. A speech in which the actor speaks directly to the audience without pretending to be speaking to himself or another character.

Dithyramb. A Greek choral lyric sung in honor of Dionysos by a chorus of fifty men accompanied by the flute and the lyre.

Domestic tragedy. Tragedy which deals with common people in a setting familiar to the audience. It is concerned with personal and family affairs rather than affairs of state and treats them in a realistic manner. Domestic tragedy exists in England in the late-sixteenth century, but the most famous example of its kind is George Lillo's *The London Merchant* (1731).

Double plot. The use of two plots interwoven throughout a play. One of these (the SUBPLOT) is frequently subordinated to the other and parallels or contrasts with it, as the Gloucester scenes in *King Lear*, for example, provide another illustration of natural and familial disorder similar to that in Lear's own family.

Downstage, down center, down left, down right. Stage directions which indicate the part of the stage in which action takes place. They are relative to the position of an actor facing the audience, and "right" and "left" are the reverse of the point of view of the spectator. The downstage area is the half of the stage nearest the audience; the half of the stage farthest from the audience is upstage.

Drama. 1. The whole body of work written for the theater, or a group of plays related by nationality, chronology, style, or content, as in Roman drama, Elizabethan drama, or the Drama of Ideas. 2. A play. A composition intended to be acted on a stage, in which a story is related by means of dialogue and action. It is important to remember that drama presupposes a theater, actors, and an audience, and that to be fully experienced it must be seen and heard, not merely read.

Drama of Ideas. Plays which are devoted to the discussion of questions of social or moral significance, usually involving persons who are struggling against oppressive customs or institutions. The Drama of Ideas may be divided into PROBLEM PLAYS, which depict the effects of some social problem on a group of characters without proposing a solution, and THESIS PLAYS (French: *pièces à thèse*), which put forth some answer to the problem. Combined with the technique of the well-made play, the Drama of Ideas became the dominant form of English drama at the end of the nineteenth century due to the influence of Ibsen and the practice of Henry Arthur Jones, Arthur Wing Pinero, and George Bernard Shaw. See WELL-MADE PLAY.

Dramatic image. In poetic drama, a dramatic symbol which duplicates or reinforces the imagery of the poetic dialogue itself. In Shakespeare's *Richard the Second*, for example, King Richard speaks the following lines as he descends from the walls of Flint Castle to meet his victorious opponent, Bolingbroke, in the courtyard below:

> Down, down I come, like glist'ring Phaeton,
> Wanting the manage of unruly jades.
> In the base court? Base court, where kings grow base,
> To come at traitors' calls and do them grace!

Here the physical descent of Richard from his high position symbolizes his failure to control his nobles and retain his kingship, and it is reinforced by the reference to Phaeton and the pun on the "base court" in the poetry of the dialogue.

Dramatic irony. The condition in which the audience is made aware of information unknown to some of the characters. This information may be the true identity of a character, his real intentions, or the outcome of the action, but the fact that the audience possesses knowledge which the characters do not permits the audience to measure the words and deeds enacted before it against a clear standard. See ASIDE, CONFIDANT.

Dramatic metaphor. The juxtaposition of scenes in such a way that comparisons between them are suggested to the spectators. Many of the humorous scenes formerly thought to be only comic relief in tragedy, for example, are presented to illustrate the significance of surrounding action which is soberer in tone.

Dramatic symbol. A visual sign, presented either in the costumes, properties, settings, or action of a play, which has significance in itself and also relates to some larger meaning, such as the essence of a character or the theme of the play.

Dramatis personae (Latin: "the masks of the drama"). 1. The characters in a play. 2. A list of the characters.

Dramatist. See PLAYWRIGHT.

Dramaturgy. The art of writing plays.

Drame bourgeois. See BOURGEOIS DRAMA.

Drawing-room drama. See CUP-AND-SAUCER DRAMA.

Drop curtain (drop cloth). A canvas backcloth or curtain, painted for scenic effect, which is suspended from the flies and raised and lowered by means of a roller.

Dumb show. A scene which is enacted without words. Dumb shows were employed frequently in Elizabethan drama, where they were characteristically allegorical and symbolic, to parallel and to interpret the main action of the play.

Eccyclema. See GREEK THEATER.

Empathy. The experience in which the spectator *unconsciously* identifies himself with the object he is observing. It is the process of projecting his emotions into the actions and characters before him and of seeming to participate in their physical movements and emotions. The opposite of empathy is SYMPATHY, which is not feeling *with* something but feeling *for* something. When we sympathize with other persons, our pity and emotion is aroused by their situation, but we are conscious that we do not share their experience.

Epic drama. The term used by Bertolt Brecht to describe drama, particularly his own, which attempts to arouse the spectator's detached thought about, rather than his emotional involvement in, the action before him. Like the epic poem, epic drama consists of loosely connected episodes and deals with themes having large social implications. Brecht called the stage technique by which he aroused this detached thought the *Verfremdungseffekt* or alienation effect. It attempts to break down the spectator's involvement through utilizing choral interludes, lantern slides, signs, formalized action, masks, and scenery which only suggests locale, to interrupt the action and to call attention to the unrealistic quality of the performance.

Epilogue. 1. A concluding speech or poem, appended to a play after the last scene. It is frequently an appeal for applause, but it often has no relation to the subject matter of the play. 2. The actor who speaks the Epilogue.

Episode (Greek: *epeisodion*). See GREEK COMEDY and GREEK TRAGEDY.

Epode. See GREEK TRAGEDY.

Excursion. See ALARUM.

Exit, Exeunt. Stage directions, from the Latin meaning "he/she goes out" and "they go out." *Exeunt omnes* means "they all go out." Exit, however, has also become an English word, used either as the verb "to exit," meaning "to go out," or as a noun denoting the place where one goes out.

Exodos. See GREEK COMEDY, GREEK TRAGEDY.

Exposition. The process of providing the background information necessary for an understanding of the developing action.

Expressionism. The literary movement which seeks to present experience as it is seen in the mind of the characters. Expressionistic drama shatters the normal movement in time and place and frequently employs dream sequences which move unrealistically from one setting to another. Settings are distorted and represent the theme of the action rather than the locale. Characters are symbolic and wear masks or emblematic costumes. As a movement, expressionism was strongly influenced by the symbolic drama of August Strindberg (1849–1912) and achieved its greatest success in Germany between the two World Wars.

Fable. The plot of a play.

Falling action. The action of the play which follows the climax.

Farce. A type of comedy whose sole purpose is to provoke laughter, usually by depicting one-dimensional characters in absurd situations. It frequently employs slapstick or broad physical humor and ignores the usual considerations of motivation and probability in order to gain the maximum comic effect.

Flat. A rectangular wooden frame covered with canvas and painted. It has been the basic element in most systems of scenery since the middle of the seventeenth century.

Flies. The space above the stage where scenery is stored by being "flown" or raised by ropes.

Foil. A character used to provide a contrast which will set off the qualities of another character, as Ismene's fear of defying the orders of Creon contrasts with Antigone's determination to honor her brother.

Forestage. The part of the stage in front of the proscenium arch. In the seventeenth and early-eighteenth century it was the principal acting area.

Fourth wall. The term applied to the proscenium opening when it is imagined to be the wall of an interior set through which the audience views the action.

Greek comedy. The origin of Greek comedy, like that of Greek tragedy, seems to have been intimately connected with the worship of Dionysos. The first comic contest in Athens was celebrated at the City Dionysia in 486 B.C. Comedy of the fifth century, generally called Old Comedy, is known to us primarily through the first nine of Aristophanes' eleven extant plays. These plays exhibit a structure designed to exploit the mixture of fantasy, political and satiric allusion, farce, and lyric poetry of which they are composed. The ridiculous central idea is introduced in the *prologos* or opening passage of exposition, which is followed by the *parodos*, the entrance song of the chorus, who are dressed fantastically in costumes representing birds, frogs, etc. The idea is debated by the adversaries in the *agōn* or dispute, and the chorus comes forward in the *parabasis* to explain the theme of the play directly to the audience and to speak for the poet. This elaborate debate is succeeded by several *epeisodia* (episodes) which illustrate the central idea in amusing situations. The play is ended in the *exodos* or final scene of rejoicing. This pattern was altered after 400 B.C. by the ascendance of Middle Comedy, which emphasized social, rather than political themes and burlesqued stories from mythology. New Comedy, prevalent after 336 B.C., was concerned almost exclusively with the manners and romantic adventures of the Athenian upper middle class. Its chief practitioners were Diphilus and Philemon, whose plays are now known only through their titles, and Menander, of whose work two plays and some fragments are known to be extant. See DIONYSOS.

Greek theater. Greek drama was written to be performed in large open-air theaters which were set in the sides of hills and could accommodate as many as 16,000 spectators. These theaters took their shape from the requirements of the choral dithyramb, from which drama originated. At their center was a circular dancing area (the *orchēstra*) which contained an altar about which the chorus danced. The area for the spectators (the *theatron*, "seeing-place") nearly surrounded the dancing area in a kind of horseshoe and consisted of tiers of seats which rose in concentric circles. Behind the orchēstra and facing the audience was the *skēnē* (originally a temporary "tent of hides"), a wooden building with three doors through which the actors made their entrances and exits. At the end of the skēnē short wings (*paraskēnia*) extended toward the audience. The chorus entered between these paraskenia and the theatron. The area in front of the skēnē was known as the *proskēnion*, and it possibly contained a low stage on which the actors acted. There are references to three stage devices: the *ekkyklēma* ("wheel out"), probably a platform on wheels rolled out of the central door of the skēnē to reveal bodies or set scenes; the *mēchanē* or crane used to lower gods; and *periaktoi*, revolving prisms which had different scenes painted on their various surfaces and which were turned to indicate a change in the location of the action.

Greek tragedy. Tragedy seems to have developed by the addition, possibly under the influence of Thespis, of acted parts to the choral dithyramb in honor of Dionysos. The history of Greek tragedy is largely the story of the tragic contests at Athens, held twice yearly as part of the ceremonies for the god. Each of the three competing poets contributed three tragedies and a satyr-play. Performances began at sunrise on the grounds of the temple of Dionysos, and the cost of the actors was paid by the state. The expense of training the chorus was borne by the *choragi* (singular: *choragos*), prominent wealthy citizens specially chosen by lot. Actors were restricted in number first to two, then to three. The structure of Greek tragedy clearly reveals the influence of the ritual elements from which it developed. The opening speech of exposition or *prologos* is succeeded by the entrance song of the chorus or *parodos*. Each of the scenes containing the actors (the *epeisodia*) is followed by a *stasimon*, a lyric sung by the chorus which develops the general significance of the action depicted in the epeisodia. The stasimon is divided into the *strophē*, sung while the chorus moves to the left, the *antistrophē*, sung while the chorus returns to the right, and the *epode*, sung while the chorus stands still. After the last episode, the play concludes with the *exodos* or final song. See CHORUS, DITHYRAMB, DIONYSOS, SATYR-PLAY.

Groundling. The term used by the Elizabethans to denote the persons who paid the lowest admission and stood in the yard around the stage.

Hamartia. See TRAGEDY.

The heavens. The area above the stage in the Elizabethan theater, where the machinery for raising and lowering gods and producing the sound effects for thunder was located.

Heavy. 1. A serious leading role, particularly that of a villain. 2. An actor who consistently plays such roles.

Hero (Heroine). 1. The central character or protagonist. 2. The leading romantic character. The good moral connotations associated with the term sometimes cause some ambiguity in its use. In Shakespeare's *Richard the Third*, for example, Richard is the protagonist in the moral tragedy, but Henry of Richmond emerges as the hero at the end of the play.

Heroic drama. A type of play initiated by William Davenant's *The Siege of Rhodes* (1656) and popular throughout the Restoration period. It depicts a noble hero, caught in a struggle between love and honor; it is set in a locale which is remote and exotic; and it generally makes lavish use of spectacle and music. The plot is a series of peripeties (reversals) which generally produces a happy outcome for the protagonist and his love after bloody action in which many other characters die.

History play (chronicle play). A play whose source is an historical account or chronicle and which treats its source material with fidelity to historical fact and purpose. The classification was suggested by the division of Shakespeare's plays into *Comedies, Histories, and Tragedies* on the title page of the 1623 Folio. The distinction is a difficult one to maintain, however, because many of the characteristics of history plays are similar to those of moral tragedy. History plays were quite popular in the Elizabethan period, when their patriotism and morality appealed to the spirit of the age. There have been some attempts to revive the type in the modern theater, particularly by Maxwell Anderson, and George Bernard Shaw called *Saint Joan* a chronicle play.

Hubris (*hybris*). See TRAGEDY.

Humor (Latin: "moisture, fluid"). By extension, from the amusing behavior of humour characters, humor has come to denote that quality which arouses man's comic sense and excites laughter. It may take verbal forms, such as wit; it may arise from the presentation of absurd and embarrassing situations; or it may take broader, rougher forms such as slapstick. See HUMOUR CHARACTER, WIT, SLAPSTICK.

Humour character. A type of characterization originated by George Chapman and developed most fully in the comedies of Ben Jonson and his seventeenth-century imitators and disciples. Jonson uses the term to apply to two classes of characters: (a) characters whose temperament is determined by one of the four humours or elemental fluids of the body (blood, choler, black bile, phlegm), so that they are either sanguine, choleric, melancholy, or phlegmatic; and (b) by metaphor, to characters whose dispositions and actions are dominated by a particular quality, such as jealousy, avarice, or pride. A third group of Jonson's characters, though not strictly humour characters, affect humours, that is, pretend to have a quality or social grace that they do not naturally possess.

Induction. In Elizabethan drama, a short introductory scene which precedes the Prologue.

Inner stage. The curtained enclosure at the rear of the platform stage in the Elizabethan theater. In some playhouses it appears to have been a temporary structure which could be erected when it was necessary to present interior scenes which were discovered by drawing a curtain.

Irony of fate. See COSMIC IRONY.

Legitimate drama. Plays which depend almost entirely on acting and spoken dialogue, as opposed to other dramatic forms such as opera and pantomime. The distinction arose in the period 1660–1843, when there were only two theaters in London licensed to perform stage plays.

Liturgical drama. Medieval religious drama originating in the liturgy of the Church. It began originally as an expansion of the antiphons (choral responses sung alternately by two parts of the choir) for the Christmas and Easter services. Actors were added who played the parts of the shepherds seeking the new-born Christ or of the three Marys visiting His tomb and the angels who spoke to them. Originally, they spoke only the Latin lines of the liturgy, but more and more action was introduced, and the Latin was eventually replaced by the language of the people. Temporary stage houses or mansions were set up in various parts of the church to represent different localities. When the action became too complex for the church proper, the plays were moved outside. See MYSTERY PLAYS.

Manet, Maneunt. Stage directions, from the Latin meaning "he/she remains" and "they remain" used to indicate the continual presence of a character on the stage when the others depart, especially at the end of a scene.

Mansions. Structures made of wooden frames and canvas to represent stage houses or locations, frequently used in simultaneous settings. See MULTIPLE SETTING.

Mask. 1. A covering, either for the whole head or for part of the face, worn by an actor to conceal his features. Masks were worn by all actors in Greek and Roman drama, since they permitted the actor to double in more than one role. The masks in classical drama were standardized and represented both characters of different social standings (hence the term *dramatis personae*, "the masks of the drama") and also different emotions of the same character. With the rise of symbolic and non-realistic drama in the twentieth century, such playwrights as Yeats, O'Neill, and Brecht have again begun to employ masks in their plays. 2. In Elizabethan terminology, a disguise or entertainment presented at court by masked noblemen and ladies.

Mechane. See GREEK THEATER.

Melodrama. 1. Plays produced with a great deal of music at the unlicensed theaters in London in order to evade the ban on drama at theaters other than the two legitimate ones. (See LEGITIMATE THEATER). 2. Since these plays were often sensational in nature, the term was extended to mean a play which involves the protagonist in violent, unmotivated action, introduced only for sensational effect, and which ends happily through a surprising last-minute development. In the sense of a serious action imitated only for the thrills it produces, the term may be applied to drama from any period, such as Euripides' *Medea*, but nineteenth-century melodrama developed characteristics of its own. It had a set of stock characters—sailors, farmers, rent collectors—who were drawn from everyday life. It frequently depicted the conflict of social classes, but in such a way that the virtues of poverty were extolled and patriotism and moral values were stressed.

Middle Comedy. See GREEK COMEDY.

Miles gloriosus. See BRAGGART SOLDIER.

Morality play. An allegorical drama whose characters signify the virtues and the vices or other moral abstractions. The central figure of the play, who frequently represents Mankind, is depicted as torn between the choice of good or evil. After the Reformation, the morality play was employed for political purposes to depict the choice between the forces of Catholicism and the forces of Protestantism. See VICE.

Motivation. The grounds or causes which prompt a character to action. These may be economic, psychological, or moral, but it is required in serious drama that they be clearly established for each character and that his actions be based on consistent motives. When the characters in comedy lack motivation, it becomes farce; in tragedy, it becomes melodrama.

Multiple setting (simultaneous setting). A stage setting in which different locations are represented by stage houses or mansions which are disposed about the acting area and ignored by the audience when not in use. Multiple setting was the standard stage technique in Medieval liturgical drama, and it seems to have survived in the Elizabethan private theaters and the French theater until well into the seventeenth century.

Mystery plays (craft cycles). Mystery plays were Medieval religious plays dramatizing an episode from Old or New Testament history or from the lives of the saints. They developed gradually from the simple liturgical plays as they were expanded into a survey of the significant acts of God in human history. They were eventually grouped in cycles which depicted the history of the relationship of God and man from the fall of Lucifer until the Judgment Day. In England, they are often called craft cycles, because each of the craft guilds (associations of skilled workmen and businessmen) in the town where a cycle was given was reponsible for performing a play which was appropriate to their trade: the shipwrights performed the play about Noah's Ark, for example. The cycles were quite long (the York cycle contains forty-eight plays), and for the convenience of the spectators the plays were mounted on wagons or pageants, which were rolled to the different locations around the city where the performances were given. See LITURGICAL DRAMA, PAGEANT.

Myth. A story, generally involving the supernatural, which is of unknown origin and which explains the beginning of life, religious practice, social institutions, or natural phenomena. Together with legend, stories which are believed to be historical fact but are transmitted by tradition and cannot be verified, myth is one of the primary sources of subject matter for early drama. It provides the poet with material which is known to his audience and is of cosmic significance. Both Greek drama and Medieval drama developed from attempts to give myth a dramatic form, to make it more immediate for worshipers. See RITUAL.

Naturalism. Like realism in its attempt to reproduce the world of experience as closely as possible, naturalism differs from it in its philosophical basis. Its underlying assumption is that man is shaped by his inherited traits, his natural needs and impulses, and the social and economic forces of his environment. Naturalism is essentially pessimistic. The protagonist in naturalistic drama is usually defeated, but without even having the opportunity to avoid his fate by the exercise of his will which is given to the protagonist of classical tragedy. See REALISM.

Neoclassicism. The term "neoclassic" refers both to a period (the second half of the seventeenth and the earlier eighteenth century) and to a set of assumptions about art. The most important of these assumptions is that the surest way to achieve excellence in art is to observe certain well-tested rules, founded on reason and exemplified most clearly in the writings of the ancient Greeks and Romans. In the drama this meant a renewed emphasis on the unities and the adherence to certain other rules, such as the necessity of verse and a five-act structure for tragedy. Neoclassic playwrights also turned to classical literature for subject matter, and many of the myths of Greek tragedy and the characters and plots of Roman comedy were employed by French and English dramatists of the neoclassic period. In England the irregular tragedy of Shakespeare was extensively revised to fit the new stage requirements, and much of the comedy in the period was modeled on that of Ben Jonson, the leading classicist of the previous age.

New Comedy. See GREEK COMEDY.

Obligatory scene (French: *scène à faire*). A scene which the audience expects, either because the action it depicts is a necessary part of a well-known legend or because the dramatist has led the audience to anticipate it.

Off stage. The term used in stage directions to indicate that part of the stage which is not visible to the audience.

Old Comedy. See GREEK COMEDY.

On stage. The term used in stage directions to indicate any part of the acting area which is visible to the spectators.

Orchestra. 1. The circular dancing area in the Greek theater. 2. In the Renaissance theater, the seating space for the nobility (as in the Swan theater drawing). 3. The seating area on the ground floor of a modern American theater (called the "Stalls" in Britain). 4. The group of musicians who play in a theater. See GREEK THEATER.

Pace. The speed at which a play or part of a play is acted.

Pageant. 1. A stage on wheels used in the presentation of religious drama in the Medieval processions. The pageant consisted of two levels: an open acting area on the upper level and a curtained lower level, used as a dressing room. The two levels could also be used to represent Heaven and Earth or Earth and Hell if necessary. 2. An entertainment or procession which employs pageant wagons, generally carrying tableaux in dumb show.

Panorama. 1. A landscape or other scene painted on canvas and unrolled on cylinders at the rear of the stage so as to present a continuous moving background. 2. A cyclorama.

Parabasis. See GREEK COMEDY.

Parodos. See GREEK COMEDY, GREEK TRAGEDY.

Paraskenia. See GREEK THEATER.

Parquet. The part of the main floor of the auditorium not covered by balconies.

Pastoral drama. A type of Elizabethan play, influenced by Italian dramas based on pastoral poetry, in which the characters are shepherds and shepherdesses, the setting is rural, and the subject is love.

Pathos (Greek: "suffering, feeling"). The quality in a speech or scene which arouses pity, sorrow, or tenderness in the spectators. It is used especially to describe the suffering of helpless or innocent persons, such as women and children.

Periaktoi. See GREEK THEATER.

Peripety (Greek: *peripeteia*). A sudden reversal in the fortunes of the protagonist, either from good to bad or from bad to good. See TRAGEDY.

Picture-frame stage. A stage which is separated from the audience and framed by a proscenium arch.

Pièce à thèse. See DRAMA OF IDEAS.

Pièce bien faite. See WELL-MADE PLAY.

Pit. 1. A sunken area for musicians beneath or in front of the stage. 2. In British terminology, the ground floor of the theater auditorium or, in modern usage, the seats on the ground floor behind the higher priced stalls.

Platform stage. An acting area which extends into the auditorium and is surrounded on three sides by spectators.

Play. A dramatic composition. See DRAMA.

Playhouse. See THEATER.

Play-within-a-play. The presentation of a play within the action of a drama itself, such as the performance Hamlet arranges for the King to test his guilt in Act III, Scene ii of *Hamlet*. The main plot of some plays, such as Shakespeare's *The Taming of the Shrew* and Beaumont and Fletcher's *The Knight of the Burning Pestle*, is entirely set within the framework of the play-within-a-play.

Playwright. One who composes plays. Note that the origin of the word defines the dramatist as a play*maker* rather than a play*writer*, for he must consider the total effect of sound, color, movement, and stage grouping as well as that of dialogue.

Plot. The story or the total actions which a dramatic work relates. In this sense, the plot includes actions which occur offstage as well as on stage and actions which occur before the events that the spectators witness begin, such as Polyneices' death and the proper burial which Antigone gives him in Sophocles' play. Do not confuse plot with structure. See STRUCTURE.

Poetic drama. Drama composed in verse. The term itself would at one time have been unnecessary, for all European drama was originally poetic. Comedies written entirely in prose were introduced in the seventeenth century, while poetry remained the language of tragedy until well into the nineteenth century, when the advent of realistic drama concerned with social problems caused it to be abandoned in favor of prose. There have been notable attempts to revive poetic drama in the twentieth century commercial theater, particularly by T. S. Eliot, W. H. Auden, Christopher Isherwood, and Christopher Fry, and experimental drama has frequently employed verse or free-verse dialogue.

Poetic justice. The rewarding or punishing of characters in proportion to their virtue or vice. It frequently implies that the reward or punishment is related by nature, as well as by degree, to the action committed.

Problem play. See DRAMA OF IDEAS.

Prologos. See GREEK COMEDY, GREEK TRAGEDY.

Prologue. 1. An introductory speech or poem, preceding the first scene of a play. Originally the portion of the play which provided the exposition (see GREEK COMEDY, GREEK TRAGEDY), it later was used to summarize the plot, to appeal for the audience's attention, to explain the dramatist's purposes, or to comment on social, political, and dramatic conditions in general. In the Restoration period and the eighteenth century, both the Prologue and Epilogue usually have little relation to the subject matter of the play. 2. The actor who speaks the Prologue.

Property (prop). An object essential to the action of the play, with the exception of costumes, scenery, or lighting effects. Small objects which are held by actors, such as books, swords, knitting, etc., are known as hand-props.

Proscenium. From the Greek *proskēnion*—literally, the space "before the scene"—meaning the area or stage in front of the actors' dressing room. (See GREEK THEATER.) 1. In the seventeenth century, the forestage or the part of the stage in front of the curtain, then the principal acting area. 2. By extension, the whole surroundings of the stage opening.

Proscenium arch. The frame through which the audience views the stage setting. The proscenium arch divides the modern theater into two main sections—one in which the audience views the action and one in which the action takes place. See FOURTH WALL.

Proscenium balcony. A balcony above a proscenium door, overlooking the forestage.

Proscenium doors. Originally, the several pairs of doors facing each other on either side of the forestage, through which the actors made their entrances and exits. When the stage area behind the curtain became more important as an acting area in the eighteenth century and the actors entered in the scene itself, the doors were reduced in number to one pair and became part of the proscenium frame facing the audience.

Proskenion. See GREEK THEATER.

Protagonist. 1. In Greek tragedy, the first actor (of the three to which the dramatist was restricted). The second and third actors were known as the DEUTERAGONIST and the TRITAGONIST respectively. 2. By extension, the central figure in any dramatic work.

Psychical distance. See AESTHETIC DISTANCE.

Realism. The literary mode which attempts to depict the world objectively, without imposing artificial patterns on experience. It reproduces as closely as possible a "slice of life" in which the characters are commonplace and the events are ordinary experiences. In drama, realism also employs representational staging and naturalistic acting to create the illusion of exact reality. Care is paid that details of speech, manner, costume, and setting are as much as possible like the characters and locales of the actual life being depicted. The term is also used in its adjectival form, "realistic," to indicate any aspect of a play or production which is presented with verisimilitude. See REPRESENTATIONAL STAGING.

Renaissance. The period of European history (roughly 1450–1650) which witnessed the Reformation, the alteration of the accepted view of the world and the physical universe through scientific discoveries, and the rediscovery of classical thought and literature and its integration into the culture of Western Europe. In the drama, the Renaissance period is significant for its return to classical models. Senecan tragedy and Plautine and Terentian comedy were both translated and imitated. The Unities were formulated. Classical dramatic conventions, such as the chorus, the five-act structure, and stock characters, and new dramatic types, such as revenge tragedy and intrigue comedy, were joined with the native dramatic traditions to form one of the most creative and flourishing periods in the history of the theater. See UNITIES.

Representational staging. Staging which aims at a high degree of realism or verisimilitude in the presentation of action. Thus, actors eat real food and drink real beverages in stage settings arranged to look as much as possible like real dining rooms when a play includes a dinner scene. Representational staging employs sets which have workable doors and windows, and properties that actually work. It attempts to reproduce, rather than to suggest, the locale in which the action takes place.

Revenge play. An Elizabethan dramatic form which developed from the imitation of the Roman tragedies of Seneca (c. 4 B.C.–A.D. 65). Its characteristics are revenge as the motive for the protagonist's action, the appearance of the ghost who calls for revenge on his murderers, the use of disguises and elaborate plots to discover and torment the guilty persons, the play-within-a-play, and violent, bloody action. The vogue for the revenge play was begun by Thomas Kyd's *The Spanish Tragedy* (c. 1586); the most famous revenge play is, of course, Shakespeare's *Hamlet* (1600).

Rising action. That portion of the play which precedes the climax.

Ritual. Ritual is the *form* of religious observance, the ceremony with which believers worship. Just as early drama takes its subject matter from religious myth, so it takes its structure from religious ritual. Thus, the form of Greek tragedy was influenced by the choral dithyramb from which it originated, and the episodic structure of Medieval drama is due to the way in which the choral responses of the Christian liturgy were amplified into dramatic presentations. Ritual elements, in the sense of formalized patterns by which religious and social beliefs are expressed, are continually present in drama. Both Thornton Wilder's *The Skin of our Teeth* and T. S. Eliot's *Murder in the Cathedral*, for example, contain ritual elements. See GREEK TRAGEDY, LITURGICAL DRAMA.

Romantic comedy. Comedy whose subject matter is drawn from or is similar to prose and verse romances. It is characterized by distant settings or unrealistic atmosphere, noble characters, love-at-first-sight, and plots which involve disguises and other difficulties but which end happily.

Romanticism. The literary movement dominant in the early nineteenth century. No one satisfactory definition can be given, but romantic drama is characterized by the rejection of the neoclassic rules, by settings distant both in time and space, by idealized and rebellious heroes who defy society, and by freer and more violent action than that in eighteenth-century drama. The adjective "romantic" is also used to describe drama from any period which stresses the distant, the exotic, the courageous, and which moves freely in time and space. See NEOCLASSICISM.

Rules. See NEOCLASSICISM.

Satire. The use of ridicule and laughter as a weapon to criticize or to expose human behavior. It is distinguished from comedy in that its aim is generally asserted not to be the amusement of its audience but the correction of folly and vice by making it contemptible and ridiculous. Although it is occasionally used for personal purposes, it is usually stated to be directed not at persons but at general faults.

Satyr-play. A Greek play whose chorus was composed of performers dressed like satyrs—the half-human, half-animal figures who accompany Dionysos in his revels. Each competing poet in the tragic contests supplied a satyr-play which was performed after the three tragedies. Satyr-plays seem to have burlesqued myth by introducing mythological heroes, frequently those in the earlier tragic trilogy, in ludicrous situations. Both the language and the gestures were often obscene, and the chorus wore a phallus and a horse's tail and ears as part of their costume. See DIONYSOS, GREEK TRAGEDY.

Scene (from the Greek *skēnē;* see GREEK THEATER). 1. The stage setting or some part of it. 2. The locale or place in which the action of the play or part of the play is located. 3. A formal division of the play's structure, shorter than an act and usually encompassing an episode which takes place in one locale. 4. A portion of a play in which the stage is occupied by an unchanging group of actors. The entrance of new characters or the exit of ones already present thus changes the scene.

Scène à faire. See OBLIGATORY SCENE.

Scenery. The components of the stage decoration, especially those made of wood and canvas, used to suggest the locale of the action or to hide parts of the stage from the audience's view.

Sentimental. The term used to describe the excessive indulgence in the tender emotions of sympathy and pity beyond the degree warranted by the situation.

Sentimental comedy. A type of comedy popular in the eighteenth century. It attempts to inculcate moral principles by arousing the tears and pity of the audience for the plight of virtuous heroes and heroines who suffer through four acts of tribulation at the hands of wicked characters only to be delivered from suffering and injustice in the last act.

Setting (set). 1. Originally used to denote a "set scene" or a scene which was prepared in advance and revealed by opening a curtain or a shutter. 2. By extension, the complex of scenery, furniture, and properties arranged to form the locale for a scene.

Shutter. A large flat, set in a groove in the stage floor and used in pairs so that, when pushed together, they form a continuous scenic background. See WING.

Simultaneous setting. See MULTIPLE SETTING.

Skene. See GREEK THEATER.

Slapstick. 1. A paddle made of slats so that it creates a loud noise when used to strike another actor. 2. Humor which depends for its effect on physical assault and boisterous action.

Soliloquy. Lines spoken by an actor as if speaking his thoughts aloud to himself.

Solus. A stage direction, from the Latin meaning "alone," which indicates the entrance of a character by himself.

Spectacle. A stage display employing elaborate costume and scenery.

Stage. A platform, generally raised above the level of the spectators, on which action takes place in a dramatic performance.

Stage direction. A statement in the text or script of a play which indicates either an actor's movements or scenery and stage effects necessary at that time.

Stagy. Theatrical; an adjective used to describe action which depends heavily on stage effect and which reminds the spectator that he is seeing the representation of reality and not the reality itself.

Stalls. In British terminology, the seats on the ground floor of the theater auditorium. Those closest to the stage are known as the orchestra stalls.

Stasimon. See GREEK TRAGEDY.

Strophe. See GREEK TRAGEDY.

Structure. The selection of incidents from the plot and their arrangement into the order in which they are presented to the audience. See PLOT.

Style. The manner or mode of expression used by an artist or a performer. It is possible to speak not only of a playwright's style, but also of an actor's style or of the style in which scenes or costumes are designed. A distinction should be made between style in general and works or performances which are "stylized," that is, written or performed in such a way as to call attention to the artifice or the extreme manner of their presentation.

Subplot. See DOUBLE PLOT.

Suspense. Uncertainty over the outcome of the action or the anticipation of an event which is expected but delayed. It is frequently used by both tragic and comic dramatists to intensify the action, as in *Antigone*, where the uncertainty about Antigone's fate which is created by Creon's last-minute attempt to stop her execution increases the tragic force of the ending, and in the *Mostellaria*, where the humor of Acts III and IV depends upon the precarious success of Tranio's plotting.

Symbolism. The use of dramatic symbols to suggest the significance or theme of a play. Symbolism has always been present in the theater, but in the modern theater it is used extensively by such naturalistic playwrights as Chekhov and Ibsen, and by such expressionistic playwrights as Strindberg. The plays of William Butler Yeats (1865–1939), which do not fit easily into either of these categories, are also primarily symbolic.

Sympathy. See EMPATHY.

Tableau (French: *tableau vivant*). A picture created by the formal arrangement of actors who are both silent and motionless, particularly at the end of an act or scene when the curtain drops and then raises immediately for applause.

Tempo. See PACE.

Theater (Greek: "seeing-place"). A building designed for seeing and hearing dramatic performances. Every theater is divided into three main areas: an auditorium or room for the spectators; an acting area or stage; and a backstage area used by the actors to dress and to store properties, scenery, and costumes.

Theatron. See GREEK THEATER.

Thesis play. See DRAMA OF IDEAS.

Thespis. A Greek poet who won the prize in the first tragic contest at Athens in 534 B.C. He apparently was the first poet to introduce an actor into the performance of the chorus and its leader, and he is therefore considered to be the founder of tragedy.

Tiring house. The backstage area of the Elizabethan theater, in which costumes (attire) were donned and scenery and properties were stored.

Tragedy. In general, tragedy is a serious play which ends with the death or defeat of the protagonist. This unhappy outcome is caused by some fault or tragic flaw (Greek: *hamartia*) in the protagonist's character. Essential to tragedy is the recognition (Greek: *anagnōrisis*) of this fault or error by the protagonist, but he arrives at this recognition when his faults have carried him beyond a compromise with the forces opposing him so that a fortunate ending is impossible.

Critical discussion of tragedy has been largely dominated by Aristotle, although he did not intend the analysis of tragedy in the *Poetics* as rules which must be followed. Aristotle considers tragedy to be the representation of a serious action centering on a protagonist who is superior to most men and involving a sudden reversal or peripety (Greek: *peripeteia*) in his fortunes. This change could be from bad to good fortune, but in most tragedies it is from good to bad and results from some tragic flaw, frequently pride (Greek: *hybris*), which leads the protagonist to ignore moral or divine law. Aristotle considers the aim of tragedy to be the purgation or catharsis (Greek: *katharsis*) of the emotions of pity and fear which leaves the audience relieved and almost elated even though the action they view is unfortunate.

Although Aristotle's terms can be applied to many tragedies, they are not applicable to all serious drama. Much Elizabethan tragedy was influenced by the Medieval Christian conception of tragedy as the sudden downfall which attends the foolish subjection of the self to the rule of Fortune rather than reason. In the nineteenth and twentieth centuries, the increasing concern of the drama with social and psychological themes and the deterministic view of naturalism has led to a broadened interpretation of the usual concepts of tragedy. See DOMESTIC TRAGEDY, GREEK TRAGEDY, NATURALISM.

Tragic flaw (Greek: *hamartia*). See TRAGEDY.

Tragicomedy. A play serious in tone in which grave events threaten an unfortunate outcome that is averted at the last moment by skillful plotting. It retains the noble characters and the motivation common to tragedy, but it arouses emotion by a series of shocking incidents and then relieves it by an unexpected compromise between the opposing forces. The term is also frequently applied to plays with two plots, one of which is tragic and the other of which is comic, or to plays which mix the two attitudes freely.

Traps. Openings in the stage floor through which entrances and exits can be made or through which properties and scenery can appear or disappear.

Tritagonist. See PROTAGONIST.

Unities. The three rules of dramatic construction formulated by Italian Renaissance critics. The Unity of Time demands that the action cover a period of no more than twenty-four hours. The Unity of Place restricts action to one city and preferably to one locale. The Unity of Action requires that no extraneous events be included in the plot and that comedy not be mixed with tragedy. The authority of Aristotle was frequently claimed for these rules, but in fact, the only Unity which he insists on in the *Poetics* is the Unity of Action, although he does mention in passing that most tragedies are restricted in time to twenty-four hours or less. See NEOCLASSICISM.

Upstage. 1. The rear half of the stage. 2. A transitive verb: to detract attention from another actor's performance, generally by moving upstage so that he must turn his back on the audience to speak his lines. See DOWNSTAGE.

Upper stage. The balcony and the chamber above the inner stage in the Elizabethan theater.

Verfremdungseffect. See EPIC DRAMA.

Vice. The comic antagonist of the Medieval morality play. Symbolically, he represents a combination of one of the Seven Deadly Sins attempting to destroy the proper relationship between the protagonist, who represents Mankind, and God or virtue. But the disorder he introduces is a farcical one, and he is frequently carried off by a devil at the end of the play.

Well-made play (French: *pièce bien faite*). A type of play created by the French playwright, Eugène Scribe (1791–1861). It is characterized by careful preparation for each incident, which must develop logically from the preceding action. Character is subordinate to plot. The well-made play generally manipulates a series of simple type characters through a difficult situation toward marriage. Inanimate objects, such as letters, play an important part in the plot, which is planned to provide a maximum of suspense and exciting reversals in the situation.

Wing. A flat placed at the side of the stage, facing toward the audience, in order to conceal the offstage area. A series of wings, each set in a groove so that it may be shifted easily, is generally employed on each side of the stage in conjunction with a backdrop or shutter to provide scenes of varying depths. This method of staging was the dominant one in the European theater until the latter half of the nineteenth century, when it was replaced by the Box Set to meet the demand for an increasingly realistic setting.

Wit. A verbal form of humor, whose comic effect is created by the clever turn of a sentence or expression so as to surprise the hearer.

Yard. The area for standing spectators around the platform stage in the Elizabethan theater. Its name reflects the development of the theaters from temporary stages set up in London inn yards.

BIBLIOGRAPHY

BIBLIOGRAPHY

HISTORIES OF THE STAGE AND CONTRIBUTORY ARTS

CHEYNEY, SHELDON, *The Theatre: Three Thousand Years of Drama, Acting, and Stagecraft*, New York, 1929.

FREEDLEY, GEORGE, AND J. A. REEVES, *A History of the Theatre*, New York, 1941.

HARTNOLL, PHYLLIS, *The Oxford Companion to the Theatre*, New York, 1951.

MACGOWAN, KENNETH, AND W. MELNITZ, *The Living Stage*, New York, 1955.

NAGLER, A. M., *A Source Book in Theatrical History*, New York, 1959.

SOUTHERN, RICHARD, *The Seven Ages of the Theatre*, New York, 1961.

DRAMA, HISTORY AND CRITICISM

CLARK, BARRET H., *European Theories of the Drama*, New York, 1947.

FERGUSSON, FRANCIS, *The Idea of a Theater*, New York, 1953.

GASSNER, JOHN, *Masters of the Drama*, New York, 1954.

NICOLL, ALLARDYCE, *World Drama*, New York, 1950.

DRAMA: BY PERIOD AND INDIVIDUAL AUTHOR

Classical

BOWRA, C. M., *Sophoclean Tragedy*, Oxford, 1945.

DECHARME, PAUL, *Euripides and the Spirit of His Dramas*, New York, 1906.

DUCKWORTH, GEORGE, *The Nature of Roman Comedy*, Princeton, 1952.

KITTO, H. D. F., *Greek Tragedy*, New York, 1954.

LUCAS, F. L., *Euripides and His Influence*, Boston, 1923.

MURRAY, GILBERT, *Euripides and His Age*, New York, 1913.

NORWOOD, GILBERT, *Plautus and Terence*, New York, 1932.

WALDOCK, A. J. A., *Sophocles the Dramatist*, Cambridge (Eng.), 1951.

WHITMAN, C. H., *Sophocles: A Study of Heroic Humanism*, Cambridge (Mass.), 1951.

Oriental

BOWERS, FAUBION, *Theatre in the East,* New York, 1960.
DAS GUPTA, H., *The Indian Stage,* Calcutta, 1934–8.
KEITH, A. B., *The Sanskrit Drama,* Oxford, 1924.
SHEKHAR, Q., *Sanskrit Drama, Its Origin and Decline,* Leiden, 1960.

Medieval

BEVINGTON, DAVID M., *From Mankind to Marlowe,* Cambridge (Mass.), 1962.
CHAMBERS, E. K., *The Mediaeval Stage,* Oxford, 1903.
CRAIG, HARDIN, *English Religious Drama of the Middle Ages,* Oxford, 1955.
FARNHAM, WILLARD, *The Medieval Heritage of Elizabethan Tragedy,* Berkeley, 1936.
SOUTHERN, RICHARD, *The Medieval Theatre in the Round,* London, 1957.

XVI–XVII Centuries

BOGARD, TRAVIS, *The Tragical Satire of John Webster,* Berkeley, 1955.
BORGERHOFF, E. B. O., *The Freedom of French Classicism,* Princeton, 1950.
DORAN, MADELEINE, *Endeavors of Art,* Madison, 1954.
DOWNER, ALAN S., *British Drama,* New York, 1950.
FERNÁNDEZ, RAMÓN, *Molière, The Man Seen through the Plays,* New York, 1958.
LEECH, CLIFFORD, *John Webster, A Critical Study,* London, 1951.
LEWIS, D. B. WYNDHAM, *Molière, The Comic Mask,* New York, 1959.
PARROTT, T. M., AND R. H. BALL, *A Short View of Elizabethan Drama,* New York, 1943.

XVIII Century

LYNCH, J. J., *Box, Pit, and Gallery: Stage and Society in Johnson's London,* Berkeley, 1953.
NETTLETON, G. H., *English Drama of the Restoration and Eighteenth Century,* New York, 1914.
THALER, A., *Shakespeare to Sheridan,* Cambridge (Mass.), 1922.
WARDLE, R. M., *Oliver Goldsmith,* Lawrence (Kansas), 1957.

XIX–XX Centuries

BRADBROOK, M. C., *Ibsen the Norwegian,* London, 1946.
CLARK, BARRETT H., AND GEORGE FREEDLEY, *A History of Modern Drama,* New York, 1947.
DOWNER, ALAN S., *Fifty Years of American Drama,* Chicago, 1951.
GROSSVOGEL, DAVID, *The Self-Conscious Stage in Modern French Drama,* New York, 1958.

HINGLEY, RONALD, *Chekhov, A Biographical and Critical Study,* London, 1950.

INSKIP, DONALD, *Jean Giraudoux, The Making of a Dramatist,* Oxford, 1958.

LE SAGE, LAURENT, *Jean Giraudoux, His Life and Works,* University Park (Pa.), 1959.

MAGARSHACK, DAVID, *Chekhov the Dramatist,* London, 1952.

SIMMONS, E. J., *Chekhov, A Biography,* Boston, 1962.

STARKIE, W., *Luigi Pirandello,* New York, 1937.

WEALES, GERALD, *American Drama Since World War II,* New York, 1962.

WEIGAND, H. J., *The Modern Ibsen, A Reconsideration,* New York, 1929.

WELLAND, DENNIS, *Arthur Miller,* Edinburgh, 1961.

WILDER, THORNTON, "Some Thoughts on Playwriting," in *The Intent of the Artist,* ed. A. Centeno, Princeton, 1941.

Book and cover design by Gayle Jaeger
Set in The Times *New Roman*
Composed by Santype Limited
Printed by Murray Printing Co.
Bound by American Book - Stratford Press
HARPER & ROW, PUBLISHERS, INCORPORATED